lonely planet

South Pacific

Errol Hunt
Jean-Bernard Carillet
Kate Galbraith
Robyn Jones
Nancy Keller

James Lyon
Rowan McKinnon
Denis O'Byrne
Leonardo Pinheiro
Tony Wheeler

LONELY PLANET PUBLICATIONS
Melbourne • Oakland • London • Paris

SOUTH PACIFIC

120°E, 20°N   *130°E*   *140°E*   *150°E*   *160°E*

Mariana Islands

NORTHERN MARIANA ISLANDS
At church fiestas you can join in
on the music, dancing and
Chamorro feasts.

**NORTHERN
MARIANA
ISLANDS**

MANILA

*PHILIPPINE
SEA*

PHILIPPINES

Saipan

GUAM
(USA) Guam

FEDERATED STATES OF MICRONESIA

10°N

PALAU

Yap

Yap

Caroline

C h u u k

Pohnpei

Koror

M

Weno

Islands

Pohnpei

I

C

FEDERATED STATES OF MICRONESIA
The sunken ruins of the
ancient city of Nan Madol
are a delight to explore by canoe.

R

O

Equator

PALAU
The Rock Islands are a maze of
green, mushroom-shaped islands,
offering some of the world's
finest snorkelling and diving.

SOLOMON ISLANDS
Bustling Honiara city on
Guadalcanal Island will astound
you with its shops,
restaurants and hotels.

Choiseul

Santa Isabel

I   N   D   O   N   E   S   I   A

**PAPUA NEW
GUINEA**

*Solomon
Sea*

Malai

*Arafura
Sea*

New Georgia
Islands

Guadalcanal

10°S

PORT MORESBY

Makira

Rennell &
Bellona

*TIMOR
SEA*

*Gulf
of
Carpentaria*

VANUATU
On Pentecost Island, the land-diving
(naghol) ceremony is carried
out every year to ensure a good
harvest and inspire the world's
bungy jumpers.

*CORAL
SEA*

**NEW
CALEDO**
(France)

**Northern
Territory**

Tropic of Capricorn

AUSTRALIA

NEW CALEDONIA
In the rugged mountains near
Koné are opportunities for
epic horse trekking expeditions.

**Western
Australia**

**South
Australia**

Queensland

Brisbane

*Lord Howe
Island
(Australia)*

**New South
Wales**

Sydney

CANBERRA

Victoria

Melbourne

SOUTHERN   OCEAN

120°E, 40°S   *130°E*   *140°E*   *150°E*   *160°E*

Contents – Text

NEW CALEDONIA 567

SOLOMON ISLANDS 633

VANUATU 704

MICRONESIA 780

FEDERATED STATES OF MICRONESIA 782

GUAM 813

Contents – Maps

FIJI

NEW CALEDONIA

SOLOMON ISLANDS

VANUATU

FEDERATED STATES OF MICRONESIA

GUAM

US TERRITORIES

KIRIBATI

MARSHALL ISLANDS

NAURU

NORTHERN MARIANA ISLANDS

PALAU

The Authors

Errol Hunt

After growing up in Whakatane, Aotearoa (New Zealand), Errol left
for the big smoke (Hamilton) where he bluffed his way through a
physics degree. Moving to Australia, he bluffed his way through 5½
years as a research scientist for a mining company before joining
Lonely Planet's Melbourne office as an editor – he is still bluffing.

In this book, Errol wrote the introductory and Tokelau chapters
and acted as coordinating author.

Jean-Bernard Carillet

After a degree in translation and in international relations, Jean-
Bernard joined Lonely Planet's French office in 1995 as an editor
and is now a full-time author. Diving instructor and incorrigible
traveller, he will decamp at the slightest opportunity to travel
round the world, but always returns to his native Lorraine in the
east of France. Jean-Bernard wrote the New Caledonia chapter of
this guide, and assisted with the French Polynesia chapter. He has
also contributed to Lonely Planet's *Tahiti & French Polynesia*,
Corsica, and the French-language guides to *Martinique*, *Dominique et Sainte-Lucie* and *Guadeloupe et ses îles*.

Kate Galbraith

Kate is a freelance writer who graduated from Harvard with a
degree in English literature, and has since worked mostly in
Eastern Europe. Covering the nations of Micronesia for this book
was rather a change from her last Lonely Planet assignment
(Bosnia) and her next (Latvia). Hourly applications of sunscreen
stopped Kate from frying in the tropical sun, and she's also proud
to have survived vulturous Kiribati immigration authorities. Kate
now lives in London.

Robyn Jones

As a teenager Robyn traded farm life in rural Victoria, Australia,
for a year as an exchange student in the Brazilian megalopolis of
São Paulo. While studying for a degree in architecture she tripped
around Australia and Europe, and later returned to Brazil for a while,
to get to know her future in-laws. She has worked on Lonely
Planet's *Brazil*, *South America* and *Fiji*. In this book, Robyn and
Leonardo Pinheiro wrote the Fiji and Tuvalu chapters. In between
travels Robyn works as an architect in Melbourne. Robyn and
Leonardo's son Alex makes their travelling much more interesting!

Nancy Keller

Born and raised in northern California, Nancy worked in the alternative press for several years, doing every aspect of newspaper work from editorial and reporting to delivering the papers. She returned to university to earn a master's degree in journalism, graduating in 1986. She's been travelling and writing ever since. Nancy is author or co-author of many Lonely Planet books including *Rarotonga & the Cook Islands*, *Tonga* and *New Zealand*. Nancy updated the Cook Islands and Tonga chapters in this book.

James Lyon

A sceptic by nature, and a social scientist by training, James worked as an editor in Lonely Planet's Melbourne office, then jumped at the chance to update Lonely Planet's guide to *Bali & Lombok*. His interest in island cultures has also taken him to the Maldives, and for this book he covered Rapa Nui, better known as Easter Island, the most enigmatic island of all.

Rowan McKinnon

Born in country Victoria, Australia, Rowan spent some early years on Nauru, then grew up in outer bayside Melbourne. He worked as a kitchen-hand, poster putter-upper, taxi driver, packer, warehouse keeper, carpenter and rocket scientist, while studying philosophy and playing bass with an arty band called Not Drowning Waving. After 10 years, he gave up the life of airports, tour buses, and rehearsal rooms to get a 'real job' with Lonely Planet as an editor. Rowan wrote the Solomon Islands chapter – he has also contributed to Lonely Planet's *Papua New Guinea*.

Denis O'Byrne

Denis was born and bred in country South Australia and received his first taste of overseas travel as a surveyor in the Australian Army. Since then he's earned a living as a mine surveyor, national park ranger, plant operator, builder's labourer and building consultant. He has travelled in Europe, Southern Africa, New Guinea and New Zealand and lived in Zimbabwe for a time. Currently a travel writer most of the time, Denis lives in Darwin in Australia's Northern Territory.

Denis wrote the Vanuatu chapter for the *South Pacific* guidebook. He has also worked on Lonely Planet's *South Australia*, *Vanuatu*, *Australia* and *Outback Australia*.

Leonardo Pinheiro

Leonardo was born and raised in Rio de Janeiro, Brazil. From age 15 onwards he travelled as much as his pocket money and time would allow throughout Brazil. After tertiary studies in agricultural science he came to Sydney to do a master's degree in biotechnology and to check out the Australian surf. He met Robyn, and moved to Melbourne where they now live. As well as the Fiji and Tuvalu chapters in this book, Leonardo has also worked on Lonely Planet's *Brazil*, *South America* and *Fiji*. He is currently studying for a PhD in biochemistry.

Tony Wheeler

Tony was born in England but grew up in Pakistan, the Bahamas and the USA. He returned to England to study engineering, worked as an automotive design engineer, completed an MBA then set out with his wife, Maureen, on an Asian overland trip that ultimately led to them founding Lonely Planet in Australia in 1973. They have been travelling, writing and publishing guidebooks ever since.

For this book Tony wrote the French Polynesia, Niue, Pitcairn Islands and Wallis & Futuna chapters.

FROM THE AUTHORS

From Errol

Lonely Planet's guide to the South Pacific was a long time coming. Thanks to the readers who kept bugging us and finally made it happen.

Gathering information about Tokelau would have been impossible without the help of Val Leno of the Tokelau Office in Wellington, Alepano Savelio, also in Wellington, and Makalio Ioane on Nukunonu Atoll. *Faka fetai.*

Jacinta Kearney and Kim Shearman at the Victorian EPA, Gareth Walton and 'Claire' of Greenpeace and Mike Atkinson of Diamantina Technology helped with global warming information. Ron Schaeffer at Bishop Museum helped track down images.

Thanks to all the authors, who were a delight to work with. Thanks finally to Maui Tikitiki a Taranga – for inspired fishing.

From Jean-Bernard

Thanks to the staff of the tourist offices in Noumea, to all the dive instructors, and to all the Kanak people I met – they provided new perspectives to a stranger they saw dashing through their marvellous country. I admire also the people who took me to the abandoned Thiebaghi mine. I am indebted to Greg Alford and Mary Neighbour for their confidence in the 'Frenchie' from an overseas office, and to Errol for having ensured a smooth process all the way.

From Kate

Countless thanks go to Ben of the Marshall Islands Visitors Authority. On Nauru, great thanks to Ellamaine of Air Nauru. Thanks to the tourist office on Tarawa for their generous assistance, and the same to Simeon at Chuuk Visitors Bureau and Tony at the Guam Visitors Bureau. On Guam, Ron Jewell also helped out. In Palau, my gratitude goes to the Tmetuchl family, for the wonderful hospitality, food and company, and to James Woods. Also thanks to Mary Neighbour and Errol at LP, and Mike and Sheela. And to the innumerable others who offered me guidance and company, my deepest gratitude.

From Robyn & Leo

In Fiji, thanks to: Bob for getting us around Kadavu; the Bulou family in Navala; Leslie and Bruce from Suva; John for agreeing to our crazy schedule in the Mamanucas; baby Georgia for letting Alex have her helicopter; Abe from the FVB in Nadi; Abdul in Nadi; Tups from the FVB in Suva; Mike in Ovalau; Helen for dive tips; Michelle in Korotogo; Travis and friends for a fun time in the Yasawas; Peter and David in Nadi; Noreen in Waiyevo; and Mum for again paying our bills while we were away! A special *vinaka vakalevu* to all the people who gave Alex lots of attention along the way!

For Tuvalu thanks to Lene and Bob at the Ministry of Tourism, Mema and Titivalu at the Vaiaku Hotel, Tataua and Claudia at the Town Council, John at Radio Tuvalu, Mataia at the Ministry of Environment, Hellani at AusAID, Vitoli and Aunise.

From Nancy

Many thanks to everyone who helped with the Cook Islands and Tonga chapters. *Meitaki maata* to Papatua Papatua of the Cook Islands Tourism Corporation for helpfulness as always, and *meitaki maata* to Raina Mataiapo. Thanks also to Errol for our lively exchange of interesting ideas, stories and conversation, making this book even more fun.

From James

On Easter Island, thanks to Sandra, who drove us, helped us, informed us and was wonderfully hospitable. At Lonely Planet, thanks to Errol, for his thorough briefing, persistent good humour, and professional editorship. Finally, thanks to Pauline, my partner and muse, who helped so much on this trip.

From Rowan

Thanks to the Solomon Islanders for their welcome and generosity. Thank you also to Jim and Sunny Vicars, Christian, Hazel Clothier, Dick Anning, Dennis Anii, Alice and Telissa Djernov, Mia Morton, Robert Soekeri, Hudson Arek and Prime Minister

Bartholomew Ulufa'alu. Special thanks go to Danny and Kerrie Kennedy and Morris Kuikakea.

At the Planet thanks to Mary Neighbour and Errol Hunt. Thank you to Lewis, Eadie and Deb. To Jane Hart – for love, support and help on the road and at home – and to our intrepid two-year-old daughter, Lauren Rose, thank you for everything, always.

From Denis

Max Herman and the various members of VIBA – particularly Father Luke Dini, Laan Douglas, Peter Fidelio, William Mete, Chief Willy Orion, John Eddie Saitol and George Thompson – gave generously of their time and helped smooth my path. Thanks to the Environment Unit for providing information about Vanuatu's dugongs. Special thanks also to Annie (Island Safaris), Chief Aiairandes, Max Aru, Cathy Clarkin, Kate (Lands Planning Office), Kathy Fry, Roy and Fran Hills, Jane Laycock, Chief Alben Reuben, Kevin White, Sonny Whitelaw and Dave Woods. A huge thanks to Vanair for their assistance on numerous flights throughout the archipelago. Last, but by no means least, thanks to Julianne Donnelly for her kind hospitality.

From Tony

In French Polynesia my thanks go to Jonathan Ray and to the dive staff at Tahiti Plongée, Bathy's Club and Bora Diving Centre. Geoff Green and the other expedition staff and the Russian crew of the *Akademik Shuleykin* deserve a special thank you for a fascinating trip which took me to the Pitcairn Islands and to Mangareva, Rapa, Raivaevae and other islands in French Polynesia. On Niue, Kevin and Carrie Fawcett of Niue Dive were enormously helpful (great diving too) and Ida Talagi-Hekesi and the other staff of the Niue Tourism Office made my work much easier. On Wallis & Futuna thank you to Monika and Jacques Bilco, Bernard Riou, Michelle Lombard, Fabrice Le Corre and Claire Moyse-Faurie.

This Book

This is the first edition of Lonely Planet's guide to the South Pacific. Most of the region was researched anew 'on the ground' for this guide. However, we also acknowledge the excellent work done by the authors of the various Pacific islands guides, including Dorinda Talbot (*Samoa*), Leanne Logan & Geert Cole (*New Caledonia*), Mark Honan (*Solomon Islands*), Glenda Bendure & Ned Friary (*Micronesia*) and Wayne Bernhardson (*Chile & Easter Island*).

From the Publisher

The production of the *South Pacific* was coordinated in-house by Jenny Joy Jones (design and mapping) and by Errol Hunt (editing). Jenny was assisted with the maps by Helen Rowley, Kusnandar and Corinne Waddell. The book's editors and proofers were Hilary Erickson, Anne Mulvaney, Bruce Evans, Jane Thompson, Joanne Newell, Lara Morcombe, Lyn McGaurr, Martine Lleonart, Miriam Cannell, Rowan McKinnon and Rebecca Turner.

The title page illustrations were drawn by Mick Weldon. In the South Pacific Gateways chapter, Paul Harding wrote and researched the Australian territories, Rowan wrote the Papua New Guinea section, Martine wrote Hawai'i and Errol wrote New Zealand.

The myriad travel possibilities in the region were researched by Leonie Mugavin. Quentin Frayne beat the language sections into shape. Matt King and Val Tellini tracked down illustrations and slides, and Indra Kilfoyle designed the book's cover.

Scope of the Book

This book does not cover all the islands of the Pacific Ocean – partly to keep the book to a manageable size and partly because these places are covered in other substantial Lonely Planet titles. The Pacific island states not included in this book (Papua New Guinea, New Zealand and Hawai'i) are included in the South Pacific Gateways chapter, but to get the full story, see their individual guidebooks. Norfolk and Lord Howe islands (also in South Pacific Gateways) are covered more substantially in our *New South Wales* guide. Easter Island is also covered in our guide to Chile. With so much to be said about each of these destinations, we hope you'll be thankful that we've saved you lugging the extra text around the Pacific.

THANKS
Many thanks to the travellers who used the last edition and wrote to us with helpful hints, advice and interesting anecdotes. Your names appear in the back of this book.

Foreword

ABOUT LONELY PLANET GUIDEBOOKS

The story begins with a classic travel adventure: Tony and Maureen Wheeler's 1972 journey across Europe and Asia to Australia. Useful information about the overland trail did not exist at that time, so Tony and Maureen published the first Lonely Planet guidebook to meet a growing need.

From a kitchen table, then from a tiny office in Melbourne (Australia), Lonely Planet has become the largest independent travel publisher in the world, an international company with offices in Melbourne, Oakland (USA), London (UK) and Paris (France).

Today Lonely Planet guidebooks cover the globe. There is an ever-growing list of books and there's information in a variety of forms and media. Some things haven't changed. The main aim is still to help make it possible for adventurous travellers to get out there – to explore and better understand the world.

At Lonely Planet we believe travellers can make a positive contribution to the countries they visit – if they respect their host communities and spend their money wisely. Since 1986 a percentage of the income from each book has been donated to aid projects and human rights campaigns.

Updates Lonely Planet thoroughly updates each guidebook as often as possible. This usually means there are around two years between editions, although for more unusual or more stable destinations the gap can be longer. Check the imprint page (following the colour map at the beginning of the book) for publication dates.

Between editions up-to-date information is available in two free newsletters – the paper *Planet Talk* and email *Comet* (to subscribe, contact any Lonely Planet office) – and on our Web site at www.lonelyplanet.com. The *Upgrades* section of the Web site covers a number of important and volatile destinations and is regularly updated by Lonely Planet authors. *Scoop* covers news and current affairs relevant to travellers. And, lastly, the *Thorn Tree* bulletin board and *Postcards* section of the site carry unverified, but fascinating, reports from travellers.

Correspondence The process of creating new editions begins with the letters, postcards and emails received from travellers. This correspondence often includes suggestions, criticisms and comments about the current editions. Interesting excerpts are immediately passed on via newsletters and the Web site, and everything goes to our authors to be verified when they're researching on the road. We're keen to get more feedback from organisations or individuals who represent communities visited by travellers.

Lonely Planet gathers information for everyone who's curious about the planet – and especially for those who explore it first-hand. Through guidebooks, phrasebooks, activity guides, maps, literature, newsletters, image library, TV series and Web site we act as an information exchange for a worldwide community of travellers.

Research Authors aim to gather sufficient practical information to enable travellers to make informed choices and to make the mechanics of a journey run smoothly. They also research historical and cultural background to help enrich the travel experience and allow travellers to understand and respond appropriately to cultural and environmental issues.

Authors don't stay in every hotel because that would mean spending a couple of months in each medium-sized city and, no, they don't eat at every restaurant because that would mean stretching belts beyond capacity. They do visit hotels and restaurants to check standards and prices, but feedback based on readers' direct experiences can be very helpful.

Many of our authors work undercover, others aren't so secretive. None of them accept freebies in exchange for positive write-ups. And none of our guidebooks contain any advertising.

Production Authors submit their raw manuscripts and maps to offices in Australia, USA, UK or France. Editors and cartographers – all experienced travellers themselves – then begin the process of assembling the pieces. When the book finally hits the shops, some things are already out of date, we start getting feedback from readers and the process begins again ...

WARNING & REQUEST

Things change – prices go up, schedules change, good places go bad and bad places go bankrupt – nothing stays the same. So, if you find things better or worse, recently opened or long since closed, please tell us and help make the next edition even more accurate and useful. We genuinely value all the feedback we receive. Julie Young coordinates a well travelled team that reads and acknowledges every letter, postcard and email and ensures that every morsel of information finds its way to the appropriate authors, editors and cartographers for verification.

Everyone who writes to us will find their name in the next edition of the appropriate guidebook. They will also receive the latest issue of *Planet Talk*, our quarterly printed newsletter, or *Comet*, our monthly email newsletter. Subscriptions to both newsletters are free. The very best contributions will be rewarded with a free guidebook.

Excerpts from your correspondence may appear in new editions of Lonely Planet guidebooks, the Lonely Planet Web site, *Planet Talk* or *Comet*, so please let us know if you *don't* want your letter published or your name acknowledged.

Send all correspondence to the Lonely Planet office closest to you:

Australia: Locked Bag 1, Footscray, Victoria 3011
USA: 150 Linden St, Oakland, CA 94607
UK: 10A Spring Place, London NW5 3BH
France: 1 rue du Dahomey, 75011 Paris

Or email us at: talk2us@lonelyplanet.com.au

For news, views and updates see our Web site: www.lonelyplanet.com

HOW TO USE A LONELY PLANET GUIDEBOOK

The best way to use a Lonely Planet guidebook is any way you choose. At Lonely Planet we believe the most memorable travel experiences are often those that are unexpected, and the finest discoveries are those you make yourself. Guidebooks are not intended to be used as if they provide a detailed set of infallible instructions!

Contents All Lonely Planet guidebooks follow roughly the same format. The Facts about the Destination chapters or sections give background information ranging from history to weather. Facts for the Visitor gives practical information on issues like visas and health. Getting There & Away gives a brief starting point for researching travel to and from the destination. Getting Around gives an overview of the transport options when you arrive.

The peculiar demands of each destination determine how subsequent chapters are broken up, but some things remain constant. We always start with background, then proceed to sights, places to stay, places to eat, entertainment, getting there and away, and getting around information – in that order.

Heading Hierarchy Lonely Planet headings are used in a strict hierarchical structure that can be visualised as a set of Russian dolls. Each heading (and its following text) is encompassed by any preceding heading that is higher on the hierarchical ladder.

Entry Points We do not assume guidebooks will be read from beginning to end, but that people will dip into them. The traditional entry points are the list of contents and the index. In addition, however, some books have a complete list of maps and an index map illustrating map coverage.

There may also be a colour map that shows highlights. These highlights are dealt with in greater detail in the Facts for the Visitor chapter, along with planning questions and suggested itineraries. Each chapter covering a geographical region usually begins with a locator map and another list of highlights. Once you find something of interest in a list of highlights, turn to the index.

Maps Maps play a crucial role in Lonely Planet guidebooks and include a huge amount of information. A legend is printed on the back page. We seek to have complete consistency between maps and text, and to have every important place in the text captured on a map. Map key numbers usually start in the top left corner.

Although inclusion in a guidebook usually implies a recommendation we cannot list every good place. Exclusion does not necessarily imply criticism. In fact there are a number of reasons why we might exclude a place – sometimes it is simply inappropriate to encourage an influx of travellers.

Introduction

The islands of the Pacific Ocean have had a reputation as an untouched paradise ever since 18th century European explorers took home romantic stories about South Sea islands and islanders.

Modern visitors to the region are often surprised to discover bustling cosmopolitan cities, universities, libraries and, of course, tourist resorts by the hundreds. However, there really are places in the Pacific that conform to the tropical paradise myth: some seem entirely untouched by western society and others unaffected by humans at all. From the mountain rainforests of the high islands to perfect beaches, underwater worlds and thriving coral reefs, the region's natural beauty is spectacular and accessible.

The Pacific Ocean is huge, as large as all the world's other oceans put together. Yet its landmasses are relatively small – tiny dots of land separated by enormous distances of open sea. It's hardly surprising then that the cultures of the Pacific islands – conveniently divided into Polynesia (Many Islands), Melanesia (Black Islands) and Micronesia (Small Islands) – are so diverse. What is surprising is that these cultures also have many similarities in their religion, languages and customs.

The history of oceanic voyaging that produced these similarities has amazed westerners from the time of James Cook. Since the successive waves of Lapita settlement from as early as 1500 BC, the Pacific Ocean has been criss-crossed by innumerable journeys by canoe. Later, during the 18th and 19th centuries, these criss-crossings were intersected by the paths of curious, proselytising or entrepreneurial Europeans.

The Pacific's history as a place of journeying is a tradition that has continued into our own age. With few mineral resources or other economic options, the journeys of modern-day travellers now form a mainstay of the economies of many Pacific nations.

This is one industry in which the islands excel, with a natural advantage over many other places. Tourist infrastructure varies, but the natural beauty of the islands is unrivalled and traditional cultures are strong and proudly displayed. Remnants of the ancient Pacific remain, with stone statues and monuments still standing in many places (those of Easter Island are among the world's most famous). Modern artists can be seen honouring their past, re-creating and reinterpreting ancient themes in their artwork. Meanwhile traditional rites, dances and feasts are performed throughout the region, restating the vitality of its many cultures.

The islands offer countless opportunities for yachting, kayaking, bushwalking, swimming, diving and snorkelling. There's no obligation to do any of these activities, though. The paralysis that afflicts Pacific travellers is legendary, and it doesn't take long to get used to lengthy spells under the shade of a tree reading a good book between leisurely dips in the crystal-clear sea.

Where is the South Pacific?

When the Spanish conquistador Balboa gazed south from Central America in 1513, he named the ocean he had discovered 'Mar del Sur', the South Seas – a name printed on many maps of the 16th and 17th centuries. Even after Magellan named the ocean the 'Pacific' in 1521 for the calmness of its water, the 'South Seas' and 'South Sea Islanders' were still associated with the tropical Pacific and its people both north and south of the equator. Modern regional institutions have continued this tradition, even if they include countries north of the equator, for example the University of the South Pacific. In 1999 the inter-governmental South Pacific Forum decided to correct the error, renaming itself the Pacific Islands Forum in recognition of its northern members.

Facts about the South Pacific

HISTORY

It was about 50,000 years ago that people first reached the Pacific islands, arriving in New Guinea from South-East Asia via Indonesia. These people, now known as Papuans, share ancestry with those of Australia's first Aboriginals. Moving slowly east, the Papuans were halted in the northern Solomon Islands about 25,000 years ago, lacking the technology and skills to cross the increasingly wide stretches of open ocean. Subsequent people, collectively known as Austronesians, moved into the area from the west, mingling with the Papuans and eventually becoming the highly diverse group of people we conveniently group together as 'Melanesians'. New Guinea and the Solomons were the only inhabited islands in the Pacific for many thousands of years.

The wider seas from the Solomons to Vanuatu were finally crossed in about 1500 BC. An Austronesian people now known as the Lapita (see the boxed text in the 'South Pacific Arts' special section) finally developed the technology and the skills to cross open seas and quickly expanded through New Caledonia, Fiji, Tonga and Samoa. In Fiji, Tonga and Samoa the Lapita developed the culture we now know as Polynesian.

The Melanesians of New Guinea and the Solomons mingled a little with the Lapita and followed them east across the Pacific. In time Melanesians came to dominate New Guinea, the Solomons, Vanuatu, New Caledonia and Fiji.

The Lapitas' descendants, the Polynesians of Samoa and Tonga, 'paused' there for about a thousand years, until even more advanced ocean vessels and skills were developed. They crossed the longer ocean stretches to the east to the Society and Marquesas island groups (in modern French Polynesia) some time around 200 BC. From there, voyaging canoes travelled south-west to Rarotonga and the southern Cook Islands, south-east to Rapa Nui (Easter Island; 300 AD), north to Hawai'i (400 AD) and south-west past Rarotonga to Aotearoa (New Zealand; 900 AD).

The myriad islands and atolls of Micronesia, north of the Solomons and New Guinea, were populated by several groups of people over a long period. Western Micronesia was reached by Asian people island-hopping through the Philippines in about 1500 BC. Melanesians moved north into central Micronesia (1000 BC), and eastern Micronesia was settled by Polynesians spreading outwards from their base in Fiji, Samoa and Tonga (1-500 AD).

Although the predominant direction of human movement was from west to east, population pressure and the occasional religious disagreement prompted a constant movement of people across the oceans. There are Polynesians in Melanesia's eastern islands as well as in eastern Micronesia. Largely-Melanesian Fiji is also home to many Polynesians and Micronesians.

The settlement of the Pacific Ocean was the most remarkable feat of ocean sailing up to that time. All but the furthest-flung islands of the Pacific were colonised by 200 BC – 1200 years before the Vikings crossed the Atlantic.

Melanesians embarked on regular trade routes and some war missions, but it was Micronesians and, to a lesser degree, Polynesians who travelled the broadest stretches of open ocean (see the boxed text 'Voyaging & Navigation'). Almost no Pacific islands were cut off entirely from other cultures. The presence of the *kumara* (sweet potato) in the Pacific islands confirms that at least some journeys were made as far east as South America, probably from the Marquesas. Traditional stories also indicate exploratory journeys into Antarctic waters 'not seen by the sun'.

There is more information about ancient Pacific cultures in the Society & Conduct and Religion sections later in this chapter.

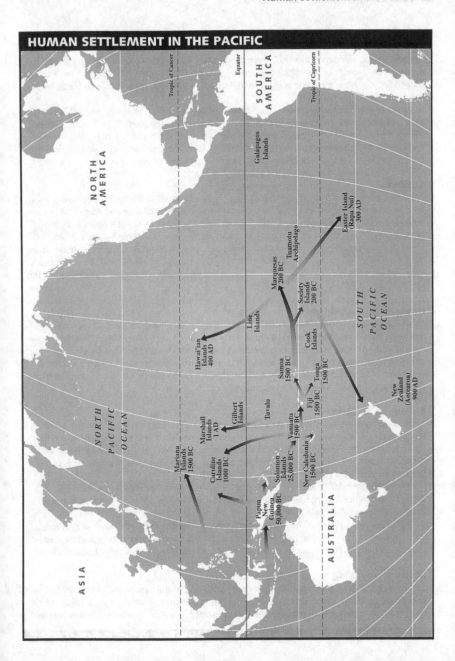

HUMAN SETTLEMENT IN THE PACIFIC

Voyaging & Navigation

Ancient Pacific islanders' voyages were motivated by war, trade, colonisation, the search for resources or sometimes merely by curiosity and pride. The Tongans – 'Vikings of the Pacific' – ruled Samoa, Niue and eastern Fiji with an iron fist, and raided from Tuvalu to the Solomon Islands, 2700km to the west!

At the time of European contact, prodigious feats of navigation and voyaging still occurred, although not on as grand a scale as previously. The navigator-priest Tupaia, who boarded Cook's *Endeavour* in Tahiti, could name around 100 islands between the Marquesas and Fiji, and he directed Cook's search for islands west of Tahiti. For the entire circuitous journey to Java in Indonesia, Tupaia could always point in the direction of his homeland.

Canoes

The term 'canoe' *(vaka* or *va'a)* is misleading. The same word describes small dugouts used for river navigation, giant war vessels accommodating hundreds of men and 25m-long ocean-voyaging craft. Ocean-voyaging vessels, either double canoes or single canoes with outriggers, carried one (or more) masts and sails of woven pandanus. James Cook and contemporary observers estimated that Pacific canoes were capable of speeds greater than their own ships; probably 150 to 250km/day, so that trips of 5000km could be comfortably achieved with available provisions. See Books in the Regional Facts for the Visitor chapter for literature about Pacific canoes.

Navigation Techniques

Initial exploratory journeys would often follow the migratory flights of birds. Once a new land had been discovered, the method of rediscovery was remembered and communicated mostly by way of which stars to follow. Fine tuning of these directions was possible by observing the direction from which certain winds blew, the currents, wave fronts reflecting from islands and the flights of land birds. In Micronesia, elaborate stick charts (see the boxed text in the Marshall Islands chapter) were used to record sailing instructions.

European Theories

Many European explorers were unable to believe that a stone age culture without a written language or use of the compass could have accomplished such amazing feats of navigation. Some assumed that an earlier, more advanced culture must have existed. They proposed that islanders were the barbaric survivors of this ancient empire, living on the mountain tops of the sunken continent of Mu.

Once the continent of Mu was discounted, a wide range of possible origins for Pacific islanders was considered, including India, Israel and the Americas. Others proposed that the islands had been settled quite accidentally, as fishermen were blown off course and lost at sea.

The majority of evidence, however, points towards mostly-deliberate west to east migration. This conclusion rests on linguistic, genetic, anthropological and archaeological studies, vegetation patterns, computer modelling of wind and currents, and a study of oral traditions.

Modern Voyaging

The voyaging skills of Pacific islanders may not match that of their ancestors, but the traditional knowledge of navigational methods is still being put to everyday use. Not only small inter-island trips, but long-distance voyages have been used to test many theories about ocean voyaging.

Voyaging & Navigation

Probably the most famous such voyage, that of Thor Heyerdahl's *Kon Tiki* from South America to the Tuamotus in 1947, was made in an attempt to prove the now discredited theory that Polynesia was populated from South America.

In the last few decades, a resurgence of long-distance voyages along traditional routes has refined theories about canoe construction and navigational methods. Among such journeys, the 25m-long outrigger canoe *Tarratai* was sailed from Kiribati 2500km south to Fiji in 1976. That same year the voyage of the 20m *Hokule'a*, which used traditional navigation methods for the 4250km trip from Hawai'i to Tahiti, sparked a resurgence of interest in traditional navigation.

Other voyaging canoes include the 21m *Hawaiki Nui*, which sailed 4000km from Tahiti to Aotearoa in 1985. More recently, in 1995 *Te Au o Tonga*, captained by the former prime minister of the Cook Islands, Sir Thomas Davis (Papa Tom), sailed from Rarotonga to Tahiti, on to Hawai'i, and back to Rarotonga. Part of the cargo on the last leg was less than traditional: Papa Tom's new 1200cc Harley Davidson.

The *Hokule'a* and *Te Au o Tonga*, among other great vaka, continue to make long voyages. See also the boxed text 'Mau Piailug' in the Federated States of Micronesia chapter.

BY PERMISSION OF THE NATIONAL LIBRARY OF AUSTRALIA

'Pacific Ocean – a native canoe meeting strangers off the Murray Islands'. Painted by Edwin Augustus Porcher (watercolour, 1845). Driven by two sails and steered by paddle, this form of medium-sized canoe was used for inter-island travel.

European Explorers

Like Pacific islanders, European explorers came in search of resources (gold and spices initially), and were driven often by curiosity or national pride. However, Europeans were also inspired by one overpowering myth: the search for *Terra Australis Incognita*, the unknown Great Southern Continent.

Scientific philosophies since the time of Ptolemy have predicted the presence of a huge landmass in the southern hemisphere to counter the Earth's northern continents. Otherwise, it was believed, the globe would be top heavy and would fall over! Belief in this southern continent was unqualified; explorers were not asked to confirm its existence, but to chart its coasts and parlay with its people. In the absence of hard facts, Terra Australis was peopled with strange heathens and magical creatures, and rumoured to be rich in gold. The biblical tale of King Solomon required the presence of vast gold mines in some unknown location. What could be a better spot than Terra Australis?

Spanish In 1521 the Portuguese Ferdinand Magellan led a Spanish expedition that discovered, at the southern tip of the Americas, an entrance to the ocean he named 'Mar Pacifico', the Pacific Ocean, for the calmness of its seas. With extraordinary bad luck, and lacking the island-finding skills of Pacific islanders, Magellan saw only two small uninhabited islands until he had sailed north-west across almost the entire ocean to Guam in Micronesia.

On Guam the first contact between Pacific islander and European followed a pattern that was to become all too familiar. The Micronesian (and Polynesian) attitude was that all property was shared. Guam's islanders helped themselves to one of the expedition's small boats and Magellan retaliated – seven islanders were killed. Magellan himself was killed two months later while in the Philippines, but not before he became the first person to circumnavigate the globe (having previously visited the Philippines from the other direction).

Spaniard Don Alvaro de Mendaña sailed twice, in 1567 and 1595, in search of Terra Australis. On his first voyage he sailed west across the Pacific to the Solomon Islands, which he named for King Solomon's gold. Here, conflict with the locals arose when islanders were unable to supply the resources Mendaña needed to reprovision.

It took Mendaña nearly 30 years to gain approval for his disastrous second voyage. An estimated 200 islanders were killed in the Marquesas when conflict broke out; there was more conflict with locals when they reached the Solomons, and fighting spread to the crew. Mendaña himself died of malaria, and the expedition returned to Peru under the command of the more humane Pedro Fernández de Quirós.

Quirós led another expedition to the Pacific in 1605, discovering the Tuamotu Islands and Vanuatu (see the boxed text about Quirós in the Vanuatu chapter).

Dutch Le Maire and Schouten's 1616 expedition, again searching for Terra Australis, revealed to Europe the Tongan islands and Futuna. Jacob Roggeveen spotted Bora Bora in the Society Islands in 1722, and Tutuila and Upolu in Samoa. Abel Tasman became the most famous Dutch explorer after charting Tasmania and the east coast of New Zealand in 1642, then sailing on to make contact with the southern islands of Tonga and the islands of Fiji.

English In 1767, Samuel Wallis – *still* searching for Terra Australis – landed on Tahiti and claimed it for England, but the greatest of the English explorers was James Cook (see the boxed text).

Following the most famous of maritime mutinies, Fletcher Christian captained the *Bounty* to discover Rarotonga in the southern Cook Islands in 1789. See the boxed text 'Mutiny on the Bounty' in the Pitcairn Islands chapter.

French The most famous French explorer, Louis-Antoine de Bougainville, came upon Tahiti and claimed it for France in 1768. He went on to the Samoan islands, which he

Captain James Cook

James Cook (1728-79) was born in Yorkshire, the son of a farm labourer. He showed early aptitude for maths, joined the navy aged 27 and went on to become England's most famous explorer and the most methodical navigator and map-maker the Pacific ever saw.

During Cook's three journeys to the Pacific (in 1768-71, 1772-75 and 1776-79), he charted New Zealand, New Caledonia and the east coast of Australia. He also landed at Tahiti and Tonga (see the boxed text 'Cook's 'Friendly Islands' in the Tonga chapter). Although he spotted a few new islands, Cook's greatness was in the accuracy of his maps and scientific observations. And his greatest contribution to exploration science was something he did not add to his maps – the fabled *Terra Australis Incognita*.

Cook's instructions were to map and claim the Great South Land, but instead

MICK WELDON

he was finally to prove it did not exist. After Cook had sailed from west to east at 60° south, only a fool could still believe such a land existed. Such fools did exist, and they launched vicious attacks on Cook's methods, but they could no longer persuade governments and companies to finance exploratory voyages.

With the final dismissal of the Terra Australis myth, interest in Pacific exploration diminished. As one Frenchman said: 'Cook left his successors with little to do but admire his exploits.'

On his third and last voyage, the newly-promoted Captain Cook revisited New Zealand and Tahiti, then sailed north to map Hawai'i. On Kealakekua, in the Hawai'ian islands, Cook was killed while making a last attempt to teach locals the European concept of property.

---

named the Navigator Islands for the skills of the canoeists sailing circles around his ship. He went on to Vanuatu and discovered Australia's Great Barrier Reef. Bougainville's impact was greater than dots on a map, however; his accounts of the South Pacific sparked massive interest in Europe and created the myth of a southern paradise.

In 1827, Dumont d'Urville sailed the Pacific searching for his lost countryman, the Comte de La Pérouse, who had sunk in the Solomon Islands in 1788 (see the boxed text 'Disaster on the Reef' in that country's chapter). D'Urville's writings of this and another journey, ten years later, were to establish the concept of the three great subdivisions of the Pacific: Melanesia, Micronesia and Polynesia.

Missionaries

After a few largely unsuccessful Spanish Catholic forays into Micronesia during the 17th century, the first major attempt to bring Christianity to the Pacific was by English Protestants. Horrified – and inspired – by tales of cannibalism, human sacrifice, promiscuity and infanticide, the newly formed London Missionary Society (LMS) outfitted missionary outposts on Tahiti, Tonga and in the Marquesas in 1797. These first holy crusades were no roaring success – within two years the Tongan and Marquesan missions were abandoned. The Tahitian mission did survive but its success was limited. For a decade only a handful of islanders were tempted to join the new religion.

Other Protestant groups soon joined the battle. The new players were the Wesleyan Missionary Society (WMS), fresh from moderate victory in New Zealand, and the American Board of Commissioners for Foreign Missions (ABCFM), following great success in Christianising Hawai'i. The WMS and ABCFM both failed miserably in the Marquesas, but fared marginally better in Tonga.

In the 1830s, French Catholic missionaries established missions in the Marquesas and on Tahiti. Catholic missionaries were often as pleased to convert a Protestant as a heathen, and the fierce rivalry between the different denominations extended to their islander converts. Religious conflicts fitted easily into the already complex political melee of Pacific society, and local chiefs gleefully used the two Christian camps for their own purposes.

Despite the slow start, missionary success grew, and by the 1820s missionary influence on Tahiti was enormous. The Bible was translated into Tahitian, a Protestant work ethic was being instilled, tattooing was discouraged, promiscuity was guarded against by nightly 'moral police' and the most 'heathen' practices such as human sacrifice were unknown. From Tahiti, Tonga and Hawai'i, Christianity spread throughout the Pacific.

Missionaries' success was due to three major factors. Clever politics played a part, particularly the conversion of influential Tongan chief Taufa'ahau and the Tahitian Pomare family. Another factor was the perceived link between European wealth and Christianity: missionaries sought to 'civilise' as well as Christianise, and islanders desired European tools and skills. Finally, the message of salvation fell on especially attentive ears because of the massive depopulation occurring through the spread of disease.

Two rather remarkable missionaries had enormous influence on the Christianisation of the region: the 'plodding and laborious' John Thomas (WMS), who arrived in Tonga in 1826, and the extraordinary John Williams (LMS), who travelled between many islands from 1818 until his death in Vanuatu in 1839. Many Polynesian converts also took up missionary work themselves.

Missionaries changed the Pacific forever. While traditional culture was devastated and customs such as tattooing banned, human sacrifice and ritual warfare – ancient traditions about which it is harder to be nostalgic – were also curtailed. Missionaries shielded islanders from the excesses of some traders, and it was missionary pressure that finally put an end to the blackbirding trade (see later in this section). Putting Pacific languages into written form, initially in translations of the Bible, was another major contribution. While many missionaries deliberately destroyed 'heathen' Pacific artefacts and beliefs, others diligently recorded myths and oral traditions that would otherwise have been lost. A substantial portion of our knowledge of Pacific history and traditional culture comes from the work of missionary-historians.

Manoeuvrings by both missionary and islanders resulted in substantial political changes. Ruling dynasties in Tonga, Tahiti and Fiji all owed some of their success to missionary backing – just as missionary success owed a lot to those dynasties.

Trade

Whaling European whalers enthusiastically hunted in the Pacific from the late 18th century. The trade peaked in the mid-19th century, then declined rapidly as whale products were superseded by other materials. The effect on the Pacific's whale population was catastrophic, but the effect on Pacific islanders was complex. There were many opportunities for trade as ships resupplied, and many Pacific islanders took the opportunity to travel on whaling ships. Some islanders, however, travelled without consenting, and conflict was common; whalers of the Pacific were not the most gentle of men.

Beches-de-Mer Also known as trepang, sea cucumbers or sea slugs, the beche-de-mer is a marine organism related to starfish and urchins. An Asian delicacy, Pacific beches-de-mer were sought by early 19th century European traders to exchange for Chinese tea. Beches-de-mer were relatively abundant, and important trading relations were forged with islanders. For the most part the trade was mutually beneficial, with islanders trading eagerly for metal, cloth, tobacco and muskets. In contrast with the sandalwood trade, the trade in beches-de-mer was largely nonviolent.

Sandalwood Nineteenth century Europeans trading with China found another Pacific resource in fragrant sandalwood, used in China for ornamental carving and cabinet-making, as well as for burning as incense. By the 1820s, traders had stripped the sandalwood forests of Hawai'i, and forests on islands to the south were sought. Fiji, Vanuatu, the Solomons and New Caledonia's extensive sandalwood forests became the focus for traders keen to satisfy the demands of the Chinese market.

On each new island, payment for sandalwood was initially low. A small piece of metal, a goat or a dog was sometimes sufficient to buy a boatload of the aromatic wood. But as the supply of slow-growing sandalwood dwindled, the price rose – islanders demanded guns, ammunition, tobacco or assistance in war as payment.

While the sandalwood trade in Fiji was fairly orderly under the supervision of local chiefs, spheres of chiefly influence in the Solomons, Vanuatu and New Caledonia were much smaller and traders had difficultly establishing lasting relationships with islanders. The sandalwood trade was the most violent of any trades in the Pacific, and Melanesians' savage reputation in Europe was not improved. There were many attacks on ships' crews, sometimes motivated by a greed for plunder, but often these attacks were a response to previous white atrocities. Melanesians assumed that all Europeans belonged to the one kin group, and thus were accountable for one-another's crimes.

The sandalwood trade was far from sustainable. Island after island was stripped of its forests, and the trade petered out in the 1860s with the removal of the last accessible stands.

Blackbirding

In the late 19th century, cheap labour was sought for various Pacific industries such as mines and plantations. Pacific islanders were also 'recruited' to labour in Australia, Fiji, New Caledonia, Samoa and Peru. Satisfying the demand for labour was a major commercial activity from the 1860s.

In some cases islanders were keen to sign up, seeking to share the benefits of European wealth. Often, though, they were tricked into boarding ships, either deceived about the length of time for which they were contracted, or sometimes enticed aboard by sailors dressed as priests. In many cases no pretence was attempted: islanders were simply herded onto slaving ships at gunpoint.

The populations of many small, barely viable islands were devastated by blackbirders – Tokelau lost almost half its population to Peruvian slaving ships in 1863, while the Tongan island of 'Ata lost 40% of its population, and as a result is today uninhabited. People were also taken as slaves from Tuvalu, New Caledonia, Easter Island, Vanuatu and the Solomons.

Similar recruitment practices – trickery and deceit – were common when Indian labourers were transported to Fiji in the 1870s. See History in the Fiji chapter for more details.

Blackbirding was finally halted at the end of the 19th century after persistent lobbying by missionaries. Their campaigns in the UK and Australia finally resulted in the banning of overseas labour recruitment to Australia (in 1904), Samoa (in 1913) and Fiji (in 1916). Some islanders were restored to their homelands but many never returned. A sizeable Melanesian population remains in Australia's Queensland, and there is, of course, a huge Indian population in Fiji.

Epidemics & Depopulation

A population of a certain size is required for a contagious disease to establish itself. For the most part, Pacific islands lacked that population. The larger landmasses of Melanesia had (and still have) malaria, but the smaller islands of Micronesia and Polynesia knew only mild outbreaks of leprosy and filariasis (a form of elephantiasis).

The squalid cities of 17th century Europe bred diseases (and resistant survivors) rather more effectively. The infection-ridden vessels of explorers, missionaries and traders brought diseases to which the peoples of the Pacific had little resistance: cholera, measles, smallpox, influenza, pneumonia, scarlet fever, chicken-pox, whooping cough, dysentery, venereal diseases and even the common cold all took a terrible toll.

Almost all Polynesian populations fell by at least half, while Micronesian and Melanesian populations suffered even more. Some Micronesian islands were reduced to 10% of their previous population level, and some islands of Vanuatu dropped to just 5%.

Most recently, the post-WWI influenza epidemic of 1918-19 devastated Tonga (killing 8% of the population), Nauru (16%), Fiji (5%) and Western Samoa, where 22% of the population died within a few months.

European Colonialism

Once European traders were established in the Pacific, many began agitating for their home countries to intervene and protect their interests. Some missionaries also lobbied for colonial takeover, hoping that European law would protect islanders from the lawless traders! Gradually, and sometimes reluctantly, European powers acted by declaring protectorates and then by annexing Pacific states.

Germany, one country which was *not* reluctant, annexed the Marshall Islands, northern Solomons, Nauru, the Marianas, Palau, the Carolines (now in the Federated States of Micronesia) and Western Samoa between 1878 and 1899. The treaty that gave Germany Western Samoa in 1899 ceded American Samoa to the US. This added to the Phoenix Islands (now in Kiribati), which the US and Britain had claimed in 1836.

After annexing French Polynesia (1840s) and New Caledonia (1853), the French lost interest for a while before claiming Wallis & Futuna (1880s) and going into partnership with the UK in Vanuatu in 1906.

Contrary to popular opinion, Britain was a reluctant Pacific empire builder. However, it ended up with the largest of all Pacific empires after being forced by various lobby groups to assume responsibilities for the Phoenix Islands in 1836, then Fiji, Tokelau, the Cooks, the Gilbert & Ellice Islands (modern Kiribati and Tuvalu), the southern Solomons and Niue between 1874 and 1900, and finally Vanuatu in 1906. Between 1900 and 1925, the UK happily offloaded the Cooks, Niue and Tokelau to eager New Zealand.

WWI & WWII

WWI had little effect in the Pacific, except to exchange German colonial rulers in Micronesia, Samoa and Nauru for Japan, New Zealand, Australia and the UK. Germany was more concerned with events in Europe and didn't resist these Pacific takeovers. When the USA joined the war, the German gunboat *Cormoran* was scuttled by its crew in Guam's harbour to avoid its capture.

In contrast, the Pacific was a major arena of conflict during WWII. The war with Japan was fought through the Micronesian territory Japan had won from Germany in WWI, in Papua New Guinea (PNG) and in the Solomon Islands.

Initially Japan expanded south and southwest from its Micronesian territories almost unhindered until 1942, when it was turned back from PNG at the Battle of the Coral Sea and in the north Pacific at the Battle of Midway. From 1944 the USA pushed the stubbornly defending Japanese back island by island. Despite such defence the Japanese were pushed out of Micronesia and eventually back to Japan by US attacks. US bombers based in the Marianas punished Japanese cities for ten months until 6 August 1945, when the *Enola Gay* took off from Tinian to drop an atomic bomb on Hiroshima. Days later another was dropped on Nagasaki, and the Pacific war was over.

Not surprisingly, the suffering of islanders during the Pacific war was immense. Japanese forces in Micronesia, seemingly without motive, forced the transport of large numbers of islanders between various islands. People were concentrated in areas without adequate food, thousands died from hunger and thousands more were executed by the Japanese as an Allied victory became apparent. It is difficult to establish the frequency of rape of islanders by both Japanese and Allied forces, but it is undeniable that it happened.

Many Pacific islanders fought in the war, fighting in the Pacific, Africa and Europe. Soldiers from Fiji, the Solomons, Western and American Samoa, Tonga, Palau, Pohnpei, French Polynesia and New Caledonia served in the armed forces. Their valour cemented relations with white allies. Fijian Corporal Sefania Sukanaivalu was posthumously awarded the Victoria Cross in 1943.

WWII had a lasting effect on the region. Most obviously, Japan's Micronesian colonies were taken over by the USA, becoming the Trust Territory of the Pacific Islands. However, there were also more widespread and subtle effects of the war. There was a huge improvement in roads and other infrastructure on many islands. There was also an input of money, food and other supplies

that contributed towards the development of so-called 'cargo cults' (see Religion later in this chapter).

WWII hastened the end of traditional colonialism in the Pacific, the relative equality between white and black US soldiers prompting islanders to question why they were still subservient to the British and the French. Many independence leaders were influenced at this time.

Postwar History

From Western Samoa in 1962 through to Vanuatu in 1980, most of the Pacific island states gained independence (or partial independence) from their former colonial rulers. This was a relatively bloodless transition, with colonial masters as keen to ditch their expensive responsibilities as islanders were to gain independence. It took longer for the USA to dismantle its Trust Territory of Micronesia, slowed by the 'need' to maintain a military presence. Between 1975 and 1990, however, each of those Micronesian states except Guam achieved some level of independence. At the end of the 20th century only a handful of Pacific territories were still in the hands of the USA, France, Chile, and New Zealand. See Government & Politics later in this chapter.

GEOGRAPHY

The Pacific Ocean is huge – it covers 165,250,000 sq km (64,500,000 sq miles), which is a third of the world's surface, and is larger than all the Earth's land combined. The thousands of islands of the Pacific, however, have a total land area of less than 1,300,000 sq km – the bulk of which (1,100,000 sq km) is in the relatively massive islands of New Guinea, New Zealand and Hawai'i.

The French explorer Dumont d'Urville conveniently divided the Pacific – largely along racial and cultural grounds – into three major subdivisions: Melanesia (Greek for the 'Black Islands'), composed of New Guinea, the Solomons, Vanuatu, New Caledonia and Fiji; Micronesia (Small Islands), the atolls and small islands north and northeast of New Guinea and the Solomons; and Polynesia (Many Islands), the huge triangle

SIMON ROWE

Saipan, in the Northern Mariana Islands, is littered with rusting WWII debris.

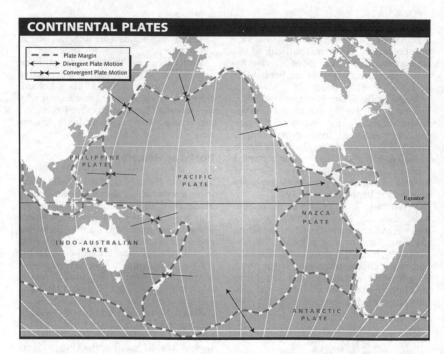

CONTINENTAL PLATES

Plate Margin
Divergent Plate Motion
Convergent Plate Motion

PHILIPPINE
PLATE

PACIFIC
PLATE

Equator

NAZCA
PLATE

INDO-AUSTRALIAN
PLATE

ANTARCTIC
PLATE

of islands bounded by Hawai'i, Easter Island and New Zealand. Although the divisions are artificial, it is a useful and relevant partitioning of the Pacific. The characteristics of the three areas (Polynesia, Melanesia and Micronesia) are summarised in introductions to each of the three supra-chapters in this book.

Three main island types occur in the Pacific: continental, high and low. Large, continental islands exist only in Melanesia and New Zealand. And of the smaller islands, 'high' islands are usually the peaks of volcanoes, whether extinct or active, while 'low' islands are generally formed by coral growth on sinking submarine volcanoes (see the boxed text 'Coral Atolls' later in this chapter).

GEOLOGY

The surface of the Earth is composed of ten interlocking continental and oceanic plates, which float on the planet's molten mantle. The floor of the Pacific Ocean is largely composed of one enormous plate (called the

Pacific plate). The much smaller Nazca plate is in the Pacific's south-eastern corner.

The boundary between the two plates is a 8000km-long line of submarine volcanoes called a 'constructive fault', running roughly north-south at the longitude of Easter Island. From this fault, newly ejected material adds to the two plates. This pushes the Pacific plate north-west at about 17cm per year, and pushes the Nazca plate south-east.

Where the Pacific's oceanic plates meet neighbouring continental plates, the heavier oceanic plates are forced hundreds of kilometres down into the Earth's molten magma. Deep trenches are formed along the seams, the world's deepest being the Mariana Trench (see the boxed text in the Northern Mariana Islands chapter). Molten, mineral-rich material from the diving plate rises to form volcanic archipelagoes such as the Mariana Island chain. The line where the Pacific plate meets the Indo-Australian plate can be followed north along the island

Coral Atolls

The first person to recognise that atolls are made from coral growth built up around the edges of submerged volcanic mountain peaks was Charles Darwin. (See the boxed text 'How the Islands Formed' in the Tuvalu chapter.)

Submarine volcanoes are common on the ocean floor, and some of them grow above the sea's surface to become islands. Once an island exists, coral (see Flora & Fauna later in this chapter) begins to grow around its coast. If subsequent plate movement causes the volcano to sink again, the coral continues to grow in order to stay close to the sea's surface (coral requires sunlight and cannot live in water deeper than 40m). As the central island sinks, a fringing lagoon forms between the island and the reef. A coral atoll is formed when the island finally sinks completely, leaving a ring of coral encircling an empty lagoon.

The long conversion of these coral islets to inhabitable islands begins with coral sitting above the sea's surface being broken up by waves, eventually forming a coarse, infertile soil. Seeds blown by the wind, carried by the sea or in the bowels of birds can then take root. Initially, only the most hardy of plants, such as coconut trees, can survive in this hostile, barren environment. Once the pioneering coconuts have established a foothold, rotting vegetative matter forms a more hospitable soil for other plants.

The people of the Pacific islands have learned how to eke out an existence from even the smallest of coral atolls. Vegetables brought from other islands, such as taro and *kumara*, supplement what grows naturally, and fish from the seas and the lagoon provide protein. However, atoll populations live a precarious existence. Resources are scarce and atolls are vulnerable to droughts, storms and tsunamis.

If geological activity lifts a coral atoll entirely above the water's surface, the resulting island is known as a *makatea* after one such island in French Polynesia.

Step 1
A new volcano rises from the sea bed high enough to become an island.

Step 2
The volcano becomes extinct; meanwhile a coral reef forms around its coast (eg Tahiti).

Step 3
As the island erodes and sinks, the coral grows to stay near the water's surface; a lagoon forms between reef and island (eg Bora Bora).

Step 4
The old volcano sinks entirely, leaving a ring of coral to mark the ancient coastline (eg Aitutaki).

chain of New Zealand to Tonga and Samoa, then north-west through Fiji and the other Melanesian islands.

A glance at a map of the Pacific reveals a number of parallel island chains. These are 'hot spot' volcano chains. Volcanoes form where hot spots exist in the Earth's mantle; then, as the ocean floor moves away to the north-west, these volcanoes become extinct, often sinking beneath the sea. In the Pacific's hot-spot island chains, the youngest, still-active volcanoes are in the south-east and older submarine volcanoes or coral atolls are in the north-west. The Hawai'ian islands, and the Tuamotus and the Australs in French Polynesia are classic examples of hot-spot island chains.

New volcanoes are constantly being formed. Failing a new island fortuitously appearing within sight, active volcanism is most visible at Mt Yasur in Vanuatu.

The seismic activity of the area is also manifested in earthquakes, such as the one that hit Guam in 1993, and in tsunamis (often incorrectly called tidal waves). Huge walls of water propelled by underwater earthquakes, tsunamis can do massive damage to low-lying islands and coastal towns: 3000 people were killed by the tsunami that hit Aitape, PNG, in 1998.

CLIMATE

Apart from the cool highlands of some Melanesian islands, and temperate New Zealand, Easter Island and Pitcairn, the tropical Pacific islands are humid, and air temperatures are high and generally uniform throughout the year (21 to 28°C or 70 to 83°F). The year is divided into a dry season and a wet season. South of the equator, the dry season is from May to October and the wet season (including the cyclone season in some regions) is from November to April. North of the equator, in Micronesia, seasons are reversed. See the climate charts in an appendix at the back of this book.

Most Pacific islands are well-watered, but some regions are drier and can experience long droughts. Coral atolls, lacking rivers or streams and with little ground water, are particularly vulnerable to droughts.

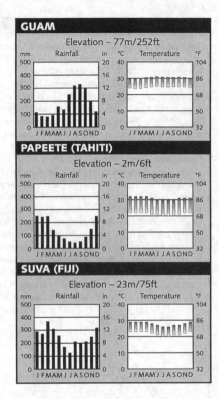

In the tropics, air flowing towards the equator is deflected west by the Earth's rotation. Called the trade winds, these winds blow from the south-east in the southern hemisphere, and from the north-east in the northern hemisphere. The climate of islands facing these cool rain-carrying trade winds changes from one side of the island to the other. Villages and towns on Pacific islands are more likely to be found on the sheltered leeward coast than the cloudier and wetter windward side.

The region where the trade winds meet at the equator is referred to as the doldrums, and this region gets little or no wind. About Christmas time each year the prevailing easterlies of the trade winds weaken, then reverse for a time and blow from the west.

Tropical Cyclones

Called hurricanes in the Atlantic and typhoons in the western Pacific, tropical cyclones are large systems of winds rotating around a centre of low atmospheric pressure. Their winds, which can reach as high as 200km/h, torrential rains and high waves are a hazard to shipping and can cause extensive damage to crops and buildings.

Cyclones can occur at any time but are most common during the wet season, and they only form in certain regions. Only Melanesia, western Micronesia and western Polynesia are likely to experience cyclones. (However, patterns change with El Niño and La Niña events, and may be affected by global warming.)

It's worth checking for cyclones before you head off on a Pacific holiday, even if you're not yachting. Some options include the Internet and travel agents.

The worst cyclones of recent times include cyclones Ofa and Val, which hammered Polynesia in 1990 and 1991. Also see the boxed text 'Supertyphoon Paka' in the Guam chapter.

El Niño

In the tropical Pacific, the prevailing easterly trade winds, driven by the Earth's rotation, normally pile up the warmer surface water towards the western Pacific. The resulting warm water in the west causes more rain in that region, so that the western Pacific (Melanesia, Australia and New Zealand) experiences more rain than the east.

An El Niño (more correctly El Niño/ Southern Oscillation, or ENSO) event occurs when the annual Christmas-time reversal in wind direction combines with high air pressure in the western Pacific and low pressure in the east. The self-perpetuating system that is created blows the warm surface water back towards the eastern Pacific.

As the warm water moves east, it carries rain with it. Western Pacific countries experience droughts while eastern islands suffer unusually heavy rains or cyclones. Although El Niño ('The Boy' or 'The Christ Child') develops in the Pacific, its effects are felt as far afield as Africa and India.

An El Niño usually lasts for about a year, and recurs irregularly about every four or five years. Although only recently understood, El Niño is no recent development. Evidence shows that El Niños have occurred for at least hundreds, and probably thousands, of years. The most recent El Niño (1997-98), the strongest on record, was followed, as often happens, by a weaker related event called La Niña ('The Girl'), which reverses El Niño – bringing storms to the western Pacific and droughts to the east.

ECOLOGY & ENVIRONMENT

The most severe ecological danger to the nations of the Pacific comes not from their own actions but from the developed world (see the boxed text 'Global Warming' later in this chapter). Less threatening but more visible an ecological problem is the presence of trash – particularly on beaches where the trash of an island's population adds to that drifting ashore from fishing vessels.

Fishing

The Pacific Ocean's commercial fishing fleet catches about half of the world's annual 100 million tonnes of fish. While the ocean's vast size lulls many people into thinking of it as an infinite resource, many claim this catch is unsustainable. Critics point out that despite the ever increasing number of vessels in the world's fishing fleets, their annual catch is decreasing. A UN study, which found that most commercially exploited fisheries were being fished beyond their capacity to recover, said the industry 'is globally nonsustainable' and that 'major ecological and economic damage is already visible'.

If you want to avoid eating fish that are at risk, abstain from swordfish, marlin, southern bluefin tuna (albacore tuna is fine) and gemfish.

It is not only fish caught for consumption that are endangered; fishing fleets worldwide claim a 'bycatch' of almost 30 million tonnes per year. These are unwanted species, such as dolphins, sharks and turtles, that are pulled up along with the target species and then dumped. The infamous drift nets,

Global Warming

Since the Industrial Revolution in the 18th century, the concentration of greenhouse gases in the Earth's atmosphere has risen dramatically – particularly carbon dioxide from burning fossil fuels. These gases increase the Earth's natural greenhouse effect, reducing the loss of heat to space and raising the Earth's temperature. The predicted increase in average temperature may seem small – about 4°C (6°F) in the next 100 years – but this rate of increase is vastly faster than any change in the last 10,000 years.

One of the most obvious effects of global warming will be a rise in sea level from thermal expansion of the oceans and the melting of polar icecaps – a 0.5 to 1m (1½ to 3 feet) increase in the next 100 years is a conservative estimate. Other important effects are an increase in the severity of storms in some regions, an increase in the frequency of droughts in other areas, and coral bleaching (see Effects).

Although it is difficult to accurately calculate the causes and effects of global warming, there is no longer any doubt that it is occurring. It's accepted that global temperatures are increasing and polar ice breaking up, but claims of increasing storm severity and the exact cause of coral bleaching events are hotly debated. Some claim the Earth's warming is a natural event.

There are people who express doubt about the whole issue of global warming – and they're not *all* groups with vested interests, such as oil companies. Some doubters claim the risks are being exaggerated by extreme 'green' movements. However, these dire predictions are sourced from the United Nations Environment Program, the Intergovernmental Panel on Climate Change, and the South Pacific Regional Environment Program, and have been accepted by the international insurance community and even British Petroleum – hardly the lunatic left!

Effects

Rising sea levels will cause devastating sea flooding and coastal erosion in many Pacific countries, most disastrously on low-lying coral atolls. However, even on 'high' islands most agriculture, population centres and infrastructure tend to be in low-lying coastal areas. As well as the loss of land, higher seas will increase the effects of storms and cyclones, and the rising seawater table will poison crops and reduce the available fresh groundwater.

It has been found that even small increases in sea temperatures can kill off coral reefs (coral cannot survive in water warmer than 28°C). Called 'coral bleaching', the first symptom of the process is the expulsion of the colourful symbiotic algae that lives within coral. Colourless, dead coral is left behind. As well as meaning the loss of precious fisheries, the absence of coral reefs will decrease islands' protection against storms already worsened by the rising sea level.

Freshwater contamination, land erosion, increased storms, lost fisheries and lost agricultural land will make some marginal, resource-poor atolls uninhabitable, forcing the relocation of large numbers of 'greenhouse refugees'.

'High' island countries, such as those in Melanesia, will be able to relocate people and infrastructure inland, although at enormous financial cost. Countries with both high and low islands, such as the Cook Islands, can relocate atoll dwellers to the higher islands. People in countries composed only of atolls and low-lying islands, such as Tokelau, Tuvalu, Kiribati and the Marshall Islands, will have no choice but to emigrate entirely to other countries – risking the extinction of their unique cultures. These countries may not survive the next century.

Ironically, the developed Pacific rim countries that will probably bear the brunt of relocation (the USA, Canada, Australia and New Zealand) are among the world's worst producers of greenhouse gasses per capita.

A View in Otaheite [Tahiti] – oil painting by Augustus Earle, 1820

A depiction of the discoveries of Cook and La Pérouse (engraving by Antoine Phelippeaux, 1799)

The traditional Polynesian canoe, *Hokule'a*, has sailed thousands of kilometres across the Pacific.

Another replica – a tallship off Bora Bora in the Society Islands

which are legally limited to 2.5km in length but are often much longer, have a huge by-catch. Remnants of drift nets are often found wrapped around dead whales that wash ashore. Nets and lines that have broken loose continue to drift through the oceans, catching and killing as they go. Longlines drifting loose on the surface of the South Pacific kill over 40,000 albatross per year, bringing some species near to extinction. Closer to the coast, blast fishing and cyanide fishing – both illegal – kill everything nearby rather than just their target species.

To resource-poor Pacific islands, selling licences to fish their relatively large Exclusive Economic Zones (EEZ) is one of their few economic options. Their governments' discussions in the South Pacific Forum (SPF; see Government & Politics) reflect an increasing concern that fisheries are managed in a sustainable fashion.

Mining

The best known mines in the Pacific are the phosphate mines of Nauru. Mined since 1907, Nauru's little remaining phosphate will run out within ten years. Like Kiribati's Banaba (Ocean Island), which was mined by British interests from 1900 to 1979, much of Nauru is uninhabitable as a consequence of the mining.

Melanesia's large continental islands are rich in minerals. New Caledonia and Fiji have extensive mines providing important income for those countries.

Deforestation

Rapa Nui (Easter Island) led the world in its efforts of deforestation a thousand years before Magellan sailed into the Pacific. The resources put into the famous statues of Easter Island turned the island into a desolate wasteland.

In modern times, many South Pacific countries are sacrificing long-term viability for short-term gains by intensive logging. Condoned by Pacific governments with few economic options, logging is often undertaken by offshore companies with few long-term interests in the island. Only the larger islands, such as the Solomons, Vanuatu, New Caledonia, Fiji and Samoa, have sufficient forestry reserves to hold the interest of such companies. However, even small-scale logging on the smaller islands can have a devastating effect.

As well as the loss of habitat for native birds and animals, the effects of deforestation include massive soil loss, particularly serious on small coral islands, such as Niue, which have never had good soil quality. Increased runoff from deforested land can lead to pollution of vital waterways and muddying of coastal waters can severely retard the growth of coral.

Nuclear Issues

The Pacific Ocean has seen more than its fair share of nuclear explosions. The world's only hostile use of nuclear weapons, on Hiroshima and Nagasaki in 1945, were launched from the Northern Marianas (see the boxed text 'Little Boy & Fat Man' in that chapter). Subsequently, US nuclear tests were conducted on or near Johnston Island (still a US military territory), Rongelap, Enewetak and Bikini in the Marshall Islands, and on Christmas Island (in Kiribati). The UK also carried out tests on Christmas and Malden in Kiribati.

The nuclear testing issue loomed large at the first meeting of the SPF in 1971. The French certainly didn't reduce anti-nuclear feeling in 1985, when they sank Greenpeace's *Rainbow Warrior* in Auckland's Waitemata Harbour, killing photographer Fernando Pereira. In 1986, the SPF's Treaty of Rarotonga established the South Pacific Nuclear-Free Zone, banning nuclear weapons and the dumping of nuclear waste. This was ratified ten years later by the nuclear powers France, the USA and Britain.

France's Pacific nuclear testing program commenced with atmospheric tests in 1966 at Moruroa and Fangataufa in French Polynesia. Their early atmospheric tests caused measurable increases in radiation in several Pacific countries – as far away as Fiji, 4500km to the west. Atmospheric testing was abandoned in 1974 under severe international pressure, but underground testing continued until 1996.

The effects of atmospheric nuclear testing have rendered Rongelap and Bikini uninhabitable (although short-term visits are fine); their people live in unhappy exile on neighbouring islands. Fragile coral atolls were always a dumb place to detonate underground nuclear weapons, and the French have recently confirmed the appearance of cracks in the coral structure of Moruroa and Fangataufa atolls, and leakage of plutonium at Moruroa. The effect of large amounts of radioactive material leaking into the Pacific Ocean would be catastrophic and far-reaching. Claims of high rates of birth defects and cancer on neighbouring islands are denied by the French, and are impossible to confirm because of the secrecy attached to government health records.

FLORA & FAUNA

Most species of both vegetation and wildlife in the Pacific islands have historically moved across the ocean from west to east. This is confirmed by the reduction of numbers of species from the western to the eastern Pacific. In part the spread of flora was a natural process, with seeds and fruits borne across the sea by winds, in bird droppings and by ocean currents. But early Pacific settlers also deliberately carried with them many plants such as kava, coconut, breadfruit and taro.

The higher islands (Samoa, Melanesia and western Micronesia) have greater variety and numbers of flora and fauna. Smaller coral atolls and low islands, on the other hand, can be almost desolate.

Flora

Coconut If there is a symbol of the Pacific islands, it is the coconut tree. The coconut *(Cocos nucifera)* originated in South-East Asia and its migration west across the Pacific was probably a mixture of natural processes (coconut fruit floats freely) and deliberate introduction by ancient settlers.

Without the coconut tree many small Pacific atolls and islands would never have become inhabitable. Coconuts are tolerant of sandy soils and are the only large tree that will grow on a sandy atoll islet without human assistance. Coconuts broke the

NEVILLE PEAT

'Feed the backs' – a game of rugby in Tokelau, using a coconut for the ball

ground for later vegetation on many small coral atolls.

As well as food, coconuts historically provided drinking water for long ocean voyages, and the tree's wood was the main building material for voyaging canoes. On land coconuts were vital for house and roofing materials, and the fibres were used for rope, weaving and fire-making. The coconut is still economically important to many Pacific countries, providing income from sales of crude oil, coconut cream and copra. A further use of the coconut in Polynesia can be seen whenever a group of boys or young men find themselves lacking a football and wanting a quick game of rugby.

Kumara While most Pacific vegetables and trees originated in the west and migrated east, the kumara *(kumala* or *'umala)* or sweet potato originated in South America – it is known as *kumar* in Peru.

The east to west movement of the kumara was a foundation of the alternative theory that the Pacific was settled from the Americas. That theory quickly fell into disfavour as the bulk of other evidence mounted towards the west-to-east migration (see the earlier History section). It's now believed that the kumara was introduced to the Pacific by Polynesians, probably Marquesans, voyaging to South America. From the Marquesas it was carried westwards, reaching western Polynesia fairly quickly and Melanesia by the 16th century.

The kumara's effect on Pacific societies was enormous; it is easy to grow in tropical climates and to transport by canoe. The kumara revolutionised food in the Pacific.

Fauna

The only land mammal that made its own way to the Pacific islands was the flying fox, or fruit bat, although there are also possums in the Solomons. However, the domestic chicken, dog and pig have been present for thousands of years, introduced on the canoes of ancient settlers. Since European contact, other introduced animals include cattle, horses, sheep, goats and cats.

Stowaways on voyaging canoes included the Polynesian rat and the small lizards that are now ubiquitous in the region – that flicker of movement on the bedroom wall may not be a trick of the kava, it may be a lizard keeping the mosquito population under control. Apart from the small lizards, land reptiles are confined to a few snakes and monitor lizards in western Melanesia and Micronesia. Palau, the Solomon Islands and – occasionally – Vanuatu have saltwater and freshwater crocodiles. Adult saltwater crocs, which can exceed 4m in length, have been known to supplement their fish diet with humans.

Birdlife is dominated by migratory seabirds. One of the more interesting bird types is the megapode; see the boxed text in the Solomon Islands chapter.

Domestic Animals As settlers moved into the Pacific, they were careful to bring domesticated dogs, chickens and pigs with them. As ready sources of protein, many of them probably did not survive the voyage, but enough did to spread the three species across the Pacific.

These animals were widespread by the time Europeans arrived, although on many islands one or more of the domestic trio was missing: only chickens made it to Easter Island and only dogs to New Zealand. Chickens, dogs and pigs were reserved for feasting in most societies, rather than used for everyday food.

Of the three, pigs and chickens are still widespread, and the pig has an important role in many Melanesian rituals. (See The Nimangki under Society & Conduct in the Vanuatu chapter for an illustration of pigs' importance in that country.) The Pacific dog, however, has died out, wiped out by interbreeding and competition from European dog species.

As well as humans, the introduction of dogs and rats had a major environmental impact on isolated islands. Birds that previously had no natural predators now contended with several. In many cases extinction was the result. The later introduction of cats, very efficient killing machines, caused even more extinctions.

Marinelife Many thousands of species of fish live in the Pacific Ocean. It's impossible to describe here every species you might see; some guides to fishes of the Pacific are listed under Books in the Regional Facts for the Visitor chapter. Also in that chapter, see the boxed text 'Venomous Marinelife' and Swimming under Dangers & Annoyances for a few fish you might want to avoid.

Mammals Whales were plentiful in the Pacific until the arrival of whaling fleets in the 18th century. Their numbers are recovering now, although slowed by the continuing Japanese and Norwegian whaling industries. Attempts to establish a South Pacific whale sanctuary continue despite strong opposition, and not only from the whaling nations. Pacific island countries such as the Solomon Islands are wary of a whale sanctuary, which would cut off whaling licences as a prospective source of income. In many Pacific countries, whale-watching tours are a win-win alternative (see the boxed text 'Singing Whales' in the Tonga chapter).

Dolphins abound, and follow ships in the Pacific with the same enthusiasm they show elsewhere in the world. The source of the mermaid myth (those sea journeys must have been long indeed), the dugong, or sea cow, thrives in the western Pacific. Swimming with dugongs is a popular tourist activity in Vanuatu; see the boxed text 'The Gentle Dugong' in that chapter.

Reptiles Sea turtles, including hawksbills, green turtles and leatherbacks, which are all endangered species, lay eggs on uninhabited sandy beaches throughout Micronesia. They've been an important native food for centuries, and both turtles and their eggs are still occasionally eaten, particularly on more remote islands.

Colourful sea snakes, highly venomous but non-aggressive, are common throughout the Pacific.

Coral Although coral looks and behaves like a plant, it's actually a tiny primitive carnivorous animal. Coral reefs are made up of millions of tiny rock-like limestone structures, which are coral skeletons. Coral draws calcium from the water, then excretes it to form a hardened shell to protect its soft body. As coral polyps reproduce and die, new polyps attach themselves in successive layers to the empty skeletons already in place. In this way, a coral reef grows by about 15cm per year. Only the outer layer of coral is alive, and it is algae, living in a symbiotic relationship within the coral's tissue, that gives it colour. So not only is it environmental vandalism to pluck vivid coral from the ocean, it's futile because it loses its colour when dead.

Coral is a fussy wee beast. It requires waters between 21 and 28°C, and the algae needs abundant sunlight, so the water must be mud free and shallow (less than 40m). Coral reefs form in three varieties: as a fringing reef close to the land, as a barrier reef separated from the land by a stretch of water, and as a coral atoll (see the boxed text

earlier in this chapter). Coral reefs thrive with fish, and are one of the most biodiverse habitats found on earth. Thus, of course, they make excellent fishing grounds.

Corals catch their prey by means of stinging nematocysts (a specialised type of cell). Some corals can give humans a painful sting, so they should be given a wide berth. Despite the seemingly robust nature of many types, all corals are fragile and can be damaged by the gentlest touch. Take care to stay well back from coral growths when diving or snorkelling on the reefs (see Responsible Diving in the 'South Pacific Diving' special section), and avoid reef walking.

National Parks

Parks and reserves are listed under individual country chapters. There are three UNESCO-listed World Heritage Sites in the Pacific: East Rennell Island, in the Solomons, Henderson Island, near Pitcairn, and the Parque Nacional Rapa Nui, on Easter Island. With Rennell Island a stepping stone to the Lapita people's settlement of the Pacific, and Henderson and Easter among the last islands to be settled, these sites have important anthropological as well as ecological significance.

GOVERNMENT & POLITICS

After the rash of independence that broke out in the Pacific between 1962-80 (see Postwar History under History earlier in this chapter), Pacific island states largely adopted the British model of parliamentary government, incorporating varying degrees of traditional customs and hierarchies. Conflicts between traditional authorities (chiefs) and modern, elected officials are common.

One of the most traditional systems of government is that of Tonga. The Tongan royal family, descended from a chiefly line that is hundreds of years old, wields enormous power over that country's parliament. In Samoa, only *matai* (village elders) can be elected into parliament. In Fiji, Kiribati and Vanuatu, councils of chiefs have important roles in advising central government. In other countries, traditional chiefs wield their power at local government level. Even

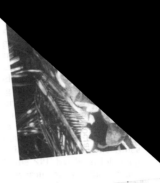

now, Pacific island politics are to a large degree dependent on kinship, family and *wantok* ties (see the boxed text in the Solomon Islands chapter).

The representation of women in Pacific governments is minimal, except at a local government level. Relative to the rest of the Pacific, the situation is slightly better, but still poor, in Polynesia.

The only 'foreign' countries still administering or claiming Pacific territories are Chile (Easter Island), France (French Polynesia, New Caledonia and Wallis & Futuna), the USA (American Samoa, Guam, Hawai'i and several small military islands) and New Zealand (Tokelau). In addition, the USA has some responsibilities for defence and foreign policy in its old Micronesian territories, and New Zealand has a similar arrangement with Niue and the Cook Islands.

There is little agitation in Chile's Easter Island towards independence. Tokelau is moving slowly but surely towards autonomy. In French Polynesia and New Caledonia, recent calls for more independence are finally being addressed by the French government. See History and Government & Politics in the New Caledonia chapter.

Secretariat of the Pacific Community (SPC)

The South Pacific Commission, recently retitled the Secretariat of the Pacific Community, was established in 1947 by the region's colonial powers to ensure the stability of the island nations and territories. Island governments became frustrated by colonial powers, particularly France's blocking of discussion of the nuclear testing issue, and formed the South Pacific Forum in 1971. With the establishment of the SPF, the SPC was reduced to the role of an information agency, providing technical assistance, advice and training.

South Pacific Forum (SPF)

Founded in 1971 (see the SPC entry), the SPF has 16 members, who are the heads of state of all the independent Pacific island countries, plus Australia and New Zealand. Unlike the SPC, the Netherlands, UK, USA, France and France's Pacific colonies are not

m...
ce...
of...

an...
est...
con...
Pac...
adm...
Trea...
the S...
the I...
the ...
posed ... ...y global warming
(see the boxed text earlier in this chapter). Unfortunately, Australia restrains these discussions just as France once blocked the SPC's efforts to discuss nuclear testing.

In late 2000 the SPF will be renamed the Pacific Islands Forum to recognise its north and central Pacific member countries.

ECONOMY

The gross domestic product (GDP) per capita in Pacific countries varies widely, from as high as $US10,000 in New Caledonia and French Polynesia, to about US$800 in Kiribati and Tuvalu. In countries where foreign aid forms a significant part of the economy, GDP is a poor indicator of relative wealth of the people (eg in Tokelau, where foreign aid is five times more than GDP).

The larger Melanesian nations – the Solomons, Vanuatu, New Caledonia and Fiji – are in relatively strong economic positions. Rich in mineral resources, they have large areas available for agriculture and large Exclusive Economic Zones (EEZs) for fisheries. Their wide range of industries include forestry, agriculture, minerals, tourism and selling fishing rights.

At the other end of the scale, tiny Tuvalu and Kiribati have few resources and lack the infrastructure to fully exploit their EEZs or tourism. Industry in these countries is largely subsistence agriculture and fishing.

Small Pacific island economies are particularly vulnerable to external influences. The Asian financial crisis of the late 1990s, combined with a particularly severe El Niño event, caused havoc in Pacific economies.

NED FRIARY

Coconuts shells are left out in the sun to dry before being processed to make copra.

Individual islands can take years to recover from droughts, cyclones or tsunamis.

Agriculture

Although not as important as it was historically, agriculture still forms a large part of all Pacific economies. This ranges from subsistence-level agriculture on the smaller islands to large scale growth of cocoa, vanilla, taro, kava and coconuts. The all-important coconut is vital to small (and some large) Pacific economies, forming a substantial proportion of export earnings from oil, cream and copra.

Aid & Remittances

In many South Pacific countries, trade imbalances are compensated for by foreign aid. It is difficult to put a figure on the amount paid: the definition of aid is nebulous, and the amount paid varies each year depending on needs in the Pacific and politics in the donor country. However, the South Pacific region receives the world's highest aid payments per capita – about US$200 per annum

on average, and over US$1300 in some territories. The money is unevenly distributed; major donors are New Zealand (mostly to those Polynesian states with which it has historical links), Australia (to PNG) and the USA (to its old Micronesian territories). The European Union, and organisations such as the UN and the SPF, provide development and emergency funds.

Many Pacific island emigrants living in the USA, New Zealand and Australia, motivated by a strong family commitment, send a proportion of their earnings back home. Some Pacific countries depend heavily on these remittances. In 1997, remittances to Samoa were worth about 15% *more* than export earnings.

Fishing

In addition to feeding their own population, the relatively large EEZs of small Pacific nations provide an income from the licensing of international fishing fleets – about US$50 million per year. The importance of fisheries as a food source as well as an income source, makes it vital to ensure that they are managed sustainably; see Ecology & Environment earlier in this chapter.

Mining

The only long-term mining industries in the Pacific are in the larger Melanesian countries: New Caledonia (mostly nickel) and Fiji (gold), and there are some undeveloped mineral deposits in the Solomons. Nauru is a special case, having become very wealthy by mining phosphate (the phosphate is expected to be exhausted in the next few years).

On the Pacific sea bed, enormous deposits of minerals, including manganese, copper and nickel, have been discovered. However, the technology required to mine these deposits does not yet exist.

Tourism

Tourism is a significant industry in many Pacific countries. About three million tourists visit the Pacific islands each year, providing US$3 million in foreign exchange. Almost half of these tourists are Japanese visiting

Guam and the Northern Mariana Islands. Other significant tourist origins are the USA, Australia, Korea, New Zealand and France. The most popular destinations are Guam (1,406,000 visitors in 1998), the Northern Marianas (660,000), Fiji (366,000) and French Polynesia (190,000).

Tourism has many attractions for Pacific governments. Properly managed, it is sustainable, unlike logging or mining, and generates significant employment; over 20% of jobs in Fiji are generated by tourism. On the downside, interaction with affluent western tourists introduces new social stresses, and tourism increases vulnerability to overseas economies. If not properly managed, tourism can also have severe environmental effects.

Financial Miscellanea

Several Pacific islands have branched into 'financial services'. Vanuatu, the Cook Islands, Nauru and Samoa offer tax havens for overseas businesses.

A handful of Pacific islands received something of a windfall with the popularity of the Internet. Countries that have profited from the sales of their top level domain (the last two letters in a URL or email address) include Niue (.nu), Tonga (.to), Tuvalu (.tv) and the Federated States of Micronesia (.fm). See the boxed text 'The .tv Get-Rich-Quick Scheme' in the Tuvalu chapter.

In very small economies, such as those of Pitcairn or Tokelau, items such as handicrafts can form a significant proportion of the economy. Small obscure countries have been able to profit from their own obscurity by the sales of postage stamps and coinage.

The public service is the major employer on many Pacific islands; such a large public service is often only made possible by foreign aid.

POPULATION & PEOPLE

The population of the Pacific islands (not including New Zealand, Hawai'i, or PNG) is 2.3 million, divided into 1.4 million, 500,000 and 400,000 people in Melanesia, Polynesia and Micronesia respectively. Individual country populations range from Fiji at 775,000 to Pitcairn at 50.

Most populations are coastal – a trend that began in the 18th century when people migrated to coastal areas for easier access to Europeans trade. As well, populations are increasingly concentrated on one island or in one main town. This is most prevalent in Micronesia (Nauru being almost exclusively an urban community). Melanesian countries have the highest proportion of rural dwellers, eg 80% in Vanuatu.

Population density varies from as low as eight people per sq km in Vanuatu to 430 on Nauru. Tiny Ebeye Islet on Kwajelein Atoll in the Marshall Islands has an incredible 40,000 per sq km! (More than 13,000 people on 31 hectares of land.) Annual population growth is about 2.3%, with the highest rates in Melanesia and Micronesia.

Pacific islanders have always been travellers, and a large number of islanders live abroad. About 15% of Pacific islanders live in other countries around the Pacific rim, in New Zealand (210,000), mainland USA (154,000), and Australia (65,000). In many island nations, emigration relieves population pressure, but in some, for example Niue, there is a net population loss; almost 90% of ethnic Niueans now live in New Zealand. Islanders living abroad do their best to maintain their community and language, and to maintain contact with family on the island (also see Remittances under Economy). The traffic between Pacific islands and developed nations, with islanders visiting family and family getting an 'island fix', speeds the spread of western influences through Pacific societies.

EDUCATION

Literacy rates in the Pacific are high (above 90% in most countries), but the rate is very low in two of the most populous countries: the Solomon Islands (23%) and Vanuatu (64%).

University of the South Pacific (USP)

Established in 1968, the USP is jointly owned by 12 countries: the Cook Islands,

Fiji, Kiribati, Marshall Islands, Nauru, Niue, Solomon Islands, Tokelau, Tonga, Tuvalu, Vanuatu and Samoa. The university is based in Suva, Fiji, with campuses in Vanuatu (law) and Samoa (agriculture). Students also study humanities, science and economics. Learning in any particular discipline includes an emphasis on the Pacific region.

ARTS

See the 'South Pacific Arts' special section for the object-based arts, such as sculpture, and information about common themes in Pacific arts.

The Pacific's premier cultural gathering is the Festival of Pacific Arts, where arts and crafts of all kinds, including dance, song, weaving and carving, are celebrated. Held every four years in a different country, the festival attracts large numbers of tourists from outside the region. See Special Events in the Regional Facts for the Visitor chapter.

Traditional dancers from tiny Ifalik Atoll in Yap, Federated States of Micronesia.

ASTRID WITTE & CASEY MAHANEY

Western artists influenced by the Pacific include Paul Gauguin, who lived in French Polynesia between 1890 and 1903. See the boxed text 'Paul Gauguin' in the French Polynesia chapter.

Dance & Song

Traditional dance is still strong across the Pacific. The expectation of many tourists to see something like the Hawai'ian *hula* has persuaded many islanders to adopt that familiar sway and wobble, but dancing for tourists also provides the young with a strong financial incentive to learn the ancient skill. Dances may be performed by groups or by individuals; group dancing is more common at large village ceremonies.

One of the most successful contemporary bands incorporating a Pacific feel into their songs recently has been the Tokelauan group Te Vaka, who are based in New Zealand but tour internationally (see www.tevaka.com).

Literature

Pacific island authors are listed in the Institute of Pacific Studies' *South Pacific Literature – From Myth to Fabulation*. See Books under Facts for the Visitor in the individual country chapters for contemporary Pacific island authors. Probably the most successful is the Samoan writer Albert Wendt – see the Samoa chapter.

Many 19th century European authors were inspired to write about the Pacific islands. Among them James Michener and Jack London (see Books in the Regional Facts for the Visitor chapter). Other authors were moved enough to relocate to the islands themselves, either temporarily or permanently. Among them, in Samoa, Robert Louis Stevenson. See that country's chapter for more information.

SOCIETY & CONDUCT

Although the phrase *faka Pasifika* has been used to describe a Pacific culture, there are more differences between Pacific cultures than there are similarities. However, there are some common features identifying Melanesian, Polynesian and Micronesian cultures.

Traditional Society

A huge diversity of cultures had evolved across the Pacific by the time of contact with Europeans. Not surprisingly, considering the poor resources of their island homes, Pacific islanders remained in a stone age culture – it's difficult to run an iron foundry on a coral atoll. In the absence of metal tools, voyaging canoes, houses and artwork were fashioned largely with stone tools.

Only the design of ocean-going craft and navigation skills attained a high degree of scientific rigour (see the boxed text 'Voyaging & Navigation' earlier in this chapter). In the absence of other high technology, emphasis shifted to refining oral skills and cultural systems, creating rich mythologies and intricate cultural rules.

The status of women in traditional and modern Pacific societies seems to improve as you move east. In eastern Polynesia, chiefly titles are almost as likely to be held by women as by men, but there are very few female chiefs in the central Pacific, and almost none in Micronesia or Melanesia.

While European contact changed forever the cultures of the Pacific, it did not lead to a complete loss of culture. Many elements of tradition continue to be practised, or else they have been rejigged to accommodate the modern world of the Pacific.

Melanesian The remarkable cultural and linguistic diversity of Melanesia is partly a product of the region's many thousands of years of settlement. This has been attenuated by the rugged topographical nature of the islands: travel between villages even a short distance apart has always been made difficult by high mountain ranges and deep valleys.

Melanesian social groups were generally small – less than a few hundred people. Each group was (and still is) ruled by a man known as a 'bigman'. Hereditary factors were important in selecting a bigman, but the individual's ambition and skills in politics and war were equally important.

Men who displayed prowess in war or village affairs, or who showed a special affinity with the spirit world, could ascend the social hierarchy by stepping up through successive 'grades'. Feasting and displays of wealth were central to grade-taking ceremonies, which are still held today. See Nimangki under Society & Conduct in the Vanuatu chapter.

The concept of reciprocity is central to Melanesian culture. Assistance, whether in the form of food or labour, was given out of a sense of duty and was given with the expectation of the favour being returned in the future. Trade was a basis of the culture, and the relationships involved in exchange rituals between individuals and between clans were very complex. In a culture with many hundreds of languages spoken by small groups of people, allegiance to kin was paramount, and it was possible to include all speakers of one language in the wider group to which one owed allegiance. See the boxed text 'The Wantok System' in the Solomon Islands chapter for more details.

So-called 'ancestor worship' and sorcery pervaded every aspect of Melanesian life. Magical spells and rituals were necessary to guarantee success in war, fishing, agriculture and good health. Success in war was particularly important; the concept of reciprocity extended to an enthusiastic exacting of revenge for past wrongs. Head-hunting was common and cannibalism (see the boxed text in the Fiji chapter) was practised on a ritual basis as well as being a food source – in some areas until the 1950s.

More than other Pacific islanders, Melanesians have retained their culture in the face of western influence. Almost 80% of Solomon Islanders and Ni-Vanuatu still follow a subsistence-agriculture lifestyle. While Melanesians use modern technology for fishing, agriculture and other pursuits, this is still supplemented with sorcery and rituals. The concepts of *kastom* and reciprocity remain important in modern Melanesia, providing unique difficulties for western businesses trying to operate there.

Kastom (Custom) You will hear the word kastom used constantly in the Solomon Islands and Vanuatu when villagers refer to traditional beliefs and land ownership. If something is done in a certain way 'because of kastom', this means it has always been done this way, and people consider it right to continue doing it this way. Breaches of kastom are always deplored.

Polynesian Ancient Polynesian society was strongly hereditary, with seniority determined by descent through the male side of the family. The most senior male, the paramount chief or *ariki* (sometimes *ari'i* or *ali'i*), ruled over sub-chiefs and commoners. Chiefly families formed a class of their own, having minimal contact with lower classes. Proving chiefly genealogy was vital, and in the absence of a written language, oral histories evolved a high significance, with the ability to recite one's ancestry an important part of any political debate.

Along with the ruling chief, power was shared by a class of experts or priests known as *tohunga (tohu'a* or *kahuna)*, who were the repository of knowledge and often the interpreter of the gods' wills for the village. Obviously, this was a position of some political power!

The degree to which Polynesian societies were stratified by hereditary class varied from island to island. In egalitarian Samoa, chiefs (matai) were selected on political nous and ability rather than on lines of descent. At the other end of the scale, social class in Hawai'ian, Tongan and Tahitian societies was strictly hierarchical. Soon after European contact, all three of these later cultures came to be ruled by single leaders.

Religious beliefs were remarkably consistent across ancient Polynesia. The worship of a pantheon of gods – ruled by

Maui's Fish

A person common to many Pacific legends is the demigod known as Maui – trickster, fool, hero, Polynesian Prometheus and a damn fine fisherman.

Many cultures of the Pacific tell a traditional tale wherein one or more of their islands is fished up out of the ocean depths by Maui. Each island has its variations on the story: in Tokelau, Maui hauled up each of the three atolls in that group; while fishing up Rakahanga in the Cooks he is said to have baited his hook with coconuts and leaves; in Aotearoa (New Zealand) he used a fish-hook fashioned from the jawbone of his grandmother, and baited it with blood from his own nose; and on various islands of French Polynesia his bait was either his own ear or sacred crimson feathers. However the hook was baited, it was effective. The hook caught onto the largest fish ever seen.

Maui's struggles to haul this enormous catch to the surface were aided by various magical chants and spells – and his prize was a fish so large that it formed the island of Rakahanga or Tongatapu, or whichever island is appropriate to the teller of the tale.

Maui's other contributions to mankind include stealing fire from the gods, slowing the path of the sun and creating the first dog. One of his major appeals to Polynesian society seems to be the use of trickery to defeat force. Whether Maui was ever a real person is unknown, but if so he must have lived long ago, since his tales are so widespread.

MICK WELDON

Tangaroa (Tangaloa or Ta'aroa) – spread from the Society Islands throughout Polynesia. The gods shared responsibilities for the seas, the forests, war, cultivated crops and other departments.

The importance of warfare in Polynesian society was universal. The shortage of land was a contributing factor, and revenge was often demanded for long-remembered feuds. Cannibalism was common, and was the ultimate revenge against one's enemy.

Ancient hierarchies and the power of hereditary chiefs are greatly diminished in modern Polynesia, although Tonga retains its powerful monarchy, and in Samoa (one the most resilient Polynesian societies) only chiefs are eligible for election to parliament. The concepts of *tapu* and *mana* (see later in this section) remain important.

Marae The word marae (or *malae*) varies in meaning in different Polynesian cultures. In western Polynesia, it refers to the grassy area at the centre of a village, the central point of village life. Towards the east, the same word is used for sacred sites and temples, such as Marae Taputapuatea in French Polynesia. See also Production in the 'South Pacific Arts' special section.

Micronesian As in Polynesia, one's position in Micronesian society was based largely on hereditary factors, in most cases traced through the female line. Society was structured in multi-family clans, usually scattered over several islands, and there were obligations to protect and assist all other clan members.

On many islands, particular clans were the traditional rulers. Chiefly clans ruled lasting empires on Pohnpei and Kosrae, where society was heavily stratified. The Pohnpei empire built the remarkable monuments and artificial islands of Nan Madol (see the Federated States of Micronesia chapter). Other societies were less structured; in the western Carolines, clan seniority was based simply on prior settlement. Oral histories were important in establishing a clan's history on the island and thus rank in that island's society.

Ancestral spirits were the major recipients of worship. These spirits inhabited objects that could be kept close at hand, thus ensuring that the assistance of ancestors could be quickly accessed. Warfare was common, based largely on clan allegiances and on the struggle for land of communities on small resource-starved atolls.

Micronesian culture remains strongest now on Yap and the small atolls of the Carolines. Chiefs remain powerful in many cultures, eg Palau and the Marshalls, but the ultimate authority of chiefs in Kosrae and Kiribati no longer exists.

Tapu

Also present in Polynesian-influenced Micronesia and in Melanesia, the concept of *tapu* (pronounced 'ta-bu' in many Pacific languages, and the source of the English word 'taboo') is common to all of Polynesia. There are many common themes, like the ability of women and cooked food to remove *tapu*, but there are also many variations. See the individual country chapters for local interpretations.

Mana

More important in Polynesia, the concept of mana (personal spiritual power) is common to many Pacific cultures. Mana is a quality possessed by all people, and the degree of one's mana depends not only on hereditary factors but on one's achievements. A chief (or politician) without mana could not – and can not – rule effectively.

Dos & Don'ts

Certain rules of etiquette have their origins in ancient custom, while others are the direct result of Christianity. Special allowances are made for visitors, especially in major cities and touristy centres, where even many of the locals ignore established traditions. But those who learn and respect local traditions will be more readily accepted, especially in rural areas.

Apart from one or two affluent countries, the average Pacific islander is not wealthy by western standards. To avoid resentment, don't flash expensive cameras or other equipment around. Both tipping for service and bargaining for better prices can cause offence in Pacific countries. See also Buying Art in the 'South Pacific Arts' special section and Money in the Regional Facts for the Visitor chapter.

Few Pacific places are exactly uptight about clothing standards, but complying with regional customs will usually get a much better reception from the locals. Dressing like a slob won't endear you to anyone – it's rarely appropriate for men to go bare-chested in town, and women's dress conventions are even stricter (see Women Travellers in the Regional Facts for the Visitor chapter). If you visit a church, even more care should be taken with your clothes.

Public displays of affection between men and women, even two tourists, are often inappropriate. Flirting with the locals can also get you into a *lot* of trouble; there are some very serious expectations attached to what may appear to be casual affairs. Despite the writings of western visitors from Bougainville to Margaret Mead, the Pacific is *not* a playground of free love.

Avoid becoming visibly frustrated when things don't go your way. Causing someone to lose face because they have failed you is an unforgivable sin.

Many tourists wish to see traditional villages, and visitors are usually welcomed with a remarkable hospitality. (See Accommodation in the Regional Facts for the Visitor chapter.) Bear in mind, though, that such visits can be extremely disruptive in a traditional society. Guidelines are often quoted in tourist publications in the islands, and some are repeated here for the benefit of intending visitors.

- Shoes are usually removed when entering a home. Sit cross-legged on the floor, not with your feet pointing out. Don't enter a house during prayers.
- Behave yourself especially carefully on a Sunday. For example, it's best not to arrive in a village on Sunday.
- Be careful not to walk between two people in conversation. Try to remain on a lower level than a chief. Do not eat food while walking around a village.

RELIGION

Ancient Pacific religion is discussed under Traditional Society in the Society & Conduct section earlier in this chapter. Ancestor worship and magic were prevalent in Melanesia and some parts of Micronesia, while a rich pantheon of gods ruled Polynesia and still other parts of Micronesia. However, neither powerful ancestors nor Tangaroa were strong enough to resist the new religion that arrived in the early 19th century.

In many cases traditional religion has been incorporated into modern beliefs, but it is Christianity that dominates religious life in the Pacific today. Only Fiji, with its large Hindu and Muslim Fijian Indian population, has significant numbers of non-Christians.

Christianity

Following the efforts of missionaries in the Pacific in the last century, the islands of the South Pacific adopted Christianity with a passion, Polynesia especially. The area is famous now for the fervency of believers.

The Church of the Latter Day Saints (Mormon Church) arrived in the Pacific in 1888. They were at least partly inspired by the Book of Mormon's assertion that Pacific islanders are the children of the Israelite refugee Hagoth, who sailed into the Pacific from the American mainland in 53 BC. The Mormon Church has been fairly successful in the Pacific; it shares a family focus with islanders, allows believers to baptise heathen ancestors, and puts some effort and resources into schooling. Other Christian denominations include the Seventh Day Adventists, who arrived in Samoa in 1890.

Cargo Cults

During WWII, Pacific islanders were introduced to huge western material wealth, but when US troops left the Pacific, most of this wealth disappeared with them (or was dumped into the sea in many cases). In Melanesia, cargo cults formed to encourage and prepare for the return of these riches, which were known as 'cargo'. One of the best known cargo cults is the Jon Frum movement in Vanuatu (see the boxed text in that chapter).

Only your best hat will do for attending church in Papeete (French Polynesia).

LANGUAGE

The Austronesian family of languages is the most widely distributed in the world. It includes all Polynesian and Micronesian languages, many Melanesian and South-East Asian languages as well as the Malagasy language from Madagascar, off the African coast. While the words for common concepts such as 'land', 'ancestors' or 'fish' are the same in many Pacific languages, there is also considerable diversity, particularly in ancient, culturally-diverse Melanesia, where over a thousand different languages exist.

At the other end of the scale, the last area to be settled, Polynesia, is the most linguistically homogenous. Here, inter-island voyaging ensured that the languages of Polynesia are almost dialects of one language. James Cook's Tahitian translator, Tupaia, had little trouble understanding Maori in the Cook Islands or New Zealand, and travellers to the Pacific may find that they have a head start in a new Polynesian language if they've already learned a few words in another.

Micronesian languages are more complex: western Micronesia forms one language group, which is related to languages of the Philippines. The central Micronesian language group reflects those people's Melanesian influence, and southern/eastern Micronesian languages are strongly influenced by Polynesia.

Prior to the arrival of the missionaries, no written languages existed in the Pacific (with the possible exception of the rongorongo script of the Rapa Nui; see the boxed text 'Rongorongo' in the Easter Island chapter). Without a written language, oral traditions were very important in all Pacific cultures.

A common feature of Polynesian and Micronesian languages is the dropped consonant; an effect similar to that heard in the Cockney accent, where the letter 't' is not pronounced when it falls within a word, eg 'butterfly' is pronounced 'bu-er-fly', and 'bottle' is pronounced 'bo-ul'. The space that's left in the word is called a glottal stop, and is written as an apostrophe. Thus in Tahiti, where the 'k' sound is dropped, the place name Havaiki becomes Havai'i (ha-vai-ee) and kumara becomes *'umara*. Cook Islanders drop 'h', so that Havaiki becomes 'Avaiki.

Another feature of Pacific languages that troubles English speakers is the soft 'ng' sound. This is pronounced as the 'ng' in the English word 'singer' – without pronouncing the hard 'g' as in 'finger'. For example the country name Tonga is pronounced 'tong-ah' not 'ton-gah'. To make it even more difficult, some Pacific languages spell this sound simply 'g' (the Samoan word *palagi* is pronounced 'pah-lang-i').

English is spoken widely across the Pacific, and will be understood in the main towns and cities of almost every country. Exceptions are the French territories (New Caledonia, Wallis & Futuna and French Polynesia, including Tahiti), where French is the first or second language.

The hundreds of languages of Melanesia have led to the development of 'business' or pidgin languages for communication across language barriers. PNG, the Solomon Islands and Vanuatu all use pidgin languages that mix English, French and German with Melanesian words.

No Pacific languages use an 's' to denote plurals (as the English language does). Although this rule is happily broken almost everywhere – for example a Samoan hotel owner will offer to show you around their *fales* (huts), or a Vanuatuan trader will offer to sell you some *tamtams* (slit drums) – we have stuck to the rules in this book and relied on the context to make the meaning clear.

For useful phrases in Pacific languages, see the Language section in individual country chapters. Some French (even bad French) is very useful in that country's territories; an extensive French language guide is given in an appendix of this book.

For a more comprehensive overview of the languages of the region, get a copy of Lonely Planet's *South Pacific* and *Pidgin* phrasebooks.

SOUTH PACIFIC ARTS

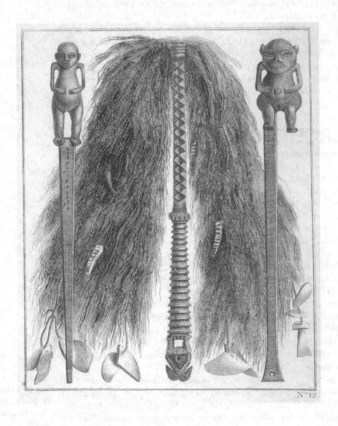

South Pacific art is very varied, and it can be incredibly beautiful and potent. Some objects of art from the South Pacific are highly sought after by collectors. However, this is not 'art' in the traditional western sense of the word. Rather, in the Pacific islands traditional art objects were (and often still are) utilities that might invoke *mana* (spiritual power) in war, assist passage into the afterlife, forge relationships of exchange, bring juveniles into adulthood, or just serve as a stool or a bowl. All these pieces of 'art' were entirely practical objects whether their purposes were 'spiritual' or more mundane.

The meanings that we look for in Pacific art are complicated, because it is necessary to look beyond the superficial appearance of the artwork and explore the social organisation and contexts in which the work was produced. Although artifice and decoration are traditional, art for its own sake is a new idea in most cultures of the Pacific islands.

PERCEPTIONS

Europe was abuzz when explorers returned with traditional artefacts and stories of South Sea islands in the late 18th century. The islands were described as places of loose morals and free love, as well as being earthly paradises uncorrupted by the modern world and its vices. These perceptions gave rise to the idea of the 'noble savage' who practised 'primitive art', and motivated many European artists and travellers to visit the Pacific or even settle there (most famously Paul Gauguin, W Somerset Maugham and Robert Louis Stevenson). Back in Europe, Picasso and Braque's cubism was greatly influenced by Pacific art pieces.

However, the ideas of 'noble savage' and 'primitive art' do not provide us with any satisfying meanings of Pacific art, and they are inherently patronising. The term 'primitive art' is also a misnomer, because it refers to things that are not primarily art, but rather ceremonial objects, stories or motifs with real and immediate powers and vivid histories. In traditional Pacific societies all these objects of 'art' were interconnected, just as religion, culture, politics and tribal affairs were.

Traditionally, the manufacture of these art-objects was (and often still is) highly ceremonial and ritualised – in Melanesia, rigidly organised secret men's councils still build figures or masks to be presented in elaborate funerary rites or initiation ceremonies. Men and boys fell trees, prepare materials and build the artefacts under strict rules and according to their well-defined traditional roles. The production of art in these cultures is very unlike the way art is produced in the west.

Title page: *Fly flaps, South Sea Isles*. Engraving by J Hawkesworth, 1773 (by permission of the National Library of Australia).
Polynesian chiefs used ornaments such as this Tahitian fly whisk as symbols of their power.

CONTEXTS

In Melanesia, honouring ancestors was more important than honouring the gods, and the spirit world was ever-present. 'Bigmen' (chiefs) provided feasts for the clan, and the display of wealth and the accumulation of ceremonial objects conferred much prestige upon the sponsor. Much Melanesian art was produced for these ceremonies – which were rites of passage for the living and the dead. Ancestors were powerful protectors and benefactors, whose presence was manifested in the process of producing art as well as in the artefact itself.

In most traditional cultures in the Polynesian region, the most noble of hereditary chiefs and aristocrats (ariki) were themselves semi-deities, and spiritual power and knowledge came to them through their splendid feather-worked regalia, fly-whisks and ornaments. In Polynesia, art was primarily produced for this elite group and objects of art were preserved and inherited by successive generations, bringing with them the mana of their ancestors. These heirlooms had enormous prestige and power, and were preserved with much reverence.

Micronesia is more a geographic grouping than an easy cultural one, but here too the islands were largely dominated by hereditary elites. Influences from both Melanesia and Polynesia are clear, but some of the earliest settlers came from the Philippines. Seafaring and navigation were important to Micronesian islanders who built 'maps' of cane and shell – these look almost like late-20th century minimalist twig sculptures. Shells represent islands and the cane lengths are currents; see the 'Stick Charts' boxed text in the Marshall Islands chapter. Micronesian artworks are generally smaller in scale.

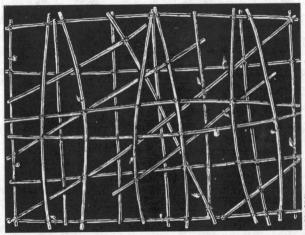

Right: Cane stick charts were used by Micronesian navigators to record the instructions for long inter-island canoe journeys.

KATE NOLAN

Lapita

The Lapita people are thought to be responsible for the wide distribution of Austronesian languages in the Pacific. Coming from the Bismark Archipelago in far-north Papua New Guinea (PNG) from around 1500 BC, they were the first to populate the islands from Vanuatu east to New Caledonia, Fiji, Samoa and Tonga. It was in Tonga and Samoa that the Lapita developed into the people we now call Polynesians.

The Lapita people had an enormous influence over a vast area of the Pacific from 1500 to 500 BC, and their influence has been traced through the reverberations of their unique pottery. This earthenware was tempered with sand and fired in open fires, and decorated with rows of curvilinear patterns stamped into the unfired clay. Polynesian tattooists took up these motifs, using chisels to scrape or puncture the skin, and *tapa* (bark-cloth) decoration across the Pacific bears similar patterns. In some areas Lapita-style pottery is still produced.

The first ancient ceramic fragments (later to be identified as Lapita) were discovered on Watom Island in Papua New Guinea, by a missionary in 1909. The name Lapita comes from an archaeological dig at Lapita in New Caledonia in 1952. Shards of Lapita pottery have been found throughout Melanesia, in parts of Micronesia and in western Polynesia in Tonga, Samoa and Futuna. More recently, a distinctive Lapita style has been identified in certain adzes and other implements.

They were highly skilled sailors and navigators, able to cross hundreds of kilometres of open sea, and trade and settlement were important to their culture. They were also agriculturists and practised husbandry of dogs, pigs and fowls. Regarded as the first cultural complex in the Pacific, the Lapita were a highly organised people who traded obsidian (volcanic glass used in the production of tools) from New Britain (PNG) with people up to 2500km away in Tonga and Samoa.

Today Pacific art is dizzying in its variety of form, execution and purpose, but perhaps its most unifying thread is the patterns, motifs and techniques it inherits from these ancient people.

Left: This fragment of distinctive Lapita pottery was found in the Santa Cruz Islands, Solomon Islands.

PRODUCTION
War Objects

Warfare and killing were central to many Pacific cultures, and were often highly ritualised. In the Solomon Islands they were part of a cycle that linked with good fortune and fecundity. Skulls of head-hunters' victims were used in the consecration of canoes

KATE NOLAN

and men's houses, and for the mourning of recently dead chiefs. In many Melanesian cultures the over-modelled skulls of war victims were used in funeral rites, and violence was often engaged in purely to produce ceremonial objects. Vanuatu is famous for its over-modelled skullwork in vivid ochre colours, which forms the basis of much effigy making. (Over-modelling is the technique of building up materials like clay and fibres over a skull. The surface is decorated with eyes, hair and teeth, and sometimes with ornaments like earrings and headbands.)

In Fiji and western Polynesia warfare was associated with expansionism and rivalry. Marquesan war clubs, known as *u'u*, are highly prized among collectors and feature extraordinary fine-relief carving (often a double-sided human face, a Janus-figure form which proliferates through the Pacific). These weapons were carved from solid hardwoods and were very heavy, and very deadly. The massive Fijian clubs *(sali)* are recognisable by their 'lip' or barb, and a warrior wielding such an implement would have been very formidable indeed. Warriors from Kiribati wore full-body armour and helmets that were woven from vegetable fibres and human hair, and used swords of shark's teeth.

Weapons, shields and war canoes were decorated with motifs that imbued them with powers. Ancestors, spirits and legends assisted warriors in combat – coming alive in their tools.

KATE NOLAN

Top: In Melanesia, the skulls of enemies killed in war often ended up as ceremonial artworks.

Bottom: The carved heads of Marquesan war clubs *(u'u)* incorporated designs also used in traditional tattoos.

The Body

'Tattoo' is an Oceanic word, which comes from the Polynesian word *tatau*. Up until the 18th century, full-body tattoos were common through the Cook, Marquesas, Austral and Society islands. Early observers assumed that tattoos were a sign of rank, and this was partly true but some people of the highest rank were not tattooed at all. A person began acquiring tattoos in their childhood and initiation into adulthood was usually accompanied by special markings. Tattooing is a painful and arduous process, but this 'hardens' the body and the motifs have protective properties – warriors were often covered in motifs that inspired fear in their enemies and, like their weaponry, gave them the powers of their ancestors and spirits.

Polynesian tattooing reached its zenith in the war-torn Marquesas, where no part of a warrior's skin was left unembellished (even his eyelids and tongue were tattooed), giving him a second skin and a bewildering visual 'armour'. Marquesan warrior tattoos featured an extraordinary density and number of designs. Marquesan noble people bore complex and elegant tattoos also, although theirs were not so all-covering. Tattooed skin was sometimes removed from a person after their death. In Tahiti, Samoa and Tonga tattoos were usually restricted to the buttocks and thighs. Here, dense areas of pigment were broken up with curvilinear designs and spots.

Below: *Inhabitant of the Island Nuku Hiva* (engraving by S Halle, 1810). Shows Marquesan warriors' intricate 'clothing' of tattoos.

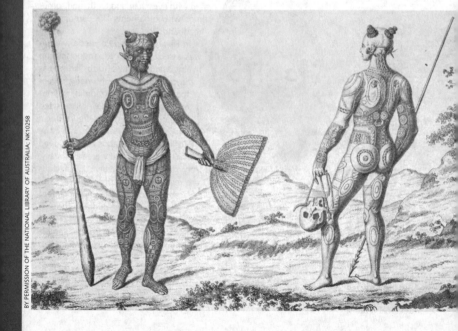

Tattoo Goes to Europe

Although tattooing was practised in many cultures throughout the world, it only took off in Europe after British officers and crewmen returned from Pacific voyages in the late 18th and early 19th centuries, and bared their flesh. Sir Joseph Banks had tattoos done in Tahiti, as did the *Bounty* mutineers. It became fashionable for seamen to have tattoos, and Europe's repressed underclasses took up the habit. Soon tattoos had become a furtive fashion among the European aristocracy – kings of England and Norway, Russian Tsars, Bourbons of France and many men and women of royal and social rank had themselves tattooed (some profusely). Yet the fashion bypassed the middle class.

By the 20th century, missionary activity had virtually killed off Polynesian tattooing. The tradition remained strong in Samoa, however, and is now being revived in areas of French Polynesia and elsewhere. In Fiji, where tattooing had strong associations with sexuality, the repression by the Christian church means that a revival is unlikely.

Rather than tattooing, scarring of the body was more commonly practised in Melanesia where ochre pigments don't show so well against darker skin. Techniques varied somewhat but scarification (keloid decoration) served much the same role, in terms of bestowing symbols of rank and/or status, as tattooing did in lighter-skinned people.

Male Cults & Men's Houses in Melanesia & Micronesia

Throughout Melanesia secret councils of men convene to practise 'the arts'. The production of objects within these societies – for funerary rituals, initiations etc – is done in accordance with strict rules, and is itself highly ceremonial. Much Melanesian art was traditionally produced to allow rituals to be performed properly, and it was sometimes produced collectively or by a master and his apprentices.

Men's houses are widespread throughout Melanesia and Micronesia and, before the towering church edifices were built, were a village's dominant structure and often its most sacred place. In many places men still move through various grades or social ranks, and feasts, gifts, body adornment, sculpture, and song and dance remain important components of these ceremonies. The best known grade-taking societies are on the northern islands of Vanuatu (Ambrym, Malekula and Pentecost islands; see The Nimangki under Society & Conduct in the Vanuatu chapter). Males are allocated a place within the *nakamal* (men's house) according to their rank, and they seriously transgress if they step into an area of a man of higher rank.

The men's house contained the most sacred objects – often the revered over-modelled skulls of ancestors were kept here, although sometimes they were kept in other *tapu* (taboo or *tabu*) structures, such as canoe houses. Throughout Melanesia and Micronesia, the structure of the men's houses universally symbolise woman and fecundity. They are often great artworks themselves with towering facades and detailed interiors, and are built using complex joinery without a nail or a screw. Western observers find it ironic that all things exclusively male, magic and *tapu* to women happen inside a female form. The relationship between the aloof and exclusive men's council and the ever-present feminine symbol is very complicated, but connects with ideas of rebirth, grade-taking and initiation.

The *bai* houses in the Caroline Islands feature carved-relief narrative scenes – telling the clan history and mythology – which is very unusual in Pacific art. Traditionally, Pacific artforms were loosely representational and narrative depictions were very rare, confined to the beams and facades of Micronesian bai houses and to storyboards from the Sepik region of Papua New Guinea. (A direct extrapolation of bai artwork, storyboards, are now common in Micronesia also. See the boxed text in the Palau chapter.)

Below Left & Right: The colourful murals painted on the front of Palau's famous *bai* (men's houses) depict traditional stories.

NED FRIARY

NED FRIARY

Nan Madol

Aptly described as the 'Venice of the South Seas', Nan Madol was an 80 hectare city built upon 92 man-made islands in the lagoon of Pohnpei Island in the modern Federated States of Micronesia (FSM).

Remnants of this megalithic architectural style exist elsewhere nearby, but Nan Madol is the greatest testament to this unique architecture and to the royal family (the Saudeleleurs) who commissioned it in the early 13th century. Huge basalt stones, some in excess of 50 tonnes, were quarried on the main island and floated on rafts to the site. Nan Madol prospered under the Saudeleleurs until its decline in the early 17th century. The last residents left Nan Madol around 1820, after which it was occasionally used for religious ceremonies.

See the boxed text 'The Saudeleurs' Demise' in the FSM chapter.

Marae in Polynesia

The principal social structure and meeting place in eastern Polynesia was the *marae* (or *malae*). It was very unlike a Melanesian men's house (being gender neutral), but had a similar monumental status within the community. Villages might have several marae, each for a different function and devoted to different gods. Nobles and royal families would have their own marae.

In western Polynesia, marae were little more than village greens, sometimes merely a clearing marked off by walls. In the east they developed a religious significance and could be elaborate structures. The ancient marae in Easter Island, the Societies, Australs and Marquesas must have been extraordinary – they were massive open-air, paved temples with altars, carved-stone seating, platforms and walls. The scale of the remaining petroglyphs and carved-stone figures attest to some awesome temples.

In the Marquesas the *me'ae*, a structure of basalt blocks, was *tapu* to all but the most noble people and high priests. Here priests would engage in high religious acts involving sacrifice and cannibalism.

Women's Business – Tapa Cloth, Baskets & Mats

When the early European voyagers arrived in the Pacific, mulberry and breadfruit trees were plentiful and tapa anvils proliferated. Although tapa was ubiquitous, the early Europeans did not collect much. Women's art was largely undervalued and misunderstood. Weaving looms were not known outside of the Caroline Islands and the Santa Cruz Islands, although free-hand pandanus weaving was used to produce sleeping mats and sails for voyaging canoes.

Tapa was the only form of cloth and was used for garments as well as for mats. But its significance is wholly misunderstood if it's seen merely as a crude fibrous material – the importance of tapa cannot be overstated. In both Polynesia and Melanesia the exchange of tapa was (and often still is) crucial in forging relationships. By accepting gifts the receiver was indebted to the giver and was required, over time, to honour the debt. These relationships were bound not so much by the 'financial' transaction but by a moral contract that invoked spirits of ancestors or gods – the exchange of gifts was symbolic of a much more profound agreement. Certain kinds of tapa were valued in these exchanges above all other things.

Tapa, baskets and mats were often produced collectively; this was an important women's institution in much the same way (though not so grandiloquently) as men's councils were in producing their objects. *Buka* baskets, originally from Buka and Bougainville islands, PNG, are now emulated all over the Pacific and woven pandanus mats of various kinds are still commonly made.

Tapa was produced by great numbers of women in massive sheets for royal occasions and for the most sacred of ceremonies. Significantly, the most sacred Polynesian tapa cloths were fine, white and

PATRICK HORTON

Left: A traditional pattern is painted onto a piece of tapa in Tonga.

unadorned (similarly the most sacred demigod chiefs of Polynesia were usually not tattooed) – in some Pacific contexts, decoration is trivial. Meanings in Pacific art are not to be found in an object's motifs, but rather in the context in which the art is produced and the cultural structure in which it operates. When Tonga's Queen Salote said 'our history is written in our mats', she was referring to the role that tapa had always played in exchange and kinship relationships, rather than stories of Tonga's history being literally painted onto tapa.

In Tahiti, tapa was prepared in huge sheets – up to 3m wide and sometimes hundreds of metres long. These sheets were rolled up, stored and preserved in chiefs' houses. This way chiefs accumulated wealth, status and holy power, and when they died they and their mausoleums were wrapped in this sacred cloth for the duration of funerary rites.

The introduction of European calico and the influence of missionaries quickly brought about the virtual abandonment of tapa making in much of Polynesia. Tapa is still produced in Tonga and in Samoa, where it is called *siapo*. It is worn for special occasions and sometimes to visit town. In Melanesia tapa is still widely produced.

Canoes

All Pacific cultures built and sailed canoes. It was (and often still is) the primary means of transport. Canoes traversed vast distances of open sea in the early migrations, plied trade routes and were used on fishing expeditions and for warfare. See the boxed text 'Voyaging & Navigation' in the Facts about the South Pacific chapter. Canoe prows were the subject of much creative energy, but many other parts of the canoe – paddles (both genuine and symbolic), sterns, bailers and splash boards – were decorated with symbolic motifs that conferred power and protection onto the craft and the voyage. The canoe is also an important element in mythology, and a recurring motif in Pacific art. The canoe shape – stylised, in profile and often bearing a mast – is represented in countless artworks.

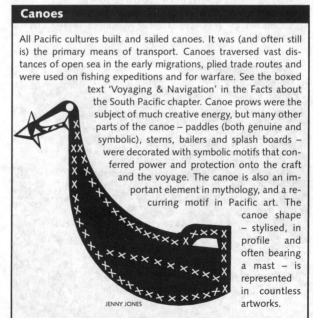

JENNY JONES

Right: An example of a canoe shape design from the Solomon Islands.

Money

Certain valuables act as currency in ceremonies (eg brideprice) or in trade. Currencies among interconnected Pacific peoples are complicated – a currency may be made by one group for use by another group, or it may only be valid tender in certain kinds of transactions. Money can enter a cyclical trade route between islands hundreds of kilometres apart, from which it never leaves.

The materials were usually hard to get, such as deep-water shells, obsidian and rare feathers, and were often worked on to produce the currency. Red-feather money, axe heads and shell money were traditional currencies in the Solomons, as were objects made from the teeth of dogs and dolphins. Rare shells, for example deep-water oyster shells, would often be cut and ground into tiny discs and threaded along a string. Leaf money was widely used in Melanesia, and in New Caledonia a certain kind of women's skirt is still used as a traditional currency in particular transactions.

Perhaps the most unusual, and certainly the most unwieldy, was the stone money from Yap called *rai*. Round disks were carved from a single piece of stone that could be 2 to 3m in diameter, weighing up to 5 tonnes. A hole was bored through the disc's centre making it look like a wheel. Rai is no longer made on Yap, but many village paths are still lined with stone money (this is called a rai bank).

There are boxed texts about traditional money in the Solomon Islands chapter, the Federated States of Micronesia chapter, and the Palau chapter.

KATE GALBRAITH

Left: No one can steal your lunch money when it weighs a cool 3 tonnes – enormous stone *rai* were used to store wealth in Yap (FSM)

Ornament

In pre-European times Pacific chiefs and nobles wore splendid regalia that confirmed their status and imbued them with the powers of ancestors and spirits. Chiefs sat on artfully carved chiefly stools and ate from beautifully made vessels. The Polynesian nobles developed a penchant for delicate fly-whisks made from rare feathers, human hair and shells set on finely carved handles (it's commonly thought that the fly was introduced by Europeans). Nobles' staffs, feather capes and *lei* (necklaces) were not just stately symbols of prestige, but were vehicles through which the holy elite participated in the world of the gods – feathers were thought to be a particularly good conduit between the worlds. The feather capes and feather-god sculptures collected for Europoean museums from the Marquesas and Hawai'i are extraordinary – vividly coloured and made with the feathers of thousands of birds.

Shells were widely used in breastplates in Melanesia, and necklaces, armlets and ornaments associated with piercings in the earlobes and nose all displayed a person's status. The *kapkap*, an open-worked turtle shell over a white shell disc, is worn on the forehead or as a necklace, and is a classic form that appears in a vast area throughout the Solomons and New Ireland (PNG). The bones of animals, head-hunters' victims and ancestors had different spiritual properties, and were often carved into personal ornaments, or objects such as combs. The most splendid personal ornamentation was reserved for special ceremonies

Right: An ornamental *kapkap* from the Solomon Islands.

JANE HART

Masks, Sculptures & Headdresses

The most abundant manifestation of aesthetic energy in the Pacific are masks and sculptures. Most 'masks' were never meant to be worn but were a form of iconographic sculpture representing a face. These objects were produced for a variety of reasons grounded in the local religion and mythology. Sometimes they were built to be destroyed in funeral pyres, and sometimes they were preserved for hundreds of years and used in on-going rituals. Sometimes masks were built to ward off malevolent spirits or to invoke benevolent ones. Some effigies and masks were built for long-dead ancestors to inhabit and watch over the clan – they were placed in special areas and had much *tapu* associated with them. Especially in Melanesia, the making of these kinds of artefacts was highly ritualised in secret men's councils.

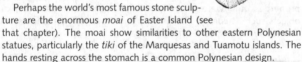

Perhaps the world's most famous stone sculpture are the enormous *moai* of Easter Island (see that chapter). The moai show similarities to other eastern Polynesian statues, particularly the *tiki* of the Marquesas and Tuamotu islands. The hands resting across the stomach is a common Polynesian design.

Ceremonial activities were often accompanied by dancers in costumes and headdresses. Dancers were important to the rites performed at the ceremony, and were sometimes temporarily possessed by spirits (the *dukduk* rituals in New Ireland and New Britain, PNG, are a striking example of this). Such costumes are not likenesses of spirits, but, within the ceremony, they are the very embodiment of spirits in the real world.

COMMON THEMES

There are themes that echo through Pacific art, but they are more to do with the role of artefacts and their production than in any motifs and icons used. Objects were created for similar reasons (islanders were exposed to similar elements) and out of the same materials, but there is no identifiable style that represents Pacific art. Resonances of Lapita pottery decoration arguably exist in much Pacific art, particularly their curvilinear dot-rendered style and simple figurative renderings of humans.

Migrations too have made it complicated. People moved east first, but some Polynesians turned back west and north-west, and Micronesians came south to settle islands off northern PNG. With long sea journeys common, there was massive cross-pollination of stories, ideas, forms, motifs and meanings in Pacific art.

Top: A 19th century wooden mask from Malekula in Vanuatu, which was designed to be worn by a dancer.

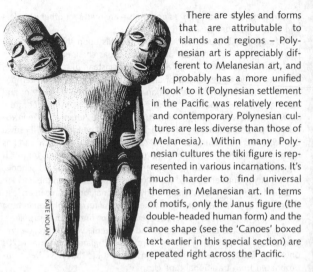

KATE NOLAN

There are styles and forms that are attributable to islands and regions – Polynesian art is appreciably different to Melanesian art, and probably has a more unified 'look' to it (Polynesian settlement in the Pacific was relatively recent and contemporary Polynesian cultures are less diverse than those of Melanesia). Within many Polynesian cultures the tiki figure is represented in various incarnations. It's much harder to find universal themes in Melanesian art. In terms of motifs, only the Janus figure (the double-headed human form) and the canoe shape (see the 'Canoes' boxed text earlier in this special section) are repeated right across the Pacific.

MODERN TRANSLATIONS

The influence and impact of European visitors on the production of art was remarked upon by Cook during his second and third voyages; tiki figures were much more widely available. Ever since, there's been a tourist trade of sorts and Europeans brought new metals, tools and materials that have long since been incorporated.

The influences on contemporary Pacific people are numerous, complicated and sometimes quite contradictory. Some purists argue that western society has contaminated indigenous art, which patronisingly suggests that Pacific islanders are unable to properly assess the value of their traditional forms, and meaningfully incorporate contemporary influences. As elsewhere, Pacific culture has not remained static, and few islanders are interested in being stone-age primitivists just to keep the purists happy.

Missionaries killed off countless traditional art forms in their attempts to convert heathens, and reorganised people around different institutions. The production of some women's art – tapa, baskets, mats – is now often organised around Christian women's groups, and Christian motifs are incorporated in the design.

Oddly, modern textile designs have also taken on commercial images such as the Coca Cola and Pepsi emblems, and even the logos of banks and outboard motor manufacturers. Images of western pop artists and film stars proliferate as T-shirt prints, and television, western trash culture and a consumer society prevails among many urbanised islanders.

Top: A Tahitian Janus figure – double-headed humans were a popular theme in Pacific sculpture, particularly in Tahiti.

Tourist art (see Buying Art) is produced in large volumes in places such as Fiji, New Caledonia and Tahiti, but elsewhere the tourist trade is too small to generate a proper industry. Many of the most attractive utilitarian objects – bowls, bags and mats – are made for other islanders and sold in the markets.

Although contemporary Pacific art still calls upon the histories and legends of islanders, its place in the culture has changed. The production of art is now often an individual activity instead of a collective one, and the notion of ownership of artworks has arisen. Some contemporary art is an adaptation of traditional forms, for example pottery and carving, but new media, materials and tools have been incorporated. Travelling exhibitions to Australia, Europe and the Americas have introduced a broad audience to Pacific art, and since the four-yearly Festival of Pacific Arts was inaugurated in 1972, the renaissance of Pacific art has become the source of great pride for islanders and the impetus for much regional tourism. National governments have been funding art schools, community groups and public works (mural art is popular in the Pacific).

Especially in Polynesia, where many traditional forms have been lost, the rebirth of creative energy has taken on new forms. Polynesian tapa is mostly a lost art, but these days *tivaevae* (or *tifaifai*) has supplanted tapa. These are applique works and the needlework technique was introduced by missionary wives from New England from the 1820s onwards. Tivaevae bear some designs and motifs that have been appropriated from traditional tapa cloth.

Tattooing has experienced a major rebirth in parts of French Polynesia (especially the Societies and Marquesas) but the stories and

Below Left & Right:
Modern Tahitian mural frescoes incorporate traditional designs and tales from mythology.

JEAN-BERNARD CARILLET

JEAN-BERNARD CARILLET

meanings behind many of the traditional designs have been lost. This is true too in New Zealand where traditional Maori tattoos have become very popular, but in many cases their application has become more ad hoc and original meanings may be lost. Designs that were reserved for a chief or noble family may now exist in the public domain.

Nuclear testing in the Pacific is a strong theme in much modern art. In areas where independence and indigenous rights struggles are current (for example in New Caledonia and French Polynesia) modern art is highly political.

Among the internationally recognised South Pacific artists are Eddie Daiding Bibimauri, from Malaita in the Solomons, who is a Honiara-based graphic artist and muralist; Kiribati's Tekiraua Urio; New Zealand-based John Pule, a Nuiean artist who inventively reworks the traditional art of tapa; and painters Alio Pilioko and Nikolai Michoutouchkine from Vanuatu. Contemporary artists such as these rely on support from governments, cultural centres, art collectors and tourists.

BUYING ART

In the popular tourists destinations (Fiji, New Caledonia and Tahiti) artworks are abundant and specialist shops sell quasi-traditional artefacts, T-shirts and various other souvenirs. In most other areas of the South Pacific there are not enough tourists to support this.

The biggest market for modern artists are the tourists that come and stay in the international hotels, and artists often sell works outside. Carvers and other traditional artists also sell pieces outside the hotels. Usually these are pieces produced for sale to tourists, but that doesn't mean they're poorly made or trashy souvenirs – some of the objects

Buying South Pacific Art

There are three important points about buying art in the South Pacific:

- Try to buy from the maker rather than a shop owner, so that the maker collects the full sale value. In cash-poor communities your tourist dollars can make a real difference.
- Don't haggle about the price. Bargaining is not natural in the South Pacific (an exception is the Indian community in Fiji) and it's rare for an artefact maker to over-inflate the price to give room for negotiation. While it is becoming increasingly common for artisans to offer a 'second price' in the bigger cities and around international hotels, protracted bargaining is considered rude, especially in Melanesia. If you can't afford it, buy something else.
- Don't buy objects that incorporate rare shells, corals or turtle shells.

are produced by masters using traditional forms or derivatives and honouring time-old traditions. Needless to say there are plenty of poorly made trashy souvenirs too. Some local markets have artefacts for sale, and the bigger hotels often sell objects (at a substantial mark-up).

Out of the big cities and in the more remote places, artists and artefacts makers will often be hanging around the airport waiting for you to step off the plane, or they'll be waiting by the wharf. Sometimes in these areas the vendor won't speak English well (if at all), but will have no trouble communicating the terms of the transaction.

You may prefer to buy one object that you really like, rather than countless small carvings and inferior pieces. This piece may be quite expensive, but it will be a much more potent and enduring reminder of your journey than a bunch of disposable souvenirs. Consider, too, how you will get it home in one piece – many carvings are heavy, unwieldy items that won't travel well. Or they might be incredibly delicate. Objects made from animal materials – skin, teeth, hair – will probably be subject to quarantine restrictions in your home country.

Look carefully at the details and the materials used. Inferior timbers are sometimes rubbed down with shoe polish or stain to pass them off as quality ebony (which is rare these days). Feel the weight in the timber and look carefully for the carver's deft touches in the details and the finish. Expect to pay for what you get – a good piece will be beautiful but it may be expensive.

FURTHER READING

There are many excellent books available on South Pacific art. Some that were published as early as the 1950s are out of print, but perhaps available from libraries.

The most comprehensive and beautifully presented pictorial book must be Anthony JP Meyer's hardback, two-volume *Oceanic Art* with explanatory text in English, French and German. Artefacts are singly photographed under studio lighting and there are various asides and archival photographs.

Anne D'Alleva's *Art of the Pacific* is also excellent. The fine colour pictures are secondary to the arguments developed in the text, which provide an excellent deconstruction of art in Pacific societies. This book provides some fascinating insights into the religious structures in which art was made.

From the World of Art series, *Oceanic Art* by Nicholas Thomas is splendid. Although it's an academic work, the book is very readable and the selection of pictures complements Thomas' compelling arguments.

Rowan McKinnon

Carved wooden panel, Marquesas Islands, French Polynesia

Small wooden *tiki*, Marquesas

Palisade of carved totems in Vao, on New Caledonia's Île des Pins

Cute carving, New Caledonia

Kerosene-wood bowl from Western Province, Solomon Islands

Beating *tapa* cloth, Marquesas Islands

Woodcarver, Loyalty Islands, New Caledonia

Roof beams in a *fale fono* (meeting house), Futuna

Applique fabric from Atiu, Cook Islands

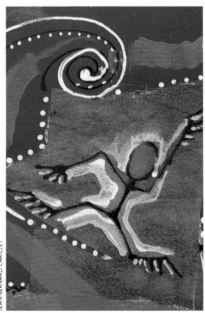

Painting with Polynesian motifs

Regional Facts for the Visitor

The Best & Worst

The Best

The Pacific is an enormous and diverse region and no list of highlights can hope to please everyone. But it's fun to compile one anyway, so we asked our authors to list their personal Pacific highlights. The results are as follows:

- Participating in a game of *kirikiti* – a form of all-in cricket – in Samoa, French Polynesia or Tokelau
- Trekking through Rarotonga's rugged mountain interior
- Attending a feast and cultural show and watching traditional dancing
- Scuba diving in magnificent Chuuk Lagoon (FSM), the Rock Islands (Palau), the wreck of the SS *President Coolidge* (Vanuatu) – hell, diving anywhere in the Pacific!
- Staying with a Pacific family
- Seeing the famous stone *moai* (statues) of Easter Island
- Watching the ancient *naghol* (land diving) ceremony on Pentecost Island in Vanuatu
- Getting a formal invite to a traditional kava-drinking ceremony

The Worst

It's not all kava & skittles. The authors were also asked to nominate the worst aspects of the South Pacific. Their list included:

- Tinned meat and other highly processed foods and drinks
- Mosquitos!
- Shonky sweatshops in American Samoa and the Northern Mariana Islands
- The relentless heat and humidity at certain times of the year
- Exorbitant prices designed to drain the last *franc* out of tourists in Noumea and Tahiti
- Constant harassment of western women in Chuuk – making it difficult to venture out alone
- Piles of plastic trash, aluminium cans – and much much worse – littering beaches and lagoons

PLANNING

Despite appearances to the contrary, things can change quickly in the Pacific. A cyclone can knock out all accommodation (not to mention roads, electricity and telephones) and local disputes can close off an area.

The number one rule for a Pacific holiday is to be flexible. The Pacific attitude to time is more relaxed than in many western cultures, so you shouldn't set your heart on getting to destinations or getting things done in any great hurry. See Time later in this chapter, and the boxed text 'Last Bus to Paradise' in the Samoa chapter for a typical experience.

Inter-Island Travel

Unlike Europe or Africa, in the Pacific you usually can't just decide which country you'd like to visit next and arrange travel on the spot – unless, of course, you have your own yacht! If, like most Pacific tourists, you're travelling by air, the only reasonable way to travel to more than one or two countries is by buying an air pass (see Air in the Getting Around the Region chapter). Otherwise, costs for inter-country flights will quickly break the bank.

Most air passes have to be bought well in advance, and many of them must be purchased before you commence travel. So decide where you want to go before you do anything else.

When to Go

Most Pacific islands tourists time their visit according to the weather. Namely, they avoid the wet season. Being in the tropics, the temperature doesn't vary much – it's *always* hot – but during the wet season, heat, humidity and persistent rain can combine to make a holiday a bit uncomfortable. However, most of the rain falls at night, and the wet season is the time when other tourists will not accompany you in plague proportions.

South of the equator, the dry season runs from May to October and the wet season (including the cyclone season in some areas; see

Climate in the Facts about the South Pacific chapter) is from November to April. These seasons are more-or-less reversed north of the equator, ie in Micronesia. In the individual country chapters, see Climate under Facts about the Country, and When to Go under Facts for the Visitor. Also use the Climate Charts at the back of the book to compare the weather in different destinations.

During peak tourist times, prices can be high, accommodation fully booked and the attractions packed. You'll find much better deals and far fewer crowds in the shoulder seasons (either side of the dry season) in October and May. Around Christmas time, many flights and boats are fully booked by islanders returning home from overseas to spend time with their families.

See Public Holidays and Special Events in this chapter and in the individual country chapters for information on holidays and festivities in your destination country.

What Kind of Trip

'If it's Monday, we must be in Nuku'alofa.' Though often ridiculed, the mad dash that crams six countries into a month does have its merits. If you've never visited the Pacific islands before, you won't know which islands you'll like, and a quick 'scouting' tour will give an overview of the options. An air pass offering unlimited travel within a set period of time is the best way to do this. See the Getting Around the Region chapter.

But if you know where you want to go, or where you can find a place you like, the best advice is to stay put for a while, discover some lesser known sights, make a few local friends and settle in. It's also cheaper in the long run.

It's possible to incorporate an island holiday while en route from North America to Australasia or to Asia. Often this can be done without any extra cost to your air fare. If you have access to a yacht, either your own or someone else's, an island-hopping holiday can take in some of the more remote islands.

Maps

No map covering an area as huge as the Pacific Ocean can provide enough detail of any one island to be really useful on the ground (or on the water). However, a map of the Pacific – there are several on the market – can provide you with some idea of 'context' if that's important to you.

The maps in this book will help you get an idea of where you might want to go, and will be a useful first reference when you arrive in a country. However, if you're driving or cycling, proper road maps are essential. (See Planning under Facts for the Visitor in the individual country chapters for good local maps.) Tourist offices often provide free maps, while government lands departments are a good source for better quality, more detailed maps.

It is possible to get maps from some international organisations – some will post you a free catalogue on request. The US Geological Survey (USGS; ☎ 888-275 8747, fax 303-202 4693, infoservices@ usgs.gov), PO Box 25286, Denver Federal Bldg, Denver, CO 80225, USA, provides slightly dated maps for many US and ex-US territories. Its maps are listed on the Internet at http://mapping.usgs.gov/mac/ maplists/selectstatelist.html (select 'Pacific Islands' and 'Full List'). The US National Ocean Service (NOS; ☎ 301-436 8301, fax 436 6829, distribution@noaa.gov), 6501 Lafayette Ave, Riverdale, MD 20737-1199, USA, publishes nautical maps of the territories. Its international sales agents are listed on the Internet (http://acc.nos.noaa .gov/Nau/NautAgents.html).

Similarly, New Zealand's Terralink (☎ 04-470 6020, fax 495 8450, info@terralink .co.nz), 103 Thorndon Quay, Wellington, maps the Cook islands, Niue and Tokelau. Its Pacific maps are listed online (www.maps .co.nz). France's Institut Géographique National (IGN; ☎ 01 43 98 80 00, fax 01 43 98 85 89, Minitel 3615 IGN), 107 Rue Boétie, Paris 75008, publishes an excellent range of maps for the French territories.

What to Bring

The Pacific is no shopping paradise. As the locals will tell you, it can be really difficult to find some items when you're not in the capital – and sometimes even when you are!

The general rule of travelling, that it's better to start with too little rather than too much, doesn't apply quite so much in the Pacific. Clothes are easy to buy in large centres, but anything else you *need*, you should bring with you.

A backpack is still the most popular method of carrying gear, as it is convenient, especially for walking. On the down side, a backpack doesn't offer much protection for your valuables, the straps tend to get caught on things and some airlines may refuse to accept responsibility if the pack is damaged or tampered with.

Travelpacks, a combination backpack/shoulder bag, are very popular. The backpack straps zip away inside the pack when they're not needed, so you almost have the best of both worlds. Some packs have sophisticated shoulder-strap adjustments, making them comfortable even on those long hikes into town when the buses have stopped for the day. Backpacks or travelpacks can be made slightly theft-proof with small padlocks.

As for clothing, the climate will have a bearing on what you take along. Remember that insulation works on the principle of trapped air, so several layers of thin clothing are warmer than a single thick one (and will be easier to dry). You'll also be much more flexible if the weather suddenly turns warm. Be prepared for rain at any time of year.

A minimum packing list could include:

- underwear, socks and swimming gear
- pair of long trousers and shorts or a skirt
- an ankle-length skirt for formal occasions
- a few T-shirts and shirts
- one warm pullover
- a pair of solid walking shoes
- sandals or thongs (flip flops) for showers and hot days
- a lightweight raincoat
- medical kit and sewing kit
- a padlock
- Swiss Army-type knife
- soap and light-weight towel
- toothpaste, toothbrush and other toiletries

A padlock is useful to lock your bag to a luggage rack in a bus; it may also be needed to secure your hostel locker. A Swiss Army knife comes in handy for all sorts of things. *Any* pocketknife is fine, but make sure it includes such essentials as scissors, a bottle opener and strong corkscrew. Soap, toothpaste and toilet paper are readily obtainable, but you'll need your own supply of paper in many public toilets and 'open air facilities' (behind a tree). Tampons are available at pharmacies and supermarkets in all but the most remote places. Condoms are similarly available.

A tent and sleeping bag are vital if you want to save money by camping, but see Accommodation later in this chapter for restrictions on camping in the Pacific. If you're not camping, it's probably better to save the space in your backpack and leave the sleeping bag at home.

Other optional items include a compass, a torch (flashlight), a pocket calculator for currency conversions, an alarm clock, an adapter plug for electrical appliances (such as a cup or immersion water heater to save on expensive tea and coffee), a universal bath/sink plug (a film canister sometimes works), portable short-wave radio, sunglasses or a few clothes pegs.

Also, consider using plastic carry bags or bin liners inside your backpack to keep things separate but also dry if the pack gets soaked.

RESPONSIBLE TOURISM

Being the perfectly responsible tourist sometimes feels like picking your way through a minefield. You may have to pick your battles and decide where you want to concentrate your efforts.

As background information for your crusade, you could read: Fishing, under Ecology & Environment in the Facts about the South Pacific chapter; Buying Art, in the 'South Pacific Arts' special section; and the boxed texts 'Responsible Bushwalking' (later in this chapter), 'Responsible Diving' in the 'South Pacific Diving' special section and finally 'Responsible Yachting' in the Getting Around the Region chapter. Phew!

TOURIST OFFICES

See the Facts for the Visitor sections of individual country chapters for local tourist offices.

The Tourism Council of the South Pacific (TCSP) is an intergovernmental organisation based in Suva, Fiji, that fosters regional co-operation in the development and promotion of tourism in the Pacific.

The TCSP serves as a tourist office for many countries, and can provide information and brochures about travel, accommodation and things to do. It has a website (www.tcsp.com), and offices around the world include:

France
   (☎ 04 76 70 06 17, fax 04 76 70 09 18, 100772.1160@compuserve.com)
   13 Rue d'Alembert, 38000 Grenoble
Fiji
   (☎ 304 171, fax 301 995, tcsphq@is.com.fj)
   PO Box 13119, Suva
Germany
   (☎ 030-42 25 60 26, fax 42 25 62 87, 100762.3614@compuserve.com)
   Petersburger Strasse 94, Berlin 10247
UK
   (☎ 020-8392 1838, fax 8878 0998)
   375 Upper Richmond Rd West, London SW14 7NX
USA
   (☎ 530-538 0152, fax 538 0154, SoPacTour@cs.com)
   PO Box 7440, 475 Lake Blvd, Tahoe City, CA 96145

VISAS & DOCUMENTS
Travel Insurance
A travel insurance policy to cover theft, accidental loss and medical problems is a good idea. Some policies offer various medical-expense options; the higher ones are chiefly for countries, such as the USA, that have extremely high medical costs. There is a wide variety of policies available, so check the small print.

Some policies exclude 'dangerous activities', which can include scuba diving, motorcycling, even trekking. A locally acquired motorcycle licence is not valid under some policies.

You may prefer a policy that pays doctors or hospitals directly rather than you having to pay on the spot and claim later. If you have to claim expenses later, make sure you keep all documentation. Some policies ask you to call back (reverse charges) to a centre in your home country, where an immediate assessment of your problem is made.

Check that the policy covers ambulance transportation and/or an emergency flight home.

Driving Licence & Permits
Prior to travelling, check whether you need an International Driving Permit to drive in the countries you are visiting. Bring your scuba-certification card if you plan to do any scuba diving.

Photocopies
All important documents (passport data page and visa page, credit cards, travel insurance policy, air/bus/train tickets, driving licence etc) should be photocopied before you leave home. Leave one copy with someone at home and keep another with you, separate from the originals.

EMBASSIES & CONSULATES
Your home country embassy or consulate as well as those of the Pacific nation in question are listed in the Facts for the Visitor section of individual country chapters.

Your Own Embassy
It's important to realise what your own embassy – the embassy of the country of which you are a citizen – can and can't do to help you if you get into trouble.

Generally speaking, it won't be much help in emergencies if the trouble you're in is remotely your own fault. Remember that you are bound by the laws of the country you are in. Your embassy will not be sympathetic if you end up in jail after committing a crime locally, even if such actions are legal in your own country.

In genuine emergencies you might get some assistance, but only if other channels have been exhausted. For example, if you need to get home urgently, a free ticket home is exceedingly unlikely – the embassy would expect you to have insurance. If you have all your money and documents stolen, it might assist with getting a new passport, but a loan for onward travel is out of the question.

Some embassies used to keep letters for travellers or have a small reading room with home newspapers, but these days the mail holding service is usually defunct and even newspapers tend to be out of date.

CUSTOMS

If you are travelling with expensive camera or computer equipment, carry a receipt to avoid hassles when returning home. Importing vegetable matter, seeds, animals or dairy produce to isolated island nations can introduce diseases with the potential to lay waste to local agriculture. Importing such items without a licence is usually prohibited.

Naturally, taking firearms or drugs through customs is frowned upon every-

where. See the individual country chapters for any particular customs rules. Many countries prohibit taking coral, shells or artefacts out of the country.

MONEY
Exchanging Money

The most easily exchanged currencies in the Pacific are the US, Australian and New Zealand dollars, and the Pacific franc (the Cour de Franc Pacifique; see the French Polynesia or New Caledonia chapters for exchange rates). Exactly which is best depends on the particular country (see Money in the individual country chapters). Approximate exchange rates are given in the table below.

Exchange Rates

US Dollar Exchange Rates

country	unit		US$
Australia	A$1	=	$0.65
Canada	C$1	=	$0.67
Easter Island	Ch$100	=	$0.19
euro	€1	=	$1.10
Fiji	F$1	=	$0.51
France	10FF	=	$1.60
Germany	DM1	=	$0.52
Japan	¥100	=	$0.91
New Zealand	NZ$1	=	$0.53
Pacific franc	100 CFP	=	$0.89
PNG	K1	=	$0.40
Samoa	ST1	=	$0.33
Solomon Islands	S$1	=	$0.20
Tonga	T$1	=	$0.66
UK	£1	=	$1.60
Vanuatu	100VT	=	$0.77

Australian Dollar Exchange Rates

country	unit		A$
Canada	C$1	=	$1.05
Easter Island	Ch$100	=	$0.29
euro	€1	=	$1.60
Fiji	F$1	=	$0.78
France	10FF	=	$2.40
Germany	DM1	=	$0.81
Japan	¥100	=	$1.40

country	unit		
New Zealand	NZ$1	=	$0.81
Pacific franc	100 CFP	=	$1.40
PNG	K1	=	$0.52
Samoa	ST1	=	$0.50
Solomon Islands	S$1	=	$0.30
Tonga	T$1	=	$1.05
UK	£1	=	$2.50
USA	US$1	=	$1.50
Vanuatu	100VT	=	$1.20

NZ Dollar Exchange Rates

country	unit		NZ$
Australia	A$1	=	$1.20
Canada	C$1	=	$1.30
Easter Island	Ch$100	=	$0.36
euro	€1	=	$1.90
Fiji	F$1	=	$0.96
France	10FF	=	$3.20
Germany	DM1	=	$0.99
Japan	¥100	=	$1.70
Pacific franc	100 CFP	=	$1.70
PNG	K1	=	$0.66
Samoa	ST1	=	$0.62
Solomon Islands	S$1	=	$0.37
Tonga	T$1	=	$1.20
UK	£1	=	$3.20
USA	US$1	=	$1.90
Vanuatu	100VT	=	$1.50

You lose out through commissions and customer exchange rates every time you change money, so if you only visit Guam, for example, you may be better off buying US dollars straight away if your bank at home can provide them. If banks charge a flat rate, you are better off changing larger amounts less frequently.

All Pacific currencies are fully convertible, but you may have trouble exchanging some of the lesser-known ones at small banks, while currencies of countries with high inflation face unfavourable exchange rates. Try not to have too many leftover notes of Pacific currencies at the end of your trip; no bank outside the Pacific will touch them.

Most airports and big hotels have banking facilities that are open outside normal office hours, sometimes on a 24-hour basis. Post offices often perform banking tasks and outnumber banks in remote places; they also tend to have extended hours of operation. Be aware, though, that while they always exchange cash, they might balk at handling travellers cheques.

The best exchange rates are generally offered at banks. *Bureaux de change* usually offer worse rates or charge a higher commission. Hotels are almost always the worst places to change money. American Express and Thomas Cook offices usually do not charge a commission for changing their own cheques, but may offer a less favourable rate than banks.

Cash Nothing beats cash for convenience ... or risk. If you lose it, it's gone forever and very few travel insurers will come to your rescue. Those that will, limit the amount to somewhere around US$300. A money belt under your clothes is not a bad precaution.

Travellers Cheques The main reason for carrying travellers cheques rather than cash is the protection they offer from theft, though they are losing their popularity as more travellers deposit their money in their bank at home and withdraw it as they go along through automatic teller machines (ATMs).

American Express and Thomas Cook travellers cheques are widely accepted and have efficient replacement policies. If you're going to remote places, it's worth sticking to American Express, since small local banks may not always accept other brands.

When you change cheques, don't look at just the exchange rate; ask about fees and commissions as well. There may be a service fee per cheque, a flat transaction fee or a percentage of the total amount irrespective of the number of cheques. Some banks charge fees (often exorbitant) to change cheques and not cash; others do the reverse.

Keep a record of cheque numbers; without them, replacement of lost cheques will be a slow and painful process. Many institutions charge a per-cheque fee, so most of your cheques should be in large denominations, say US$100. It's only at the end of your stay that you might want to change a US$10 or US$20 cheque just to get through the last day or two. The exchange rate for travellers cheques is often better than that for cash.

Plastic Cards & ATMs Ask your bank to explain the workings and relative merits of credit, credit/debit, debit, charge and cash cards.

A major advantage of credit cards is that they allow you to pay for expensive items (eg airline tickets) without your having to carry great wads of cash around. They also allow you to withdraw cash at selected banks or from the many ATMs that are linked up internationally. However, if an ATM in Fiji swallows a card that was issued in Germany, it can be a major headache. Also, some credit cards aren't hooked up to ATM networks unless you specifically ask your bank to do this. ATMs are common in major Pacific centres, but unknown in the outer islands or rural areas.

Cash cards, which you use at home to withdraw money directly from your bank account or savings account, can be used at ATMs linked to international networks like Cirrus and Maestro.

Credit and credit/debit cards, such as Visa and MasterCard, are widely accepted. However, these cards often have a credit limit that is too low to cover major expenses like long-term car rental or airline tickets and can be difficult to replace if lost abroad. Also, a cash advance against your Visa or MasterCard credit card account incurs a transaction fee and/or finance charge. With some issuers, the fees can reach as high as US$10, *plus* interest per transaction, so it's best to check with your card issuer before leaving home and compare rates.

Charge cards, such as American Express (Amex) have offices in many countries that will replace a lost card within 24 hours. However, Amex offices in the Pacific are limited to Australia, French Polynesia, New Caledonia, New Zealand and the Northern Mariana Islands. Charge cards are not widely accepted off the beaten track.

The best advice is not to put all your eggs in one basket. If you want to rely heavily on bits of plastic, go for two different cards – an American Express or Diners Club, for instance, along with a Visa or MasterCard. Better still is a combination of credit or cash card and travellers cheques so you have something to fall back on if an ATM swallows your card or the banks in the area are closed.

A word of warning: fraudulent shopkeepers have been known to quickly make several charge slip imprints with your credit card when you're not looking, and then simply copy your signature from the one that you authorise. Try not to let your card out of sight, and always check your statements upon your return.

Transfers through International Transfers Telegraphic are inexpensive but can be quite slow. Specify the name of the bank and the name and address of the branch where you'd like to pick it up.

You can wire money via an American Express office (US$60 for US$1000). Western Union's Money Transfer system (available at post offices in some countries) and Thomas Cook's MoneyGram service are also popular.

Costs

The Pacific is *not* a bargain location for travellers. Accommodation is relatively expensive; hostels may be fairly common in most regions but low cost options such as camping are often not possible (see Accommodation

later in this chapter). Much of the food is imported, and is therefore pricey. In remote areas transport costs force food prices up even further. The most expensive countries to visit are French Polynesia and New Caledonia, while the cheapest are Samoa and Fiji.

Costs vary enormously. Look through Places to Stay and Places to Eat in the appropriate country chapters to get some idea of local prices. About US$30 per day will allow you to live like a monk (or a nun) in New Caledonia (staying in the hostel, eating bread and cheese), or have a pretty good time in Samoa (mid-range accommodation, car hire and some restauranting).

Because of the price of fuel, travel costs can be particularly high, whether by car, air or speedboat. Some careful planning can reduce travel costs substantially. Hiring a bicycle or hitch-hiking is worth considering.

One money-saving strategy is preparing your own meals; it's worth looking at accommodation with access to a kitchen. Avoid expensive tinned goods in favour of locally grown fruit and vegetables. Markets are usually the cheapest way to buy any kind of food. At the very least, avoid trendy tourist restaurants and look for the places catered by locals.

The more time you spend in any one place, the lower your daily expenses are likely to be as you get to know your way around. Travelling with someone else is another way to save money.

Activities such as scuba diving, organised tours and car hire will push costs up considerably.

A general warning about the prices we list in this book: they're likely to change, usually upward, but if the last holiday season was particularly slow, or the local economy crashes, they may remain the same or even come down a bit. Many Pacific economies, particularly in Micronesia, were badly affected by the Asian economic crisis of the late 1990s. In these countries prices have already dropped dramatically, and when their economies recover, prices will rise. Nevertheless, relative price levels should stay fairly constant: if Hotel Ay costs twice as much as Hotel Bee, it's likely to stay that way.

Tipping & Bargaining

Attitudes to tipping vary in the Pacific but in general, tipping is not expected and in some cases it may even cause offence. It's far better to keep your 'tip' to a smile of thanks. In Melanesian societies, a tip is a gift that creates an obligation that the receiver must reciprocate, and they can't do this if you're passing through. Tipping is becoming more common in US-influenced Micronesia, and in cities like American Samoa's Pago Pago or French Polynesia's Papeete.

The Pacific is not Asia; bargaining is not the practice in any Pacific countries and may cause offence. Although it is becoming more common in the tourist shops of major cities, village people will often take their produce back home from market rather than accept a lower price than what's asked. See Buying Art in the 'South Pacific Arts' special section.

Occasionally, people in isolated areas will quote you grossly inflated prices for artefacts or accommodation, usually because they have no idea what the current price should be. When this happens, explain that you can't afford that much and then tell them what it would cost in the city. If they don't accept it, you'll have to either pay the first price or try elsewhere.

POST & COMMUNICATIONS
Post

You can collect mail at poste restante counters in all major post offices. Ask friends writing to you to print your name clearly and to underline your surname. Then mark the envelope 'Poste Restante (General Delivery)' with the name of the city and country. When collecting mail, you may be required to present identification and you may have to pay a small fee. Check under your first name as well as your surname. Post offices usually hold letters for about a month.

If you're arriving by yacht, letters should have the name of the vessel included somewhere in the address. Mail is normally filed under the name of the vessel rather than by surname.

Telephone

At the time of writing, it wasn't feasible to take a mobile phone on holiday in the Pacific. Public telephones are a bit of a rarity, but it's usually not too hard to find a shop owner who will let you borrow their phone for local calls if you smile nicely. Some top-end hotels charge pretty steeply for the privilege of using their phones.

International telephone codes are listed in an appendix of this book.

Email & Internet Access

Travelling with a portable computer is a great way to stay in touch with life back home. Remember that the power supply voltage in the countries you visit may vary from that at home. See Electricity later in this chapter and under Facts for the Visitor in the individual country chapters.

Your modem may not work once you leave your home country – you won't know for sure until you try. The best option is to buy a reputable 'global' modem before you leave home, or buy a local modem if you're spending an extended time in one country. Keep in mind that the telephone socket in each country you visit will probably be different from that at home, so take at least a US RJ-11 telephone adapter that works with your modem. (You can almost always find an adapter that will convert from RJ-11 to the local variety.) For more information on travelling with a portable computer, see www.teleadapt.com or www.warrior.com.

The major international Internet service providers, such as AOL, CompuServe and IBM Net, have very few dial-in nodes in the South Pacific. You're better off relying on cybercafes and other public access points to collect your mail.

As well as a handful of cybercafes, you may also find public Internet access in post offices, telecom offices, libraries, hostels, hotels or universities. See individual country chapters for information about Internet access in that country.

If you use cybercafes to access your home email account, you'll need three pieces of information: your incoming (POP or IMAP) mail server name, your account name and your password. Your ISP or network supervisor will be able to give you these. With this information you should be able to access your account from any Internet-connected machine in the world, provided it runs some kind of email software (Netscape and Internet Explorer both have mail modules). It pays to become familiar with the process for doing this before you leave home. Another option for collecting mail through cybercafes is to open a free web-based email account such as HotMail (www.hotmail.com) or Yahoo! Mail (mail.yahoo.com).

INTERNET RESOURCES

The Internet is a rich resource for travellers. You can research your trip, hunt down bargain air fares, book hotels, check on weather conditions or chat with locals and other travellers about the best places to visit (or avoid!).

There's no better place to start your explorations than the Lonely Planet website (www.lonelyplanet.com). Here you'll find succinct summaries on travelling to most places on earth, postcards from other travellers and the Thorn Tree bulletin board, where you can ask questions before you go or dispense advice when you get back. You can also find travel news and updates to many of our most popular guidebooks, and the sub-WWWay section links you to the most useful travel resources elsewhere on the web.

Many airlines have their own websites; see Airlines in the Getting Around the Region chapter. Tourist office websites are a good source for relevant links, see the individual country chapters. Some other useful and reliable websites providing information on the Pacific are:

Air Promotion Systems
  www.pacificislands.com
  (regional airlines, air passes and a calendar of Pacific events)
Australian National University
  http://sunsite.anu.edu.au/spin/wwwvl-pacific
  (comprehensive collection of Pacific links)
Greenpeace
  www.greenpeace.org
  (information about environmental issues affecting the oceans, including the greenhouse effect, nuclear testing and over-fishing)

Polynesian Voyaging Society
  http://leahi.kcc.hawaii.edu/org/pvs/
  (the history of Polynesian voyaging and contemporary voyages)
South Pacific Environment Program
  www.sidsnet.org/pacific/sprep
  (environmental issues in the Pacific)
Teldir
  www.teldir.com/pacific/
  (telephone directories)
Tourism Council of the South Pacific (TCSP)
  www.tcsp.com
  (a summary of tourist information about most of the countries in the region)
United Nations
  www.unep.ch/iuc/submenu/infokit/factcont.htm
  (global warming and rising sea levels)
University of Hawai'i
  http://pidp.ewc.hawaii.edu/PIReport/
  (the excellent daily Pacific Islands Report)
  www2.hawaii.edu/~ogden/piir/
  (a collection of Pacific island Internet resources)
University of the South Pacific Book Centre
  http://maya.usp.ac.fj/~bookcentre/
  (Pacific books and publications)
US State Department
  http://travel.state.gov/travel_warnings.html
  (mildly paranoid official travel warnings)
World Climate
  www.worldclimate.com
  (average climate trends)

BOOKS

Only the larger towns on main islands are likely to have much in the way of bookshops. It's also worth trying public and college (high school) libraries. In the Pacific region you'll find large Pacific collections in libraries in Honolulu, Suva and Auckland. The website of the University of the South Pacific (USP) lists many Pacific books. See the individual country chapters for more books.

Publishers

Most books are published in different editions by different publishers in different countries. As a result, a book might be a hardcover rarity in one country but readily available in paperback in another. Fortunately, bookshops and libraries search by title or author, so your local bookshop or library is best placed to advise you on the availability of our recommendations.

If a title is out of print, try public or university libraries.

Lonely Planet

A guidebook covering an area as vast as the South Pacific can only hope to scratch the surface. For more detailed information about your destination see Lonely Planet's comprehensive list of South Pacific titles. Single-country guidebooks of the region are *Rarotonga & the Cook Islands*, *Chile & Easter Island*, *Tahiti & French Polynesia*, *Samoa*, *Tonga*, *Fiji*, *New Caledonia*, *Solomon Islands* and *Vanuatu*. In addition, we publish the multicountry guide *Micronesia*, and guides for the Pacific islands not included in this book: *Hawaii*, *Papua New Guinea* and *New Zealand*.

Pacific travellers might also find Lonely Planet's phrasebook series useful: the *South Pacific* phrasebook includes Cook Islands Maori, Kanak, Niuean, Pitkern, Samoan, Tahitian and Tongan. The *Pidgin* phrasebook includes the languages of the Solomon Islands and Vanuatu.

Lonely Planet's Pisces series includes guides to *Great Reefs of the World*, *Sharks of Tropical & Temperate Seas*, *Venomous & Toxic Marine Life of the World* and *Watching Fishes*. Individual Pisces guides to diving and snorkelling in the Pacific islands are listed in the 'South Pacific Diving' special section.

In the Journeys travel literature series is Isabella Tree's *Islands in the Clouds – Travels in the Highlands of New Guinea*.

Guidebooks

The natural history and environmental aspects of Pacific (and Carribbean) islands is given in Frederic Martini's *Exploring Tropical Isles and Seas*. Dick Watling's *Birds of Fiji, Tonga and Samoa* is excellent, and includes colour illustrations of all the region's endemic and migratory birds. A useful Melanesian bird guide is the *Field Guide to the Birds of the Solomons, Vanuatu and New Caledonia*, by Chris Doughty.

A guide to the marinelife of the region is Ewald Lieske & Robert Myers' *Coral Reef Fishes*. Another good guide is *Sharks of Polynesia*, by RH Johnson. If you prefer killing fish to just looking at them, Peter Goadby's *Big Fish and Blue Water – Gamefishing in the Pacific* might be for you.

See Books under Sea in the Getting Around the Region chapter for a couple of excellent guides to cargo ships and yachting.

Travel

The first travelogue about the Pacific was Simon Winchester's *The Pacific* – an entertaining but rather hastily assembled account of his journalistic journeys around the region. Far superior is Julian Evans' *Transit of Venus – Travels in the Pacific* – a well written account of his shoestring journey by boat through the Pacific.

Slow Boats Home by Gavin Young is the sequel to his earlier book *Slow Boats to China*. These books recount the author's 1979 voyage around the world on a wide range of maritime transport. The second book includes the Pacific part of the journey.

The perpetually miserable Paul Theroux's *The Happy Isles of Oceania – Paddling the Pacific* is anything but 'happy'. Poor old Paul complained of a wretched time and eventually had to return to the USA.

The classic *A Reporter in Micronesia*, by EJ Kahn, is a very readable log of Kahn's travels around the islands. His journeys were mostly by field ship, as Micronesia then had no jet traffic, no tourist hotels and very few visitors.

Fiction

After a flurry of novels about the Pacific islands at the start of the 20th century, other regions became more fashionable and it is now difficult to find a contemporary novel set in the region. Most famous among the oldies, *Tales of the South Pacific*, *Rascals in Paradise* and *Return to Paradise*, by James Michener, are collections of short stories and essays dealing with life in the South Pacific from WWII onward. The first title sparked a revival of western interest in the Pacific, won a Pulitzer Prize, and was made into a Broadway show and a film; see the Films entry in this chapter.

Jack London (*South Sea Tales*; 1911), Somerset Maugham (*The Trembling of a*

Leaf; 1921) and Robert Louis Stevenson (see Books in the Samoa chapter) were other European authors whose Pacific island short stories became famous.

Contemporary Pacific island novelists include Sir Thomas Davis (see Pre-European History & Voyaging books), Albert Wendt (see Books in the Samoa chapter) and 'Epeli Hau'ofa (see the Tonga chapter).

The work of Pacific island authors is comprehensively described in the Institute of Pacific Studies' *South Pacific Literature – From Myth to Fabulation*.

General

Ian Campbell's *A History of the Pacific Islands* is an good, short summary of the Pacific region from the time of the original inhabitants through to the 1980s. *Tides of History*, edited by KR Howe *et al*, is a superb collection of essays covering the same period, though from a variety of perspectives.

The Cambridge History of the Pacific Islands, edited by Donald Denoon *et al*, is an excellent recent study of the Pacific. Ferry Howe's popular *Where the Waves Fall* is a history of the islands from first settlement through to colonial rule.

History of Micronesia, edited by Rodrigue Levesque, is a comprehensive but expensive 10 volume history of the region, told through colourful source documents. *An Introduction to the Peoples & Cultures of Micronesia* by G Alkire, an authority on Micronesian societies, is a comprehensive study resulting from Alkire's fieldwork in the islands.

Pre-European History & Voyaging

The most comprehensive text on the Lapita precursors of Polynesians is Patrick Kirch's *The Lapita Peoples*. Peter Bellwood discusses the arrival and migration of the Polynesian islanders from South-East Asia through the islands in his *Man's Conquest of the Pacific*.

A great compilation of Pacific mythology and legends is *Vikings of the Sunrise* by Te Rangi Hiroa (Sir Peter Buck).

One of the best books about ancient Pacific voyaging is *Polynesian Navigation*, edited by Jack Golson. Jeff Evans' *The Discovery of Aotearoa* describes the ancient journeys from the Society and Marquesas islands to New Zealand, and the modern journey of the *Hawaiki-Nui*, a traditional *vaka* (canoe), along the same route.

We, the Navigators and *The Voyaging Stars – Secrets of the Pacific Island Navigators*, both by meticulous researcher David Lewis, are excellent studies of traditional navigation methods, though difficult books to find. Lewis' more easily located *From Maui to Cook* is very readable. It includes European exploration in the Pacific and describes the modern journey of another traditional vaka, the *Hokule'a*.

Thor Heyerdahl's *Kon Tiki Expedition* is a rip-snorting adventure story of the author's 1947 journey from Peru to the Tuamotus in a balsa raft. While Heyerdahl's scientific methods may have been less than rigorous, he writes a good adventure. The popularity of Heyerdahl's east-to-west theories probably owe much to the appeal of this Boy's Own escapade.

Vaka, by Sir Thomas Davis (Pa Tuterangi Ariki), is a fictional account of ancient Polynesian voyaging to the Cook Islands from Havaiki and Samoa. The author writes from personal experience: see the boxed text 'Voyaging & Navigation' in the Facts about the South Pacific chapter.

Contact

Glyndwr William's *The Great South Seas* is a fascinating and often amusing study of European explorers in the Pacific. Archibald Grenfell Price's *The Explorations of James Cook* is a worthy summary of Cook's journals. Miriam Estensen's *Discovery – The Quest for the Great South Land* is a good history of the search for *Terra Australis Incognita*.

An interesting work about 19th century trade in the south-west Pacific is Dorothy Shinberg's *They Came for Sandalwood*. The blackbirding trade is described in *Slavers in Paradise* by HE Maude – an account of the tragic events surrounding the kidnapping of Pacific islanders by Peruvian slave traders in the early 1860s. The continuing effect of the blackbirding trade in Solomon Islander populations in Samoa is told in Malama Meleisea's short book *O Tama Uli – Melanesians In Western Samoa*.

One of the most influential books written on the impact of colonialism in the South Pacific, *The Fatal Impact – The Invasion of the South Pacific 1767-1840*, by Alan Moorehead, critically assesses the havoc wreaked on the Pacific by early European explorers and fortune-seekers. Much less pessimistic is Nicholas Thomas in *Colonialism's Culture* and *Entangled Objects*; he argues that despite the lasting impact of colonialism, Pacific cultures are resilient and that a complex system of cultural exchange took place (and continues to). Another book on this subject, Ron Crocombe's *The South Pacific – an Introduction*, discusses the potential of the Pacific nations as independent countries and the changes to their cultures and identities since white settlement.

Micronesia – Winds of Change, edited by Francis X Hezel *et al*, is a colourful, wonderfully illustrated history from the accounts of early explorers and missionaries between 1521 and 1951. *Nan'yo – The Rise & Fall of the Japanese in Micronesia, 1885-1945* by Mark R Peattie is one of the best books about the Japanese colonial empire in Micronesia.

For books about the mutiny on the *Bounty*, see the boxed text in the Pitcairn Islands chapter.

Contemporary Issues

The definitive source for hard facts about Pacific countries is the comprehensive *Pacific Island Yearbook*, published by the USP. However, despite the name, it is not an annual publication and such facts quickly become out of date.

A number of books have been written about the Pacific arena during WWII, including Eric Bergerud's *Touched With Fire – The Land War in the South Pacific* and Colonel Joseph Alexander's *Utmost Savagery – The Three Days of Tarawa*.

The enthusiastic Oliver Sacks' *The Island of the Colour-Blind* is a typically well researched study of anthropology, genetics and disease on three Micronesian islands – more riveting than it sounds.

The USP's *Pacific Tourism as Islanders See It* contains essays by islanders regarding the increase in tourism and, consequently, in outside influences on their cultures and ways of life. *Pacific Women – Roles and Status of Women in Pacific Societies*, also by the USP, assesses the changing status of women in the Pacific. Robert Stewart's *Pacific Profiles* is a fascinating compilation of very short stories by a hundred Pacific islanders.

For an insight into Micronesian society, pick up *The Edge of Paradise* by PF Kluge, a perceptive account of the effects of cultural imperialism on Micronesians written by a former Peace Corps volunteer. *Micronesia – A Trust Betrayed* by Donald McHenry is an insightful history of the Trust Territory and the events leading up to the Compacts of Free Association.

A modern and wide-ranging political guide is the USP's excellent *New Politics in the South Pacific*. Less up-to-date, David Robie's angry *Blood on Their Banner* describes nationalist struggles in New Caledonia, French Polynesia, Palau and Fiji.

Also looking at France's role in the Pacific is *France's Overseas Frontier* by Robert Aldrich & John Connell. In the same genre is Stephen Henningham's *France & the South Pacific*, a very readable paperback dealing individually with each of the French territories, as well as with the issue of French nuclear testing. Henningham also wrote *The Pacific Island States*, which concentrates on conflict and security issues in the modern Pacific.

The nuclear testing program in the Pacific is the topic of many books, including Jane Dibblin's *Day of Two Suns* – a well researched and readable study of the lasting effects of US nuclear tests in Micronesia – and *Moruroa, Mon Amour* by Bengt Danielsson.

Global warming is discussed in John Houghton's *Global Warming – The Complete Briefing*, Ian Lowe's *Living in the Greenhouse*, Stewart Boyle & John Ardill's *The Greenhouse Effect* and many other books. If you have access to a good reference library, look for publications by the United Nations Environment Program (UNEP) and the Intergovernmental Panel on Climate Change (IPCC). Some excellent websites giving up-to-date details about both nuclear testing and the greenhouse effect are listed earlier in this chapter under Internet Resources.

FILMS

The better-known Pacific films show little of Pacific culture and these days may be of more comedy value than social. Two of James Michener's novels were made into films: *Return to Paradise* (1953) and *South Pacific* (1958). The former was filmed in Samoa, where Return to Paradise Beach became a popular tourist destination. See the boxed text 'Mutiny on the Bounty' in the Pitcairn Islands chapter for movies about that famous mutiny.

Recently, the blockbuster war film *The Thin Red Line* showcased the beautiful singing of the Solomon Islanders, and the stunning scenery of Guadalcanal. For a much less successful Hollywood view of the islands, see the boxed text 'The Movie of the Island of the Statues' in the Easter Island chapter.

Recent short films by award-winning Sima Urale include *O Tamaiti* (The Children; 1996), and her innovative documentary *Velvet Dreams* – about kitschy velvet paintings of dusky Pacific maidens. Cinta Kaipat's *Lieweila – A Micronesian Story* (1997), about traditional life on the Mariana Islands, has also done well at world film festivals.

Lonely Planet's *The Pacific Islands* video depicts Fiji, Vanuatu and the Solomons. Other commercially available videos include *The Eastern Pacific*, in the OceanLife series; and *Wayfinders – A Pacific Odyssey*, a documentary about traditional voyaging and the *Hokule'a* canoe (see the film's website at www.pbs.org/wayfinders).

NEWSPAPERS & MAGAZINES

If you want to keep up with issues in the Pacific, your two best sources are a couple of regionally published magazines. To subscribe to *Pacific Island Monthly* (☎ 304 111,

fax 303 809) write to them at PO Box 1167, Suva, Fiji; for subscriptions to *Pacific Magazine* (fax 808-852 6325) write to PO Box 37551, Honolulu, Hawai'i 96837.

The *Pacific Daily News* (☎ 477 9711) and *Isla – A Journal of Micronesia Studies* are published in Guam and widely distributed in Micronesia.

RADIO & TV

In addition to the easy-listening music and Christian dogma of local stations, if you have a shortwave radio, you can pick up several useful broadcasts across the Pacific. Some of the stations broadcasting international and Pacific news include:

BBC World Service
  www.bbc.co.uk/worldservice/freq/
Radio Australia
  www.abc.net.au/ra/swave.htm
Radio France Outre-Mer (French language)
  www.rfo.fr
Radio New Zealand International (English and Pacific languages)
  www.rnzi.com
Voice of America
  www.voa.gov/allsked.html

Frequencies change depending on the time of day: higher frequencies (15 to 17MHz) are used during daylight hours, lower frequencies (6 to 7MHz) are used at night and intermediate frequencies (9 to 14MHz) are used during the early morning or evening (local time). Check broadcasters' websites, the magazine *Monitoring Times*, the annual *World Radio Handbook* or the *Passport to World Band Radio* for frequency schedules.

Most major Micronesian islands have access to US cable and CNN television. Other Pacific islands carry a combination of foreign feeds and local television.

VIDEO SYSTEMS

If you want to record or buy video tapes to play back home, you won't get a picture unless the 'image registration' system is the same. Three systems are used in the world, and each one is completely incompatible with the others. The three formats are NTSC, used in North America and Japan;

PAL, used in Australia, New Zealand and most of Europe; and SECAM, used in metropolitan France.

As a general rule, South Pacific countries associated with the USA use NTSC, a handful of French colonies use SECAM and the rest use PAL.

NTSC
Easter Island, American Samoa, Federated States of Micronesia, Guam, Kiribati, Marshall Islands, Palau

PAL
Cook Islands, Niue, Pitcairn Island, Samoa, Tokelau, Tonga, Tuvalu, Fiji, Solomon Islands, Vanuatu, Nauru

SECAM
French Polynesia, Wallis & Futuna, New Caledonia

PHOTOGRAPHY & VIDEO
Film & Equipment
The availability of film and photographic/video equipment varies from country to country. In most cases you will be able to buy film in the main town or city but not in more remote areas. Often though, even if film is available it is heinously expensive, so it's usually best to buy at least a few duty-free films, if not all your film, before you arrive.

Processing film is easy in the major cities of most countries although developing black-and-white print film and slide film may not be possible until you get back home.

Useful equipment to bring includes a small flash, spare batteries, polarising filter, lens cleaning kit and silica-gel packs to protect equipment from the high humidity. Film in the tropics needs to be protected from both heat and humidity. Sachets of silica crystals will protect your equipment from moisture, but it's more important to keep your camera and film in a cool place.

Photography Tips
Avoid taking pictures in the midday sun. The best times for photography are before 9.30 am and after 4 pm. Otherwise, you may have to underexpose your shots slightly to avoid glare.

Automatic cameras and light meters are often fooled by the Pacific's strong light. If your camera is automatic it may overcompensate, causing dark-skinned faces and rainforest views to come out shadowy. This can be a real problem if you're photographing subjects against a bright background, such as a white sand beach. In these situations, use manual settings. It's often best to deliberately overexpose by 1.5 stops (eg use f11 instead of f16/22). Conversely, it's a good idea to underexpose by the same amount if taking close-ups of dark-skinned faces and other dark subjects.

Slides have less latitude for using the wrong exposure. If you're taking slides, one option is to bracket exposures (take extra photos half a stop over and half a stop under the reading set by the camera's meter) as some guarantee of success.

Use a flash to take photos in house interiors, for close-ups in the jungle dimness and at evening cultural dances (remember that kava makes the drinker's eyes sensitive to light, so go easy in these situations). A telephoto lens – 100mm is recommended – is invaluable when something interesting is going on but you'd prefer to remain unobtrusive. Use a polarising filter for dramatic effects and maximum colour saturation, particularly if shooting over the sea.

Underwater Photography
In recent years, underwater photography has become a much easier activity. There is a variety of reasonably priced and easy-to-use underwater cameras available. The cheapest and most convenient option is the disposable one-roll underwater camera. These cost around US$15 and will be available at only the biggest towns and cities in the region.

As with any basic camera, the best photos are likely to be straightforward snapshots. You are not going to get superb photographs of fish and marine life with a small, cheap camera; however, photos of your fellow snorkellers can be terrific.

More than with other types of photography, the results achieved underwater can improve dramatically if you spend more on equipment, particularly on artificial lighting. As you descend natural colours are quickly absorbed, starting at the red end of the spectrum. The deeper you go the more 'faded' and blue your photos will look. The brain fools us to some extent by automatically compensating for this colour change, but the camera doesn't lie. If you are at any depth, your photos will look cold and blue.

To put the colour back in, you need a flash, and to work effectively underwater it has to be a much more powerful and complicated flash than you'd use out of water. Thus newcomers to serious underwater photography soon find that having bought a Nikonos camera, they have to lay out as much money again for flash equipment to go with it. With the right experience and equipment the results can be superb. Generally, the Nikonos cameras work best with 28 or 35mm lenses; longer lenses do not work so well underwater. Although objects appear closer underwater, with these short focal lengths you have to get close to achieve good results. Patience and practise will eventually allow you to move in close to otherwise wary fish. Underwater photography opens up a whole new field of interest to divers, and the results can be startling. Flash photography can reveal colours that simply aren't there for the naked eye.

Video Tips
Video cameras have very sensitive microphones, and you might be surprised how much sound is picked up. This can be a problem if there is a lot of ambient noise – filming by the side of a busy road might seem OK at the time, but back home you'll find a cacophony of traffic noise.

Try to film in long takes, and don't move the camera around too much. If your camera has a stabiliser you can use it to obtain good footage while travelling on bumpy roads. Make sure you keep the batteries charged and have the appropriate charger, plugs and transformer (see Electricity in the individual country's chapter). In most countries it is possible to obtain video cartridges easily in big towns, but make sure you buy the correct format (see Video Systems earlier). It is usually worth buying at least a few cartridges duty-free to start off your trip.

Photographing People
The perfect 'people shot' poses some specific challenges in the Pacific. While most islanders will enjoy being photographed, others will be put off and some people may be superstitious about your camera or suspicious of your motives.

Some kids will bug you so hard to take their photo that you'll eventually resort to pretending to click the shutter to keep them happy. Others will refuse unless they get something in return. Usually you'll find it hard to get a 'natural' shot, and people will want to pose for you – even to the point of changing into their best clothes before you take their photo!

Always respect the wishes of the locals. Ask permission to photograph if a candid shot can't be made and don't insist or snap a picture anyway if permission is denied.

TIME
Local time relative to Greenwich Mean Time (GMT; which is the same as UTC) is given in the At a Glance box at the start of individual country chapters. Since this is the tropics, there's no daylight saving (summer time) on most of the Pacific islands – the exceptions are Fiji, Pitcairn Island and Easter Island.

Time zones in the Pacific are made more complex by the International Dateline, which splits the region in half. When you cross from the east to the west, you go forward one day. The Dateline runs along the 180° latitude, detouring 800km to the east around Fiji and Tonga, and 3600km to the east to accommodate all of Kiribati in one day (see the boxed text 'Millennium' in the Kiribati chapter). The following times are valid when it is midday in Fiji:

GMT-0600 (6 pm, previous day)
  Easter Island
GMT-0830 (3.30 pm, previous day)
  Pitcairn Island
GMT-0900 (3 pm, previous day)
  Gambier Archipelago
GMT-0930 (2.30 pm, previous day)
  Marquesas Islands
GMT-1000 (2 pm, previous day)
  Hawai'i, Tokelau, Cook Islands, Society
  Islands including Tahiti

GMT-1100 (1 pm, previous day)
  Samoa, American Samoa, Niue
GMT+1400 (2 pm, same day)
  Kiribati's Line Islands
GMT+1300 (1 pm, same day)
  Kiribati's Phoenix Islands, Tonga
GMT+1200 (midday, same day)
  Marshall Islands, FSM's Kosrae, Nauru,
  Tuvalu, Wallis & Futuna, Kiribati's Gilbert
  Islands including Tarawa
GMT+1100 (11 am, same day)
  FSM's Pohnpei, Solomon Islands, Vanuatu,
  New Caledonia
GMT+1000 (10 am, same day)
  Northern Mariana Islands, FSM's Chuuk and
  Yap

New York: 7 pm, previous day
Los Angeles: 4 pm, previous day
New Zealand: midday, same day
Sydney: 10 am, same day
Tokyo: 9 am, same day
Singapore: 8 am, same day
Berlin, Paris: 1 am, same day
London: midnight, same day

Note that daylight saving may apply in some of these last countries. It's worth checking your airline tickets and itinerary very carefully if a country on your route is starting or finishing daylight saving.

Throughout the Pacific you'll hear such terms as 'Tongan time', 'Fijian time' or 'island time'. This could be translated to a wish for tourists to 'relax, it'll happen eventually'. The concept of time is a bit fluid in the tropics and you'll find it a lot less stressful to adopt the same relaxed approach rather than try to change the Pacific single-handedly. It's also worth building some flexibility into your plans; don't plan on split-second transfers from bus to ferry, and if you need government approval for anything, be prepared to wait for it.

ELECTRICITY

The electricity supply in each Pacific country largely reflects its historical associations. The three plug shapes used in the Pacific are: Australasian (Australia and New Zealand), European (used everywhere in the west except in Britain and North America), and US-style. Many resorts have outlets for 240V or 110V shavers and hair dryers.

230/240V AC; 50Hz; Australasian-style plug (two or three flat blades)
  Cook Islands, Fiji, Kiribati, Nauru, Niue, Samoa, Solomon Islands, Tokelau, Tuvalu, Vanuatu
220V AC; 60Hz; European-style plug (two round prongs)
  French Polynesia
220V AC; 50Hz; European-style plug (two round prongs)
  Easter Island, New Caledonia, Wallis & Futuna
110V/120V AC; 60Hz; US-style plug (two flat blades)
  American Samoa, all of the Micronesian countries except Kiribati and Nauru

A universal AC adapter will enable you to plug in anywhere without frying the innards of your equipment. You'll also need a plug adapter for each country you visit – they're often easier to buy before you leave home. While adapters can transform voltage or connect one type of plug with another type of socket, frequency (Hz) conversion is impractical, and a clock or computer designed for one frequency *will not operate* under another.

Power supply in some countries may be unreliable – especially away from the main centres – and some form of surge protection may be desirable if you are going to operate sensitive equipment such as a computer.

WEIGHTS & MEASURES

The metric system (kilometres, kilograms and degrees Celsius) is used in most South Pacific countries. The few who still cling to the imperial system (miles, pounds, degrees Fahrenheit) are the places where the US influence is greatest – the Micronesia region (except Kiribati and Nauru) and American Samoa. In each chapter of this book, we give distances in the appropriate units. See the table inside the back cover of this book if you're having trouble with conversions.

TOILETS

Public toilets are rare or nonexistent in most Pacific towns and cities. In town you will be able to pop into hotels, restaurants and cafes if you ask permission; if you're travelling off the beaten track, you may on occasion have to nip behind a banyan tree (coconut trees can be hazardous due to falling coconuts, and filling out the travel insurance medical claim form would be embarrassing). Bury your paper afterwards, and carry spare toilet paper with you.

Although most toilets are of the western sit-down variety, many villages still don't have flush toilets (water is supplied in a separate container) or may just use the nearby bush or reef. Sustainable development projects in several countries include the establishment of composting toilets.

HEALTH
How healthy you are while travelling depends on your predeparture preparations, your daily health care and how you handle any medical problem that develops. While the potential dangers can seem quite frightening, in reality few travellers experience anything more than an upset stomach.

Predeparture Planning
Immunisations Although there are no required vaccinations for travellers to any countries in the South Pacific, there are some that are recommended. Plan ahead for vaccinations: some require more than one injection, while some vaccinations should not be given together. Note that some vaccinations should not be given during pregnancy or to people with allergies – discuss with your doctor.

Seek medical advice at least six weeks before travel. Be aware that there is often a greater risk of disease with children and during pregnancy. Carry proof of your vaccinations; this is sometimes needed to enter a country.

Discuss your requirements with your doctor, but vaccinations you should consider for this trip include the following (for more details about the diseases themselves, see the individual disease entries later in this section).

Diphtheria & Tetanus Vaccinations for these two diseases are usually combined and are recommended for everyone. After an initial course of three injections (usually given in childhood), boosters are necessary every 10 years.

Polio Everyone should keep up to date with this vaccination, which is normally given in childhood. A booster every 10 years maintains immunity.

Hepatitis A & B Hepatitis A vaccine (eg Avaxim, Havrix 1440 or VAQTA) provides long-term immunity (10 years) after an initial injection and a booster at six to 12 months.

Alternatively, an injection of gamma globulin can provide short-term protection against hepatitis A – two to six months, depending on the dose given. It is not a vaccine, but is ready-made antibody collected from blood donations. It's reasonably effective and, unlike the vaccine, it is protective immediately, but because it is a blood product, there are concerns about its long-term safety.

Hepatitis A vaccine is also available in a combined form, Twinrix, with hepatitis B vaccine. Three injections over a six-month period are required, the first two providing substantial protection against hepatitis A.

You should consider vaccination against hepatitis B for long trips, or if visiting countries with high levels of hepatitis B infection, where blood transfusions may not be adequately screened or where sexual contact or needle sharing is a possibility. Vaccination involves three injections, with a booster at 12 months. More rapid courses are available if necessary.

Typhoid Vaccination against typhoid is now available either as an injection or as capsules to be taken orally. Seek advice about the current status of typhoid in the Pacific.

Rabies Vaccination should be considered by those who will spend a month or longer in a country where rabies is common, especially if they are cycling, handling animals, caving or travelling to remote areas, and for children (who may not report a bite). Pre-travel rabies vaccination involves having three injections over 21 to 28 days. If a vaccinated person is bitten or scratched by an animal, they will require two booster injections of vaccine; those not vaccinated require more.

Tuberculosis (TB) The risk of TB to travellers is very low, unless you're living with, or are closely associated with, local people. Vaccination against TB (BCG) is recommended for children and young adults living in at-risk areas for three months or more.

Malaria Antimalarial drugs do not prevent you from being infected but kill the malaria parasites and significantly reduce the risk of getting very ill or even dying. Expert advice should be sought, as there are many factors to consider, including the area to be visited, the risk of exposure to malaria-carrying mosquitoes, the side effects of medication, your medical history and whether you are a child or are pregnant. Travellers to isolated areas in the Solomon Islands and Vanuatu may like to carry a treatment dose of medication for use if symptoms occur.

Travel Health Guides

If you're planning to be travelling in remote areas for a long period of time, you may like to consider taking a detailed health guide.

CDC's Complete Guide to Healthy Travel. The US Centers for Disease Control & Prevention (CDC) recommendations for international travel.

Healthy Travel – Australia, New Zealand & the Pacific, Lonely Planet Publications. Need-to-know information about general travel health in the region.

Travellers' Health, Dr Richard Dawood. Comprehensive, easy to read, authoritative and highly recommended, although it's rather large to lug around.

Where There Is No Doctor, David Werner. A very detailed guide intended for someone, such as a Peace Corps worker, going to work in an underdeveloped country.

There are also a number of excellent travel health sites on the Internet. From Lonely Planet's home page, there are links at www.lonelyplanet.com/weblinks/ep.htm#heal to the World Health Organization (WHO) and the CDC.

Medical Kit Check List

Following is a list of items you should consider including in your medical kit – consult your pharmacist for brands available in your country.

- ☐ **Aspirin** or **paracetamol** (acetaminophen in the USA) – for pain or fever
- ☐ **Antihistamine** – for allergies, eg hay fever; to ease the itch from insect bites or stings; and to prevent motion sickness
- ☐ **Antibiotics** – consider including these if you're travelling well off the beaten track; see your doctor, as they must be prescribed, and carry the prescription with you
- ☐ **Loperamide** or **diphenoxylate** –'blockers' for diarrhoea; **prochlorperazine** or **metaclopramide** for nausea and vomiting
- ☐ **Rehydration mixture** – to prevent dehydration, eg due to severe diarrhoea; particularly important when travelling with children
- ☐ **Insect repellent, sunscreen, lip balm** and **eye drops**
- ☐ **Calamine lotion, sting relief spray** or **aloe vera** – to ease irritation from sunburn and insect bites or stings
- ☐ **Antifungal cream** or **powder** – for fungal skin infections and thrush
- ☐ **Antiseptic** (such as povidone-iodine) – for cuts and grazes
- ☐ **Bandages, elastic plasters** and other wound dressings
- ☐ **Water purification tablets** or **iodine**
- ☐ **Scissors, tweezers** and a **thermometer** (note that mercury thermometers are prohibited by airlines)
- ☐ **Syringes** and **needles** – in case you need injections in a country with medical hygiene problems. Ask your doctor for a note explaining why you have them.
- ☐ **Cold** and **flu tablets, throat lozenges** and **nasal decongestant**
- ☐ **Multivitamins** – consider for long trips, when dietary vitamin intake may be inadequate

Other Preparations

Make sure you're healthy before you start travelling. If you are going on a long trip make sure your dental health is OK. If you wear glasses take a spare pair and a copy of your prescription.

If you require a particular medication take an adequate supply; it may not be available locally. To make getting replacements easier, take part of the packaging showing the generic name rather than the brand. It's a good idea to have a legible prescription or letter from your doctor to show that you legally use the medication.

See Travel Insurance under Visas & Documents earlier in this chapter.

Basic Rules

Food Vegetables and fruit should be washed with purified water or peeled where possible. Beware of ice cream sold on the street or anywhere that it might have melted and been refrozen; if there's any doubt (eg a power cut in the last day or two), steer well clear. Shellfish such as mussels, oysters and clams should be avoided as well as undercooked meat, particularly in the form of mince. Steaming does not make shellfish safe for eating.

If a place looks clean and well run and the vendor also looks clean and healthy, then the food is probably safe. In general, places that are packed with travellers or locals will be fine. The food in busy restaurants is cooked and eaten quite quickly, and is unlikely to have sat around or been reheated.

Water The number one rule is *be careful of the water* and especially ice. If you don't know for certain that the water is safe, assume it's not. Bottled water or soft drinks are generally fine, although bottles may be refilled with tap water. Only use water from containers with an unbroken serrated seal – not tops or corks. Take care with fruit juice, particularly if water may have been added. Milk should be treated with suspicion as it is often unpasteurised, though boiled milk is fine. Tea or coffee should be OK, since the water will have been boiled.

See Health in the individual country chapters for the local water-purity situation.

Water Purification The simplest way of purifying water is to boil it thoroughly. However, you could consider purchasing a water filter for a long trip. There are two main kinds of filter. Total filters take out all parasites, bacteria and viruses and make water safe to drink. They are expensive, but they can be more cost effective than buying bottled water. Simple filters (which can even be a nylon mesh bag) take out dirt and larger foreign bodies from the water so that chemical solutions work more effectively; if water is dirty, chemical solutions may not work at all. It's very important when buying a filter to read the specifications, so that you know exactly what it removes from the water and what it doesn't. Simple filtering will not remove all dangerous organisms, so if you cannot boil water it should be treated chemically.

Chlorine tablets will kill many pathogens, but not some parasites like giardia and amoebic cysts. Iodine, available in tablets, is more effective. Follow the directions carefully; too much iodine can be harmful.

Medical Problems & Treatment

Self-diagnosis and treatment can be risky, so you should always seek medical help. Ask an embassy, consulate or five-star hotel to recommend a local doctor or clinic. Although we give drug dosages in this section, they are for emergency use only. Correct diagnosis is vital. In this section we have used the generic names for medications – check with a pharmacist for brands available locally.

Note that antibiotics should ideally be administered only under medical supervision. Take only the recommended dose at the prescribed intervals and use the whole course, even if the illness seems to be cured earlier. Stop immediately if you experience any serious reactions and don't use the antibiotic at all if you are unsure that you have the correct one. If you are allergic to commonly prescribed antibiotics, such as penicillin, carry this information (eg on a bracelet) when travelling.

Everyday Health

Normal body temperature is 37°C (98.6°F); more than 2°C (4°F) higher indicates a high fever. The normal adult pulse rate is 60 to 100 per minute (children 80 to 100, babies 100 to 140). As a general rule the pulse increases about 20 beats per minute for each 1°C (2°F) rise in fever.

Respiration (breathing) rate is also an indicator of illness. Count the number of breaths per minute: between 12 and 20 is normal for adults and older children (up to 30 for younger children, 40 for babies). People with a high fever or serious respiratory illness breathe more quickly than normal. More than 40 shallow breaths a minute may indicate pneumonia.

Environmental Hazards

Heat Exhaustion & Heatstroke Dehydration and salt deficiency can cause heat exhaustion. Take time to acclimatise to high temperatures, drink sufficient liquids and do not do anything too physically demanding. Salt deficiency is characterised by fatigue, lethargy, headaches, giddiness and muscle cramps; salt tablets may help, but adding extra salt to your food is better.

Heat exhaustion can develop into heatstroke. This serious, occasionally fatal, condition occurs when the body's heat-regulating mechanism breaks down and the body temperature rises to dangerous levels.

The symptoms include feeling unwell, sweating very little (or not at all) and a high body temperature (39 to 41°C, or 102 to 106°F). When sweating ceases, the skin becomes flushed and red. Severe headaches and lack of coordination also occur, and the sufferer may be confused or aggressive. Eventually the victim can become delirious or convulse. Hospitalisation is essential, but in the interim get the victim out of the sun, remove his or her clothing, cover with a wet sheet or towel and fan continuously. Give fluids if the person is conscious.

Prickly Heat Prickly heat is an itchy rash caused by excessive perspiration trapped under the skin. It usually strikes people who have just arrived in a hot climate. Keeping cool, bathing often, drying the skin and using a mild talcum or prickly-heat powder may help as will resorting to air-conditioning.

Sunburn You can get sunburnt surprisingly quickly, even through cloud. Use sunscreen, a hat, and a barrier cream for your nose and lips. Snorkellers, distracted by the view below them, often get sunburnt. Calamine lotion or a commercial after-sun preparation are good for mild sunburn. Protect your eyes with good quality sunglasses.

Motion Sickness Eating lightly before and during a trip will reduce the chances of motion sickness. If you're prone to motion sickness try to find a place that minimises movement – near the wing on aircraft, close to midship on boats, near the centre on buses. Fresh air usually helps; reading and cigarette smoke do not. Commercial motion-sickness preparations, which can cause drowsiness, have to be taken before the trip commences.

Diarrhoea Simple things like a change of water, food or climate can all cause a mild bout of diarrhoea, but a few rushed toilet trips with no other symptoms is not indicative of a major problem.

Dehydration is the main danger with any form of diarrhoea, particularly in children or the elderly as it can occur quite quickly. Under all circumstances *fluid replacement* is the priority. Weak black tea with a little sugar, soda water, or soft drinks allowed to go flat and diluted 50% with clean water are all good. With severe diarrhoea, a rehydrating solution is preferable to replace minerals and salts lost. Commercially available oral rehydration salts (ORS) are very useful; add them to boiled or bottled water. In an emergency you can make up a solution of six teaspoons of sugar and a half teaspoon of salt to a litre of boiled or bottled water. You need to drink at least the same volume of fluid that you are losing in bowel movements and vomiting. Urine is the best guide to the adequacy of replacement – if you have small amounts of concentrated urine, you need to drink more. Drink small amounts often, and stick to a bland diet as you recover.

Gut-paralysing drugs such as loperamide or diphenoxylate bring relief from the symptoms, but are not a cure for the problem. Only use these drugs if you do not have access to toilets, eg if you *must* travel. These drugs are not recommended for children under 12.

In certain situations antibiotics may be required: diarrhoea with blood or mucus (dysentery), any diarrhoea with fever, profuse watery diarrhoea, persistent diarrhoea not improving after 48 hours and severe diarrhoea. These suggest a more serious cause and in these situations gut-paralysing drugs should be avoided.

In these situations, a stool test may be necessary to diagnose what bug is causing your diarrhoea, so you should seek medical help urgently. Where this is not possible the recommended drugs for bacterial diarrhoea (the most likely cause of severe diarrhoea in travellers) are norfloxacin 400mg twice daily for three days or ciprofloxacin 500mg twice daily for five days. These are not recommended for children or pregnant women. The drug of choice for children would be co-trimoxazole with dosage dependent on weight. A five day course is given. Ampicillin or amoxycillin may be given during pregnancy, but medical care is necessary.

Two other causes of persistent diarrhoea in travellers, particularly those travelling off the beaten track, are giardiasis and amoebic dysentery.

Giardiasis This is caused by a common parasite, *Giardia lamblia*. Symptoms include stomach cramps, nausea, a bloated stomach, watery, foul-smelling diarrhoea and frequent gas. Giardiasis can appear several weeks after you have been exposed to the parasite. The symptoms may disappear for a few days and then return; this can go on for several weeks.

You should seek medical advice if you think you have giardiasis, but where this is not possible, tinidazole or metronidazole are the recommended drugs. Treatment is a 2g single dose of tinidazole or 250mg of metronidazole three times daily for five to 10 days.

Amoebic Dysentery Caused by the protozoan *Entamoeba histolytica*, amoebic dysentery is characterised by a gradual onset of low-grade diarrhoea, often with blood and mucus. Cramping abdominal pain and vomiting are less likely than in other types of diarrhoea, and fever may not be present. It will persist until treated and can recur and cause other health problems.

As with giardiasis, you should seek medical advice if you suspect you have amoebic dysentery. If this is out of the question, see the Giardiasis entry for interim treatment.

Infectious Diseases

Fungal Infections Fungal infections occur more commonly in hot weather and are usually found on the scalp, between the toes (athlete's foot) or fingers, in the groin and on the body (ringworm). You get ringworm (which is a fungal infection, not a worm) from infected animals or other people. Moisture encourages these infections.

To prevent fungal infections wear loose, comfortable clothes, avoid artificial fibres, wash frequently and dry yourself carefully. If you do get an infection, wash the infected area at least once daily with a disinfectant or medicated soap and water, and rinse and dry well. Apply an antifungal cream or powder such as tolnaftate. Try to expose the infected area to air and sunlight as much as possible and wash all towels and underwear in hot water, change them often and let them dry in the sun.

Hepatitis Hepatitis is a general term for inflammation of the liver. There are several different viruses that cause hepatitis, and they differ in the way that they are transmitted. The symptoms are similar in all forms of the illness, and include fever, chills, headaches, fatigue, feelings of weakness and aches and pains, followed by loss of appetite, nausea, vomiting, abdominal pain, dark urine, light-coloured faeces, jaundiced (yellow) skin and yellowing of the whites of the eyes. People who have had hepatitis should avoid alcohol for some time after the illness, as the liver needs time to recover.

Hepatitis A is transmitted by contaminated food and drinking water. You should seek medical advice, but there is not much you can do apart from rest, drink lots of fluids, eat lightly and avoid fatty foods. Hepatitis E, transmitted in the same way as hepatitis A, can be particularly serious in pregnant women.

There are almost 300 million chronic carriers of hepatitis B in the world. It is spread through contact with infected blood, blood products or body fluids, for example through sexual contact, unsterilised needles, blood transfusions or contact with blood via small breaks in the skin. Other risk situations include having a shave, tattoo or body piercing with contaminated equipment. The symptoms of hepatitis B may be more severe than type A, and the disease can lead to long-term problems such as chronic liver damage, liver cancer or a long-term carrier state. Hepatitis C and D are spread in the same way as hepatitis B and can also lead to long-term complications.

There are vaccines against hepatitis A and B, but there are currently no vaccines against the other types. Following the basic rules about food and water (hepatitis A and E) and avoiding risk situations (hepatitis B, C and D) are important preventative measures.

HIV & AIDS Infection with the human immunodeficiency virus (HIV) may lead to acquired immune deficiency syndrome (AIDS), which is a fatal disease. Any exposure to blood, blood products or body fluids may put the individual at risk. The disease is often transmitted through sexual contact or dirty needles – tattooing, vaccinations, acupuncture and body piercing can be potentially as dangerous as intravenous drug use. HIV/AIDS can also be spread through infected blood used in transfusions; some developing countries cannot afford to screen blood used for transfusions.

If you do need an injection, ask to see the syringe unwrapped in front of you, or take a needle and syringe pack with you.

Fear of HIV infection should never preclude treatment for a serious medical condition.

Intestinal Worms These parasites are most common in rural, tropical areas. The different worms have different ways of infecting people. Some may be ingested with food such as undercooked meat (eg tapeworms) and some enter through your skin (eg hookworms). Infestations may not show up for some time, and although they are generally not serious, if left untreated some can cause severe health problems later. Consider having a stool test when you return home to check for these and determine the appropriate treatment.

Sexually Transmitted Diseases (STDs) HIV/AIDS and hepatitis B can be transmitted through sexual contact – see the relevant sections earlier for more details. Other STDs include gonorrhoea, herpes and syphilis; sores, blisters or rashes around the genitals and discharges or pain when urinating are common symptoms. In some STDs, such as wart virus or chlamydia, symptoms may be less marked or not observed at all, especially in women. Chlamydia infection can cause infertility in men and women before any symptoms have been noticed. Syphilis symptoms eventually disappear completely but the disease continues and can cause severe problems in later years. While abstinence from sexual contact is the only 100% effective prevention, using condoms is also effective. The treatment of gonorrhoea and syphilis is with antibiotics. The different STDs each require specific antibiotics.

Tuberculosis TB is a bacterial infection usually transmitted from person to person by coughing but which may be transmitted through consumption of unpasteurised milk. Milk that has been boiled is safe to drink, and the souring of milk to make yoghurt or cheese also kills the bacilli. Travellers are usually not at great risk as close household contact with the infected person is usually required before the disease is passed on. You may need to have a TB test before you travel as this can help diagnose the disease later if you become ill.

Typhoid Typhoid fever is a dangerous gut infection caused by contaminated water and food. Medical help must be sought.

In its early stages sufferers may feel they have a bad cold or flu on the way, as early symptoms are a headache, body aches and a fever that rises a little each day until it is around 40°C (104°F) or more. The victim's pulse is often slow relative to the degree of fever present – unlike a normal fever where the pulse increases. There may also be vomiting, abdominal pain, diarrhoea or constipation.

In the second week the high fever and slow pulse continue and a few pink spots may appear on the body; trembling, delirium, weakness, weight loss and dehydration may occur. Complications such as perforated bowel, pneumonia or meningitis may also occur.

Insect-Borne Diseases

Malaria This serious and potentially fatal disease is spread by mosquito. If you are travelling in the Solomon Islands and Vanuatu, it's extremely important to avoid mosquito bites and to take tablets to prevent this disease. Symptoms range from fever, chills and sweating, headache, diarrhoea and abdominal pains to a vague feeling of ill-health. Seek medical help immediately if malaria is suspected. Without treatment malaria can rapidly become more serious and can be fatal.

If medical care is not available, malaria tablets can be used for treatment. You need to use a malaria tablet which is different from the one you were taking when you contracted malaria. The standard treatment dose of mefloquine is two 250mg tablets and a further two tablets six hours later. For Fansidar, it's a single dose of three tablets. If you were previously taking mefloquine and cannot obtain Fansidar, then other alternatives are Malarone (atovaquone-proguanil; four tablets once daily for three days), halofantrine (three doses of two 250mg tablets every six hours) or quinine sulphate (600mg every six hours). There is a greater risk of side effects with these dosages than with

normal use if used with mefloquine, so medical advice is preferable. Be aware also that halofantrine is no longer recommended by the WHO as emergency standby treatment, because of side effects, and should only be used if no other drugs are available.

Travellers are advised to prevent mosquito bites at all times. The best advice is:

- wear light-coloured clothing
- wear long trousers and long-sleeved shirts
- use mosquito repellents containing the compound DEET on exposed areas (prolonged overuse of DEET may be harmful, especially to children, but its use is considered preferable to being bitten by disease-transmitting mosquitoes)
- avoid perfumes or aftershave
- use a mosquito net impregnated with mosquito repellent (permethrin) – it may be worth taking your own net
- impregnating clothes with permethrin effectively deters mosquitoes and other insects

Dengue Fever This viral disease is transmitted by mosquitoes and is fast becoming one of the top public health problems in the tropical world. Unlike the malaria mosquito, the mosquito which transmits dengue is most active during the day, and is found mainly in urban areas, in and around human dwellings.

Symptoms of dengue fever include a sudden onset of high fever, headaches, joint and muscle pains (hence its old name, 'breakbone fever') and nausea and vomiting. A rash of small red spots sometimes appears three to four days after the onset of fever. In the early phase of illness, dengue may be mistaken for other infectious diseases, including malaria and influenza. Minor bleeding such as nose bleeds may occur in the course of the illness, but this does not necessarily mean that you have progressed to the potentially fatal dengue haemorrhagic fever (DHF). This is a severe illness, characterised by heavy bleeding, which is thought to be a result of secondary infection due to a different strain (there are four major strains) and usually affects residents of the country rather than travellers. Recovery even from simple dengue fever may be prolonged, with tiredness lasting several weeks.

Seek medical attention as soon as possible if you think you may be infected. A blood test can exclude malaria and indicate the possibility of dengue fever. There is no specific treatment for dengue. Aspirin should be avoided, as it increases the risk of haemorrhaging. There is no vaccine against dengue fever. The best prevention is to avoid mosquito bites at all times – see the Malaria section earlier for advice on avoiding mosquitoes.

Filariasis This is a mosquito-transmitted parasitic infection found in parts of the Pacific. Possible symptoms include fever, pain and swelling of the lymph glands; inflammation of lymph drainage areas; swelling of a limb or the scrotum; skin rashes; and blindness. Treatment is available to eliminate the parasites from the body, but some of the damage already caused may not be reversible. Medical advice should be obtained promptly if the infection is suspected.

Cuts, Bites & Stings
Cuts & Scratches Wash and treat any cut with an antiseptic (for example povidone-iodine). If possible avoid bandages and elastic plasters, which can keep wounds wet.

Coral cuts are notoriously slow to heal and if they are not adequately cleaned, small pieces of coral can become embedded in the wound. Severe pain, redness, fever or general feelings of ill-health suggest an infection and the need for immediate antibiotics as coral cuts may result in serious infections. Avoid coral cuts by not walking on reefs and try not to touch coral when swimming or snorkelling.

Bedbugs & Lice Bedbugs live in various places, but particularly in dirty mattresses and bedding, evidenced by spots of blood on bedclothes or on the wall. Bedbugs leave itchy bites in neat rows. Calamine lotion or a sting relief spray may help.

All lice cause itching and discomfort. They make themselves at home in your hair (head lice), your clothing (body lice) or in your pubic hair (crabs). Powder or shampoo treatment will kill the lice and infected

clothing should then be washed in very hot, soapy water and left in the sun to dry.

Bites & Stings Bee and wasp stings are usually painful rather than dangerous. However, in people who are allergic to them severe breathing difficulties may occur and require urgent medical care. Calamine lotion or a sting relief spray will give relief and ice packs will reduce the pain and swelling.

There are various fish and other sea creatures that sting or bite (see the boxed text 'Venomous Marinelife' later in this chapter), or which are dangerous to eat – see Ciguatera, following.

Ciguatera This is a form of food poisoning that comes from eating fish. Reefs that have been disturbed, for example by urban development, are particularly prone to the micro-organism which becomes present in reef fish, which are themselves consumed by larger fish such as rock cod, trevally and sea perch. There are no outward signs that a fish is infected.

Symptoms include vomiting, diarrhoea, nausea, dizziness, joint aches and pains, fever and chills and tingling around the mouth, hands and feet. Seek medical attention if you experience any of these symptoms after eating fish. It's always best to seek local advice before eating any reef fish as any ciguatera outbreak will be well known.

Ticks You should always check your body thoroughly if you have been walking through a potentially tick-infested area as ticks can cause skin infections and other more serious diseases. Ticks are often found in dry scrubby regions or where cattle have been living. If you find a tick attached, press down around its head with tweezers, grab the head and gently pull upwards. Avoid pulling the rear of the body as this may squeeze the tick's gut contents through its mouth into your skin, increasing the risk of infection and disease. Smearing chemicals on the tick will not make it let go and is not recommended.

Tetanus This disease is caused by a germ which lives in soil and in the faeces of horses and other animals. It enters the body via breaks in the skin. The first symptom may be discomfort in swallowing, or stiffening of the jaw and neck; this is followed by painful convulsions of the jaw and whole body. The disease can be fatal. It can be prevented by vaccination.

Women's Health
Gynaecological Problems Antibiotic use, synthetic underwear, sweating and contraceptive pills can lead to fungal vaginal infections, especially when travelling in hot climates. Fungal infections are characterised by a rash, itch and discharge and can be treated with a vinegar or lemon-juice douche, or with yoghurt. Nystatin, miconazole or clotrimazole pessaries or vaginal cream are the usual treatment. Maintaining good personal hygiene and wearing loose-fitting clothes and cotton underwear may help prevent these infections.

STDs are a major cause of vaginal problems. Symptoms include a smelly discharge, painful intercourse and sometimes a burning sensation when urinating. Medical attention should be sought and male sexual partners must also be treated. For more details see the section Sexually Transmitted Diseases earlier. Besides abstinence, the best thing is to practise safer sex using condoms.

Pregnancy It is not advisable to travel to some places while pregnant as some vaccinations normally used to prevent serious diseases are not advisable during pregnancy. In addition, some diseases are much more serious for pregnant women and may increase the risk of a stillborn child (eg malaria).

Most miscarriages occur during the first three months of pregnancy. Miscarriage is not uncommon and can occasionally lead to severe bleeding. The final three months should also be spent within reasonable distance of good medical care. A baby born as early as 24 weeks stands a chance of survival, but only in a good modern hospital. Pregnant women should avoid all unnecessary medication, although vaccinations and malarial prophylactics should still be taken where needed. Additional care should be

taken to prevent illness and particular attention should be paid to diet and nutrition.

WOMEN TRAVELLERS
Many Pacific customs, particularly in Melanesia, may look to westerners like draconian male chauvinism. Some of them might look like this to the local women too: domestic violence is a huge problem in many Pacific countries. The Secretariat of the Pacific Community (see Government & Politics in the Facts about the South Pacific chapter) has initiated studies to determine how widespread this problem is.

See also Women's Health under Health earlier in this chapter.

Safety Precautions
Rape and sexual assault are rare but do occur in the Pacific, as elsewhere. In general women travellers should have nothing to fear, but it is wise to exercise caution, as always when you are out of your element.

It is not uncommon for lone women to experience some harassment. Men will sometimes assume you are fair game if you are travelling alone. Chuuk, in the Federated States of Micronesia, is particularly bad. Finding a travelling companion, seeking the company of local women, or even just wearing a wedding ring may reduce unwanted attention.

In some countries it is against local customs for young women to be out at night by themselves. So think *very* carefully before accepting an invite to go drinking alone with local men. If you are alone at night, remain in busy areas and use a taxi for transport. Lone female tourists swimming or sunbathing at isolated beaches may also attract local Romeos. And we do not recommend that women hitchhike by themselves.

Women travelling in some parts of the Pacific may encounter a phenomenon known as 'creeping' or 'window peeking'. This un-nerving practise involves a male standing outside your window hissing, whistling or knocking on the glass. Keep curtains drawn and don't invite them inside if you're not after company overnight.

What to Wear

Pacific islanders can be a conservative bunch. They are also usually more tolerant of the peculiar ways of western males than of females. However, attitudes to women's dress are changing in the Pacific. It's common to see women wearing jeans or even longish shorts in many main centres. However, in more rural areas and outer islands the dress code will be rather more severe.

Women showing their thighs in public is *tapu* (forbidden) in most areas, so shorts should be knee-length. Sleeveless shirts and short skirts are similarly frowned upon. You should never swim or sunbathe topless or in the nude, and in some places you should even consider keeping the knee-length shorts on for swimming.

If you're visiting a church, your clothing should be even more modest. In resorts catering to westerners, rules are considerably less strict: western standards, or lack thereof, apply. Local fashions inevitably change at differing paces, so ask around and take note of what others are wearing.

The most fashionable frock in many Pacific countries, the frumpy full-length 'Mother Hubbard' dress, won't win you many admirers on the streets of Paris or New York but it will make you lots of friends in Port Vila or Nukunonu.

GAY & LESBIAN TRAVELLERS

Pacific attitudes to homosexuality are complex. Pacific cultures are conservative, and some more enthusiastic religious leaders occasionally whip themselves into a frenzy about homosexuality. However, in Polynesia, at least, there is an ancient tradition of male 'cross-dressing', which is usually, but not always, associated with homosexuality. See the boxed text 'Fakaleiti' in the Tonga chapter.

Apart from the most popular tourist centres, such as Fiji and Guam, there is little in the way of clubs or other facilities for gays and lesbians. Exceptions are those Polynesian cultures where the *fakaleiti* tradition remains strong, in Tonga, Samoa and Tahiti. See individual country chapters for more details.

There's little problem with open displays of male gay affection in most Polynesian countries, although lesbians are much less open in public. Excessive public displays of both heterosexual and homosexual affection are frowned upon in many Pacific societies.

Male homosexuality is technically illegal (although rarely enforced) in many Pacific countries, including the Cook Islands, Fiji, Kiribati, Niue, the Solomons, Tokelau, Tonga and Tuvalu. Female homosexuality only gets an official mention in Samoa, where it is also illegal. In the more liberal French colonies of New Caledonia and French Polynesia, homosexuality is legal.

DISABLED TRAVELLERS

Most Pacific nations have very poor facilities for disabled travellers. Getting around can be a real problem for wheelchair users – small domestic aeroplanes have narrow doors and shipping services may not have ramp access. What's more, hotels and guesthouses are not used to receiving disabled guests, and nautical and open-air activities are geared for the 'able-bodied'.

On the other hand, disabled people are simply part of the community in the Pacific, looked after if necessary but expected to play a useful role. You won't have people pretending you don't exist; where a Sydney taxi cab might just accelerate away, a Samoan bus driver will call someone over to help him carry you aboard.

Flash western resorts and hotels are more likely to have some facilities. If you are intending to stay at a particular resort, check if they suit your needs. It may be best to book a ground-level room until you check out the ramp situation.

For pre-trip planning advice, check the Internet and contact disabled people's associations in your home country.

SENIOR TRAVELLERS

Pacific cultures value the family above almost anything else, and the elderly are universally respected for their wisdom. You may find a holiday in the Pacific a terrifically uplifting experience.

Check with any relevant organisations before you leave home for advice and for discounted travel packages. Some countries have special discounts for senior citizens; ask at tourist offices in that country. Be aware that the medical facilities on some outer islands may be poor or nonexistent.

TRAVEL WITH CHILDREN

The climate, natural setting, aquatic games and lack of poisonous creatures make the Pacific a paradise for children. However, apart from major destinations such as Fiji, which is well set up for children, few travellers take their kids anywhere in the Pacific. In fact, some resorts and hotels ban small children for all or part of the year, so check when you make your booking. Ask about kids' discounts on everything from hotels to air fares.

Smaller towns and outer islands may have few resources for westerners wanting to pamper their kids. You will usually be able to buy disposable nappies (diapers), infant formula, long-life milk etc in the main town, but don't leave the capital without buying everything you need or checking the local situation.

Supervise your children when swimming or playing on beaches, and make sure they understand not to touch coral. Bring plenty of sunscreen and light clothes for sun protection. Make sure vaccinations are up to date and that your health and travel insurance also covers your child. It's important to keep small children well hydrated in a hot climate. Gastrolite helps prevent dehydration and also masks unpleasant tastes in the water. If your child is sensitive to the local water, you can boil drinking water or buy bottled water.

Children are highly valued in Pacific cultures. Locals will often be keen to talk to your kids, play with them and invite them to join activities or visit homes. However, local kids are expected to behave, so try (ha!) to curb your child's crying and tantrums if visiting a village. Child care is a shared responsibility in the Pacific, and locals will sometimes correct your children for you if they misbehave!

Also see Health earlier in this chapter for more advice. Lonely Planet's *Travel with Children* has useful information for travel with children anywhere in the world. It has a section on Fiji.

USEFUL ORGANISATIONS

Offices of the TCSP are listed under Tourist Offices earlier in this chapter. Yacht clubs are listed under Sea in the Getting Around section of individual country chapters.

Volunteer work is an excellent way to get to know a country but it's not an option for the casual tourist: volunteer programs require a serious and long-term commitment. Most organisations require volunteers to have tertiary qualifications or work experience in their particular field, and to hold residency in the organisation's base country. Volunteer organisations active in the Pacific region include:

Australian Volunteers International
(☎ 03-9279 1788, fax 9419 4280, ozvol@ozvol.org.au)
PO Box 350, Fitzroy Vic 3065, Australia; www.ozvol.org.au
United Nations Volunteers
(☎ 0228-815 2000, fax 815 2001, hq@unv.org)
PO Box 260 11, D-53153, Bonn, Germany; www.unv.org
US Peace Corps
(☎ 800 424 8580, fax 202-692 2201, webmaster@peacecorps.gov)
1111 20th St NW, Washington DC 20526, USA; www.peacecorps.gov/countries/pacific.html
Volunteer Service Abroad (VSA)
(☎ 04-472 5759, fax 472 5052, vsa@vsa.org.nz)
PO Box 12246, Wellington, New Zealand; www.vsa.org.nz
Voluntary Service Overseas (VSO)
(☎ 020-8780 7200, fax 8780 7300, enquiry@vso.org.uk)
317 Putney Bridge Rd, London SW15 2PN, UK; www.vso.org.uk; offices in Canada, the Netherlands and Portugal

DANGERS & ANNOYANCES

The Pacific islands are safer than many places in the world, but a certain amount of common sense is still called for. In general, you will find most Pacific islands to be just as idyllic as the tourist brochures lead you to expect and the people to be some of the friendliest you will ever meet. As anywhere, crime does exist, but with minimal caution you should have no problems. In some of the larger cities of the Pacific there have been an increase of assaults, so be aware when walking around at night, even as a couple. See Women Travellers earlier in this chapter for hassles that women may encounter.

In some areas at peak season, the sheer number of tourists can be a nuisance. But you can hardly complain about that when you're one of the tourists, can you?

Theft

Like the European explorers before you, you might run into some different attitudes to personal property while you are in the Pacific. You'll also sympathise with James Cook's dilemma: it can be difficult to stay Zen about another culture's attitude to property when someone has just run off with the ship's sextant!

Keep copies of important documents somewhere safe (see Visas & Documents earlier in this chapter) and use a money belt

Venomous Marinelife

Probably the most dangerous thing you'll have to worry about when snorkelling over a reef is sunburn. However, there are several nasty creatures worth mentioning because there's always the chance that you'll meet one.

The stonefish is an ugly looking thing that spends much of its time on the bottom pretending to be a weed-covered rock. If you tread on a stonefish's sharp, extremely venomous dorsal spines, you'll find that the pain is immediate and incapacitating. Bathing the wound in hot water reduces the pain and the effects of the venom, but medical attention should be sought urgently.

Stonefish
MARTIN HARRIS

Lionfish

The lionfish, a relative of the stonefish, is a strikingly banded, brown and white fish with large, graceful dorsal fins containing venomous spines. Lionfish are obvious when they're swimming around, but they can also hide under ledges.

Then there's the cone shell, several species of which have highly toxic venom. The bad ones have a venomous proboscis – a rapidly extendible, dart-like stinging device that can reach any part of the shell's outer surface. Cone shell venom can be fatal. Stings should be immobilised with a tight pressure bandage (not a tourniquet) and splint. Get medical attention immediately.

MARTIN HARRIS

Avoid contact with jellyfish, which have stinging tentacles – seek local advice. Dousing in vinegar will deactivate any stingers that have not 'fired'. Calamine lotion, antihistamines and analgesics may reduce the reaction and relieve the pain. Other stinging sea creatures include flame or stinging coral and sea urchins.

Cone Shell

Generally speaking, the best way to avoid contact with any of the above while you're in the water is to look but don't touch. Shoes with strong soles will provide protection from stonefish, but reef walking damages the reef, so you shouldn't be doing it anyway – you could view the stonefish as a very enthusiastic environmental protection officer.

KATE NOLAN

under your clothes to carry your passport and travellers cheques. Belongings are normally safe in hotel rooms but bear in mind that privacy is far from a sacred right in the Pacific.

And remember what happened to Captain Cook. Don't let your over-reaction to the threat of stealing spoil your holiday.

Swimming

The safest ocean swimming is within the protected waters of lagoons. However, swimmers should still be aware of tides and currents, and particularly of the swift movement of water out of a lagoon and through a pass into the open sea. Avoid swimming alone, seek local advice about the conditions and be on the alert for venomous marinelife (see the boxed text). The safest, and most responsible, approach to any sealife is to look but don't touch.

Attacks by shark are rare but not unknown in many Pacific countries. It's always wise to seek the advice of local people before taking to the water. You have some protection from sharks when swimming inside a reef. If you're approached by a shark, stay calm (as calm as possible, anyway) and swim steadily away.

Mosquitos

Even in places where mosquito-borne malaria is not a risk, the bites of mosquitos can still cause considerable discomfort. They are less of a problem around the coast where sea breezes keep them away, but inland they can be a pest. See Insect-Borne Diseases under Health earlier in this chapter for ways to avoid mosquito bites.

Conflict

Appropriately enough, the Pacific is a fairly peaceful region. The most recent conflict, in the Solomon Islands, is described in the 'Guadalcanal Revolutionary Army' boxed text in that country's chapter. Otherwise, the last decade has been pretty quiet. Conflicts in past trouble spots in New Caledonia and Fiji have been largely resolved, with only the 1996 riots in Papeete breaking the peace.

LEGAL MATTERS

The only drug you are likely to come across in the Pacific (apart from the eminently legal kava, betel nut, alcohol, coffee and tobacco) is marijuana. This is illegal in all countries of the Pacific, so extreme caution should be exercised if you are thinking about supplementing that natural Pacific high.

BUSINESS HOURS

Business hours vary throughout the islands, but 8 am to 4.30 pm Monday to Friday is fairly common. Banking hours also vary, though Monday to Thursday from 10 am to 3 pm, to 5 pm on Friday, is usual. Check this section in the individual country chapters for any local variations.

The last weeks of the year are often difficult for doing business. Not only do Christmas and New Year holidays and parties interfere, but many government employees have leftover annual leave that must be taken by the end of the year, so lots of people take a quick vacation. This goes for the day after a holiday as well: people have a habit of extending their holiday.

Every second Friday is payday on some islands, so that people leave work early (if they show up at all) to line up at the bank; it can be a major challenge to find government workers on payday.

In the devoutly Christian Pacific, many countries effectively close down on Sunday. On Sunday morning especially there are often no businesses open, and travellers who have not planned ahead can find themselves waiting a long time for breakfast. Rules are often relaxed at tourist resorts, so spending the day at a resort is one way to escape the Sunday blues. Another option is to join in; attend an island church and listen to the beautiful singing.

PUBLIC HOLIDAYS

The standard western holidays are observed in the Pacific islands. For extra national holidays, check individual country chapters.

Easter (March/April) includes Good Friday, Holy Saturday, Easter Sunday and Easter Monday. Many Catholic countries observe the Ascension 40 days after Easter

Sunday; Whit Sunday (Pentecost) is seven weeks after Easter. The Assumption is celebrated on 15 August.

The US-influenced nations may celebrate Martin Luther King Day, US Independence Day, Columbus Day, Veterans' Day and Thanksgiving. French territories celebrate Labor Day, Bastille Day, All Saints' Day and Armistice Day. Countries associated with New Zealand/Australia often celebrate Anzac Day.

The following is a list of the some standard western public holidays:

New Year's Day	1 January
Martin Luther King Day	3rd Monday in January
Easter	March/April
Anzac Day	25 April
Labor Day (French)	1 May
Whit Sunday & Monday (Pentecost)	May/June
US Independence Day	4 July
Bastille Day	14 July
Assumption Day	15 August
Columbus Day	2nd Monday in October
All Saints' Day	1 November
Veterans' (Armistice) Day	11 November
Thanksgiving	4th Thursday in November
Christmas Day	25 December
Boxing Day	26 December

If a public holiday falls on a weekend, the holiday is often taken on the preceding Friday or following Monday.

SPECIAL EVENTS
Local festivals that involve a few different countries are listed here. See this section in the individual country chapters for special events and holidays in particular countries.

October
Festival of Pacific Arts
Held every four years in a different Pacific country. The eighth festival is in New Caledonia in October/November 2000.

November
Hawaiki Nui Va'a
Held each year in French Polynesia – canoes from many Pacific countries are raced between the islands of Huahine, Raiatea, Tahaa and Bora Bora.

Sports
South Pacific Games
The South Pacific games are held every four years at a different location around the Pacific. The 2003 games are in Fiji.
Rugby
Rugby union and its spin-off, sevens rugby, is enormously popular in Polynesia. Annual Pacific island sevens tournaments, featuring as much dance and celebration as rugby, are held in the Cook Islands, Fiji and Samoa.

The Air Promotion Systems website (www.pacificislands.com) has a useful Pacific islands calendar of events.

ACTIVITIES
In the very Christian Pacific islands, many activities will not be appropriate on the Sabbath (Sunday), unless you're at a resort that is accustomed to the heathen ways of tourists, or in main cities.

Sailing
See the Getting Around the Region chapter for information about taking your own yacht to the Pacific or getting a berth on someone else's. Yacht clubs are a good first port of call (ho ho) for information about renting a yacht. In the individual country chapters, yacht clubs are listed in the Sea section of Getting There & Away. Yacht rental companies are listed under Activities

Trekking
Although a trek from one side of the island to the other may be a matter of minutes on small coral atolls, on the higher Pacific islands there are opportunities to walk through some magnificent rainforest. Many tracks cross land under customary ownership, so ask around before heading off. You may need to ask someone's permission and you may be required to pay a small fee.

Bushwalking in the heat has the potential to be a truly miserable experience. It's better to undertake long walks in the cooler parts of the year. Check Climate under

Responsible Bushwalking

Bushwalking places great pressure on the natural environment. When bushwalking consider:

Rubbish
• Carry out all your rubbish. Make an effort to carry out rubbish left by others.
• Minimise the waste you must carry out by taking minimal packaging. If you can't buy in bulk, unpack small-portion packages and combine their contents in one reusable container.
• Never bury your rubbish: digging disturbs soil and ground-cover and encourages erosion. Buried rubbish will more than likely be dug up by animals, who may be injured or poisoned by it. It may also take years to decompose.
• Don't rely on bought water in plastic bottles. Disposal of these bottles is a major environmental problem. Use iodine drops or purification tablets instead.
• Carry out sanitary napkins, tampons and condoms. They burn and decompose poorly.

Human Waste Disposal
• Contamination of water sources by human faeces can lead to the transmission of hepatitis, typhoid and intestinal parasites such as giardia and roundworms. It can cause severe health risks not only to members of your party, but also to local residents and wildlife.
• Where there are no toilets, bury your waste. Dig a small hole 15cm (6 inches) deep and at least 50m (55 yards) from any watercourse. Consider carrying a lightweight trowel for this purpose. Cover the waste with soil and a rock. Bury toilet paper with the waste.
• If the area is inhabited, ask locals if they have any concerns about your chosen toilet site.

Washing
• Don't use detergents or toothpaste in or near watercourses, even if they are biodegradable.
• Wash at least 50m (55 yards) from a watercourse. Disperse the waste-water widely to allow the soil to filter it fully before it makes it back to the watercourse. For personal washing, use biodegradable soap. For cooking utensils use a scourer or sand instead of detergent.

Erosion
• Hillsides and mountain slopes are prone to erosion. It is important to stick to existing tracks and avoid short cuts. If you blaze a new trail straight down a slope, it may turn into a watercourse with the next heavy rainfall and eventually cause soil loss and deep scarring.
• If a well used track passes through a mud patch, walk through the mud: walking around the edge will increase the size of the patch.
• Avoid removing the plant life that keeps topsoil in place.

Fires & Low Impact Cooking
• Don't depend on open fires for cooking. Cook on a light-weight kerosene, alcohol or Shellite (white gas) stove; avoid those powered by disposable butane-gas canisters.
• If you do light a fire, ensure that you fully extinguish it after use. Spread the embers and douse them with water. A fire is only safe to leave when you can comfortably place your hand in it.

Wildlife Conservation
• Don't buy items made from endangered species.
• Discourage the presence of vermin by not leaving food scraps behind. Place gear out of reach and tie packs to rafters or trees.
• Do not feed the wildlife, as this can lead to animals becoming dependent on hand-outs.

Trekking in Populated Areas
• Follow the social and cultural considerations when interacting with the local community. See Dos & Don'ts under Society & Conduct in the Facts about the South Pacific chapter.

Facts for the Visitor in the individual country chapters. Take plenty of water; see Mosquitos under Dangers & Annoyances earlier in this chapter.

Water Sports

What the Pacific islands lack in landmass, they make up for in water. See the 'South Pacific Diving' special section for information about scuba diving and snorkelling in the Pacific islands.

The sport of board surfing was invented first by the sea-loving cultures of Polynesia. The first recorded observations of surfing on a board come from Hawai'i and Tahiti in the 1770s. Some 200 years later the Pacific is still popular among surfers. Apart from the most famous beaches in Hawai'i, surfers flock to Guam, Tonga, French Polynesia and Fiji. See Activities in the relevant country chapters. Surfing over coral reefs is obviously dangerous and should only be attempted at high tide. As always, local knowledge is the best guide regarding both safety and where the best waves are to be found.

Kayaking is popular, and kayaks can be rented on several islands. There are also opportunities to windsurf and jet ski. Several islands have set up beach huts as very cheap accommodation especially to cater for the surfing crowd.

Surfing

Modern surfers will identify with James Cook's observations of a Tahitian surfer in 1777:

I could not help concluding that this man felt the most supreme pleasure while he was driven on so fast and so smoothly by the sea.

Frustrated surfers may also be interested to learn an ancient Hawai'ian chant used to make the surf rise:

Kumai!
Kumai!
Ka nalu nui mai Kahiki mai
(Arise! Arise! You great surfs from Tahiti)

SPECTATOR SPORTS

Among Pacific women, netball is the most popular game. Other sports pursued in the Pacific are soccer, boxing, athletics, basketball, volleyball, pétanque (in the French territories) and American football. Rugby union is popular throughout the Pacific, as well as the faster version rugby sevens, in which Fiji is the world's best.

The British influence can also be seen in cricket's popularity, as well as the local variation known as *kirikiti* (see the boxed text 'It's Not Just Cricket' in the Samoa chapter). Vanuatuan handball is another unique Pacific sport.

Sailing and paddling contests pay tribute to islanders' voyaging past; international contests include the annual Hawaiki Nui *va'a* (canoe) race in French Polynesia. The premier multi-sport event is the South Pacific Games, held every four years at a different location around the Pacific.

In Pacific rim countries, some of the highest profile Pacific islanders are those playing sport, such as the rugby players of New Zealand and Australia or the American football players of the USA.

WORK

See the individual country chapters for restrictions on working in the Pacific islands. Also see Useful Organisations earlier in this chapter for some volunteer organisations active in the Pacific.

ACCOMMODATION

Accommodation options vary widely in the Pacific. Some countries with thriving tourist industries, such as Fiji, have a range of choices from expensive resorts to backpacker hostels. Other popular destinations, for example New Caledonia or Guam, may only have expensive options. Countries with a small tourist trade have accordingly fewer options; see Accommodation in the individual country chapters for more information.

If you have your own tent, camping can be a cheap alternative. For example, it's an excellent way to save some precious francs on Tahiti. However, many countries actively discourage camping; check Facts for the Visitor in the individual country chapters. Before you set up your tent, it is important to seek permission from any customary owners of the land. In many cultures, camping near a village can cast shame on the villagers for failing to invite the strangers into their homes. If you do camp out, try to leave no trace of your visit; carry out everything you carry in.

Staying in Villages

The Pacific islands are famous for their hospitality, and in many countries it is almost inevitable that you will be invited to stay in the home of a local family. Not only does this provide you with an insight into local culture and lifestyle, it confers a degree of honour on the host family.

Staying with a family should not be viewed as just a cheap form of accommodation. Even the most welcome guest will eventually strain a family's resources, and although they may never ask you to leave, after a few days it may be more considerate to move on. When you leave, it is important to express your gratitude formally. Gather the family, offer your thanks with a short speech, and present a gift of some sort. Don't call it 'payment' or it may be refused. It may well be refused anyway, but you should do your best to leave it behind. Cash will not always be accepted, but kava, alcohol or shop goods (such as canned meat) may be. Souvenir items from your own homeland will be most popular.

See Dos & Don'ts under Society & Conduct in the Facts about the South Pacific chapter for some more advice about how to behave in traditional homes and villages. Bear in mind that many Pacific cultures have a relaxed attitude to property. It's best not to leave expensive gear lying around in private homes unless you share that relaxed attitude.

FOOD

The traditional diet of Pacific islanders depended heavily on vegetables; coconuts, taro, breadfruit, banana, papayas, yams and kumara provided the bulk of meals. Protein was largely gained from seafood and birds,

with dogs, pigs and fowl kept in reserve for feasting and ceremonial occasions.

Since contact with Europeans, the diet of Pacific islanders has taken a turn for the worse. Canned foods, particularly canned meat, are popular, as are heavily processed foods and drinks. Health problems related to this diet include obesity and diabetes. Popular fast-food outlets have added to the problem.

Restaurants

In most cases, Pacific islanders themselves do not have the ready cash to patronise restaurants, so they are built to serve the tourist population. As such they are concentrated in areas with a high tourist population.

The restaurants of the French territories and ex-French territories can be superb. In general, vegetarians and vegans are not very well catered for.

Self-Catering

There will be some form of shopping outlet in all but the smallest of villages. Depending on the level of isolation, the choice may be limited and the goods may be expensive. Markets are the source of the freshest and cheapest foodstuffs.

Umu

The *umu* earth oven (*ahima'a* in French Polynesia) is used throughout the Pacific. Variations are many but the common theme is that food, wrapped in wet cloth or leaves, is cooked under a layer of earth and surrounded by rocks heated red-hot in a fire. The food is steamed slowly and takes on some of the flavour of the earth. A traditional umu meal is not hard to arrange in most Pacific centres.

Coconuts

The coconut is a vital resource in the Pacific. Each of the nut's five growth stages provides a different form of food or drink. The first stage is ideal for drinking, because as yet there's no flesh inside. During the next stage, tasty jellied flesh appears inside. The best eating stage is the third, when the flesh inside is firm but thin and succulent. After this, the flesh becomes thick and hard – ideal for drying into copra. At its fifth stage, the

Kava

Kava (*'ava*, *yaqona* or *sakau*) is drunk throughout almost all of Polynesia, as well as in much of Melanesia and a few islands of Micronesia.

Drinking kava has always been a very formal process. It is still a strong social tradition at evening time in many Pacific cultures. As well as being used as a form of welcome, it's also used to seal alliances, to start chiefly conferences, and to commemorate births, deaths and marriages. If you're asked to drink some at a village, consider yourself honoured. To decline kava when it is offered is to decline friendship – so even though it may taste disgusting, you've got to gulp it down and appear impressed.

Kava is made from the roots of the *Piper methysticum* shrub, which was deliberately carried from island to island from Melanesia eastwards into Polynesia. There are many varieties of the plant growing in Melanesia: some 40 subspecies thrive in Vanuatu. Eastern Polynesia has only a few varieties.

Kava is an important cash and cultural crop in a number of Pacific Islands. Exports are largely for the benefit of islanders living overseas, but kava is now sold in tablet form in western countries as a herbal medicine for stress and sleeping disorders.

Ceremony

Traditionally, there are strict rules for preparing and drinking kava.

Preparation procedures vary throughout the Pacific. In the more traditional areas, kava root is washed, then prepared by chewing into a mush and spitting the hard bits onto leaves. The mush is then placed in a container, water is added and the ingredients are stirred with the hands. Then the mud-coloured liquid is filtered through coconut fibres. In other areas, the root may simply be pounded in a plastic bucket, or the drink may be prepared from a commercially packaged powder. As saliva releases the root's active ingredients, kava prepared by chewing is more potent than that from pounding.

Once the liquid mixture is ready for drinking, it's poured into a bowl made from an empty half-coconut shell, which serves as a cup. The order in which kava is drunk varies. Usually the chief drinks it first, followed by any honoured guests. Then the other men drink in order of precedence. Usually kava drinkers consume two to three half-coconut cupfuls in a session.

Some cultures expect drinkers to down the kava in a single gulp, any remaining liquid being poured on the ground. Sometimes, kava is drunk in silence, but some

ROBYN JONES

A traditional four-legged Fijian kava bowl.

Kava

cultures prefer a great deal of slurping to show appreciation. Sometimes your companions will quietly clap as you drink. Generally, while kava is being drunk, except for the clapping stage, conversation and loud noises are kept to a minimum. Islanders feel it's best imbibed when there's an atmosphere of quietness.

Kava makes the eyes sensitive to glare, so any strong lights, especially flashbulbs, are very intrusive. If you really want to take a photograph, ask permission and limit yourself to one or two shots.

Experiential Effects

Kava has a pungent, muddy taste. If the brew is a strong one, your lips will go numb and cold, like after a dental injection. Then your limbs will feel heavy and your speech will become quiet and slow.

You'll begin to be affected within 10 to 25 minutes. Even if it's only a mild brew, you'll probably want to do nothing more than lie down and think about life, feeling sedated and a general sense of wellbeing. You may also experience some minor perceptual changes, both in emotions and vision. If the brew is a strong one, you'll probably experience a mild form of double vision, and want to sleep for a few hours.

Some islanders claim to have repeated religious experiences after drinking kava. Many religious visions have occurred at such times!

Social Effects

In many countries, kava has helped to retain ancient customs longer. Its rituals reinforce the traditional authority of chiefs, even when villagers have moved to the towns. Many people attribute a low crime rate to the calming effects of kava. Unlike alcohol, which often produces aggressive and irresponsible behaviour, kava produces amiability, peacefulness and acceptance of life.

Medicinal Uses

Some Melanesian subspecies of kava are too strong to drink, and are used instead as bush medicines. Different kinds of kava plants produce differing effects, which are strengthened or reduced depending on whether the drink is prepared by chewing, straining or pounding.

In scientific terms, kava is an amalgam of up to 14 analgesics and anaesthetics, and has natural pain and appetite-suppressant features. The root also has antibacterial, relaxant, diuretic and decongestant properties. It's been recommended for cancer and asthma patients, and also for people suffering from stomach upsets.

No studies have fully established the effects of a lifetime of kava drinking. Plenty of elderly Pacific islanders and long-term expats who have drunk copious quantities on a daily basis for years appear to be well and mentally alert – certainly a lot healthier and sharper than the average alcoholic. However, some evidence points to heavy drinkers developing a scaly skin, hepatitis, weight loss, lung disease and/or impotence.

Female Kava Drinkers

In some parts of the Pacific, drinking kava is an exclusively male activity – some say the original kava plant sprang from the loins of a woman, hence the *tapu*. However, women are free to drink it along with the men in some areas. In major tourist areas, where customary rules are usually relaxed, an increasing number of local, expat and tourist women enjoy a regular shell.

nut begins to shoot while the milk inside goes crispy, making what is known throughout the Pacific as 'coconut ice cream'.

See Flora & Fauna in the Facts about the South Pacific chapter for more information about the coconut tree.

The Face of the Coconut

The importance of the coconut to Pacific islanders is highlighted by a widespread traditional story. Many Pacific cultures tell the tale of the man Tuna, the lover of Hina. When Tuna was killed by a jealous suitor (Maui in some tellings), he became the coconut, and his face is represented by the three black depressions at the top of the coconut's shell. Push your straw through Tuna's mouth, the only depression that pierces the shell, and you can drink the coconut's juice. It is also through Tuna's mouth that the shoot of a new coconut tree grows, providing food for the children of Hina.

MICK WELDON

DRINKS

Tap water is not always safe to drink; see Health earlier in this chapter and in individual country chapters. Fresh coconut juice is a refreshing drink on a hot day. Any small town in the Pacific will have young drinking coconuts for sale somewhere, or you can prevail upon most small boys to climb up a tree for the right price (anything from a smile to a few coins). Make sure you get permission from the owner of the land, and you'll need a large knife to hack away the green husk – or a pocket knife and a lot of patience.

Alcoholic Drinks

Attitudes to alcohol vary. Some communities, seeing the detrimental effects of alcohol, such as domestic violence, have banned alcohol completely – but in most countries it's freely available. Many countries with their own breweries brew excellent beers; a couple of the best are Samoa's Vailima and Palau's Red Rooster. Australian, New Zealand and US beers are also available in most countries.

Before drinking mixed drinks, ask if the drink has been diluted with water. In many countries the tap water should not be drunk.

Traditional Highs

Drinks made from fermented coconut sap (called coconut wine, sour toddy, *kaleve*, *tuba* or *kaokioki*) are popular on many Pacific islands. Kava is even more widespread; see the boxed text. For another nonalcoholic form of high, popular in the west Pacific, see the boxed text 'Betel Nut' in the Federated States of Micronesia chapter.

SOUTH PACIFIC DIVING

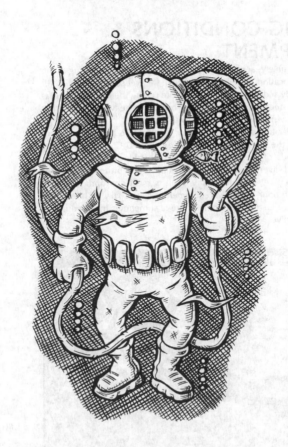

Dramatic drop-offs, pristine and sheltered lagoons, ocean dives, magnificent reefs and caves, exceptional wrecks, an incredibly rich and colourful fauna, warm tropical waters – the South Pacific has just about everything a diver could hope for. The region provides memorable dive experiences for expert divers as well as for beginners.

Most dive sites in the South Pacific are largely uncrowded and untouched compared with overexploited areas in the Caribbean and Red Sea, providing an exclusiveness which can be exciting.

DIVING CONDITIONS & EQUIPMENT

Diving is possible year round although conditions vary according to the season and location. Visibility is reduced in the wet season as the water is muddied by sediments brought into the sea by the rivers, and areas that are exposed to currents might also become heavy with particles. On average, visibility ranges from 15 to 50m.

In most Pacific countries the water temperature peaks at a warm 29°C during the rainy season, but can drop to 20°C in some areas at certain periods of the year. Though it is possible to dive without a wetsuit, most divers wear at least a lycra outsuit to protect themselves from abrasions. A 3mm tropical wetsuit is most appropriate. If you don't want to bring your own equipment it can usually be hired from the larger dive centres. Equipment hire is sometimes included in the price of the dive.

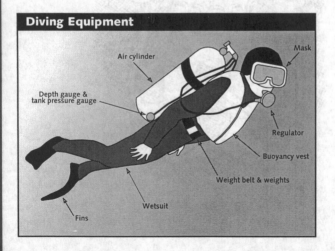

Diving Equipment

Mask

Air cylinder

Depth gauge & tank pressure gauge

Regulator

Buoyancy vest

Weight belt & weights

Wetsuit

Fins

Responsible Diving

Please consider the following tips when you're diving and help to preserve the ecology and beauty of reefs:

• Do not use anchors on the reef, and don't ground boats on coral. Encourage dive operators and regulatory bodies to establish permanent moorings at popular dive sites.

• Avoid touching living marine organisms with your body or by dragging equipment across the reef. Polyps can be damaged by even the most gentle contact. Never stand on coral, even if it looks solid and robust. If you must hold on to the reef, only touch exposed rock or dead coral.

• Be conscious of your fins. Even without contact the surge from heavy fin strokes can damage delicate reef organisms.

• Practise proper buoyancy control. Major damage can be done by divers descending too fast and colliding with the reef. Make sure you are correctly weighted and that your weight belt is positioned so that you stay horizontal. If you have not dived for a while, have a practice dive in a pool first.

• Take great care in underwater caves. Spend as little time within them as possible as your air bubbles may catch in ceiling cavities, leaving previously submerged organisms high and dry.

• Do not collect or buy corals or shells. Aside from the ecological damage, taking home marine souvenirs depletes the beauty of a site and spoils the enjoyment of others. The same goes for ship-wrecks – respect their integrity (some sites are protected from looting by law).

• Take out all your rubbish and any litter you may find as well. Plastics, in particu-lar, are a serious threat to marine life. Turtles can mistake plastic for jellyfish and eat it.

• Don't feed fish. You may disturb their normal eating habits, encourage aggressive behaviour or feed them food that is detrimental to their health.

• Minimise your distur-bance of marine animals. In particular, do not ride on the backs of turtles, as this causes them great anxiety.

MICHAEL AW

DIVE CENTRES & COURSES

On most tourist-oriented islands you'll find professional and reliable dive centres staffed with qualified instructors catering to divers of all levels. Choose a dive centre affiliated with an internationally recognised dive organisation – eg PADI, NAUI, SSI or CMAS. Like a hotel or a restaurant, each dive centre has its own personality and style. Wherever possible, it is a good idea to visit several dive centres to get a feel of each operation. Word of mouth should also let you know which ones are good. See the Activities sections in individual country chapters.

Diving in the South Pacific is expensive in comparison to most destinations in Asia, the Caribbean or the Red Sea. Expect to pay about US$40 to $50 for a single dive. Set dive packages (eg two dives or 10 dives) are usually cheaper. All types of courses are available, including introductory courses (US$40 to $70) or open-water certification courses. You'll be looking at about US$300 to $500 for a three or four day course. Once you've got your certificate, you can dive in centres worldwide.

If you're a certified diver, ensure that you have your dive certificate with you. Dive centres welcome divers regardless of their training background, provided they can produce a certificate from one of the agencies mentioned earlier.

There are decompression chambers in Suva (Fiji), Papeete (French Polynesia) and Arakabesang (Palau). However, in practice patients are usually transferred to New Zealand or Australia.

DIVE SITES

The South Pacific boasts hundreds of breathtaking dive sites. Our list is by no means exhaustive and should be considered merely a sample of some of the most renowned sites.

Cook Islands

On Rarotonga, **Matavera Wall** plunges to a sandy bottom at 60m. The major attraction, apart from the drop-off, is the abundance and variety of coral formations and fish. White-tipped reef sharks, eagle rays and sometimes whale sharks can be sighted nearby.

Close by, **Ngatangiia School** is riddled with swim-throughs and crevices that offer an ideal habitat for moray eels, lobsters, urchins, clams, lionfish, stonefish and shellfish.

Papua Passage refers to a natural opening chiselled into the lagoon, and varying in depth from 5 to 30m. Several tunnels lead off the passage, and eagle rays and turtles are regularly seen. The **Pinnacles** is rated as one of the Cooks' best sites; it's formed by a series of large rocks on the edge of the drop-off and it teems with colourful marine life.

Getting Started

The South Pacific provides ideal conditions for beginners with its sheltered lagoons, crystalline, warm water and prolific marine life. If you've always fancied diving but never taken the plunge, now's your chance.

Arrange an introductory dive with a reputable dive centre. It will begin on dry land, where the instructor will run through basic safety procedures (such as the use of sign language to indicate that everything is 'OK' or 'not OK', and ear equilibration techniques) and show you the equipment.

The dive itself takes place in a safe location and lasts between 20 to 40 minutes under the guidance of the instructor.

You'll practise breathing with the regulator above the water's surface before going under. The instructor will hold your hand under water if need be, and guide your movements to a depth of usually between 3 and 10m. Many centres start the instruction in waist-high water in a hotel swimming pool or on the beach.

There is no formal procedure but you shouldn't dive if you have a medical condition such as acute ear, nose and throat problems, epilepsy or heart disease (such as infarction), if you have a cold or sinusitis, or if you are pregnant.

If you enjoy your introductory dive, you might want to follow it up with a three to four day course to obtain a first-level certification which will allow you to dive anywhere in the world.

French Polynesia

Rangiroa Atoll in the Tuamotu archipelago is a mecca for divers. The tidal flows create exceptional diving conditions and attract numerous open-sea species. **Tiputa Pass** is a world-class drift dive. Divers immerse themselves at the edge of the reef drop-off and let themselves be sucked into the lagoon through the pass with the incoming current, accompanied by a procession of fish, including numerous grey sharks.

Off the north-western coast of Moorea is the **Tiki**, another exceptional site, renowned not so much for the seascape as for its density of marine life. Spectacular shark-feeding sessions are regularly held in less than 25m, attracting a crowd of grey sharks, black-tipped sharks and even bigger lemon sharks.

Off Bora Bora, don't miss **Tupitipiti**, one of the archipelago's most magical dive sites. It features a steep drop-off tumbled with rocks and dotted with caves and swim-throughs.

In the Marquesas, devoid of coral reefs and lagoons, the main attraction is the **Orques Pygmees**, east of Nuku Hiva Island. Here you can snorkel or dive with dozens of melon-headed whales.

Niue

Niue has no fringing lagoon, but does have several coastal caverns. The **Ana Mahaga** (or Twin Caves) is the most exciting dive site. It features two large caves connected by a horizontal tunnel, at a maximum depth of 30m. Another popular site is **Snake Gully**, famous for its incredible population of sea snakes. **Tepa Fans** is a deep dive (30 to 40m) where experienced divers will enjoy the sight of enormous gorgonian fans.

Tonga

On Tongatapu, the diving is at its best at **Beach Dive**, off Ha'atafu Beach. There is a succession of drop-offs, from 3 to 15m and from 15 to 30m. The coral supports a large amount of sea life, from small reef fish to large species, such as barracuda and tuna. The caves and fissures, worth exploring, are a bonus. On the islands north of Nuku'alofa are **Deep Reef**, on Hakaumama'o Reef, a wall exposed to currents and thus having abundant large fish, and **Barrier Reef**, near Malinoa Island, which is another excellent spot for enjoying fish action.

Fiji

The Fijian islands are the world's capital of soft corals. Off Taveuni Island, the most remarkable dive zone is **Rainbow Reef**, in the Somosomo Strait, which gets its name from the unbelievable colours of its corals. Here, all

Pre-Dive Safety

Before embarking on a diving trip, make sure it will be a safe as well as an enjoyable experience. You should:
• possess a current diving certification card from a recognised scuba diving instructional agency, or take an introductory course.
• obtain reliable information about physical and environmental conditions at the dive site (eg from a reputable local dive operator).
• be aware of local regulations and etiquette about marinelife and the environment. Ask permission of customary owners of the reef or beach if appropriate.
• Dive only at sites within your realm of experience; if available, engage the services of a competent, professionally-trained dive instructor.
• be aware that underwater conditions vary significantly from one region, or even site, to another. Seasonal changes can significantly alter any site and dive conditions. These differences may influence the way you need to dress for a dive and what diving techniques to use.

divers covet the legendary Great White Wall – a sheer drop-off starting at a depth of about 15m and ornamented with a profusion of magnificent soft corals. Tunnels and myriad small tropical fish add to the wonders of the dive.

East of Viti Levu, along Malolo Reef off the Mamanuca islands, do not miss the **Supermarket**, a dive famous for its regular shark-feeding sessions. Between 10 and 30 grey, black-tipped and white-tipped sharks run the show.

If you go through a live-aboard operation, you'll certainly dive **E6** or **Wakaya Passage**. E6 is in the channel between Vanua Levu and Viti Levu – it's a seamount rising from 1000m, renowned for its abundance of pelagics, while the passage, off Wakaya Island in the Lomaiviti Islands, offers a mix of large species (manta rays and hammerhead sharks) and the usual plethora of tropical fish.

South of Viti Levu, **Caesar's Rock**, in Beqa's lagoon, boasts several coral pinnacles carved with a few tunnels and covered with brightly coloured soft corals and sea fans. The pinnacles are a magnet for marinelife.

New Caledonia

New Caledonia boasts one of the largest lagoons in the world. Off Noumea, the huge **Passe de Boulari** is the most popular site. Pelagics, including manta rays, big wrasses and horse-eye jacks, are plentiful. Regular shark-feeding sessions maintain a large population of sharks. Nearby, *La Dieppoise* is a famous wreck, deliberately scuttled in 1988, lying at a depth of 26m.

Off the southern tip of Grande Terre, the **Aiguille de Prony** (Prony Needle), in Baie de Prony, features a unique topography, with a pyramid-shaped mineral spike rising from the sea bed, 40m below the surface, to within 2m of the surface.

Off Bourail, the stunning **La Faille de Poé** is a narrow channel

Top: Plate coral is one of the most common types of hard coral.

Right: Soft corals usually have eight tentacles.

STEVE SIMONSEN

Dive into History

No other area in the world boasts as many wrecks as the western part of the South Pacific. Vanuatu, Chuuk (Truk) lagoon and the Solomon Islands offer a fantastic variety of wrecks, dating mostly from WWII, that are a paradise for wreck-diving enthusiasts. The devastating naval battles that took place in the area during WWII wreaked havoc on the Japanese fleet. In Chuuk the airplanes, destroyers, cruisers, other vessels and even tanks and jeeps are virtually the sole attraction. All are in good to perfect condition and are festooned with soft corals and sponges that provide an eerie home for many underwater creatures.

Wrecks are a fascinating experience for divers. Most of them are accessible to novice divers who have a certification. However, entering a wreck requires specific skills and divers should always explore these war relics under the guidance of an experienced local dive master.

into the reef that runs perpendicular to the coast; it's the remnant of a former river bed and home to numerous rays, sharks and gropers.

Off northern Grande Terre, Poum reef is by far the most spectacular. It is completely unspoilt and divers will experience thrilling encounters with sharks and rays near **Passe de la Gazelle** or in **Fausse Passe**.

Off Lifou Island, **Gorgone Reef** is the most renowned site. As its name suggests, it offers an incredible diversity of brightly coloured gorgonians, sea fans and soft corals.

Off Île des Pins, try **Vallée des Gorgones**, near N'Gié Islet, northwest of the main island. You will enjoy the many gorgonians and varieties of reef life and some pelagics in less than 20m. There are also interesting arches and swim-throughs.

SIMON FOALE

Left: The spectacular orange and white rugged-finned firefish (*Pterois antennata*)

Solomon Islands

Guadalcanal Island is a wonderland for WWII buffs, with many ship-wrecks from naval battles resting close to the shore. The most popular sites, with some 50 other ships and aircraft in the aptly named Iron Bottom Sound off Honiara, include *Bonegi I*, a 172m Japanese trans-port ship, varying in depth from 3m to 55m, and *Bonegi II*, another Japanese transport ship, still partly above the water's surface, with its stern submerged to 27m. Both wrecks are adorned with excellent coral and attract masses of fish.

Seven kilometres north-west of the town of Gizo on Ghizo Island, is the *Toa Maru*, a huge Japanese freighter that sank during WWII. It rests in 18 to 36m of water and is still in perfect condition. Divers can explore the ship's holds, which contain tanks, ammunition and trucks. **Grand Central Station** is another exhilarating site, 6km further north-west, near Varu Island. Here divers just sit at 18m and watch the fish life, including rays, sharks and barracudas, pass by.

In Western Province, off New Georgia Island, near Munda, try **Shark Point**, a drop-off that is patrolled by sharks and huge schools of pelagics. In Marovo lagoon, near Uepi Island, which is still largely unspoilt, the **Elbow** features a breathtaking wall carpeted with mag-nificent corals and dropping to a depth of 600m. Sharks and barra-cudas are common.

Vanuatu

Vanuatu is also renowned for its numerous WWII wrecks. Off Espiritu Santo, the SS *President Coolidge* is one of the world's most fascinat-ing wreck dives. An impressive 654 foot luxury liner, it was used as a troop ship during WWII. It sank in 1942 after having hit two mines, but remained in perfect condition. Divers can swim through numer-ous decks to inspect the rooms and mechanical parts. Many fish have taken up residence. The depth range is 18 to 70m.

Another amazing site off Es-piritu Santo is **Million Dollar Point**, where thousands of tonnes of military paraphernalia were dumped by the US navy after the war. Divers swim among a jumble of cranes, bull-dozers, trucks and other con-struction hardware at a depth ranging from surface to 35m. This junkyard, covering more than half a hectare, attracts huge numbers of marinelife.

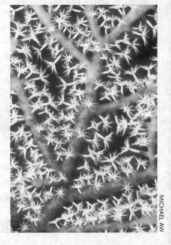

Right: A close-up of a orgonian fan, a type of ft coral, shows the tiny inging nemocysts used to catch food.

MICHAEL AW

On the nearby island of Tutuba, **Tutuba Point** has spectacular hard and soft corals and offers a combination of caves and swim-throughs at 10 to 40m. The countless varieties of fish are another attraction at this site.

Off Efate Island, enjoy diving at the *Star of Russia*, a ship that was built in the 1800s and sank in Port Vila's harbour 70 years ago. **Black Sand Reef and Caves**, also close to Port Vila, features a reef chiselled with caves and swim-throughs and with corals and reef fish in abundance. The site's sandy bottom is home to many rays.

Federated States of Micronesia
Yap

Yap is one of the few areas in the world where sightings of manta rays are guaranteed. They use the long and winding Miil Channel, at the north-western side of the island, as a cleaning station area. **Manta Cleaning Station**, **Manta Ridge** and **Miil Point** are the best sites to watch these superb creatures.

Wild Encounters

The thousands of square kilometres of reefs that dot the South Pacific harbour tropical fish of every shape, colour and size. But what makes the diving so distinctive is the density of pelagics. Virtually anywhere sightings of sharks can be expected. White-tipped, black-tipped, grey, lemon, nurse and hammerhead sharks are the most common species. In many countries, shark-feeding sessions are held by a dive instructor and allow amazed divers to watch sharks at close range in safety.

Various species of rays may also be encountered. Stingrays can be found on sandy floors everywhere and magnificent manta rays are the star attraction of Yap and of some islands of French Polynesia.

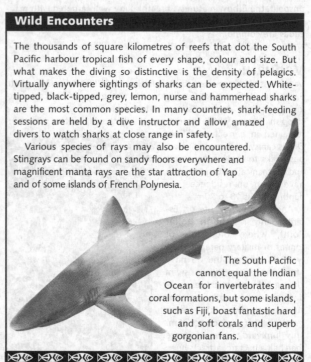

The South Pacific cannot equal the Indian Ocean for invertebrates and coral formations, but some islands, such as Fiji, boast fantastic hard and soft corals and superb gorgonian fans.

Left: Galapagos Shark, an aggressive pelagic species (photograph by Astrid Witte)

STEVE SIMONSEN

Chuuk

The lagoon floor at Chuuk (Truk) is an underwater war museum. It is covered with over 60 remarkably-intact Japanese ships sunk by the Americans during battles at the end of WWII. The best wreck is the **Shinkoku Maru**, a large freighter, about 160m long, lying at a depth of 10 to 40m. It is resplendent with corals and fish life, and sharks regularly prowl around. It also has numerous well-preserved artefacts. The **Fuji-kawa Maru**, at a similar depth range, is another great wreck dive. The ship is 145m in length and is loaded with coral life.

Guam

A major WWII battle site, Guam's Apra Harbor is full of diveable wrecks. One of the best is the 12 to 38m *Tokai Maru*, a big Japanese freighter bombed during WWII. It sank on top of the Cormoran, a

Guidebooks

Lonely Planet's Pisces series includes the following guides to the Pacific Islands:

Diving & Snorkeling Chuuk Lagoon, Pohnpei & Kosrae
Diving & Snorkeling Fiji
Diving & Snorkeling Guam & Yap
Diving & Snorkeling Hawaii
Diving & Snorkeling Palau
Diving & Snorkeling Papua New Guinea
Diving & Snorkeling Tahiti & French Polynesia
Diving & Snorkeling Vanuatu

Top: The giant flathead *(Cymbacephalus beau-orti)* is perfectly camou-flaged on a sandy seabed.

German cruiser scuttled during WWI, so at about 30m you can have a hand on each war. Another is the mysterious *Kitsugawa Maru*, resting upright at a depth of 18 to 43m.

Apart from wrecks, the finest dive in Guam is the **Blue Hole**. It consists of a vertical shaft starting at 18m and plunging to about 100m, with a large exit at 40m opening to the outer wall, allowing the diver to ascend after a free fall through the azure abyss of the shaft. Visibility is superb and large fish can be expected at the exit hole.

Marshall Islands

Within Bikini Atoll, the lagoon bed holds a unique collection of post-WWII warships. Don't miss the **USS *Saratoga***, the largest ship (275m long) of this ghost fleet laden with weaponry and resting in water between 30 to 40m.

The Northern Mariana Islands

The most renowned site is the **Grotto**, in Saipan. For experienced and fit divers only, it features a 30m cavern accessible by concrete stairs. Turtles, sharks and sometimes a manta ray keep company with divers. The currents can be quite tricky, so get a thorough briefing beforehand.

Palau

Palau offers world-class drop-offs. **Ngemelis Wall** is the most exhilarating site. It features a sheer wall starting in shallow waters and falling to depths greater than 300m. Divers can free float past a brilliant rainbow of multi-hued soft corals and sponges. Close by, the **Blue Corner** is famous for its fish action. It forms a flat area in the reef in about 15m of water before dropping off abruptly. Sharks, rays and fish life abound.

For a surreal experience, **Jellyfish Lake**, on one of the Rock Islands, is a must. Here you'll have the unique opportunity to dive with thousands of harmless jellyfish in less than 10m of water.

Jean-Bernard Carillet

WWII warplane (B17 bomber), Guadalcanal

Soft coral trees, Somosomo Straits, Fiji

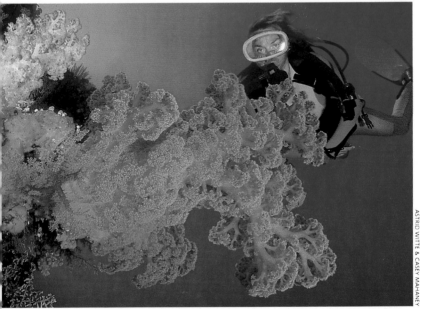

A diver admires a tree of orange soft coral, Fiji.

Regal angel fish *(Pygoplites diacanthus)*

Wide-eyed marinelife

Clown anemonefish

Decorator crab on coral

Gentle manta rays, up to 4m across, are a favourite of divers.

Getting There & Away

The first part of your journey is reaching the South Pacific. Compared to travel in Europe, this can be an expensive exercise – the smaller number of travellers in the region means that prices are generally high. The main gateways to the South Pacific region are the USA (via Hawai'i), Australasia (Australia and New Zealand) and Japan. See the South Pacific Gateways chapter for a short introduction to Hawai'i, New Zealand, Papua New Guinea and the Australian Territories.

Large international airlines flying routes between Australasia, Asia and the USA link a number of the island countries. There are also many small local airlines that only service the Pacific region. The countries covered by each airline, and relevant contact details, are listed under Airlines in the Getting Around the Region chapter.

Within countries, inter-island shipping routes can be used to reach smaller islands without air services. Cruise ships provide an expensive way of reaching the major tourist destinations. Cargo vessels, some of which carry passengers, travel between island groups and the main Pacific trading nations.

AIR

Under the different regions later in this section, we give prices to get to centres such as Guam, Honolulu (Hawai'i), Papeete (French Polynesia), Nadi (Fiji), Sydney (Australia) and Auckland (New Zealand). Travellers to the South Pacific can usually pick up connecting flights from these centres to elsewhere in the region.

Always reconfirm your onward or return bookings by the specified time – at least 72 hours before departure is standard on international flights. Otherwise, there's a real risk that you'll turn up at the airport only to find that you've missed your flight because it was rescheduled or that you've been reclassified as a 'no show' and have been 'bumped' (see the 'Air Travel Glossary' later in this chapter).

Use the fares quoted in this book as a guide only. They are based on the rates advertised by travel agents at the time of research. Most are likely to have changed by the time you read this.

Buying Tickets

An air ticket alone can gouge a great slice out of anyone's budget, but you can reduce the cost by finding discounted fares. Stiff competition has resulted in widespread discounting – good news for travellers! The only people likely to be paying full fare these days are travellers flying in 1st or business class. Passengers flying in economy can usually manage to find some sort of discount. But unless you buy carefully and have some flexibility, it is still possible to end up paying exorbitant amounts for a journey.

For long-term travel there are plenty of discount tickets valid for 12 months, allowing multiple stopovers with open dates. When you're looking for bargain air fares, go to a travel agent rather than directly to the airline. From time to time, airlines do have promotional fares and special offers but generally they only sell fares at the official listed price.

The other exception is booking on the Internet, where many airlines – full-service and no-frills – offer some excellent fares. They may sell seats by auction or simply cut prices to reflect the reduced cost of electronic selling. Many travel agents around the world have websites, which can make the Internet a quick and easy way to compare prices – a good start for negotiating with your favourite travel agency. Online ticket sales work well if you want a simple one-way or return trip on specified dates. However, online superfast fare generators are no substitute for a travel agent who knows all about special deals, has strategies for avoiding layovers and can offer advice on everything from which airline has the best vegetarian food to the best travel insurance to bundle with your ticket.

The days when some travel agents would routinely fleece travellers by running off with their money are, happily, almost over. Paying by credit card generally offers protection, as most card issuers provide refunds if you can prove you didn't get what you paid for. Similar protection can be obtained by buying a ticket from a bonded agent, such as one covered by the Air Transport Operators License (ATOL) scheme in the UK. Agents who only accept cash should hand over the tickets straight away and not tell you to 'come back tomorrow'. After you've made a booking or paid your deposit, call the airline and confirm that the booking was made. It's generally not advisable to send money (even cheques) through the post unless the agent is very well established – some travellers have been ripped off by fly-by-night mail-order ticket agents.

You may decide to pay more than the rock-bottom fare by opting for the safety of a better known travel agent. Firms such as STA Travel, which has offices worldwide, Council Travel in the USA and USIT Campus (formerly Campus Travel) in the UK are not going to disappear overnight and they do offer good prices to most destinations.

If you purchase a ticket and later want to make changes to your route or get a refund, you need to contact the original travel agent. Airlines only issue refunds to the purchaser of a ticket – usually the travel agent who bought the ticket on your behalf. It's often desirable to change your route halfway through a trip, so think carefully before you buy a ticket that is not easily refunded.

Student & Youth Fares Full-time students and people under 26 have access to better deals than other travellers. The better deals may not always be cheaper fares but can include more flexibility to change flights and/or routes. You have to show a document proving your date of birth or a valid International Student Identity Card (ISIC) when buying your ticket and boarding the plane. There are plenty of places around the world where nonstudents can get fake student cards but if you get caught using a fake card, you could have your ticket confiscated.

Frequent Fliers Most airlines offer frequent flier deals that can earn you a free air ticket or other goodies. To qualify, you have to accumulate sufficient mileage with the same airline or airline alliance. Many airlines have 'blackout periods', or times when you cannot fly for free on your frequent flier points (eg Christmas and Chinese New Year). The worst thing about frequent flier programs is that they tend to lock you into one airline, and that airline may not always have the cheapest fares or most convenient flight schedule.

Courier Flights Courier flights are a great bargain if you're lucky enough to find one. Air freight companies expedite delivery of urgent items by sending them with you as your baggage allowance. You are permitted to bring along a carry-on bag, but that's all. In return, you get a steeply discounted ticket.

There are other restrictions: courier tickets are sold for a fixed date, and schedule changes can be difficult to make. If you buy a return ticket, your schedule will be even more rigid. You need to clarify before you fly what restrictions apply to your ticket, and don't expect a refund once you've paid.

Booking a courier ticket takes some effort. They are not readily available and arrangements have to be made a month or more in advance. You won't find courier flights on all routes either – just on the major air routes.

Courier flights are occasionally advertised in the newspapers, or you could contact air freight companies listed in the phone book. You may even have to go to the air freight company to get an answer – the companies aren't always keen to give out information over the phone. *Travel Unlimited*, PO Box 1058, Allston, MA 02134, is a monthly travel newsletter from the USA that publishes many courier flight deals from destinations worldwide. A 12 month subscription to the newsletter costs US$25, or US$35 for residents outside the USA.

Another possibility (at least for US residents) is to join the International Association of Air Travel Couriers (IAATC). The membership fee of US$45 gets members a bimonthly update of air courier offerings, access to a fax-on-demand service with daily updates of last minute specials and the bimonthly newsletter the *Shoestring Traveler*. For more information, contact IAATC (☎ 561-582 8320) or visit its website at www.courier.org. However, be aware that joining this organisation does not guarantee that you'll get a courier flight.

Ticketless Travel Ticketless travel, whereby your reservation details are contained within an airline computer, is becoming more common. On simple return trips the absence of a ticket can be a benefit – it's one less thing to worry about. However, if you are planning a complicated itinerary that you may wish to amend en route, there is no substitute for the good old paper version.

Travellers with Special Needs

Most major international airlines can cater for people with special needs – travellers with disabilities, people with young children and even children travelling alone.

Special dietary preferences (vegetarian, kosher etc) can be catered for with advance notice. If you are travelling in a wheelchair, major international airports can provide an escort from the check-in desk to the plane if required, and ramps, lifts, toilets and phones are generally available. Small domestic airports and airlines can be much less well set up for disabled travellers.

Airlines usually carry babies up to two years of age at 10% of the adult fare, and a few carry them free of charge. Reputable international airlines usually provide nappies (diapers), tissues, talcum and all the other paraphernalia needed to keep babies clean, dry and half-happy. For children between the ages of two and 12, the fare on international flights is usually 50% of the regular fare or 67% of a discounted fare.

Also see Disabled Travellers and Travel with Children in the Regional Facts for the Visitor chapter.

North America

Airlines connecting North America to the Pacific islands include Air New Zealand, Air Pacific, Continental Airlines, Corsair, Hawaiian Airlines, Japanese Airlines, Northwest, Polynesian Airlines and Qantas. See Airlines in the Getting Around the Region chapter.

In general, November and December are the most expensive and congested months to travel, while the northern summer, corresponding to winter in the South Pacific (also the driest and most comfortable season to visit), is the cheapest and easiest time to get a booking.

There are some very useful air passes (see Air Passes in the Getting Around the Region chapter for prices and conditions) available for travellers leaving from North America. Circle Micronesia and Visit Micronesia are great for the Micronesian region, Pacifica and Polypass are useful for visiting the central and western Pacific, and Visit South Pacific covers pretty much everywhere.

USA Discount travel agents in the USA are known as ticket consolidators (although you won't see a sign on the door saying Consolidator). San Francisco is the ticket consolidator capital of America, although some good deals can be found in Los Angeles, New York and other big cities. Consolidators can be found through the *Yellow Pages* or the major daily newspapers. The *New York Times*, *Los Angeles Times*, *Chicago Tribune* and *San Francisco Examiner* all have weekly travel sections in which you will find a number of travel agency ads.

Council Travel, America's largest student travel organisation, has around 60 offices in the USA; its head office (☎ tollfree 800 226 8624 in the USA) is at 205 E 42nd St, New York 10017. Call for the office nearest you or visit its website (www.ciee.org). STA Travel (☎ tollfree 800 777 0112 in the USA) has offices in Boston, Chicago, Miami, New York, Philadelphia, San Francisco and other major cities. Call for office locations or visit its website (www.statravel.com).

Air Promotions Inc (☎ 310-670 7302, or ☎ tollfree 800 677 4277 within the USA, fax 310-338 0708) is the US agent for Pacific-based airlines. It has offices in Los Angeles, New York and San Francisco, and a website (www.pacificislands.com).

US travellers to the Pacific usually go via Honolulu, Papeete or Guam. A return ticket to Honolulu from the US west coast (San Francisco or LA) will cost US$520 year round. From the same cities, fares to Papeete will cost about US$1078, also a year round fare. To Guam, low/high season fares are around US$1088/2400. From the east coast (New York or Washington DC), fares to Honolulu will cost US$985/1090, while fares to Papeete start at around US$1261/1608 and fares to Guam start at US$1391/1820.

See the South Pacific Gateways chapter for information about Hawai'i.

Canada In Canada, discount air ticket sellers are also known as consolidators and their air fares tend to be about 10% higher than those sold in the USA. The *Globe & Mail*, *Toronto Star*, *Montreal Gazette* and *Vancouver Sun* carry travel agency ads and are a good place to look for cheap fares.

Travel CUTS (☎ tollfree 800 667 2887 in Canada) is Canada's national student travel agency and has offices in all major cities. Its website is www.travelcuts.com.

From Vancouver you can fly to Honolulu for C$650 year round. Fares to Nadi start at C$2060/2640 during the low/high season, and to Papeete they start at C$1651/2015. From Ottawa or Toronto, flights are generally via Chicago and Los Angeles; fares to Honolulu in the low/high season start at C$1239/1508. Fares to Nadi are around C$1963/2400 and to Papeete C$2075/2304.

Australasia

The east coast of Australia has excellent connecting flights to Melanesia, while Auckland or Wellington in New Zealand (NZ) have good connections to Polynesia. Airlines connecting Australia and NZ to the Pacific islands are Air Nauru, Air New Zealand, Air Pacific, Air Vanuatu, Aircalin, Ansett Australia, Polynesian Airlines, Qantas, Royal Tongan and Solomon Airlines.

Warning

The information in this chapter is particularly vulnerable to change: prices for international travel are volatile, routes are introduced and cancelled, schedules change, special deals come and go, and rules and visa requirements are amended. Airlines and governments seem to take a perverse pleasure in making price structures and regulations as complicated as possible. You should check directly with the airline or a travel agent to make sure you understand how a fare (and ticket you may buy) works. In addition, the travel industry is highly competitive and there are many lurks and perks.

The upshot of this is that you should get opinions, quotes and advice from as many airlines and travel agents as possible before you part with your hard-earned cash. The details given in this chapter should be regarded as pointers and are not a substitute for your own careful, up-to-date research.

Australia's east coast and NZ are both included in the Polypass, which can be a cheap option for visiting Fiji, Samoa and Tonga. The Circle South West Pacific air pass is handy for visiting the islands of Melanesia from Australia, and the Pacific Explorer or Visit Micronesia passes are good for Micronesia. See Air Passes in the Getting Around the Region chapter.

Australia Quite a few travel offices specialise in discount air tickets. Some travel agents, particularly smaller ones, advertise cheap air fares in the travel sections of weekend newspapers, such as the *Age* (in Melbourne) and *Sydney Morning Herald*.

Two well known agents for cheap fares are STA Travel and Flight Centre. STA Travel (☎ 03-9349 2411), 224 Faraday St, Carlton, VIC 3053, has offices in all major cities and on many university campuses. Call ☎ 131 776 for the location of your nearest branch or visit its website (www.statravel.com.au). Flight Centre (☎ 131 600 Australia-wide) has a central office at

82 Elizabeth St, Sydney; other Australian offices are listed at www.flightcentre.com.au.

A return ticket to Nadi, Fiji, from the east coast of Australia (Melbourne or Sydney) will cost A$809/909 during the low/high season. Fares from Brisbane are cheaper – expect to pay A$755/859. Fares to Vanuatu's Port Vila are the same year round; from Brisbane, fares start at A$670, while from Sydney they start at A$827. Fares from Australia to Papeete, in French Polynesia, are also pretty much the same year round – about A$989 for a return fare.

New Zealand The *New Zealand Herald* has a travel section in which travel agents advertise fares. Flight Centre (☎ 09-309 6171) has a large central office in Auckland, at National Bank Towers (corner Queen and Darby Sts), and many branches throughout the country. STA Travel (☎ 09-309 0458) has its main office at 10 High St, Central Auckland, and has other offices in Auckland as well as in Hamilton, Palmerston North, Wellington, Christchurch and Dunedin; its website is www.statravel.co.nz.

From Auckland it costs about NZ$775/925 to get to Nadi in the low/high season. Fares from Auckland to Port Vila are NZ$948 year round, and a low/high season fare to Papeete starts at NZ$889/1149.

See the South Pacific Gateways chapter for some information about what you can do during stopovers in Auckland.

Asia

Although most Asian countries are now offering fairly competitive air fares, Bangkok, Singapore and Hong Kong are still the best places to shop around for discount tickets. Hong Kong's travel market can be unpredictable, but some excellent bargains are available if you are lucky. Airlines flying direct to the Pacific from Asia include Air Nauru, Air New Zealand, Air Niugini, Air Pacific, Asiana Airlines, Continental, Japan Airlines, Northwest and Qantas.

South-East Asia Khao San Rd in Bangkok is the budget travellers' headquarters. Bangkok has several excellent travel agents but there are also some suspect ones too; ask the advice of other travellers before handing over your cash. STA Travel (☎ 02-236 0262), 33 Surawong Rd, is a good and reliable place to start.

In Singapore, STA Travel (☎ 737 7188) in the Orchard Parade Hotel, 1 Tanglin Rd, offers competitive discount fares for Asian destinations and beyond. Singapore, like Bangkok, has hundreds of travel agents, so you can compare flight prices. Chinatown Point shopping centre, on New Bridge Rd, has a good selection of travel agents.

Hong Kong has a number of excellent, reliable travel agencies and some not so reliable ones. One way to check on travel agents is in the phone book: fly-by-night operators aren't usually listed. Many travellers use the Hong Kong Student Travel Bureau (☎ 2730 3269), 8th floor, Star House, Tsimshatsui. You could also try Phoenix Services (☎ 2722 7378), 7th floor, Milton Mansion, 96 Nathan Rd, Tsimshatsui.

From Hong Kong and Taipei there are direct flights to Guam. Fares from Hong Kong start at around US$673 for a return ticket in the low season. From Taipei, a return low season fare is around US$454.

Japan In Japan, STA Travel has branches in Tokyo and Osaka. In Tokyo (☎ 03-5391 2922) the main branch is in the Nukariya building, 1-16-20 Minami-Ikebukuro, Toshima-Ku, Tokyo 171-0022. Other discount travel agents are listed in local *gaijin*-orientated magazines. In Tokyo, the best place to look is the *Tokyo Journal*. In the Kansai Region (Kyoto, Osaka and Kobe) check *Kansai Time Out*.

From Tokyo and Osaka, there are daily flights to Saipan. Return fares range from around ¥53,800 to ¥75,200 (US$500 to $700) for a stay of up to 21 days. There are also daily flights to Guam, return fares range from ¥59,000 to ¥80,600. Fares from Tokyo to Noumea are marginally more expensive; expect to pay from ¥73,700 to ¥109,800 for a return fare.

Most Japanese travel in the last week of April to the first week of May, a week in the middle of August and around Christmas.

Air Travel Glossary

Baggage Allowance This will be written on your ticket and usually includes one 20kg item to go in the hold, plus one item of hand luggage.

Bucket Shops These are unbonded travel agencies specialising in discounted airline tickets.

Bumped Just because you have a confirmed seat doesn't mean you're going to get on the plane (see Overbooking).

Cancellation Penalties If you have to cancel or change a discounted ticket, there are often heavy penalties involved; insurance can sometimes be taken out against these penalties. Some airlines impose penalties on regular tickets as well, particularly against 'no-show' passengers.

Check-In Airlines ask you to check in a certain time ahead of the flight departure (usually one to two hours on international flights). If you fail to check in on time and the flight is overbooked, the airline can cancel your booking and give your seat to somebody else.

Confirmation Having a ticket written out with the flight and date you want doesn't mean you have a seat until the agent has checked with the airline that your status is 'OK' or confirmed. Meanwhile you could just be 'on request'.

Courier Fares Businesses often need to send urgent documents or freight securely and quickly. Courier companies hire people to accompany the package through customs and, in return, offer a discount ticket which is sometimes a phenomenal bargain. In effect, what the companies do is ship their freight as your luggage on regular commercial flights. This is a legitimate operation, but there are two shortcomings – the short turnaround time of the ticket (usually not longer than a month) and the limitation on your luggage allowance. You may have to surrender all your allowance and take only carry-on luggage.

Full Fares Airlines traditionally offer 1st class (coded F), business class (coded J) and economy class (coded Y) tickets. These days there are so many promotional and discounted fares available that few passengers pay full economy fare.

ITX An ITX, or 'independent inclusive tour excursion', is often available on tickets to popular holiday destinations. Officially it's a package deal combined with hotel accommodation, but many agents will sell you one of these for the flight only and give you phoney hotel vouchers in the unlikely event that you're challenged at the airport.

Lost Tickets If you lose your airline ticket an airline will usually treat it like a travellers cheque and, after inquiries, issue you with another one. Legally, however, an airline is entitled to treat it like cash and if you lose it then it's gone forever. Take good care of your tickets.

MCO An MCO, or 'miscellaneous charge order', is a voucher that looks like an airline ticket but carries no destination or date. It can be exchanged through any International Association of Travel Agents (IATA) airline for a ticket on a specific flight. It's a useful alternative to an onward ticket in those countries that demand one, and is more flexible than an ordinary ticket if you're unsure of your route.

No-Shows No-shows are passengers who fail to show up for their flight. Full-fare passengers who fail to turn up are sometimes entitled to travel on a later flight. The rest are penalised (see Cancellation Penalties).

Air Travel Glossary

On Request This is an unconfirmed booking for a flight.

Onward Tickets An entry requirement for many countries is that you have a ticket out of the country. If you're unsure of your next move, the easiest solution is to buy the cheapest onward ticket to a neighbouring country or a ticket from a reliable airline which can later be refunded if you do not use it.

Open Jaw Tickets These are return tickets where you fly out to one place but return from another. If available, this can save you backtracking to your arrival point.

Overbooking Airlines hate to fly empty seats and since every flight has some passengers who fail to show up, airlines often book more passengers than they have seats. Usually excess passengers make up for the no-shows, but occasionally somebody gets 'bumped' onto the next available flight. Guess who it is most likely to be? The passengers who check in late.

Point-to-Point Tickets These are discount tickets that can be bought on some routes in return for passengers waiving their rights to a stopover.

Promotional Fares These are officially discounted fares, available from travel agencies or direct from the airline.

Reconfirmation If you don't reconfirm your flight at least 72 hours prior to departure, the airline may delete your name from the passenger list. Ring to find out if your airline requires reconfirmation.

Restrictions Discounted tickets often have various restrictions on them – such as needing to be paid for in advance and incurring a penalty to be altered. Others are restrictions on the minimum and maximum period you must be away, such as a minimum of 14 days or a maximum of one year.

Round-the-World Tickets RTW tickets give you a limited period (usually a year) in which to circumnavigate the globe. You can go anywhere the carrying airlines go, as long as you don't backtrack. The number of stopovers or total number of separate flights is decided before you set off and they usually cost a bit more than a basic return flight.

Stand-by This is a discounted ticket where you only fly if there is a seat free at the last moment. Stand-by fares are usually available only on domestic routes.

Transferred Tickets Airline tickets cannot be transferred from one person to another. Travellers sometimes try to sell the return half of their ticket, but officials can ask you to prove that you are the person named on the ticket. This is less likely to happen on domestic flights, but on an international flight tickets are compared with passports.

Travel Agencies Travel agencies vary widely and you should choose one that suits your needs. Some simply handle tours, while full-service agencies handle everything from tours and tickets to car rental and hotel bookings. If all you want is a ticket at the lowest possible price, then go to an agency specialising in discounted fares.

Travel Periods Ticket prices vary with the time of year. There is a low (off-peak) season and a high (peak) season, and often a low-shoulder season and a high-shoulder season as well. Usually the fare depends on your outward flight – if you depart in the high season and return in the low season, you pay the high-season fare.

Continental Europe & the UK

Airline ticket discounters are known as bucket shops in the UK. Despite the somewhat disreputable name, there is nothing under-the-counter about them – discount air travel is big business in London. Advertisements for many travel agents appear in the travel pages of the weekend broadsheets, such as the *Independent* (on Saturday) and the *Sunday Times*. Look out for the free magazines, such as *TNT*, which are widely available in London – start by looking outside the main train and underground stations.

For students or travellers under 26, popular travel agencies in the UK include STA Travel (☎ 020-7361 6161), which has an office at 86 Old Brompton Rd, London SW7 3LQ. STA has numerous other offices in London and Manchester, and a website (www.statravel.co.uk). USIT Campus Travel (☎ 020-7730 3402), 52 Grosvenor Gardens, London SW1W 0AG, has branches throughout the UK, and a website (www.usitcampus.co.uk). Both these agencies sell tickets to all travellers but they cater especially to young people and students. Other recommended bucket shops include:

Bridge the World
   (☎ 020-7734 7447) 4 Regent Place, London W1R 5FB
Flightbookers
   (☎ 020-7757 2000) 177-78 Tottenham Court Rd, London W1P 9LF
Trailfinders
   (☎ 020-7938 3939) 194 Kensington High St, London W8 7RG

Although London is the travel discount capital of Europe, there are several other cities in which you will find a range of good deals. Across Europe many travel agencies have ties with STA Travel, where cheap tickets can be purchased and STA-issued tickets can be altered (usually for a US$25 fee). Outlets in major cities include:

ISYTS
   (☎ 01-322 1267, fax 323 3767)
   11 Nikis St, Upper floor, Syntagma Square, Athens, Greece

Passaggi
   (☎ 06-474 0923, fax 482 7436)
   Stazione Termini FS, Gelleria Di Tesla, Rome, Italy
STA Travel
   (☎ 030-311 0950, fax 313 0948)
   Goethestrasse 73, 10625 Berlin, Germany
Voyages Wasteels
   (☎ 08 03 88 70 04, fax 01 43 25 46 25)
   11 Rue Dupuytren, 756006 Paris, France

Currently, the best fares to the South Pacific are with Air New Zealand from London. Fares remain the same whether your final destination is the Pacific islands, New Zealand or Australia. Tickets allow six free stopovers between London and Australasia, which may include Los Angeles, Hawai'i, Samoa, Fiji, Tonga, the Cook Islands or New Zealand.

A round-the-world (RTW) ticket that takes in the Pacific islands, about £1000, is value for money and you get to more places, such as Africa and Asia as well as the Pacific.

A return ticket from London to Nadi (Fiji) is around £700/1000 in the low/high season. Fares from London to Papeete (French Polynesia) start at around £650/1000, to Honolulu (Hawai'i) at around £400/700 and to Auckland at around £500/900 (from Auckland you can easily reach the Cook Islands, Samoa or Tonga).

From Paris, return fares in the low/high season are around 6750/11000FF to Papeete. A ticket from Paris to Noumea (New Caledonia) costs 7202/8907FF and to Honolulu 5272/5672FF.

From Berlin to Nadi, return fares start at DM2470/2600 in the low/high season. Fares to Papeete are around DM2000/2600 and to Honolulu DM1300/1500.

Low season is April to June and October to November. High season is July to September and Christmas/New Year.

SEA

To reach the Pacific islands by sea you can travel either on your own yacht (or on someone else's), by cargo ship or by cruise ship. All three options are discussed in more detail in the Getting Around the Region chapter.

South Pacific Gateways

The Pacific countries (and state) in this chapter, along with Japan and the Australian mainland, are the most common gateways to the destinations covered in this book.

Hawai'i

- pop 1,186,600   • area 16,757 sq km

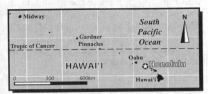

Hawai'i is the northern point of the triangle that makes up Polynesia. It was first settled from the Marquesas around 400 AD and subsequently named after an island in the Society Islands (see the boxed text 'The Ancient Homeland, Havaiki' in the Samoa chapter).

Perhaps the most famous visitor to the Hawai'ian islands was Captain James Cook, who met his grisly death here in 1779. The Hawai'ian islands were the last Pacific islands to be discovered by Cook. Shortly after Cook's death, Kamehameha the Great unified the Hawai'ian islands for the first time. The Hawai'ian royal *(ali'i)* lineage continued until 1893, when European businessmen overthrew Queen Liliuokalani's rule.

In 1959 Hawai'i became the 50th state of the USA. Today, Hawai'i has a multicultural society and, although less than 1% of the population are 'full-blooded' Hawai'ian, there has been a resurgence of interest in traditional Hawai'ian culture.

The islands of the Hawai'ian archipelago are dramatic and diverse. They include the world's most active volcano (Kilauea), the highest mountain when measured from the sea floor (Mauna Kea) and the highest sea cliffs (on Molokai). There's everything from tropical rainforest to lowland desert.

You'll find myriad activities, with something to please everyone. There's world-renowned surfing, excellent snorkelling opportunities and, believe it or not, secluded beaches to explore.

One of the leading visitor destinations in the world, Hawai'i has a massive tourism industry, but if you're willing to tread off the tourist trail, you'll find loads of untouristed areas.

Getting to Hawai'i by plane is straightforward. It's a major stopover point between the USA and Asia, Australia, New Zealand and the Pacific. Passengers on any of these routes may find that they get a free stopover in Honolulu. While stopping over in Hawai'i you can:

- Visit the observatories at Mauna Kea on the Big Island
- Go hiking in the amazing lunar landscape of the largest dormant volcano on earth. Haleakala National Park, on Maui, offers plenty of great walking and camping opportunities
- Visit Bishops Museum (☎ 808-847 3511), 1525 Bernice St, Honolulu, to see its wonderful array of Pacific artefacts. The museum is an inspiration, and its library has a great selection of books.
- Explore central Honolulu, with its fascinating mix of cultures

The Hawai'ian Visitors Bureau (☎ 808-923 1811, fax 922 8991, infooff@hvcb.org) has offices throughout Hawai'i, but the central office is in the Waikiki Business Plaza, 2270 Kalakaua Ave, Suite 801, Honolulu, HI 96815. It provides free information and will send it on request. You can also search its website (www.gohawaii.com) for information on accommodation and activities on the islands.

Currency is the US dollar and the international telephone code is ☎ 1. Hawai'i's area code is ☎ 808. If you're in Hawai'i for a while, you might like to check out Lonely Planet's *Hawaii* and *Honolulu* guidebooks, and *Diving & Snorkeling Hawaii*.

New Zealand

• pop 3,800,000   • area 226,000 sq km

At the southern point of the great Polynesian triangle, the relatively large islands of New Zealand (NZ) were among the last Pacific islands to be settled. About 1000 years ago, explorers from the Society and Marquesas islands (in modern French Polynesia) followed the track of migrating birds 4000km south-west past the Cook islands to a land they named Aotearoa (Land of the Long White Cloud). Settlers followed in a series of migratory canoes, and journeys back from Aotearoa to the homelands were not unknown.

NZ's Maori people (who make up about about 15% of the population) are closely related to the Maohi people of the Society and Marquesas islands and the Maori of the southern Cook Islands.

New Zealand was added to European maps by Tasman in 1642, and competently mapped by Cook in 1769. The historic Treaty of Waitangi, signed between England and many Maori in 1840, bought NZ into the British Empire.

In the early 20th century the NZ government, dreaming of a Pacific empire of its own, took on varying responsibilities for Niue, the Cook Islands and Tokelau. All three island states still share legislative links with New Zealand. Partly because of these historical links, Pacific islanders form about 6% of New Zealand's population. More Niueans, Tokelauans and Cook Islanders live in NZ than in their 'home' countries! Auckland, in particular, is sometimes known as the 'Capital of Polynesia' – in addition to the Maori population, another 10% of Aucklanders are Pacific islanders (up to 30% in some areas).

Flights link Auckland and Wellington with Fiji, Tonga, Samoa, the Cook Islands and French Polynesia. It's not unlikely that while waiting for a connecting flight, you'll have to spend a couple of days in NZ. Luckily, there are plenty of things to do while stopping over in Auckland:

• Visit the excellent display of Pacific voyaging canoes in the Auckland Museum
• Watch a game of Samoan *kirikiti* on Sunday at Massey Domain or at Waitakere College in Henderson
• Discover the islands of the Hauraki Gulf
• Mingle with the Maori and Polynesian crowds at outdoor food markets in Otara and Avondale
• Go bushwalking in the Waitakere Ranges
• Attend the Pasifika Festival (in March each year) – featuring performance, arts and food from many Pacific cultures

Just off Queen St in downtown Auckland, the Visitor Centre (☎ 09-366 6888, fax 366 6893, reservations@aucklandnz.com), at 24 Wellesley St, should be your first port of call when you reach town. You can also search its website (www.aucklandnz.com) for information about events, activities and accommodation.

Exchange rates for the NZ dollar (also used in the Cook Islands, Niue, Pitcairn Island and Tokelau) are given under Money in the Regional Facts for the Visitor chapter. NZ's international telephone code is ☎ 64.

If you're staying here long enough, you may also find useful Lonely Planet's *New Zealand*, *Tramping in New Zealand*, *Cycling New Zealand* and *Auckland* guidebooks.

Papua New Guinea

- pop 4,500,000   - area 462,840 sq km

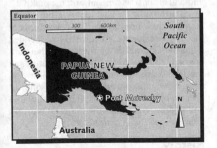

Papua New Guinea (PNG) lies between Indonesia and the Solomon Islands, just north of Australia, sharing New Guinea Island (807,400 sq km) with Indonesian Irian Jaya. More than 1400 islands make up the nation of PNG, mostly small and coral or volcanic in origin. A rugged mountainous spine runs the length of New Guinea Island, which is scoured with rivers and valleys. This rugged landscape gave rise to many isolated and distinct groups of people – PNG has over 770 languages.

The first arrivals on New Guinea Island were Papuans who island-hopped from Asia via Indonesia around 50,000 years ago. Further waves of Papuan and Melanesian migration followed.

The rest of the South Pacific was settled from the island of New Guinea. Around 25,000 years ago, people crossed the waters to the Solomon Islands. Much later (3500 years ago), Watom Island, off New Britain, was the birthplace of the Lapita culture and the launching site of their push east into the greater Pacific Ocean (see the 'Lapita' boxed text in the 'South Pacific Arts' special section).

Locals had contact with early Indonesian and Malay traders, but the Euopean discovery of the main island is credited to the Portuguese Jorge de Meneses in 1526. Over the next centuries, colonial authority was variously asserted by the Dutch, the British and the Germans.

Australia wrested control of German New Guinea in the early days of WWI, but the Japanese invaded and occupied most of PNG during WWII. There was fierce fighting between the Allies and the Japanese until Japan surrendered in 1945.

PNG's mostly Melanesian people display an intoxicating mix of cultures, traditional art and dance. However, cities like Port Moresby, Lae and Hagen can be frenetic, unruly and sometimes even intimidating – normal precautions after dark are advisable. Out in the backlands and villages you'll encounter overwhelming hospitality.

Flights link Port Moresby, the PNG capital, with Australia, the Solomon Islands, Fiji, Vanuatu, and Nauru. To properly experience PNG you'd need a few weeks, but with a few days' stopover in Port Moresby you can:

- Rub shoulders with the locals at Koki Market and nearby Koki Village, with its stilt houses over the water
- Visit the superb National Museum & Art Gallery
- Take a tour of Parliament House and catch a sitting of Parliament
- Take a day trip by small plane out to lovely Loloata Island for some terrific swimming and snorkelling, and lunch at the Loloata Island Resort
- Dive the many nearby reefs and beaches
- Take a day trip by small plane to the steep and spectacular Owen Stanley Ranges

In Port Moresby's waterfront region (known as 'Town') is PNG's Tourism Promotions Authority (☎ 320 0211, fax 320 0223), PO Box 1291, in the NIC Haus building. It can help with tour and accommodation information, and there are some good travel information links from their website (www.niugini.com).

PNG's currency is the *kina* (K1 = US$0.40) which is divided into 100 *toea*. The international phone code is ☎ 675. If you're spending more than a few days in PNG you'll find Lonely Planet's *Papua New Guinea* very useful. There's also the *Pidgin* phrasebook and *Snorkeling & Diving Papua New Guinea*.

Australian Territories

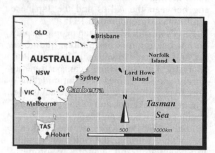

Not gateways to the Pacific, but often included in Pacific itineraries, Norfolk and Lord Howe are two tiny subtropical islands on the edge of the Pacific (Lord Howe is in the Tasman Sea). Both have volcanic origins, are Australian territories, and have tourism and kentia palm seeds as their main industries – but that's about where the similarities end.

Travel Agents

Package deals, combining flights and accommodation, are usually the cheapest way to go. A five-night package to Norfolk Island starts at around A$900/740 in summer/winter. There's more seasonal variation on Lord Howe Island (A$1000/600). In Sydney (Australia) Fastbook Pacific Holidays (☎ 02-9212 5977), Pacific Unlimited (☎ 02-9290 2260) and the Pacific Island Travel Centre (☎ 02-9244 1833) specialise in holidays to both islands. Oxley Travel (☎ 02-6583 1955), in Port Macquarie, has some of the best deals.

Fastbook also operates charter flights between Norfolk and Lord Howe on Sunday and Wednesday, but the limited seats are allocated as part of a twin-island package – a return flight from Sydney with six nights on each island costs from A$1699.

NORFOLK ISLAND
• pop 1800   • area 35 sq km
Norfolk Island is a tiny green speck some 1600km north-east of Sydney and almost 700km south of New Caledonia.

Norfolk tends to attract older Australian and New Zealand package tourists, but its historical links with the *Bounty* mutineers and a grim past as a penal outpost make it a fascinating place. The locals cling steadfastly to their unique identity (two-thirds of the 1800 residents are directly descended from the original Pitcairners) and their unhurried 'country town' lifestyle. Features of the island are its spectacular coastline and the lush vegetation, which includes some 40 species of endemic plants, the most notable and widespread being the majestic Norfolk Island pine *(Araucaria heterophylla)*.

History
Although once occupied by Polynesians, the island was uninhabited when Captain Cook sighted it in 1774. The first settlers, including 15 convicts, arrived from Port Jackson (Sydney) in 1788 and stayed until 1814. In 1825 the colonial authorities tried again, planning a penal settlement as 'a place of the extremest punishment short of death'. In 1854 the penal colony was wound up and the prisoners shipped off to Van Diemen's Land (Tasmania). This abandonment proved to be a godsend for the descendants of the *Bounty* mutineers who, having outgrown Pitcairn Island, begged England for help. They were granted Norfolk Island, and on 8 June 1856 the entire Pitcairn population of 194 arrived.

Today Norfolk Island is a self-governing external territory of Australia; the locally elected Legislative Assembly is responsible for such issues as taxation and immigration.

Information
The town of Burnt Pine contains most of the island's shopping and information services, including the Norfolk Island Visitor Information Centre (☎ 22 147), post office and banks.

The island's postcode is 2899, the international telephone code is ☎ 6723 and currency is the Australian dollar. Internet access is available in Burnt Pine; look up www.norfolkisland.nf for online information.

You get a 30 day visa on arrival at Norfolk Island, but it is an international destination and even Australians require a passport. On return to Australia (or New

Zealand) you will need a re-entry visa, or a valid Australian (or NZ) passport.

Things to See & Do

The historic settlement of Kingston, built by convicts of the second penal colony, is the island's main attraction. Most of the buildings have been restored – the finest are Quality Row. Some have been turned into small but excellent museums.

It's interesting to wander through the cemetery at the eastern end of Quality Row; many headstones bear poignant epitaphs.

The Norfolk Island National Park has some fine walking tracks and good views from Mt Pitt (320m) and Mt Bates (321m).

Places to Stay & Eat

Accommodation ranges from guesthouses to large motel-style resorts. Comfortable self-contained apartments start at around A$85 per night for a double; motel rooms are around A$140.

Places to eat range from takeaways to up-market dining. In Burnt Pine try the Brewery Bar & Bistro for cheap counter meals or James' Place for something fancier.

Getting There & Away

from Australia, Flightwest (☎ 1300 130 092) and Norfolk Jet Express (☎ 07-3221 6677) have frequent flights from Sydney (A$750 14 day advance purchase) and Brisbane (A$736). Air New Zealand (☎ tollfree 0800 737 000 within NZ) flies twice a week from Auckland (starting at NZ$629 return).

There's a departure tax of A$25, payable at the airport. There's no harbour, and no facilities for yachts or cruise ships.

LORD HOWE ISLAND

• pop 300   • area 16 sq km

Beautiful Lord Howe is a tiny boomerang-shaped island in the Tasman Sea, 770km north-east of Sydney and about 1200km south-west of New Caledonia.

Most people visit on package trips but yachts also stop (see Getting There & Away). The laid-back nature of the island is maintained by a restriction on visitor numbers – around 400 at any one time.

What Lord Howe lacks in exotic culture, it makes up for in natural beauty. A World Heritage Site, much of the island is covered in rainforest. There are some beautiful beaches, a wide lagoon sheltered by the world's most southerly coral reef and excellent fishing and snorkelling. The forests are home to 70-odd plant species that occur naturally only on Lord Howe, including the hardy kentia palm (Howea forsteriana), prized by gardeners around the world.

Lord Howe Island was first spotted by Lieutenant Henry Lidgbird Ball and the crew of the HMS *Supply* while sailing to Norfolk Island on 17 February 1788.

The first settlers arrived from New Zealand in 1834, establishing a whaling supply station at Old Settlement Beach. Tourists began arriving early in the 20th century and today the economy is almost entirely dependent on tourism, though the islanders have been successful with the export of kentia palms. The island is a dependency of NSW, with local government in the hands of the Lord Howe Island Board.

Around the Island

The settlement area at the north end of the lagoon has the Lord Howe Island Visitor Centre (☎ 6563 2114), post office, bank agents and general stores. The postcode is 2898, international telephone code ☎ 61 and area code ☎ 02.

Bushwalking is excellent, with a good network of tracks leading to some fine views. The full-day ascent of Mt Gower is the biggest challenge and must be done with a licensed guide. There's good snorkelling and a great fish-feeding ritual at Ned's Beach.

Getting There & Away

Eastern Australia Airlines (☎ 13 1313) has four flights a week from Sydney from A$554 (seven-day advance purchase).

Yachties can anchor off the island; contact the port operations manager (☎ 6563 2266, VHF channel 16 or 12) prior to arrival. The mooring fee is A$16 per night plus a once-off service levy of A$20 per person.

Getting Around the Region

AIR

In the Pacific region, air travel is the primary way of getting from country to country, and it can be expensive. As well as the major airlines, there are several airlines run by small Pacific nations that can get you to the less-accessible parts of the Pacific.

See the Air Travel Glossary in the Getting There & Away chapter for information on the types of ticket available. That chapter also includes information on travel agents in various countries around the world. For more detailed information, see the Getting There & Away section in individual country chapters.

Micronesia probably has the worst domestic air service in the Pacific because of the lack of tourists in this region, excepting to Guam and the Northern Marianas. (Tourist money is needed to support tourist infrastructure.) Local airlines and governments are doing their best to rectify this situation.

Airlines

The following airlines operate between South Pacific countries. Many also connect the South Pacific with the rest of the world, so this list will be useful both for getting to the Pacific and for getting around the region.

Many airlines also operate a domestic service around their own country. Details of domestic services are given in the individual country chapters.

Air Fiji Although it is primarily a domestic service, Air Fiji (☎ 313 666, fax 300 771, airfiji@is.com.fj), also flies to Tuvalu and Tonga.

Air France Air France (☎ 08 36 64 08 02 in France) flies from Paris to Tahiti three times per week.

Air Marshall Islands As well as domestic flights, Air Marshall Islands (☎ 625 3733, fax 625 3730, amisales@ntamar.com) flies to Kiribati.

Air Nauru The national airline of Nauru connects the Pacific with the Philippines and Australia. Around the Micronesian region, it connects Nauru to Guam, Pohnpei, Kiribati and Fiji. See the Pacific Explorer air pass entry later in this section. The central office is in Nauru (☎ 444 3141, fax 444 3705) and its international offices are listed on its website (www.airnauru.com.au).

Air New Zealand Connects the Pacific with Japan, Taiwan, Hong Kong, Singapore, Australia, mainland USA, Canada, the UK and Germany. The airline's service to Pacific islands is comprehensive: it flies from New Zealand to Vanuatu, New Caledonia, Fiji, Tonga, Samoa, Cook Islands, French Polynesia and Hawai'i. See the Pacifica air pass later in this section.

The airline has offices all over New Zealand (☎ 09-488 3700, or ☎ tollfree 0800 737 000 within NZ, fax 488 3701). Its website (www.airnz.co.nz) lists international offices.

Air Niugini Papua New Guinea's Air Niugini (☎ 325 9000, fax 327 3482) connects PNG with the Solomon Islands, as well as Singapore, the Philippines and Australia. Its international offices are listed online (www.airniugini.com.pg).

Air Pacific Fiji's Air Pacific connects with Japan, Australia, New Zealand and mainland USA. It also flies to Samoa, Tonga, Vanuatu and the Solomon Islands. The main office is in Suva (☎ 720 888, fax 722 272, airpacific@is.com.fj), and other offices are listed on its website (www.airpacific.com.au).

Air Tahiti Nui Air Tahiti Nui (☎ 310-662 1860 in the USA) flies between French Polynesia and Los Angeles.

Air Vanuatu Flying to Australia and New Zealand, Air Vanuatu (☎ 23848 in Vanuatu, fax 23250) also serves New Caledonia and Fiji, and has a comprehensive domestic air service. Its international offices are listed under Tourist Offices in the Vanuatu chapter.

Aircalin New Caledonia's Aircalin (Air Calédonie International; ☎ 26 55 00, fax 26 55 61, acinou@canl.nc) flies to Australia, New Zealand, Vanuatu, Fiji and French Polynesia. It is the only airline flying to the French colony of Wallis & Futuna. Fares and international offices are listed on its website (www.aircalin.nc).

Aloha Airlines As well as offering a domestic service around the Hawai'ian islands and weekly service to Kiribati's Christmas (Kiritimati) Island, Aloha (☎ 808-484 1111 in Hawai'i) has recently started flights to the Marshall Islands; see its website (www.alohaair.com).

Ansett Australia Although primarily a domestic airline, Ansett Australia (☎ tollfree 13 13 44 within Australia) operates flights from Australia to Fiji and to Norfolk Island. Ansett's website (www.ansett.com.au) lists its international offices.

AOM French Airlines Flying from Paris to Tahiti via Los Angeles, AOM (☎ 310-338 9613 in the USA) also flies to New Caledonia via Australia.

Asiana Airlines Korea-based Asiana Airlines (☎ 02-669 4000, or ☎ tollfree 1588 8000 within Korea) has daily flights from Seoul to the Northern Marianas and Guam.

Continental The US Continental Airlines (☎ 647 6453 in Guam, or ☎ 234 6459 in Saipan) is the main carrier in the Micronesian region. It connects the region with the USA, the Philippines, Hong Kong, Japan and Australia. Within Micronesia, the airline flies to the Marshall Islands, the Federated States of Micronesia (FSM), Guam, the Northern Marianas, and Palau. Its website is www.continental.com.

Continental's one-way and round-trip fares between Micronesia's islands are rather exorbitant. Its air passes (Circle Micronesia and Visit Micronesia; see later in this chapter) are better deals. Recently, because of the Asian financial crisis, Continental has been cutting back its Micronesian service, so check the current situation with a (well informed) travel agent.

Given its reduced flight schedule, Continental's flights tend to fill up quickly, particularly at the Guam or Honolulu ends of the route, so make your reservations early.

Canadian Airlines Connecting Fiji with Hawai'i and the North American mainland is Canadian Airlines (☎ tollfree 800 665 1177 in Canada or the USA).

Corsair A privately owned French company, Corsair (☎ 01 49 79 49 59 in France, or ☎ tollfree 800 677 0720 in the USA) flies from Los Angeles to Tahiti.

Hawaiian Airlines Connecting Hawai'i to mainland USA, Hawaiian Airlines (☎ 808-835 3700 in Hawai'i, fax 835 3690) also flies to American Samoa, Kiribati's Christmas Island, French Polynesia and the Marshall Islands. Its website (www.hawaiianair.com) has more information.

Japan Airlines JAL (☎ 03-5489 1111, or ☎ tollfree 0120 255 931 from within Japan) flies to the Northern Marianas, Guam, Hawai'i and New Caledonia. It also links eastern and South-East Asia with Europe, South Africa, Australia, New Zealand and North and South America. JAL's website is www.japanair.com.

LanChile Flying between Chile and French Polynesia, LanChile (☎ 426 455 on Tahiti, fax 421 887) also stops at Easter Island (☎ 56-32-100 279). It's website is www.lanchile.com.

Northwest Based in Minneapolis (☎ tollfree 800 447 4747 within the USA), Northwest stops at Micronesia's Northern Mariana Islands (including Guam) between Asia and mainland USA. Northwest's website is www.nwa.com.

Polynesian Airlines From Samoa, Polynesian Airlines (☎ 22737, fax 20023, enquiries@PolynesianAirlines.co.nz) flies to Australia, New Zealand and mainland USA. Among the Pacific islands, it flies from Samoa to Hawai'i, US Samoa, Fiji and Tonga. International offices, schedules and specials are listed on the airline's website (www.polynesianairlines.co.nz). See the Polypass air pass later in this chapter.

Qantas Australia's Qantas flies from Australia to South-East and east Asia, North and South America, South Africa, Papua New Guinea, New Zealand and Europe. In the Pacific, Qantas flies to New Caledonia, Fiji and French Polynesia.

Qantas has offices all around Australia (☎ 03-9285 3000, or ☎ tollfree 13 13 13 within Australia); its international offices are listed online (www.qantas.com.au).

Royal Tongan Flying from Tonga to Australia, New Zealand and Hawai'i, Royal Tongan (☎ 23414 in Tonga, fax 23559, rtamktng@kalianet.to) also flies to Fiji and Samoa, and is the only airline flying to Niue. Its website (http://kalianet.to/rta/) lists international offices.

Samoa Air As well as offering domestic flights around the Samoan islands (both independent and American Samoa), Samoa Air (☎ 699 9106 in independent Samoa, fax 699 9751, samoaair@samoatelco.com) flies to Tonga.

Solomon Airlines Connecting Melanesia with Australia and New Zealand, Solomon Airlines (☎ 20031 in the Solomons, fax 20232, solomonair@solomonairline.com .au) also flies to Papua New Guinea, Vanuatu and Fiji. It also has an extensive domestic service through the Solomon Islands. The airline's website (www .solomonairlines.com.au) lists its international offices.

Air Passes

Inter-country flights in the Pacific can be prohibitively expensive. The only really

workable way to travel to more than a handful of countries is by using an air pass.

Fortunately, there are some excellent air passes taking in several Pacific nations for a reduced price. Some passes are arranged by airlines, while others are put together by travel agents. There may be conditions attached to these passes, such as the total number of days travelling, the travel termination date or minimum stays in each country. Seating availability for heavily discounted fares can be quite limited, so book early.

If you think air pass conditions are complex, you'll be happy to hear that they often confuse airline agents too. You have to communicate your desired itinerary carefully so that the agent gets everything right, but the complexity means that things are ultimately a bit flexible. Often nobody really knows the rules; even once you have your ticket, one agent will tell you one thing, another agent something else. If you need to make a change, pull out your best negotiating skills. If your request is turned down once, it won't hurt to ask at the next office.

Prices and conditions attached to air passes change often, so check the current situation with a travel agent or the airline. Contact details for the airlines listed are given earlier in this chapter.

Boomerang This pass from Air Pacific, Ansett and Qantas provides for travel on selected south-west Pacific routes, taking in Fiji, Vanuatu, Tonga, Western Samoa, New Caledonia and the Solomon Islands. The price of the pass ranges from A$600 (for travel between two countries) to A$1800 (which takes in all countries).

The pass is only available in connection with air or sea travel to/from Australia, New Zealand or Fiji from outside the region; it's not available to residents of Australia, New Zealand, Fiji, Tonga, Samoa or Vanuatu.

Circle Excursion For A$1127 this multi-airline pass allows travel between either Fiji-Australia-New Zealand, Fiji-Australia-Vanuatu, Fiji-Tonga-Samoa or Fiji-Vanuatu-New Caledonia.

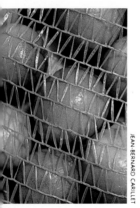

Limes

Tasty parrot fish

Aromatic frangipani flowers – put them in your hair.

The Solomon Islands' yellow-fronted lori

Heliconia

JOHN BORTHWICK

A performer at one of Papeete's island-dancing nights

JEAN-BERNARD CARILLET

Colourful *pareu* (sarongs)

JEAN-BERNARD CARILLET

Tahitian dance costume

JEAN-BERNARD CARILLET

Le Truck in Papeete

JEAN-BERNARD CARILLET

Hand-painted Tahitian *pareu*

Circle Micronesia Continental's Circle Micronesia pass is great for travellers going to several Micronesian islands, but they are only available to travellers departing from the USA.

Circle Micronesia air fares are round-trip tickets originating in Honolulu or the US west coast (Los Angeles or San Francisco). One leg is a nonstop flight between Honolulu and Guam. Another is the so-called 'island-hopper' leg between Guam and Honolulu. The plane stops in Chuuk, Pohnpei, Kosrae, Kwajalein and Majuro.

If you turn around at Guam, the base fare is US$920/1230 from Honolulu/US west coast. You can go on to Yap for an extra US$230, and from there to Koror (in Palau) for another US$100. To continue from Guam to Saipan, instead of to Yap or Koror, costs US$975/1280 from Honolulu/US west coast. Add US$300 if you're coming from the US east coast. Four 'free' stopovers are included in the base fare. Additional intermediate stops are US$50 each.

If your endpoint is Koror or Yap you cannot stopover in Saipan (and vice versa). If you wish to visit all three places, it's best to opt for Yap or Koror as your endpoint and take one of the frequent and cheap commuter planes from Guam to Saipan. (Continental's flight from Guam to Saipan is much more expensive.)

Circle Pacific Similar to round-the-world (RTW) tickets but covering a more limited region, Circle Pacific uses a combination of airlines to connect Australia, New Zealand, North America and Asia with a variety of stopover options in the Pacific islands. There are advance-purchase restrictions and limits on how many stopovers you can make.

A Circle Pacific pass is likely to be about 15% cheaper than a RTW ticket but they're better value from the USA than from Australasia. For example: LA-Tahiti-Rarotonga-Fiji-Auckland-Sydney-Hong Kong-Taipei-Chicago costs US$1695, while LA-Hong Kong-Auckland-Fiji-Tahiti-LA is US$1539. Sydney-Tokyo-LA-Tahiti-Rarotonga-Auckland-Sydney costs A$1960.

Travel agents are well informed about these tickets.

Circle South West Pacific For A$650 to $1035 (depending which countries you visit) this pass allows travel from Australia's east coast to any two of the Solomon Islands, Vanuatu, Fiji or New Caledonia. For an extra A$130 to $400 (depending on the flight), you can add an extra country.

The Solomons and Fiji are the most expensive options; flying from Brisbane is A$50 cheaper, while from Melbourne it is A$50 more expensive. High-season travel is A$50 more (A$90 to Vanuatu).

Flights are on Qantas, Aircalin, Air Pacific, Air Vanuatu and Solomon Airlines. Travel must start and finish in Australia, must be completed within 28 days, and there's a minimum stay per destination of five nights.

Pacific This pass allows for travel on Air Pacific between Fiji, Samoa, Tonga and Vanuatu for US$462. Travel must be completed within 30 days and the pass is only available in the Americas, Africa and Europe.

Pacific Explorer Offered by Air Nauru, this pass can be used to fly between the Philippines, Guam, Pohnpei, Nauru, Kiribati, Fiji and Australia. Your first three flights cost US$450 (US$50 more in high season), and subsequent legs cost US$75 each to a maximum of eight legs. Flights must be completed within 30 days.

Pacifica With this pass, a three month Los Angeles-Auckland return trip with one stopover in the Pacific costs US$1048/1298 in the low/high season; additional stopovers are US$150 each. Six-month tickets and one-year tickets are also available.

Countries included in this pass are Australia, New Zealand, Cook Islands, Tonga, Samoa, Fiji, New Caledonia, Vanuatu and the Solomons.

Flights are on Air New Zealand, Air Vanuatu, Aircalin, Ansett Australia, Polynesian Airlines, Royal Tongan and Solomon Airlines.

It must be combined with an Air New Zealand or United Airlines ticket to the Pacific from the Americas, and is not available to residents of Australia, New Zealand or Fiji.

Polypass This Polynesian Airlines pass is a cheap way to fly between Samoa, Tonga, Fiji, Australia and New Zealand. It costs US$999 for (almost) unlimited travel within 45 days, excluding the Christmas period. Linking with Hawai'i/Los Angeles costs US$150/450 extra.

Triangle Fare Air Pacific's Triangle Fare links Fiji, Vanuatu and the Solomons for US$600. The fare is only available from North and South America and travel must be completed within 30 days.

Visit Micronesia This Continental pass is for travellers who originate in Asia, Australia (Cairns) or the Americas. The pass must be purchased outside Micronesia in conjunction with an international ticket to Guam or Saipan (Northern Marianas) on Continental or Northwest airlines. It allows travel to Guam (or Saipan, depending where you start), Palau, Chuuk and Yap (the latter two in the FSM). Pohnpei and Kosrae (FSM) can be added for an additional charge.

The pass is valid for 30 days, and travel must begin within 60 days of arrival in Guam or Saipan. The price differs depending on the country from which you originate and the islands at which you stop. For example, if you're originating in the Americas, it's US$400 for Guam, Saipan, Palau and Yap (an extra US$100 for Chuuk, and another US$200 for Pohnpei and Kosrae). Your endpoint (Guam or Saipan) counts as a stopover if you stay there more than 24 hours.

For travellers originating in Australia or Asia there is no four-island option. The five-island pass (any four of Guam, Saipan, Chuuk, Yap and Palau) is US$625, and it's US$775 for the six-island pass.

Visit the South Pacific This air pass allows for any combination of flights on Air Marshall Islands, Air Nauru, Air Niugini, Air Pacific, Air Vanuatu, Aircalin, Polynesian Airlines, Royal Tongan, Solomon Airlines and Qantas.

Countries included are Australia, New Zealand, PNG, the Solomons, Vanuatu, New Caledonia, Fiji, Wallis & Futuna, Tonga, Niue, Samoa, French Polynesia, Tuvalu, Kiribati, Nauru, the Marshalls and the FSM.

It costs A$175 to $320 per sector (depending on the sector; minimum of two sectors; up to eight). The pass must be bought in conjunction with an air/sea ticket from outside the region.

SEA

There's a certain romance in the idea of doing at least some of your travel around the Pacific by sea, especially if your imagination is fired by ancient Pacific canoe voyages or tales of Captain Cook . Sea travel is much slower than flying, and usually more expensive – but if you've got lots of books you want to read, or just a love of the ocean, this could be the route for you.

Cruise Ship

The cruise ship industry has experienced a renewal in recent years. They will never be the cheapest or the fastest way from A to Z but cruise ships are not just about getting there. The facilities on board usually range from luxurious to even more luxurious. This is *not* a form of travel with a budget option.

Travel agents are always well informed about cruise ships and should be able to tell you what the options are. As always, it's best to shop around for the best prices.

Cruise-ship fares vary enormously, but prices start at about US$200 per day. Major destinations are Noumea (New Caledonia), Port Vila (Vanuatu) and Honiara (Solomons) in Melanesia – also Papeete, Moorea and Bora Bora in French Polynesia. Melanesian cruises usually depart from Australia's east coast. Other cruises depart from the US east coast, and Honolulu is another hub.

A cruise ship with an adventure theme, the *World Discoverer*, travels between Easter Island, the Pitcairns, French Polynesia, the Cook Islands, the Samoas, Tonga,

Fiji, Guam, the Solomons and Papua New Guinea. Cruises lasting from 12 to 18 days cost from US$2020 to $4760 per person. Contact Society Expeditions (☎ 206-728 9400, fax 728 2301, societyexp@aol.com), 2001 Western Ave, Suite 300, Seattle, WA 98121, USA. The company's website is at www.societyexpeditions.com.

A similar company, Marine Expeditions, departs from Valparaiso in Chile, travelling via Robinson Crusoe, Alejandro Selkirk and Easter islands (all Chilean territories), through the Pitcairn Islands to Tahiti in French Polynesia. The 27-day trip costs from US$5995, including Los Angeles-Santiago (Chile) and Papeete-Los Angeles flights. Marine Expeditions (☎ 416-964 9069, fax 964 2366) is at 890 Yonge St, 3rd floor, Toronto, Ontario, Canada M4W 3P4. Check the company's website (www.marineex.com) for more information.

Cargo Ship

It's not exactly cheap, the food can be less than excellent, and the comfort level is low, but if you've got the time, cargo ships (freighters) are a way to reach some of the less accessible Pacific islands. You can just do just one or two legs of a cargo ship journey, and combine it with air travel.

The cost per day of cargo ship travel (around US$100) is about half that of the cruise ship low-end options. The ship's number one concern is the cargo, and sudden changes to schedules are common, so build flexibility into your plans and book well ahead. The *OAG Cruise & Ferry Guide* (see Books later in this section) is a useful starting point for research.

Travel agents don't book cargo ship travel. You can either book through a freighter agent or directly with the shipping company. If you use an agent, check its margin (mark-up). Some freighter agents are:

The Cruise People
  Canada:
  (☎ 416-444 2410, fax 447 2628,
  cruise@tcpltd.com)
  1252 Lawrence Ave East, Suite 202, Don
  Mills, Toronto, Ont M3A 1C3;
  www.tcpltd.com/tcp_frat.htm

United Kingdom:
  (☎ 020-7723 2450, fax 7723 2486,
  cruise@dial.pipex.com)
  88 York St, London, W1H 1DP;
  members.aol.com/CruiseAZ/home.htm
Freighter Travel (NZ)
  (☎ 06-843 7702, fax 843 7684,
  hamishjm@ramhb.co.nz)
  250 Kennedy Rd, Napier;
  www.freightertravel.hb.co.nz
Freighter World Cruises
  (☎ 626-449 3106, fax 449 9573,
  freighters@freighterworld.com)
  180 South Lake Ave, Suite 335, Pasadena,
  CA 91101-2655; www.freighterworld.com
TravLtips
  (☎ 718-939 2400, fax 939 2047,
  info@travltips.com)
  PO Box 580188, Flushing, New York 11358,
  USA; www.travltips.com

A round trip of about 50 days from the USA taking in Fiji and Tahiti will cost around US$5000.

See the boxed text 'The Aranui' in the Marquesas section of the French Polynesia chapter for the most famous cargo ship operating in those islands.

Yacht

Between May and October the harbours of the South Pacific swarm with cruising yachts from around the world. If you have your own yacht, you've got probably the most flexible system of transport in the Pacific. Slightly less flexible options are chartering a yacht or joining the crew on someone else's yacht.

Almost invariably, yachts follow the favourable winds west from the Americas towards Asia, Australia or New Zealand.

Popular routes from the US west coast take in Hawai'i and Palmyra Atoll before following the traditional path through the Samoan islands, Tonga, Fiji and New Zealand. From the Atlantic and Caribbean, yachties access this area via Panama, the Galápagos Islands, the Marquesas, the Society Islands and the Tuamotus. Possible stops include Suwarrow (northern Cook Islands), Rarotonga or Niue.

Because of the cyclone season, which begins in November, most yachties try to clear

Fiji or Tonga and be on their way to New Zealand by the early part of that month.

The yachting community is quite friendly, especially toward those who display an interest in yachts and other things nautical. Yachties are a good source of information about world weather patterns, navigation and maritime geography. They're also worth approaching to ask about day charters, diving and sailing lessons.

Crewing Often yachties are looking for crew, and for those who'd like a bit of low-key adventure, this is a great opportunity. Most of the time, crew members will only be asked to take a turn on watch – that is, scan the horizon for cargo ships, stray containers and the odd reef – and possibly to cook or clean up the boat. In port, crew may be required to dive and scrape the bottom, paint or make repairs. In most cases, sailing experience is not necessary and crew members can learn as they go. Most yachties charge crew US$10 to $15 per day for food and supplies.

If you're trying to find a berth on someone else's yacht (or trying to find crew for your own boat) ask at local yacht clubs and look at noticeboards at marinas and yacht clubs. The west coast of the USA is prime hunting ground – San Francisco, Newport Beach and San Diego are all good. Australia's northeastern seaboard is good and so is Auckland in New Zealand. In the Pacific, it shouldn't be too difficult to find crew or a yacht in Honolulu, Papeete, Pago Pago, Apia, Nuku'alofa, Noumea or Port Vila.

The most successful passage-seekers tend to be young women who are willing to crew on boats with male 'single-handers' (ie they sail alone). Naturally, the bounds of the relationship should be fairly well defined before setting out!

Bear in mind that no-one is compatible with everyone; under the conditions of a long ocean voyage, petty rivalries are magnified many times. Only set out on a long passage with someone with whom you feel relatively comfortable, and remember that, once aboard, the skipper's judgement is law.

If you'd like to enjoy some relative freedom of movement on a yacht, try to find one that has wind-vane steering; the tedious job of standing at the wheel staring at a compass all day and all night is likely to go to the crew members of the lowest status (that's you). Comfort is also greatly increased on yachts that have a furling jib, a dodger to keep out the weather, a toilet and shower.

Yachts rigged for racing are usually more manageable than simple live-aboards. As a general rule, about 3m of length for each person aboard affords relatively uncrowded conditions.

Charts & Information This guidebook is not a comprehensive guide for yachting in the South Pacific. We can give you the cultural background and travel information, but if you don't want to see your expensive boat high and dry on a coral reef, seek the advice of people who have sailed the area before at local yacht clubs (listed under Sea in the Getting There & Away section of individual country chapters). A very useful guide to the Pacific is *Landfalls of Paradise*; see Books later in this section.

See Maps under Planning in the Regional Facts for the Visitor chapter for information about charts.

Red Tape Even on your own yacht you're not completely free to do as you please (you are if you stick to the high seas, but if you

---

Finding Atolls

As the Spanish explorer Magellan found, low-lying coral atolls can be very difficult to spot from a distance, even in calm seas. Magellan sailed almost across the entire Pacific without realising how close he had passed to several islands. Ancient Pacific navigators used reflected wave fronts, sightings of land birds and reflections of lagoons on the underside of clouds to locate a nearby atoll. If you haven't quite mastered these techniques yourself, a global positioning satellite (GPS) navigation system might be useful.

Responsible Yachting

- Don't add to the unsightly (and ecologically hazardous) trash floating up on island beaches by allowing rubbish to fall into the sea, even if you are nowhere near an island. Rubbish can float a long way!
- Many harbours are fished for food. So unless you have holding tanks or onboard sewerage treatment, use on-shore toilet facilities when you are in harbour.
- Never anchor on coral, or allow your anchor to drag through live coral.
- When in public view, observe the local customs regarding dress. Don't lounge about the deck topless on Sunday, for example!

want to take advantage of a country's facilities, you have to obey its laws). You must enter a country at an official 'port of entry' (usually the capital). If this means sailing past a dozen beautiful outlying islands on the way to an appointment with an official in a dull capital city, bad luck. Ports of entry are listed in the Getting There & Around section of individual country chapters.

When you arrive, hoist your yellow quarantine flag (Q flag) and wait for the appropriate local official to contact you. Often, you are expected to alert them by VHF radio (usually on channel 16). Ask customs officials at the port of entry about requirements for visiting other islands in the country. Bear in mind that you are legally responsible for your crew's actions as well as your own.

Ferries

Within a country, ferries are often the only way to get to some of the outer islands. See Getting Around in the individual country chapters for details about inter-island travel within a country.

Books

Published for (and available from) travel agents, the Reed Travel Group's *OAG*

Cruise & Ferry Guide is a comprehensive listing of cargo ship routes and companies around the world. It takes some work to find your route but this is an excellent aid to planning a cargo ship trip. It's pretty handy for checking cruise ship options, too.

Cadogan Guides' *Travel by Cargo Ship*, by the very enthusiastic Hugo Verlome, is also useful in planning a trip by cargo ship.

Earl Hinz's *Landfalls of Paradise: The Guide to the Pacific Islands* is a vital resource if you are travelling by yacht in the Pacific. Anchorages, fees, marinas and official procedures are described by the author, who has been sailing the Pacific for years. This book can be difficult to locate but if you're serious about Pacific yachting, it's worth writing to the publisher to secure a copy (Western Marine Enterprises, 3611 Motor Ave, Los Angeles, CA 90034, USA).

BUS

Large and populous islands will usually have some kind of bus service. However, Pacific island public transport is rarely described as ruthlessly efficient. Buses are often privately (or family) owned. It's not unusual for owner-drivers to set their own schedules, and if there aren't many people travelling on a particular day, the buses may just stop. Build flexibility into your plans, and read the boxed text 'Last Bus to Paradise' in the Samoa chapter.

CAR & MOTORCYCLE

Larger islands and tourist destinations will usually have some car or motorcycle rental companies operating. Fares and rules vary enormously; see the individual country chapters for more details.

Most Pacific countries drive on the right-hand side of the road. The exceptions are the Solomons, Fiji, Tonga, Cook Islands, Niue, Tuvalu, Kiribati and Nauru. Take extra care when you're driving on the 'wrong' side of the road – or when crossing the road on foot. The rules for getting a driving permit are explained in the individual country chapters.

In rural areas, roads may be no more than dirt tracks used mostly for foot traffic. Be wary of people or animals on the road; drive especially carefully near villages. Road conditions can be atrocious if there has been cyclone or flood damage recently (or even if there hasn't).

Make sure you get insurance rules and conditions explained when you rent a car, and ask about petrol availability if you're heading off the main routes. Check your own travel insurance policy too – some do not cover unsealed roads or riding a motorcycle (see Travel Insurance in the Regional Facts for the Visitor chapter).

BICYCLE

On flat Pacific islands, riding a bicycle can be an excellent way to get around. See Getting Around in the individual country chapters for details about renting a bike, or just ask around when you get there. Most bikes will not come with a safety helmet or a bike lock unless you ask for them.

Watch for other traffic and poor road surfaces, and check your travel insurance for disclaimers about hazardous activities. If you're bringing your own bike into the country, ask the airline about costs (it's often free) and rules regarding dismantling and packing the bike.

HITCHING

Although it has a lot going for it, hitching is never entirely safe in any country and we cannot recommend it. Travellers who decide to hitch should understand that they are taking a small but potentially serious risk. People who do choose to hitch will be safer if they travel in pairs and let someone know where they plan to go.

In some Pacific countries hitching is an accepted way of getting where you're going, and is practised by locals and tourists alike. In others it's not the local custom and only tourists are seen trying it. It is possible anywhere, however, and can be quite fast.

The main difficulty on a Pacific island is that rides generally won't be very long, perhaps only from one village to the next, and it could take you a good while to go a longer distance. Still, given the sorry state of the bus service in some regions, hitching is a way to see the area without renting a car. It's also a great way to meet the locals and is an option for getting home after the buses have stopped running, which can happen at almost any time in some areas. You might be expected to pay a small fee for a ride, so offer what you think the ride is worth (they'll often refuse the offer).

POLYNESIA

Polynesia

Usually when people think of the Pacific islands they think of Polynesia (Greek for 'Many Islands'). The largest of the three subdivisions of the Pacific, the huge triangle of Polynesia extends from Hawai'i to New Zealand to Easter Island.

All of Polynesia's islands and atolls are volcanic in origin. Many of the major island chains are evidence of hot spots beneath the moving Pacific plate.

The first people to settle Polynesia arrived in Samoa and Tonga about 3000 years ago. From here they spread eastwards to the Marquesas and Society islands in modern French Polynesia, and from there spread out to the Cook Islands, Hawai'i, Easter Island and New Zealand.

Although the distances between Polynesia's islands are enormous, there is a remarkable homogeneity of cultures. Settling the region relatively recently, Polynesians maintained contact between islands on long canoe journeys, which resulted in a relatively consistent language and religion.

It was Tahiti, the 'Isle of Love', that really fired the imagination of Europeans in the 18th and 19th centuries. These days, Tahiti is still the most popular tourist destination in Polynesia, and also the most expensive. However, other islands of Polynesia have beaches even more beautiful than those of Tahiti, along with equally spectacular diving and fascinating cultures.

Not surprisingly, travellers seeking Polynesian culture at its most untouched must venture to the most remote islands – not an easy or a cheap exercise. However, many cultures, such as that of Samoa, proudly retain a strong tradition despite the influence of the west.

Two of the corners of the Polynesian triangle, Hawai'i and New Zealand, are briefly outlined in the introductory chapter South Pacific Gateways.

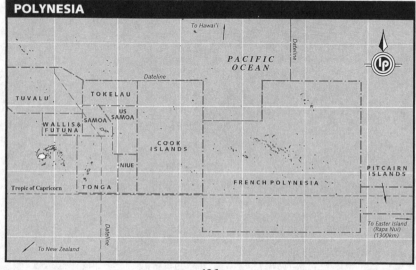

Cook Islands

The Cook Islands is an excellent destination for beach-potatoes and hardy adventurers alike. The beautiful main island of Rarotonga combines densely forested mountains and superb snorkelling reefs with excellent tourist infrastructure and a range of budget options. The second most populous island, Aitutaki rewards the effort required to reach it with one of the most beautiful lagoons in the Pacific. The isolated islands of the northern Cooks get almost no visitors except for the occasional delighted yachtie.

Facts about the Cook Islands

HISTORY
The Cook Islanders are Polynesians, a Maori people related to New Zealand (NZ) Maori and the Maohi of the Society Islands in French Polynesia. Historians believe Polynesian migrations from the Societies to the Cook Islands began around the 5th century AD, and oral history traces Rarotongan ancestry back about 1400 years. In 1997 a *marae* (ceremonial meeting ground) estimated to be about 1500 years old was found on Motutapu, off the coast of Rarotonga. Rarotonga has always been the most influential of the Cooks, and it's assumed that the culture of its early inhabitants was largely duplicated on the other islands.

European Explorers
Pukapuka, in the northern group of the Cook Islands, was the first to be sighted by a European (Alvaro de Mendaña on 20 August 1595). Eleven years later Pedro Fernández de Quirós stopped at Rakahanga, also in the northern group. There is no further record of European contact until 150 years later when James Cook explored much of the group on his 1773 and 1777 expeditions.

In an atlas published in 1835, the Russian cartographer Admiral Johann von

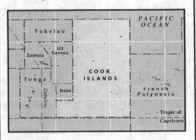

COOK ISLANDS

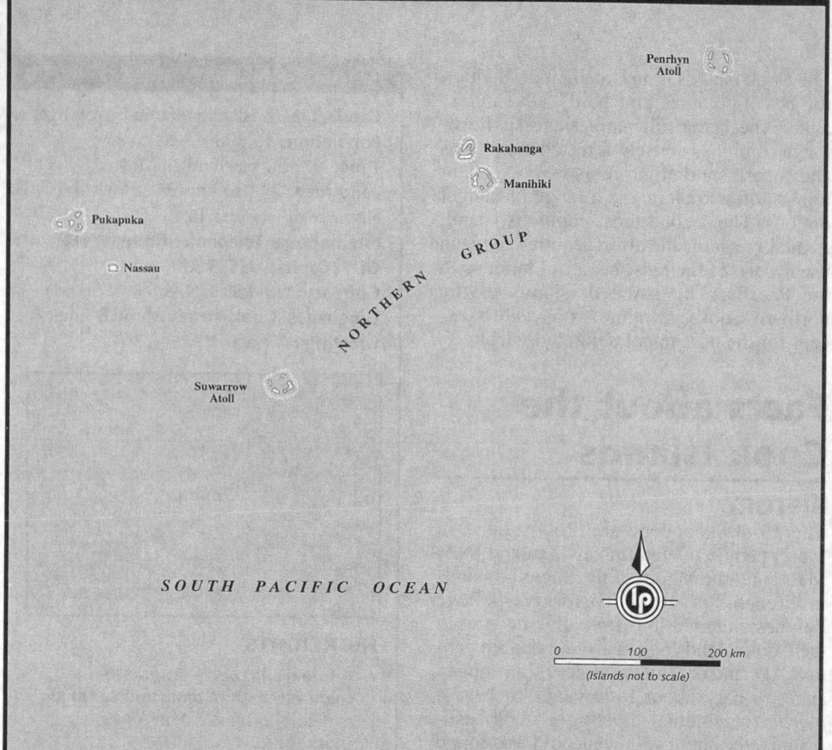

Penrhyn Atoll

Rakahanga

Manihiki

Pukapuka

Nassau

NORTHERN GROUP

Suwarrow Atoll

SOUTH PACIFIC OCEAN

0   100   200 km
(Islands not to scale)

Palmerston Atoll

SOUTHERN GROUP

Aitutaki   Manuae

Mitiaro

Takutea

Atiu

Mauke

Avarua
Rarotonga

Mangaia

Krusenstern named the southern group islands in honour of Cook. The northern group islands were called, among other names, the Penrhyn Islands and the Manihiki Islands. Early in the 20th century, when the islands were annexed by NZ, both the southern and northern groups became known as the Cook Islands.

Missionaries

Reverend John Williams of the London Missionary Society (LMS) first arrived on Aitutaki in 1821. Papeiha, a convert from Raiatea in the Society Islands, moved to Rarotonga in 1823, where he laboured for the rest of his life. In that period the missionaries established a religious control which holds strong to this day.

Government of the islands was left to the tribal chiefs, and thus the individual islands remained independent political entities. Likewise, the missionaries did not completely obliterate the island culture, as indicated by the endurance of *ariki* (the traditional hierarchical system of chiefs), the system of land inheritance (see the boxed text near Society & Conduct later) and the indigenous language.

The missionaries, however, brought with them deadly diseases such as whooping cough, measles, smallpox and influenza, leading to a long-lasting population decline. Not until early in the 20th century did a real increase in population begin. (See the Facts about the South Pacific chapter for more about missionaries in the South Pacific.)

Annexation & Independence

The Cook Islands became a British protectorate in 1888, in response to fears of French colonialism. In 1900 Rarotonga and the other main southern islands were annexed by NZ, and in 1901 all the islands were encompassed.

Prior to the takeover, the NZ government was convinced the Cooks could easily be made self-sufficient but this did not turn out to be the case. The easy-going Polynesian nature, combined with shipping difficulties, defeated all attempts to tap the agricultural richness of the islands.

During WWII the USA built airstrips on Penrhyn and Aitutaki, but essentially the Cooks remained forgotten. In 1965 the Cook Islands became internally self-governing, but foreign policy and defence were left to NZ and remain so today. Cook Islanders have NZ citizenship; the Cook Islands is precluded from taking a seat in the United Nations.

Modern Politics

Elections in 1968 installed Albert Henry, leader of the Cook Islands Party (CIP) and a prime mover in the push for independence, as the Cook Islands' first prime minister. In 1974 he was knighted, but was stripped of his title in 1980 after accusations of misappropriation of public funds following claims of electoral fraud during the 1978 election. He died in 1981.

Dr Thomas Davis (Papa Tom), leader of the Democratic Party, followed Albert Henry as prime minister. In the 1983 election, however, the Democratic Party was bundled out and the following years saw power change hands several times, including through a 1984 coalition between the Democratic Party and the CIP. In 1989, Geoffrey Henry, Albert Henry's nephew, became prime minister. He presided over the 6th International Festival of Pacific Arts (the Maire Nui) in 1992, and despite widespread discontent with his government, his CIP party won a landslide victory in 1994.

Political and economic problems persisted. A controversy concerning the Cook Islands' offshore banking industry and alleged international tax evasion ripened into an international scandal known as 'the winebox affair'; NZ was the principal complainant, although wrongdoing was never proved in court.

In April 1996 Sir Geoffrey (he was knighted in October 1992) announced severe economic measures which included a 50% reduction in government departments and ministries and the privatisation of several government-owned enterprises. Altogether about 2000 public servants were sacked and many of the newly unemployed left for NZ and Australia. Negative media coverage resulted in further economic hardship as tourism suffered a sharp decline (the industry has since gradually recovered).

The government's biggest problem remains the economy, specifically achieving a balance between the country's meagre exports and an avalanche of imports.

Following the 1999 elections and lengthy political manoeuvring, Sir Geoffrey was eventually ousted and Dr Joe Williams (CIP) became the new prime minister.

GEOGRAPHY & ECOLOGY

The Cook Islands' small land mass (just 241 sq km) is scattered over about two million square kilometres of ocean. The islands are about midway between US Samoa and Tahiti.

The islands are conveniently divided into northern and southern groups. The southern group, constituting about 90% of the Cook Islands' total land area, are younger volcanic islands, while the northern group are coral atolls which have formed on top of ancient sunken volcanoes (see the boxed text 'Coral Atolls' in the Facts about the South Pacific chapter). Only Rarotonga, the youngest island, is a straightforward volcanic, mountainous island.

Of the southern group, Atiu, Mauke, Mitiaro and Mangaia are raised islands. They have rocky coastal areas (this area is called a *makatea* in the Cooks), made of uplifted coral reefs, surrounding higher central regions of volcanic soil. All the northern group islands are coral atolls, with an outer reef encircling a lagoon.

Waste management is a big issue in the Cook Islands. Glass, plastic and aluminium are collected in special bins for recycling, but there's still a huge amount of rubbish. Septic tanks are used for sewerage waste; generally the pumped-out water is used as agricultural fertiliser. Water supply is a major concern, especially as droughts have occurred in recent years.

Land clearing, agricultural chemicals and introduced species are all influences that native flora and fauna have had to contend with, and overfishing has affected marine life in some of the islands' lagoons. The Cook Islands Natural Heritage Project is cataloguing the hundreds of species of flora and fauna on the islands, and promoting their conservation.

The biggest threat to the Cooks' northern coral atolls is global warming, which may render them uninhabitable by the end of the next century. See the boxed text 'Global Warming' in the introductory Facts about the South Pacific chapter.

CLIMATE

The Cooks has a pleasant, even climate year-round. The wettest and hottest months are usually December to March. Seasonal variations are slight, ranging from high/low temperatures of 29/23°C in February to 25/18°C from June to September. The cyclone season is from November to March.

Like the rest of the Pacific, the Cook Islands was affected by the El Niño (see Climate in the Facts about the South Pacific chapter) of 1997-98, with a long-running drought, a couple of spectacular cyclones and sustained higher-than-normal temperatures. El Niño usually brings an increased number of cyclones to the Cooks.

FLORA & FAUNA

Most noticeable in the Cook Islands are the coconut palms, and gorgeous flowers which seem to grow with wild abandon almost everywhere.

Rarotonga has a wide variety of vegetation. Communities include valley forest, native fernland, native slope forest, native ridge forest, native rock face and, highest of all, native cloud forest; the damp, mountainous central part of the island is densely covered in a luxuriant jungle of ferns, creepers and towering trees. Pandanus trees grow on the makatea of most of the southern islands, though they are now rare on Rarotonga and Atiu.

Fauna and native birds are generally few in number. The only mammal considered native is the Pacific fruit bat, found on Mangaia and Rarotonga. Rats and pigs were introduced to the islands and today there are many domestic pigs. Rarotonga has many dogs, some cats and goats, and a few horses and cattle.

On Rarotonga you have to get up into the hills to see native birds. The mynah was introduced in 1906 to control coconut stick insects and is now prolific on many southern group islands, contributing to the lack of native birds found in the lowlands. Endemic birds include the cave-dwelling Atiu swiftlet *(kopeka)* on Atiu and the Rarotonga flycatcher *(kakerori)*, which is found in a limited area of Rarotonga and is an endangered species.

GOVERNMENT & POLITICS
The Cook Islands has its own government responsible for internal affairs, while its international relations and defence matters are handled by NZ. It has a Westminster parliamentary system, with a lower house, or Legislative Assembly, of 24 members from the various districts of the islands, plus one member representing Cook Islanders living in NZ. The upper house, or House of Ariki, represents the island chiefs and has advisory powers only.

ECONOMY
The Cook Islands' economy is far from balanced – imports far exceed exports. The biggest factor in coping with the shortfall is foreign aid, particularly from NZ. Considerable amounts of money are sent back by Cook Islanders living abroad.

Pearls and pearl shell are the most lucrative exports, followed by citrus fruits, tropical fruits, vegetables and copra (dried coconut). New export items are live, fresh or chilled fish. Aromatic *maire ei* (necklaces of maire leaves) are flown to Hawai'i. Major trading partners are NZ, Australia, Fiji, Hong Kong and the USA.

Tourism is one of the country's biggest industries; it's estimated that 48,600 tourists visited Rarotonga in 1998.

POPULATION & PEOPLE
The population of the Cook Islands is about 16,800, but dropping steadily. The number of Cook Islanders living abroad is much greater – around 55,000 Cook Islanders are estimated to live in NZ, and a large number live in Australia too (Cook Islanders have residency and working rights in these countries). More than 90% of the Cooks' population lives on the southern group islands, with over 50% of the country's population on Rarotonga.

More than 90% of the population is Polynesian, though there are subtle differences between the islands' peoples. The people of Pukapuka in the north, for example, are more closely related to Samoans than to other Cook Islanders. People of European NZ, Fijian, Indian or Chinese descent are a small minority.

ARTS
Cook Islanders are reputed to be the best dancers in Polynesia, and dancing in the Cook Islands is colourful, spectacular and very popular.

Many traditional arts and crafts are still in evidence. Woven pandanus mats, baskets, purses, fans and other items are still in daily use. You'll see women going to church wearing finely woven white hats made of *rito*, an especially fine variety of pandanus; these hats are made in the northern group islands, but other islands also have distinct hat styles.

Beautifully crafted traditional ceremonial adzes and stone taro pounders are produced on Mangaia. Other arts you'll see in the Cooks include the fine textile art known as *tivaevae*, an applique-and-embroidery creation made by women and used on bedspreads, cushion covers and in home decoration. Flower art is also in daily use – you'll see people wearing an amazing variety of necklaces *(ei)* and tiaras *(ei katu)* made of flowers.

Jewellery is made from various materials, including shells. Nowadays, the black pearl is one of the Cooks' largest industries, and black pearl creations, including jewellery, are a speciality. Other pearl-related arts include jewellery and carvings made from mother-of-pearl shell.

A few painters and writers live on Rarotonga. You can see their paintings in local galleries, and find their books in local shops. Glass blowing is also getting started on Rarotonga.

Land Ownership

A law prohibiting anybody from selling or buying land makes it impossible for outsiders to own land in the Cooks. Land ownership is purely hereditary and land can only be leased, not sold, to outside parties. Because land is passed from generation to generation, people acquire curiously divided chunks of property. Families might have a house by the coast, a citrus plantation somewhere else and the odd group of papaya trees dotted here and there. It can be a full-time job commuting from one farmlet to another.

SOCIETY & CONDUCT

Beneath a western veneer, layers of Cook Islands culture survive. Every native Cook Islander is part of a family clan, and each clan is connected to the ancient system of chiefs. Rarotonga's six ariki clans are based on the original land divisions from when the Maori first arrived on the island many centuries ago. Even today, when an ariki is installed the ceremony takes place on an ancient family marae, and you will see many graves of the ancestors beside modern houses.

Friendliness and respect for others are highly valued in Cook Islands culture. Visitors are urged to dress modestly.

RELIGION

Few people today know much about the traditional religion of the Cook Islands, with its sophisticated system of 71 gods, each ruling a particular facet of reality, and its 12 levels of heaven, some above the surface of the earth and some below. Today, the Protestant Cook Islands Christian Church (CICC) attracts about 70% of the faithful, with the remaining 30% Roman Catholic, Seventh-Day Adventist, Church of the Latter Day Saints (Mormons) and various other denominations.

LANGUAGE

Cook Islands Maori (Rarotongan) is the common language, but there are some small dialectical differences between many islands and some northern islands have their own languages. English is spoken as a second (or third) language by virtually everyone. Rarotongan is a Polynesian language most similar to New Zealand Maori and Marquesan (from French Polynesia).

See Language in the Facts about the South Pacific chapter for the pronunciation of the glottal stop. In Rarotongan, the glottal stop replaces the 'h' of similar Polynesian languages, eg the Tahitian word for one, *tahi* (ta-hee), is *ta'i* (ta-ee) in Rarotongan.

Rarotongan Basics

Hello.	*Kia orana.*
Goodbye.	*Aere ra.*
How are you?	*Pe'ea koe?*
I'm well.	*Meitaki.*
Please.	*Ine.*
Thanks (very much).	*Meitaki (ma'ata).*
Yes.	*Ae.*
No.	*Kare.*
Cheers.	*Kia manuia.*

Facts for the Visitor

SUGGESTED ITINERARIES

In one week you can visit the two principal islands, Rarotonga and Aitutaki. With a little more time, it's worth visiting other islands of the southern group: Atiu, Mauke, Mitiaro and/or Mangaia. Visiting the northern group islands requires more time, as they are right off the beaten track.

PLANNING

The moderate climate means you rarely need anything warmer than a short-sleeved shirt, but bring along a jumper (sweater) or jacket, especially during the cooler months of June to September. Bring rain gear at any time of year. You'll need an old pair of running shoes for walking on the reefs and a pair of sturdy shoes for climbing on Rarotonga, or across the razor-sharp makatea of Atiu, Mauke, Mitiaro or Mangaia.

Most western commodities are readily available but somewhat expensive. A torch (flashlight) is handy on the outer islands, where the power goes off at midnight, and for exploring caves.

TOURIST OFFICES

The Cook Islands Tourism Corporation (☎ 29435, fax 21435, tourism@cookislands .gov.ck), PO Box 14, is in the centre of Avarua on Raratonga. Its website is www.cook-islands.com. Tourist information is also available from Cook Islands consulates. Overseas offices and representatives include:

Australia
(☎ 02-9955 0446, fax 9955 0447,
cookislands@speednet.com.au)
PO Box H95, Hurlstone Park, NSW 2193

Belgium
(☎ 02-538 2930, fax 538 2885)
Rue Americaine 27, 1050 Brussels

France
(☎ 04-76 90 41 63, fax 76 18 29 31)
13 Rue d'Alembert, 3800 Grenoble

Germany
(☎ 030-238 17628, fax 238 17641)
Dirkenstrasse 40, 1020 Berlin

New Zealand
(☎ 09-366 1100, fax 309 1876,
albert@tourismcookislands.co.nz)
1/127 Symonds St, PO Box 37391, Parnell, Auckland

Thailand
(☎ 652 0507, fax 652 0509,
pl_group@loxinfo.co.th)
8th Floor, Maneeya Center Bldg, 518/5
Ploenchit Rd, Bangkok 10330

UK
(☎ 020-8392 1838, fax 8392 1318)
375 Upper Richmond Rd West, East Sheen, London SW14 7NX

The Cook Islands are also represented abroad by the Tourism Council of the South Pacific (see the Regional Facts for the Visitor chapter).

VISAS & CONSULATES

No visa is required to visit the Cooks. A visitor permit, good for 31 days, is granted on arrival to people of all nationalities on presentation of a valid passport (with six months' remaining validity), an onward or return airline ticket, and honour of the prior booking arrangement (see Accommodation later in this section). Visitor permits can be extended for a maximum of six months at the Ministry of Foreign Affairs & Immigration (☎ 29347, fax 21247) in Avarua.

Foreign diplomatic representation in Avarua includes:

France
(☎ 20919, fax 22031)
Mrs Marie Melvin, Honorary French Consul

Germany
(☎ 23306, fax 23305)
Dr Wolfgang Losacker, Honorary German Consul

New Zealand
(☎ 22201, fax 21241)
NZ High Commission

CUSTOMS

Restrictions of 2L of spirits or wine or 4.5L of beer, plus 200 cigarettes or 50 cigars or 250g of tobacco apply. Bringing in plants or plant products, animals or animal products, is restricted or prohibited. Importation of firearms, weapons and drugs is prohibited.

MONEY

There's a healthy slug on top of NZ prices to cover shipping costs for imports. A 12.5% VAT (value added tax) is figured into the quoted price of most goods and services.

Tipping is not customary in the Cook Islands, and haggling over prices is considered very rude. Accommodation costs the same year-round (there are no high or low-season prices).

Currency

New Zealand paper money is used in the Cooks, while NZ and Cook Islands coins are used interchangeably. NZ dollar exchange rates are listed under Money in the Regional Facts for the Visitor chapter.

Cash & Travellers Cheques

Cook Islands money cannot be changed anywhere else in the world, so be sure to either spend it or change it into another currency before you leave the country. The only places that change money are the Westpac and ANZ banks in Avarua, the Administration Centre in Aitutaki, and some hotels. You receive about 4% more for travellers cheques than for cash; all brands of travellers cheques are cashed at the banks.

Credit Cards

Visa, MasterCard and Bankcard are readily accepted at most places in Rarotonga. The Westpac and ANZ banks in Avarua give cash advances on all three cards. American Express and Diners Club are accepted at the better hotels and restaurants.

POST & COMMUNICATIONS

Poste restante mail is held for 30 days at post offices on most islands. To collect mail at the post office in Avarua it should be addressed to you c/o Poste Restante, Avarua, Rarotonga, Cook Islands.

All southern islands have modern telephone systems. International collect calls can be made from any telephone, but only to Australia, Canada, Fiji, French Polynesia, Niue, Netherlands, NZ, Sweden, Tonga, UK and the USA. Each island has a Telecom office, also providing fax, telegram and telex services.

The international telephone code for the Cook Islands is ☎ 682. There are no local area codes and no code is required for inter-island calls. Dial ☎ 00 for direct international calls, or dial the international operator on ☎ 015 for international and inter-island operator-assisted calls. International information is ☎ 017; the local information operator is ☎ 010.

INTERNET RESOURCES

Email and Internet connections are available (see the Rarotonga Information section later for details). Useful websites about the Cooks include the Cook Islands Tourism Corporation, at www.cook-islands.com, and the Cook Islands News at www.cinews .co.ck (updated weekly).

BOOKS

Alphons MJ Kloosterman's *Discoverers of the Cook Islands & the Names They Gave* gives a brief history of each island, early legends and a record of European contact.

History of Rarotonga, up to 1853, by Taira Rere, is a short, locally written history.

One of the best-known residents of the Cooks was the late Tom Neale. In *An Island to Oneself* he wrote of the periods during the 1950s, 60s and 70s he spent living as a hermit on the isolated northern atoll Suwarrow. *How to Get Lost & Found in the Cook Islands*, by John & Bobbye McDermott, concentrates on the Cooks' many colourful characters.

Cook Islands Politics – the Inside Story is an anthology of articles by 22 writers. Presenting many points of view, it tells the story of Sir Albert Henry's topple from power, along with the historical background, the intrigues, the corruption and the bribery.

Cook Islands Legends and *The Ghost at Tokatarava and Other Stories from the Cook Islands* are both written by notable Cook Islands author Jon Jonassen. *Te Ata O Ikurangi: The Shadow of Ikurangi*, by JJ MacCauley, is another collection of legends. There are available several books of poems by Kauraka Kauraka.

Good books on arts and crafts include *Cook Islands Art* by Dale Idiens, illustrated with black and white photos, and *Tivaevae – Portraits of Cook Islands Quilting*, by Lynnsay Rongokea, which introduces 18 women from five islands and their colourful tivaevae (applique works).

The Cook Islands, by Ewan Smith, is a coffee-table book with magnificent photos and text. *Visions of the Pacific*, by David Arnell & Lisette Wolk, is a coffee-table book with exceptional colour photographs of the different peoples who gathered in Rarotonga for the 1992 Maire Nui festival.

A useful trekking/fauna and flora guide is *Rarotonga's Mountain Tracks and Plants*, by Gerald McCormack & Judith Künzle. Also look for *Rarotonga's Cross-Island Walk*, by the same authors. *Guide to Cook Islands Birds*, by DT Holyoak, has colour photos and text for identification of a number of local birds.

NEWSPAPERS & MAGAZINES

Rarotonga's *Cook Islands News*, published daily except Sunday, provides coverage of local events and a brief summary of international events. The daily *New Zealand Herald* is sold on Rarotonga the day after it's published. A small selection of foreign magazines is available in Avarua.

RADIO & TV
The AM station reaches all the islands and broadcasts local programs, Radio New Zealand news and Radio Australia's overseas world news service. The FM station is less powerful but can be received on most (but not all) of Rarotonga.

Rarotonga has one television station, CITV. Tapes of its programs are flown to some outer islands for re-broadcast. A few outer islands, notably Aitutaki, have begun to experiment with creating their own TV programming.

PHOTOGRAPHY & VIDEO
Film is only available on Rarotonga. High-speed film is useful in the densely forested interior of Rarotonga, and in the makatea of Atiu and Mauke. Bring a flash for photographing caves.

TIME
The Cook Islands is east of the International Dateline, 10 hours behind Greenwich Mean Time (GMT). The country has no daylight saving time. Making no allowances for daylight saving time in other countries, when it's noon in the Cooks the time in other places is:

London	10 pm same day
Tahiti & Hawai'i	noon same day
NZ & Fiji	10 am next day

HEALTH
The Cook Islands is generally a healthy place for visitors. Food is good, fresh, clean and readily available and there are few endemic diseases. No vaccinations are required for travel here.

Although tap water is usually safe to drink on Rarotonga and on most of the outer islands, do ask about it. In Aitutaki, for example, there are some places where you should take your drinking water from a rainwater tank, rather than from the tap.

Even on Rarotonga, tap water is not treated and has caused some visitors to experience stomach problems, although others are not bothered by it; it might be advisable to boil your drinking water.

Every island has a basic medical clinic. Outer islands patients are often sent to Rarotonga for care, where there are a hospital, an outpatient clinic and several private doctors.

DANGERS & ANNOYANCES
Theft has become quite a problem on Rarotonga. Don't leave money in your wallet on the beach while you're swimming, take clothes in from clotheslines at night, and beware of leaving hotel rooms unlocked or easy to access.

In the sheltered lagoons swimming is very safe, but be very wary of the passages and breaks in the surrounding reef, where currents are especially strong. Rarotonga has several such passages, notably at Avana Harbour, Avaavaroa, Papua and Rutaki; they exist on other islands as well, often opposite streams.

Mosquitoes can be a real nuisance in the Cooks, particularly during the rainy season (around mid-December to mid-April). Use repellent; mosquito coils are available everywhere.

BUSINESS HOURS
The usual business week is Monday to Friday from 8 am to 4 pm, and shops are also open on Saturday until noon. Small local grocery stores are often open from 6 or 7 am until 8 or 9 pm. Nearly everything is closed on Sunday, except some small grocery stores which open for a couple of hours very early in the morning and again in the evening.

PUBLIC HOLIDAYS & SPECIAL EVENTS
The Cook Islands has many public holidays, and they're good opportunities to see dancing and other activities. As well as New Year's Day, Easter, Anzac Day, Christmas and Boxing Day, there are:

Queen's Birthday	1st Monday in June

Gospel Day (Rarotonga)	26 July
Constitution Day (Independence)	4 August
Gospel Day (Cooks)	26 October
Flag Raising Day	27 October

Gospel Day is celebrated with much enthusiasm. Some of the more entertaining festivals are:

February
Cook Islands Sevens Rugby Tournament
   International and local teams

April
Island National Dance Festival Week
   Third week of April – dance competitions

August
Constitution Celebration
   Beginning the Friday before 4 August – 10 day sporting and dance festival

November
Tiare (Floral) Festival Week
   Last week of November – parades and more

ACTIVITIES
Watersports
All the islands have some sort of sheltered lagoon where you can swim, and some sandy beaches. Rarotonga and Aitutaki are excellent for **swimming**, and are especially attractive for **diving**, with a high visibility level of 30 to 60m and a great variety of sealife. Lagoon cruise operators go out to some of the best **snorkelling** spots. On Rarotonga, Muri beach has snorkelling gear, sailing boats, windsurfers and other equipment for hire.

Glass-bottom boats operate from Muri beach for viewing coral and tropical fish. Fully equipped boats for **deep-sea fishing** can be chartered on Rarotonga and Aitutaki.

Hiking, Walking & Caving
Rarotonga has rock climbing and challenging mountain treks as well as easy strolls through lush valleys, along beautiful white-sand beaches and along streams. Aitutaki, with its single small mountain Maungapu (124m) and limitless beaches and trails, is also great for walking and exploring. Atiu, Mauke, Mitiaro and Mangaia all have interesting caves to explore.

Visiting a Marae
History and archaeology buffs will enjoy visiting the historic marae on many of the islands. These traditional religious meeting places are still very significant in some aspects of culture on Rarotonga and on other islands.

ACCOMMODATION
One important stipulation for all visitors is that you are supposed to have booked accommodation before you arrive. Recently, enforcement of this rule has become more relaxed and often you can choose a hotel when you arrive at the airport. Nevertheless, the prior booking rule is officially in place and it's best to have a booking, at least for the first night.

Rarotonga has the most places to stay, including two major resort hotels, some hostel-style places and plenty of motel-style accommodation. Houses can be rented, fully furnished, for around NZ$125 to $300 a week. There's organised accommodation on Aitutaki and all the other southern group islands that have air services.

Penrhyn is the only northern group island with a guesthouse. Elsewhere you may have to stay with local people; be sure to pay your way and bring food to share.

FOOD
Rarotonga has a number of good restaurants, Aitutaki has a few, and Mangaia and Atiu each have a couple. Elsewhere, the choice of places to eat is far more limited. Fortunately, most accommodation has kitchen facilities.

You won't find much local food on restaurant menus, but 'island night' buffets or barbecues will often have local dishes. An *umukai* is a traditional feast cooked in an underground oven *(umu)*.

DRINKS
The truly local drink is coconut water and Cook Islands coconuts are especially tasty. Try also Atiu Island coffee, and fresh juices from the Frangi juice factory on Rarotonga. A wide variety of NZ and other international beers are available; Cook's Lager, Rarotonga's own beer, is quite good and the

least expensive. Liqueurs (40% alcohol) are made from local products on Rarotonga.

ENTERTAINMENT

The most typical Cook Islands entertainment is the 'island night', which starts with a buffet dinner of local food, followed by a floor show of dance, music and song. Friday night is the big night for drinking and dancing.

SHOPPING
Traditional Handicrafts

The squat, ugly, but well-endowed, figure of Tangaroa, traditional god of the sea and fertility, has become the symbol of the Cooks. You can get Tangaroa figures in forms ranging from keyring figures 2cm high to huge ones standing 1m or more. A 25cm-high figure will cost around NZ$40.

Ceremonial stone adzes with intricately carved wooden handles or stands, as well as sennit binding and stone taro pounders are made on Mangaia. Rito hats made of woven fine, bleached pandanus leaves are a Cook Islands speciality. Prices start at about NZ$50. Other pandanus products are mats, purses and fans.

Colourful and intricately sewn tivaevae are traditionally made as burial shrouds, but are also used as bedspreads and cushion covers. They take an enormous amount of time to make, so a full-size tivaevae will cost you several hundred dollars. Smaller wall hangings, cushion covers, and clothing using tivaevae-inspired patterns are cheaper.

Pearls, Shells & Shell Jewellery

Pearls are farmed on Manihiki and Penrhyn and sold on Rarotonga. Black pearls (very rare), golden pearls, white pearls, mother-of-pearl products and pearls embedded in their mother-of-pearl shells are all available. A lot of shell jewellery is produced. *Pupu ei* – long necklaces made of tiny pupu shells collected on Mangaia – are a sought-after item.

Before you rush off to buy shells remember that something has to be evicted to provide the shell, and conservationists fear some species are being collected to extinction.

Rare black pearls are an important export earner for the Cook Islands economy.

Other Souvenirs

Pure coconut oils and coconut oil-based soaps, liqueurs made from local fruits, and Atiu Island coffee are all good souvenirs. Rarotonga has a couple of resident artists and their artworks are on sale, often at very reasonable prices (see the Rarotonga Shopping section later for details).

There are also a fair number of souvenirs that don't originate from the Cooks at all, such as shell jewellery and wooden bowls made in the Philippines, and NZ Maori items masquerading as Cook Islands Maori products.

Getting There & Away

AIR

Usually, getting to the Cook Islands means flying. Air New Zealand is the only regular international airline servicing the Cooks (plus one charter service – read on), though it is still worth comparing prices and stopover options when buying your ticket. Travel agents often work out package deals (air fare plus accommodation) that cost the same or even less than the air fare alone.

It's possible to visit the Cooks as a destination in itself, as a stopover or as part of a round-the-world ticket or Pacifica air pass. (see the introductory Getting There & Away and Getting Around the Region chapters for details on these tickets). It may not cost much more to visit the Cooks in combination with other destinations than it would to visit them alone.

The low season for travel to the Cooks is from mid-April to late August, and the high season is from December to February; other times are shoulder season. There's heavy demand from NZ to the Cooks in December, and in the other direction in January.

Departure Tax

There's a NZ$25 departure tax when you fly out of Rarotonga (NZ$10 for children aged two to 12 and free for children under two).

The Americas

Flights to Rarotonga from the USA (departing Los Angeles) go via either Honolulu or Tahiti. A one-month return ticket (without stopovers) costs US$888/958/1048 in low/shoulder/high season. A three-month ticket allowing a free stopover in Honolulu or Tahiti costs US$998/1068/1268.

Flights to/from Santiago are routed via Tahiti; LanChile airline flies Santiago-Tahiti, and Air New Zealand flies Tahiti-Rarotonga. A four-month return ticket costs US$1020.

Canada 3000, a charter airline, operates a weekly flight routed Toronto-Vancouver-Honolulu-Rarotonga-Auckland and return, but only from around November to April. Its fares may be significantly lower than Air New Zealand's – it's worth checking out. Travel agents will have information. Island Hopper Vacations (see Travel Agencies in the Rarotonga section later) is Canada 3000's Cook Islands agent.

Australasia

Air New Zealand has three direct flights weekly from Auckland to Rarotonga; return fares are NZ$1056/1296 in low/high season for a one-year ticket.

Flights between Australia and Rarotonga go via Auckland. A basic return to Rarotonga, valid for four months, costs A$1167/1286 from Sydney, A$1394/1512 from Melbourne.

The Pacific

The only Pacific islands with direct flights to Rarotonga are Fiji, Tahiti (French Polynesia) and Hawai'i. If you want to visit any other Pacific island from the Cooks, you'll have to fly via one of these or NZ.

Asia

Air New Zealand's connections to/from Tokyo are via either Fiji or Auckland. Basic fare is ¥359,100 for a one-year return ticket; cheaper fares may be available through some travel agencies.

SEA

Various cruise ships stop in at Rarotonga and other islands, typically arriving in the morning and departing again in the afternoon, after quick island tours.

See the introductory Getting Around the Region chapter for information about the *World Discoverer* cruise ship, whose itinerary includes Rarotonga.

Yacht

The other sea alternative is to come by yacht, except during the November-to-March cyclone season. Once you arrive in Rarotonga, fly your Q flag and wait for the customs officials (☎ 21921). Other official ports of entry are Aitutaki, Penrhyn and Pukapuka, all of which have good anchorages. The virtually uninhabited Suwarrow Island, made famous by Tom Neale's book *An Island to Oneself*, is another favourite with yachties, but is not an official port of entry.

There's a remote chance of catching a yacht from the Cook Islands to Tonga, Samoa, Fiji, French Polynesia or NZ. Check the situation at Rarotonga's Ports Authority (☎ 21921, fax 21191) at Avatiu Harbour, and on its downstairs bulletin board where yachties often leave messages if they are looking for crew.

Getting Around

There are only two options for inter-island travel unless you have a yacht. In the southern islands you can fly on Air Rarotonga or you can take the inter-island passenger ship. In the northern islands the best option is by sea; only Manihiki, Penrhyn and Pukapuka have airstrips, and flights are expensive.

AIR
Air Rarotonga is the only commercial inter-island air service in the Cook Islands. There are several daily flights between Rarotonga and Aitutaki, several weekly flights between Rarotonga and the other southern group islands, and a weekly flight between Rarotonga and the northern islands of Manihiki and Penrhyn. There are no flights on Sunday. See the individual island sections in this chapter for details of air fares and flight times.

If you're visiting more than one of the southern group islands, ask about a discounted 45 day Island Discovery AirPass.

BOAT
Most of the northern islands are only accessible by ship. Shipping schedules are hard to pinpoint – weather, breakdowns, loading difficulties and unexpected demands can all put a kink in the plans. Ships usually stay at each island for just a few hours. Only Rarotonga and Penrhyn have wharves; at all the other islands, you go ashore by lighter or barge. Trips from Rarotonga to the northern islands often take up to 10 days as several islands may be visited.

Travel throughout the southern islands usually involves setting off in the late afternoon or early evening, and arriving at the next island early the next morning.

The *Maunga Roa* and *Taimoana* provide inter-island passenger and cargo services for the Cooks. Information, schedules and bookings are available through Taio Shipping Ltd (☎ 24905, 20535, fax 24906, risa@taio.co.ck), PO Box 2001, downstairs in the Ports Authority building at Avatiu Harbour in Avarua.

LOCAL TRANSPORT
On Rarotonga there are taxis and a bus service, and you can hire cars, Jeeps, minibuses, motorcycles and bicycles. Aitutaki has rental cars, Jeeps, motorcycles and bicycles. Atiu and Mauke have rental motorcycles and bicycles, and Atiu has a taxi service. All the islands are good for bicycling – the distances are short and the roads are quite flat.

Hitchhiking, though not the custom, is perfectly legal. You'll get some strange looks but if you're cheeky enough to try, you'll probably get a lift fairly quickly.

ORGANISED TOURS
On Rarotonga, circle-island tours are a good introduction to the island and its history, culture, people, agriculture and economy. Circle-island tours are also offered on Aitutaki, Atiu, Mauke and Mangaia. For more specialised tours (eg cave tours) see the individual island entries later in this chapter.

Day tours are available from Rarotonga to Aitutaki. Rarotonga travel agents can also organise one-island or multi-island package tours to many of the islands.

Flying in the Cooks

In the Cook Islands, people fly inter-island trips aboard 18-passenger Bandeirante turbo-prop planes. With people travelling back and forth for many different reasons, there's often quite a motley collection of passengers on any given flight.

The tradition of giving *ei* (necklaces) whenever people arrive and depart is alive and well on Rarotonga – and even more so on the outer islands, where it would be inconceivable for a guest to arrive or depart without being garlanded with flowers. The small planes sometimes seem like mobile florist shops, and the aroma can be almost overpowering!

COOK ISLANDS

Rarotonga

• pop 11,150   • area 67 sq km

Rarotonga is the main island and population centre of the Cook Islands. The interior is rugged, virtually unpopulated and untouched, while the coastal region is fertile and evenly populated. Fringing this is an almost continuous clean, white beach with clear, shallow lagoons and a protective outer reef.

History

Oral histories relate that Rarotonga was first discovered by Io Teitei, who came by canoe about 1400 years ago from Nuku Hiva in the Marquesas Islands (in modern French Polynesia). In the early 13th century, Tangi'ia, from Raiatea in the Society Islands, and Karika, from Samoa, arrived simultaneously at the head of two settlement expeditions. Tangi'ia and Karika fought each other at first, then ruled Rarotonga as joint kings.

Eventually the land was divided among six tribes, each headed by a tribal king (ariki). Inter-tribal conflicts over land and other issues were frequent, and people lived at higher elevations than they do today for easier defence. They practised agriculture and raised livestock, including pigs.

Surprisingly, considering its historical importance, Rarotonga was one of the later islands to be found by Europeans. Philip Goodenough, captain of the *Cumberland*, showed up in 1814 and spent a bloody three months on Rarotonga unsuccessfully looking for sandalwood. In 1823, the missionaries Papeiha and John Williams set out to covert the Rarotongans, and in little more than a year Christianity had taken a firm hold.

In 1865 Makea Takau, a Rarotongan ariki, fearing French expansionism in the Pacific, requested British protection for the first time, and in 1888 when a British protectorate was formally declared over the southern islands, Rarotonga became the unofficial capital of the group. The Cook Islands were annexed by NZ in 1901, eventually becoming independent in 1965.

BY PERMISSION OF THE NATIONAL LIBRARY OF AUSTRALIA; NK1224/6

Makea, King of Rarotonga, painted by the Rev John Williams (watercolour, 1830s).

Orientation

Finding your way around Rarotonga is very easy – there's a coastal road (the Ara Tapu) and another road about 500m inland (the Ara Metua) going most of the way around the island. A number of smaller roads connect these two, and a few others lead to inland valleys. The island can only be crossed on foot.

New Zealand's Department of Lands & Survey has an excellent 1:25,000 topographical map of Rarotonga (NZ$8.50) showing all the roads, a number of walking trails, the reefs and villages and a separate enlargement of Avarua. Maps are available at the post office and many shops in Avarua, and at the Cook Islands Survey Department office (☎ 29433, fax 27433).

Information

Tourist Offices The Cook Islands Tourism Corporation office (☎ 29435, fax 21435, PO Box 14, tourism@cookislands.gov.ck), in the centre of Avarua, is open weekdays 8 am to 4 pm, Saturday 8 am to noon. Its website is at www.cook-islands.com. Pick up the free *What's On in the Cook Islands*, an annual information guide.

Money Westpac is on the main road in Avarua; ANZ is tucked away in the rear of the white, three-storey building between Foodland and the police station. Both banks are open weekdays 9 am to 3 pm; Westpac is also open Saturday 9 to 11 am. Travellers cheques and major currencies in cash can be changed at some of the larger hotels.

Post & Communications The post office, just inland from the traffic circle in central Avarua, is open weekdays 8 am to 4 pm, Saturday 8 am to noon. Postal depots operate at several small shops around the island. The Telecom office, on Tutakimoa Rd in Avarua, a couple of blocks inland from Cook's Corner Arcade, is open 24 hours.

Internet and email connections are available in Avarua at the post office, Telecom, and at Pacific Computers (☎ 20727, fax 20737, email@pacific.co.ck), near the Staircase Restaurant.

Travel Agencies Useful travel agencies include:

Cook Islands Tours & Travel
    (☎ 28270, or ☎ 20270 after hours, fax 27270, raroinfo@citours.co.ck)
    (at the airport) PO Box 611, Rarotonga;
    http://cookpages.com/CookIslandsTours
Island Hopper Vacations
    (☎ 22576 or ☎ 22026, fax 22036, vacation@islandhopper.co.ck)
    (in Avarua) PO Box 240, Rarotonga;
    www.islandhoppervacations.com
Stars Travel
    (☎ 23669, fax 21569, holidays@starstravel.co.ck)
    (in Avarua) PO Box 75, Rarotonga

Bookshops The largest selection of books in the Cook Islands can be found at the University of the South Pacific (USP) centre, the Cook Islands Library & Museum Society, opposite USP, and the CITC department store, all in Avarua.

The Bounty Bookshop in the three-storey building between Foodland and the police station has a good selection of books, foreign magazines and newspapers. Island Craft Ltd and Pacific Supplies also have books about the Cook Islands.

Laundry Snowbird Laundromat has one laundry in Avarua (☎ 21952) and one in Arorangi (☎ 20952). Both are open weekdays 8 am to 4 pm, Saturday till noon.

Photography Cocophoto (☎ 29295) at the CITC Pharmacy sells colour print, slide and video film and offers same-day colour print processing.

Medical Services & Emergency The hospital (☎ 22664) is on a hill up behind the golf course, west of the airport. There's an outpatient clinic (☎ 20065) on the main road at Tupapa, about 1km east of Avarua.

The Cook Islands Police Headquarters (☎ 22499) is on the main road in the centre of Avarua. Emergency phone numbers are: police (☎ 999), ambulance and hospital (☎ 998) and fire (☎ 996).

Activities
Walking & Climbing The valley walks are easy strolls suitable even for older people or young children. Scaling the hill behind the hospital is also easy and short, although a bit steep, and provides a great view. Most of the mountain walks are hard work, often involving scrambling over rocky sections. The trails are often difficult to follow, but fortunately Rarotonga is too small for you to get really lost. If you do get lost, walk towards the coast on a ridge crest.

It is most important not to go alone, and to let someone know where you're going and when you expect to return. The valleys and bushy inland areas have plenty of mosquitoes, so bring repellent. Make sure you wear adequate walking shoes as trails can be quite slippery after rain. Also carry plenty of drinking water. See the Books section under Facts for the Visitor earlier in this chapter for recommended walking guides.

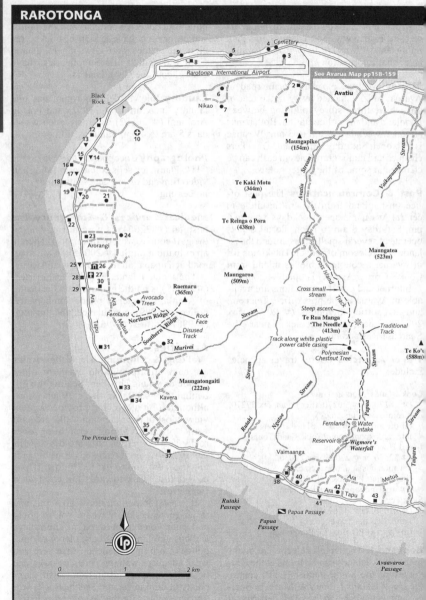

RAROTONGA

Cemetery

9
8
5
4
3
2

Rarotonga International Airport

See Avarua Map pp158-159

Avatiu

Black
Rock

6
Nikao
7

1

Maungapiko
(154m)

11
12
13
10
15
14
16
17
18
19
20
21
22
23
24

Arorangi

Te Kaki Motu
(344m)

Te Reinga o Pora
(438m)

Maungatea
(523m)

Cross Island Track

25
26
27
28
30
29

Ara
Tapu

Ara
Metua

Maungaroa
(509m)

Cross small
stream

Steep ascent

Te Rua Manga
'The Needle'
(413m)

Traditional
Track

Raemaru
(365m)

Avocado
Trees

Fernland

Northern Ridge

Southern Ridge

Rock
Face

Disused
Track

32

Murivai

Track along white plastic
power cable casing

Polynesian
Chestnut Tree

Te Ko'u
(588m)

31

Maungatongaiti
(222m)

Kavera

33
34

Stream

Stream

Stream

Papua
Stream

Taipara
Stream

35

The Pinnacles

36
37

Vaimaanga

Fernland
Reservoir

Water
Intake

Wigmore's
Waterfall

39
40
38

Ara
Metua

Rutaki
Passage

41

42
Ara
Tapu

43

Papua Passage

Papua
Passage

Avaavaroa
Passage

N

0   1   2 km

RAROTONGA

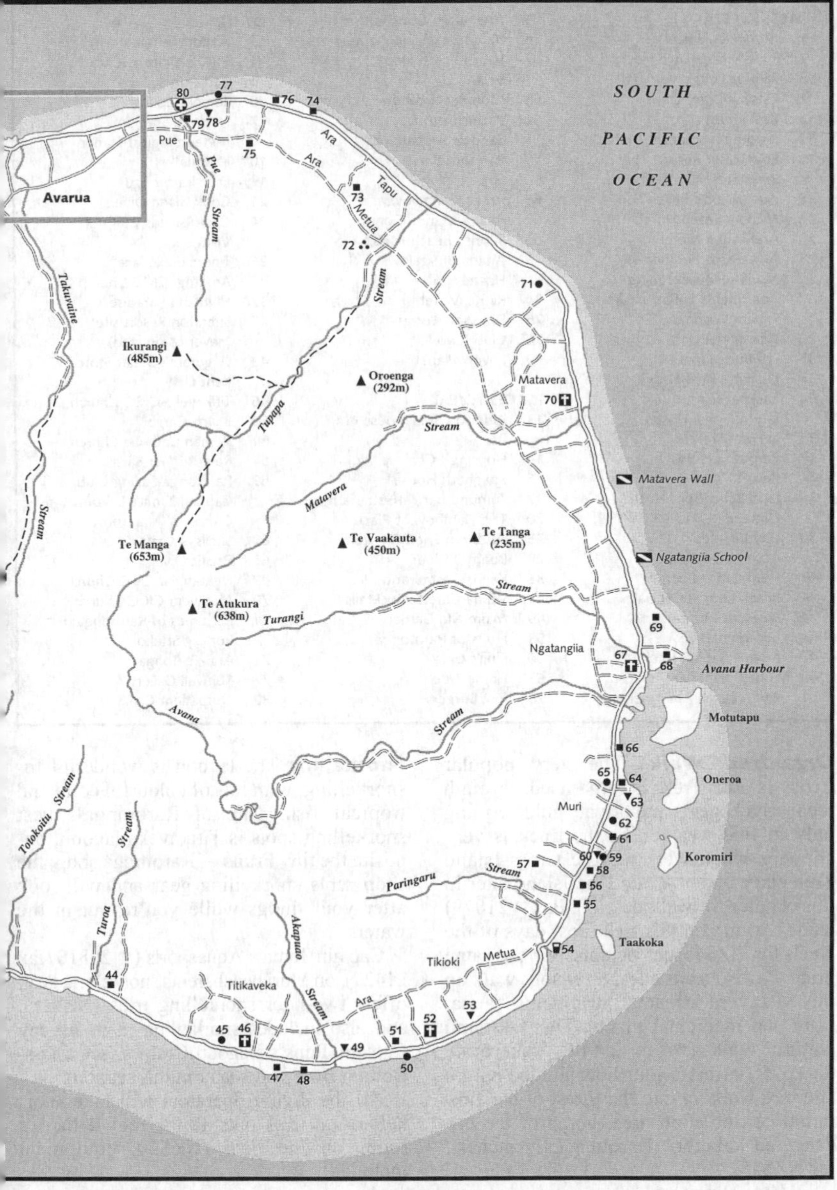

SOUTH

PACIFIC

OCEAN

Avarua

Pue

80 77
79 78 76 74
75

73

72

71

Ikurangi
(485m)

Oroenga
(292m)

Matavera

70

Matavera Wall

Ngatangiia School

Te Manga
(653m)

Te Vaakauta
(450m)

Te Tanga
(235m)

Te Atukura
(638m)

Turangi

Ngatangiia

67
68

69

Avana Harbour

Motutapu

66

65 64
63

Muri

62
61

Oneroa

Koromiri

57
60 59
58
56
55

Taakoka

44

54

Titikaveka

Tikioki

45 46

49

47 48

51

50

52

53

COOK ISLANDS

RAROTONGA

PLACES TO STAY
1   Matareka Hostel
2   Tiare Village Dive Hostel
8   Airport Lodge
11 Oasis Village; Oasis Restaurant
12 Rarotongan Sunset Motel
16 Edgewater Resort; The Brasserie; Mals Bar
18 Aunty Noo's Beach Lodge
22 Manuia Beach Hotel
23 Are-Renga Motel
28 Ati's Beach Bungalows
30 Maria's Housekeeping Apartments & Backpackers; Exham Wichman Woodcarving
31 Etu Bungalows
33 Puaikura Reef Lodge
34 Backpackers International Hostel
35 Lagoon Lodges
37 Rarotongan Beach Resort
38 Piri's Beachfront Hostel & Cottage
39 Daydreamer Accommodation
43 Palm Grove Lodge
44 Beach Lodge; Official Residence of Queen's Representative
47 Moana Sands Hotel
48 Little Polynesian
51 Raina Beach Apartments

55 Aremango Guesthouse
56 Vara's Beach House
57 Vara's Beach House Villa
58 Muri Beachcomber
61 Pacific Resort; Sandals Restaurant; Barefoot Bar
64 Sokala Villas
66 Aroko Bungalows
68 Avana Marina Condos
69 Sunrise Beach Motel
73 Ariana Bungalows & Hostel
74 Kii Kii Motel
75 Sea View Lodge
76 Club Raro
79 Lovely Planet

PLACES TO EAT
13 Alberto's Steakhouse & Bar
14 Hopsing's Chinese Wok
15 Spaghetti House
17 Tumunu Bar & Restaurant
20 The Flamboyant Place
25 Southern Fried Chicken
29 Bunny's Diner
36 Kaena Restaurant
41 Vaima Cafe & Cocktails
49 Maire Nui Gardens & Cafe
53 Fruits of Rarotonga
60 Emil's Cafe
63 Flame Tree
78 Just Burgers

OTHER
3   Airport Terminal
4   RSA & Citizens Club
5   Parliament
6   Tereora College
7   National Stadium
9   Meteorological Station
10 Hospital
19 Dive Rarotonga
21 Cook Island Divers
24 Cook Islands Cultural Village
26 Tinomana Palace
27 Arorangi CICC Church
32 Highland Paradise
40 Sheraton Resort site (never completed)
42 Wigmore's Super Store
45 Kent Hall
46 Titikaveka CICC Church
50 Beach Cargo
52 Roman Catholic Church
54 Reef Runner Bar
59 Rarotonga Sailing Club; Captain Tama's Lagoon Cruizes & Aquasports
62 Shells & Craft
65 Pacific Divers
67 Ngatangiia CICC Church
70 Matavera CICC Church
71 Perfumes of Rarotonga; Pottery Studio
72 Arai-Te-Tonga
77 Kenwall Gallery
80 Outpatient Clinic

Organised Walks The very popular Cross-Island Trek is organised through local travel agents and private guides, going only in fine weather, as the track is very slippery when wet (see the Cross-Island Trek entry under Around the Island later in this chapter for walk details). Pa (☎ 21079) leads a group on this trek most days of the week for NZ$45 per person. For the same price, Pa also leads a less strenuous walk up the Matavera stream, introducing fauna, flora and medicinal plants. The Takitumu Nature Walk (☎/fax 29906, kakerori@ tca.co.ck) offers a four hour guided nature and bird walk up into the forest of the Takitumu conservation area, home of the endangered kakerori (Rarotonga flycatcher), for NZ$35.

Snorkelling The lagoon is wonderful for snorkelling, with lots of colourful coral and tropical fish. One of Rarotonga's best snorkelling spots is Titikaveka lagoon, opposite the tiny Fruits of Rarotonga shop; the shop rents snorkelling gear and will look after your things while you're out in the water.

Captain Tama's Aquasports (☎ 20810, fax 21427), on Muri beach, rents snorkelling gear, offers two-hour snorkelling trips (NZ$25), and also includes snorkelling in its all-day Captain Tama's Lagoon Cruizes (see Glass-Bottom Boat Tours later in this section).

All the diving operators will take snorkellers on trips outside the reef if there's room on the boat (NZ$20, equipment included).

To buy your own snorkelling gear, visit The Dive Shop in Avarua.

Diving Outside the reef the diving is good. There are canyons, coral, caves and tunnels, and the reef drop-off goes from 20m right down to 4000m. Most diving is done at 3 to 30m. See the 'South Pacific Diving' special section for some of the island's best dives. Diving operators include:

Cook Island Divers
(☎ 22483, fax 22484,
gwilson@gatepoly.co.ck)
PO Box 1002
Dive Rarotonga
(☎ 21873, fax 21878,
jbateman@tumunu.co.ck)
PO Box 38
Pacific Divers
(☎/fax 22450, dive@pacificdivers.co.ck)
PO Box 110

All offer morning and afternoon trips outside the reef for certified divers (NZ$60/ 100 for one/two dives).

Cook Island Divers and Pacific Divers offer courses leading to PADI or NAUI certification (NZ$425), plus shorter courses designed to give an initial feel for diving (NZ$60). Ask about night dives.

Surfing Rarotonga doesn't offer the world's best surfing, but spots worth trying are in Avarua right in front of the traffic circle, Avana Harbour, Black Rock and Matavera. Ollies Surf Gear (☎ 20558 or ☎ 27999, fax 20202) sells surfing supplies and a map of Rarotonga's best surfing spots.

Other Watersports Muri lagoon is the best place for swimming, windsurfing, sailing and kayaking. Sailing races start from Muri beach every Saturday at 1 pm. Watersports equipment can be hired on Muri beach at Captain Tama's Aquasports; sailing and windsurfing lessons are available. Rarotongan Beach Resort also rents out watersports equipment.

Deep-Sea Fishing Right off the reef deep-sea fishing is excellent. The *Seafari*

Weddings

On Rarotonga, Captain Tama's Island Paradise Weddings (☎/fax 20810, weddings@ tamascruizes.co.ck), PO Box 3017, organises many types of weddings. Most popular are beach weddings on the *motu* of Koromiri. Music, photos, video, flowers and food can all be arranged. The Rarotongan Beach Resort arranges weddings for guests and others; Little Polynesian arranges weddings for its guests only (see Places to Stay in the Around the Island section later).

(☎ 20328, fax 20310), Pacific Marine Charters (☎ 21237, fax 25237) and Avana Charters (☎ 28270 or ☎ 20270 after hours, fax 27270, raroinfo@citours.co.ck) offer five-hour deep-sea fishing tours for NZ$85 to $95 per person. The *Angela II* (☎ 20850) costs NZ$70 for a three to four hour trip. Brent's Fishing Tours (☎ 23356, fax 23354, bafisher@oyster.net.ck) takes a tour around the island on an 8m (26 foot) glass-bottom catamaran (NZ$60). Beco Game Fishing Charters (☎ 21525 or ☎ 24125, fax 21505, beco@gatepoly.co.ck) offers four-hour catamaran fishing tours (NZ$85).

Whale-Watching Humpback whales visit the Cook Islands from July to October; you might see them just outside the reef. Pacific Divers offers whale-watching trips in season (NZ$50 per person).

Glass-Bottom Boat Tours Based at Muri beach, Captain Tama's Lagoon Cruizes (☎ 20810 or ☎ 21427, fax 21427, weddings@tamascruizes.co.ck) operates glass-bottom boat tours of the lagoon. The tours cruise out to some fine snorkelling spots (gear is provided) and then to Koromiri *motu* (island) in the lagoon for a barbecue lunch and entertainment. Tours (NZ$38) run daily except Sunday from 11 am to 3.30 pm (Sunday by arrangement).

The Reef Sub (☎ 25837) is a semisubmersible viewing vessel that goes outside the reef. Two-hour cruises (NZ$35) depart twice daily from Avatiu Harbour.

Horse Riding Aroa Pony Trek (☎ 21415), near the Rarotongan Beach Resort, offer horse riding tours. Two-hour rides cost NZ$30 (children NZ$20); bookings are essential.

Other Sports Public tennis courts are dotted around the island. Tennis courts and rental gear are available at the Edgewater and Rarotongan Beach resorts (phone for reservations – see Places to Stay under Around the Island later in this section). Lawn bowling is held at the Rarotonga Bowling Club (☎ 26277) in Avarua most Saturdays. The nine-hole Rarotonga Golf Club (☎ 20621) is just south of the airport.

The Topshape Health & Fitness Centre (☎ 21254), in Avarua, is open weekdays 6.30 am to 7 pm, Saturday 8 am to noon.

Scenic Flights A 20 minute flight with Air Rarotonga (☎ 22888) costs NZ$55 per person.

Organised Tours

Circle-island tours provide an insight into many aspects of Rarotongan history and culture. The Cook Islands Cultural Village (☎ 21314, fax 25557) afternoon circle-island tour is good value, starting with an island-style lunch and a show of traditional Cook Islands legends, song and dance (NZ$25). Raro Tours (☎ 25325 or ☎ 25324, fax 25326) offers a 3½ hour circle-island tour weekdays (NZ$25). Raro Safari Tours (☎ 23629 or ☎ 22627 after hours) does an inland 4WD Jeep expedition (NZ$45, children under 10 free) twice a day, every day. Buzz Tours (☎ 23470, fax 21907) offers excursions to the outer islands.

Reservations are essential on all tours; all run only when there are sufficient numbers.

Getting Around

Air Raro Tours (☎ 25325 or ☎ 25324, fax 25326) operates an airport shuttle service (NZ$10/20 one way/return).

Bus Bus services run around the coast road in both directions, departing from the bus stop at Cook's Corner Arcade in Avarua. Clockwise buses depart hourly 7 am to 4 pm weekdays, 8 am to 1 pm Saturday. Anti-clockwise buses depart hourly 8.25 am to 4.30 pm weekdays, 8.30 to 11.30 am Saturday. Night buses operate on a more limited schedule. Fares are NZ$2.50 for one ride, NZ$4 return, and NZ$17 for a 10-ride ticket. Cook's Island Bus (☎ 25512, or ☎ 20349 after hours) has information and timetables. You can flag the bus down anywhere along its route.

Car, Motorcycle & Bicycle To rent a motor vehicle you must obtain a local driving licence (NZ$10) from the police station in Avarua, a straightforward procedure. Your home driving licence or passport is needed for identification. Driving is on the left-hand side of the road.

Car rental costs around NZ$60 to $70 per day, Jeeps NZ$75 to $85; significantly cheaper for several days or per week.

Hire motorcycles from car rental agencies for NZ$20 to $25 per day, NZ$90 to $120 per week. Many hotels also rent motorcycles.

Mountain bike rentals cost around NZ$5 to $10 per day, NZ$40 per week. Many of the companies listed here rent bicycles, as do many hotels.

Rental companies include:

Avis Rental Cars
 (☎ 22833, fax 21702) Avarua
BT Bike Hire
 (☎ 23586) Arorangi
Budget Rent-A-Car & Polynesian Bike Hire
 (☎ 20895, fax 20888) Avarua
Hogan's Service Centre
 (☎ 22632, fax 23632) Arorangi
Rarotonga Rentals
 (☎ 22326, fax 22739) Avatiu
Tara's Rental Bikes
 (☎ 20757) Muri
Tipani Rentals
 (☎ 22328 or ☎ 21617, fax 25611) Arorangi
Vaine's Rental Bikes
 (☎ 20331) Muri

Taxi Local taxi operators include:

A's Taxis
 (☎ 27021) in Avarua

BK Taxis
   (☎ 20019) in Ruatonga
JP Taxis
   (☎ 26572) in Arorangi
Muri Beach Taxis
   (☎ 21625) in Muri
Ngatangiia Taxis
   (☎ 22238) in Ngatangiia
Parekura Taxis
   (☎ 26490) in Avarua

Rates are around NZ$1.50 per kilometre; it costs around NZ$20 to go from Muri to the airport.

AVARUA
• pop 10,900

Avarua, the capital of the Cook Islands and Rarotonga's principal town, lies on the middle of the north coast, about 2km east of the airport. This relaxed town has all the basic services and some interesting places to visit. If you're looking for nightlife, Avarua is probably where you'll find it.

Orientation & Information

There's only one main road, the Ara Maire Nui, and it's right along the waterfront, with a strip down the middle with plenty of shady trees. An obvious landmark is the traffic circle near the Takuvaine stream and the Avarua Harbour entrance. West along the main road is Avatiu Harbour, where the inter-island passenger cargo ships are based. The airport is 1km or so further west.

For information about Avarua see Information under Rarotonga, earlier.

Thing to See

Cook Islands stamps, coins and banknotes are all international collectors' items. The Cook Islands **Philatelic Bureau** (☎ 29336), next door to the post office, sells uncirculated mint and proof sets of coins and banknotes, plus collectors' editions of Cook Islands stamps. It's open weekdays 8 am to 4 pm.

Rarotonga Breweries (☎ 21084) produces Cook's Lager. Free 15-minute tours operate Monday, Wednesday and Thursday at 2 pm, including a free glass of the amber liquid.

South of the traffic circle, on Takuvaine Rd, is **Papeiha Stone**, upon which Papeiha

stood in 1823 when he preached the gospel in Rarotonga for the first time; it sits atop a raised traffic circle near its original site.

Half a block east of the main traffic circle on the inland side of the main road are the **Para O Tane Palace** and **Taputapuatea**, the palace area of Makea Takau who was the ariki of this district in 1888 when the British officially took control of the Cook Islands. The palace is the residence of Takau's descendent, Makea Ariki, and is not open to the public. Named after a temple on Raiatea in the Society Islands, Taputapuatea was one of the largest and most sacred marae on Rarotonga before it was destroyed by the missionaries.

One long block east of the traffic circle, the **Beachcomber Gallery** (☎ 21939) displays arts and crafts in a building constructed in 1845 by the LMS for its Sunday school. You can visit the workshop here to see black pearl jewellery and shell carvings being made.

The fine, white-painted **CICC church** building, south of the Beachcomber Gallery, was built of coral in 1853. The **graveyard** around the church is worth a leisurely browse. At the front is a monument to Papeiha and just to the left (as you face the church) is the grave of Albert Henry, the first prime minister of the Cook Islands. The main church service is held Sunday at 10 am.

Inland behind the Para O Tane Palace, the small **Cook Islands Library & Museum Society** (☎ 26468) houses a collection of rare books and literature on the Pacific, which you may be able to inspect. You can apply for a temporary library card. The small museum (admission NZ$2) has an interesting collection. The library and museum are open Monday to Saturday 9 am to 1 pm, plus Tuesday from 4 to 8 pm.

The Fiji-based **University of the South Pacific** (USP; ☎ 29415, fax 21315) has its Cook Islands Centre opposite the library. A wide selection of books on the Pacific, published by the university, is on sale.

Another small museum and library are the **National Museum** and **National Library** (☎ 20725), at the front of the National Auditorium complex.

AVARUA

PLACES TO STAY
49 Paradise Inn
56 Central Motel
64 Atupa Orchid Units

PLACES TO EAT
2   Southern Fried Chicken
3   Palace Takeaways
14 Ronnie's; The First Club
16 Mana Court – Black Pearl
    Cafe; The Dive Shop
20 Mama's Cafe; Foodland
    Supermarket
29 Banana Court Bar; Blue Note
    Cafe; Arasena Gallery; Island
    Hopper Vacations
34 Breez'n Cafe
36 Trader Jack's
37 Browne's Arcade – Metua's
    Café; TJ's Nightclub; Tuki's
    Pareu
41 Staircase Restaurant/Bar;
    Topshape Health & Fitness
    Centre
46 Portofino

OTHER
1   CITC Wholesale Supermarket;
    CITC Liquor Centre
4   Paradise Bar
5   Ports Authority; Taio Shipping
6   Ingram House
7   Odds & Ends; Rarotonga

Rentals; DHL
8   Punanga Nui Outdoor Market
9   Children's Playground
10 Pacific Supplies; June's
    Boutique; June's Pearls; South
    Seas International; Kenwall
    Gallery
11 St Joseph's Catholic Cathedral
12 Meatco Supermarket
13 Budget Rent-A-Car
15 Vonnia's General Store
17 Linmar's Department Store
18 Island Craft Ltd
19 Westpac Bank
21 Stars Travel; ANZ Bank; Bounty
    Bookshop; Ollies Surf Gear;
    Budget Rent-A-Car
22 Police Station
23 The Energy Centre Petrol Station
24 Bus Stop; Cooks Corner
    Arcade – Alliance Française de
    Rarotonga; Cook's Corner
    Cafe; Simone's Bistro; Tangee's
    Hideaway Bar; The Pearl Shop
25 CITC Shopping Centre – CITC
    Department Store; Pharmacy &
    Duty-Free; Cocophoto
26 Avis Rent-A-Car
27 Cook Islands Tourism
    Corporation
28 Pearl Factory; Dr Wolfgang
    Losacker
30 Post Office; Philatelic Bureau;

New Zealand High Commission
31 Ministry of Foreign Affairs &
    Immigration
32 Takitumu Conservation Area
33 Seven-in-One Coconut Tree
35 T-Shirt Factory
38 Empire Theatre
39 Snowbird Laundromat
40 Para O Tane Palace &
    Taputapuatea Marae
42 Beachcomber Gallery
43 The Bakery
44 Perfumes of Rarotonga; Pearl
    Hut
45 Cook Islands News
47 Are Tiki Shop
48 Vakatini Palace
50 National Museum
51 National Library
52 National Auditorium
53 Avarua CICC Church
54 University of the South Pacific
    (USP)
55 Cook Islands Library &
    Museum Society
57 Rarotonga Breweries
58 Papeiha Stone
59 Telecom
60 Prime Minister's Office
61 Rarotonga Bowling Club
62 Petrol Station
63 The Perfume Factory
65 Michael Taveoni's Studio

AVARUA

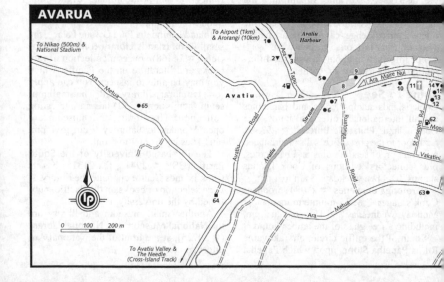

Places to Stay

The 14-unit **Central Motel** (☎ 25735, fax 25740, stopover@centralmotel.co.ck, PO Box 183), half a block inland from the post office, is very well kept and costs NZ$76 per night. **Paradise Inn** (☎ 20544, fax 22544, paradise@gatepoly.co.ck, PO Box 674) is just a short walk east on the main road. Although the beach here is not good for swimming, the amenities are good. Single/double/triple units cost NZ$73/80/93, budget singles NZ$47, family units NZ$99.

Places to Eat

Trader Jack's (☎ 26464 or ☎ 25464), on the seafront near the traffic circle, is one of Rarotonga's most popular bar-and-grill restaurants and both indoor and deck tables have great sea views. Lunch is served Monday to Saturday, dinner nightly. **Metua's Cafe** (☎ 20850), hidden away in Browne's Arcade, is an inexpensive open-air restaurant/bar open Monday to Thursday from 7.30 am to 10 pm, until 2 am Friday, midnight Saturday.

A little further east, **Staircase Restaurant/Bar** (☎ 22254), upstairs behind the Topshape fitness centre, is a family restaurant serving quality food at low prices. It's open Wednesday to Friday from 6.30 pm; reservations preferred.

Portofino (☎ 26480) on Avarua's east side is one of the best restaurants on the island, with an eclectic international menu and an extensive, reasonably priced winelist. It also has a takeaway menu with free delivery around the island. It's open Monday to Saturday 6.30 to 9.30 pm, until midnight on Friday.

For snacks and takeaway try popular **Mama's Cafe**, beside the Foodland supermarket (it has an ice-cream counter), and **Black Pearl Cafe**, a few doors down in the Mana Court. **Blue Note Cafe**, on the verandah of the Banana Court, is a fine place for coffee or lunch.

At Avatiu Harbour, **Palace Takeaways** is a favourite with locals and is open long hours – 8 am until midnight most days, until 2 am Saturday night and 4 am Friday night. Opposite this, **Southern Fried Chicken** is also popular and is open Monday to Saturday from 8 am to 10 pm.

CITC Wholesale Supermarket, near Avatiu Harbour, is Rarotonga's largest supermarket and has the widest selection. **Foodland** supermarket, in the centre of Avarua, also has a good selection.

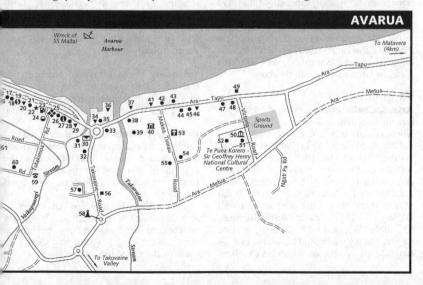

AVARUA

Fresh local produce and foods are available Saturday mornings at **Punanga Nui outdoor market** beside the waterfront near Avatiu Harbour. Early on any morning whole fresh fish is often sold here.

Entertainment

Piri Puruto III (☎ 20309) zips up coconut trees, demonstrates traditional firemaking and gives an entertaining one hour performance (NZ$12, children NZ$6) at various locations. He also offers a popular Sunday umukai and show, a fish barbecue, and other entertainment throughout the week.

The **Empire Theatre** shows films every night for NZ$5 (children NZ$2.50).

There are a variety of bars, many with entertainment. Typically they stay open until around midnight (until 2 am on Friday night). Many of the restaurant/bars have live music, including **Trader Jack's** (Thursday and Friday) and **Staircase Restaurant/Bar** (Wednesday and Friday). The intimate **Tangee's Hideaway Bar**, in Cook's Corner Arcade, has live music on Wednesday, Friday and Saturday.

TJ's Nightclub, a disco with super-loud music and flashing lights, is popular with young people. **Ronnie's** restaurant/bar is a popular drinking spot, especially on Friday night.

Two friendly bars featuring rousing live music for dancing on outdoor patios are **Paradise Bar**, at Avatiu Harbour (Wednesday, Friday and Saturday), and **Metua's Cafe**, in Browne's Arcade (Friday).

Shopping

Arts & Crafts Island Craft Ltd (☎ 22009) has an excellent selection of high-quality Cook Islands arts and crafts, including a collection of masks and spears. The Beachcomber Gallery (☎ 21939) has a wide selection of excellent weavings, tivaevae, paintings and jewellery. Local artists' works are displayed at Arasena Gallery (☎ 23476) at the Blue Note Cafe and at Kenwall Gallery (☎ 25527), beside Pacific Supplies. Exham Wichman (☎ 21180), a fine carver, has a shop behind his house in Arorangi. Michael Taveoni shows his excellent wood and stone carvings at his studio on the Ara Metua, behind the airport; stop when you see the large stone carvings. Judith Künzle (☎ 20959), one of Rarotonga's best artists, sells watercolours of local land and seascapes, and drawings and paintings of Cook Islands dancers.

Pearls & Jewellery For pearl jewellery, loose pearls, pearls still embedded in their shells, carved mother-of-pearl and other creations, go to The Pearl Shop in Cook's Corner Arcade, The Pearl Factory near the Banana Court Bar, the Beachcomber Gallery, Maui Pearls and June's Pearls.

Shells & Shell Products You'll find shell jewellery at many of the arts and crafts places mentioned earlier in this section. Necklaces, handbags, fans, wind chimes, statues, jewellery boxes and other items are sold at Island Craft Ltd and the Beachcomber Gallery.

Perfumes, Soaps & Coconut Oil Pure coconut oil (scented or plain) and locally made perfumes and soaps made from pure coconut oil are sold at The Perfume Factory, on the Ara Metua road just behind town, heading west, and at Perfumes of Rarotonga, which has one shop in Avarua and another on the main road in Matavera village. You can taste and buy locally produced liqueurs at either place.

Tattooing Michael Taveoni practises this traditional Polynesian art form at his studio in Atupa, behind the airport. Or there's T's Tatts (☎ 23576), operated by Tetini Pekepo.

Pareu & T-Shirts Colourful tie-dyed and printed *pareu* (sarongs) are sold at many shops around Avarua. Tuki's Pareu, on the east side of town, and Punanga Nui outdoor market, beside Avatiu Harbour, offer good selections.

The T-Shirt Factory has an outlet in Avarua beside the traffic circle. Visitors are welcome to stop by the factory, behind the airport at the Tangaroa Shopping Centre, to see how the printed shirts are made.

AROUND THE ISLAND

Most island attractions are on or near the Ara Tapu coastal road. If you hire a vehicle or take a circle-island tour on the Ara Metua (running slightly inland parallel to the Ara Tapu) you'll see another side to the island – swamp taro fields, goats and pigs grazing in pawpaw patches, citrus groves, men on ancient tractors and ancestral graves beside houses.

The following description moves around the island anticlockwise, starting from Avarua. Distances indicated are from the centre of Avarua.

Cemetery (2.5km)

Opposite the airport terminal is a small graveyard, known locally as the 'brickyard'. The controversial Australian cancer-cure specialist Milan Brych set himself up here after being thrown out of Australia. Cancer patients who died despite his treatment are buried in the graveyard. Tom Neale, the hermit of Suwarrow Atoll, is also buried here.

Black Rock (6.5km)

Black Rock (Tuoro) is said to be the departure point from where the spirits of the dead commence the voyage back to the legendary homeland of 'Avaiki. This is also where the missionary Papeiha is supposed to have swum ashore, clasping the Bible over his head. Actually he was rowed ashore in a small boat!

Arorangi (8km)

On Rarotonga's west coast, Arorangi was the first missionary-built village and was conceived of as a model for all the other villages on the island. Its main place of interest is the 1849 CICC church. Papeiha is buried here. Rising up behind Arorangi is the flat-topped peak of Raemaru (365m).

Carver Exham Wichman's arts shop (☎ 21180) is behind his house in Arorangi (see the Budget entry under Places to Stay in the Around The Island section later).

Cultural Village (7km)

Visiting the Cook Islands Cultural Village (☎ 21314, fax 25557) on Arorangi's back

road is a delightful experience. Guided tours, beginning weekdays at 10 am, visit traditional huts and include demonstrations of many aspects of Cook Islands culture; reservations are essential. Tours are followed by a feast of traditional foods, a show of music, dance and chants, and an optional afternoon round-the-island tour.

Highland Paradise (9km)

High atop a slope behind Arorangi, Highland Paradise is on the site of the village where the Tinomana people lived before the introduction of Christianity. The Pirangi family, descendants of Tinomana Ariki, telling stories of the old days, take visitors on a two hour tour of the site, which is followed by a traditional umukai lunch. Tours cost NZ$30 per person (or NZ$35 including transport); bookings are essential (☎ 20611).

Muri (9.5km)

Muri beach, on Muri lagoon on the southeast side of the island, is particularly beautiful. The shallow water has a sandy bottom dotted with countless sea cucumbers and some coral formations. Out towards the reef are four small motu: Taakoka, Koromiri, Oneroa and Motutapu. Taakoka is volcanic; the others are sand cays.

Shells & Craft (☎ 22275), on the main road, has a remarkable array of shells for sale.

Matavera (5.5km)

The old CICC church here is especially lovely at night when the outside is lit up. The scenery inland between Matavera and Avarua is particularly fine. Perfumes of Rarotonga (☎ 25238) is on the main road in Matavera. There's a pottery shop at the rear. Jillian Sobieska (☎ 21079) has an art studio on a back road in Matavera.

Arai-Te-Tonga (3.5km)

Just before you arrive back in Avarua a small sign points off the road to the most important marae site on the island, Arai-Te-Tonga. A great marae is on your right as you go down the small road heading inland towards Arai-Te-Tonga. When you meet the

Ara Metua there's a stone-marked *koutu* (ancient open-air royal courtyard) site in front of you; walk down the Ara Metua to your left and you'll see on your right yet another ceremonial ground.

Cross-Island Trek

This three to four hour trek, from the north to south coasts via the 413m Te Rua Manga (the Needle), is the most popular walk on Rarotonga. It can also be done as a shorter walk from the north end to the Needle and back again. It's important that you do the walk in a north-south direction, as the chances of taking a wrong turn are greater if you try it from the other direction. Be sure to wear adequate shoes and to take plenty of drinking water and mosquito repellent. Parts of the walk get extremely slippery in wet weather.

The road to the starting point runs south from Avatiu Harbour. The public bus will drop you at the harbour, from where you can begin the walk; you can flag the bus down when you reach the coast road at the end of the track. Note that on Saturday the last daytime bus departs from Avarua at 1 pm, and there are no more buses until the night bus schedule starts at 6 pm. There is no service on Sunday. If you come on an organised trek across the island, hotel transfers are provided at both ends (see Organised Walks earlier in this chapter).

If you're driving, continue on the road up the valley by the Avatiu Stream, until you reach a prominent sign announcing the beginning of the walk and that vehicles cannot be taken past this point. A private vehicle road continues for about 1km.

A footpath takes off from the end of this vehicle road. After about 10 minutes it drops down and crosses a small stream. Avoid following the white plastic power-cable track up the valley; instead pick up the track beside the massive boulder on the ridge to your left, after the stream crossing.

From here the track climbs steeply all the way to the Needle, (about 45 minutes). At the first sight of the Needle there's a boulder in the middle of the path – a nice place for a rest. A little further on is a T-junction.

Te Rua Manga is a 10 minute walk to the right. Up to now you've been ascending a ridge running in a north-south direction; at this junction it intersects with a ridge running in an east-west direction. This is an important junction and you will return to it after visiting the Needle.

Actually climbing the Needle is strictly for very serious rock climbers – it's high and sheer. You can, however, scramble around the north side to a sheer drop and a breathtaking view from the north-western corner. Take care on this climb: the ledge is very narrow and there's a long unprotected drop which would be fatal if you slipped. Do *not* try to climb around to the southern side of the Needle – it offers no view and is extremely dangerous.

Retrace your steps back to the T-junction, from where the left fork heads east. Just before you reach the T-junction you'll come to a path along a white plastic electric-cable casing heading to the right (south). Some guides take this way, as the traditional track is slightly more difficult. However, from the T-junction, take the traditional track, which drops slightly and then climbs to a small peak that gives you the best view of the Needle. From here the track leads down a long, slippery ridge for about half an hour. This long descent can be positively treacherous in wet weather.

After about 30 minutes the track meets the Papua stream and follows it down the hill, zigzagging back and forth across the water. After about 45 minutes, the track emerges in fernland. Here it veers away from the stream to the right, passing through the fernland. Be sure to stick to the main track; there are several places where newer, minor tracks seem to take off towards the stream but these end at dangerous spots upstream from the waterfall. After about 15 minutes the main track turns back towards the stream, bringing you to the bottom of the beautiful **Wigmore's Waterfall** – the mosquitoes here are particularly nasty. The pool under the fall is a real delight for a dip. A rough dirt road leads from the south coast up to Wigmore's Waterfall. It's about a 15 minute walk down this road to the coast road.

Places to Stay

Rarotonga has places to stay in every budget range. Most places have cooking and laundry facilities for guests and most provide free airport pick-up. All prices given here include VAT (12.5%).

Places to Stay – Budget

Lovely Planet (☎/fax 25100, PO Box 711) offers budget accommodation for NZ$20 per person (negotiable). *Tiare Village Dive Hostel* (☎ 23466, ☎/fax 21874, tiarevil@gatepoly.co.ck, PO Box 719), a comfortable backpackers haven famous for its hospitality, is on Kaikaveka Drive, about 3km from the centre of Avarua. Nightly per-person cost is NZ$18 in triple rooms in the main house, NZ$20 in single/double rooms in chalets, and NZ$25 in double poolside units, with special weekly rates. There's also a TV room, board games and a library.

Aunty Noo's Beach Lodge (☎ 21253, fax 23629, PO Box 449) is in Arorangi, close to the beach – dorms/doubles cost NZ$8/10 per person.

Maria's Housekeeping Apartments & Backpackers (☎ 21180, PO Box 777) is a pleasant duplex behind the family home of Exham and Maria Wichman in Arorangi. Self-contained units/dorm beds cost NZ$18/15 per person.

Backpackers International Hostel (☎ 21849, fax 21847, annabill@backpackers.co.ck, PO Box 878), in Kavera, is an old favourite. With discounts for stays of four days or more, singles/doubles or twins cost NZ$26/15 per person. Triples and an eight person dorm cost NZ$14 per person.

Piri's Beachfront Hostel & Cottage (☎/fax 20309, PO Box 624) is on a beautiful stretch of beach at Vaimaanga on the island's south. Rates are NZ$12.50 in the dorm, NZ$14 in a twin or double with shared facilities, NZ$15 with private bath, and NZ$20 for a single room.

Vara's Beach House (☎ 23156, fax 22619, backpack@varasbeach.co.ck, PO Box 434) has one house on Muri beach, and a luxurious villa and cottage up the hill. Rates are NZ$18 per person in dorms, NZ$33/42 for single/double rooms, NZ$60 for double rooms with private bath. The cottage can be booked as a self-contained house (NZ$80 for two people).

Spacious double and triple rooms at Muri's popular *Aremango Guesthouse* (☎ 24362, fax 22739, aremango@hotmail.com, PO Box 714), on the coast road, cost NZ$16.50 per person.

The *Beach Lodge* (☎ 28270 or ☎ 20270 after hours, fax 27270, raroinfo@citours.co.ck, PO Box 611) is beside the official residence of the Queen's Representative (QR) in Titikaveka, in a beautiful spot opposite a white sandy beach good for swimming and snorkelling. Three self-contained two-bedroom apartments, sleeping up to five people, cost NZ$50 a night each.

Places to Stay – Mid-Range

Kii Kii Motel (☎ 21937, fax 22937, PO Box 68, relax@kiikiimotel.co.ck), about 2km east of Avarua on the beach, has a swimming pool as the beach here is not good for swimming. Prices range from NZ$68/84 in budget singles/doubles to $115/143 in rooms overlooking the sea.

Ati's Beach Bungalows (☎ 21546, fax 25546, bungalows@atisbeach.co.ck, PO Box 693) is on a good stretch of beach in Arorangi. Self-contained studio units cost NZ$80 (no view), beachside studio bungalows cost NZ$132.

Daydreamer Accommodation (☎ 25965, fax 25964, byoung@daydreamer.co.ck, PO Box 1048), opposite a fine beach at Vaimaanga, has pleasant one-bedroom units (NZ$100) and also a two-bedroom unit (NZ$150).

Aroko Bungalows (☎ 23625 or ☎ 21625, fax 24625, aroko@bungalows.co.ck, PO Box 850), in a tranquil setting by Muri lagoon, has garden/beachfront bungalows for NZ$90/100.

Lagoon Lodges (☎ 22020, fax 22021, des@lagoon.co.ck, PO Box 45) is on the coast road opposite the beach, 400m from the Rarotongan Beach Resort. The lodges are set back from the road, and are safe for children. Prices for spacious bungalows set around a garden cost from NZ$135 to $190 for larger units.

In Titikaveka on the south-east of the island are two pleasant places with rooms facing directly onto a fine beach with great snorkelling. *Little Polynesian* (☎ 24280, fax 21585, littlepoly@beach.co.ck, PO Box 366) is private, secluded and intimate, with eight beachfront studio units (NZ$195) and a lagoonside cottage (NZ$235), each with a full kitchen; children over 12 years welcome. *Moana Sands Hotel* (☎ 26189, fax 22189, beach@moanasands.co.ck, PO Box 1007) has 12 rooms without kitchen for NZ$179/199.

Places to Stay – Top End
Pacific Resort (☎ 20427, fax 21427, thomas@pacificresort.co.ck, PO Box 790), on Muri beach, is probably Rarotonga's most attractive medium-sized resort. Self-contained units cost from NZ$273, including breakfast.

Sokala Villas (☎ 29200, fax 21222, villas@sokala.co.ck, PO Box 82) is an assortment of seven self-contained timber villas right on Muri beach, all excellently appointed. It's especially popular for couples and honeymooners – children under 12 years not accepted. Prices range from NZ$295 to $440 – ask about 'early bird' discounts.

Avana Marina Condos (☎ 20836, fax 22991, avanaco@oyster.net.ck, PO Box 869), on Muri lagoon, overlooks Avana Harbour. It has its own jetty and the units come with a boat, plus there's a private beach. Children are welcome. The cost is NZ$350 per night.

Large Resorts The 'rack rates' at the two resorts are high, but most business comes from package holidays, which makes the rates cheaper.

The *Rarotongan Beach Resort* (☎ 25800, fax 25799, info@rarotongan.co.ck, PO Box 103), on the south-west corner of the island, has its own beach, beachfront swimming pool and spa pool, activities and dining areas. Singles/doubles range from NZ$240 (garden rooms) to $480 (suites). The resort is wheelchair accessible, and some rooms have facilities for travellers with disabilities.

Edgewater Resort (☎ 25435, fax 25475, stay@edgewater.co.ck, PO Box 12), on the beachfront at Arorangi, has a beachfront swimming pool and a travel desk for booking activities. Prices range from NZ$210 (garden rooms) to $390 (deluxe suites).

Places to Stay – Renting a House
A fully equipped two bedroom house usually costs around NZ$125 to $300 per week. *Cook Islands Commercial Realty Brokers Ltd* (☎ 25264, fax 25265, property@realty.co.ck, PO Box 779) rents houses for a minimum of three nights (early bookings advised). *Cook Islands Tours & Travel* (☎ 28270 or ☎ 20270 after hours, fax 27270, raroinfo@citours.co.ck, PO Box 611) rents houses, apartments and beach cottages.

Kii Kii Holiday Cottages (☎ 21937, fax 22937, relax@kiikiimotel.co.ck, PO Box 68) rents self-contained two-bedroom cottages around the island, opposite sandy beaches, each sleeping up to four people, for NZ$395 per week, plus power. Also check the classified ads in the *Cook Islands News*.

Places to Eat
Restaurants Restaurants are scattered at distances around the island, with more on the west than on the east side. Reservations are generally a good idea.

In Arorangi, *Oasis Restaurant* (☎ 28213), specialising in chargrilled steaks, is simple but pleasant, and the food is delicious. It's open Monday to Saturday from 6 pm. *Alberto's Steakhouse* (☎ 23597) in Arorangi is another very pleasant steakhouse. *Hopsing's Chinese Wok* (☎ 20367), also in Arorangi, serves Chinese and European dishes; it's open nightly from 6 pm.

At the entrance to the Edgewater Resort, *Spaghetti House* (☎ 25441) has air-con and tasty Italian food to eat there or take away; it's open nightly from 5 pm.

Tumunu Bar & Restaurant (☎ 20501), beside the Edgewater, has a pleasant outdoor barbecue area and an indoor restaurant/bar with attractive Polynesian touches. The menu includes vegetarian and children's meals. It's open nightly from 6 pm.

Muri has two fine moderately-priced restaurants. *Flame Tree (☎ 25123 after 3 pm)*, with an excellent international menu and artistic decor, is regarded by many as the best restaurant on the island; it's open for dinner nightly from 6.30 pm (reservations recommended). *Sandals Restaurant (☎ 20427)* at the Pacific Resort serves a continental buffet breakfast daily, and dinner from 6.30 pm nightly; the resort's *Barefoot Bar* is open daily for lunch and snacks.

Island Buffets *The Brasserie* at the Edgewater Resort *(☎ 25435)* in Arorangi has a weekly schedule of 'island night' buffets and theme dinners (NZ$25 to $40). *Ati's Beach Bungalows (☎ 21546)*, also in Arorangi, has an all-you-can-eat Sunday dinner buffet at 6.30 pm; book by Saturday. *Backpackers International Hostel (☎ 21849)* has its island buffet on Saturday; book by 4 pm Friday. The entertainer Piri Puruto III (☎ 20309) hosts a traditional Cook Islands umukai every Sunday. You can participate in the preparation and learn how it's done, and also see his entertaining show; book by 6 pm Saturday. See also Entertainment later in this section.

Snacks & Takeaways In Arorangi, *The Flamboyant Place* in the little shopping centre opposite Dive Rarotonga has inexpensive takeaways. It's open daily from 8 am until 1 or 2 am, Friday night till 4 am. Also in Arorangi, *Bunny's Diner* has basic breakfasts, burgers, sandwiches and groceries.

Maire Nui Gardens & Cafe (☎ 22796) in Titikaveka, on the south side of the island, has a beautiful, peaceful garden atmosphere and tasty food. It's open Monday to Saturday 8 am to 5 pm, Sunday noon to 5 pm.

Fruits of Rarotonga (☎ 21509) in Tikioki, also on the south side of the island, features reasonably priced home-made fruit products like jams, chutneys and relishes. It also serves morning and afternoon teas and sandwiches, and is opposite the island's best snorkelling spot.

Emil's Cafe (☎ 24853), on the main road at Muri, is a favourite with locals and visitors alike for its good food and coffee and its pleasant atmosphere; eat there or take away. It's open Monday to Saturday from around 9 am to 9 pm, Sunday 5 to 9 pm.

Markets & Supermarkets *Wigmore's Super Store* in Vaimaanga has a good selection of foods, good prices, and a wide variety of produce fresh from Wigmore's farm.

Entertainment

Island Nights Quoted prices for island nights at hotels – around NZ$35 – include buffet 'island meals'. To see the show only will cost NZ$5 to $10. The shows start about 8.30 or 9 pm, and afterwards there's usually a live band. *Rarotongan Beach Resort*, *Edgewater Resort*, *Pacific Resort* and *Club Raro* all hold island nights at least once or twice a week.

Bars At the Edgewater Resort, *Mals Bar* has entertainment every night. Nearby, the *Tumunu Bar & Restaurant* is cosy and has a weekly darts competition.

Aitutaki Atoll

• pop 2332   • area 20 sq km

Aitutaki is the Cooks' second most populated island and the second most visited by tourists. The hook-shaped island nestles in a huge triangular lagoon, measuring 12km across its base and 15km from top to bottom. The outer reef of the lagoon is dotted with beautiful motu.

Ask at your hotel if you should boil your drinking water. At some places, the water comes from underground and should be boiled first; at others it comes from a special rainwater tank.

History

Various legends tell of the first Polynesian settlers arriving at Aitutaki by canoe. The first settler was Ru, from 'Avaiki, who arrived with wives and family at the Akitua motu (now occupied by the Aitutaki Lagoon

AITUTAKI ATOLL

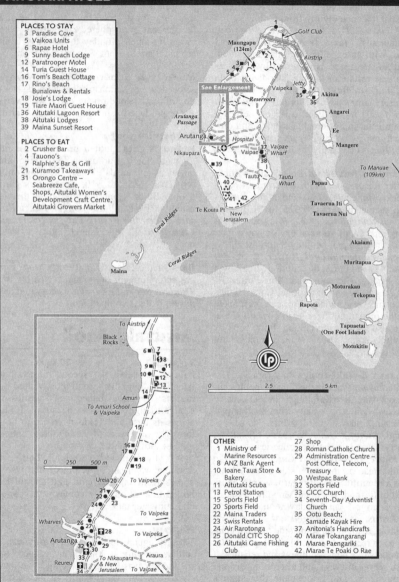

PLACES TO STAY
3 Paradise Cove
5 Vaikoa Units
6 Rapae Hotel
9 Sunny Beach Lodge
12 Paratrooper Motel
14 Turia Guest House
16 Tom's Beach Cottage
17 Rino's Beach
   Bunalows & Rentals
18 Josie's Lodge
19 Tiare Maori Guest House
36 Aitutaki Lagoon Resort
38 Aitutaki Lodges
39 Maina Sunset Resort

PLACES TO EAT
2 Crusher Bar
4 Tauono's
7 Ralphie's Bar & Grill
21 Kuramoo Takeaways
31 Orongo Centre –
   Seabreeze Cafe,
   Shops, Aitutaki Women's
   Development Craft Centre,
   Aitutaki Growers Market

OTHER
1 Ministry of
   Marine Resources
8 ANZ Bank Agent
10 Ioane Taua Store &
   Bakery
11 Aitutaki Scuba
13 Petrol Station
15 Sports Field
20 Sports Field
22 Maina Traders
23 Swiss Rentals
24 Air Rarotonga
25 Donald CITC Shop
26 Aitutaki Game Fishing
   Club
27 Shop
28 Roman Catholic Church
29 Administration Centre –
   Post Office, Telecom,
   Treasury
30 Westpac Bank
32 Sports Field
33 CICC Church
34 Seventh-Day Adventist
   Church
35 Ootu Beach;
   Samade Kayak Hire
37 Anitonia's Handicrafts
40 Marae Tokangarangi
41 Marae Paengariki
42 Marae Te Poaki O Rae

Resort). Aitutaki's original name was Ararau 'Enua o Ru ki te Moana (Ru in Search of Land over Sea) – the present name, *a'i tutaki*, means 'to keep the fire going'.

Aitutaki's European discoverer was Captain William Bligh, who arrived on the *Bounty* on 11 April 1789 (17 days before the famous mutiny). In 1821 Christian converts Papeiha and Vahapata arrived. The 1850s saw Aitutaki become a favourite port of call for whaling ships. During WWII the island went through great upheaval when a large US contingent built two long runways.

Orientation

You can make a tour of Aitutaki in just a few hours. The road runs near the coast most of the way, and passes through several pleasant villages. Arutanga, about halfway down the west coast, is the island's main settlement.

The New Zealand Department of Lands and Survey produces a 1:25,000 topographical map of Aitutaki showing the island's roads and trails and the coral formations in the lagoon. *What's On in the Cook Islands* and Jason's publications contain maps of Aitutaki.

Information

Money In the Administration Building, at the intersection of the two main roads in Arutanga, is the Treasury, where foreign currency and travellers cheques can be exchanged weekdays, 8 am to 3 pm. Westpac has a branch opposite the Administration Building, open on Wednesday only, 9.30 am to 3 pm. The ANZ bank agent, beside Ralphie's Bar & Grill in Amuri, is open weekdays but changes only New Zealand dollar travellers cheques.

Post & Communications Also in the Administration Building, the post and Telecom offices are open weekdays from 8 am to 4 pm. Aitutaki issues its own postage stamps.

Activities

Swimming & Snorkelling The best swimming, snorkelling and beaches are out around the lagoon motu. From beside the old

---

Aitutaki Gets a Mountain

According to legend, Aitutaki was once just a low atoll. The inhabitants decided they needed a mountain, so they went off across the sea in search of one. Coming to Rarotonga, they spotted Raemaru, the mountain behind the village of Arorangi, and decided it would be perfect. It was rather large for Aitutaki, however, so they decided they'd take just the top off and bring that home.

Late at night, they encircled Raemaru, thrust their spears in until they had severed the top from the bottom, and took off with it. When morning came, the Arorangi villagers set off in hot pursuit to reclaim their mountain. But the fierce Aitutakian warriors, holding the mountain aloft between them with their spears, beat the Rarotongans back with their single free hands. After bringing the mountain top to Aitutaki they placed it in the northern part of the island.

Back on Rarotonga, Raemaru today has a distinctly cut-off, flat-topped appearance.

Rapae Hotel you can walk all the way out to the outer reef on a natural coral causeway which starts 50m from the shore. There are interesting coral rockpools and places for snorkelling just inside the outer reef.

The snorkelling is pretty good along this stretch of coast all the way up to the airstrip, and is also good in the channel separating Akitua motu from the main island.

Diving Diving outside the lagoon is very relaxed, with small groups and warm water. Suitable for everyone from novices to experts, it's mostly drop-off diving, with visibility averaging 40m most days.

Neil Mitchell at Aitutaki Scuba (☎ 31103, fax 31310, scuba@aitutaki.net.ck) is a professional dive operator. One-tank dives cost NZ$70 (NZ$60 if you bring your own gear). Snorkellers are welcome (space permitting) at NZ$20 per person. A variety of PADI and NAUI diving certification courses are available. Contact Neil upon arrival.

Lagoon Cruises Several operators offer trips on the lagoon and to the motu. Most are full-day cruises and include transport to and from your accommodation, snorkelling gear and a barbecue fish lunch on the motu. Prices are around NZ$40 to $50 per person. Operators using motorised boats include Bishop's Lagoon Cruises (☎ 31009, fax 31493, bishopcruz@aitutaki.net.ck) and Ru's Cruise (☎ 31164).

Outrigger reef canoes are available at Tauono's (☎ 31562). A poled and guided tour, including snorkelling, swimming, fishing and a reef walk, costs NZ$25. Samade (☎ 31526) at Ootu beach offers catamaran lagoon cruises (NZ$70 for two) and sea kayak rental (NZ$15/20 per half/full day).

Paradise Islands Ltd (☎ 31248, fax 31398, lagoon@aitutaki.net.ck) offers lagoon cruises on the big 21m (69 foot) *Titiai-tonga* catamaran for NZ$65 per person, including barbecue lunch and snorkelling gear.

Fishing Aitutaki Sea Charters (☎ 31281) and Clive Baxter (☎ 31025) take big-game fishing trips outside the reef for NZ$105 per person, including all gear. Barry Anderson (☎ 31492) offers full-day fishing trips inside the lagoon (NZ$150/180 for one/two people).

Aitutaki's fishermen congregate at the Aitutaki Game Fishing Club near the wharf; open Wednesday to Saturday, 4 pm until late. Thursday and Friday nights are the best for socialising (see Entertainment later in this section); if you're keen to go fishing, stop by.

Organised Tours Chloe & Nane's (☎ 31248) offers circle-island tours Monday to Saturday (NZ$30 per person).

Getting There & Away
Air Rarotonga (☎ 31888 in Aitutaki) operates three flights a day to Aitutaki (NZ$136 one way, 50 minutes), except Sunday. The Super Saver fare (NZ$109 one way) applies to certain flights. All the Rarotonga travel agencies offer package deals to Aitutaki. The Air Rarotonga office on the main road in Arutanga is an agent for Air New Zealand.

Air Rarotonga also offers day trips to Aitutaki (NZ$349), departing Rarotonga airport at 8 am and returning by 6.30 pm. Book through Air Rarotonga (☎ 22888, fax 20979) or Rarotonga travel agencies.

See the introductory Getting Around section earlier in this chapter for information on passenger cargo ship services to Aitutaki. Trips between Rarotonga and the northern group islands often stop on Aitutaki.

Getting Around
A bus (☎ 31379) connects with all arriving and departing flights; it costs NZ$5 into town.

In Arutanga, Swiss Rentals (☎ 31600, fax 31329) rents mountain bikes (NZ$5 per day), motorbikes (NZ$20/100 per day/week) and cars (NZ$50). Rino's Rentals (☎ 31197, fax 31559) in Ureia rents bicycles (NZ$8), motorbikes (NZ$20) and Jeeps (NZ$70).

AROUND THE ISLAND
Arutanga
Arutanga is a pleasant, sleepy little town. A weathered **CICC church** is picturesquely situated by the playing fields beside the harbour. Built in 1828, it is the oldest church in the Cooks, and has beautiful carved wood painted red, yellow, green and white all around the ceiling, more dark woodcarving over the doorways, simple stained-glass windows, and an anchor placed on the ceiling.

New Jerusalem
On the south coast, New Jerusalem village was built in the early 1990s entirely of native materials, in the style of a traditional Cook Islands village. The residents of New Jerusalem are pretty much all members of the Free Church.

Marae
Aitutaki's marae are notable for their large stones. Orongo marae used to sit where the Seabreeze Cafe is today, in Arutanga. The main road goes right through a big marae at the turn-off to Aitutaki Lodges; the stones are along both sides of the road. On the inland road between Nikaupara and Tautu, the

signs saying 'Marae' and 'Marae/Jerusalem' will direct you to some of the most magnificent marae on the island: Tokangarangi, Taravao, Te Poaki O Rae and Paengariki. These marae may have been cleared, or may be overgrown; check for information before you go looking for them.

Aitutaki Lagoon
This marvellous lagoon is large, colourful and full of life, and the snorkelling is magnificent. The lagoon is dotted with sandbars, coral ridges and 21 motu.

Maina motu at the south-west corner of the lagoon offers top snorkelling on the coral formations near its shore and around the large powder-white sandbars just to its north and east. Akaiami is where the old flying boats (now known as seaplanes) used to land to refuel. Tapuaetai, or One Foot Island, is the best-known motu, with its lovely white stretch of beach and brilliant, pale-turquoise water.

Tauono's
At Tauono's (☎ 31562) a wide variety of organic fruits, vegetables and herbs can be picked to order from the lush garden; deepsea and reef fish, Cakes, coffee and herbal teas are also sold. The operators, Tauono and Sonja, will do a traditional umukai on request (minimum 10 people).

Places to Stay – Budget
Paradise Cove (☎ 31218, fax 31456), on the island's north-west, is on a beautiful stretch of beach with good snorkelling. Singles/doubles cost NZ$20/30 in a large house, NZ$25/40 in rustic bungalows. This is the only place we saw in the Cook Islands where you can sleep in a traditional *kikau* (thatch-roofed) hut.

Further south, *Vaikoa Units* (☎/fax 31145) has self-contained studio-apartment units for NZ$30/50/80 a single/double/triple. It's on a lovely white beach good for swimming and snorkelling.

Tom's Beach Cottage (☎ 31051, fax 31409, papatoms@aitutak.net.ck) in Amuri is a relaxed beachfront place with rooms for NZ$32/48/58, bungalows NZ$76/86.

Places to Stay – Mid-Range
The pleasant *Paratrooper Motel* (☎ 31563 or ☎ 31523), on the main road in Amuri, has several self-contained houses. A one bedroom unit costs NZ$60 per night (minimum stay three nights). Two-bedroom units cost NZ$100 per night (ask about discounts).

On the beach, *Rino's Beach Bungalows & Rentals* (☎ 31197, fax 31559) has four self-contained studio units for NZ$65/85/115 a single/double/triple, two beachfront rooms for NZ$105/135/165, two deluxe beachfront rooms with great views for NZ$85/130, and a three-bedroom house (NZ$250 per week).

Places to Stay – Top End
Aitutaki Lodges (☎ 31334, fax 31333, aitlodge@aitutaki.net.ck), on the east coast, has A-frame chalets with splendid views of the lagoon and motu. Singles/doubles/triples cost NZ$186/192/237, including breakfast and airport transfers.

Aitutaki Lagoon Resort (☎ 31201 or ☎ 20234, fax 31202, akitua@aitutaki.net.ck) on Akitua motu (joined to the main island by a footbridge) has standard/deluxe garden bungalows (NZ$305/350), lagoonview bungalows (NZ$472) and deluxe beachfront suites (NZ$665).

Places to Eat
In the Orongo Centre in Arutanga, *Seabreeze Cafe* is a pleasant open-air cafe/bar, with entertainment on Friday night. *Kuramoo Takeaways* on the main road is similarly simple and inexpensive.

Ralphie's Bar & Grill (☎ 31418) in Amuri is open daily, with 'island night' entertainment on Friday night.

On the north side of the island, the *Crusher Bar* (☎ 31283) is a true island-style restaurant/bar, with a thatched-roof, open-air dining room, lots of island decor, a popular 'island night' on Thursday (NZ$25.50, reservations essential), and dinner, live music and dancing every night except Friday.

Also on the north side, *Tauono's* (see separate entry earlier) serves European-style cakes, coffee, fresh fruits and vegetables, fish, traditional Maori umukai meals

Manuae

- pop 0   • area 6.8 sq km

The tiny unpopulated islets of Manuae and Te Au O Tu, jointly known as Manuae, belong to the people of Aitutaki. These islets are the only parts of a huge volcanic cone to break the ocean's surface. The cone measures 56km from east to west, 24km north to south. The other high point on the rim of this vast cone is the Astronomer Bank, 13km west of Manuae, which comes to within 300m of the ocean's surface.

Copra-cutting parties visit Manuae from Aitutaki occasionally, as they have done for a century or more. In 1823 the missionary John Williams visited the island and found about 60 inhabitants. There were only a dozen or so in the late 1820s, and missionaries took them to Aitutaki. Later various Europeans made temporary homes. The best-known was William Marsters, who in 1863 was moved to Palmerston with his three wives.

and more, with a garden cafe scheduled to open in 1999.

The *Aitutaki Growers Market* at the Orongo Centre has locally grown produce; around 7 or 8 am you may also find freshly caught fish. The *Ioane Taua Store & Bakery*, opposite Aitutaki Scuba, has freshly baked bread and other goods.

Entertainment

The *Crusher Bar*, *Ralphie's* and *Seabreeze Cafe* (see Places to Eat earlier) are the popular entertainment spots.

Aitutaki Game Fishing Club at the foot of the wharf in Arutanga is a simple place to enjoy a cheap beer, a friendly and relaxed atmosphere, and a beautiful sunset view. It's open Wednesday to Saturday from 4 pm (see the Fishing entry earlier in this section).

The upmarket *Aitutaki Lagoon Resort* (see Places to Stay earlier) has entertainment on Wednesday and Saturday nights, with a buffet starting at 7 pm, and a floor show and dancing afterwards. Prices start from NZ$38

per person, including entertainment; there's no charge for the show only.

Shopping

Island crafts are available at the Aitutaki Women's Development Craft Centre and at several other shops in the Orongo Centre, by the wharf in Arutanga. Aitutakian crafts include woven pandanus purses, bags, mats and hats, shell-and-rito fans, white rito church hats, shell jewellery, wooden drums, ukuleles and colourful pareu. In Vaipae, Anitonia's makes wooden drums, ukuleles and other handicrafts.

Palmerston Atoll

- pop 49   • area 2.3 sq km

Palmerston is far to the north-west of the other southern islands, and is sometimes treated as part of the northern group. The lagoon is 11km wide at its widest point and 35 small islands dot the reef.

The island's most famous resident was the prolific breeder William Marsters (died 1899), who, along with his three wives, is an ancestor of many Cook Islanders here and on several other islands.

Palmerston is a quiet little place. There is no organised accommodation, although Reverend Bill Marsters can arrange accommodation with local families. There are no flights to Palmerston, and inter-island passenger cargo ships stop very infrequently.

Atiu, Mauke & Mitiaro

Atiu, Mauke and Mitiaro are often collectively referred to as Nga Pu Toru (The Three Roots) and the links between the people of the three islands have been strong for many centuries. The islands are similar geographically, characterised by a narrow lagoon, a raised coral reef (makatea) around the outside edge, and a higher interior.

Modesty standards on these outer islands are more conservative than on Rarotonga;

locals will be upset by anyone going shirt-less or wearing swimming gear in town.

Electricity operates every day from 5 am to midnight.

Getting There & Away

The three islands can easily be visited as a group. Rarotonga travel agents can organise package tours to Atiu, Mauke and Mitiaro, either singly or in combination. See the individual island sections for more details on air travel.

For details on passenger cargo ships, see the Getting Around section of this chapter.

ATIU

● pop 960   ● area 26.9 sq km

The third largest of the Cook Islands, Atiu is noted for its makatea. Atiu's five villages – Areora, Ngatiarua, Teenui, Mapumai and Tengatangi – are all close together in the centre of a hill region, radiating out on five roads from the administrative centre and the CICC church.

Atiu has some fine beaches, magnificent scenery, excellent walks, ancient marae and limestone caves. Many visitors stay only a couple of days, but the island is worth a longer visit.

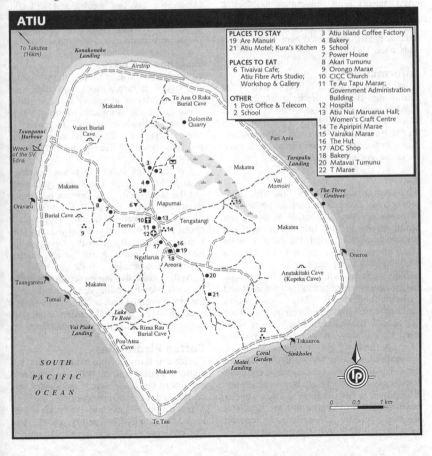

ATIU

PLACES TO STAY
19 Are Manuiri
21 Atiu Motel; Kura's Kitchen

PLACES TO EAT
6 Tivaivai Cafe;
   Atiu Fibre Arts Studio;
   Workshop & Gallery

OTHER
1 Post Office & Telecom
2 School
3 Atiu Island Coffee Factory
4 Bakery
5 School
7 Power House
8 Akari Tumunu
9 Orongo Marae
10 CICC Church
11 Te Au Tapu Marae;
   Government Administration
   Building
12 Hospital
13 Atiu Nui Maruarua Hall;
   Women's Craft Centre
14 Te Apiripiri Marae
15 Vairakai Marae
16 The Hut
17 ADC Shop
18 Bakery
20 Matavai Tumunu
22 T Marae

History

Atiu's traditional name is Enua Manu, which can be translated as 'Land of Birds' or 'Land of Insects'. Atiuans were the warriors of the Cook Islands and their colourful and bloody history includes many raids on neighbouring islands.

The European discovery of Atiu is credited to James Cook on 3 April 1777. In the early 1820s two Polynesian Christian 'teachers' were sent here from Bora Bora in the Society Islands, but their mission was unsuccessful. Later, Rongomatane, the leading Atiuan chief, was converted by the missionaries John Williams and Papeiha. The chief quickly ordered all the idols on the island burnt. Williams' and Papeiha's arrival is still celebrated here with Gospel Day each 19 July.

Information

Foreign currency can be exchanged at the administration centre in the island's centre. Cash advances on Visa, MasterCard and Bankcard are available from the ADC shop in Areora village. The post and Telecom offices, in the same building in Mapumai village, are open weekdays 8 am to 4 pm.

Caves

The coastal makatea is riddled with limestone caves, complete with stalactites and stalagmites. You'll stumble across many small caves in any ramble through the makatea so take a torch (flashlight). Wear good shoes as the coral is razor sharp; a walking stick is a great help also.

You must go with a guide to visit the major caves, which are on private land and difficult to find. The place where you're staying can help you arrange this (see Organised Tours later). Many caves were used for burials – do not move or take any of the bones.

Anatakitaki, also known as the Kopeka cave, is Atiu's most famous and frequently toured cave. A hauntingly large and beautiful cave, it is the home of the rare kopeka bird (a small bird similar to a swift) which lives only on Atiu. The cave can be reached by a longish walk from the plateau road.

The **Te Ana O Raka** burial cave, south of the airstrip, is just off the road and very easy to find, but you must go with a guide. Aue Raka (☎ 33086) offers tours of the cave and other local sights.

In the south-west, the **Rima Rau** burial cave is reached by a vertical pothole. There are many bones in this cave and nearby there's a very deep sinkhole with a cold pool at the bottom.

Lake Te Roto is noted for its eels, a popular island delicacy. On the western side of the lake, a cave leads right through the makatea to the sea. Vaine Moeroa goes eeling here every few weeks, and will take visitors; ask at the place where you're staying to be put in touch with him. Be prepared to get very muddy.

Beaches & Coast

Atiu's reef is close to shore – the surrounding lagoon is rarely more than 50m wide and the water is generally quite shallow. You can swim in **Taunganui Harbour**, where the water is clear and deeper. Thatch-roofed shelters have been erected near several beaches including Taungaroro, Matai and Takauroa.

On the west coast, **Oravaru** beach is thought to be where Cook's party landed. On the south-east coast **Oneroa** beach has beautiful shells. South of Oneroa is the turn-off to **Takauroa** beach. If you walk about 100m back along the rugged cliff face there are some sinkholes deep enough for good snorkelling, safe only at low tide or when the sea is calm.

At low tide, the lagoon from Takauroa beach to Matai Landing drains out through the sinkholes and fish become trapped in a spot known as the **Coral Garden**, which becomes a fascinating natural aquarium.

Coffee Plantations

Coffee was introduced to Atiu by early 19th century traders and missionaries. After a century of ups and downs, the industry was revitalised by German-born Juergen Manske-Eimke in the mid-1980s. He established the Atiu Coffee Factory, and the Atiu Coffee Growers Association was formed.

Tumunu

When English whalers came to Atiu to provision their ships over 200 years ago there was no alcohol, only kava (see the boxed text in the Regional Facts for the Visitor chapter). Atiu was covered with oranges and it was not long before a wild brew was concocted with the help of the whalers. It is still drunk to this day.

The *tumunu* came into existence during the period when missionaries attempted to stamp out kava-drinking in the Cooks and men would retreat to the bush to drink home-brewed 'orange beer'. The tumunu is the hollowed-out coconut-palm stump traditionally used as a container for brewing the beer. Drinking kava was always a communal activity with a ceremony involved – despite the change in the potion, the ceremony continued.

Today Atiu has eight tumunu (bush beer schools) that survived the missionaries. All retain some of the ancient ceremonies associated with drinking kava, although the container is likely to be plastic nowadays and the beer may be made from imported hops. Technically, however, bush beer schools are still illegal.

The staff at the place where you're staying can arrange an invitation to visit the local tumunu. Traditionally it is for men only, and women rarely participate, but the rules relax somewhat for tourists and any visitor, male or female, is welcome. Just be wary of over imbibing – bush beer is very strong.

Juergen gives tours of the coffee plantations and factories (NZ$10 per person). Bookings can be made either through your accommodation, or directly (☎ 33031, fax 33032, adc@adc .co.ck).

Atiu Fibre Arts Studio

The Atiu Fibre Arts Studio (☎ 33031, fax 33032, adc@adc.co.ck) specialises in tivaevae. The cost of a machine-sewn double to queen-size tivaevae is NZ$500 to $1100; a hand-sewn one, requiring countless hours to make, costs NZ$1300 or more.

The studio also produces a variety of other textile arts. Products are exhibited in its gallery, workshop and cafe building in Teenui, on weekdays from 8 am to 4 pm, Saturday to 1 pm.

Organised Tours

Atiu Tours (☎ 33041) offers tours of the Kopeka cave (NZ$15 per person). Guides James and Sarah Humphreys are very knowledgeable about plant life and the kopeka; a highlight is a swim in a candle-lit water hole. For NZ$25 per person they offer an excellent three hour plus tour to historical sites and places of interest, which includes

explanations about plants and nature, and a visit to a beach where they serve light refreshments. Bookings can be made directly or through your accommodation.

Places to Stay

Are Manuiri (☎ *33031, fax 33032, adc@adc.co.ck*), in the centre of Areora village, is a pleasant three-bedroom house. Prices are NZ$25 per person for a shared room, NZ$50 for a room to yourself and NZ$66 for the family room. Return airport transfers are NZ$10 per person.

Atiu Motel (☎ *33777, fax 33775, atiu@ gatepoly.co.ck*), about 1km out of Areora on the road leading to the beach, has four delightful A-frame chalets made from local materials and costing NZ$90/100/110 a single/double/triple.

Places to Eat

Tivaivai Cafe at the Atiu Fibre Arts Studio serves Atiu Island coffee, home-made cakes, breads and jams, good breakfasts and fresh fruit juice. It's open weekdays 8 am to 4 pm, Saturday to 1 pm. *Kura's Kitchen* at the Atiu Motel provides evening meals; book before 3 pm.

Atiu has several *trade stores*, two *bakeries* and three *doughnut makers*. *Maroro* (flying fish), an Atiuan delicacy, is caught in butterfly nets a week or so after the new moon from June to December.

Entertainment
Dances are held in the thatched open-air pavilion bar at the *Atiu Motel* every Saturday night from around 9 pm. Dances are also held on occasional Friday nights at the *Atiu Nui Maruarua Hall* opposite the CICC church.

Shopping
Woodcarving is popular on the island, and many carvers sell from their homes. You can see workshops along the road as you pass through the villages. Atiu Island coffee and goods from the Atiu Fibre Arts Studio are popular souvenirs.

Getting There & Away
Atiu's airport is in the north-eastern corner of the island. Air Rarotonga (☎ 33888) flies between Rarotonga and Atiu daily except Sunday (NZ$146/209 one way/return, 40 minutes). Flights also connect Atiu with Mauke and Mitiaro (NZ$83). By sea, stops in Atiu are often made in conjunction with stops at Mauke and Mitiaro.

Getting Around
You will need transport to get around Atiu. Both accommodation places rent motorcycles (NZ$25 per day). Are Manuiri also rents mountain bikes (NZ$10). Clara George (☎ 33115) provides a taxi service.

MAUKE
• pop 646   • area 18.4 sq km

Mauke is the easternmost of the Cook Islands, and one of the more easily visited since there are regular flights. Inland from its encircling fossil coral reef, a band of swampland surrounds the flat, fertile central land.

A couple of the island's highlights are the **Divided Church** and **Kea's Grave**. Ask locals for the fascinating stories behind these two places.

Information
The Telecom and post offices, in the same building in Ngatiarua village, in the centre of the island, are open weekdays 8 am to 2 pm.

Caves
Mauke has makatea riddled with limestone caves, many filled with cool water and wonderful for a swim. The easiest cave to reach, and also one of the larger ones for swimming, is **Vai Tango**, a short walk from Ngatiarua village. You'll probably need someone to guide you there the first time.

Other interesting caves in the north of the island, a short walk off the main road, are **Vai Ou**, **Vai Tunamea** and **Vai Moraro**. **Motuanga Cave** (or the 'Cave of 100 Rooms', each room with its own pool) is Mauke's best-known cave. It is entered on land and extends out towards the sea and under the reef.

Marae
Mauke's best preserved marae, still used for stylised ceremonial functions, is the **Puarakura Marae**. There's a triangular area enclosed within a rectangle within another rectangle, with seats for the ariki, the *mataiapo* (heads of sub-tribes) and the *rangatira* (nobles).

Out past the old airstrip is **Marae Rangimanuka**, the marae of Uke, Mauke's ancestor and namesake. It's hidden in an overgrown area but is not difficult to get to with a guide. **Paepae'a** is an impressive marae built in 1997.

Beaches
An 18km-long road runs around the coast of the island. The fringing reef platform is narrow but Teoneroa beach is fairly good, as is the beach at Arapaea. Beaches on the southern side, such as Anaokae, are pleasantly secluded. Others like Anaraura and Teoneroa have picnic areas with thatched shelters.

South of Tiare Holiday Cottages, the first turn-off towards the sea leads to **Kopupooki** (Stomach Rock) beach. Past the last outcrop visible from the beach is a lovely cave full of fish, good for swimming and snorkelling. It's accessible only at low tide. Many more

MAUKE

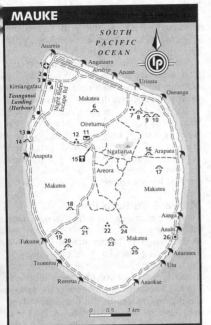

MAUKE

PLACES TO STAY & EAT		22	Marae Rangimanuka (Uke's Marae)
3	Mauke Cove Lodge	26	Kea's Grave
13	Tiare Holiday Cottages		
		CAVES	
		6	Vai Tango
OTHER		8	Vai Ou
1	Hospital	9	Vai Moraro
2	Sports Field	10	Vai Tunamea
4	Air Rarotonga	14	Kopupooki
5	Marae O Rongo;		(Stomach Rock)
	Government	16	Vai Mutu
	Administration	17	Cave
	Building; CAO	18	Caves
	Residence	19	Tukume Cave
7	Paepae'a Marae	20	Vai Mau
11	Post Office &	21	Caves
	Telecom	23	Cave
12	Puarakura Marae	24	Vai Moti
15	Ziona – The	25	Motuanga Cave
	Divided Church		(Cave of 100
	(CICC)		Rooms)

little caves and beaches are dotted around the island.

Places to Stay & Eat
Tiare Holiday Cottages (☎ 35083, fax 35102), on the coast near the village, has three simple cottages costing NZ$30/35 a single/double, and one self-contained unit (NZ$50). *Mauke Cove Lodge* (☎ 35130 or ☎ 35888, fax 35094, aguinea@gatepoly .co.ck), on the northern edge of Kimiangatau village, has rooms for NZ$30/50.

You can do your own cooking at either place, or arrange for meals to be prepared. Island and cave tours, fishing trips and other activities can be arranged. Both hotels rent motorcycles (NZ$20 per day) and bicycles (NZ$10), and provide airport transfers.

Shopping
Mauke is noted for its woven pandanus mats, purses, hats and baskets. Bowls shaped like the leaves of the breadfruit tree

and carved from miro wood are another traditional craft. To buy handicrafts, ask at the place you're staying.

Getting There & Away
Mauke has an airstrip on the north coast. Air Rarotonga (☎ 35888) flies between Mauke and Rarotonga each weekday (NZ$136/299 one way/return). Flights also connect Mauke with Mitiaro and Atiu (NZ$83). See Getting There & Away earlier in this chapter for details of passenger ships to the island.

MITIARO
● pop 319   ● area 22.3 sq km
Mitiaro is not one of the Cooks' most beautiful islands, but you can pass a pleasant few days here. The people are very friendly, and all live in one small village on the west side of the island. To see the sights, especially the caves and the marae, you'll need a local person to guide you. This can easily be arranged at the place where you stay.

Mitiaro has a raised coral limestone outer plain. The interior of the island is very flat and much of it is swampland, with two sections deep enough to be called lakes: Te Rotonui (Big Lake) and Te Rotoiti (Small Lake).

MITIARO

SOUTH
PACIFIC
OCEAN

0   0.5   1 km

CAVES
1 Vaiai
3 Vai Marere
4 Vai Nauri
5 Vai Tamaroa
6 Tepito-O-Kare Pool

MARAE
2 Karangarua Marae
7 Te Pare Fort & Marae

Kaapoto
Okaraua
Orongomai
Airstrip Cemetery
Okore
Tevaikuku
Makatea
Atai
Kovea Auta
Omutu Mangarei
Landing Takabe
Atai & Auta
Peat & Hard Fern
Te Rotoiti
Taurangi
Peat & Hard Fern
Te Rotonui
Tiaara
Mangarei
Parava
Peat & Hard Fern
Takaue
Makatea
Te Rua te Pui
Te Unu
Oavea Te Kokenga

Many handicrafts are still made on Mitiaro, and traditional customs are still practised. Women weave long pandanus strips into floor mats, fans, handbags and other items. Big bowls are carved from solid wood and canoes are still made in the traditional way. Fishing and planting are timed by the phases of the moon, and traditional arts are taught to both boys and girls.

Information
The post and Telecom offices, in one building, are open weekdays 8 am to 4 pm. You'll need to change money before you arrive on Mitiaro.

Mosquitoes are a real pest here. Bring repellent, sturdy shoes for walking across the makatea and sunglasses, as the white road-surfaces are extremely reflective.

Beaches, Caves & Pools
A 10 minute walk from the village on the Takaue road, **Vai Marere** is the only sulphur

pool in the Cook Islands. All you can see from the road is a big hole in the ground but it opens up into a large cave with stalactites. The water is refreshingly cool.

Vai Tamaroa, on the eastern side of the island, is about a 15 minute walk across sharp makatea from the coast road. You'll need a local guide because the trail is faint. A road to **Vai Nauri**, also on the eastern side, has been cut so you can drive right up to it. Vai Nauri is a large, brilliantly clear pool in a big cave. The women hold gatherings known as *terevai* at both Vai Tamaroa and Vai Nauri, where they gather to swim and to sing the bawdy songs of their ancestors.

Marae & Te Pare Fort
There are marae in the inland areas where the villages used to be, although many are overgrown. The **Takero marae** in the old Takaue village area has been excavated and the huge stone seat of the ariki, which was found broken in two, has been rejoined. There are several old graves near the marae. **Karangarua marae** in the old Atai village area has also been excavated.

In the south-east part of the island are the stone remains of the ancient **Te Pare fort**, built as a defence against Atiuan raids. An underground shelter was large enough for the people to congregate in during times of danger, while above was a lookout tower from which approaching canoes could be seen.

To visit the Te Pare fort and marae, you must first ask permission of Tiki Tetava Ariki, to whom the marae belongs. His speaker will take you to the fort.

Plantations
In the 1800s, the islanders moved their houses to the seaside village, but continued to use the fertile, peat-laden plantation areas in the island's centre. There are roads across the makatea to the plantations, although many people still make the long trip on foot.

CICC Church
The white-painted CICC church with its blue trim, parquet ceiling decorated with black and white stars, and stained-glass

windows is a fine sight, and the singing on Sunday is superb.

Cemetery

The cemetery on the north side of the island has a few modern-style cement tombs and many older graves marked simply by upright slabs of coral. At almost every grave, possessions of the dead person have been left at the headstone, along with eating utensils in case the sprit of the deceased is hungry.

Lakes

Except in one spot, where there is a road leading to the shore of **Te Rotonui**, the lakes are hard to approach as the surrounding area is exceedingly soggy. Where the road arrives at Te Rotonui the ground is firm, and there's a boat landing and a pleasant picnic spot.

You can also approach the lakes from the Taurangi plantation area, which is quite easy since there is no makatea to cross. If you have a motorbike you can take it all the way to the end of the Taurangi area pathway. From there it's a 15 minute walk to the lake, across a wide strip of very black mud.

Places to Stay & Eat

Sea Breeze Lodge (☎ 36153, fax 36683), in Atai, charges NZ$55 per night, including meals and airport transfers. Bicycles (NZ$10 per day) and motorbikes (NZ$25 per day) are available. Limited food supplies are sold at the small village *food shops*.

Getting There & Away

Air Rarotonga (☎ 36888 at the airport) flies to Mitiaro three times a week (NZ$136/299 one way/return, 50 minutes). Flights also connect Mitiaro with Atiu and Mauke (NZ$83). For details on passenger cargo ships to the islands, see this chapter's Getting Around section.

Mangaia

• pop 1104   • area 51.8 sq km

The second-largest of the Cook Islands, Mangaia is not much smaller than Rarotonga, although its population is far smaller

and has declined sharply in recent years. The island's central hills are surrounded by an outer rim of makatea. The lagoon inside the fringing coral reef is very narrow and shallow. The island rises rapidly from the coast and in most places it drops as a sheer wall to the inner region.

Scrub, ferns, vines and coconut palms grow on the makatea. Taro swamps are found around the inner edge and in the central valleys. Mangaia pineapples are justly famous – big, sweet and juicy.

History

A Mangaian legend relates that the island was not settled by canoe. Instead, Rangi, Mokoaro and Akatauira, the three sons of the Polynesian god Rongo (also known as Lono or Ro'o), simply lifted the island up from the deep, becoming its first settlers and the ancestors of the Nga Ariki tribe.

James Cook sailed by in 1777 but met an unfriendly reception and quickly moved on. Missionary John Williams was similarly not welcome in 1823 but subsequent Polynesian missionaries had more success.

Orientation

The three main villages are all on the coast: Oneroa in the west, Ivirua in the east and Tamarua in the south. Oneroa, the main village, has three parts: Tava'enga and Kaumata on the northern and southern parts of the coast respectively, and Temakatea above. The airstrip is in Mangaia's north.

Information

Mangaia's tourist office (☎ 34289, fax 34238), PO Box 10, in the Ministry of Outer Islands Development building at the bottom of the Temakatea road cutting, is open weekdays 8 am to 4 pm.

The post office is in the government building opposite the tourist office; it's open weekdays, 8 am to noon and 1 to 4 pm. The Telecom office, in Temakatea, is open weekdays 7.30 am to 4 pm. Pokino's Store in Oneroa is an agent for the ANZ bank.

The electricity supply operates daily from 5 am to midnight.

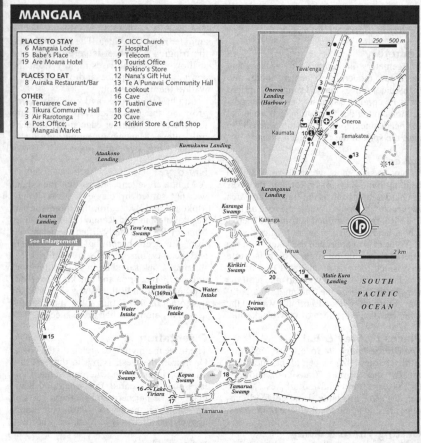

MANGAIA

PLACES TO STAY
6 Mangaia Lodge
15 Babe's Place
19 Are Moana Hotel

PLACES TO EAT
8 Auraka Restaurant/Bar

OTHER
1 Teruarere Cave
2 Tikura Community Hall
3 Air Rarotonga
4 Post Office;
   Mangaia Market

5 CICC Church
7 Hospital
9 Telecom
10 Tourist Office
11 Pokino's Store
12 Nana's Gift Hut
13 Te A Punavai Community Hall
14 Lookout
16 Cave
17 Tuatini Cave
18 Cave
20 Cave
21 Kirikiri Store & Craft Shop

Churches & Marae

There are typical, old CICC churches in
Oneroa, Ivirua and Tamarua. The Tamarua
church, surrounded by shady trees, is beautiful – look for the woodcarving and the
sennit-rope binding on the roof beams.

Mangaia has 24 pre-missionary marae,
but you'll need a local expert to find them
(see Organised Tours under Getting There
& Around, later in this section).

Rangimotia

The highest point on the island, Rangimotia (169m) isn't really a peak – more of a

high plateau. But there are excellent views
from the top. From the Oneroa side of the
island there's an old dirt road, suitable for
4WDs, motorcycles or mountain bikes,
right to the top, plus easy hiking tracks. The
track forks at the top and you can follow either fork down to the coast.

Caves

Mangaia has many spectacular caves, including some burial caves where you can
still see ancient human skeletons (see Organised Tours under Getting There &
Around later in this section).

Organised Tours Clarke's Island Tours
(☎ 34303) offers various tours, including a
3½ hour inland and around-the-island tour,
which includes Rangimotia (NZ$50), a 1½
hour tour of the Tuatini (Labyrinth) cave
(NZ$30), and a 1½ hour tour of Lake Tiri-
ara and its Tangiia cave, which is entered
by boat (NZ$30).

Tere Tauakume (☎ 34223) offers an en-
thralling four hour cave tour, including
lunch (NZ$35). Mana Samuel (☎/fax
34261) leads a 1½ hour tour through Tuatini
cave on the outskirts of Tamarua (NZ$20).
Island tours and other cave trips can also be
arranged through the Are Moana Hotel,
Babe's Place, or by asking at the tourist
office.

Places to Stay

All the places to stay on Mangaia make
some provision for their guests to eat. Most
accommodation is in Oneroa.

Mangaia Lodge (☎ 34206 or ☎ 34260),
near the hospital in Temakatea, has three
very large bedrooms in a sprawling old
colonial-style home (NZ$20 per person).

Babe's Place (☎ 34092, fax 34078), in the
Kaumata section of Oneroa, has a large
house plus new motel-style units. Singles/
doubles/triples cost NZ$75/120/150, which

includes airport transfers and meals. Dances
are held on Friday and Saturday nights.

In Ivirua, *Are Moana Hotel (☎ 34278,
fax 34279)* has tiny cabins for NZ$70 per
person, including breakfast and dinner.

Places to Eat

Clean and friendly, *Auraka Restaurant/Bar
(☎ 34281)* is on the back road behind the
hospital, and also operates a bakery and
sells fresh eggs. *Babe's Place* and *Are
Moana Hotel (☎ 34278)* will prepare meals
for casual diners – just ring ahead.

Clarke's Tours offers an *umukai* for
groups of four people or more (NZ$20 per
person). *Pokino's Store*, near the coast in
Oneroa, and *Akeke Trading*, further inland
in Oneroa, are well-stocked shops.

Shopping

Nana's Gift Hut (☎ 34254) is in a traditional
hut by the side of the road in Temakatea.
Handicrafts include hats, purses, bags, fans
and mats all made from pandanus, as well as
pupu ei and shell jewellery. In Ivirua village
is the Kirikiri Store & Craft Shop (☎ 34133).

Tuaiva Mautairi (☎ 34001) makes Mangaian ceremonial adzes in the traditional
style, as well as crystal rock taro-pounders,
carved wooden drums and jewellery. Glenn

A traditional Mangaian hut – the thatched roof uses leaves of the *kikau* palm.

Tuara of Rapeuru Stone Carving (☎ 34227) makes stone taro-pounders.

Teremoana Ruatoe (☎ 34010) makes tivaevae, cushions and pillow cases. Tako Ruatoe (☎ 34010) and Teremoana Tutu make baskets, pandanus mats and long fishing baskets.

Getting There & Around

Air Rarotonga (☎ 34888) flies between Mangaia and Rarotonga four times weekly (NZ$122/209 one way/return, 40 minutes).

See the introductory Getting Around section to this chapter for details on passenger cargo ships from Rarotonga to Mangaia.

Babe's Place and Are Moana Hotel rent motorbikes (NZ$20 to $30). Clarke Mautairi (☎ 34303) rents a 4WD Jeep (NZ$60).

The Northern Group

The northern islands are low-lying coral atolls scattered in a vast expanse of sea. Despite their idyllic appearance, life on these atolls is hard. Fish may be abundant in the lagoon but atoll soil is only marginally fertile and the range of foodstuffs which can be grown is limited. Fresh water is always a problem. Today, returning islanders and radios have whetted the locals' appetites for the outside world and consequently the population of the northern islands is in decline.

Getting There & Away

To visit the northern group you can fly to Manihiki, Penrhyn or Pukapuka, a 3½ to four hour flight from Rarotonga (NZ$546 one way to/from Manihiki, NZ$605 one way to/from Penrhyn or Pukapuka). Flights are scheduled for only once a week, and are sometimes cancelled due to bad weather, limited fuel supplies, lack of passengers, and other adverse conditions. Rarotonga travel agents recommend you take out travel insurance to cover such unavoidable delays.

The only other regular transport to the northern group islands is on the inter-island passenger cargo ships. For more information, see the Getting Around section at the beginning of this chapter.

MANIHIKI ATOLL
● pop 662   ● area 5.4 sq km

Manihiki has a reputation as one of the most beautiful atolls in the South Pacific. Nearly 40 islands, some only tiny motu, encircle the 4km-wide, totally enclosed lagoon. The main village is Tauhunu; there is a second village, Tukao. Manihiki has no safe anchorage for visiting ships, which consequently stay offshore.

The famous **Manihiki black pearls** are the economic mainstay of the island and a significant export. The abilities of the island's pearl divers are legendary – they can dive to great depths and stay submerged for minutes at a time.

Cyclone Martin struck Manihiki with full force on 1 November 1997, causing major destruction and the loss of 19 lives. The pearl industry survived, but most of the island's buildings were damaged or totally destroyed. At the time of writing this book, rebuilding was continuing, but was proceeding very slowly. The population was much reduced, the guesthouse was no longer operating, and the island was not accepting visitors.

Air Rarotonga flies to Manihiki (NZ$546 one way, 3½ hours) once per week. Flights may be routed through Pukapuka or Penrhyn. Travel agents on Rarotonga were offering packages to Manihiki before the cyclone; but check with them for current options.

RAKAHANGA ATOLL
● pop 249   ● area 4.1 sq km

Only 42km north of Manihiki, this rectangular atoll consists of two major islands and a host of smaller motu, almost completely enclosing a central lagoon about 4km long and 2km wide at its widest point.

Without the pearl wealth of Manihiki, Rakahanga is conspicuously quieter and less energetic. The population is concentrated in the village of Nivano on the southwestern corner of the atoll. Copra is the only export product. The rito hats woven on Rakahanga are particularly fine.

Rakahanga has an airstrip but there are no regular flights to the island. The only way to reach Rakahanga is by boat.

PENRHYN ATOLL
● pop 600 ● area 9.8 sq km

Penrhyn, often still called by its traditional Maori name, Tongareva, is the northernmost of the Cook Islands. Its lagoon is unlike most of the other Cook atolls in that it is very wide and easily accessible.

Penrhyn was once famous for its natural mother-of-pearl, which is still found. More recently, Penrhyn has joined Manihiki in the lucrative business of pearl farming. Some interesting shell jewellery is produced on the island. Penrhyn is also noted for its fine rito hats.

Soas Guesthouse (☎ 42019) in Omoka village offers basic, clean accommodation with shared facilities for NZ$61 per person, including three meals and airport transfers. The Tini family operates the guesthouse and will assist with activities.

Air Rarotonga operates weekly flights (NZ$605 one way, four hours). The flights may be routed through Aitutaki or Manihiki. Penrhyn is also served by inter-island shipping services.

PUKAPUKA ATOLL
● pop 780 ● area 1.3 sq km

Shaped like a three-bladed fan, Pukapuka Atoll has an island at each 'blade end' and another in the middle. The only landing place is accessed via narrow and difficult passages through the reef on the western side of Wale Island.

There are three villages – Ngake, Roto and Yato – all on Wale Island. Copra and smaller quantities of bananas and papayas are grown. Due to their relative proximity to Samoa, the islanders' customs and language are more closely related to Samoa's than to the rest of the Cooks'. There's a

well known decorated Catholic **church** on the island and excellent **swimming** and **snorkelling**, particularly off the central island of Kotawa. Pukapuka is noted for its finely woven mats.

During the 20th century, South Seas character Robert Dean Frisbie lived for some time on the island and wrote *The Book of Puka-Puka* and *The Island of Desire*.

Getting There & Away
Air Rarotonga operates flights to/from Rarotonga on an irregular basis (NZ$605 one way).

Pukapuka is served by passenger cargo ships from Rarotonga; see this chapter's introductory Getting Around section. There is some boat traffic between Pukapuka and Samoa.

SUWARROW ATOLL
● pop 4 ● area 0.4 sq km

Suwarrow Atoll is one of the best-known atolls in the Cook Islands, due to a prolonged visit by New Zealander Tom Neale. Between 1952 and his death in 1977, Neale lived on the island for extended periods as a virtual hermit. His book *An Island to Oneself* is a South Seas classic.

Neale's memory lives on and yachties often call at the atoll, one of the few in the northern Cooks with an accessible lagoon. Neale's room is furnished just as it was when he lived here and visitors fill in a logbook left in the room.

Suwarrow has been declared a national park (the Cook Islands' only national park) to preserve its pristine natural character; it is inhabited only by a caretaker and family.

Suwarrow can only be reached by infrequent shipping services or by private yacht.

Easter Island

Tiny Easter Island is one of the most isolated places on earth – the nearest populated landmass is the even tinier Pitcairn Island, 1900km west, while the South American coast is 3700km east. World famous for its enigmatic stone statues, the island attracts a growing number of visitors, but remains unspoiled and sparsely populated. A Chilean territory since 1888, it's officially known by its Spanish name, Isla de Pascua, but it retains an essentially Polynesian character. Locally, it is called Rapa Nui and also Te Pito o Te Henua, 'The Navel of the World'.

Facts about Easter Island

HISTORY

It's generally accepted that the Pacific Islands were settled by people moving by sea south and east from Asia (see the Facts about the South Pacific chapter). But because Easter Island is the most southeasterly corner of Polynesia, some theories have linked the ancestral Easter Islanders to the South American mainland (a mere 3700km away). Local folklore has it that King Hotu Matua brought the original settlers, but that there was a period of rivalry between two different peoples, intriguingly called the Long Ears and the Short Ears.

Thor Heyerdahl's 1947 *Kon-Tiki* expedition proved that it was possible to cross to the Pacific islands from South America on balsa-wood rafts, and Heyerdahl visited Easter Island in 1955 to seek more evidence of links to South America. He speculated that the oral tradition could be reconciled with separate migrations of the Short Ears from Polynesia and the 'more advanced' Long Ears from South America. Heyerdahl's adventures and ideas had great popular appeal, but modern linguistic and cultural studies conclude that the Rapa Nui people are of Polynesian ancestry, and that

AT A GLANCE

Capital City: Hanga Roa
Population: 2800
Time: Six hours behind GMT
Land Area: 117 sq km (45 sq miles)
Number of Islands: One (plus some small islets near the coast)
Telephone Code: ☎ 56-32
GDP/Capita: Not applicable
Currency: Chilean peso (Ch$100 = US$0.19)
Languages: Spanish & Rapa Nui
Greeting: *Hola* (Spanish) or *'Iorana* (Rapa Nui)

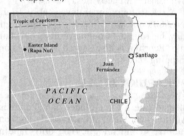

HIGHLIGHTS

- **Rano Raraku volcano** – where statues grow from the ground and freeze in time

- **Moai** – sad, stern and stoic stone faces

- **Rapa Nui culture** – one of the world's most isolated cultural groups

the first of them arrived from the Marquesas islands about 400 AD.

The Rapa Nui developed a unique civilisation, characterised by the construction of many stone monuments, notably the stone platforms called *ahu* and the distinctive Easter Island statues called *moai* (see the Archaeology section later). Easter Island is

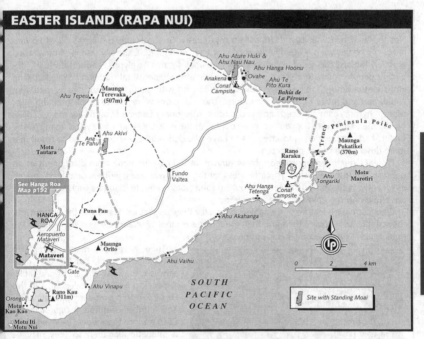

EASTER ISLAND (RAPA NUI)

also unique in the Pacific for the development of a form of writing – the hieroglyphic script engraved on wooden *rongorongo* tablets (see the boxed text 'Rongorongo'). The population probably peaked at around 15,000 in the 17th century, when the people were working on ever larger moai. A conflict late in the century, possibly over dwindling resources, nearly exterminated the Long Ears. More recent warfare, between peoples of the Tuu and Hotu-iti regions, resulted in the progressive destruction of the ahu, and all the moai were ultimately toppled.

Early Europeans

When the Dutch admiral Jacob Roggeveen arrived on Easter Sunday 1722, the islanders were living a healthy subsistence from intensively cultivated gardens of sugar cane, sweet potatoes, yams and taro. At this stage many of the great moai were still standing, but there was no sign of any

modern implements, suggesting the islanders did not trade with the outside world.

In 1774, the English navigator James Cook found the Rapa Nui people poor, small, lean, timid and miserable, and noted that many moai had been damaged and many topknots had fallen – apparently as a result of inter-tribal wars. Fourteen years later, the doomed French explorer La Pérouse (see the boxed text 'Disaster on the Reef' in the Solomon Islands chapter) found the people prosperous and calm, suggesting a quick recovery. In 1804, a Russian visitor reported more than 20 standing moai, but later accounts suggest further disruption.

Contact with outsiders nearly annihilated the Rapa Nui people. A raid by Peruvian blackbirders (slavers) in 1862 took a thousand islanders away to work the guano deposits of Peru's Chincha islands, where about 900 of them perished. After intense pressure from the Catholic Church, some

Rongorongo

Not the least of Easter Island's unsolved mysteries is the undeciphered script called *ko hau motu mo rongorongo* – literally 'lines of script for recitation'. Carefully inscribed on shaped wooden tablets, the script comprises rows of small figures or glyphs, about 1cm high, depicting people, animals, stylised plants and geometric shapes. Oral tradition has it that King Hotu Matua brought rongorongo tablets to the island with the first settlers, and learned men could read and recite from the inscriptions. The recitations were said to be of three different types – hymns, criminal deeds and war stories. Missionary Eugene Eyraud saw many tablets on the island in the 1860s, but no-one could read the script. Within a few years, many of the tablets had disappeared, and attempts to have islanders read the script seemed to result in a mere description of the characters.

Only 21 original rongorongo tablets survive, including one made from a fragment of an oar from a British Navy ship. This indicates that the script was being written, or at least copied, as recently as the early 18th century, but no rongorongo-literate islanders survived the 1862 slave raid and the epidemics that followed.

One fascinating feature of the tablets is the way they are written. Starting in the bottom left, the script reads across to the right, then the tablet is rotated 180° and the next line reads to the right again – every second line is upside down.

JAMES LYON

Rongorongo characters include many that are human-shaped and some with the heads of birds.

There have been many attempts to decipher the script, but the only consensus is that a small part of one tablet appears to be a lunar calendar, and this corresponds to a modern lunar almanac. The number of different figures (some 200) is more than would be needed for a phonetic alphabet, so they may be ideographs, like Chinese characters.

Alternatively, the characters may be a series of prompts to assist in the recitation of a ritual chant or story, and not really a true written language.

Despite much fanciful speculation, the rongorongo script is not related to any form of writing from the Indus Valley, ancient Egypt or anywhere else – it is truly unique to Easter Island.

survivors were returned to Easter Island, but many of them had contracted smallpox and died on the ship. Only 15 of the islanders made it back, and they carried smallpox with them. In a final tragedy, the resulting epidemic reduced the local population to just a few hundred.

A brief period of French-led missionary activity saw most of the surviving islanders converted in the 1860s. In 1870, Jean-Baptiste Dutroux-Bornier, established a sheep farming operation and had many islanders sent away to work on plantations in Tahiti. There was some conflict with the missionaries, who were at the same time deporting islanders to missions in Mangareva. Dutroux-Bornier was assassinated by an islander in 1877, and his estate was contested in litigation until the time of the Chilean takeover.

Chilean Rule

After its defeat of Bolivia and Peru in the War of the Pacific (1879-84), Chile entered an expansionist phase, and its navy annexed Easter Island in 1888, believing it might have potential as a strategic naval base. In fact, the island was almost devoid of naval stores and located far from any trade routes. Chile soon leased the whole place to Williamson, Balfour & Company, a British-Chilean farming and grazing enterprise. This company managed the island through its Compañía Explotadora de la Isla de Pascua (CEDIP), which was the de facto government until the 1950s, though islander welfare was a low priority and there were several uprisings against the company.

In 1953, the Chilean government revoked CEDIP's lease and the navy took charge. After 1967, a civilian administration proved more benevolent and there were improvements to water and electricity supply, medical care and education. In 1985, the airport was expanded and improved as an emergency landing site for the US space shuttle. Though there were some local objections, the larger runway enabled the establishment of a regular commercial air service, which strengthened links with the mainland and made tourism feasible for the first time.

ARCHAEOLOGY

The most common archaeological remains are the ahu – some 245 of these stone platforms surround the coast. Originally, ahu were village burial sites and ceremonial centres and are thought to derive from altars in French Polynesia. The *ahu moai* supported massive carved figures, which probably represented clan ancestors; ancestor deification being common in Polynesia. From 2 to 10m tall, these stony-faced statues stood with their backs to the Pacific Ocean, looking over villages of oval, boat-shaped houses. Some statues were even crowned with a large red *pukao*, or 'topknot', which may represent the traditional Polynesian 'top-knot' hair style (or may have been just an over-the-top sculptural fashion). Although this style of statue is unique in the Pacific, there are similarities with the stone *tiki* of the Marquesas islands, and the ahu are similar to the carved backs of ceremonial seats found elsewhere in Polynesia.

How were the moai moved from where they were carved at Rano Raraku volcano to their ahu around the coast? Legend says that priests moved the moai by the power of their *mana* alone (personal spiritual power), with the statues themselves 'walking' a short distance each day. US archaeologist William Mulloy proposed that a sledge was fitted to the moai, which was then lifted with a bipod and dragged forward (or 'walked'?) a short distance at a time. Heyerdahl and 180 islanders managed to pull a 4m moai across a field at Anakena and he figured that they could have moved a larger one with wooden runners and more labour. The use of timber to help move the statues may partly explain the island's deforestation.

Many stone structures have been demolished, damaged, recycled or rebuilt, both during tribal conflicts and under CEDIP. For example, the pier at Caleta Hanga Roa is built on stones from dismantled ahu. Several moai, and numerous smaller artefacts, have been taken by collectors and museums. Some moai have been completely restored, while others have been re-erected but are eroded. Many more lie on the ground, toppled over near an ahu, or abandoned on the long drag from Rano Raraku. Most of them lie face down, but the newest ones, freshly carved only 300 years ago, are buried up to the shoulders in the grassy slopes of the old volcano.

GEOGRAPHY

Easter Island is roughly triangular in shape, with an extinct volcanic cone in each corner – Maunga (Mount) Terevaka, in the northwest corner, is the highest point at 507m. Much of the interior of Easter Island is grassland, with cultivable soil interspersed with rugged lava fields. Wave erosion has created steep cliffs around much of the coast, and Anakena, on the north shore, is the only sandy beach. The volcanic soil is quite fertile, but so porous that water quickly drains underground – there are no permanent streams.

EASTER ISLAND

CLIMATE

Just south of the Tropic of Capricorn, Easter Island has a mild climate with average daily temperatures around 20 to 25°C. Annual average rainfall is about 1235mm, distributed fairly evenly throughout the year. The island is hottest in January and February and coolest (but still warm) in July and August. May is the wettest month, but downpours can occur at any time.

ECOLOGY

The lack of trees on the island is usually attributed to the earlier use of timber for scaffolds and rollers to make and move the stone statues, though this is supposition – more recent agricultural activities may also be partly responsible. Deforestation is also cited as a reason for the islanders' isolation, because there were no trees big enough to make an ocean-going canoe. Several parts of the island are now being replenished, mostly with eucalyptus trees, which are growing strongly.

FLORA & FAUNA

Deforestation and grazing has seen the loss of nearly all the distinctive local vegetation, and most of the island is now covered in grassland. Lakes in some of the volcanic cones have thick growths of *tora* reeds – they are very similar to some South American types (eg in Lake Titicaca), but their presence here pre-dates any human arrivals. There are no endemic bird or animal species, but chickens, rats, sheep, cattle and horses have been introduced.

GOVERNMENT & POLITICS

Administratively, the island is part of Chile's fifth region, Region V, with its capital at Valparaíso on the mainland. The Chilean government owns most of the land and appoints Easter Island's governor. The mayor and locally elected council have very limited powers. An indigenous organisation, the Consejo de Ancianos (Council of Elders), represents the traditional families of Easter Island, and has split into two factions: Consejo de Ancianos #1 and the more radical Consejo de Ancianos #2. In early 1999, members of Consejo de Ancianos #2 occupied government and National Commission of Indigenous Development (CONADI) premises in protest at the organisation of CONADI elections. In April 1999, Alberto Hotus Chavez of Consejo #1 was elected as president of the Consejo de Ancianos and now serves on the island's Development Commission along with five other elected members.

Indigenous politics experience a dilemma between the desire for more local autonomy and a recognition that the island is economically dependent on mainland Chile. There is a demand for more control over the land and greater administrative autonomy, but complete independence is not on the agenda.

ECONOMY

Cattle and sheep grazing, fishing and market gardens supply local needs, but tourism is the only activity that brings money to the island. Easter Island receives substantial economic support from the mainland, and the thousand or so residents from mainland Chile *(continentales)*, mostly government employees, also bring some income to the island's economy.

POPULATION & PEOPLE

The population is about 2800, of whom about 1000 are non-Rapa Nui people (mostly from the Chilean mainland). About 800 people are recognised as indigenous adults, eligible to vote for CONADI. The population figure probably includes a substantial number of Rapa Nui who are actually living, permanently or temporarily, off the island.

ARTS

Apart from the famous stone statues (and the numerous miniature replicas made for souvenirs), the island has a number of distinct styles, notably the *moai kavakava*, or 'statues of ribs', said to represent ghosts. Some wood carvings have features similar to New Zealand tiki faces, while others are reminiscent of the petroglyphs found at sites around the island.

The first *moai kavakava* depicted two ghosts seen by an ancient Rapa Nui king.

There is an indigenous Rapa Nui music, which may be derivative of other South Pacific sounds but is nevertheless distinctive. The music is enjoyable and cassettes are available locally. You can hear a sample on the Internet at the Easter Island website – see Internet Resources later in this chapter.

The folkloric group Kari Kari gives regular music and dance performances. You might catch them at the Kona Koa bar, or even at the airport when planes arrive.

SOCIETY & CONDUCT

Despite its unique language and history, contemporary Rapa Nui does not give the impression of being a 'traditional' society – its continuity was totally shattered by the near extinction of the population in the last century. Nevertheless, the Rapa Nui people identify more as Pacific islanders than Latin Americans, and visitors should be aware that the relationship between local people and the mainland can be a sensitive subject.

At most archaeological sites it's forbidden to climb on any stonework. The moai in particular are made of quite soft stone, and can easily be damaged.

RELIGION

The island was converted by French missionaries in the 1860s, and most Easter Islanders are still at least nominally Catholic.

LANGUAGE

Spanish is the official language, but the indigenous language is Rapa Nui, an Eastern Polynesian dialect closely related to the languages of French Polynesia and Hawai'i. There is some concern that the Rapa Nui language may become extinct.

Those in regular contact with Tahiti may speak French and many people in the tourist business speak English. While speaking some Rapa Nui might impress the locals, Spanish would be more useful for visitors.

Spanish Basics

Hello.	*Hola.*
Goodbye.	*Adiós.*
How are you?	*¿Como estás?*
I'm well (thanks).	*Bien (gracias).*
Please.	*Por favor.*
Thanks.	*Gracias.*
Yes.	*Sí.*
No.	*No.*

Rapa Nui Basics

Hello.	*'Iorana.*
Goodbye.	*'Iorana.*
How are you?	*Pehe koe?*
I'm well.	*Rivaria.*

EASTER ISLAND

Facts for the Visitor

SUGGESTED ITINERARIES
A not-too-strenuous itinerary is to allow a day for the sites near Hanga Roa, another day for a circuit of the north-east of the island, and perhaps a short day to see the Rano Kau volcano, the bird-man sites and Ahu Vinapu. The north-east circuit has the best sites, so do that first if the weather is fine. If you have more time and energy, consider a circuit of the island on foot or by horse.

PLANNING
When to Go
The weather will probably be OK at any time of the year, but most visitors to the island come in late December-January (the South American summer holidays), in February for the Semana de Rapa Nui festival, and in August-September (the northern hemisphere summer holidays). Allow at least three days to see the major sites.

Maps
The outstanding 1:30,000-scale *Isla de Pascua-Rapa Nui: Mapa Arqueológico-Turístico* is available at local shops for about US$10. JLM Mapas publishes the excellent *Isla de Pascua Trekking Map*, at 1:32,000, also available locally for US$10. The annotated Easter Island map by ITM, at 1:30,000, is also excellent.

TOURIST OFFICES
Sernatur, Chile's national tourist service, provides some information on the island and has an office in Hanga Roa (☎ 100 255) on Tuu Maheke.

VISAS & EMBASSIES
Visa requirements are the same as for mainland Chile. Passports are obligatory and are essential for checking into hotels, cashing travellers cheques and for other routine activities. Most nationalities receive a 90 day tourist card on arrival, though some nationalities, eg New Zealanders, need advance visas. Check with a Chilean embassy for the latest information. There's no consular representation on the island, but many countries have an embassy in Santiago.

To rent a car on Easter Island, you'll need an International Driving Permit.

CUSTOMS
There are no currency restrictions. Duty-free allowances include 400 cigarettes or 50 cigars or 500g of tobacco; 2.5L of alcoholic beverages; and perfume for personal use.

MONEY
Easter Island uses the Chilean *peso* but the US dollar is also readily accepted. In Hanga Roa, the Banco del Estado, next to Sernatur, changes US dollars at reasonable rates, but charges a US$7 commission on travellers cheques. The gas station may change travellers cheques at reasonable rates without charging a commission. Many businesses accept cash dollars, though some use very approximate exchange rates. If you're coming from the Chilean mainland, it's handy to bring some currency with you. There is no automatic teller machine (ATM) on Easter Island.

Exchange Rates
Exchange rates for the US dollar are given under Money in the Regional Facts for the Visitor chapter. Approximate rates for the Chilean peso are listed below.

country	unit		peso
Australia	A$1	=	Ch$340
Canada	C$1	=	Ch$360
euro	€1	=	Ch$550
Fiji	F$1	=	Ch$270
France	10FF	=	Ch$840
Germany	DM1	=	Ch$280
Japan	¥100	=	Ch$510
New Zealand	NZ$1	=	Ch$280
Pacific franc	100 CFP	=	Ch$470
Samoa	ST1	=	Ch$170
Solomon Islands	S$1	=	Ch$100
Tonga	T$1	=	Ch$350
UK	£1	=	Ch$860
USA	US$1	=	Ch$530
Vanuatu	100VT	=	Ch$410

POST & COMMUNICATIONS

Easter Island is under Chile's international telephone code (☎ 56), and one area code (☎ 32) covers the whole island. International calls (dial ☎ 00) are expensive: US$2 per minute minimum. See under Hanga Roa later for details of the post office and telephone office.

INTERNET RESOURCES

The Easter Island homepage, www.netaxs .com/~trance/rapanui.html, has some background facts about the island and comprehensive links to information on everything from local politics to archaeological tour operators.

BOOKS

On geography and environment, the most thorough source is Juan Carlos Castilla's edited collection (in Spanish) *Islas Oceánicas Chilenas*, which also covers the Juan Fernández Islands.

Thor Heyerdahl's *Aku-Aku – the Secret of Easter Island* is well known, though his theories aren't taken too seriously these days. The Bavarian priest Sebastian Englert, a longtime resident, retells Easter Island's history through oral tradition in *Island at the Center of the World*. Grant McCall's *Tradition and Survival on Easter Island* (1994) is an ethnography of contemporary Rapa Nui.

RADIO & TV

Chilean programs are beamed to Easter Island via satellite.

TIME

Easter Island is two hours behind mainland Chile, six hours behind GMT, or five hours behind GMT in summer (daylight saving time).

HEALTH

There is no malaria, dengue fever or any other particular health risks. The local water supply is OK, but short-term visitors would be wise to stick to bottled water because their stomachs will not have time to adapt to the local micro-organisms.

DANGERS & ANNOYANCES

The weather can be hot and there is little shade or fresh water available outside town. On excursions, bring water bottles, a long-sleeved shirt, sunglasses, a hat and sun block.

BUSINESS HOURS

Office hours are pretty much 9 am to 5 pm, with some places closing for an hour at lunch time. Restaurants tend to close early if business is slow.

PUBLIC HOLIDAYS & SPECIAL EVENTS

Chilean public holidays include New Year's Day, Semana Santa (Holy Week; the week before Easter), Asunción de la Virgen (the Assumption), Columbus Day, Todos los Santos (All Saints' Day) and Navidad (Christmas) – see the Regional Facts for the Visitor chapter for these dates. In addition there is:

Día del Trabajo (Labor Day)	1 May
Glorias Navales (Naval Battle of Iquique)	21 May
Corpus Christi	30 May
Día San Pedro y San Pablo (St Peter's & St Paul's Day)	29 June
Día de Unidad Nacional (Day of National Unity)	September
Día de la Independencia Nacional (Independence Day)	18 September
Día del Ejército (Armed Forces Day)	19 September
Inmaculada Concepción (Immaculate Conception)	8 December

For 10 days in late January and early February, the Semana de Rapa Nui (Tapati festival) presents cultural and sporting events with a South Pacific flavour.

ACTIVITIES

Surfing

Three main surf breaks in the south corner of the island can get good swells at any time of year, but are not very reliable.

Diving

Steep drop-offs, abundant marine life and clear water make for good diving. Centro de

EASTER ISLAND

Buceo Orca (☎ 100 375) is the only dive operator. Dives cost from US$50 to US$80 and packages with three or five dives can be arranged.

Getting There & Away

AIR

LanChile, the only airline serving Easter Island, has four flights per week to/from Santiago, and three per week to/from Papeete (French Polynesia), but it's an expensive detour. A standard economy round-trip fare from Santiago costs US$865, with promotional excursion fares from US$584. From Papeete to Easter Island, the cheapest excursion air fare, good for a stay of seven to 21 days, is around US$259 (29,900 CFP).

It's much cheaper to do a stopover at Easter Island as part of a trip to South America or in conjunction with other flights around the Pacific. From Asia or Australia you can fly via Auckland (New Zealand) and join a Qantas flight to Papeete, connecting with LanChile's Papeete-Easter Island-Santiago service. There's a free Easter Island stopover on this route. Easter Island can be included in any round-the-world (RTW) or Circle Pacific deal that involves LanChile, and is a possible stopover on some fares from North to South America via the Pacific.

See the Getting There & Away and Getting Around the Region chapters for RTW tickets, air passes and airline contact details. Flights can be heavily booked, especially in summer, so reconfirm at both ends. The airport departure tax is US$8.

SEA

Few passenger services go to Easter Island, but see Cruise Ships in the Getting Around the Region chapter. A few yachts stop here, mostly in January, February or March. Anchorages are not well sheltered, and coming ashore can be difficult. The only official entry port is Hanga Roa – Hanga Piko is used for emergencies only.

ORGANISED TOURS

Organised tours of Easter Island are usually offered in conjunction with a South American package and are typically an expensive add-on option. It is so easy to arrange accommodation and local tours on the island that it hardly seems worth paying the extra cost of a tour organised from your home country. For more information, contact one of the following operators that specialise in South American travel:

Journey Latin America (JLA)
  (☎ 020-8747 8315, fax 8742 1312)
  12 & 13 Heathfield Terrace, Chiswick,
  London W4 4JE, UK;
  www.journeylatinamerica.co.uk
*M*I*L*A*
  (☎ 847-249 2111, or ☎ tollfree 800 367 7378
  in the USA, fax 847-249 2772)
  S. Greenleaf Ave, Gurnee, IL 60031-3378,
  USA; www.a2z.com/a2z/mila/milachil
South America Travel Centre
  (☎ 03-9642 5353, fax 9642 5454)
  104 Hardware St, Melbourne, Vic 3000,
  Australia

For an in-depth cultural examination of the island, Far Horizon Archeological and Cultural Trips (☎ 505-343 9400, fax 343 8076), PO Box 91900, Albuquerque, NM 87199-1900, USA, organises a limited number of specialist tours guided by highly qualified archaeological authorities. A seven day trip will cost from US$3000 to US$3500 per person, plus air fares.

Getting Around

CAR & MOTORCYCLE

Agencies and bigger hotels rent out Suzuki jeeps for US$90 per day in peak season, but locals and some guesthouses do it for as little as US$50 per eight hour day. A 24 hour day is up to US$80 or US$90, but you can get a few consecutive days for US$50 per day. On Policarpo Toro, try Easter Island Rent-a-Car (☎ 100 328), Comercial Insular (☎ 100 480), Puna Pau Rent-a-Car (☎ 100 978) or Te Aiki (☎ 100 366, at Tekena Inn); or look for signs in windows. Outside the high season, prices are negotiable. Insurance is not usually included and some cars are far from perfect.

Motorbikes are rented out for about US$20 per eight hours; US$30 to $35 a day. Given rough roads and occasional tropical downpours, a jeep is more convenient, and more economical, for two or more people.

BICYCLE

Bikes can be rented at a few places for around US$20 per day – try Comercial Insular. LanChile has few restrictions on carrying bikes, and if you bring your own, you may be able to sell it on the island.

TAXI

Taxis cost a flat US$2 for most trips around town. Longer trips can be negotiated, with the cost depending mainly on the time – an all-day trip will be expensive.

HORSE

For sites near Hanga Roa, horses can be hired for about US$20 to US$25 per day. Horse gear is very basic and potentially hazardous for inexperienced riders. Hotel Hotu Matua (☎ 100 242) or Hotel Hanga Roa (☎ 100 299) can organise riding excursions with proper saddles, bridles and guides. Residencial Ana Rapu (☎ 100 540) runs five-day horseback camping tours around the island from around US$250 per person.

ORGANISED TOURS

Plenty of small operators run tours of the sites for around US$35 to US$40 per person for a full day; US$20 to US$25 for a half day.

Around Easter Island

HANGA ROA
● pop 2700

Nearly all the islanders live in Hanga Roa, a sprawling town with irregular, uncrowded streets. Tourism, fishing, retailing and the

provision of government services are the main sources of income, but the tourist sector is so informal that the town doesn't seem touristy at all.

Orientation

Only a few of the main streets are paved, none have street signs, street numbers are nonexistent and houses are often hidden behind overgrown gardens. But everyone knows everyone else and is happy to give directions, and the place is so small that you'll learn your way around in a day or so. Avenida Policarpo Toro, the main north-south road, has the island's few shops and several eateries. The bank, tourist office, school and some other public buildings are in the blocks between Policarpo Toro and the small bay called Caleta Hanga Roa. Only small fishing boats can enter the bay, which has a nice little surf break and a protected swimming area. Ahu Tautira, a restored moai, stands with its back to the bay, looking over the football field.

Information

Tourist Offices Sernatur (☎ 100 255), near Caleta Hanga Roa, is open 9 am to 1 pm and 2 to 7 pm weekdays, and on Saturday from 9 am to 1 pm. Some staff speak English, French or Rapa Nui, but most information is in Spanish.

Post & Communications The post office is on Avenida Te Pito o Te Henua, and is open 9 am to 5 pm weekdays, and on Saturday morning from 9 am to noon. The Entel telephone office, with its conspicuous satellite dish, is in a cul-de-sac opposite Sernatur, and is open 8 am to 6 pm daily. See under Post & Communications earlier in this chapter for telephone country codes and charges.

Medical Services The hospital (☎ 100 131) is one long block east from the church.

Conaf The Chilean National Forests Authority (Conaf) is responsible for the national park that covers most of the island. The Conaf office (☎ 100 236) is south of

EASTER ISLAND

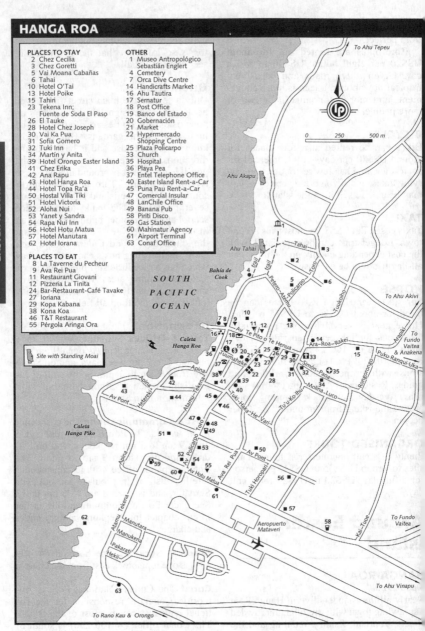

HANGA ROA

PLACES TO STAY
- 2 Chez Cecilia
- 3 Chez Goretti
- 5 Vai Moana Cabañas
- 6 Tahai
- 10 Hotel O'Tai
- 13 Hotel Poike
- 15 Tahiri
- 23 Tekena Inn;
  Fuente de Soda El Paso
- 26 El Tauke
- 28 Hotel Chez Joseph
- 30 Vai Ka Pua
- 31 Sofia Gomero
- 32 Tuki Inn
- 34 Martin y Anita
- 39 Hotel Orongo Easter Island
- 41 Chez Erika
- 42 Ana Rapu
- 43 Hotel Hanga Roa
- 44 Hotel Topa Ra'a
- 50 Hostal Villa Tiki
- 51 Hotel Victoria
- 52 Aloha Nui
- 53 Yanet y Sandra
- 54 Rapa Nui Inn
- 56 Hotel Hotu Matua
- 57 Hotel Manutara
- 62 Hotel Iorana

PLACES TO EAT
- 8 La Taverne du Pecheur
- 9 Ava Rei Pua
- 11 Restaurant Giovani
- 12 Pizzeria La Tinita
- 24 Bar-Restaurant-Café Tavake
- 27 Ioriana
- 29 Kopa Kabana
- 38 Kona Koa
- 46 T&T Restaurant
- 55 Pérgola Aringa Ora

OTHER
- 1 Museo Antropológico
  Sebastián Englert
- 4 Cemetery
- 7 Orca Dive Centre
- 14 Handicrafts Market
- 16 Ahu Tautira
- 17 Sernatur
- 18 Post Office
- 19 Banco del Estado
- 20 Gobernación
- 21 Market
- 22 Hypermercado
  Shopping Centre
- 25 Plaza Policarpo
- 33 Church
- 35 Hospital
- 36 Playa Pea
- 37 Entel Telephone Office
- 40 Easter Island Rent-a-Car
- 45 Puna Pau Rent-a-Car
- 47 Comercial Insular
- 49 LanChile Office
- 58 Pirti Disco
- 59 Gas Station
- 60 Mahinatur Agency
- 61 Airport Terminal
- 63 Conaf Office

own on the road to Orongo and can give advice on hiking and camping.

Museo Antropológico Sebastián Englert

This moderately interesting museum concentrates on Rapa Nui people and their history, with many photographs depicting their encounters with European culture since the mid-19th century. It also displays the strange moai kavakava and replica rongo-rongo tablets. The museum is north of town near Ahu Tahai and opens 9.30 am to 12.30 pm and 2 to 5.30 pm Tuesday to Friday; 9.30 am to 12.30 pm on weekends (US$2).

Places to Stay

Inexpensive *residenciales* (guesthouses) charge about US$25/40 for a single/double room, including breakfast, for most of the year. Many offer full board for around US$45/75, but it's probably better to have a picnic lunch at the archaeological sites and to try the Hanga Roa restaurants for dinner. Note: neither streets nor residenciales are well signposted, and buildings rarely have numbers, so locate places by referring to the map, or with the help of a taxi driver.

Reservations are only necessary in the peak times of August and January-February, when prices may be 30 to 50% higher. It's considerably more expensive to book accommodation through agents on the mainland. Hosts often meet incoming flights with a discount offer, including transport to town. Representatives of the better, more expensive lodgings are allowed to solicit business inside the terminal, while those from the cheaper guesthouses wait outside. These people are usually reliable and are the easiest and most common way to find budget accommodation.

Camping There are Conaf camping areas near the Rano Raraku volcano and at Anakena on the north coast – ask first about the water supply. In town, you can camp in the grounds of some residenciales, including *Chez Cecilia* and *Ana Rapu*, for about US$8 per person per night.

Residenciales One of the cheapest is *Residencial Tahai* (☎ 100 395), off Policarpo Toro, at US$14/25 for a single/double with shared bathroom; better rooms with private bath cost US$25/40. Friendly *Residencial Ana Rapu* (☎ 100 540), near the bay, is the backpackers' choice, with rooms from US$15/20 per person with shared/private bath. It has facilities for campers, arranges car and horse rentals, conducts tours and does the occasional Rapa Nui barbecue.

Other popular residenciales include the centrally located *El Tauke* (☎ 100 253), up a steep driveway on the south side of Avenida Te Pito o Te Henua, and *Tekena Inn* (☎ 100 289) on Policarpo Toro; quiet places on the outskirts like *Tuki Inn* (☎ 100 859) and *Martín y Anita* (☎ 100 593), both on Simón Paoa; and those closer to the airport like *Yanet y Sandra* (☎ 100 365) on Policarpo Toro and the well-recommended *Rapa Nui Inn* (☎ 100 228), also on Policarpo Toro. They all cost around US$25/50 for singles/doubles with breakfast and bathroom and they may give discounts in the off season. Plenty of other guesthouses (most are marked on the map) have similar standards and prices and they might have someone meet you at the airport.

Other comfortable places near the northern end of Policarpo Toro include *Chez Goretti* (☎ 100 459) from US$30/50; the new *Vai Moana Cabañas* (☎ 100 626) with sea views for US$40/60; and the comfortable *Chez Cecilia* (☎ 100 499) at US$40/70. Other places include the attractive *Residencial Sofía Gomero* (☎ 100 313) on Tu'u Ko Ihu at US$35/60; *Hotel Poike* (☎ 100 283) on Petero Atamu, with a family atmosphere and pretty gardens from US$40/60; *Hostal Villa Tiki* (☎ 100 327) on Avenida Pont, which has a beautiful outlook, for US$45/70; *Hotel Chez Joseph* (☎ 100 373), off Ava Rei Pua, on a hilltop near the middle of town, for US$45/85 (get a room facing outwards); and *Chez Erika* (☎ 100 474) on Tuki Haka He Vari, with bungalow rooms in a spacious garden from US$35/70.

Hotels Some so-called 'hotels' are just oversized guesthouses with slightly better

EASTER ISLAND

facilities. An interesting one is the *Hotel Victoria* (☎ 100 272), on a hilltop near the middle of town, with good rooms from US$40/60. It has some character, though the service can be idiosyncratic.

The better hotels have swimming pools and are quite expensive. *Hotel O'Tai* (☎ 100 250, fax 100 482) on Avenida Te Pito o Te Henua opposite the post office is OK for US$59/94, with friendly management, good food and a nice outlook to the sea. *Hotel Manutara* (☎ 100 297, fax 100 768), on Avenida Hotu Matua near the airport, is a well run, motel-style place with comfortable rooms for US$78/121.

Hotel Hotu Matua (☎ 100 242, fax 100 444) is in an uninspiring location on Avenida Pont at the airport end of town. Rooms with all the usual comforts and conveniences start at US$60/110, but the place is pretty low on charm. *Hotel Iorana* (☎ 100 312) on Atamu Tekena is between the ocean and the end of the airport runway – the ocean views are spectacular and there are only a few flights per week! The rooms are OK, but some parts of the hotel look like they are due for renovation. Prices start at US$85/118.

Hotel Hanga Roa (☎/fax 100 299) on Apina has a great position handy to town and overlooking the ocean. Rooms start at around US$90/110 with individual cottages at around US$220. One of the Chilean-owned Panamericana chain, it's the largest hotel on the island (60 rooms), and was being upgraded at the time of writing.

Places to Eat
Food is quite expensive and nothing special, though the seafood and vegetables are fresh. If you're camping or cooking your own food, get provisions at general stores and bakeries on Policarpo Toro. The *open-air market* is good for vegetables, and the new *Hypermercado*, opposite, has a fair variety of cheese and spam.

Inconspicuous *Restaurant Giovani* just off Avenida Te Pito o Te Henua is one of the cheapest eateries and is popular with locals – you eat what is served (a set meal). To find it, walk up the lane beside *Pizzeria La Tinita*.

A few places along Policarpo have adequate food in a convivial atmosphere – try *Fuente de Soda el Paso*, *Ioriana*, or the *T&T Restaurant*.

Bar-Restaurant-Cafe Tavake is OK for hot dogs and snacks, but pricey for main meals. *Kopa Kabana* on Avenida Te Pito o Te Henua serves some typical Rapa Nui dishes and other excellent offerings in a pleasant indoor/outdoor setting. *Pérgola Aringa Ora*, on Avenida Hotu Matua opposite the airport, is also recommended.

The French-run *La Taverne du Pecheur* on Atamu-Tekena at the entrance to the harbour area, has a rustic seaside setting, some excellent dishes and high prices – main courses are well over US$10.

Entertainment
Kona Koa (☎ 100 415) near the Entel office on a cul-de-sac south of Tuu Maheke, is a somewhat pricey restaurant, with a popular bar and regular Rapa Nui folkloric shows.

The *Banana Pub* on Policarpo Toro attracts young locals with off-beat decor inside and a surfboard outside. Other nightspots are *Playa Pea*, on Atamu-Tekena near the seafront and the popular *Piriti Disco*, on Avenida Hotu Matua opposite the airport – both open Thursday to Saturday nights.

Shopping
For crafts, the best selection and price (open to some negotiation) are at the recently reconstructed handicrafts market opposite the church. (A morning craft market was operating on Policarpo Toro during the building work.) The classic souvenir is a miniature carved stone moai, usually sold with a red stone topknot. Smaller ones cost from about US$15 and are not too heavy. Stuffed moai soft toys are a cuddly variant. Wooden moai kavakava and rongorongo tablets are also good, as are jewellery and necklaces of obsidian or seashells.

PARQUE NACIONAL RAPA NUI
Since 1935, much of Easter Island's land and all the archaeological sites have been a national park administered by Conaf. The park has been a World Heritage Site since 199?

Non-Chileans are supposed to buy admission tickets (US$10) at Ahu Tahai or Orongo, valid for the whole park for the length of their stay, but the fee is not always collected.

Though Chilean government agencies have promoted tourism and enabled the restoration of some moai, many islanders view the park as a land grab. Some sections of the Consejo de Ancianos (Council of Elders) want the park (about a third of the island's area) returned to its aboriginal owners, who control almost no land outside Hanga Roa.

Near Hanga Roa

Several sites of interest are close to town, and all can be seen in a few hours by car or motorbike. By bicycle, the circuit would make a full day. Walking, you could get around everything in a long day, except the Puna Pau topknot quarry.

Ahu Tahai A short hike north of town, this site contains three restored ahu, especially photogenic at sunset. Ahu Tahai proper is in the middle, with a solitary moai. Ahu Ko Te Riku is to the north, with a topknotted and eyeballed moai. Ahu Vai Uri has five eroded moai of varying sizes.

Ahu Akapu A solitary moai stands here, on the coast just north of Ahu Tahai. It's another great sunset spot.

Ahu Tepeu Four kilometres on a rough but scenic road north of Tahai, this large ahu has several fallen moai and an extensive village site. Walk around to find foundations of *hare paenga* (elliptical houses) and the walls of several round houses.

Ana Te Pahu Off the dirt road between Akivi and the west coast, Ana Te Pahu is a former cave dwelling where the entrance is an overgrown garden of sweet potatoes, taro and bananas. The caves here are lava tubes, created when rock solidified around a flowing stream of molten lava.

Ahu Akivi Unusual for its inland location, this ahu has seven restored moai. They are the only ones that face towards the sea, but like all moai they overlook the site of a village, traces of which can still be seen.

Puna Pau The soft, red, stone of this volcanic hill was used to make the reddish, cylindrical pukao (topknots) that were placed on many moai. Half-finished topknots have been rolled down the hill, and remain in a scattered line. Look for the partly hollow underside designed to slot onto a moai's head. Puna Pau is only a couple kilometres east of town, but it's only accessible via a rough and very roundabout road.

The North-East Circuit

This loop takes in the three finest sites on the island and can be done in a long day with motorised transport. It's good to go anticlockwise, because Rano Raraku is a magnificent highlight in the late afternoon. Heading north-east from the airport, a smooth paved road runs 13km to the north coast.

Anakena The legendary landing place of Hotu Matua, Anakena has several caves and is popular for swimming and sunbathing. The curving, white-sand beach is a perfect backdrop for **Ahu Nau Nau**, with its fine row of moai. A 1979 excavation and restoration

Fifteen restored moai watch over the site of an ancient village at Ahu Tongariki.

revealed that the moai were not 'blind' but had inlaid coral and rock eyes – 'eyes that look to the sky', in a Rapa Nui phrase.

On a rise south of the beach stands **Ahu Ature Huki** and its lone moai. Heyerdahl and a dozen islanders took nine days to lever up this statue with wooden poles and ropes.

You can stay overnight at the small Conaf campsite, just inland from the beach, but bring supplies from Hanga Roa. Ask in town whether water is available.

Ovahe Just east of Anakena, this cove has a sandy beach, small caves, a ruined ahu, rough water and the occasional shark.

Ahu Te Pito Kura Here, beside Bahía de La Pérouse Bay, a massive 10m moai lies face down with its neck broken. It is the largest moai ever moved from Rano Raraku and erected on an ahu. Its resemblance to the incomplete figures at Rano Raraku suggests that this moai is also one of the most recent.

The Movie of the Island of the Statues

The 1994 movie *Rapa Nui* is B-grade matinee material at best. Famous for having Kevin Costner as its co-producer, the film was hardly a hit at the box office and made little impression on the critics, but it had a huge impact on Easter Island. The filming itself, over several months of 1993, involved hundreds of the islanders as extras and brought a valuable injection of cash to the economy (though stories that every islander bought a car are exaggerated). Inevitably there were romances between local women and the visiting film crew, and fears of permanent disruption to island life and permanent damage to archaeological sites. In the end, the film company paid for a thorough cleanup and made a substantial donation to the national park; the statues suffered no real damage and island life resumed pretty much as before.

While the film may have stimulated local pride in the island's culture, it presents some unflattering and inaccurate images. For example, the film has islanders clad in skimpy 'caveman'-

A Rapa Nui chieftan in ceremonial cloak and head-dress

style loincloths, portraying them as primitive even as they created the fine stone statues for which the island is so famous. The impression of the islanders as savages is reinforced in scenes of mindless deforestation, and in the depiction of the 'birdman' ritual as a brutal, cut-throat contest. The main inaccuracy is that events that occurred over several centuries are shown as happening in just a few years of film time. While the film takes great liberties with historical fact, its impact depends on it being seen as a true story, not fiction. Just as Heyerdahl's theories suggested (wrongly) that Rapa Nui's culture did not derive from a Polynesian heritage, so this film can be seen as the distortion of an indigenous history to satisfy the western taste for a stimulating yarn.

On a positive note, the film's scenery has all the rugged and remote appeal of the island itself. This may be good publicity for the local tourism industry, but unless the tourists show more respect for Rapa Nui heritage than this film does, tourism may be a mixed blessing.

Poike Peninsula Easter Island's eastern corner is a peninsula formed by the extinct volcano Maunga Pukatikei. Legend says that the Long Ears retreated to Poike and built a km defensive trench that was filled with wood and set ablaze, though recent tests do not indicate that there was a fire here.

Ahu Tongariki In 1960, a tsunami demolished several moai and scattered topknots far inland from this, the largest ahu ever built. A Japanese project has restored the 15 imposing moai at this stunning oceanside location. The statues gaze over a large, level village site, with ruined remnants scattered about and some petroglyphs nearby.

Rano Raraku This volcano, where moai were cut from the porous grey rock, is a wonderfully evocative place. Groups of moai are partly buried, their heads grouped on the grassy slopes. Others are in the early stages of carving and seem to be sleeping in niches in the cliffs – the largest is a 21m giant, but most range from 5.5 to 7m. Over 300 of these figures stand and lie around Rano Raraku, and a number are scattered face-down in an irregular line to the south-west, never to reach their ahu on the coast.

Most were carved face up, horizontal or slightly reclined. Be sure to walk up and around to the inside of the crater, which has a reedy lake and an amphitheatre full of handsome heads. Climb right to the top for a fabulous 360° view.

There are no facilities at the site, but Conaf maintains a shady campsite on a side track a little to the south-west. Rano Raraku is a detour off the rugged south coast road, about 18km from Hanga Roa. There are several ruined ahu along the way.

The South-West
The south-west corner of the island is dominated by the Rano Kau crater. On its seaward slopes, the low stone houses of **Orongo ceremonial village** were used during the rituals of the 'bird cult' in the 18th and 19th centuries.

The climax of the rituals was a competition to retrieve an egg of the sooty tern *(Sterna fuscata)*, which breeds on the small *motu* (islets) just offshore. Young men climbed down the steep cliffs and swam out to the islands to search for an egg. The egg was then tied to the forehead for the return swim and climb. Whoever returned first with an intact egg won the favour of the god Makemake and great community status. Also (as if that were not enough), local lore has it that seven virgins became birdman groupies for the whole year. Birdman petroglyphs are visible on a cluster of boulders between the cliff top and the crater's edge. Orongo is a steepish 2km climb from town, or a short scenic drive.

Ahu Vinapu Beyond the eastern end of the airport runway, a road heads south past some large oil tanks to Ahu Vinapu. Several toppled moai lie around, but Vinapu is most famous for its tight-fitting stonework, which some claim is similar to a style found at Inca sites on the South American mainland.

French Polynesia

Better known by the name of its main island of Tahiti, French Polynesia and its islands have come to epitomise the Pacific dream. There are beautiful reef-fringed islands, palm trees and vividly blue lagoons, stunning diving, sensuous hip-swinging dancers and outrigger canoes propelled by powerful tattooed men. The islands comprise five distinctly different groups, scattered over an area as big as Europe.

French Polynesia is well known for the beauty of the islands, whether it's mountainous islands like Bora Bora or low-lying coral atolls like Rangiroa. Unfortunately it's equally well known for hitting visitors with some of the highest prices in the Pacific. Fortunately the beauty is real and the high prices are not always as bad as they seem. Visitors looking for island luxury and fine food – and equipped with industrial-strength credit cards – may decide French Polynesia is worth the expenditure. Travellers on a tighter budget will be pleasantly surprised to find there are backpacker resorts and low-key local pensions, moderately priced places to eat and excellent shipping services between the most popular islands of the Society Islands.

Facts about French Polynesia

HISTORY
It was almost a millennium after people reached Samoa and Tonga before the next great migration wave, in 200 BC (some believe it may have been as late as 300 AD), east to the Society and Marquesas islands of modern-day French Polynesia.

Here they called themselves the Maohi and their culture bloomed. The island of Raiatea (then known as Havaiki) became the cultural and religious centre of the vast region of Polynesia. When migrations began again in earnest (in about 300 AD), Raiatea

AT A GLANCE

Capital City (& Island): Papeete (Tahiti)
Population: 220,000
Time: 10 hours behind GMT (Tahiti)
Land Area: 3500 sq km (1360 sq miles)
Number of Islands: 118
International Telephone Code: ☎ 689
GDP/Capita: US$12,750
Currency: Cour de Franc Pacifique (100 CFP = US$0.89)
Languages: Tahitian, French & English
Greeting: *Ia ora na* (Tahitian) or *Bonjour* (French)

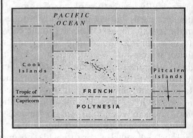

HIGHLIGHTS
- **Ua Huka** – riding on horseback through the desolate landscape of the isle of horses

- **Society Islands** – the fun and festivities of the spectacular annual Hawaiki Nui canoe race

- **Hiva Oa** – Iipona displays the most significant remains of pre-European civilisation in the Marquesas Islands

- **Bora Bora** – superb snorkelling with lagoon marine life

- **Papeete after dark** – eating alfresco from *les roulottes* and taking in the nightlife of colourful waterfront Blvd Pomare

FRENCH POLYNESIA

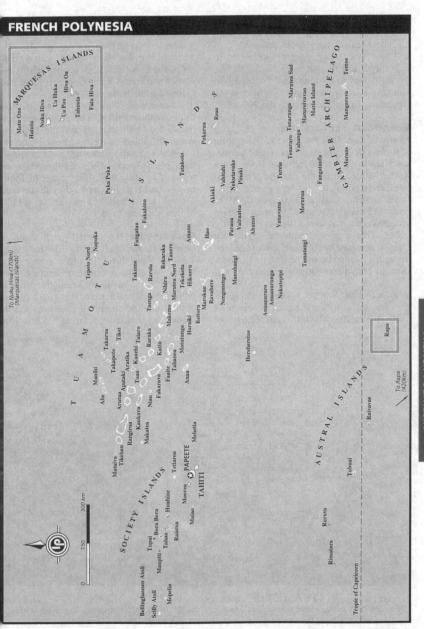

MARQUESAS ISLANDS

Motu One
Hatutu
Nuku Hiva
Ua Huka
Ua Pou   Hiva Oa
Tahuata
Fatu Hiva

To Nuku Hiva (1700km)
(Marquesas Islands)

T U A M O T U   I S L A N D S

GAMBIER ARCHIPELAGO

Reao
Pukarua
Vahitahi
Nukutavake   Akiaki
Pinaki
Vairaatea
Ahunui
Paraoa
Hao
Amanu
Tatakoto
Fakahina
Fangatau
Napuka
Tepoto Nord
Takume
Raroia
Tenararo   Tenarunga   Marutea Sud
Vahanga   Maturei'vavao
Maria Island
Turcia   Fangataufa
Morane
Morurou   Temoe
Vanavana   Mangareva
Tematangi

Tenaga
Kauehi   Taiaro
Takapoto   Tikei
Takaroa
Manihi
Ahe
Raraka
Katiu   Nihiru   Rekareka   Tauere
Makemo   Marutea Nord
Tahanea   Tekokota
Hikueru
Motutunga   Retoru
Haraiki
Marokau
Ravahere
Nengonengo
Manuhangi
Nukutepipi
Anuanuraro
Anuanurunga
Hereheretue

Mataiva
Tikehau
Rangiroa
Makatea
Arutua
Apataki
Kaukura
Niau
Fakarava
Faaite
Toau
Anaa
Puka Puka

Bellinghausen Atoll
Scilly Atoll
Mopelia

Manuae   Bora Bora
Tupai
Tahaa   Huahine
Maupiti   Raiatea
Maiao
Moorea   Tetiaroa
Mehetia
PAPEETE
TAHITI
SOCIETY ISLANDS

A U S T R A L   I S L A N D S

Rapa

To Rapa
(420km)

Raivavae
Tubuai

Rurutu
Rimatara

Tropic of Capricorn

0   150   300 km

FRENCH POLYNESIA

was the hub for the expansion. Legends claim that temples built on each new island all incorporated stones from Raiatea.

These last voyages went south-west to Rarotonga and the southern Cook Islands, north to Hawai'i, south-east to Rapa Nui (Easter Island) and via Rarotonga to Aotearoa (New Zealand) around 900 AD.

European Exploration

Mendaña & Quirós In 1595 Alvaro de Mendaña de Neyra came upon the Marquesas Islands on his second search for *Terra Australis Incognita*, the non-existent Great Southern Continent. Mendaña named the islands after his patron, Marquesas de Mendoza, but his visit resulted in open warfare and 200 islanders were killed.

Mendaña's pilot, Pedro Fernández de Quirós, returned in 1606 and discovered the Tuamotu Islands before sailing to Vanuatu. (See the boxed text 'Quirós' in that chapter.)

Wallis In 1767 Samuel Wallis on the HMS *Dolphin* came to the Pacific in search of Terra Australis – which of course he never found. More usefully, he and his crew became the first Europeans to visit Tahiti.

The *Dolphin* anchored in Tahiti's Matavai Bay for a few weeks, with a quarter of the crew sick with scurvy. Wallis renamed the island King George's Land and claimed it for Britain.

After some initial conflict, a friendly trade was carried on. The crew were desperate for fresh supplies and the Tahitians were delighted to receive metal knives, hatchets and nails in exchange. At this point the *Dolphin*'s crew also took the first steps towards creating the lasting image of Tahiti as a sexual paradise when they discovered a single nail would buy sex just as readily as it would buy food.

Bougainville The great French explorer Louis-Antoine de Bougainville arrived at Tahiti in April 1768, less than a year after Wallis. When he returned to Europe his reports of 'noble savages', Venus-like women with 'the celestial form of that goddess' and of the Tahitians' uninhibited attitude towards matters sexual swept through Paris like

The Natives of OTAHEITE attacking CAPT. WALLIS in the Dolphi

The *Dolphin*'s crew defend themselves against a Tahitian attack. After relations improved, Wallis' crew discovered the amazing purchasing power of a single iron nail (engraving 1786).

Jean Baret

When Bougainville arrived in 1768, his ship's naturalist, Dr Philibert Commerçon, was accompanied by a young valet named Jean Baret. When Baret came ashore the Tahitians, pretty cluey about these matters after centuries of the *mahu* tradition, immediately took a great interest in him. They stripped his clothes off to reveal that Baret was actually a woman! Commerçon was extremely embarrassed, but Baret became not only the first European woman to visit Tahiti but also the first woman to circumnavigate the world.

wildfire. Not having heard of Wallis' claim, Bougainville claimed Tahiti for France while he was there.

Cook One of Cook's tasks in the Pacific (the first was to chart Terra Australis) was to observe from Tahiti the transit of Venus as it passed across the face of the sun. Cook's meticulous observations of Tahiti brought the wonders of the island to an appreciative European audience.

Cook arrived in April 1769 and stayed for three months before sailing south to New Zealand (NZ). His scientists and artists surveyed the flora and fauna and described traditional society and Maohi customs. Cook returned to Tahiti during his second (1772-75) and third (1776-80) expeditions.

Boenechea In 1772 the *Aguilla*, under the Spaniard Don Domingo de Boenechea, sailed from Peru to Tahiti Iti and, for the third time, the island was claimed by a European nation. When Boenechea returned in 1774 he established Tautira – the first long-term European settlement on Tahiti.

Completely unsuccessful at converting the heathens, the Spanish missionaries returned to Peru in 1775. Thus ended the Spanish role in Tahiti. When Cook returned in 1777 he found the Spanish cross in front of the abandoned mission house, carved with the year of its establishment. On the back of the cross

Cook added the list of Tahitian visits by his own and Wallis' expeditions.

The *Bounty* Mutineers

In 1779 the infamous mutiny on the *Bounty* occurred after Bligh's crew had spent six long comfortable months in Tahiti. The boxed text in the Pitcairn Islands chapter tells the *Bounty* story.

The mutineers returned to Tahiti and Tubuai in the Austral Islands after the mutiny, then some of them sailed off to find a more remote hideaway on Pitcairn. Sixteen mutineers stayed behind in Tahiti, however, with long-lasting effects.

Prior to the arrival of Europeans, power had been a local affair. No ruler was strong enough to extend control very far, and Tahiti was divided into a number of squabbling groups. When they realised the importance of European weaponry, Tahitians pressed the *Bounty* mutineers to take sides in local conflicts. The mutineers offered themselves as mercenaries to the highest bidder – which was the Pomare family.

Before the arrival of the *Bounty*, the Pomares had been just one of a number of important families. But the mutineers and their weapons were the first step towards the Pomare destiny as rulers of the islands. Pomare I, known as Tu, controlled most of Tahiti by the time he died in 1803 – his son Pomare II took over.

Whalers, Missionaries & Depopulation

The London Missionary Society (LMS) landed at Point Venus in March 1797. Success was not immediate – the missionaries' influence rose and fell along with their patron, Pomare II. However, once they had a foothold, dancing, 'indecent' songs, tattoos, nudity, indiscriminate sex and even wearing flowers in hair were all banned.

Whalers and traders arrived in Polynesia in the 1790s, inadvertently spreading diseases, encouraging prostitution and introducing alcohol and more weapons.

Plagued by diseases against which they had no natural immunity, the population plummeted. When Cook first visited, the population of Tahiti was probably about 40,000. In 1800 it was less than 20,000 and by the 1820s it was down to around 6000. In the Marquesas the situation was even worse – the population dropped from 80,000 to only 2000 in one century.

The Pomares & the Missionaries

After 1815 the Pomares ruled Tahiti, with Protestant missionaries advising them on government and laws and attempting to keep whalers and Australian traders at arm's length. Pomare II died in 1821 and his son, Pomare III, who died in 1827, was succeeded by the young Queen Pomare IV.

The new queen's missionary advisers saw her only as an interim ruler until the arrival of the next king, so they turned a blind eye to some of her youthful excesses. The new queen was not averse to a little singing and dancing, and even visiting passing ships. Queen Pomare ruled over Tahiti for 50 years.

MANOLO MYLONAS

The long-ruling Queen Pomare IV (1827-77) was the last to rule an independent Tahiti.

English Protestant missionaries were the major advisers to chiefs in the Society, Austral and Tuamotu islands. But in the Gambiers and Marquesas, French Catholic missionaries were in control. In 1836 two French missionaries, Laval and Caret, from the Gambiers came to Papeete and were promptly arrested and deported.

The French Takeover

The deporting of the two missionaries was treated as a national insult by France. Demands, claims, counterclaims, payments and apologies shuttled back and forth until 1842, when Admiral Dupetit-Thouars turned up in the ship *La Reine Blanche* and pointed his guns at Papeete. Queen Pomare was forced to yield and French soldiers promptly landed, along with Catholic missionaries.

The French arrested and deported George Pritchard, the British missionary who was consul and unofficial chief adviser to the queen. The queen, still hoping for British intervention, fled to Raiatea in 1844 and a guerrilla rebellion broke out on several islands. Eventually the rebels were subdued and by 1846 France had control over Tahiti and Moorea. The queen returned to Tahiti in 1847, although as a mere figurehead, as the French were in command.

Queen Pomare died in 1877 and her son, Pomare V, had little interest in the position, abdicating in 1881. French power extended to include most of the other Society Islands in 1888, although rebellions rumbled on in Raiatea until almost the end of the century. The Gambiers were annexed in 1881 and the Australs in 1900-01.

20th Century & Beyond

Soon after the turn of the century, an economic boom attracted colonists, mostly French. By 1911 there were about 3500 Europeans in the islands, adding to Chinese immigration, which had begun in 1864 with the production of cotton at Atimaono. The foundations of a multiethnic society were in place.

French Polynesia was directly involved in both world wars. In WWI almost 1000 Tahitian soldiers fought in Europe and on 22 September 1914 two German cruisers patrolling the Pacific sank the French cruiser *Zélée* and shelled the Papeete market. In WWII Bora Bora was a base for 5000 US soldiers, and a 2km runway was built in 1943. Tahitian volunteers in the Pacific Battalion fought in North Africa and Europe.

In 1946 the islands became an overseas territory within the French Republic, but the first signs of a push for emancipation from France also took shape. A political party, the Democratic Assembly of Tahitian Populations (RDPT), took centre stage on the political scene for about 10 years.

On 22 July 1957 the territory officially became French Polynesia. Three events in quick succession had a considerable impact. In 1961 the construction of Faaa airport opened French Polynesia to the world. Shortly after, the Tahiti filming of *Mutiny on the Bounty* poured millions of dollars into the island's economy. In 1963, with the establishment of the Pacific Experimentation Centre (CEP) at Moruroa and Fangataufa, French Polynesia entered the nuclear age.

In addition to the controversy raised by the experiments – violent protests shook Papeete in 1987 and 1995 – the CEP overturned the socioeconomic structures of Polynesia, thrusting it into a market economy.

From 1977 to 1996 French Polynesia took over internal management and autonomy. Independence is still a future possibility but it would bring with it great social and economic challenges.

GEOGRAPHY

French Polynesia's five island groups are distinctly different. The Society Islands are mountainous high islands with lagoons protected by barrier reefs, sometimes dotted with small fringing islets known as *motu*. Subdivided into the Windward and Leeward islands, the Societies are home to over three-quarters of French Polynesia's population. The administrative capital of Polynesia, Papeete, is on Tahiti.

The Tuamotus are classic low-lying coral atolls. The remote Marquesas are rugged high islands. Finally, there are the even more remote and scattered Australs and the tiny Gambier Archipelago.

CLIMATE

French Polynesia's hot and humid wet season runs from November to April and the cooler dry season runs from May to October. Temperatures are rarely impossibly high and do not vary a great deal through the year.

French Polynesia is in the South Pacific cyclone zone. In 1997-98, there were eight cyclones including Osea (which caused great damage on Maupiti in November 1997) and Alan (which did enormous damage to Bora Bora, Raiatea, Tahaa and Huahine in April 1998).

ECOLOGY & ENVIRONMENT

Atolls are ecologically fragile places, highly susceptible to environmental damage, and French Polynesia has been slow in ensuring environmental protection. Tourism, the region's main resource, depends on the integrity of the natural heritage.

The biggest potential environmental problem for French Polynesia, one that dwarfs the garbage floating in lagoons and poor quality sewerage treatment, is the legacy of the nuclear tests on Moruroa and Fangataufa. In 1998 the French government confirmed the presence of cracks in the coral structure of the two atolls and leakage of plutonium into the sea at Moruroa. Claims of birth defects and cancer in the Tuamotus are impossible to confirm, with a tight lid kept on health records in the territory. (Also see Ecology & Environment in the Facts about the South Pacific chapter.)

The only reserve is Scilly Atoll in the Leeward Society Islands, although several species of marine life are protected, notably rays and turtles.

French Polynesia has many low-lying coral atolls, all of which would be threatened by the rising seas predicted under global warming models. (See the boxed text under Climate in the Facts about the South Pacific chapter.)

FLORA & FAUNA

Almost all the Pacific's flora and fauna migrated east from South-East Asia, becoming less varied as you move east across the

Pacific towards French Polynesia. Numerous plant and animal species have been introduced by humans at different times.

Flora

The most luxuriant flora, particularly on the high islands, is recent and has been introduced by humans. Ancient Polynesian navigators brought with them plants, fruits and domestic animals. These were supplemented in the 19th century, as missionaries and settlers imported other plants of ornamental and commercial value.

Vegetation varies significantly from one archipelago to another. On the atolls, where the soil is poor and winds constant, bushy vegetation and coconut palms predominate. On the high islands, plant cover is more diverse and varies according to altitude.

Fauna

Like the flora, the fauna of French Polynesia's is poor compared to regions in the west Pacific.

Ancient settlers bought the first domestic animals: pigs, chickens and dogs. Horses have bred on the Marquesas and goats are also common, roaming almost free.

There are about 100 species of *manu* (birds) in French Polynesia. On the low islands, many nest on the ground or in bushes. The feathers of certain birds were once much sought after for head-dresses and chieftains' belts.

Sea birds include terns, petrels, noddies, frigatebirds, boobies and the superb tropicbirds (phaethons) with long red or white feathers in their tails. On Ua Huka, the number of *kaveka* (sooty terns) nesting on two islets is estimated at nearly one million. In the Tuamotus there are numerous islands inhabited only by birds.

Marinelife includes the *kaveu* (coconut crab), which can reach an impressive size, *rori* (sea cucumber), sharks, *ono* (barracuda), manta rays, moray eels and dolphins. Swimming with whales is a popular activity in the Australs.

On the islands, the waterways are home to eels and freshwater shrimps – highly valued in local cuisine.

GOVERNMENT & POLITICS

French Polynesia is a French overseas territory. France, represented in the territory by a high commissioner, has control of defence, law and order, foreign affairs, immigration and justice. The territory itself looks after local administration, education, taxation and foreign trade.

The president of the French Polynesian government is elected by the assembly which is composed of councillors elected from the five archipelagos under universal suffrage every five years. There are three representatives of French Polynesia in the French Parliament.

On one side of local politics is the Tahoeraa Huiraatira (Gathering of the People) party, which is currently in power. On the other side is Tavini Huiraatira (To Serve the People), the pro-independence party that wants to break all ties with France and return to Polynesian principles.

ECONOMY

Money from France is the mainstay of the economy, with a large civil service paid at European salary levels. This artificial economy is a key reason for the high prices in French Polynesia. From the early 1960s the French nuclear testing program was a large factor in the imported economy but it's now being wound back.

Beautiful black pearls are a key export, and recently the wonders of therapeutic *noni* juice have become another important money maker. Pineapples are the only other major agricultural product. As in other Pacific islands, copra plantations are on a downward trend.

Tourism is an important source of income and employment, although it's worth noting that all the hotel rooms in French Polynesia wouldn't add up to a single mega-hotel on Hawai'i's Waikiki Beach!

POPULATION & PEOPLE

Of the population of 220,000, 86% live in the Society Islands (nearly half in the city of Papeete). The remaining 14% are split between the Marquesas, Tuamotus, Gambiers and Australs. Ethnic Polynesians and part-Polynesians account for 83% of the population, Europeans 12% and Asians 5%.

ARTS
Dance
All early European explorers commented on the excitement and erotic explicitness of Tahitian dancing, so of course it was one of the first things the missionaries banned. It continued clandestinely, and since the 1950s has been revived to become one of the best ambassadors for Polynesian culture.

Music
Traditional music is still strong and often accompanies dance performances, with guitars, ukuleles and percussion instruments playing a large part. Song, either secular or religious, is also important.

Architecture
The *fare* (house) is the traditional dwelling, constructed from plant materials and built directly on the ground without foundations. The framework is coconut wood and the roof either woven coconut palms or pandanus leaves. Paradoxically, it's at luxury hotels where you are most likely to find traditional architecture with frames and rafters in ironwood, thatched roofs and walls covered in plaited bamboo.

Today, the traditional *fare* style is often built with modern materials. Less picturesque perhaps, but more permanent and resistant to cyclones.

Painting
A number of predominantly European artists have sought inspiration in French Polynesia, most famously, of course, Paul Gauguin (see the boxed text). Apart from Matisse, who made a short stay in Tahiti, the best known is Jacques Boullaire. Mention must also be made of Christian Deloffre, François Ravello, Michèle Dallet, Bobby André Marere (also known as a singer and musician, he died in 1991), Jean Masson, Yrondi, Noguier and Erhart Lux.

Sculpture
The best known contemporary sculptors are the potter Peter Owen on Huahine and Woody on Moorea. Traditional sculptural craftwork is particularly dynamic in the Marquesas (see that section of this chapter) where fine *tiki* (large human figures), bowls, mortars and pestles, spears and clubs are carved from rosewood, *tou* wood or in stone.

Handicrafts
See Shopping in the Facts for the Visitor section for more information on crafts.

Clothing Like South-East Asia's sarong, or Samoa's *lavalava*, the *pareu* is a single piece of cloth colourfully decorated and usually worn by women, although equally appropriate for men. Woven hats made from pandanus leaves or thin strips of bamboo and often decorated with flowers or shells, are worn by Polynesian women, particularly at Sunday church services. The mission dress (or Mother Hubbard) is a style of long dress that arrived with the missionaries. Generally

Woven hats and printed *pareu* for sale at a market in Papeete.

Paul Gauguin

MANOLO MYLONAS

If one thing is responsible for Polynesia's enduring reputation as a paradise lost, it is the evocative paintings of Paul Gauguin (1848-1903).

After a childhood in Peru and France, Gauguin joined the navy as an officer cadet, and from 1868 to 1871 roamed the seas. He began to paint his first landscapes while working as a stockbroker in Paris. One of these was shown at the Salon Art Exhibition in 1876, and he exhibited with the Impressionists in 1879. The collapse of the stock market in 1882 put an end to Gauguin's business career and, leaving his wife and children, he devoted himself exclusively to painting. The following years were particularly difficult, and he lived for a long while in virtual poverty.

After some limited success, In 1890 Gauguin left France to cultivate his art in Tahiti. In Mataiea, where the Gauguin Museum now stands, he concentrated on capturing images of daily life, and in 1892-93 he painted *Te Nave Nave Fenua* (Delicious Land), *Manao Tupapau* (Spirit of the Dead Watching) and *Arearea* (Amusements). Exuberant settings and flamboyant colours, with yellow, red and blue predominating, increasingly pervaded the artist's painting.

But Gauguin sold few canvases, and to escape poverty he sailed for France in 1893. In November of that year, a large exhibition devoted solely to his work opened in Paris. He took up ceramics and embarked on writing a narrative, *Noa Noa*, inspired by his Tahitian period and designed to make the public understand his work. Disappointed with the results, he set off for the South Seas again in 1895.

His most powerful compositions, *Te Arii Vahine* (The Royal Woman; 1896), *Nevermore* (1897) and *Where Do We Come From? What Are We? Where Are We Going?* (1897), date from this second and final stay in French Polynesia, which was marked by illness and distress. After a failed suicide attempt, he took refuge on the island of Hiva Oa in the Marquesas, where he is fondly remembered for defending the inhabitants against the colonial administration and the all-powerful Catholic mission. Although weakened, he did not stop writing, drawing, sculpting and painting until his death. It was during this period that he produced one of his most beautiful nudes, entitled *Barbaric Tales* (1902).

worn by older women, they're decorated in floral styles and often trimmed with lace.

Tifaifai are large patchwork cloths, usually decorated with stylised flowers or fruit designs, which are used as tablecloths, bedspreads and curtains. Shells are used to make necklaces, traditionally used to garland people arriving at and departing the islands. *Monoi* is an oil made from coconuts and perfumed with crushed flowers (tiare, jasmin, santal and the like). It's used for hair oil, ointment, sunscreen and even mosquito repellent.

Tapa The ancient technique of making *tapa* (or *hobu*) from the bark of breadfruit, banyan or *aute* (paper mulberry) trees was practised by women throughout the Pacific. (See the 'South Pacific Arts' special section for an explanation of its significance.) Nowadays, tapa is almost disappearing – replaced by woven fabrics. Only on Fatu Hiva, in the Marquesas, is this ancient technique still practised.

Plaiting & Basketwork This craft is the domain of women who make baskets, hats and the panels used for roofing and walls of houses. The best work comes from the Austral Islands.

SOCIETY & CONDUCT

Some traditions of French Polynesia survived the attentions of the missionaries and there has been a revival of Polynesian culture in recent years, partly inspired by the tourist trade and by a rising pride in Polynesian accomplishments.

French Polynesia is generally very easy going and there are few pitfalls for the unwary visitor. *Aita pe'a pe'a* (No problems) is a common expression. You'll sometimes encounter people who are *fiu*, a temporary state like the Samoan *musu* or the western 'blues', when they are distant and unreceptive. Don't show your impatience; it won't get you anywhere.

See Society & Conduct in the Facts about the South Pacific chapter for information about Polynesian tradition and see Accommodation in the Regional Facts for the Visitor chapter for advice about staying in Polynesian homes.

Religion permeates everyday life and, contrary to popular myth, Polynesian women are very chaste. Local women usually wear shorts and T-shirts in the water and nudity on the beach is only permissible on isolated islets. Bikini tops are not required at big hotel beaches and swimming pools but elsewhere going topless is inappropriate.

Respect archaeological sites. For many Polynesians these are living places and these people will be deeply offended if you move stones or tiki around on *tapu* (sacred, taboo or prohibited) sites.

Tipping is not expected and bargaining (except for pearls) is not practised. Respect private-property signs, which often indicate that entry is *tapu*. Most waterfront land is privately owned, so ask permission before making your way down to the water. Fruit trees are almost always private property, so never pick fruit without asking first.

The Family System

The extended family, including uncles, aunts, cousins, and grandparents, is the *fetii*.

In addition to natural children, there are *faaamu* (adopted) children. It is also common for children to be entrusted to other relatives or neighbours, and it is becoming increasingly common for westerners to adopt Polynesian children.

Role of the Vahine

Eastern Polynesians practised sexual equality well before the 20th century. The appointment of Tahiti's Queen Pomare IV in 1827 is one example of power being passed to either *vahine* (women) or men without discrimination.

Nowadays, women are very well represented in the tertiary sector and they fill up to 80% of posts in commerce, hotels, health, insurance and social services. Arts and crafts are also their stronghold, except on the Marquesas where the sculptors are mostly male.

In the private domain, women generally take charge of children's schooling, domestic chores, administrative tasks or social and cultural responsibilities. They are often the family land-holders.

RELIGION

Missionaries did their best to obliterate the pre-European religion, destroying stone tiki and other religious images and demolishing many *marae* (the traditional temples). However, archaeologists have repaired much of the damage and there's a great deal to be seen of the old religion.

Some pre-Christian rituals and superstitions survive. In some dwellings a light is left on overnight for fear that *tupapau* (spirits of the dead) or *varua ino* (malevolent spirits) might be on the prowl. Ancient *tapu* sites are respected and feared. Few Maohi would dare to move a tiki or marae stone and on occasion they will consult a *tahua* (a traditional healer).

The first LMS ship arrived in 1797 and established Protestantism so thoroughly that Catholicism has never been able to overtake it. Today about 55% of the population is Protestant and 30% Catholic. Mormons, various other Christian sects, Buddhism and Confucianism constitute the rest.

FRENCH POLYNESIA

LANGUAGE

Tahitian and French are the official languages of French Polynesia although Tahitian is spoken much more than it is written. Much of the tourist industry uses English, but if you venture to the more remote and less touristy islands it's useful to know some French. Fortunately, bad French is readily accepted in French Polynesia. See the French Language appendix for some useful phrases.

Tahitian, known as Maohi, is a Polynesian language very similar to Hawai'ian and Cook Islands Maori. Other languages in the islands include Austral, Marquesan and Tuamotuan.

In Tahitian, a glottal stop (see Language in the Facts about the South Pacific chapter) replaces the consonants 'k' and 'ng'. The Polynesian word *vaka* (canoe) is *va'a* in Tahitian. The glottal stop is not usually written in place names (strictly speaking, Papeete is Pape'ete).

Tahitian Basics

Hello.	*Ia ora na, nana.*
Goodbye.	*Parahi, nana.*
Welcome.	*Maeva, manava.*
How are you?	*E aha te huru?*
Thanks.	*Mauruuru roa.*
Yes.	*E, 'oia.*
No.	*Aita.*
My name is	*To'u i'oa 'o ...*
I don't understand.	*Aita i ta'a ia'u.*

Facts for the Visitor

SUGGESTED ITINERARIES

Don't expect to see everything – French Polynesia's five archipelagos cover an expanse of ocean larger than Europe.

In one week you could visit Tahiti, Moorea and Bora Bora, with a quick visit to one of the Tuamotus (flying direct from Bora Bora to Rangiroa). Two weeks is the minimum time to have a decent look around the Society Islands (about two days on each island) and visit one of the Tuamotus.

In three weeks you could explore several islands in depth. You could visit all the main islands of the Society group by air or sea and continue to the Tuamotus (Rangiroa, Tikehau and Manihi) or the Australs (Rurutu and Tubuai) by air. Or else allow a week for the Society Islands, then take a 10 to 12 day cruise on the *Aranui* to the Marquesas.

A whole month would give you time to see the Society Islands, two or three atolls in the Tuamotus and several islands in the Marquesas. Fly from Bora Bora to Rangiroa in the Tuamotus and Rangiroa to Nuku Hiva (Marquesas).

PLANNING
When to Go

For many tourist activities you need good weather and the period from November to April statistically gets lots of rain. May through October is drier and slightly cooler but from June to August the intermittent *maraamu* trade winds can bring blustery weather and rain from the south. During that period it's often better on the more sheltered northern sides of the high islands.

School holidays are the same as in France, adding to crowds at resorts and making flights more difficult to get. There are lots of tourists around Christmas and New Year since that's also the start of the southern hemisphere holiday period.

The month of activities and festivals in July draws big crowds. It's not only popular locally but is also one of the most popular times of year for international visitors to French Polynesia, so plan ahead.

Diving and surfing are popular year-round, but sailing is best if you avoid the November to March tropical depressions. Walking is also better in the dry season – some of the trails are impassable when wet.

Maps

The map *Tahiti Archipel de la Société* (IGN No 3615) at 1:100,000 is readily available in Papeete and from map specialists abroad. It covers the Society Islands and is the one really useful map for tourists. IGN also publishes maps at 1:50,000 for every island of the archipelago. For the Tuamotus the SHOM navy maps are the best available. For the Marquesas there are SHOM maps or IGN maps at 1:50,000 for Hiva Oa, Nuku

Hiva and Ua Pou. You can find these maps at Prince Hinoi Centre, Ave Prince Hinoi or at Klima on Rue Jeanne d'Arc in Papeete, or in Paris from the Librairie Maritime et d'Outre Mer (☎ 01-46 33 47 48).

TOURIST OFFICES
Local Tourist Offices
Tahiti Tourisme (GIE; ☎ 50 57 00, fax 43 66 19, tahiti-tourisme@mail.pf) is based in Papeete. It has information on accommodation and local tourist operators and a website at www.tahiti-tourisme.com. There are visitors' bureaux on many of the islands.

Tourist Offices Abroad
Offices of the Tahiti Tourisme include:

Australia
    (☎ 02-9281 6020, fax 9211 6589,
    paramor@ozemail.com.au)
    12 Ann St, Surry Hills, NSW 2010
Chile
    (☎/fax 02-251 2826, tahiti@cmet.net)
    Ave 11 de Septiembre 2214, OF 116, Box
    16057, Santiago 9
France
    (☎ 01 46 34 50 59, fax 01 43 25 41 65,
    tahitipar@calva.net)
    Office du Tourisme de Tahiti et ses Îles, 28
    Blvd Saint-Germain, Paris 75005
Germany
    (☎ 69-97 14 84, fax 72 92 75)
    Bockenheimer Landstr 45, 60325
    Frankfurt/Main
Japan
    (☎ 03-3265 0468, fax 3265 0581,
    tahityo@mail.fa2.so-net.ne.jp)
    Sankyo Bldg (No 20) 8F-802, 3-11-5 Ild-
    abashi, Chiyoda Ku, Tokyo 102-0072
New Zealand
    (☎ 09-360 8880, fax 360 8891,
    lolac@tahiti-tourisme.co.nz)
    Villa Tahiti, 36 Douglas St, Ponsonby,
    Auckland
Singapore
    (☎ 732 1904, fax 732 3205,
    cti-network@pacific.net.sg)
    c/o CTI Network Pte. Ltd, 09-01 Orchard
    Shopping Centre, 321 Orchard Rd, Singapore
    238 866
USA
    (☎ 310-414 8484, fax 414 8490,
    tahitilax@earthlink.net)
    300 Continental Blvd, Suite 160, El Segundo,
    CA 90245

French Polynesia is also represented overseas by the Tourism Council of the South Pacific (TCSP). See the Regional Facts for the Visitor chapter for offices.

VISAS & DOCUMENTS
Passport & Visas
Except for French citizens anyone visiting French Polynesia needs a passport, and if you need a visa to visit France then you'll need one to visit French Polynesia (check with a French diplomatic office or travel agent). Most visitors must have an onward or return ticket.

Visa Extensions & Exemptions Travellers who wish to extend a one month visa should contact the Police aux Frontières (Frontier Police, formerly known as DICILEC) at Faaa airport, from 8 am to noon and 2 to 5 pm Monday to Friday, at least one week before the visa or exemption expires.

Travellers with a three month visa who wish to extend their stay must complete a form at the Direction de la Réglementation et du Contrôle de la Légalité (DRCL; ☎ 54 27 00), Blvd Pomare. Apply during the second month of your stay in the territory. Extensions are not automatically given.

Stays by foreign visitors (without a residence permit) may not exceed six months in any 12 month period.

EMBASSIES & CONSULATES
French Embassies & Consulates
French Polynesia is represented overseas by France's embassies and consulates:

Australia
    Embassy:
    (☎ 02-6216 0100, fax 6273 3193)
    6 Perth Ave, Yarralumla, ACT 2600
    Consulate:
    (☎ 03-9820 0944, fax 9820 9363)
    Level 4, 492 St Kilda Rd, Melbourne, Vic 3004
    Consulate:
    (☎ 02-9262 5779, fax 9283 1210)
    20th floor, St Martin's Tower, 31 Market St,
    Sydney, NSW 2000
Canada
    Embassy:
    (☎ 613-789 1795, fax 789 0279)
    42 Sussex Drive, Ottawa, Ontario K1M 2C9

FRENCH POLYNESIA

Consulate:
(☎ 514-878 4385, fax 878 3981)
1 Place Ville Marie, 26th floor, Montreal, Quebec H3B 4S3
Consulate:
(☎ 416-925 8041, fax 925 3076)
130 Bloor St West, Suite 400, Toronto, Ontario M5S 1N5
Germany
Embassy:
(☎ 0228-955 6000, fax 955 6055)
An der Marienkapelle 3, 53179 Bonn
Consulate:
(☎ 030-885 90243, fax 885 5295)
Kurfürstendamm 211, 10719 Berlin
Consulate:
(☎ 089-419 41 10, fax 419 41 141)
Möhlstrasse 5, 81675 Munich
New Zealand
(☎ 04-472 0200, fax 472 5887)
1-3 Willeston St, Wellington
Spain
Embassy:
(☎ 91-435 5560, fax 435 6655)
Calle de Salustiano Olozaga 9, 28001 Madrid
Switzerland
Embassy:
(☎ 031-359 2111, fax 352 2191)
Schosshaldenstrasse 46, 3006 Berne
UK
Embassy:
(☎ 020-7201 1000, fax 7201 1004)
58 Knightsbridge, London SW1X 7JT
Consulate:
(☎ 020-7838 2000, fax 7838 2001)
21 Cromwell Rd, London SW7 2DQ. The visa section is at 6A Cromwell Place, London SW7 2EW (☎ 020-7838 2051, fax 7838 2001). Dial ☎ 0891-887733 for general information on visa requirements.
USA
Embassy:
(☎ 202-944 6000, fax 944 6166)
4101 Reservoir Rd NW, Washington DC 20007
Consulate:
(☎ 212-606 3688, fax 606 3620)
934 Fifth Ave, New York, NY 10021
Consulate:
(☎ 415-397 4330, fax 433 8357)
540 Bush St, San Francisco, CA 94108

Embassies & Consulates in French Polynesia

Since French Polynesia is not an independent country there are no foreign embassies,

only consulates, and many countries are represented in Papeete only by honorary consuls, not by the regular diplomatic services. Canada, the USA and Japan don't have diplomatic representation in French Polynesia. If you need a US visa, the nearest place to inquire is Fiji. If you're Canadian and you lose your passport, the Australian consulate may be able to help.

Australia
(☎ 43 88 38, fax 41 05 19)
c/o Qantas, Vaima Centre, BP 1695, Papeete
Austria
(☎ 43 91 14, fax 43 21 22)
Rue de la Cannonière-Zélée, BP 4560, Papeete (also represents Switzerland and Liechtenstein)
Belgium
(☎ 82 54 44, fax 83 55 34)
École Notre-Dame des Anges, BP 6003, Faaa
Chile
(☎ 43 89 19, fax 43 48 89)
Rue du Général de Gaulle, BP 952, Papeete
Germany
(☎ 42 99 94, fax 42 96 89)
Rue Gadiot, Pirae, BP 452, Papeete
Italy
(☎ 43 45 01, fax 43 45 07)
Punaauia, Punaruu Valley, BP 380 412, Tamanu
Netherlands
(☎ 42 49 37, fax 43 56 92)
Mobil Bldg, Fare Ute, BP 2804, Papeete
New Zealand
(☎ 54 07 47, fax 42 45 44)
c/o Air NZ, Vaima Centre, BP 73, Papeete

CUSTOMS

No live animals can be imported (if you bring them in on a yacht they must stay on board) and certification is required for any plants bought into the territory. The duty free allowance is 200 cigarettes (or 100 cigarillos, 50 cigars or 250g of tobacco), 50g of perfume and 2L of spirits.

MONEY
Currency

The unit of currency is the Cour de Franc Pacifique (CFP), also called the Pacific franc and used in New Caledonia and Wallis & Futuna as well as French Polynesia. There are coins of 1, 2, 5, 10, 20, 50 and 100 CFP and notes of 500, 1000, 5000 and 10,000 CFP.

Exchange Rates

The CFP is tied to the French franc (FF) at a fixed rate, with 1 CFP equal to 0.055FF.

country	unit		franc
Australia	A$1	=	73 CFP
Canada	C$1	=	77 CFP
Easter Island	Ch$100	=	21 CFP
euro	€1	=	120 CFP
Fiji	F$1	=	58 CFP
France	10FF	=	180 CFP
Germany	DM1	=	60 CFP
Japan	¥100	=	110 CFP
New Zealand	NZ$1	=	60 CFP
PNG	K1	=	38 CFP
Samoa	ST1	=	37 CFP
Solomon Islands	S$1	=	22 CFP
Tonga	T$1	=	75 CFP
UK	£1	=	180 CFP
USA	US$1	=	110 CFP
Vanuatu	100VT	=	88 CFP

Exchanging Money

The most common bank is the Banque Socredo. Banks are rare in the outer islands: only one island in the Tuamotus, three in the Marquesas and two in the Australs have permanent banking services. Banks are typically open Monday to Friday with a break for lunch. On the main islands of the Society group there are ATMs (*distributeurs automatiques de billets*, or DABs in French).

Taxes

In 1998, the VAT (value added tax, also known as GST or goods & services tax) was introduced at hotels. In 1999 it stood at 2% and it is scheduled to go up every year until it reaches 5%. VAT also applies to restaurants, but it's hidden in the prices so customers don't see it directly. Big hotels also have a government tax of 8%. On some islands there's another tax simply for being there. Moorea, Bora Bora, Rangiroa and Tikehau charge 50 to 150 CFP per adult per day depending on whether it's a guesthouse or hotel.

Unless you're changing French francs there are hefty bank charges for changing money or travellers cheques. Typically it's 350 or 400 CFP. Top end and mid-range hotels, restaurants on the tourist islands, souvenir and jewellery shops, dive centres, major supermarkets and Air Tahiti all accept credit cards.

POST & COMMUNICATIONS

Post

Mail to Europe, the USA or Australia takes about a week and the postal system is generally quite efficient. There are post offices on all the main islands. There is no door-to-door mail delivery, so mail is usually addressed to a BP (*boîte postale*; post office box) number.

To collect mail at the post office in Papeete it should be addressed to you c/o Poste Restante, Papeete, Tahiti, French Polynesia. American Express card or travellers cheque holders can have mail sent care of the local American Express agent: Tahiti Tours, BP 627, Papeete, Tahiti, French Polynesia.

Telephone

The telephone system is modern, widespread and rather expensive for international calls. Public phone boxes are found even in surprisingly remote locations. Most require phonecards rather than coins. Cards can be bought from post offices, retail shops or vending machines at Faaa airport. A 5000 CFP card will give you half an hour from a public phone box to the USA. You can send faxes from post offices.

Local Calls There are no area codes in Tahiti. Local phone calls cost 32 CFP for four minutes, while inter-archipelago calls cost 40 CFP per minute.

International Calls French Polynesia's international telephone code is ☎ 689. To call overseas from French Polynesia dial ☎ 00. If you have any difficulty, call information on ☎ 3612. The ☎ 19 service (international communications by operator) is accessible only from private phones. To make a reverse-charge call, ask for *un appel* *payable à l'arrivée*. International call prices can be astronomical from a hotel room.

Email & Internet Access

Only the big hotels and some of the pearl trade specialists have email addresses or websites. There is a cybercafe in Papeete, a computer shop with Internet access in Raiatea and an Internet cafe in Bora Bora.

INTERNET RESOURCES

Useful websites include: Tahiti Tourisme (www.tahiti-tourisme.com), Tahiti Nui Travel (www.tahiti-nui.com), Tahiti Communications (www.tahiti.com) and Tahiti Explorer (www.tahiti-explorer.com).

BOOKS

There is a wide range of literature on French Polynesia and a number of excellent bookshops in Papeete. Some of the most interesting titles are only readily available in French Polynesia and some are only available in French.

History

One of the few Polynesian accounts of pre-European religion is Teuira Henry's *Ancient Tahiti* (1928). For a concise, highly readable account of the collision between Europe and Polynesia, David Howarth's *Tahiti – A Paradise Lost* is hard to beat.

Many other early visitors from Captain Wallis to Morrison (the boatswain's mate on the *Bounty*) wrote their accounts of Tahiti, but you would have to use a major library to find them.

Travel Literature

A remarkable number of renowned writers have written books either using French Polynesia as a setting or describing their own visits. Herman Melville, Pierre Loti, Robert Louis Stevenson, Jack London and Somerset Maugham all paid visits.

Melville was the first important visitor, writing about his escapes from whaling ships. His first novel, *Typee* (1846), was an instant success. He followed it up with *Omoo* (1847), based on his further adventures on another whaling hell-ship, an attempted mutiny, his arrest by the French, imprisonment in Papeete and a spell on Moorea.

French literature's primary contribution to the Tahiti bookshelves was Pierre Loti's 1876 novel *The Marriage of Loti*, which contributed to the romantic Tahitian myth.

Robert Louis Stevenson's visit to the Marquesas, the Tuamotus and Tahiti resulted in the book *In the South Seas* (1900). Somerset Maugham visited Tahiti to research his 1919 novel *The Moon and Sixpence*, which was loosely based on Gauguin's life.

Art & Culture

The Art of Tahiti by Terence Barrow is a succinct introduction to the art of the Society, Austral and Cook islands.

There are countless books on Gauguin and his works. *Noa Noa – The Tahiti Journal of Paul Gauguin* is his autobiographical account of life in Tahiti.

Tatau – Maohi Tattoo by Dominique Morvan is a fascinating account of the resurgence of traditional tattooing in French Polynesia.

Hiva Oa – Glimpses of an Oceanic Memory by Pierre Ottino & Marie-Noëlle de Bergh-Ottino (Département Archéologie, Papeete, 1991) is a locally-produced book on the archaeology and art of the Marquesan island of Hiva Oa.

In 1999 publisher Le Motu launched a series on local artists with a short introductory text in English and French. The first three titles were *Dubois, Deloffre* and *Boullaire*.

Guidebooks

Lonely Planet's Pisces series includes *Diving & Snorkeling Tahiti & French Polynesia*. A series of booklets by Nouvelles Éditions Latines in Paris and the Société des Océanistes include *Moorea, Huahine, Wings over Tahiti* (the history of aviation in French Polynesia), *Sacred Stones & Rites* (about Polynesian temples), *Pomare – Queen of Tahiti* and *Bougainville in Tahiti*.

The Marquesas Islands – Mave Mai by Chester, Baumgartner, Frechoso & Oetzel was published in 1998. The small book *Birds of Tahiti* by Jean-Claude Thibault & Claude Rivers (Les Éditions du Pacifique) is worth a look.

FILMS

Tahiti's role as a movie backdrop is almost exclusively tied up with the *Bounty*. Three times Hollywood has despatched Bligh, Christian and the *Bounty* back to Tahiti to relive the mutiny (see the boxed text about the mutiny in the Pitcairn Islands chapter).

Tabou (1931) is the only decent film shot in Polynesia that has nothing to do with the *Bounty*. This 80 minute work of fiction shows the inhabitants of Bora Bora in their natural environment.

NEWSPAPERS & MAGAZINES

In Papeete, Le Kiosque, in the Vaima Centre, and the Polygraph bookshop have a wide selection of international newspapers and magazines. There are other well-stocked newsstands in Papeete, but elsewhere around the islands local TV is probably the best way to keep up to date with world events.

Tahiti Beach Press is a free English-language weekly tourist paper with some local news coverage.

RADIO & TV

About 15 independent radio stations broadcast mainly musical programs, a few interviews and news in French and Tahitian. Broadcasting is mainly from Tahiti and Moorea, with some on the Leeward Islands. Radio France Outre-Mer (RFO) broadcasts many local programs in Tahitian, as well as news in French.

RFO also broadcasts on two television channels: Télépolynésie and Tempo. In addition to these, on Tahiti only, are Canal+ and Téléfenua, a cable package including CNN. The Australs, Tuamotus and Marquesas have to make do with Télépolynésie.

PHOTOGRAPHY

Film is expensive in French Polynesia. For 36 exposure film in Papeete count on 1700 CFP for slide film and 1000 CFP for print film. Film gets more difficult to find and even more expensive as you get further from Papeete. Fast developing and printing is easy to find on Tahiti and the other touristed islands.

TIME

Tahiti (and neighbouring islands) are 10 hours behind GMT. The Marquesas are half an hour ahead of the rest of French Polynesia (noon in Tahiti is 12.30 pm in the Marquesas) but check flight schedules carefully: Air Tahiti departures and arrivals for the Marquesas may run to Tahiti time.

ELECTRICITY

The electricity supply is at 220V AC, 60Hz. Sockets are French-style, requiring a plug with two round pins. Some deluxe hotels have a 110V supply for electric shavers.

LAUNDRY

Laundry can be a real problem in French Polynesia. Big hotels will wash clothes at exorbitant prices. Laundrettes are just about unknown outside Papeete and even there prices are frightening (US$8 per load and the same again to dry it). You'll need to wash some clothes if you're doing anything other than lazing back in air-conditioned comfort.

HEALTH

French Polynesia is generally a healthy place for locals and visitors alike. Food and water are good, there are few endemic diseases and the most serious health problem that visitors are likely to experience is sunburn.

Some urban areas may have very rudimentary sanitation facilities. Avoid swimming or walking barefoot on beaches that may not be clean and be wary of seafood caught near such communities.

If you need medical care, the facilities in French Polynesia are generally of a high standard. Papeete has a public hospital and two private clinics, as well as numerous pharmacies. On all tourist islands you will find at least a medical cabinet with one or more physicians and on Moorea, Raiatea, Bora Bora, Nuku Hiva and Hiva Oa there are small medical centres. Even the most remote islands possess a clinic. The price of a consultation with a doctor is about 3000 CFP. French visitors can get the fee refunded when they return home, citizens of the European Union should obtain an E-111 form before leaving home.

Malaria does not exist in French Polynesia, but there have been outbreaks of dengue fever and filariasis. Ciguatera also occurs. See Health in the Regional Facts for the Visitor chapter for more information.

Water
Tap water is only completely safe in Papeete and on Bora Bora. On some islands, particularly low-lying atolls, rainwater is collected and stored separately from well water, which can be tainted by sea water. Bottled spring water or mineral water is readily available.

Bites & Stings
Take care on some walking routes where wasp nests sometimes overhang the path. Large centipedes can give a painful or irritating bite but it's no more dangerous than a bee or wasp sting, despite the strange dread Polynesians have of these creatures.

GAY & LESBIAN TRAVELLERS
There are no networks or associations for gays or lesbians in French Polynesia but French law prevails, so there is no legal discrimination against homosexuals. Homophobia is uncommon; in fact, a fine old Polynesian transgender tradition is still alive and well here. *Mahu* are men who dress and act as women from childhood. They are similar to the *fakaleiti* of Tonga (see the boxed text in that country's chapter). Most, but not all, mahu are homosexual and many are *rae rae* (transvestites). The Scorpio disco behind the Vaima Centre in Papeete is a popular centre for western gays, mahu, rae rae and heteros alike. HIV testing is available at the Mamao Hospital and the Malardé Institute in Papeete.

DISABLED TRAVELLERS
As elsewhere in the Pacific, travellers with restricted mobility will find very little in the way of helpful infrastructure. With narrow flights of steps on boats, high steps on le trucks and difficult boarding on Air Tahiti aircraft, the disabled traveller's itinerary in French Polynesia resembles a bit of an obstacle course.

Those who are not put off by these obstacles should contact the Polynesian Association of War Invalids & Military Pensioners (☎ 43 17 89) for advice and assistance.

SENIOR TRAVELLERS
Seniors will have no problems in French Polynesia. Air Tahiti gives reductions to over 60s once they have obtained a Troisieme Age (Third Age) card. The card requires a photo and ID; it costs 1000 CFP and takes three days to obtain.

TRAVEL WITH CHILDREN
Nappies (diapers) are very expensive, even in the Papeete supermarkets. Medical facilities are widespread and Mamao Hospital has a modern paediatric department.

If you're travelling with kids, you will have priority when boarding Air Tahiti aircraft. A *carte famille* (family card) costs 2000 CFP, requires identity photos of the parents and takes up to five days to obtain. It entitles you to significant reductions on some flights. At hotels and guesthouses, children under 12 generally pay only half the adult rate.

USEFUL ORGANISATIONS
Te Fare Tahiti Nui (☎ 54 45 44 or ☎ 54 45 40) is at 646 Blvd Pomare, Papeete, at the western exit from the city. It is devoted to promoting cultural events. In addition to the traditional Heiva, it organises concerts and craft exhibitions and plays in French and Tahitian. Cultural weeks or gatherings are held there regularly. Beginners and advanced Tahitian language courses are also available. Te Fare Tahiti Nui is open from 8 am to noon and 1 to 5 pm weekdays (Friday to 4 pm).

DANGERS & ANNOYANCES
The most unhappy encounters with wildlife in French Polynesia are likely to be with mosquitoes and *nono* (sandflies) rather than sharks or any other serious threats.

Swimming
Swimming in French Polynesia is usually within the protected waters of a lagoon, but

FRENCH POLYNESIA

swimmers should still be aware of tides and currents, particularly where the lagoon water passes swiftly into the open sea. Around Papeete, beware of the dangers of untreated sewerage contaminating the water.

Mosquitoes & Nono

Mosquitoes are usually not a problem around the coast, where sea breezes keep them away, but inland they are a pest. Standing to read an explanatory noticeboard at a historic marae site can test anyone's enthusiasm for scholarship! The tiny nono (sandflies) of the Marquesas are even worse.

Dogs & Roosters

Some guesthouses are very quiet until 3 am, when you discover that they are completely surrounded by roosters who keep up a nonstop symphony until 4 am. The only solution is to change guesthouse.

On some islands, particularly the Tuamotus, dogs should be treated with caution. Some have no interest in obeying their masters; if you go out for a sunset stroll, carry a stick.

Theft & Violence

Despite recent increases in theft and petty violence, even busy Papeete is relatively safe compared to US or European cities. Nevertheless, there are occasional robberies and pickpocketings. Theft is less of a problem on the outer islands but take care in cheaper hotel rooms. Don't leave anything of value on view in a rented car.

Violence is rarely a problem. Intoxicated youths are the most likely troublemakers and it rarely gets beyond shouting at tourists that they're *titoi* (wankers). Ignore them. As anywhere, it's a good idea to keep well clear of unfriendly drunks. The bars that are most likely to be trouble spots are those frequented by French army personnel.

Yacht Security

Yacht crews should take care in popular yachting centres like Bora Bora or in the Marquesas, where theft from yachts has been a problem.

BUSINESS HOURS

Shops and offices are open from 7.30 or 8 am to 5 pm weekdays, although many places close an hour earlier on Friday. A long, leisurely lunchbreak is not uncommon. Some food shops and supermarkets stay open late in the evening.

Shops open on Saturday morning only and almost all are closed on Sunday. Food shops and supermarkets are the exception. Even on the smaller islands they tend to stay open every day.

PUBLIC HOLIDAYS & SPECIAL EVENTS

French Polynesia has the same major public holidays as France. In addition to New Year's Day, Easter, Ascension Day, Labor Day, Pentecost, Bastille Day, Assumption Day, All Saints' Day, Armistice Day and Christmas (see the Regional Facts for the Visitor chapter for the dates of these holidays), the following extra holidays are celebrated in the territory:

Arrival of the first Missionaries	5 March
May Day	1 May
VE Day	8 May
Autonomy Day	29 June

Other major events include:

January
Chinese New Year
Usually falling between late January and mid-February, the Chinese new year is ushered in with dancing, martial arts displays and fireworks.

February
International Marathon
The Moorea Marathon takes place in late February for anyone keen to run around most of the island.

March
Arrival of the First Missionaries
On 5 March the landing of the first LMS missionaries is re-enacted at Point Venus. There are celebrations at Protestant churches on Tahiti and Moorea and in Tipaerui (Tahiti) and Afareaitu (Moorea). (Actually, the missionaries arrived on 4 March but they did not know about the International Date Line.)

April/May
Beauty Contests
Many beauty contests are held in April and May leading up to the Miss Tahiti and Miss Heiva i Tahiti contests in June. (Mr Tahiti contests are also held.)

July
Heiva i Tahiti
This major Polynesian festival is held annually in Papeete, and includes many traditional demonstrations throughout the month. Mini-Heiva events take place on other islands in August.

September
Annual Flower Show
Held in Bougainville Park, Papeete
Surfing Contest
A major competition held at Punaauia (Tahiti)

October
Stone Fishing Contest
Traditional stone fishing celebrations take place in Bora Bora (see the boxed text in that section).
Carnival
At the end of October there are parades with floats decked with flowers.

November
Hawaiki Nui Canoe Race
The major sporting event of the year – a three day outrigger canoe race from Huahine to Raiatea, Tahaa and Bora Bora.
All Saints' Day
Graves are cleaned and decorated and families sing hymns in the candle-lit cemeteries on 1 November.

December
Tiare Tahiti Days
The national flower is celebrated on 1 and 2 December.
The Marquesas Festival
A major arts festival at Ua Pou with the accent on the Marquesan identity

ACTIVITIES
Surfing
Tahiti has several surf shops, board shapers and a healthy local surfing scene. Tahiti, Moorea and Huahine are the three main islands for surfing. Windsurfing has a wide following and many resorts offer instruction and equipment.

Boating
Raiatea is the main yachting base in French Polynesia. There are a number of yacht charter operations with a flotilla of modern monohulls and catamarans. You can rent small boats with outboards to explore the lagoons on some islands. Game-fishing boats are available for charter.

Hiking & Cycling
The high islands of French Polynesia offer some superb walks, although the tracks are sometimes hard to follow and a guide may be necessary. Tahiti and Moorea are the main islands for walking but there are also possibilities on Raiatea, Bora Bora and Maupiti. The Marquesas have huge untapped potential: as of yet the only popular walk is on Nuku Hiva.

On many islands it's possible to rent bicycles and the rough roads leading into the interior are perfect for mountain biking.

Horse Riding
There are equestrian centres on the larger Society Islands. They offer jaunts of a few hours or longer excursions to explore the island interiors. On the Marquesas, horses are part of the landscape and there are various places to rent horses, with or without a guide. Ua Hika is sometimes known as 'the island of horses'.

Diving
Scuba diving is enormously popular in French Polynesia. The water temperature varies between 26 and 29°C, and visibility is excellent almost everywhere. The region's varied marine life includes hammerhead sharks and manta rays.

Some of the territory's most spectacular dives, in the Tuamotu, Society and Marquesas islands, are spotlighted in this book's 'South Pacific Diving' special section. For even more information look for Lonely Planet's Pisces guide, *Diving & Snorkeling in Tahiti & French Polynesia*.

There are about 20 professional dive centres in the territory, catering to beginners and experienced divers. All are at least level 1 on the French CMAS scale and most have at least one PADI instructor. There are almost always staff who speak English. Operators are listed under Activities in island sections later in this chapter. Unless mentioned, the prices quoted include equipment rental but not the 6% VAT. Almost all dive centres accept credit cards.

Snorkelling

Without any training and with minimal equipment that you can easily pack yourself, snorkelling is a delightful and (usually) free way to experience the amazing underwater world of the territory. The coral reefs and numerous outcrops that dot the lagoons are perfect for snorkelling. You can join a lagoon tour by pirogue (outrigger canoe) or rent an outboard powered boat to explore the lagoon yourself.

Other Sports

There are squash and tennis courts in Tahiti; (ask at the tourist office). On other islands tennis courts can be found at the larger hotels. Tahiti has the only golf course in French Polynesia. Tahiti's soaring mountains promise interesting hang-gliding and there are facilities for this sport. Jetskis are also popular on some islands.

ACCOMMODATION

French Polynesia has a wide range of accommodation, from camping and hostel dormitories to five star luxury. However, in all categories the balance between price and quality can be discouraging. Levels of service and comfort often fall well short of the price being asked.

Many cheaper places don't supply towels or soap. Even some quite expensive places may not have air-con, although you'll find that a fan is usually adequate. Check if credit cards are accepted; they're welcome at luxury resorts but a surprising number of mid-range places want cash only. There's usually an 8% government tax on the mid-range and top end places.

Camping & Hostels

Campsites may not exist but some guesthouses have places where you can erect a tent and use the facilities. Count on 800 to 1800 CFP per person. Be prepared to shift if the rain is too hard and make sure your tent is mosquito-proof.

There are no youth hostels, but there are guesthouses with dormitory facilities (for about 1500 CFP a bed) on the larger of the Society Islands.

Guesthouses & Pensions

Staying with a family in a guesthouse or pension means either a room in the family house, or an independent bungalow. The cheapest bungalows are equipped with shower, toilet, bed with a screen to keep the mosquitoes at bay and a ceiling fan. Hot water is rarely available. Guesthouses often offer motu picnics, island tours, fishing trips and pearl-farm visits. If they don't organise their own they'll certainly put you in touch with local operators.

Prices vary widely from island to island. Guesthouses often include *demi-pension* (half-board; breakfast and dinner) which typically costs 5000 to 6000 CFP per day in the cheaper places, 9000 CFP in a mid-range place. *Pension complète* (full board) adds 1500 to 2000 CFP. Children under 12 usually pay half tariff and credit cards are rarely accepted. The tourist office produces a booklet about guesthouses.

Small Inns & Resorts

This mid-range group can offer excellent lodging. Generally they are well situated and more comfortable than the guesthouses. The rooms are usually well-equipped independent bungalows in traditional Polynesian style with modern comforts. The tariff is typically US$80 to $150 per night. Meals are not included but there will often be a restaurant on the site. Most places in this category accept credit cards and some are subject to an 8% VAT and a nightly tourist tax.

Deluxe Hotels

These four or five star establishments are usually sited in the most beautiful parts of the island. They will generally have restaurants, bars, a swimming pool, boutique, jewellery shop specialising in black pearls and sporting facilities. They organise activities on land and water and usually put on a Polynesian dance performance with a buffet meal two or three times a week.

Typically bungalows range from US$300 to $800 a night. You can add another US$50 to $80 a day for meals (plus 8% tax). Overwater bungalows, standing on stilts and reached by walkways, are always the most expensive.

These complexes are not isolated fortresses. If you buy a drink at the bar or a meal in the restaurant you will be welcome to use the beach or watch a dance performance.

FOOD

Good news: you will eat well in French Polynesia. The cuisine is multi-ethnic, with traditional Polynesian specialities happily coexisting with French, Chinese and Italian cuisine. From a classic pizza to chow mein to *mahi mahi* (fish in coconut milk), the repertoire is varied. Nevertheless, western favourites such as hamburgers and soft drinks are increasingly popular. Prices listed apply to Papeete; transport costs can push prices up on other islands.

Local Food

Traditional cuisine, based on fresh produce, is called *maaa Tahiti* in the Society Islands and Tuamotus and *kaikai enana* in the Marquesas. Maaa Tahiti is traditionally eaten with the fingers.

Fish & Seafood Dishes Open-sea fish and lagoon fish feature prominently in traditional cuisine. *Poisson cru*, raw fish in coconut milk, is the most eaten local dish. It is also eaten grilled or poached, accompanied by lime, coconut milk or vanilla sauce. *Fafaru* (raw fish soaked in seawater) is renowned for its particularly strong smell. Lobsters, crayfish, sea urchins and freshwater shrimps are highly prized, usually served in curry. The seafood on offer is limited in variety, compared to cooler climates, and there are no restaurants specialising in seafood. Salmon, trout, lobsters and prawns may be imported.

Fruit & Vegetables Available fruit includes mangoes, grapefruit, green lemons, watermelons, pineapples and bananas. *Pamplemousse* (grapefruit) is the large, thick-skinned South-East Asian variety, rather than the grapefruit common in Europe or North America. The rambutan, another South-East Asian introduction, is a red spiny-skinned cousin to the lychee.

Baked papaya is a succulent dish, as is *poe* (small pieces of crushed papaya or banana mixed with starch, wrapped in a banana leaf and baked in the oven with a vanilla pod split down the middle). The whole thing is then sprinkled with coconut milk.

Uru or *maiore* (breadfruit) is eaten cooked. On the Marquesas, the basic dish is *popoi* (a sweet-and-sour dish, which looks like a yellow paste). It consists of cooked uru crushed with a pestle, mixed with uru pulp, left to ferment and coconut milk is then added. The whole thing is covered with a *purau* leaf. To western tastes, taro and other local staples can be rather bland and

Temporary, quickly woven baskets at the markets hold a healthy supply of fruit.

tasteless. They are usually boiled but additional flavouring can make them more palatable. *Fei* (a sort of plantain banana) is only eaten cooked and has a bittersweet taste. Taro root is eaten cooked, as are sweet potato and manioc (cassava).

Meat *Pua* (suckling pig) is the preferred meat for a traditional underground oven known as an *umu* or *ahimaa*. On the Marquesas, goats are eaten and dog is still eaten on the remote atolls of the Tuamotus. Unfortunately, turtle is still eaten, despite being protected. Refusal to eat it may help to end this practice.

The most common accompaniment is coconut milk (not to be confused with coconut juice), obtained by grating the white flesh inside the nut and wringing it in a cloth.

Breads *Faraoa coco* (coconut bread) is a tasty cake. *Firifiri* (sweet fritters) are generally shaped like a figure eight or a plait. *Ipo* is Tuamotu bread and has a heavy consistency. The flour is mixed with coconut juice, sugar and grated coconut.

Other Cuisines

Among the Chinese specialities, *maa tinito* consists of a mixture of pieces of pork and red beans. *Chaomen* (chow mein) is a mixture of rice, noodles, red beans, vermicelli, vegetables and fried pork. Rice is found everywhere and pizza and pasta are common on the tourist islands. French cuisine is especially common on Tahiti and on the tourist islands. French bread, croissants and snacks are available everywhere.

Fast Food

Casse-croûte (French-bread sandwiches) are great value, usually costing from 100 CFP as 'snacks' or takeaways, or 200 CFP to eat in. Snack bars are all around the island. Dishes such as delicious Polynesian poisson cru (raw fish in coconut milk) cost from 800 CFP. *Les roulottes* (vans with kitchens and fold down counters each side for customers) also offer bargain-priced dining. The nightly gathering of roulottes on the quay side in Papeete is an institution.

Restaurants

Most restaurants are in Papeete and on the most touristy islands. They serve French, Polynesian and Chinese specialities and prices vary considerably. Count on about 1500 CFP for a typical main course.

Try to have at least one meal in the sumptuous setting of a luxury hotel. The prices can be surprisingly reasonable, often no higher than regular restaurants. Several times a week they put on superb buffets with seafood, Polynesian or international cuisine as a theme. Accompanied by a Polynesian dance performance, they cost 4000 to 6500 CFP.

Self-Catering

Markets are laden with vegetables, fruit, meat and fish. Papeete's central market opens at 5 am and has products from all the archipelagoes. The Pirae market also deserves a detour. Traditional grocery stores can be expensive.

The biggest and best-supplied supermarkets on Tahiti are the Continent Hypermarket (Arue and Punaauia), Tropic Import (Papeete) and Cash & Carry (Faaa). If you're restocking a yacht, this is where to come. On other islands you're at the mercy of cargo ship schedules. Avoid European imports; cheese air-freighted from France can be incredibly expensive.

Most islands have at least one bakery. A French baguette costs less than 50 CFP and a *pain au chocolat* costs about 120 CFP. Small food stalls along the road, particularly on Tahiti, sell fruit and vegetables.

DRINKS
Nonalcoholic Drinks

Some delicious bottled fruit juices, coconut juice and mineral water are all available to quench your thirst. Coffee (surprisingly, in a Gallic territory, this is usually of the instant variety) costs 200 to 300 CFP.

Alcoholic Drinks

Beer The local Hinano brand of *pia* (beer) is available in glass 500mL bottles, 330 and 500mL cans and on tap. Allow at least 350 CFP in a bar or restaurant.

FRENCH POLYNESIA

Wine & Spirits Papeete's supermarkets have plenty of French wine from around 800 CFP. Restaurants sell wine for 1500 to 3000 CFP per bottle. *Maitai*, a local speciality, is a cocktail made with brown rum, white rum, pineapple, grenadine and lime juice, coconut liqueur and sometimes Grand Marnier or Cointreau.

ENTERTAINMENT
On the weekend, Papeete is the only place with a really active nightlife. On other islands a drink in a bar and Polynesian dance performance in a big hotel is about as active as it gets. Family events with friends, known as *bringues*, are an interesting slice of life.

SPECTATOR SPORTS
Polynesian kids are a sporting bunch and you may catch a volleyball or football event. The national sport is pirogue racing, especially on Tahiti. You will certainly have the opportunity to admire the pirogue teams training on the lagoon. Tahiti has hosted events in the world surfing championship.

SHOPPING
There are plenty of souvenir shops and craft outlets waiting to lure you. Beware of local souvenirs that aren't local at all – the colourful wood carvings probably come from Bali or Colombia. Nevertheless, there are some excellent local crafts and many of them can be found on Tahiti, especially in the Papeete market.

There are duty-free shops in Papeete and at Faaa airport. Stamp collectors will find some interesting and very colourful stamps on sale. The Papeete post office has a section for philatelists.

Weaving, Cloth & Tapa
Coconut palm leaves are used for rough-woven work such as the walls of a *fare*, but for finer work, such as hats and mats, pandanus leaves are used. Some of the finest work comes from Rurutu in the Austral Islands.

Brilliantly coloured tifaifai (patchwork blankets) are produced on a number of islands, including Rurutu. Flowers or fruit are often used in tifaifai patterns and production can be a community activity.

Tapa rapidly disappeared when European cloth became available, but it is still produced (particularly on Fatu Hiva in the Marquesas) for ceremonial use and for collectors. Tapa can be bought in Papeete.

Sculpture & Woodcarving
These crafts are particularly renowned in the Marquesas. Tiki, *umete* (wooden dishes), spears, hair pins and other personal adornments are sculptured in wood, stone or bone.

Specialist galleries in Papeete sell sculptors' work at higher prices. Twice a year Marquesan sculptors have an exhibition and sale in the Territorial Assembly building, usually in June and November.

Black Pearls
Black pearls, cultivated in the Tuamotus, are sold in jewellery shops in Papeete and on other islands. They can cost from 5000 CFP to more than 200,000 CFP.

Getting There & Away

Occasionally a cruise ship calls in and there's a steady trickle of cruising yachts, but visitors to French Polynesia generally arrive by air.

AIR
There are plans for an international airport on Nuku Hiva in the Marquesas but at the time of writing Papeete's Faaa airport is the only arrival point from overseas.

Airlines flying to French Polynesia include Aircalin, Air France, Air New Zealand, Air Tahiti Nui, AOM (Air Outre-Mer), Corsair, Hawaiian Airlines, LanChile and Qantas. For local airline phone numbers, see Getting There & Away under Papeete in the Tahiti section.

There are direct connections with Los Angeles, Honolulu and Auckland (with onward connections to Australia) and to a number of other Pacific islands. Tahiti is a popular stop on round-the-world (RTW) tickets and is included in several air passes; see the introductory Getting Around the Region chapter for details.

The Pacific

New Caledonia's Aircalin has two weekly flights from Noumea: one via Fiji, the other via Wallis & Futuna. Noumea costs 78,000/92,200 CFP low/high season return. A stopover in Fiji or Wallis costs 111,400/124,000 CFP. Tahiti to Fiji return costs 81,400/93,600 CFP. Tahiti to Wallis return costs 77,300/87,600 CFP.

LanChile flies Papeete-Easter Island-Santiago three or four times weekly for 56,000/59,000 CFP.

From Papeete to Fiji costs 59,000/69,000 CFP return in the low/high season; Rarotonga is 39,000/59,000 CFP

There are also direct flights to Hawai'i – see USA & Canada. Connections to any other Pacific islands require a change at Rarotonga, Fiji or NZ.

USA & Canada

Fares to Tahiti from the USA are seasonal; late December to mid-June is the low season.

Hawaiian Airlines flies every week from Honolulu to Papeete with connections to/from Los Angeles (direct), San Francisco, Seattle and Las Vegas. Honolulu-Papeete return costs US$629/829 in the low/high season.

Air France, Corsair, Air New Zealand, AOM and local Air Tahiti Nui all fly to Papeete from Los Angeles (Corsair also from Oakland). Hawaiian Airlines flies via Hawaii. See Airlines in the introductory Getting Around the Region chapter for contact details. Los Angeles to Papeete return is about US$700. From Canada you have to connect on the west coast or in Hawai'i.

Australasia

Air New Zealand flies from Auckland to Papeete three times weekly: once direct, once via Rarotonga (Cook Islands) and once via Fiji and Rarotonga. Qantas flies Sydney-Auckland-Papeete three times per week. Both airlines have flights to Papeete

from other Australian cities, all routed via Auckland.

Auckland to Papeete costs NZ$1211/1417 return in the low/high season. Discount agencies can offer the fare below NZ$900. From Sydney, Papeete return costs A$1285/1429. Discount tickets are available at around A$1000.

South America

LanChile has three or four weekly flights to Santiago (Chile) via Easter Island. Tahiti and Easter Island can be attractive stopovers on the way to Chile from Australia, NZ or the USA.

Flying from Australia via Tahiti and Easter Island to Santiago costs A$2200 return. From the USA, Santiago via Tahiti and Easter Island costs around US$1800 return.

Japan & Asia

Air Tahiti Nui flies once or twice weekly between Papeete and Tokyo. Other connections are via Australia or New Zealand with a Circle Pacific fare (see Air Passes in the introductory Getting Around the Region chapter). Circle Pacific is also the best way to reach Tahiti from other countries in Asia.

Europe

The three direct routes from Europe to Tahiti are from Paris, Frankfurt and London – RTW tickets or connections from the USA are another option.

Three airlines fly from Paris to Papeete: Corsair, AOM and Air France. You can also fly Air New Zealand with reasonably priced connecting flights to Frankfurt or London from where they depart (with possibilities for extending trips as far as NZ). All airlines stop briefly at Los Angeles. These airlines have agencies in Switzerland and Belgium, offering connecting flights to Paris at reduced fares.

Only Air New Zealand flies from London to Papeete (via Los Angeles and on to Auckland and Australia, with the option of stopovers in the Cook Islands and Fiji). Fares from London can be as low as £1000 – not much less than a RTW fare incorporating Tahiti.

SEA
Cruise & Cargo Ships

There are no regular passenger shipping services to French Polynesia and cruise ships are infrequent visitors. Travel on occasional freighter ships is, however, making a comeback. See Cargo Ship under Sea in the introductory Getting Around the Region chapter.

There are two shipping companies that operate in French Polynesian waters (see Cruise Ship under Sea in the introductory Getting Around chapter): Marine Expeditions travels from Chile to Robinson Crusoe, Alejandro Selkirk and Easter islands; the Pitcairns, Mangareva, Rapa, Raivavae, Rurutu and Moorea to Tahiti for US$5995 including air connections to Los Angeles.

The *World Discoverer* does loops from Papeete through various islands of French Polynesia; or to Easter Island via islands of the Tuamotus and Marquesas, Mangareva and the Pitcairns. A typical 17 to 20 day Papeete-Easter Island trip costs US$7400 including connections to Los Angeles.

Yacht

Sailors are subject to the same passport and visa requirements as those arriving by air or by cruise ship. Unless you have a return air ticket, each crew member must post a bond equivalent to the price of an airline ticket to their country of origin.

Advise the Frontier Police at Papeete when you are to depart and they will issue a bond release. This release document must be presented to the gendarmerie on the last island at which you call, where you collect your bond.

The first port of call, if not Papeete, must be one of those with a gendarmerie: Afareaitu (Moorea), Uturoa (Raiatea), Fare (Huahine), Vaitape (Bora Bora), Taiohae (Nuku Hiva, Marquesas), Hakahau (Ua Pou, Marquesas), Atuona (Hiva Oa, Marquesas), Mataura (Tubuai, Australs), Moerai (Rurutu, Australs), Rairua (Raivavae, Australs), Avatoru (Rangiroa, Tuamotus) or Rikitea (Mangareva, Gambiers). Advise the gendarmerie of your arrival and departure and any change of crew.

The boat and equipment on board are considered duty free for six months, which can be extended for a further six months on application to the director of customs. If the skipper works anywhere other than on the boat, they are no longer entitled to this exemption and must pay import duty on the boat.

Before arriving at Papeete, announce your arrival on VHF channel 12. Two anchorages are provided: the quay or the beach. Report to the *capitainerie* (harbour master's office) to complete an arrival declaration. Moorage at the quay costs 110 CFP per metre of boat length per day, plus 100 CFP per day for water, 288 CFP per day for electricity and 1000 CFP per month for garbage disposal, with a minimum of 5000 CFP. At the beach, but moored to shore, you pay a daily fee of 55 CFP per metre of boat length.

In Papeete, the offices of the Frontier Police and the harbour master are in the same building on the seafront, 50m from the tourist office. They're closed at the weekend, so report on Thursday if you're departing at the weekend. On the other islands, the gendarmerie are the relevant authority.

ORGANISED TOURS

There's a variety of tour packages available from travel agents in all western countries. In France there are also agencies specialising in diving tours. Packages typically include flights, accommodation, diving fees and diving tours on the main islands.

Getting Around

Getting from island to island involves flights or boat travel and, thanks to French government financial support, travel to the larger and more densely populated islands is relatively easy and reasonably priced. Getting to the remote islands can be harder. On some islands there are paved roads, on others there are just rough tracks, but only around Papeete and its suburbs do you find reasonably comprehensive public transport. Renting a car or even a bicycle may be the best bet for other places.

AIR FARE CHART

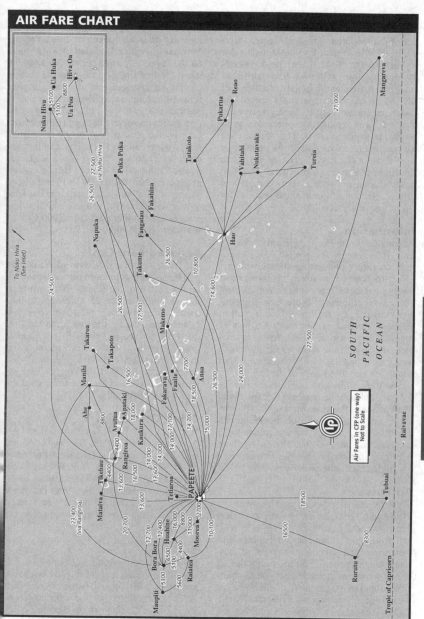

Air Fares in CFP (one way)
Not to Scale

SOUTH PACIFIC OCEAN

FRENCH POLYNESIA

AIR

Apart from smaller charter-style operations and Tahiti-Moorea with Air Moorea, anywhere else in French Polynesia means Air Tahiti Nui (☎ 86 42 42, or on weekends ☎ 86 41 84 or ☎ 86 41 95, rtahitim@ mail.pf). It flies to 38 islands in all five of the major island groups and some of the distances are so long it's hardly surprising that the fares are high despite heavy government subsidies. The best bargains are the air passes that allow you to visit a number of islands for one fare. Papeete is very much the flight hub and you'll generally have to pass through Papeete between island groups. See the relevant island sections for flight frequency details.

Information

Theoretically, the free baggage allowance is only 10kg, except for international passengers on direct connecting flights who get 20kg. In practice, overseas visitors almost always get 20kg but going over that limit can cause problems. There is an (expensive) left-luggage facility at Faaa airport in Papeete. Reconfirmation is not officially required, but is a good idea. Leave your contact details with the local agent; in remote locations schedules sometimes change. No shows are penalised 25% of the fare.

See the sections on the relevant islands for Air Tahiti phone numbers or contact the head office in Papeete. Air Tahiti publishes a very useful flight schedule booklet that's essential reading for anyone planning a complex trip around the islands. At most Air Tahiti offices or agencies you can pay for flights by credit card.

Air Passes

Six different island-hopping air passes are available offering inclusive fares to a number of islands.

Travel must commence in Papeete and there are restrictions on the number of transits through Papeete. You are only allowed one stopover on each island but you can transit an island so long as the flight number does not change. If you stop at the island to change flights, it counts as a stopover. The tickets are

valid for a maximum of 28 days and all flights (except Papeete-Moorea or Moorea-Papeete) must be booked at the beginning. You can use either Air Tahiti or Air Moorea on the Papeete-Moorea sector. Once you've taken the first flight on the pass the routing cannot be changed and the fare is non-refundable. Flights are classified in ascending order as blue, white or red and there are restrictions on which flights you can use, particularly the popular peak period red flights.

The passes all start from Papeete; they include a Discovery Pass (four Society Islands; 21,000 CFP), a Bora Bora Pass (all six Society Islands; 30,500 CFP) and a Bora Tuamotu Pass (add three islands in the Tuamotus; 45,500 CFP). You can add the Marquesas to any other pass for 45,000 CFP or the Australs for 20,000 CFP.

Reduced Fare Cards

Air Tahiti has several cards available that let you buy tickets at reduced prices depending on the colour of the flight – blue, white or red. If you're under 25 a *Jeunes* (Youth) card, or if you're over 60 a *Troisieme Age* (Third Age), card gives you up to 50% reductions and costs 1000 CFP. A *Famille* (Family) card gives the family members up to 50% (adults) and 75% (children) discount and costs 2000 CFP. You need a passport and photos and for the Family card the kids' birth certificates.

Other Companies

Wan Air (☎ 85 55 54, fax 85 55 56) and Air Archipels (☎ 81 30 30, fax 86 42 99) are based at Faaa airport. Héli Inter Polynésie (☎ 81 99 00, mobile ☎ 77 80 08, fax 81 99 99) and Héli Pacific (☎ 85 68 00, fax 85 68 08) charter helicopters. Héli Inter Polynésie (☎/fax 67 52 59) offer the same service on Bora Bora and Héli Inter Marquises in the Marquesas.

BOAT

It's no problem getting from one island to another in the Society group. Between Tahiti and Moorea high-speed, regular ferries shuttle back and forth. For the other major islands of the Society group the ultra-quick

Parau na te Varua Ino (Words of the Devil), oil painting by Paul Gauguin, 1892

JEAN-BERNARD CARILLLET

A weathered stone *tiki* still stands guard

JEAN-BERNARD CARILLLET

Incredible views on the climb to Tahiti's Mt Aor

JEAN-BERNARD CARILLLET

Opunohu on Moorea, where ancient *marae* (temples) have spectacular views over the bay

Ono-Ono offers a reliable and speedy service specifically aimed at tourists. In fact the popular *Ono-Ono* is more like an aircraft than a ship with fast turn arounds and speeds of 35 knots (65km/h). Leaving Tahiti at 9 am, you can reach Bora Bora at 4 pm that afternoon. In Papeete, bookings for the *Ono-Ono* (☎ 45 35 35, fax 43 83 45, onoono@mail.pf) can be made at the company's office on the Moorea ferry quay where credit cards are accepted.

In the other archipelagoes the situation is much more difficult, as there are no ships specifically for passenger transport. The cargo ships, known as *goélettes* (schooners) from the time when they were propelled by sail, are principally involved in freight transport although they generally take passengers. Island hopping on these cargo ships can be a fascinating experience but it's equally likely to be a very uncomfortable one. The level of comfort is rudimentary, some ships don't even have passenger cabins and you have to travel deck class, providing your own bedding which you simply unroll on the deck. You will get wet and cold. And then there's seasickness.

Furthermore, schedules are always uncertain – a notice posted at Chez Guynette in Huahine sums up the situation: 'The boats arrive when they are here and leave when they are ready.'

Other Ships

See the relevant sections for information on the ships that operate to each island. Apart from the *Ono-Ono*, the main ship through the Society group is the *Vaeanu*, which is slower but regular and popular with shoestring travellers. The *Maupiti To'u Aia* does a regular service from Papeete to Maupiti and there's a high-speed service between Bora Bora, Tahaa, Raiatea and Maupiti with Maupiti Express.

There are about 10 ships operating through the Tuamotu Islands and they can be contacted in the Motu Uta port area in Papeete. Take le truck No 3 from the town hall. Ships include the *Dory* (☎ 42 30 55), *Cobia I* (☎ 43 36 43), *Hotu Maru* (☎ 41 07 11), *Saint Xavier Maris Stella* (☎ 42 23 58),

Mareva Nui (☎ 42 25 53), *Vai-Aito* (☎ 43 99 96), *Aurra'Nui 3* (☎ 43 92 40), *Kura Ora* (☎ 45 55 45) and the *Rairoa Nui* (☎ 48 35 78).

See the boxed text 'The Aranui' in the Marquesas section of this chapter for information about this popular ship, which makes stops in the Tuamotus en route to the Marquesas. The *Taporo IV* (☎ 42 63 93) also goes via the Tuamotus. For the Australs try the *Tuhaa Pae II* (☎ 43 15 88) or the *Vaeanu II* (☎ 41 25 35, fax 41 24 34). The *Nuku Hau* (☎ 45 23 24) sails to the Gambier Archipelago via remote islands of the eastern Tuamotus.

Cruise Ships

The enormous 156m-long, 320-passenger *Paul-Gauguin* departs Papeete every week for a seven day cruise around the Society group. In French Polynesia contact SCAT (☎ 54 51 00, fax 45 52 66). In France, contact the Compagnie Maritime de Croisière (☎ 01-40 67 77 95, fax 40 67 77 71). In the USA, the cruise is marketed by Radisson Seven Seas Cruises (☎ 402-498 5072). In other countries contact a good travel agent. Renaissance Cruises (☎ 954-463 0982, fax 463 9216, renaissance_cruises@rcruises .com) in the USA operates two ships named *Renaissance* (the *R3* and *R4*) around the Society Islands.

Local company SPM (☎ 43 43 03, fax 42 99 14, haumana@mail.pf) operates the *Haumana*, a magnificent 36m catamaran that can accommodate 40 to 60 people, between Raiatea, Tahaa and Bora Bora. Moorea-based Archipels Croisières (☎ 56 36 39, BP 1160, Papetoai, Moorea) does trips through a variety of islands with large 18m sailing catamarans.

The *World Discoverer* of Society Expeditions and the Russian polar vessels of Marine Expedition make trips through the remote islands of French Polynesia. See Getting There & Away earlier in this chapter and the Getting Around the Region chapter for more details.

French Polynesia is an enormously popular yachting destination. It's also possible to rent a yacht here. There are a number of yachting operations that offer bare-boat charters (you provision and crew the boat yourself) and crewed or cabin charters (somebody else sails it). Stardust Marine (☎ 66 23 18, fax 66 23 19, stardustRaiatea@ mail.pf) and the Moorings (☎ 66 35 93, fax 66 20 94) in Raiatea are two of the most popular operations.

Local Boats

In several places it's possible to rent small outboard-powered boats for which no permit is necessary. This can be a great way to explore the Bora Bora and Raiatea lagoons for example. Lagoon tours by pirogue are good value for two or more people. In French Polynesia, if you need to get across a lagoon, there will always be someone available with the appropriate boat. Just ask!

CAR

Well-maintained coastal roads trace much of the coast of each major island in the Society group, while rougher 4WD roads lead inland into the mountains. Tahiti has an exciting 4WD track traversing the rugged centre of the island between the north and south coasts.

In the Austral Islands, a sealed road encircles Tubuai and there are reasonable stretches of sealed road on Rurutu. Otherwise, roads are fairly limited and little transport is available. There are far more boats than wheeled transport in the Tuamotus. Except in towns, there are hardly any sealed roads in the Marquesas. Tracks, suitable for 4WD vehicles only, connect the villages.

It's often worth renting a car even though the rates are high and fuel is expensive. Fortunately distances are short, even Tahiti is not much over 100km around. Count on US$60 to $80 per day for a small car, including insurance and unlimited kilometres. Fuel costs 113 CFP a litre (about US$5 a gallon). Off-road excursions into the interior are usually off-limits to anything except 4WDs. On the Marquesas, rental vehicles are mainly 4WD and come complete with a driver. Driving is on the right, the standards are not too bad and traffic is light almost

---

Le Truck

Le truck is the public bus service of French Polynesia – as its name suggests it's a truck with a bench seat down each side. Riding le truck is something every visitor to French Polynesia should do, but only in Tahiti are the services reliable enough to make them a worthwhile form of public transport.

---

everywhere apart from the busy coastal strip around Papeete in Tahiti.

Scooters & Bicycles

Scooters can be rented on a number of islands. It's a good way of get to around (when it doesn't rain), but rates are only slightly lower than for small cars.

French Polynesia is an ideal region to explore by bicycle. Apart from on Tahiti, traffic is rarely a problem and on most islands the distances are relatively short. You can ride a complete circuit of many of the islands in a morning or afternoon and the coast roads are generally flat. Bicycles can be rented on many of the islands, typically for 1000 to 1500 CFP per day and many guesthouses have bicycles for their guests, sometimes for free. A mountain bike is ideal for some of the rougher roads and it's even worth bringing your bike with you – they're accepted on all the inter-island ships.

Taxi

Tahiti, Moorea, Huahine, Raiatea and Bora Bora all have taxi services, but they are all very expensive. If you pre-book a hotel, staff may offer to pick you up and even if they charge it's still likely to work out much cheaper than a taxi.

Hitching

Hitching is never entirely safe in any country. But on the less touristed islands and on islands where public transport is limited, hitching is a widely accepted way of getting around, although the very light traffic can be a problem.

ORGANISED TOURS

Many of the more touristed islands have regularly scheduled tours that can be excellent value, particularly if you're on your own. They can vary from minibus tours or 4WD trips to lagoon tours by pirogue.

Society Islands

The Society Islands, subdivided into the Windward (eastern) and Leeward (western) islands, are home to over 80% of French Polynesia's population and are the destination for most visitors – Tahiti is the arrival and departure point for the overwhelming majority of visitors. Most of the Societies are high islands, in some cases very high indeed. Bora Bora and Moorea in particular are spectacular.

Tahiti

● **pop 150,000**   ● **area 1045 sq km**

It's common to speak of Tahiti as if it were the whole colony; in fact it is merely the largest island, the site of the capital (Papeete) and the only international airport (Faaa). Tahiti doesn't match its reputation; the beautiful beaches on local postcards are on islets out from other islands, the glamorous overwater bungalows on brochures are at hotels on Bora Bora, the underwater glimpses of sharks cruising past colourful reefs are in the Tuamotus. Even Gauguin's paintings are mostly of the Marquesas, not Tahiti.

Most visitors soon head to the other islands, but Tahiti deserves more than a cursory glance. This is the economic centre of French Polynesia and it has a historic dimension no other island can match, whether it's the remains of ancient marae or the first contact with European explorers. It was here that Cook and Bougainville first anchored.

The downside is that there are crowds, traffic jams, few beaches and often mediocre accommodation – and it's expensive. The upside is that there's a balance between the joys of the lagoon and a wild and uninhabited interior, with secret valleys, impressive peaks and volcanic massifs reaching over 2000m and waiting to be explored on foot or by 4WD. The lagoon and reef have plenty of interest for surfers and divers , while everybody should make a circuit of the island to discover its historic places, its small museums and the untouched wilderness of Tahiti Iti.

Finally, there's Papeete with its always active and intriguing waterfront. It's a good place to sip a sunset cocktail, dine in a restaurant, do some shopping or catch a great dance performance. Tahiti deserves better than a quick stopover.

History

Like other islands in the Society group, Tahiti is the creation of volcanic eruptions. The larger circle of Tahiti Nui probably came into existence around 2½ to three million years ago, while smaller Tahiti Iti was created less than two million, perhaps less than a million, years ago.

FRENCH POLYNESIA

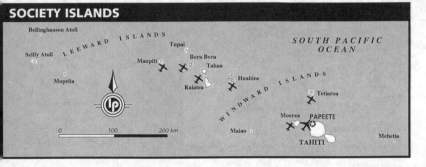

SOCIETY ISLANDS

SOUTH PACIFIC OCEAN

Bellinghausen Atoll

LEEWARD ISLANDS

Scilly Atoll

Mopelia

Tupai

Maupiti

Bora Bora
Tahaa

Raiatea

Huahine

WINDWARD ISLANDS

Tetiaroa

Moorea PAPEETE

Maiao

TAHITI

Mehetia

0   100   200 km

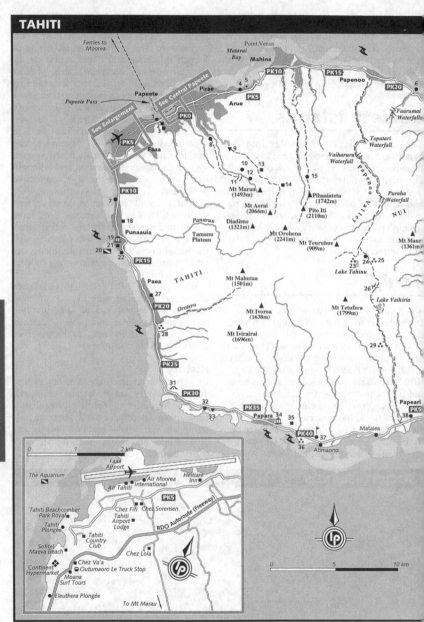

TAHITI

FRENCH POLYNESIA

TAHITI

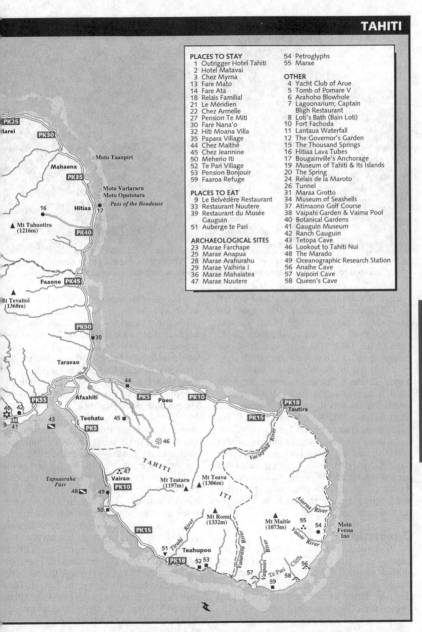

PLACES TO STAY
1 Outrigger Hotel Tahiti
2 Hotel Matavai
3 Chez Myrna
13 Fare Mato
14 Fare Ata
18 Relais Familial
21 Le Méridien
22 Chez Armelle
27 Pension Te Miti
30 Fare Nana'o
32 Hiti Moana Villa
35 Papara Village
44 Chez Maïthé
45 Chez Jeannine
50 Meherio Iti
52 Te Pari Village
53 Pension Bonjouir
59 Faaroa Refuge

PLACES TO EAT
9 Le Belvédère Restaurant
33 Restaurant Nuutere
39 Restaurant du Musée Gauguin
51 Auberge te Pari

ARCHAEOLOGICAL SITES
23 Marae Farchape
25 Marae Anapua
28 Marae Arahurahu
29 Marae Vaihiria I
36 Marae Mahaiatea
47 Marae Nuutere

54 Petroglyphs
55 Marae

OTHER
4 Yacht Club of Arue
5 Tomb of Pomare V
6 Arahoho Blowhole
7 Lagoonarium; Captain Bligh Restaurant
8 Loti's Bath (Bain Loti)
10 Fort Fachoda
11 Lantaua Waterfall
12 The Governor's Garden
15 The Thousand Springs
16 Hitiaa Lava Tubes
17 Bougainville's Anchorage
19 Museum of Tahiti & Its Islands
20 The Spring
24 Relais de la Maroto
26 Tunnel
31 Maraa Grotto
34 Museum of Seashells
38 Vaipahi Garden & Vaima Pool
40 Botanical Gardens
41 Gauguin Museum
42 Ranch Gauguin
43 Tetopa Cave
46 Lookout to Tahiti Nui
48 The Marado
49 Oceanographic Research Station
56 Anaihe Cave
57 Vaipoiri Cave
58 Queen's Cave

FRENCH POLYNESIA

A Dance in Otaheite – engraving by JK Sherwin, 1784. The Arioi society, a group which seemed to be devoted to lascivious dances and great feasts, was *not* a great friend of the missionaries.

Tahiti's rise to central importance started in 1767 when Samuel Wallis made the European 'discovery' of the island. He was soon followed by Bougainville then Cook, who made Tahiti the favoured base for European visitors. It was this European presence that led to Tahiti's rise to Polynesian power. It was a fleeting moment, for soon Tahiti became a minor pawn in the European colonial quest and it was only a generation from Tahiti's takeover by Pomare II (in 1815) to its annexation by France (1842).

Today, Tahiti's population is about 150,000, about 70% of French Polynesia's population. The growth in recent years has been dramatic and Papeete has become the region's 'big city', the place of bright lights and fragile prospects that sucks in the hopeful and helpless from other islands.

Orientation

Tahiti divides neatly into two circles: the larger Tahiti Nui is connected by a narrow isthmus to small Tahiti Iti. From the narrow coastal fringe, where the vast majority of the population is concentrated, the land sweeps rapidly upwards to a jumble of soaring, green-clad mountain peaks.

The mountainous centre of Tahiti Nui is effectively a single huge crater, with the highest peaks arrayed around the rim. The highest of all is Mt Orohena (2241m) on the western side of the crater rim. Dense vegetation and crumbling ridgelines make Mt Orohena difficult to climb, but a ridge runs west from the summit to Mt Aorai (2066m), a popular ascent. The ridge continues to the spectacular rocky Diadème (1321m) and Mt Marau (1493m). A number of valleys run down to the coast from the mountains, the most impressive being the wide Papenoo Valley to the north, which cuts through the ancient crater rim. Tahiti Iti's highest point is Mt Ronui (1332m), and its eastern end finishes with steep cliff faces in the Te Pari district although there is a difficult walking track around the east coast of the island.

A fringing reef encloses a narrow lagoon around much of the island but parts of the coast, particularly the north coast from Mahina to Tiarei, are unprotected. There are no less than 33 passes through the reef, the most important of which is the Papeete Pass into Papeete's fine harbour. Less than 10km east is Matavai Bay, the favourite anchorage point of many early explorers.

Activities

Trekking Tahiti offers the best walking in French Polynesia, with walks into the mountainous interior that can reach over 2000m altitude. The walk up the Fautaua River to the waterfall takes about two hours from **Loti's Bath**. You need permission from the Service de l'Hydralique (☎ 43 02 15). Mt Aorai (2066m) is the third-highest peak on the island and is a straightforward ascent. It's best to stay overnight at the hut near the top and arrive at the top at dawn. The **Hitiaa Lava Tubes** are an exciting expedition through long tunnels off the road at PK40 (*pointe kilométrique*, ie 40km from Papeete). A trip to **Te Pari** (The Cliffs), at the eastern end of Tahiti Iti, is another excursion taking a couple of days.

Guides include Tiare Mato (☎ 43 92 76, fax 42 21 03) and Polynesian Adventure (☎/fax 43 25 95). Presqu'Île Loisirs (☎ 57 00 57) and Le Circuit Vert (☎ 57 22 67) specialise in Tahiti Iti.

Surfing Tahiti has some classic surf spots, including Matavai Bay and Point Venus (PK10) and several breaks at Papenoo (PK13 to PK15.5) on the north coast of Tahiti Nui. On the south coast, Papara (PK39), Fisherman's Point at the Museum of Tahiti (PK15) and Taapuna (PK12) are popular. On Tahiti Iti the Big and Small Vairao Pass and Teahupoo attract international surfers. Tura'i Mataare's surfing and bodyboarding school in Tahiti offers courses by the day (4500 CFP per person) or a program of 10 half-day lessons for 26,500 CFP. Contact Kelly Surf (☎ 45 44 00) in Fare Tony in Papeete.

Diving Tahiti's scuba centres include: Scuba Tek Tahiti (☎/fax 42 23 55) at the Arue Marina Yacht Club at PK4; Dolphin Sub (☎/fax 45 21 98, dolphin.sub@usa.net) at Fare Ute; Aquatica Dive Center (☎ 53 34 96, fax 43 10 65) has two bases, one in the Beachcomber Parkroyal, the other in the Paea Marina at PK27; Eleuthera Plongée (☎ 42 49 29, fax 41 04 09) is at the Taina Marina in Punaauia; Tahiti Plongée (☎ 41 00 62, fax 42 26 06, plongee.tahiti@ mail.pf) is

beside the lagoon at PK7.5. Iti Diving International (☎/fax 57 77 93, itidiving@ hotmail.com) at the Puunui Marina in Vairao at PK6 is the only centre on Tahiti Iti.

Popular sites include the **Cliffs of Arue** in Matavai Bay, the **Aquarium** in the lagoon near the Faaa airport, which is a delight for beginners, and **The Spring** in front of Fisherman's Point at Punaauia. Tahiti Iti has superb sites, such as the aptly named **Hole in the Lagoon** and the **Tetopa Cave**.

Swimming Tahiti's beaches are nothing flash. The beach by the Hotel Sofitel Maeva is just 8km from Papeete and right by the Outumaoro le truck stop. On the other side of town, 3km east in the suburb of Pirae, there's a stretch of not very inspiring black-sand beach by the Royal Tahitien Hotel.

There are better beaches out of town. Along Tahiti Nui's north coast, beaches are principally black sand. **Point Venus**, 10km from Papeete, is one of the most popular beaches close to the city. There are short stretches of black-sand beach further along, such as the small bay just past the **Arahoho Blowhole** (22km from Papeete). On the south coast, there are white-sand beaches between 10 and 15km from Papeete, at Punaauia.

Organised Tours

Hotels, numerous Papeete travel agencies and a number of independent operators offer island circuit tours by minibus for about 4500 CFP. Other activities include horse riding, with Ranch Gauguin (☎ 57 51 00) at PK53 in the Papeari area, or golf, at the Olivier Bréaud Golf Course (☎ 57 40 32) at PK42 in Atimaono.

PAPEETE
● pop 80,000

Tahiti's busy metropolis has a reputation as an ugly and overpriced port town, blighted by tasteless concrete development and heavy traffic. However, Papeete is not really that bad. Amble along the waterfront watching yachts, ferries and cargo boats come and go, return at night to sample the mobile restaurants known as les roulottes, soak up

PAPEETE

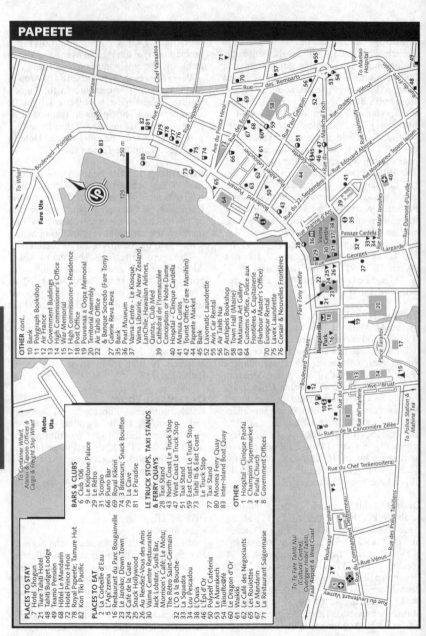

PLACES TO STAY
1 Hotel Shogun
21 Tiare Tahiti Hotel
48 Tahiti Budget Lodge
49 Teamo Pension
68 Hôtel Le Mandarin
72 Hôtel Prince Hinoi
78 Royal Papeete; Tamure Hut
82 Kon Tiki Pacific

PLACES TO EAT
2 La Corbeille d'Eau
5 L'Api'zzeria
16 Restaurant du Parc Bougainville
23 Le Janoko; Down Town
24 Café de la Gare
25 Snack Hollywood
26 Au Rendez-Vous des Amis
30 Vaima Centre Restaurants:
   Jack Lobster, Sushi Bar,
   Morrison's Café; Le Motu;
   The Rétro Saint-Germain
32 L'O à la Bouche
33 La Squadra
34 Lou Pescadou
38 L'Oasis
46 L'Epi d'Or
50 Polyself Cafeteria
53 Le Marrakech
54 Le Dragon d'Or
60 Le Retro
61 Waikiki
62 Le Café des Negociants
65 Les Roulottes
67 Le Mandarin
71 La Restaurant Saïgonnaise

BARS & CLUBS
6 Club 106
9 Le Kiriptone Palace
29 Le Rétro
31 Scorpio
66 Piano Bar
69 Royal Kikiriri
74 3 Brasseurs; Snack Bouffon
79 La Cave
81 Le Paradise

LE TRUCK STOPS, TAXI STANDS & FERRY QUAYS
28 Taxi Stand
43 North Coast Le Truck Stop
47 West Coast Le Truck Stop
51 Taxi Stand
59 East Coast Le Truck Stop
73 Tahiti Iti & East Coast
   Le Truck Stop
77 Taxi Stand
80 Moorea Ferry Quay
83 Inter-Island Boat Quay

OTHER
1 Hospital - Clinique Paofai
3 Champion Supermarket
4 Paofai Church
8 Government Offices

OTHER cont..
10 Bank
11 Polygraph Bookshop
12 Air France
13 Government Buildings
14 High Commissioner's Office
15 War Memorial
17 High Commissioner's Residence
18 Post Office
19 Pouvanaa a Oopa Memorial
20 Territorial Assembly
22 Air Tahiti Office
27 Galerie Reva Reva
   & Banque Socredo (Fare Tony)
35 Bank
36 Pearl Museum
37 Vaima Centre - Le Kiosque,
   Vaina Librairie, Air New Zealand,
   LanChile, Hawaiian Airlines,
   Qantas, Club Med
39 Cathédral de l'Immaculée
   Conception or Notre Dame
40 Hospital - Clinique Cardella
41 Manuia Curios
42 Tourist Office (Fare Manihini)
44 Papeete Market
45 Bank
52 Lavomatic Laundrette
55 Avis Car Rental
56 Air Tahiti Nui
57 Archipels Bookshop
58 Town Hall (Mairie)
63 Matamua Art Gallery
64 Customs Office, Police aux
   Frontières & Capitainerie
   (Harbour Master's Office)
70 Europcar Rental
75 Lavex Laundrette
76 Corsair & Nouvelles Frontières

To Container Wharf
Aranui Shipping Office &
Cargo & Freight Ship Wharf

Motu Uta

Fare Ute

To Fare Tahiti Nui
(Cultural Centre);
Outrigger Hotel Tahiti;
Faa'a Airport & West Coast

To Police Station & Mahina Tea

the Polynesian atmosphere in the busy Papeete Market, sip a coffee in a sidewalk cafe while you watch the world go by and plan visits to other islands. Approached this way, Papeete can be a very enjoyable town.

History

The capital and largest city of Tahiti and French Polynesia, Papeete was a European creation. In 1769, when Cook anchored 10km east in Matavai Bay, there was no settlement in Papeete. The arrival of the LMS missionaries and the role of the young Queen Pomare made it a religious and political centre, and visiting whaling ships made it an increasingly important port. It became the administrative headquarters for the new French protectorate in 1842. By 1860 the town had already taken its present form, with a straggling European settlement between the waterfront and the street, then known as 'the Broom' and now as Rue du Commandant Destremeau, Rue du Général de Gaulle and Rue du Maréchal Foch.

Chinese merchants and shopkeepers started to trickle in to Papeete, but the population was still less than 5000 at the beginning of the 20th century. A disastrous cyclone in 1906 and a German naval bombardment in 1914, which destroyed the central market, took their toll but during WWII the population reached 10,000 and by the early 1960s it was over 20,000. The city's growth and change accelerated in the 1960s with the opening of Faaa airport, but it was nuclear testing operations which really encouraged the flood of people from remote islands. Today Papeete and its suburbs have more than 100,000 people and spread for 30km along the coast.

Orientation

Central Papeete curves around an almost enclosed bay and the downtown district is a compact area, easily covered on foot. Blvd Pomare follows the waterfront and most of the central businesses, banks, hotels and restaurants are concentrated along this busy street or in the few blocks back from the water's edge. The Vaima Centre marks the centre of the city but it's the waterfront, with its constant shipping activity, which is the city's true heart. The port zone, Fare Ute and Motu Uta, is easily visible across

MANOLO MYLONAS

A ship is unloaded at the busy Papeete docks.

FRENCH POLYNESIA

the harbour to the north. The city centre is noisy and crowded during the day but quickly empties in the late afternoon, until the roulottes open up on the waterfront for the evening bringing some energy back.

Greater Papeete forms a vast conurbation, squeezed between the mountains and the lagoon for 30km along the north coast of Tahiti. The westward sprawl of Papeete extends beyond the airport, in the unattractive suburb of Faaa, to Punaauia. The coast road west is complemented by the Route de Dégagement Ouest (RDO), French Polynesia's *autoroute* (freeway) which runs slightly inland from the western edge of central Papeete to just beyond Faaa airport where it rejoins the coastal road. On the other side of Papeete two roads, Ave du Prince Hinoi and Ave Georges Clémenceau, run east through the suburb of Pirae before joining at Arue.

Information

Tourist Offices The Tahiti Tourist Board (or GIE) has its tourist office (☎ 50 57 00, fax 43 66 19, tahiti-tourisme@mail.pf) in Fare Manihini on Blvd Pomare. The office has a large collection of information sheets detailing cheaper accommodation, island by island, and also distributes brochures and leaflets from a host of tourist operators. There is an information desk at the airport but it's often unstaffed.

Money Banque Socredo, Banque de Tahiti and Banque de Polynésie are all found in Papeete and its suburbs. Most Papeete branches will change money or travellers cheques and most have ATMs that accept Visa and MasterCard for cash advances or let you withdraw money from your home account. Outside of the Papeete area the only ATMs are in Taravao. On the Quai d'Honneur, in the same building as the capitainerie, there's a foreign exchange bureau open Monday to Saturday. The Banque Socredo branch in the Fare Tony Centre on Blvd Pomare has a machine that changes foreign bills.

Post & Communications Papeete's main post office fronts on to the waterfront Blvd Pomare, next to Bougainville Park. For normal postal services go upstairs from the Blvd Pomare entrance. Poste restante (general delivery) service is downstairs. The post office also offers phone, fax and telegram services.

Tahiti Tours (☎ 54 02 50, BP 627, Papeete, Tahiti) at 15 Rue Jeanne d'Arc, next to the Vaima Centre, is the American Express agent and will hold clients' mail.

Email & Internet Access Tikisoftc@fe (☎ 77 44 34, tikisoft@mail.pf) is a convivial and *branché* (connected) cybercafe on the Pont de l'Est roundabout, close to the *mairie* (town hall). Check its website (www.tikisoft.pf) for more information.

Bookshops & Newsagencies Papeete has several excellent bookshops with special sections for Polynesia and the Pacific. Try Archipels (☎ 42 47 30), at 68 Rue des Remparts to the east of the centre; Prince Hinoi Centre (☎ 54 05 04), on Ave du Prince Hinoi; Vaima Librairie (☎ 45 57 44), in the Vaima Centre; and the Klima bookshop (☎ 42 00 63), at 13 Place Notre Dame. For newspapers and magazines check Le Kiosque at the front of the Vaima Centre.

Medical Services & Emergency For the hospital or a doctor in an emergency, call ☎ 15. You can call SOS Médecins on ☎ 42 34 56. The Mamao Hospital (☎ 46 62 62, or for 24-hour emergencies ☎ 42 01 01), on Ave Georges Clémenceau, is the biggest hospital in French Polynesia. There are two 24-hour private clinics: Cardella (☎ 42 81 90), on Rue Anne-Marie Javouhey behind the cathedral, and Paofai (☎ 46 18 18), at the junction of Blvd Pomare and Rue du Lieutenant Varney. They're more expensive than the Mamao Hospital – during the day a consultation costs 3000 CFP; at night or on Sunday it jumps to 7000 CFP.

Things to See & Do

Papeete would be a rather charmless and dull town were it not for the **waterfront**. Rows of visiting yachts, cargo ships loading and unloading and the arrivals and departures of the inter-island ferries make the waterfront a colourful and always-interesting strip. After dark the waterfront car park becomes the home of les roulottes, the mobile restaurants which are not only the cheapest places to eat in Papeete but also the most fun. To complete the picture, the eastern end of Blvd Pomare, the waterfront road, is also the entertainment district, with bars, clubs and, at night, rae rae.

Start a waterfront stroll along the four-lane Blvd Pomare from the west. Shaded by overhanging trees and brightened by hibiscus, it's attractive, colourful and busy. Close to the metal footbridge on the lagoon side of the road is the imposing **Te Fare Tahiti Nui building**, the Polynesian-style cultural centre. Various exhibitions and cultural events are regularly staged here.

The imposing pink and white Protestant **Paofai Church** is a colourful scene at Sunday services, with a congregation arriving and departing beneath a flotilla of wide-brimmed white hats and belting out rousing *himene* (hymns). It marks Papeete's birthplace, as the first Protestant church, built on this site in 1818, effectively signalled the town's creation.

Across the road from the church is a **monument** to the great double-canoe *Hokule'a*, which emulated the feats of the legendary Polynesian navigators by sailing from Hawai'i to Tahiti in 1967. As you walk east there are racing pirogues, the outrigger canoes that Tahitians paddle with a vengeance, stacked up under trees on the quayside. Local teams can be seen practising some afternoons and every Saturday morning. Past Ave Bruat, cruising yachts from both sides of the Pacific as well as local boats give Papeete an international flavour. On the inland side of the road is **Bougainville Park** and the adjacent post office. The park is fronted by a bust of the great French navigator and naval guns from the German WWI raider the *Seeadler* , wrecked at Mopelia in the Leeward Islands, and the French vessel *La Zélée*, sunk during the German raid in September 1914.

Next up on the island side is the glossy **Vaima Centre**, with shops, airline offices,

restaurants and, on the Rue Jeanne d'Arc side, the **Pearl Museum** (π 45 21 22), which was created by the pearl magnate Robert Wan. It's open from 8 am to 7 pm daily (from 9 am on Sunday) and entry is 600 CFP. On the harbour side Fare Manihini is the home of the Tahiti Tourist Board, perched on the **Quai d'Honneur**.

Late in the afternoon fishing boats land the day's catch at the quay, and at night les roulottes line the carpark from here to the **Moorea ferry quay**. On the inland side of Blvd Pomare the sometimes seedy but always energetic entertainment district starts just south of Ave du Prince Hinoi and extends north past Ave du Chef Vairaatoa.

Tourism and entertainment fades out further along the waterfront as the road continues through the docks and industrial zone of **Fare Ute** (which becomes Motu Uta after the bridge). This is the sweaty working part of the harbour where the copra boats unload their cargoes from the islands and the sweetish smell of coconut hangs in the air. Pallets of cargo – from building materials to crates of Hinano beer, from drums of fuel to shiny new Taiwanese bicycles – are loaded on the ships to transport to the outer islands.

Behind the Vaima Centre the **Cathédrale de l'Immaculée Conception** (or Cathedral of Notre Dame) dominates. It had a chequered construction history but was completed in 1875. From the cathedral, Ave Monseigneur Tepano Jaussen leads into the **Mission Quarter**, originally known as Tepapa Valley. Papeete's principal Chinese temple, the 1987 **Kanti de Mamao**, is on Ave Georges Clémenceau and Ave du Commandant Chessé. It replaced a century-old Chinese temple. There's a **synagogue** just off Ave du Prince Hinoi and an imposing **Seventh-Day Adventist church** just south of Ave Georges Clémenceau, on the Route du Fautaua, the road leading to Loti's Bath.

Behind Bougainville Park the **Territorial Assembly** and other government buildings occupy the former site of the Pomare palace. On Rue du Général de Gaulle in front of the assembly building is a **statue** of Pouvanaa a Oopa, a Tahitian patriot and WWI volunteer.

His espousing of Tahitian nationalism earned him a prison sentence after riots shook Papeete in 1958 and he remains a potent symbol of Tahitian aspirations.

Papeete's **municipal market** is colourful, appetising and very Polynesian. Early Sunday morning, when local residents flock from around Papeete, is the prime occasion. The **mairie** (town hall or hôtel de ville) is a block north of Papeete Market. It was completed in 1990, in vague imitation of the old Queen's Palace which was replaced by the modern Territorial Assembly building.

From east of the centre, the Route de Fautaua runs inland through lower-income dormitory suburbs to **Loti's Bath** (Bain Loti), 2.5km inland. It was here in Pierre Loti's 1880 novel *The Marriage of Loti* that the beautiful Rarahu met the novel's hero. The pool is no longer the pleasantly rural scene Pierre Loti enjoyed but it remains a favourite meeting place and swimming hole for local youngsters and a bust of Pierre Loti still overlooks the scene. From there a walking path leads inland, see Activities earlier in this section.

Directly across from Faaa airport, a road signposted Saint-Hilaire runs inland, under the autoroute and up towards the summit of **Mt Marau** (1493m) – the rough road really requires a 4WD. From the end of the road it is only a half-hour walk to the top of Mt Marau.

Places to Stay

There's a range of accommodation but bargains are rare and the balance between price and quality is not good. Central Papeete has cheaper places, business-style, mid-range hotels and some fading establishments from an earlier tourist era. The luxury beachside hotels are all outside the city, mostly beyond the airport. Reserve ahead during the Heiva festivities in July when many hotels are completely booked out.

Places to Stay – Budget

Papeete If Papeete is the first place you stay in French Polynesia, you're likely to be disillusioned, the choice is pretty basic; OK for a night or two but convenience is their sole advantage. *Tahiti Budget Lodge* (☎ 42 66 82, fax 43 06 79) is on Rue du Frère Alain, about a 10 minute walk from the waterfront in a quiet district. A dormitory bed costs 2000 CFP, rooms for one or two people are 4000 or 5000 CFP with toilet and shower. It's pricey considering its rustic nature but there's a shared kitchen, you can leave luggage for 1000 CFP per week and credit cards are accepted.

Teamo Pension (☎ 42 00 35, fax 43 56 95) is only a couple of minutes' walk away and has dorm beds from 1300 to 1600 CFP. Rooms with shared bathroom cost 3700 CFP for singles or doubles; those with attached bathroom cost 4200 CFP. It's pretty basic but there's a shared kitchen and credit cards are accepted.

The *Mahina Tea* (☎ 42 00 97, BP 17, Papeete, Tahiti) is more like a cheaper hotel than the two backpacker favourites. It's on Route de Sainte Amélie, only 10 or 15 minutes' walk from Ave Bruat in the centre. There are 16 very plain rooms from 4000 CFP, dropping to 3500 CFP for stays of three days or longer. Other rooms are in the 4700 to 6000 CFP bracket, while the studio apartments with kitchen facilities are 10,000 CFP. Credit cards are not accepted.

The *Shogun Hotel* (☎ 43 13 93, fax 43 27 28) at 10 Rue du Commandant Destremeau, just west of the Ave Bruat junction, is strictly a last resort.

Chez Myrna (☎/fax 42 64 11), half a kilometre from the Matavai Hotel in the Tipaerui Valley, is the only place offering really acceptable standards in this category. There are two well-kept rooms for 3500/4500 CFP including breakfast. There's a two night minimum stay, airport transfers cost 1000 CFP each way and credit cards are not accepted. There's no sign for the guesthouse.

Around Papeete Most places on the city periphery are on the west coast between Faaa and Punaaiua. There are frequent Papeete-Faaa-Outumaora le trucks during the day and even at night. Except for the big hotels, nowhere on this stretch has a beach or swimming place. Places beyond PK8 are covered in the Tahiti Nui section, later in this chapter.

The *Heitiare Inn* (☎ 83 33 52) is at PK4.3, just a kilometre or so from the airport towards Papeete. Free transfers are provided from the airport or you can walk there in 15 minutes, but this is a somewhat noisy and not particularly attractive area. Singles/doubles are 4500/5000 or 6000/7000 CFP with air-con and attached bathroom.

Chez Fifi (☎ 82 63 30) is across from the airport and offers a good balance between price and quality. Take the small road beside the Mea Ma laundry across from the airport car park. There's a sign and the guesthouse is 150m on the left. Dorm beds are 2000 CFP and rooms are 3500/6000 CFP, including breakfast. *Chez Sorensen* (☎ 81 93 25) is just 50m away and owned by the same people. Dorm beds are 2500 CFP or rooms with shared bathrooms 3500/5500 CFP.

Chez Lola (☎/fax 81 91 75) is also near the airport but inland from the previous guesthouses, in the Saint-Hilaire district. Rooms, including breakfast and airport transfers, are 4000/5500 CFP. The Saint-Hilaire le truck passes close by about every hour during the week but it's easier to ask the owners to take you down to the main road, about 1.5km away. The *Tahiti Airport Lodge* (☎ 82 23 68, fax 82 25 00) is also perched up above Faaa, overlooking the airport and about 100m from the coast road. There are a dozen or so rooms for 3500/5500 CFP or for 7500 CFP with bathroom. Airport transfers and breakfast are included and this can be a pleasant place, provided the owner is in a good mood.

Vaimana Fare (☎/fax 48 07 17, fax 43 87 27), one of the rare addresses east of the city, is at PK10.5 in Mahina and has bungalows at 6500 CFP.

Places to Stay – Mid-Range & Top End
Papeete Mid-range hotels are mainly city business hotels and all accept credit cards. The well-kept *Hôtel Le Mandarin* (☎ 42 16 33, fax 42 16 32, mandarin@chris.pf) has a very central location on Rue Colette, right

beside the mairie and only a short stroll from Papeete Market. Its air-con rooms cost from 12,960/15,120 CFP.

Three other mid-range hotels are along the quayside Blvd Pomare in the centre of town. Overlooking the Moorea ferry wharf from Blvd Pomare, the bland rooms at the *Kon Tiki Pacific* (☎ 43 72 82, fax 42 11 66) are not bad value at 7540/10,260 CFP. The *Royal Papeete* (☎ 42 01 29, fax 43 79 09) is a bit worn around the edges at 9000/10,700 CFP – or 10,500/12,000 CFP for deluxe rooms. Continue towards the centre and the *Hotel Prince Hinoi* (☎ 42 32 77, fax 42 33 66) is at the junction of Blvd Pomare and Ave du Prince Hinoi. Featureless but efficient rooms are reasonable value for 12,545 CFP.

The friendly *Tiare Tahiti Hotel* (☎ 43 68 48, fax 43 68 47) is further along Blvd Pomare, near the post office. Its comfortable rooms cost 12,000 to 15,500 CFP. The *Mataiva Hotel* (☎ 42 67 67, fax 42 36 90) is towards the western edge of the city, on Route de Tipaeru, 200m from the Total station. It's nondescript but modern rooms cost 12,000/16,000 CFP. There's a restaurant, bar, swimming pool and tennis courts.

The beach-side *Royal Tahitien Hotel* (☎ 42 81 13, fax 41 05 35) is about 3km east of the centre, in Pirae. It has rooms at 10,800 CFP. Le truck stops less than 100m from the hotel.

Around Papeete The *Tahiti Country Club* (☎ 42 60 40, fax 41 09 28) is about 6km from Papeete, west of the airport, just beyond the Beachcomber Parkroyal Hotel and on the slopes of Punaauia Hill. The 40 air-con rooms are very straightforward and cost 8640 CFP. There's a bar, swimming pool and tennis courts.

Papeete's four luxury hotels all lie to the west, one on the city edge, two immediately beyond the airport and one at PK15. All are right on the lagoon and have all the amenities you'd expect. Several times a week they offer Polynesian dance performances by the best dance groups on the island. The *Outrigger Hotel Tahiti* (☎ 86 48 48, fax 86 48 40, reservation@outrigger.pf) is at PK2, just 500m beyond the city exit. It has 200 rooms from 29,700 to 70,200 CFP.

The *Tahiti Beachcomber Parkroyal* (☎ 86 51 10, fax 86 51 30, tahiti@parkroyal .pf) is 8km from the centre of Papeete, just 2km beyond the airport. The 300-plus rooms range from 31,664 to 52,380 CFP for the lagoon bungalows. One of the swimming pools even has a sand beach.

The *Sofitel Maeva Beach Hotel* (☎ 42 80 42, fax 43 84 70) is less than a kilometre past the Tahiti Beachcomber Parkroyal, beside the roundabout where the autoroute from Papeete meets the coast road. The Outumaoro le truck terminus is immediately beyond the roundabout. It's older and more traditional and tariffs range from 21,600 to 43,200 CFP. Some of the rooms look a little tired.

Le Méridien (☎ 47 07 07, fax 47 07 28, sales@lemeridien-tahiti.com), the most luxurious hotel on the island, is beside the lagoon at PK15, not far from the Museum of Tahiti. The 138 rooms range from 34,020 to 52,164 CFP for the over-water bungalows.

Places to Eat

Papeete has a range of international cuisines and there are classic restaurants, snack bars and Tahiti's famed roulottes. Sunday is the closing day for most establishments, when finding a meal can be difficult. For breakfast go to one of the numerous snack bars where, from 5.30 am, you can get coffee, baguettes and croissants. If you're preparing your own food, Papeete has several large and well-stocked supermarkets.

Restaurants Most places in this category accept credit cards. At *Le Marrakech* (☎ 42 80 00) on the Pont de l'Est near the mairie you can even finish with a traditional Moroccan mint tea. It's open Monday to Saturday. Credit cards are accepted.

In the Vaima Centre, on the Blvd Pomare side, *Jack Lobster* (☎ 42 50 58) is American style, from its red-and-white checked tablecloths to the background music and, of course, the Tex-Mex and steak menu. It's open Monday to Friday for lunch and dinner, Saturday for dinner only. The *Sushi Bar*, directly above Jack Lobster, is a chic and stylish Japanese 'rotating sushi bar', where you sit at a bar and small dishes of sushi float by on little pirogues. It's open Monday to Thursday for lunch, Friday and Saturday for lunch and dinner.

Le Café des Negociants (☎ 48 08 48) is on narrow Rue du Commandant Jean Gilbert, leading back from Blvd Pomare to Rue Leboucher. It's a good place for a drink and has a varied and inventive menu. It's open Monday to Friday from breakfast through dinner, Sunday just for dinner.

Lou Pescadou (☎ 43 74 26) on Rue Anne-Marie Javouhey is an institution and its exuberant owner Mario, usually presiding over the pizza oven at the front, is certainly part of its fame. Pizzas from 600 to 980 CFP are what it's all about, but there are other choices. It's open until 11 pm Monday to Saturday. *La Squadra* (☎ 41 32 14) is right behind Lou Pescadou on Passage Cardella and offers standard Italian dishes. It's closed Monday and Tuesday evenings and all day Sunday. The apostrophes seem to have gone walkabout at *L'Api'zzeria* (☎ 42 98 30), another popular pizzeria just west of the Paofai Church. It's open Monday to Saturday.

Le Mandarin (☎ 42 16 33) on Rue des Écoles, just round the corner from the hotel of the same name, has hardly changed since the early 1960s and its Chinese menu has 180 dishes. It's open every day. *Le Dragon d'Or* (☎ 42 96 12), next to Le Mandarin Hotel and across from the town hall on Rue Colette, is another classic Chinese restaurant. It's open Tuesday to Sunday.

The excellent *La Restaurant Saïgonnaise* (☎ 42 05 35) on Ave du Prince Hinoi is the only Vietnamese restaurant in Papeete. It's open Monday to Saturday.

In the more expensive category *L'O à la Bouche* (☎ 45 29 76), right in the centre of town on Passage Cardella, is a real surprise – very stylish and not exceptionally expensive. The menu has a modern French flavour and there's a good winelist. It's closed Saturday lunch time and Sunday.

Morrison's Café (☎ 42 78 61), atop the Vaima Centre, takes its name from Jim (not

Les Roulottes

Good food, good fun and the best prices in town: that's *les roulottes*, quayside in downtown Papeete every evening until around 1 am. A roulotte is a van turned into a mobile diner. Flaps lowered on each side become the counters, stools are set up for the customers and the staff inside the van prepare the food.

Roulottes turn out pretty much everything you'll find at regular restaurants but at lower prices. Typically, a roulotte meal will be in the 800 to 1000 CFP bracket.

Roulottes' names tell what they're all about; the cast may change from night to night but you may come across mobile pizzerias (would you believe a wood-fired pizza oven on wheels?) like Vesuvio Pizza, Pizza Napoli and even the Pizza Hut (should that be Pizza Van?). There's steak and chips at Chez Roger or steak and pizza at Le Romain, complete with Roman columns to support the van's side flaps and a cut-out figure of a centurion. Of course there are plenty of Chinese roulottes *(spécialités chinoises)* like Chez Michou, Chez Lili, Pacifique Sud Roulotte or Hong Kong (a specialist in *chao men*).

Van) and the rock & roll continues, with live music several times a week. Main courses are 1900 to 2800 CFP and there's a good winelist. It's closed Saturday lunch time and Sunday.

Traditional French restaurants include *L'Excuse (☎ 53 13 25)*, on Rue du Maréchal Foch, and *La Petit Auberge (☎ 42 86 13)*, close to the Pont de l'Est roundabout. *La Corbeille d'Eau (☎ 43 77 14)*, further west on the waterfront Blvd Pomare, regularly wins accolades as the home of fine French dining in Papeete and is a favourite for Papeete business people and politicians.

Snacks & Light Meals Papeete Market has some good places but there's nowhere to sit down. Close to the post office, *Restaurant du Parc Bougainville* in Bougainville Park serves various Chinese and Polynesian specialties. *Le Janoko* and *Down Town* are in the Fare Tony shopping centre.

In the centre of town, the Vaima Centre has a number of cheap-eats possibilities as well as more expensive restaurants. The *Rétro Saint-Germain*, accessible from Rue

Georges Lagarde, serves classic French dishes. It's closed on Sunday afternoon.

L'Oasis (☎ 45 45 01), on Rue du Général de Gaulle, on the opposite corner of the Vaima Centre to Le Rétro and looking across the street to the cathedral, is a popular breakfast and lunch spot but it's closed on Sunday. Also on the Rue du Général de Gaulle side of the Vaima Centre, on the corner of Rue Lagarde, *Le Motu* has a great selection of *casse-croûte* from 200 to 450 CFP. There are no places to sit but there are tables for standing. Along Rue Lagarde is *Au Rendez-Vous des Amis* and *Snack Hollywood*, both good for light meals and snacks. *Café de la Gare (☎ 42 75 95)* is round the corner on Rue du Général de Gaulle. It looks authentically Parisian, is open Monday to Saturday and is a little pricey.

Other snack-bars are aimed at office workers grabbing lunch. The self-service *Polyself Cafeteria*, in Rue Paul Gauguin, is a good example. *Waikiki* is a Chinese restaurant on Rue Albert Leboucher with a varied menu and low prices. It's closed Monday evenings and Sunday lunch time.

FRENCH POLYNESIA

L'Épi d'Or, on Rue Colette in front of the station for trucks to the west coast, is another lunch place.

On Blvd Pomare, just beyond the Hotel Prince Hinoi, the *3 Brasseurs* is a very popular boutique brewery with various restaurant dishes. Next door is the minuscule *Snack Buffoon*, ideal for a take-away meal and open every day until midnight. Right on the Pont de l'Est roundabout is *Tiki-softc@fé*, which has various reasonably priced snacks and Internet access. It's open 7 am to 11 pm during the week, until 1 am on the weekend.

Entertainment

Pubs & Bars On a balmy tropical evening the first question is where to go for a cold Hinano or a well poured cocktail. At the ever-popular *Le Rétro* (☎ *42 86 83*), on the waterfront side of the Vaima Centre, a *pression* (draught) Hinano will set you back 430 CFP. It also serves food. A block from the waterfront *Café de la Gare* (☎ *42 75 95*) looks like it was beamed straight from the centre of Paris, complete with chain Gauloise smokers. *Le Café des Negociants*, just off Blvd Pomare, has about 50 beers on offer and cocktails at 850 CFP. Jazz groups play from time to time. *Morrison's Café*, upstairs in the Vaima Centre, is a trendy spot to drink.

Popular places along the nightlife strip of Blvd Pomare include *3 Brasseurs*, with its excellent boutique brewery beer on tap for 400 CFP. For local ambience try the *Royal Kikiriri* on Rue Colette. Of course the *Outrigger Tahiti*, *Tahiti Beachcomber Parkroyal*, *Sofitel Maeva Beach* and *Le Méridien* bars are great places to enjoy the ocean breezes and nibble on peanuts.

Discos & Clubs After a stay on other islands where nightlife is nonexistent, Papeete could almost pass for a wild and abandoned city – although actually it only gets busy on the weekends. The waterfront Blvd Pomare is the main centre – from the Tahitian waltz to techno, it's all there. Entry ranges from 1000 to 2000 CFP, it usually includes a drink and sometimes

only applies to men. Places typically close around 3 or 4 am.

Popular locations include the *Scorpio* to the rear of the Vaima Centre with its eclectic clientele. The *Piano Bar* is on Rue des Écoles and it's certainly a place to get an education. *Le Paradise*, on Blvd Pomare next to the Hotel Pacific, attracts a slightly older crowd.

If you want a more local atmosphere head to *La Cave*, beside the Royal Papeete on Blvd Pomare. Next door the *Tamure Hut* offers the same music and style, while the *Royal Kikiriri* on Rue Colette is the main centre for Tahitian dancing. *Le Kriptone Palace*, Ave Bruat, next to the New Port, is the favourite hangout of the town's wealthy youngsters. The clientele is older at *Club 106*, just beyond Ave Bruat.

Cinemas Papeete has a number of cinemas showing films either dubbed in French or with subtitles. The letters VO *(version originale)* indicate that if the film started life in English it will still be in English, with subtitles rather than dubbed audio.

Dance Performances Superb Polynesian dance performances take place around 8 pm in the big hotels, lasting about 45 minutes. They're accompanied by a 5000 to 6500 CFP buffet dinner although a drink at the bar will sometimes get you in. The *Captain Bligh Restaurant* (☎ *43 62 90*) at the Lagoonarium at PK11 in Punaauia also has an island-night performance on Friday and Saturday nights for only 4200 CFP.

Shopping

You can buy products from all over French Polynesia here. Pearls produced in the Tuamotus, wood carvings made in the Marquesas and hats and baskets woven in the Australs are all on sale.

The Te Fare Tahiti Nui (Territorial Cultural Centre), at the western end of Blvd Pomare, organises regular exhibitions of traditional and contemporary Polynesian art. Just beyond the centre, before the footbridge, the Tipaerui craft centre displays local crafts. A wide variety of handicrafts is on sale in Papeete Market, particularly up-stairs where you'll find sculptures, monoi (oil) products, pareu (sarongs), clothes, shells, engraved mother of pearl, jewellery and basketwork. There are numerous craft and souvenir shops along Blvd Pomare and Rue du Général de Gaulle and in the Vaima and Fare Tony centres. Manuia Curios (☎ 42 04 94), at Place Notre Dame, beside the cathedral and Ganesha (☎ 43 04 18), in the Vaima Centre, have handicrafts from French Polynesia as well as other Pacific centres.

Papeete has a number of art galleries showing the work of Polynesian artists. They include Galerie des Tropiques (☎ 41 05 00), at the junction of Blvd Pomare and Rue Cook; Gallery Matamua (☎ 41 34 95), on Blvd Pomare in front of the Quai d'Honneur; Galerie Reva Reva (☎ 43 32 67), at 36 Rue Lagarde near the Vaima Centre; and Gallery Winkler (☎ 42 81 77), at 17 Rue Jeanne d'Arc close to the cathedral.

You'll find local music CDs in city music shops and hypermarkets. There are many jewellery shops and pearl specialists in Papeete, particularly in the Vaima Centre.

Getting There & Away

Papeete is the flight and shipping hub for all of French Polynesia.

Air At Faaa (pronounced 'fa-ah-ah') airport (☎ 82 60 61) international check-in is at the eastern end of the terminal. Air Tahiti domestic check-in is at the western end and Air Moorea is in a separate small terminal just to the east of the main terminal.

The Air Tahiti office (☎ 86 40 00, or on weekends ☎ 86 41 84 or ☎ 86 41 95) is up-stairs in the Fare Tony Centre, which ex-tends between Blvd Pomare and Rue du Général de Gaulle and is open Monday to Friday. There's also an Air Tahiti office open daily at the airport, in the domestic flights area. Qantas (☎ 43 06 65, or ☎ 83 90 90 at the airport prior to flights), Air New Zealand (☎ 54 07 47), LanChile (☎ 42 64 55, or ☎ 82 64 57 at the airport prior to flights) and Hawaiian Airlines (☎ 42 15 00) all have offices in the Vaima Centre. Other phone numbers are Aircalin (☎ 85 09 04),

Air France (☎ 42 22 22), Air Moorea (☎ 86 41 41, Air Tahiti Nui (☎ 45 55 55), AOM (☎ 54 25 25) and Corsair (☎ 42 28 28).

Boat Papeete is the shipping centre for French Polynesia. Moorea ferries and the high speed *Ono-Ono* to the main islands of the Society group moor at the ferry quay at the north-east end of Blvd Pomare. Cruise ships and other visitors moor at the Quai d'Honneur, close to the tourist office and capitainerie (harbour master). The numer-ous cargo ships to the different archipela-goes work from the Motu Uta port zone, to the north of the city and reached by le truck route 3 from the mairie.

Getting Around

To/From the Airport The airport is less than 6km west of the centre of Papeete, but a taxi into town costs a hefty 1600 CFP during the day or 2500 CFP at night (from 8 pm to 6 am). Even to nearby hotels, it's 1000 CFP (1500 CFP at night). Le truck, the public transport alternative, is easy to use and very economical but very infrequent in the early hours, when most international flights arrive at and depart from Papeete. If you arrive at a reasonable hour, walk across the car park, cross the road and catch any east-bound le truck (to your left as you emerge from the terminal). The 15 minute trip into the city will cost 120 CFP (200 CFP at night). Dri-vers can ask for an additional 100 CFP for your baggage. From Papeete catch a le truck heading for Faaa and Outumaoro – the des-tination will be clearly posted on the front.

Local Transport Not only is le truck cheap and convenient, it's also very much a part of the Polynesian experience. Services on Tahiti are comprehensive and well organised, and le trucks have their route number and the final destination posted on the front. From Papeete to Faaa airport, for example, you want an Outumaoro le truck, heading for a terminus just beyond Faaa. There are official le truck stops, complete with blue signs and sometimes with canopies and seats, but les trucks will gen-erally stop for anybody who hails them.

On weekdays, le truck operates from dawn until about 5.30 pm, except for the Papeete-Faaa-Outumaoro line which operates 24 hours (getting very quiet after 10 pm). On weekends, and particularly on Sunday, the service is less frequent. Fares for the shortest trips, eg from Papeete to a little beyond the airport, start from 120 CFP. Out to about 20km from Papeete the fare increases in stages to around 200 CFP. Getting to the other side of the island might cost 400 CFP.

Papeete has several le truck stops. The red Faaa airport stop is on Rue du Général de Gaulle by Papeete Market and les trucks for some other destinations in that direction also depart from there. North coast destinations go from the blue stop, opposite the Tahiti Tourist Board on Blvd Pomare. The yellow stop for Tahiti Iti is further along Blvd Pomare, opposite the Moorea ferry quay. The green stop beside the town hall handles various destinations including the tomb of Pomare V and the Motu Uta cargo ship area.

Taxis are metered but flagfall is 800 CFP (1200 CFP at night) plus 120 CFP (240 CFP at night) per kilometre – more than US$10 just to turn the meter on at night! To phone for a taxi call the nearest taxi rank: Faaa airport (☎ 86 60 66), Vaima Centre (☎ 42 33 60), Papeete Market (☎ 43 19 62) or Jasmin Station, Hotel Prince Hinoi (☎ 42 35 98).

Since le truck services rapidly fade as you leave Papeete, and taxis are so expensive, many visitors rent cars. Once out of Papeete traffic is light and the driving isn't too scary. Count on 7500 to 8000 CFP per day for a small car with unlimited distance and insurance. Agencies include Avis at Rue des Remparts and Ave Georges Clémenceau (☎ 41 93 93, fax 42 19 11), Quai des Ferries (☎ 43 88 99) and Faaa airport (☎ 85 02 84). Daniel Rent-a-Car is at Faaa airport (☎ 82 30 04, fax 85 62 64). Europcar is at Ave Prince Hinoi and Rue des Remparts (☎ 45 24 24, fax 41 93 41), Faaa airport (☎ 86 60 61) and Quai des Ferries (☎ 45 24 24). Hertz is at Tipaerui (☎ 42 04 71) and Faaa airport (☎ 82 55 86).

Hitchhiking is still possible on Tahiti, particularly when you get to the far end of the island where le truck services are infrequent. The worldwide rules for hitching apply: it's not the safest means of travel, and women should never hitch alone.

TAHITI NUI
Tahiti Nui (Big Tahiti) is by far the larger of Tahiti's two landmasses.

Tahiti Nui's Coastal Road
The 114km road that circles Tahiti Nui is marked with 'PK' signs, recording the distance from Papeete. The circuit described below is clockwise from Papeete and lists the appropriate PK marker numbers.

On Point Outuaiai in Arue is the **Tomb of Pomare V** (PK4.7), the last of the Pomare dynasty. Pomare II demonstrated his new Christian enthusiasm by constructing a gigantic church at this point, on the site of an equally large marae. The church was replaced in 1821 and again around 1900. Today's building was built in 1978. Pomare's tomb, which looks like a stubby lighthouse made of coral boulders, was actually built for Queen Pomare IV. Pomare V, her ungrateful son, had her remains evicted a few years after her death in 1877 and when he died in 1891 it became his tomb.

Taharaa Point (PK8.1) is the western boundary of Matavai Bay, the favourite locale of early European explorers. There are fine views towards Papeete. **Point Venus** (PK10), the promontory which marks the eastern end of Matavai Bay, was the site of Cook's observatory. Until Papeete began to develop around the 1820s, Matavai remained the principal anchorage for visiting European ships. There's a memorial to the arrival of the pioneering LMS missionaries in 1797 at this point, and the popular beach with its shady trees is overlooked by an impressive lighthouse.

There's an often crowded surfing break just before the headland that signals the start of the small village of **Papenoo** (PK17). A long bridge crosses the Papenoo River at the far end of the village and the 4WD route up the Papenoo Valley, cutting through the ancient crater rim to the **Relais de la Maroto**, starts up the west side of the river. See the Tahiti Nui's Centre section for more information. Appropriate swell conditions produce a geyser-like fountain of water from the **Arahoho Blowhole** (PK22) just before Tiarei. When the blowhole really performs people have been washed right off the rocks, so take care. Just beyond the blowhole there's a fine sliver of black-sand beach. Near here a road turns off to the three **Faarumai Waterfalls** (PK22.1).

A plaque on the bridge at **Hitiaa** (PK38) commemorates the visit to Tahiti in 1768 by the French explorer Louis-Antoine de Bougainville, who anchored near the tiny islets of Variararu and Oputotara. There's a charming **abandoned church** in Hitiaa.

Strategically situated at the narrow isthmus connecting Tahiti Nui with smaller Tahiti Iti, the town of **Taravao** (PK54) has been a military base on and off since 1844, when the first French fort was established. It's a good place for a mid-circuit lunch break, and from Taravao roads run along the north and south coasts of Tahiti Iti.

Tahiti's fine 137 hectare Botanical Gardens and the interesting Gauguin Museum share an entrance road and car park at PK51. The **Botanical Gardens** are open from 9 am to 5 pm daily; entry is 400 CFP. Interestingly, the gardens concentrate more on exotic vegetation than on Tahiti's own lush plant life. The **Gauguin Museum** is open the same hours; entry is 600 CFP. It's more a museum of his life than a gallery of his work. The museum gardens are home to three superb tiki from Raivavae in the Austral Islands.

The **Vaipahi Garden & Vaima Pool** (PK49) are beside the road and the **Vaipahi Waterfall** is a few minutes' walk inland. At PK47.5 is the turn-off for the rough track up to Lake Vaihiria, the Relais de la Maroto and across the island to the north coast. During his first visit to Tahiti Gauguin lived in **Mataiea**, near PK46, between 1891 and 1893. The Mataiea district ends with the **golf course** at Atimaono at PK42, the site of the abortive Terre Eugénie cotton plantation in the 1860s.

Just east of Papara village, **Marae Maha-iatea** (PK39.2) was the most magnificent marae in Tahiti at the time of Cook's first visit. It measured 80 by 27m at its base, rising in 11 great steps to a height of 13m, but today it's just an impressively large heap of rubble. The turn to the unmarked site is between the roadside Beach Burger restaurant and the PK39 sign.

In the village of Papara the **Museum of Seashells** (PK36) is open from 8 am to 5 pm daily and admission is 300 CFP for adults. A variety of flowers and tropical plants are assembled in the **Mataoa Garden** (PK34.5). Entry is 400 CFP, including a glass of fruit juice, and it's open from 10 am to 4 pm weekdays, 1.30 to 4 pm on weekends. At the **Maraa Grotto** (PK28.5) a manicured path beside the road runs through a garden past a series of overhung caverns, with crystal-clear pools and ferny grottoes.

In the Paea district the **Marae Arahurahu,** at PK22.5, is the best looking marae on the island, although it was only a secondary marae, of no great significance. Not only has it been restored, it has also been embellished with impressive tiki and the lushly photogenic site is used for performances, particularly during July's Heiva festivities. The village is centred around the **Orofero River** at PK20, a popular surfing site.

The **Museum of Tahiti & Its Islands** (☎ 58 34 76) in Punaauia (PK15.1) has one of the best collections in the Pacific. It's right on the coast, several hundred metres' walk from the coast road after the Punaruu bridge. From Papeete a Punaauia le truck will drop you at the road junction for 160 CFP. The museum is open from 9.30 am to 5.30 pm Tuesday to Sunday and entry (via a bookshop) is 500 CFP. It's in a large garden and if you get tired of history, culture and art, you can wander out to the water's edge to watch the surfers at one of Tahiti's most popular breaks.

The museum is divided into four sections: geography and natural history, pre-European culture, the European era and outdoor exhibits. Highlights include a wonderful display of tiki and petroglyphs, many of them from the Australs and Marquesas. They include a huge wooden tiki and a very expressive stone tiki, both from the Marquesas.

Ancient Polynesian archery equipment, surfboards and the enormously heavy stones used in stone-lifting contests are displayed.

There are good beaches between PK15 and PK10 through **Punaauia**. Well into the Papeete urban sprawl, the **Lagoonarium** (PK11) is a pleasant little tourist trap, just in case you don't get to see a shark for real on a snorkelling trip.

Tahiti Nui's Centre

Although several roads and tracks climb a little way into the central highlands, there is only one route which extends right across Tahiti. It's a wonderful, but quite rugged, 39km route from Papenoo in the north to Mahaiatea in the south, via the Relais de la Maroto and Lake Vaihiria. Several 4WD operators offer this excursion for a completely different look at Tahiti: not lagoons but mountains, waterfalls, a lake and mysterious archaeological sites.

From Papenoo, the track follows the wide **Papenoo Valley**, passing the **Topatari Waterfall**, **Vaiharuru Waterfall** and the **Puraha Waterfall**. The track passes the **Bassin Vaituoru** (Vaituoru Pool) and finally reaches the Relais de la Maroto.

From the Relais de la Maroto, tracks fan out to several hydro dams and the marae that were restored during the dam's construction. The extensive **Marae Farehape** site is almost directly below the ridgeline on which the Relais de la Maroto perches. The Vainavenave Dam looks like a huge marae wall and the beautifully restored **Marae Anapua** perches up above the dam reservoir. There are some fine natural swimming pools and striking waterfalls nearby.

Driving along Tahiti Nui's south coast, the turn-off to the cross-island road is at PK47.5, just beyond the Seventh-Day Adventist church and just before the Tahiria bridge and a small settlement. Turning left, the track follows the river upstream to a small catchment lake and **Marae Vaihiria I**. There is a second small catchment lake before the road climbs quickly to the major **Lake Vaihiria**, then descends steeply to a road junction where you turn left to the Relais de la Maroto.

Tahiti Safari Expedition (☎ 42 14 15, fax 42 10 07) and Freddy Adventure (☎ 41 97 99, fax 53 21 22) do trips across the centre for 6000 to 7000 CFP per person but it's wise to book in the high season. You can also do the trip in a rented 4WD but check the track conditions before you start out; in the rainy season this route can be truly perilous. You can walk across in a couple of days or ride across on a mountain bike.

Places to Stay

There are remarkably few places to stay once you've left Papeete.

Coastal Tahiti Nui The only place on the north coast between Papeete and Taravao is *Fare Nana'o (☎ 57 18 14, fax 57 76 10)* on the water's edge at PK52, only a few kilometres before Taravao. It's six bungalows range from a tree house to Polynesian-style over-water bungalows (5500 to 7500 CFP). Transfers from the airport cost 3000 CFP and there's a pirogue for guests to use.

There are a number of quiet places in the Punaauia-Paea-Papara sector, close to some unexceptional black sand beaches. During the day there are regular le truck services but they dry up towards 4 or 5 pm. *Chez Va'a (☎/fax 42 94 32)* is in Punaauia (PK8), on the mountain side of the Sofitel, and has two rooms for 3500/5000 CFP, including breakfast and airport transfers. *Moana Surf Tours (☎/fax 43 70 70)*, aimed at visiting surfies, is on the mountain side of the road at PK8.3 and has dorm beds from 6000 CFP, including transport to surf breaks on Tahiti and Moorea.

The *Relais Familial (☎/fax 45 01 98)*, at PK12.5 in Punaauia, 200m inland from the coast road, has two rooms for 3500/4500 CFP (airport transfers 1000 CFP per person). *Chez Armelle (☎ 58 42 43, fax 58 42 81)* is on the lagoon side of the road at PK15.5 in Punaauia, just beyond the Tahiti Museum and Le Méridien. The eight rooms are 4500/6000 CFP, including breakfast. There's also a dormitory at 2000 CFP a night. *Le Bellevue (☎/fax 58 47 04)* at PK16 is a possibility if you're staying at least one week. An equipped studio costs 23,000 CFP for two, including airport transfers.

The friendly and popular *Pension Te Miti* (*☎/fax 58 46 61, or mobile ☎ 78 60 80*) is on the mountain side of the main road at PK18.5 in Paea, about 200m from the shore. Dorm beds are 1800 CFP and rooms are 4500 to 6000 CFP, all including breakfast.

Fare Opuhi Roti (*☎ 53 20 26*) at PK21 has a simple *fare* for 6500 CFP and a room for 2500/5000 CFP, including breakfast and airport transfers. The *Hiti Moana Villa* (*☎ 57 93 33, fax 57 94 44*) is on the lagoon side at PK32 in Papara and has a swimming pool. The four bungalows are impeccable and cost 8160 CFP for two.

Papara Village (*☎ 57 41 41, fax 57 79 00*) is at PK38, perched on the hillside 800m off the coast road. The small Marae Tetaumatai is on the site which has fantastic views of the lagoon and the mountains. The well-equipped bungalows cost 7000/10,000 CFP.

Central Tahiti Nui The popular *Relais de la Maroto* (*☎ 43 97 99, fax 57 90 30, maroto@mail.pf*), which originally served as accommodation quarters for workers on the hydro-electricity project, has rooms for 4400 CFP per person plus meals. The wine cellar is exceptional.

Places to Eat

There are snack bars dotted round the coast while Taravao, the mid-point on the circuit, has quite a collection of snack bars and restaurants including *Ahki Vairua* (*☎ 57 20 38*), a modest but authentic Chinese place. *L'Escale Restaurant* (*☎ 57 07 16*) does fine French cuisine in a classic setting, while the rotunda-shaped *Te Hono* (*☎ 57 21 84*) does Chinese specialities; both are closed Monday. *Snack Restaurant Chez Myriam* (*☎ 57 71 01*) is across the road and has an indoor restaurant section and outdoor tables for snacks. It's closed Sunday.

Continuing from Taravao there's a larger choice of restaurants along the south coast. *Restaurant Baie Phaéton* (*☎ 57 08 96*) at PK59 has a superb view across Phaéton Bay from its terrace built over the lagoon and a moderately priced, predominantly Chinese menu. The *Restaurant du Musée*

Gauguin (*☎ 57 13 80*) is half a kilometre after the Gauguin Museum and firmly aimed at tourist groups. The *Atimaono Golf Club House* (*☎ 57 40 32*) at PK40.2 is open for lunch everyday. The *Restaurant Nuutere* (*☎ 57 41 15*) at PK32.5 in Papara is easily located by its extravagantly painted facade and has a good reputation for its French specialities. It's closed Tuesday.

The chic suburbs around Punaauia have many restaurants. *Coco's Restaurant* (*☎ 58 21 08*) has a magnificent setting beside the sea at PK13 and fine food. The *Venezia* (*☎ 41 30 56*) is nearby at PK12.7 and serves pizzas from 990 to 1250 CFP and other dishes at higher prices.

The tourist-oriented *Captain Bligh Restaurant* (*☎ 43 62 90*), at the Lagoonarium at PK11.4, has a Friday and Saturday evening buffet and dance performance (4200 CFP) with one of the best island dance groups on Tahiti. *L'Auberge du Pacifique* (*☎ 43 98 30*), beside the lagoon at PK11, has become an institution for its French-Polynesian menu. It's open Monday to Saturday.

TAHITI ITI

Tahiti Iti (Small Tahiti) is the smaller landmass of Tahiti's figure eight shape. There are roads along the northern and southern coasts and a short road up the centre of the island. The north and south roads do not meet and, although walking trails extend around the coast from the ends of both roads, the sheer Te Pari cliff-faces cut off the trails, so walking right around the coast is very difficult. There are, however, some superb walks on Tahiti Iti, including a fine walk from Tautira to a series of marae and petroglyphs in the Vaiote River valley.

Around Tahiti Iti

The north coast road ends just beyond **Tautira**. A good walking track leads round the coast for another 12km or so before reaching **Te Pari** beyond the **Vaiote River**. There are some noted petroglyphs on boulders near the coast and a series of marae in the valley.

The central route climbs to a **lookout** about 10km east with superb vistas across the isthmus of Taravao to the towering mountains of Tahiti Nui.

The south coast road runs past beaches and bays to **Vairao** and the small settlement of **Teahupoo**, passing a turn-off at PK9.5 which leads a short distance inland to **Marae Nuutere**, restored in 1994. The road stops abruptly at the **Tirahi River** at PK18 and from here it is an easy 2½ hour walk to **Vaipoiri Cave**.

Places to Stay

Fare Nana'o is only a couple of kilometres north of Taravao, so it's another alternative if you want to explore Tahiti Iti. *Chez Maïthé (π/fax 57 18 24)* is at PK4.5, on the north coast, facing the Nono Islet and has two rooms at 6500 CFP for two people. *Chez Jeannine (π/fax 57 07 49)* is at PK4 on the plateau road and has rooms at 4000 CFP or large bungalows at 6000 CFP. Airport transfers are 1000 CFP per person.

There are three establishments along the south coast. *Meherio Iti (π 57 73 56)*, beside the lagoon at PK11.9, has well-equipped bungalows for 6000/8000 CFP a single/double. Airport transfers cost 1000 CFP per person. *Te Pari Village (π/fax 42 59 12)* is 10 minutes by boat from the Teahupoo pier, in the middle of a magnificent coconut grove beside the lagoon. The four traditional-style bungalows have bathrooms and cost 8500 CFP per person with all meals and transfers from the Teahupoo pier.

Popular with surfers, *Pension Bonjouir (π 57 02 15, π/fax 43 69 10)* is a little beyond Te Pari Village. A tent site is 500 CFP (this is the only campsite on Tahiti), a dorm bed is 2500 CFP, simple bungalows are 4500 CFP for two or the family bungalow is 14,500 CFP.

Places to Eat

The Taravao restaurants and snack bars are easy to reach. On the south coast *Auberge Te Pari (π 57 13 44)* is in Teahupoo, right at the end of the road, and is open for lunch Saturday through Thursday and for dinner on demand. Chez Jeannine, on the road to the plateau at PK4, has the *Eurasienne Restaurant (π 57 07 49)* which turns out some Asian specialities.

Other Society Islands

MOOREA
● pop 11,965   ● area 132 sq km

Mountains that leap out of the lagoon, fine beaches, terrific scuba diving, some interesting marae, a number of excellent walks, a pleasantly unhurried pace of life and absurdly easy access from Tahiti all combine to make Moorea the second most popular destination in French Polynesia.

History

Moorea means 'yellow lizard' and it's speculated that this was the name of one of the ruling families of the island. Marae Umarea at Afareaitu is the oldest marae on the island, dating back to 900 AD, but the Opunohu Valley has the greatest number of marae and in the pre-European era it was heavily populated.

Moorea had long been a refuge for Tahitians on the losing side of power struggles.

Archery in Ancient Times

Archery, as it existed before the arrival of Europeans, was not a wartime activity but a sacred game, reserved exclusively for the male elite of *ari'i* (high chiefs) and *ra'atira* (middle-ranked chiefs). It involved complex religious rituals and very strict rules. There was no specific target at which to aim – archers simply had to shoot an arrow the longest possible distance. Several referees validated shots and announced results by waving flags. Archery was only practised in the Society Islands and Mangareva (Gambier). The best archery platforms are found on Moorea, in the Opunohu Valley.

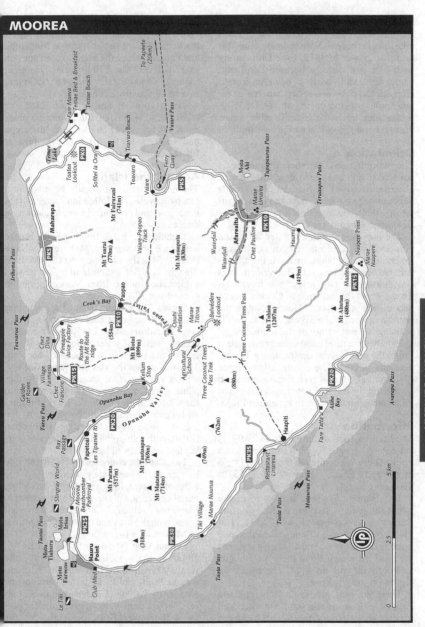

MOOREA

FRENCH POLYNESIA

In 1808 Pomare II retreated to Moorea, settled at Papetoai, befriended the LMS missionaries here and, when he mounted his return to power in 1815, took Christianity with him – it quickly became dominant. Copra and vanilla have been important crops in the past, and today Moorea is the pineapple-growing centre of French Polynesia. Tourism is the island's other major business and it continues to grow rapidly.

Orientation

The mountainous, untouched interior is covered in dense *mape* forests, the gigantic chestnut trees of Polynesia. Two roads beginning from the two bays run into the interior; they meet and climb up to the Belvédère lookout.

The population is concentrated in coastal villages. With its frenetic ferry quay, Vaiare is the busiest centre but Afareaitu is the administrative headquarters. Tourist development is concentrated in two strips: one from Maharepa down the east side of Cook's Bay to Paopao, the other around Hauru Point on the north-west corner of the island. The airport is at the north-east corner of the island.

Beaches are rare; good ones are at Hauru Point, the main tourist centre, and at Temae, near the airport. The pointe kilométrique (PK) markers start at zero at the airport and go around the coast clockwise to Haapiti at PK24 and anticlockwise to Haapiti at PK35.

Information

The Moorea Tourist Bureau (☎ 56 29 09) is at Le Petit Village shopping centre at Hauru Point. There is a counter at the airport (☎ 56 26 48) and a ticket window (☎ 56 38 53) at the Vaiare ferry.

The Banque Socredo across from the wharf at Vaiare has an ATM. Another Banque Socredo branch with ATM is at PK6.3 in Maharepa, a Banque de Tahiti and Banque de Polynésie branch are right across the road. At Hauru Point there's a Banque de Polynésie with an ATM. The banks are closed on the weekend.

There are post offices at Maharepa and Papetoai. There are many supermarkets and smaller shops around the island. Most are open Sunday morning and accept credit cards. TOA at Vaiare is the biggest supermarket; there are fish markets at Maharepa and Paopao, where the night's catch goes on sale at dawn. The Commercial Centre at Maharepa and Le Petit Village at Hauru are two small shopping centres.

The Moorea Hospital (☎ 56 23 23 or ☎ 56 24 24) is in Afareaitu. There's a pharmacy (☎ 56 10 51) at PK6.5 in Maharepa and another shortly after Tiki Village at PK31 heading north.

Around the Island

The island circuit can easily be made in a day by bicycle. The following route starts at the airport and proceeds in an anticlockwise direction.

Technicolour pareu floating in the breeze announce the start of **Maharepa village** (PK4 to 5) at the Lili Shop. At PK5 **Maison Blanche** is a fine example of a *fare vanira*, a plantation house from Moorea's vanilla boom from 1900 to 1915.

Cook's Bay is somewhat of a misnomer since Cook actually anchored in Opunohu Bay. Backdropped by Mt Rotu it's a spectacular stretch of water. Cook's Bay is also one of the two tourist centres of Moorea. The road passes the **van der Heyde Gallery**, with a collection of Oceanic art. Further along is the **Cook's Bay Gallery**, across from the Club Bali Hai. It has a small museum with items from all over Polynesia. At the top of Cook's Bay is the village of **Paopao** (PK9), with a shipping dock, a popular market and a variety of shops.

Two **Catholic churches** (PK10) stand side by side on the west side of Cook's Bay. The older of the two, long abandoned, has a fine mural depicting Polynesian-featured Joseph, Mary, the Archangel Gabriel and the infant Jesus, with the lush and mountainous profile of Moorea as a background.

Kellum Stop (☎ 56 18 52) is at PK17.5, almost at the top of the bay. In 1925 the wealthy Medford Kellum brought six scientists to Tahiti and kick-started some of the pioneering Polynesian archaeological studies. Kellum Stop welcomes visitors for personal tours weekdays, preferably in the mornings. The stroll round the garden costs 300 CFP.

At PK18 a road turns off inland from the bay along the Opunohu Valley to the several valley marae, the Belvédère lookout and the walking route to the Three Coconut Trees Pass.

The coast road rounds **Hauru Point** (PK25 to 30), the north-west corner of the island and one of the island's major tourist enclaves. The tourist strip starts with the big Moorea Beachcomber Parkroyal, quickly followed by the equally sprawling Club Méditerranée, along with a host of smaller establishments, restaurants and shops. **Tiki Village** at PK31 marks the end of the strip and is open from 10.30 am to 3 pm Tuesday to Sunday. It presents various facets of traditional Polynesian culture for tourists. Entrance costs 2000 CFP and a small dance performance is put on around 3 pm. At 11 am Friday and Sunday historical events are replayed for 3000 CFP.

Hauru Point has one of the best **beaches** on the island; the narrow but sandy stretch extends for about 5km. Finding your way to the beach is not easy because of the continuous nature of beachside developments. All beaches, however, are public property in French Polynesia and the hotel proprietors along this popular strip do not seem to mind if you walk through their grounds.

The neglected but evocative **Marae Nuurua** (PK31.5) is on the lagoon side at the end of a football field. It marks the start of the less developed side of Moorea. **Haapiti** (PK24) boasts two churches and Matauvau Pass has a popular surf break. **Atiha Bay** (PK18) is a sleepy fishing village which also attracts some surfers.

Nuupere Point is immediately south of Maatea village and the scant remains of **Marae Nuupere** (PK14) are just 100m or so south of the point – but the marae stands on private property. About 100m south of Chez Pauline in Afareaitu, **Marae Umarea** (PK10), thought to date from about 900 AD and the oldest marae on the island, is a long wall of coral boulders right along the waterfront.

The constant arrival and departure of ferries makes **Vaiare** (PK4) the busiest patch of

real estate on Moorea. There's good snorkelling in the shallow water at **Teavaro Beach** where the expensive Sofitel Ia Ora hotel is located. The island road climbs away from the coast to the **Toatea Lookout**, with great views over to Tahiti. A road on the lagoon side of the runway extends around **Temae Lake**, one of the rare breeding grounds for the only species of duck found in French Polynesia.

Paopao & Opunohu Valleys

From Moorea's two great bays, valleys sweep inland, meeting south of the coastal bulk of Mt Rotui. Today settlements are creeping up the Paopao Valley but the principal activity is still agriculture, with many hectares of pineapple plantations. In the pre-European era the valleys were densely populated and the Opunohu Valley was dotted with marae, some of which have been restored and maintained.

The oldest structures date from the 13th century. From the car park beside the huge **Marae Titiroa** a walking track leads through a dense forest to **Marae Ahu-o-Mahine**, with an imposing three-stepped *ahu* (raised altar). A short distance further up the road from Marae Titiroa is **Marae Afareaito** and an adjacent **archery platform**.

Beyond Marae Afareaito the road continues to climb steeply, winding up to the excellent **Belvédère lookout** on the slopes of Mt Tohiea (1207m).

Activities

MUST (☎ 56 17 32, ☎/fax 56 15 83, mustdive@mail.pf) at Cook's Bay, Moorea Fun Dive (☎ 56 40 38, ☎/fax 56 40 74, fundive@mail.pf) at the Moorea Beach Club, Scubapiti (☎/fax 56 20 38) next door at Les Tipaniers and the big Bathy's Club (☎ 56 31 44, bathys@mail.pf) at the Beachcomber Parkroyal are the Moorea dive centres. Most dive sites are along the north shore, and include the well-known **Le Tiki**, a popular shark feeding centre, **Stingray World** (Bathy's Club only), where you'll have the chance to frolic with stingrays, the **Ray Passage** and, for more experienced divers, the **Garden of Roses**.

Hauru Point has white sand beaches and good snorkelling. For the best snorkelling join a lagoon tour; the pirogue trips around the lagoon usually make a snorkelling stop. Aqua Blue (☎ 56 53 53, fax 56 42 51) at the Beachcomber Parkroyal does 'diving helmet' excursions on the lagoon bottom – a half-hour stroll costs 10,000 CFP.

Tours of Moorea's magnificent lagoon typically visit the two bays, stop to feed the sharks, swim with the rays and picnic and snorkel on Motu Fareone. Shark Tour at Moorea Camping is the cheapest operator at 1000 CFP. Others include Albert Tours (☎ 56 13 53) and Te Aho Nui (☎ 56 31 42).

Several operators organise half-day Safari 4x4 excursions in open Land Rovers, including Inner Island Safari Tours (☎ 56 20 09), Ron's Tours (☎ 56 42 43) and Tefaarahi Safari Tours (☎ 56 41 24).

Moorea has some great walking possibilities, including the two hour walk from the ferry quay at Vaiare, up over the crater ridge into the central valley, emerging at Cook's Bay. The climb from near the agricultural school in the Opunohu Valley to the Three Coconut Trees Pass is spectacular but the trail can be hard to follow (despite the red trail markers) so you may need a guide. Tiare Mato (☎ 43 92 76, fax 42 21 03), Polynesian Adventure (☎/fax 43 25 95) and Derek Grell of Chez Tefaarahi Safari Tours (☎/fax 56 41 24) all organise guided walks and climbs.

Dolphin Quest (☎ 55 19 48) at the Beachcomber Parkroyal has dolphin swims for 10,500 CFP. Dr Michael Poole at the Centre Océanographique du Moorea operates Moorea Dolphin Watch (☎ 56 14 70), doing dolphin and whale research trips around Moorea for 5000 to 6000 CFP per person. The money goes to finance scientific research. Tiahura Ranch (☎ 56 28 55) at Hauru Point offers various guided horse rides. Other activities include game fishing, parasailing, jetski tours, water-skiing and helicopter flights.

Places to Stay

Although there is accommodation scattered around the island, most of it's concentrated between PK5 to PK9 on the east side of Cook's Bay and from PK26 to PK31 around Hauru Point. Both these centres are very spread out. Moorea has superb overwater bungalows but also the best selection of economical (by local standards) accommodation in French Polynesia. More expensive places take credit cards.

Cook's Bay The bay looks magnificent but there is no beach. *Motel Albert (☎ 56 12 76, fax 56 58 58)* at PK7 has 19 simple *fare* with kitchens from 4000 CFP for two people There's a 1000 CFP one night supplement

The *Bali Hai Moorea (☎ 56 13 59, fax 56 19 22)*, just past PK5, is one of the longest established tourist hotels in French Polynesia. The cheapest rooms at 12,960 CFP are depressing little boxes but much better the bungalows (from 15,120 CFP) are much better *Club Bali Hai (☎ 56 13 68, fax 56 13 27)* is right on the bay at about PK8 and has 42 rooms and bungalows from 7560 CFP.

Also on the lagoon, the *Kaveka Hotel (☎ 56 50 50, fax 56 52 63, kaveka@mail.pf)* has 23 functional units from 10,260 CFP Round-trip transfers to the airport or ferry quay are 1200 CFP.

Cook's Bay to Hauru Point *Chez Dina (☎ 56 10 39)* at PK12.5 has three *fare* with kitchenettes for 5000 CFP for up to three people. At the time of writing *Hotel Moorea Lagoon* was under construction at PK14. *Village Faimano (☎ 56 10 20, fax 56 36 47)* is also at PK14 and has seven bungalows beside the lagoon from 7500 CFP.

Les Tipaniers Iti (☎ 56 12 67, fax 56 29 25) is associated with the popular Les Tipaniers at Hauru Point and has five very pleasant bungalows with kitchens for 8424 CFP. There's no beach but the lagoonside setting at PK21 is very attractive.

Hauru Point Unlike Cook's Bay this sector has a pleasant beach, although it's rather narrow and access is not easy since there are so many places along the water's edge The two islets directly offshore are very easy to reach.

There are two very popular backpacker centres on big beachfront sites with a wide range of accommodation possibilities. Don't expect a hint of luxury or even a friendly welcome at either – setting and price are their only assets. And add 20% for a one night stay. *Chez Nelson & Josiane* (☎ 56 15 18) at PK27 has tent sites (700 CFP per person), dorm beds (1020 CFP), beach cabins (from 2244, or 3060 CFP for two). There are clean shared toilets and showers and a well-kept kitchen and dining area. *Moorea Camping* (☎ 56 14 47, fax 56 30 22) at PK27.5 has tent sites (800 CFP), dorm beds (1000 CFP), tiny, spartan rooms (2200 CFP) and functional bungalows (from 4500 CFP).

Fare Auti Rua is across from Moorea Camping and has six comfortable bungalows with kitchens from 7000 CFP.

The *Moorea Beach Club* (☎ 56 15 48, fax 41 09 28) is the first place along the Hauru Point strip after the big Beachcomber and has 40 identical motel-like rooms in two-storey blocks by a swimming pool for 9720 CFP. At the same location *Fare Condominium* (☎ 56 26 69, fax 56 26 22) has 43 spacious but functional units with kitchenettes from 13,500 CFP. Prices go up for more than two people.

Hotel Hibiscus (☎ 56 12 20, fax 56 20 59, hibiscus@tahiti.net email) at PK27, next to Club Med, has 29 slightly Spartan bungalows in a pleasant garden from 12,960 CFP. *Moorea Village* (☎ 56 10 02, fax 56 22 11), on the beach side of the road at PK28, is also known as Fare Gendron. Ideal for families it has 80 functional bungalows, some with kitchenettes, from 8640/9720 CFP.

Fare Mato Tea (☎ 54 14 36, fax 56 32 54) at PK28.7 has nine simple family-style beach cabins from 8500 CFP. A minimum stay of two nights is required. *Fare Manuia* (☎ 56 26 17, fax 56 10 30) has a pleasant stretch of beach at PK30 with six family bungalows from 8000 CFP. There's a two night minimum stay.

Hauru Point starts with the big and luxurious *Moorea Beachcomber Parkroyal* ☎ 56 19 19, fax 56 18 88, moorea@ parkroyal.pf), where 147 rooms wind around an artificial lagoon complete with resident dolphins. Nightly costs range from 29,160 to 44,280 CFP for the over-water bungalows. The hotel has bars, restaurants, sporting facilities and a dive centre.

The *Club Méditerranée Moorea* (☎ 55 00 00, fax 55 00 10) at Hauru Point is the largest resort in French Polynesia. It's a typical activity-related Club Med facility. Daily costs, including all meals with drinks and all activities except scuba diving, are around US$100 to $130 per person in a double room. There is a Club Med office in the Vaima Centre in Papeete.

Around the Island Popular with surfers, *Fare Tatta'u* (☎/fax 56 35 83), at PK21.3 in Haapiti, is well away from the tourist crush with dorm beds at 1200 and 1500 CFP and miniature cabins at 4000 CFP (5000 CFP for one night).

At Afareaitu, 5km south of the Vaiare ferry quay, *Chez Pauline* (☎ 56 11 26) has a historic but decidedly Spartan charm, and a restaurant which specialises in Tahitian cuisine. Rooms are 2500/4000 CFP.

The *Sofitel Ia Ora* (☎ 56 12 90, fax 56 12 91) looks across to Tahiti from Temae Beach. It vies with the Beachcomber Parkroyal for the title of Moorea's most luxurious hotel with 110 bungalows from 25,812 CFP.

Near the public beach at Temae, *Temae Bed & Breakfast* (☎/fax 56 42 92) has a double room for 6000 CFP including a big breakfast. *Fare Maeva* (☎/fax 56 18 10) has three attractive bungalows for 6500 CFP for two.

Places to Eat

Moorea has *crêperies*, snack bars, seafood specialists, pizzerias, Polynesian restaurants and many others. Most places close towards 9 pm and on Sunday the choice can be surprisingly restricted. Some establishments will collect you from your accommodation and return you after your meal. If you're fixing your own food there are plenty of food shops.

Cook's Bay *Crêperie-Snack Sylésie*, in the Maharepa shopping centre, is an ideal place for breakfast or a snack. It's open from 6 am to 6 pm. *L'Ananas Bleu* (the Blue Pineapple) is on the inland side of the road and is recommended for breakfast or lunch, served on its pleasant verandah. There are several small snack-bars in Paopao, including *Snack Chez Michèle* and *Snack Rotui*.

Le Mahogany (☎ 56 39 73) is a pleasant little place in Maharepa with a French and Chinese menu. *Le Cocotier* (☎ 56 12 10) is just before the PK5 marker and is a popular and well-run restaurant specialising in French cuisine.

The cuisine at *La Case* (☎ 56 42 95), across the road and a little further along, has shifted from Caribbean to Swiss, although the decor – colourful chairs and posters – remains Caribbean! It's closed Wednesday.

Caprice des Îles (☎ 56 44 24), shortly after the Club Bali Hai, looks like an enormous Polynesian *fare* with a menu varying from French via Chinese to Tahitian. It's open Wednesday to Monday. *Alfredo's* (☎ 56 17 71), on the mountain side of the road near the end of the bay, is a popular Italian restaurant with a pleasant open air dining area. It's closed Sunday.

Opunohu Valley & Papetoai En route to the Belvédère or the archaeological sites, stop at the agricultural school where a small *fare* sells delicious ice creams. In Papetoai *Chez Serge* (☎ 56 13 17) is right by the turn-off to the octagonal church and specialises in traditional Polynesian dishes.

Hauru Point *Le Motu* is in the first small shopping centre, across from Club Med and has light meals Tuesday to Saturday and Sunday morning. There are two snack bars in Le Petit Village centre. *Lagoon Café* is open Monday to Saturday while the *Garden* is open Tuesday through Sunday morning. Other places for a snack include *Coco d'Îsle* and *Pitcairn*. The Beachcomber Parkroyal (☎ 56 51 10) has several restaurants including the poolside *Fare Hana* and the fancier *Fare Nui*.

Les Tipaniers Restaurant (☎ 56 12 67), at the hotel of the same name, combines French-Italian food with a Tahitian flavour

and has a great reputation. It's a moveable feast with breakfast and lunch at the beach while at dinnertime it shifts to the main road.

The beachfront *Sunset Restaurant* (☎ 56 12 20) at the Hotel Hibiscus has a great location and turns out good pizzas and other dishes. The restaurant at the *Fare Vaimoana* (☎ 56 17 14) has a pleasant beachside setting while the adjacent *Restaurant Tumoana* (☎ 56 37 60) serves attractively priced Chinese dishes.

Around the Island *Le Linareva* (☎ 56 15 35), at PK34.5 in Haapiti, is a floating restaurant installed at the end of the wharf. The food is essentially French and the restaurant enjoys an excellent reputation so reservations are recommended. *Pizzas Daniel*, a little north of the Linareva restaurant, is a straightforward place which is closed Thursday.

In Afareaitu *Chez Pauline* (☎ 56 11 26) requires advance reservations and offers Polynesian specialities in a simple family setting. At Vaiare you won't starve while you wait for your ferry to depart as there are roulottes. At the Sofitel Ia Ora there's *La Pérouse* and the *Molokai*.

Entertainment

There are some good places for a sunset drink. The *Club Bali Hai*'s bar offers a magnificent panorama of Cook's Bay, while *Le Cocotier* is another good place for a drink at Cook's Bay. At Hauru Point *Les Tipaniers* and the *Sunset Restaurant* have popular beachside bars. The floating *Le Linareva* at PK34.5 is a great place to watch the sunset with a cocktail.

The *Tiki Theatre Village* (☎ 56 18 97, fax 56 10 86, tikivillage@mail.pf), just south of Hauru Point at PK31, has an excellent troupe of 60 professional dancers who perform on Tuesday, Wednesday, Friday and Saturday at 8.45 pm. The performance alone costs 3000 CFP. There are also Polynesian music and dance performances by local groups at the big hotels.

Only *Club Med* has any nightlife There's a disco every night, although it's particularly busy on Friday and Saturday nights. Entrance, which includes a string of beads to buy drinks, costs 2000 CFP on the weekend, 1000 CFP during the week.

Shopping

For pareu (sarongs), T-shirts and other curios, try the Lili Shop, Maison Blanche and Vaimiti, between the airport and Cook's Bay. At Cook's Bay, stop at Honu Iti and L'Atelier du Santal behind the Blue Pineapple snack bar.

Moorea has a number of art galleries, such as that of painter Christian Deloffre (☎ 56 21 56) at PK5.5 and Galerie van der Hyde at Cook's Bay. Further along the Cook's Bay Gallery (☎ 56 25 67) is in part of a museum while close to the Kaveka Hotel the Teva Yrondy Gallery displays his pottery. The major black-pearl specialists have outlets in Moorea.

Getting There & Away

Crossing the 20km that separates Moorea from Tahiti is dead easy. It takes less than 10 minutes by plane, or half an hour by high-speed ferry.

Air Air Moorea (☎ 86 41 41 on Tahiti, or ☎ 56 10 34 on Moorea) flies from Faaa airport on Tahiti to Moorea about every half an hour or less. The trip takes less than 10 minutes and there's no need to book – just turn up and if there's a surfeit of passengers they'll just put on more flights. The one-way fare is 2700 CFP. At Faaa airport, Air Moorea is in a separate small terminal, a short stroll east of the main terminal.

Air Tahiti (☎ 86 42 42 on Tahiti, ☎ 56 10 34 on Moorea) also flies to Moorea, but chiefly for passengers making onward connections to other islands in the Society group. There's usually only one to three flights a day. Onward fares to Huahine or Raiatea are 11,000 CFP; to Bora Bora it is 16,000 CFP.

Sea Between Papeete and Moorea there are two high-speed and two slower services. First departures are usually around 6 am, last trips around 4.30 to 5.30 pm. Passengers

pay 1020 CFP one way on any of the ferries, cars cost from 2040 CFP.

Le Prado (☎ 43 76 50 in Papeete, or ☎ 56 13 92 on Moorea) has the fast *Corsair* and the ferry *Tamarii Moorea VIII H*.

Degage (☎ 42 88 88 in Papeete, or ☎ 56 31 10 on Moorea) operates the *Aremiti* catamaran and the *Aremiti Ferry*.

From Papeete, departures take place from the ferry wharf, about 300m north-east of the tourist office and the Vaima Centre. On Moorea, at the Vaiare wharf, les trucks wait for passengers after every boat arrival and make a half tour of the island, there are vehicles going in both directions, stopping where requested for a standard 200 CFP. You can buy tickets at the ticket counter on the wharf just a few minutes before departure.

Getting Around

The Cook's Bay hotels are 5 to 9km from the airport while the Hauru Point establishments are 25 to 30km away. It's a further 5km from the Vaiare wharf.

A bus shuttle service theoretically meets all the boat arrivals and departures and costs just 200 CFP to or from any of the Cook's Bay or Hauru Point hotels.

Air Moorea offers a 100 CFP minibus service to any of the island hotels after each flight. This recent introduction is such a bargain it seems unlikely it will last! Otherwise you could walk about 500m to the road and wait for the shuttle to come by from the wharf.

Taxis are horribly expensive, even by French Polynesian standards. Flagfall is 600 CFP. A trip from the airport to the Beachcomber Parkroyal at the very start of Hauru Point costs about 3400 CFP. They can be found at the airport (☎ 56 10 18) from 6 am to 6 pm and at the taxi rank in front of Club Med at Hauru Point (☎ 56 33 10).

Public transport is not very reliable or convenient. If you're not doing a tour, this is an island where having your own wheels is very useful. Rental-car operators can be found at the Vaiare boat quay, at the airport, at some of the major hotels and dotted around the Cook's Bay and Hauru Point tourist centres. There are petrol stations near the Vaiare ferry wharf, close to the airport, beside Cook's Bay and at Le Petit Village. Europcar (☎ 56 34 00, fax 56 35 05), Avis (☎ 56 32 61, fax 56 32 62) and Albert Rent-a-Car (☎ 56 19 28) are the main operators.

Tehotu Renting (☎ 56 52 96) at the Vaiare ferry wharf rents out scooters, Albert Rent-a-Car has bicycles as does Rando Cycles (☎ 56 35 02) at Club Med, and a number of other hotels.

Loca Boat (☎ 78 13 39), on the beach at the Moorea Beach Club, has boats to rent. this is an ideal way to explore the lagoon and the small islets by yourself.

OTHER WINDWARD ISLANDS

Tahiti and Moorea are the only major islands in the Windward group; there are also two small high islands and a single atoll.

Tetiaroa Atoll
● pop 50   ● area 6 sq km

Owned by Marlon Brando, Tetiaroa Atoll is a dozen sandy islets dotted around a 7km diameter lagoon. It is picture-perfect, with beautiful beaches, clear water and a population comprised mainly of birds.

Tetiaroa's hotel, indeed the only habitation, is on Motu Onetahi. *Hotel Tetiaroa Village* (☎ 82 63 02, fax 85 00 51) has nine beach bungalows in less than prime condition. Two days and one night on Tetiaroa costs 37,400/58,600 CFP for one/two people, leaving Faaa at 8.15 am and returning at 4 pm the next day. Bookings can be made at the Air Moorea terminal at Faaa airport.

Air Moorea operates regular 20-minute flights. The round-trip fare, including lunch and an excursion to the Tahuna Rahi bird island, is 24,300 CFP. There are quite a few day trips by boat, including Nouvelles Frontiéres (☎ 77 64 46) who do several day trips each week for 12,500 CFP including lunch. Jet France (☎/fax 56 15 62) has a catamaran crossing three times weekly for 9500 CFP (bring your own lunch). Pacific Charter (☎ 77 39 77) costs 15,500 CFP, including meals and drinks.

During the high season it's wise to book some days in advance, but note that trips are sometimes cancelled if the weather forecast is bad. Come prepared for sharp coral underfoot and harsh sunlight overhead.

Maiao
● pop 250   ● area 9 sq km

Maiao's small population prizes its isolation and has vigorously resisted the construction of an airstrip. Nouvelles Frontiéres (☎ 77 64 46, fax 56 40 60) organises two-day trips which cost from 25,500 CFP per person.

Mehetia
● pop 0   ● area 3 sq km

Geologically the youngest island in the Society group, uninhabited Mehetia is 100km east of Tahiti, 1.5km across and rises steeply from the sea.

HUAHINE
● pop 5411   ● area 75 sq km

The easternmost of the leeward Islands, Huahine's two islands are Huahine Nui (Big Huahine) to the north and Huahine Iti (Little Huahine) to the south. Legend relates that the split came about when the god Hiro ploughed his mighty canoe into the island, creating deep, majestic Bourayne Bay to the west and Maroe Bay to the east. Huahine is green, lush and beautiful and its easy-going atmosphere entices visitors to kick back and relax. There are some fine beaches to the south, some excellent and easily accessible islets, great snorkelling and diving, popular surfing breaks and, in the village of Maeva, the most extensive complex of pre-European marae in French Polynesia.

History

Just north of Fare, archaeological excavations have revealed some of the earliest traces of settlement in the Society Islands. There were bitter struggles when the French tried to take over, including a pitched battle in 1846. Although the French kicked the Protestant English missionaries out, the island remains predominantly Protestant.

Orientation

A 60km road, not all of it sealed, follows the coast most of the way around both islands.

HUAHINE

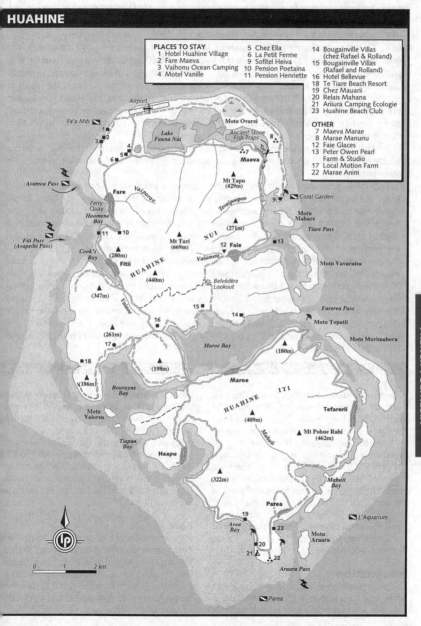

PLACES TO STAY
1 Hotel Huahine Village
2 Fare Maeva
3 Vaihonu Ocean Camping
4 Motel Vanille
5 Chez Ella
6 La Petit Ferme
9 Sofitel Heiva
10 Pension Poetaina
11 Pension Henriette
14 Bougainville Villas (chez Rafael & Rolland)
15 Bougainville Villas (Rafael and Rolland)
16 Hotel Bellevue
18 Te Tiare Beach Resort
19 Chez Mauarii
20 Relais Mahana
21 Ariiura Camping Ecologie
23 Huahine Beach Club

OTHER
7 Maeva Marae
8 Marae Manunu
12 Faie Glaces
13 Peter Owen Pearl Farm & Studio
17 Local Motion Farm
22 Marae Anini

Airport

Fa'a Miti

Motu Ovarei

Lake Fauna Nui

Ancient Stone Fish-Traps

Maeva

1
2
3
4
5
6
7
8

Avamoa Pass

Fare

Vaiparao

Mt Tapu (429m)

Tevaipoopoo

9 Coral Garden

Motu Mahare

Tiare Pass

Ferry Quay
Haamene Bay

Fiti Pass (Avapeihi Pass)

11
10

NUI

(271m)

Cook's Bay

(280m)

Fitii

HUAHINE

Mt Turi (669m)

12 Faie

Vaiumete

13

Motu Vavaratea

(440m)

(347m)

Belvédère Lookout

15

14

Farerea Pass

Motu Topatii

Motu Murimahora

Vaitoa

16

17

(261m)

Maroe Bay

(180m)

18

(186m)

(198m)

Maroe

Bourayne Bay

Motu Vaiorea

HUAHINE   ITI

Tefarerii

(409m)

Mt Pohue Rahi (462m)

Tiapaa Bay

Haapu

Mahuti

(322m)

Mahuti Bay

Parea

19
Avea Bay

23

L'Aquarium

20

21   22

Motu Araara

Araara Pass

Parea

0   1   2 km

Hawaiki Nui Canoe Race

In French Polynesia the big event – the sporting spectacular that has the entire nation glued to its TV sets and talking passionately about favourites and challengers – is a canoe race. The three-day, four-island, 116km Hawaiki Nui Va'a race pits 60-odd of the islands' best six-man pirogues against each other and against any paddlers brave enough to turn up from overseas.

The first day of the race, held in late-October to mid-November, starts on the island of Huahine and goes out of the lagoon and across 44.5km of open sea to Raiatea. The canoes are a superb sight, dramatically televised live for the four-hour crossing. The brawny paddlers, often sporting vivid Tahitian tattoos, paddle three on each side for about 10 strokes then switch sides with precise timing and lightning speed.

Day two takes the canoes on a 20km sprint within the lagoon between the twin islands of Raiatea and Tahaa. Plan on completing this leg in under 1½ hours if you want to remain in contention.

Day three, finishing on a Saturday, is the big one: a 52km crossing of open sea to Bora Bora. Starting around 6.30 am the leading canoe arrives at the finish line at Matira Beach about four hours later. It's a fantastic sight with thousands of cheering spectators lining the beach and wading out to greet the arriving canoes. Drummers pound out an encouraging rhythm from a float by the finishing line, TV camera crews wade out into the water to film the excitement and happy supporters wait with flower *lei* to garland their teams.

Faaa is one of the local favourites, the supermen from the airport suburb of Papeete have won several times, but there's always great interest in overseas competitors, particularly from Hawai'i. So far the local paddlers have remained supreme but there's increasing international interest in the race and more iron men turn up every year. There's also a women's Hawaiki Nui race, known as the Vaa Hine, a pun on *va'a* (canoe) and *vahine* (woman). Other major pirogue marathons include a little jaunt from Papeete across the open sea to Moorea, and then right around Moorea and then back to Tahiti! This 100km+ race takes place during the Heiva festival in July.

A series of islets stretches along the east coast of the two islands, while around the north coast is Lake Fauna Nui, an inlet from the sea. It almost cuts off the northern peninsula, with the airport, from the rest of Huahine Nui. There are only a few beaches.

Fare, the principal town, is on the west coast of Huahine Nui and looks out on Haamene Bay, which has two passes out to the sea. Faie and Maeva, on the east coast, and Fitii, on the west, are the other main settlements on Huahine Nui. There are four villages around Huahine Iti: Haapu, Parea, Tefarerii and Maroe.

Information

Chez Guynette's noticeboard in Fare is one of the best information sources on the island. Fare has a Banque de Tahiti branch opposite the wharf and a Banque Socredo branch on the bypass road, both with ATMs. The town also has a post office, two private medical centres (☎ 68 82 20) and a clinic and a pharmacy across from the quay. Chez Guynett has a laundrette and charges guests 750 CF for a 6kg load. Each year in October or November, Huahine is the starting point for the international Hawaiki Nui canoe race; see the boxed text.

Fare

Fare is the image of a sleepy South Sea port, where people sit on the wharf waiting for boats to arrive while children tumble into the water and splash around. There's a colourful little waterside market, roulottes, shops, some nice restaurants and a selection of hotels and pensions.

aapiti church, French Polynesia

haa, French Polynesia

A group of *moai* (stone statues) at Ahu Tongariki on Easter Island

aditional-style double canoe – Cook's Bay, Moorea, in French Polynesia's Society Islands

A tiny, uninhabited island in Tonga's Vava'u Group

Polynesian cricket on Wallis Island

The elaborate church of St Joseph, Wallis Island

Crystal-clear waters at Avaiki Cave, Niue

Traditional flute – Rarotonga, Cook Islands

Around Huahine Nui

This 60km circuit of the larger island starts at Fare and goes around the island in a clockwise direction.

Fare to Maeva The old Hotel Bali Hai, just north of Fare, closed after a cyclone in 1998 but its original construction in 1972 revealed a fascinating **archaeological site**.

Towards the seaward end of **Lake Fauna Nui** (also known as Lake Maeva), near Maeva village, there are a number of ancient, but still utilised, stone **fish traps** or parks.

Maeva Village & Marae Nearly 30 marae are found along the shoreline, scattered among the modern buildings of the village and up the slopes of Matairea (Pleasant Wind) Hill. Bring mosquito repellent, drinking water and sunscreen when you set out to explore the site.

The defence wall on the Fare side of the village may have been built by Polynesian resistance forces in their struggle with the French in 1846. From here a trail goes uphill to the multi-tiered complex **Matairea Huiarii**. This area included marae, houses and agricultural terraces, was occupied from around 1300 to 1800, and there are indications of an early settlement around 900 AD. A side path winds on through the forest to **Marae Tefano**, where a massive banyan tree overwhelms one end of the ahu.

Further on, a trail branches off downhill to **Marae Matairea Rahi**. From here you can catch glimpses of the lagoon. Retrace your steps to the main trail and continue to the turn-off to **Marae Paepae Ofata**, a steep climb above the main trail. It's worth the effort: the marae is perched on the edge of the hill with fine views down the hillside and across Motu Papiti to the outer lagoon. Retrace the route to the main path, which continues over a second part of the marae and winds on around the hillside to **Marae Tamata Uporu**, before dropping to the road.

The path emerges just south of the lagoonside **Marae Te Ava**. A short walk east leads to the lagoonside **Marae Fare Miro**, which has some particularly neat stonework

and a fine setting. The massive **Marae Manunu** stands on the motu, across the bridge from the main Maeva complex. Nearby is a monument to the battle with French forces in 1846.

The coast road turns inland beside narrow Faie Bay to the village of **Faie**. Huahine's famous blue-eyed eels can be seen in the river immediately downstream of the bridge. Climb to the **Belvédère lookout** on the slopes of Mt Turi. From the high point the **Route Traversière** drops even more steeply to the shores of Maroe Bay.

Around Huahine Iti

This route also circles the southern island in a clockwise direction. The village of Maroe stands on the south side of **Maroe Bay**.

At the southern tip of Huahine Iti is the important **Marae Anini**, a community marae echoing the role of Marae Manunu on the larger island. Constructed of massive coral blocks this large coastal marae was dedicated to Oro (the god of war) and Hiro (the god of thieves) but the site is sadly neglected. Some of the best **beaches** around Huahine are found on the southern peninsula and along its western shore around Auea Bay.

Activities

Pacific Blue Adventure (☎ 68 87 21, fax 68 80 71), right on the quay at Fare, and Centre Nautique Oiri (☎ 68 81 46, fax 68 85 86), in the Huahine Beach Club at the south of the island, are the two dive operators. There are good dive sites at both ends of the island.

Huahine has some of the best and most consistent surf in French Polynesia and attracts a steady stream of surfers.

Walking possibilities on the island are limited, there are no clearly marked trails and the occasional paths in the interior are quickly grown over if they're not maintained. Horse riding is a popular activity and La Petite Ferme (☎ 68 82 98) offers an interesting variety of guided horse-riding trips.

Fare has a pretty, sandy beach by the site of the old Bali Hai Hotel, just north of the town, but further north the island's fringing reef means there is no beach or place to swim until you get right around to the Sofitel Heiva.

The Huahine lagoon is superb and includes many untouched motu accessible only by boat. A variety of lagoon tours are offered with stops for snorkelling, swimming, fish feeding and a picnic on a motu. Try Vaipua Cruises (☎ 68 86 42) in the Arts Polynésiens shop in Fare or the Sofitel.

There are numerous tours by 4WD or minibus and they're good for people who want a quick view of the island without renting a car. Operators include Huahine Land (☎ 68 89 21), Huahine Discovery Tours (☎ 68 75 18) and Huahine Explorer (contact Étienne, the manager of Vaihonu Ocean Camping).

Places to Stay
Most of Huahine's accommodation is concentrated in and around Fare, with a handful further afield on each island. Airport transfers are usually 500 CFP each way.

Fare *Chez Guynette* (☎/fax 68 83 75) is one of the most popular backpacker centres in French Polynesia so reserve ahead – it's often booked out. It's right on the colourful main street of Fare and has seven simple but comfortable rooms, costing 3400/4000/4600 CFP a single/double/triple. There's also an eight bed dormitory at 1400 CFP per person.

Hotel Huahine (☎ 68 82 69), on the corner where the street turns away from the sea, has an 'old South Seas hotel' feel. Popular with surfies, it has dorm beds for 1000 CFP, double rooms with toilet and shower for 3500 CFP. The *Taahitini Supermarket* (☎ 68 89 42), immediately south of the town on the coast, 100m from the main street, has featureless rooms for 5000 CFP.

Meri Pension (☎ 68 82 44, fax 68 85 96, pension_meri@unforgettable.com), five minutes from the centre, behind the Banque Socredo, has well-equipped units and bungalows for 6500 or 7000 CFP for up to four people. There's a three day minimum stay.

North of Fare There are a number of places between Fare and the airport, 2.5km

to the north. Several of them are on the coast although there is not much of a beach

Chez Lovina (☎/fax 68 88 06) is popular with surfers and close to the sea. Tent space costs 1000 CFP per person and dorm bed 1200 CFP. There are five small bungalows for 3000/5000 CFP single/double and three family bungalows from 5000/6500 CFP.

La Petite Ferme (☎ 68 82 98), a popular horse-riding centre by the road, has simple dormitory beds for 1650 CFP, small double rooms at 1950 CFP per person or bungalows at 5000/7500 CFP. Transfers to the airport or the quay in Fare are free.

Pension Fare Maeva (☎ 68 75 53, fax 68 77 51) is accessible by the track beside La Petite Ferme. There are 10 functional bungalows with kitchens and bathrooms for 6000 CFP including airport transfers. They do a room plus rent-a-car deal for 12,900 CFP per day.

Vaihonu Ocean Camping (☎ 68 87 33, fax 68 77 57, vaihonu@mail.pf) is 150m further along, by the water, and has camping space (1000 CFP per person) and an eight bed dormitory at 1200 CFP per person. Simple cabins are 2000/3000 CFP, better equipped chalets cost from 5200 CFP. There are bicycles available free for guests use and airport transfers are included. *Chez Ella* (☎ 68 73 07, or ☎ 83 75 29 in Papeete, BP 71, Fare, Huahine), at the intersection of the coast road and the turn-off to the airport, also has a variety of options from 5500 CFP for two.

Motel Vanille (☎/fax 68 71 77) is hidden in vegetation across from Chez Ella and about 1km from the coast. There are five bungalows with bathrooms and verandah around a swimming pool for 7200 CFP per double. Simpler and smaller rooms are 4800 CFP. Credit cards are accepted.

Just south of Fare, *Pension Poetani* (☎/fax 68 89 49) is big and rather peculiar looking and has functional doubles from 7500 CFP. Breakfast and airport transfers are included and there's a two night minimum.

Maeva Area *Camping Vanaa Delor* (☎ 68 89 51) is on a pleasant beach near the Maeva fish traps. Minimal huts cost 2500

CFP per person, including breakfast, or you can camp for 1000 CFP per person.

At the opposite extreme the beachside *Sofitel Heiva* (☎ 68 86 86, fax 68 85 25), 8km from Fare at the southern tip of Motu Papiti, is the biggest hotel on the island. The well-equipped units range from 24,300 CFP. Round-trip airport transfers are 1900 CFP and there's a swimming pool, the Manuia Bar and the poolside Omai Restaurant.

South of Fare The *Hotel Bellevue* (☎ 68 82 76, fax 68 85 35) is rather a long way from anywhere and has eight rooms at 3780/4860 CFP a single/double and 12 bungalows at 6480 to 7560 CFP. Airport transfers are 500 CFP per person each way.

The *Te Tiare Beach Resort* (☎ 60 60 50, fax 60 60 51, tetiarebeach@mail.pf) is a pricier hotel at the south-west corner of Huahine Nui, a good location for a complete getaway. Accessible only by sea, this appealing complex has traditional but luxurious bungalows from 32,400 CFP. Airport transfers cost 4000 CFP round trip.

Villas Bougainville, *Oiseau de Paradis* (Bird of Paradise), *Chaouia* and *Saint Mandrianus* are four furnished, fully equipped, comfortable villas in a garden setting to the north of Maroe Bay, close to the coast road. They can accommodate up to six people and cost from 16,500 CFP for two or three people, including the use of a car and a boat – ideal for getting out to idyllic Motu Topati. They're also known collectively as Rafaël and Rolland. For Bougainville and Bird of Paradise phone ☎/fax 68 81 59 in Huahine and ask for Rafaël. For Chaouia and Saint Mandrianus phone ☎ 82 49 65 in Papeete.

Huahine Iti *Chez Mauarii* (☎/fax 68 86 49) is an excellent place in a beautiful seafront garden. There are impeccable garden bungalows for 9500/10,000 CFP a single/double and beach bungalows from 15,000 CFP for two. Round-trip airport transfers are 1800 CFP.

The beachside *Ariiura Camping Ecologie* (☎ 68 85 20) is excellent for people on a low budget looking for a relaxed atmosphere. It's

also close to a prime surfing location. There are tent sites at 1200 CFP per person and some utilitarian 'camping *fare*' for two (3500 CFP). The cabins don't lock and even the toilet facilities are local style!

The *Huahine Beach Club* (☎ 68 81 46, fax 68 85 86) is beside the beach looking across to Motu Araara and has bungalows from 15,120 CFP. Use of pirogues and kayaks is free. Transfers cost 900 CFP per person each way.

Places to Eat

Fare For cheap eats and late eats the wharfside roulottes are Huahine's best bargain. There are a number of places to eat along the main street of Fare. The pleasant open-air area at the front of *Chez Guynette* is good for breakfast or a light lunch.

The *Snack Bar Te Manava* (☎ 68 76 02), at the end of the street, is more a restaurant than snack-bar. Pleasantly situated on the beach it has an interesting and reasonably priced menu. It's closed Friday. *Pension Enite* (☎ 68 82 37) has a restaurant with an excellent reputation and a charming setting beside the lagoon but bookings are essential. The Huahine Hotel's ground floor *snack bar* does some moderately priced dishes. It's closed on Sunday.

Te Vaipuna Restaurant (☎ 68 70 45) is opposite the wharf and serves excellent Chinese food. It's open Monday to Friday for lunch and dinner, Saturday for dinner only. The *Tiare Tipanier* (☎ 68 80 52) is very popular, offering an excellent blend of price and quality for lunch or dinner. *Fare Pizza* (☎ 60 60 01) is next to the Taahitini store.

If you're preparing your own meals, fruit, vegetables, fish and other fresh supplies are available from the impromptu quayside *marketplace* and there are several *food shops*.

Around Huahine There aren't too many places to eat around the island, apart from at the hotels. The pleasant *Omai* at the Sofitel Heiva has a varied menu. In the south-west corner of Huahine Nui *Local Motion* (☎ 68 86 58) is a local fruit farm and orchard with delicious cool fruit juices and set meals. It's closed on Sunday. *Faie Glaces (☎ 68 87 95)*, on the exit from Faie, at the start of the Route Traversière, does great home-made ice cream. It's also closed on Sunday.

The *Restaurant Mauarii (☎ 68 86 49)*, in the pension of the same name on Huahine Iti, has some of the best food on the island, perhaps on all the Leeward Islands, including many Polynesian specialities. It's right by the lagoon and is open for lunch and dinner every day.

The *Huahine Beach Club* restaurant offers light meals at lunch time. *Relais Mahana* also has a restaurant, which faces the lagoon. There are small shops with variable opening hours around the island, at Maeva and Fitii on Huahine Nui and at Haapu and Parea on Huahine Iti.

Entertainment

Entertainment on Huahine is very limited. The *Sofitel Heiva* has twice-weekly buffet dinners with good traditional dance performances from 5000 to 6000 CFP.

Shopping

Lots of places sell souvenirs and local crafts in and around Fare. Rima'i Te Niu Taue, Souvenirs des Îles, Photographe Jojo and Faahotu Arts Creation sell souvenirs and local crafts along the town's main street.

Getting There & Away

Westbound from Tahiti it's 170km to Huahine, the first of the Leeward Islands. The twin islands of Raiatea and Tahaa lie a further 35km to the west.

Air Air Tahiti connects with Papeete (8800 CFP; 35 minutes) two to four times daily, with onward flights to Raiatea (4400 CFP; another 15 minutes) and/or Bora Bora (6500 CFP). Connections to Maupiti (7700 CFP), are more complex, usually requiring a change of aircraft at Raiatea or Bora Bora. The Air Tahiti office (☎ 68 82 65) is at the airport.

Boat The high-speed *Ono-Ono* can be booked through the office (☎ 68 85 85) on the quay in the centre of Fare. It takes just 3½ hours to get to Papeete (4895 CFP) or 45 minutes to Raiatea (1676 CFP) with continuations to Tahaa and Bora Bora. The *Taporo IV* also operates to Huahine.

Getting Around

You could walk the 2.5km to town from the airport if you were really intent on saving money, but pensions and hotels in Fare will arrange taxi transfers which are sometimes included in their tariffs. The extreme shortage of public transport is Huahine's biggest drawback. A le truck belonging to each district shuttles in to Fare early each morning and returns to the various villages late in the morning for 300 CFP. Pension Enite (☎ 68 82 37), Felix Tours (☎ 68 81 69) and one or two other agencies can organise taxis.

Avis-Pacificar (☎ 68 73 34, fax 68 73 35) and Europcar (☎ 68 82 59, fax 68 80 59) are the two car rental operators in Huahine. Discounts of 10% are easy to get and credit cards are accepted. There are two service stations in Fare, one or the other will be open on Sundays and early mornings.

Europcar rents bicycles for 1900 CFP a day, Avis for 1800 CFP. Chez Huahine Lagoon (☎ 68 70 00), on the waterfront at the north end of the main street of Fare, charges 1200 CFP a day for a mountain bike. Across the road is Chez Jojo (☎ 68 89 16) which charges 1500 CFP. Some guesthouses and hotels have bicycles for guests. For scooters check with Europcar or Avis – both charge 5900 CFP for 24 hours.

RAIATEA

● pop 10,057   ● area 170 sq km

Largest of the Leeward Islands, Raiatea has some fine beaches on its many islets and its yachting marinas make this the sailing centre of French Polynesia. The large lagoon is ideal for diving and pirogue tours while the mountainous interior is the place for walks and horse rides. Uturoa, the principal town is the administrative centre for the Leeward Islands. The rest of the island is wild and lightly populated. The island had a central role in ancient Polynesian religious beliefs. Marae Taputapuatea, in the south-east of the

sland, is the largest marae in French Poly-
esia and one of the most important in all of
'olynesia.

Only 3km separates Raiatea from Tahaa
nd the islands share a common lagoon.
'isitors to either island will usually come to
Raiatea first since the airport is there and
most inter-island ships dock at Uturoa.

History

Raiatea, known as Havai'i in ancient times
see the boxed text 'The Ancient Homeland,
Havaiki' in the Samoa chapter), was the
religious centre of the Society Islands and it
was from here that the great Polynesian
navigators are said to have continued the
voyages to colonise other islands in the
Pacific. Early legends relate that Raiatea
nd Tahaa were the first islands to be set-
led, from Samoa, far to the north-west.

The pioneering missionary John Williams
urned up in Raiatea in 1818 and the island
remained under British missionary influence
ong after Tahiti came under French control.
t was not until 1888 that the French at-
empted a real takeover and not until 1897
hat French troops were sent in to put down
he final Polynesian rebellion.

Orientation

Raiatea's encircling road hugs the coast all
he way around. The interior is mountainous
nd includes the 800m-high Temehani
Plateau. The highest peaks are Mt Tefatua
1017m) and Mt Tepatuarahi (945m).

The Raiatea airport, which also serves
Tahaa, is at the northern tip of the island.
The town of Uturoa is just south-east of the
airport and extends almost continuously to
he entrance of Faaroa Bay, but the rest of
he way around the island there are only
mall, scattered villages.

Information

At the time of writing there were plans to
move the tourist office (☎ 66 23 33) to the
ock terminal. The airport desk (☎ 66 23
4) handles flight arrivals. The Hawaiki Nui
anoe race (see the boxed text in the
Iuahine section) passes through Raiatea
nd Tahaa.

All three local banks have branches in
Uturoa and the Banque Socredo and
Banque de Tahiti have ATMs. The post office is just north of the centre towards the
airport. Raiatea's health facilities include a
hospital (☎ 66 35 03), in front of the post
office, several doctors and a pharmacy
(☎ 66 34 44) on the main street.

Eloy Informatique (☎ 66 35 85, fax 66 14
05, eloyinfo@tahiti.net) is between the
Uturoa marina and the airport. It offers various services for travellers and yachties, including Internet access, fax use, email and
poste restante. It's open Monday to Friday.

The Bleu des Îles laundry is in the Tahina
Commercial Centre, on the inland side of
the airport road, behind the Afo store. The
Jacqueline Laundrette (☎ 66 28 36) is 200m
before the Apooiti Marina clubhouse when
coming from Uturoa. Uturoa has several
well-stocked supermarkets that accept
credit cards. They're used to supplying
yachts. For films and photo developing go
to Photo Gauguin next to the Hotel Hinano.

Uturoa

Raiatea's busy port is the second largest
town in French Polynesia. The presence of
the Chinese community is demonstrated by
the many shops and restaurants and the Kuo
Min Tang Association building. The Protestant church on the north side of the town
centre has a memorial stone to pioneer missionary John Williams. Uturoa is overlooked
by Mt Tapioi, topped by TV-relay masts and
offering fine views over the lagoon.

Around the Island

The following island circuit starts from
Uturoa and goes clockwise.

Uturoa blends seamlessly into **Avera**, site
of the final battle between the French and
local rebels in 1897. At 12.5km the road
passes **Stardust Marina**, a major yacht-
charter operation. Soon after you reach the
turn-off to the south coast and the **Faaroa
River**. If you turn right at the turn-off, the
road climbs to the **Belvédère lookout**
(26.5km) with views down towards the coast
and of the surrounding mountains. Turning
left takes you to Marae Taputapuatea.

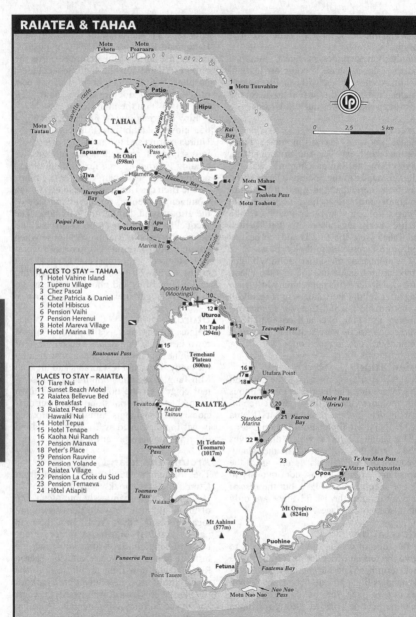

RAIATEA & TAHAA

0   2.5   5 km

PLACES TO STAY – TAHAA
1 Hotel Vahine Island
2 Tupenu Village
3 Chez Pascal
4 Chez Patricia & Daniel
5 Hotel Hibiscus
6 Pension Vaihi
7 Pension Herenui
8 Hotel Mareva Village
9 Hotel Marina Iti

PLACES TO STAY – RAIATEA
10 Tiare Nui
11 Sunset Beach Motel
12 Raiatea Bellevue Bed
    & Breakfast
13 Raiatea Pearl Resort
    Hawaiki Nui
14 Hotel Tepua
15 Hotel Tenape
16 Kaoha Nui Ranch
17 Pension Manava
18 Peter's Place
19 Pension Rauvine
20 Pension Yolande
21 Raiatea Village
22 Pension La Croix du Sud
23 Pension Temaeva
24 Hôtel Atiapiti

Motu Tehotu
Motu Poaraara
Motu Tuuvahine
Motu Tautau
TAHAA
Patio
Hipu
Rai Bay
Vaipuru
Track Traversière
Vaitoetoe Pass
Mt Ohiri (598m)
Faaha
Tapuamu
Tiva
Haamene
Haamene Bay
Motu Mahae
Toahotu Pass
Motu Toahotu
Hurepiti Bay
Paipai Pass
Poutoru
Apu Bay
Marina Iti
navette route
Navette Route

Apooiti Marina (Moorings)
Uturoa
Mt Tapioi (294m)
Teavapiti Pass
Rautoanui Pass
Temehani Plateau (800m)
Utufara Point
Avera
Maire Pass (Iriru)
RAIATEA
Tevaitoa
Marae Tainuu
Stardust Marina
Faaroa Bay
Tepuatiare Pass
Mt Tefatua (Toomaru) (1017m)
Te Ava Moa Pass
Tehurui
Faaroa
Opoa
Marae Taputapuatea
Toamaro Pass
Vaiaau
Mt Aahinui (577m)
Mt Oropiro (824m)
Puohine
Punaeroa Pass
Point Tauere
Fetuna
Faatemu Bay
Motu Nao Nao
Nao Nao Pass

Marae Taputapuatea (42km) had great importance to the ancient Polynesians. Any marae constructed on another island had to incorporate one of Taputapuatea's stones as a symbol of allegiance – even a new marae in the Cook Islands or Hawai'i! The main part of the marae is a large flag-stoned platform with a long ahu stretching down one side. At the very end of the cape is the smaller Marae Tauraa, a *tapu* (sacred) enclosure with the tall 'stone of investiture' where young *ari'i* (chiefs) were enthroned.

Continuing past Taputapuatea the road passes the village of **Puohine**, then continues through the village of **Fetuna** (68km).

The road continues through Tehurui then Tevaitoa village, where massive stone slabs stand in the 50m long wall of **Marae Tainuu** (95km), behind the church. Turn-offs lead to the Temehani Plateau on the stretch to the **Apooiti Marina** (107km), also known as Marina Moorings. From the marina the road passes the airport and returns to Uturoa.

Activities

Hémisphère Sub (☎ 66 12 49, fax 66 28 63) at the Apooiti Marina and Raiatea Plongée (☎ 66 37 10, fax 66 26 25) at the Hotel Tepua are the two dive centres. The wreck of the **Nordby**, one of French Polynesia's few shipwrecks, and the superb **Teavapiti Pass** are popular dives. There's splendid swimming and snorkelling on some of the reef motu, such as Motu Iriru to the west of the island and Motu Noa to the south. Several companies do pirogue lagoon tours with motu picnics and snorkelling and swimming stops. Manava Tours at the Pension Manava (☎ 66 28 26) and Raiatea Safari Tours (☎ 66 37 10) at the Hotel Tepua do tours to Tahaa and to Faaroa River with a visit to Marae Taputapuatea.

Walking possibilities are limited and apart from Temehani plateau walks with a guide, the short climb up Mt Tapioi, dominating Uturoa, is the only real interest. The well-respected Kaoha Nui Ranch (☎/fax 66 25 46) offers a variety of guided horse-riding excursions.

Several companies organise 4WD island tours for 4000 to 5000 CFP per person.

Contact Raiatea 4x4 (☎ 66 24 16), Raiatea Safari Tour (☎ 66 37 10), Anapa (☎ 66 20 50) and Jeep Safari Raiatea (☎ 66 15 73). Tariffs oscillate between 4000 and 5000 CFP per person and you should reserve a place as soon as you arrive. Almost Paradise Tours (☎ 66 23 64) rather proudly announces on its leaflet that its minibus tours are 'in English only'.

Places to Stay

Most accommodation is in or close to Uturoa. Raiatea has several places where you can camp.

Uturoa & Around The *Hotel Hinano* (☎ 66 13 13, fax 66 14 14) is right in the centre of Uturoa with motel-style rooms at 4600/5700 CFP a single/double or 5700/6800CFP with air-con. Airport transfers are included and credit cards are accepted.

On the lagoon edge at PK2, just south of the centre, the luxurious *Raiatea Pearl Resort Hawaiki Nui* (☎ 66 20 23, fax 66 20 20, h.Raiateapearl@mail.pf) has rooms ranging from ordinary studios (15,120 CFP) through to garden and lagoonside bungalows to over-water bungalows (34,560 CFP).

At PK2.5, beside the lagoon, the *Hotel Tepua* (☎ 66 37 10, fax 66 26 25) offers a variety of accommodation: dorm beds are 1300 CFP, simple rooms with a shared bathroom are 4500 CFP and comfortable and well-equipped bungalows are 8000/9000 CFP single/double.

Perched high above the north side of Uturoa, the quiet and relaxing *Raiatea Bellevue Bed & Breakfast* (☎/fax 66 15 15) has extraordinary views, a swimming pool and five small but tidy rooms for 5500/6500 CFP with breakfast. Transfers cost 1250 CFP per person round-trip.

Around the Island The *Kaoha Nui Ranch* (☎/fax 66 25 46) is a charming equestrian centre on a large, green and pleasant property with simple rooms with shared facilities for 1900 CFP per person. There's a better equipped room and a bungalow for 5800 CFP a double. Airport or dock transfers are free and meals are available.

The friendly *Pension Manava* (☎ *66 28 26, fax 66 16 66)* has rooms at 4000 CFP for two and pleasant bungalows from 5000 CFP. *Peter's Place* (☎ *66 20 01)*, just beyond Pension Manava at PK6.5, offers camping space for 800 CFP per person, or there are very spartan rooms at 1200 CFP per person.

Three places are on the lagoon side of the road around the PK8.5 to 10 mark, just before the road turns inland along Faaroa Bay. *Pension Rauvine* (☎*/fax 66 25 50)* has rooms with shared bathroom at 4000/4500 CFP and bungalows at 5500 CFP, all including transfers. *Pension Yolande* (☎*/fax 66 35 28)* is a large house with four functional rooms at 5000 CFP. Transfers cost 1500 CFP for the car per journey. *Raiatea Village* (☎ *66 31 62, fax 66 10 65)* is a small resort right on the water's edge that has bungalows with bathrooms and kitchens for 5940/7020 CFP. Airport or ferry-quay transfers cost 1080 CFP per person round-trip.

Opposite Stardust Marina on Faaroa Bay, 12km from Uturoa, *Pension La Croix du Sud* (☎*/fax 66 27 55)* has a fine setting, small swimming pool, good food and rooms at 6000/6500 CFP, including breakfast and transfers. At *Pension Temaeva* (☎*/fax 66 37 28, temaeva@mail.pf)* at PK24, 7km before Marae Taputapuatea, you can camp for 1500/2000 CFP for one/two people and there are comfortable bungalows at 5500/6000 CFP. Both options include breakfast, and there's a swimming pool.

Hotel Atiapiti (☎*/fax 66 16 65)* is right next to Marae Taputapuatea in a flower bedecked garden. Bungalows cost from 9180 CFP for two; airport transfers are 2000 CFP per person round-trip and credit cards are accepted.

The *Hotel Tenape* (☎ *60 01 00, fax 60 01 01, raiatea@spmr.com)*, 4km from the airport, has great views from its mountain side location, a restaurant, bar, swimming pool and rooms at 15,120 CFP. Credit cards are accepted.

Places to Eat

On the waterfront in Uturoa *Snack Moemoea* is a pleasant, busy little cafe with an open terrace and modest prices. *Restaurant*

Michèle (☎ *66 14 66)*, in the Hinano Hotel offers a mix of Chinese, Tahitian and standard French dishes. It's open all day Monday to Friday, but only until lunch on Saturday

Uturoa has two popular Chinese restaurants. The *Restaurant Moana* (☎ *66 27 49* above the Leogite store is closed lunch time Sunday and all day Monday and the *Jade Garden Restaurant* (☎ *66 34 40)*, which is also on the main street, is closed Sunday and Monday.

The *Raiatea Pearl Resort Hawaiki Nui* serves very reasonably priced meals right beside the swimming pool and the lagoon. The *Kaoha Nui Ranch* at PK6 does lunch and dinner in a pleasant small *fare*. At PK9.5 *Snack Iriru* is open Monday to Saturday for lunch and dinner.

Near the airport, *Havai'i Snack* offers a varied menu but is closed Sunday evening and all day Monday. The *Club House* (☎ *66 11 66)* offers free transport. At the end of the marina, facing Tahaa, the snack restaurant *Tamaa Maitai* is open Wednesday to Sunday and Monday for lunch only

Entertainment

It's difficult to find a reason for a late night on Raiatea. You could sip a sunset drink at the Apooiti Marina *Club House*. On weekends Restaurant Moana, above the Leogite store, metamorphoses into *Le Zénith* disco

Shopping

In Uturoa, Arii Boutique (☎ 66 33 53 specialises in Polynesian tapa. Head for La Palme d'Or (☎ 66 23 79) for black pearls or the adjacent Anuanua Gallery for arts and crafts. The Te Fare boutique (☎ 66 17 17) in Uturoa and the Art-Expo Gallery (☎ 66 1 83) at the Apooiti Marina are other outlets Local women sell their crafts, particularly shellwork and pareu, in the airport building

Getting There & Away

Raiatea is 220km north-west of Tahiti 40km south-east of Bora Bora and separated from Tahaa by a 3km-wide channel.

Air Air Tahiti flies to Raiatea two to seven times daily from Papeete (10,100 CFP directly (40 minutes) or via Moorea and/or Huahine. There are also daily connections with Bora Bora (5100 CFP) and Huahine (4400 CFP) and three times weekly with Maupiti (5600 CFP, either directly or via Bora Bora). The Air Tahiti office (☎ 66 32 50) is at the airport.

Boat Tahaa Transport Services (☎ 65 67 10) operates two *navettes* (shuttle boats) between Uturoa, on Raiatea, and various stops on Tahaa – Iti Marina, Poutoru, Tiva, Tapuamu, Amaru quay and Haamene. The services operate Monday to Friday and Saturday morning. The one-way fare is 850 CFP and there are two to four services a day depending on the destination on Tahaa.

The same company offers a charter 'taxiboat' between the two islands and can transfer customers directly from the airport quay to the marinas, Uturoa quay or any of the quays on Tahaa. Charter rates start at 2000 CFP but prices jump 50% on Sunday and 24 hour advance booking is required.

The *Tamarii Tahaa* (☎ 65 65 29 or ☎ 65 60 18) goes to the west coast of Tahaa twice daily from the Uturoa quay, Monday to Friday and on Saturday morning. Fares are 500 CFP to Marina Iti and 700 CFP for the one-hour trip to Patio.

Further afield the fast *Ono-Ono* sails from Papeete through to Bora Bora. Huahine to Raiatea takes barely an hour and costs 1795 CFP, it's one hour and 45 minutes to Bora Bora, also for 1795 CFP. Papeete-Raiatea costs 5554 CFP. The office (☎ 66 24 25) is on the waterfront next to the Champion store.

Getting Around

There are taxis at the airport (about 1000 CFP to Uturoa), but most island accommodation will pick you up, although you may be charged. It's only 3km to the centre of Uturoa. Around the island you can rent a car or hitchhike – hitching appears to be fairly acceptable as a result of the low-key tourism and lack of public transport. Don't count on le truck; they circulate mainly in the morning, between outlying districts and Uturoa then return in the early afternoon.

Check that there will be a return trip if you don't want to get stuck at your destination. There's a taxi stand by the market (☎ 66 20 60) and taxis can also be found at the airport but they're very expensive.

Europcar (☎ 66 34 06, fax 66 16 06), Avis (☎ 66 34 35, fax 66 15 59) and Motu Tapu (☎ 66 33 09, fax 66 29 11) are rental car operators. Cars can always be delivered to the airport. Europcar has scooters for 5300 CFP and bicycles for 2120 CFP. Some hotels and guesthouses have bicycles for their guests and sometimes for outsiders as well. Europcar rents boats with outboards.

TAHAA

- pop 4470   • area 90 sq km

Raiatea may be quiet but Tahaa is even quieter. The island is an undiscovered jewel, little known by tourist operators, accessible only by boat and with a village atmosphere. Like its southern sister, there are no beaches to speak of on the main island and the tourist facilities are even more basic. A coast road encircles most of the island but traffic is very light and there is no public transport. Vanilla cultivation and pearl farming are important activities. The main tourist attraction is the string of beautiful islets along the northern reef edge.

History

Tahaa was once known as Kuporu ('Uporu or 'Upolu), and was named after an island in Samoa. Tahaa was at times a pawn in struggles between neighbouring Raiatea and the fierce rulers of Bora Bora. The first missionaries arrived from Raiatea in 1822 and the island came under French control at the same time as Raiatea.

Orientation & Information

The population is concentrated in eight main villages on the coast. Tapuamu has the main wharf, Patio is the main town while Haamene is where the roads round the south and north part of the island meet, forming a figure eight. Apu Bay to the south, Haamene Bay to the east and Hurepiti Bay to the west are deep inlets offering sheltered anchorages for yachts.

Tahaa's only bank branch, the Banque Socredo in Patio, is open weekdays. Bring credit cards and enough cash.

Around the Island

It's 70km, most of it on crushed coral road, around the island. Starting from the Marina Iti, the first navette stop from Raiatea, the road sticks to the coast around Apu Bay. At the top of the bay the round-the-island route leaves the coast and climbs up and over to the larger village of **Haamene**. The **Maison de la Vanille** (☎ 65 67 27) and **Alfred** (☎ 65 61 16) are vanilla producers on this side of Haamene.

Tapuamu is the site of the island's main wharf, where the *Ono-Ono* docks. From here the chain of motu that fringe the northern coast of the island come into view. **Patio** is the administrative centre of the island. More motu, including the luxurious resort motu of **Vahine Island**, come into view as the road passes copra plantations to **Faaha** and Faaha Bay. OfaifOfaifa (☎ 65 69 77) and Motu Pearl Farm (☎ 65 69 18) are two **pearl farms** on the north side of the bay.

The road climbs over a headland and drops down to Haamene Bay. Turn east to Hotel Hibiscus where the **Foundation Hibiscus** is dedicated to saving turtles which have become entangled in local fishers' nets. The turtles are transferred to remote Scilly Atoll (see Other Leeward Islands). From the Hotel Hibiscus the coast road goes round the north side of the bay to Haamene, passing the pearl farms of **Patricia & Daniel** (☎ 65 60 83) and Rooverta Ebbs' **Poerani** (☎ 65 60 25). The road then continues along the south side of the bay and winds in and out of seemingly endless small bays before coming back to the Marina Iti.

Activities

There's no diving centre in Tahaa but the dive centres on Raiatea regularly dive east of the island by the Toahotu Pass and will collect you from hotels at the south of the island. There are no beaches – you have to go to the motu for swimming and snorkelling.

You can walk the little-used 7km track across the centre of the island from Patio to

Haamene but otherwise there's very few trails into the Tahaa interior. There are dazzling views of Haamene Bay from the Vaitoetoe Pass.

Places to Stay

Tahaa's places to stay are dotted around the coast and it's wise to make reservations so that you're collected from the appropriate village quay or even the airport on Raiatea.

On the Island *Hotel Marina Iti* (☎ 65 61 01, fax 65 63 87, radio VHF 68) on Toamaro Point has a popular restaurant. The comfortable garden and lagoonside bungalows cost 13,260 CFP a double. The hotel offers a variety of tours and credit cards are accepted. Round-trip transfers from the airport on Raiatea cost 3060 CFP per person.

Across the bay and near the next navette stop at Poutoru, the *Hotel Mareva Village* (☎/fax 65 61 61) has six spacious and sturdily built bungalows with kitchens and terraces for 7560 CFP a double, 8640 CFP a family or 10,800 CFP for two couples.

There are two places on the north shore of Haamene Bay. *Hotel Hibiscus* (☎ 65 61 06, fax 65 65 65, VHF 68) has well-equipped bungalows for 5000 CFP per person or simpler ones at 8250 CFP for two. *Chez Patricia & Daniel* (☎/fax 65 60 83) is just east and is popular with travellers. Bungalows cost 6000 CFP for two. Airport transfers cost 1500 CFP per person round-trip.

On the south side of Hurepiti Bay *Pension Vaihi* (☎ 65 62 02) offers isolation and tranquillity; bungalows with bathrooms cost 6000 CFP a double. The Uturoa-Tahaa ferry will drop you at this pension's pontoon.

Shortly after Tupuamu heading north, the turn-off towards the island interior brings you to *Chez Pascal* (☎ 65 60 42), the cheapest place on the island. Four small bungalows with shared toilet and showers cost 2500 CFP per person. If you are really penniless *Restaurant Louise* (see Places to Eat) might have a dormitory bed available for just 1500 CFP with breakfast.

The only place on the north shore of the island is *Tupenu Village* (☎ 65 62 01), about 1.5km west of Patio. There's a big two-level *fare* with five rooms sharing two hot-water bathrooms for 6000 CFP double.

Off the Island *Hotel Vahine Island* (☎ 65 67 38, fax 65 67 70, vahine.island@usa.net, VHF 70) occupies a motu on the outer reef to the north of Tahaa. Beach bungalows are 32,400 CFP; over-water are 48,600 CFP. Transfers from the airport in Raiatea cost 5000 CFP per person round-trip. Credit cards are accepted.

Places to Eat

There are shops in each village but the dining possibilities are very limited. The well known restaurant at the *Marina Iti* features French specialities and the *Hotel Hibiscus* restaurant also has a good reputation. If you want something more local try *Restaurant Louise* (☎ 65 66 68) at Tiva; it enjoys an excellent reputation. On Wednesday lunch time there's a Tahitian oven organised for customers of the *Haumana* catamaran cruise for 3000 CFP with musical entertainment. Reservations are essential.

Getting There & Away

The airport on Raiatea is only 15 minutes across the lagoon and some hotels will pick up their guests on Raiatea. See the Getting There & Away section under Raiatea for information on the navette service. This local ferry service shuttles back and forth between Uturoa and a variety of stops on Tahaa and costs 850 CFP one way.

Inter-island ships between Raiatea and Bora Bora stop at Tapuamu on Tahaa, but not on every voyage. If your trip doesn't stop at Tahaa it's easy enough to disembark at Uturoa and take the navette across. The *Ono-Ono* stops at Tahaa between Raiatea and Bora Bora.

Getting Around

There is no public transport on Tahaa and traffic is very light. Renting a car or a mountain bike are the only ways to see the island by yourself. The coast road is 70km in length and although not all of it is sealed it's quite OK. If you decide to tackle it by bicycle there are some steep stretches in

the south of the island that you may find trying.

The Marina Iti (☎ 65 61 01) and Monique Location (☎/fax 65 62 48) rent small cars and bicycles. Europcar (☎ 65 67 00, fax 65 68 08) also has cars while the Hotel Hibiscus has bicycles for its customers only. If you want a scooter you could rent one on Raiatea and bring it across on the shuttle. There are petrol stations in Patio and Tapuamu.

BORA BORA

● pop 5767   ● area 38 sq km

The postcard views of Bora Bora are the stuff of South Pacific dreams – sandy, palm-fringed islets around a deep blue lagoon with a central island of mountains and peaks. The lagoon is simply superb and waiting to be explored by pirogue or sailboat, or by snorkelling or diving. There are a number of small archaeological sites and some reminders of WWII, but a Polynesian dance performance at a luxury hotel is also part of the Bora Bora experience.

History

Land pressures, due to the shortage of level ground, helped to create a warlike population that campaigned against other islands in the Society group. Only Huahine managed to resist the warriors of Bora Bora at their most expansive. An LMS missionary station was established on the island in 1820 and to this day Bora Bora remains chiefly Protestant. WWII had a huge effect on Bora Bora, when a major US supply base was established on the island. Until Faaa airport opened in Tahiti in 1961, the airport they left was French Polynesia's main connection with the outside world.

Orientation

A road encircles the island, which is about 9km north to south and 4km across. Vaitape, on the western side, is the main settlement, looking directly out to the Teavanui Pass, the only entry to the lagoon. Larger inter-island boats dock at Farepiti, north of Vaitape and the airport is on Motu Mute at the north of the outer reef. Connecting boats transfer airline passengers to Vaitape.

BORA BORA

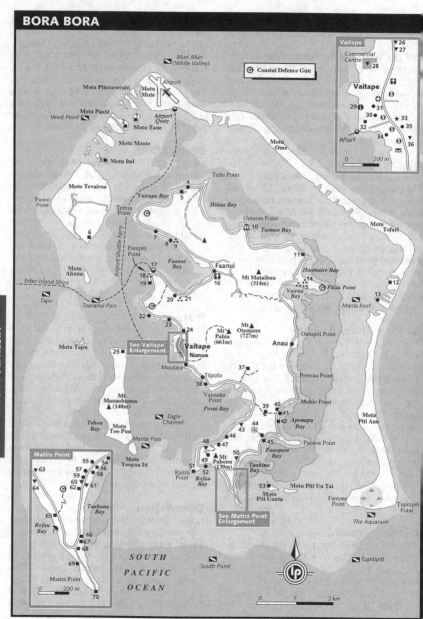

Muri Muri
(White Valley)

Coastal Defence Gun

Motu Pitoraverahi

Motu Mute

Airport

Airport Quay

Motu Paahi

West Point

Motu Tane

Motu Moute

Motu Ome

Motu Itel

Taihi Point

Motu Tevairoa

Vairupe Bay

Hitiaa Bay

Paoeo Point

Tereia Point

Outurau Point

Taimoo Bay

Motu Tofari

Motu Ahuna

Farepiti Point

Faanui Bay

Faanui

Mt Mataihua (314m)

Haamaire Bay

Fitiu Point

Motu Tapu

Vairau Bay

Manta Reef

Inter-Island Ships

Tapu

Teavanui Pass

Airport Shuttle Ferry

Outipiti Point

Mt Pahia (661m)

Mt Otemanu (727m)

Anau

See Vaitape Enlargement

Vaitape

Nunue

Moutara

Tiipoto

Pererau Point

Vaiotaha Point

Povai Bay

Mohio Point

Motu Tapu

Mt Mauaohunoa (148m)

Eagle Channel

Aponapu Bay

Motu Piti Aau

Tehou Bay

Motu Too Pua

Manta Pass

Paoaoa Point

Motu Toopua Iti

Mt Pahonu (139m)

Faaopore Bay

Raititi Point

Rofau Bay

Taahina Bay

Motu Piti Uu Tai

Motu Piti Uuuta

Fareone Point

Tupitipiti Point

The Aquarium

SOUTH

PACIFIC

OCEAN

South Point

Tupitipiti

Vaitape

Commercial Centre

Vaitape

Wharf

0   200 m

Matira Point

Taahana Bay

Rofau Bay

Matira Point

0   200 m

0   1   2 km

BORA BORA

PLACES TO STAY
1   Motu Tane Island
2   Le Paradis
3   Mai Moana Island
5   Bora Bora Condos
6   Bora Bora Pearl Beach
    Resort
11 Revatua Club
12 Méridien Bora Bora
19 Bora Bora Yacht Club
23 Topdive (hotel & dive centre)
24 Au Lait de Coco
25 Bora Bora Lagoon Resort
37 Chez Ato
38 Blue Lagoon
40 Bora Bora Lagoonarium
41 Chez Stellio & Henriette
42 Chez Téipo
45 Club Med
46 Chez Rosina
47 Village Pauline
51 Hotel Bora Bora
53 Sofitel Motu
54 Hotel Sofitel Marara
56 Beach Club Bora Bora
58 Bora Bora Motel

62 Maitai Polynesia Bora Bora
65 Hotel Matira &
    Restaurant
66 Pension Maeva – Chez
    Rosine Masson
67 Pension Temanuata
68 Moana Beach Parkroyal
69 Chez Nono
70 Chez Robert & Tina

PLACES TO EAT
26 Le Cocotier
27 Snack Michèle
28 L'Appetisserie
36 Brasserie Manuia
43 Bamboo House Restaurant
48 Bloody Mary's
50 Snack Patoti
60 La Bounty Restaurant
61 Snack de la Plage
63 Ben's Place
64 Snack Matira

OTHER
4   Hyatt Remains
7   Seaplane Ramp

8   Submarine Dock
9   Marae Fare-Opu
10 Marine Museum
13 Lagoonarium
14 Marae Taharuu
15 Marae Aehua-tai
16 Faanui Church
17 Farepiti Quay
18 Marae Marotetini
20 Faanui Power Station
21 Marae Taianapa
22 Old Club Med
29 Tourist Office
30 Alain Gerbault Memorial
31 Craft Centre
32 Air Tahiti Office
33 Police Station
34 Town Hall (Mairie)
35 Europcar
39 Telephone Tower
44 Belvédère (Lookout)
49 Television Tower
52 Bora Bora Diving Center
55 New World
57 Tiare Market
59 René & Maguy

Information

The Bora Bora Visitors' Bureau (π/fax 67 76 36) has an office on the wharf at Vaitape, open Monday to Friday and some Saturday mornings. There are branches of Banque de Tahiti, Banque Socredo and Banque de Polynésie (the former two with ATMs) in Vaitape. The post office is also centrally located and telephones are scattered all around the island. L'Appetisserie (see Places to Eat) offers Internet and email services, usually in the morning. Count on 500 CFP for 15 minutes surfing or sending emails.

Vaitape has several well-supplied supermarkets. Across from the Bora Bora Motel near Matira Point the Tiare Market is the only supermarket at the south end of the island. There's a local craft centre, the Centre Artisanal de Bora Bora, in the same building as the tourist office. In Vaitape, Cathina (π 67 65 27) will do a load of laundry for 1800 CFP.

If you need medical assistance inquire at your hotel. There is a medical centre in Vaitape (π 67 70 77) or you can contact Dr Juen (π 67 70 62). There's a pharmacy in Vaitape open every day although only briefly on Sunday.

Vaitape

Vaitape, the island's main settlement, is not the most attractive centre but there are some cheaper places to stay and most of the tourist services are here. It gets very quiet by late afternoon.

Around The Island

Bora Bora's 32km coast road hugs the shoreline almost all the way around the island passing several old marae and assorted WWII remnants. Only at Fitiiu Point and just east of Club Med at Paoaoa Point does the road rise slightly above sea level. Since it's so level, doing the circuit by bicycle is easy, although motor scooters and cars can also be rented. The tour that follows commences at Vaitape and goes anticlockwise around the island.

Just 3km south of Vaitape and just past the Alain & Linda art gallery the **overland** road shortcuts across the island, an overgrown footpath crossing the top of the ridge bringing you out by Chez Stellio at Anau on the other side. At 6km the luxurious and expensive Hotel Bora Bora at Raititi Point marks the start of the pleasant sandy stretch of **Matira Beach**. From the eastern edge of the Hotel Matira property, a walking trail runs up the hill to a battery of WWII **coastal defence guns**.

The Moana Beach Parkroyal Hotel sign at 7.5km points the way to the small road which runs out to **Matira Point**. The public beach is on the west side of the point and the annual Hawaiki Nui inter-island canoe race ends here. From Matira Point, the coast road passes a busy little collection of shops, restaurants and hotels, rounds the point and passes Club Med (9km) on its own bay and with its own Belvédère lookout atop the ridge above the bay. Just past Chez Stellio (10.5km) is the office for the Lagoonarium where motu excursions and island tours are organised.

At Fitiiu Point (15km), the road climbs briefly away from the coast. Just as the road starts to climb, a track peels off and runs down to **Marae Aehua-tai** at the water's edge. The road beyond Fitiiu Point traverses the most lightly populated stretch of coast on the island as it rounds Haamaire and Taimoo bays. The middle-of-nowhere Revatua Club at 16.5km on Taimoo Bay is a good place for a lunch or drink stop on a circuit of the coast.

The small private **Marine Museum** (☎ 67 75 24) at 21km has an interesting collection of ship models. Entry to the museum is free but a donation is appreciated; it's generally open on weekends or during the week if the proprietor is at home. Just before **Taihi Point** (22km) a steep and often very muddy track climbs up to an old WWII radar station atop Popotei Ridge and on to a lookout above the village of Faanui.

A seaplane ramp and an old ferry jetty, more **WWII reminders**, pop up around 24km. At the end of Tereia Point, a rectangular concrete water tank marks the position of another coastal gun. There's no path: just clamber straight up the hill behind the

tank for a couple of minutes. Immediate before the Faanui village and speed-lim signs, **Marae Fare-Opu** is squeezed be tween the roadside and water's edge 26km. Two of the slabs are clearly marke with turtle petroglyphs. Turtles were sacre to the ancient Polynesians and similar stor designs can be seen at numerous other site in the Society Islands.

Faanui Bay This bay (27km) was the si of the main US military base during WW and there is still much evidence of th wartime operations. From the picturesqu church at the head of the bay an often ver muddy road runs directly inland and u over the ridge to drop down to Vairau Ba just south of Fitiiu Point. **Marae Taianap** (28km) is a fairly large marae on the inlan side of the road past Faanui village. Inter-is land ships dock at Farepiti wharf (29km) a the western end of Faanui Bay. **Mara Marotetini** is just beyond the wharf, a fin 50m-long shore marae restored by Dr Yosi hiko Sinoto in 1968. The Bora Bora Yach Club is just beyond the marae so there ar often yachts moored offshore from the point

Activities

Diving is a prime activity in Bora Bora, wit sharks, rays and other marine life inside an outside the lagoon. The friendly Bora Div ing Centre (☎ 67 71 84, ☎/fax 67 74 83) Nemo World (☎/fax 67 63 33, divebora@ mail.pf) and the high-tech Topdive (☎ 60 5(50, fax 60 50 51, topdive@mail.pf) are th local dive centres. Anau, with its regular vis its by manta rays, is one of the most popu lar lagoon sites. Others are Too Pua an Toopua Iti. Outside the lagoon Muri Muri just north of the airport, is a superb site.

Allow five hours round-trip for the tough ascent of Mt Pahia (661m), directly over looking Vaitape. Ato at Chez Ato (☎ 67 77 27) or Otemanu Tours (☎ 67 70 49) wil lead a group of five to the summit fo 15,000 CFP. Tupuna Mountain Safar (☎/fax 67 75 06) run popular guided tours by 4WD including visits to the American WWII sites and the archaeological sites For horse riding on Motu Piti Aau, contact

Stone Fishing Festival

The annual stone fishing festival takes place in the last week of October. Events include singing and dancing, agricultural and craft displays, local sporting events (including fruit-carrying races!), fishing contests and canoe races. A fire-walking ceremony is a highlight of the festivities before the final event, the stone fishing festival. Flower-bedecked pirogues fan out across the lagoon and the surface of the water is beaten with stones to herd the fish into an enclosure.

Ranch Reva Reva (☎ 60 44 61); for parasailing, contact Société Parasail (☎ 67 70 34, fax 67 61 73). For fishing and sailing trips and even helicopter flights, contact Héli-Inter Polynésie (☎ 67 62 59).

Matira Point is the best stretch of beach on the main island and the marine reserve off Hotel Bora Bora has good snorkelling.

Places to Stay

Bora Bora accommodation ranges from backpacker campsites and hostels up to some of the most luxurious (and expensive) resorts in the Pacific. It's spread right around the island although the main concentration extends from Raititi Point past Matira Point to Faaopore Bay, from 6 to 9km from Vaitape. Recently there's been a spate of luxury hotel construction on the islets. Mid to top end places generally accept credit cards but cheaper places don't; exceptions are noted.

Vaitape & Around The main settlement is simply a business centre, there's no beach or other attractions. *Au lait de Coco (☎ 67 67 66)* is north of the centre and has dorm beds at 2000 CFP and rooms at 5000 and 6000 CFP for one or two. There's nothing fancy about it but there is an equipped kitchen. *Topdive (☎ 60 50 50, fax 60 50 51, topdive@mail.pf)* is also north of Vaitape and is a diving centre with bungalows from 14,580 CFP for two people.

Blue Lagoon (☎/fax 67 65 64) is simple but great value with five fan-cooled rooms at just 2000 CFP per person. There's a restaurant with a terrace on to the lagoon. Turn off the main island coast road just over 2km from Vaitape and go inland about half a kilometre to *Chez Ato (☎ 67 77 27)* in a lush green setting on the mountain slope. The main accommodation block has five rooms around a central open area, which share shower and toilet facilities and cost 5000 CFP for one or two people. There are also bungalows at 60,000 CFP a month and a big fully equipped *fare* for 15,000 CFP a night. Transfers to the Vaitape wharf are free.

Chez Rosina (☎/fax 67 70 91), on the mountain side of the road, 4.5km from Vaitape, is warm and friendly with rooms at 5000/6000 CFP single/double. Each of the four rooms has an attached bathroom and costs 5500/7000 CFP. Right after Chez Rosina is *Village Pauline (☎ 67 72 16, fax 67 78 14)*, the most popular spot for budget travellers. The well-kept mini-village has tent sites at 1800 CFP per person, dorm beds at 2500 CFP, and bungalows from 6000 CFP for one or two people. Transfers from the ferry quay are 500 CFP, from the Vaitape quay 300 CFP. They have bicycles, scooters and kayaks to rent.

Around Matira Point – Budget Matira Point, the eastern end of the best sweep of beach on the main island, has several budget-priced guesthouses. Beachside *Chez Nono (☎ 67 71 38, fax 67 74 27)* has singles/doubles at 5500/6500 CFP with shared bathrooms and a large kitchen and lounge area downstairs. The rooms are quite comfortable, although the walls are paper thin. There are also two small bungalows from 8500 CFP. *Chez Robert & Tina (☎ 67 72 92)* is at the end of the point and has simple rooms with shared bathroom and kitchen facilities at 4000 CFP.

Pension Maeva – Chez Rosine Masson (☎/fax 67 72 04), by the water, just beyond the Matira Point turn-off, is full of the late Jean Masson's exuberant paintings and has dorm-style beds at 2500 CFP, and rooms from 5500 CFP.

FRENCH POLYNESIA

Around Matira Point – Mid-Range

Right on Matira Beach and just before Matira Point, the *Hotel Matira* (☎ 67 78 58, fax 67 77 02) has a restaurant and simple bungalows with bathrooms and terraces (some with kitchenettes) from 22,203 CFP. Just after the Matira Point turn-off *Pension Temanuata* (☎ 67 75 61, fax 67 62 48) is behind the restaurant of the same name and has five comfortable bungalows for up to three people from 8500 CFP.

The beachfront *Bora Bora Motel* (☎ 67 78 21, fax 67 77 57) has studios for 13,000 CFP for one or two people and separate apartments and a beach bungalow for 17,000 CFP. The *Beach Club Bora Bora* (☎ 67 71 16, fax 67 71 30), between the Bora Bora Motel and the Hotel Sofitel Marara, has rooms from 19,440 CFP.

Around Matira Point – Top End

On Raititi Point, *Hotel Bora Bora* (☎ 67 44 60, fax 60 44 66/60 44 22) has terrific views and a good beach. Prices start at 48,600 CFP. The restaurant overlooking the lagoon is one of the best places to eat on the island and there's a bar and restaurant down towards the beach.

On the east side of Matira Point the 51 room *Moana Beach Parkroyal* (☎ 60 49 00, fax 60 49 99, borabora@parkroyal.pf) is relatively small but very classy. Costs start at 50,898 CFP and there's a bar, two restaurants and a swimming pool. The *Maitai Polynesia Bora Bora* (☎ 60 30 00, fax 67 66 03, maitaibo@mail.pf) sprawls across both sides of the road, just beyond the Matira Point turn-off and offers a good balance between luxury and price. Rooms cost from 22,680 CFP.

The *Hotel Sofitel Marara* (☎ 67 70 46, fax 67 74 03) is at the end of Taahina Bay and has bungalows from 33,480 CFP, plus an extra 1500 CFP in the high season.

Around the point is *Club Med* (☎ 60 46 04, or in Papeete ☎ 42 96 99, fax 60 46 10, cmbora@mail.pf) on Faaopore Bay, just before Paoaoa Point. Meals and most activities are included at no extra cost, so after-dinner drinks are the only cost on top of the typical US$220 to $260 per person per day

if you've pre-booked. If you just turn up count on upwards of 16,924/30,830 CFP a single/double, including all meals and depending on the season.

Around the Island The rest of the island, past Club Med, is much quieter. *Chez Téipo* (☎ 67 78 17, fax 67 73 24, teipo@tahiti .net), also known as Pension Anau, is good value with single/double bungalows at 6500/7500 CFP, or there's a more spacious bungalow with hot water and space for three for 10,500 CFP.

At the entrance to Anau village *Chez Stellio & Henriette* (☎ 67 71 32) is the cheapest place on the island with camping space at 1000 CFP, dorm beds at 1500 CFP and rooms from 4000 CFP, all sharing the communal kitchen. Just beyond Chez Stellio, the *Bora Bora Lagoonarium* (☎ 67 71 34, fax 67 60 29) has rooms at 6000 CFP for one or two people, or a small lagoonside *fare* with bathroom for 8000 CFP.

The most isolated outpost on the island is the pink and white *Revatua Club* (☎ 67 71 67, fax 67 76 59). The hotel usually picks up its guests directly from the airport. There's a pleasant bar and restaurant by the lagoon and fan-cooled rooms for 10,573/12,355 CFP. There's also one villa on the lagoon side.

The *Bora Bora Condos* (☎ 67 71 33) are 10km from Vaitape, at the north end of the island. This long-term accommodation starts from 15,000 CFP a day in the low season. Credit cards are not accepted. Only 3km from Vaitape, almost completing the island circuit, the *Bora Bora Yacht Club* (☎ 67 70 69) has comfortable bungalows for up to four people from 10,000 CFP.

On the Motu Staying on one of the motu, the islands around the outer reef, ensures tranquillity, a complete escape and great views. Free shuttle boats run between the islets and the main island for the luxury resorts. Credit cards are accepted at all these places. *Motu Tane Island* (☎/fax 67 74 50) is on tiny Motu Tane, very close to the airport motu. There's a fine beach and good swimming around the motu and the two *fare* each have a double bedroom, living room, ining room, equipped kitchen and bathroom and cost 20,500 CFP for two people, including airport transfers.

Le Paradis (☎/fax 67 75 53), on Motu Paahi, the next island to the south, is probably the most affordable motu resort with five local-style, shared-bathroom *fare* in a lagoonside coconut plantation at 5000 CFP per person. Two *fare* with private bathrooms cost 15,000 CFP for up to three people. Airport transfers are included. *Mai Moana Island* (☎ 67 62 45, fax 67 62 39) on Motu Ite, a few islands south, has a dreamlike setting, with costs for two people starting at 28,000 CFP.

On Motu Tevairoa, the *Bora Bora Pearl Beach Resort* (☎ 60 52 00, fax 60 52 22, nfo@SPMhotels.pf) is equally luxurious, with bungalows starting at 49,680 CFP. There's a magnificent swimming pool and an over-water restaurant.

The *Bora Bora Lagoon Resort* (☎ 60 40 00, fax 60 40 01, bblr@mail.pf) is on Motu Toopua, looking across the lagoon to Vaitape and across the Teavanui Pass. It's one of the most luxurious resorts on the island, costing from 52,000 CFP.

The Sofitel Marara's *Sofitel Motu* is on Motu Piti Uuuta, five minutes by dugout from the Marara. The 30 bungalows are perched on a hillside among the coconut trees, on the beach or over-water and combine Polynesian design with modern technology. On the long motu to the north-east side of the lagoon, the *Méridien Bora Bora* (☎ 60 51 51, fax 60 51 52, sales@emeridien-tahiti.com) combines style and setting with prices starting at 62,400 CFP.

Places to Eat

Bora Bora doesn't have a great choice of restaurants and they generally shut around 9 pm. Some places offer a free transfer service to/from your hotel. There are several small supermarkets for those who prefer to prepare their own food.

Vaitape & Around Vaitape has good places for breakfast, a snack or a cheap meal. *L'Appetisserie* (☎ 67 78 88) is a pleasant little open-air snack bar and *pâtisserie* in the Commercial Centre near the quay, which is also the Bora Bora Internet centre. Near to the Banque de Polynésie the *Brasserie Manuia* offers breakfast and light meals but is closed on Monday. Facing it is the *Snack Bora Bora Burger* with very cheap burgers.

The simple *Snack Richard* specialises in Chinese takeaways. Next to the pharmacy *Pizza Bora* (☎ 67 68 00) does pizzas and waffles. Both are closed on Monday. On the north side of the town *Le Cocotier* snack bar is another Chinese specialist. In the evenings several *roulottes* take up positions across from the artist market.

The *Bamboo House Restaurant* (☎ 67 76 24), about 3.5km from Vaitape towards Matira Point, has great food and a tourist menu for 3800 CFP. Free transport is provided and credit cards accepted. *Bloody Mary's* (☎ 67 72 86), 5km from Vaitape or 1km before the Hotel Bora Bora, is one of the best-known restaurants in the Pacific. It's very pricey and inordinately proud of the list of celebrities who have dined there. One variety of fish costs 2400 CFP and the price steps up to 4000 CFP for lobster. Dinner for two can easily cost 12,000 to 15,000 CFP but they do provide free transport. It's closed on Sunday.

Around Matira Point The well-stocked Tiare *market* will save the long trip to Vaitape if you're fixing your own food. Between the Hotel Bora Bora and Matira Point, *Ben's Place* is a popular little cafe with a straightforward menu and variable hours. Just beyond Ben's Place and beside the lagoon, *Snack Matira*, also known as *Chez Julie*, is simple, but the prices are low and it's just a few steps from the beach. It's open from 10 am to 6 pm daily except Monday.

Right on the beach, between the Maitai Polynesia and La Bounty, you can enjoy the wonderful location at the *Snack de la Plage* for a very modest price. Across the road *La Rôtisserie* is a minuscule *fare* where you can get take-away chicken dishes and sandwiches, Monday to Saturday from 9 am to 6 pm. Near the last Sofitel bungalows, but on the inland side of the road, *Snack Patoti* has a small but interesting menu and is open from 7.30 am to 2 pm and 6 to 9 pm Monday to Saturday.

Restaurant Matira (☎ *67 70 51)*, between the Hotel Bora Bora and Matira Point, has a magnificent beachfront site and reasonably priced Chinese food. Immediately beyond the turn-off, *Temanuata* (☎ *67 62 47)* has a garden setting at the guesthouse of the same name and lots of fish dishes. It's open Monday to Saturday and free transport is offered. *La Bounty Restaurant* (☎ *67 70 43)* is a popular place with great food from 1000 to 1500 CFP served in a pleasant open *fare*. It's open Monday to Saturday, free transport is offered and credit cards are accepted.

All the big hotels have dance performances with buffet dinners several times a week. Count on 4000 to 6500 CFP. The Hotel Bora Bora's *Matira Terrace* (☎ *60 44 60)* offers excellent food in a romantic open-air setting looking out over the point and the prices are fairly reasonable. The *Noa Noa* at the Moana Beach Parkroyal has an especially attractive setting on the beach. The *Haere Mai* restaurant at the Maitai Polynesia Bora Bora is also worth trying, while *La Pérouse* at the Hotel Sofitel Marara has a lunch-time snack menu with sandwiches and burgers and a more elaborate dinner menu.

Around the Island *L'Espadon Restaurant* at the Revatua Club (☎ *67 71 67)* has a good reputation for fish and other seafood dishes. Credit cards are accepted and transport can be arranged. At the *Bora Bora Yacht Club* (☎ *67 70 69)* the pleasant waterfront setting and nautical decorations are complemented by good food.

Motu Restaurants Free shuttles, which generally operate until midnight, allow you to enjoy the restaurants at the motu hotels. Like their competitors on the main island, they offer evening performances with dinner buffets several times a week. Reservations are advisable.

Le Méridien Bora Bora has the superb surfboard-shaped *Tipanie* restaurant right by the lagoon with set menus from 5100 to 6100 CFP and a smaller restaurant beside the swimming pool. The shuttle operates from the Anau quay.

The *Otemanu* restaurant at the Bora Bora Lagoon Resort is probably the most chic spot on the island and a great place for a candlelit dinner over the lagoon. The prices match the romance! Shuttles operate from the Vaitape quay. The Bora Bora Pearl Beach Resort has two lagoonside restaurants.

Entertainment

A Sunset Drink Bora Bora does not have a lot of nightlife. Any of the luxury hotels will provide a good cold beer or a 1000 to 1300 CFP cocktail in an attractive lagoonside setting. Some even have a happy hour and for the motu hotels free shuttle services operate until about midnight.

The waterside bar of the *Bora Bora Yacht Club* is the perfect place for a sunset drink. On the opposite side of the island, the bar at the *Revatua Club* also has a great waterside setting. The famous *Bloody Mary's* is a good all-hours hangout.

On the edge of Vaitape, heading towards Matira Point, the *Blue Lagoon* has an unexciting setting but there's a pleasant terrace and beer is just 600 CFP for a half-litre.

Tahitian Dancing & Discos Don't miss a traditional dance performance by a local group in one of the luxury hotels. You can usually get in for the price of a drink at the bar, or for around 6000 CFP combine the evening with a buffet dinner. Performances take place two or three times weekly. Ask at the reception desks about the schedule and entry policy.

The only other night-time entertainment worthy of the name is the Club Med disco, which is open to all for 2300 CFP (includes one drink) and operates until the heady hour of 11.30 pm!

Shopping

The Centre Artisanal de Bora Bora in the tourist office by the Vaitape wharf has pareu, basketwork and other crafts produced by island women. Several shops in Vaitape sell souvenirs and craftwork. There are some black-pearl specialists on the island.

Getting There & Away

Bora Bora is 270km north-west of Tahiti, only 15km north-west of Tahaa.

Air Air Tahiti (☎ 67 70 35) connects Bora Bora five to nine times daily with Papeete, sometimes direct in about 45 minutes, other times via Moorea (16,000 CFP), Huahine (6500 CFP) or Raiatea (5100 CFP), or some combination of those islands. There are twice-weekly connections with Maupiti (5300 CFP). Bora Bora offers the only connections to the Tuamotus apart from via Papeete, with flights to Rangiroa (one hour 20 minutes; 20,700 CFP) with an onward connection to Manihi (23,400 CFP). The Air Tahiti office is on the wharf at Vaitape.

Boat Inter-island boats dock at the Farepiti wharf, 3km from Vaitape. The high speed *Ono-Ono* (☎ 67 78 00, or ☎ 45 35 35 on Tahiti) zips out to Bora Bora three times a week from Tahiti (6676 CFP), taking as little as seven hours for the trip with stops en route at Huahine (3142 CFP), Raiatea (1795 CFP) and Tahaa (1346 CFP). The cheaper cargo ship *Vaeanu* makes three trips a week between Papeete and the Leeward Islands.

The Maupiti Express (☎ 67 66 69) makes regular trips between Bora Bora and Maupiti, departing the Vaitape wharf at 8.30 am on Thursday and Saturday. The return departure is at 4 pm the same day. The fare is 2000/3000 CFP one way/return.

There are 17 moorings off the Bora Bora Yacht Club for visiting yachts and free showers if you eat there. Always take all valuables and documents with you when leaving the boat.

Getting Around

The airport is on Motu Mute at the northern edge of the lagoon and free transfers are made to/from the Vaitape wharf on two large catamaran ferries. You need to be at the wharf at least 1¼ hours before the flight departure. Some hotels transfer their visitors directly to/from the airport, others pick them up at the wharf.

Although there's no regular le truck service there often seems to be one going some-where at the appropriate times, particularly for flight and boat departures. There's a regular service for Village Pauline (300 CFP) and the Matira Point guesthouses (500 CFP).

Europcar (☎ 67 70 15, fax 67 79 95) has an agency opposite the wharf in the centre of Vaitape plus desks in several hotels. Other agencies are Fredo Rent-a-Car (☎ 67 70 31, fax 67 62 07), which is also in Vaitape and at several of the hotels, and Fare Piti Locations (☎ 67 65 28, fax 67 65 29), in Faanui and across from the Hotel Sofitel Marara.

Scooters and bicycles are available. Bora Bora's back roads cry out for a mountain bike but some of the bicycles available are either French village single-speeders or American-style cruisers. You will find bikes for rent at Europcar, Fredo and Fare Piti.

Renting a boat is a good way to explore the lagoon. René & Maguy (☎ 67 60 61, fax 67 61 01), next to La Bounty Restaurant, rents outboard-powered boats for 6360/7420/10,600 CFP for three hours/half day/full day, including fuel. Village Pauline has kayaks for 1000 CFP per hour. Jetski rentals are available for accompanied trips.

MAUPITI

• pop 1271   • area 11 sq km

The smallest and most isolated of the Society high islands, Maupiti has impressive soaring, rocky peaks with slopes tumbling down to the lagoon, cloaked in the waving green of coconut plantations. Like Bora Bora there's a shimmering, shallow lagoon edged by a string of islets flaunting white-sand beaches. The difference is size (it's 32km round Bora Bora's coastal road, just 10km around Maupiti's) and the pace of life (Maupiti is unsophisticated and very low key).

History

Sites on Motu Paeao, at the northern end of the lagoon, are some of the oldest in the Society Islands. The European discovery of Maupiti is credited to the Dutch explorer Jacob Roggeveen in 1722. The French arrived late in the last century, but missionaries and local chiefs continued to wield power until after WWII. Cyclone Osea ravaged the island in 1997 and many houses have been replaced by less interesting (but much safer) modern buildings.

Orientation & Information

There's just one road encircling the island and the string of buildings along the east side technically constitutes two villages, Fararuu and Vaiea, but they're difficult to separate. The main shipping wharf is at the south-east corner of the island, directly across from the Onoiau Pass. The small airport wharf is halfway up the east side of the island, just south of the church. Many motu fringe the lagoon with the airport on Motu Tuanai. The main island's only beach is at Tereia Point, but the motu have fine white sand beaches.

The church in the middle of the village is the most notable landmark. The town hall, post office, Air Tahiti office and Banque Socredo office are all together in one neat little group immediately north. The bank is only open when a representative comes to the island, so don't plan to change money.

Around the Island

You can walk around the island in just a few hours. Heading north, anticlockwise, from

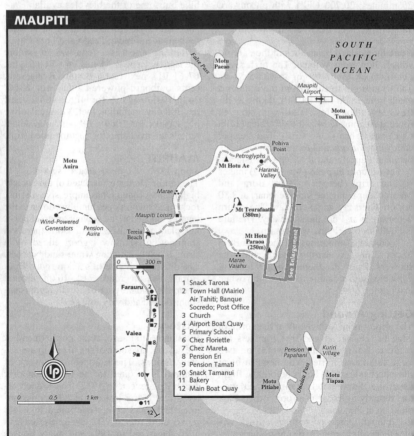

MAUPITI

SOUTH PACIFIC OCEAN

False Pass

Motu Paeao

Maupiti Airport

Motu Tuanai

Pohiva Point

Petroglyphs

Mt Hotu Ae

Harana'i Valley

Motu Auira

Marae

Mt Teurafaatiu (380m)

Maupiti Loisirs

Mt Hotu Paraoa (250m)

Wind-Powered Generators

Pension Auira

Tereia Beach

Marae Vaiahu

See Enlargement

0   300 m

1 Snack Tarona
2 Town Hall (Mairie)
   Air Tahiti; Banque
   Socredo; Post Office
3 Church
4 Airport Boat Quay
5 Primary School
6 Chez Floriette
7 Chez Mareta
8 Pension Eri
9 Pension Tamati
10 Snack Tamanui
11 Bakery
12 Main Boat Quay

Fararuu

Vaiea

Pension Papahani

Kuriri Village

Onoiau Pass

Motu Pitiahe

Motu Tiapaa

0   0.5   1 km

the neat little villages you'll pass the church basketball court into the Haranae Valley and, just before the sign for Tahiti Yacht Charter on the mountain side and just after the green MTR house, a track heads inland to a small pumping station. Follow the stream and after only 100m on the left you'll find boulders cut with **petroglyphs**. The biggest and most impressive is a turtle image on a flat boulder just to the right. If you follow the rocky riverbed further inland for a few hundred metres it leads to a ruined marae.

The west coast, from Pohiva Point to Puoroo and Tereia points, is dotted with **coastal marae**. Between Tereia and Puoroo points, at the western end of the island, **Tereia Beach** is the finest on the island for white sand and swimming. It's easy to walk across the lagoon to Motu Auira, particularly at low tide, but beware of stingrays lying in the sand.

In Atipiti Bay on the south side of the island, just north-west of the main wharf, the area known as Tefarearii, the 'House of Kings'. The island's nobility once lived here and **Marae Vaiahu** is a large coastal site with a wide expanse of paving-like stones. Just beyond the marae a sheer rock face rises up, overlooking the shipping quay at the south-east corner of the island. Traces of a fortified *pa* have been discerned atop this imposing outcrop.

Maupiti has some good walking, including the short clamber up to the ridge high above the two villages. The track to the top starts just south of Pension Eri, and from the top you can easily see Bora Bora and beyond to Raiatea and Tahaa. It's a superb climb to the summit of **Mt Teurafaatiu** (380m), also known as Mt Nuupere, the highest point on the island. Allow three hours for the round trip. The walk starts from the high point where the road crosses the ridge above Tereia Point and generally sticks firmly to the ridgeline.

The Lagoon & the Motu

The island guesthouses will organise picnic trips to Maupiti's many motu. Motu Paeao, at the northern end of the lagoon, was the site for the important archaeological discovery of a series of 1000 year old burial sites. There are marae sites on Motu Tiapaa and Motu Auira.

Snorkelling is particularly good around the Onoiau Pass. Richard (☎ 67 80 62) at Tahiti Yacht Charter organises half-day lagoon tours, including snorkelling stops for 2000 CFP, or 3000 CFP with lunch.

Places to Stay

Everything is family-style although the motu resorts are a little more sophisticated. Most visitors opt for demi-pension, which means a room plus breakfast and dinner, or pension (ie all meals). There's only one place with hot water and credit cards haven't arrived at Maupiti.

On the Island There are four guesthouses in the village (none with identifying signs) and one near Tereia Beach. South of the airport dock Chez Floriette and Chez Mareta are side by side, backing on to the well-used basketball court. *Chez Mareta (☎ 67 80 25)* has a peaked blue roof and is the cheapest place on the island at 1000 CFP per person, 1500 CFP with breakfast or 3000 CFP halfboard. *Chez Floriette (☎ 67 80 85)* is the most popular, with a bungalow at 4500 CFP per person half-board or 5500 CFP with all meals, including airport transfers.

Pension Eri (☎ 67 81 29), 200m south and also on the lagoon side of the road, is a well run place with four rooms sharing bathrooms, kitchen and living room. Half-board costs 4500 CFP per person.

The pleasant *Maupiti Loisirs (☎ 67 80 95)* is close to Tereia Beach and has two rooms at 2000 CFP per person, add another 1000 CFP to use the kitchen facilities. You can camp here but the cost is the same. Airport transfers cost 1000 CFP return.

On the Motu The resorts out on the motu exchange the low-key bustle of village life for the pleasures of isolated white-sand beaches, but don't expect swimming pools, water-sports equipment or diving trips. *Pension Auira (☎/fax 67 80 26)*, on the east side of Motu Auira, is also known as Chez Edna and has a 'beach' bungalow at 8000

CFP half-board per person and very basic bungalows at 7000 CFP.

At the northern end of Motu Tiapaa is **Pension Papahani** (☎ *67 81 58, BP 1, Vaiea, Maupiti*), right on the beach beside the pass. It's also known as the Pension Vilna and has bungalows with bathrooms for 6500/7500 CFP per person half/full board. Return transfers from the airport are 2000 CFP per person. Further south and on the ocean side of the island is **Kuriri Village** (☎/fax *67 82 23, hcc@tahiti.com*), which has four traditional-style bungalows with bathrooms at 9500/12,000 CFP per person half/full board. The food here has an excellent reputation and airport transfers are included.

Places to Eat
The village has several small and simple snack bars that are open irregular hours with uncertain provisions. Try **Snack Tarona** or **Chez Chanel** at the north end of the village or **Snack Tamanui** to the south. There are several small **shops** with basic supplies and soft drinks.

Getting There & Away
Maupiti is 320km west of Tahiti and just 40km west of Bora Bora.

Air Air Tahiti has about three flights a week between Papeete (12,700 CFP) and Maupiti, via Raiatea (5600 CFP) and/or Bora Bora (5300 CFP). The Air Tahiti office (☎ 67 80 20) is beside the mairie and post office.

Boat Onoiau Pass, at the southern end of the lagoon, is the only entry point to the Maupiti lagoon and strong currents and a tricky sand bar means the narrow pass can only be navigated by smaller ships. Maupiti Express (☎ 67 66 69) operates to Maupiti from Bora Bora on Thursday and Saturday for 2000/3000 CFP one way/return. Departing Vaitape (Bora Bora) at 8.30 am the ship arrives in Maupiti at 10 am, then departs for the return trip at 4 pm. The schedule allows enough time to look around Maupiti and return to Bora Bora on the same day although the crossing can be rough.

The small *Maupiti To'u Aia* makes weekly Papeete-Maupiti trip, via Raiatea o alternate weeks (2300 CFP one way).

Getting Around
If you're not met at the airport there's boat which takes the Air Tahiti staff and an hangers-on back to the main island. Th one-way fare for the 15 minute trip is 40 CFP. Boat departure times for outgoin flights are posted at the Air Tahiti office Motu transfers from the airport typicall cost from 1000 CFP return. Many of the vi lage guesthouses organise a weekly mo picnic trip for a minimal cost. Count on 50 to 1000 CFP between a motu and the mai island or 2000 CFP for a lagoon excursio Guesthouses and Snack Tamanui rent bicy cles for 500 CFP per half-day.

OTHER LEEWARD ISLANDS
There are four other Leeward Islands in th Society group, all of them atolls. Walli sighted Mopelia and Scilly in 1767, but di not pause to investigate them. Mopelia the only one of these Leeward atolls with pass for ships to enter its lagoon. All fo atolls are important breeding grounds fc green turtles, which lay their eggs on th beaches from November each year.

Tupai Atoll
Ancient Polynesian beliefs held that th souls of the dead had to pass through Tupa on their way to the afterworld (see also th boxed text 'Gateway to the Underworld' the Samoa chapter). Also known as Mot Iti, the tiny atoll is only 16km north of Bor Bora. There is an airstrip on the island bu no pass big enough to allow ships to ente the lagoon.

Mopelia Atoll
● pop 100   ● area 4 sq km
Mopelia Atoll (also known as Maupihaa) 160km south-west of Maupiti. The atoll roughly circular, with a diameter of abou 8km. In 1917 the German raider *Seeadle* was wrecked here when it paused for re pairs. Mopelia's population are statione there purely to harvest pearl oysters. Th

toll is also noted for its many bird species nd abundant turtles.

The atoll's tricky pass is just wide nough for small ships to enter the lagoon nd the *Maupiti To'u Aia* sails from Maupiti o Mopelia every two weeks. Yachts occa-ionally call into Mopelia – the only atoll in he Society Islands with a navigable pass.

Scilly Atoll

Tiny, remote Scilly (also known as Manuae) s a marine reserve and home to green tur-les and oysters. It's about 60km north-west of Mopelia and is covered in coconut palms.

Bellinghausen Atoll

Bellinghausen (also known as Motu One) was 'discovered' in 1824 by the Russian ex-plorer of that name. Four low-lying islands ncircle the reef but there is no entrance to he lagoon.

Tuamotu Islands

The Tuamotu Islands form the heart of French Polynesia, 77 atolls stretching 1500km north-west to south-east and 100km east to west. The total land area of he Tuamotus is only about 700 sq km, but he narrow chains of low-lying islets mak-ng up the islands encircle around 6000 sq km of sheltered lagoons – more than 1000 sq km in the vast Rangiroa lagoon alone.

The atolls are fragile and vulnerable places. Their lack of height offers no pro-ection against cyclones and the poor soil nd freshwater makes agriculture difficult. Named the 'Dangerous Islands' by Boug-inville, they've long remained in the shadow of the Society Islands although ecently tourism and black pearl cultivation as brought some of the islands more into he mainstream.

History

The history of the Tuamotu archipelago is a mystery; stories from the early navigators, archaeological vestiges and fragments of ancient traditions are the only historical sources. European explorers first chanced upon the Tuamotus in 1521, when Ferdi-nand Magellan chanced upon Puka Puka. Later European explorers were less than complimentary about the group – Le Marie and Schouten in 1616 spoke of the 'Islands of Dogs', the 'Islands without End' or sim-ply the 'Islands of Flies'.

At the same time as the first explorers touched on the islands, the central and west-ern areas of the Tuamotus were being torn apart by intense wars with the ferocious war-riors of Anaa Atoll, who spread terror across the whole region. Through much of the 19th century the only Westerners established in the archipelago were missionaries, and souls were fiercely contested for in the Tuamotus. As a result there are numerous fine churches today, including Catholic, Protestant, Mor-mon, Adventist and Sanito.

Copra plantations, pearl diving and mother-of-pearl became important activi-ties, but from 1911 until 1966 phosphate mining on the island of Makatea was vitally important. Then for a long time the econ-omic spillover from nuclear testing was the mainstay of the local economy.

Activities

Activities in the lagoons are what counts and diving is number one. You can visit pearl farms and also walk on the reef, snorkel, explore archaeological sites and visit bird reserves on remote islets or fish parks. The best beaches are often on remote islets but picnic trips or islet drop-offs are easy to organise. Definitely bring a mask and snorkel.

Accommodation

Only Manihi and Rangiroa have inter-national-class hotels. Family run guest-houses and pensions are the usual accommodation options in the Tuamotus. Because there are not many restaurants most visitors opt for half-board (breakfast and dinner) or full board (all meals). A room with half-board typically costs 5500 to 6000 CFP per person but fish and rice can quickly pall unless your hosts have exceptional tal-ents in the kitchen.

FRENCH POLYNESIA

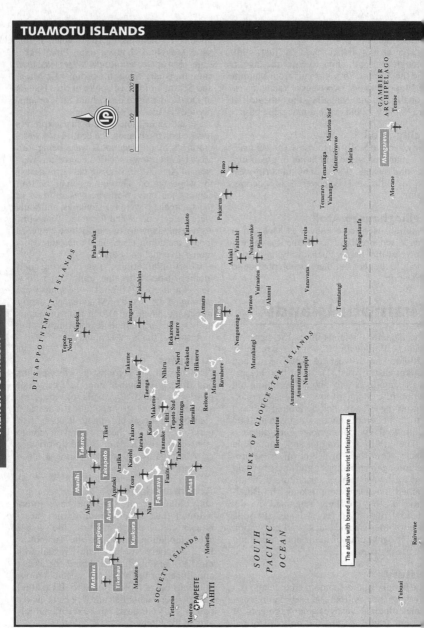

TUAMOTU ISLANDS

GAMBIER ARCHIPELAGO

Temoe

Mangareva

Morane

Maria

Marutea Sud

Matureivavao

Vahanga

Tenararo Tenarunga

Reao

Pokarua

Tatakoto

Akiaki Vahitahi

Nukutavake Pinaki

Fangataufa

Moruroa

Tureia

Vairaatea

Paraoa Ahunui

Vanavana

Manuhangi

Nengonengo

Tematangi

Amanu

Hao

Fakahina

Fangatau

Poka Poka

Napuka

Tepoto Nord

DISAPPOINTMENT ISLANDS

Rekareka Tauere

Marokau Ravahere

Hikueru

Teikokota

Marutea Nord

Nihiru

Takume

Raroia Taenga

Makemo

Katiu

Tuanake Hiti

Tepoto Sud

Motutunga

Tahanea

Faaite

Reitoru

Haraiki

Anaa

DUKE OF GLOUCESTER ISLANDS

Anuanuraro

Anuanurunga

Nukutepipi

Hereheretue

Tikei

Takaroa

Takapoto

Aratika

Kauehi Taiaro

Rarika

Iosu Niau

Apataki

Ahe

Manihi

Arutua

Fakarava

Rangiroa

Kaukura

Makatea

Mataiva

Tikehau

Tetiaroa

Moorea

PAPEETE

TAHITI

Mehetia

SOCIETY ISLANDS

SOUTH PACIFIC OCEAN

Raivavae

Tubuai

The atolls with boxed names have tourist infrastructure

0   100   200 km

Don't expect professional hotel standards in local guesthouses and note that lagoonside doesn't necessarily mean right by the water. With the exception of a few hotels and guesthouses in Rangiroa and Manihi, credit cards are not accepted and only Rangiroa has any permanent banking services.

Getting There & Away

Air There are 27 atoll airstrips and although most traffic is with Papeete there are also connections with Bora Bora, the Marquesas Islands and the Gambier Archipelago. Within the Tuamotus, Rangiroa and Hao are the two principal flight centres. If you're visiting an island, always give the Air Tahiti representative a contact address or phone number because schedules are subject to change.

Boat The *Saint Xavier Maris Stella*, *Dory*, *Cobia I*, *Mareva Nui*, *Vai-Aito*, *Auura'Nui 3*, *Rairoa Nui*, *Kura Ora*, *Hotu Maru*, *Taporo IV* and *Aranui* all serve the archipelago from Papeete and most take passengers. On islands without wharves, loading and unloading is done by whaleboat.

Getting Around

The road networks on the Tuamotu Islands are often just crushed coral or sand tracks, perhaps just a few kilometres long. There is very little public transport. Airports are sometimes near the villages, sometimes on remote islets, but if you have booked accommodation, your hosts will come and meet you although transfers aren't always free.

RANGIROA ATOLL

- **pop 1913**   • **area 40 sq km**

Rangiroa is the second-biggest atoll in the world, outranked only by Kwajalein in the Marshall Islands. The enormous (1640 sq km) lagoon measures 75 by 25km and could contain the whole island of Tahiti. From the edge of the lagoon, it is impossible to see the opposite bank. This is the most populated atoll in the Tuamotu archipelago and in two decades has established itself as a terrific tourist destination. Its reputation is based on diving and excursions on the idyllic lagoon. Apart from tourism, fishing and pearl production have provided additional income for the inhabitants.

History

Marae and cultivation pits reveal evidence of many population centres spread around Rangiroa Atoll: at Tereia, Fenuaroa, Otepipi, Tevaro, Tiputa and Avatoru.

Historically, Rangiroa has had to contend with two types of threat: raids from Anaa Atoll in the south-east and devastating cyclones. A tsunami is said to have destroyed the human settlements in the west of the atoll in 1560. Raids by the fierce warriors of Anaa Atoll in the 1770s forced the Rangiroa survivors into exile on Tikehau or Tahiti. They were able to return to Rangiroa in 1821 and repopulate the atoll.

Although discovered by the Dutchman Le Marie in 1616, Rangiroa saw the first European settlers only in 1851.

Orientation & Information

The atoll's coral belt is no more than 200 to 300m wide but the long circuit of islands, islets and channels stretches for more than 200km. The lagoon opens to the ocean via three passes. The village of Avatoru is on the eastern side of the Avatoru Pass. A 10km string of islets, separated at high tide and with the airport around the mid point, separates Avatoru Pass from Tiputa Pass. Most of the places to stay are along this string but the village of Tiputa is just across the Tiputa Pass, on its eastern side. A few people live on a motu south of the lagoon, in the vicinity of Hotel Kia Ora Sauvage.

The Banque de Tahiti and Banque Socredo have agencies in Avatoru and Tiputa, open on designated days. They change travellers cheques and make credit card cash advances. There are also post offices and telecard phones, medical centres, a private clinic and an infirmary.

Avatoru & Tiputa

Avatoru has shops, churches and a fishing and research centre specialising in cultured

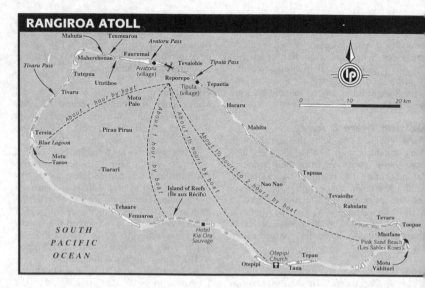

RANGIROA ATOLL

pearl research. Rangiroa College is about 3.5km east of the village and has more than 400 students from the northern Tuamotu Islands. Although Tiputa is quieter and less touristy it's actually the administrative centre not just for Rangiroa but also Makatea, Tikehau and Mataiva. After leaving the village a track continues through coconut plantations until you're halted by the next pass.

Around the Lagoon

The huge Rangiroa Atoll is worth exploring but it takes at least an hour to cross to the opposite side, an uncomfortable hour if the sea is rough. Tours depend on enough people signing up and the state of the lagoon and weather conditions.

The **Blue Lagoon** is one hour away by boat on the western edge of the atoll, close to Motu Taeoo. A string of islets and coral reefs have formed a natural pool on the edge of the main reef, thereby creating a lagoon within a lagoon.

The magnificent 'pink sand beach' of **Les Sables Roses** is on the south-eastern edge of Rangiroa's lagoon near Motu Vahituri, 1½ to two hours from Avatoru by boat.

On the south of the atoll, an hour by boat from Avatoru, is **L'Île aux Récifs** (Island of Reefs), also known as Motu Ai Ai. It lies in water dotted with raised coral outcrop called *feo*, weathered shapes that have been chiselled by erosion into strange petrified silhouettes.

There are a few scattered motu in the lagoon, rather than around the edge. They include Motu Paio and they are **bird sanctuaries**. **Otepipi Church** is on a motu on the south-east side of the atoll, about 1½ hours by boat, which once had a village. Today, only the church remains.

Lagoon and motu trips typically cost 6000 to 9000 CFP and are organised by Hiria Arnoux of Atoll Excursion (☎ 96 07 88), Tetiare Excursion (☎ 96 85 85), Ariitini Excursions at Chez Félix & Judith (☎ 96 04 41), Punua Excursions (☎ 96 84 73), Gatien Guitteny (☎ 96 72 14) and Alban of Chez Cécile (☎ 96 05 06).

Activities

Paradive (☎ 96 05 55, fax 96 05 50), the Raie Manta Club (☎ 96 84 80, fax 96 85 60) and the Six Passengers (☎/fax 96 02 60) are the Rangiroa dive operators. Rangiroa is ne of the best-known dive sites in the Pacific, with a worldwide reputation, although in fact there are not many sites and the coral is relatively poor. It is the powerful currents running through the passes and the exceptional density of sharks that those currents attract which accounts for Rangiroa's fame. Divers enter on the ocean side and drift with the current into the lagoon. The zodiac follows the divers and picks them up them at the end of the dive. This type of dive is strictly for the experienced.

Snorkelling through the passes is also popular and Rangiroa Activities (☎ 96 03 31) and Oviri (☎ 96 05 87) both organise trips. Société Parasail (☎ 96 04 96) offer 15-minute parasails over the lagoon while Matahi Tepa (☎ 96 84 48) has a glass-bottom boat.

Rangiroa has several pearl farms which you can visit and even buy pearls. Try Gauguin's Pearl (☎/fax 96 05 39) or the small operations run by the Tetua family (contact L'Atelier Corinne on ☎ 96 03 13) or Heipoe Ura (☎ 96 04 35).

Places to Stay

The choice and price range is wide at Rangiroa, from dorm beds to luxury over-water bungalows. Most visitors opt for half or full board since the choice of places to eat is limited. Mid-range and top end places generally take credit cards, budget ones usually don't.

Places to Stay – Budget

Chez Henriette (☎ 96 84 68, fax 96 82 85), in Avatoru village, has three rudimentary bungalows for 5150/6170 CFP half/full board per person. *Chez Punua & Moana* (☎/fax 96 84 73), directly opposite, costs from 3500 CFP per person including breakfast. *Pension Herenui* (☎ 96 84 71, BP 31 Avatoru, Rangiroa) is next to the Raie Manta Club and also costs 3500 CFP including breakfast.

Rangiroa Lodge (☎ 96 82 13, Avatoru, Rangiroa) is another place for those on a tight budget, with dorm beds for 1500 CFP and rooms at 2500 CFP per person, all squeezed into one *fare*. *Pension Hinanui* (☎ 96 84 61, BP 16 Avatoru, Rangiroa) is 200m further on and has three well-designed

bungalows for 4000/7000 CFP a single/double. Credit cards are accepted.

Pension Loyna (☎/fax 96 82 09) is on the ocean side of the road and costs 5500/6500 CFP half/full board. Next to it is *Pension Henri* (☎/fax 96 82 67) with three comfortable bungalows for 8000/10,000 CFP half/full board. *Chez Nanua* (☎ 96 83 88, BP 54, Avatoru, Rangiroa) is the cheapest place on Rangiroa, with five rustic bungalows for 3000 CFP per person half-board, 4000 CFP for the two with bathroom. You can camp for 1000 CFP per person.

The popular *Chez Cécile* (☎ 96 05 06, BP 98, Avatoru, Rangiroa) is halfway between the airport and the village and costs 6000/7000 CFP half/full board. Cécile's cooking is superb and meals are taken in a communal hut in a garden setting. Credit cards are accepted. *Turiroa Village* (☎/fax 96 04 27) has bungalows for 8000 CFP that accommodate up to four people.

Chez Martine (☎ 96 02 53, ☎/fax 96 02 51) has bungalows for two to four people for 6000/7000 CFP half/full board per person. Next door, *Chez Félix & Judith* (☎ 96 04 41, BP 18, Avatoru, Rangiroa) has comfortable and pleasantly-situated bungalows for 6000/6500 CFP half/full board.

Pension Teina & Marie (☎ 96 03 94, fax 96 84 44), at the end of the Avatoru string of islets and on the edge of the Tiputa Pass is very popular with divers. The bungalows start at 5500/6500 CFP per person for half/full board. Meals are delicious and generous and are taken in a large *fare*, opposite the lagoon.

The *Chez Glorine* guesthouse (☎ 96 04 05, fax 96 03 58), next to the wharf at the end of the Avatoru string of islets, does particularly good food. The well-maintained bungalows are 6500/7500 CFP half/full board. Call first.

Across the pass, *Chez Lucien* (☎ 96 73 55, BP 69, Tiputa, Rangiroa) in Tiputa, has well-maintained bungalows for 5000/6000 CFP.

Places to Stay – Mid-Range & Top End

Miki Miki Village (☎ 96 83 83, fax 96 82 90) has charming bungalows at 6000 CFP, including breakfast. At *Pension Tuanake* (☎ 96 04 45, fax 96 03 29) half-board costs from 8000 CFP a single; the food has a good reputation.

The *Raira Lagoon* (☎ 96 04 23, fax 96 05 86, rairalag@mail.pf) has 10 excellent single/double bungalows at 11,000/14,000 CFP with half-board, and a terrific restaurant. The *Rangiroa Beach Club* (☎ 96 03 34, fax 96 02 90) is 150m from the lagoon and has 11 tidy and attractive bungalows that cost from 10,260 CFP (often booked out).

The Tuamotus' most luxurious hotel, the *Kia Ora Village Hotel* (☎ 96 03 84, fax 96 04 93) has 60 bungalows in a coconut plantation on the lagoon's edge, 2.5km east of the airport. Extravagance starts at 21,600 CFP (up to 55,080 CFP for an over-water bungalow). There's a good restaurant over the lagoon and activities include diving, lagoon excursions, tennis and windsurfing. *Kia Ora Sauvage* is an annexe on Motu Avearahi, on the south side of the lagoon (one hour by boat). Traditional-style *fare* cost 36,720 CFP for two plus 7000 CFP per person (full board). Round trip boat transfers are included.

Places to Eat

Avatoru and Tiputa have a few well-stocked *shops* if you want to prepare your own food. Snack bars include the popular *Snack Manuragi* in Avatoru, and *Chez Béatrice* (☎ 96 04 12), about 5km east of Avatoru. *Pizzeria Vaimario* (☎ 96 04 96), near the Rangiroa Beach Club, has pizzas to eat there or take away – they'll even deliver! At *Pâtisserie Afaro* (☎ 96 04 91), on the ocean side 1.5km east of Avatoru Village, orders must be placed the day before. At Tiputa the restaurant of the *CETAD technical school* offers lunch prepared by the students twice a week. Phone ☎ 96 72 96, or ☎ 96 02 68 at the weekend, to book.

Several guesthouses offer good meals from 1500 to 2500 CFP, try *Chez Glorine*, *Teina & Marie*, *Raira Lagoon*, *Pension Tuanake* and *Chez Lucien*. It's also worth trying the more expensive hotels such as the *Rangiroa Beach Club*, which has good meals from 1250 CFP. The cuisine at *Kia Ora Village Hotel* is great; dinner dishes start from 2000 CFP. There's a twice weekly barbecue buffet and Polynesian dance performance for 4250 CFP. *Miki Miki Village* has an open terrace looking out on the lagoon and a set dinner menu at 2500 CFP.

Shopping

A few shops around Avatoru sell souvenirs, postcards, hand-painted pareu, film and a few local handicrafts. Try Paréo Carole, Ocean Passion, Le Coquillage and the shops in the Kia Ora Village and the Rangiroa Beach Club.

Getting There & Away

Rangiroa is 350km north-east of Tahiti and is an important link for air and sea communication, located at the mid-point between the Society Islands and the Marquesas.

Air The airport is 5.5km east of Avatoru village and Air Tahiti (☎ 96 03 41) is inside the air terminal building. Rangiroa is connected to Tahiti (13,600 CFP), Bora Bora (20,700 CFP), the Marquesas (24,500 CFP) and other atolls in the Tuamotus. There are several flights between Papeete and Rangiroa. There's direct connections with the Leeward Islands via the three or four times weekly Bora Bora-Rangiroa-Manihi flight. In the other direction it only operates once a week. There's a weekly Marquesas connection (Papeete-Rangiroa-Nuku Hiva) but only in that direction.

Boat The *Dory*, *Mareva Nui*, *Vai-Aito*, *Saint Xavier Maris Stella* and *Rairoa Nui* load and unload freight at the wharf in Avatoru Pass and at the wharf close to Chez Glorine on the other end of the motu string, as well as the Tiputa wharf next to the town hall.

The *Aranui*, on the way back from the Marquesas, also stops at Rangiroa for half a day.

Getting Around

If you have booked accommodation, your hosts will be at the airport, 5.5km east of

Avatoru, to welcome you. Transfers are not automatically included in the accommodation price.

A sealed road runs the 10km from Avatoru village to the Tiputa Pass. There is no regular service crossing the pass separating the Avatoru islets from Tiputa village although from time to time speedboats travel between the wharf next to Chez Glorine and the Tiputa landing platform. During the school term you can take the school ferry for 500 CFP, or ask at Chez Glorine.

Rangi Location (☎ 96 03 28), part of the Europcar group, rents cars, those curious little three-wheeler fun cars, scooters and bicycles. Several guesthouses have bicycles and scooters at the same rates. Paréo Carole (☎ 96 82 45) and Kia Ora Village also have bicycles and scooters.

MAKATEA
- **pop 84**   • **area 30 sq km**

The only high island in the Tuamotus, Makatea is a bean-shaped plateau with precipitous cliffs 80m high forming its outer edge. These cliffs are in fact a former barrier-reef and the plateau was once the basin of a lagoon where vast amounts of phosphate accumulated.

In 1908 a company was created to exploit the phosphate deposits and by 1960 phosphate was the mainstay of the French Polynesian economy. In 1962 the population was 3071, making Makatea the most populous island in the Tuamotus but in 1966 the phosphate was exhausted and it was all over. Today the island's population make their living from copra production and the sale of *kaveu* (coconut crabs).

TIKEHAU
- **pop 400**   • **area 15 sq km**

Tikehau is a ring-shaped atoll, 26km on its longest axis. Dotting the lagoon are a number of islets that provide nesting-grounds for birds. Tikehau's population is grouped in the village of Tuherahera, on the southwest of the atoll. The atoll is becoming popular with visitors who are looking for a quieter alternative to Rangiroa.

Diving is a great reason to visit Tikehau.

Rangiroa's Raie Manta Club has an offshoot at Tikehau Village (☎ 96 22 86) with a single dive master. Dives are made in the magnificent Tuheiava Pass where manta rays and sharks are regularly encountered.

There is no bank in Tikehau but there is a post office.

Places to Stay & Eat
There are *guesthouses* in the village and close to the airport, less than 1.5km from Tuherahera.

North of the village, close to the lagoon, the *Chez Maxime* guesthouse (☎ 96 22 38) has basic rooms from 3500 CFP per person with half-board, fairly ordinary food and a lot of mosquitoes. *Chez Isidore & Nini* (☎ 96 22 89), near the village entrance coming from the airport, charges the same prices and has a beautiful garden. About 100m away in the village *Chez Colette* (☎ 96 22 47) has an equipped kitchen and is brilliantly clean, with rooms at 3000/5000 CFP per person half/full board

Pension Hélène (☎ 96 22 52, fax 96 22 00 at the post office), at the village entrance on the left track coming from the airport, is a great place for 4500/5500 CFP. Hélène,

TIKEHAU

Teavatia · Puaea · Taa
Temaruopapahia
Teoparapara
Motuhiraumaine
Hararu
Oeoe
Piuta · Aramaruru
Tuheiava Pass
Motu Puarua
Ohihi
Matiti
Motuiore
Motura
Paeatohora
Rafarua
Motupiro
Motutohino
Tohuarei
Motumauu
Tavararo
Pohueava
Aua
Tuherahera · Ohotu

SOUTH PACIFIC OCEAN

0   5   10 km

the post office agent, also has a small chalet and a three room house on a private motu for 1500 CFP per person. There's an outrigger canoe for your use.

Halfway between the village and airport the attractive *Tikehau Village* (☎ 96 22 86) has nine bungalows from 6000/7000 CFP. Meals include local specialities and there are bicycles for guests' use. The lagoonside *Pension Tematie* (☎/fax 96 22 65) is nearby; nightly cost is 4500/6500 CFP.

Chez Justine (☎ 96 22 88), on the edge of the lagoon, 1.5km from the village entrance and 500m on the right coming from the airport, has bungalows at 5500/6500 CFP half/full board.

The most remote of the guesthouses is *Kahaia Beach* (☎ 96 22 77, fax 96 22 81) on a motu to the north-east of the airport. Four lagoonside bungalows cost 5000/7000 CFP.

Apart from the guesthouses, there are not that many places to eat on Tikehau. The *Chez Maui* and *Chez Rosita* are shops with general supplies and the village's only *bakery* has coconut bread some days each week. *Chez Hélène* does meals for 2500 CFP but you must book ahead. The *Tikehau Village* has a restaurant in a superbly situated beachfront *fare* where lunch costs 1500 CFP and dinner 2000 CFP.

Getting There & Away
The airport is little more than 1km east of the village entrance. Air Tahiti (☎ 96 22 66) has four weekly flights between Papeete and Tikehau (13,600 CFP), direct or via Rangiroa (4400 CFP).

The *Rairoa Nui*, *Mareva Nui*, *Saint Xavier Maris Stella* and the *Dory* all stop in Tikehau and tie up at the wharf on the lagoon side.

Getting Around
A 10km track goes around the motu on which Tuherahera is situated and passes by the airport. Your hosts can hire or lend you bicycles.

MATAIVA ATOLL
The structure of Mataiva's lagoon gives it a special appearance: the coral constructions

at the surface of the water create wall which divide the lagoon into about 7 basins of 10m depth.

The village of Pahua is divided by a pas only suitable for very small boats, it's just a few metres wide and no deeper than 1.5m A bridge spans the pass and links the tw parts of the village. Nine channels, thi trickles of water, provide small links be tween the lagoon and the ocean. Mataiv (Nine Eyes) is named after these channels Mataiva has superb beaches, numerou snorkelling spots and one of the few note worthy archaeological sites in the Tua motus. There's no bank but Pahua has couple of shops and a post office.

Things to See & Do
Le Rocher de la Tortue (the Rock of th Turtle, or Ofai Tau Noa) is a remnant of former uplifted coral reef. Take the trac that starts at the bridge on the northern sid of the pass, follow it for 4.7km, then tak the secondary track on the left, whic crosses the coconut plantation to the ocean There are many fine beaches along th edge of the lagoon to the south of the atoll Marae Papiro is a well-kept marae with th legendary throne of the giant Tu. It's on th edge of a channel, about 14km from the vil lage, south-east of the atoll at the end of th track.

Île aux Oiseaux (Bird Island), a crescent shaped coral tongue covered in small shrub to the east of the lagoon, is a favourite ex cursion. According to legend a rock on th surface of the lagoon, next to Île au Oiseaux, is the Nombril de Mataiva (th Mataiva Papa, or navel of Mataiva).

Mataiva also has a **shipwreck** stuck in th middle of the coconut plantation. It's said t have been wrecked in the 1906 cyclone an blown onto the land by cyclones in late years. Follow the track for about 3km, the take the secondary track which turns righ towards the ocean. After 450m, you wil come to a fork, from where you can catch glimpse of the ocean. Don't head toward the ocean, instead follow the other track t the left for 250m. You will then find your self facing the shipwreck.

Places to Stay

There are three very similar guesthouses and all the prices listed below include airport transfers. The only guesthouse north of the pass, 150m from the bridge and right on the pass, is Edgar's *Mataiva Village* (☎ 96 32 33, ☎/fax 96 32 95), with six clean and comfortable bungalows for 4000/6000 CFP per person half/full board. Crayfish are a speciality in the large dining room on stilts, but it's worth asking for a mosquito coil if you're dining here.

Super Mataiva Cool (☎ 96 32 53) is south of the bridge, also right on the edge of the pass, and has units from 5500/10,000 CFP a single/double with half-board, 7000/13,000 CFP with full board. The *Ava Hei Pension* (☎ 96 32 39) is close to the lagoon about 5km from the village. The beach location is perfect and the three traditional-style bungalows cost 7000 CFP per person with all meals.

Getting There & Away

Mataiva is 350km north-east of Tahiti and 100km west of Rangiroa. The Air Tahiti (☎ 96 32 48) representative is the proprietor of the Mataiva Village. At least twice a week there are flights from Papeete (13,600 CFP) via Rangiroa (4400 CFP).

Mataiva is on the route of the *Mareva Nui* and *Saint Xavier Maris Stella*.

Getting Around

A good-quality track goes almost all the way around the atoll, in the middle of the coconut plantation. To the north, the track finishes at Marae Papiro, about 14km away. To the south, allow about 10km to the end. On this dead-flat atoll, cycling is an excellent way of getting around. The Mataiva Village and Super Mataiva Cool guesthouses, rent out bicycles for about 1000 CFP per day. Cars can be rented for 2000 to 3000 CFP per day, with driver. Inquire at the guesthouses.

All the guesthouses have motor boats and will suggest a visit to the Île aux Oiseaux, the fish parks and the Nombril de Mataiva. Allow 2000 to 3000 CFP for the day, including a picnic.

MANIHI ATOLL

Some 175km north-east of Rangiroa, Manihi (population 770) has acquired an international reputation in the field of pearl production and the lagoon is now scattered with large-scale family and industrial pearl production farms. The ellipse-shaped atoll is 28km long and 8km wide, with only one opening, the Tairapa Pass in the south-west. The exhilarating beauty of the lagoon and the riches of its underwater world were quickly recognised and an international hotel was built in 1977.

Information

There is no bank on the atoll but the Manihi Pearl Beach Resort may be able to change money in emergencies. The post office is in Paeua village, opposite the marina. There are card-operated public telephones on the ground floor of the post office building, at the airport and at the Manihi Pearl Beach Resort. The village also has a hospital.

Things to See

Unlike other atoll villages, **Paeua** is charmless and the activity is all in pearl farms. The first pearl farm was set up in Manihi in 1968 and there are now about 70 pearl farms. The best idea is to visit a small family farm and a larger industrial farm, but avoid holiday periods, particularly Christmas, when the workers may be away.

The Manihi Pearl Beach Resort is the main organiser of pearl farm visits, usually combined with a picnic and village excursion for 2544 CFP. You can go to the village and ask to see a pearl farm, but remember these are businesses not tourist sites. Prices tend to be lower than in Papeete or abroad.

Activities

Manihi Blue Nui (☎ 96 42 17, fax 96 42 72) is in the Manihi Pearl Beach Resort and, like the hotel, is luxurious and immaculate. Dives cost 6000 CFP and there are four sites in the immediate vicinity of the Tairapa Pass, just 10 minutes from the dive centre. **Le Tombant** (the Drop Off), on the ocean side, is a dizzy wall that topples towards the abyss. The **Tairapa Pass** forms a passageway about 70m wide and 20m in depth; you simply let yourself be sucked into the lagoon by the current, observing the amazing density of marine life as you slip past. This dive ends at the **Circus**, inside the lagoon, where there's an entanglement of pinnacles from 20m depth right up to the surface, the whole thing peppered with coral fish. **The Cliffs** is another ocean dive at a fracture in the reef, where divemasters engage in shark feeding.

Places to Stay

Reasonably priced accommodation is difficult to find in Manihi and the facilities are scattered all over the atoll. *Jeanne & Guy Huerta* (☎ 96 42 90, fax 96 42 91) is on the lagoon side on Motu Taugaraufara, about 9km north-east of the airport. They have two well-equipped bungalows on the beach at 8000 CFP per person full board and one over-water bungalow for 12,000 CFP, including airport transfers. Credit cards are accepted and lagoon tours are organised.

Vainui Perles (☎ 96 42 89, fax 96 42 00 at the post office) is on Motu Marakorako, east of the village and about a half-hour by boat from the airport. There are six rooms with shared bathrooms for 8000 CFP per person per day, including all meals, airport transfers and fishing and picnic excursions. Credit cards are accepted.

Two minutes from the airport, at the south-west end of the lagoon, *Manihi Pearl Beach Resort* (☎ 96 42 73, or ☎ 43 16 10 in Papeete, fax 96 42 72) is a luxury resort with 41 rooms in an idyllic natural setting of coconut groves and white-sand beaches beside the magnificent lagoon. The rooms range from 30,240 CFP for a beach bungalow to 49,680 CFP for an over-water bungalow. Add 6100/8400 CFP per person for half/full board in the Poe Rava Restaurant.

Places to Eat

Apart from the guesthouses and hotels, there are hardly any other places to eat. In Paeua, the self-service *Jean-Marie*, near the marina, has good supplies. The restaurant at the *Manihi Pearl Beach Resort* has reasonable prices, especially at lunch time.

Getting There & Away

The Air Tahiti office (☎ 96 43 34, or ☎ 9 42 71 on flight days) is in Jean Marie supermarket in Paeua. On flight days it's a the airport. There are nearly daily connections with Papeete (16,500 CFP, direct or via Ahe or Rangiroa (8800 CFP). Manihi i also linked to Bora Bora, via Rangiroa three times weekly in the Bora Bora-Manih direction and weekly for Manihi-Bora Bor (23,400 CFP).

The *Mareva Nui*, *Saint Xavier Mari Stella* and *Vai-Aito* service Manihi. Loadin and unloading takes place at the Paeu wharf in the pass.

Getting Around

The only track links Taugaraufara to the air port and is about 9km long. Getting aroun the atoll requires some ingenuity! Th Manihi Pearl Beach Resort can sugges where you can rent a bicycle for around 50 CFP per day.

The airport is at the south-west end of th atoll, near the Manihi Pearl Beach Resor To get to the village you have to hitch a boa ride from the wharf next to the airport *fare* To get to the dive centre from the village you can use the Manihi Pearl Beach Resor staff shuttle, which generally leaves th Paeua marina at about 6 am. If they're going to the airport or the village, resor owners will generally take you across to th dive centre. For other points around th atoll talk to boat owners in the village.

AHE ATOLL

Situated 15km west of Manihi, Ahe wa 'discovered' by the Englishman Wilkes i 1839. Ahe's large lagoon is 20km long b 10km wide and is entered by the Tiarero (or Reianui) Pass in the west. The village o Tenukupara is on the south-west side. Th atoll (population 380) is 15km west o Manihi and is well-known to yachties.

Air Tahiti connects Ahe two to thre times weekly with Papeete (16,500 CFP) The return flight sometimes goes vi Manihi. The *Saint Xavier Maris Stella Mareva Nui* and *Vai-Aito* are ships tha service Ahe.

TAKAROA ATOLL

The atolls of Takaroa (Long Chin) and Takapoto are labelled the King George Islands on marine maps.

Rectangular Takaroa Atoll (population 990) is 27km long by 6km wide and has only one pass, in the south-west, into the lagoon. The atoll's only village, Teavaroa, is on the edge of this pass. Ninety percent of the population belongs to the Mormon church and alcohol is prohibited. There is no bank but there is a post office and a shop.

Things to See

Sleepy quietness emanates from **Teavaroa** village. There are two **marae** close to the village, but they have been neglected and all you can see is a shapeless mass of fallen rock, covered in *miki miki* bushes.

The imposing rusty **wreck** of a four-masted vessel that ran into the coral reef at the beginning of the century is 6km along the track from the airport *fare*, going in the opposite direction from the village. Takaroa's lagoon has numerous coral formations near the beach, which are wonderful for snorkelling around. Ask village kids about accompanying them when they go spear fishing.

Places to Stay

Chez Vahinerii (☎ 98 23 05) has impeccably clean rooms for 3000 CFP for one or two people. The house faces the Mormon temple and the bathroom is shared. There's also a bungalow beside the lagoon, about 800m from the airport, for 5000 CFP for two people, without meals.

Pension Poe Rangi (☎ 98 23 82, or ☎ 98 23 77 at the weather station) is on the other side of the pass, 10 minutes by boat from the village, and has bungalows with at 6000/7000 CFP half/full board, including airport transfers. It will rent kayaks and organise all sorts of activities.

Getting There & Away

Takaroa is 575km north-east of Papeete and less than 100km east of Manihi. The airport is 2.5km north-east of the village and there are at least three weekly connections with Papeete (1½ hours, 18,000 CFP) and Takapoto (4400 CFP), as well as less frequent connections to Manihi.

The *Mareva Nui* and *Saint Xavier Maris Stella* service the atoll. They draw up to the wharf in the pass.

Getting Around

The only track goes from the village to Paul Yu's pearl farm through the airport – in all about 10km. Your hosts will arrange picnics on the lagoon motu for 2500 to 3500 CFP per person. To rent a bicycle, ask at the Pension Vahinerii.

TAKAPOTO ATOLL

Takapoto (Short Chin) is 9km south of Takaroa. It is 20km long and 6km across at its widest point and doesn't have a pass. The atoll was one of the first in the Tuamotus to be used for pearl farming. Pearl farms, beaches and some archaeological remains could one day make the atoll a popular tourist attraction. Takapoto (population 610) has no bank but there is a post office.

Things to See & Do

The little village of **Fakatopatere** spreads right across the reef crown, with sandy tracks criss-crossing around a Catholic church. The atoll has a number of pearl farms and numerous idyllic **white-sand beaches** that are easily accessible by a track. In the village itself, there is a small beach close to Pimati Toti's house. Follow the track through the coconut grove until you come to the white building on the left, less than 5km from the village. Walk for 700m and turn off at the path on the left that crosses the coconut grove towards the lagoon. You'll find several fishers' *fare* and the beach of your dreams. Follow the north-east track to the end, about 9km at **Teavatika**, to a fish park built of coral blocks in a *hoa* (a shallow channel). This public park is a rare example of its kind.

The **Marae Takai** archaeological site is north-west of Fakatopatere and well hidden but it's worth the long walk. Follow the track which goes past the cemetery at the village exit for 15km. You will see a channel

FRENCH POLYNESIA

spanned by a stone bridge. Cross this bridge and immediately on the right, walk 60m along the channel towards the lagoon. Turn left for about 30m, clearing your way through *kahaiai*, miki miki bushes and coconut trees and you will come upon the three marae in a little clearing.

Places to Stay

Étienne Heuea (☎ 96 65 09) is close to the post office and has a well-equipped chalet for 4000 CFP per person per day. *Takapoto Village* (☎ 98 65 44) is on a small yellow-sand beach beside the lagoon, south-east of the village, and has a comfortable bungalow (4500 CFP per person half-board) and a room (3500 CFP).

Getting There & Away

Takapoto is 560km north-east of Papeete and less than 100km east of Manihi. The airport is just a stone's throw to the south-east of the village and there are three weekly flights, connecting Takapoto (1½ hours, 16,500 CFP) and Papeete and, on certain days, Manihi.

The *Saint Xavier Maris Stella* and *Mareva Nui* serve Takapoto. *Taporo IV* and *Aranui*, en route to the Marquesas Islands, also stop there. The transfers by whaleboat take place at the landing stage next to the Nadine shop.

Getting Around

There are two tracks from the village. The first one goes in a north-easterly direction for about 9km, to a fish park made of coral blocks. The other goes in a north-westerly direction. It's fine as far as Marae Takai, 15km out, but then reaches some uncrossable channels.

The ideal way to discover the atoll is by bicycle (500 CFP a day) or scooter (1500 to 2000 CFP). Most guesthouses organise picnics on deserted islets, reached by speedboat. Allow 2000 CFP per person.

ARUTUA ATOLL

This almost circular atoll (population 620) is nearly 25km in diameter. The lagoon waters meet the ocean through the small Porofai Pass in the east, near the village o Rautini. The village is on a motu south o the airport, half an hour away by boat.

Chez Neri (☎ 96 52 55) has two rooms a 6000 CFP per person per day with all meals plus 3000 CFP per person for round-trip air port transfers.

Arutua is about 375km north-east o Tahiti but only 30km from the easter extremity of Rangiroa. There are thre flights weekly between Papeete and Arutu (14,000 CFP) and two of the return fligh stop at Rangiroa (4400 CFP). Getting t Rautini from the airport, at the west of Mot Tenihinihi, takes half an hour by boat.

The *Saint Xavier Maris Stella*, *Marev Nui*, *Dory* and *Cobia I* serve Arutua.

KAUKURA ATOLL

Kaukura (population 380) is oval shapec measuring 50km by 14km at its wides point, with only one pass into the lagoor Kaukura, together with Tikehau, is th biggest provider of fish to the Papeete mar kets from the Tuamotus. Raitahiti village i on the north-west side of the lagoon.

Places to Stay

Pension Rekareka (☎ 96 62 40) has si rooms at 6000 CFP per person per day, ful board. There are also five bungalows o Motu Tahunapona, 15 minutes by boat fror the village. Airport transfers are included.

Getting There & Away

The airport is 2km from the village an there are twice weekly flights from Papeet (1 hour 40 minutes; 14,000 CFP) via Rangi roa (4400 CFP).

The *Saint Xavier Maris Stella*, *Marev Nui*, *Cobia I* and *Dory* have stopovers a Kaukura.

FAKARAVA

Fakarava is the second-largest atoll in th Tuamotu archipelago. The opening of permanent airstrip here in 1995 has helpe to open up this magnificent atoll to tourism Fakarava has amazing diving in the pas through the reef and the atoll is visited by several dive cruise operators.

Most of the population of 470 is in Roto-ava village at the north-eastern end, 4km east of the airport. A handful of inhabitants also live in Tetamanu village, on the edge of the southern pass.

Activities

Te Ava Nui (☎ 82 08 05) runs dives to the staggering **Garuae Pass** with its dense population of sharks, dolphins, rays, barracudas and lesser marine life.

Places to Stay

Relais Marama (☎ 98 42 25), on the ocean side of the motu at Rotoava, has rooms and bungalows at 4800/6500 CFP per person for half/full board with shared bathroom. *Pension Paparara* (☎ 98 42 40 and leave a message for M Ato Lissant) is beside the lagoon, about 5km south of the village, and has bungalows for 6500 CFP per person full board plus 1000 CFP for airport transfers.

Tetamanu Village (☎ 43 92 40, fax 42 77 70) is at the other end of the atoll, beside the Tumakohua Pass, and makes for a remote escape at 40,000 CFP per person, including all meals and activities for three days.

Getting There & Around

The airport is about 4km from the village, west towards the pass, and there are flights from Papeete (14,700 CFP) three or four times a week, via Rangiroa (4400 CFP).

The *Saint Xavier Maris Stella*, *Vai-Aito* and *Mareva Nui* serve Fakarava. *Auura'Nui 3*, whose owner also owns Tetamanu Village, stops at Tetamanu.

From Rotoava, a track goes to the southwest of the atoll for about 40km. Boat excursions are arranged by both guesthouses.

ANAA ATOLL

Anaa Atoll (population 425) is just 28km long and 5km wide, and is made up of 11 islets scattered on the reef circumference. There is no pass into the lagoon. In ancient times, Anaa was known for the ferocity of its inhabitants, who extended their domination over the northern part of the Tuamotu archipelago, pillaging the atolls they conquered.

Pension Maui Nui (☎ 98 32 75) is close to the airport and the lagoon and costs 4000/6000 CFP per person half/full board. *Pension Toku Kaiga* (☎ 98 32 69), also near the airport, has a bungalow and a *fare* with bathroom for 5500/6500 CFP half/full board.

Papeete-Anaa flights are once or twice a week and the 1 hour and 10 minute flight costs 15,000 CFP. It's also on the shipping route of the *Auura'Nui 3* and *Kura Ora*.

RAROIA ATOLL

Raroia (population 184) is east of the central Tuamotus. It was on the southern part of the Raroia reef that Thor Heyerdahl's *Kon Tiki* ran aground in 1947. Raroia is served by the *Auura'Nui 3* and *Kura Ora*.

PUKA PUKA ATOLL

Described by Magellan in 1521 and by Le Marie in 1616, who gave it the name of Houden Eiland (Island of Dogs), this atoll (population 175), at the easternmost boundary of the Tuamotus, has a small lagoon in the process of filling in and drying up. The *Auura'Nui 3* and *Kura Ora* serve the atoll.

NUKUTAVAKE

The lagoon of Nukutavake (population 190) has been entirely filled by sand and limestone particles from the external reef.

Pension Afou (☎ 98 72 53), on the seashore in the village of Tavananui, 1km from the airport, has three local-style bungalows at 7000 CFP per person full board.

Air Tahiti serves Nukutavake via Hao at least once a week (27,500 CFP).

HAO ATOLL

Established as an administrative centre for the Moruroa nuclear testing, Hao had a population of up to 5000 during the testing era of the 1960s (now it's 1300). Hao is the air traffic centre for the southern Tuamotus.

In Otepa, *Chez Amélie* (☎ 97 03 42, fax 97 02 41) has four rooms with bathrooms at 5500 CFP per person, or 6500 CFP with air-con.

Air Tahiti fly Papeete-Hao (2 hours 20 minutes; 24,000 CFP) three or four times a week via Anaa or Makemo. There are also connections to Takume, Fangatau, Fakahina, Takapoto, Tureia, Vahitahi, Nukutavake, Pukarua and Reao.

The ships *Auura'Nui 3* and *Kura Ora* serve Hao.

MORUROA ATOLL

Moruroa (Mururoa) Atoll, 1250km southeast of Tahiti, will be forever synonymous with nuclear testing. Also see Ecology & Environment in the Facts about the South Pacific chapter.

During the tests it was equipped with ultra-modern electricity production installations, a desalinisation plant and an airport which handled large transport planes. Restaurants, cinemas, sports grounds and an internal radio and TV channel were there for the military staff. Today there's just a small contingent of French legionnaires.

Marquesas Islands

Te Henua Enana (The Land of Men) is the Marquesans' name for their archipelago. This is the most northerly archipelago of French Polynesia. Only six of the 15 Marquesas Islands are inhabited (total population 8000) and travelling within the archipelago, which stretches 350km north-west to southeast, can be difficult. The islands are divided into northern and southern groups.

Unlike the high Society Islands, these islands have no sheltering reefs or lagoons to soften the assault of the waves. As a result, necks, needles and peaks towering to more than 1000m stand side by side with high plateaus bordered by steep cliffs. This sharp relief is ridged with deep valleys covered with luxuriant tropical vegetation. There's a wealth of archaeological remains, many of which are still to be catalogued. Horse riding is a popular local activity but the nono, an incredibly annoying small, biting, fly, spoils the fun of a visit to the beach.

History

The Marquesas, with the Societies were among the first islands in this region to be

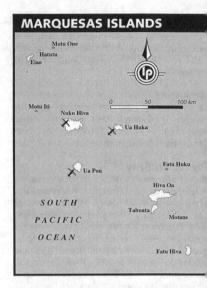

MARQUESAS ISLANDS

Motu One
Hatutu
Eiao

Motu Iti
Nuku Hiva
Ua Huka

Ua Pou
Fatu Huku

Hiva Oa
Tahuata
Motane

SOUTH
PACIFIC
OCEAN

Fatu Hiva

0   50   100 km

settled and served as a dispersal point to the rest of Polynesia. There are numerous archaeological remains that have survived to modern times, including *tohua* (meeting places), *me'ae* (the Marquesan equivalent of marae), *pae pae* (paved floors or platforms) and tiki.

The Marquesas' isolation was broken in 1595, when Mendaña sighted Fatu Hiva and christened the island group in honour of the viceroy of Peru.

The French took possession of Tahuata in 1842 but the Marquesas were quickly marginalised in favour of Papeete for geographic, economic and strategic reasons. Upon contact with western influences, the foundations of Marquesan society collapsed. Whalers brought alcohol, firearms and syphilis, while the colonial administration and missionaries paid little attention to the ancestral values of the Marquesan people. The population fell from an estimated 18,000 in 1842 to 2100 in 1926.

This century, the experiences of the painter Paul Gauguin drew world attention to the Marquesas. More recently, the development of transport and telecommunications infrastructures have helped to lessen the archipelago's isolation, while archaeological discoveries have underlined the significance of Marquesan civilisation.

Activities
The Marquesas offer excursions to historic and archaeological sites, on foot or by 4WD. There are also opportunities to shop for high quality crafts, to dive at Nuku Hiva, and on a number of islands there are walking and horse riding possibilities.

Accommodation
There are several good hotels on Nuku Hiva and Hiva Oa, particularly in Taiohae and Atuona, the main towns. More frequent flights and cheaper fares should spur more hotel room construction. In Ua Huka, Ua Pou, Tahuata and Fatu Hiva there are guesthouses, rooms in homes and sometimes independent bungalows.

Shopping
Marquesan handicrafts enjoy an excellent reputation, particularly sculpture, for which a school has been opened at Taiohae on Nuku Hiva. Tiki, pestles, umete (bowls), adzes, spears, clubs, fishhooks and other work is done in miro or tou wood, bone or volcanic stone. You will also find necklaces, Marquesan *umu hei* and the famous tapa cloth of Fatu Hiva, made from beaten bark and decorated with traditional designs. In most villages, there are small craft *fare* with items for exhibition and sale but they may only be open when requested or, of course, when the *Aranui* is in port. Bring enough cash – you cannot pay with credit cards.

Getting There and Away
Air There are direct flights between Papeete and the Marquesas and, once weekly, a direct flight from Rangiroa, in the Tuamotus, to Nuku Hiva. There are airports at Nuku Hiva, Hiva Oa, Ua Huka and Ua Pou. There are also flights from Papeete to Hiva Oa, while Nuku Hiva is linked three times weekly to Ua Pou and once weekly to Ua Huka. It takes about three hours to fly from Tahiti to the Marquesas. Don't forget that

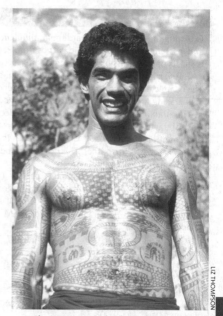

In the Marquesas Islands, traditional-style tattoos are still proudly worn.

LIZ THOMPSON

FRENCH POLYNESIA

the Marquesas are half an hour ahead of Tahiti time.

Boat The *Taporo IV* and *Aranui* serve the Marquesas from Papeete via Rangiroa and/or Takapoto in the Tuamotus. The *Aranui* does about 15 trips a year while the *Taporo IV* departs every two weeks. Taiohae, Hakahau and Atuona are the only places with wharfs where the ships can actually dock, at other ports unloading is done with whaleboats.

Getting Around
Getting around the Marquesas is difficult, whether by sea or land. The valleys are isolated from each other, making it virtually impossible to do island tours by road, and only the main towns or villages have sealed roads. Some villages have no landing stage and the sea is often rough, making landings difficult. The introduction of helicopter shuttles within the northern and southern

The Aranui

Exploring the Marquesas aboard the *Aranui* (Great Path) is an excellent adventure. The cargo-and-passenger vessel does 16-day trips from Papeete to the Marquesas and Tuamotus. Cargo is still its primary mission – passengers are a secondary consideration – but that's half the fun.

The ship is quite comfortable – there's a mini-swimming pool, good food and plenty of wine. The complete cruise costs from US$1762 (depending on the cabin). At each stop, while the ship is unloading and loading, passengers make excursions ashore which are included in the tariff.

The *Aranui* also carries local islanders on deck class. Visitors are dissuaded from using this class of travel, but it is usually possible for short trips. Contact the tour guides at the stopovers and count on about 20,000 CFP from Tahiti to the Marquesas or 3000 CFP from one island in the Marquesas to another. This doesn't include meals (so don't try and join the other tourist passengers!) or excursions.

Bookings are necessary and peak periods (July-August and December) are booked out months in advance. Contact your travel agent or go to the shipowner, the Compagnie Polynésienne de Transport Maritime (CPTM; ☎ 42 62 40 or ☎ 43 76 60, fax 43 48 89, aranui@mail.pf), BP 220, Papeete. The CPTM is open Monday to Friday, 7.30 am to 5 pm (closed for lunch) and is at the entrance to the Motu Uta port zone. Take le truck No 3 from the city hall. You can find out more about the *Aranui* on its website (www.aranui.com).

In France contact Quotidien Voyages (☎ 01-41 92 08 30, fax 46 24 34 88), 103 Ave Charles-de-Gaulle, 92200 Neuilly. In the USA contact CPTM (☎ 650-574 2575, cptm@aranui.com), 2028 El Camino Real South, Suite B, San Mateo, CA 94403.

MANOLO MYLONAS

---

groups has improved inter-island transport, which was previously only possible with Air Tahiti or by irregular passing boats.

Island to Island Nuku Hiva in the north and Hiva Oa in the south are the hub islands; travel between the two is regular and reliable, but further afield can be more difficult. The difficulty of inter-island transport in the Marquesas is one of the major obstacles to tourism development. Visitors should definitely not expect things to go to schedule. There are Air Tahiti flights, helicopters, *bonitiers* (old whaleboats) and the cargo ships *Taporo IV* and *Aranui*.

Around the Islands Land transport requires a 4WD because the roads are rough and the terrain spectacularly steep and divided by numerous valleys. There's no public transport and helicopters are the main means of getting around the island. By sea, bonitiers and speedboats usually link the villages much more rapidly than 4WDs.

NUKU HIVA
● pop 2372 ● area 340 sq km

The main island of the northern group and the largest in the archipelago, Nuku Hiva (also known as The Chevrons) is the administrative and economic capital of the

Marquesas, outshining its traditional rival, Hiva Oa, in the southern group. Settlement is concentrated in Taiohae on the south coast, Hatiheu on the north coast and Taipivai in the south-east. Hamlets such as Anaho, Hooumi, Aakapa and Pua are home to only a handful of inhabitants.

Orientation

Nuku Hiva was formed from two volcanoes, stacked one on top of the other to form two concentric calderas. The top of the main caldera forms a jagged framework that surrounds the Toovii plateau. The highest point is Mt Tekao (1224m). To the south of this plateau, the broken-mouthed caldera of the secondary volcano reaches its highest point at Mt Muake (864m) and outlines a huge natural amphitheatre. At its foot is a vast natural harbour, around which curls Taiohae, the main town on the island. Deep bays cut into the south and east coasts. On the north coast, erosion by wind and rain has shaped impressive basalt *aiguilles* (needles).

Information

The tourist office (☎/fax 92 03 73) in Taiohae is by the town hall. Rose Corser, head of the Keikahanui Nuku Hiva Pearl Lodge, has established a small museum dedicated to Marquesan culture and has several explanatory booklets. The Banque Socredo (☎ 92 03 63) is on the seafront. The post office (OPT) is on the eastern side of the bay, opposite the police station. For laundry inquire at d'Archipels Croisières at the marina or the Marquesas Dive Centre.

Around the Island

The main centre is **Taiohae**, which hugs Taiohae Bay for nearly 3.5km. Climbing the Meau Valley for less than a kilometre you reach a restored **me'ae**, with a small contemporary tiki figure. To the west of the town stands the **Herman Melville memorial**. Approaching the centre, 700m further along, is the **Piki Vehine Pae Pae**, also known as Theme, an open-air museum in the form of an *ah* (traditional house).

The summit of **Mt Muake** (864m) can be reached on foot or by 4WD along a picturesque track. At an average height of 800m the **Toovii Plateau**, which you cross by taking the Taiohae-Terre Déserte (airport) track, looks surprisingly like the mountains of Bavaria.

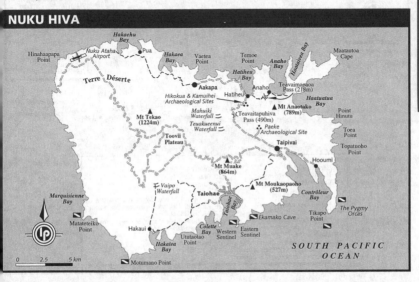

NUKU HIVA

Map showing: Hakaehu Bay, Hinahaapapa Point, Nuku Ataha Airport, Pua, Hakaea Bay, Vaetea Point, Temoe Point, Anaho Bay, Huaaiveet Bay, Maatautoa Cape, Terre Déserte, Hatiheu Bay, Teavaimaoaoa Pass (218m), Aakapa, Hikokua & Kamuihei Archaeological Sites, Hatiheu, Anaho, Haatuatua Bay, Mahuiki Waterfall, Mt Anaotako (789m), Point Hinutu, Mt Tekao (1224m), Teavaitapuhiva Pass (490m), Teuakueenui Waterfall, Paeke Archaeological Site, Toovii Plateau, Taipivai, Toea Point, Topatuoho Point, Hooumi, Mt Muake (864m), Vaipo Waterfall, Taiohae, Mt Moukaopaoho (527m), Contrôleur Bay, The Pygmy Orcas, Marquisienne Bay, Taiohae Bay, Tikapo Point, Matateteiko Point, Hakaui, Ututaotao Point, Colette Bay, Western Sentinel, Eastern Sentinel, Ekamako Cave, Hakatea Bay, Motumano Point, SOUTH PACIFIC OCEAN

0   2.5   5 km

About 8km west of Taiohae, the **Hakaui Valley** forms a great gash in the basalt platform. Vertical walls rise to nearly 800m on either side of the river and the **Vaipo Waterfall**, one of the highest in the world at 350m, flows vertically into a basin. Almost uninhabited today, a paved road, which was once an **ancient royal way**, goes up the valley following the river past pae pae, tohua and some tiki hidden behind a tangle of vegetation. From Taiohae, the valley can be reached by speedboat (about 20 minutes), on foot or on horseback by a 12km bridleway. The path includes stretches of the ancient paved royal way. When you return to Hakaui Bay walk 100m east to the magnificent Hakatea Beach.

Scottish writer Robert Louis Stevenson succumbed to the charm of **Hatiheu** in the north of the island, 12km from Taipivai and 28km from Taiohae. The town's focal point is the wooden church, and the tiny town hall on the seafront houses a small **museum**

with a collection of traditional Marquesa artefacts. From Taipivai, follow the mai road inland and west. The track deteriorate as it climbs to the **Teavaitapuhiva Pas** (490m), with magnificent views of Hatihe Bay and, on the left, the waterfalls o Teuakueenui and Mahuiki. Shortly befor Hatiheu is the **Hikokua archaeological site** where modern tiki have been added to th old ones and the vast **Kamuihei & Tahaki archaeological site**.

Taipivai lies 16km north-east of Taiohae At the eastern end of the village the rive rushes into Contrôleur Bay. Allow 1½ hour by 4WD to reach Taipivai from Taiohae From the village take the road toward Hatiheu for 1.5km to the turn-off where steep 20 to 30 minute walk takes you to th **Paeke archaeological site**.

The charming hamlet of **Hooumi**, sur rounded by luxuriant vegetation, is abou 4km east of Taipivai. The village has a pic turesque small timber church and there's a

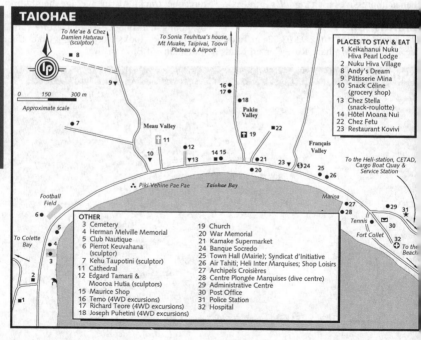

TAIOHAE

To Me'ae & Chez Damien Haturau (sculptor)
To Sonia Teuhitua's house, Mt Muake, Taipivai, Toovii Plateau & Airport

Approximate scale
0   150   300 m

Meau Valley

Pakiu Valley

Français Valley

To the Heli-station, CETAD, Cargo Boat Quay & Service Station

Piki Vehine Pae Pae   Taiohae Bay

Football Field

Marina

To Colette Bay

Tennis
Fort Collet
To the Beach

PLACES TO STAY & EAT
1 Keikahanui Nuku Hiva Pearl Lodge
2 Nuku Hiva Village
8 Andy's Dream
9 Pâtisserie Mina
10 Snack Céline (grocery shop)
13 Chez Stella (snack-roulotte)
14 Hôtel Moana Nui
22 Chez Fetu
23 Restaurant Kovivi

OTHER
3 Cemetery
4 Herman Melville Memorial
5 Club Nautique
6 Pierrot Keuvahana (sculptor)
7 Kehu Taupotini (sculptor)
11 Cathedral
12 Edgard Tamarii & Mooroa Hutia (sculptors)
15 Maurice Shop
16 Temo (4WD excursions)
17 Richard Teore (4WD excursions)
18 Joseph Puhetini (4WD excursions)
19 Church
20 War Memorial
21 Kamake Supermarket
24 Banque Socredo
25 Town Hall (Mairie); Syndicat d'Initiative
26 Air Tahiti; Heli Inter Marquises; Shop Loisirs
27 Archipels Croisières
28 Centre Plongée Marquises (dive centre)
29 Administrative Centre
30 Post Office
31 Police Station
32 Hospital

tunning, but nono-plagued, white-sand beach opposite one of the two inlets of Contrôleur Bay.

Anaho can be reached by speedboat from Hatiheu in less than 10 minutes or on foot along a picturesque track. It's about a 45 minute walk to reach Anaho Beach. At the Teavaimaoaoa Pass (218m) there's an unbroken view over Anaho Bay and the descent, right through the middle of a huge coconut plantation, is quite steep. **Aakapa**, west of Hatiheu, has a superb natural setting and can be reached by the path from Hatiheu or by speedboat.

Activities

Centre Plongée Marquises (☎/fax 92 00 88) in Taiohae is the dive centre for the Marquesas.

Visibility is not fantastic but encounters with dolphins, hammerhead sharks and many other species more than compensate for those who are keen on diving. Popular sites include **Pygmy Orcas**, **Tikapo**, **Sentry of the Hammers**, **Ekamako Cave**, **Motumano Point** and **Matateiko Point**.

There are good walking tracks all over the island including the hikes to the Hakaui waterfall, Colette Bay and to Anaho from Hatiheu. From Taiohae, it is easy to reach Colette Bay on horseback. Other popular rides are to the Hakaui waterfall, along the track between Hatiheu and Aakapa and on the Taiohae ridgeline. In Taiohae ask at your hotel or contact Patrice Tamarii at Le Ranch (☎ 92 06 35) or Louis Teikiteetini (☎ 92 02 37). In Hatiheu contact Yvonne Katupa at the Chez Yvonne guesthouse.

Experienced parasailers might want to have a go on this magnificently mountainous island – there's a *parapente* club in Taiohae. Phone Roland (☎ 92 05 30) for more details. Héli Inter Marquises operates scenic 20-minute flights for a minimum of five people at 14,500 CFP each.

Pua Excursions, run by Monsieur Taupotini (☎ 92 02 94, fax 92 01 35) offers three and four-day tours with English-speaking guides. Alternatively contact André Teikiteetini of Andy's Dream (☎ 92 00 80) in Taiohae.

Places to Stay

Taiohae *Chez Fetu* (☎ 92 03 66, BP 22, Taiohae, Nuku Hiva) is the only good budget place with simple rooms for 2000 CFP per person. It's 200m along the small path that starts from the west side of the Kamake store. Right in the centre of Taiohae on the seafront, the more upmarket *Hôtel Moana Nui* (☎ 92 03 30, fax 92 00 02) has rooms at 5000/5500 CFP a single/double with breakfast. Credit cards are accepted. At the western end of Taiohae Bay, the *Nuku Hiva Village* (☎ 92 01 94, fax 92 05 97) has 15 sparkling-clean traditional *fare* for 7020/8100 CFP. Credit cards are accepted.

The luxurious *Keikahanui Nuku Hiva Pearl Lodge* (☎ 92 03 82, fax 92 00 74, or in Papeete ☎ 43 90 04, fax 43 17 86, info@spmhotels.pf) overlooks the western extremity of Taiohae Bay. It has air-con bungalows for 28,080 to 37,800 CFP and a swimming pool.

Andy's Dream (☎/fax 92 00 80) is a little out of the centre and has bungalows for 2500 CFP per person with breakfast.

Around the Island In Taipivai, the riverside *Chez Martine Haiti* (☎ 92 01 19, fax 92 05 34), about 400m past the church, has rooms and a charming bungalow at 2000 CFP per person, including breakfast. Give several days warning, as not many people come here. Hatiheu has the excellent *Chez Yvonne* (☎ 92 02 97, fax 92 01 28) with small local-style bungalows for 2600 CFP per person with breakfast.

Places to Eat

There are shops in several villages. Taiohae has a roulotte permanently stationed on the waterfront, attached to the small *Chez Stella fare*, and *Pâtisserie Mina* (☎ 92 00 86) does excellent pizzas and other light meals.

Restaurant Kovivi (☎ 92 03 85), hidden by lush vegetation beside the Banque Socredo, adds tropical influences to classic French cuisine. It's closed Sunday night and all of July. The restaurants at the *Hôtel Moana Nui* and the *Nuku Hiva Village* are worth trying and there's a restaurant at the *Keikahanui Nuku Hiva Pearl Lodge*.

The airport at Terre Déserte has a snack bar. At Taipivai, try the restaurant at *Chez Martine Haiti* or at Hatiheu the *Hinakonui* restaurant at Chez Yvonne, which has a deservedly good reputation.

Shopping
In Taiohae, some curios and pareu are on sale at the Kanahau Shop and Shop Loisirs. Several important sculptors work on Nuku Hiva. In Taiohae visit Pierrot Keuvahana (☎ 92 06 14), Edgar Tamarii (☎ 92 01 67) or Mooroa Hutia, who lives nearby. The best-known sculptor is Damien Haturau (☎ 92 05 56), who lives in the Meau Valley.

Marcel Taupotini (☎ 92 02 42), known as Kehu, lives in the Hoata Valley.

Getting There & Away
Air Nuku Hiva is the flight hub of the Marquesas. Air Tahiti's office (☎ 92 03 41) shifts to the airport (☎ 92 01 45) on days when there is a flight. There are five to seven Papeete-Nuku Hiva flights (26,500 CFP) a week, one of which stops at Rangiroa (Tuamotus) while flying in the Papeete-Nuku Hiva direction only. Papeete to the Marquesas takes three hours.

Within the Marquesas there are flights from Nuku Hiva to Hiva Oa (8800 CFP), Ua Huka (5100 CFP) and Ua Pou (5100 CFP). Frequencies vary but all these flights connect to/from Papeete.

Héli Inter Marquises (☎/fax 92 02 17, or ☎ 92 00 54 at the heli-station, or ☎ 92 04 40 at the airport) provides regular shuttle services to Ua Pou, the 15 minute trip costs 12,000 CFP.

Boat In Taiohae, Xavier Curvat, the director of the dive centre (☎/fax 92 00 88) on the marina quay, operates a ferry to Ua Pou twice weekly for 5000 CFP one way. Laurent (Teiki) Falchetto (☎ 92 05 78) is also in Taiohae and has a bonitier which can be chartered. You can also try the owner of the speedboat *Dina*. The *Aranui* and the *Taporo IV* serve Nuku Hiva and they dock at the end of the bay in Taiohae. The *Aranui* goes to Taipivai and Hatiheu, as well as Taiohae.

Getting Around
A network of tracks link the airport, Taiohae, Taipivai, Hooumi, Hatiheu and Aakapa. It's only 18km from Taiohae to Nuku Ataha airport at Terre Déserte but it takes at least two hours along the bumping, winding track. If it has been raining it's wise to ensure you're being picked up either by your accommodation or by a 4WD taxi: try Joseph Puhetini (☎ 92 03 47), Maxime or Sonia Teuhitua (☎ 92 02 22) or Temo (☎ 92 04 13). The airport-to-Taiohae run costs 4000 CFP by day or 5000 CFP by night per person. Alternatively take the helicopter (eight minutes; 7000 CFP).

4WDs can be rented with or without a driver. From Taiohae count on 3000 to 5000 CFP to Muake, 12,000 CFP to Taipivai, 20,000 CFP to Hatiheu, 25,000 CFP to Aakapa. In Taipivai contact Henri Taata (☎ 92 01 36); in Hatiheu contact Yvonne Katupa (see Places to Stay). Count on 6000 CFP between Hatiheu and Aakapa. Charles Mombaerts at the Hôtel Moana Nui has a two-seat Suzuki available for 9000 CFP a day – good value if you're solo.

The owner of the *Dina* (☎ 92 04 78), Léonard Hokaupoko (☎ 92 00 16) and Francis Falchetto (☎ 92 01 51) have speedboats. Through Yvonne Katupa at Chez Yvonne, it costs 6000 CFP to make the Hatiheu-Anaho crossing or 7000 CFP for Hatiheu-Aakapa.

UA HUKA
● pop 571   ● area 83 sq km
Ua Huka is 50km east of Nuku Hiva and 56km north-east of Ua Pou, and for some reason it's rarely visited. The Vaikivi Plateau occupies the northern edge of the island, while the island's three villages – Vaipaee, Hane and Hokatu – nestle around the edges of steep-sided valleys on the south coast. Mt Hitikau (855m) is the high point. Ua Huka is the driest island in all French Polynesia and the desolate scenery is accentuated by the free-ranging herds of semi-wild horses, hence the nickname 'Island of Horses'.

The island boasts archaeological treasures, such as the ancient Hane tiki and the Vaikivi petroglyphs, and the Marquesas' first museum devoted entirely to archaeology was established in Vaipaee.

Vaipaee

The island's main town is at the end of aptly named Invisible Bay. When the *Aranui* comes in, it manoeuvres in a space the size of a pocket handkerchief and ties up to the rock face with hawsers. The **museum** in the centre of Vaipaee has great symbolic value for the heritage-proud Marquesans. Entry is free but donations are appreciated. The **arboretum** offers a striking contrast between the wealth of plants and the relative aridity of the island.

Around the Island

Hane was said to be the first Polynesian settlement in the Marquesas and has a small marine museum. Less than 30 minutes walk from the village, the **Meiaute archaeological site** is one of the major attractions on Ua Huka, with tiki, pae pae and me'ae. Peaceful **Hokatu** is about 3km east of Hane in a sheltered bay. Tupapau (ghosts) are said to haunt **Footstep Cave**, slightly west of Point Tekeho, between Vaipaee and Haavei Bay. Thousands of *kaveka* (sooty terns) have taken up residence on the islands of **Hemeni** and **Teuaua**, near the south-west point of Ua Huka. They lay a huge number of eggs every day, which the islands' inhabitants regularly gather.

Ua Huka has the most beautiful beaches in the Marquesas, although the sandflies spoil the pleasure. Accessible by speedboat or 4WD, **Manihina Beach**, between Vaipaee and the airport, is fringed with fine white sand. **Hatuana Beach** is in the west of the island; there are petroglyphs nearby. **Haavei Beach** is a beautiful inlet but ask the owners, who live on the coconut plantation, for permission before you plunge in. **Motu Papa**, a popular picnic and snorkelling spot, is just offshore from the airport, between Vaipaee and Hane but you have to swim ashore. The little-visited **Vaikivi petroglyphs** site on the Vaikivi Plateau is worth the detour, if only for the walk or horse ride to get there. The well-restored petroglyphs are engraved on a grey stone.

Activities

Horses are an important part of activities on Ua Huka and there are varied itineraries. The most popular is the ride from Vaipaee to Hane, passing the arboretum, airport and wind-swept arid plateaus before reaching the cliff road, which plunges down towards Hane. Ask at your accommodation about where to find horse owners. A ride typically costs 5000 CFP, with guide.

It's a beautiful three hour walk inland to the Vaikivi petroglyphs from Vaipaee or Hane. The path climbs the long face of the ancient volcano caldera. Take a guide, as it's a long way and the trail is indistinct; a guide will charge from 3000 to 5000 CFP. Ask at your accommodation, or contact Léonard Teatiu or Napoléon at Vaipaee town hall, Gilles Brown at Vaipaee or Patrick Teiki at Hokatu. The coastal route, between Haavei to the west and Hokatu to the east, offers spectacular views and is worth doing.

Places to Stay & Eat

Considering the small number of visitors, Ua Huka has a surprising number of guesthouses. In Vaipaee, *Chez Alexis Scallamera* (☎ 92 60 19) has doubles for 1500 CFP per person including airport transfers. *Chez Christelle* (☎ 92 61 08) is also 1500 CFP per person with airport transfers. At the exit from the village towards Hane the *Mana Tupuna Village* (☎/fax 92 60 08, manatupuna@marquises.com) has three local-style bungalows for 5500/10,000 CFP for one/two people with half-board.

In Hane *Auberge Hitikau* (☎ 92 60 68) has simple but clean rooms for 2000/3000 CFP a single/double. In Hokatu *Chez Maurice & Delphine* (☎/fax 92 60 55, delphine@marquises.com) has rooms for 1200 CFP per person, and two more private bungalows perched above the edge of town for 2000/3000 CFP. In Haavei Bay, about 5km west of Vaipaee, *Chez Joseph Lichtlé* (☎ 92 60 72) has various bungalows and rooms at 5500 CFP full board, including transfers to the airport.

The food at the guesthouses is good and includes Marquesan specialities. The only true restaurant is the *Auberge Hitikau* in Hane.

Getting There & Away

There's a weekly flight from Nuku Hiva (5100 CFP), with connections to Papeete (27,500 CFP). Air Tahiti has an office in Vaipaee (☎ 92 60 85) and at the airport (☎ 92 60 44).

In Hokatu, Maurice Rootuehine and Paul Teatiu (☎ 92 60 88) have speedboats and can take you to Ua Pou or Nuku Hiva. The *Aranui* and the *Taporo IV* serve Ua Huka.

Getting Around

A 13km track links Vaipaee to Hokatu via Hane, the stretch from Vaipaee to Hane is surfaced. Haavei is also accessible by the track from Vaipaee. The airport is on a dry plateau, next to the road between Vaipaee and Hane above Motu Papa. Transfers are usually included in guesthouse charges.

For 4WD rentals (10,000 CFP per day with driver) in Vaipaee contact Alexis Scallamera at the guesthouse of the same name or Jean-Baptiste Brown (☎ 92 60 23). In Haavei, the Lichtlé's have a 4WD. In Hane, contact Céline Fournier at the Auberge Hitikau; in Hokatu, contact Chez Maurice & Delphine. For bonitier rentals (10,000 CFP a day) contact the Fournier family in Vaipaee, Céline Fournier in Hane and Maurice Rootuehine in Hokatu.

UA POU

• pop 2013   • area 125 sq km

Hakahau, Ua Pou's main settlement, is home to most of the population. A few villages nestled in the steep-sided valleys are dotted along the east and west coasts. Ua Pou is noted for its culture and arts. The island was the site of an ancient settlement, estimated to have been established around 150 BC, and fascinating archaeological remains can be seen in the Hakamoui and Hohoi valleys.

Information

Rosita Teikitutoua (☎ 92 53 36) is the head of the tourist office. The Banque Socredo (☎ 92 53 63) is in the Hakahau town hall.

The post office is to the west of the bay. Restaurant-Pension Pukuéé will do laundry.

Around the Island

The recently built stone-and-timber Catholic church in the south of Hakahau houses some noteworthy sculptures by local artisans. The admirably restored Tenei pae pae in the middle of the village is a platform of massive stone blocks supporting a shelter of plant material.

Charming Hakahetau is noted for its red church tower near the waterfront. A 15km track snakes between the bare plateaus of the island's north-west, and along the section between Hakahau and Aneou airport you will see wild horses and goats on either side of the road. In the background, due south, the slender profile of Mt Oave (1203m) appears, while in the north you can make out the contours of Nuku Hiva.

The tiny end-of-the-world village of Haakuti is the terminus of the 22km track

UA POU

SOUTH PACIFIC OCEAN

0   2.5   5 km

Hakanai Bay
Aneou Airport
Hatukoemo Point
Tepapaki Point
Hakahetau
Hakahau
Anahoa Beach
Motu Mokohe
Panahu Point
Haakuti
Mt Poutemoka (683m)
Matatihotea Point
Vaiehu Bay
Mt Oave (1203m)
Hakamoui Valley
Archaeological Site
Poava Point
Hakamaii
Hohoi
Tekotake Point
Hikeu
Paaukoheputa Point
Hakaohoka Archaeological Site
Hakataō
Mt Tekataihiko (433m)
Motu Papati
Motu Tamuko
Motu Takaae
Motu Tehuaki
Motu Oa

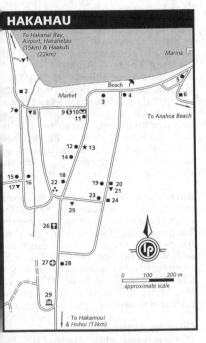

HAKAHAU

PLACES TO STAY & EAT		9	Banque Socredo
1	Snack Vehine		Town Hall (Mairie);
2	Tepano Kohumoe-	10	Post Office
	tini	12	Grocery Shop &
6	Restaurant-Pension		Boutique
	Pukuéé	13	Police Station
8	Snack-Pâtisserie	14	Eugène Hapipi
	Vaitiare		(sculptor)
11	Chez Marguerite	15	William (sculptor)
	Dordillon's	16	Aimé Kohumoetini
17	Snack Guéranger		(sculptor)
20	Pension Vehine	18	Grocery Shop
21	Snack Vehine	19	Joseph B Shop
24	Chez Samuel &	22	Tenei Pae Pae
	Jeanne-Marie		(archaeological
25	Chez Rosalie		site)
		23	Boutique; Air Tahiti
OTHER		26	Church
3	College	27	Medical Centre
4	CETAD	28	Fara Shop
5	Fare Artisanal	29	Museum
7	Honey for Sale		

from Hakahau. **Hakamaii**, with its one street, is only accessible by boat – a difficult manoeuvre at times, as visitors have to reach the shore by tiny pirogue. The facade of the town's stone church, facing the ocean, has unusual yellow, blue and red painted wooden panels. Minute **Hakatao** is the most remote place on the whole island and is accessible by boat or by the track from Hohoi.

Picturesque little **Hohoi** in the south-east of the island is 13km from Hakahau and has two pae pae and a curious pagoda-shaped church. The famous flowering pebbles of Hohoi, pieces of phonolite which have crystallised to form amber-coloured flower shapes, can be found on the beach.

The **Hakamoui Valley archaeological site** includes pae pae, bas reliefs and some tiki. From Hakahau take the road to Hohoi for about 3km, take the left fork descending eastwards towards the ocean and a kilometre further on, on the right and set back

from the track, is a pae pae. The **Hakaohoka Valley archaeological site** is in the southeast of the island running back 2km from Hohoi Bay. There's a map of the site on the pebbly beach at Hohoi where you should pay 1000 CFP to the site custodian.

Ua Pou has some good beaches but bring repellent for the accursed sandflies. Whitesand **Anahoa Beach** is 25 minutes walk east of Hakahau. **Hakanai Bay** is a popular picnic spot called Plage aux Requins (Shark Beach). The black-sand **Puamau Beach** is popular with young surfers.

You can rent horses from Francis Aka (☎ 92 51 83) or, in Hakahetau, from Tony Tereino or Étienne Hokaupoko (see Places to Stay). There are many hiking possibilities, including simply following the tracks from one village to another. If you intend to leave the tracks it's advisable to take a guide.

Places to Stay

Hélène and Doudou, who run the *Restaurant-Pension Pukuéé* (☎/fax 92 50 83) in Hakahau, are well-known to the yachties who anchor in the bay. They have singles/doubles for 3000/5500 CFP. *Chez Marguerite Dordillon* (☎ 92 51 36) has well-equipped rooms for a very reasonable 2000/3000 CFP. *Pension Vehine (☎ 92 53 21)* costs 2000/3000 CFP and for a meal you only have a 20m walk to Snack Vehine.

Chez Samuel & Jeanne-Marie (☎ 92 53 16) is nearby and run by the same family. A straightforward room is 4500 CFP per person with all meals. Towards the western end of Hakahau Bay *Tepano Kohumoetini (☎ 92 53 88, BP 61, Hakahau)* is comfortable enough and costs 2000 CFP per person per day.

In Hakahetau, Étienne Hokaupoko, owns *Pension Vaekehu (☎ 92 51 03, BP 120, Hakahetau)*; he speaks good English and is a font of local knowledge. Rooms cost 2000 CFP per person. You can also stay with sculptor Apataroma Hikutini for 1000 CFP per person, possibly the cheapest *guesthouse* in French Polynesia.

There's no official guesthouse at Hakamaii but check with Agnè Huuti in the *house* overlooking the church, near the waterfront.

Places to Eat

The only real eating places are in Hakahau. In the other villages, you can go to a guesthouse or make do with a few provisions from the *shops* and *grocers*. Hakahau has a couple of shops and *Snack Guéranger*, which is more of a grocer's but also sells a few reasonably priced takeaways. *Snack-Pâtisserie Vaitiare* is open at lunch time and in the evening.

Chez Rosalie (☎ 92 51 77) only opens when the *Aranui* is in port but its Marquesan feast (3000 CFP) is definitely worth trying. The *Chez Adrienne* snack bar *(☎ 92 53 60)* has a relaxed family atmosphere. *Snack Vehine (☎ 92 53 21 or ☎ 92 50 63)* is open for lunch Monday to Saturday and for dinner on demand. The owners of the Restaurant-Pension Pukuéé have a covered *terrace restaurant* looking out over the seafront and the quay and do great Marquesan cuisine.

Shopping

Many of the region's most respected artisans come from Ua Pou. In Hakahau, contact Alfred Hatuuku (☎ 92 52 39), William

Aka (☎ 92 53 90), Eugene Hapipi (☎ 92 5 28 at his sister's, in the neighbouring house or Marcel Bruneau (☎ 92 50 02).

Getting There & Away

Air The Air Tahiti office (☎ 92 53 41) is i Hakahau, or at Aneou airport (☎ 92 51 08 on flight days. There's a weekly flight t Nuku Hiva (5100 CFP one way) with con nections from there to Papeete (26,50 CFP) and Hiva Oa (8800 CFP). Héli Inte Marquises, based in Nuku Hiva, has regu lar Taiohae-Hakahau-Taiohae services an the 15 minute flight costs 12,000 CFP.

Boat In Hakahau, contact Joseph Tamari (☎ 92 52 14). He charges 40,000 CFP t charter his bonitier (for up to 10 people) fo Taiohae, and the Hakahau communal boni tier (☎ 92 53 17) can also be hired at thi rate. Manu Guéranger (☎ 92 51 49), at th snack bar of the same name, charges 45,00 CFP. The *Aranui* and *Taporo IV* serve U Pou. Sailing from Hakahau the *Aranui* als stops at Hakahetau.

Getting Around

On the east cost, a track connects Hakahau with Hohoi (13km) and continues t Hakatao on the west coast. On the wes coast, Hakahau is connected to Hakahetau (15km), Haakuti (22km) and Hakamaii. The track doesn't make a complete circuit of the island but there is a plan to extend the track from Hakamaii to Hakatao. Aneou airport is about 10km west of Hakahau, and if you've booked accommodation your hosts will collect you. Otherwise it costs 500 to 1000 CFP per person for the transfer.

Transport in a 4WD can be arranged in Hakahau with Patricia Guéranger (☎ 92 51 49) at Snack Guéranger, Rudla Klima (☎ 92 53 86) or the owners of the Pension-Restaurant Pukuéé. In Hakahetau, get in touch with Étienne Hokaupoko or Apataroma Hikutini.

Boats can be hired in Hakahau from Manu Guéranger (☎ 92 51 49), Joseph Tamarii (☎ 92 52 14) or Alain Alho (☎ 92 52 80). In Hakamaii, contact Jules and Charles Tissot or José Kautai.

HIVA OA

- pop 1829
- area 320 sq km

Hiva Oa is the most important island in the southern group. The slopes of Mt Temetiu (1276m) and Mt Feani (1126m) form a vast amphitheatre, at the base of which is Atuona, the island's capital. For the French painter Paul Gauguin this was the last stop on his wanderings. On the north-east coast, Puamau has the most important archaeological remains discovered to date in the Marquesas Islands. A site at Taaoa, in the south-west, is another archaeological treasure.

Information

The Atuona Tourist Board (☎/fax 92 75 10) is in the craft *fare* behind the museum, in the centre of Atuona. The Banque Socredo (☎ 92 73 54) is next to the Air Tahiti office. There is a post office in Atuona and in Puamau. In Atuona, the hospital (☎ 92 73 75) is behind the town hall.

Atuona

Atuona is at the north of Taaoa Bay, at the mouth of the Vaioa River, and stretches back up the valley for about 1.5km. Gauguin lived here from 1901 to 1903, and

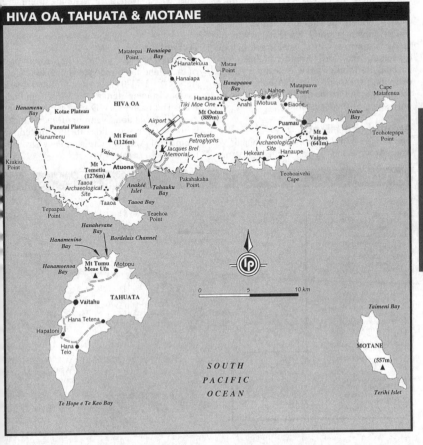

HIVA OA, TAHUATA & MOTANE

FRENCH POLYNESIA

singer-poet Jacques Brel until 1978. To one side of the small **museum** is a faithful, but empty, replica of Gauguin's **House of Pleasure**. The museum is open Monday to Friday, 7.30 to 11.30 am, admission is 400 CFP. Gauguin and Brel are buried in the small **Calvaire Cemetery** which dominates Atuona Bay.

Tohua Pepeu is a restored *tohua* (communal site) in the centre of town. It includes a reconstructed *hae* (traditional house). The **Jacques Brel Memorial** is near the airport, where the famous singer had intended to build a house. Ask for directions; it's better to walk there than go by 4WD, as the track is very bad.

The **Tehueto petroglyphs** in the Faakua Valley makes a good walk from Atuona along a narrow, little used track which crosses a small ford. Another archaeological site, the **Tohua Upeke**, is near the village of Taaoa 7km south-west of Atuona and has more than 1000 stone platforms, or pae pae, only some of them restored.

Around the Island

The village of **Puamau** is a 2½ hour drive from Atuona and has an elegant seafront and the most beautiful archaeological site in the Marquesas. Discovered by ethnologists and archaeologists last century, the **Iipona site** is one of the most important testimonies to pre-contact Marquesan civilisation. Iipona, featuring five monumental tiki in the central and rear parts of the site, is about 1.5km from Puamau and there's a 200 CFP entry fee. In the village **Tohua Pehe Kua** is the tomb of the valley's last chief.

Hanapaaoa is a tiny village in an area of wild beauty two hours drive from Atuona. A 15 minute walk away is the strange **Tiki Moe One** – you'll probably need a guide to find it. As well as at Atuona, there are beaches at Puamau, Hanamenu and Hanatekua.

Activities

Some old bridleways cross the western part of the island from Taaoa to Hanamenu. Colliano (☎ 92 71 04) in Atuona rents horses, as does Étienne Heitaa (☎ 92 75 28) in Puamau. The island's 4WD tracks are good for easy hikes but don't venture off these tracks without taking a guide. In the immediate vicinity of Atuona there's an easy stroll to the Tehueto petroglyphs.

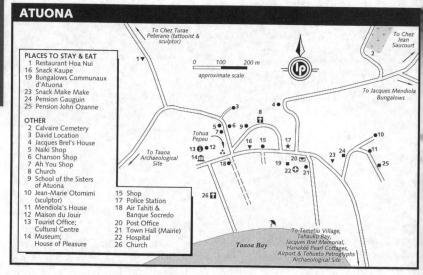

ATUONA

PLACES TO STAY & EAT
1 Restaurant Hoa Nui
16 Snack Make Make
19 Bungalows Communaux d'Atuona
23 Snack Make Make
24 Pension Gauguin
25 Pension John Ozanne

OTHER
2 Calvaire Cemetery
3 David Location
4 Jacques Brel's House
5 Naiki Shop
6 Chanson Shop
7 Ah You Shop
8 Church
9 School of the Sisters of Atuona
10 Jean-Marie Otomimi (sculptor)
11 Mendiola's House
12 Maison du Jouir
13 Tourist Office; Cultural Centre
14 Museum; House of Pleasure
15 Shop
17 Police Station
18 Air Tahiti & Banque Socredo
20 Post Office
21 Town Hall (Mairie)
22 Hospital
26 Church

To Chez Turae Peterano (tattooist & sculptor)

To Chez Jean Saucourt

To Jacques Mendiola Bungalows

Tohua Pepeu

To Taaoa Archaeological Site

To Temetiu Village, Tahauku Bay, Jacques Brel Memorial, Hanakéé Pearl Cottages, Airport & Tehueto Petroglyphs Archaeological Site

Taaoa Bay

0   100   200 m
approximate scale

Places to Stay

Bungalows Communaux d'Atuona (☎ 92 73 32 at the town hall, fax 92 74 95) has seven fully-equipped bungalows from 2000 CFP for one person, plus 500 CFP for each additional person. Booking is recommended.

Jacques Mendiola (☎ 92 73 88, BP 60, Atuona, Hiva Oa) has two superb bungalows in the Atuona hills. They're well-equipped, have superb views and cost 5000 CFP.

Chez Jean Saucourt (☎/fax 92 73 33) has two excellent bungalows for 4000 CFP on the hillside above Taaoa Bay but they're usually rented by the month. Also east of Atuona on the hillside is the wonderfully peaceful *Pension John Ozanne* (☎/fax 92 73 43), with simple rooms for 3500 CFP per person half-board and bungalows for 2500 CFP for the room only.

Pension Gauguin (☎/fax 92 73 51), in the east of Atuona Bay, is very popular with travellers and costs 6000/11,000 CFP a single/double half-board. Also popular and similarly priced but on the Tahauku Bay side, a 20 minute walk from Atuona, is the *Temetiu Village* (☎/fax 92 73 02). Credit cards are accepted.

The *Hanakéé Pearl Cottages* (☎ 43 90 04, fax 43 17 86, info@spmhotels.pf) is perched on the hillside in Tahauku Bay, above the cargo ship quay. There are 20 fine bungalows with air-con for 28,080 to 37,800 CFP and there is a swimming pool.

Chez Marie-Antoinette (☎ 92 72 27) in Puamau is the only place not in Atuona and it costs 3500 CFP per person half-board. There's an archaeological site with several tiki and tombs on the guesthouse land.

Places to Eat

Atuona and Puamau have *shops*, and *roulottes* sometimes appear near Tohua Pepeu in Atuona. The *Hoa Nui restaurant* (☎ 92 73 63) specialises in Marquesan cuisine and puts on a feast when the *Aranui* is in port. The *Temetiu Village* offers meals with a view of Tahauku and Taaoa bays. More expensive is the restaurant at the *Hanakéé Pearl Cottages* at Tahauku Bay. In Puamau *Bernard Heitaa's* is a good place for lunch.

Getting There & Away

Air Tahiti (☎ 92 73 41 in Atuona, ☎ 92 72 31 at the airport) has connections to Papeete, Nuku Hiva and Ua Pou. Papeete-Nuku Hiva-Atuona flights go five times a week and cost 27,500 CFP.

Ozanne Rohi and Médéric Kaimuko (☎ 92 74 48) charter bonitiers for 15,000 CFP to Tahuata, or 55,000 CFP to Fatu Hiva. The Tahuata communal bonitier connects Vaitahu (Tahuata) with Atuona twice a week. The *Aranui* and *Taporo IV* stop at Hiva Oa.

Getting Around

The airport is 13km from Atuona. If you have booked your accommodation, your host will collect you for about 1500 CFP; the journey takes 25 minutes. It's also possible to hitch a ride.

Excursions by 4WD cost from 8000 CFP to Taaoa, 12,000 CFP to Hanaiapa, 15,000 CFP to Hanapaaoa and 15,000 CFP to Puamau.

Contact André Teissier of the Pension Gauguin, Gaby Heitaa of the Temetiu Village guesthouse, Serge Lecordier of the Hanakéé Pearl Cottages, Ozanne Rohi or Ida Clark (☎ 92 71 33). In Puamau, ask for Étienne Heitaa (☎ 92 75 28). David Location (☎ 92 72 87), in a small street a stone's throw from the Chanson, Ah You and Naiki shops have Suzukis for 12,000 CFP a day.

TAHUATA
- pop 637　　　● area 70 sq km

Separated from Hiva Oa by the 4km wide Bordelais Channel, Tahuata is the smallest inhabited island in the archipelago. Oriented along a north-south ridgeline, it has numerous inlets, two of which shelter the island's main villages, Hapatoni and Vaitahu.

Around the Island

On the hill that dominates tiny **Vaitahu** village are a few remains of the **French Fort**. The seafront stone **Catholic church**, opened in 1988, includes a wooden statue which is a masterpiece of modern Marquesan art. There is a small Polynesian art and history **museum** in the town hall.

On a wide bay **Hapatoni** is several kilometres south of Vaitahu by boat or bridleway and has a 19th century royal road and a magnificent **me'ae** in the middle of the village. **Motopu**, to the north, has a few dozen inhabitants and is accessible by 4WD by the vehicle track that crosses the island's interior. Enchanting **Hanamoenoa Bay** is a favourite anchorage for yachts between March and August. The track which joins Vaitahu and Motopu, a distance of about 17km, is an ideal place for riders and Simon Timau, known as Kiki, in Vaitahu, has several horses (with wooden saddles). Check also with the owner of the Chez Jeanne guesthouse. In Hapatoni, contact Frédéric Timau (☎ 92 92 55). Count on 5000 to 10,000 CFP for the Vaitahu-Hanahevane-Motopu ride and return, with a guide.

Places to Stay & Eat

Chez Jeanne (☎ 92 92 24 at the school, or ☎ 92 92 19 at the town hall) in Vaitahu has rooms for 5000 CFP per person with full board, but it's not open during school vacations. At the edge of the village *Chez Nicolas Barsinas (☎ 92 92 01)* has a room for 2000 CFP.

Getting There & Away

Tahuata is not served by aircraft. The *Te Pua O Mioi* communal bonitier (☎ 92 92 19) runs a Vaitahu-Atuona-Vaitahu ferry service on Tuesday and Thursday for 1000 CFP per passenger round trip; the crossing time is about one hour.

Yves-Bertrand Barsinas (☎ 92 92 40) and Louis Timau (☎ 92 92 71) also carry people by bonitier (from 20,000 CFP to Vaitahu or Hapatoni to Atuona).

The *Aranui* and *Taporo IV* serve Tahuata.

Getting Around

A 17km 4WD track crosses the island's interior to link Vaitahu with Motopu. Contact Louis Timau or Yves-Bertrand Barsinas (see Getting There & Away) for 4WD hire (15,000 CFP per day with driver).

Hapatoni is less than 15 minutes away by speedboat from Vaitahu. For speedboat hire in Vaitahu, contact Célestin Teikipupuni (☎ 92 92 13), Yves-Bertrand Barsinas, Louis Timau, Donatiano Hikutini or Nicolas Barsinas. In Hapatoni, ask for Liliane Teikipupuni (☎ 92 92 46) or Frédéric Timau. It cost about 6000 CFP to hire the boat between Vaitahu and Hapatoni return, 7000 to 10,000 CFP between Vaitahu and Hanahevane.

FATU HIVA
● pop 631   ● area 80 sq km

Fatu Hiva is an island of superlatives: the most remote, the furthest south, the wettest, the lushest and the most authentic. It was also the first island in the archipelago to be seen by the Spanish navigator Mendaña on 21 July 1595.

About 75km south of Hiva Oa, Fatu Hiva consists of two craters, forming arcs open to the west. Between the flanks of the caldera are two valleys, in which nestle the only villages on the island: Hanavave in the north and Omoa in the south, 5km apart. Thor Heyerdahl, of *Kon Tiki* fame, used his 18 month stay on here from 1937 as the basis for his evocatively-titled work *Fatu Hiva the Return to Nature*.

Around the Island

The red roofed church with the white facade and slender spire dominates **Omoa**. Ask someone to take you to the giant **petroglyph** at the edge of the village, near the river: it's an enormous fish carved on a block of rock. **Hanavave** is on the seashore, at the mouth of a steep-sided valley leading onto the beautiful **Bay of Virgins**.

You can walk or ride to the Bay of Virgins from Omoa along the island's only track. On foot it's a several hour walk with no particular difficulties except the climb to the pass separating the two valleys. The route can be followed by horse or by 4WD if it's not too muddy. Roberto Maraetaata (☎ 92 80 23 at the town hall) has two horses but needs several days warning.

A favourite for passing yachties, the phallic protuberances of Hanavave Bay caused it to be named Baie des Verges (Bay of Penises). Outraged, the missionaries hastened to add a redeeming 'i' to make the name Baie des Vierges (Bay of Virgins).

Places to Stay & Eat

n Omoa *Pension Heimata (☎ 92 80 58)* las rooms for 4000 CFP per person half-board. *Chez Norma Ropati (☎ 92 80 13)* is near the beach in a separate house. The six double rooms with shared bathroom (hot water) cost 1500 CFP per person or 5000 CFP full board. In front of it is *Chez Cécile Gilmore (☎ 92 80 54)* which costs 3500 CFP half-board.

Chez Marie-Claire (☎ 92 80 75 or call the town hall on ☎ 92 80 23 and ask for Henri, Marie-Claire's husband) offers double rooms for 3000 CFP with shared bathroom (cold water) and kitchen. *Chez Lionel Cantois (☎/fax 92 80 80)* is the last house in the village, beside the river and in the middle of a beautiful tropical garden with rooms for 4000 CFP for two.

Shopping

Arts and crafts are the island's major activity and Fatu Hiva prides itself on being the only island in French Polynesia where tapa is still made according to ancestral methods. Guesthouse owners Cécile Gilmore and Norma Ropati are well known for their work.

In Omoa Charles Seigel is a carved coconut specialist and Joseph Pavaouau is one of the last stone sculptors.

You will have no difficulty in finding the artisans, either at their homes or at the craft centre in each of the two villages.

Getting There & Away

Fatu Hiva is the most difficult island to get to in the entire archipelago. Theoretically there's a local catamaran between Omoa and Atuona once a week but it has not been operating for some time. That only leaves the *Aranui* and the *Taporo IV* or the possibility of chartering a private bonitier.

Getting Around

A 17km road links Hanavave with Omoa. It's impassable in wet weather, so journeys between villages are often undertaken by motorised pirogue instead. Ask at your accommodation for some advice on renting a 4WD.

Austral Islands

South of the Society Islands, the scattered islands of the Austral group run 1300km northwest to south-east. There are five inhabited and two uninhabited islands in the group, with a total population of just 6500. Two of the islands have airports and regular flight connections with Papeete, the other inhabited islands are served by regular but infrequent cargo-passenger ships and are very occasionally visited by passing yachts. All the inhabited islands have guesthouses. There are ancient marae, hilltop fortresses, limestone caverns and annual visits by migrating whales.

History

The Austral Islands were the last in French Polynesia to be settled and it is believed the first arrivals came from Tahiti between 1000 and 1300 AD. James Cook was the first European visitor, sighting Rurutu in 1769, but it was not until 1811 that the whole chain had been 'discovered'. The French did not take over the last of the Australs until 1901 and as a result of the early English missionaries the islands are still overwhelmingly Protestant.

Getting There & Away

Rurutu and Tubuai have Air Tahiti connections three times weekly in the low season, nearly every day in the high. One flight goes Tahiti-Rurutu-Tubuai-Tahiti while the next goes Tahiti-Tubuai-Rurutu-Tahiti. The one-way fare Tahiti-Rurutu is 16,500 CFP,

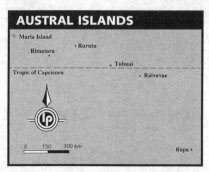

AUSTRAL ISLANDS

Maria Island
Rimatara
• Rurutu
Tubuai
Tropic of Capricorn
• Raivavae

0   150   300 km

Rapa •

Tahiti-Tubuai 18,500 CFP and Rurutu-
Tubuai 8300 CFP.

Two passenger-carrying cargo ships
serve the Austral Islands. The *Tuhaa Pae II*
does three trips a month while the *Vaeanu
II* does two.

RURUTU

● pop 2015   ● area 36 sq km

Rurutu is fringed by a continuous reef but
it's rarely more than a stone's throw from
the shoreline so there's not much beach and
little opportunity to swim. A road encircles
the island and there are limestone caverns
and some ancient marae. A network of
minor tracks wind into the island's dense
patchwork of plantations and ascend to the
highpoint, Mt Taatioe (389m). Rurutu has
a local dance troupe which regularly wins
inter-island dance competitions. This is
also the centre for stone lifting competitions, the men's stone weighs a back-
breaking 130kg.

RURUTU

Orientation & Information

There are three main villages, Moreai is the
largest and has the cargo ship dock, a post
office and a Banque Socredo branch. It's
36km around the island, about one third of
it sealed. Air Tahiti (☎ 94 03 57) is at the
airport. The Tauraatua Pass near Moerai is
the only pass of any size.

Things to See & Do

Moreai is 4km south-east of the airport and
has a picturesque little Protestant church
dating from 1865-72. Éric de Bisschop, the
island's most famous resident, was a French
version of Thor Heyerdahl, dedicated to
perilous voyages in unsuitable craft. Bisschop's adventures were ultimately less succesful than Heyerdahl's though – his
gravestone is in the village cemetery.

Around the island there are many indications of Rurutu's formation as an upthrust
reef. Going clockwise, south of **Arei Point**,
which has one of Rurutu's impressive elevated reef cliffs, the road climbs inland then
drops back to the coast at **Hauti**, the second
of the island's three villages. Continuing
from Hauti the road runs along what was
once the ancient lagoon bottom, looking
west from this road the range of hills is the
old barrier reef, now well above sea level.
Near **Toataratara Point**, the southern tip of
the island, there's the small **Poreopi Marae**.

After turning north and passing the village of **Avera**, the road leads to **Marae Vi-
taria**, once an extensive marae although
only remnants survive. Nearby is the huge
Teanaeo Grotto. The coast road continues
past the Rurutu Village Hotel and skirts the
airport runway before rounding **Anamani-
ana Point** and arriving back at Moerai.

It's easy to climb the three highest peaks.
Whales come close inshore from July to
October; the Raie Manta Club diving
centre organises **whale watching** trips.

Places to Stay & Eat

The four places to stay all provide free airport transfers. *Chez Catherine (☎ 94 02 43,
fax 94 06 99)* is in the centre of Moerai. It's
friendly, well run and has single/double
rooms with bathrooms for 3000/4500 CFP

and a small restaurant and bar. The *Rurutu Village Hotel* (☎ 94 03 92, fax 94 05 01) is not in a village but right on the beach on the island's north-west coast, about 1km from the airport. It has comfortable bungalows with bathrooms for 4000/5000 CFP, a restaurant, bar and swimming pool. It accepts credit cards.

Pension Ariana (☎ 94 06 69), near the Rurutu Village Hotel, has rooms for 4500 CFP for two. *Pension Temarama* (☎/fax 94 02 17), about 1km from the village, has rooms from 3000 CFP for one or two people.

There are various small shops, particularly in Moerai where you will also find *Snack Tetua* by the sports field.

Getting Around

The Rurutu Village Hotel, Chez Catherine and Pension Temarama rent bicycles for around 1000 CFP a day, Chez Catherine and Pension Temarama have cars for 6000 CFP. They all offer island and cave tours.

TUBUAI

● pop 2049 ● area 45 sq km

Tubuai has a wide but shallow lagoon with some pretty motu. The first LMS missionaries arrived in 1822 and the population of around 3000 fell to less than 300 later in the century before slowly recovering.

Orientation & Information

Mataura, 4km from the airport, is the main village and has a post office, a branch of the Banque Socredo and a handful of shops. Air Tahiti (☎ 94 03 57) is at the airport.

Things to See & Do

Travelling clockwise around the island from **Mataura** the coast road passes through **Taahuaia**, the island's second village and an empty patch of green, which is the only trace of the site of the *Bounty* mutineers' **Fort George** where they holed up for a few months before heading back to Tahiti. The three larger **islets** are visible at the edge of

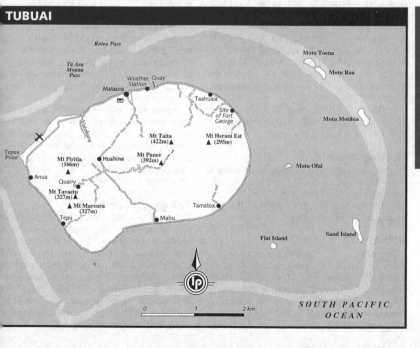

TUBUAI

Rotea Pass

Ta Ara Moana Pass

Weather Station

Quay

Mataura

Taahuaia

Site of Fort George

Motu Toena

Motu Roa

Motu Motihia

Mt Taita (422m)▲

Mt Herani Est ▲ (295m)

Tepuu Point

Mt Piritia (166m) ▲

Huahine

Mt Panee (392m)

Motu Ofai

● Anua

Quarry

Mt Tavaetu (327m) ▲

▲ Mt Mareura (327m)

Tamatoa

Tepu

Mahu

Flat Island

Sand Island

0 1 2 km

SOUTH PACIFIC OCEAN

FRENCH POLYNESIA

the lagoon as you round the long, even curve of the island's east end. The third village of **Mahu** marks the southern end of the Route Traversière (the cross-island route).

There are better beaches around the southern end of the island plus the good little beach at the **Ta Ara Moana Pass**, just west of Mataura. The Mormon church has made a major onslaught on Tubuai and their modern, functional churches are sprinkled all around the coast road.

From the Route Traversière a 4WD track and then a walking trail climbs to the top of Mt Taita (422m), from where there are good views.

Places To Stay & Eat

There's a small supermarket and one other reasonable-size store in Mataura, plus a scattering of smaller stores around the island. However, the choice of goods will be wider and the prices lower in Tahiti, so you may want to bring supplies with you. Come prepared for mosquitoes as well. Don't count on using credit cards on Tubuai.

Chez Doudou (☎/fax 95 06 71) is close to the shipping wharf Mataura and has 20 rooms with bathrooms for 3000/4500 CFP a single/double. *Chez Sam & Yolande* (☎/fax 95 05 52) is right by the sea in Mataura and has five rooms with bathrooms for 6000/ 7500 CFP.

In Taahuaia, *Le Bounty* (☎ 95 03 32, fax 95 05 58) is connected with the college and has *fare* for 3000/5000 CFP.

Getting Around

Island pensions will collect their guests from the airport or dock if you book ahead. Bernard Le Guilloux (☎ 95 06 01) in Mataura has cars to rent for 4000 CFP a day, or ask at the guesthouses.

RIMATARA

● pop 929   ● area 8 sq km

Tiny Rimatara is a rough circle 4km in diameter, rising to 83m Mt Uahu (or Vahu) in the centre. Spaced around this low mountain are the three villages of Anapoto, Amaru and Mutuaura, linked by a road running some distance inland from the coast.

Like Rurutu, the island is circled by a fringing reef and the narrow Hiava Pass let small boats in to land on the beaches in front of Amaru and Anapoto. Traditionally arriving visitors must pass through the smoke of a purifying fire as they step ashore.

The most densely-populated of the Austral Islands, Rimatara is about 600km south-west of Tahiti and about 150km west of Rurutu. Only small boats can enter the island pass so goods are transferred from cargo ships to shore on whaleboats which land right on the beach.

Places to Stay

The only place to stay is *Umarere* (☎ 83 2, 84 in Papeete), a two-room fully equipped house for 2000 CFP per person per day. You've got to fend for yourself so bring supplies.

RAIVAVAE

● pop 1049   ● area 16 sq km

Proclaimed as one of the most beautiful islands in the Pacific, Raivavae (pronounced 'rye-vie-vie') is encircled by a motu-dotted reef. Rairua is the site of the island's main shipping quay but Mahanatoa is the largest of the villages. There is no airport on Raivavae but the ship *Tuhaa Pae II* comes by about twice a month.

At the time of contact with Europeans Raivavae had a population of around 3000 people with a reputation as excellent sea farers (they regularly visited the Society Islands). In 1826 the same European fever that nearly wiped out Tubuai reduced the population to just over 100.

Things to See & Do

Raivavae was once noted for the many massive stone tiki which once stood in the island's several marae. But at the site of the principal marae, near Rairua, there is only one great tiki left today. Its relations stand in the gardens of the Gauguin Museum on Tahiti, but the island's sole remaining tiki is a powerful figure emanating great *mana* (supernatural power). At the other end of the island is Marae Maunauto.

Places to Stay

Chez Annie Flores (☎ 95 43 28) in Rairua village, where the boats dock, has two rooms, bathroom facilities and an equipped kitchen for 2000 CFP per person. Chez 'aite (☎ 95 42 85) in Mahanatoa has a house with three rooms for 4000/7000 CFP single/double. Also in Mahanatoa Pension Moana (☎ 95 42 66) costs 2000 CFP per person per day.

RAPA

pop 521 • **area 22 sq km**

Rapa is the most remote and isolated island of French Polynesia – even its nearest inhabited neighbour in the Australs, Raivavae, is 500km distant. This far south there are no coral reefs or coconut palms, and temperatures as low as 5°C have been recorded in winter.

Although it's believed that Rapa was only settled by Polynesians around 1000 to 1300 AD, it was once densely populated and divided into warring kingdoms whose mountain-top forts, or pa, were similar to those of the New Zealand Maori. The island is also known as Rapa Iti (Little Rapa) to distinguish it from Rapa Nui (Big Rapa; Easter Island).

Like other islands, Rapa was devastated by European diseases post-contact and its population fell from about 2000 at the time of contact with Europeans, to a mere 150. A raid on the island by a Peruvian slave ship compounded the agony.

The Tuhaa Pae II visits Rapa about once a month. The wide Haurei Bay is the easiest bay to enter and the most sheltered anchorage in the Australs.

Things to See & Do

The population is concentrated in the villages of Haurei and Area, on opposite sides of Haurei Bay, and generally linked by boat since there is only a rough road round the bay. At its peak there were about a dozen villages scattered across the island. Morongo Uta, between Haurei and Airi bays, is the best preserved of Rapa's ancient fortresses. The great pa has terraces separated by deep moats around the central fortress, which has a perimeter of over 300m and is overlooked by a double-pyramid watchtower. Directly overlooking Haurei is the Tevaitau pa, restored in 1960. Other pa can be found along the mountain ridge or at the passes from one valley to another. They typically have flat terraces and a lookout tower.

Places to Stay & Eat

Chez Cerdan Faraire (☎ 95 72 84) in Haurei is the only family-run pension that takes guests; it charges 4000 CFP per person per day with all meals.

OTHER AUSTRAL ISLANDS

Furthest north-west of the Austral chain, uninhabited **Maria Island** is an atoll with four motu on a triangular-shaped reef. The atoll is about 200km north-west of Rimatara and about 400km east of the Cook Islands. The Tuhaa Pae II makes occasional stops at Maria Island and visitors from Rurutu and Rimatara come here from time to time to harvest copra.

At the other end of the chain **Marotiri**, also known as Bass Rocks, are nine uninhabited rocky spires rising from the sea about 70km south-east of Rapa. Although even landing on the rocks is difficult, the largest one has a saddle between its two pinnacles and this saddle is defended by a miniature pa!

Gambier Archipelago

• **pop 1087** • **area 27 sq km**

The most remote of the French Polynesian island groups, the Gambier Archipelago lies at the extreme south-east end of the long arc of the Tuamotus. Unlike the Tuamotu atolls, these are high islands and islets within an encircling reef. Mangareva (Floating Mountain) is the largest within the group and the only populated island. It was the centre for the obsessive missionary activities of Father Honoré Laval between 1834 and 1871.

FRENCH POLYNESIA

History

The Gambier Archipelago was populated in three waves around the 10th to the 13th century. A Catholic mission was established here in 1834 and quickly converted the population. Father Honoré Laval and his assistant François Caret transformed the islands, building wide roads, a massive cathedral, nine churches and chapels, monuments, lookout towers, wharves and a prison. Laval and Caret found time to pop over to Tahiti to attempt to carry Catholicism to that bastion of Protestantism. Their subsequent clash with Queen Pomare IV and the English missionaries was the excuse for the French takeover of Tahiti.

Although France established a protectorate over the archipelago in 1844, it continued as a semi-independent entity until being annexed in 1881. When Laval arrived the population may have been 5000 to 6000, spread across the four main islands, but it had fallen to 463 by 1887, largely due to European diseases.

Orientation & Information

The wide lagoon is protected by a 90km coral barrier with 25 motu dotted along the northern edge and three passes into the lagoon. Within the lagoon there are 10 volcanic high islands but, apart from a handful of people, the population is all on Mangareva.

Well to the south, the islands have a relatively mild climate and in winter it can actually get cool. The Gambier Islands are one hour ahead of Tahiti. Rikitea, the town on Mangareva, has shops and a post office.

GAMBIER ARCHIPELAGO

SOUTH PACIFIC OCEAN

Fallout Shelter (Maison Nucleaire)

Totegegie

Mangareva

Rouru Convent • Rikitea Tararu Roa

Taravai

Aukena

Agakauitai

Akamaru

Makaroa

Manui

Kamaka

0   5   10 km

St Michael's Cathedral on Mangareva – one legacy of a very enthusiastic priest.

QUIS UT AΩ DEUS?

Things to See & Do

At the south-west end of the town o Rikitea, on the slopes of Mt Duff (441m the **Cathedral of St Michael**, built in 1839 48, is the ultimate symbol of Laval's single minded obsession. The cathedral ca accommodate 1200 people – more than th population of the island! The cathedral ha twin blue-trimmed towers and an altar dec orated with mother-of-pearl. It was built o the site of Mangareva's greatest marac which once featured a coral-decorated ah and an adjacent 30m royal house with a roc supported by decorated columns.

Other Laval constructions include th coastal **watchtowers and turret** from th 'palace' Laval built for the island's las king. The island's **Rouru Convent** once ha 60 Mangarevan nuns, although it's sai Laval would hide the entire female popula tion of the island in the convent whenever whaling ship paid a visit. An overgrow path built in Laval's era leads uphill to th convent, passing a hollowed out rock poc known as the **Queen's Bath**, finally enterin the nunnery through a triumphal arch.

On the north coast of the island is the rust ing ruin of the **maison nucleaire**, a fallou

helter from the 1966-74 atmospheric testing
period at Moruroa, 400km away. Island resi-
ents were squeezed into this windowless
omb for up to three days at a time.

Aukena has reminders of the missionary
period, including the 1839 **Church of St
Raphaël** and the hexagonal **lookout tower**,
prominent landmark, on the south-west
ip of the island. Akamaru was the island
where Laval first arrived and his 1841 **Our
ady of Peace Church** still stands on the ut-
erly deserted island.

Places to Stay & Eat

Chez Pierre & Mariette Paemara (☎ 97 82
7), just 100m from the docks in Rikitea,
as three rooms and costs 2000 to 6000
CFP per day with all meals. Also in the vil-
age *Chez Terii & Hélène Paemara* (☎ 97
2 80) offers similar facilities at a similar
rice.

Chez Benoît & Bianca (☎/fax 97 83 76)
s 1km from the quay, offers fine views
cross the bay to Aukena and costs 5500
CFP per person half-board, 7350 CFP full

board. *Chez Jojo* (☎/fax 97 82 61) is by the
water, 5km from the quay and costs
4500/6000 CFP half/full board or you can
camp here for 1000 CFP per day.

There's a small *bakery* by the waterfront
in Rikitea.

Getting There & Away

The Gambier Archipelago has Air Tahiti connections about once a week (27,500 CFP).
The *Nuku Hau* sails via the eastern Tuamotus to the Gambiers every three weeks.

Getting Around

The airport is on Motu Totegegie on the
eastern side of the lagoon. Local boats meet
every flight and charge 500 CFP for the 45
minute journey.

Chez Benoît & Bianca and Chez Pierre
& Mariette organise island tours from 2500
CFP per person. Chez Benoît & Bianca
also rents bicycles for 1000 CFP per day
while Chez Pierre & Mariette rent a car for
5000 CFP per day. Chez Jojo will organise
fishing trips.

Niue

Known to the islanders as 'the rock', although the name actually means 'Behold the Coconut', Niue (pronounced '**new**-ay') stands alone and isolated midway between New Zealand (NZ) and French Polynesia. The closest neighbours are the islands of Tonga, about 600km south-west, and Rarotonga, 1000km south-east. NZ is 2400km to the south-west.

One of the smallest Pacific nations, Niue is a quiet and easy going place with amazing cave formations, a dramatic rocky coast and superb scuba diving. The island is a textbook example of a *makatea*, an upthrust coral reef, hoisted up above sea level by some primeval upheaval.

Facts about Niue

HISTORY

Niue's first settlers arrived about 1000 years ago. The Niuean language is based on both Samoan and Tongan, with traces from Pukapuka in the Cook Islands. But whether the Samoans or the Tongans arrived first is open to dispute. Possibly the settlers came in waves from both directions.

Captain Cook stopped by in 1774 on his second Pacific voyage, but his attempts to land were repulsed three times. He dubbed Niue the 'Savage Island' in contrast to Tonga which he had christened the 'Friendly Islands' (see the boxed text in the Tonga chapter). Although Niueans insist that Cook's unfriendly reception might simply have been a strong 'challenge' rather than outright hostility, it frightened off future visitors for many years.

The pioneering missionary John Williams came by in 1830, but continued on his way. It was not until 1846 that Peniamina, a Niuean who had been converted to Christianity in Samoa, established the first Christian (London Missionary Society; LMS) foothold on the island. He was followed in 1849 by Paulo, a Samoan missionary. Apart

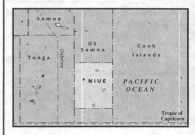
from visits by whalers and Peruvian slav ships, Niue's major problem in the late years of that century was exactly the sam as it is today – a continuing exodus of is landers looking for employment abroad The missionaries had the island firml under control when Niue briefly became British colony in 1900, before being hande over to NZ the next year. The Niueans wer not consulted about this imperial handove

NIUE

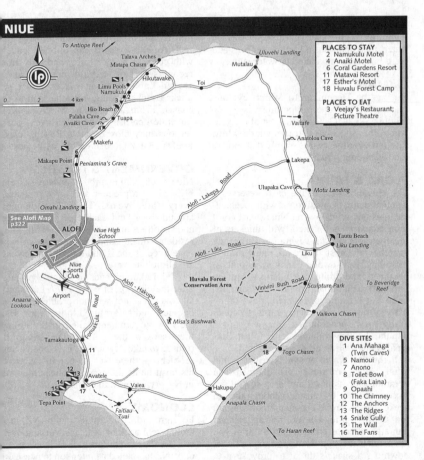

NIUE

PLACES TO STAY
2 Namukulu Motel
4 Anaiki Motel
6 Coral Gardens Resort
11 Matavai Resort
17 Esther's Motel
18 Huvalu Forest Camp

PLACES TO EAT
3 Veejay's Restaurant;
  Picture Theatre

DIVE SITES
1 Ana Mahaga
  (Twin Caves)
5 Namoui
7 Anono
8 Toilet Bowl
  (Faka Laina)
9 Opaahi
10 The Chimney
12 The Anchors
13 The Ridges
14 Snake Gully
15 The Wall
16 The Fans

but they protested loudly when NZ proposed lumping their island in with the Cook Islands group.

Niue remained a quiet backwater through the first half of the 20th century, until, after WWII, pressure began for independence. However, Niueans, aware that their economy was heavily dependent upon NZ aid and remittances from relatives living in NZ, were in no hurry to expedite independence. Independence finally arrived in 1974, and Niue is now in 'free association' with NZ. Niueans, like Cook Islanders, hold NZ citizenship.

GEOGRAPHY & ECOLOGY

Niue is a makatea or 'raised atoll' island, like Rurutu in French Polynesia or Atiu in the Cook Islands. It's one of the largest upthrust coral atolls in the world, with two tiers, one rising 20m sheer from sea level and the second as high as 65m. There are few beaches and no rivers but many caves, chasms, ravines and gullies around the coast. There's a fringing reef around much of the island but no offshore lagoon.

The island limestone is extremely porous and rainfall simply disappears on contact. At various points around the island fresh

NIUE

water can be seen percolating into the sea. Although there is no permanent surface water, the island has a huge water lens and there is usually an adequate water supply.

CLIMATE

During the December to March cyclone season the average temperature is 27°C, dropping to 24°C during the rest of the year when the south-east trade winds blow. Rainfall over the year is evenly distributed, totalling about 200cm.

FLORA & FAUNA

The Huvalu forest in the east preserves a patch of dense tropical forest with spectacular trees and wildflowers. Niue's east coast is particularly untouched, with thickets of impenetrable coastal vegetation and shady stretches of forest. There are many birds – including *weka* (wood hens), swamp hens, parakeets and white tailed terns – but the only native mammals are rats and fruit bats. Feral cats are a major problem, devastating native wildlife, particularly birds. Coconut crabs (*uga*; pronounced 'ung-a'), are a popular delicacy found in dense forest. Butterflies are prolific all over the island.

In the clear waters around Niue you'll find a full selection of tropical fish but the island is famous for its black and grey striped sea snakes, *katuali* in Niuean. Although the sea snakes have a strong venom their mouths are too small to bite. They're not aggressive, although often as curious about you as you are about them. You'd have to shove a finger down a sea snake's throat to provoke it to bite you. Visitors soon become accustomed to swimming in what could be described as 'snake infested waters'.

Pods of small spinner dolphins are found along the island, including off the coast at Alofi. The name comes from their practice of spinning around when they jump clear of the water. Humpback whales breed in Niue's waters between June and November, when they migrate north from the Antarctic.

Niue's coastal waters are protected by legislation. Fishing with explosives or poisons is banned and no marine creatures can be taken using scuba equipment. Also, net fishing has never caught on in Niue. Tradition requires that the popular *ulihega* ba fish (roundeye scad) can only be caug with coconut bait or lures, and only fron recognised bait fishing areas, usuall around canoe landing places down se tracks (tracks leading from the road to th coast). From January to May, *kaloam* (juvenile goatfish) and *atule* (bigeye scad seasons may close Avatele Beach, Avaik Reef and Utuko Reef areas. Signs are poste

GOVERNMENT & POLITICS

Niue elects a 20 member legislative assem bly, led by a premier and three minister every three years. The 14 settlement around the island each elect one membe and six others are elected island-wide. Onl resident Niueans and New Zealanders wh have lived on the island for over three year are eligible to vote.

Sani Lakatani became Niue's premie after the election of early 1999. Lakatani' takeover was not without problems: whe one defeated MP refused to leave her sea the new government called in the police then sacked the police chief when h refused to take any action. This created ne problems – there was no-one to take ove his position as the deputy police chief wa in NZ giving birth to twins!

ECONOMY

Foreign aid, principally from NZ, an money sent back by Niueans working over seas are the twin pillars of the island's econ omy. NZ has stated its intention to phase ou aid by 2003, forcing Niue's leaders to con sider other aid options.

The old copra trade has long gone; cotto and bananas once had short spells as ex port products; and sewing footballs for th NZ market has also died. Niuean honey i excellent, but today's production is a frac tion of what it was in its heyday. A little tar is exported, there are some pretty stamp for collectors and the tourist 'flow' is mor of a trickle. One of the few bright spots i the economy is the quarantine station. Here neatly inverting the old Peruvian blackbird ing business, alpacas imported from Peru

The Rat & the Octopus

One day, long before people arrived in Niue, a rat was foraging on the reef and became so pre-occupied it failed to notice the incoming tide. Trapped on the reef edge with the waves lapping its paws the rat squeaked for help and a kindly octopus popped up and offered to transfer the rat to shore. Balanced precariously on the octopus' head the rat was soon back on dry land, but, being a rat after all, instead of thanking the octopus for its kindness the unpleasant rodent did something distinctly ratty. It defecated on the octopus' head as it hopped off. Not surprisingly the octopus was outraged and announced that in future any rat that ventured on to the reef risked being hauled under and drowned.

MICK WELDON

Many years later, when the island had been populated, someone heard the tale of the ungrateful rat and devised an unbeatable octopus lure. Simply take one tiger cowrie and one mourning cowrie shell and tie them back to back to look like a rat's body. Add a stick for the tail, some straw to form the head and whiskers and no octopus can resist it. Tie the lure on a fishing line, lower it over the edge of the reef and it's certain death for any octopus.

---

re quarantined before being sent on to Australia and Canada.

There is some small scale agriculture and an experimental farm working on adapting temperate-climate plants to the tropical climate. Every night hordes of outrigger canoes sally out to fish the fringing reefs and there's also much line-fishing from the reef edge.

POPULATION & PEOPLE

There are more Niueans off island than on. At the turn of the century the population was around 4500, at independence in 1974 it was still around 4000 although it had probably been higher in the intervening years. Now it's down to 2000 or less and falling. There are about 18,500 Niueans living in NZ and another 2000 to 3000 in Australia. All around Niue you'll see empty and abandoned houses; some villages have more uninhabited than inhabited homes.

ARTS

There's a little wood carving and pandanus weaving but no large-scale production. NZ artist Mark Cross is married to a Niuean and

his large, dramatic, almost surreal, canvases can be seen in the Niue Hotel and Matavai Resort lobbies or at Tahiono Arts in the Commercial Centre in Alofi.

SOCIETY & CONDUCT

Niue is still a traditional Polynesian society in many respects – and the people are very conservative, as you will observe on Sunday when church and quiet are the order of the day. On that day no boats are allowed to go to sea between 4 am and 9 pm – so there's no scuba diving or fishing. The radio station shuts down, swimming is only permitted at a couple of beaches and after church your choices are a long afternoon siesta or watching videos.

Traditional customs continue, such as the kaloama spawning season when a number of beaches and reef swimming holes are closed. A *fono* – ban on fishing – is declared by a village council and signs are posted on the sea tracks and at the beaches and canoe landings. Teenage boys enter adulthood with a hair-cutting ceremony, and there's a similar ear piercing ceremony for girls.

NIUE

RELIGION

Churches of the Protestant Ekalesia Niue, related to the original LMS, are found in every village. Since WWII Roman Catholic, Latter Day Saint (Mormon), Seventh-Day Adventist, Baha'i and Jehovah's Witness churches can also be found. Sunday is taken seriously – see the Society & Conduct section – and it's worth catching a church service as the singing is fantastic.

LANGUAGE

The Niuean language is similar to Tongan and also has Samoan influences. The letter 'g' is pronounced 'ng' as in Samoan. Most people speak English as a second language but a few words of Niuean will go down well.

Niuean Basics

Hello.	*Fakaalofa atu.*
Goodbye.	*To feleveia.*
How are you?	*Malolo nakai a koe?*
I'm well (thanks).	*Malolo (fakaaue).*
Please.	*Fakamolemole.*
Thank you.	*Fakaaue lahi.*

Facts for the Visitor

TOURIST OFFICES

The friendly Niue Tourism Office (☎ 4224, fax 4225, niuetourism@mail.gov.nu), PO Box 42, Alofi, is at the Commercial Centre. It has a website at www.visit.nu. Niue is represented abroad by the Tourism Council of the South Pacific (see the Regional Facts for the Visitor chapter).

VISAS & EMBASSIES

A passport is required to enter Niue. There are no visa requirements for stays of less than 30 days, so long as you have an onward ticket and 'sufficient' funds.

CUSTOMS

Don't bring fresh food with you – there are strict quarantine regulations on the island.

MONEY

The NZ dollar (see Exchange Rates in the Regional Facts for the Visitor chapter) is used in Niue. The Westpac bank change travellers cheques and exchanges foreig currency, but charges NZ$10 for credit car advances on Visa or MasterCard. It's ope weekdays from 9 am to 3 pm. You can us credit cards at the pricier hotels, car rent agencies and the dive shop.

POST & COMMUNICATIONS

The post office is in the Commercial Centr and has some pretty stamps and a philateli centre, but mail to or from Niue can be ver slow. There's no cybercafe in Niue yet.

Niue's international telephone code i ☎ 683. The Telecom office is in the Com mercial Centre and is open 24 hours. I charges NZ$1.90 per minute for a call t NZ, NZ$2.30 to Australia or NZ$4.20 t North America or Europe. The internationa access code is ☎ 00.

INTERNET RESOURCES

Many businesses have email addresses an even websites. The 'sin' in Niuean ema addresses stands for Savage Island Net work. See Tourist Offices earlier.

BOOKS

Terry Chapman's *Niue – A History of the Is land* (1982) tells the full story of the islan and can be bought in Niue. Treat it wit caution, as dates may be inaccurate. *Niue The Island & Its People*, by S Percy Smit is a recent reprint of a study of the islan first published in 1902. Novels by Niuea John Pule include *The Shark that Ate th Sun* and *Burn My Head in Heaven.*

There's a library with a good Pacific sec tion opposite the hospital.

MEDIA

Niue Radio broadcasts at 91MHz an 102MHz FM from 6 am. TV broadcast start at 6 pm; both radio and TV shut dow around 11 pm. On Sunday both start broad casting in the evening. The weekly *Niu Star* keeps you up to date on island events

TIME

Niue is east of the dateline and is 11 hour behind GMT. When it is noon in Niue it i pm in Los Angeles, 11 pm in London and 1 am the next day in Auckland.

LECTRICITY

here's 24 hour 240V AC, 50 Hz electric-y; the plugs and sockets are the three-lade style used in Australia and NZ.

HEALTH

he government's brochure suggests that nce the water is untreated it should be oiled as a precaution. However, everybody eems to drink it without any problems.

The hospital (☎ 4100) is in south Alofi.

DANGERS & ANNOYANCES

iue is a very quiet and safe place but you hould take care walking or climbing round the coast and caves. Even a small all on the island's sometimes razor-sharp oral rocks would be an unpleasant experi-nce. The knife-edge rocks wreck shoes ith remarkable speed.

Dial ☎ 999 for police, fire or ambulance.

BUSINESS HOURS

hops are generally open 8 am to 4 pm Monday to Friday, and in the morning and ate afternoon on Saturday.

PUBLIC HOLIDAYS & SPECIAL EVENTS

iue celebrates New Year's Day, Easter, Anzac Day and Christmas (see Public Holi-ays in the Regional Facts for the Visitor hapter for dates). In addition, Niue's inde-endence is marked by the Constitution Cel-brations around 19 October, with singing, ancing, sports events and handicraft isplays. The Monday of these celebrations s Peniamina Day, celebrating the arrival of Christianity in 1846. Each village has its own how day during the year, and the island has surprising number of golf tournaments.

ACTIVITIES

Niue's active Hash House Harriers ☎ 4052) run on Monday afternoon. Visitors re welcome at the Niue Sports Club's nine ole golf course, across from the airport ter-inal. The club also has tennis courts.

Niue is small enough, the traffic light enough and some of the sea tracks rough enough to make Niue a great place for mountain biking.

Snorkelling

Niue Dive (☎ 4311) operates snorkelling trips and the Snake Gully site is equally interesting for snorkellers and divers. There's good snorkelling at the Limu Pools and the Matapa Chasm while just north of Hio Beach is an idyllic little rock pool, ideal for snorkelling at low tide. On the east coast, Vaitafe also has a reef-top pool with good snorkelling. There are places around the island where snorkellers can swim out-side the reef but you need to be a confident swimmer and should seek local advice about entry points and water conditions be-fore venturing offshore. The Omahi sea track, just north of Alofi, is a good entry point, as is Avatele Beach.

Diving

Niue Dive (☎ 4311, or ☎ mobile 3483, fax 4028, niuedive@dive.nu) is the island's dive shop and charges NZ$140 for a two dive boat trip with full gear. It's a good operation: the equipment is top quality, moorings are used at the dive sites and there's no fish feeding. See its website at www.dive.nu.

Niue has no rivers running into the sea so visibility is stunning. Especially in the April to November dry season, 40m visibility is the norm. The water is warm too – peaking at 29°C in January, and only falling to 25°C in August. All diving is on the west coast.

Caves and sea snakes are Niue's two prime dive attractions. Directly offshore from the Limu Pools is **Ana Mahaga** (or Twin Caves), where two chimneys plummet down through the reef then turn through 90° to emerge as huge caves on the reef edge. A horizontal tunnel joins the two caves to make this one of Niue's most spectacular dives. It's nearly 30m deep at the cave floors. South from this dive are **Namoui** and **Anono**, a marine reserve where turtles are often encountered.

Directly off from Alofi the **Chimney** drops from 5m at the top over 20m straight

NIUE

down before emerging as a reef cave. Also off Alofi are **Opaahi** and a dive known as the **Toilet Bowl** or, more politely, Faka Laina after the sea track that leads down to the coast at this point. The dive features a twisting series of gullies, ravines, chasms and caves leading out to reef ridges extending into deeper water. The toilet bowl moniker comes from a shore entry point that rises and falls like a flushing toilet.

Outside the pretty little bay at Avatele there are several popular dives including the **Ridges** and the **Anchors**, with a number of old anchors embedded in the reef, and **Snake Gully** where divers will encounter all the sea snakes they might ever hope to meet in a lifetime. On the surface snakes are constantly popping up to grab a breath before heading down again. From below it resembles a collection of snake elevators constantly wriggling up or down. Down in the gully there are snakes winding along the bottom, snakes seemingly sleeping and snakes snarled up in what looks like a sea snake tangle.

A little further south the **Fans** features wonderful gorgonian fans below 30m, but this dive cannot be made if there is a current running around Tepa Point. The **Wall** stretches back from the Fans towards Snake Gully.

Beaches & Swimming

Niue has none of those long sweeps of golden sand that you find on Pacific postcards. In fact even finding a place you can go for a swim can be difficult. Around most of the coast waves beat straight on to the reef only a stone's throw from the towering cliffs that edge the island. There are, however, a few tiny patches of beach and some delightful natural rock pools – ideal for a swim or snorkel, though often only accessible at low tide. On Sunday swimming is only allowed at the Limu Pools and Matapa Chasm. Swimming may also be banned at some places during the January to May *kaloama* spawning season.

Fishing

Horizon Charters (☎ 4067 or ☎ 4106, fa 4010) and Wahoo Charters (☎/fax 434 wahoo@sin.net.nu) will take you fishin for wahoo, tuna and mahimahi in the wate around the island.

SHOPPING

Some handicrafts and T-shirts are availabl from shops in the Commercial Centre, suc as Taoke Prints.

Getting There & Away

AIR

Not many people visit Niue so flights hav been an off and on proposition. Royal Tong an (see Airlines in the introductory Gettir Around the Region chapter) flies fro Auckland, NZ, on Monday, crossing th International Dateline to arrive in Niue thre hours later on Sunday and continuing t Nuku'alofa in Tonga (fast forward to Mor day again) with connections back to NZ. O Saturday it flies Nuku'alofa-Vava'u-Niue arriving on Friday, and back. Fares to Niu are expensive: around NZ$1300 return fro NZ or T$340 from Tonga.

In Alofi, reconfirm your flight with Pele ni's Travel Agent. Niue is very relaxed, th approved way of departing is to check i early, get your boarding pass, pay the de parture tax (NZ$20), get your passpo stamped by immigration and then scoo back to town for lunch or a last swim.

SEA

There are no regular shipping services t the island but many yachts turn up durin the April to December season. Visitin yachties are advised that it's preferable t arrive on weekdays rather than at the wee end. There is no accessible pier or wharf Niue but moorings are available at a cost o NZ$5/10 per day for a small/large yacht.

The Niue Yacht Club (yachtclub(sin.net.nu), PO Box 140, Alofi, has a websi at www.visit.nu/yachting.html.

Yachties are also subject to the NZ$20 departure tax.

ORGANISED TOURS

Helen's Tours (☎ 4307, or ☎ 4167 after hours, fax 4308) operates round-the-island tours, village visits, walking tours, canoe trips and the like. Niue Dive (☎ 4311) does glass-bottom boat trips. Herman Taga-oailuga (☎ 3106) is an expert on shells who leads reef walks, and Tamafai Fuhiniu (☎ 4394) is a canoe maker who will tell you all about traditional Niuean *vaka* (canoes) and take you out on one.

The Ulupaka and Anatoloa caves are on Tali Magatogia's (☎ 4337 or ☎ 3405, fax 4010) family land and he does tours to either or both caves. Wear old clothes as there's a bit of crawling to do and you will get pretty dirty. The Ulupaka Cave trip takes about 1½ hours and includes a squeeze through the 'keyhole'; the Anatoloa trip is slightly shorter. Both caves have spectacular stalagmites and stalactites and, refreshingly, they are not commercialised. Prices depend on the number of people visiting and caves visited; count on around NZ$25.

Misa, a friendly Niuean, does forest walks (☎ 4394) for NZ$25. In a couple of hours wandering through the dense forests in the centre of the island you will learn to identify different plants and trees, see how to construct an *uga* (coconut crab) trap, hear about traditional ways of catching fruit doves and starlings (you need 15 to 20 for a square meal!) and find out about Misa's childhood in the forest.

Getting Around

AIR

Hanan, Niue's airport, is about 3km south-east from the centre of Alofi. There are taxis at the airport for the twice-weekly flights and Helen's Tours (see Organised Tours, earlier) charges NZ$6 for a trip to the Alofi hotels and NZ$10 to any places further afield. However, most accommodation places on the island will collect you from the airport.

ROAD

Niue has over 100km of paved road but no public transport. A variety of vehicles can be rented from Alofi Rentals (☎/fax 4017, alofirentals@sin.net.nu), Niue Rentals (☎ 4216, fax 4065, niurentals@sin.net.nu) and Ama's Rentals/Budget Rent-a-Car (☎ 4307, fax 4308). Usually there are plenty of vehicles available but it may be wise to make advance reservations.

Car rental is NZ$40 to $50 a day, motorcycles NZ$25, scooters NZ$20 and mountain bikes are NZ$5; they're all cheaper by the week. The roads are uncrowded and the driving is pleasantly conservative: driving is on the left-hand side of the road and the speed limit is 40km/h in town and 60km/h out of town – but many people stick to 40km/h everywhere. Watch out for jaywalking chickens during daylight hours and crabs on wet nights. Visitors must present their driving licence to the police to obtain a local licence for NZ$2. Hitching is relatively easy although traffic is light, particularly on the east coast.

TAXI

There are a number of taxis around town including Alofi Rentals (☎ 4017, ☎ 4373 after hours, or ☎ 1107 mobile). Count on 50c a kilometre.

Around Niue

ALOFI
• pop 730

Alofi consists of one street stretching for several kilometres along the coast. Right by the airport turn-off is the **Huanaki Cultural Centre & Museum**, with interesting displays on the island's history and traditional life. It's open Monday to Friday, 9 am to 4 pm, and admission is by donation.

The **Opaahi Landing**, right in the middle of Alofi, is the best known of the places where Captain Cook tried, unsuccessfully, to come ashore in 1744. Alofi has several other traditional canoe landing spots; opposite the police station the **Utuko sea track** leads down to a pocket-handkerchief-sized beach.

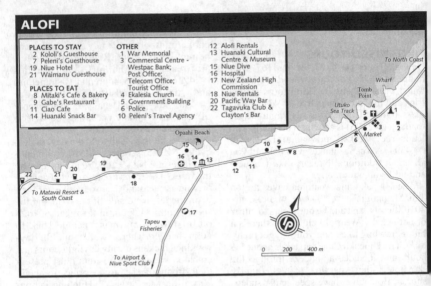

ALOFI

PLACES TO STAY
2 Kololi's Guesthouse
7 Peleni's Guesthouse
19 Niue Hotel
21 Waimanu Guesthouse

PLACES TO EAT
8 Mitaki's Cafe & Bakery
9 Gabe's Restaurant
11 Ciao Cafe
14 Huanaki Snack Bar

OTHER
1 War Memorial
3 Commercial Centre - Westpac Bank; Post Office; Telecom Office; Tourist Office
4 Ekalesia Church
5 Government Building
6 Police
10 Peleni's Travel Agency

12 Alofi Rentals
13 Huanaki Cultural Centre & Museum
15 Niue Dive
16 Hospital
17 New Zealand High Commission
18 Niue Rentals
20 Pacific Way Bar
22 Tagavuka Club & Clayton's Bar

In north Alofi the **Omahi sea track** leads to a point where you can swim outside the reef if conditions are suitable. At low tide you can walk out on the reef from the wharf, looking for natural pools in the reef flat.

Towards the northern end of town the **Ekalesia Church** is on Tomb Point, opposite the Commercial Centre and overlooking the island wharf. Headstones outside the church mark the graves of two island kings, Tuitoga (pronounced 'tui tonga'; ruled 1876-87) and Fataaiki (ruled 1888-96). Niue's government consisted of separate chiefdoms prior to the missionary period and these first two kings were actually elected. Fataaiki was only a part-time king, reckoning his other job, as a schoolteacher, was more important. The grave of NZ Resident Commissioner Hector Larsen is also here. He was murdered in 1953, a time when the island was in great turmoil over proposals to allow cargo ships to be unloaded on Sunday and other changes to long-held traditions.

Ships anchor offshore from the wharf and even containers are wrestled ashore by barge. Opposite the wharf area there's a **war memorial**, beside which were the seats vertical stone slabs which were the seats used for the coronation of kings Tuitoga and Fataaiki.

AROUND THE ISLAND

Almost all the island's attractions are on the coast and getting to them may involve a bit of scrambling or walking. It's 60km right round the island on the coast road, and the distances which follow are in an anticlockwise direction from the junction by the police station in the middle of Alofi. Along the east coast, between Mutalau at the northern end of the island and Vaiea in the south, there's about 20km of unsealed road. Cyclists intent on making the complete trip around the island should start early, and carry plenty of fluids to cope with the heat and humidity.

All around Niue you'll see signs to 'sea tracks', the roads or paths leading down to canoe landings on the coast. Some of the landings are floodlit at night when much of the island fishing takes place.

There are many gravestones around Niue; people are usually buried on their family land. The marker is new at **Peniamina's Grave** (4.7km from Alofi), the site commemorating Nukai Peniamina he islander credited with introducing Christianity to Niue in 1846. He died in 1874.

The **Avaiki Cave** (7km) is clearly signposted from the road, and a path leads down through a narrow gorge to an impressive coastal cavern sheltering a beautiful rock pool filled with crystal clear water, just to the north of where the trail emerges on the coast. Swimming in the pool is forbidden on Sunday and when the kaloama spawn. Legends relate that the first canoe bringing Niuean settlers to the island landed here. Only 200m further on is the **Palaha Cave**. There's no rock pool here but there are impressive stalagmites and stalactites.

Probably the finest (and longest) stretch of sand on the island, **Hio Beach** (10.5km) is reached by a wooden stairway down the cliffside. At low tide you can walk across the reef about 100m north to an idyllic snorkelling pool inside the reef. The winding chasm is full of tropical fish, fringed with coral and features not only small overhangs and caves but two swim-throughs. This is snorkelling at its finest.

At one of the island's most popular swimming and snorkelling spots, fresh water percolates into the **Limu Pools** (9.9km), creating an out-of-focus effect and making the water noticeably cooler than the sea, particularly at low tide. Apart from colourful fish you may also see black and grey striped sea snakes in the pools. The second pool is just to the north, with a natural bridge between it and the sea. Just off shore from the Limu Pools is Ana Mahaga, one of the island's most spectacular scuba diving spots.

At 11.7km a turn-off in Hikutavake village leads to two attractions. Take the right fork first for the 15 minute walk to the **Talava Arches**. Here there are a series of huge arches and deep caves but you can only reach the main cavern, with its impressive limestone formations, at low tide. A light can also be useful. Just five minutes down the left fork trail enjoy a refreshing dip in the **Matapa Chasm**. This narrow channel, running straight out to the sea, is blocked off by a rock formation that almost seals the chasm. As at the Limu Pools, there's a

steady influx of freshwater creating a curious temperature inversion where the surface water is much cooler than the salt water a metre or two below.

Across from the village green at **Mutalau** (18.6km) is a memorial commemorating Peniamina's return to the island in 1846 and the arrival of the Samoan Paulo three years later. Opposite, the sea track leads down to the **Uluvehi Landing**, passing a display panel recounting the dramatic events of Christianity's coming to Niue.

A sign clearly points the way to **Vaitafe** (22.1km). Leave your car at the road; the rough track only goes for a short distance before becoming a walking track. It takes about 20 minutes to reach the coast with one short drop followed by a longer tumble down a picturesque narrow rocky corridor fringed with bright green vegetation. Finally there's a couple of metres of rock climbing before the track spills out on the reef. At low tide you can walk along the reef for some distance north and south, but head north to a huge swimming pool in the reef. Fresh water filters into this pool, creating a greasy look to the water and causing strange temperature variations. It doesn't seem to worry the fish which are colourful and abundant.

The **Anatoloa Cave** (23.6km), just before the village of **Lakepa** (24.7km), and the **Ulupaka Cave** (25.9km), just after the village, are extensive limestone cave systems complete with stalactites and stalagmits. They're on private property and you can only visit them with Tali's Cave Tours (see Organised Tours). If you continue down the Ulupaka Cave track a steep pathway drops down to **Motu Landing**. A long ladder makes the final descent to the reef.

From the seaward side of the village green in **Liku** (30km) a driveable sea track runs down to the sea, where there are several pretty little beaches but nowhere to swim except some small rock pools at low tide. Look for the curious green-coloured grave figure on the inland side of the road just south of the village. A little further south is the eccentric **Sculpture Park** (32.2km) with strange creations and a barbecue.

NIUE

The trail to the **Vaikona Chasm** (33.7km) is not always distinct but it's marked with red trail arrows so it's easy to follow as long as you pay attention. A 20 minute walk through shady forest drops down through a maze of paths through dead coral pinnacles, suddenly bringing you up beside a huge hole in the ground; way below is the chasm. The trail continues round to the other side of the chasm where a sign warns you, in no uncertain terms, that the cave leading to the chasm is unsafe and you enter at your own risk.

If you decide to take the risk it's a relatively easy clamber down through the sloping cave to orange ropes leading to the chasm floor. There's a small freshwater pool at this end of the chasm but a little further in is a much larger pool. Green ferns contrast with the brilliant blue of the pool and high above there's an oval of sky fringed with green. It's a magical place and if you swim to the end of the long pool and dive under the wall you will come up in a large and rather dark cave. Making one dive into the dark is scary enough but for the truly brave it's said that there's an ongoing series of caves beyond the first. A mask and snorkel and an underwater light are required.

After leaving the chasm you can walk on to the coast, but take care as the red arrows give out. It's advisable to mark where you emerge on the cliffs as the scenery looks remarkably similar. The trail is difficult to find and clambering over razor-sharp, crumbling limestone rocks and beating your way through the tangled vegetation is seriously unpleasant.

The **Togo Chasm** (36.5km; pronounced 'tong-oh') is very easy to find. The trail is well kept and the 20 minute walk through the green forest is followed by a sharp descent through a jagged forest of threatening pinnacles. A long ladder takes you down to a picturesque little oasis – a sandy-floored ravine with palm trees. Unfortunately, this postcard-perfect beach isn't on the sea. The far end of the ravine is cut off by a pool of stagnant green water. If you make your way behind the boulders at the ladder end, a cave leads through to the sea, where waves crash onto the rocks at the entrance. Back at the top of the ladder continue a few steps to the cliff edge where you can look down into the chasm, the sea cave or along the dramatic coastline.

At the village of Hakupu (40.7km) the driveable sea track takes you to within a few minutes walk of the **Anapala Chasm**. A long flight of steps descends between the narrow ravine walls to a long freshwater rock pool, traditionally used as a water source in times of drought. Once you've swum up to the other end you can turn round, swim back and climb back up that long flight of steps.

Turn towards the coast at **Vaiea** (45.6km) and take the clearly marked Vaiea sea track to the site of the **Fatiau Tuai deserted village**. After a short distance the road forks, take the right fork – the village was located at the next fork in the road. Take the left fork from the village site to reach the rugged coastline. The villagers were relocated to Vaiea in the 1950s and there are only scattered remains of the old village.

The road drops steeply to the village of **Avatele** (48.6km; pronounced 'avasele') where there's a pretty, but rocky, little beach on a sheltered bay. There are some popular diving sites just offshore from the bay, including the aptly named Snake Gully. Just beyond Avatele is the **Matavai Resort** (50.4km) and the village of **Tamakautoga** (51km), with a nice little beach at the end of the sea track.

The final attraction before completing the circuit is the **Anaana Lookout** (54.3km) with stirring views back along the rocky and rugged coastline towards Tepa Point, just beyond Avatele.

PLACES TO STAY

Apart from the Niue Hotel and the Matavai Resort, accommodation generally includes kitchen facilities – shared in the cheaper places – and laundry facilities. Places that don't have their own email address can be contacted via info@mail.gov.nu.

There's no real backpacker accommodation on Niue apart from the *Huvalu Forest Camp*, which is a long way from anywhere on the remote eastern side of the island, just south of the trail to the Togo Beach. There are rather basic cooking and bathroom facilities. You can camp here or use the bunkroom; count on NZ$10 to $15 a night.

In Alofi the *Waimanu Guesthouse* (☎ 4224, fax 4225) is at the southern end of town, perched on the cliff edge and close to the Amanau sea track, leading down to a natural pool inside the reef. There are four rooms with shared facilities at NZ$40/55 for singles/doubles in the high season, NZ$30/45 in the low. A larger room with an attached bathroom costs NZ$65 and there are two self-contained units with kitchen facilities for NZ$80.

Kololi's Guesthouse (☎ 4258, fax 4010) is centrally located but set well back from the main road. There are four rooms with shared bathroom facilities. Three of them are twin rooms at NZ$35, one is a slightly larger double room for NZ$42. Upstairs there's a room with an attached bathroom and an adjoining smaller bedroom for NZ$50. There's a communal kitchen, laundry and lounge room with TV.

In the centre *Peleni's Guesthouse* (☎ 4135, fax 4322, tokes@sin.net.nu) is slightly back from the road, opposite the gym. There are three rooms with shared bathroom, kitchen and laundry facilities at NZ$35.

Heading up the coast north from Alofi are three small places. *Coral Gardens Resort* (☎ 4235, fax 4222, sguest@sin.net.nu) is 5km north of Alofi and has five pleasant separate *fale* each with an attached bathroom, a small kitchen, ceiling fan, TV and verandah for NZ$80/100. There's a bar on the cliff edge. Right in the middle of the grounds is a spectacular sinkhole with a pool where you can swim in the right conditions; steps and a ladder lead down to the waterline. The resort also has a fine sunset view deck at the Makapu Point lookout.

Another 2km brings you to the simpler *Anaiki Motel* (☎ 4321, fax 4320), adjacent to the Avaiki Cave. Rooms cost from around NZ$60 for a single. Continue up the coast to the *Namukulu Motel* (☎ 4052, fax 3001, namukulu_motel@mail.gov.nu), 10km from

the centre of Alofi. There are three very well-designed fale, each with a double room and a couple of single beds in the entrance lounge area. They also have a bathroom, kitchen, ceiling fan and verandah and there's an attractive swimming pool. At low tide you can walk along the reef to Limu or there are bicycles available for free. Rooms cost NZ$125/95 in the high/low season.

In Alofi's south, the *Niue Hotel* (☎ 4092, fax 4310, niuehotel@sin .net.nu) is on the cliff edge with standard motel-style rooms. Each has a fridge, TV, ceiling fan, verandah and an attached bathroom and cost NZ$65. There's a licensed bar, a popular restaurant and a swimming pool.

Niue's newest and biggest development, the *Matavai Resort* (☎ 4360, fax 4361, matavai@mail.gov.nu) is 10km south of Alofi between Tamakautoga and Avatele. The rooms all have a bathroom, fridge, TV, ceiling fan, verandah, ISD phone and access to the guest laundry and cost NZ$100. There's a restaurant, bar and two swimming pools spectacularly perched on the cliff edge. From the car park a short bushwalk leads down to the reef.

Just beyond the Matavai, in the attractive little village of Avatele, *Esther's Motel* (☎ 3708, fax 4010) has three rooms for NZ$40 to $45.

PLACES TO EAT
Some accommodation includes cooking facilities but if you plan to prepare your own food bring some supplies for the first few days. Flights only arrive on Friday and Sunday and shops (there are several small supermarkets in Alofi) are generally closed over the weekend so you may have to wait until Monday to shop. Don't bring fresh food, as it may be subject to quarantine regulations. The weekly market, on Friday morning, is very inconveniently scheduled for visitors arriving by air. Get there early – it's busy from dawn and the good stuff soon sells out. Around the island most villages will have a small shop, although you will need to ask where it is.

Apart from the Matavai Resort and the Hakupu village feast, all the following places are in Alofi. If you're eating out it's wise to plan ahead or plan to diet. Lunch time, when various places open during the noon to 1.30 pm peak period, is not so bad.

The *Huanaki Snack Bar* (☎ 4071) is in the Huanaki Museum compound and has a variety of burgers at around NZ$4.50, sandwiches at NZ$2.50 and other light meals. It has a burger night on Friday. *Mitaki's Cafe & Bakery* features fish, pies, sausages and the like, all with chips. It is open late on Saturday and they also bake bread. *Tapeu Fisheries* (☎ 4106), on the airport road, is the island fish and chip specialist, but recently it has only been opening on Friday nights for their excellent NZ$7 fish, chips and salad deal. There are several places selling fast food (pies, fish, chips) in the stores and at the Commercial Centre.

At night the restaurants at the *Matavai Resort* and the *Niue Hotel* are the most reliable. The Matavai Resort's restaurant is open every night except Wednesday and does a popular Saturday night barbecue. On other nights its menu features main courses in the NZ$18 to $22 range, good food and very substantial serves. The Niue Hotel restaurant is usually open if it has guests who want to eat in. Its excellent NZ$20 Sunday night buffet is a major island attraction.

Emanuela Sabatini's *Ciao Cafe* (☎ 4316) probably has the best food on the island. This Italian outpost does lunch Monday to Friday, with individual pizzas for up to NZ$8 and family-size up to NZ$14. There are also pasta dishes for NZ$5 and focaccia at NZ$2 to $4. Tuesday is the evening you're most likely to find them open, followed by Thursday and Wednesday, but it will open any time if four or more people book. The five course dinner – antipasto, soup, pasta dish, main course and dessert – costs just NZ$24 and you can wash it down with Italian wine. You can also order the courses individually; the main course is NZ$15.

Gabe's Restaurant (☎ 4379) does lunch most days of the week and on Wednesday puts on a popular seafood buffet with lots of local food (taro, breadfruit and sweet potato) and Western dishes. It costs NZ$15, including dessert, and it's wise to book ahead. An island group plays and a karaoke session often concludes the evening.

Hakupu puts on a regular *fiafia* (dance) night (☎ 4394), usually on Wednesday, if a minimum of seven people book. The cost per person is NZ$30, or NZ$35 including transport. There's a delicious selection of Niuean dishes cooked *umu* style (in an underground oven). A traditional welcome by the village women, music and dances accompany the food. *Ota*, raw fish marinated in coconut milk and lime juice, and uga (coconut crab) are island specialities.

ENTERTAINMENT

New Zealand beers are NZ$2 or $2.50 a can at island bars. The *Pacific Way Bar*, next to the Waimanu Guesthouse on the south side of Alofi, and the *Tagavuka Club & Clayton's Bar*, a stone's throw further south behind the K-Mart supermarket, are the popular local bars. The *Top Club*, at the Niue Sports Club golf course, welcomes visitors. You can also get a beer at the *Niue Hotel* in Alofi, the *Coral Gardens Resort* and *Veejay's*, to the north, and the *Matavai Resort* to the south. Friday and Saturday night are dance nights in Niue and the islanders will be stepping out at a number of the island bars.

The picture theatre next to Veejay's, 9km north of Alofi, shows fairly current films for NZ$5.

NIUE'S REEFS

Niue consists of just the single island but there are also three reefs in its territorial waters. **Beveridge Reef** is 300km south-east of Niue, and the huge horseshoe-shaped reef has a 5km sandspit on its north-west side. There's also a wreck of an old tuna fishing boat, washed high and dry on the east side of the reef. There's impressive scuba diving in the reef pass, which is wide enough to allow boats to sail into the deep and open lagoon.

The other reefs are Antiope and Haran.

NIUE

Pitcairn Islands

Tiny Pitcairn Island, with a population you could easily seat in a city bus, is most famous as the hideaway settlement for the notorious *Bounty* mutineers. Now, over 200 years later, it is one of the last remnants of the British Empire. As well as Pitcairn itself – a beautifully green and lush high island – the Pitcairn group includes two low-lying atolls and a *makatea* island (see Geography & Geology later in this chapter), which is a World Heritage Site due to its virtually untouched environment and endemic birdlife.

Facts about the Pitcairn Islands

HISTORY

These islands have always had a close connection with Mangareva in the Gambier Archipelago and at one time a Polynesian trading triangle operated between Mangareva, Pitcairn and Henderson. Mangareva's lagoon had abundant supplies of black-lipped pearl oyster shells, which made fine scrapers or scoops and could be cut to make fish-hooks. Pitcairn had the only stone quarry in south-eastern Polynesia for adzes and spear points. Henderson's tiny population supplied red tropicbird feathers, green turtles and other 'luxury' goods. Then over-population devastated Mangareva, deforestation removed the trees used for making the great seagoing canoes and, in a classic ecological disaster, the downfall of Mangareva led to the abandonment of both Henderson and Pitcairn.

See the individual island sections for the Polynesian settlements on Henderson and Pitcairn and for the colourful and tragic history of Pitcairn's *Bounty* settlers. See also the boxed text 'Mutiny on the *Bounty*' for the full story of the mutiny.

The four Pitcairn Islands would probably have been annexed by the French along with the Tuamotu and Gambier islands were

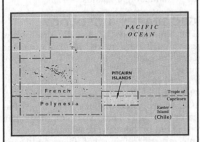

HIGHLIGHTS

- **Ducie** – the beautiful lagoon and the amazing collection of flotsam on the beach (an academic paper noted that Suntory whisky bottles were the most numerous bottles).

- **Henderson** – the classic *makatea* geology of the island, and its four endemic bird species

- **Pitcairn** – reminders of the island's *Bounty* history include Fletcher Christian's Bible and the *Bounty* models for sale, carved by a mutineer's descendant

- **Polynesian petroglyphs** – Pitcairn's pre-European history is carved into the rocks at Down Rope

PITCAIRN ISLANDS

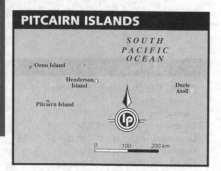

SOUTH PACIFIC OCEAN

Oeno Island

Henderson Island

Ducie Atoll

Pitcairn Island

0   100   200 km

it not for the British settlement. Henderson, Oeno and Ducie were annexed in 1902 and appropriate signs were erected on each of these uninhabited islands.

GEOGRAPHY & GEOLOGY

The four islands of the Pitcairn group, essentially outliers of the Tuamotu and Gambier islands of French Polynesia, comprise 43 sq km of land scattered over a vast tract of ocean; it's more than 500km from Oeno in the west to Ducie in the east. The islands are three distinct types. Tiny Pitcairn is a high island, the tip of a mountain rising out of the sea. The island has only an intermittent fringing reef. Oeno and Ducie are classic atolls, a scatter of low-lying sandy islets on a coral reef fringing a central lagoon. Henderson, by far the largest island in the group, is a makatea island, an ancient coral reef that geological forces have pushed up above sea level.

Pitcairn lies 2100km east of Easter Island, or some 5350km north-west of New Zealand (NZ). The nearest inhabited island is Mangareva in French Polynesia.

CLIMATE

Pitcairn enjoys a very mild and equable climate, the mean monthly temperatures varying from 19°C in August to 24°C in February. The lowest temperature ever recorded is 10°C; the highest 34°C. Rainfall averages about 1800mm per year, spread fairly evenly, although July and August are usually the driest months and November the wettest.

ECONOMY

Although the islanders are essentially self sufficient for food they have become used to many imported goods. Fuel is needed for their motorcycles, for outboard motors and for the island's electricity generator. Island homes are typically equipped with washing machines, microwaves, electric cookers, fridges, stereo equipment, VCRs and deep-freezes. To pay for this some islanders have government jobs but the postmaster, for example, isn't paid much since the post office is only open for one hour on Sunday, Tuesday and Thursday (plus extended hours around the arrival and departure of a mail-carrying vessel).

Most income comes from selling the island's famous stamps to collectors, or curios to passing ships or by mail order. From time to time the British government funds major infrastructure projects. For example, in 1998 an apiculture program was funded by its Department for International Development. The program has been successful, in fact more so than anticipated, with Pitcairn's apiarists exporting their honey worldwide.

POPULATION & PEOPLE

Only Pitcairn is populated although Henderson has had Polynesian populations of perhaps a few dozen in the past. The population of Pitcairn is currently around 50 although there are many more Pitcairners resident overseas. There are major concerns that the island cannot maintain a viable population and may eventually be deserted. The people of Pitcairn are descendants of the original *Bounty* mutineers and their Tahitian companions, plus other arrivals over the years. The *Bounty* family names, Adams, Young and Christian, are still common.

RELIGION

In 1887 a Seventh-Day Adventist missionary arrived from the USA and converted the whole island so Saturday is observed as the Sabbath, alcohol is ostensibly banned (that ban seems to be slipping) and the islanders are supposed not to eat pork (that ban can be a bit loose as well) or fish that do not have scales (which means the island's large

upply of lobsters are used only for bait).
Declining interest in religion has been an is-
and problem of recent years.

LANGUAGE

Pitcairners communicate quite happily in
English but among themselves lapse into
Pitkern, which could be described as 18th
century seafaring English spiced with an
assortment of Polynesian words. So when
Pitcairners go out to shoot goats they do it
with *muskets*, the goats end up as *wekle*
(victuals), houses have a *deck* and if a Pitcairn party consumes too much of that
banned beverage it's possible that *all hands*
(everyone) may *capsize* (fall over).

Facts for the Visitor

VISAS

No visa is necessary for visitors while their
ship is present. If you want to stay on Pitcairn after your ship leaves, however, your
stay must be approved by the islanders and
a six month stay permit issued.

The islands are administered by the Pitcairn Islands Administration at the British
Consulate-General in Auckland, NZ, and
applications should be made to that office.
Think up a good reason for your stay before
you bother applying and allow six months
for the application to be considered. You
must have in your possession NZ$175 for
each week you intend to stay. The application fee is NZ$10, and the licence itself
NZ$150 (NZ$75 for visitors under 18).

MONEY

New Zealand dollars (see Exchange Rates
in the Regional Facts for the Visitor chapter) are the official currency of Pitcairn Island although other major currencies will be
happily accepted. Don't count on using
credit cards though.

You could survive on NZ$160 a week,
but budget on about NZ$180 to $200.

POST & COMMUNICATIONS

You can phone or fax Pitcairn Island
through INMARSAT, but the charges are

based on satellite time so you get billed for
dialling and connection times whether or
not the phone is answered. Count on about
NZ$15 a minute. You can expect the phone
(the *only* phone) to be answered between
1800 and 0530 GMT Sunday to Friday – on
Saturday the service is unreliable. The telephone number (following your country's
international access code) is ☎ 872-144-
5372. The fax number is 5373.

To write to anybody on Pitcairn Island,
address mail to: the resident's name, Pitcairn Island, South Pacific Ocean (via NZ),
and count on about three months each
way. A number of Pitcairners are ham
radio amateurs.

INTERNET RESOURCES

There's an informative Pitcairn government
website at http://users.iconz.co.nz/pitcairn.
For information on World Heritage-listed
Henderson Island, visit http://winthrop.
webjump.com/hender.html or www.unesco
.org/whc/sites/487.htm.

BOOKS

A Guide to Pitcairn is the official government publication about the islands. It was
most recently updated in 1990 and is available from the Pitcairn Island Administration
(see Useful Organisations later in this chapter); it costs NZ$8.50, or NZ$12.50 (including post and packaging) if you're ordering
from Australia.

Dea Birkett's *Serpent in Paradise* (1997)
is an account of a three month stay on Pitcairn in 1991. After its publication a
Fletcher Christian descendant commented,
'It's not quite a *fatwah*, but she's not welcome [on Pitcairn]'.

The *Pitcairn Miscellany* is the island's
monthly newsletter. Overseas subscriptions
are available by writing to the Editor, *Pitcairn Miscellany*, South Pacific (via NZ);
annual subscriptions are NZ$8. Reading be-
tween the lines will confirm some of the
local tensions which Dea Birkett found her-
self embroiled in.

Some books about the famous mutiny are
listed in the boxed text 'Mutiny on the
Bounty' later in this chapter.

TIME

Pitcairn is 8½ hours behind GMT (9½ hours during daylight saving).

USEFUL ORGANISATIONS

Pitcairn Islands Administration (☎ 64-9-366 0186, fax 366 0187, pitcairn@iconz.co.nz) is located in Auckland, NZ. Its postal address is: Office of the Commissioner for Pitcairn Islands, Pitcairn Islands Administration, Private Box 105 696, Auckland.

The Pitcairn Magistrate (☎ 872-7612-24115, fax 244116, or via the INMARSAT numbers given under Post & Communications) can be contacted by post at: Pitcairn Island, South Pacific Ocean (via NZ).

Getting There & Away

See the introductory Getting Around the Region chapter for information about Pacific cruises stopping at Pitcairn.

Cargo vessels that stop at Pitcairn usually do not anchor, they simply pause to transfer cargo or passengers to the Pitcairn longboats. The British Consulate-General in Auckland, NZ, advises on schedules for Panama Canal-Auckland cargo ships that will take passengers. The standard fare per person is US$800 to $1000 one way. Getting off the island requires waiting until a ship comes by – it can be a long wait.

If you simply want to hang loose and hope a Pitcairn-bound yacht comes by, Mangareva would be the best place to try your luck. Visiting yachties should be aware that while the Pitcairners are happy to sell fresh fruit, which they grow on the island, other supplies generally have to be imported from NZ and may be in short supply. Although the Pitcairners may appear generous they may secretly resent demands from ill-equipped yachties. There is no sheltered anchorage at Pitcairn and boats must be moved when the winds change.

There is currently much discussion about building an airstrip on Pitcairn. There is sufficient flat land on the island's central plateau to construct a short airstrip, and there are already infrequent but regular flights between Papeete and Mangareva, only 550km away. Air connections would end the islanders' current fears of medical emergencies, would attract more tourism and might help to slow or reverse the population decline. On the other hand it would signal the end of Pitcairn as the isolated, romantic island at the end of the world.

Landings on Pitcairn are notoriously difficult and intending visitors should note that it's not unknown to travel all the way to the island and then be unable to set foot on land due to rough seas.

Pitcairn Island

● pop 50   ● area 5 sq km

Pitcairn Island is so tied up with the *Bounty* story that it's easy to overlook the fact that although it was uninhabited when the *Bounty* mutineers showed up in January 1790 it had, in the past, been settled by Polynesians. The small, green and fertile island rises precipitously from the surrounding sea.

The island is noted for its curious array of place names, which confronts the visitor immediately on arrival at the Bounty Bay landing. The accurately named Hill of Difficulty is the steep trail that leads up to Adamstown, perched 120m above the sea on the Edge. Houses in Adamstown are either 'upside' or 'downside' of the main road through the small settlement.

The island's power generator is turned on for two hours during the morning and for four hours in the evening. The island has a primary school but children move to NZ for secondary schooling.

History

It is believed there was a Polynesian settlement on the island between the 12th and 15th centuries, and there may have been an earlier settlement as long as 2000 years before. As the mutineers were to prove, small though it was, Pitcairn provided all the basic necessities of life. For the Polynesian settlers the island also had the only quarry in this part of

PITCAIRN ISLAND

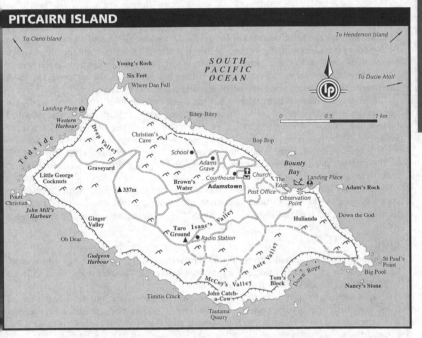

Polynesia where they could flake off the sharp-edged stones needed to make adzes and other cutting tools. The Polynesian Pitcairners carried on a busy trade with the stoneless islanders on Mangareva and Henderson islands; during that time inhospitable Henderson also supported a small resident Polynesian population. In 1606, however, when the explorer Pedro Fernández de Quirós (see the boxed text in the Vanuatu chapter) chanced upon Henderson, the island was uninhabited and presumably Pitcairn Island had also been evacuated.

Pitcairn's European discovery had to wait until 1767 when Philip Cartaret sailed by on HMS *Swallow*. Cartaret decided to name it Pitcairn's Island after Major Pitcairn of the marines, whose son first spotted it. They were unable to land. Finding it was one thing, relocating it would turn out to be quite another; Cartaret misrecorded both the latitude and longitude, mischarting the island by 300km.

In January 1790 the *Bounty* mutineers arrived at Pitcairn after a long search for a remote hideaway, far from the long arm of British naval justice. Led by Fletcher Christian the party was made up of eight other mutineers, six Tahitian men, 12 Tahitian women and a child. Once settled on the island the *Bounty* was burnt, both to prevent escape and to escape detection. The first years of the island's post-*Bounty* history saw a disastrous sequence of violence due to the English mutineers' condescending treatment of the Tahitians and the imbalance in male and female numbers. When a mutineer's partner died in a fall and he demanded that one of the Tahitians give up his wife, a cycle of murder and revenge commenced during which all six Tahitian men and five of the nine mutineers, including Fletcher Christian, were killed by 1794. Only Young, Adams, Quintal and McCoy survived.

A few peaceful years followed before McCoy discovered how to produce a killer

Mutiny on the Bounty

In April 1789, off the island of Tofua in Tonga, Captain William Bligh and 18 crewmen of the HMS *Bounty* were involuntarily relieved of their duties and set adrift in an open boat with a minimum of supplies. The most famous naval mutiny in history, the incident made the *Bounty* a household name, and gave Bligh a centuries-long reputation for bad-tempered cruelty. It also inspired several Hollywood extravaganzas and a plethora of books.

The *Bounty*'s mission was to fetch breadfruit from Tahiti to feed England's African slave population in the Caribbean. Under the command of Bligh, an expert navigator who had trained under Cook, the expedition arrived in Tahiti in September 1788 after a particularly arduous 10-month journey. Breadfruit season was over and they had to wait six months in Tahiti before returning. Three weeks into the return journey, on 28 April 1789, the crew, led by the master's mate Fletcher Christian, mutinied and set Bligh adrift on an open longboat with 18 loyal crew members.

Traditionally Bligh has been painted as the brutal villain in the incident, with Christian the crew's saviour. While Bligh certainly had some anger-management issues, it's likely that the six months in Tahiti, and the Tahitian brides taken by many of the crew, were also strong motivation for the mutineers.

Bligh

Whatever problems Bligh had with people skills, he was a brilliant navigator. Against the odds, he managed to get the longboat, and most of his loyal crew, 7000km from Tonga to Timor in the Dutch East Indies (modern-day Indonesia).

They landed in Tonga briefly, hoping to secure some provisions, but local unrest forced them to cast off after loading only the most meagre of rations. Quartermaster John Norton was attacked and killed by islanders. Sailing west, they were the first Europeans to sight Fiji, and charted several unknown islands in Vanuatu.

They finally reached Timor in the Dutch East Indies on 14 June. Bligh, determined to get that breadfruit, returned to Tahiti in 1792. This time he sensibly bought along 19 marines – in case of further morale problems. In 1806, Bligh was governor of New South Wales in Australia when the so-called 'rum rebellion' overturned his government. Bligh was exonerated from blame … again.

The Mutineers

Under Christian's command, the mutineers returned to Tahiti then attempted to settle on Tubai in the Austral Islands. Meeting local resistance on Tubai, they split into two groups: Fletcher taking a group of sailors and Tahitians off in search of Pitcairn Island (see History, earlier in this chapter), and a second group of 16 sailors staying behind on Tahiti.

The Pursuit

After Bligh returned to England, Captain Edward Edwards (a tyrant who made Bligh look like a saint) was sent in the *Pandora* to search for the mutineers.

Edwards sailed past Ducie Island in the Pitcairn Islands group, but didn't see the larger island 470km to the west where Christian's small troupe had settled. However, Edwards did find and capture 14 of the 16 mutineers who had remained on Tahiti. He stuffed them into a cage on the *Pandora*'s deck before heading back for England. Sadly Edward's sailing skills were not up to Bligh's standards. He ended up sinking the *Pandora* on the Great Barrier Reef off Australia. Of the surviving prisoners, three were ultimately hanged for the mutiny.

Mutiny on the Bounty

Books

The American duo of Nordhoff & Hall wrote three books on the *Bounty* mutiny and its aftermath in 1934. The first of the three, *Mutiny on the Bounty*, provided the plotline for the first two Hollywood versions of the story (see later). *Men against the Sea* follows Bligh's epic open-boat voyage, while *Pitcairn Island* follows Fletcher Christian and his band to Pitcairn.

Two other sources are Richard Hough's *Captain Bligh and Mr Christian* (1973) and Greg Dening's *Mr Bligh's Bad Language* (1992).

More recently, *Fragile Paradise* by Glynn Christian (Fletcher's great-great-great-great-grandson) is a well-researched, if a little speculative, investigation of the mutiny and the story of the mutineers on Pitcairn.

Films

The first, and perhaps the worst, film about the mutiny was *In the Wake of the Bounty* (1933) – a low-budget flick filmed in Pitcairn, Tahiti and Australia and memorable only for being Errol Flynn's first film (as a noble Fletcher Christian). Simultaneously, Hollywood was making *Mutiny on the Bounty* (1935) with Clark Gable in the same role – neither film was too concerned with historical correctness.

The 1962 remake *Mutiny on the Bounty*, starring Marlon Brando as the good guy, was slightly less inaccurate. The film injected huge amounts of cash into the economy of Tahiti, where it was made.

Based on Hough's book, *The Bounty* (1984) is a surprisingly good re-enactment of the tale, with magnificent scenes of Moorea in French Polynesia. Anthony Hopkins plays a more likeable and complex Captain Bligh and Mel Gibson plays Fletcher Christian.

SCREENSOUND AUSTRALIA

Fletcher Christian (Errol Flynn) looks stern as a seaman is flogged for poor dress sense.

Reading the Land

There's a straightforward, down-to-earth approach to everything Pitcairnese and the island's place names are certainly simple, descriptive and rather worrying. Over the years it appears the islanders have had a disturbing propensity for falling right off Pitcairn, many of them tumbling down a sheer cliff face while gathering bird eggs, chasing goats or fishing. So right in Adamstown you find a spot with the dire name, Where Dick Fall. A little further to the west, below Christian's Cave, the cliffs must be particularly dangerous since the map lists: Where Dan Fall, Johnny Fall, McCoy's Drop and the succinct Tom Off. It's no better on the west coast, Where Warren Fall, or the east coast, Where Freddie Fall. But the south coast has the most enigmatic and worrying warning of all – Oh Dear.

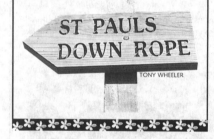

TONY WHEELER

spirit from the roots of the *ti* plant. By 1799, under the influence of the drink, McCoy had thrown himself into the sea with a rock tied around his neck and Quintal had become so crazed under the drink's influence that Adams and Young had killed him in self-defence. A year later Young died of asthma and John Adams was the sole survivor of the 15 men who had arrived 10 years earlier.

This left Adam with 10 women, 23 children and his recent discovery of religion. Adamstown was a neat little settlement of God-fearing Christians when Captain Mayhew Folger of the American sealing ship *Topaz* rediscovered Pitcairn, solving the 19 year mystery of what had happened to Christian and the *Bounty* after the mutiny.

By this time British attention was focuse on the struggle with Napoleon and there wa no interest in a mutineer, guilty of a crim now nearly 30 years old. The next visitors the British ships HMS *Briton* and *Targus* i 1814, arrived unaware of Folger's earlie visit but decided there was no point in tak ing any action against the lone mutineer.

Ship visits became more frequent, and b the time Adams died in 1829 there was con cern that the island would become over populated.

In 1831 the British government relocate the islanders to Tahiti, but within months 1 of the Pitcairners, lacking immunity to variety of diseases, had died – including Thursday October Christian, the son o Fletcher Christian and the first child to b born on Pitcairn. By the end of the year the 65 survivors were all back on Pitcairn. Th island became a British colony in 1838, bu when the population grew beyond 150 ther were once more fears of overpopulation. I 1856 the entire population, then numbering 194, was moved to Norfolk Island, an unin habited former Australian prison-islan between Australia and NZ (See Australia Territories in the South Pacific Gateway chapter). Not all the settlers were conten with their well equipped new home and, i 1858, 16 of them returned to Pitcairn, jus in time to prevent the French annexing i to their Polynesian colony. More familie returned in 1864, bringing the population back to 43.

During the later days of John Adams and right up to the mid-1870s, Pitcairners were staunch followers of the Church of England However, the arrival of a box of Seventh-Day Adventist literature from the USA in 1876 saw the beginnings of religious change. A decade after receiving the avidly consumed material, the arrival of a Seventh-Day Adventist missionary her alded real conversion from the teachings of Pastor Simon Young. A mission ship wa sent out to Pitcairn from the USA in 189(and the happy proselytes were baptised with a dousing in one of the island's rock pools and its pigs were swiftly killed to remove the temptation of pork.

Over the last century the island's problems can be summed up as people and ships. Although the population grew to a peak of 223 just before WWII, depopulation rather than overpopulation has become the major concern. In 1956 the figure was 161, in 1966 it was 96 and in 1976 Pitcairners numbered 74. Through the past two decades the figure has generally been in the 40s and 50s. There are many empty homes and fears that lack of opportunities will finally force the population below a viable level.

Ships have been part of the problem. For years after the *Bounty* settlement's discovery there were regular visits by sealing ships, and when they became a thing of the past the opening of the Panama Canal put Pitcairn directly on the Panama-NZ passenger ship route. Passing ships were important in provisioning the island, but they also transported curious Pitcairners to the world beyond.

The decline in visiting ships, due to modern air travel, has, however, increased the island's isolation, reducing contacts to visiting yachts, to cargo ships that can be persuaded to stop and to the occasional cruise ship.

Things to See

There are many reminders of the island's *Bounty* origins, including Fletcher Christian's *Bounty* Bible, kept in a glass case in the church. It was actually sold in 1839, but returned to the island in 1949. The *Bounty's* anchor, salvaged by Irving Johnson in 1957, stands between the court house and post office, and there's a *Bounty* cannon further

Fletcher Christian's bible – open to the passage: 'thou shalt not mutiny'.

along the road. The anchor from the *Acadia*, wrecked on Ducie Atoll, is displayed on the Edge, overlooking Bounty Bay.

The only **mutineer's grave** is that of John Adams. There was no such name on the original ship's register; he changed his name from Alexander Smith, perhaps hoping to avoid arrest if the feared naval squad ever turned up. **Fletcher Christian's cave**, overlooking the settlement, is where the leading mutineer is said to have hidden, either to watch for pursuing ships or to evade the killings that swept the island in the early years of the new settlement. Each year on 23 January the *Bounty*'s demise is commemorated by towing a burning model of the ship across Bounty Bay.

Petroglyphs on the rock face at the bottom of Down Rope are reminders of Pitcairn Island's pre-*Bounty* Polynesian habitation. The island's important Polynesian stone quarry is at Tautama, a kilometre west round the coast. When the mutineers arrived there were also *marae* platforms and stone images, which the devoutly-Christian mutineers promptly tossed in the sea. The road to Down Rope continues to **St Paul's Pool**, a beautiful natural pool fed and drained by the sea. Turpin or Mr T, the island's **Galapagos tortoise**, is the survivor of a pair left here by a visiting yacht in the 1940s.

Places to Stay

The island has no guesthouse or hotel. Longer term visitors are accommodated with islanders, typically paying about NZ$125 to $130 a week for room and board. Accommodation has to be confirmed before the administration will issue you with a visitor licence; applications for accommodation can be made through the island magistrate (see Useful Organisations in the Facts for the Visitor section earlier in this chapter).

Shopping

The islanders do a busy trade in turning out curios for visiting ships. They include woven pandanus bags and a variety of sharks and dolphins carved out of miro wood as well as the famous models of the

Bounty. Limited food supplies are available in the Co-op Store, which opens three times a week for a few hours.

Getting Around

Tin, *Tub* and *Moss* are the three longboats used for transport between Bounty Bay and boats anchored offshore, and for the occasional trip to Oeno and Henderson. Their wooden predecessor was *Stick*. Three and four-wheeled fat-tyred motorcycles, or ATVs, are the usual means of transport around the island; Pitcairners rarely walk. The island's six or so kilometres of dirt roads turn into famously sticky mud when it rains.

Other Islands

OENO ISLAND

* pop 0   * area 1 sq km

Captain James Henderson, who gave his name to Henderson Island, also came across Oeno Island in 1819, but it was an American whaling ship which gave Oeno its name in 1824.

Two narrow passages enter the central lagoon; the outer reef is about 4km across with one larger palm-covered island a few kilometres long on the western side. It points towards a smaller sandbank islet beside the narrow pass through the reef. For a time in the early 1990s a sandspit actually joined the two islands. The Pitcairners make occasional visits here for pandanus leaves to weave into bags, and sometimes just for a spell of beach vacationing.

Over the years Oeno was the site of a number of shipwrecks, including one which had disastrous results for Pitcairn. In 1893 the *Bowden* was wrecked on the island, but there were no casualties and the captain and crew made their way to Pitcairn in the ship's boat. The islanders made four trips to Oeno, to salvage the *Bowden*, but after working in the filthy bilge water, clearing out the canned goods and barrels of beef, one of them contracted typhoid fever. Back on Pitcairn the infection raced through the islanders, killing 13 people.

HENDERSON ISLAND

* pop 0   * area 36 sq km

Largest of the four islands in the Pitcairn group, uninhabited Henderson Island is 168km east-north-east of Pitcairn. At 9.6km long by 5.1km wide, it is nearly eight times as big as Pitcairn itself. Henderson is a classic example of a makatea island. The island is believed to have been uplifted by three undersea volcanoes – Adams, Young and Bounty – to the south-east of Pitcairn Adams has grown to within 20m of sea level.

A new fringing reef has grown up around two-thirds of the island's 26km coastline – the sheer 15m-high cliffs, which run all the way around the island, are simply the seaward face of the old coral reef. The interior of the island rises to a 30m flatland with a central depression which was once the lagoon inside the old reef. The fossilised coral that makes up the island contributes to its extreme inhospitability. Climbing the coral cliff face is difficult, and the sharp, crumbling ground in the interior is carpeted with a dense thicket of waist-to-shoulder high pisonia brush. The interior shelters stands of the fine miro wood, much loved by Pitcairn Island woodcarvers. Since Pitcairn has been denuded of miro trees the islanders make occasional trips to harvest those of Henderson. Over the years they have taken the easily accessible stands.

There are no native land mammals on the island although there are Polynesian rats. Henderson has four endemic land birds: the flightless Henderson rail, the colourful Stephen's lorikeet, the Henderson fruit dove

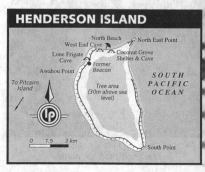

HENDERSON ISLAND

North Beach
West End Cave — North East Point
Lone Frigate Cave — Coconut Grove Shelter & Cave
Awahou Point — Former Beacon
To Pitcairn Island
Tree area (30m above sea level)
SOUTH PACIFIC OCEAN

0   1.5   3 km

South Point

d the Henderson warbler. The fruit dove
territorial, unlike other fruit doves, and
ards its own little patch of fruit trees, in-
ecting the fruit they bear every day and
ting each fruit on the very day it ripens.
ne seabird species breed on the island and
x other types have been seen there. Green
a turtles also nest occasionally on the is-
nd. The island has beaches on the north,
rth-west and north-east sides. The long
rth-eastern beach is littered with flotsam
d jetsam, brought in with the prevailing
inds. Pitcairners normally land on this
ach because it's easier and is closer to the
iro wood stands. During certain tides
ere may be a freshwater spring in a cave
the north of the island.

Henderson is unusual for a raised atoll in
at it has not been dramatically altered by
xploitation for phosphate reserves. Be-
ause of this unique condition and its rare
rdlife the island was declared a UNESCO
/orld Heritage Site in 1988. As part of the
nservation management plan a licence,
hich is dependent on approval by the Pit-
airn Island Council, is required in order to
sit the island.

History

espite its unwelcoming topography Hen-
erson was settled by Polynesians between
e 12th and 15th centuries and there may
ven have been earlier habitation between
round 900 and 350 BC. Since freshwater
pplies were limited, agriculture must have
een nearly impossible with the lack of soil,
nd even fishing was complicated by the
ifficult reef entries. Henderson was clearly
ot an easy place to live. Nevertheless the
lenderson settlement traded with the settle-
ent on Pitcairn Island, supplying them
ith fish, turtles and the island's flightless
nd birds and nesting seabirds. Scientists
elieve three species of land birds and three
five types of seabirds disappeared from
e island during its Polynesian habitation.

Around 1450 AD, trade between the is-
nds ceased, and Henderson was certainly
ninhabited when Portuguese explorer
uirós, sailing under the Spanish flag, visit-
d in 1606. Quirós renamed the island San

Juan Bautista and it was promptly forgotten
until it was rediscovered by the *Bounty*
mutineers in 1790, en route to their new
home on Pitcairn. It was discovered yet
again in 1819 by Captain James Henderson
of the British merchant ship *Hercules*.

The island's next brush with the history
books took place in 1820-21 when the crew
of the whaling ship *Essex* ended up shipwrecked on the island after their ship was
charged and sunk by a sperm whale near the
Marquesas. This episode is believed to have
provided the inspiration for Herman
Melville's *Moby Dick*. Most of the 20 survivors carried on, hoping to reach South
America, but, enduring a nightmare voyage,
only five survived and then only by revert-
ing to cannibalism. The mate and two others
stayed on the island until rescued by the
Surrey three months later. During their enforced stay the men discovered a cave with
six, some reports say eight, skeletons. Over
a century later, in 1958, a visiting party from
Pitcairn found six more skeletons in a cave.
Although extensive investigations con-
cluded that the skeletons were probably of
European rather than Polynesian origin, it
was never determined if they were the same
skeletons from the *Essex* visit.

A year earlier Henderson had made the
news when a passenger on a passing ship
thought they had seen someone on the
beach. The Pitcairn Islanders confirmed
that it wasn't one of their people and sent a
party to investigate. They found Robert
Tomarchin, an American, and his chim-
panzee Moko! At first Tomarchin claimed
he had been deliberately marooned on the
island, but later it turned out he had asked
to be dropped there. He stayed on the island
about six weeks, then stayed briefly on Pitcairn, but Moko made a longer visit before
eventually being returned to the USA.

In the early 1980s another American, the
wealthy Arthur M 'Smiley' Ratcliffe (or
Ratliff), offered to buy or lease the island,
intending to flatten the vegetation, turn it
into a cattle ranch and build a home and
airstrip. This scheme sounds extremely
unlikely but it was a major factor in the
island's subsequent World Heritage listing.

There have been a number of investigations into the island's natural history, including that of a Smithsonian party in 1987 and the year-long Sir Peter Scott Commemorative Expedition in 1991-92. A bronze plaque on the island's North Beach records the latter party's stay there. Archaeological excavations have been conducted by various people, including Yosihiko Sinoto whose 1971 visit found six caves with evidence of occupation between 1250 and 1425 AD (plus or minus 105 years).

DUCIE ATOLL

- **pop 0**   • **area 1 sq km**

Discovered, like Henderson, by Quirós in 1606 and named Encarnacion, Ducie was rediscovered by Edward Edwards on the *Pandora* in 1791, during his *Bounty* hunt. It was named after his patron, Lord Ducie. The island is a classic coral atoll with one larger and three smaller *motu* (islands) arrayed around a lagoon. The main island, Acadia, stretches for over 3km around the lagoon, but it's only around 100m wide. It is home to Polynesian rats, lizards, tens of thousands of seabirds, including masked boobies, various petrels, pretty little fairy terns, tropi birds and frigate birds and very little els there are no palm trees and the vegetation limited to just two hardy types. There is accessible pass into the lagoon, but on eastern side gentle whirlpools drain wat straight out to the open sea.

Notable shipwrecks on the island includ the British ship *Acadia* in 1881. The cre made a nightmare 13 day voyage to Pitcai in the ship's boat and two of them marrie Pitcairners. Until quite recently Coffin w a familiar Pitcairn family name from one those shipwrecked sailors, Phillip Coffin.

The usual landing point on Acadia Islan is marked by a memorial, which notes th recovery of the *Acadia*'s main anchor i 1990. The wreck of the ship is directly of shore from the **monument** in about 10m water. A short distance to the west a marke trail wanders across the island to the lagoo side. An alarming variety of flotsam litter the island, including countless glass bottle plastic debris of every type and hundreds fishing-net floats.

Samoa

The Samoan islands are a homogenous nation politically divided. On both sides of the 171st median – which divides the independent Samoa (until recently known as Western Samoa) from the US territory of American Samoa – people speak the same language and practise the same customs.

The common features of the two entities, including their history up till partition in 1900, are given in this chapter. American Samoa has its own chapter, which follows this one.

Independent Samoa's two mountainous islands bear the scars of recent volcanic activity and the scenery is nothing short of magnificent. The capital city, Apia, on smaller Upolu Island, is one of the most enchanting of Pacific ports, and has enough creature comforts for all but the most demanding traveller. But as even the most sophisticated residents of Apia will tell you with pride, a visit to Samoa is not complete without visiting the larger island of Savai'i. Samoan culture has been remarkably resilient to western influences.

Facts about Samoa

HISTORY
The Samoan islands were initially settled by the 'Lapita' culture (see the boxed text in the 'South Pacific Arts' special section), from Fiji and Tonga in about 1500 BC. Many old Samoan legends have Fijian kings and princesses as their heroes.

In 950 AD warriors from nearby Tonga invaded and established rule on Savai'i, the nearest island to Tonga, then moved on to Upolu. They were eventually repelled by Malietoa Savea, the chief of the Samoas, whose title was derived from the shouted tributes of the retreating Tongans to this *malie toa* (brave warrior). A treaty of peace between the two countries was drawn up and the Samoans were left by the Tongans to pursue their own course.

SAMOA

AT A GLANCE

Capital City (& Island): Apia (Upolu)
Population: 161,298
Time: 11 hours behind GMT
Land Area: 2934 sq km (1145 sq miles)
Number of Islands: Nine
International Telephone Code: ☎ 685
GDP/Capita: US$865
Currency: Samoan *tala* (ST$1 = US$0.33)
Languages: Samoan & English
Greeting: *Malo*

HIGHLIGHTS

- **Falealupo Peninsula, Savai'i** – a remote area combining lovely wild beaches with a beautiful rainforest reserve that protects Samoa's unique vegetation as well as fruit bats and a variety of birds. An aerial walkway takes you through the rainforest canopy and up into a banyan tree.

- **Fatumea Pool, Upolu** – a clean freshwater pool and cave offering a cool and refreshing break on a hot day

- **Pulemelei Mound & Olemoe Falls, Savai'i** – Polynesia's largest ancient monument and Samoa's most beautiful waterfall and tropical pool

- **Taga Blowholes, Savai'i** – one of the world's largest and most impressive marine blowholes

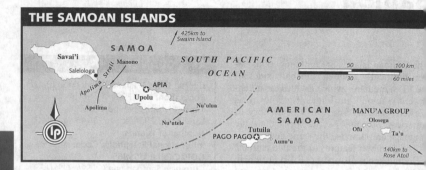

THE SAMOAN ISLANDS

The earliest known evidence of human occupation in the islands is the Lapita village, partially submerged in the lagoon at Mulifanua on the island of Upolu. Carbon tests have tentatively dated the site at 1000 BC. Undecorated pottery, known as Polynesian plainware, of a comparable age has been found at Aoa on the island of Tutuila and at To'aga on the island of Ofu.

At numerous other sites on Upolu, Savai'i and Tutuila (and to a lesser extent on Manono and Ta'u), archaeologists have discovered odd platforms, with stone protrusions radiating from their bases, that have been dubbed 'star mounds'. Information gathered from oral traditions and archaeological studies suggests that these structures were used in the ancient sport of pigeon-snaring (see the boxed text 'Star Mounds of Ancient Power' in the American Samoa chapter).

On Savai'i, near the village of Palauli, is the pyramid of Pulemelei, the largest ancient structure in Polynesia.

European Contact

Although whalers, pirates and escaped convicts had landed in the islands earlier, the first European on record to approach the Samoan islands was the Dutchman Jacob Roggeveen in 1722. Louis-Antoine de Bougainville also passed through Samoan waters (1768), bartering with the inhabitants of the Manu'a Islands. The ill-fated La Pérouse (1787; see the boxed text 'Disaster on the Reef' in the Solomon Islands chapter) and *Bounty*-mutineer-hunter Captain

Edward Edwards (1791) both had ski mishes with the locals.

By the 1820s quite a few Europeans ha settled in the islands, most of them escape convicts and retired whalers. The Europea settlers established a society in Apia and minimal code of law in order to govern the affairs, all with the consent of Upolu chief who maintained sovereignty in their ow villages.

The Missionaries

Encouraged by the similarity of Christia creation beliefs to Samoan legend, and by prophecy by Nafanua the war goddess tha a new religion would take root in the i lands, Samoans were quite well prepared accept the message of Christian mission aries, who arrived in the early 19th centur The wondrous possessions of the *palag* (white men) were also seen as evidence tha their god was more generous than the o Samoan gods.

Squabbling Powers

There were (and still are) four 'paramount families – equivalent to royal dynasties – i Samoa: the Malietoa, Tupua Tamases Mata'afa and Tu'imaleali'ifano. During th 1870s, a civil dispute between two king one in the east and one in the west, divide Samoa. Much land was sold to Europea by Samoans seeking to acquire armamen to settle the matter.

The British, Americans and Germans se about squabbling over Samoan territor with an eventual compromise being me with the drawing up of the Tripartite Treaty in 1899. This gave control of western Samoa to the Germans and that of eastern Samoa to the Americans. Britain stepped out of the picture altogether in exchange for renunciation of all German claims to Tonga, the Solomon Islands and Niue.

Twentieth Century

For information on American Samoa see History in the following American Samoa chapter.

In February 1900, after the bitter colonial power struggle between the US, Britain and Germany left the latter in control of Western Samoa, Dr Wilhelm Solf was appointed governor and the new caretakers of the colony settled in to rule. Although the Germans had agreed to rule 'according to Samoan custom', they hardly kept their word. Solf continued to ignore Samoan tradition in favour of personal and European interests, causing a breakdown in communications between the Samoans and their colonial rulers.

By 1908 many Samoans had decided they could take it no longer. An official resistance force, the Mau a Pule (Mau Movement), was organised on Savai'i by Namulau'ulu Lauaki Mamoe, the talking chief of Fa'asalele'aga district. Fearing violence, Germany sent warships and in January 1909 Namulau'ulu and company were exiled to the island of Saipan in the Northern Mariana Islands (at the time a German colony).

At the outbreak of WWI, Britain persuaded nearby New Zealand (NZ) to seize German Samoa. Preoccupation with affairs on the home front prevented Germany from resisting.

When the Mau Movement leaders in Saipan heard of the NZ takeover they decided it would be necessary to learn English if they wanted to deal with the new administration at home. The leader at the time, 'Iga, built an outrigger canoe on Saipan and escaped to the American colony on Guam, arriving after only two days at sea. In honour of this crossing, the strait between Saipan and Guam became known as 'Iga Pisa.

Still under NZ administration, Samoa suffered a devastating outbreak of influenza in 1919. Almost a quarter of the population (8500 people) died, and it was many years before NZ was forgiven for the administration's tragic mismanagement of the epidemic.

Discontent with the NZ administration, and an increasing call by the Mau Movement for independence, culminated in the authorities opening fire on a demonstration at the Court House in Apia in 1929. Eleven Samoans, including the Mau leader Tupua Tamasese Lealofi III, were killed.

Following a change of government (and policy) in NZ, Western Samoa's independence was acknowledged as inevitable and even desirable. During the 1940s and 1950s Western Samoa's government was reorganised in preparation, in 1959 Prime Minister Fiame Mata'afa was appointed, the following year a formal constitution was adopted, and on 1 January 1962, independence was finally achieved.

GEOGRAPHY & ECOLOGY

Samoa, with a total land area of 2934 sq km, consists primarily of the two large islands of Savai'i (1700 sq km) and Upolu (1115 sq km), both of volcanic origin. The Samoas' highest peak, Mt Silisili in Savai'i, rises to 1858m.

Samoa's other two inhabited islands, Manono and Apolima, lie in the 18km-wide strait separating Upolu and Savai'i. A few other rocky islets and outcrops are found to the south-east of Upolu.

Deforestation is the most serious of all the environmental challenges facing Samoa. Forest now accounts for less than 37% of the country's land area. The current rate of forest depletion is estimated to be about 3000 hectares per year – 80% due to agriculture and other activities; 20% the result of logging.

In 1993 the South Pacific Regional Environment Programme (SPREP), funded by the United Nations, put together a detailed national environment and development management strategy to pave the way towards sustainable development in Samoa.

SAMOA

CLIMATE

There is a distinct wet season (summer) between November and April and a dry season (winter) from May to October. The driest and most comfortable period to visit the Samoas is between May and October. The average temperatures range from 21 to 32°C (70 to 90°F). Year-round humidity averages about 80%. The Samoas lie squarely within the South Pacific cyclone belt; cyclone season is between November and April.

FLORA & FAUNA

On the heights of Savai'i, Upolu, Ofu, Olosega and Ta'u one finds temperate forest vegetation: tree ferns, grasses, wild coleus and epiphytic plants. The magnificent banyan tree dominates the landscape of the higher areas of these islands, especially on Savai'i and Upolu. Other parts of the Samoas are characterised by scrublands, marshes, pandanus forests and mangrove swamps. The rainforests of Samoa are a natural apothecary, home to some 75 plant species.

Because the Samoan islands are relatively remote, few animal species have managed to colonise them. The Lapita bought with them domestic pigs, dogs and chickens as well as the ubiquitous Polynesian rat. But apart from two species of fruit bat and the small, sheath-tailed bat, mammals not introduced by humans are limited to the marine varieties. Whales, dolphins and porpoises migrate north and south through the Samoas, depending on the season. Most common are the pilot whales that are frequently seen in the open seas around the islands.

Skinks *(pili)* and geckos *(mo'o)* can be seen everywhere. The harmless Pacific boa *(gata)* is found only on Ta'u Island and various types of turtles are rare visitors to the islands.

Almost 900 species of fish and nearly 200 species of coral have been documented. There are also several shark species, which generally don't pose much of a risk to humans.

Fifty-nine species of bird have been recorded in American Samoa. The numerous species of seabirds include petrels,
white-tailed tropicbirds, boobies, bla noddies, curlews, frigate birds and tern Other species include the nearly flightle banded rail and the beautiful blue-crown lory, which Samoans call the *sega* or parro

National Parks

One of only two fully fledged nation parks in the Samoan islands, O Le Pup Pu'e National Park is on the southern sho of Upolu. An increasing number of villag in Samoa are establishing their own co servation areas. Protected areas includ Palolo Deep Marine Reserve, Mt Va Scenic Reserve, Aleipata Islands Mari Reserve, Uafato Conservation Area, Satao Sa'anapu Conservation Area, Manor Island Marine Reserves, Tafua Rainfore Preserve, Falealupo Rainforest Reserv and the Sasina & Letui Conservation Are

In American Samoa the 4000 hectare N tional Park of American Samoa (NPS) co sists of three distinct areas on three separa islands. Other protected areas in America Samoa are Fagatele Bay National Mari Sanctuary on Tutuila Island and Rose Ato which is a wildlife refuge for nesting s turtles and seabirds.

GOVERNMENT & POLITICS

For information on American Samoa see t following chapter.

The national government of Samoa ope ates under a British-based parliamentar system, revised to accommodate local cu tom and Christian principles.

Until recently, voting rights in th country were restricted to the 20,000 o ficial *matai* (chiefs), but unfortunate their selections were often influenced mo by cronyism, obligation or family ties tha by professed beliefs, policies or abilit After a referendum in 1990, universal su frage was extended to all citizens 21 yea of age or over, but only matai have the rig to stand for election.

There are currently two political parti represented in the *Fono* (Parliament) – th ruling Human Rights Protection Part (HRPP) under Prime Minister Tuilaep Sailele, and the opposition Samoan Nation evelopment Party (SNDP) led by Tupua amasese Efi, the son of the Mau leader lled in 1929.

A scandal hit Samoan politics in 1999 hen two Cabinet ministers, Vitale and ukuso, were arrested for conspiracy in the ssassination of another minister, Luagalau amu. Vitale's son was convicted of the ctual shooting.

CONOMY

ee the following chapter for information egarding American Samoa's economy.

Since independence, Samoa has concentrated on developing a modern economy ased on traditional village agriculture and rimary products. Subsistence agriculture ill supports around 75% of the population. he primary sector employs more than half e workforce and accounts for 50% of DP and about 80% of export earnings. bout 30% of the workforce is employed y the government. Despite huge investments in agriculture, fisheries and forestry, ere has been a continuing decline in the xport of primary products and, at the same me, a rise in imports.

The economy continues to depend heavy on foreign aid, provided by NZ, Austra-a, the European Economic Community, apan and China. Remittances from amoans working overseas is another important source of foreign exchange.

Emigration to Australasia and North merica remains high, and though this provides much-needed foreign exchange, it lso results in a loss of skilled workers.

Wages in Samoa are extremely low relative to local living costs.

Tourism is of increasing importance to e economy of Samoa and in recent years e government has promoted the development of light manufacturing industries.

OPULATION & PEOPLE

1996 the population of Samoa was 51,298 people, the huge majority of them thnic Polynesians.

The population of American Samoa is round 58,000, with 95% living on the ain island of Tutuila and the remaining 5% living on the Manu'a islands. Tutuila has an annual population growth rate of 3.7%, one of the highest in the world.

Samoans are citizens of an independent country, while American Samoans are US nationals. The latter may not vote in presidential elections until they opt to become US citizens, which they are free to do at any time. There are more than 150,000 ethnic Samoans from both sides of the border living in NZ, Australia and the USA (especially Hawai'i). Many were born outside the Samoas.

ARTS
Dance & Fiafia

Originally, the *fiafia* was a village play or musical presentation in which participants would dress in a variety of costumes and accept money or other donations. These days the term 'fiafia night' refers to a lavish presentation of Samoan dancing and singing staged at the larger hotels, usually accompanied by a huge buffet dinner.

Most of the dancing, including the *sa sa*, is performed by groups to the rhythm of a beating wooden mallet. The popular *siva* is a slow and fluid dance performed by one or two women acting out impromptu stories with their hands and expressions.

Traditionally, the final dance of the evening was the *taualuga*. It was normally a siva danced by the *taupou* (ceremonial virgin), dressed only in *siapo* (artistically decorated bark cloth, made from the mulberry tree), her body oiled seductively.

Music

Songs are written to tell stories or commemorate events, most of which are sad and stirring. Love songs are the most popular, followed by patriotic songs extolling the virtues of the Samoas.

Another highly respected institution is the brass band and musical competitions between villages are common.

Architecture

The most prevalent manifestation of traditional – and practical – Samoan architecture is the *fale*, a wooden thatch-roofed house

SAMOA

with rounded ends and posts instead of walls. Although houses are now built with more-sturdy materials, the traditional fale shape can be seen in modern buildings.

Every village has one prominently elevated fale, the *fale talimalo*, in which the village council meets. It is the responsibility of the village women's committee to keep it clean and brightly decorated. The women skewer hibiscus, frangipani and ginger flowers on little pales to decorate the surrounding grounds.

Siapo & Fine Mats

The bark cloth known as siapo, or tapa, made from the inner bark of the paper mulberry tree *(u'a)*, provides a medium for some of the loveliest artwork in the Samoas.

Woven from pandanus fibres split into widths of just a couple of millimetres, fine mats *(toga)* take months of painstaking work and, when finished, have the look and feel of fine linen or silk. Although never really used as mats, toga, along with other woven mats, siapo and oils, make up 'the gifts of the women' that must be exchanged at every formal Samoan ceremony. Agricultural products comprise 'the gifts of the men'.

SOCIETY & CONDUCT
Traditional Culture

The *fa'amatai* (matai system of government) is practiced throughout the Samoas and has its roots in ancient Polynesian culture. Each *nu'u* (village) comprises a group of *'aiga* (extended families) that include as many relatives as can be claimed. The larger an 'aiga, the more powerful it is and to be part of a powerful 'aiga is the goal of all tradition-minded Samoans.

The 'aiga is headed by a chief, called a matai, who represents the family on the *fono* (village council). Matai, who can be male or female, are normally elected by all adult members of the 'aiga, but most candidates hold titles of some description and many inherit office automatically.

The fono consists of the matai of all the 'aiga associated with the village. The highest chief of the village, or *ali'i*, sits at the head of the fono. In addition, each village has one *pulenu'u* (a combination of mayor and police chief), and one or more *tulafale* (talking chiefs). The pulenu'u is elected every three years and acts as an intermediary between the village and the national (or territorial, in the case of American Samoa) government. The tulafale is an orator who liaises between the ali'i and outside entities, carries out ceremonial duties and engages in ritual debates.

Beneath the matai, members of a village are divided into four categories. The society of untitled men, the *aumaga*, are responsible for growing the village food and traditionally were the warriors of the village. The *aualuma* is the society of unmarried, widowed or separated women. They are responsible for providing hospitality and producing toga (women's wealth) in the form of fine mats, siapo and oils. Married women are called *faletua ma tausi*. Their role revolves around serving their husband and his family. The final group is the *tamaiti* (the children). Close social interaction is generally restricted to members of one's own group.

Dos & Don'ts

Although many visitors to the Samoas wish to see traditional villages, such visits can be extremely disruptive in a traditional society. It's best not to arrive in a village on a Sunday. The presence of a foreigner unknown to the village will interrupt the smooth customary flow of religious and family activities.

Shoes should be removed when entering a fale and you should never enter during prayers or meetings. Don't make noise or commotion in the area while prayers are being said.

Throughout the Samoas, women are best advised to wear knee-length skirts or *lavalava* (sarongs) and should avoid wearing shorts or bathing gear away from the beach no matter what the temperature. Men would do best to wear knee-length, baggy shorts (or lavalavas) and should always wear shirts while walking in the streets. Also see Society & Conduct in the Facts about the South Pacific chapter.

a

a, which means 'sacred', is the nightly espers. Sometime between 6 and 7 pm a illage gong sounds (usually an empty ropane tank), signifying that the village hould prepare for sa. All activity comes to n abrupt halt and motor and pedestrian affic stops. When the second gong is ounded, sa has begun. When a third gong sounded, usually after about 10 or 15 inutes, sa is over and activities may be re- med. If you're caught out in a village dur- g sa, stop what you're doing, sit down nd quietly wait for the third gong to sound. hese rules do not apply in Apia or the Pago ago Harbor area.

raditional Medicine

raditional healers are typically women who earn their methods during a long appren- ceship. An apprentice must learn to recog- ise several hundred species of rainforest lants, each with its own medicinal value. 1odern healers are taught to take notes and keep a close and accurate record of each atient's symptoms, their diagnosis, treat- ent and response.

As a general rule, there are four types of amoan healers: the *fa'atosaga* or mid- ives; those who practise *fofo* or massage;

the *fofogau* or orthopaedists (normally men capable of setting broken bones); and the *taulasea*, herbalists who utilise the diversity of Samoan rainforest flora in their treatment of disease. Other related types of healers in- clude those who effect love potions or ban- ish troublesome *aitu* (spirits).

The Fa'afafine

By traditional definition, a *fa'afafine* is a male who opts to dress and behave as a fe- male, for whatever reason. The word means simply 'like a woman' and is similar to the Tahitian *mahu* or Tongan *fakaleiti* (see the boxed text in the Tonga chapter).

Tattooing

Samoa is the last Polynesian nation where traditional tattooing is still widely prac- tised (against the wishes of many religious leaders). When a boy is born his grand- mother will start collecting the dye for his tattoo *(pe'a)*. The dye is presented to the grandson when he reaches puberty.

Tattoos normally cover the man's body from the waist to the knees. On occasion, women also elect to be tattooed, but their designs cover only the thighs.

The skills and tools of the *tufuga pe'a*, the tattoo artist, are traditionally passed

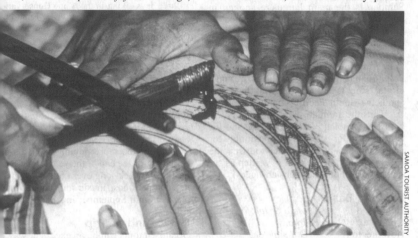

Many hands make art-work – a *tufaga pe'a* (tattooing artist) and his apprentices at work.

SAMOA TOURIST AUTHORITY

SAMOA

from father to son. Sharpened sharks' teeth or boars' tusks are used to carve the intricate designs. The man being tattooed must not be left alone in case the aitu take him away. A special language is used when addressing the tufuga and he is assigned an off-limits, sacred fale for use as a resting place. Once begun, the tattoo must be completed or the young man will bring shame upon himself and his 'aiga. In most cases the procedure will take a month to complete.

'Ava Ceremony

'Ava (or kava) is a drink derived from the ground root of the pepper plant. See the boxed text 'Kava' in the Regional Facts for the Visitor chapter. The 'ava ceremony is a ritual in the Samoas, and every government and matai meeting is preceded by an 'ava ceremony. You'll see many 'ava circles at Maketi Fou (the central market) in Apia.

RELIGION

Half of all Samoans belong to the Congregational Church, which is derived from the London Missionary Society. About 25% are Catholics, 12% are Methodists and most of the remainder are Mormons.

LANGUAGE

Samoan is the main language spoken in both independent and American Samoa although most people speak English as a second language. Samoan, similar to Tongan, is one of the oldest Polynesian languages.

In Samoan, 's' replaces the 'h' of other Polynesian languages, 'l' replaces 'r', and a glottal stop (see Language in the Facts about the South Pacific chapter) replaces 'k'. Thus the Tahitian word for 'one', *tahi*, is *tasi* in Samoan, *rua* (two) is *lua*, and *ika* (Rarotongan for 'fish') is *i'a*. Seemingly for no reason except to confuse tourists, the soft 'ng' sound in Samoan is written as 'g' (palagi is pronounced 'pah-lah-ngee').

Samoan Basics

Hello.	*Malo* or *talofa*.
Goodbye.	*Tofa*.
How are you?	*O a mai 'oe?*
I'm well (thanks).	*Manuia (fa'afetai)*.
Please.	*Fa'amolemole*.
Thanks (very much).	*Fa'afetai (tele)*.
Yes.	*Ioe*.
No.	*Leai*.
Two beers please.	*E lua pia fa'amole mole*.

Facts for the Visito

For specific information relating to Ame. can Samoa, see the following chapter.

SUGGESTED ITINERARIES

Depending on the length of your stay a your particular interests, you might want see and do the following things:

One week
  Tour the 'Big Island of Savai'i' – include overnight stop in the banyan tree at Falealup a couple of days on the beach at Tanu or Sat iatua and a hike on the Tafua Peninsula.
Two weeks
  Add to the above: a visit to Manono Island, excursion into the Uafato Conservation Ar on Upolu, a couple of days on the beach Aleipata and a visit to the Sataoa/Sa'ana Wetlands Conservation Area.
Three weeks
  Extend any of the above and/or add: two three days hiking in the A'opo Conservati Area on Savai'i or in the O Le Pupu-Pu National Park on Upolu.
One month
  Add to the above: a visit to the islands Aunu'u and Ofu in American Samoa.

PLANNING
When to Go

Weatherwise, the most comfortable time visit the Samoas is between May and Oct ber, during the dry season.

Some of the more popular festivals a held towards the end of the year – the Teui Festival, a week-long event featuring spor ing competitions, music and dance, tak places in mid-September in Apia, Samoa.

What Kind of Trip

Organised tours can be an excellent way learning about a place, particularly in

ace like Samoa that demands a certain
mount of cultural awareness from visitors.
here are a number of interesting tours on
ffer that focus on natural history and vari-
is 'eco-friendly' outdoor activities. See
rganised Tours in this chapter's Getting
round section for a list of options.

Anyone going to the Samoas for more
an just a short break should consider visit-
g both Samoa and American Samoa – not
nly for the stunning scenery they both
ffer but for the opportunity to witness an
ncient culture evolving in different direc-
ons. It's worth factoring in some time for
tting around doing nothing.

Maps

he most up-to-date map of Samoa is the
195,000 map published by South Pacific
laps in 1996 and distributed worldwide
rough Hema Maps (☎ 61-7-3290 0322,
x 3290 0478, manager@hemamaps.com
u), 24 Allgas St, Slacks Ck, QLD 4127,
ustralia. The Visitors Bureau in Apia sells
pies of the Hema map for ST10.

The University of Hawai'i publishes a
rger scale map of both Samoas. In Apia,
u can sometimes buy it at Aggie's Gift
op; in Pago Pago, try the Transpac Store
the Nu'uuli Shopping Centre.

TOURIST OFFICES
Local Tourist Offices

he Samoa Visitors Bureau (☎ 20180, fax
)886, samoa@samoa.net), PO Box
!72, Apia, is housed in a modern fale on
e reclaimed area behind Beach Rd. The
ffice is open from 8 am to 4.30 pm Mon-
y to Friday and on Saturday from 8.30 am
noon. The bureau publishes a free
onthly newspaper, *The Visitor*, and has a
ebsite at www.samoa.co.nz.

Tourist Offices Abroad

amoa has visitors bureau offices in the
llowing countries:

Australia
(☎ 02-9824 5050, fax 9824 5678,
samoa@ozemail.com.au)
PO Box 361, Minto Mall, Minto, NSW 2566

New Zealand
(☎ 09-379 6138, fax 379 8154,
samoa@samoa.co.nz)
Level 1 Samoa House, 283 Karangahape Rd,
PO Box 68423, Newton, Auckland
UK
(☎ 020-8392 1838, fax 8392 1318,
samoa@samoa.net)
375 Upper Richmond Rd, London SW14 7NX
USA
(☎ 916-538 0152, fax 583 0154,
sdsi@compuserve.com)
Lake Blvd 475, PO Box 7740, Tahoe City,
CA 96145

Samoa is represented abroad by offices of the
Tourism Council of the South Pacific (see the
Regional Facts for the Visitor chapter).

VISAS & EMBASSIES

Visitors entering Samoa require a valid
passport and an onward ticket. You're also
required to provide a contact address
within the country. Visas may be extended
by several weeks at a time by the immigration office in Apia.

Samoan Embassies & Consulates

In countries without Samoan diplomatic
posts, Samoa is represented by NZ and
British diplomatic missions. Samoa has
diplomatic representation in the following
countries:

Australia
(☎ 06-286 5505, fax 286 5678)
PO Box 3274, 13 Culgoa Circuit, O'Malley,
ACT 2606
New Zealand
(☎ 04-720 953, fax 712 479)
1A Wesley Rd, Kelburn, PO Box 1430,
Wellington
United Nations Mission
(☎ 212-599 6196, fax 599 0797)
820 2nd Ave, Suite 800, New York, NY 10017,
USA

Embassies & Consulates in Samoa

Australia
(☎ 23411)
High Commission, NPF Building, Apia
UK
(☎ 21895)
Consul, 2nd Floor, NPF Bldg, Apia

SAMOA

New Zealand
(☎ 21404)
High Commission, Tamaligi, Apia
USA
(☎ 21631)
Embassy, John Williams Building, Apia

CUSTOMS

Visitors can bring in a 1L bottle of spirits and up to 200 cigarettes duty free. Plant material, vegetables and meat may not be imported without a permit from the quarantine section of the Department of Agriculture.

MONEY
Currency

The Samoan *tala* (dollar), which is divided into 100 *sene* (cents), is the unit of currency in independent Samoa. (The US dollar is used in American Samoa.)

In 1999 it became illegal to use foreign currencies in Samoa's shops, much to the chagrin of Samoans who receive cash remittances from overseas family.

In Apia, most middle to upper range hotels, car rental agencies, upmarket restaurants and craft shops will accept major credit cards.

Exchange Rates

country	unit		tala
Australia	A$1	=	ST2.00
Canada	C$1	=	ST2.10
Easter Island	Ch$100	=	ST0.57
euro	€1	=	ST3.10
Fiji	F$1	=	ST1.50
France	10FF	=	ST4.80
Germany	DM1	=	ST1.60
Japan	¥100	=	ST2.90
New Zealand	NZ$1	=	ST1.60
Pacific franc	100 CFP	=	ST2.70
Solomon Islands	S$1	=	ST0.60
Tonga	T$1	=	ST2.00
UK	£1	=	ST4.90
USA	US$1	=	ST3.00
Vanuatu	100VT	=	ST2.30

Exchanging Money

The most acceptable foreign currencies for exchange are the US, NZ and Australian dollars (see Exchange Rates in the Region. Facts for the Visitor chapter), and poun sterling. Travellers cheques fetch about 4° more than cash.

The three main banks in Samoa and thos that change travellers cheques and foreig currency are the Bank of Samoa, the Pacif Commercial Bank and the new Nation. Bank of Samoa. All have their main offic in central Apia, plus subsidiary branches i Salelologa on Savai'i. They're open weel days from 9 am to 3 pm. The National Ban of Samoa has a branch near the main ma ket in Apia that is open on Saturday fro 8.30 am to 12.30 pm.

When you're leaving Samoa, excess ta may be re-exchanged for foreign currenc (normally limited to US, NZ and Australia dollars) in the banks or at the exchang branches at Faleolo airport, which are ope to conicide with incoming and outgoin flights.

Costs

Samoa is one of the cheapest places t travel in the South Pacific. With car hir mid-range accommodation and up-mark eating, two people could travel in Samc on a minimum of about ST160 each pe day.

Tipping & Bargaining

Tipping and bargaining is not encouraged i Samoa.

Taxes

There is a hotel tax of ST1 per person pe night but it is normally included in th quoted price of the room. There's also 10% GST on goods and services, which usually included in marked prices.

POST & COMMUNICATIONS
Post

The main post office is on Beach Rd, Api one block east of the clock tower. Post services are available between 9 am an 4.30 pm.

To post an item to anywhere in the Pa cific islands (including Australia and NZ the rate is 70 sene for up to 10g. To Nort

merica and Asia, it's 90 sene for 10g. To
urope, the Middle East and Latin Amer-
a, you'll pay 95 sene for 10g. Aero-
ammes to anywhere in the world cost 85
ne. An airmail parcel weighing 1kg costs
out ST24 to NZ, Australia and North
merica; ST37 to the UK; and from ST46
mainland Europe.

Poste restante is located in a separate of-
ce just down Post Office St behind the
ain lobby. The address for the service is
oste Restante, Chief Post Office, Apia,
amoa.

elephone, Telex & Fax

djoining the post office, the ITB is open
r phone and telex services from 8 am to
) pm daily. Fax services are available up-
airs from 8 am to 4.30 pm weekdays.
here is a useful online phone directory at
ww.samoa.co.uk/phone.html. Samoa's
ternational telephone code is ☎ 685
American Samoa's is ☎ 684).

TERNET RESOURCES

he local service provider in Samoa is
ww.samoa.net. You can visit their office
the Lotemau Centre in Apia to access the
ternet for a fee. A good site to visit is
ww.samoa.co.uk, which has visitor infor-
ation and many good links. The visitors
ureaus in independent Samoa (www
amoa.co.nz) and American Samoa (www
amoanet.com) both have useful websites.

OOKS

ain, the most famous story in W Somer-
t Maugham's collection *The Trembling
f a Leaf*, is set in the Samoas. Robert
ouis Stevenson's novels *The Ebb-Tide
d The Wrecker* and his short story *The
each of Falesaá* were all written at the
ailima estate above Apia during the last
ur years of the author's life.

Coming of Age in Samoa, by Margaret
ead, is perhaps the most famous work
er written about the Samoas. This contro-
rsial, and these days thoroughly discred-
d, cultural study was made on the island
Ta'u in the Manu'a group. Derek Free-
an's *The Fateful Hoaxing of Margaret

Mead thoughtfully but methodically dis-
mantles Mead's research and writings.

The oral tradition of recounting myths,
legends, histories and fables is still very
much alive in Samoa. *Tala o le Vavau – The
Myths, Legends and Customs of Old Samoa*
is a good collection of Samoan legends, as
is *Fagogo – Fables from Samoa in Samoan
and English* by Richard Moyle.

Albert Wendt is Samoa's most renowned
author. His novels include *Leaves of the
Banyan Tree, Flying Fox in a Freedom
Tree, Pouliuli, Birth and Death of the Mir-
acle Man, Inside Us the Dead, Shaman of
Visions* and *Sons for the Return Home*.

Samoan performance poet and writer Sia
Figiel uses traditional storytelling forms in
her work. Her powerful first novel is *Where
We Once Belonged* (1996). Another recom-
mended novel is *Alms for Oblivion* by Fata
Sano Malifa (1993). *Tatou Tusi Tala* (Let's
Write Stories) is an anthology of Samoan
writing.

NEWSPAPERS & MAGAZINES

Perennially in trouble with Samoa's
criticism-sensitive government, the *Samoa
Observer* (☎ 23078, fax 21195), PO Box
1572, Apia, comes out daily except Monday
and Saturday. The *Sunday Newsline* is published weekly and the government-run
paper *Savali* comes out twice a week. The
local news magazine *Taluma*, PO Box
1321, Apia, is published monthly.

RADIO & TV

Samoa has two radio stations. Magic 98FM,
which broadcasts from 6 am to midnight,
plays a good range of popular music. The
government-run AM station Radio 2AP
operates on two channels – the English-
language channel broadcasts from 5 pm to
11 pm weekdays, the Samoan channel from
6 am to 11 pm daily. TV Samoa mainly
broadcasts overseas programs.

ELECTRICITY

Samoa's power supply is 230/240V AC,
50Hz. The Australasian-style plug (two or
three flat blades) is used and power fluctu-
ations (or outages) are not uncommon.

SAMOA

WEIGHTS & MEASURES

Independent Samoa uses the metric system.

LAUNDRY

Laundry prices are quite high relative to other costs. Most middle and upper-range hotels offer same-day laundry services.

HEALTH

There is no malaria in the Samoan islands; the only infectious diseases you should be aware of are occasional cases of dengue fever and filariasis (see Health in the Regional Facts for the Visitor chapter).

The National Hospital in Apia (☎ 996) is inland on Ifiifi St in the village of Leufisa. Health treatment is free to Samoan citizens and legal residents but foreigners must pay a small fee. Anyone suffering serious medical problems should probably head to Hawai'i or NZ.

There is a chemist opposite the public library on Beach Rd, but supplies are limited.

Don't drink the water – and that includes ice. If you don't know for certain that the water is safe assume the worst.

WOMEN TRAVELLERS

Thanks to western and Asian videos, which are extremely popular in the Samoas, foreign women have a reputation for easy availability, whether or not they are single. To avoid the measure of attention that a lone foreign woman is likely to attract, modest dress is recommended – see how young Samoan women dress and do likewise.

DANGERS & ANNOYANCES

Violent crime and alcohol-related incidents seem to be more prevalent in American Samoa than in Samoa. Theft isn't a huge problem, but remember that the concept of personal property is a recent introduction to Samoan society – it's worth keeping an eye on your things.

Beware of scams that involve people asking for a custom fee to access a site. While this is often legitimate, sometimes individuals who are in no way related to the village council get away with collecting money from unwary or foolish travellers. If you

are in doubt about a particular fee, ask t see the pulenu'u before paying.

BUSINESS HOURS

As a general rule, banks are open weekday from 9 am to 4 pm. In Samoa, governmen offices open from 8 am to noon and 1 t 4.30 pm. In American Samoa, they're mo likely to open at 9 am and close at 5 pm.

Shops in both countries remain open fro 8 am to noon and from 1.30 or 2 pm to 4.3 pm. Restaurants and takeaway shops opera between 8 am and 4 pm if they serve breal fast and lunch or from 6 to 10 pm if the serve only the evening meal. Saturday shop ping hours are from 8 am to 12.30 pm.

Markets open about 6 am. In America Samoa they close at about 3 pm, but th Maketi Fou in Apia is active 24 hours a da The big market day is Saturday.

On Sunday, everything not directly relate to the tourist industry is closed.

PUBLIC HOLIDAYS & SPECIAL EVENTS

Public holidays celebrated in both Samoa include New Year's Day, Good Frida White Sunday (the second Sunday in Oct ber), and Christmas. In addition, indeper dent Samoa celebrates the day after Ne Year's Day, Boxing Day and:

Anzac Day	25 April
Flag Day	17 April
Aso o Tina (Mothers' Day)	May
Independence Celebrations	1 to 3 June
Labor Day	4 August
White Monday	October
Palolo Day	October/Novembe

A well-attended annual event is the Teui Festival, which takes place from the first t the second week of September. (A simila but lower-key festival, Tourism Week, tak place in American Samoa in early July.)

ACTIVITIES

Whatever you do in Samoa, whether it bushwalking, surfing, or snorkelling, b sure to ask the local owners before usir their land, beach or lagoon.

norkelling

here is no shortage of snorkelling possibilities in Samoa, but not many places hire ut gear, so you might want to bring your wn mask and snorkel. One of the best and asiest places to catch a glimpse of the nderwater scene is at Palolo Deep near pia (you can hire gear here).

The best areas for inexperienced snor-ellers are along the Aleipata coast at the astern end of Upolu and around the islands ' Manono and Apolima on the far western nd. Just off the south coast, near Poutasi, Nu'usafe'e Islet, which offers some of the ost diverse corals and fish around Upolu. rong swimmers and snorkellers can also ckle the turbulent waters en route to the xcellent snorkelling around Nu'utele and u'ulua islands and between Malaela vil-ge and Namu'a Island, all in the Aleipata strict.

The dive centres mentioned here offer rganised snorkelling trips to sites around polu. Expect to pay around ST40 per rson:

cific Quest Divers
(☎ 24728, pqdivers@samoa.net)
Operates from Beach Rd, Apia, across from
Aggie Grey's Hotel
moa Marine
(☎ 22721, fax 20087, pmeredith@samoa.net)
PO Box 4700, Apia; located on Beach Rd
opposite the main wharf
vama Divers
(☎/fax 24858, tourism@samoa.net)
PO box 843, Apia; has an office above the
Pasifika Inn

urfing

allow waters, sharp reefs, treacherous cur-nts and inconsistent breaks make surf con-tions in Samoa difficult. Well known surf ots on Upolu include Solosolo, 10km east Apia; the break near Nu'usafe'e Islet on e south coast and nearby 'Boulders' break f Cape Niuato'i. Two of the best spots on vai'i are at Fagamalo on the north coast d at Satuiatua on the south-west coast.

For advice about surfing spots, talk to the cals. An excellent source is Cyril Curry, e manager of the Seaside Inn in Apia.

Hiking

Hiking possibilities on Upolu include the coastal and rainforest walks in O Le Pupu-Pu'e National Park, the coastal route from Falefa Falls to Fagaloa Bay, the rugged hike between the village of Uafato and Ti'avea, the short but steep walk to the summit of Mt Vaea to see the graves of Robert Louis and Fanny Stevenson, and the muddy but rewarding trek to Lake Lanoto'o in the central highlands.

On Savai'i, there's even more scope. Shorter possibilities include the hike to Ole-moe Falls and the mysterious Pulemelei Mound, to the blowholes south of Salelologa and into the rainforest at Sasina. Longer day-hikes might include exploration of the Mt Matavanu area, the Tafua Rainforest Pre-serve or the Falealupo Rainforest Preserve (with an overnight stop in a banyan tree).

For more of an expedition, you can hire a guide and climb up into the Cloud Forest Preserve on Mt Silisili, the highest point in the Samoas. Guided walks (among other activities) are offered on tiny, traditional Manono Island.

Kayaking & Canoeing

Sea kayaking is an excellent way to explore the islands and one of the only ways to ac-cess some of the more remote parts of the coastline. Tours are available with Eco-Tour Samoa (see Organised Tours under Getting Around later in this chapter) and a number of villages offer traditional outrigger canoe tours. Sinalei Reef Resort and Coconuts Beach Club, on the south coast of Upolu, offer a variety of organised boat tours.

Fishing

The reefs and their fishing rights are owned by villages so you can't just drop a line anywhere; seek permission first.

Samoa Marine (see under Snorkelling) operates pricey, deep-sea fish charters on a no-fish-no-pay scheme.

ACCOMMODATION

Compared to more developed Pacific is-lands such as Hawai'i and Fiji, accommo-dation options in the Samoas are fairly

SAMOA

limited. Samoa offers a range to suit most budgets, but 'budget' accommodation is not necessarily cheap and, though there are several expensive resorts to choose from, don't expect anything too sophisticated.

Budget

You can stay in a beachside fale on Upolu, Savai'i and Manono in Samoa for about ST15.

In Apia's guesthouses and cheaper hotels, decent singles/doubles start at around ST44/55, and dormitory beds at around ST20. Most places only have cold-water facilities.

In American Samoa, decent 'budget' accommodation starts at US$35 for a single room. Most places have hot water. At the time of writing there were no beachside fale to rent in American Samoa.

Though there are a couple of designated camping areas on Upolu (and some guesthouses will allow camping in their grounds) there are few other opportunities for camping. More than 80% of Samoan land is under customary ownership and to camp anywhere, even on seemingly secluded beaches, you must ask permission from the traditional owners.

Mid-Range & Top End

In Samoa there are quite a few smaller hotels and bungalow-style resorts in the middle bracket, where rooms range from ST100/110 to around ST160/180.

In American Samoa, there are only three or four hotels in this category with single or doubles starting at around US$60. You won't find any five-star hotels in Samoa but there are a couple of up-market hotels in Apia where prices range from ST200 for a standard double to more than ST300 for 'deluxe' rooms.

Staying in Villages

In Samoa, home and village stays can be organised through Safua Tours (☎ 51271, fax 51272) in Lalomalava on the island of Savai'i.

In American Samoa, the Office of Tourism runs an official home-stay program

known as *Fale, Fala ma Ti* (House, Mat and Tea). It provides the option of staying with Samoan host families for US$25 to US$45 per night. For information contact the Office of Tourism (☎ 684-633 1091, fax 633 1094), PO Box 1147, Pago Pago, American Samoa 96799.

See Dos & Don'ts under Society & Conduct earlier in this chapter and in the Facts about the South Pacific chapter for some pointers on visiting traditional homes and villages.

FOOD
Local Food

Traditional Samoan food is very good and some excellent dishes are made from tropical crops. Meals consist mostly of such items as root vegetables, coconut products *(niu and popo)*, taro *(talo)*, breadfruit *(fuata)*, fresh fruit, pork *(pua'a)*, chicken *(moa)*, fish (i'a) and – yum! – corned beef *(pisupo)*. The best way to sample the local cuisine is to stay in a village, be invited into a Samoan home or take part in an *umu* feast. An umu is a traditional Polynesian earth oven (made above the ground in Samoa) and some of the most interesting and delicious traditional concoctions are prepared in it. The midday Sunday meal, to'onai is almost always cooked in an umu – wreathing the hills around Apia with the smoke of hundreds of umu fires.

Most restaurants are in Apia and Pago Pago, with Apia having the widest choice. Restaurants range from cheap cafes to upmarket places. Chinese food is very popular in both Samoas and reasonable Mexican and Korean food is available in American Samoa. Vegetarians are not well catered for and vegans, in particular, might find it difficult to maintain a decent protein intake.

In Samoa, a cheap meal costs from around ST10, an upmarket feed from ST2? In American Samoa, you'll pay US$5 for cheap meal, US$30 for a splurge.

The cheapest food of all is to be found the markets in Apia, Salelologa (Savai'i) and Pago Pago.

Every village has a small grocery store where you can buy basic goods such bread, eggs, tinned fish, corned beef and local beer. Look out for sticky coconut buns, they're a delicious treat.

Fast Food

Local people, especially those in American Samoa, are facing serious health problems as junk food replaces the healthy diet to which Samoans have long been accustomed.

DRINKS

Despite the variety of fruit on hand, fresh juices aren't terribly popular – sugary cordial is much easier to find. A delicious Samoan drink is *koko Samoa*, a chocolate drink made with locally grown roasted cocoa beans, sugar and water. An unusual hot drink you might come across is *vaisalo*, which is made from coconut milk and flesh thickened with starch.

Samoa's locally brewed lager, Vailima, is very good and is available just about everywhere – except on Sunday of course.

ENTERTAINMENT

Bars and nightclubs are very popular with urbanised Samoans. Pago Pago has one or two nightclubs and a couple of modern cinemas showing current mainstream movies.

SPECTATOR SPORTS

The most popular sports are netball and rugby (Samoa's national rugby team, Manu Samoa, has reached the rugby world cup quarter finals twice, in 1991 and 1995). Most afternoons, Samoans gather on *malae* (village greens) to play rugby, volleyball and a unique brand of cricket, *kirikiti* (see the boxed text 'It's Not Just Cricket').

SAMOA

It's Not Just Cricket

No discussion of Samoan sporting tradition would be complete without a mention of *kirikiti*, the national game. A bizarre version of cricket, kirikiti is played by apparently flexible rules known only to the players. Missionaries introduced the game to Samoa (and other Polynesian countries such as Tokelau and Wallis & Futuna) early in the 20th century as a way to get entire villages involved in one activity.

The balls are handmade of rubber and wrapped with pandanus. The three-sided bat also keeps things interesting – nobody, not even the batter, has a clue where the ball will go.

The scoring system is also unique – not only to Samoa but to the particular village where the game is being played. If a church stands closeby, then hitting the ball to the church might be worth one point. Beyond the church into someone's garden might be worth two points, the coconut plantation three or four and lodging the ball in a tree could be worth six.

Lack of pads and any face protection adds to the element of risk – and disputed calls have resulted in death by cricket bat. This certainly isn't Lords!

Since everyone in the village wants to be involved in a typical afternoon game, Samoans don't limit participation to teams of 11 aside. Forty or fifty on each side is not uncommon! Serious competitions go on for days and, once a team has lost, it can always buy its way back into the match by paying a fee to the host village, which is responsible for catering for the entire tournament.

The game is played year-round, with frequent Saturday matches throughout the year and practice games held nearly every day. There are male, female and mixed teams. The main season for inter-village matches is from April to June, while the national play-offs are held in August in preparation for the national championships. These take place during the Teuila Festival in the second week of September.

If you'd like to have a look at cricket, Samoan-style, or even participate in a game, wander through the rural villages of Upolu or Savai'i in the mid-afternoon. You'd be hard-pressed to find a *malae* (village green) where a match is not in progress.

SHOPPING

In Apia, there are several craft stores, a couple of interesting art galleries and a large flea market where you can look for local arts and crafts. Pago Pago has a few craft outlets, but prices are likely to be substantially higher than in Samoa.

Getting There & Away

AIR

The majority of visitors to the Samoas arrive on scheduled flights at Faleolo airport 35km west of Apia on Upolu, or at Pago Pago airport at Tafuna on Tutuila.

From NZ, Australia, Fiji, Tonga, Hawai'i and Los Angeles, access to Samoa is fairly straightforward. From anywhere else, however, travelling to the Samoan islands will entail first reaching one of these connecting points. Auckland and Nadi/Suva are the most convenient and best-served runs. See the introductory Getting There & Away and Getting Around the Region chapters.

Airlines

The major carriers to the Samoan islands are Air New Zealand and Polynesian Airways. Other options are Hawaiian Airlines, Air Pacific, Royal Tongan Airlines and Samoa Air (which flies between the two Samoas as well as to the Vava'u group in Tonga). Several air passes that include Samoa are listed in the introductory Getting Around the Region chapter.

Airline offices in the Samoas are:

Air New Zealand
  (☎ 685-20825)
  Lotemau Centre, Apia, Samoa
Air Pacific
  (☎ 685-22693, fax 20023)
  Beach Rd, Apia, Samoa
Hawaiian Airlines
  (☎ 684-699 1875)
Polynesian Airlines
  American Samoa:
  (☎ 684-699 9126, fax 699 2109)
  PO Box 487, Pago Pago, American Samoa

Samoa:
  (☎ 685-22737, fax 20023,
  enquiries@PolynesianAirlines.co.nz)
  NPF Bldg, Beach Rd, PO Box 599, Apia;
  www.polynesianairlines.co.nz
Samoa Air
  American Samoa:
  (☎ 684-699 9106, fax 699 9751,
  samoaair@samoatelco.com)
  Tafuna Airport, PO Box 280, Pago Pago
  Samoa:
  (☎ 685-22901, fax 23851)
  Beach Rd, PO Box 599, Apia

Departure Tax

There is a departure tax of ST20 when flying out of Samoa, payable at the airport at the time of check-in. The American Samoa departure tax is US$3 but it's included in the price of airline tickets.

North America

The main hub for travel between North America and the Pacific is Honolulu and most travellers to the Pacific islands will have to pass through here.

Australasia

Travelling to the Samoas from Australia or NZ is reasonably straightforward, but not necessarily inexpensive. Polynesian Airlines operates six weekly flights direct from NZ to Samoa – five out of Auckland and one from Wellington. Air New Zealand flies three times weekly from Auckland and once from Wellington.

Polynesian Airlines flies twice weekly to Apia from Sydney, once via Auckland and once via Auckland and Tonga, plus one weekly flight from Melbourne via Wellington (Australia to Samoa direct flights are planned). Air New Zealand flies twice weekly from Sydney and once weekly from Melbourne and Brisbane, all via Auckland.

The Pacific

Within the central Pacific region, island hopping isn't very difficult or expensive but some routes will present scheduling problems. Samoa Air flies between Pago Pago and the Vava'u group of islands in Tonga four times weekly for US$300 return. Royal Tongan Airlines operates weekly flights between Pago Pago and Nuku'alofa in Tonga for around the same price. Tickets can be booked through Samoa Air.

Polynesian Airlines flies once a week from Apia to Nuku'alofa. Between them, Polynesian and Air Pacific run three weekly flights from Apia to Fiji for around US$300 return. Air New Zealand and Polynesian both have weekly flights from Apia to Honolulu for around US$600 return. To get to or from Niue, the Cook Islands or French Polynesia, you'll have to fly via Tonga, NZ, Fiji or Hawai'i. Though Polynesian Airlines offers a couple of good-value Pacific fares, in general you'll get far better deals by applying through a travel agency specialising in independent travel.

See Air Passes in the introductory Getting Around the Region chapter.

Europe
See the introductory Getting There & Away chapter for information about getting to Samoa from Europe.

SEA
Cargo Ship
The newspapers in Pago Pago, Apia, Nuku'alofa, Suva and Honolulu list the sailing schedules and routes of various lines up to three months in advance. Agencies in American Samoa include:

Polynesia Shipping Services
(☎ 633 1211, fax 633 1265)
PO Box 1478, Pago Pago 96799
Samoa Pacific Shipping
(☎ 633 4665, fax 633 4667)
Pago Pago 96799

The once-monthly cargo ship that sails between Apia and remote Tokelau, provides Tokelau's only passenger link with the rest of the world. For sailing dates and fares, contact the Tokelau Apia Liaison Office (☎ 20822) in Apia.

Yacht
Yachts travelling to the Samoas almost always follow the trade winds west from the northern Cook Islands or from French Polynesia. Often, yachts will anchor in Pago Pago Harbor to stock up on provisions at the local supermarkets; American Samoa has the lowest grocery prices between Venezuela and South-East Asia. From there, most of them stop at Apia and a few cruise around Savai'i before moving on to Tonga.

The only official ports of entry into the two countries are Apia and Pago Pago.

Apia Harbour Yachts arriving in Apia Harbour should pull up inside the basin rather than outside where they may block large freighters. The entrance fee is ST15. Pull up alongside the wharf at Apia Harbour with the quarantine flag raised. Port quarantine officials will come aboard and may check for yellow fever vaccination certificates, although these aren't officially required unless you're coming directly from Africa or South America. When the yellow quarantine flag is lowered, customs officials will board and check documentation, which must include a certificate of clearance from your previous port of call and five copies of the crew list.

Crew members must be guaranteed onward passage with the yacht or have an air or ferry ticket out of Samoa. (An air ticket out of Pago Pago will normally also suffice.) Visits to other harbours in Samoa require permission from the Prime Minister's office (☎ 23636).

The Apia Yacht Club (☎ 21313) is near the end of Mulin'u Peninsula.

Pago Pago Harbor The anchorage at Pago Pago Harbor is free for seven days. After that you are charged about US$15 per month, more or less, depending on the length of your yacht. Those arriving by yacht from Hawai'i must present a US customs clearance document from Honolulu. Though improved filtering has cut down the nose-wrenching fumes from the tuna canneries, boats leave the 'fertile' harbour covered with a worm-like tubular scum that grows to unbelievable thicknesses in a matter of days and fouls depth sounders, anchor chains, through-the-hull fittings and propellers after only a short visit.

The Pago Pago Yacht Club, 2km east in Utulei, is a friendly place to gather information about local yachting conditions.

Getting Around

This section contains information relevant to both Samoas. There are separate Getting Around sections at the beginning of the sections dealing with the individual islands of Samoa and American Samoa.

AIR

The main inter-island transport in the Samoas is provided by Samoa Air and Polynesian Airlines. The former flies between Apia (from Fagali'i airport just east of town) and Pago Pago; between Pago, Ofu and Ta'u and between Pago and Savai'i. Polynesian flies between Pago Pago, Apia and Savai'i.

Samoa Air runs three to six daily flights between Apia and Pago Pago. Polynesian does the 20-minute hop from Apia's Fagali'i airport to Savai'i's Maota airport on the south-east side of the island three times daily. They also fly once a day to Savai'i's new airport at Asau in the north-west of the island. Samoa Air flies twice weekly between Pago Pago and Maota airport.

Another option is Inter Island Air (☎ 684-699 5700, fax 699 5850, iia@samoanet.com) in Pago Pago.

BUS

Travelling by public bus is the most common method of getting around. In Samoa, bus services operate at the whim of the drivers. If your driver feels like knocking off at 1 pm, he does, and passengers counting on the service are left stranded. Never, under any circumstances, rely on catching a bus after about 2 pm. Buses are scarce on Saturday afternoon and Sunday.

In American Samoa, the island of Tutuila is served by small 'aiga-owned buses. The buses theoretically run until early evening, but if you want to head back to town after visiting outlying villages, make

sure you leave by 3.30 or 4 pm at the latest. It's difficult to find transport after about 2 pm on Saturday, and on Sunday the only buses running are those taking people to church.

To stop a bus in either Samoa, wave your hand palm down, as the bus approaches. To signal that you'd like to get off the bus, either knock on the ceiling or clap loudly. Pay the fare to the driver or leave the money on the dash as you leave. Try to have the exact change for the driver.

CAR

Getting around by car in the Samoas is quite straightforward. You'll normally get by using your driving licence from home but occasionally visitors to independent Samoa will be required to get their licence endorsed at the court house in Apia (ST10).

In independent Samoa, the speed limit within Apia and villages is 40km/h (25mph); outside populated areas, it's 55km/h (35mph).

In American Samoa, the speed limit is 24km/h (15mph) through villages and 40km/h (25mph) outside populated areas. In both independent and American Samoa, vehicles drive on the right – most of the time.

You must be at least 21 years of age to hire a car in Samoa and tariffs on hire cars are regulated by the government. Petrol costs about ST1.20 per litre in Samoa and about 36c per litre in American Samoa.

BICYCLE

For fit, experienced cyclists, touring Upolu and Savai'i by bicycle can be great. The roads are generally in very good condition and traffic is minimal.

The island of Tutuila in American Samoa is much less suitable for cycling; Although smaller than Upolu or Savai'i, Tutuila is more mountainous, and the traffic is heavier

BOAT
Ferry

Ferries and launches connect all the main Samoan islands except Manu'a. The largest car ferry, the *Queen Salamasina*, runs between Pago Pago Harbor and Apia once a

Last Bus to Paradise (and Back if You're Lucky)

On the big island of Savai'i, public transport is limited and buses seem to operate on a schedule known only to their drivers. For example, in Asau I visited the owner/driver of one vehicle to find out what time the following morning the first bus to Salelologa would leave. He told me that passengers should be waiting at the petrol station at 3 am.

I turned up at 2.30 am, however, because the previous day I'd missed the 6 am bus, which for some reason had departed at 5.40 am. Of course there was no-one else waiting when I arrived at the petrol station and when the 3 am bus finally turned up (at 4.30 am) there was still no-one else waiting. I soon learned why.

We pulled up in front of a house. The driver got out, knocked on the door, and the lights came on. There was evidence of people bustling around inside and then, 15 min-

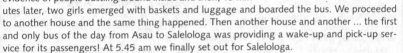

MIC LOOBY

utes later, two girls emerged with baskets and luggage and boarded the bus. We proceeded to another house and the same thing happened. Then another house and another ... the first and only bus of the day from Asau to Salelologa was providing a wake-up and pick-up service for its passengers! At 5.45 am we finally set out for Salelologa.

The bus was scheduled to return to Asau at noon (leaving me only three hours in Salelologa), so at precisely 12 I was waiting beside the road. Two hours passed, then three. The ferries between Savai'i and Upolu had been undergoing repairs so there was no way of knowing if there might be a bus to meet a ferry. Everyone I asked about the matter had a different answer. Since traffic is thin on Savai'i after about 2 pm, I realised it was time to begin hitching. After several short rides and many kilometres of walking, I arrived back in Asau well after dark.

Later, I learned from a friend that the driver of the Asau bus had decided to stay in Salelologa to play pool and drink with his buddies that night and that no afternoon ferry had ever arrived.

The moral of the story is that you shouldn't set out between any two points without leaving your options open. If you have a plane to catch in Apia the following day, don't count on the bus getting you to the wharf or the airport, and for that matter, don't depend on the plane or the ferry getting you back to Upolu in any reasonable amount of time either. Go back a day early – or even two days early – if you'd rather not risk missing an international flight.

Welcome to paradise!

Deanna Swaney

week. The trip takes about eight hours each way.

The ship isn't all that clean and the sight of people puking and the general smell and trashy nature of the ship may have an affect even on those not usually prone to seasickness. Travellers on overnight ferries should carry a ground cover and sleeping bag if they plan to do any sleeping on the boat. For information on the ferry between Upolu and Savai'i, see Getting There & Away at the end of the Savai'i section.

Yacht

The yachtie route through the Samoan islands begins in Pago Pago and runs west to

Apia Harbour and to the three anchorages on Savai'i. Private yacht owners who intend to cruise around Savai'i should apply for a cruising permit at the Prime Minister's office in Apia. The permit will be issued in one or two days. If you're leaving Samoa from Savai'i, check out of the country in Apia before leaving the harbour or you'll have to sail back against prevailing winds to do so.

ORGANISED TOURS

There are several excellent organised tours in Samoa. Those in American Samoa are much more limited in scope and about twice the price. The following are just a few of the many companies offering different types of tours:

Eco-Tour Samoa
  (☎/fax 22144, info@ecotoursamoa.com)
  PO Box 4609 Matautu-uta, Samoa; offers an action-packed safari (US$137 per person per day) taking visitors (maximum of 15) to Upolu, Namua, Manono and Savai'i. Seven nights are spent in villages. It also runs a seven day tour (US$210 per day), with three nights in hotels and four nights in villages; sea kayaking tours overnighting in villages (US$137 per day); and educational tours for student groups (from US$79 per day). It's website is www .ecotoursamoa.com.

Safua Tours
  (☎ 51271, fax 51272)
  Lalomalava, Savai'i, Samoa; provides excellent cultural, educational and scenic tours, including a half day tour to Pulemelei Mound and an excellent clifftop walk from Cape Paepaeoleia on the Tafua Peninsula. Home and village stays are also offered.

Samoa Tours & Travel
  (☎ 633 5884, fax 633 1311)
  PO Box 727, Pago Pago, American Samoa 96799; offers tours around Tutuila Island, village visits and island feasts.

Upolu

• **pop 115,000**   • **area 1119 sq km**
Upolu is the second-largest island of Samoa. About 40% of the island is characterised by relatively gentle volcanic slopes rising to crests of around 1000m. The highest peak is

Mt Fito (1158m), which lies within the O L Pupu-Pu'e National Park. The interior of the island is covered in indigenous rainfores which accounts for about 20% of the tota land area.

Around 30% of Upolu is customary lan (ie owned by extended families and unabl to be sold), the bulk of which is cultivate for subsistence agriculture. Though most o Upolu's villages lie along the coast, ther are several villages and settlements scat tered around the central highlands.

A fairly good system of roads makes a parts of the island easily accessible from th national capital and hub of activity, Apia which is situated roughly in the centre o the north coast.

Getting There & Away

Flights for Savai'i and Pago Pago leav from Fagali'i airport, a few kilometres eas of Apia. The bus fare between the airpor and Apia is ST1.50. Taxis between Fagali' airport and central Apia cost ST5.

Taxis from Apia and Faleolo airport cos ST30 – quite high by local standards.

Getting Around

Bus Buses connecting Apia with other part of Upolu leave from the central market, th Maketi Fou, off Fugalei St, and from th bus area behind the flea market.

If you'd like to visit a remote spot – sa Lefaga or Aleipata – and return the same day be at the Maketi Fou in Apia by 6 or 7 am.

From Apia, fares to the western end o Upolu (Mulifanua and Manono-uta) or Muli vai are ST1.50. To Si'umu or Lefaga they'r ST2 and to Aleipata, ST3. Getting aroun Apia and its environs will cost between 4 and 80 sene.

Car Three good cross-island roads pas over the east-west central ridge and divid the island roughly into quarters. The centra one begins in Apia at Falealili St before be coming The Cross Island Rd farther south

The north-eastern section of Upolu is th most rugged; you'll need a 4WD to negoti ate the track to Fagaloa Bay. The Fagalo Bay track and the tracks leading off th southern Main Coast Rd down to Aganoa Beach, Nu'uavasa Beach and Matareva Beach can get pretty muddy after heavy rain.

Prices start at around ST100 per day for a Suzuki 4WD jeep. Discounts are offered for longer term rental. There are plenty of agencies, so ring around for the best deal.

Avis Car Rentals
  (☎ 20486, fax 26069)
Budget Car Hire
  (☎ 20561, fax 22284)
Hibiscus Rentals
  (☎ 27039, fax 20162)
Teuila Rentals
  (☎ 20284, fax 24179)

Bicycle The Seaside Inn (☎ 22578) and the Rainforest Cafe (☎ 25030), both on Beach Rd, and the Outrigger Hotel (☎ 20042) at Vaiala Beach, all have bicycles to rent from around ST20 per day. For information on cycling around the islands see the Getting Around section earlier.

Taxi Taxis are cheap and plentiful. To travel anywhere in Apia the charge is about ST3. You'll pay around ST40 for half a day's sightseeing for up to four or five people. The following companies are recommended:

Airport City Cabs
  (☎ 25420 or ☎ 21600)
Magic 98FM Taxis
  (☎ 20808)
  corner of Beach Rd and Matautu St
Samoan Lager Taxis
  (☎ 25909)

APIA
• pop 40,000

With its run-down colonial buildings, big old pulu trees and easy-going pace, Apia still retains a certain shabby and romantic charm.

Orientation

Apia is the only place in Samoa that could conceivably be called a city but it would be more accurately described as an agglomeration of urbanised villages. From the centre of town, Apia's neat villages spread west along the level coastal area and climb up the gentle slopes towards the hills and into the valleys. Apia is the service centre of Samoa and it is here that you'll find shops, supermarkets, communications offices, tourist information, travel agencies and so on. The bulk of Samoa's hotels and restaurants are located in Apia, too.

Most of the activity is spread along Beach Rd between Aggie Grey's Hotel and the flea market, with the business district spreading south from the clock tower into the area known as Chinatown. The central market and main bus station are a couple of blocks south of the clock tower, between Fugalei and Saleufi Sts. The wharf lies at the eastern end of the harbour. The marine reserve, Palolo Deep, is just beyond the wharf.

Information

Tourist Offices The Samoa Visitors Bureau (☎ 20878, fax 20886, samoa@ samoa.net) is on Beach Rd. A good map of Samoa, which includes a plan of Apia, is available for ST10. The office is open from 8 am to 4.30 pm weekdays and from 8.30 am to noon on Saturday.

Money Samoa's three main banks, the Bank of Samoa (☎ 22422), the Pacific Commercial Bank (☎ 20000) and the new National Bank of Samoa (☎ 23076), are open from 9 am to 3 pm weekdays. The National Bank branch near the market is open from 8.30 am to 12.30 pm on Saturday. Aggie Grey's Hotel and the Hotel Kitano Tusitala offer currency-exchange services.

Post & Communications The main post and telephone office is on Beach Rd. Postal services are available at the counter between 9 am and 4.30 pm. For poste restante, go to the separate office two doors down Post Office St from the main lobby. The telephone office (which has the only two public telephones in Samoa) is open from 8 am to 10.30 pm daily. Fax services are available upstairs from 8 am to 4.30 pm weekdays. The international telephone code for Samoa is ☎ 685.

SAMOA

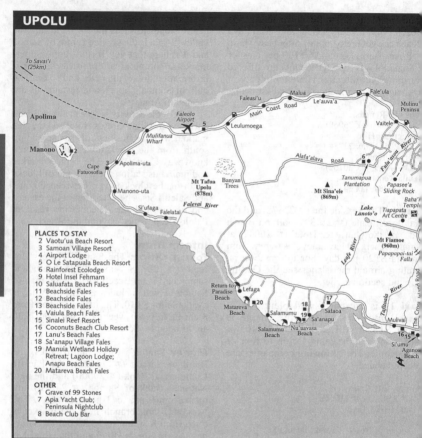

UPOLU

To Savai'i (25km)

Apolima

Manono

PLACES TO STAY
2 Vaotu'ua Beach Resort
3 Samoan Village Resort
4 Airport Lodge
5 O Le Satapuala Beach Resort
6 Rainforest Ecolodge
9 Hotel Insel Fehmarn
10 Saluafata Beach Fales
11 Beachside Fales
12 Beachside Fales
13 Beachside Fales
14 Vaiula Beach Fales
15 Sinalei Reef Resort
16 Coconuts Beach Club Resort
17 Lanu's Beach Fales
18 Sa'anapu Village Fales
19 Manuia Wetland Holiday
   Retreat; Lagoon Lodge;
   Anapu Beach Fales
20 Matareva Beach Fales

OTHER
1 Grave of 99 Stones
7 Apia Yacht Club;
  Peninsula Nightclub
8 Beach Club Bar

Travel Agencies Two recommended local agencies are Island Hopper Vacations (☎ 26940, fax 26941), PO Box 2271, in the Lotemau Centre, and Oceania Travel & Tours (☎ 24443, fax 22255), PO Box 9339, near the Hotel Kitano Tusitala.

Bookshops The Wesley Bookshop in the Wesley Arcade has branches in Salelologa and Asau on Savai'i and in Pago Pago, American Samoa. You'll also find a limited number of titles at the Educational Bookshop, near the corner of Mt Vaea and Vaitele Sts, and at Aggie's Gift Shop, on Beach Rd.

Libraries The Nelson Public Library, on Beach Rd, allows travellers to borrow books for ST5 plus a ST15 refundable deposit. The library is open from 9 am to 4.30 pm Monday to Thursday, from 8 am to 4 pm Friday, and from 8.30 am to noon Saturday.

Universities Originally established in 1984, the National University of Samoa (☎ 20072, fax 20938, nus@samoa.net) opened a new campus in 1997 at Malifa, just south-east of the town centre. The University of the South Pacific, which is based in Suva, Fiji, has its Agriculture

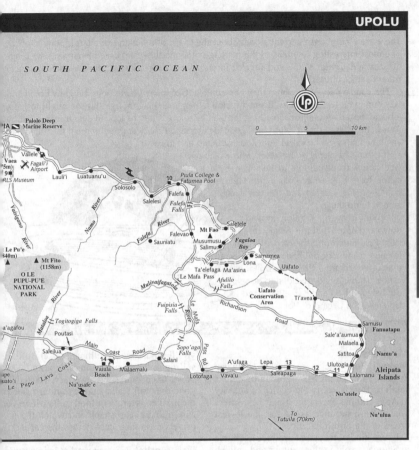

Department (☎ 21671) in Alafua, on the outskirts of Apia.

Laundry The most convenient of the several laundrettes in Apia is Sapolu's Laundry & Legal Services (!) on Matautu St near Beach Rd, only five minutes walk from town. It charges ST2.50 to wash and ST4 to dry; washing powder costs ST1. Lily's Laundromat, also on Matautu St, is a bit cheaper.

Medical Services The following private medical and dental services, all in the Apia area, have been recommended by the Samoa Visitors Bureau:

Apia Medical Clinic (☎ 20942)
Faletoese Clinic (☎ 23344)
Dr John Atherton (☎ 26113)
Dr Kome Kuresa (☎ 20365)
LTP Surgery (☎ 21652)
So'onalole Dental Surgery (☎ 21145)
T&T Medical Centre (☎ 24946)

Emergency In an emergency, call one of the following: ambulance (☎ 999), fire (☎ 994), police (☎ 995), National Hospital (☎ 996).

SAMOA

How a Lazy Lad Put Upolu on the Map

There are a number of ancient stories about the origin of the name Upolu (properly 'Upolu). The most interesting one tells of the marriage of an earthly chief called Beginning, to Timuateatea, a daughter of the god Tagaloa (pronounced '**tung**-a-low-a', and called Tangaroa in other Pacific cultures).

The couple had a son whom they named Polu. Like many young boys, he grew bored and lazy during his teenage years. Being a typical father, Beginning thought his son ought to get a job and looked around for something for the boy to do. When he looked over towards nearby Savai'i, he realised that it might be a good idea to send Polu over there to see if the island had any inhabitants. So he called Polu and instructed him to pay a visit to his heavenly grandfather, who would provide him with carpenters to help him build a canoe for the journey. Polu initially refused but Beginning insisted and the boy finally agreed to do the job.

Up in heaven, Tagaloa looked down and noted that the initially reticent Polu had found the carpenters uninterested and lazy, but had nevertheless managed to urge them to build his canoe. Thus, Tagaloa decided to honour his grandson and name his island Upolu – 'The Urging of Polu'.

MICK WELDON

Markets

Maketi Fou The main market, between Fugalei and Saleufi Sts a couple of blocks south of Beach Rd, is the centre of activity in Apia and has the biggest and best selection of fresh produce as well as the lowest prices in the South Pacific.

Every kind of meat and produce available in Samoa is sold in this vibrant and colourful place. Here, matai gather to chat and drink 'ava and the general public comes to socialise. You'll find drinking coconuts for sale, kiosks selling ready-made *palusami* (coconut cream wrapped in taro leaves), *fa'ausi* pudding, cakes and koko Samoa. You can also get cheap meals of meat and traditional vegetables. At the back of the main market are shops selling tinned foods, bread and other dry goods.

Flea Market Apia's flea market is housed in the old central market building down on Beach Rd, west of the clock tower. Here

you'll find cheap clothing and craft stalls selling everything from siapo and 'ava bowls to coconut shell jewellery. Tucked beyond the craft stalls, on the northern side of the market, is a row of food stalls where you can grab a cheap snack and watch the taxi drivers push their cabs across the carpark.

Fish Market The fish market is in a building just east of the flea market. It's open every day, but Sunday morning is the busiest time with everyone rushing in to buy fish for the Sunday umu before hurrying off to attend church. Look out for Coke bottles full of sea slug innards (a Samoan delicacy).

Churches

Apia's many churches reflect the major role that Christianity plays in Samoan life. The landmark of the city's waterfront is the chunky Madonna-topped **Catholic cathedral** (☎ 20400) on Beach Rd. The **Wesleyan church** nearby is also an imposing structure

Also on Beach Rd, the **Congregational Christian church** on the corner of Falealili St is a site of some historical interest. The missionary John Williams, who succeeded in bringing Christianity to Samoa in 1830, was killed and eaten in Vanuatu nine years later. His bones (slightly gnawed) are buried in this church and a monument to Williams stands across the road.

A lovely, unassuming building is the **Anglican church,** on Ifiifi St not far from the National Hospital. There is some impressive glasswork in the stained-glass windows.

Two kilometres south-west of Apia, the **Mormon temple** is a large striking building surrounded by an educational complex. The Baha'i Temple is also worth a look (see the Central Upolu section).

Clock Tower
The clock tower in the centre of town is a landmark for anyone who's ever tried to give directions around Apia.

Government Buildings
The most imposing addition to the Apia skyline is the seven-storey **government office building**, which towers above the area, reclaimed from the sea, behind the Samoa Visitors Bureau.

The two-storey knocked-about colonial building on the corner of Beach Rd and Ifiifi St is home to the **court house**.

The **police station** is just across the road on Ifiifi St and at 7.45 am every weekday, the Police Band marches from here to the government building to commemorate Samoa's independence. Vehicle and pedestrian traffic is stopped and the national anthem is played while the flag is raised.

Samoa's modern parliament building, the traditionally-shaped **Fale Fono**, is towards the end of the Mulinu'u Peninsula.

Madd Gallery
One of Samoa's best known contemporary painters, Momoe von Reiche, set up the Madd Gallery (☎ 25494), on Ifiifi St opposite the hospital, in 1984. The gallery is open from 9 am to 4 pm Monday to Friday and to noon Saturday.

Memorials
On the eastern side of Mulinu'u Peninsula, near the observatory, are the **tombs of Malietoa Tanumafili I** and **Malietoa Laupepa**, the father and grandfather, respectively, of the present ceremonial head of state. Gardens are planted around the tombs as a mark of respect. At the very end of the peninsula are two more tombs, the **mausoleum of Tupua Tamasese** and the magnificent seven-tiered **tomb of the Tu'imaleali'ifano dynasty**.

Palolo Deep National Marine Reserve
Past the wharf on Beach Rd, near the palagi enclaves of Matautu and Vaiala, is Palolo Deep National Marine Reserve. There's magnificent snorkelling here, as well as several shady, comfortable fale for picnicking and relaxing.

The real attraction at Palolo Deep is the sudden drop from the shallow reef into a deep blue hole which is flanked by walls of coral and densely populated by colourful species of fish. The reserve is open between 8 am and 6 pm daily. Admission is ST2 per person and snorkelling gear can be rented here.

Places to Stay
All prices are subject to the addition of 10% GST except where stated that tax is included.

Places to Stay – Budget
The *Samoan Outrigger Hotel* (☎/fax 20042, outrigger@samoa.net, PO Box 4074) is a spacious old colonial house at Vaiala Beach, a short walk from Palolo Deep. Dorm beds (two rooms with three bunks each) cost ST25; singles/doubles without shower will cost you ST55/66; and single/double or triple rooms with shower and toilet are ST66/88, including tax. Breakfast is included. There is no hot water as yet, but there are plans to install solar panels. The hotel has a fully equipped kitchen with two big dining tables, a reading room with maps and pool table, a laundry room (ST4 for a load of washing),

APIA

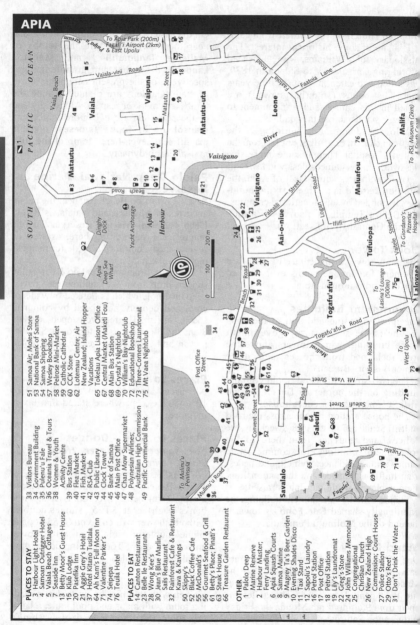

To Apia Park (200m)
Fagali'i Airport (2km)
& East Upolu

Vaiala-vini Road

PACIFIC OCEAN

SOUTH

Vaiala Beach

Matautu

Vaiala

Vaipuna

Matautu-uta

Leone

Malifa

To RSL Museum (2km)
& South Coast

Faatoia Lane

River

Vaisigano

Vaisigano

Maluafou

Beach Road

Apia Harbour

Dinghy Dock

Yacht Anchorage

Apia Deep Sea Wharf

Aai-o-niue

Falealili Street

Logan Road

Ifiifi Street

Tufuiopa

Vaitele Street

To Giordano's;
Pizzeria;
Hospital

Togafu'afu'a Road

Togafu'afu'a

To Lasina's Lounge
(500m)

Lalovaea

To West Upolu

Matautu Street

Malinu'u Stream

Beach Road

Post Office Street

Mt Vaea Street

Convent Street

Saleufi Street

Savalalo

Saleufi

Fugalei Stream

Savalalo

Fugalei Street

To Mulinu'u Peninsula

Matautu Street

Atinae Road

0   100   200 m

PLACES TO STAY
3   Harbour Light Hotel
4   Samoan Outrigger Hotel
5   Vaiala Beach Cottages
7   Seaside Inn
13 Betty Moor's Guest House
15 Klub Lodge
20 Pasefika Inn
37 Aggie Grey's Hotel
64 Hotel Kitano Tusitala
71 Vh Kam's Full Moon Inn
74 Valentine Parker's
76 Teulia Hotel

PLACES TO EAT
14 Canton Restaurant
23 Belle Ile Restaurant
28 Wong Kee's
30 Jean's Blue Marlin;
    Sails Restaurant
32 Rainforest Cafe & Restaurant
    Kava & Kavings
50 Skippy's
52 Black Coffee Cafe
55 McDonald's
56 Gourmet Seafood & Grill
61 Betty's Place; Pinati's
63 Steak House
66 Treasure Garden Restaurant

OTHER
1   Palolo Deep
    Marine Reserve
2   Harbour Master;
    Ferry Landing
6   Apia Squash Courts
8   Samoa Marine
9   Magrey Ta's Beer Garden
10 Evening Shades Disco
11 Taxi Stand
12 Sapolu's Laundry
16 Lily's Laundromat
17 Petrol Station
18 Petrol Station
19 Greg's Store
24 John Williams Memorial
    Congregational
    Christian Church
25 New Zealand High
    Commission; Court House
26 Police Station
29 Otto's Reef
31 Don't Drink the Water

33 Visitors Bureau
34 Government Building
35 Pulenu'u Fale
36 Oceania Travel & Tours
38 Women & Youth
    Activity Centre
39 Bus Station
40 Flea Market
41 Fish Market
42 RSA Club
43 Public Library
44 Clock Tower
45 Main Post Office
46 Bank of Samoa
47 Chan Mow Supermarket
48 Polynesian Airlines;
    Australian High Commission
49 Pacific Commercial Bank
51 Samoa Air; Moles Store
53 National Bank of Samoa
54 Samoa Shipping
57 Wesley Bookshop
58 Pelrose Mini-Market
59 Catholic Cathedral
60 CCK Store
62 Lotemau Centre; Air
    New Zealand; Island Hopper
    Vacations
65 Tokelau Apia Liaison Office
67 Central Market (Maketi Fou)
68 Main Bus Station
69 William's Bay Nightclub
70 Crystal's Nightclub
72 Educational Bookshop
73 Three-Corners Laundromat
75 Mt Vaea Nightclub

elephone/fax service and two outrigger anoes that guests can hire. Snorkelling ear is available for hire, and dive lessons re available. The manager of the hotel also uns three local tours each week (including Matareva, Aleipata and Piula Cave).

The **Seaside Inn** (☎ *22578, fax 22918, PO Box 3019, Apia*) continues to be a popular choice with budget travellers. With its outdoor terrace and small, friendly bar, a good place to meet and mix with other travellers. Dorm beds cost ST25, while clean rooms with shower (cold) and toilet cost ST45/55/65. Breakfast is included. The Seaside has a kitchen that guests can use, laundry facilities, fax and telephone service, bicycles for ST15 per day and Suzuki jeeps from ST100 per day. The manager, Cyril Curry, is an excellent source of knowledge on surfing.

South of the centre and tucked away among village houses is **Seipepa** (☎/fax *25447, seipepa@samoa.net, PO Box 1465 Lalovaea, Apia*), a delightful 'Samoan Travel Home'. Guests have the choice of sleeping in one of the two small fale (one with a double mattress and one with two single mattresses) or in a double or twin room inside the house. There are spotless communal showers (cold) and toilets. Seipepa is a great place to sample traditional food (eaten sitting on the floor), especially on Sunday when a midday umu is prepared. There are no set accommodation rates here – guests simply pay what they feel to be fair. English, German, Swedish and Samoan are spoken.

Places to Stay – Mid-Range

Pasefika Inn (☎ *20971, fax 23303, pinn@ samoa.net, PO Box 4213*) is just off Beach Rd on Matautu St. The inn offers comfortable, air-conditioned single/double rooms with spa baths for ST120/140 and smaller, but equally comfortable, air-con rooms with shower and toilet for ST100/120. You can choose to go without the air-conditioning and pay just ST50/60 (with the luxury of hot water, this is possibly the best deal in town). All rooms have a fridge and telephone. Dormitory beds (one room with four

bunks) are also available for ST22 per person. All room prices, unless you're sleeping in the dorm, include breakfast. The inn has a big, fully equipped communal kitchen, a TV and video room, same-day laundry service and fax and Internet service. Every Sunday afternoon the Pasefika offers an excellent traditional Sunday dinner, to'ona'i, for around ST30 per person.

The pleasant **Le Godinet Beachfront Hotel** (☎ *25437, fax 25436, PO Box 9490*) is out on the quiet Mulinu'u Peninsula. Air-con rooms with private facilities cost ST107/133/160. Le Godinet is better known for being one of Apia's finest restaurants.

The **Rainforest Ecolodge** (☎/fax *22144, info@ecotoursamoa.com, PO Box 4609 Matautu-uta*) is a small B&B in the cool foothills 10 minutes west of Apia. There are three large rooms opening onto a wooden balcony that overlooks a lush tropical garden. Rooms cost US$20 per person per night, with a shared (hot water!) bathroom, cooking and laundry facilities. The lodge is run by Steve Brown and Funeali'i Lumaava Sooaemalelagi, who also offer excellent environmental and cultural tours.

Places to Stay – Top End

A very pleasant upmarket option, which actually straddles the middle and upper price ranges, is **Vaiala Beach Cottages** (☎ *22202, fax 22008, PO Box 2025, Apia*), close to Vaiala Beach. Family-sized cottages with bathroom, ceiling fans and cooking facilities (gas stove) will cost you ST158/183/ 207/244 for singles/doubles/ triples/quads. The cottages, set in spacious gardens overlooking the sea, can sleep up to three adults and two children. Vaiala offers a laundry service and traditional fofo massage on request.

The three-storey **Hotel Insel Fehmarn** (☎ *23301, fax 22204, PO Box 3272, Apia*), at Moto'otua on Falealili St, has large air-con rooms, balconies, TV and private facilities; it is a quiet but rather stark alternative to the hotels nearer the shore. Rooms with air-conditioning, bathroom and kitchen facilities cost ST158/183; the 3rd floor rooms are the nicest, affording views across Apia and out to sea. The hotel

SAMOA

also has a swimming pool, tennis court, laundrette, restaurant and live music every Saturday.

The busiest upmarket hotel in Apia is *Aggie Grey's Hotel* (☎ 22880, fax 23626, aggiegreys@talofa.net, PO Box 67), on Beach Rd. Well-appointed rooms and cute individual fale are gathered around a tropical garden and swimming pool. A standard room costs US$95/100/105, with discounts for children under 12. For fale accommodation, add US$20 per night to the above prices. Rooms in the new wing at the front (no children under 16 permitted) cost another US$25. To all these rates, add 10% GST. The comprehensive meal plan costs an additional US$50 per person per day.

The hotel has two bars, and offers nightly Polynesian musical entertainment. On Wednesday, don't miss the famous fiafia with spectacular dancing, drumming and singing. The show, with buffet dinner, costs ST44; tickets for the show only are ST11.

Places to Eat
Snacks & Cheap Meals One of the best places for a cheap meal, particularly breakfast, is the *Maketi Fou* or the food stalls behind the *Flea Market*. Look out for delicious palusami and drinking coconuts.

The *Black Coffee Cafe* (☎ 26528), on Convent St, is one of the cheapest and most pleasant sit-down places in town. The food is fresh, well made and served in Samoan-sized portions. A breakfast of pancakes with papaya and banana and two large mugs of coffee costs around ST7. A few tala more will get you a special 'hangover breakfast' of steak and the works served on a platter. The cafe also does excellent fruit shakes and a range of cakes. Lunch and dinner menus (daily specials from ST7) feature authentic curries, spicy food, fresh pasta, seafood, steaks and chicken dishes. Vegetarians can be catered for. The cafe has a BYO licence and is open for breakfast, lunch and dinner from 6 am weekdays and for breakfast and lunch on Saturday.

Another of Apia's favourite restaurants is *Gourmet Seafood & Grill* (☎ 24625) on the corner of Convent and Post Office Sts, open

from 7 am to 9.30 pm Monday to Saturday. It has a pleasant, relaxed feel and offers a good range of simple dishes.

Giordano's Pizzeria (☎ 25985), opposite the Insel Fehmarn Hotel, offers excellent pizzas in a pleasant courtyard setting. For a pizza large enough for two people, you'll pay around ST15. It's open from 3 to 10 pm Monday to Saturday and from 5 to 9 pm on Sunday.

There are plenty of cheap takeaway places around town, including a McDonald's on the corner of Convent and Mt Vaea Sts. *Betty's Place* and *Pinati's*, both opposite McDonald's on Convent St, offer cheap Samoan and Chinese dishes. Pinati's does a filling meat and vegetable soup for ST2.

Restaurants *Rainforest Cafe & Restaurant* (☎ 25030), on Beach Rd, has breakfast items including fresh blended fruit juices, cappuccino, French toast and pancakes (from ST5). Lunch specials – excellent salads, curries, fish and chicken dishes and huge sandwiches – range from ST9 to ST15. Main courses at dinner start at ST18. The restaurant is closed on weekends.

Lesina's Lounge (☎ 20836), in a great location overlooking Apia, specialises in Japanese, Samoan and continental dishes. Starters (palolo on toast, or oysters) range from ST10 to ST15; main courses start at around ST25. There's an adjoining bar with a large deck area and pool table, and live music every Friday and Saturday evening. The restaurant is open from 4.30 to 11.30 pm Monday to Saturday (lunchtime opening is on the cards).

The elegant *Le Godinet's* (☎ 23690), on the Mulinu'u Peninsula, is best known for its seafood and Friday night Polynesian buffet. Seafood dishes with deliciously prepared vegetables cost from ST26; lobster thermidor is ST32. Book ahead, if possible in the early afternoon.

Fale Restaurant and *Le Tamarina* at Aggie Grey's Hotel are also good; there's also a *coffee lounge* at the hotel.

There are quite a number of Chinese restaurants around town. *Oriental Restaurant* (☎ 25171), below Fiasili's Guesthouse

SAMOA

& Backpackers Centre opposite the Mormon temple, is the most popular and probably the best value, offering lunch specials from just ST5. A full meal at dinner will cost between ST20 and ST25. It's open for lunch from noon to 2 pm weekdays, and for dinner from 6 to 10 pm every evening. Other Chinese restaurants in Apia include *Canton*, *Treasure Garden*, *Hua Mei Restaurant* and *Wong Kee's*.

Sunday Lunch One of the best places for a traditional Sunday lunch is *Pasefika Inn* (☎ 20971), on Matautu St. A typical spread includes baked fish and other seafood (freshwater prawns, crabs, octopus cooked in coconut milk), suckling pig, baked breadfruit, bananas, palusami, salads, curry dishes and more. For ST30 per person, it's excellent value.

Dave Parker's Silver Streams (☎ 24426), up in the hills above Apia, puts on Sunday lunch in the rainforest. *O Le Satapuala Resort* (☎ 42212), 25 minutes drive west of Apia, also stages a well-attended to'ona'i for ST30 per person.

Self-Catering For fresh produce, the best place to head is *Maketi Fou*, off Fugalei St, or the *Fish Market*, just east of the Flea Market, which also has a few fruit and vegetable stalls. You'll find a reasonable selection of groceries at *Chan Mow Supermarket*, near the clock tower; the *Molesi Store*, farther west on Beach Rd; *Greg's Store*, next to the Belle Ile Restaurant up near Aggie Grey's; *Lynn Netzler's Store* (☎ 20272), on Salenesa Rd near the hospital; and *CJ's Deli*, in the Lotemau Centre.

Entertainment
Bars & Nightclubs *Don't Drink the Water*, on Beach Rd, is an air-conditioned, no-smoking cocktail bar that serves huge cocktails for very reasonable prices. *Otto's Reef* and *Magrey Ta's Beer Garden*, both on Beach Rd, sometimes feature bands on the weekends.

Seaside Inn is a good place to meet other travellers, locals and the occasional salty old sailor. The *Fale Bar* at Aggie Grey's

Hotel has live Polynesian-style music nightly and a pleasant atmosphere. Slightly more elegant, Aggie's *Le Kionasina* bar, at the front of the hotel, is open from 3 to 11 pm Monday to Saturday.

The *Ocean Terrace Bar* at the Hotel Kitano Tusitala stages live music and dancing until midnight nightly, Monday to Saturday. On the south coast, the upmarket Sinalei Reef Resort and Coconuts Beach Club have *bars* open to nonguests (see Places to Stay & Eat under The South Coast later). Traditional Samoan music is played in the beach bar at Coconuts every Tuesday to Friday evening and on Saturday and Sunday afternoons.

Peninsula Nightclub is built on the edge of the mangrove forest on the Mulinu'u Peninsula, next to the petrol storage tanks. The large open dance floor is nicely lit, there's a good mixture of ages (20s to 50s) and beyond the dance floor and bar, there are tables and chairs gathered beneath enormous pulu trees. Further south, the *Beach Club Bar* also has live music.

In the evenings the *RSA Club*, on Beach Rd near the clock tower, transforms from a big rattling pool hall and bar into a popular nightclub – thanks mainly to an excellent band and enthusiastic use of ultraviolet lighting. There's a younger crowd and more serious beer drinking here.

Fiafia The fiafia at *Aggie Grey's Hotel* is staged on Wednesday evening. Dinner and show cost ST44; the show only costs ST11. The *Kitano Tusitala's* fiafia is on Thursday. The fiafia and buffet cost ST45; the show only is ST10. *Sinalei Reef Resort* stages a fiafia on Friday evening and *Coconuts Beach Club* puts on its show on Saturday.

AROUND THE ISLAND
Upolu is the archetypal tropical island, with beaches, reefs, rainforests, mountains and quiet villages.

North-Eastern Upolu
Uafato Conservation Area The north-eastern coastal region of Upolu is the wildest and least visited part of the island,

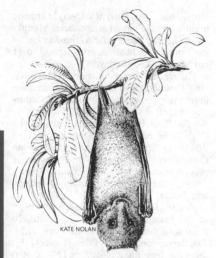

The *pe'a fanua* (flying fox or fruit bat) was once a prized delicacy but is now protected.

containing some of the best scenery. A 4WD track follows the rugged coastline as far as the picturesque village of Uafato, where 14 sq km of the surrounding rainforest and coastal waters have been declared a conservation area. This is believed to be one of the few areas left in Samoa where there is an intact band of rainforest stretching from the sea to the interior uplands. The area also contains one of the largest remaining stands of *ifilele*, the tree used for carving kava bowls, as well as a range of bat and bird species, including the rare *manumea* or tooth-billed pigeon.

From Uafato, a coastal walking track continues eastward to Ti'avea (about four hours), which is connected by road to the Richardson Rd, just above Aleipata. Although there is no formal accommodation in Uafato, it is possible to stay overnight. Ask to speak to the pulenu'u when you arrive.

To drive to Uafato, take the 4WD track that leads eastward off Le Mafa Pass Rd at Falefa Falls; heading from Apia, look out for a sharp left over a precarious-looking bridge. The track meanders above the coastline with numerous beautiful views

through the rainforest and down to the sea. A shorter 4WD track (about 10km) leads over the mountain from Le Mafa Pass to the village of Taelefaga. If you have plenty of time, this makes an excellent walk. The track isn't signposted; look for a sharp turn by a small roadside fale. From Apia, this route is occasionally served by buses marked Fagaloa.

Piula College & Fatumea Pool Usually known simply as 'Piula Cave Pool', Fatumea Pool lies beneath Piula Methodist Theological College 18km east of Apia. It's a wonderful spot to spend a few hours picnicking, swimming in the clean, clear springs and exploring the water-filled caves. Just metres from the sea, the freshwater pool is separated from salt water by black lava rock. At the rear of the first cave you'll see light through the wall under the water. A 3m swim through the opening will take you to the second cave pool. If you don't fancy a James Bond-type swim, follow the path leading to the opening on the seaward side of the second cave. There's a ST1 custom fee to use the pool and 'obscene languages' are not allowed.

Central Upolu

Robert Louis Stevenson Museum & Mt Vaea Scenic Reserve Just 4km inland from Beach Rd, off the Cross Island Rd, is the beautifully restored home (☎ 20798, fax 25428) of Robert Louis Stevenson, who spent the last four years of his life in Samoa. Stevenson and his wife, Fanny, are buried on top of nearby Mt Vaea.

The museum is open from 9 am to 3.30 pm weekdays and from 8 am to noon Saturday. Tickets cost ST15/5 for adults/children under 12, including a guided tour around the house.

If you'd like to walk up to the Stevensons' tomb (a relatively short but very steep climb), or spend some time wandering around the botanical gardens and rainforest trails in addition to seeing the museum, allow a good half day or more.

To get to Mt Vaea, follow the trail down to the Vailima Stream, cross the stream and turn left (the trail to the right leads to a waterfall).

fter a few minutes you'll come to a fork
here a sign announces that the short trail to
e top will take 35 minutes and the left fork,
e long route, will require 55 minutes. The
ails can be very muddy and slippery after
avy rain. The tombs, on a plateau just
low the summit, look down onto Vailima
d out to the surrounding mountains.

A taxi from Apia to Vailima should cost
ound ST6. To go by bus, take the Mulivai
Salani bus from the Maketi Fou or wave
down on Falealili St around the Hotel
sel Fehmarn.

aha'i Temple From near the highest point
The Cross Island Rd, the 28m Niue lime-
one dome of the Baha'i House of Worship
☎ 24192) points skyward. Designed by
anian Husain Amanat in 1984, this impos-
g and very beautiful structure is one of
ven Baha'i houses of worship in the world.
Visitors are welcome. There is an adjoin-
g information centre, where attendants will
appily answer your questions. The well-
oomed lawns and gardens are worth a visit,
o. Services are held on Sundays at 10 am.

ake Lanoto'o Known also as Goldfish
ake, Lake Lanoto'o is an eerie, pea-green
ater lake in the central highlands of Upolu.
nyone keen on the unusual should make a
oint of visiting this little-known spot.

To get there, take The Cross Island Rd
eyond the Baha'i temple until you see a
icrowave relay tower on a low hill to
our right. Ask the driver to drop you at the
anoto'o Rd turn-off. Walk west on this
ad for about 3km, at which point it will
arrow into a track at a turn-off to the left.
on't turn, however. Continue straight
ead for about another kilometre to where
e track makes a 90° turn to the left. Fol-
w it until the array of radio towers and a
tellite dish are visible on your left.

If you have your own car, you can drive
this point. From here, look to the right
d you should be able to make out a badly
vergrown track leading away across a
uddy bog-like area. This is the route.
fter several hundred metres the trail im-
oves considerably, becoming slippery red

clay. Follow it for about 40 minutes until it
climbs a hill. The murky green lake is in
the volcanic crater ahead. Lake Lanoto'o is
full of wild goldfish that congregate
around the shore. Locals used to collect
them for pets until the government banned
it. It's a great place for a swim too, but a
little spooky because of alternating warm
and cold currents, and the fact that the bottom of the lake has never been found.

Very few visitors ever see this lovely and
unusual spot. In order to avoid the multiple
unpleasantries of ankle-deep mud, thorn
bushes, sleeping grass (which stings like
nettle) and leeches, hikers should wear long
pants and sturdy, covered shoes.

Papapapai-Tai Falls About 3km south of
the Baha'i temple, look out for a small parking area on your right. This is the overlook
for the spectacular 100m Papapapai-Tai
Waterfall which plunges into a dramatic,
forested gorge.

Papasee'a Sliding Rock A trip to the
Papasee'a Sliding Rock is obligatory for
every visitor to Samoa, although once there,
many can't seem to muster the nerve to
enjoy the star attraction, a 5m slide down a
waterfall into a jungle pool. If the big one
puts you off, though, there are three other
smaller ones to choose from. Don't miss
this place! Take the Se'ese'e bus from the
Maketi Fou and ask to be dropped off at the
intersection for Papasee'a. It's a good idea
to remember the route the bus takes to get
to this point because drivers divert from
their standard route to drop visitors close to
the park and you'll probably have to walk
out to the paved road to catch a bus back to
town. Walk 2km up the hill to the entrance.
Admission to the park is ST2, but pay only
the women at the entrance and not the children who hound you as you approach.

Tanumapua Plantation The Tanumapua
Tropical Plantation (☎ 27037), a few kilo-
metres inland from Vaitele just west of
Apia, is a pleasant rural outing from town.
You can spend an afternoon strolling
around the planted areas and tropical

flower gardens and seeing examples of tropical crops such as coffee, bananas, papayas, pineapples, kava and cacao. You can also see the plantation on horseback.

If you'd like to stay in these lush surroundings, bed and breakfast is available at the *Rainforest Ecolodge (☎/fax 22144)*, an original plantation house located in Tanumapua. From town, the plantation is about 8km along Alafa'alava Rd on the right hand side. To get to Alafa'alava Rd, take the first left turning west of the Mormon Temple. A taxi from Apia costs about ST18.

The West

Leulumoega Church On the stretch of road between Apia and Faleolo airport there are more than 60 multicoloured churches representing numerous denominations. One of the most interesting of these is the Congregational Christian (London Missionary Society) church at Leulumoega, 5km east of the airport, the design of which is unique on the island. While you're in Leulumoega, visit the School of Fine Arts, beside the Maloa Theological College, where you can appreciate some wonderful woodcarvings and other artwork by students.

Places to Stay & Eat At Cape Fatuosofia on the western tip of Upolu is the *Samoan Village Resort (☎ 46028, fax 46098, PO Box 3495)*, which offers 10 deluxe self-contained fale, all with excellent sea views. The beach is picturesque, but not great for snorkelling or swimming. All the fale have a fully equipped kitchen, separate living room, bedroom, bathroom and verandah. The living rooms have hideaway queen-sized beds so the fale can sleep up to four adults. Prices range from ST220 to ST366 for single or double occupancy, plus ST20 for each additional person. The resort has a small restaurant and bar, swimming pool and spa. A taxi from the airport will cost about ST20.

A couple of kilometres east along the coast is the new *Airport Lodge (☎ 45583, fax 45584, airportl@samoa.net)* which has small double or twin units with bathroom, fridge and small fan. There is a

well-equipped separate kitchen. Room cost ST122/134. Fishing charters and bo tours can be arranged.

Just 1km east of Faleolo airport is *O* ▮ *Satapuala Beach Resort (☎ 42212, fɑ 42386, PO Box 1539, Apia)*. Enclos beach fale with fans, kitchens and priva facilities cost ST59/79. Basic open-side fale *(faleo'o)* cost ST20 per person. Cam ing on the site costs ST5 per person and meal plan is available for ST50 per day. you'd prefer a cultural experience, hom stays can be arranged for around ST50 p person, including bed, transport and meal On Fridays, there's a ST5 barbecue and Sundays, the resort prepares a well-attende Samoan umu lunch for ST30.

The South Coast

South Coast Beaches Along with t Aleipata Islands area and Manono Islan the south coast of Upolu offers plenty beautiful palm-fringed beaches where wouldn't be difficult to pass a week or tw Custom fees may vary slightly but, in ge eral, access to beaches costs ST10 for buse ST5 for cars, ST3 for motorcycles and bic cles, and ST2 for pedestrians. Some beach offer basic fale accommodation.

In the Lefaga district is the idyllic Retu to Paradise Beach, where the film of t same name was filmed in 1951. To get the by public transport, catch the bus at t Maketi Fou in Apia.

The next beach east of Return to Paradi is Matareva, a series of delightful cov with safe, shallow snorkelling and lots rock pools to explore. There are a couple basic overnight fale, showers and a sho Access from the main road is down a 2.5k dirt track. The seclusion of Matareva being threatened, however, with plans build a 300 room luxury hotel nearby.

A couple of kilometres east is anoth good spot, Salamumu Beach, about 5km o the main road. About 15km farther east Aganoa Black Sand Beach. Unlike most the beaches around Upolu, the water here deep enough for swimming (it's shelter and safe) and there's good snorkelling at t far end of the bay.

ataoa & Sa'anapu Conservation rea In an effort to preserve one of Upolu's ost important coastal wetland areas, the angrove forests around the villages of Sa- oa and Sa'anapu on the south coast have en declared a conservation area. Man- oves provide a vital habitat for the breed- g of fish and crabs, and help to keep osion in check. The bark is used to make tural dyes, and the leaves and bark are ed in traditional medicine. The local con- rvation committee maintains the nature ail that winds through the mangroves for a uple of kilometres and offers excellent trigger canoe tours for ST20. Guided trips nearby Anaseao Cave can be arranged d there are good opportunities for **bird- atching**. The villages provide basic fale commodation. Sataoa and Sa'anapu are gnposted off the Main Coast Rd about 2km to the west of The Cross Island Rd.

Le Pupu-Pu'e National Park O Le pu-Pu'e is Samoa's only fully-fledged na- onal park. The name means 'from the coast the mountain top', which is a fair de- ription of its 29 sq km. The northern undary is formed by a ridge between vol- nic 840m Mt Le Pu'e and 1158m Mt Fito. the south is the rugged O Le Pupu Lava oast. The park entrance is near Togitogiga cenic Reserve, which lies just east of the ark. There are three **hiking** trails in the park d two basic campsites. Campers need to ing all their own supplies, including food d water. The park ranger can provide uides up to Pe'ape'a Cave for ST10; ST20 r the day. Hikers are expected to provide od for the guide.

The main inland trail, which begins to the uth-west of the car park and leads past the nger's house, will take you up through ick rainforest to Pe'ape'a Cave. The return alk will require a minimum of three hours. he large pit-like cave – actually a lava tube is full of circling *pe'ape'a* (swallows). It's ossible to explore the cave with a torch but careful climbing down into the pit on the ossy, slippery rocks. From the cave, the ew Kalati's Trail heads north for another km to Ofa Waterfall. This is an overnight

trek; campsites are located halfway along the trail and by the waterfall. The trail criss-crosses a stream at several points.

At the far western boundary of the park a 4km track leads south from the Main Coast Road to the magnificently rugged O Le Pupu Lava Coast. It's possible to drive most of the way down. There's a car park to the left of the track just before the trail hits the coast. A coastal trail leads eastwards for about 25 minutes.

Togitogiga Falls The falls lie just outside O Le Pupu-Pu'e National Park, up a dirt track from the park entrance. Several levels of falls are separated by pools, all great for swimming, and you can jump from the cliffs into the churning water below the largest one. There's a basic campsite here.

Sopo'aga Falls On Le Mafa Pass Rd, just south of the turn-off to the southern Main Coast Rd, is a lovely garden, picnic site and overlook to the 50m Sopo'aga Falls and its immense gorge. The custom fee is ST3 per car; ST1 if you're on foot. Just west of the falls lookout, along the road, an unassuming concrete bridge crosses the uppermost reaches of the Sopo'aga Falls gorge and the view down is quite impressive.

Places To Stay & Eat About 10km east of the O Le Pupu-Pu'e National Park, on a decent beach at Tafatafa, are the *Vaiula Beach Fales* (☎ 22808, fax 20886, PO Box 6600, Apia). There are five beach fale which cost ST15 per person. Meals can be provided. Camping in your own tent costs ST5 per tent including use of facilities, and picnickers are charged ST5 per car. If you just want to swim or lie on the beach, you'll pay ST5 per car. There are two basic *campsites* in the O Le Pupu-Pu'e National Park, for those who are interested in hiking up to Pe'ape'a Cave and Ofa Waterfall. Facilities are minimal and campers will need to bring all their own food and water.

Next up on the south coast is the luxurious *Sinalei Reef Resort* (☎ 25191, fax 20285, sinalei@samoa.net, PO Box 1510, Apia). Set in 13 hectares of landscaped grounds, Sinalei

SAMOA

offers 25 very comfortable self-contained units, many of which overlook Sinalei's picturesque stretch of beach. It is possible to snorkel here but the waters are very shallow and subject to strong currents. All the units have a private veranda, air-conditioning, tea and coffee-making facilities, fridge, telephone, and a partially open-air bathroom. Garden-view fale cost US$180 plus tax for single or double occupancy; ocean-view fale are US$190; and fale suites cost US$270. Meal plans cost US$55 for lunch and dinner. The resort features a huge traditionally built dining fale, swimming pool, bar and gift shop. The restaurant and bar are open to nonguests. Light lunch dishes start at around US$6; main courses at dinner start at US$12.

Sinalei hosts a Friday night fiafia followed by a buffet barbecue dinner (US$12 for dinner and the show) and a Sunday to'ona'i that costs US$10/5 for adults/children under 12. The resort also offers various tours and activities including canoe tours through the mangroves, glass-bottom boat tours, diving and deep-sea fishing.

Coconuts Beach Club Resort (☎ 24849, fax 20071, PO Box 3684, Apia) has magical upper-level rooms, all with large private balconies, air-conditioning and double bathtubs, which cost ST340/365 for singles/doubles, while rooms on the lower floor are ST217/241. If you prefer the sand at your front door, individual beachfront fale start at ST583/607. The enormous beach villa, with two bedrooms, two bathrooms, sitting room, kitchen and private terrace costs ST680/705. Built out on a jetty, they have some over-the-water fale, with their very own glass bottoms, costing ST705/729. All rates include a full American breakfast and use of snorkelling gear.

Even if Coconuts is beyond your accommodation budget, it's well worth visiting Sieni's **3-Stool beach bar** and Mika's excellent **American Bistro** restaurant, where you'll find a variety of US and European dishes, including the best lobster you'll ever taste (we promise). Lunch prices start at around ST16; main courses at dinner start at ST30. There are set-price barbecues at lunch time on Wednesday and Sunday. Traditional Samoan music is played in the beach b Tuesday to Friday evening and on Saturda and Sunday afternoons. Coconuts' fiafia held on Saturday night. The swimming po complete with swim-up bar, is open nonguests.

The resort has its own diving a snorkelling shop and tour company, Coc nuts Watersports. Tours include a jung boat cruise aboard the *African Que* through the beautiful mangrove-line waterways around the village of Muliv and self-guided kayak trips through th mangroves or along the south coast.

About 12km west from Coconuts, sig posted off the main road, is the Sataoa a Sa'anapu Conservation Area, where vis tors have the chance to stay in a *tradition village* (see earlier). The villagers of Sata and Sa'anapu are making a concerted effo to preserve their mangrove forests, whic among other things, provide a vital habit for the breeding of fish and crabs. Reven raised through village accommodation a various activities, such as guided walk canoe tours and fishing trips, will help maintain and protect the mangroves.

The village of Sa'anapu is on the oth side of the estuary, accessible from th main road down a 1km paved road. Whe you arrive in the village ask to speak to member of the conservation committee ar they'll organise accommodation for you.

A short walk along the beach fro Sa'anapu is the **Manuia Wetland Holid** **Retreat** (☎ 26225, PO Box 900, Apic which has beachside fale (ST20 per perso and three self-contained bungalows f ST80/120/150. The homely bungalow have a double and single bed, fridge, sma electric stove and cold-water shower. You need to bring your own food, though yc can buy fresh fish from the locals. Ther are three barbecue areas and if you're stay ing in a fale you may be able to use th cooking facilities in one of the bungalow The retreat has a small beach bar.

Lagoon Lodge (☎ 20196, fax 22714 right next to Manuia, has five bungalow each containing cold-water shower, g cooker and fridge; one sleeps up to six, th others sleep a maximum of three. Rooms cost ST30/80 on weekends; ST30/50 from Monday to Thursday. Meals can be provided.

A couple of kilometres farther west and 2km or so down a rough dirt track is *Matareva Beach Fales*. Here you'll find several basic fale (ST10 per person) set in well-kept gardens beside a lovely beach. You'll need to provide your own food; tank water is sometimes available. The area is popular with locals on the weekend. Beach fees are ST5 per car, ST3 per motorcycle or bicycle and ST2 if you're on foot.

Aleipata District

The reefs in the Aleipata district at the easternmost end of the island are 50m or so offshore and the water is a remarkable turquoise-blue, making for the loveliest beaches and the best **swimming** on Upolu. The snorkelling is excellent, but beware of the numerous cone shells found here (see the boxed text 'Venomous Marinelife' in the Regional Facts for the Visitor chapter). The offshore islands of Nu'utele and Nu'ulua also offer good snorkelling.

The village of Ulutogia is part of the conservation area and it has committed itself to becoming fully sustainable by 2000. Sagapolotele Uitime of Ulutogia can organise tours around the area and trips across to the islands. Vaitoa Amituanar of Lalomanu can also organise sightseeing and snorkelling trips to the islands. Ask for him at the house opposite the church. A half-day tour will cost from ST10 per person. The first bus leaves the Maketi Fou for Lalomanu around 5 am.

Places to Stay & Eat At Lalomanu village in the Aleipata district, along one of the finest beaches in Samoa, you'll find *Litia Sini's Beach Fales*; *Tafua Beach Fales*, with a small store and snorkelling gear for hire; *Sieni & Robert's Beach Fales*; *Romeo's Beach Fales* and the welcoming *Talo Beach Fales*. There are at least half a dozen more places around Lalomanu and there's not a great deal of difference between them. All charge ST20 per person and between ST20 and ST25 for three meals,

depending on what you have. In all cases, sleeping mats and mosquito nets are supplied. Some fale have electric lights, others provide oil lamps. Make sure owners can provide a secure storage area for valuables – theft from open fale can be a problem.

There's a store at Cape Tapaga, just south of Lalomanu, which sells basic supplies and petrol. Up the road, by the shore in the village of Satitoa, is *Joseph's Coffee Shop*.

West of Lalomanu, near the villages of Saleapaga and Lepa, are several more bunches of *fale*. Granted, they're situated on a lesser beach, but the accommodation is identical to those at Lalomanu and prices are a bit cheaper. *Boomerang Creek*, built on the hillside at Saleapaga, has four enclosed fale which cost ST50/80, including meals.

Manono

● pop 1500   ● area 3 sq km

The tiny, traditional island of Manono harks back to an earlier Polynesia. With no vehicles, no roads, no dogs, no noise and little evidence of the 20th century anywhere, it's a magical and extremely relaxing spot to spend a few days. You can walk all the way around it in 1½ hours. People live almost exclusively in thatched fale and have a semi-subsistence lifestyle.

Things to See & Do At around 6.30 am the sound of a conch shell signals that it's time for the island's fishers to set off for work, trawling by outrigger canoe around the limpid waters of Manono. Early in the morning is the best time to stroll around the island. Wending its way between the sea and the bottoms of people's gardens, the main track is less a road and more a garden path.

At Lepuia'i village is the **Grave of 99 Stones**, which dates back to the late 19th century. The story goes that high chief Vaovasa, who reportedly had 99 wives, was killed by villagers as he tried to escape from Upolu with his 100th wife. His body was brought back to Manono in his *fautasi* (longboat) for burial. A grave was to be built with 100 stones, but remains unfinished. You can see a large gap where the final stone was to be placed.

How Shame Made a Name

In ancient times, according to legend, an old man called Vaotuua found a young brown noddy bird, or *gogo* (pronounced 'ngo-ngo'), on the shore of Manono. He cared for the bird until it was old enough to fly. But when the noddy was ready to fly away, it was ashamed *(ma)* because it didn't have a gift for Vaotuua to show appreciation of his kindness. As the ashamed bird *(ma-gogo)* disappeared, Vaotuua decided to call the island Magogo (now spelt Manono).

At Faleu village near Matasiva Point, there's a **monument** commemorating the landing of the Methodist missionary Reverend Peter Turner on Manono in 1835.

On top of Mt Tulimanuiva (110m) is a large, 12 pointed **star mound**, thought to have been used in the ancient competitive sport of pigeon-snaring (see the 'Star Mounds of Ancient Power' boxed text in the American Samoa chapter). Nearby is the grave of Afutiti, who was buried standing up to keep watch over the island.

You can take a **guided tour** around the island, including a visit to the star mound, for ST30 per person including lunch. It costs less without lunch or for groups. Outrigger canoe **fishing trips** and **canoe tours** to uninhabited Nu'ulopa Island can be arranged from ST40 per person. For ST10 you can join village women in traditional **weaving, cooking** and **craft making**. For any of these activities, contact Willie or Tauvela at the Vaotu'ua Beach Resort on ☎ 46077. Eco-Tour Samoa (see Organised Tours under Getting Around earlier in this chapter) offers **sea kayaking trips** to Manono. A portion of the income from all of these activities goes into an environmental conservation fund for Manono Island. The island is well protected by coral reef and all around are lovely **beaches** and excellent **snorkelling** opportunities. Each of the four villages has declared its waters to be marine reserves.

Places to Stay & Eat Not far from the launch landing is the laid-back *Vaotu'ua Beach Resort* (☎ 46077). Three open-sided fale, shaded by enormous talie trees, sit by the water's edge. One large fale sleeps groups and has a rustic dining room attached. The other two fale sleep one or two people. Rates are ST45 per person including dinner and breakfast. Tauvela's excellent dishes include turkey noodle soup, deep-fried eggplant and fresh fried fish.

There are no shops on Manono, so if you're thinking of staying for a few days, bring supplies from Apia.

Getting There & Away To visit Manono take the Falelatai bus from Apia and get off just south of the Samoan Village Resort at the western end of Upolu (ST1.70). From there, small launches leave for Manono. You'll pay about ST1 each way if there are more than several people waiting or a bit more if there are only a couple of passengers. If you miss the regular morning runs, special charters will cost as much as ST20 for the entire boat.

Apolima
- pop 150   • area 1 sq km

Samoa's fourth island, Apolima, lies in the Apolima Strait, outside the reef that encircles Upolu and Manono. The remnant of a volcanic crater, it meets the sea in high steep cliffs, and there's only a tiny and difficult entrance from the sea through to the single, hardly touched village.

Getting There & Away If you're keen to get to Apolima, seek out Mr Sa'u Samoa at the village of Apolima-uta on Upolu, who can arrange transport and permission for you to visit.

Savai'i

- pop 50,000   • area 1707 sq km

Much of Savai'i – the largest island in Polynesia outside NZ and Hawai'i – still remains uninhabited and pristine. This is part of the island's appeal, along with the fact that

avai'i has retained its traditional ways even
ore than Upolu. Scattered across the island
e numerous archaeological sites – fortifi-
tions, star mounds and ancient platforms
many of which have been swallowed up
/ the nearly impenetrable jungle.

rientation & Information

he Samoas' largest island is also its wildest.
string of volcanic craters, some active, ex-
nd along the central ridge of the island
om the east coast at Tuasivi to within 5km
' Samoa's westernmost tip at Cape Muli-
'u. At 1858m, Mt Silisili is the highest
int in the Samoan islands. The north coast
' Savai'i is punctuated by lava fields.
There are basic hospitals at Tuasivi,
afotu, Sataua and Foailalo.

etting There & Away

ir Flying between Upolu and Savai'i is
ghly recommended – the flight isn't very
xpensive and the bird's-eye view of the

islands is wonderful. From Fagali'i airport
near Apia, Polynesian Airlines flies to
Ma'ota airport on the south coast of Savai'i
three times a day. The fare is ST34/60.50
one way/return. Polynesian Airlines
(☎ 22737 in Apia) flies from Apia to Asau
airport on the north coast of Savai'i once a
day (ST55/90 one way/return). Samoa Air
(☎ 51387 in Apia) flies between Pago Pago
in American Samoa and Ma'ota airport
every Friday and Sunday morning.

Boat The Samoa Shipping Corporation
(☎ 51477 in Salelologa, ☎ 45518 in Mulifanua) operates a vehicle and passenger
ferry between Mulifanua Wharf on the
western end of Upolu and Salelologa,
Savai'i. It runs two or three times daily. You
can buy tickets from the Shipping Samoa
office on the corner of Mt Vaea and Convent Sts in Apia, or at either dock. The fare
is ST6 each way for foot passengers, ST30
each way for jeeps and taxis, and ST65 for

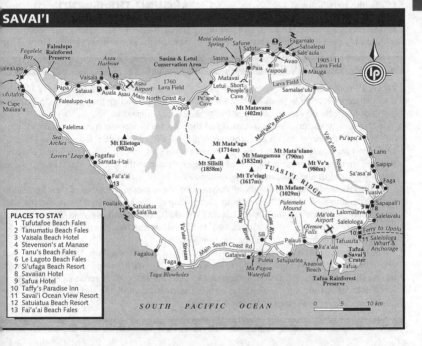

SAVAI'I

PLACES TO STAY
1 Tufutafoe Beach Fales
2 Tanumatiu Beach Fales
3 Vaisala Beach Hotel
4 Stevenson's at Manase
5 Tanu's Beach Fales
6 Le Lagoto Beach Fales
7 Si'ufaga Beach Resort
8 Savaiian Hotel
9 Safua Hotel
10 Taffy's Paradise Inn
11 Savai'i Ocean View Resort
12 Satuiatua Beach Resort
13 Fai'a'ai Beach Fales

SOUTH   PACIFIC   OCEAN

0   5   10 km

trucks and buses. The 22km crossing takes one to 1½ hours.

Getting Around

To/From the Airport By taxi from Ma'ota to Salelologa, the fare is ST7; to Lalomalava, ST15; and to Tuasivi, ST22. From Asau airport in the north-west to Safotu the taxi fare is ST55; to Falealupo, ST25; and to Satuiatua, ST60.

All Savai'i hotels offer airport transfers, provided you book in advance. Public buses are very convenient for getting to Salelologa from the airport but if you're travelling to Lalomalava, Tuasivi or further north, you'll have to change buses at Salelologa.

Bus The market near the Salelologa wharf is the main terminal for regular buses to Lalomalava, Tuasivi, Palauli and Gataivai.

The fare from Salelologa to Palauli and Lalomalava is only 50 sene. To either end of the main road – Asau or Safotu/Sasina – it's ST5. To the blowholes at Taga costs ST2.

Car The roads are quiet but keep an eye out for kids, stray pigs and kirikiti games. Petrol is available at Salelologa, at Avao in the north-east and at Vaisala in the north-west. The Savai'i Travel Centre (☎ 51206) and the West End Co (☎ 51415), both just up the road from Salelologa's wharf, have jeeps to rent from about ST100 per day. You can bring hire cars across on the ferry from Upolu (see Getting Around under Upolu).

Bicycle The Savaiian Hotel (☎ 51206) Lalomalava has mountain bikes to rent from ST20 per day.

Boat Yachties wanting to travel around Savai'i must first obtain a cruising permit from the Prime Minister's office in Apia. There are anchorages at Fagamalo, Salelologa Wharf and Asau Harbour.

Organised Tours Safua Tours at the Safua Hotel offers four different types of tour taking in various sites around the island.

AROUND THE ISLAND

South-Eastern Savai'i

Information The Bank of Samoa in Salelologa is open weekdays until 3 pm

---

The Ancient Homeland, Havaiki

When, in about 200 BC, travellers from Samoa settled the Marquesas and Society islands, they carried with them legends of their ancient homeland, including the name of 'the largest island of the leeward group', which at the time was called Havaiki.

In the Society Islands, the largest island of the leeward group was named Havaiki in honour of their homeland (much as European explorers did a millennium later). 'New Havaiki' (the island now called Raiatea) became ancient Polynesia's holy land, and the island's sacred temple Taputapuatea became the hub of further expansion to the Cook Islands, Hawai'i, Rapa Nui (Easter Island) and Aotearoa (New Zealand).

As they expanded to new islands, all Polynesians remembered the name of their homeland – often naming new islands in its honour. Depending on the local dialect the homeland was remembered as Havai'i (in the Society Islands), 'Avaiki (Cook Islands), Hawaiki (Aotearoa) and of course Hawai'i (in the Hawai'ian islands). In Samoa, where 'h' is pronounced as 's' and 'k' is dropped, the original island's name became Savai'i.

For many, the name 'Havaiki' represents not only a physical location, the homeland, but also a mythical promised land to which souls return after death. In Aotearoa and the Cooks this results in a situation where Havaiki is said to lie in the east (the direction of Raiatea, from whence those islands were settled) but also in the west (towards the setting sun, the traditional direction in which departing spirits travel).

he post and telephone office is about
00m outside Salelologa village towards
he airport. The post office is open from 9
m to noon and from 1 to 4.30 pm week-
ays. The telephone office is open from 8
m to noon and from 1 to 4.30 pm daily.
eside the Big Island CCK, the largest store
n the island, you'll find the new OK
aundromat. The main police station, the
nmigration office and other government
ffices are in Tuasivi. For travel arrange-
ents try the Savai'i Travel Centre
☎ 51206, fax 51291) in Salelologa.

alelologa Beside the market, the only
al points of interest in the Salelologa area
e the **blowholes** on the lava coast south of
e wharf. To get there follow the coast
uth from the wharf. There are two ancient
ar mounds just north of the Main Coast
d, about 200m west of its intersection with
e wharf road, and across the street there
e two **platform mounds**. They're over-
rown and difficult to find, so you may
eed directions from locals.

uasivi Ridge The Tuasivi ridge begins
ar the village of Tuasivi and rises in a sees of craters that form the spine of Savai'i,
ding just inland of the village of Falealupo.
The Samoans named it the enchanted ridge
cause they believed it possessed super-
tural powers to harm and kill those who
alt with it improperly: pregnant women
d to walk up to it three times before pro-
eding across it or the child would die.
The crater of **Mt Asi**, the one nearest the
a, is said to be the mark left when an inland
ountain wandered towards the sea to fetch
me water to make palusami. Asi didn't
ant to be second from the sea so he threw
breadfruit in the other mountain's face as
approached; where it fell, a crater was
rmed. There are two ancient terraces and
platform atop Mt Asi.

eaches All along the east coast between
lelologa and Pu'apu'a, there are nice
aches and good **snorkelling**. Most of the
lages will charge custom fees of about
5/2 per car/person to use their beaches.

The best are at Faga and Lano. The area also
has numerous freshwater pools and springs.

Pu'apu'a In the village of Pu'apu'a are
two freshwater bathing **pools** maintained by
the local women's committee. The pool on
the eastern side of the road is for women
and the one on the western side for men.
Ask villagers' permission before jumping
in. Just south of Pu'apu'a are several other
springs, including Vaimanuia, whose name
means 'Healthy Waters'.

Tafua Rainforest Preserve The Tafua
Rainforest Preserve occupies much of the
Tafua Peninsula in Savai'i's south-east. In
addition to one of Samoa's most accessible
and beautiful stands of rainforest, it contains beautifully rugged stretches of lava
coast, which are studded with cliffs, sea
arches, lava tubes and blowholes. On the
western coast of the peninsula is a track
leading south to the lovely Ananoa dark-
sand **beach**. There are strong currents here,
however, so ask locals about conditions and
swim with care. Custom fees are ST10/5/2
per bus/car/cyclists and pedestrians. The
beach is open from 8 am to 6 pm.

The village of Fa'a'ala, at the top of the
track, shares responsibility for the conservation area with Salelologa and Tafua, and
can offer visitors village accommodation
and local guides.

Another highlight of the preserve is the
extinct, forest-choked **Tafua Savai'i crater**,
which harbours a large colony of flying
foxes (fruit bats). To reach the crater, take
the 5km paved road off the Main South
Coast Rd to the village of Tafua on the
coast. From there, a 20 minute track will
take you up the steep southern slope of the
crater.

In Tafua, chief Ulu Taufa'asisina and his
wife Anita (☎ 50041) can organise guided
walks and local accommodation for visitors. The Tafua village council is building a
rainforest information centre which will
house a library with ecological information
to teach village children and visitors about
rainforest conservation issues. Donations
are welcome.

SAMOA

SAMOA

Places to Stay & Eat Near the market, *Taffy's Paradise Inn* (☎ 51544 or ☎ 51534) is a small and slightly shabby nine-room guesthouse (ST33 per person). Breakfast costs ST12, set-menu lunches ST15 and dinners are ST25.

Closer to the wharf is the *Savai'i Ocean View Hotel* (☎ 51258, fax 51377), where reasonable singles/doubles with facilities cost ST77/99.

The *general store* opposite the Ocean View serves good fish and chips, Chinese buns, curry and rice and other basic dishes. It's open weekdays. *OK's Takeaway Food Bar* in the CCK store serves similar meals and is also closed on the weekend. Inside the market are a number of *food stalls* serving very passable local dishes for rock-bottom prices. Behind the market is a whole bank of little general stores where you'll find inexpensive staple items.

Safua Hotel (☎ 51271, fax 51272), just 5km north-east of Salelologa at Lalomalava, is one of the most pleasant places to stay on Savai'i. Fale-style bungalows with shower (cold water) and toilet cost ST77/88. There are two family rooms that can sleep up to six for ST110. It's ST165/215 with the three meal plan. If you'd prefer to stay in a village, they can arrange accommodation in private homes for ST30 per person. In addition to its typically fabulous meals, the hotel stages a fiafia on Friday and Saturday nights and an umu feast at noon on Sunday.

Savaiian Hotel (☎ 51206, fax 51291, PO Box 5082, Lalomalava, Salelologa) has rooms with air-conditioning, cooking facilities and hot showers for ST105/125. Fale with shower and toilet cost ST35/50.

Another favourite travellers' haunt is the very friendly *Siufaga Beach Resort* (☎ 53518, fax 53535, PO Box 8002, Tuasivi), which is in the village of Faga immediately north of Tuasivi. The hotel consists of six self-contained fale, each with shower (one has hot water), toilet and cooking facilities. The fale, set in a large grassy lawn, sleep three or four. Camping is also permitted. The real draw card, however, is the white and sandy Si'ufaga Beach across the road, which is safe for swimming and snorkelling. Fale cost ST100/110/122; campers pay ST15 per person. There is also a restaurant and bar.

North-Eastern Savai'i

Lava Field Between Samalae'ulu and Sale'aula, the Main North Coast Road crosses the lava field and passes a couple of interesting sites. Just east of the road the village of **Mauga** (literally 'Mountain' pronounced 'mow-nga'). It is built in a circular pattern around a nearly perfect crater.

Just north of Mauga, about 100m east of the road, in a large hole in the lava, is the partially built **Methodist church** that 'miraculously' survived the lava flow.

Members of the local women's committee are generally on hand to guide people around. There's a custom fee of ST2 per person. The sites are signposted just north of Mauga. To get up this way by bus, take the Lava Fields Express that runs regularly between Salelologa and Fagamalo.

Satoalepai Wetlands The village of Satoalepai, 5km north-west of the lava field, is one of a growing number of Samoan villages committed to the sustainable development of their local resources, and to this end offers visitors village accommodation, local guides and **canoe tours** through the wetland (ST3 per person). Look out for a signpost the **turtle wetlands** where you'll find some picnic fale and a large pond inhabited by several enormous sea turtles.

Fagamalo Immediately west of Satoalepai is Fagamalo, which is known as an excellent spot for **surfing** and **windsurfing**. There's a marginal anchorage here, too. You'll find comfortable bungalow accommodation on the beach just west of the village.

Safotu The long, strung-out village of Safotu has several **churches** and freshwater **pools** for bathing or swimming. Some are for men and some for women, so be sure to ask which is which rather than make assumptions. Just to the east of Safotu a pleasant **beaches**, a new upmarket reso

Gateway to the Underworld

Falealupo Peninsula figures prominently in local legend. The natural beauty of the area belies the dark significance it holds for Samoans, who believe that the gateway to the underworld of the *aitu* (spirits) is found at the place where the sun sets in the sea. During the night, these spirits wander abroad, but at daybreak they must return to their hellish home or suffer the unpleasant consequences of being caught out by daylight.

According to tradition, there are two entrances to the underworld, one for chiefs and another for commoners. One entrance is through a cave near Cape Mulinu'u and the other – repeating a theme found in ancient cultures from the Pacific to Britain – is over the sea towards the setting sun.

Falealupo's role as gateway to the underworld is duplicated at the western (or northern) point of many other Polynesian islands: the souls of Tahitian dead are said to depart from Tupai Atoll, in the Cook Islands they must leave from Black Rock (Tuoro) on Rarotonga. In New Zealand it is Cape Reinga, while in Kiribati it is Nakaa's Beach on Makin Island.

nd the most popular budget accommodaton on the island.

Mt Matavanu Crater Walk From afotu, the crater is a pleasant day walk but an be done in about five hours if you can atch a lift as far as Paia village. Once you et to Paia, you may want to stop to have a ook at the **ancient fort and mound** atop the ill there. The mound is about 4m high and as several fales on top. The fort, which is urrounded by a ditch, is just to the north of e mound. Expect to pay a custom fee of T2 to pass through Paia en route to the rater, but be sure to pay only the pulenu'u. ou can also ask the pulenu'u for a guide.

From Paia, follow the plantation road outh. After a little more than an hour of alking you should enter the lava field. learly another hour on, the lava field gives ay to heavier bush and clumps of acacias. t the point where the road begins to dip for e first time, you'll see a trail to the left eading uphill through a forest (if you reach e end of the road, you've gone too far). everal hundred metres up the trail (keep to e left) is the rim of the immense crater of It Matavanu. If you continue to follow the ack around the crater to the left, it will wing downhill and turn into a route down e lava field to the village of Vaipouli. It's est to go back the way you came. Access the crater up this route from Vaipouli is

also possible, but don't go without a guide from the village.

Mata'olealelo Spring This ample freshwater spring in the village of Safune bubbles up through a pool into the sea – perfect for a refreshing swim. Be sure to ask permission before plunging in.

Sasina & Letui Conservation Area The villages of Sasina and Letui are part of a large coastal rainforest conservation area that extends from the coast up to the inland village of A'opo. Just outside Sasina is a pleasant rainforest walk. Take the signposted track that leads past the village and after about 1km you'll see a well-maintained path leading off to the right. Ask the village pulenu'u for access and a guide. Both Sasina and Letui offer basic village accommodation for around ST20 per person.

Places to Stay & Eat Apart from the conservation villages of Satoalepai, Sasina and Letui, there are three accommodation options in north-east Savai'i. Situated on a beautiful beach immediately west of Fagamalo village is *Le Lagoto Beach Fales* (☎ 58189, fax 58249, PO Box 34, Fagamalo), which offers four bungalows and a large beach house. The bungalows, with shower (hot water), toilet, kitchenette, TV and standing fan, cost ST134/161/187/214. The beach house, which

SAMOA

DORINDA TALBOT

Modern furniture in a traditional thatched-roof family *fale* (house) on Savai'i: *faka Samoa* (the Samoan way of life) meets western technology.

sleeps up to seven, costs ST150 per night. There is a restaurant, bar and shop. Breakfast costs ST12, lunch from ST10 and dinner between ST25 and ST35.

Just west of Manase is **Tanu's Beach Fales** (☎ 54050), one of the most popular spots for budget travellers in all of Samoa. Basic fale cost ST50 per person, including lunch and dinner. Showers (cold) and toilets are communal. There are outrigger canoes for guests to use, a couple of jeeps for rent, a small shop on the premises and fiafia nights every Friday and Monday.

Just up the road from Tanu's is the more upmarket **Stevenson's at Manase** (☎ 58219, fax 54100, PO Box 210 Apia), which offers air-con rooms with private shower from ST146 for single or double occupancy – somewhat overpriced for what you get. Across the road is a large and very comfortable air-conditioned beachfront villa, which sleeps two adults and up to three children for ST305. Also on the beach are several basic fale for ST25 per person. The hotel has a pleasant restaurant and bar, paddle boats and outrigger canoes for guests and fiafia nights on Friday and Saturday.

Northern & Western Savai'i

A'opo Conservation Area & Mt Silisili

The three day trip up Mt Silisili takes you through some stunning and rarely visited **rainforest**, although the peak itself is nondescript. Speak to the pulenu'u of A'opo who will arrange a guide for the trek. The charge is ST30 per person per day. You'll need to carry food and water for three days and provide supplies for the guide.

Asau & Vaisala Asau, 15km west of A'opo, is the main anchorage on Savai'i and service centre for the western end of the island. Asau airport, which was completely destroyed by Cyclone Ofa in 1990, has only recently been rebuilt. There's a store here selling groceries and crafts and a post office. At Vaisala, 5km farther up the road, there's a petrol station, a branch of the Pacific Commercial Bank and the Vaisala Hotel. In the village of Auala, between Asau and Vaisala, the local women's committee looks after a large pond full of protected **sea turtles**.

Falealupo Peninsula At the north-western end of Savai'i is the wild and beautiful

lealupo Peninsula, where you'll find **rock
ools**, **caves**, ancient **star mounds**, a hand-
l of romantic beachside fale and any
mber of spectacular sunsets. Take great
re swimming around Cape Mulinu'u,
ough; there's a strong rip and if you're not
reful you could end up in the Solomons.
ere's a good **swimming beach** at Papa on
e north-eastern side of the peninsula, not
r off the Main North Coast Rd. Beach fees
the peninsula are ST20/5/2 per
s/car/pedestrian. If you're not driving,
u'll have to walk or take a taxi the 7km
m the main road at Falealupo-uta to the
d of the peninsula.

lealupo Rainforest Preserve Consid-
ed sacred by the villagers of Falealupo, the
,000 hectares of lowland rainforest on the
rthern side of the peninsula became the
st customary-owned conservation area in
moa in 1989.

nopy Walkway The Falealupo Canopy
alkway not only provides the opportunity
climb to the top of a stately banyan tree,
t if you feel so inclined you can sleep up
ere too. There are meals for treehouse
ests and it costs ST50 per person to sleep
the tree (the platform can hold a maxi-
m of six people, but facilities are mini-
l), including breakfast and dinner, and
20 to just visit the walkway. You can
ok tree accommodation in advance
rough the Vaisala Hotel. The walkway is
gnposted off the Falealupo Rd, beside the
lage primary school.

ck House About 300m inland from the
lage of Falealupo are the two closely
sociated lava tubes known as the Rock
use. Inside is a very crude stone arm-
air and there are stone benches around the
es. There's a custom fee of ST5 per
up to visit the Rock House.

a Arches A couple of kilometres south-
st of Falelima are two impressive natural
arches, caused by the pounding waves.
out 300m east of the large arch at Fale-
a is an odd **blowhole** that shoots blasts

of warm air. It's known as – you guessed it
– Moso's Fart.

Beaches There are pleasant beaches at
Fai'a'ai, about 20km south-east of the
Falealupo Peninsula, and nearby at Foailalo
and Satuiatua. Fai'a'ai and Satuiatua both
offer basic beachside accommodation;
Foailalo has several picnic fale. Satuiatua,
which is about one hour by bus (ST2.30)
from Salelologa, has some of the best **surf** in
Samoa. The custom fee is ST2 per person.

Places to Stay & Eat The *Vaisala Beach
Hotel* (☎ 58016, fax 58017), at Vaisala on
the north-west coast, clings to a slope right
above a lovely white-sand beach. Often
used as a base for surfers, basic single/
double/triple rooms with shower (some
rooms have hot water!) cost ST73/89/100
including tax. Breakfast is available from
ST9, toasted sandwiches cost ST5 and set-
menu dinners are ST27.50.

A space on the *banyan tree* plus two meals
costs ST50 per person. You can book through
the Vaisala Hotel, or just turn up at the tree.

On the edge of the Falealupo Peninsula is
Tanumatiu Beach Fales. The four traditional beach fale are situated on one of the
most idyllic beaches in Samoa. The fale are
supplied with comfortable mattresses, bedding, mosquito nets and oil lamps. There's
a toilet and outside shower on the site. Beyond the family house is an ancient star
mound. The fale cost ST40 per person, including two meals. The custom fee for
beach use is ST5 per car.

There are a couple of *fale* on the beach
next to Tanumatiu for around the same
price, and two more on the other side of
Cape Mulinu'u at Tufutafoe. It costs ST15
to stay overnight at Tufutafoe and another
ST15 for two meals.

The *Fai'a'ai Beach Fales* (☎ 56023) are
perched on the clifftop just off the Main
South Coast Rd. A well-maintained path
leads down the escarpment to a pleasant
palm-fringed beach. The two large fale
sleep up to about six people; the overnight
charge is ST15 per person plus ST15 for
two meals.

SAMOA

About 7km farther down the coast is **Satuiatua Beach Resort** (*☎/fax 56026, PO Box 5623 Salailua, Savai'i*), another spot travellers return to time and again. There are four large beachside fale, which sleep six to eight people, and three small fale. The beach is good for snorkelling and has some of the best surf on the island. Fale cost ST20 per person, ST50 with two meals. There's a small restaurant here and a shop selling basic supplies. Satuiatua is about one hour by bus (ST2.30) from Salelologa.

Southern Savai'i

Olemoe Falls Olemoe Falls is a lovely jungle waterfall that plunges into the crystalline waters of a deep blue **pool**, which is marvellous for swimming and diving.

To reach it, take the bus west from Salelologa to just past the bridge across the Falealila River near Palauli. About 200m west of the bridge, a small plantation track leads inland. Follow it across a ford, past the plantation house, and continue 300m up the hill until you reach the second break in the stone wall. Take a sharp right here and head through a gentle valley of friendly cows and horses. On the far side of the pasture there's a steep 20m walk down to the river bed. Just upstream are the falls and pool. The track leads around to the western side of the pool.

Pulemelei Mound Polynesia's largest ancient structure is Pulemelei Mound (marked on the Hema map as Tia Seu Ancient Mound), not far from Olemoe Falls, also on the Letolo Plantation. This large pyramid measures 61m by 50m at the base and rises in two tiers to a height of more than 12m. The main approaches to the summit are up ramps on the eastern and weste slopes. Smaller mounds and platforms a found in four directions away from the ma structure. There is a relatively large pl form about 40m north of the main pyram connected by a stone walkway.

Unfortunately, this impressive monume is naturally obscured by jungle growth, unless it has been cleared recently, it is most impossible to locate. We recomme hiring a guide to help you find anything, at least getting someone to point the w from the road.

Gataivai The beautifully situated villa of Gataivai sits beside a veritable wat garden of cascades. Here, the waters Samoa's greatest river rush down to th climax at **Mu Pagoa Waterfall**, where th plunge 5m into the sea. The approach the falls is from the subvillage of Gautav beside the Main South Coast Rd on the posite (left) bank of the river.

Taga Blowholes This is not just anoth set of blowholes. There's little to equ them anywhere else in the world. At the v lage of Taga, pay the custom fee (ST5 car; ST2 for those on foot) and walk do the hill and west along the coast for abc 10 minutes. You'll emerge from the coco plantation with a clear view across the bla lava coast and before the blowholes.

It's possible to walk a farther 5km or around this stretch of coast to the village Fagaloa; to be sure of the way take a gu from the village. About 5km north-west Taga, just north of the road, is a large jung covered **Polynesian mound** at least 10 years old, possibly from the time of Tong domination. Fashioned of coral and la blocks it is divided by a low wall.

American Samoa

e US territory of American Samoa forms
e other half of the politically divided
moan islands. With almost identical lan-
age and culture, and a shared history up
1900, the two countries obviously have
ot in common. Information relevant to
th countries is given in the introductory
ctions of the preceding independent
moa chapter.

The rugged islands of American Samoa
ve some areas of magnificent native for-
. In contrast, the capital, Pago Pago, con-
nts the traveller with fast-food, American
otball and cable TV. It may not have suf-
ed the high-rise building mania and con-
minium developments of Honolulu, but
Pago Pago, *fa'a Samoa* (the Samoan
y) has largely given way to the American
eam. However, once off the beaten track,
u will encounter traditional open-hearted
moan hospitality – as well as some of the
st breathtaking scenery in the Pacific.

acts about
merican Samoa

STORY
5 Military Rule

e formal annexation of eastern Samoa by
USA took place in 1900, when a deed of
ssion was signed by all the chiefs of the
ands involved.

Thus, under the jurisdiction of the US
partment of the Navy, the territory be-
me a naval station. The USA agreed to
otect the traditional rights of the indi-
nous Samoans in exchange for the mili-
y base and coaling station. The
ritory's inhabitants acquired the status of
nationals but to this day are denied a
te or representation in Washington.

n 1905, the military commander of Tutu-
was given the title of governor and the
ritory officially became known as Ameri-
n Samoa.

AMERICAN SAMOA

383

Moves for More Democracy

Between 1967 and 1975, lack of sufficient funds from Washington to maintain the new amenities introduced in the previous decade caused the whole system to fall into disrepair or go awry for one reason or another. In a series of referenda, American Samoans voted to continue under the direction of appointed governors. However, with some US coercion, a subsequent referendum determined that the American Samoans were ready for democratically elected leadership and some measure of autonomy.

GEOGRAPHY & ECOLOGY

American Samoa is comprised of seven islands and a few rocky outcrops. Its land area is 77 sq miles, 57 of which belong to the main island of Tutuila.

Aunu'u Island is a small volcanic crater off the south-east coast of Tutuila. The Manu'a group, about 60 miles east, consists of the three main islands of Ta'u, Ofu and Olosega, with 15½, 2½ and 2 sq miles, respectively.

Sixty miles east of Manu'a is tiny Rose Atoll, which comprises the two sandy islets of Rose and Sand.

The biggest issues affecting the environment in American Samoa are its population growth rate of 3.7% per year (which means a doubling in less than 20 years), the increased preference for western goods and equipment, increased generation of waste, greater pressure on treated-water supplies and the development of land for uses such as housing.

GOVERNMENT & POLITICS

American Samoa is an unincorporated and unorganised territory of the United States. It is unincorporated because not all provisions of the US Constitution apply to the territory. It is the only territory whose residents are nationals, rather than citizens, of the USA and who are not governed (as all other US territories are) by an act of the US Congress.

Instead, American Samoa has remained an 'unorganised' territory – that is, with its own constitution but under direct US federal government supervision. The territory's 1960 Constitution established thr branches of government: executive, leg lative, and judicial.

Though American Samoans are not aut matically granted US citizenship, they m freely apply for it. Their status as nationals allows freedom of entry into t USA.

ECONOMY

About one-third of American Samo workforce is employed by the governme The two tuna canneries on Tutuila empl another third of the workforce, with t remaining third employed in retail and s vice enterprises.

American Samoa's territorial status lows all businesses based there, such as t tuna canneries and textile manufacturers, export their goods duty-free to the US This is an important consideration, American Samoa is not required to adhe to US minimum-wage standards.

The US Department of Interior provid operating and capital improvement pr jects (CIP) grants to the American Samo Government.

In 1997-98, the American Sam Government was allocated an operatio grant of US$23 million, a CIP grant US$10 million and a technical assistan grant of about US$1 million for educatio related programs.

Facts for the Visito

TOURIST OFFICES

The American Samoa Office of Touris (☎ 633 1092, fax 633 1094, samoa samoatelco.com), PO Box 1147, Pago Pag American Samoa 96799, USA, off brochures and a basic map of Tutuila and harbour area. Some accommodation deta are listed on their website at www.samoa .com/americansamoa.

The National Park Visitor Informati Center (☎ 633 7082, fax 633 708 NPSA_Administration@nps.gov), in Pa Plaza, Pago Pago, has an informati brochure about the national park, includi ood maps of Tutuila and the Manu'a lands. There is some useful information on eir website (www.nps.gov/npsa).

American Samoa is represented abroad y offices of the Tourism Council of the outh Pacific (see addresses in the Regional acts for the Visitor chapter).

ISAS & DOCUMENTS
o visas are required of visitors to American amoa but US citizens need proof of citi- nship and everyone else must have a valid assport (citizens of independent Samoa quire an entry permit). Everyone, includ- g US citizens, must have an onward ticket.

isa Extensions
pplications for visa extensions, work per- its and long-stay permits must be organ- ed through the immigration office in the xecutive Office building in Utulei.

MBASSIES & CONSULATES
ll American Samoan diplomatic affairs are andled by the USA. There are no consu- tes or embassies in American Samoa (there e some in independent Samoa).

USTOMS
ustoms and immigration are handled at the rport and at the port facility in Fagatogo. e prepared for fairly thorough customs arches. Visitors can bring in one gallon .8L) of liquor and up to 200 cigarettes uty free.

ONEY
urrency
he US dollar (see Exchange Rates in the egional Facts for the Visitor chapter) is the rrency used in American Samoa.

xchanging Money
he Bank of Hawaii and the Amerika amoa Bank both have automatic teller ma- ines (ATMs) and can give cash advances major credit cards. The latter charges a S$5 commission on travellers cheques. here's also an ATM and branch of the ank of Hawaii in Pava'ia'i. Banks are en from 9 am to 3 pm weekdays, with a

service window open until 4.30 pm on Fri- day. The Tafuna branch of the Amerika Samoa Bank is open from 9 am to noon on Saturday.

There is no exchange office at the airport.

Credit Cards Visa, American Express and MasterCard are all accepted at the Rain- maker and Motu-o-Fiafiaga hotels, as well as tourist-oriented shops and restaurants on Tutuila. Both banks give credit card cash advances.

Costs
As might be expected, costs in American Samoa are quite a bit higher than in inde- pendent Samoa. There's little choice of accommodation and what is available is rel- atively expensive.

Tipping & Bargaining
Tipping and bargaining are not encouraged.

Consumer Taxes
There is a 2% territorial sales tax on con- sumer goods, which is not included in advertised prices.

POST & COMMUNICATIONS
Post
US stamps are used and US postal rates apply. The zip (postal) code for all of American Samoa is 96799.

The main post office is on the ground floor of the Lumana'i building, the same building the Bank of Hawaii occupies. It is open from 8 am to 4 pm weekdays and from 8.30 am to noon Saturday.

Travellers who wish to receive corres- pondence by poste restante should have mail addressed to themselves care of Gen- eral Delivery, Pago Pago, American Samoa 96799.

Telephone, Telex & Fax
The communications office is open 24 hours a day for local and international calls. Telex and fax services are also available. The international telephone code for Ameri- can Samoa is ☎ 684. Local calls cost just 10c each.

AMERICAN SAMOA

NEWSPAPERS & MAGAZINES

The *Samoa News* (☎ 633 5599) is published weekdays and the *Samoa Journal* is published weekly on Friday.

RADIO & TV

Radio WVUV (AM 1640kHz) plays a variety of music 24 hours a day, with brief news programs hourly. Broadcasts are in Samoan and English. Radio KSBS (FM 92.1MHz) plays a similar selection of popular music from 6 am to midnight. The government-owned TV station, KVZK, broadcasts on two channels: Channel 2 shows local and noncommercial programmes from the USA, while Channel 4 broadcasts commercial US programs. There's also US cable TV for subscribers.

ELECTRICITY

The power supply is 110V AC, 60Hz. US-style plugs (two flat blades) are used.

WEIGHTS & MEASURES

American Samoa uses the imperial system of measurement, so distances in this chapter are given in miles. See the table inside the back cover of this book for conversion between metric and imperial units.

HEALTH

There's no malaria in American Samoa. The only real health risks are occasional cases of dengue fever and filariasis (see Health in the Regional Facts for the Visitor chapter).

The LBJ Tropical Medical Center in Faga'alu can provide basic medical services but anyone suffering serious medical problems is advised to go to Hawai'i or New Zealand. Emergency doctors are on duty at all hours and the LBJ clinic is open from 8 am to 4 pm weekdays. Patients are charged a small fee. The emergency telephone number is ☎ 911. There is a good pharmacy close to the harbour area in the Samoa Sports building in Fagatogo.

The main water supply in Pago Pago is OK to drink. Untreated village water, however, should be avoided. Bottled water is widely available.

PUBLIC HOLIDAYS & SPECIAL EVENTS

See the preceding Samoa chapter for public holidays common to both Samoas. In addition, American Samoa has Martin Luther King Day, US Independence Day, Columbus Day, Veterans Day (for these holiday dates, see Regional Facts for the Visitor), Tourism Week in early July, and the following extra holidays:

President's Day	3rd Monday in February
Flag Day	17 April
Memorial Day	Last Monday in May
Arbor Day	November

ACTIVITIES

Snorkelling & Swimming

Some of the best snorkelling is to be found in the National Park of American Samoa (NPS) on the rugged little island of Ofu. The best spots for swimming and snorkelling on Tutuila are along the south coast near the western and eastern ends of the island and along the north coast. Always ask permission from local villagers before using the beach, and bring your own snorkelling gear.

Diving

On the northern and western ends of the island, corals are prolific and visibility is excellent. John Harrison (Divemaster), who runs the Tutuila Dive Shop (☎ 699 284, Tutuiladiveshop@samoatelco.com), PO Box 5137, Pago Pago, at Vaitogi, west of the airport, can organise dives for those interested.

Surfing & Windsurfing

Some of the best surfing is found just beyond the reef near Faganeanea, but if the trade winds are blowing and the tides aren't right, surfing is impossible. The rest of the time it is still very risky.

Other breaks worth investigating include those at Poloa, Amanave, Sliding Rock, Nu'uuli, Lauli'ituai, Alofau and Tula. During the winter months, conditions in Pago Pago Harbor are favourable for windsurfing but the hazards are obvious – watch out for cargo ships, longliners and yachts.

iking

ere are limited opportunities for hiking
American Samoa. Anyone intending to
ke in the national park should contact the
ational Park Visitor Information Center in
go Pago (see Tourist Offices earlier in
s section).

The well-established 3 mile trail to the
p of Mt Alava above Pago Pago Harbor is
sily accessible and offers excellent views
the harbour and the rugged north-west
ast. A continuation of the trail, from Mt
lava to Vatia, was under construction at
e time of writing. The remote island of
'u offers some very wild and untouched
enery. Sections of the coast are accessible
nd inland walks to Judds Crater (six hours)
d Mt Lata (overnight trek) are possible.
u'll need to take a local guide.

olf

he Illi'ili Golf Course, south of Pago Pago
rport, is very scenic and quite cheap.

CCOMMODATION

ccommodation options are extremely
mited throughout American Samoa. At
e top end, Rainmaker Hotel monopolises
e market but represents very poor value
r money. There's not much at all in the
ay of formal budget accommodation,
ough local villagers living close to the
ational park are being encouraged to pro-
de inexpensive lodging for visitors. At the
me of writing, there were no basic beach-
de *fale* ('far-ley'; traditional thatched-roof
uts) to rent anywhere in the islands.

The tourist office runs a home-stay pro-
ram called Fale, Fala ma Ti (House, Mat and
ea). Accommodation may be in western-
yle homes (as the vast majority are in
merican Samoa) or in traditional
atched-roof open-sided guesthouses, or
le talimalo. Space for campers is also of-
red. Prices range from US$25 to US$35
r person per night.

HOPPING

he Senior Citizens' Handicraft Fales and
e Jean P Haydon Museum sell locally
ade items.

Getting There & Around

See the preceding independent Samoa chapter for information about getting to and
around American Samoa, including airline
offices in Pago Pago, yachting information,
buses, car rental and organised tours.

Tutuila

- pop 52,250   • area 57 sq miles

Tutuila is by far the largest of the seven islands of American Samoa. The dramatic
landscape of Tutuila is dominated by steep,
rugged and lush forested mountains that
branch out from the central ridge, confining
most of the development to a narrow strip
along the south coast. The north coast is so
wildly eroded that only a few tributary
roads connect it with the long highway that
snakes around the south coast.

Matafao Peak, just west of Pago Pago
Harbor, above Fagatogo, is the highest
point, at 2142 feet (653m). Immediately to
the east of the harbour is 1718-foot-tall
Rainmaker Mountain.

Tutuila's most important feature these
days is Pago Pago Harbor, which is all that
remains of the volcanic crater that created
Tutuila in the first place.

History

Archaeological finds near the villages of Tula
and Aoa on the far eastern tip of Tutuila, and
at To'aga on the island of Ofu, reveal that
the islands have been inhabited for more
than 3000 years.

Getting Around

Bus The main bus terminal is at Fagatogo
market. 'Aiga buses (family-owned trucks,
converted to carry passengers) leave every
couple of minutes from early morning to
about 6 pm eastbound for Tula (US$1),
and westbound for Tafuna and the airport
(50c), and Leone (75c). Less frequently,
buses go to Fagasa (50c), A'oloaufou on
the central ridge (75c), Amanave (US$1),

AMERICAN SAMOA

TUTUILA

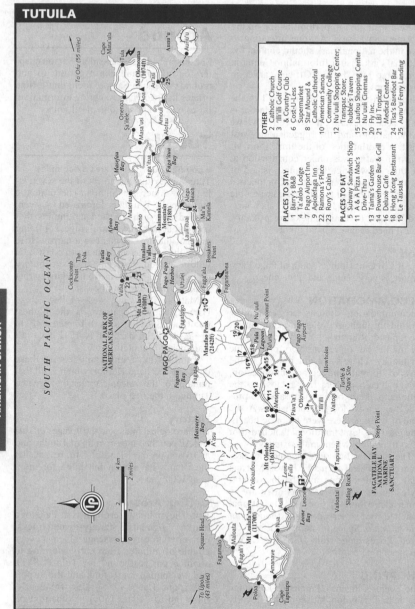

OTHER
2 Catholic Church
3 'Ili'ili Golf Course & Country Club
6 Cost-U-Less
8 Supermarket
Star Mound & Catholic Cathedral
10 American Samoa Community College
12 Nu'uuli Shopping Center; Transpac Store; Rubble's Tavern
15 Laufou Shopping Center
17 Nu'uuli Cinemas
20 Fly Inc.
21 LBJ Tropical Medical Center
24 Tisa's Barefoot Bar
25 Aunu'u Ferry Landing

PLACES TO STAY
1 Barry's B&B
4 Ta'alolo Lodge
7 Pago Airport Inn
9 Apiolefaga Inn
22 Ramona's Place
23 Rory's Cabin

PLACES TO EAT
5 Subway Sandwich Shop
11 A & A Pizza Mac's Drive-Thru
13 Taima's Garden
14 Powerhouse Bar & Grill
16 Deluxe Cafe
18 Hong Kong Restaurant
19 Le Tausala

AMERICAN SAMOA

d Fagamalo in the west (US$1.25).
u'll be lucky to catch a bus after 2 pm
Saturday, and on Sunday the only buses
nning will be those taking people to
urch.

r Tutuila's one main road (signposted
ute 1) follows the twisty coastline from
gamalo in the west of the island to
enoa in the north-east, a distance of
und 30 miles. The rental agencies
ted here charge about US$50 per day
us insurance. Petrol costs about US$1.45
r gallon (36c per litre).

is Car Rental
(☎ 699 2746, fax 699 4305)
Airport
yal Samoan Rent-a-Car
(☎ 633 4545, fax 633 2197)
Rainmaker Hotel
rifty Car Rental
(☎ 633 7482, fax 633 2953)
Rainmaker Hotel

xi Expect to pay about US$1 per mile for
taxi on Tutuila. This works out to US$10
om the harbour area to Pago Pago airport
Tafuna.

AGO PAGO
pop 3520

go Pago (**pa**-ngo **pa**-ngo) is an alluring
ixture of the seedy and the dramatically
autiful. The picturesque harbour is sur-
unded by high, almost wicked-looking
ountains that plunge straight into the sea.
nfortunately, on a 'bad tuna day' the smell
om the massive tuna canneries on the
rthern side of the bay will take your
eath away.

formation

ourist Offices The tourist office in Pago
ago (☎ 633 1092; see Tourist Offices in
acts for the Visitor earlier) is next to the
acht club at Utulei, just south of the Rain-
aker Hotel. It is open from 7.30 am to 4
m weekdays.

In Pago Plaza at the western end of the
arbour is the National Park Visitor Infor-
ation Center (☎ 633 7082; see Tourist

Offices earlier). The centre is open from 8
am to 4.30 pm weekdays and until noon on
Saturday.

Money The Bank of Hawaii and the
Amerika Samoa Bank, both near the *malae*
(town square) in Fagatogo, have exchange
facilities and ATMs.

Post The post office is by the malae on the
ground floor of the Lumana'i building. It is
open from 8 am to 4 pm weekdays and from
8.30 am to noon Saturday.

Bookshops The gift shop at the airport, the
Wesley Bookshop in Fagatogo, the Rainmaker Hotel gift shop and the Transpac
Store at the Nu'uuli Shopping Center all
stock a handful of Samoan and Pacific titles.

Libraries The Feleti Pacific Library in
Utulei near the Rainmaker Hotel has a reasonable selection of books, but you can't
get a library card unless you're a resident.

Laundry There are dozens of laundrettes in
town. Mary's, across the lane from Herb &
Sia's Motel, is one of the best.

Mt Alava

Towering above Pago Pago Harbor is 1610
foot Mt Alava. The National Park Service
maintains the 3 mile trail that follows the
ridge to the top of Mt Alava. It's an excellent walk, with the summit offering spectacular views.

The trail begins at Fagasa Pass about
three-quarters of a mile south-west of the
park's visitor information centre.

Jean P Haydon Museum

Across the road from the post office in
Fagatogo is the Jean P Haydon Museum.

The museum houses numerous artefacts
of early Samoa, including the *va'a* and
alia (bonito canoes and war canoes) that
inspired the old name for Samoa, the Navigator Islands.

Also fascinating is the display of native
pharmacopoeia used by the early Polynesians. The museum is open from 10 am to

PAGO PAGO HARBOR

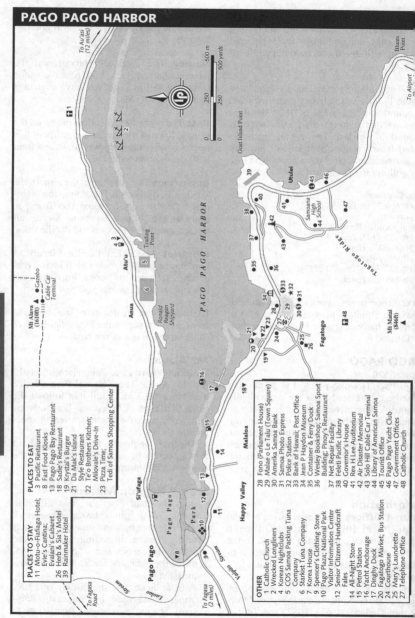

PLACES TO STAY
11 Motu-o-Fiafiaga Hotel;
    Evie's Cantina;
    Evalani's Cabaret
26 Herb & Sia's Motel
39 Rainmaker Hotel

PLACES TO EAT
3 Pacific Restaurant
8 Fast Food Kiosks
13 Pago Pago Bay Restaurant
18 Sadie's Restaurant
19 Krystal's Burger
21 Da Mak's Island
    Style Restaurant
22 Te'o Brothers Kitchen;
    Milovale's Drive-In
23 Pizza Time;
    Tedi of Samoa Shopping Center

OTHER
1 Catholic Church
2 Wrecked Longliners
4 Korean Nightclubs
5 COS Samoa Packing Tuna
   Company
6 Starkist Tuna Company
7 Korea House
9 Spencer's Clothing Store
10 Pago Plaza; National Park
   Visitor Information Center
12 Senior Citizens' Handicraft
   Fales
14 All-Night Store
15 Petrol Station
16 Yacht Anchorage
17 Dinghy Dock
20 Fagatogo Market; Bus Station
24 Courthouse
25 Mary's Laundrette
27 Telephone Office
28 Fono (Parliament House)
29 Malae o Le Talu (Town Square)
30 Amerika Samoa Bank
31 Samoa Photo Express
32 Police Station
33 Bank of Hawaii; Post Office
34 Jean P Haydon Museum
35 Container & Ferry Dock
36 Wesley Bookshop; Samoa Sport
   Building; Pinoy's Restaurant
37 Net Repair Facility
38 Feleti Pacific Library
40 Governor's House
41 Rex H Lee Auditorium
42 Air Disaster Memorial
43 Solo Hill Cable Car Terminal
44 Library of American Samoa
45 Tourist Office
46 Pago Pago Yacht Club
47 Government Offices
48 Catholic Church

pm weekdays. Admission is free. The museum has a small gift counter selling locally made items. **Kava ceremonies** and weaving and **woodcarving demonstrations** sometimes take place in the fale next to the museum.

The Fono

The large and impressive group of buildings beside the museum is the *fono* (parliament house), where American Samoan law-makers convene and legislate.

Market

The market and 'aiga bus station is near the western end of Fagatogo village. Here, local growers come to sell their bananas, coconuts, breadfruit and other fresh produce. The big market day is Saturday, but arrive before 7 am if you want to get a decent selection. Fresh fish is available at the Star of the Sea fish market, near the shore behind the main market.

Tuna Canneries

The two tuna canneries are in the mile-long industrial complex on the north coast of the harbour. Nearest to Pago Pago is Starkist. The other is COS Samoa Packing.

Flowerpot Rocks

The Flowerpot Rocks, or Fatumafuti, are found along the highway, near the village of Faga'alu. The legend says that Fatu and Futi were lovers living on the Manu'a Islands. They wanted to marry but were forbidden to do so because tradition prevents members of the same 'aiga marrying. Fatu, the woman, built a coconut raft and set off for Tutuila. When Futi learned that she had gone, he was distraught and set out after her. Both their boats were destroyed by a tsunami as they approached Tutuila and the two lovers were stranded on the reef, where they remain to this day. The area around Fatumafuti is nice for picnics.

Places to Stay

Herb & Sia's Motel (☎ 633 5413, fax 699 9557) has very basic singles/doubles/triples for US$35/40/60 with shared bathroom (cold water). You can stay in equally basic rooms with private cold shower for an extra US$5.

Motu-o-Fiafiaga Hotel (☎ 633 7777, fax 633 4767) is a comfortable mid-range option, which offers air-conditioned rooms with shared (hot) shower for US$60 for single or double occupancy. All rooms have queen-sized beds and TV. *Lavalava* (sarongs) are provided for guests and a breakfast of Samoan pancakes, fruit and coffee is included. The hotel also has a small workout room and sauna. Adjoining the hotel is a bar and restaurant specialising in Mexican food.

The government-run *Rainmaker Hotel* (☎ 633 4241, fax 633 5959, PO Box 996) has a reputation as one of the worst hotels in the South Pacific. Standard rooms with private bathroom (bath and shower) cost from US$72; VIP fale (huts) cost US$90, and executive fale cost US$150. A third bed costs US$15. The hotel has a dining room, a pleasant coffee shop that serves cheaper meals, a bar and a swimming pool.

Also see Places to Stay & Eat in the Around the Island section for options outside Pago Pago.

Places to Eat

Snacks & Cheap Meals One place where you can get traditional Samoan dishes, as well as Hawai'ian and Chinese dishes, is *Da Mak's Island Style Restaurant*. It's open for breakfast and lunch from 6.30 am to 4 pm weekdays. A cooked breakfast costs US$3.75; lunch, which may include Hawai'ian-style *palusami* (coconut cream wrapped in taro leaves) with pork or Chinese roast duck, costs from US$3 to US$6. There are a few other places near the market which serve decent cheap meals. *Te'o Brothers Kitchen* and *Milovale's Drive-In*, next to each other on the eastern side of the market, offer fish and chips, curries, barbecue lamb and chicken, hot dogs and sausage, taro and chop suey for about US$4 for a heaped plateful. They're both open from around 5 am to 3 pm Monday to Saturday. Milovale's is open 24 hours on Friday.

Krystal's Burger is a popular chain serving some of the best burgers in the territory as well as a variety of other meals. *Pizza Time (☎ 633 1199)* sells pizzas (US$10 for medium size) and other fast foods. Call for deliveries.

Evie's Cantina specialises in Mexican food. Dishes start at around US$5 and go up to US$15 for steaks. It's open daily for lunch and dinner, and has karaoke nightly. The *Pago Pago Yacht Club* in Utulei serves lunch from 11.30 am weekdays. For about US$4 you'll get a burger or hot dog, chips and coleslaw. On Friday night during happy hour (5 to 7 pm), it serves similar fare.

In Pago Park at the head of the harbour you'll find a cluster of bargain-basement *fast food kiosks* selling all sorts of Korean, Chinese and pseudo-Samoan dishes. About US$3 will buy you a plateful of food big enough for a Samoan football player. The kiosks often run out of food around 2.30 pm.

Restaurants With its period décor and atmosphere, *Sadie's Restaurant (☎ 633 5981)* is the most elegant and expensive restaurant in the territory. The menu features lots of seafood and most main courses hover at around US$18, going up to US$26 for lobster tails. It's open Monday to Saturday for lunch and dinner.

The *Pago Pago Bay Restaurant*, a favourite with yachties, overlooks the water near the west end of the harbour. The menu (cheaper than Sadie's) features US, Chinese and Samoan dishes.

For very good, inexpensive Filipino-style meals featuring lots of vegetables, try *Pinoys*. Also good is the Korean food at the *Pacific Restaurant*.

Self-Catering If you want locally grown fresh fruit and vegetables, the *Fagatogo market* is the place to go. It is open Monday to Saturday. Fresh fish is available nearby at the *Star of the Sea* fish market, near the shore behind the main market. You'll find plenty of **supermarkets** and small Korean-run **stores** on Tutuila that sell more or less the same fare available on the mainland for only slightly higher prices. *Fly inc.* in Nu'uuli sells a good range of groceries for reasonable prices. Other favourites for provisions are *Kruse* at Leo village and *Haleck's* at Pava'ia'i.

Entertainment

Bars & Nightclubs Local nightclubs clo at 2 am. You can expect to pay around US for a drink.

Adjoining Motu-o-Fiafiaga Hote *Evalani's Cabaret* is open Monday to Sa urday nights. There's karaoke until 10 p *Sadie's Restaurant* has an elegant ba which occasionally has live music. Ne Pago Pago Park is the *Player's Sports Clu* with a bar, pool tables, dart boards ar giant-screen video.

West of Pago, *Rubble's Tavern* i Nu'uuli is a pleasant place for a cold bee (and good food). The *Country Club* at th golf course has a big US-style sports b with pool, darts and TV sport. *Silver Bro* a popular nightclub near the turn-off to th airport, features live Polynesian-style roc and roll most nights.

About 6 miles east of Pago Pago (50c b bus), *Tisa's Barefoot Bar (☎ 622 7447)* i character-full fale bar on Alega Beach. It open from 10 am until midnight seven day a week.

Cinemas The new multiscreen cinem complex on the main road in Nu'uuli, ju east of the Deluxe Cafe, screens lates release commercial movies.

AROUND THE ISLAND

In rural Tutuila, everything moves at a mor Polynesian pace than in the capital.

Eastern District

National Park of American Samo Bounded by the Maugaloa Ridge to th south, this section of the park covers 247 acres of land (most of which is covered i lowland and montane rainforest) as well a 1185 acres of offshore waters.

At the time of writing, the 3 mile trai from Fagasa Pass to Mt Alava (see Mt Alav in the Pago Pago section) was the only offi cial hiking trail in this part of the park. Any one wanting to explore the national park should contact the superintendent (see ourist Offices under Facts for the Visitor earlier in this chapter).

Amalau Valley Between Afona and Vatia is the secluded Amalau Valley, which is home many forest **bird** species and the Samoan Islands' two rare species of **fruit bat**.

Vatia Situated on the edge of a wide, coral-fringed bay, Vatia is a charming and friendly village that seems a million miles away from the big smoke over the ridge. From Vatia you can view The Pola, a tiny uninhabited island just offshore whose magnificent sheer cliffs rise more than 400 feet straight out of the ocean. The craggy cliffs are home to numerous **seabirds** including frigate birds, boobies, white terns, tropicbirds and noddy terns. To get there, go to the end of the road through the village and then walk a quarter of a mile along the coral rubble beach.

Vatia offers basic accommodation for visitors who would like to sample village life, as well as boat and fishing tours. (See Places to Stay & Eat later.) 'Aiga buses go to Vatia (US$1.50) from Pago Pago several times a day. It will soon be possible to walk to Vatia from Mt Alava above Pago Pago (ask the NPS for advice).

Rainmaker Mountain (Pioa) Rainmaker (1718 feet) is Tutuila's best example of a volcanic plug associated with the major fissure zone that created the island. Although it appears as one peak from below, the summit is actually three-pronged. The separate peaks are North Pioa, South Pioa and Sinapioa. Rainmaker Mountain and its base area are designated a national landmark site due to the pristine nature of the tropical vegetation on the slopes.

Alega Beach One of Tutuila's finest beaches, Alega Beach is just 10km east of Pago Pago (50c by 'aiga bus). It's a great place to **swim** and **snorkel** but check currents and conditions with locals first.

Masefau & Sa'ilele Near the village of Faga'itua, another cross-island road goes over to the north coast. At the pass, this one

splits. The left fork leads down to the beautiful bay and village of Masefau. The right fork goes to the tiny settlement of Masa'usi and then through dense forest to Sa'ilele, which has one of the loveliest **beaches** on the entire island. On a track east of the village of Sa'ilele is a **burial ground** of reasonable interest where some *ali'i* (high chiefs) are buried.

Au'asi Falls Above the village of Au'asi is a pleasant waterfall, a nice place to cool off on a hot day. It can be reached by walking up the stream for about half an hour.

Aoa Although the road between Amouli and Aoa is scenically rather uninteresting, more than 40 ancient **star mounds** have been discovered, but not yet excavated, in the bush near the spine of the island. In addition to the star mounds, Polynesian plainware (a type of undecorated pottery) has been found in the Aoa area. Some estimates date the pot shards found here from as early as 1000 BC, but the figure currently accepted by the scientific community is 500 BC.

Tula Tula, the easternmost village on Tutuila, is a quiet and laid-back place with a pleasant white **beach**. It is the end of the bus line east, but if you have a reliable vehicle or feel like a nice walk, you can continue around the end of the island to Cape Mata'ula and Onenoa, a beautiful area of high cliffs, small plantations and forested slopes. As in all traditional villages, it's a good idea not to wander into Onenoa on Sunday, but the area between the villages has plenty of places to picnic, especially above the cliffs.

Places to Stay & Eat North-east of Pago and tucked away in the family plantation above Vatia is *Rory's Cabin* (☎ 644 1416, PO Box 3412, Pago Pago), where the self-sufficient can reside in rustic splendour for as little as US$10 per night. There's an outside shower and toilet and basic cooking facilities. The garden, which is crammed with exotic fruits and vegetables, is home to dozens of fruit bats. Rory West also runs North Shore Tours, which offers boat and

AMERICAN SAMOA

Star Mounds of Ancient Power

More than 140 distinctive earthen, and sometimes stone, mounds, dating back to late prehistoric times, are scattered across the Samoan archipelago. Dubbed 'star mounds', the structures range from 20 to 100 feet in length, are up to 9 feet high and have from one to 11 ray-like projections radiating from their base.

It is highly probable that these mounds were used for catching the revered Pacific pigeon (*lupe*), which isn't as pedestrian as it may sound. An extremely important sport of *matai* (chiefs), it had a five month season, from June until the end of September, and involved nearly the entire population of the islands. The people would follow their matai into the forest to observe and support competitions.

Archaeologists have found strong evidence to suggest that though the structures were used primarily for pigeon-catching, they also served a much more complex function in Samoan society as sites for rituals related to marriage, healing and warfare. The star mounds also reflected the status of the matai, and pigeon hunting was the field in which personal ability and *mana* (personal supernatural power) could be expressed. Star mounds (sometimes called *tia seu lupe*) were therefore places of immense power.

fishing tours around the northern side of the island. Also in Vatia, **Ramona's Place** (☎ 644 4976, PO Box 5222, Vatia) is a family home with inexpensive rooms.

Western District
Virgin Falls A three-quarters of a mile walk past the LBJ Tropical Medical Center in Faga'alu leads to a small rock quarry. From there, a rough trail climbs past a series of waterfalls. Some of the **pools** beneath the falls are suitable for bathing. The surrounding vegetation is beautifully lush so you may have to make your own trail in some sections. Watch for sudden rock slides, as the ravine is quite steep in areas. Allow a couple of hours for the return walk if you plan to climb all the way to the top fall.

Matafao Peak At 2142 feet, Matafao Peak is the highest point on Tutuila. Above the 1150 foot level, the mountain is designated a national landmark site.

Nu'uuli Nu'uuli is primarily a loosely defined shopping area along the main road between Coconut Point and the airport turnoffs. There are quite a few restaurants along here (see Places to Stay & Eat later), as well as the Nu'uuli Shopping Center, the Laufou

Shopping Center and the Nu'uuli Cinema complex.

Tia Seu Lupe American Samoa's Historic Preservation Office maintains a particularly well-preserved ancient Polynesian star mound, *tia seu lupe* (literally 'earthen mound to catch pigeons'), near the Catholic cathedral at Tafuna. The mound has a unique connecting platform and views across to Matafao Peak. Call the Historic Preservation Office (☎ 633 2384) for a personalised tour of the site. Adjoining the site is a small **rainforest reserve**. The nearby **cathedral** contains some beautiful wood carving and a fabulous photo-realist painting of a traditional Samoan family by Duffy Sheridan.

Fagatele Bay National Marine Sanctuary Fagatele Bay is a submerged volcanic crater surrounded by steep cliffs. The area contains the last remaining stretch of coastal rainforest on the island.

The sanctuary is also home to several marine mammal species. Southern humpback **whales** winter here from August to November, several varieties of **porpoise** occasionally visit and sperm whales have been seen. Threatened and endangered species of **marine turtles**, such as hawksbill and

reen sea turtles, also use the bay. Other less
equent visitors include the leatherback, the
ggerhead and the olive Ridley sea turtle.

The rocky cliffs surrounding the bay are
ome to numerous **seabirds**. All but tradi-
onal fishing methods are prohibited in the
nner bay, the taking of invertebrates is pro-
bited and historical artefacts found in the
ay are protected. It is possible to **dive**,
norkel and **swim** in the bay, but access is
fficult. Contact the Marine and Wildlife
esources Office (☎ 633 7354, fax 633
355), down by the market in Fagatogo, to
rrange transport.

liding Rock The sliding rock, near Leone
n the side road between Taputimu and
ailoatai, is on an interesting coast of black,
able-flat volcanic terraces. The tilted one
arthest from the road is the sliding rock.
t's nondescript when dry, but when it's wet,
ocal children use it as a slippery slide.

eone Leone village has a post office, and
bakery that is a nice place to stop for some-
hing gooey. 'Aiga buses direct to Leone
eave every couple of minutes from the main
erminal in Fagatogo, but Leone is the turn-
round point. If you'd like to travel beyond
here on the main road, you'll have to wait
n front of the church for a westbound bus.

eone Falls & Ancient Quarry The
mall waterfall and ancient stone quarry
omplex behind Leone village is close to
3arry's B&B. To get to the waterfall go up
he road past the white Catholic church near
he town centre to the end of the pavement,
hen follow the short walking track to the
ead of the valley, where a ribbon-like
waterfall plunges into a moss-covered
asin. An artificial catchment barrier cre-
tes a freshwater pool at the bottom. It's a
ool and pleasant spot, but wear strong
ootwear for the brief walk as the track can
e extremely muddy.

The basalt quarry, known as Tataga
Matau (Hit the Rock), above Leone is one
f the most important archaeological sites
n the South Pacific. Surveys carried out
uring the past 10 years have identified 10

John William's church in Leone – the oldest
church in American Samoa.

quarry sites on Tutuila and archaeologists
believe the island was the centre of a large
trade network that stretched across the
South Pacific. Artefacts made of stone from
the Tutuila quarries have turned up as far
away as the Solomon Islands.

There's also a **star mound** at the Leone
quarry similar to those found at Aoa.

Massacre Bay The hiking trail down to
A'asu at Massacre Bay leaves from the village of A'oloaufou, high on the spine of
Tutuila, above Pava'ia'i on the main road.
Massacre Bay is the site where, on 11 December 1787, 12 men from La Pérouse's
ships *La Boussole* and *Astrolabe*, as well as
39 Samoans, were killed in a skirmish. An
obscure **monument** in A'asu commemorates
the European crew members who died there
(for more about La Pérouse, see the boxed
text 'Disaster on the Reef' in the Solomon
Islands chapter).

To get to A'oloaufou, take a Leone-bound
bus from the market in Fagatogo to Pava'ia'i
(75c) and wait on the corner there for one
headed up the hill.

Across from the large park in A'oloaufou
is a colourful garden. The trail to A'asu takes
off downhill just east of that garden and
continues for about 2½ miles to the beach.

AMERICAN SAMOA

The first three-quarters of a mile of the track is a little intimidating; it's a veritable mudhole, and you'll be slogging in slippery, shoe-grabbing, ankle-deep ooze, so lace up your shoes tightly or remove them altogether.

There is only one family living in the old deserted village of A'asu. On arrival, it's best to introduce yourself and ask for permission to use their **beach**. The worn-out admonition not to go on Sunday again holds.

For this trip, strong hikers should plan on one hour to walk down and half again as long for the climb back up. There is no road outlet from Aasu. Also from A'oloaufou (which means 'New A'oloau') you'll find a trail to the **abandoned village** of A'oloautuai (Old A'oloau) and another down the ridge to Fagamalo, where there are infrequent buses back to town.

Cape Taputapu The village of Amanave lies at the end of the beaten path. A short distance beyond the village on Loa inlet is a lovely white-sand beach, generally known as **Palagi Beach**. It's just east of Cape Taputapu, which is Tutuila's westernmost point and a national natural landmark site.

You can walk to the beach via the track above the shoreline. Allow about 10 or 15 minutes to get to the beach. You can paddle and **snorkel** in the small pool by the offshore island but be mindful of strong currents.

Beyond Amanave, the road climbs steeply and winds up and down to the small villages of Poloa, Fagali'i, Maloata and Fagamalo, where the road ends. There are some spectacular views of the wild and trackless north coast of Tutuila.

Places to Stay & Eat The following establishments are in western Tutuila.

Barry's B&B (☎ 688 2488, fax 633 9111) is a comfortable modern home outside Leone offering singles/doubles with shared bathroom for US$35/40. Barry can provide evening meals for guests, a free laundry service and custom-made island tours, which range from gentle outings to strenuous five-hour hikes.

Near Masepa, the *Apiolefaga Inn (☎ 699 9124, fax 699 4892)* has large, air-con rooms with private bathroom (bath and showe fridge and TV for US$50/60. Breakfast not included. The inn has a bar, swimmi pool and two kitchens that guests can use

A stone's throw from the airport is the ne *Pago Airport Inn (☎/fax 699 6333, PO B 783, Pago Pago)*, which has air-con roo with private bathroom, TV, fridge and te phone for US$75/85. The inn is a 20 minu walk or US$3 taxi ride from the airport.

Eating options in Tutuila's west inclu the *Deluxe Cafe (☎ 699 4000)*, a very plea ant, air-con US-diner-style place open f breakfast, lunch and dinner seven days week. Lunch and dinner specialities inclu fresh local fish, salads and imported steak

Rubble's Tavern (☎ 699 4403) is ve popular with locals and expats alike and a good option for a relaxed lunch or supp washed down with a cold beer. The lun menu features very US-style items. The di ner menu includes fresh fish (US$15) well as pasta dishes (US$13). Rubble's open from 11 am to midnight seven days week, with happy hour from 4.30 to 6 p

The most popular Chinese restaurant the island is the *Hong Kong Restaura (☎ 699 1055)*, in Nu'uuli, which offers extensive menu featuring carefully pr pared Chinese favourites. A full meal wi rice costs around US$12, but you can ord a very good vegetable deluxe for as little US$6. It's open for lunch and dinner seve days a week.

AUNU'U
● pop 500   ● area 1.2 sq miles

Tiny Aunu'u Island, off the south-easter end of Tutuila, is a treasure house of natur phenomena and is a tranquil and pristin place. The waters around the island ar clear and blue and the village is spaciou and unspoilt.

Pala Lake
Heading north from the village, you wi arrive at Pala Lake after walking abou half a mile. This beautiful and deadly look ing expanse is a sea of fiery-red quicksan and it's a safe bet to say you'll never hav seen anything like it before. During th

iny season, the sand thins out and is in-
bited by grey ducks.

ed Lake

ed Lake lies in the middle of Fa'imulivai
arsh, which is in the middle of Aunu'u's
onounced volcanic crater. It is filled with
els and **tilapia fish**. The water of the lake
ally is reddish – the colour of weak tea.
' you want to get a look at it and the eels,
ou can walk out to the edge on the sedges
at surround the marsh. To get there, fol-
w the track past Pala Lake and up the hill
the crater. There is a well-groomed track
ound the crater, but access to the lake is
little tricky, since it necessitates a bit of
ushwhacking on the approach. The best
ace to have a go at it is from the western
de of the crater north of the intersection
f the village trails. If you'd like a local
uide to come with you, ask around in the
illage.

Ma'ama'a Cove

his bowl in the rocks is a cauldron of surf
at boils, pounds and sprays dramatically
ver, through and around the rocks. The
ave action here seems to be completely
ndom and is good for entertainment, but
on't venture too close to the edge.

Pisaga

he Pisaga is a region just inside the crater,
elow Fogatia Hill. Here people are for-
idden to call out or make loud noises lest
ey disturb the *aitu* (spirits) that inhabit
is place. The Samoans believe that those
ho make noise may be answered by an ir-
table spirit. For a superb view over Red
ake, as well as Aunu'u village, climb up
ast the water tank on the slopes of Foga-
a Hill.

Places to Stay & Eat

here is no formal accommodation availble on Aunu'u. You'll need to make
rrangements before you arrive. Find some-
ne on Tutuila who can sponsor you with an
unu'u family. There's a **bush store** in the
illage where you can buy soft drinks and
asic supplies.

Getting There & Away

Take the bus to the harbour at Au'asi (fare
US$1 from Pago Pago). From here, a ferry
travels frequently to and from Aunu'u Harbor for US$2 per person. If you can't be
bothered waiting for the ferry, you can charter a boat from the bush store at Au'asi for
US$10 each way for as many people as will
fit. The trip takes about 15 minutes and can
get a bit hairy through the strait, especially
if the wind is blowing.

SWAINS ISLAND

• **pop 15**   • **area 1.3 sq miles**

Swains Island is situated about 220 miles
north-north-west of Tutuila, but both historically and geographically it is one of the
Tokelau Islands (Tokelauans know it as
Olohega).

It is not possible to visit Swains Island
without permission from the resident Jen-
nings family. If you're interested, contact
the Marine and Wildlife Resources Office
(☎ 633 7354, fax 633 7355), near Fagatogo
market.

The Manu'a Islands

The three small islands of the Manu'a group
(Ofu, Olosega and Ta'u) lie 60 miles east of
Tutuila. As well as the most stunning
scenery in either Samoa – sparkling white
beaches, soaring cliffs, crystal lagoons and
mountain peaks – they are the most traditional islands of American Samoa.

Almost touching, Ofu and Olosega islands
are a complex of volcanic cones that have
been buried by lava from two merging shield
flows. Deep valleys were carved out, leaving
very high, sheer cliffs around the islands.

Remote Ta'u Island's sea cliffs are some
of the highest in the world, rising 3170
feet to Mt Latu. More than 4900 acres of
the dense rainforest of Ta'u is national
park, and the island is dotted with inactive
volcanic cones and craters.

History

The Tu'i Manu'a was the paramount chief of
these islands and many supernatural powers

AMERICAN SAMOA

have been ascribed to holders of the title down through history. Some of the *tu'i* were credited with the ability to fly and to become invisible. All, of course, had exceptional prowess at war. The last Tu'i Manu'a ceded the islands in 1904, but in his will he stipulated that his title would die with him.

Orientation & Information

Although the lack of transport will slow you down considerably, that's just what the Manu'a Islands do best. If you're not pressed for time, Manu'a can absorb a lot of it. You can sit for hours relaxing or reading on a 2½-mile-long deserted white beach, go snorkelling over the reefs, gaze at seabirds riding thermals over sheer cliffs, climb rainforested peaks and meet the people in the tiny, still-traditional villages. Manu'a is American Samoa at its best, and it promises to remain that way for a long time to come. Bring your own snorkelling equipment, reading material and any particular foods you may need for your stay. There are no banks or restaurants on the islands. Ofu village has a basic medical clinic.

Getting There & Around

Air Ofu airport is at Va'oto on the south coast. Fortunately for travellers heading for Ta'u, the old nightmare airstrip – which had a cliff on one end, a mountain at the other and lots of quirky air currents in between – has been decommissioned and replaced by a flash new facility in a more suitable location at Fiti'uta, 4½ miles east.

Samoa Air flies twice a day between Tutuila and the Manu'a Islands. The planes stop at both Ta'u and Ofu whenever there are passengers to be picked up or dropped off. The schedule changes all the time, however, so make prior arrangements if you want to fly between Ofu and Ta'u or vice versa on a particular day. Between Pago Pago and either of the Manu'a airstrips, the fare is US$44 each way or US$86 return. Phone and make a reservation (☎ 699 9106 in Pago Pago, ☎ 655 1103 in Ofu, ☎ 677 3569 in Ta'u) then reconfirm the return flight upon arrival. The trip between Ofu and Ta'u is US$22 each way.

Boat Water transport to the Manu'a Islan is at present limited to private yachts. Cru ing yachts arriving from the east must ste into Pago Pago before they're permitted land at Manu'a, and once they've arrived Pago Pago, they face a fierce beat into t wind to get back to Manu'a. Ofu and Ta harbours are marginal, and can prove disa trous in the event of any carelessness.

OFU

● pop 400   ● area 2 sq miles

Ofu is the most dramatic and beautiful the Manu'a Islands. It's the easiest to vis and the one most often seen by outsiders

The Beach

Ofu's crown jewel is the beach along tl south coast. Two and a half miles of shi ing, palm-fringed white sand, and the on footprints to be seen other than your ov are those of birds and crabs.

The strip of beach stretching from Va'o Lodge to the beginning of the Ofu-Olose; bridge plus 350 acres of offshore wate comprise the Ofu section of the nation park. With your own snorkelling equi ment, parts of the stretch offshore are dee enough for some excellent viewing of cor and **tropical fish**. Almost 300 species of fi have been identified and the reef is believe to contain about 150 species of coral. C out at low tide (at high tide, waves brea over the reef and wash into the lagoon) a watch out for stinging flame coral.

On both Ofu and Ta'u, plants are still co lected for traditional medicinal purpos and the narrow strip of land that comprise the Ofu unit of the national park is a important source of medicinal plants for tł villages of Ofu and Olosega.

To'aga Site

About three-quarters of a mile north-east Va'oto Lodge, behind Ofu Beach, is tł To'aga site, where in 1987 archaeologis found an unprecedented array of artefact ranging from the earliest times of Samoa prehistory (1000 BC) to modern times.

The site also has legendary and spiritua significance for Samoans. In fact, the enti

And God Created Samoa

Samoans accept the scientific theory that Polynesians originally migrated to the islands from South-East Asia by way of Indonesia. However, they believe this applies to all Polynesians except themselves. Their land, they claim, is the 'cradle of Polynesia.'

Samoa, they say, was created by the Polynesian sky god Tagaloa (Tangaroa). Before the sea, earth, sky, plants or people existed, Tagaloa lived in the expanse of empty space. He created a rock, commanding it to split into clay, coral, cliffs and stones. As the rock broke apart, the earth, sea and sky came into being. From a bit of the rock emerged a spring of fresh water.

Next, at Saua in the Manu'a Islands, Tagaloa created man and woman, whom he named Fatu and 'Ele'ele ('Heart' and 'Earth'). He sent them to the region of fresh water and commanded them to people the area. He ordered the sky, which was called Tu'ite'elagi, to prop itself up above the earth. Using starch and *teve*, a bitter-root plant and the only vegetation then available, he made a post for it to rest upon.

Tagaloa then created Po and Ao (Night and Day), which bore the 'eyes of the sky' – the sun and the moon. At the same time he made the nine regions of heaven, inhabited by various gods, most famously Rongo (or Ro'o), the god of agriculture, and Oro, the god of war.

In the meantime, Fatu and 'Ele'ele were doing as they were told and 'peopling the area'. Tagaloa, reckoning that all these people needed some form of government, sent Manu'a, another son of Po and Ao, to be the chief of the people. The Manu'a Islands were named after this chief, and from that time on, Samoan kings were called Tu'i Manu'a tele ma Samoa 'atoa ('King of Manu'a and all of Samoa).

Next, the countries were divided into islands or groups of islands. The world now consisted of Manu'a, Viti (Fiji), Tonga and Savai'i. Tagaloa then went to Manu'a and noticed that a void existed between it and Savai'i. Up popped Upolu and then Tutuila.

Tagaloa's final command, before he returned to the expanse, was: 'Always respect Manu'a; anyone who fails to do so will be overtaken by catastrophe.' Thus, Manu'a became the spiritual centre of the Samoan islands and, to some extent, of all Polynesia.

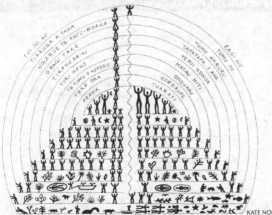

KATE NOLAN

This diagram (first drawn in 1869) shows nine regions of heaven above
the Earth – although most Polynesian cultures named only eight.

area of bush between the road and Ofu Beach is strongly believed to be infested with devilish aitu (spirits). Wander down here alone in the dark and you're likely to agree. Archaeologists reckon that virtually all the coastal flatlands and broad upland slopes of the Manu'a Islands are dotted with **archaeological sites** and features. Tito Malae of Va'oto Lodge can take visitors to some of the major sites on Manu'a.

Ofu Village

Just 1¼ miles north of the airstrip is Ofu village. Along the shore is a calm **lagoon** for swimming (ask permission), but avoid the pass between Ofu and Nu'utele Island just offshore as the currents are dangerous.

Mt Tumutumu

The road to the summit of Mt Tumutumu (1621 feet) leaves from near the wharf and twists and climbs up to the TV relay tower atop the mountain. The road can be negotiated by a sturdy 4WD vehicle. More usually, the trip to the top involves a hot and sweaty 3 mile climb on foot, but the vegetation and views make it well worthwhile. If it's hot, allow a full day and don't forget to carry all

the food and water you'll need as nothing available anywhere above the village.

Places to Stay & Eat

The friendly **Va'oto Lodge** (☎ 655 1120) conveniently located beside the airstrip a a few steps from the beach. The rooms, a with electric fan, hot shower and toilet, a clean and quiet. You'll find cold beer, boo and TV in the large dining/common room. you're not on the strictest of budgets, it's perfect place to relax for a few days. Singl double rooms cost US$35/40, with di counts for longer stays. Dinner costs US$ per person, lunch is US$2 and a cook brekkie costs US$5. In Ofu village itse **Peau's Place** (☎ 655 1110) has five roor with private shower (cold) for US$35/4 plus US$15 for three meals.

OLOSEGA

● pop 400   ● area 1.2 sq miles

Olosega (oh-lo-**seng**-a) is Ofu's twin islar – when viewed from the sea the two appe to be almost mirror images of each othe Olosega lies only 450 feet from Ofu and joined to it by a cyclone-proof bridge. The are both encircled by the same reef. Olose

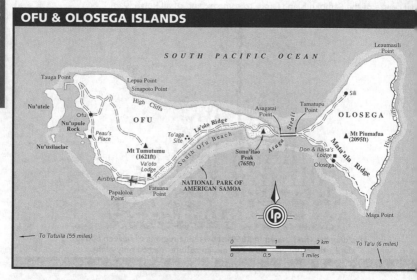

OFU & OLOSEGA ISLANDS

as a very nice beach along its south-west coast between the pass and Olosega village. There's another small settlement at Sili on the north-western side of the island.

Places to Stay & Eat

Don & Ilaisa's Lodge (☎ 655 1212) in Olosega village has pleasant rooms for US$20 per person, less for a family. Meals are available if ordered in advance and there's a kitchen that guests can use. Three of the five rooms have private shower (hot) and toilet. Basic, albeit expensive, supplies are available at the *store* in Olosega village.

Getting There & Away

Since there is no harbour or airstrip, access to Olosega is on foot or by vehicle from Ofu. To walk from Ofu village to Olosega village will take about two hours.

TA'U

• pop 3500   • area 15 sq miles

Mt Lata, the sacred mountain of Ta'u, is the highest point in American Samoa (3170 feet).

It was in Luma that the young Margaret Mead researched and wrote her controversial work *Coming of Age in Samoa* in 1925. Ta'u and the island's other two villages, Fiti'uta and Faleasao, were rebuilt after being flattened by Cyclone Tusi in 1987.

Ta'u feels seriously remote. The coastline is extremely wild and rugged and so untouched in parts that it's not difficult to imagine you've just been dropped off by a whaling boat.

The island sees very few visitors and isn't really set up for tourists; if you'd like to spend a couple of days exploring, bring food supplies with you. It's fairly easy to hitch a ride between the eastern and western ends of the island. Traffic is sparse, but if someone is going your way they're sure to offer a lift.

Fiti'uta Village

At the north-eastern corner of Ta'u is the tiny, sleepy village of Fiti'uta. The airstrip is here, along with the only official place to stay, a small video shop and a store selling basic supplies.

National Park of American Samoa

The Ta'u unit of the national park comprising most of the uninhabited southern half of Ta'u, and 990 acres of offshore waters. There is a spectacular escarpment along the southern side and cliffs as high as 3000 feet.

Ta'u's protected lowland and montane rainforest provide excellent habitats for **fruit bats** and many native **birds**. Species include black noddies, white terns, Tahiti petrels, Audubon's shearwaters, the Fiji shrikebill, the friendly ground dove and the culturally important Pacific pigeon, or *lupe*. Other native wildlife includes the Pacific boa, which lives only on Ta'u and in very small numbers; 13 species of amphibians and reptiles, most of which are geckos and skinks; and 20 species of land snail. Endangered sea turtles nest along the remote shorelines of Ta'u. There are plans to build an elevated canopy walkway in the rainforest of Ta'u, similar to the one which has been built in the Falealupo Rainforest Preserve on Savai'i. In the meantime, we highly recommend that you find a local guide for any bushwalk.

Saua Site Claimed by some to be the birthplace of Polynesian culture, there are the remains of an **ancient village** near Saua, and numerous grave sites between Saua and Si'u Point. This is where the god Tagaloa (**tung-a-lo-a**) created the first Polynesians, and where the first Tu'i Manu'a was crowned.

Laufuti Stream A rough plantation track follows the east coast as far as Tufu Point, and from here it's possible to hike 1¼ miles along the shoreline to Laufuti Stream where there's a **waterfall** and a nearby spring. The southern coastline of Ta'u is so wild and pristine that it's worth a look even if you don't want to walk all the way to the stream. You may be able to find local transport from Fiti'uta to Tufu Point. Anyone going beyond Si'u Point will certainly need a guide.

Mt Lata & Judds Crater Walks into the cloud forest on Mt Lata and to Judds Crater

AMERICAN SAMOA

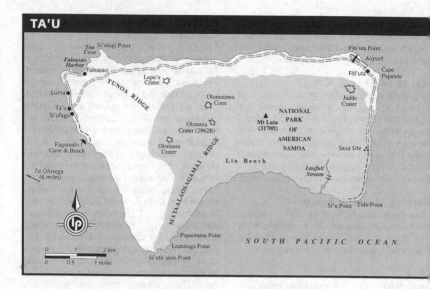

TA'U

are possible with a local guide; organise them through the National Park Visitor Information Center in Pago Pago (☎ 633 7082). Judds Crater, above Fiti'uta, is a three hour climb; the overnight climb to Mt Lata requires a sleeping bag, tent and warm clothing.

Ta'u Village

The main settlement on Ta'u consists of the twin villages of Luma and Si'ufaga at the north-western corner of the island. In Luma are the **tombs** of the last Tu'i Manu'a and several other early politicians.

There are basic stores scattered around the villages. The waters off the north-west coast are treacherous. There are three ancient **star mounds** on the ridges above Faleasao.

Fagamalo Cove

From Ta'u village, the walk south to the **beach** at secluded Fagamalo Cove is a pleasant way to pass a couple of hours. The track along the west coast can be muddy at times but it offers some nice views of the cliffs above and pounding surf below.

Places to Stay & Eat

The main place to stay is the *Fiti'uta Lodge* (☎ 677 3155 or ☎ 677 3501), a slightly run-down, western-style house near the airport in the village of Fiti'uta. Basic rooms with shared bathroom (hot water) cost US$23 per person. Meals are not available, but there is a kitchen in the house. Next door is a *shop* that sells basic supplies.

There are no facilities for camping on Ta'u, and no restaurants. Bring any food or supplies you'll be needing from Tutuila.

ROSE ATOLL

● pop 0   ● area 19 acres

Tiny Rose Atoll, only 10 feet high at its highest point, is a US national wildlife refuge. Permission to visit, which is very difficult to obtain, must be secured from the controlling agency in Hawai'i.

Tokelau

The three small atolls of Tokelau (the name is a Polynesian word for the north wind) lie in a rough line 480km north of their nearest neighbour, Samoa. The three atolls are separated not only from the rest of the world but from each other; it is 92km between Nukunonu and Atafu, and 64km between Nukunonu and Fakaofo.

Each of the atolls is a ribbon of tiny *motu* (islands) surrounding a lagoon. Tokelau's people, about 500 per atoll, crowd into one small village perched on the main motu of each atoll – although Fakaofo Atoll has a smaller cluster of homes on a second island. These three atolls house a small population of hardy souls living what amounts to a subsistence lifestyle.

Facts about Tokelau

HISTORY
The atolls of Tokelau have been populated by Polynesians for about 1000 years, and traditional tales link the original settlers with Samoa, the Cook Islands and Tuvalu.

Tokelau was no more than a collection of fiercely independent atolls until the Tokelau wars of the 18th century. Fakaofo conquered Atafu and Nukunonu, bringing them under the rule of the god Tui Tokelau and creating the first united entity of Tokelau. Soon afterwards, Tokelau came to the attention of those sailing by on various English and US ships. Whalers frequented the group in the 1820s, and in the middle of the 19th century missionary groups started paying attention to the spiritual wellbeing of the Tokelauans. Catholic Samoan missionaries converted the people of Nukunonu Atoll in the 1840s and Protestant Samoans converted Atafu in 1858. The two groups later battled for the souls of Fakaofo.

The French missionary Pierre Bataillon transported 500 reluctant Tokelauans to Wallis Island in the 1850s because he feared they would otherwise die of starvation, and

Peruvian slave traders seized about 250 of the atolls' population in the 1860s. Together, missionaries, slaving and disease reduced Tokelau's population to 200. At the request of the Tokelauans themselves, the UK annexed the group in 1889 into the Gilbert & Ellice Islands Colony (see History in the Kiribati and Tuvalu chapters).

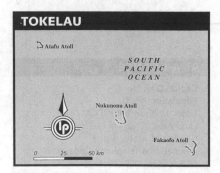

TOKELAU

Atafu Atoll

SOUTH PACIFIC OCEAN

Nukunonu Atoll

Fakaofo Atoll

0   25   50 km

In the early 20th century, large numbers of Tokelauans left their homes to work the phosphate mines of Banaba (Ocean Island) in the Gilbert & Ellice Islands. After New Zealand (NZ) took over responsibility for Tokelau in 1925, the flow of emigration shifted to Western Samoa (then also a NZ territory). Samoa's independence in 1962 prompted Tokelauans to shift to NZ instead.

In recent years Tokelau has been moving towards independence, with government and administration increasingly based in Tokelau itself instead of in NZ and Samoa. To make this possible, recent improvements in infrastructure have included a reliable telephone system and an inter-atoll ferry.

GEOGRAPHY

The three atolls of Tokelau (Atafu, Fakaofo and Nukunonu) are classic coral atolls: thin necklaces of small islets surrounding central lagoons (see the boxed text 'Coral Atolls' in the Facts about the South Pacific chapter). Like all coral atolls, Tokelau's soil is thin, infertile and holds water poorly.

The low-lying islands have a maximum elevation of only 5m above sea level, and the land area is tiny: only 12.2 sq km over

all three atolls. No islets are more than 200m wide.

CLIMATE

Tokelau's climate is tropical, with an average temperature of 28°C and heavy but irregular rainfall. Tokelau is at the northern limit of the South Pacific cyclone zone, so tropical storms are rare. However, cyclones Ofa (1990) and Val (1991) caused extensive damage. See the Tokelau climate chart in the appendix to this book.

Consisting of low-lying coral atolls, Tokelau faces great risk from global warming. It is possible that all three atolls will be uninhabitable by the end of the 21st century! See the boxed text 'Global Warming' in the Facts about the South Pacific chapter.

GOVERNMENT

Tokelau's local government is composed of the three village councils (called the *taupulega*) comprising the male heads *(matai)* of each family group. Each atoll elects a village mayor *(pulenuku)* as well as one atoll representative *(faipule)*. A number of delegates from each atoll serve with the pulenuku and the faipule on Tokelau's legislative council, the General Fono. The three faipule form the cabinet, and one of their number becomes Tokelau's head of government *(Ulu o Tokelau)* on a rotating basis.

Tokelau is a non-selfgoverning territory under NZ administration. The United Nations (UN) has long been pushing the Tokelauans towards full independence however, with substantial financial assistance, easy access to NZ schools and free emigration to relieve the pressure of over crowding, many Tokelauans prefer their current status. Negotiations with NZ and the UN continue towards increasing autonomy.

ECONOMY

Foreign aid from NZ forms the bulk of Tokelau's economy: NZ$4 million per year or NZ$2700 per head, which swamps the gross domestic product of NZ$1.2 million. Exports are minimal: stamps, coins and some handicrafts bring in a meagre income. Revenue is also raised by selling licences to

Population & Area

Atoll	Pop	Land	Lagoon
Atafu	499	3.5 sq km	17 sq km
Fakaofo	578	4 sq km	50 sq km
Nukunonu	430	4.7 sq km	98 sq km

Guardian Spirits

Each of Tokelau's three atolls has one special blessing setting it apart from the other two atolls. On Fakaofo Atoll it is fresh water; Fakaofo has the best reserves of fresh groundwater under the coral. Nukunonu's particular blessing is its pandanus trees *(kie)*, from which the fibres are used for weaving. Atafu's blessing is its stands of *kanava* trees, whose wood is an excellent building material for houses and canoes.

A favourite Tokelauan story tells how Fakaofo got its special blessing – a spirit from Fakaofo stole the fresh water from Nukunonu. In revenge, a Nukunonu spirit stole Fakaofo's pandanus. Fakaofo, historically the most aggressive of the atolls, represents men in this story; while Nukunonu represents women, as pandanus weaving is a woman's task. Following the Tokelau wars (see the History section), Atafu, whose entire population had fled the atoll, was repopulated by a Fakaofo man (Tonuia) and a Nukunonu woman.

Years later, Tonuia's death was caused by Atafu's sacred kanava trees. Tonuia defied instructions not to touch certain kanava trees, so he was killed at sea by two female spirits.

sh in Tokelau's Exclusive Economic Zone EZ). Tokelau's isolation adds to the country's financial woes – telecommunications nd transport cost 25% of the yearly budget. ll medical supplies, equipment and many oodstuffs are imported.

The public service is the main source of egular income for Tokelauans; these jobs re rotated among villagers and a village ax is imposed on wages. The other major ource of income is from the *aumaga*, or illage workforce (see Society & Conduct). Payment for aumaga work, which as traditionally unpaid, provides an income for young Tokelauans who would therwise have to look overseas for work. emittances from Tokelauan relatives living overseas is another source of income.

OPULATION & PEOPLE

here are approximately 500 people on each f Tokelau's three atolls. Tokelauans are olynesian, closely related to Tuvaluans, amoans and Cook Islanders. A liberal prinkling of European surnames in the lands is the legacy of some enthusiastic halers and beachcombers of the late 19th entury.

Land shortages have long forced emigrations from Tokelau, and many now live in amoa and NZ. In fact there are almost 000 Tokelauans in NZ – three times as any as in Tokelau itself!

EDUCATION

Three schools (one on each atoll) provide primary and secondary education, and many youngsters receive government scholarships to study in NZ, Fiji, Samoa, Tonga or Niue. Adult education programs are conducted to improve awareness of health, environmental and dietary issues.

SOCIETY & CONDUCT

Tokelau's isolation from the rest of the world, as well as NZ's 'hands-off' approach to administration, has resulted in *faka Tokelau* (the Tokelauan way) being preserved to a far greater degree than indigenous culture has been elsewhere in the Pacific. However, the large numbers of Tokelauans living abroad has resulted in an ever-increasing awareness of the benefits of modern *palagi* (western) culture – whether perceived or real.

Partly because of the difficulty of travel between the atolls, Tokelau society is still compartmentalised into the three atolls and their single village. The one name describes both the atoll and the village: eg Atafu Atoll/Atafu village. Village unity *(maopoopo)* is paramount in Tokelau. Beyond that, villages are divided into two *faitu* – or sides – on a roughly territorial basis. The two sides compete enthusiastically in fishing, action songs, dancing, sports and, most importantly, in *kilikiti* (see Spectator Sports later in this chapter). Each family group

TOKELAU

Work Well Done

In times past, when a cash economy was unknown in Tokelau, contributing to the unpaid village work force (aumaga) was compulsory. Even if too old to assist with manual work, elders were expected to be present and would suffer subtle community rebuke if they were absent without good reason.

Accompanying fishermen in their canoes would be inconvenient for all, so elders waited on the beach to offer praise and comment when canoes returned. If the aumaga was busy on land, elders could watch the men at work, occasionally offering the ritual encouragement 'malo te galue' (work well done), to which the stylised response was 'malo te tapuaki' (encouragement well given).

(kau kaiga) is led by the senior male, or matai.

The elderly are awarded enormous respect in Tokelau, with the three taupulega (village councils of elders and matai) ordering daily life. Elders are still expected to contribute to the community; both through attendance at the taupulega and by encouraging the younger workers at their tasks.

Each village taupulega administers the aumaga (workforce), which gathers fish, harvests crops and maintains village buildings. Almost all males over school age, except for public servants, join the aumaga. The female equivalent is the komiti a fafine (women's committee), whose responsibilities include inspections to ensure village cleanliness and health.

Under Tokelau's socialist inati (sharing) system, resources are divided between families according to need. Inati still operates – each day the village's catch of fish is laid out on the beach and apportioned by the taupulega – but it is under increasing pressure from the cash economy. Steps have been taken to ensure that employed Tokelauans, mainly public servants, do not receive unfair benefits though this principle of sharing.

The inati system grew from necessity in an environment where resources are scarce, community cooperation is vital. Individualism is not a virtue in these circumstances, nor is it really an option. Neither is privacy: Tokelau's islands are cramped beyond belief. On Fakaofo Atoll even with emigration to NZ and the large island of Fenuafala relieving some of the population pressure, there are still some 40 people living on tiny (4 hectare) Fale island. Fale's population density, one of the highest in the Pacific, is such that the island's numerous domestic pigs (puaka) live on the reef rather than on land.

There are only nine police officers in Tokelau, and no imprisonment system. In Tokelau's closely knit society, punishment takes the form of public rebukes, fines or labour.

Dos & Don'ts

Tokelau is a staunchly Christian country – the percentage of the population that does not belong to one of the two main churches is tiny – so criticising Christianity will not win you any friends. Sunday is devoted almost entirely to church activities, with some time off for a large meal and a midday snooze. If you attend church yourself you'll be better accepted by the community – and it will give you something to do on Sunday. Work and many activities are forbidden on Atafu and Fakaofo on Sunday. Nukunonu is less strict.

A conservative dress code is appropriate in all of the villages. Wearing bikinis or other skimpy swimwear is considered rude and should be saved for the outer islets.

Resources are scarce in Tokelau, so don't help yourself to things like coconuts. Tokelauan society is very similar to Samoa – see Dos & Don'ts in that chapter for more pointers.

RELIGION

Prior to Christianity, Tokelauans worshipped a god called Tui Tokelau – personified in a slab of coral still standing in Fakaofo's village. The usual pantheon of Polynesian gods was acknowledged here, too.

The Tokelauan Fale

The traditional Tokelauan *fale* (house) has all but disappeared. Following damage from cyclones Ofa and Val, new housing was built with sturdy concrete in the hope that modern materials would withstand future cyclones more successfully than the traditional coral pebbles and *kanava*. With rain run-off from roofs being the major source of fresh drinking water, pandanus-leaf thatching has given way to corrugated iron as a roofing material.

More traditional Atafu still has a number of traditional *fale*, partly because that atoll has a better supply of the excellent building wood, kanava.

The largest and most ornate building on each atoll is the church, or three churches in Fakaofo's case. Other community focal points are the village cricket pitch and the village hall *(fale fono)*. Tokelau's three *fale fono* are radically different from each other, ranging from Fakaofo's traditional open-sided *fale* to Nukunonu's pragmatic cargo shed.

❋ ❋ ❋ ❋ ❋ ❋ ❋ ❋ ❋ ❋ ❋ ❋

Tokelau's modern religious distribution reflects the arrival of Samoan missionaries of different denominations during the 19th century: Atafu is almost completely Protestant, Nukunonu is largely Catholic, and Fakaofo, where Catholic and Protestant missionaries arrived almost simultaneously, is split between the two faiths. Even in Fakaofo, though, inter-denominational conflict is rare, as it runs contrary to the supreme concept of village unity (maopoopo).

LANGUAGE

Tokelauan is a Polynesian language, closely related to Tuvaluan and Samoan. Because of frequent contact with NZ, most Tokelauans speak some English – and some 100 New Zealanders speak Tokelauan.

Tokelauan pronunciation is similar to other Polynesian languages, except that 'f' is pronounced as a soft 'wh', and 'g' is pronounced 'ng' (a soft sound).

Tokelauan Basics

Hello.	*Malo ni* or *taloha.*
Goodbye.	*Tofaa.*
How are you?	*Ea mai koe?*
I'm well.	*Ko au e lelei.*
Please.	*Faka molemole.*
Thank you.	*Faka fetai.*
Yes.	*Io.*
No.	*Heai.*

Facts for the Visitor

PLANNING

The best months to travel to Tokelau are from April to October. Between November and January ships are usually full of scholarship students and other Tokelauans living abroad, returning to spend Christmas with their families. December to March is cyclone season, when the trip from Samoa could be rough.

VISITOR PERMITS

The Tokelau Apia Liaison Office (TALO) in Samoa (see Useful Organisations later in this section) issues visitor permits. Accommodation must be arranged prior to departure (either at a hotel or with a local family) and a return ticket to Samoa must be booked. Also, consent must be given by the village taupulega. A visitor permit for a one month stay in Tokelau costs NZ$20.

MONEY

Tokelauan coinage is largely aimed at the collector market. The NZ dollar (see Exchange Rates in the Regional Facts for the Visitor chapter) and the Samoan tala (see the Samoa chapter) are used instead. There are no banks in Tokelau.

COMMUNICATIONS

As part of the improved infrastructure necessary for independence, Tokelau was connected with the international phone system in 1994. The telephone code is ☎ 690.

BOOKS

Judith Huntsman & Antony Hooper's huge *Tokelau – A Historical Ethnography* is the

TOKELAU

Tokelau Telephones

While septic tanks are becoming more common in Tokelau, most people still make use of small huts perched above the lagoon. Such huts serve more than one purpose; they are a common meeting venue, and several men (or women) will gather in the one hut to swap gossip and discuss the busy day's events. This is why they're called 'Tokelau telephones'.

The Tokelau telephones have an obvious drawback. The atolls' lagoons are already under ecological pressure: garbage disposal directly into the lagoon is common (despite education programs encouraging composting and recycling) and the toilet huts add to this waste. Tokelau's telephones will eventually be phased out, their two functions replaced by sewerage tanks and modern telecommunications.

definitive text about Tokelau, telling you all you ever wanted to know about Tokelau and its people. With Allan Thomas & Ineleo Tuia, Huntsman has also compiled an interesting collection of tales called *Songs and Stories of Tokelau – An Introduction to the Cultural Heritage*. More easily found than either of these books is Neville Peat's short *Tokelau – Atoll Associate of New Zealand*.

ELECTRICITY

The power supply (240V AC; 50 Hz; two or three-pin plugs of the Australian/NZ style) is dependent on community-owned, diesel-operated generators that in turn are dependent on parts brought in on the infrequent cargo ship from Apia. Power outages are not uncommon.

USEFUL ORGANISATIONS

In Samoa, the Tokelau Apia Liaison Office (TALO; ☎ 20822 or ☎ 71805, fax 21761), PO Box 865, Apia, should be the first port of call for all inquiries. It handles bookings on the monthly cargo ship (see Getting There & Around, later in this chapter) and visitor permits.

In NZ, the Tokelau Office (☎ 04-49 8514) is at the Ministry of Foreign Affair & Trade, Private Bag 18-901, Wellington.

ACTIVITIES

Diving inside the atolls' lagoons is fantasti There is almost nothing in the way of searc and rescue facilities though, so diving ou side the reef should be undertaken with max imum caution. Talk to the locals to find o where the safest diving spots can be foun The nearest decompression chamber is so fa away (Fiji) that it might as well be on Mar

Ask the local men whether you can ac company them on fishing trips, but be awar that they are working and won't always b able to accommodate your wishes.

You probably couldn't drop kick a rugb ball from the sea to the lagoon across mos of the islands, but trying will give yo something to fill your days.

FOOD

The traditional method of cooking in Toke lau, most popular on Fakaofo, is the eart oven or *umu*, which will be familiar to any one who has spent some time in the Pacifi Most households, however, cook o kerosene stoves. The traditional diet of fish *kumala* (sweet potato), breadfruit, taro, pig and fowl is supplemented by processe foods brought in on the monthly cargo shi to the village-owned co-op stores. Canne meat, which will also be familiar to an Pacific traveller, is in plentiful supply.

DRINK

As on all coral atolls, fresh water is scarce The porous coral soil drains quickly, so de spite the heavy rainfall there are fe groundwater reserves except on Fakaof Instead, rainwater is collected from roof into rain-water tanks. Tank water tends t taste somewhat brackish, perhaps explainin the preference for 'cold stuff' (beer). Coco nuts are plentiful, but make sure you hav permission before grabbing one to drin from; such resources are limited in Tokela

Cold stuff, when available, is sold at th co-op stores on Fakaofo and Nukunonu. I sale is strictly rationed on more-traditiona tafu Atoll. Tokelau's isolation means that supplies of *hostuff* ('hot stuff'; spirits) and old stuff can be unreliable. *Kaleve*, made from fermented coconut sap, is also drunk.

ENTERTAINMENT
There is not much in the way of a night-club culture in Tokelau. In fact, as any young Tokelauan who has spent some time in NZ will tell you, life in Tokelau can be pretty dull. However, community discos are popular on all three atolls – involving cold stuff, loud music and dancing.

Although gambling for money is illegal, weekly bingo games are extremely popular with women. Prizes include boxes of washing powder and bottles of shampoo.

SPECTATOR SPORTS
Tokelauans play similar sports to those played in Samoa and NZ. Rugby and netball are popular. In the Polynesian form of village cricket (called kilikiti in Tokelau; see the boxed text 'It's Not Just Cricket' in the Samoa chapter), each side fields as many players as are available – 50 per side is not uncommon. A shot into the ocean or lagoon is a confirmed 'six'.

Getting There & Around

Isolated Tokelau has no airstrip, so the only way to get there is by sea. A monthly cargo ship, the *Forum Tokelau*, from Apia in Samoa is the only way travellers without their own yacht can get to Tokelau. Because of the hazards of anchoring, yachting to Tokelau is no easier.

Cargo Ship
Bookings on the monthly *Forum Tokelau* are made through the TALO (see Useful Organisations earlier in this chapter). Allow plenty of time to process your booking, and be aware that tourists are a lower priority than locals.

The trip to Fakaofo (the closest atoll to Samoa) takes about 36 hours, and travellers have a choice between cabin fare (NZ$528 return) and deck fare (NZ$286). In either case there will be plenty of company on the voyage, as Tokelauans from Samoa and NZ return to Tokelau to see their families.

There is no harbour on any of the atolls. The ship waits offshore while passengers and cargo are transferred via small boats and dinghies: a hair-raising experience if seas are heavy.

Apparently, the *Forum Tokelau* 'sometimes' sails to the northern Cook Islands. Check this with TALO and don't plan your life around it.

Yacht
Seek advice about the voyage to Tokelau from someone who has been there, and see the introductory Getting Around the Region chapter for more information about sailing in the Pacific.

Tokelau's atolls are low-lying and make difficult visual targets. There are no harbours and anchoring offshore is difficult, especially in an offshore wind. The sea floor drops off sharply outside the coral reef and the water is too deep for most anchor chains. There is one anchorage beyond the reefs at each atoll, but leave a crew member aboard in case the anchor doesn't hold. The channels blasted through the coral are shallow and are intended for dinghies only.

If you're heading to Tokelau on your own yacht you still need to apply for a visitor permit (see that section) in Apia.

Getting Around
Unlike their ancestors, modern Tokelauans are forbidden to travel independently between Tokelau's three atolls; the potential for broken-down outboard motors to cause loss is deemed too risky. The *Tu Tolu*, a large purpose-built catamaran, travels between the atolls fortnightly and this is the only method of crossing from one atoll to another (for a small charge).

Travel between islands on an atoll is usually accomplished with a small aluminium dinghy, although more-traditional *kanava* outrigger canoes are still preferred on Atafu.

TOKELAU

Atafu, Fakaofo & Nukunonu

Information

There are minimal facilities on the atolls. Each has a small co-op store (closed weekends) supplying basic needs. There is a hospital on each atoll, but serious health problems can easily become life threatening. Medical supplies are difficult to come by and specialist care is days away in Apia.

Places to Stay & Eat

Accommodation must be arranged prior to your arrival in Tokelau (see Visitor Permits). There are a limited number of official places to stay in Tokelau. You may be able to arrange accommodation in a private home but it won't be easy without contacts on the appropriate atoll.

Nukunonu is a relative goldmine of options, with *two* places to stay. Hete Perez manages the *Luana Liki Hotel (☎ 4140)*, a family-run hotel with six rooms for guests. The Nukunonu village runs the *Fale Fa Resort (☎ 4139)*. Inquiries should be directed to Iosefa Aselemo, the village clerk.

On Atafu, master fisherman Feleti Lopa runs a small *accommodation house (☎ 2146, fax 2108)*. The Fakaofo village may soon open a small hotel there.

Confirm the rates with TALO in Apia. Despite the optimistic names, these are not flash tourist resorts. Facilities are basic; all that is provided is a bed, meals and a bar.

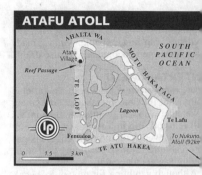

ATAFU ATOLL

Only one island (or two in the case Fakaofo) is occupied at each atoll. Some the more remote islets are quiet retrea where, if you have a tent, the days can passed camping out or just sitting under t trees contemplating life. This shouldn't viewed just as a cheap accommodation o tion, though. All the islands are owned either a family or the village, and it's i portant to get permission to visit. Howeve this is an option you could consider claustrophobic village life is getting ye down.

Restaurants Only joking! If you're sta ing with one of the establishments list above, or with a local family, your fo needs will be looked after. Processed fo (and other supplies) can be bought from t small co-op stores on each atoll. Supplies fresh fish, vegetables and drinking cocon should be negotiated with someone fro the taupulega.

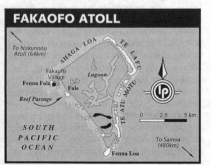

FAKAOFO ATOLL

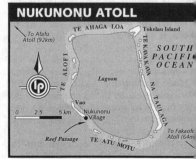

NUKUNONU ATOLL

TOKELAU

How the Islands Formed

The Traditional Version

Tuvalu's islands were created by the mythological beings Te Pusi (The Eel) and Te Ali (The Flounder). They were trying to carry home a heavy rock, however the friendly competition of strength turned into a fight. Te Pusi, who had magic powers, turned Te Ali flat, like the islands of Tuvalu, and made himself round like the coconut trees. Te Pusi threw the rock, which was coloured black, white and blue, into the air – and there it stayed. With a magic spell it fell down but a blue part remained above to form the sky. Te Pusi threw it up again, and its black side faced down, forming night. With another spell the rock fell down on its white side and formed day. Te Pusi broke the rest of the rock into eight pieces, forming the eight islands of Tuvalu. With a final spell he threw the remaining pieces of blue stone and formed the sea.

The Scientific Version

After his Pacific voyages in 1835-36, Charles Darwin proposed that coral atolls were were built on slowly sinking volcanic rock, which at the same time was being built up by new deposits of coral. The subsidence theory explained why coral rock was found at depths far greater than those at which coral polyps can survive (deeper than about 40m). See the boxed text 'Coral Atolls' in the Facts about the South Pacific chapter. Darwin's theory was controversial at the time – others believed that the reefs grew on underwater platforms that had been raised by volcanic action.

Darwin proposed that a coral atoll be drilled for samples and Tuvalu achieved fame in the scientific world when the Royal Society of London sent expeditions to Funafuti. After three 'boring' expeditions, in 1898 scientists managed to obtain atoll core samples from 340m below the surface. When analysed back in London, they showed traces of shallow water organisms, thus supporting Darwin's hypothesis. It was fifty years later, on Eniwetok in Micronesia in 1952, before it was possible to drill to a depth of 1290m, right through the coral structure and actually reach volcanic rock.

As part of the traditional Polynesian religion, people were occasionally sacrificed to honour the gods and ancestor spirits. Each *sologa* (family) had a particular specialty or community responsibility, such as building, fishing and farming, healing, dancing and singing, or defence. Knowledge and skills were passed down by word of mouth and it was *tapu* (taboo) to leak this information to other families.

Land was considered a family's most valuable asset and was passed down through the male side of the family. Communal lands were set aside to support and maintain those in need. Once married, a woman became part of her husband's family. As long as he could maintain his family, a man could marry as many women as he liked.

Outside Influences

The Spanish explorer Alvaro de Mendaña sighted the islands in 1568, but the first European contact wasn't until 1781, with another Spaniard, Francisco Antonio Mourelle, at Niutao. In 1819 an American explorer, De Peyster, named Funafuti 'Ellice's Island', after an English politician friend. By the 1830s all of the islands had been charted.

In the 1820s whalers and other traders began to visit the islands, and traditional Tuvaluan society began to change with the introduction of alcohol, money and new tools and goods. The aliki were seen to lose their *mana* (power) as people lost respect for their leaders' often drunk and disorderly behaviour. While most *palagi* ('pah-lung-ee'; white people) lived peacefully with the

TUVALU

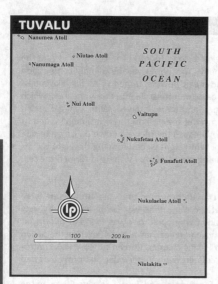

TUVALU

Nanumea Atoll

Niutao Atoll

Nanumaga Atoll

SOUTH PACIFIC OCEAN

Nui Atoll

Vaitupu

Nukufetau Atoll

Funafuti Atoll

Nukulaelae Atoll

0   100   200 km

Niulakita

islanders, many earned a reputation of being dishonest and possessive. This opinion worsened in 1863 when 'blackbirders' (slavers; see History in the Facts about the South Pacific chapter) raided the southern islands for labourers for the Peruvian guano mines. They were aided by a resident American beachcomber, who coaxed the islanders on to the ship by promising knowledge of Christianity. The blackbirders succeeded in taking 250 people from Nukalaelae and 171 from Funafuti.

The Samoan missionaries from the London Missionary Society (LMS) who arrived in 1865, had an even greater impact. They managed to oust the traditional religion while building on its influence. The new pastors began to dominate the aliki and take over their positions of authority and privilege. The Tuvaluan language was represented with Samoan orthography and sermons were delivered in Samoan. Ancestral shrines were replaced by churches, new laws were introduced, and polygamy and sacrifices were forbidden. Use of the men's narrow woven pandanus loincloth was suppressed. The quick rhythmic dancing of the *fakanau* was banned by pastors who

regarded it as sexually stimulating and 'evil' dancing. The custom of 'night-creeping' (nocturnal visits by courting males to young women's houses) was discouraged.

In 1886 the imperial powers of Britain and Germany divided up most of the western and central Pacific, each claiming a 'sphere of influence'. Tuvalu fell within British 'influence', along with Kiribati and the southern Solomon Islands.

On Funafuti, in September 1892, the British representative, Captain Gibson, met with the elders and the resident missionary who agreed to Tuvalu becoming a British protectorate. By this time the traditional power structure had lost most of its influence but not all were happy with Britain claiming their islands. Tuvalu was incorporated into the Gilbert & Ellice Islands Protectorate, partly to deter US influence in the area. Thus Tuvalu and Kiribati (and later Tokelau), although ethnically and culturally different, were arbitrarily joined. See the Kiribati chapter and the boxed text 'Independence for Tuvalu' in this chapter for more about the Gilbert & Ellice union.

In 1894 the foreign authority introduced new laws, including the banning of sour toddy (the local coconut brew) and working on Sunday.

The Colonial Period

Due to the wealth generated by phosphate mining on Banaba (Ocean Island in modern-day Kiribati), in 1916 Britain raised the status of the Gilbert & Ellice Island to Crown colony. Between 1900 and 1979 an average of 200 Tuvaluans were employed on Banaba at any given time, on two-year work contracts. Phosphate mining was hard work and in 1926 the entire Tuvaluan labour force went on strike for higher wages; everyone was repatriated.

Laws imposed on the colony became increasingly strict and paternalistic, however there was little direct palagi influence. Authoritarian boarding schools were established by DG Kennedy, a New Zealand (NZ) schoolteacher who arrived in 1923. He also introduced the *fusi* (island co-op stores) and radio, and served as district officer until

1939. In 1930 regulations were imposed on dancing, feasting, domestic animals and night fishing – even sleeping in an eating house attracted a fine.

During WWII, Tuvaluan workers were trapped on Banaba when the Japanese invaded. From Kiribati the Japanese had intended to move south to Tuvalu. US forces set up base on Funafuti and also had airfields at Nukefetau and Nanumea in the north. From this strategic location the USA was able to bomb Japanese bases in Kiribati, Nauru and the Marshall Islands. There were more than 6000 Americans in Tuvalu at this time.

The locals of Fongafale were shifted to Funafala and Papaelise islets for the duration of the war, and contact between camp and village was controlled. Funafuti was attacked nine times during 1943, although few people were killed. On 23 April 1943, 680 people hid in the Funafuti church until an American soldier persuaded them to shelter in the dugouts. Ten minutes later the church was blasted. Generally though, islanders gained material benefits from the occupation and saw the war as an exciting time.

Postwar changes were significant. Some islanders chose to leave their overcrowded islands and use their war compensation money to migrate. Some of the people of Nanumaga shifted to Tonga and the Carolines. Others moved from Vaitupu to Kioa in Fiji. The colony headquarters was set up at Tarawa in the Gilberts (Kiribati) and many Tuvaluans went there for work or study.

In response to UN calls for decolonisation, the first House of Representatives was established in 1967. Representation of Kiribati outnumbered Tuvalu by 18 to five, and Tuvaluans felt that their islands were being neglected. Wary of remaining joined to Kiribati as a minority group in an independent country, Tuvaluans overwhelmingly supported separation in a 1974 referendum.

Independence

Tuvalu separated from Kiribati in 1975, becoming a British dependency with its own government. The country, however, was virtually bankrupt on separation. While Tuvalu's

TUVALU

Independence for Tuvalu

The Gilbert & Ellice islands' union was largely an artificial construct of British rule. While Tarawa's independence movement was growing in the mid-1960s, Ellice Islanders began agitating strongly for their own independence. The Ellice feared that the more populous Gilbert Islands would have greater political clout. This became apparent in the 1967 House of Representatives, when the Gilberts were allotted 18 seats and the Ellice just five. The Gilbertese, meanwhile, resented the Ellice Islanders' disproportionate hold on civil service positions.

In a 1974 referendum, Ellice Islanders voted overwhelmingly for separation from the Gilberts. Official separation came in October 1975, though administration remained under Tarawa until 1 January 1976. In 1975-76, Ellice Islanders departed Tarawa en mass for their homeland, though a few hundred remain today on Tarawa.

On 1 October 1978 the Ellice Islands became the independent nation of Tuvalu.

people wanted British support they also wanted the freedom to negotiate foreign aid from other countries. So in 1978 Tuvalu became an independent constitutional monarchy; England's Queen Elizabeth II is the head of state, represented by a governor general.

Aid money came flowing in. The Funafuti hospital was built in 1978 with NZ aid, and in 1981 the deep-water wharf and cargo storage facilities were built with Australian money. In 1987 Australia, NZ and the UK, together contributed A$24.7 million for a Tuvalu Trust Fund. Earnings from this fund average A$2.6 million annually. Taiwan financed the new Vaiaku Lagi Hotel, completed in 1993, and there is currently a French aid project at the Nauti primary school. Tuvalu has also come up with some interesting money-making schemes as it attempts to survive on its meagre resources (see the boxed text 'The .tv Get-Rich-Quick Scheme' later in this chapter).

GEOGRAPHY & ECOLOGY

Tuvalu is an archipelago of seven coral atolls and two islands spread over 800km of ocean. Funafuti, the capital, is about 1100km north of Fiji, and the northern islands are about 250km south of Kiribati. Funafuti, Nukufetau, Nanumea, Nui and Nukulaelae are classic atolls, each with a continuous rim of reef at or near the water surface surrounding a lagoon. The others are single coral islands with only land-locked lagoons or swamp. With a total land area of only 26 sq km, Tuvalu is one of the world's smallest countries. The highest land is a mere 5m above sea level.

As an atoll nation, the major ecological threat to Tuvalu comes from global warming (see the boxed text in the Facts about the South Pacific chapter) and rising sea levels.

More locally, nearly half the population is squeezed on the narrow Fongafale Islet, one of the islands of Funafuti Atoll. With a rapidly increasing population, and the movement away from traditional resource conservation and subsistence to a cash economy, there is concurrent environmental degradation (see the boxed text 'Funafuti's Fragile Environment' later in this chapter). Changes in eating habits and an increasing dependence on packaged imports, have led to severe garbage disposal problems on all of the inhabited atolls and islands.

CLIMATE

Tuvalu has a tropical maritime climate. The temperature varies little throughout the year, ranging mostly from 28 to 31°C. Rainfall is high, up to 3500mm in the south (including Funafuti), and is usually brief and heavy. The wettest season is between November and February. From May to October winds are light and from the south-east (the trade winds) changing to west-northwest during the 'cyclone season' (November to April). While Tuvalu is considered just outside the tropical cyclone belt, there were severe cyclones in 1894, 1972 and 1990. Three bad cyclones (Gavin, Hina and Keli) hit Tuvalu during the last El Niño period (March 1997 to April 1998) with heavy rains and strong winds. The increased frequency of cyclones

has been linked (although inconclusively) with global warming.

FLORA & FAUNA

Tuvalu's infertile atoll soils support coconut palms, pandanus, salt-tolerant ferns and some atoll scrub. Mangrove areas are rare. There are about 50 endemic plant species. Cultivated plants include banana, cassava, taro and breadfruit. Vegetation has an important role in foreshore protection and degradation is quite severe. Large tree species traditionally used for canoes and building are rare in many areas.

Marine life is diverse, with dolphins and manta rays commonly seen in the Funafuti lagoon. Turtles born in Tuvalu migrate to other Pacific countries and return to lay their eggs. There are some indigenous birds, insects, lizards, frogs and land crabs, but no native land mammals. Rats, domestic dogs, cats and pigs have been introduced. Many protected bird species are still commonly eaten on the outer islands. Wildlife within the Funafuti Conservation Area is protected.

GOVERNMENT & POLITICS

Tuvalu has a Westminster-style parliamentary democracy with a 12 member elected parliament and a four year term. In April 1999 Prime Minister Bikenibeu Paeniu was ousted by a vote of no confidence. He was replaced by Ionatana Ionatana. Each island is represented in the parliament and has its own *falekaupule* (island council).

ECONOMY

Most of the population relies on subsistence farming and fishing, and each island has a fusi (co-op store). Apart from coconuts and pandanus, there are limited crops. Money is increasingly important as people become more reliant on imported food, petroleum building materials and manufactured goods mostly from Australia and Fiji. Most paid jobs are with the government.

Income is derived from the sale of stamps, the sale of fishing licences to foreign ships, copra exports and returns on money invested in the Tuvalu Trust Fund. Remittances from Tuvaluans overseas

The .tv Get-Rich-Quick Scheme

Tuvalu has seen some novel money making schemes. In the late 1970s government money was tied up with speculative American land developers, and in the late 1990s the government was making millions by leasing out unused telephone lines to international providers. There was a setback when it was discovered the lines were being used for sex chat, presenting a moral problem for the strongly Christian Tuvaluans.

But never mind! Thanks to technological wonders, in 1998 the government contracted a Canadian company to market Tuvalu's rights of its Internet suffix '.tv'. It was thought that companies worldwide, mostly television networks, would pay big money for the rights. Figures thrown around (up to an annual revenue of US$100 million) proved overly optimistic. Euphoria turned to bitter disappointment when, by the end of 1998 the total revenue generated by the company was only about US$200,000 – well under the promised advance payment of US$50 million. In May 1999 the deal with the Canadian company collapsed, but the government is pursuing negotiations for a similar deal with other companies.

Meanwhile, Tuvalu has some other interesting projects in mind, such as the licensing of Tuvalu's upper airspace, and the sale of Tuvaluan passports in return for investment in the country.

mostly seamen employed on international ships or phosphate miners on Nauru, also contribute. Tuvalu is remote and air fares are expensive, so there is very little tourism. Most of the 1000 or so annual overseas visitors are aid workers, consultants and government workers.

External aid, mainly from Australia, NZ, the European Union, Taiwan and Japan, is a major source of income. Australian aid to Tuvalu was expected to be A$2.9 million in 1998-99, most of it used in education and training. Taiwan is intending to fund the proposed $7 million, multi-storey government buildings in Vaiaku (Fongafale).

POPULATION & PEOPLE

Over 90% of Tuvaluans are of Polynesian origin, although most of Nui's 600 people have Micronesian ancestors. Tuvalu's 1998 resident population was estimated at 10,900 people, with 42% living on Funafuti and 58% spread over the rest of the country. Tuvaluans living overseas include about 750 contract workers on Nauru in the phosphate mining industry, a couple of hundred students and about 500 seamen.

Tuvalu has a very high population density, currently averaging 419 people per sq km over its tiny land area. The population is most concentrated in the capital, Funafuti, which has a density of about 1600 people per sq km! At the current growth rate of 1.7% per year, the population is expected to double in 41 years. When the phosphate runs out on Nauru and the workers return, the problem will only worsen.

Tuvalu has one the highest infant mortality rates of the region: 41 babies in 1000 die before their first birthdays.

EDUCATION

After separation from Kiribati, students started to go to Fiji for higher education, and there are now extension courses available through the University of the South Pacific (USP) on Funafuti. Education is free and compulsory; literacy is 93%. All islands have primary schools, but for high school the children have to board on Vaitupu.

ARTS

Traditional handicrafts are usually time-consuming and make imaginative use of limited materials. Expect to pay a bit more for intricately woven items of fine white *taa* (the youngest coconut leaves), the preparation of which is painstaking. It can take two women a day to prepare just a handful of the raw material. Dyes of red,

TUVALU

ROBYN JONES

Woven disks of cowrie shell and coconut fibre
decorate shell necklaces *(tuilili)*.

yellow, black and brown are obtained from
natural materials.

Pandanus sleeping, floor and ceremonial
mats are highly valued in Tuvaluan society.
The creation of ceremonial mats is often
competitive, producing imaginative, brightly coloured applied designs. Sitting mats
take up to a week to make, while sleeping
mats can take five to ten weeks.

Handicrafts include ornamental stars,
woven pandanus balls, model *fale* (traditional wooden thatch-roofed houses), model
canoes, shell necklaces, hairclasps, brightly
coloured dancing-skirts and woven fans of
varied design. Utilitarian items include
baskets and trays, carved fish hooks and
coconut-fibre rope. Wooden articles, such as
drums made from hollow trunks (similar to
the Fijian *lali*) and *toluma*, fishermen's round
tight-topped boxes, are now fairly rare.

Traditional song and dance are practised
on festive occasions in the *maneapa* (open-
air community meeting-halls). The dancers
wear pandanus-strip skirts and flower gar-
lands and use familiar Polynesian hand

movements. The accompanying music
drumming – banging on the floor or on
low wooden stand. The young, howeve
prefer international music and 'twists' (di
cos) at the nightclubs.

SOCIETY & CONDUCT

Tuvaluans traditionally live in fale, whi
have coral floors or raised wooden pla
forms. On Funafuti, however, most hom
are western style, inappropriately designe
for the climate. People usually have litt
furniture and few possessions apart fro
woven mats. Maneapa are the meetir
places where all special events are hel
Parliament sits at the large maneapa ne
the airport in Vaiaku.

Women spend much of their time o
handicrafts, especially weaving mats. Whe
a fale is being built in the village it is cor
mon for many women to contribute k
preparing thatching material. Both sex
enjoy wearing headdresses of flower
shells and coconut leaves, not just f
adornment but also for the perfume.

While much traditional culture has bee
retained, the family unit is being broke
down as people are attracted to the ca
economy on Funafuti. National indeper
dence and the accompanying dependenc
on foreign aid, has brought an increasir
number of palagi, mostly aid workers ar
volunteers. It is becoming more difficult
live by traditional subsistence fishing ar
agriculture in the high-density areas.

There are no longer chiefs in Tuvalu, b
certain families are privileged and influer
tial, and have greater access to money ar
further education. There is an increasir
economic divide between the relatively fe
wage-earning indigenous people (most
government workers) and the grass-ro
villagers. The remote outer islands see litt
of the overseas aid.

Dos & Don'ts

Traditionally men are allowed to do prett
much anything, but there are lots of rule
for women. Women should cover up t
below the knee or risk negative vibes fro
the old people. Unmarried girls usuall

bathe fully clothed or in shorts under a *sulu* (wraparound cloth or sarong).

There are many things to be aware of when visiting a maneapa. No-one should walk across the inner circle – traditionally women were not even allowed to enter or speak. The poles of a maneapa also have symbolic meaning and the place at either pole is reserved for important people. Sit down cross-legged, but never show the bottom of your feet or flash your thigh, and avoid walking in front of people.

When visiting a home leave your shoes at the door and try not to walk over the pandanus mats, especially the small ones which are used for sleeping.

When visiting an outer island it is customary to give presents to your hosts. Useful things such as groceries, clothing and toys are sure to be appreciated.

RELIGION
Traditional Tuvaluan religious beliefs were ousted by the Samoan missionaries who arrived in the 1860s. Church is the main event on Sunday, which is a day of rest. Most people (97% of the population) belong to the Protestant Church of Tuvalu (Ekalesia Kelisiano o Tuvalu), which is derived from the LMS. Seventh-Day Adventists account for another 1.4% of the population, followed by Baha'i at 1%.

Religion is especially influential on the outer islands. In the past every *mataniu* (family estate) had to supply goods and support for community projects. The old men and people in the maneapa would assess how much each was to contribute. It seems that the church has incorporated this tradition and it now demands money from parishioners for its projects.

LANGUAGE
English is widely spoken, especially on Funafuti. Tuvaluan is a Polynesian language closely related to Tokelauan. Tuvaluan uses 'l' where some Polynesian languages use 'r' - so the name for a chief, *ariki* in the Cook Islands, is aliki in Tuvalu. When missionaries put the language into written form they used Samoan orthography, so as in Samoa,

the letter 'g' is usually used for the soft 'ng' sound.

Tuvaluan Basics
Hello.	*Talofa.*
Goodbye.	*Tofa.*
How are you?	*E a koe?*
I'm well.	*Malosi.*
Please.	*Fakamolemole.*
Thank you.	*Fakafetai.*
Yes.	*Io* or *Ao.*
No.	*Ikai.*

Facts for the Visitor

SUGGESTED ITINERARIES
If you have plenty of time and feel adventurous, tackle a trip to the outer islands. While on Funafuti be sure to include a visit to the conservation area, and consider spending a couple of days on Funafala Islet.

PLANNING
You will probably need a few days to accept Funafuti for what it is, to start enjoying the laid-back pace and appreciate the culture. You need plenty of time and flexible plans to visit the outer islands. The boat timetable is notoriously unreliable, so you can easily get stranded for weeks – or even months!

Bring your own toiletries and medical supplies as availability is limited here and things often run out. Nappies (diapers) and sanitary pads are generally stocked, but not tampons. Photographers should take their own film and snorkellers their own gear.

Excellent maps of the atolls are available at the Lands & Survey Department (☎ 20 170), on Funafuti. Alternatively try the South Pacific Applied Geoscience Commission (SOPAC; ☎ 381 139, fax 370 040) in Suva, Fiji.

Tuvalu is relatively expensive, compared to neighbouring Fiji, and air fares are high.

TOURIST OFFICES
Tuvalu has little infrastructure for tourism. There are no tourist offices, but see Information in the Funafuti section. Tuvalu is represented abroad by the Tourism Council

of the South Pacific (see the Regional Facts for the Visitor chapter for offices).

VISAS & EMBASSIES

Visitors do not require a visa and are granted a one month entry permit on arrival. You need a valid passport and a return ticket – and a valid yellow fever certificate if you have come from an infected area. Visa extensions, available at immigration (☎ 20 706), are granted for a maximum of three months.

The only overseas consulate in Tuvalu is that of the Republic of China (Taiwan). Tuvalu has an embassy in Fiji (☎ 301 355, fax 301 023), 16 Gorrie St, PO Box 14449, Suva.

MONEY

Australian currency is the legal tender (see Exchange Rates in the Regional Facts for the Visitor chapter), but there are also Tuvaluan 5c, 10c, 20c, 50c and $1 coins. The National Bank on Funafuti is the country's only bank (see Money in the Funafuti section later). A 10% government tax on accommodation is included in prices listed in this chapter. Tipping isn't expected.

POST & COMMUNICATIONS

The capital, Funafuti, has a post office and the Tuvalu Philatelic Bureau. Postal rates are 60c to Australia and 90c to the USA, Europe and South America.

Tuvalu's international telephone code is ☎ 688.

The Funafuti Telecom office has a public fax (20 800) and telex (1800). International calls are sometimes difficult to connect. Calls per minute cost: Australia A$1.15; North America and Europe A$4; Fiji A$2. Local calls are 10c per minute and calls to outer islands 60c. Faxes cost $4, plus the regular per-minute telephone charge. There is no minimum charge using the direct dial international access code ☎ 00. For operator calls dial ☎ 012 for international; ☎ 010 for local. The capital has cardphones; phonecards come in A$2, $5, $10 and $20 value. The outer islands have phone operators 8 am to nnon and 1 to 4 pm on weekdays, 11 am to 2 pm weekends.

INTERNET RESOURCES

'Tuvalu Online', at http://members.xoo .com/tuvaluonline, is an excellent si with interesting links. It is produced by Canadian/Tuvaluan family, and has photo news headlines and general informatio about the country.

BOOKS

There are a few books about Tuvalu avai able at the USP (☎ 20 811, fax 20 704) o Funafuti. *Tuvalu, A History* (1983) wa written by a team of Tuvaluans with th assistance of the Institute of Pacific Studie USP. *The Material Culture of Tuval* (1961), by Gerd Koch, concentrates on th islands of Niutao and Nanumega. *Th Autobiography of Frank Pasefika* (1990) quite an interesting read. Try *Strateg Atolls, Tuvalu and the Second World Wa* (1994), by Peter McQuarrie, if you have special interest in WWII. Tuvaluan diction aries are available at the National Bank o Funafuti.

NEWSPAPERS & MAGAZINES

The Broadcasting and Information Offic (☎ 20 731, fax 20 732) on Funafuti pub lishes a monthly national newspaper i English and Tuvaluan – the *Tuvalu Echoes*

TIME

Tuvalu is 12 hours ahead of Greenwic Mean Time (GMT). When it's noon in Tu valu, it's noon the same day in Fiji, 10 a the same day in Sydney, Australia, and 2 p the previous day in Hawai'i.

RADIO & TV

Radio Tuvalu has programs in English an Tuvaluan. There is no local TV broadcast however videos are popular. In addition, 24 hour satellite TV service is available fre of charge to virtually anyone with a TV set

ELECTRICITY, WEIGHTS & MEASURES

The generator-supplied electricity supply i at 240V AC, 50 Hz.

Tuvalu officially uses the metric system although imperial units are still widel sed, especially by older people – it's a ood idea to be aware of this when inter- reting directions.

HEALTH

uvalu is malaria-free. Common health roblems include staphylococcal skin infec- ons, tuberculosis, filariasis, scabies and in- cted cuts. Always boil your drinking ater, or use bottled water. Groundwater is enerally brackish and rainwater is stored in dividual tanks. There is no organised sew- rage disposal.

Tuvalu's only hospital is on Funafuti. he outer islands have trained nurses, but ery limited facilities and drug supplies. ften patients have to wait months for ansport to Funafuti hospital, and compli- ated cases are referred to Fijian hospitals.

DANGERS & ANNOYANCES

e careful with your feet, both in and out of ne water! On Funafuti you are likely to ome across broken glass and open cans – nd some people use the beach as a public o. The rough exposed ocean side of the toll is very risky for swimming. Otherwise, ne only things to be careful of are the nopeds swerving along the potholed roads.

Inter-island ship transfers can be difficult see Getting Around later).

BUSINESS HOURS

Government offices are open weekdays 8 m to 4.15 pm (to 1 pm on Friday).

PUBLIC HOLIDAYS & SPECIAL EVENTS

n addition to New Year's Day, Easter, Christmas and Boxing Day (see Regional acts for the Visitor), Tuvalu celebrates:

unafuti Youth Day	11 February
Commonwealth Day	March
Bomb Day (Japanese bombing Funafuti)	23 April
Gospel Day	2nd Monday in May
Queen's Birthday	early June
Children's Day	early August
ndependence Day	early October

Hurricane Day (1972 Cyclone Bebe)	21 October
Prince Charles' Birthday	early November

ACTIVITIES

Once in Tuvalu, you have no option but to get into the slow swing of things since there is not much to do, and no reason to hurry! See Things to Do in the Funafuti section later.

ACCOMMODATION

Funafuti has one fairly ordinary hotel with nice lagoon views. Standards here are below those of most mid-range hotels in Fiji. There are less expensive guesthouses, varying from stuffy small rooms to simple but reasonably comfortable self-contained units. Most of the outer islands have coun- cil guesthouses, but make sure you give advance warning of your arrival.

FOOD

Staple foods include coconut, pandanus fruit, bananas and fish, especially tuna. Breadfruit is boiled, or fried as chips, and *pulaka* (a variety of swamp taro) is eaten boiled or roasted. Eating habits are chang- ing for the worse as locals become depen- dent on tinned corned beef and other imports. There is a corresponding increase in diet-related disease.

On Funafuti the restaurant meals are limited in variety. Fresh fruit and vegetables are a bit of a treat, but you may find some at the fusi co-op.

DRINKS

Coconut milk and coconut toddy (fermented coconut-tree sap) are traditional drinks. Cans of mango and pineapple juice, soft drink and beer are imported. Powdered and long-life milk are also available, although you may have to search several shops to find either.

ENTERTAINMENT

Feasts and dancing are held at the maneapa on special occasions, such as weddings and VIP visits. There are volleyball and soccer

TUVALU

TUVALU

Ano: The Ball Game

To play the Tuvaluan game *ano* you need two round balls about 12cm in diameter and woven from dried pandanus leaves. (similar cubic 'balls' are used for other ball games). The two opposing teams face each other about 7m apart in five or six parallel rows of about six people, and nominate a captain (*alovaka*) and a catcher (*tino pukepuke*) who stand in front of each team.

Team members can hit the ball to each other with the aim of eventually reaching the catcher. Only the catcher can throw the ball back to the captain to hit back to the other team. To keep the game lively, two balls are used simultaneously.

When either ball falls to the ground the other team scores a point and the first to ten points wins the game.

competitions and cricket and *ano* (a local ball game; see the boxed text) are played on special occasions – you might be able to join in. See the Things to Do and Entertainment entries in the Funafuti section for more information on entertainment.

SHOPPING

Each island has a fusi co-op, and Funafuti has a few stores with a very limited supply of imported goods. Excellent handicrafts can be purchased at the Women's Handicraft Centre and the craftswomen's stalls at Funafuti airport.

Getting There & Away

AIR

Tuvalu's International Airport is on Funafuti. Air Fiji (☎ 313 666 in Fiji, fax 300 771, airfijireserve@is.com.fj) took over the Suva-Funafuti route from Air Marshall Islands in March 1999 (F$530 one way; Monday and Thursday). Make sure you

reconfirm, as seats are usually in high demand and you could get stranded.

Departure Tax

An international departure tax of A$20 applies to all visitors over 12 years old.

SEA

The government-owned cargo/passenger ship the MV *Nivaga II* travels to Suva, Fiji every three months or so (the trip takes five days). Fares are A$57.40/172.20 for deck/double cabin, without meals. You have to pay the return fare regardless. The ship also does very rare charter trips to Tokelau via Samoa. Pacific Forum Line (☎ 315 444 in Fiji) is the agent for the *Nivaga II* in Suva.

The cargo boat *Nei Matagare* makes irregular trips between Tuvalu, Tarawa (Kiribati) and Fiji. Suva-Funafuti deck class, including meals, is A$99 one way. William & Goslings (☎ 312 633 in Fiji) are the Suva agents for the *Nei Matagare*.

Irregular cargo boats also link Funafuti with NZ, Australia, Wallis & Futuna.

Getting Around

CAR & MOTORCYCLE

Motorcycles and mopeds are the most popular means of land transport, and are available for rent on Funafuti. The capital has a minibus and taxi service. Driving is on the left side of the road.

BOAT

All inter-island transport is by boat. Only Funafuti and Nukufetau have reef passages large enough for ships to enter their lagoons. This means ships must load and unload into a small boat which can be hazardous in rough seas – not for those who aren't confident swimmers. The inter-island ship MV *Nivaga* typically visits each of the outer islands once every three or four weeks. The southern trip takes about three days, the northern trips about four. Don't expect too much comfort: it's often crowded with chickens and pigs as well as people, toilets overflow and passengers are often seasick

A trip to the northern islands costs about A$100 for 1st class, including food, and A$17 deck class without food.

For bookings and schedule confirmation contact Marine Travel on Funafuti (☎ 20 44) or the Telecom representative on the outer islands. Printed schedules are pretty unreliable as the boat is often off for maintenance, or detouring to pick up VIPs.

It is also possible to visit the outer islands by chartering a government fishing boat (about A$1000 per day, including meals). Make arrangements with the Fisheries Department on Funafuti (☎ 20 344).

Visiting yachts have to check in at Funafuti for immigration and customs clearance on arrival, and before leaving Tuvalu. Therefore few yachts visit the outer islands.

Funafuti Atoll

FUNAFUTI ATOLL

• pop 4500   • area 2.8 sq km

Funafuti (pronounced 'foo-**nah**-foo-ti') Atoll is the country's capital, with the administrative centre and airport at Vaiaku village on Fongafale Islet. The vast lagoon, about 24km long and 18km wide, has four reef passages. Funafala Islet at the southern end of the atoll has simple accommodation, and the Marine Conservation Area on the western side is well worth a visit. Excellent maps of the atoll (A$10) are usually available from the Lands & Survey Department (☎ 20 170), south of Vaiaku Lagi Hotel on the waterfront in Vaiaku.

FONGAFALE ISLET

Fongafale (also spelt Fogafale or Fagafale) is the largest of Funafuti's islets. It's a long snake-like slither of land, 12km long and between 10 and 400m wide, with the Pacific Ocean on the east and the protected lagoon on the west. The airstrip runs from north-east to south-west on the widest part of the island with the village and administrative centre of Vaiaku on the lagoon side. None of the roads are signed. The deep water wharf is 1.7km north of the hospital; the main road continues north and at times is almost half the islet's width!

During WWII, Fongafale was the main base for the American bombers in Tuvalu. Most of the population was relocated to Funafala Islet for the duration of the war. Fongafale has many small, man-made lagoons known as 'borrow pits', where coral material was extracted for the construction of the airstrip.

Information
Tourist Offices Tuvalu receives few tourists. Funafuti Town Council (☎ 20 754 or ☎ 20 489, fax 20 664), north of the fusi, manages and arranges transport to the conservation area. Radio Tuvalu (☎ 20 731, fax 20 732), opposite the Vaiaku Lagi Hotel, has friendly helpful staff and is a good place to get the latest on what is happening. Otherwise, try the hotel and guesthouses.

The Ministry of Tourism, Trade & Commerce (☎ 20 182 or ☎ 20 191, fax 20 829), between the church and the fusi, may also be worth trying.

Money The National Bank is opposite the airport building in Vaiaku. It changes travellers cheques (A$1 commission per 10 cheques) and does cash advances on Visa and MasterCard; otherwise credit cards are not accepted in Tuvalu. Banking hours are 10 am to 2 pm Monday to Thursday, 9 am to 1 pm Friday. The hotel will accept payment by travellers cheque.

Post & Communications The post and Telecom offices are both near the airport building in Vaiaku.

You can make calls from the Telecom office (public fax 20 800) or by public phone outside. The town has a few other cardphones, but at the time of writing only one was working. You can buy phonecards from the Telecom office and the Vaiaku Lagi Hotel. See Facts for the Visitor earlier in this chapter for postal and telephone rates.

The Tuvalu Philatelic Bureau (☎ 20 223, fax 20 712), at the southern end of town, sells stamps to international collectors. The themes are Tuvaluan, but they are designed and printed overseas.

Travel Agencies See the Travel Office (☎ 20 737, fax 20 757) at the airport for ticketing and reconfirmation of flights. Manu Travel Services (☎ 20 649, fax 20 648) is also near the airport. Contact the Marine Travel Office (☎ 20 744) at th deep-sea wharf for information on bo services.

Libraries The Library and Archives Offic is near the Philatelic Bureau at the south ern end of town. It is open weekdays 8 a to 4 pm (closed for lunch 12.30 to 1.3 pm) and on Saturday 10 am to noon. Th USP extension centre also has a library.

The University of the South Pacifi The USP Extension Centre (☎ 20 811, fa 20 704) is just south of the hospital at th northern end of town. It caters for abou 260 extension students and specialises i accounting, economics and managemen They have a few books about Tuvalu fc sale.

Emergency & Medical Service Princess Margaret Hospital (☎ 20 750) ha about 30 beds, but is understaffed and th pharmacy often runs out of some drug weeks or months before the next suppl ship arrives. It has an ambulance servic and there are visiting specialists from tim to time.

Funafuti's Fragile Environment

About 4500 people (nearly half of Tuvalu's population) are squeezed onto Funafuti's long skinny 2.8 sq km Fongafale Islet. Only about a third of the islet is habitable – large areas are taken up by the airfield and by 'borrow pits', where material was excavated for its construction. With a growing population, and the trend away from subsistence agriculture towards a cash economy, pressure on Funafuti's meagre resources is mounting.

The most obvious environmental problem is the lack of garbage disposal. While traditional throw-away attitudes remain, there is an increasing dependence on imported packaged food. On a place this tiny it is obvious where every tin and piece of plastic ends up.

The high-density living is also impacting in other ways: causing pollution and depletion of the ground water; coastal erosion as sand and aggregate is extracted for construction; and contamination from household chemicals, pesticides and petroleum products. Industrial and commercial waste from the hospital, airport, port, power house, and fuel terminal is also a threat. The lack of water and sewage treatment and waste-disposal facilities led to outbreaks of disease in 1985 and 1990.

With these constraints on sustainable development, tourism, apart from small-scale, will just contribute to the problem. Hopefully the findings of the many studies, reports, committee meetings, and the negotiations for aid money, will be applied for a more sustainable environment.

The Police Station (☎ 911) is opposite the
Vaiaku Lagi Hotel.

Things to See & Do

Just wander around the town or hire a
moped or motorbike to explore the islet.
Every few blocks there is a **maneapa**; Parliament meets at the one adjacent to the airport. Most of houses are concrete-block
hotboxes but people escape to their outdoor
fale umu (kitchen huts) for some breeze,
and even watch videos from outside!

Housing is fairly dense and boundary
disputes are becoming common. As more
people need to squeeze on less land, there are
communal plots where banana plantations
and crops are planted. The airfield takes up
about 20 hectares of previously productive
land. About 2800 coconut palms were felled
and pulaka and taro-growing land was covered up. In between planes the airfield is
used as the town's sporting ground.

At midday the streets are fairly deserted
its the time for **inaction** – lying down in
the fale umu or some other shaded spot.
Early morning is the best time for a walk,
when the motorbikes are zipping around,
people are out sweeping the breadfruit
leaves from their yards and the roads, and
children are heading off to school in their
brightly coloured uniforms. Locals enjoy
hanging out at the fusi co-op.

The vast Funafuti **lagoon** is stunning;
perhaps ask someone for a paddle in their
outrigger canoe. Initially visitors don't find
swimming here particularly inviting
though, after seeing the tins, glass, plastic
and assorted rubbish littering the beach,
which is also used as a toilet. Nevertheless,
joining the locals and floating in the lagoon's turquoise waters is lovely at the end
of a scorching day – just avoid touching the
bottom! The concrete pier just south of the
hotel is a good spot to enter.

Late in the 19th century, coral-drilling
expeditions from England came to Funafuti
to investigate Darwin's theory of atoll formation (see the boxed text 'How the Islands
Formed' in this chapter). The site, known as
David's Drill, isn't particularly exciting in
itself: just a concrete base with a small hole

in it. It is at the northern end of the town,
not far from the hospital.

Take a trip to the far **northern end** of the
island to feel just how narrow the islet is
and witness the problems of rubbish disposal on such a tiny place. WWII reminders
include the **borrow pits** (now used as dumping grounds or for pigsty drainage), and a
rusting old **tank** near the deep-water wharf.
There is also an underground **bunker** near
the far-northern end of Fongafale. On the
way you'll see a rusting Japanese fishing
boat, wrecked here during Cyclone Bebe in
1972.

Fongafale's beaches are nothing special –
for cute islets with lovely beaches take a
trip to the **conservation area** and **Funafala
Islet** (see later).

Places to Stay

Hotels *Vaiaku Lagi Hotel* (☎ *20 733, fax
20 504)* is about 100m north-west of the airport on the edge of the lagoon. Tuvalu's
only hotel, it has 16 air-con rooms. The upstairs rooms have stunning sunset views
over the lagoon. Cleanliness and facilities
are pretty ordinary for A$88/99/109 singles/
doubles/triples, but its staff are friendly and
it accepts travellers cheques. Most guests
are on official business. Friday and Saturday are 'twist' nights, with loud music until
midnight. Drinks are cheaper in the old bar
next door.

Guesthouses Guesthouses are a more
economical option. *Filamona House* (☎ *20
983)* is a new guesthouse run by Penieli
Metia, conveniently located across from the
Vaiaku Maneapa. It has four fan-cooled
rooms downstairs, although air-con is on
the cards. It was being completed at the
time of writing and appeared to be a good
deal (A$44 per room). It has a good com-
munal lounge and kitchen, and a verandah
upstairs. A restaurant and fale umu were
also being built.

Solomai Guesthouse (☎ *20 572)* is a
block east of Vaiaku Lagi Hotel. Mr Luka
has two simple rooms with shared bathroom
in his home downstairs. The self-contained
flat upstairs is better, with a lounge, two

TUVALU

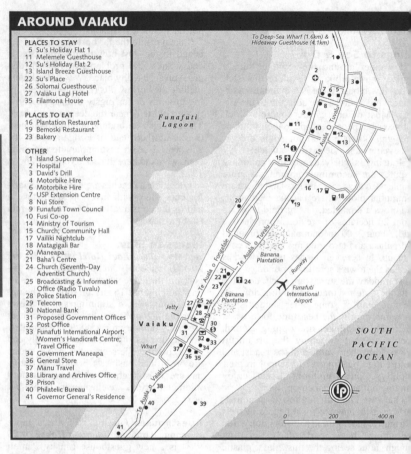

AROUND VAIAKU

PLACES TO STAY
5 Su's Holiday Flat 1
11 Melemele Guesthouse
12 Su's Holiday Flat 2
13 Island Breeze Guesthouse
22 Su's Place
26 Solomai Guesthouse
27 Vaiaku Lagi Hotel
35 Filamona House

PLACES TO EAT
16 Plantation Restaurant
19 Bemoski Restaurant
23 Bakery

OTHER
1 Island Supermarket
2 Hospital
3 David's Drill
4 Motorbike Hire
6 Motorbike Hire
7 USP Extension Centre
8 Nui Store
9 Funafuti Town Council
10 Fusi Co-op
14 Ministry of Tourism
15 Church; Community Hall
17 Vailiki Nightclub
18 Matagigali Bar
20 Maneapa
21 Baha'i Centre
24 Church (Seventh-Day
   Adventist Church)
25 Broadcasting & Information
   Office (Radio Tuvalu)
28 Police Station
29 Telecom
30 National Bank
31 Proposed Government Offices
32 Post Office
33 Funafuti International Airport;
   Women's Handicraft Centre;
   Travel Office
34 Government Maneapa
36 General Store
37 Manu Travel
38 Library and Archives Office
39 Prison
40 Philatelic Bureau
41 Governor General's Residence

Funafuti Lagoon

To Deep-Sea Wharf (1.6km) &
Hideaway Guesthouse (4.1km)

Te Ausla o Tuvalu

Te Ausla o Forogatale

Te Ausla o Tuvalu

Banana Plantation

Banana Plantation

Jetty

Vaiaku

Wharf

Te Ausla o Vaiaku

Runway

Funafuti International Airport

SOUTH PACIFIC OCEAN

0   200   400 m

bedrooms and verandah. It costs A$38 per room, A$76 for the whole flat.

Su's Place (☎/fax 20 612) is about 300m north of the airport building. It has three simple, single fan-cooled rooms for A$33 with shared bathroom. Two can be interconnected (A$64 for a maximum of five). The one air-con room costs A$41. There is a communal area and a fridge. Guests can cook for themselves, although Sue is good cook (see Places to Eat, later). She can also arrange activities, such as motorbike picnics at the end of the islet (A$15 per person) and fishing trips (A$150 for six hours).

Su's Holiday Flats (☎/fax 20 612) a good options for self-caterers. The small air-con unit is about 1.2km north of the a port near the fusi. It is clean, has a we equipped kitchen and costs A$66. T other unit, about 150m further south on t same road, is A$33 per room with shar bathroom.

Melemele Guesthouse (☎ 20 471 or ☎ 493) is a good option. It is about 1km nor of the airport on the lagoon side and clo to the fusi. It is clean and well maintaine although it's a pity the adjacent beach used as dump. It has a clean commur kitchen, lounge, TV/video and fans. Single/double rooms with en suite cost A$40/70. The two twin rooms with shared toilet/bathroom are A$27.50 per person. Three other rooms were being built at the time of writing.

Island Breeze Guesthouse (☎ 20 606, fax 20 674), 1km north of the airport, has three small, musty fan-cooled rooms with two beds in each. The low ceilings are a bit claustrophobic. Singles/doubles cost from A$30/35 to $40/45. Dorm beds cost A$25. Meals can be arranged for under A$7. It also arranges boat trips to Tepuka Islet (A$80 for up to five people).

Probably the nicest place to stay on the islet is *Hideaway Guesthouse* (☎/fax 20 865), run by Rolf, a German ex-pat, and his Tuvaluan wife Emily. It is out of town, about 2.5km north of the wharf. The stretch of the lagoon opposite is a good spot for swimming. It has a bright, mosquito-screened apartment with a kitchen and pleasant lounge for A$44/55/60.50. There are also two good, fan-cooled rooms with en suites, for A$33/44/50. There are regular minibuses to the deep-sea wharf; from where it's about a half-hour walk. On weekdays there is a morning and afternoon bus to the door (60c).

Places to Eat

The *restaurant* at Vaiaku Lagi Hotel serves good, if repetitive, meals. Usually there's a choice of fish, chicken or sometimes lobster, and a few vegetables. Lunches are good value for A$4.50. Dinner is much the same thing but nearly triple the price. *Plantation Restaurant*, about 700m north of the airport, serves large Chinese-style dishes for around A$5 (lunch and dinner) and *Bemoski Restaurant* further south also has cheap Chinese meals. *Su's Place* serves meals for guests as well as nonguests, for around A$9 per dinner: book in advance. Check if the Filamona House *restaurant* has opened. The airport *kiosk* has sandwiches (usually canned corned beef) and soft drinks. Some of the places to stay will prepare picnic lunches to take on excursions to the islets.

Self-catering is a good option if you can find enough fresh ingredients from the *fusi*

co-op. Watch out for the women pushing around *wheelbarrows* of fresh tuna. There is another *supermarket* and a few other *grocery shops*, and a small *bakery* just north of the airport. Food can be pretty scarce if the supply boat has been delayed.

Entertainment

Special occasions, such as weddings, are held at many of the maneapa, and involve feasts and traditional dancing. Visitors may be invited along. The hotel organises traditional dancing for VIPs.

If you stay here too long you'll probably develop the curious habit of waiting for planes (we did!). It is so popular in fact that it is seen to be a problem: here's an excerpt from the local paper:

Civil servants ... tend to make a habit of going to the Terminal to see who is coming in by plane, thus leaving their offices empty and customers waiting to be served ...

Most bars have billiard tables, and weekend 'twists' (discos). *Vaiaku Lagi Hotel* is the mellowest, followed by *Vailiki Nightclub* and the more seedy *Matagigali Bar* (a bouncer was killed here in 1998). The latter two are near the northern end of the airstrip; it's probably best to go with locals.

Shopping

Fongafale has few shops. The island supermarket and the fusi, both at the northern end of town, have a limited range of imported goods (see Planning in the Facts for the Visitor section earlier). The post office and the Philatelic Bureau have a few postcards and the Nui store opposite the USP Extension Centre sells regional magazines.

The best place to buy handicrafts is the Women's Handicraft Centre (☎ 20 852, fax 20 643) at Funafuti airport. Most of the items are traditional designs in natural materials and are good quality. It often has crafts from the outer islands and restocks weekly. *The Handicrafts of Tuvalu* booklet is available here. The centre opens for flights and on weekdays 8 am to noon and 1.30 to 4 pm. Local craftswomen also have stalls near the Funafuti airport and sell brightly coloured, less labour-intensive items made especially for Tuvalu's small number of travellers. These are made with bright plastic yarn and shells. Departing loved ones or important guests are laden with farewell necklaces. See Arts, earlier, for more on handicrafts.

Getting There & Away

Air Funafuti International Airport is a small wooden building with its letters falling off, built in 1993 with Australian and European Union aid. At the time of writing Air Fiji had just begun regular flights between Suva and Funafuti (see the Getting There & Away section earlier).

Boat Funafuti lagoon has two reef passages large enough for ships to enter, and a deep-water wharf north of Vaiaku. The cargo/passenger ship the MV *Nivaga II* makes occasional voyages to Fiji (see the Getting There & Away section earlier in this chapter). For bookings and schedule confirmation contact the Marine Travel Office (☎ 20 744) at the deep-sea wharf.

Getting Around

Bus Fongafale has a minibus service (40c for the length of the town), which is more like a mobile disco! The service runs from about 6.30 am to 7 pm; on Sunday only for church. There are weekday buses to the northern end of the island (60c), early in the morning and at about 4 pm.

Car & Motorcycle Vehicles are in very short supply. Motorbikes and mopeds are the most popular transport and are available for rent (A$10 to $15 per day). The hotel pick-up and driver can be hired outside flight arrival/departure time (A$10 to end of the island).

Taxi The taxi costs A$4 from the hotel to the deep-water wharf, and A$2 from the hotel to the southern end of the islet near the governor general's residence. The taxi is based at the Island Breeze Guesthouse (☎ 20 606).

Bicycle The motorbike rental places have the odd bicycle for hire. It's a nice pace for exploring the islet – try to avoid the midday heat.

Boat The easiest way to see the lagoon and some of the smaller islets is with the Funafuti Town Council (☎ 20 754 or ☎ 20 489). Its boat costs A$80, including driver and guide, for a maximum of four passengers. You may be lucky enough to score a free ride if the conservation park workers are doing a survey. The hotel can arrange a boat for A$100 – expensive unless you share with a group. Otherwise you could negotiate with locals yourself. Don't expect any lifejackets or safety gear though!

FUNAFALA ISLET

Funafala is a beautiful islet at the southern end of the atoll. When the Americans took over Fongafale in WWII the villagers were relocated here. Most moved back after the war, but there is still a small community (40 people) here. It is a lovely remote place with a more traditional village lifestyle. It gives a taste of what the outer islands are like, and is good for a day-trip escape or a for a few days relaxation. The village has a tidal sand beach.

Funafala is about one hour by boat from Vaiaku (see Getting Around earlier in this section). There is a tiny fibro *guesthouse* with two beds, louvre windows and solar electricity, but no mosquito screens. It cost A$15 per person. It's next to a maneapa on the water's edge and has a toilet block and a water tank. Take your own food as there are no shops. Book through the Funafuti Town Council (☎ 20 754 or ☎ 20 489).

FUNAFUTI CONSERVATION AREA

The Funafuti Conservation Area project began in 1996, and is funded by the South Pacific Regional Environment Program (SPREP). It covers 33 sq km of lagoon, reef, channel, ocean and island habitats, on the western side of Funafuti Atoll. There are six islets: Tepuka Vilivili, Fualopa, Fuafatu, Vasafua, Fuagea and Tefala. It is home eabirds and provides nesting sites for the green turtle. There are many species of sh, hard coral, algae and invertebrates and ne islets have 40% of the atoll's remaining ative broadleaf forest. The objective of the roject is to conserve marine and land-ased biodiversity and allow for sustainable se of the atoll's natural resources.

The project is administered by the Funa-ati Conservation Area Department (☎ 20 39) and is open to visitors for sightseeing, icnicking and swimming. It's a great place or snorkelling, with excellent visibility. ring your own gear. We saw manta rays, nd a group of dolphins raced the boat. It osts $80 for the boat, including driver and uide, for a maximum of four passengers. ook in advance.

MATUKU ISLET

matuku Islet is about 10km north of Vai-ku. A boys' mission school was started here the late 1890s, before being transferred to aitupu. The Tuvalu Maritime School was tablished here in 1979 with the assistance f the Australian government. The training cilities are isolated to simulate ship opera-ons. Tuvaluan seamen have a good reputa-on and easily find work with international ipping companies. Most send their wages ack to their families, and their contribution an important part of Tuvalu's economy.

Outer Islands

uvalu's remote outer islands and atolls are eautiful and pristine, but have very little in-astructure for visitors and are only acces-ble by irregular cargo boat (see this apter's Getting Around section). Give ad-ance warning of your arrival and come epared to be pretty much self-sufficient.

UKUFETAU ATOLL

pop 750 • area 3 sq km
his atoll is the closest to Funafuti, about 00km to the north-west. During WWII rge cargo ships and warships anchored in e lagoon, and it had an airstrip on Motu-lo Islet. There are plane wrecks and other

WWII reminders of the American presence. Ring the local island council on ☎ 36 005 if you wish to stay with a local family.

VAITUPU

• pop 1200 • area 5.6 sq km
Vaitupu Island has the largest land area in Tuvalu. In 1947 some families migrated from the overcrowded island to the island of Kioa in Fiji. It has Tuvalu's only secondary school and over 600 students between the ages of 13 and 21 board here for most of the year. Waste disposal is a big problem.

Aliki Guest House (☎ 20 606, fax 20 674) costs A$15/25 for singles/doubles. Meals can be provided (A$5 to $7). Contact the Island Breeze Guesthouse (☎ 20 606, fax 20 674) on Funafuti.

The local island council (☎ 30 005) also has a *guesthouse* charging A$10 per person, plus meals for A$8.50 to $15.50.

The Funafuti-Vaitupu trip on the *Nivaga* takes about 8½ hours and costs about A$100 return (deck class with meals). Passengers are transferred to a small boat and shuttled through the reef to the island. If seas are rough this can be hair-raising, even for the agile.

NUI ATOLL

• pop 600 • area 2.9 sq km
Nui Atoll has 11 main islets along the eastern side of its lagoon. There are several coconut-fringed, white-sand beaches and at low tide it is possible to walk between islets. Gilbertese is also spoken here as some of the people are of Micronesian descent. Contact the local island council (☎ 23 005) if you want to stay at the *guesthouse*.

NIUTAO ATOLL

• pop 750 • area 2.6 sq km
In 1949 Niutao acquired Niulakita and families were settled there to relieve over-population on the home atoll. The people are known for their traditional handicrafts. Its people retain some traditional beliefs, and until 1982 they had among them a woman who had inherited the power to make rain. Niutao has a *guesthouse*: ring the island council on ☎ 28 005.

TUVALU

NANUMEA ATOLL

● pop 820   ● area 3.9 sq km

Nanumea is Tuvalu's northernmost atoll and the clcsest to Kiribati. It is also one the most beautiful, with a **fresh-water pond** (which is unusual for atolls) and a large **church** with a tall steeple and stained-glass windows. It suffered several Japanese attacks during WWII. Plane **wrecks** and a wrecked cargo ship near the main settlement serve as reminders. The old runway took up one-sixth of the land area and its construction involved felling almost half of the existing coconut trees. The Americans also blasted a passage in the reef and the lagoon is now a sheltered **anchorage** for yachts. Contact the island council (☎ 26 000) about the *guesthouse*.

NUKULAELAE ATOLL

● pop 360   ● area 1.9 sq km

This atoll has two main islets, Niouku and Tumuiloto, on the eastern side of the lagoon. It is about 120km south-east of Funafuti and is Tuvalu's eastermost atoll. There is a preChristian **archaeological site** on the islet of Niuoka – an 'altar' stone which is thought to be a religious site, and was probably used for sacrificial purposes. In 1863 two-thirds of its population were kidnapped by blackbirders and forced to work as slaves in Peruvian mines. The people were misled by the promise of meeting a superior god. Today, the people from Nukulaelae have a reputation their **dancing** and **singing**. Visitors can stay the island council *guesthouse* (☎ 35 005).

NANUMAGA ATOLL

● pop 650   ● area 2.8 sq km

Nanumaga (nah-noo-mah-nga) Atoll is ov shaped with a landlocked lagoon and a na row fringing reef. It has two clans, Tonga the south and Tokelau in the north, who le relatively separate lives. Respect for the ders suffered in 1979 when they spent most all of the atoll's funds purchasing po land in Texas! Contact the island council 33 005) about their *guesthouse*.

NIULAKITA

● pop 100   ● area 0.5 sq km

Tuvalu's ninth, most southern landmass the tiny coral island of Niulakita. It is a little higher elevation than the other islan with fertile soils and lush vegetation. It h white-sand **beaches** within a close ring re Nuilakita was not considered part of eight islands of olden-day Tuvalu as it nev had a permanent population. It had vario foreign 'owners' and in the late 19th ce tury was exploited for its guano and later a copra plantation. In 1949 it was taken ov by the people of Niutao.

There is no guesthouse but you could to arrange to stay with one the local fan lies. Contact the island council on ☎ 21 02

Wallis & Futuna

The territory's name should have been Uvea & Futuna but Captain Samuel Wallis, fresh from 'discovering' Tahiti, dropped by and his name stuck. Later the French scooped up these two remote islands and there they sit today: forgotten specks in the immense Pacific blue with regular flights, plenty of red wine and virtually no tourists. In fact there's little connection between the islands, 230km apart, except for their French ownership: Wallis is the creation of volcanic eruptions and surrounded by a wide lagoon, while its people have ancestral connections with Tonga; Futuna and Alofi are the result of geological upheavals and neither has a lagoon, while the people of Futuna (Alofi is uninhabited) trace their ancestry back to Samoa.

Facts about Wallis & Futuna

HISTORY

Wallis and Futuna were populated when the great Lapita settlement-wave moved across the Pacific between 1500 and 500 BC. Objects found on Futuna have been dated to 800 BC although it's probable that there are even older sites. These early settlers practiced agriculture and fishing, and they brought the first pigs to the islands. Later Futuna came under the influence of Samoa while Wallis suffered repeated invasions from Tonga, starting around 1400 AD. The recently excavated archaeological sites at Talietumu and Tonga Toto in the south of Wallis are fortified Tongan settlements, established by invading forces around 1450. The ferocity of the Tongan invasions ensured their position in the island's oral histories.

The Dutch explorers Jacques le Maire and William Schouten chanced upon Futuna in 1616 and a famous illustration was made of their boat, *L'Eendracht*, anchored in the harbour of Sigave. They named the island Horn, after their home port (the same Horn

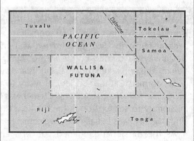
WALLIS & FUTUNA

after which Cape Horn at the southern tip of South America is named). It was 150 years later in 1767 when the next visitor, the English navigator Samuel Wallis who had recently discovered Tahiti, arrived at Uvea. Again the island was renamed but Wallis' name, unlike Hoorn, has stuck. More visitors followed, including Captain Edward Edwards of the *Pandora* in 1791, with a boxful of captured *Bounty* mutineers on board en route to his disastrous encounter with the Great Barrier Reef (see the boxed text 'Mutiny on the Bounty' in the Pitcairn Islands chapter).

In the first half of the 19th century the islands became popular stops for whaling ships and these rough and ready mariners were followed by traders, beche-de-mer gatherers and, inevitably, missionaries.

The first Marist missionaries, includi Pierre Bataillon on Wallis and Pierre Chan on Futuna, arrived in 1837 In 1841 Chan was murdered by King Niuluki, an actio which probably had more to do with loc politics than religion but which, neve theless, was to make St Pierre Chanel t Pacific's first saint – see the boxed te 'Saint Pierre Chanel of Oceania'. In the se ond half of the century France gradual began to assume control of the islands, o ficially taking control over the years 18 to 1888.

Things remained quiet until WWII wh Wallis & Futuna was the only Fren colony to side with the collaboration Vichy government, despite pressure fro New Caledonia. The arrival of war in t Pacific ended that phase and in May 19

Saint Pierre Chanel of Oceania

Pierre Louis Marie Chanel was born into a French peasant family in 1802, and trained as a priest. He was always fascinated by the idea of being a missionary and embarked for the Pacific islands with the newly-formed Catholic Society of Mary (Marist) in 1836. The following year Pierre Chanel was the first missionary to set foot on Futuna, where the ruling king, Niuluki, was initially very welcoming.

As the missionaries gained converts and thus decayed the traditional power structure of the island, Niuluki became less keen on the newcomers. When Niuluki's own son asked to be baptised, the king issued an edict that the missionaries cease their activities. On 28 April 1841 a band of warriors, probably condoned by Niuluki, attacked Pierre Chanel and killed him.

Despite this (or perhaps because of it) the island became fully Christian within a few years as other Marist priests took up the challenge.

Pierre Chanel was declared venerable in 1857, beatified in 1889 and finally canonised as the patron saint of Oceania in 1954. He is also recognised as the first martyr to lay his life down for Oceania (Rev. John Williams had been dead two years at this stage but he was a Protestant – and that doesn't count).

Church of the Sacred Heart, in Faga'uvea, Wallis Island

e 5000 Wallisians suddenly found 2000
merican forces coming ashore.

Two airstrips were built on Wallis, the
ie at Hihifo is still in use today. At its peak
ere were 6000 Americans on Wallis, and
ere was, briefly, a movement after the
ar to cut ties with France and switch to
·ing an American colony! The American
·esence caused a huge upheaval on Wallis
utuna was relatively untouched); it took
ore than a decade for the tremors to subside.
Today Wallis & Futuna is the most iso-
ted French Pacific colony with an econ-
ny almost totally based on French
onomic assistance.

EOGRAPHY & GEOLOGY

idway between Fiji and the Samoas, the
·oup consists of three major islands and
·out 20 islets. Wallis is the main island; it
low lying and rises to a maximum height
145m at Mt Lulu Fakahega.

Wallis is volcanic in origin, a fact clearly
·ested to by the many small volcano
aters, most of them now lakes. Its wide
goon is entered by four passes, only the
·onikulu Pass to the south is safe for large
·ats, and there are about 20 small islets
·tted around the edge or inside the lagoon.
·e lagoon is generally very shallow and
·ere are only a few beaches, none of them
able, on the main island. The lagoon is-
·ids are on the north, east and south sides
·the lagoon. Some of them are volcanic
·gh islands, some of them classic sandy
·tu (islands).

Futuna and its close neighbour Alofi lie
·0km to the south-west of Wallis. Futuna
·much more mountainous than Wallis,
·mbing to 524m at the top of engagingly
·med Mt Puke. Unpopulated Alofi is
·ually precipitous with Mt Kolofau
·17m) the highest point.

·Unlike volcanic Wallis, Futuna and Alofi
·the result of geologic upheaval pushing
·islands above the ocean level. There are
·lagoons around the islands and in some
·ices the mountainous interior plunges
·aight into the sea.

The islands are close to the meeting
·int of the Pacific and Indo-Australian

continental plates and are still subject to
earthquake activity, most recently in the
disastrous quake of 1993.

CLIMATE

The hot tropical climate is tempered by sea
breezes during the May to October dry season, so average temperatures are remarkably even at around 27°C. In fact for the
past 30 years the temperature has never
fallen below 17°C or climbed above 33°C.
November to April is the hotter rainy season
but in fact the rainfall, too, is pretty even.
The cyclone season is November to April.

ECOLOGY & ENVIRONMENT

Deforestation is the major ecological problem in the territory. Only a fraction of the
original forests remain intact. It's not because forestry is big business, the islands
are too small to interest any large international logging companies. The problem is
merely that the islands are so small and
wood has always been the main fuel source.
The deforested land, particularly on the
steep slopes of Futuna is particularly prone
to erosion, and increased runoff into the
oceans poses a threat to coral reefs and vital
fisheries.

All three islands have a major problem
with the large African snails that first arrived
20 years ago, hitchhiking in on the bottom of
containers from New Caledonia. Today they
are proving impossible to eradicate and they
cause great damage to local crops.

FLORA & FAUNA

There are no native animals or plants of
particular significance although Wallis does
have an endemic lizard.

Pigs were bought to the islands with the
first settlers almost a thousand years ago and
these days pigs, domestic and semi-wild, are
the most common animals. They probably
outnumber the human population and play a
key role in many festivals and activities –
their role is to be sacrificed. Until the late
1980s the pigs ranged freely and were simply rounded up each evening. Now they're
required to be penned, although on uninhabited Alofi they still roam free.

WALLIS & FUTUNA

GOVERNMENT & POLITICS

Wallis & Futuna is a straightforward colony and France calls all the shots, but there are three kings – one from Wallis and two from Futuna, where the island is subdivided into the Sigave and Alo districts – as well as a 20 member territorial assembly, elected for a five year term.

The Council of the Territory is effectively a six member government cabinet consisting of the three kings and three other members appointed by the French High Administrator with advice from the territorial assembly. Wallis & Futuna elects one senator to the French Senate and one deputy to the French National Assembly.

ECONOMY

The government figures for Wallis & Futuna's exports are 'negligible' – an armful of copra, a basketful of trocchus shells and a handful of tourist handicrafts. Imports, however, are plentiful. Lots of shiny new cars, lots of cans of Foster's beer from Australia (more Foster's cans litter the roadsides than any other beer brand), lots of food from New Zealand and lots of fine wine from France. Balancing the books on that equation is the French government and its employees and the many citizens of Wallis & Futuna who have left the islands. Apart from fishing and subsistence agriculture, working on the islands essentially means working for the government. There are, however, many people from Wallis & Futuna working overseas, principally in New Caledonia, and their remittances are the other mainstay of the economy.

POPULATION & PEOPLE

The islands have a population of approximately 14,000; 9000 on Wallis and 5000 on Futuna, but there is an even larger population living overseas. It's estimated there are about 17,000 people from Wallis & Futuna living in New Caledonia.

As well as the inigenous population, there are about 800 French people living on Wallis and 100 on Futuna.

A large proportion of the indigenous population on Wallis and Futuna still live in traditional, oval-shaped, open-sided, thatch roofed *fale* (houses). Social organisation o Wallis is matrilineal; property is hande down on the female side of the family.

ARTS

Some beautiful *tapa* (cloth made from mu berry and breadfruit trees) is produced o both islands although the designs are qui different. Futuna tapa is marked with pr dominantly geometric patterns where Wallis tapa specialises in more mode 'land and sea' designs.

Wood carving is an important activity majestically large *tanoa*, the multilegge wooden bowls used for making kava, a carved on Futuna.

RELIGION

Wallis & Futuna are quiet, conservative a Catholic; Futuna even more so than Wall A Sunday church service (mass is usually 7 am) is well worth attending: lots of colo lots of flowers and wonderful singing.

The huge number of often impressive large churches found all around Wallis a Futuna are a clear indication of the stro hold the Catholic religion has on the loc population. Even uninhabited Alofi and t small islands around the Wallis lagoon ha chapels and oratories.

LANGUAGE

Virtually no English is spoken on Wal and even less on Futuna, so being able speak some French really helps. See t French Language appendix in this book f some useful phrases.

Reflecting the historical connections the islands, Wallisian is very similar Tongan and Futunan is similar to Samoa

Wallisian Basics

Hello (in the morning).	*Malo te ma'uli.*
Hello (later).	*Malo te kataki.*
Goodbye (to someone who is leaving).	*'Alu la.*
Goodbye (if you are leaving).	*Nofo la.*
How are you?	*'E lelei pe?*
I'm well.	*Ei, 'e lelei pe.*

ank you.	Malo te ofa.
es.	Ei.
o.	Oho.

utunan Basics

ello (in the morning).	Malo le ma'uli.
llo (later).	Malo le kataki.
dbye (to someone	
is leaving).	'Ano la.
e (if you are	
ng).	Nofo la.
ow ar you?	E ke malie fa'i?
m well.	Io, e kau malie
	fa'i.
ease.	Fakamalie.
ank you.	Malo.
es.	Io.
o.	E'ai.

acts for the Visitor

UGGESTED ITINERARIES

ith only very limited numbers of flights
ming through Wallis & Futuna each
eek, there's not much flexibility to visit-
g the islands. A day is sufficient to 'see'
ther island, although, of course, lazing on
e beach can stretch those time limits.

OURIST OFFICES

ere are no tourist offices on Wallis &
tuna. There are very few tourists.

ISAS & EMBASSIES

ere are no overseas diplomatic represen-
ives on Wallis or Futuna, and since this is
French colony, not an independent coun-
, French embassies abroad represent the
ands. See the French Polynesia chapter
r diplomatic representation in Papeete and
her countries, and the New Caledonia
apter for representation in Noumea.

Immigration regulations are the same as
ance's other Pacific colonies; see the New
ledonia chapter. There are also quaran-
e regulations concerning fresh foods.

ONEY

in French Polynesia and New Caledonia,
e Cour de Franc Pacifique (CFP) is the

local currency, tied to the French franc. See
the Money section in the New Caledonia
chapter for exchange rates. It's wise to
bring CFP with you since there is no bank
at the Wallis airport and the one bank in
Mata Utu, the main centre, is only open on
weekdays.

The Banque de Wallis et Futuna (BWF)
branch can advance up to 30,000 CFP a
week to Visa card and MasterCard holders.
It will change foreign currency but exacts a
horrific 1000 CFP commission on each
travellers cheque exchange. Futuna has a
BWF branch in Sigave, which is only occasionally open; officially it also charges a
heavy commission but in practice seems
quite relaxed.

You can use credit cards at one restaurant
and one hotel on Wallis and at car rental
places.

POST & COMMUNICATIONS

There are post offices in Mata Utu, on
Wallis, and Sigave, on Futuna, and in several other centres.

Public phones require a Wallis & Futuna
telecard, available in 1000 and 3000 CFP
denominations. Dial ☎ 00 and you're on
your way to anywhere in the world. The
international telephone code for Wallis &
Futuna is ☎ 681.

INTERNET RESOURCES

Well, where doesn't have a website? Wallis & Futuna's official website (www
.wallis.co.nc) is for Francophones only
however. A useful site for English speakers
is http://wallis-islands.com/index.gb.htm.
Don't plan to send emails from Wallis &
Futuna unless you can talk yourself into the
administration office or find somewhere
else with Internet access.

BOOKS

Wallis et Futuna – Hommes et Espaces
(CTRDP, Noumea, 1994) is an excellent
and moderately priced book on the colony,
written in French. It can be bought from the
administrative centre in Wallis, or ask the
manager of the Hôtel L'Albatros who has a
small stock on hand.

WALLIS & FUTUNA

NEWSPAPERS & MAGAZINES

The colony's French language newspaper *Te Fenua Fo'ou* is published every Friday. French magazines are available in several supermarkets.

RADIO & TV

RFO (Radio France Outre Mer) operates a local radio station and one TV channel broadcasting from 4.40 am to around midnight every day.

TIME

Wallis & Futuna are just west of the International Dateline and 12 hours ahead of GMT. When it is 12 noon on Wallis & Futuna it is also 12 noon in Auckland, 10 am in Sydney, 12 midnight in London (ie just coming into the same day) and 4 pm the previous day in Los Angeles.

ELECTRICITY, WEIGHTS & MEASURES

Electricity is 220V AC, 50Hz, and sockets are the European two circular-pin type. The metric system is in use.

HEALTH

There is a public hospital in Mata Utu on Wallis, and in Sigave on Futuna.

DANGERS & ANNOYANCES

Boredom? There's not much else to worry about on either island, although a lot of beer gets knocked back on weekends and if a Wallisien ever did get drunk and unfriendly it's worth noting that they are very large.

BUSINESS HOURS

Shops are open Monday to Friday and many are open on the weekends, but they tend to shut for a long, lazy lunch.

PUBLIC HOLIDAYS & SPECIAL EVENTS

Most holidays and festivals are the French dates also celebrated in New Caledonia and French Polynesia (see this section in the Regional Facts for the Visitor chapter). It's amusing to listen to children on the other side of the world from France practising *La Marseillaise* for 14 July, with its stirring militaristic lines about fertilising our fiel with impure (ie German) blood!

St Pierre Chanel Day is 28 April. Ho days for the three Wallis parishes are May, 29 June and 15 August.

ACTIVITIES

The islands could clearly inspire lots of a tivities – diving, for example – if there we enough visitors to make them worthwhi Wallis has a six hole golf course, althou by playing the same holes in different dire tions they manage to make it feel bigg French or not, one of the most popul sports on Wallis is cricket. This is the Po nesian version of the sport (called *kilikir* with 40 or more people on the field. A sin lar game is played in French Polynes Tokelau and Samoa (see the boxed text 'I Not Just Cricket' in the Samoa chapter).

ACCOMMODATION

There are fewer than 50 hotel rooms in t island group; most of them are on Wall Booking secures you a room, but equa important, it means you get picked up at t airport.

FOOD

There are regular reminders that these lands are a French colony – you do eat we Opportunities to sample the local cuisi are limited; you're more likely to be brea fasting on a baguette or croissant and stro coffee and enjoying an equally Frenc influenced lunch or dinner.

The supermarkets and smaller shops a well stocked with food from Europe, oth Pacific centres, Australia and New Zealan There are no markets on either island a you will not see any local products on sa in the shops. If you catch a fish and do need to eat it yourself it's simply given t friend or neighbour, who in turn will te you a bunch of bananas or a basketful taro. As a result the pork in a supermar freezer or the fish served in a restaura may come from France or New Zealan even though the islands are overrun by p and surrounded by endless sea.

RINKS

he water is drinkable without being eated on Wallis but not on Futuna. A cold an of beer in a bar or restaurant will be 50 CFP or 400 CFP. Australian Foster's ger is the beer most commonly drunk on 'allis although you also see VB (from the ame Melbourne brewery), Heineken, umber One (from New Caledonia) and arious other beers.

NTERTAINMENT

'allis has several video shops and the one otel on Futuna has some videos. There ay be the occasional dance performance d Wallis has a couple of weekend discos.

Getting There & Away

'allis is about 300km west of Samoa and 00km north-east of Fiji. However, there e no regular connections with either of ose close neighbours; if you want to catch flight out of Wallis & Futuna your only tions are the other two French territories. 's 2100km west-south-west to New Cale- nia or 2900km east to Tahiti.

IR

ircalin (Air Calédonie International; ☎ 72 80 in Mata Utu, fax 72 27 11) has two nnections each week from New Caledonia. ne flight is Noumea-Wallis-Noumea; the her goes Noumea-Wallis- Papeete-Wallis- oumea.

It takes about three hours between oumea (New Caledonia) and Wallis, about hours 40 minutes (crossing the Dateline) tween Papeete (Tahiti, French Polynesia) d Wallis. An economy class one-way fare tween Noumea and Wallis is around ,000 CFP and between Papeete-Wallis it around 52,000 CFP.

See the introductory Getting Around the egion chapter for interesting possibilities flying via Wallis. Round-the-world TW) tickets are a good way of including allis & Futuna in a wider itinerary.

SEA

Although cargo ships come through Wallis & Futuna a couple of times a month (deliv- ering all that Foster's beer and French wine) there are currently no regular facilities for taking passengers. Ships from New Cale- donia take four days to Futuna and a further 12 hours to reach Wallis. Yachts don't visit Wallis that often either, despite its wel- coming lagoon. Because there isn't much room around the Mata Utu wharf, yachts are encouraged to moor near the petroleum wharf at Halalo in the south of Wallis.

Getting Around

AIR

Aircalin (☎ 72 28 80, fax 72 71 11 in Wal- lis, fax 73 32 04 in Futuna) makes the 45 minute flight between the islands five times a week. The flights will soon be replaced by a catamaran service. Check the current situ- ation in Mata Utu.

LAND

There is no public transport on either island; if you want wheels you'd better rent a car. There are lots of motorcycles and scooters (the Vespa is the two wheeler of choice on Wallis and Futuna) but very few bicycles.

Wallis Island

• pop 9528   • area 74 sq km
Surrounded by an island-dotted barrier reef, Wallis is the larger and more heavily populated of the Wallis & Futuna duo. The lagoon islands, the churches and the per- fectly shaped crater lakes are all interesting, but Wallis also has one of the largest and most extensive archaeological sites in the Pacific. It's remarkable that a site as im- posing as the one at Talietumu in the south of the island is so little known.

INFORMATION

There is no tourist office or other infor- mation source. The BWF is in the Uvea Shopping Centre and is open 8 am to 12.15

WALLIS & FUTUNA

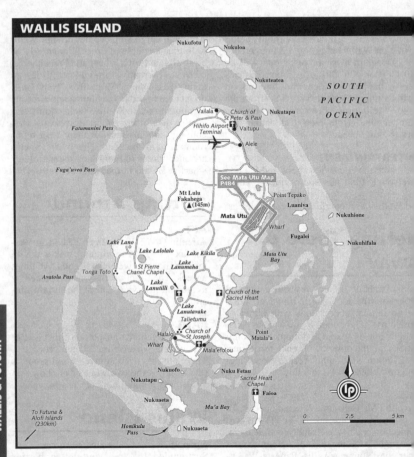

WALLIS ISLAND

(Map labels)

Nukufotu
Nukuloa
Nukuteatea

SOUTH
PACIFIC
OCEAN

Vailala
Church of St Peter & Paul
Nukutapu
Hihifo Airport Terminal
Vaitupu
Fatumanini Pass
Alele

Fuga'uvea Pass

See Mata Utu Map P484

Mt Lulu Fakahega ▲(145m)
Point Tepako
Luaniva
Nukuhione
Mata Utu
Wharf
Fugalei
Nukuhifala

Lake Lano
Lake Lalolalo
Lake Kikila
Mata Utu Bay

Avatolu Pass
Tonga Toto
St Pierre Chanel Chapel
Lake Lanumaha
Lake Lanutili
Church of the Sacred Heart

Lake Lanutavake
Talietumu

Halalo
Church of St Joseph
Point Matala'a
Wharf
Mala'efo'ou

Nukuofo
Nuku Fetau
Nukutapu
Sacred Heart Chapel
Faioa
Nukuaeta

To Futuna & Alofi Islands (230km)
Mu'a Bay
Honikulu Pass
Nukuaeta

0   2.5   5 km

---

pm and 1.30 to 4 pm, Monday to Friday.
There's a pharmacy, supermarket (with Foto
Express department) and the Perle d'Uvea, a
miniature department store, in the complex.

MATA UTU
• pop 1137

Matu Utu is the main centre, a small town
sprawling up the hill from the lagoon; it's a
long walk from anywhere to anywhere. The
waterfront is dominated by the **Matu Utu** or
Our Lady of Good Hope Cathedral, looking
across the open green to the lagoon. The
twin-towered cathedral is a grey and stolid

looking building but inside it's surprisin[g]
light and bright. The Maltese cross cent[re]
between the two towers is the royal insig[nia]
of Wallis. The adjacent **King's Palace**, w[ith]
its two-storey verandahs running all [the]
way around, almost looks like an Austral[ian]
country residence.

AROUND THE ISLAND
Mt Lulu Fakahega, towering to all of 14[5m]
in the centre of the island, makes a go[od]
lookout over the whole island. You can [ac]
tually drive all the way to the top, wh[ere]
there's a small abandoned chapel. Footpa[ths]

Wall of St Joseph Church painted in a 'sea and land' tapa design – Mala'efo'ou, Wallis Island

eander down to the west coast road from
e summit.

The 35km island circuit road is unsealed
d at times fairly rough for about 12km
wn the west coast. It never actually runs
ong the coast although in a few places there
e detours that run along the water's edge.
arting from Mata Utu and going clock-
ise around the island, the route passes **Lake
kila** (2km), the only lake that is not in a
lcano crater. Built in 1991 the **Church of
e Sacred Heart** (4.5km) at Faga'uvea is
missable – it's like a multitiered light-
use towering up beside the road.

In Mala'efo'ou (8km) the **Church of St
seph** is the oldest church on the island. It
s a beautiful interior covered in a kaleido-
ope of decorations, from random patterns
biblical scenes, to illustrations of the fish
the lagoon. Many of them are inspired by
ditional 'land and sea' tapa designs. Just
yond the village at around 9km, a side
ad, after several twists and turns and an-
er turn-off, leads to the impressive **Talie-
mu** archaeological site (the Talietumu

residence within the Koloniu Fort). This
huge and beautifully restored site was a
fortified Tongan settlement, dating from
around 1450 AD. A wide defensive wall with
entrance passages surrounds tree-dotted
lawns and a number of other structures,
including large platforms and a circular
stockade base. The archaeological work at
this site, as well as much other work on both
islands, was led by Daniel Frimigacci.

At around 11.5km the road through the
centre of the island branches off. A short
distance up this road the striking **Lake
Lanutavake** lies just off the road to the left
(west). This turn-off climbs past the lake to
the **St Pierre Chanel Chapel**, overlooking
another crater lake.

Back on the circuit route, the sealed
road ends at 14km and the road edges close
beside **Lake Lalolalo** (16km), the most spectacular of the Wallis crater lakes. The eerie
lake is an almost perfect circle with sheer
rocky cliffs falling 30m down to the inky,
80m-deep lake waters. Tropic birds are
often seen gliding effortlessly across the

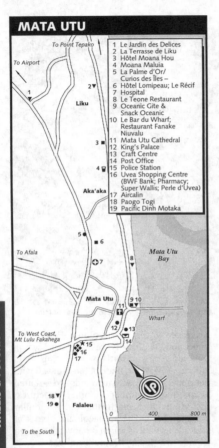

MATA UTU

To Point Tepako
To Airport
Liku
Aka'aka
To Afala
To West Coast, Mt Lulu Fakahega
To the South
Mata Utu Bay
Mata Utu
Wharf
Falaleu

1 Le Jardin des Delices
2 La Terrasse de Liku
3 Hôtel Moana Hou
4 Moana Maluia
5 La Palme d'Or/ Curios des Îles –
6 Hôtel Lomipeau; Le Récif
7 Hospital
8 Le Teone Restaurant
9 Oceanic Gite & Snack Oceanic
10 Le Bar du Wharf; Restaurant Fanake Niuvalu
11 Mata Utu Cathedral
12 King's Palace
13 Craft Centre
14 Post Office
15 Police Station
16 Uvea Shopping Centre (BWF Bank; Pharmacy; Super Wallis; Perle d'Uvea)
17 Aircalin
18 Paogo Togi
19 Pacific Dinh Motaka

0   400   800 m

lake. It's said that the American forces dumped equipment into the lake at the end of WWII. Just beyond the lake a side road branches off to the west, passing close by another crater, this one without a lake. There's another crater lake a short walk north of the track.

After about 2km this detour reaches the coast where there are several quite pretty little beaches. Unfortunately the water here is very shallow, the bottom is muddy and it's a favourite basking spot for stingrays, which are not a good idea to step on. The attraction here is the **Tonga Toto** archaeological site,

still being excavated at the time of writing. The name could be translated as 'the block of Tongans'; an alternative name for the are is the *marais sanglant* or 'swamp of blood', all indicating that the Tongan invasion wa not an easy one. This fortified settleme includes impressive walls and a paved foo path running down to the water.

Back on the main island circuit you ca cut back to Mata Utu from the junction 18km or continue up to the northern end the island. A turn-off (26.5km) leads to th coastal village of **Vailala** where there's a b of beach, and on to Vaitupu with the larg **Church of St Peter & Paul**.

AROUND THE LAGOON

Some lagoon islands are high volcanic i lands, others are sandy-reef-created mot Since there are virtually no useable beache on the main island, the lagoon islands a popular excursions for swimming and pi nics. None of the lagoon islands are inha ited but many of them have small chapels oratories. **Faioa** at the southern end of th lagoon probably has the finest beaches b it's less frequently visited, simply becau it's a long way from Mata Utu. The **Sacre Heart Chapel** is on the northern tip.

Nukuhione, with its long, curving san spit, is a more popular excursion and lies the eastern edge of the reef. Just south **Nukuhifala**, which also has good beach and the Chapel of St John the Baptist. Up the northern end of the lagoon, **Nukufotu** noted for its bird population.

PLACES TO STAY

If you book ahead, a person from your hot will meet you at the airport – a good id because there is no airport transport.

Oceanic Gite (☎ 72 24 00) is part of t Snack Oceanic and Oceanic shop comple at the wharf road junction in Mata U There are rooms with shared bathroom cilities for 5000 CFP.

Hôtel Lomipeau (☎ 72 21 20, fax 72 95) is by the main road in Mata Utu, up the hill looking down over the lagoo There are 15 single/double rooms with a con, private bathrooms and with terrac overlooking the lagoon for 9500/10,500 CFP, including breakfast. The Récif Restaurant is at the hotel and there are plans for a swimming pool. This is the only accommodation that takes credit cards.

Hôtel Moana Hou (☎ 72 21 35, fax 72 21 35) is by the coast, but on the inland side of the road, just over a kilometre north of Mata Utu in Liku. There are 15 comfortable rooms at 5000/7500 CFP.

Hôtel L'Albatros (☎/fax 72 18 27) is by the airport. It has five single rooms, all with air-con and bathroom, in the main building for 10,000 CFP including breakfast. There are three larger bungalows alongside the swimming pool for 15,000 CFP single or double. There's no sign for the hotel; turn left out of the airport and it's the large white building about 100m on the right.

PLACES TO EAT

There are a number of smaller shops and a number of well-stocked supermarkets. If you've visited islands where a few cans of tinned meat and fish and the odd packet of noodles is all there is on offer to find a supermarket with an excellent wine department is a definite shock. There are a number of small snack bars dotted around the island but most dining takes place close to Mata Utu, the main settlement.

At *Snack Oceanic (☎ 72 21 92)*, at the upper road junction in Mata Utu, there's a small cafe with sandwiches for 300 CFP and meals such as chicken with ginger (900 CFP) or steak with French fries (1100 CFP). At the start of the pier there's *Le Bar du Wharf* and the adjacent *Restaurant Fanake Fiuvalu (☎ 72 24 55)* offering a variety of meals of the 'steak or fish with French fries' variety.

Le Récif (☎ 72 20 21), in the Hôtel Lomipeau, specialises in seafood and has a pleasant dining area looking out over the lagoon from its hillside setting. Just south of the centre, *Paogo Togi (☎ 72 26 48)*, in the Pacific Dinh compound, has a predominantly Chinese menu with meals from 850 CFP to 1500 CFP, including rice.

Only a stone's throw north from the centre of Mata Utu is the waterfront *Le Teone*

Restaurant (☎ 72 29 19). It has an open-air dining area, a menu with all the French regulars and, on weekends after 11 pm, it becomes the number one disco on Wallis. Things also kick along until late on weekends at the *Moana Maluia* nightclub a bit further north on the coast. Until *l'aube*, dawn, on Saturday night/Sunday morning.

La Terrasse de Liku (☎ 72 27 37) is nearly 2km north of Mata Utu, in Liku, and has an airy, open dining area looking across the road to the lagoon. Main courses from the fairly extensive menu are 1200 to 1400 CFP, there's a good winelist, they accept credit cards and it's open every day for lunch and dinner. Also about 2km north of Mata Utu, but on the main island circuit road, at the crossroads with the Liku-Afala road, *Le Jardin des Delices (☎ 72 20 90)* has a similar menu.

By the waterfront at the Halalo petroleum wharf at the southern end of the island *Akakeeno* is an irregularly-open restaurant, serving typical Wallisien food if you arrange it in advance. There's no sign and you may not even find anybody around.

SHOPPING

You can even get Wallis & Futuna postcards in the Perle d'Uvea or in La Palme d'Or/Curios des Îles, the latter a neat little shop with some island craftwork and books. Look for paintings, prints and T-shirts by the island naive artist Soane Patita Takaniua. He painted the wall in the Paogo Togi restaurant.

GETTING AROUND
To/From the Airport

Wallis' Hihifo airport has a neat and very modern little terminal, but there's no tourist office, no bank or other way of changing money, no taxis or other transport and although there is a phone, it's a cardphone and there's nowhere to buy a phone card. So bring some CFP with you (easy to do if you come from Noumea or Tahiti) and pre-book a hotel so that you will be picked up. It's 6km between the airport and Mata Utu and if you are stuck somebody will certainly offer you a ride into town.

Island Transport

Since there's no public transport, it's a case of rent wheels or walk. Pacific Auto Location (☎ 72 28 32, fax 72 29 33), in Hihifo, has three Suzuki Vitara 4WDs at 7000 CFP a day or 7500 CFP with air-con. If they're all out you can fall back on Pacific Dinh Motoka (☎ 72 26 57, fax 72 26 57), just south of Mata Utu, which can usually provide some sort of vehicle, not always in the best condition, for a similar price. You could probably rent a scooter or bicycle if you ask around.

Futuna & Alofi

Although Futuna (still marked as Hoorn Island on some maps) may seem at first glance to be merely a quieter version of Wallis, in fact there are many differences. For a start the island is more mountainous than Wallis and has no lagoon, and the population

Futuna & Alofi

Island	Pop	Land Area
Futuna	5000	64 sq km
Alofi	0	51 sq km

has strong Samoan links, in contrast to Wallis' ties with Tonga. The languages betray these connections although the people of the two islands understand each other quite easily. Equally important, Futuna is a much more traditional island, less influenced by the modern world.

Kava drinking is still an important everyday event on Futuna and if you drive around the island soon after dusk you'll see open fale after open fale, with men involved in the ritualistic preparation and drinking of the popular Pacific intoxicant (see the boxed text 'Kava' in the Regional Facts for the Visitor chapter).

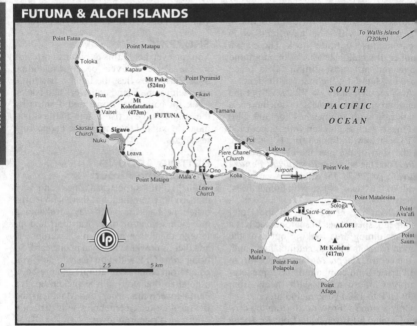

FUTUNA & ALOFI ISLANDS

Uninhabited Alofi could easily be dubbed the 'Island of Pigs', although it's probable the quoted figure of 10,000 pigs on the island is a wild over-estimate. A strait less than 2km wide separates the two islands. The lack of an adequate fresh water suppply on the island has kept permanent human settlers away.

INFORMATION

Everything of note is concentrated in Sigave. There are several shops, including a couple of reasonably sized supermarkets, the island's only petrol station, a branch of the BWF that is open from time to time, the island administrative headquarters (there's even a library), the police station and so on.

AROUND THE ISLANDS

The island circuit is 33km; half solid concrete, half unsealed. This route starts at Sigave, the island's major centre, on the south coast, and proceeds in a clockwise direction.

The rather Disneyish **Sausau Church**, at the western end of the town, is an impressive sight with its three circular towers. It was built in just eight months after its predecessor was destroyed in the catastrophic 1993 earthquake.

On the island circuit look for the many *fale fono*, the oval-shaped, open-walled structures where village men gather in the evening to prepare and drink kava. Many of them are utilitarian concrete and corrugated-iron structures, but 2km from Sigave on the water's edge, the fine fale fono in the village of **Vaisei** is totally traditional with substantial wood pillars and beams, lashed together with *sennit* (intricately patterned rope made from coconut fibre) and topped by a coconut palm roof.

The north point of the island is reached at 8km, and at 13km the road passes the natural rock formations at Matapu Point. Further along the coast is **Point Pyramid** and at 18km, at Poi, there's the green-trimmed, three tiered tower **Pierre Chanel Church**, with enough pews to easily seat a couple of thousand worshippers. The chapel includes relics of the saint, including some of his clothes and the war club said to have dispatched him.

Soon after Poi the road climbs away from the north coast over the hills to drop down to the south coast just west of the airport. At 25km the impressive blue-and-white trimmed **Leava Church** has a fine ceiling with carved wood figures of men. The figures lean out from the side walls, and each supports the roof rafters with an outstretched arm. Like much Futuna wood carving, a chainsaw was a principal instrument. At 29km there's a less inspiring sight, a seaside dump where garbage is tipped down the cliffside in an unsightly, smelly example of administrative stupidity.

No road crosses the interior – apart from at the eastern end of the island where the circuit road temporarily abandons the coast to cross the hills – but there is a network of footpaths winding up into the central hills. With enough time you might even find a way to the top of **Mt Puke**.

Boats run across to uninhabited **Alofi** from the beach beside the airport; count on spending 3000 CFP to 4000 CFP for the whole boat, roundtrip. Alofi has a positively idyllic beach; all elements of the postcard ensemble of white sand, clear water and shady trees are there. People come over from Futuna to tend gardens and to keep an eye on their pigs. There's a series of open fale, each one with a solar cell to provide lighting, for overnight accomodation. But the 2km crossing only takes 10 to 15 minutes to complete, so people usually just stay for the day. Alofi even has a small **church**.

PLACES TO STAY
Hotel Fiafia (☎ 72 32 45; pronounced 'fee-ah-fee-ah') has four comfortable air-con rooms at 7000 CFP. The rooms are around a lounge area and there is a large terrace facing the lagoon. There are two shared bathrooms and toilets and a communal kitchen area. Downstairs you'll find a restaurant and bar.

PLACES TO EAT
The shops and supermarkets may not be quite as well stocked as on Wallis Island,

but compared to almost any other Pacific island of this size they're quite amazing. Will a choice of four different champagnes, including Möet et Chandon, suffice? The only consistent place to eat is the **Restaurant Fiafia**, at the hotel, where food is served in almost overwhelmingly large quantities at 2000 CFP for a very complete meal. Other places come and go; there may be one by the waterfront near the fuel station.

SHOPPING

Futuna is noted for its tapa work and wood carving. A number of places around the island display artisan's signs. Tanoa sell for about 5000 CFP to 10,000 CFP per 10cm-diameter

bowl, so a half metre bowl would cost 25,000 CFP to 50,000 CFP. In the fale fono there a often tanoa measuring more than a metre diameter! This is obviously a boy thing 'you think yours is big? You should see t size of my kava bowl!' In the village of Ko near the airport ask for the village chief, T Savaka – you'll probably find this cheerf large gentleman hacking out handsomel finished tanoa using a chainsaw.

GETTING AROUND

Futuna's grass airstrip is 12.5km fro Sigave. Ask at the hotel about renting a c or contact Depann' Futuna (☎/fax 72 15); count on about 4000 CFP a day.

MELANESIA

Melanesia

The French explorer Dumont d'Urville named Melanesia (Black Islands) for the dark colour of its inhabitants' skin. Although its boundary with Polynesia is blurred, Melanesia's culture and even geography is distinctive.

In contrast to the rest of the Pacific, Melanesia's islands are huge. Formed by the action of the Pacific tectonic plate diving beneath the Indo-Australian plate, the continental material comprising the islands towers as high as 2000m above sea level. The difficult terrain – high mountains and deep valleys – of these islands reduced contact between tribes and is partly responsible for the remarkable cultural diversity of the region, along with the length of time that the area has been settled.

Melanesia was the first part of the Pacific to be settled by humans: people arrived here about 25,000 years ago – 22,000 years before any humans reached Polynesia or Micronesia! Ancient Melanesians did not need to be long-distance seafarers

as Micronesians and Polynesians did, be cause the islands of Melanesia lie relativel close to each other. But well-establishe inter-island trade routes were as much a pa of Melanesian culture as they were a mear of gaining material wealth.

Initially, Europeans judged Melanesian inferior to the lighter races of the easter Pacific. In part this was simply racis based on the darkness of Melanesians' ski but Europeans also had trouble establishin relationships with the fragmented an somewhat xenophobic Melanesian peopl

Fear of the Melanesians, and the malari endemic along Melanesia's coasts, delaye European trade and missionary activity i the region. And, even now, Melanesian so ciety remains highly traditional; the ma jority of people still live a rural lifestyl and the laws of Melanesian *kastom* rule a aspects of life.

Melanesia's proximity to Australia ha opened it up to tourism, and cruise ship departing from Australia's east coast ar

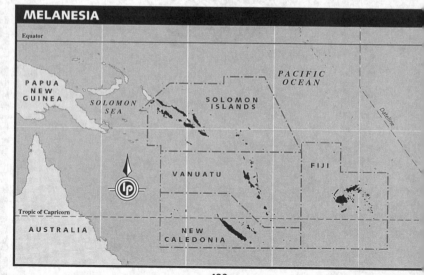

equent visitors to, for example, Vanuatu's ort Vila and New Caledonia's Noumea.

Fiji, a country with almost as many Polyesian traits as Melanesian, is as close to a eographical and cultural 'centre' as exists n the Pacific islands. In the modern Pacific, nany regional organisations are based in iji, and most Pacific airlines pass through Nadi. Nowhere else in the Pacific has as many air connections to other islands, making Fiji an almost compulsory stop on any Pacific itinerary.

The largest and oldest Melanesian country, Papua New Guinea, is briefly described in the introductory South Pacific Gateways chapter.

Fiji

Beaches. Transparent waters. Mountains. Great food. An amazing cultural mix. As one of the Pacific's most popular tourist destinations, Fiji has something special for travellers on any budget.

Fiji's position in the central Pacific, its large land areas and its rich resources make it one of the most influential of Pacific nations. It is here that the South Pacific Forum and University of the South Pacific are based. And with one of the best tourist infrastructures in the region, Fiji keeps attracting travellers who want both to 'chill out' and to soak up the culture of this remarkable archipelago.

Facts about Fiji

HISTORY
Vitian Culture
The name Fiji comes from the Tongan name for these islands. Before the arrival of Europeans, the inhabitants called their home Viti. Vitian culture was shaped by Polynesian, Melanesian and some Micronesian peoples over 35 centuries of settlement. The Lapita people, coming from Vanuatu and the eastern Solomon Islands, arrived in about 1500 BC. They were mainly coastal dwellers who relied on fishing. About 500 BC there was a shift towards agriculture, an increase in population along with an increase in tribal feuding. Cannibalism became common and in times of war villages moved to fortified sites.

The village chief was considered *tabu* (sacred) and had immense influence. Chiefs were polygamous and this led to complex interrelationships. Normally the position of chief passed through a generation of half-brothers before turning to their sons, but rivalry and power struggles were common.

Arrival of the Europeans
The archipelago's treacherous reefs and the Fijians' reputation as formidable warriors

AT A GLANCE

Capital City (& Island): Suva (Viti Levu)
Population: 775,077
Time: 12 hours ahead of GMT
Land Area: 18,300 sq km (7140 sq miles)
Number of Islands: 300
International Telephone Code: ☎ 679
GDP/Capita: US$1170
Currency: Fijian dollar (F$1 = US$0.51)
Languages: English, Fijian & Hindi
Greeting: *Bula* (Fijian) & *kaise* (Hindi)

HIGHLIGHTS

- **Snorkelling & diving** – Fiji's fantastic coral reefs

- **Fiji's cannibal history** – visit the Fiji Museum, the Tavuni Hill Fort and the Naihehe Cave

- **Kayaking & rafting** – through the gorges and wilderness of the Namosi Highlands

- **Taveuni** – walk the beautiful Lavena Coastal track and the Vidawa Forest

- **The Yasawas** – cruise, sail or kayak its azure waters

- **Levuka** – the wild and lawless capital of the 19th century

- **Abaca National Park** – spectacular views from the mountains

- **Sigatoka** – windswept sand dunes

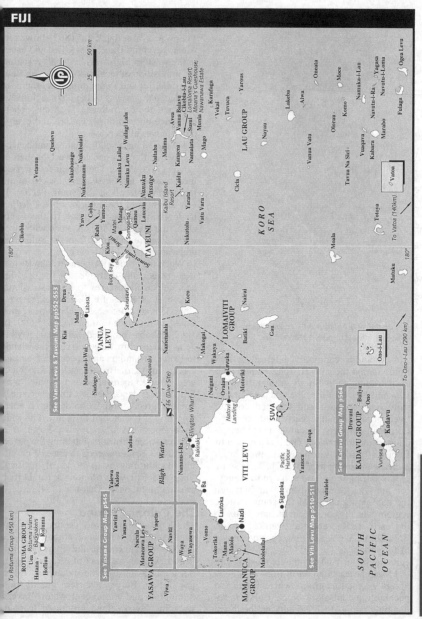

FIJI

BY PERMISSION OF THE NATIONAL LIBRARY OF AUSTRALIA; NK1178/2

Portrait of a Fijian Man – engraving by JD MacDonald, 19th century

and ferocious cannibals deterred sailors from visiting the islands. Tongans had long been trading with Fijians and during the 17th and 18th centuries the odd deserting or shipwrecked sailor and escaped convict lived here. From the early 19th century, Europeans whalers, sandalwood and beche-de-mer traders arrived. The introduction of firearms by the Europeans resulted in an increase in violent tribal warfare, with some chiefs selling their land and even villagers for guns and ammunition. War between the competing chiefs of the south-eastern regions was the norm from the late 1840s to the early 1850s, and the eventual victor, Ratu Seru Cakobau of Bau, became known to foreigners as Tui Viti (King of Fiji), despite having no real claim over most of Fiji.

Missionaries entered Fiji from Tahiti and Tonga via the Lau group, where Tonga had become the controlling force. Cakobau reluctantly adopted Christianity on the threat of withdrawal of Tongan military support, and those under his influence followed. There was a setback in 1867, however, when Reverend Baker was killed and eaten in the western highlands by locals resisting the imposition of ideas associated with Bau. Missionaries and Fijian ministers gradually displaced the priests of the old religion and assumed their privileged positions. Their influence on traditional culture and everyday life was all pervasive.

By the 1830s a small whaling and beachcomber settlement had been established at Levuka on Ovalau. The foreigners married local women and Levuka became one of the main ports of call in the South Pacific. It was a centre of the notorious blackbirding trade (slaving; see History in the Facts about the South Pacific chapter), with most of the labourers coming from the Solomons and Vanuatu.

When the home of American John Brown was accidentally destroyed by fire, and locals helped themselves to his possessions, Cakobau, as 'King of Fiji', was held responsible. This set a precedent and claims against Cakobau rose to an inflated US$45,000. In 1862, Cakobau proposed that Britain pay his debts and in return he would cede the islands to Britain. Rumours and speculation caused a large influx of British settlers who bickered between themselves and disputed with Fijians over land. Levuka town became a lawless, greedy outpost bordering on anarchy. In 1871 Cakobau formed a Fiji-wide government based at Levuka, however it was not successful at maintaining the peace.

In 1873 Britain agreed to annex Fiji, citing blackbirding as its principal justification, and Fiji was pronounced a British crown colony on 10 October 1874.

The Colonial Period

The local economy was depressed by the slump in the cotton market at the end of the US Civil War. Unrest and epidemics followed, with an outbreak of measles wiping out about a third of the indigenous Fijian population. Europeans were greatly outnumbered and the recent Maori-Pakeha wars in New Zealand prompted fears o

FIJI

cial war. Like the missionaries before it, e colonial government sought the collaboation of the chiefs. To reinforce the chiefs' aditional support, governor Sir Arthur ordon introduced an administration that corporated the existing Fijian hierarchy. ijian land rights were protected by forbiding sales to foreigners. Today 83% of the nd is still owned by indigenous Fijian ommunities.

Levuka's geography hindered expansion, the administrative capital was moved to uva in 1882. Under increasing pressure to ake the Fijian economy self-sufficient, the olonial government turned to sugar plantaons, which demanded large pools of cheap bour. Since blackbirding was under conol, slavery abolished and the employment f Fijians as plantation labourers prohibed, Gordon established an indenturedbour system using Indian workers. A total f 60,537 Indians were transported to Fiji om 1879 to 1916, under five-year conacts. While some Indians joined as a way escape poverty, they discovered the hard ality of heavy work allocations, low ages, unjust treatment, rationed food and vercrowded accommodation. Crime, suiide and disease were common. Despite nis, the vast majority decided to stay in iji. Interaction between Indians and Fijians as discouraged by the colonial governent. Indians could not buy land and intead moved into small business, trade and ureaucracy, or took out long-term leases as ndependent farmers.

By the mid-1930s Australian dominance n the Fijian economy had extended beyond ugar into gold-mining. Europeans had the nonopoly on freehold land and power and nfluence in the civil service. Labour laws vere unfair and the trade union movement ragmented along racial lines.

ndependence

he 1960s saw the formation of a ministeral government, voting rights for women, he establishment of political parties and onstitutional changes. On 10 October 1970 iji became independent after 96 years of olonial administration. The constitution

followed the British model of two houses with a senate, however political seats and parties were racially divided.

In the first few years after independence, Fijians were optimistic. However, as the economy worsened underlying racial tensions became more apparent. Competition in business, education and employment tended to be seen in purely racial terms, despite the fact that most Indians, like most Fijians, belonged to the poorer working classes. In 1975 the nationalist movement's leader called for the repatriation of the entire Indian community, despite most being fourth-generation Fijians. In the 1977 elections Fijian votes were divided, allowing the Indian National Federation Party (NFP) to win. Its victory was short lived, however, as the governor general called for a new election and the Alliance Party regained its majority.

Military Coups

Greater unity among the working classes led to a shifting of loyalties and the formation of the Fiji Labour Party (FLP), led by Dr Timoci Bavadra. In the 1987 elections an FLP-NFP coalition defeated the Alliance Party. Despite having a Fijian prime minister and a cabinet with an indigenous-Fijian majority, the new government was labelled 'Indian dominated' and racial tensions rose. The extremist Taukei movement, supported by eastern chiefs and the Fijian elite, launched a deliberate destabilisation campaign, playing on Fijian fears of losing land rights and of Indian domination. There were demonstrations and violent incidents against Fiji-Indian-owned businesses and petrol bombs were thrown into the government offices in Suva. On 14 May 1987, a month after the elections, parliament was invaded by armed soldiers led by Lieutenant Colonel Sitiveni Rabuka. He arrested Dr Bavadra and his cabinet and formed a civil interim government with himself as military member.

Talk of new elections led to more violent protests by Taukei extremists and in September 1987 Rabuka again intervened with military force. The 1970 constitution was

FIJI

invalidated and Fiji declared a republic. Rabuka proclaimed himself head of state and appointed a new council of ministers, which included leaders of the Taukei movement and army officers. Arrests of community leaders and academics followed, a curfew was imposed in urban centres, newspapers were closed and all political activities were restricted. Fiji was dismissed from the Commonwealth.

Post-Coup Politics & Constitutional Changes

The economic consequences of the coups were drastic. Fiji experienced negative growth in gross domestic product (GDP), a devalued dollar, inflation and wage cuts. The coups benefited only a minority of Fijians and tensions within the Fijian community itself were exposed. The economy's two main sources of income, sugar and tourism, were seriously affected and aid from overseas was suspended. Large numbers of people, especially Fiji Indians, emigrated.

The new 1990 constitution increased the political power of the Great Council of Chiefs and the army and reserved the position of prime minister and a majority of seats in the house of representatives for indigenous Fijians. Those involved in the coups were given immunity from legal prosecution. An electoral gerrymander advantaged the eastern chiefly elite and compulsory Sunday observance imposed Christian religious values on the whole population. Indian political leaders denounced the new constitution as racist and undemocratic, claiming it condemned Fiji Indians to perpetual minority status.

Prior to the 1992 general election, Rabuka gave up his military career to head the Soqosoqo-ni-Vakavulewa-ni Taukei (SVT). To win votes he changed his hardline approach, promising to repeal labour laws affecting trade unions, to review the constitution and to extend Fiji-Indian farmers' land leases. The SVT won by seeking coalition partners in Fiji-Indian members who he had expelled in the 1987 coup and by promising to initiate a review of the constitution. In the 1994 election Rabuka was

again appointed as prime minister and leader of the SVT-GVP (General Voters Party) coalition.

In 1995 the National Bank of Fiji was confirmed bankrupt, the Sunday observance decree was lifted and in 1996 a Constitutional Review Commission (CRC) called for a return to a multi-ethnic democracy. A new constitution was declared in 199 with the position of president reserved for an indigenous Fijian, but no provision of ethnicity for the prime minister.

In the May 1999 elections Fijian voters rejected Rabuka and the SVT. The FLP won the majority of seats and formed a coalition with the Fijian Association Party. Fiji now has a Fiji-Indian prime minister, Mahendr Chaudhry. There was initial apprehension that history could repeat itself, with an organised demonstration in the weeks that followed. Rabuka has since resigned from parliament and become chairman of the Great Council of Chiefs.

GEOGRAPHY & ECOLOGY

The Fiji archipelago has about 300 islands varying from a few metres in diameter to Viti Levu (Great Land), at 10,390 sq km. Only about one-third are inhabited. The smaller islands are generally of coral or limestone formation, while the larger ones are of volcanic origin. Vanua Levu still has some thermal activity. Fiji's highest peak is Mt Tomanivi (Mt Victoria) at 1323m, on Viti Levu.

Viti Levu is about 146km from east to west and 106km from north to south. Suva, the country's capital, largest city and main port, is on the eastern side. The main international airport, however, is in the west at Nadi, with Lautoka, Fiji's second largest city and second port, nearby. Nadi and Suva are linked by the fully sealed Queens Road along the southern perimeter of Viti Levu (221km), and by Kings Road (mostly sealed) around the northern side of the island (265km). There are many minor unsealed roads leading to isolated coastal areas or into the highland interior.

Since the 1960s more than 100,000 hectares (between 11 and 16%) of Fiji's orests have been cleared. However, in laces such as Taveuni and Abaca villagers ave turned to ecotourism as an alternative ɔ logging. Waste management is a national roblem and marine pollution near Suva is evere. Over-fishing and destructive fishng techniques are commonly employed vithout much control. Conservation roups based in Suva include the South 'acific Action Committee for Human Ecolgy and Environment (SPACHEE), the Vorld Wildlife Fund and Greenpeace.

CLIMATE

iji has mild average temperatures of round 25°C. Hot summer days can reach 1°C and during the coolest months, July nd August, the temperature can drop to etween 18 and 20°C. Humidity is high, with verages ranging from 60 to 80% in Suva nd 60 to 70% in Lautoka. The wet season is November to April and the dry season from May to October, but rainfall occurs throughut the year. November to April is also the yclone season. Fiji has been hit by an averge of 10 to 12 cyclones per decade, with wo or three of these being very severe.

All the large islands have mountain anges lying across the path of the prevailng winds (the easterly and the south-east rade winds), resulting in frequent cloud nd greater rainfall on the windward eastern ides. Most of the resorts are concentrated n the sunny south-western side of Viti evu and the Mamanuca group, while Suva s notorious for its cloudy, wet weather. It as an average rainfall of around 3100mm er year while Nadi, on the western side of 'iti Levu, gets just under 2000mm.

FLORA & FAUNA

Much of Fiji's indigenous flora and fauna is elated to that of Indonesia and Malaysia.

Fiji has over 1000 identified species of ndemic plants. The national flower, the agimoucia or *Medinilla waterhousei*, only rows at high altitudes on the island of Taveni and on one mountain of Vanua Levu.

The richest diversity of fauna is underwar. Bats are the only terrestrial native mammals and the most common wild animals are the small Indian mongoose and the cane toad, both introduced to control pests in the sugar-cane plantations. The ancestors of Fiji's crested iguana are thought to have floated to Fiji on vegetation from South America.

Fiji has about 23 endemic species of birds. The Fiji pelegrine falcon, Fiji petrel, pink-billed parrot finch, red-throated lorikeet, long-legged warbler and the silktail are all rare species. Taveuni, Kadavu and Vanua Levu are the best islands for bird-watching.

GOVERNMENT & POLITICS

The Republic of Fiji is presently governed by the FLP-Fijian Association Party (FAP) coalition, led by Prime Minister Mahendra Chaudhry. Of the new multiracial cabinet, four of the ministers are women. The president of Fiji is Ratu Sir Kamisese Mara. Chiefs make decisions at a local level as well as being influential at a national level through the Great Council of Chiefs; the former prime minister, Sitiveni Rabuka, is now chairman of the council.

ECONOMY

Sugar has been the mainstay of the economy for most of the 20th century. Tourism and sugar are Fiji's main earners, together employing about 80,000 people. The country receives about 350,000 visitors per year, however a high proportion of Fiji's tourism revenue is diverted overseas to foreign investors. Fiji also exports molasses, gold, timber, fish, copra and coconut oil, clothing, forest wood chips, sawn timber, leather products and furniture. Many villagers live a semisubsistence lifestyle. Fiji has long been reliant on overseas aid from Australia and New Zealand, and more recently Japan.

POPULATION & PEOPLE

Fiji has a total population of about 775,100, about half of which is under the age of 20. About 39% are urban dwellers and 75% of the people live on Viti Levu, followed by Vanua Levu with 18%, with the remaining 7% over 100-odd islands.

The population is the most multiracial of the South Pacific countries. Indigenous

FIJI

Fijians are predominantly of Melanesian origin, but have a strong Polynesian influence both physically and culturally. Most Fiji Indians are descendants of indentured labourers. From the late 1940s until the military coups of 1987, indigenous Fijians were outnumbered by Fiji Indians. Indigenous Fijians presently account for about 50% of the population and Fiji Indians for about 45%. After the coups, large numbers of Fiji Indians emigrated to New Zealand, the USA and Canada.

There are about 4500 so-called 'Europeans' born in Fiji, and over 10,000 'part-Europeans', many of them descendants of 19th century traders or planters. The 8600 Fijians from Rotuma are of Polynesian origin. Among the other 9000 Pacific islanders in Fiji are Tongans and Samoans and 3000 Banabans (Micronesians). There are also more than 8000 descendants of blackbirder labourers from the Solomon Islands. About 0.7% of the population (5000 people) are Chinese or part-Chinese, the majority of whose ancestors arrived early in the 20th century to open small businesses.

Education is not officially segregated, but schools are run by the major religions which results in segregation anyway. The literacy rate is high (87%).

ARTS

Fijian villagers still practise traditional arts and crafts, such as making *masi* (bark cloth, also known as *tapa*), wood carving and pottery, dance and music. Some arts remain an integral part of the culture, others are practised solely to satisfy tourist demand.

Visitors are often welcomed with a *meke*, a dance performance enacting stories and legends. The movements and arrangement of the dance group each have a significance. Guitar is the most commonly used instrument. Popular local musicians include Seru Serevi, the Black Roses, Danny Costello and the more mellow Serau Kei Mataniselala.

SOCIETY & CONDUCT
Traditional Culture
Indigenous Fijians Indigenous Fijian culture is predominantly a Melanesian culture

with strong Polynesian influences. Man aspects of the communal way of life are sti strong. Most indigenous Fijians live in vil lages in *mataqali* (extended family groups and acknowledge a hereditary chief who i usually male. Each mataqali is allocate land for farming and also has communa obligations. *Yaqona*, or kava, is an infusio prepared from the mildly narcotic root o *Piper methysticum*. It is still an importan social ritual and clans gather on specia occasions for *lovo* feasts (traditional Fijia banquets in which food is slowly prepared i an underground oven) and for meke.

Village life is now only semisubsisten cash is needed for school fees, communit projects and imported goods.

Concepts such as *kerekere* (obligator sharing) and *sevusevu* (a gift in exchang for an obligatory favour) are still strong especially in remote areas. Many youn people travel to the cities for educatio employment or to escape the restriction of village life. However, competition fo jobs is tough and the social structure les supportive.

Fiji Indians Most Fiji Indians are fourth o fifth generation descendants of indenture labourers. While traditional culture and so cial structure have been eroded over th years, there has been a resurgence of inter est in maintaining cultural values, arts an language.

Extended families often live in the sam house, but the trend is towards nuclea families. Females generally have a stricte upbringing than boys and in rural areas is common for girls to marry at a youn age and these marriages are ofte arranged. Many women wear traditiona dress, although dress codes are more cosmo politan in Suva.

Dos & Don'ts
Thanks to the missionaries, modest dress the rule. Don't swim or sunbathe naked o topless (for women), unless perhaps at a exclusive resort. When in a village, don wear hats, caps or sunglasses, or carry cam eras or bags over the shoulder. Shoulder

ntricately decorated doors on a Hindu temple

nould be covered and women should wear
nee-length skirts or *sulu* rather than long
rousers or shorts.

Village Visits & Kava Ceremonies Try
ot to show up to a village uninvited, or, if
ou do, ask the first person you meet to in-
roduce you to the chief. Always take a
evusevu of about 500g (F$15 to $20) of
ounded kava or a bundle of roots.

The chief will usually welcome you with
small kava ceremony (see the boxed text
Kava' in the Regional Facts for the Visitor
hapter, and ask locals about the Fijian cus-
oms relating to the ceremony).

RELIGION
eligion is extremely influential and im-
ortant in all aspects of Fijian society. Only
.4% of the population are nonreligious.
Different Christian denominations together
ommand the largest following (53% of the
opulation), followed by Hindus (38%),
Muslims (8%), Sikhs (0.7%) and other reli-
ions (0.1%).

LANGUAGE
Most local people who come into contact
vith tourists can speak English, and all
igns and official forms are also in English.
At the same time, for almost all local people
English is not their mother tongue – the
najority of Fijians speak Fijian at home and
he second largest ethnic group, the Indians,
peak Fijian Hindi.

In this guide a macron over a vowel (eg
) indicates that it has a long sound; a tilde
eg ĩ) indicates that the vowel is nasalised.

Fijian Basics

Hello.	*Bula!*
Hello. (reply) (more respectful)	*Io, bula/ Ia, bula.*
Good morning.	*Yadra.*
Goodbye. (if you don't expect to see them again)	*Moce.*
See you later.	*Au sā liu mada.*
Yes.	*Io.*
No.	*Sega.*
Thank you (very much).	*Vinaka (vakalevu).*

Fijian Hindi Basics

Hello. ('How are you?')	*kaise*
Fine. (response)	*tik*
Farewell.	*fir milegā*
Yes.	*hã*
No.	*nahĩ*

There are no equivalents for 'please' and
'thank you' in Fijian Hindi. To be polite in
making requests, people use the word *thoṛā*
('a little') and a special form of the verb
ending in *nā*, eg 'Please pass the salt.' *thoṛā
nimak denā*

Facts for the Visitor

SUGGESTED ITINERARIES
Day trips from Nadi
• The Mamanucas for watersports
• Abaca National Park
• Nausori Highlands by 4WD or organised tour
• Queens Road (Sigatoka Sand Dunes and Tavuni Hill Fort)
• Natadola Beach
• Organised tour (rafting in the Namosi Highlands and the Navua River; visiting waterfalls or caves).
One week
• Explore Viti Levu for at least four days: Natadola beach; Tavuni Hill Fort; Sigatoka Sand Dunes; the Coral Coast; Suva; Kings Road and Rakiraki; 4WD or bus to Navala/ Nausori Highlands. Spend two days on an offshore island (Mamanucas or Nananu-i-Ra).
Two weeks
• Spend one week exploring Viti Levu, and the other in Taveuni, the Yasawas, Kadavu or Ovalau.

FIJI

One month or more
• Combine more of the above, and add eastern
  Vanua Levu. Western Vanua Levu is not a
  high priority, but Vanua Levu is interesting to
  explore by 4WD.

PLANNING

The best time to visit is during the so-called
'Fijian winter' or dry season, which runs
from May to October. Pack lightweight
clothes, good walking sandals and perhaps
walking boots.

If you are going directly to a remote budget place it may be best to bring your personal needs from home.

TOURIST OFFICES

The Tourism Council of the South Pacific
has an office in Suva (see information in the
Suva section) and numerous offices abroad
(see Tourist Offices in the Regional Facts
for the Visitor chapter).

Local Visitors Bureau offices are:

Suva
   (☎ 302 433, fax 300 970,
   infodesk@fijifvb.gov.fj)
   Thomas St, GPO Box 92; www.bulafiji.com
Nadi
   (☎ 722 433, or ☎ tollfree 0800 721 721, fax
   720 141, fvbnadi@is.com.fj)
   Nadi Airport Concourse, Box 9217, Nadi
   Airport

The Fiji Visitors Bureau (FVB) has overseas offices and representatives in:

Australia
   (☎ 02-9264 3399 or ☎ tollfree 1800 25 1715,
   fax 9264 3060)
   Level 12, St Martins Tower, 31 Market St,
   Sydney 2000
Canada
   (☎ tollfree 1800 932 3454,
   fiji@primenet.com)
Germany
   (☎ 30-4225 6026, fax 4225 6287,
   100762.3614@compuserve.com)
   Petersburger Strasse 94, 10247 Berlin
Japan
   (☎ 03-3587 2038, fax 3587 2563)
   NOA Building, (14th floor), 3-5, 2 Chome
   Azabudai, Minato-Ku, Tokyo 106

New Zealand
   (☎ 09-373 2133, fax 309 4720)
   5th floor, 48 High St, PO Box 1179,
   Auckland
UK
   (☎ 020-7584 3661, fax 7584 2838,
   fijirepuk@compuserve.com)
   34 Hyde Park Gate, London SW7 5BN
USA
   (☎ 310-568 1616 or ☎ tollfree 1800 932 345
   fax 670 2318)
   5777 West Century Blvd, Suite 220, Los
   Angeles, CA 90045

VISAS & EMBASSIES
Passport & Visas

Tourist visas of four months are granted (
arrival to citizens of most countries, incl
ding most countries belonging to the Cor
monwealth, North America, Weste
Europe, Israel and Japan. There is no char
for the initial visa. Visa extensions (F$
fee) will be granted for up to two mont
provided you have a passport valid for thr
months after the expected date of departu
a return ticket and proof of sufficient func
Apply at the Department of Immigratio
Nadi airport (☎ 722 263); Nausori airpo
(☎ 478 785); Lautoka (☎ 661 706) or Su
(☎ 312 672). Those wishing to work w
need to apply through a Fijian High Cor
mission prior to arrival.

Foreign Embassies & Consulate
in Fiji

Australia
   (☎ 382 211, fax 382 065,
   austembassy@is.com.fj)
   37 Princes Rd, Tamavua, Suva, PO Box 214
European Union
   (☎ 313 633, fax 300 370)
   4th floor, Fiji Development Bank Centre,
   Victoria Parade, Suva
Federated States of Micronesia
   (☎ 304 566, fax 304 081)
   37 Loftus St, Suva
France
   (☎ 312 233, fax 301 894)
   7th floor, Dominion House, Thomson §
   Suva
Japan
   (☎ 302 122, fax 301 452)
   2nd floor, Dominion House, Thomson St, Su

Marshall Islands
(☎ 387 899, fax 387 115)
41 Borron Rd, Samabula
PO Box 2038, Government Buildings, Suva
Nauru
(☎ 313 566, fax 302 861)
7th floor, Ratu Sukuna House, PO Box 2420,
Government Buildings, Suva
New Zealand
(☎ 311 422, fax 300 842, nzhc@is.org.fj)
10th floor, Reserve Bank Building, Pratt St,
Suva, PO Box 1378
Tuvalu
(☎ 301 355, fax 301 023)
16 Gorrie St, Suva, PO Box 14449
UK
(☎ 311 033, fax 301 046, ukinfo@bhc.org.fj)
Victoria House, 47 Gladstone Rd, Suva, PO
Box 1355
USA
(☎ 314 466, fax 300 081)
31 Loftus St, Suva, PO Box 218

MONEY

The local currency is the Fiji dollar (F$). All
prices quoted herein are in F$ and inclusive
of VAT (value added tax), a 10% sales tax
on goods and services.

Travelling here can be cheap or expensive, depending on how careful you are.
Most restaurants charge from F$5 to $15 for
main meals; the more upmarket charge
$15 to $30. Accommodation prices vary
enormously, from backpacker beds around
$10 to luxury resorts for up to F$2000 per
night! Many of the upmarket resorts increased their prices significantly after the
1998 devaluation.

Bank business hours are 9.30 am to 3 pm
Monday to Thursday (to 4 pm on Friday).
The ANZ at Nadi airport provides 24-hour
service. Travellers cheques can be changed
in most banks, exchange houses, larger hotels and duty-free shops. American Express,
Visa and Thomas Cook travellers cheques
are readily accepted as are the major credit
cards. Some resorts charge an additional 5%
on a credit card transaction. Many budget
places, however, only accept cash. Take
cash if travelling to outer islands and remote areas. The ANZ and Bank of Hawaii
have automatic teller machines (ATMs) in
Suva, Nadi and Lautoka.

At the time of writing the exchange rates
were as follows:

country	unit		dollars
Australia	A$1	=	F$1.30
Canada	C$1	=	F$1.40
Easter Island	Ch$100	=	F$0.37
euro	€1	=	F$2.10
France	10FF	=	F$3.20
Germany	DM1	=	F$1.10
Japan	¥100	=	F$1.80
New Zealand	NZ$1	=	F$1.04
Pacific franc	100 CFP	=	F$1.80
PNG	K1	=	F$0.68
Samoa	ST1	=	F$0.65
Solomon Islands	S$1	=	F$0.39
Tonga	T$1	=	F$1.30
UK	£1	=	F$3.20
USA	US$1	=	F$1.96
Vanuatu	100VT	=	F$1.50

POST & COMMUNICATIONS

Post offices are open from 8 am to 4.30 pm
weekdays. Most have fax services.

Public telephones require a phonecard,
which can be purchased at post offices,
some pharmacies and newsagents. Email
and Internet access is available at cybercafes in Suva, Lautoka and Nadi. Vodaphone (☎ 312 000, fax 312 007) operates a
digital mobile communication service.

The international telephone code for Fiji
is ☎ 679, followed by the local number.
There are no area codes. To use IDD (International Direct Dial) dial ☎ 05 plus the
country code.

INTERNET RESOURCES

The following are useful Internet sites:

Fiji Village
www.fijivillage.com
(FM 96 radio news, and excellent links including music, movies and sport)
Fiji Visitors Bureau
www.bulafiji.com
(accommodation, activities, getting around,
links and an email directory)
Internet Fiji
www.Internetfiji.com
(many links and newsbytes from *The Fiji
Times*)

FIJI

BOOKS

Also published by Lonely Planet are the Pisces guide *Diving and Snorkeling Fiji* and the *Fijian Phrasebook*, which is an excellent aid to talking with locals.

Yalo i Viti – A Fiji Museum Catalogue by Fergus Clunie, 1986, explains the significance of Fijian artefacts, and *Matanitu – The Struggle for Power in Early Fiji* by David Routledge, 1985, covers Fiji's early history. *Life in Feejee, or Five Years Among the Cannibals* by A Lady (Mary Davis Wallis), 1851, reprinted in 1983, is the memoirs of the wife of a Yankee trading captain. *My Twenty-One Years in the Fiji Islands* by Totaram Sanadhya, 1991, is a first-hand account of the indenture system. Books about the military coups include: *Power and Prejudice – The Making of the Fiji Crisis* by Brij V Lal, 1988, and *Rabuka – No Other Way* by Eddie Dean & Stan Ritova, 1988.

Paddy Ryan's *Fiji's Natural Heritage*, 1988, and *The Snorkeller's Guide to the Coral Reef*, 1994, are good for nature enthusiasts. Photography books include Glen Craig's *Children of the Sun*, Frederico Busonero's *Fiji – The Uncharted Sea* and *Rotuma, Fiji's Hidden Paradise* by Ian Osborn. *Myths and Legends of Fiji and Rotuma* by AW Reed & Inez Hames, 1967, is light reading.

The indigenous-Fijian oral tradition of telling tall stories, myths and legends around the kava bowl is still strong, and there is a small but strong community of poets, playwrights and other writers. Contemporary literature includes works by Joseph Veramu, short-story writer Marjorie Crocombe, poet Teresia Kieuea Teaiwa and playwrights Rotuman Vilsoni Hereniko and Jo Nacola. Fiji-Indian writers include Subramani, Satendra Nandan, Raymond Pillai, Prem Banfal and poet Mohit Prasad.

NEWSPAPERS & MAGAZINES

The main newspapers are the *Fiji Times*, founded in Levuka in 1869 and now owned by Rupert Murdoch, and the *Daily Post*, established in 1987. *Pacific Islands Monthly* and *Island Business* magazines cover regional issues, while *The Review* is Fiji-oriented. Australian newspapers (at least a few days old) are available at some newsagents in Suva.

RADIO & TV

Radio stations include the government-sponsored Radio Fiji 3 and FM 104, the commercial station FM 96, and Radio Pacific (FM 88.8), run by the Student's Association of the University of the South Pacific. Fiji has one television station, since 1992, and Sky satellite TV in some resorts and bars.

TIME

The International Dateline doglegs east around Fiji. Fiji is 12 hours ahead of GMT. Daylight saving was introduced in 1998.

HEALTH

There are occasional outbreaks of the mosquito transmitted diseases filariasis and dengue fever. Water is usually safe to drink in the main towns. The best hospitals are in Suva and Lautoka.

DANGERS & ANNOYANCES

Fiji is a very safe and friendly place to travel; however, crime is on the rise in the larger towns. Be careful when walking around at night, and don't hitchhike alone. Sword sellers can be a pest: if anyone becomes overly friendly and begins carving your name on a piece of wood, just walk away.

BUSINESS HOURS

Most businesses open weekdays from 8 am to 5 pm, and some from 8 am to 1 pm Saturday. Government offices are open from am to 4.30 pm weekdays (to 4 pm on Friday). Many places close for lunch from 1 to 2 pm, and practically nothing happens on Sunday.

PUBLIC HOLIDAYS & SPECIAL EVENTS

Fiji observes the standard western holidays (New Year's Day, Easter Friday/Monday and Christmas); see the Regional Facts for the Visitor chapter for dates. Other holidays in Fiji include:

ational Youth Day   March
atu Sir Lala Sukuna Day May
ueen's Birthday   June
ohammed's Birthday   July
onstitution Day   July
ji Day (Independence)   Early October

ew Year's celebrations are comprehen-
ve, while Ratu Sir Lala Sukuna Day in-
udes cultural shows and games. Other
jian festivals include:

ebruary or March
indu Holi or Festival of Colours
  Best to celebrate this in Lautoka. People squirt
  coloured water at each other.

arch or April
am Naumi (Birth of Lord Rama)
  Hindu festival on the shores of Suva Bay.

uly
ula Festival – Nadi

ugust
ibiscus Festival
  Suva: floats and processions.
dian Fire Walking
  Maha Devi Temple, Howell Rd, Suva.

eptember
autoka's Sugar Festival

ctober or November
iwali Festival (Festival of Lights)

CTIVITIES

iti Levu and Taveuni are the best islands
r trekking: you need to ask permission, be
vited or go on a tour. Abaca Cultural &
ecreational Park and Colo-i-Suva Forest
ark on Viti Levu, and the Lavena Coastal
'alk and Bouma Falls on Taveuni, have
arked trails and don't require guides.

Snorkelling is a definite highlight and as
any reefs are very close to the coast, it is
relatively inexpensive pastime. There are
eat sites just about everywhere although
many places, such as Viti Levu's Coral
oast, you can only swim at high tide and
annels can be dangerous.

Diving here can be fantastic and divers
n choose between budget, mid-range or
luxury accommodation. Prices range from
F$85 to $180 for a two-tank dive and F$350
to $600 for an open-water certification
course. Most operators belong to the Fiji
Dive Operators Association (FDOA), which
requires its members to abide by international diving standards and to support the
Fiji Recompression Chamber Facility. Contact the FDOA (☎ 850 620, fax 850 344,
seafijidive@is.com.fj), PO Box 264,
Savusavu. Some places have half-price dive
specials from mid-January to the end of
March.

Some of Fiji's most magnificent dive
sites, such as E6 in the channel between
Viti Levu and Vanua Levu, are spotlighted
in the 'South Pacific Diving' special section earlier in this book.

Sea kayaking tours are available during
the drier months between May and November: refer to individual island sections later
in this chapter for details.

Surfing usually requires boat trips as the
majority of breaks are on offshore reefs.
The best spots are in barrier-reef passages
along southern Viti Levu (Frigate Passage)
and in the southern Mamanucas (Malolo
and Wilkes passages group). There are a
few places along Queens Road on Viti
Levu's Coral Coast where you can paddle
out to the surf, including the beach-break at
the mouth of the Sigatoka River and in front
of Hideaway Resort.

ACCOMMODATION

There is no shortage of accommodation options, ranging from dorm beds with rock-
bottom prices to world-class exclusive
resorts charging up to F$2000 per night!
Prices often vary (February and March is the
low season). Always inquire if there are
'walk-in' rates and if you are staying in the
country for a while, ask about 'local rates'.
Mid-range amenities usually include a
reasonably comfortable mattress, air-con,
tea and coffee-making facilities and a
restaurant, bar and pool. Some of the budget
places allow camping, otherwise you will
need the permission of village land owners.

There are many budget and mid-range
hotels, especially in the Nadi/Lautoka area,

FIJI

the Coral Coast and Suva on Viti Levu. In Nadi you can either stay downtown, at the 'beach' or close to the airport; many places have free airport transfers. The town has restaurants and good infrastructure for travellers. Alternatively, Lautoka is quieter and easier to get around.

The term 'resort' is used very loosely in Fiji and can refer to any accommodation anywhere near the sea, ranging from backpacker style to exclusive luxury. Budget places usually offer simple thatched-roof *bure* (thatched dwellings) and rudimentary facilities. For those who happy to spend up to a few hundred dollars per day for extra comfort, services and activities, there are many resorts in the Mamanucas, on Viti Levu's Queens Road (Coral Coast) as well as on more remote islands. Mainland resorts have the advantage of more options for tours, entertainment and shopping, however with the exception of beautiful Natadola Beach, offshore islands usually have better beaches. Often resorts offer pre-booked package deals. Expect to get about 25% discount off rack rates (the normal room rates without discounts) for packages or 'walk-in' rates.

FOOD

Fiji's food is a blend of Fijian, Polynesian, Indian, Chinese and Western styles. Traditional foods include *tavioka* (cassava), *dalo* (taro) roots and leaves, seafood in *lolo* (coconut cream), and *kokoda*, raw fish marinated in coconut cream and lime juice. Every large town has supermarkets and a fresh fruit-and-vegetable market. Village shops only have a limited range of food as villagers grow their own fresh produce.

Suva, Nadi and Lautoka all have a variety of restaurants ranging from cheap cafes to fine dining. It can be difficult to find traditional Fijian food in restaurants, however resorts often have lovo nights. Suva and Lautoka have vegetarian restaurants and most places have some vegetarian dishes; even McDonald's has vegetarian burgers.

DRINKS

Mineral water and long-life milk are readily available. Fresh juices of local fruit are great, though 'juice' on a menu often mean cordial. Fiji Bitter and Fiji Gold are locall brewed beers. Kava (or yaqona) is the na tional drink, and is an integral part of Fijia life. It is mildly narcotic, looks like mudd water and you won't escape trying it!

ENTERTAINMENT

Not much happens on Sunday so it's a goo idea to organise activities in advance or to a tend a Fijian church service to hear som great singing. Suva has many bars, nightclu and live music venues and the larger mai land resort hotels have discos, live band meke, lovo nights and fire-walking perfo mances. In small towns and remote areas th popular pastime is kava-drinking. These se sions are often accompanied by guitar pla ing, singing and story telling till the we hours. They can be fun and are a great way meet locals. Every village has a rugby fie and the major towns have cinemas that hav Indian 'Bollywood' films as well as the mai stream English-language productions.

SHOPPING

Nadi, the Coral Coast and Suva have mar souvenir shops. Popular mementos incluc bula shirts (in colourful tropical prints Indian saris and jewellery, traditional art facts such as war clubs, spears, chiefly ca nibal forks, yaqona bowls and tapa clot woven pandanus (a tropical plant wi sword-shaped leaves) mats, shell button pottery, and sandalwood/coconut soap.

Getting There & Away

AIR

Most travellers arrive in Fiji at Nadi inte national airport and a lesser number at Na sori airport near Suva. Both airports als have domestic flights.

At Nadi international airport passenge are greeted by guitar serenading and a se of smiling faces, mostly representatives local accommodation and travel agencie The best source of information is the FV

ffice (☎ 722 433, fax 720 141) next to the
24-hour ANZ bank. There are many travel
agencies, airline and car-rental offices, and
near the departures area there is a restaurant
(upstairs), a cafeteria, a duty-free shop, a
newsagency and luggage storage. The airport is 9km north of central Nadi (about
$6 taxi fare). There are frequent local
buses (45 cents) and the bus stop is just out-
ide the Queens Road entrance.

A few flights from nearby Pacific coun-
ries also land at Nausori airport near Suva
and Air Pacific now has a direct route to
Nausori from Sydney. The airport has limited facilities: see the Nausori section later in
his chapter.

Fiji is a popular stopover between
Canada, the west coast of the USA (LA and
Santiago) and Australia and New Zealand,
and for travellers on round-the-world
(RTW) tickets. Air Pacific, Qantas and
Ansett fly the Australia/Fiji route, and Air
Pacific and Air New Zealand service
Fiji/New Zealand. Air Pacific, Canadian
Airlines International and Air New Zealand
fly to Fiji from Vancouver via Honolulu.
Both Air Pacific and Air New Zealand fly
to/from Japan. Most flights to South-East
Asia go via Australia or New Zealand.

Fares to Nadi from Canada are around
C$1963/2400 in the low/high season; from
Australia's east coast (Melbourne or Sydney) it costs A$809/909 (or A$755/859
from Brisbane); and from Auckland expect
to pay about NZ$775/925.

There are many airline connections between Fiji and other Pacific countries: Air
Nauru flies to Nauru; Air Fiji flies to Tuvalu
and Tonga; Air Calédonie flies to New
Caledonia and French Polynesia; Solomon
Airlines flies to the Solomons; Royal Tongan
flies to Tonga and Hawai'i; Air Pacific flies
to the Solomons, Samoa, Vanuatu and
Tonga; and Air New Zealand flies to Vanuatu, the Solomons, Samoa and Tonga.

The following international airlines have
representatives in Fiji:

Aircalin (Air Calédonie)
    Nadi (☎ 722 145)
Air Fiji
    Nadi (☎ 722 521, fax 720 555)

Suva (☎ 313 666, fax 300 771,
airfiji@is.com.fj)
Air Nauru
    Nadi (☎ 722 795)
Air New Zealand
    Nadi (☎ 722 955, 722 472, fax 721 450)
    Suva (☎ 313 100, fax 302 294)
Air Pacific
    Nadi (☎ 720 777, 722 272, fax 720 126,
    airpacific@is.com.fj)
    Suva (☎ 304 388, fax 304 153)
Air Vanuatu
    Nadi (☎ 722 521, fax 720 555)
Ansett Airlines International
    Nadi (☎ 722 870, fax 720 351)
Canadian Airlines International
    Nadi (☎ 722 400, fax 722 523)
Polynesian Airlines
    Nadi (☎ 722 521, fax 720 555)
Qantas Airways
    Nadi (☎ 722 880, fax 720 444)
Royal Tongan Airlines
    Nadi (☎ 724 355, fax 724 810)
    Suva (☎ 315 755)
Solomon Airlines
    Nadi (☎ 722 831)

Fiji is included in a large number of air
passes. See the introductory Getting Around
the Region chapter for more information.

Departure Tax

An international departure tax of F$20 ap-
plies to all visitors over 12 years old.

SEA

Travelling to Fiji by sea is difficult unless
you're on a cruise ship or yacht: see Cargo
Ship in the introductory Getting Around the
Region chapter for other options.

Visiting yachts must first call at a designated port of entry (Suva, Lautoka,
Savusavu or Levuka) to be cleared by customs, immigration and quarantine. Present
a certificate of clearance from the previous
port of call, a crew list and passports. Approval is needed to visit some of the outer
islands. Contact the Department of Fijian
Affairs (☎ 304 200) in Suva, or the district
offices in Lautoka, Savusavu or Levuka.
Departing, you'll need to complete clearance formalities, provide inbound clearance papers, your vessel's details and your
next port of call, and have paid all port

FIJI

dues and health fees. Yacht Help (☎ 667 222) publishes the *Yacht Help Booklet, Fiji*.

ORGANISED TOURS

While travelling independently is easy in Fiji, many visitors pre-arrange some type of package tour. It may be the ideal option if you have limited time, prefer an all-inclusive upfront price, wish to stay in a particular resort or want to persue special interests and activities such as diving. Most travel agents will be able to organise this type of trip and can often arrange cheap deals. Alternatively, some Pacific cruises such as P&O's *Fair Princess* include Fiji on their itineraries.

Getting Around

By using local buses, carriers and ferries you can get around Fiji's main islands relatively cheaply and easily. There are also air-conditioned express buses, rental vehicles, charter boats and small planes.

AIR

Air Fiji and Sunflower Airlines both have regular flights by light plane. Prices on shared routes are almost identical: see the Fiji Air Fares chart.

Air Fiji
    (☎ 722 521, fax 720 555) Nadi
    (☎ 313 666, fax 300 771, airfiji@is.com.fj) Suva
    (☎ 478 077) Nausori airport
    (☎ 811 188, fax 813 819) Labasa;
    www.airfiji.net
Sunflower Airlines
    (☎ 723 016, fax 723 611, sunair@is.com.fj) Nadi Airport
    (☎ 315 755, fax 305 027) Suva
    (☎ 477 310) Nausori airport
    (☎ 811 454, fax 281 9542) Labasa;
    www.fiji.to/sage/

Charter services and joyflights are available with:

Island Hoppers (☎ 720 410, fax 720 172, Nadi Airport, islandhopper@is.com.fj) by helicopter
Turtle Airways (☎ 721 888, fax 720 095, southseaturtle@is.com.fj) by seaplane

Air Passes

Air Fiji has a 30 day Discover Fiji Pass f... US$236. It is only sold outside Fiji in co... junction with an international air fare. The... are set itineraries linking Viti Levu wi... Taveuni and Kadavu or Taveuni, Savusav... and Levuka or Savusavu, Kadavu an... Malololailai. Both Sunflower and Air Fi... have excursion fares (minimum one da... maximum seven) on some routes that a... about 20% less than the normal return fa...

BUS

Local buses are a cheap and fun way to g... around the larger islands. While often nois... and smoky, they are perfect for the tropic... with open unglazed windows offering a... excellent view of the passing countryside... everyone on board helps to pull down th... large tarpaulins over the windows when... starts raining.

The main bus stations on Viti Levu are... Lautoka, Nadi and Suva. Express buses an... minibuses operate along Queens Road an... Kings Road. Viti Minibuses also shuttl... along Queens Road between Lautoka (pic... up near the bus station) and Suva (pick u... near the market). They charge F$10 p... person, but the drivers are notorious f... speeding.

Bus companies on Viti Levu include:

Pacific Transport Limited
    (☎ 660 499 in Lautoka, ☎ 304 366 in Suv... This company has regular buses (open-a... type) serving Queens Road. There are regula... express buses (about F$9; six/five hours). Th... first bus leaves Lautoka at 6.30 am; the la... about 6 pm.
Sunbeam Transport Limited
    (☎ 662 822 in Lautoka, ☎ 382 122 in Suv... Sunbeam has Lautoka-Suva express servic... via the Kings Road (F$11; about six hours) a... well as Queens Road (F$9.70; five hours). Th... Kings Road route is scenic, especially fro... Rakiraki and the unsealed section to Korovo...
UTC (United Touring Fiji)
    (☎ 722 811, fax 720 389) Nadi Airport;
    (☎ 312 287) Suva
    UTC has a daily express air-con coach servic... between Suva and Nadi along Queens Roa... stopping at the larger hotels along the wa... (F$27 from Nadi Airport to Suva).

FIJI

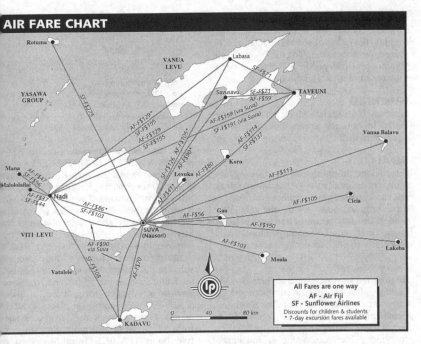

AIR FARE CHART

Rotuma

VANUA
LEVU
Labasa

SF-F$71

YASAWA
GROUP

Savusavu   SE-F$21
AF-F$59   TAVEUNI

SF-F$275

AF-F$129*
SF-F$155
SF-F$129
SF-F$155

AF-F$159 (via Suva)
SF-F$191 (via Suva)

Vanua Balavu

AF-F$105*

AF-F$114
SF-F$137

Mana

AF-F$47
SF-F$26

AF-F$126, AF-F$105*

AF-F$90

Koro

Malololailai
Nadi

AF-F$37
SF-F$44

SF-F$126, AF-F$105*

Levuka   AF-F$80

AF-F$41*

AF-F$113

AF-F$86*
SF-F$103

AF-F$56

Gau

AF-F$105

Cicia

VITI LEVU

AF-F$90
via Suva

AF-F$70

AF-F$150

SUVA
(Nausori)

AF-F$103

Lakeba

Vatulele

SF-F$108

Moala

KADAVU

| All Fares are one way |
| AF - Air Fiji |
| SF - Sunflower Airlines |
| Discounts for children & students |
| * 7-day excursion fares available |

0   40   80 km

CAR & MOTORCYCLE

Ninety percent of Fiji's 5100km of roads are on Viti Levu and Vanua Levu, and about one-fifth of those roads are sealed. Both of these islands are easy to explore by car. Driving is on the left-hand side of the road as in Australia and New Zealand. The speed limit is 80km/h on the open road; 50km/h in town areas. As a rule, local drivers are maniacs, so take care, especially on gravel or pot-holed roads. Avoid driving at night as there are many pedestrians and wandering animals. In cane-cutting season sugar trains have right of way. A current driving licence from any English-speaking country is valid here.

Rental

Renting cars or 4WD vehicles is a good way to explore the larger islands, especially if you can split the cost with a group. Consider support service, insurance, VAT, exclusions and the excess/excess waiver amount (they

vary greatly) and whether you can take the vehicle on unpaved roads.

Reliable car-rental agencies include:

Avis
(☎ 722 233, fax 720 482) Nadi Airport
(☎ 478 963) Nausori Airport
(☎ 850 195, fax 850 430) Savusavu
Budget Rent a Car
(☎ 722 735, fax 722 053) Nadi Airport
(☎ 479 299) Nausori Airport
(☎ 850 799) Savusavu
(☎ 811 999) Labasa
(☎ 880 297) Taveuni

BICYCLE

Fiji's larger islands have good potential for cycling, although some areas are too hilly and rugged and Fijian drivers can be pretty manic. The best time to go would be in the 'drier' season. Good spots for cycling include the scenic Coral Coast on Viti Levu, and on Vanua Levu from Savusavu along the unsealed Hibiscus Highway to Buca

FIJI

Bay, from where you can take the ferry to Taveuni. Ovalau also has a scenic unsealed (mainly flat) coastal road. Bicycles can be rented on the Coral Coast, Taveuni and Ovalau, and Independent Tours near Sigatoka runs mountain-bike tours.

HITCHING

Hitching is still relatively safe in Fiji, especially in country areas. Locals pay the equivalent of the bus fare to the driver.

BOAT

Inter-island hopping for sightseeing and transfers is available in the Mamanucas, and the Yasawas have organised cruises: see these sections later in this chapter. Often though, the only means of transport between islands is by small, ill-equipped local boats, especially to the backpacker resorts.

Ferry

Regular ferry services operate between Viti Levu, Vanua Levu and Taveuni between Viti Levu and Ovalau. Patterson Brothers', Beachcomber Cruises' and Consort Shipping's boats are large roll-on, roll-off ferries, carrying passengers, vehicles and cargo. Ferry timetables are notorious for changing frequently. Boats often leave at odd hours and there is usually a long waiting period for stopovers. The worst thing about the long trips is that the toilets can become disgusting: take your own toilet paper. There are irregular boats that take passengers from Suva to Lau, Rotuma and Kadavu: see the respective sections.

Beachcomber Cruises
(☎ 307 889, fax 307 359) Taina's Travel Service, Suite 8, Epworth Arcade, Suva;
(☎ 880 216, fax 880 202) Raj's Tyre Repair Naqara, Taveuni;
(☎ 661 500, fax 664 496) Lautoka;
(☎ 850 266, fax 850 499) Savusavu
Consort Shipping
(☎ 302 877, fax 303 389) Dominion House Arcade, Thomson St, Suva;
(☎ 850 279, fax 850 442) Savusavu;
Emosi's Shipping
(☎ 313 366) 35 Gordon St, Suva;
(☎ 440 057, 440 013) Levuka

Patterson Brothers Shipping
(☎ 315 644, fax 301 652) Suite 1&2, Epworth Arcade, Nina St, Suva;
(☎ 661 173) Lautoka;
(☎ 880 382) Lesuma Holdings, Waiyevo, Taveuni;
(☎ 850 161) Savusavu;
(☎ 812 444) Labasa;
(☎ 440 125) Levuka
The *Yabula*, previously the *Grace*
(☎ 880 134) Taveuni

Suva-Savusavu-Taveuni Consort Shipping's MV *SOFE (Spirit of Free Enterprise)* does weekly voyages Suva-Koro-Savusavu (F$34/60 for economy/cabin; 13 hours) and Suva-Koro-Savusavu-Taveuni (F$37/70 for economy/cabin; about 6 hours extra). The stop at Koro is about one hour and the Suva-Taveuni trip involves a 13 hour stopover in Savusavu.

Beachcomber Cruises' 500 passenger ship the *Adi Savusavu (Dana Star)* has better facilities than the *SOFE* and has Suva-Savusavu voyages three times a week (F$28/47 for economy/1st class; about 11 hours). Once a week the ferry continues from Savusavu to Taveuni, taking an extra five hours (F$20/28 from Savusavu or F$43/50 from Suva).

Patterson Brothers also has a once or twice daily (except Sunday) service from Savusavu-Buca Bay-Taveuni (F$5.50 per person), involving 1½ hours by bus to Natuvu, Buca Bay and 1¾ hours by ferry to Waiyevo. There are bus connections to Labasa.

There are also daily (except Sunday) Taveuni-Buca Bay-Savusavu services by ferry (F$7) across the Somosomo Strait and bus (F$2.95) aboard the *Yabula*. It also does weekly Taveuni-Rabi trips.

Lautoka-Ellington Wharf-Nabouwalu-Labasa Patterson Brothers provides this trip three times a week (F$43.10). It involves a bus (3½ hours) from Lautoka, the *Ashika* ferry (3¾ hours) and a bus to Labasa (four hours).

Suva-Natovi-Nabouwalu-Labasa Patterson Brothers has this trip daily (except

unday) (F$43.00). It involves bus (1½
ours) from Suva, ferry (4½ hours) and bus
• Labasa (four hours).

uva-Natovi-Buresala-Levuka The Pat-
rson Brothers' service, daily except Sun-
ay (F$23.60), involves a bus (1½ hours)
om Suva to Natovi Landing followed by a
erry to Buresala Landing (one hour) and
us to Levuka (one hour).

uva-Bau Landing-Leluvia-Levuka
moisi's Shipping, (☎ 313 366 in Suva, or
• 440 057 in Levuka) has a daily (except
unday) minibus/small boat service from
uva to Leluvia, via Bau Landing (F$20/40
ne way/return). Three times a week the
oat continues to Levuka (F$25/50).

acht
achting is a great way to explore the Fiji
rchipelago: see the Getting There & Away
ection earlier in this chapter for more
nformation. It is also possible to charter
oats or hitch a ride on cruising vessels.

OCAL TRANSPORT
axi
he main towns have plenty of taxis, al-
ough many of them are rickety old dino-
aurs. Only in Suva do they use their meters,
o always confirm the price in advance.

RGANISED TOURS
iji has many companies providing tours
ithin the country, including trekking, cy-
ling, kayaking, diving, bus and 4WD tours.
'ruises to the outer islands such as the Ma-
anucas and Yasawas are popular. Viti
.evu has the most tours, with some on
valau, Taveuni and Vanua Levu.

/iti Levu: Nadi,
_autoka & Around

'adi town and Lautoka are 33km apart on
e western coast of Viti Levu. The airport
• 9km from Nadi and 24km from Lau-
ka. Sugar cane, well suited to the hot
and relatively dry climate of western Viti
Levu, is grown extensively. A high proportion of Fiji Indians live here.

NADI
● pop 30,884
Nadi (pronounced 'nan-di') is Fiji's third-
largest city and the country's tourism hub.
While not particularly appealing in itself, it
is a convenient base to organise trips around
Viti Levu or to offshore islands. There are
many organised day trips that pick up from
Nadi hotels.

Orientation
Queens Road heads south from Lautoka
into Nadi, passing by Nadi airport (see the
Getting There & Away section earlier in
this chapter) and crossing the Nadi River,
to become Nadi town's main street, which
terminates in a T-junction at the ornate
Hindu **Swami temple**.

Between the mosque and the Nadi River
bridge, just north of town, Narewa Rd leads
west to **Denarau Island**, 6km off Queens
Road. Nadi's two most upmarket resorts
and most tours and boat services to the
Mamanuca Islands depart from the **Denarau
Marina**.

Wailoaloa Rd also turns west off the
Queens Road near the West's Motor Inn.
Wailoaloa Beach is about 1.75km from the
highway.

Viti Levu

● pop 581,300   ● area 10,390 sq km

Viti Levu (Great Land) is Fiji's largest island,
the home of 75% of the population and
the two largest cities: Suva and Nadi.

Roughly oval in shape, Viti Levu is dominated by the mountain range running
north-south through its centre. The mountains, topped by Fiji's highest peak,
Tomanivi (1323m), divide the island into
the eastern region, which bears the brunt
of the south-eastern trade winds, and the
dryer western region.

FIJI

VITI LEVU

Waya

YASAWA GROUP — Wayasewa

Bligh Water

Vatia Point

Tavua — Korovou
Rab

Vomo

Vatukoula — Nadele

Kings Road

Nailaga — Ba — Ba Back Road — Nadar

Yanuya — Tokoriki

Vitogo — Vakabuli
Lololo Pine Forest

Ba River

Matamanoa
Mana

Saweni Beach — Lautoka

Beachcomber Island — Treasure Island — 2 — Abaca — Toge — Navala

Viseisei
Lomolomo — Abaca Cultural & Recreational Park — Mt Koroyanitu (Mt Evans) Koroyanitu National Park — Balevuto

Nagatagata

Navini — Vuda Point — Garden of the Sleeping Giant — Koro — Na

MAMANUCA GROUP

Castaway Island — Malolo — Naboutini — *Vaturu Dam* — Nanoko — Rairaima Platea

Malololailai (Plantation Island) — Denarau Island — Nadi International Airport — Bukuya — Nubuta

Malolo Barrier Reef — Naisali — Nawaka — *Nadi River* — Nad Plat

Namotu — Tavarua — Uciwai Landing — Nadi — Nausori — Korolevu — Monava (913m)

Nausori Highlands — Keiyasi

Momi Bay — Old Queens Rd — Koroba (1076 m) — Naihehe Cave

Tuvutau (Mt Gordon) (933m)

3 — Tau — Vunimoli — Narewa — *Sigatoka River* — VITI LEVU

Lomawai Rd — Tubairata

Likuri — Tilivalevu — Sigatoka Valley — *Upper* Nabukelev

Natadola Beach — Sanasana — Nakabuta — Lawai — Nadrala

Coral Coast Scenic Railway — Cuvu Beach — Cuvu — 4 — Sigatoka — Naroro (Tavuni Hill Fort) — Korotogo

Kolukulu — Biasevu — *Warwick*

Sigatoka Sand Dunes — 5 — 6 — 7 — Naboutini

Korolevu — 8 — Korovis

9 — Seru

CORAL COAST

0 — 10 — 20 km

VITI LEVU

Ferry to Nabouwalu
To E6 (Dive Site)
Ferry to Nabouwalu

Nananu-i-Ra
Nananu-i-Cake
Ellington Wharf
Malake
Rakiraki
Vaileka
Togowere
Kings Road
Vatukacevaceva
Nakauvadra Range
Viti Levu Bay
Nasau
Nanukuloa
Naiserelagi
Naseyani
Namarai
Matawailevu
Nayavutoka
Burelevu
Vanuakula
Dama
Mt Tova (647m)
Silana
Naigani
LOMAIVITI GROUP
Devokula
Tomanivi (Mt Victoria) (1323m)
Nalalawa
Dawasuma
Rukuruku
Namara
Soa
Ovalau
Levuka
Monasavu Dam
Koro-ni-O
Wairuarua
Nagai
Nasau
Lodoni
Natovi Landing
Buresala Landing
Lovoni
Draiba
Tokou
Laselevu
Wailotua
Waterfall
Naivicula
Motoriki
Yanuca
Yanuca Levu
Navuniyasi
Natokalau
Dakunivuna
Caqelai
Naitauvoli
Waiqa Gorge
Vunidawa
Naiuwai
Leluvia
Korovou
Naivucini
Serea
Nasava
Sote
Ucunivanua
Kumi
Wainimakatu
Savu
Baulevu
Kasavu
Viwa
Bau
Wainikoroiluva River
Nabukaluka
Rewa River
Nausori
Bau Landing
Cautata
Toberua
Saliadrau
Waivaka
Sawani
Nambua
Nakavika
Colo-i-Suva Forest Park
Nausori Airport
Nuku
Namuamua
Namosi Highlands
Mt Korobaba (429m)
Tamavua
Lokia
Nasilai Landing
Nasilai Reef
Wainadiro
Nukusere
Lami
Nakelo Landing
To Savusavu & Taveuni
mbogi
Navua River
Kalokolevu
Orchid Island
Suva Harbour
SUVA
Laucala Bay
Wainibokasi Landing
Nabukavesi
Nakavu
Waiyanitu
Navua
Queens Road
Pacific Harbour
Nukulau
Qaloa
Deuba
Beqa Passage
Yanuca
Beqa
Beqa Lagoon
rigate assage

1 Wananavu Beach Resort
2 First Landing Resort
3 Seashell Surf & Dive Resort
4 Fijian Resort
5 Tambua Sands Resort
6 Hideaway Resort
7 Naviti Resort
8 Warwick Fiji Resort
9 Waidroka Bay Resort
10 Marlin Bay Resort

Information

Tourist Offices The FVB (☎ 722 433, fax 720 141, fvbnadi@is.com.fj) is a good information source for travellers. The office is on the left as you come out of arrivals just after the ANZ bank, and is open to meet all international flights.

Nadi town and airport have several travel agencies, however, it is best to have a look at the FVB before booking anything. Some agencies specialise in budget accommodation and offer good deals, but be careful with the arrangements. Avoid paying too much up front, and get information on details such as the safety of the transport (especially if it includes small-boat trips), the cleanliness and facilities, and the type and price of food available. If possible, quiz other travellers or browse through the FVB comments book to get the current picture of a place.

Money The ANZ bank at the airport is open 24 hours every day. It charges F$2 per transaction to change foreign currency and travellers cheques. The ANZ, Westpac, Bank of Hawaii and National Bank are on the Main St in Nadi and do not charge transaction fees. Many hotels also change money but normally they pay a bit less than the banks.

Post & Communications The post office and the telephone exchange (Telecom) are in downtown Nadi near the market. There is also a post office at Nadi airport, across the car park from the arrivals area, near the cargo sheds. Public phones are not usually hard to find.

Email & Internet Access You can surf the Internet at the Bedarra Booking Office (☎ 725 130, fax 725 131, bedarra@is.com .fj) on Queens Road in Martinar opposite Ed's Bar in Martinar. It is open from 9 am to 5 pm daily. The West Coast Cafe next to Ed's Bar also has email and Internet services and stays open until 10 pm daily.

Medical Services For medical treatment, contact:

Dr Ram Raju Surgical Clinic
(☎ 700 240, ☎ 976 333) 2 Lodhia St, Nadi

Nadi Hospital
(☎ 701 128) Market Rd, Nadi
Namaka Medical Centre
(☎ 722 288) Namaka Lane (off Queens Roa‹ Namaka

Emergency Emergency phone numbe‹ include:

Emergency (☎ 000)
FVB emergency hotline (☎ 0800 721 721)
Police (☎ 700 222)
Ambulance (☎ 701 128)

Visiting the Interior

See the Viti Levu Highlands section later this chapter for information on visiting t‹ mountains independently. Abaca is an ea‹ day trip from Lautoka. Organised tours ca also be an OK way to have a look at t‹ high country and visit interior village‹ Rivers Fiji have rafting on the Navua Riv‹ (see Namosi Highlands, in the Viti Le‹ Highlands section later); Adventures Paradise has waterfall and cave tours ar Independent Tours has guided bike tours the Highlands (see Korotogo & Korolevu the Viti Levu's Queens Road section later this chapter). Rosie Tours (☎ 722 755, fa 722 607) has daily (except Sunday) full da trekking to the Nausori Highlands fro‹ Nadi for F$58 including lunch. It also offe more expensive six-day, five-night tours the Central Highlands.

Diving

Inner Space Adventures (☎/fax 723 883) Wailoaloa offers good value budget div trips to the Mamanuca sites. It charges F$8 for a two-tank dive trip, and provides pick-up service from hotels in the Na‹ area. Open-water courses cost F$320. Alte natively, Dive Tropex (☎ 701 888), based the Sheraton, has better boats and covers wider range of dive sites in the Mamanuca A two-tank dive trip costs F$141; F$61 for open-water.

Jet-Boat Trip

Shotover Jet Fiji (☎ 750 400, fax 750 66‹ has a noisy, hair-raising jet-boat trip (F$5‹

Traditional Vale & Bure

A traditional family house was called a *vale* (pronounced 'vah-ley' not 'vail'), while men's houses were known as *bure*. These buildings were dark and smoky inside with no windows and usually only one low door. Vale had hearth pits where the women cooked, and the packed earth floor was covered with grass or fern leaves and then pandanus or coconut- leaf mats. Sleeping compartments were at one end, behind a bark-cloth curtain. Finely-woven mats and wooden headrests were used for sleeping. Storage was in baskets hanging from walls, on overhead racks and suspended multipronged wooden hooks with broad-rimmed rat guards. Coconut-fibre string was used for lashing and decorating the roof structure. Houses were mostly rectangular, but in Western Viti Levu some were round or, later, square with conical roofs supported on a central post (thought to be a New Caledonian influence). In eastern Fiji, rounded gable ends were a Tongan influence.

Traditional *bure* (thatch-roofed hut) near the town of Cautata, near Nadi on Viti Levu

er person; half hour) of the Nadi River mangroves. It departs from Denarau Mana and there's a courtesy minibus transfers from hotels.

Golf & Tennis

The Denarau Golf & Racquet Club (☎ 750 077, fax 750 484) has an 18 hole golf course with bunkers in the shape of sea creatures. The club house has a restaurant and bar, pro-golf shop, meeting and change rooms. Green fees are F$85 for 18 holes and F$50 for nine holes. The all-weather and grass tennis courts fees are F$18 per hour and racket hire is F$8 per person.

Garden of the Sleeping Giant

These landscaped gardens have the Sabeto Mountains (or Sleeping Giant Ridge) as a backdrop, and are a peaceful place to have a picnic or spend a couple of hours relaxing among the orchids. Admission is F$9.90/ 90 for adults/children. It opens daily from am to 5 pm or Sunday by appointment

(☎ 722 701). The gardens are about 6km north of Nadi airport. From Queens Road turn inland on the gravel Wailoko Rd for about 2km. A taxi from Nadi will cost about F$12.

Scenic Flights

Most domestic flights are scenic, especially on a clear day. The islands, coral reefs and blue-green waters are gorgeous from above, and flights over the Nausori Highlands and the Sigatoka Valley are also spectacular. Easy day trips include Nadi to Malololailai and Mana in the Mamanucas.

Joy flights are available with Turtle Airways (☎ 722 389) in seaplanes (departing Newtown Beach or Denarau Sheraton) and with Island Hoppers by helicopter (☎ 720 410) departing from Denarau Island.

Cruises to the Mamanucas & Yasawas

Day trips and cruises to the stunning Mamanuca and Yasawa islands are very popular;

FIJI

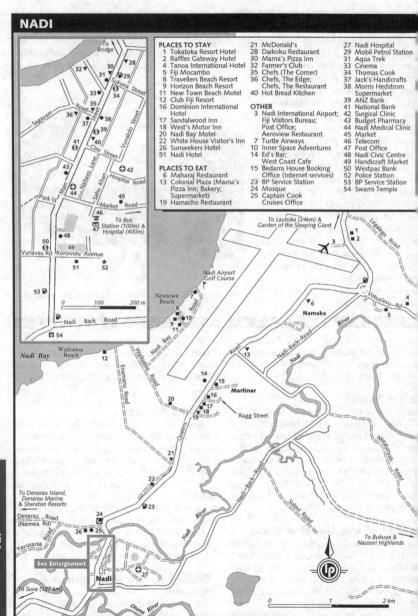

NADI

PLACES TO STAY
1 Tokatoka Resort Hotel
2 Raffles Gateway Hotel
4 Tanoa International Hotel
5 Fiji Mocambo
8 Travellers Beach Resort
9 Horizon Beach Resort
11 New Town Beach Motel
12 Club Fiji Resort
16 Dominion International Hotel
17 Sandalwood Inn
18 West's Motor Inn
20 Nadi Bay Motel
22 White House Visitor's Inn
26 Sunseekers Hotel
51 Nadi Hotel

PLACES TO EAT
6 Maharaj Restaurant
13 Colonial Plaza (Mama's Pizza Inn; Bakery; Supermarket)
19 Hamacho Restaurant

21 McDonald's
28 Daikoku Restaurant
30 Mama's Pizza Inn
32 Farmer's Club
35 Chefs (The Corner)
36 Chefs, The Edge; Chefs, The Restaurant
40 Hot Bread Kitchen

OTHER
3 Nadi International Airport; Fiji Visitors Bureau; Post Office; Aeroview Restaurant
7 Turtle Airways
10 Inner Space Adventures
14 Ed's Bar; West Coast Cafe
15 Bedarra House Booking Office (Internet services)
23 BP Service Station
24 Mosque
25 Captain Cook Cruises Office

27 Nadi Hospital
29 Mobil Petrol Station
31 Aqua Trek
33 Cinema
34 Thomas Cook
37 Jack's Handicrafts
38 Morris Hedstrom Supermarket
39 ANZ Bank
41 National Bank
42 Surgical Clinic
43 Budget Pharmacy
44 Nadi Medical Clinic
45 Market
46 Telecom
47 Post Office
48 Nadi Civic Centre
49 Handicraft Market
50 Westpac Bank
52 Police Station
53 BP Service Station
54 Swami Temple

e the island sections for more information. Malololailai, Mana and Castaway islands ke day-trippers.

Places to Stay – Budget

onsider whether you want the convenience f staying close to downtown (where there re more options for places to eat), at the lack-sand Wailoaloa Beach (fairly isolated ut peaceful) or along Queens Road beveen the airport and downtown Nadi.

Along the Highway The *Nadi Bay Motel* (☎ *723 599, fax 720 092, nadibay@is om.fj)*, on Wailoaloa Rd about 400m off Queens Road, is a good option for budget ccommodation. Dormitory accommodation ere is F\$12 a bed; try the one upstairs, hich may get more light and breezes. ooms with shared facilities are F\$35/45 for ngles/doubles, and those with private bathom are F\$56/68. Rooms are reasonably lean and have fans but no cooking facilies. The hotel has a pleasant outdoor sitting rea, a swimming pool and a reasonably riced restaurant. Credit cards are accepted.

The budget rooms at *West's Motor Inn* n Queens Road can be a good option (see etails under Places to Stay – Mid-Range, ter in this section). Next door, on the corer of Ragg St, the *Sandalwood Inn* (☎ *722 44, fax 720 103, sandalwood@is.com.fj)* is n OK budget option. Rooms with shared acilities are F\$28/35. Rooms with private acilities cost F\$35/42 and air-con versions ost F\$55/62. The *Sandalwood Lodge* (☎ *722 044, fax 720 103, sandalwood@ .com.fj)*, 200m further down Ragg St, is etter maintained with good value self-ontained units. The units feature a small itchen, TV, phone, private balcony and cute wimming pool for F\$70/77/83 for singles/ oubles/triples.

The *White House Visitor's Inn* (☎ *700 22, fax 702 822, 40 Kennedy Ave)* is closer • the town centre. Small four or five-bed an-cooled dorms here cost F\$11 a bed. ooms with fans and private facilities are \$33/44 for singles/doubles. A small breakast is included in the price. The restaurant erves Chinese meals for F\$6 to \$14.

At the Beach There are several budget options at Newtown Beach off Nadi Bay Rd, and another at Wailoaloa Beach at the end of Enamanu Rd. Both beaches are about 5km north of Nadi town. The beach is fairly unattractive, but is an alternative to the town. The disadvantage of staying here is that food options and transport are limited. To get to town you can either catch a local bus (50c) or taxi for about F\$3. A taxi to the airport costs F\$7 but normally the resorts provide free airport transfers. Buses depart Wailoaloa Beach every hour till 11.30 am and less frequently in the afternoon until the last one at 5.30 pm. Boats leave from here to Mana Island backpacker 'resorts'.

The *Horizon Beach Resort* (☎ *722 832, fax 720 662)* has friendly staff and a small swimming pool. Dorm rooms cost F\$10 per person and can get crowded, but are usually clean and have hot showers. Fan-cooled rooms are F\$28/30 for singles/doubles, but sea-view, air-con rooms are bigger, and better value for F\$37/40. There are no cooking facilities, and meals cost around F\$6/9 for lunch/dinner. *New Town Beach Motel* (☎ *723 339, fax 720 087)* is quieter and more homey. Its fan-cooled, five bed dorm costs F\$13.70 per person, and double rooms are F\$38. Meals cost F\$6/8 for lunch/dinner and the motel also has a swimming pool and deck in the back garden.

Travellers Beach Resort (☎ *723 322, fax 720 026)* is the largest of the three beach resorts, but has the least atmosphere. The dorm rooms are OK and sleep a maximum of four at F\$11 per person. Standard rooms with fans are F\$33/38.50 for singles/ doubles or F\$38.50/49.50 with air-con, but it is possible to bargain. It also has kitchenette villas, with fans, microwave and TV, which sleep four people for F\$66. The hotel has a restaurant, a small pool and deck on the beach. It accepts Visa and MasterCard.

Club Fiji Resort (☎ *702 189, fax 720 350)*, at Wailoaloa Beach off Enamanu Rd, has more of a resort feel, but seems a bit misplaced on this stretch of dark sand bay. There are 24 fan-cooled bure, a swimming pool and a large dining/bar bure. The resort has a tour desk, bar and restaurant (main meals F$11 to $20) and a diving operation. There is a daily shuttle bus to downtown Nadi at 10 am, returning at 1 pm, or a taxi ride costs F$5. Prices are F$85.80/66/42.90 for a beachfront/oceanview/garden bure. Two bure with 10 beds crammed in each are used as dormitories and cost F$11/14.50 per person without/with breakfast. Newer beachfront rooms in a double storey block are good, with bay views and balconies for F$132 for doubles.

Downtown Nadi The *Sunseekers Hotel* (☎ 700 400) is conveniently located near the north end of town on the Narewa Rd to Denarau Island. The hotel houses up to 100 guests, but is reasonably clean and organised, and is a good option for budget travellers. Dorm beds cost F$8.80 a night. Prices for fan-cooled private rooms are in the range of F$27 to $38. Some rooms have toilet and shower. The hotel also has tourist information, a small shop, bar, outdoor deck with tables, swimming pool (by accounts not always full) and a small restaurant.

The *Nadi Hotel* (☎ 700 000, fax 700 280), on Koroivolu Ave, is right in town near the post office, market and bus station. It offers budget accommodation in a two storey building, with a garden and swimming pool. The male and female dorms are on opposite sides of the pool and are not bad for F$15. Standard fan-cooled rooms are OK but a bit musty and cost F$35/40 for singles/doubles. If choosing air-con rooms, pick the deluxe versions in the newer building for F$50/60, though it can be noisy with the disco next door.

Places to Stay – Mid-Range
Most of the mid-range hotels are located on Queens Road near the airport, an important consideration given the very early morning departure times of many international flights. The disadvantage is their distance from most restaurants and entertainment. Ask about 'walk-in rates'. Day rooms (for those awaiting night-time flights) are usually about half-price.

The *Raffles Gateway Hotel* (☎ 722 444, fax 720 620), directly opposite the airport,

is convenient and good value. Standa[rd] rooms are F$44 for doubles (rooms upstai[rs] are better). There are also spacious delu[xe] rooms for F$116.60. Up to two childre[n] under 16 years can share with parents f[or] free. Restaurant meals cost around F$15.

Tokatoka Resort Hotel (☎ 720 222, f[ax] 720 400, tokatokaresort@is.com.fj), al[so] opposite the airport, is just a kilometre fu[r]ther north towards Lautoka. It has 74 vill[a] style units ranging from studios and vil[la] studios for F$137/151 doubles/up to fo[ur] better-value villa apartments for F$193 (u[p] to four people) and full villas for F$3[00] (maximum seven people). All units ha[ve] cooking facilities. The atmosphere a[nd] facilities are good for families and it has [a] restaurant and bar, and a large swimmi[ng] pool with water slide.

The *West's Motor Inn* (☎ 720 044, f[ax] 720 071, westsmotorin@is.com.fj), [on] Queens Road, has the same owners as Tok[a]toka. It has been recently refurbished and [is] good value. Standard air-con rooms co[st] F$55 and the bigger deluxe versions arou[nd] the swimming pool cost F$99. Try aski[ng] for reduced walk-in rates. The hotel has [a] bar and the restaurant has meals for F$14 [to] $19.50.

The Dominion (International Hote[l, ☎] 722 255, fax 720 187, dominionint@[is] .com.fj) is on Queens Road about 4.5k[m] from Nadi airport. Standard air-con room[s] here (called superior) are F$110/115 f[or] singles/doubles, but deluxe versions are be[t]ter value for F$130/135. Amenities inclu[de] a swimming pool and tennis courts. Resta[u]rant dinners cost from F$12.50 to $29.50.

Places to Stay – Top End
Near the Airport There are two expe[n]sive hotels near the airport, both offeri[ng] pretty standard hotel rooms without mu[ch] character. Both have swimming pools a[nd] 24 hour cafes. The *Fiji Mocambo* (☎ 7[22] 000, fax 720 324, mocambo@is.com.fj) o[n] Votualevu Rd is managed by Shangri-[La] Hotels, but don't expect the same standar[d] here. Most rooms have mountain view[s,] air-con, TV and refrigerator. Standar[d] (called superior) rooms cost F$186/198 f[or]

ngles/doubles. The hotel has a nine hole olf course, tennis, and live bands 'ednesday to Saturday nights. The *Tanoa* *ternational Hotel (☎ 720 277, fax 720 91, tanoahotels@is.com.fj)* off Votualevu d used to be a Travelodge but is now lo- ally owned. Air-con studio (superior) oms are F$180 for doubles; F$200 for eluxe versions.

enarau Island The *Sheraton Royal 'enarau Resort (☎ 750 000, fax 750 259)*, reviously the Regent Fiji, was Fiji's first uxury hotel. It has 273 rooms in spacious rounds. Prices range from F$402 for gar- enview rooms to F$633 for beachfront oms. The *Sheraton Fiji Resort (☎ 750 77, fax 750 818)* has 292 rooms, all with cean views, from F$534 to F$727 for singles/ oubles. The Royal has a traditional feel ith buildings blending in with the luxur- nt gardens, while the Sheraton Fiji has ore of a modern Mediterranean style. rices quoted are rack rates: there are sea- onal price variations and most people range some sort of package deal or dis- ount. The new *Sheraton Villas (☎ 750 77, fax 750 818)*, part of the Sheraton Fiji esort, are a good option if you prefer a elf-contained apartment.

Denarau Island is a reclaimed mangrove rea and the beach is dark grey sand, which ay be disappointing for some. It is an up- arket world in itself with many restau- nts and bars, a golf and tennis club, fitness entres, water aerobics and beach masseurs. here are snorkelling and fishing trips; rindsurfing; sailing and scuba diving; and ruises from the marina. Motorised water ctivities cost extra. The resorts cater well r young families, with a daily entertain- ent program for children.

laces to Eat

adi has a variety of restaurants and eating laces. Most places serve a mixture of Chi- ese, Indian, Fijian and Western dishes. here are lots of lunch-time eateries down- wn. Try small restaurants around the Nadi ivic Centre; while they may not be particu- rly clean, they have good, cheap food and

are popular with locals. A fast-food alterna- tive is *McDonald's* on Queens Road.

'Chefs' has three different places to eat, all on Sagayam Rd, just off the main street in Nadi. All have air-con: *Chefs (the Cor- ner)* has good value quick meals and snacks; *Chefs, the Edge* is a medium-priced restau- rant, while *Chefs, the Restaurant (☎ 703 131)* is one of the most expensive restau- rants in Nadi, offering international cuisine and candle-lit dinners; closed on Sundays.

For pizza and pasta, a good inexpensive option is *Mama's Pizza Inn* downtown on Main St or at the Colonial Plaza in Namaka on Queens Road. The large pizza is huge and costs F$13 to $22, or try the vege- tarian bolognaise spaghetti for F$6. *Maha- raj (☎ 722 962)*, on Queens Road near the airport, serves good Indian food. It is not conveniently located, but also does take- away. The *Farmer's Club* downtown has OK curries and welcomes visitors.

Nadi has two good Japanese restaurants. *Daikoku Restaurant (☎ 703 622)*, down- town near the bridge, is best avoided if on a budget. The *Hamacho (☎ 720 252)*, on Queens Road near the Capricorn Hotel, has a comfortable bar, and table seating offering a la carte small serves from F$4 to $8. If you are craving a good steak and are pre- pared to spend a bit more on food and taxis, try the *Wet Mongoose (☎ 750 900)* at the Denarau Marina.

The upmarket resort hotels on Denarau Island have fine dining restaurants, which are open for visitors. If you are at the air- port, the *Aeroview* restaurant and bar has air-con and accepts credit cards.

Self-Catering Nadi has a large produce *market*, which sells lots of fresh fruit and vegetables. Good quality meat, however, is fairly difficult to come by. There are sev- eral large *supermarkets* and *bakeries* downtown.

Entertainment

Nadi has nowhere near the variety of nightlife of Suva, however, the upmarket hotels usually have something happening at weekends. *Ed's Bar* on Queens Road in

FIJI

Hindu Symbolic Rites

ROBYN JONES

Fearless Ganesh, guardian of entrances and patron of travel authors

A Hindu temple symbolises the body, the residence of the soul. Union with God is achieved through prayer and by ridding the body of impurities (meat cannot be eaten before entering a temple and shoes must be removed).

Water and fire are used for blessings. Water carried in a pot with flowers is symbolic of the Mother, while burning camphor symbolises the light of knowledge and understanding. When illuminated the soul merges with the Great Soul. The trident represents fire the protector and the three flames of purity, light and knowledge.

The breaking of a coconut represents the cracking of three forms of human weakness: egotism (the hard shell), delusion (the fibre) and material attachments (the outermost covering). The white kernel and sweet water represent the pure soul within

Firewalking is a means to become as one with the Mother. Hindus believe that the body should be enslaved to the spirit, and denied all comforts. They believe life is like walking on fire and that a disciplined approach, like the one required in the ceremony, helps them to achieve balance, self-acceptance and to see good in everything.

Martinar is a good place for a drink; it's open until 1 am daily.

Shopping

Nadi's Main St is largely devoted to souvenir and duty-free shops, including Jack's Handicrafts and Sogo. There is an outdoor handicraft market open every day near the Civic Centre.

Getting There & Away

See the Getting There & Away section earlier in this chapter for information on Nadi international airport and the Getting Around section for inter-island air and boat services, and car rental.

Getting Around

There are regular local and express buses that travel along Queens Road. There are local buses to Newtown Beach but not to Denarau Island. Taxis are plentiful in Na but they do not use meters, so prices shou be confirmed in advance.

VUDA POINT

Vuda Point is a peninsula between Nadi a Lautoka where the first Melanesians we thought to have arrived to populate Fiji. now has a marina, a couple of resorts and oil terminal.

Places to Stay & Eat

The *First Landing Resort* (☎ 666 171, f 668 882, firstland@is.com.fj), near the m rina, has 13 air-con cottages with mosqu nets and verandah for F$198 for up to fo people including breakfast. It has a love free-form swimming pool and a pleasa beachfront restaurant. Meals on offer i clude wood-fired-oven pizza, seafood a steak dishes, from F$14 to 26. The mari next door has a good cafe serving cheap snacks.

Getting There & Away

The Queens Road now bypasses the turn-off to Vuda Point. The turn-off is about 10km south of Lautoka – the Vuda Point Marina is a further 3.5km.

LAUTOKA

● pop 43,274

Lautoka, the administrative centre of the Western Division, is Fiji's second port and largest city after Suva. While not an especially interesting city, it is a simpler place to get around on foot than Nadi. The town has a large produce and handicraft market near the bus station. Buses leave here for Kings Road to the north and Queens Road to the south.

There are several banks downtown, including ANZ, Westpac and National Bank, where you can change money and travellers cheques. The Cathay Hotel will also change money at bank rates. The post office, where there are a few public telephones, is on the corner of Vitogo Parade and Tavewa Ave. The Lautoka Hospital (☎ 660 399) is on Thomson Crescent.

Lautoka has a cybercafe (The Last Call) with email and Internet services – see Places to Eat later in this section.

The **Abaca Cultural & Recreational Park**, in the mountains about 10km south-east of Lautoka, is a great place for trekking and has budget accommodation and village stays: see the Viti Levu Highlands section later in this chapter.

Places to Stay

The *Sea Breeze Hotel* (☎ 660 717) is at the end of Bekana Lane on the waterfront, in a quiet cul-de-sac, close to the market and bus station. Rooms with en suites and aircon cost F$37/44 for singles/doubles. Rooms with ceiling fan are F$30/35 but

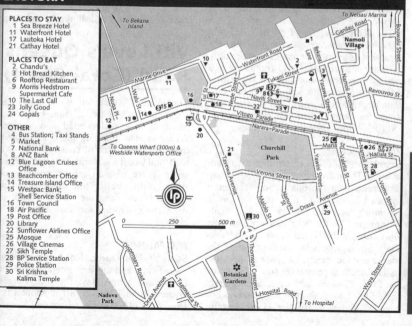

LAUTOKA

PLACES TO STAY
1 Sea Breeze Hotel
11 Waterfront Hotel
17 Lautoka Hotel
21 Cathay Hotel

PLACES TO EAT
2 Chandu's
3 Hot Bread Kitchen
6 Rooftop Restaurant
9 Morris Hedstrom
   Supermarket Cafe
10 The Last Call
23 Jolly Good
24 Gopals

OTHER
4 Bus Station; Taxi Stands
5 Market
7 National Bank
8 ANZ Bank
12 Blue Lagoon Cruises
   Office
13 Beachcomber Office
14 Treasure Island Office
15 Westpac Bank;
   Shell Service Station
16 Town Council
18 Air Pacific
19 Post Office
20 Library
22 Sunflower Airlines Office
25 Mosque
26 Village Cinemas
27 Sikh Temple
28 BP Service Station
29 Police Station
30 Sri Krishna
   Kalima Temple

To Bekana Island
To Nelsau Marina
Namoli Village
Waterfront Road
Marine Drive
Tukani Street
Naviti Street
Vitogo Parade
Narara Parade
To Queens Wharf (300m) &
Westside Watersports Office
Churchill Park
Verona Street
Mana St
Nacula St
Botanical Gardens
L Hospital Road
To Hospital
Nadovu Park

0   250   500 m

FIJI

these are often booked out. Despite being a bit expensive for the budget traveller, this hotel is a good option for getting rid of jet lag. It has a breakfast room upstairs, a quiet bar and TV lounge downstairs, and a swimming pool.

In the old wing of the *Lautoka Hotel* (☎ 660 388, fax 660 201, 2-12 Naviti St) are budget rooms, fairly grungy but spacious, for F$16.80/22 with shared bathroom. Dormitory rooms are F$8.80/11 per person with fan/air-con. Most rooms don't have external windows. There is a swimming pool, a reasonably good restaurant, a bar and a TV lounge, with a friendly, easy-going atmosphere.

The *Cathay Hotel* (☎ 660 566, fax 660 136, cathay@fiji4less.com), at Tavewa Ave up from the post office roundabout, is another option for budget accommodation. It has a swimming pool and bar, a TV lounge and a restaurant, serving OK meals. Fan-cooled rooms with private bathrooms cost F$29/38.50, and air-con rooms with private facilities cost F$40/47. A bed in one of its various dorms (up to four people in each) costs F$9.50.

The *Waterfront Hotel* (☎ 664 777, fax 665 870, tanoahotels@is.com.fj) is the only upmarket hotel in Lautoka, catering mainly to business travellers. Its 47 rooms are in a modern two storey building on Waterfront Rd. It has a spacious lounge and bar, outdoor deck, a pool and a good restaurant. Rates for doubles are not bad value at F$110/128 for superior rooms/suites.

Places to Eat

Lautoka has far fewer restaurants than Nadi or Suva. There are, however, various cheap restaurants near the bus station that serve Indian, Chinese and Fijian fare for lunch. *Chandu's*, opposite the station, has meals for around F$6 for both lunch and dinner. *Jolly Good* at the corner of Naviti and Vakabale Sts is a popular outdoor venue for snacks and ice cream. The *cafe* at the Morris Hedstrom supermarket has good value fast food; it's open until 7 pm. Self-caterers should try Lautoka's produce *market*. For vegetarian meals, try the Hare Krishna

restaurant *Gopals* on the corner of Yasaw and Naviti Sts, open from 9 am to 6 pr Both the Morris Hedstrom cafe and Gopa are closed on Sunday.

The Last Call (☎ 650 525, 21 Tui St) is a Italian restaurant/cybercafe on the wate front, quite a contrast with the outside su roundings. It serves pasta (F$10 to $13 pizza ($F4 to $16), salads, coffee, cakes an homemade gelati. Some of the dishes are bit pricey but generally the food is goo The *restaurant* at the Lautoka Hotel offe OK main meals from F$7 to $12.

Getting There & Away

Lautoka is 33km north of Nadi. Local buse shuttle between the two towns every 1 minutes during the day and less frequent during the evening. There are also regul express buses along Kings Road ar Queens Road (see the Getting Around se tion earlier in this chapter), as well as carr ers and Viti minibuses to Suva.

Getting Around

It is easy to get around Lautoka on foc Taxis are plentiful and short rides are chea

Viti Levu's Queens Road (Coral Coast)

The Queens Road follows the souther perimeter of Viti Levu, from Lautoka Suva. It is a sealed road and a scen drive/bus ride, hugging the coast most the way. The stretch of coastline known a the Coral Coast has a wide fringing reef of shore. There are many accommodation op tions. Both Pacific and Sunbeam hav regular buses along the Queens Road: se the Getting Around section earlier in th chapter.

MOMI BAY

South of Nadi, Queens Road winds throug cane fields, and the first interesting detou is towards Momi Bay, the old unseale Queens Road. The turn-off is about 18k from Nadi (46.3km from Lautoka).

laces to Stay

here is budget accommodation at *Seashell urf & Dive Resort* (☎ 706 100, fax 706 94, seashell@is.com.fj), about 1km south-est of Nadi off the old Queens Road. amping is F$12 per tent. Dorm rooms naximum five people) with fans and lock-rs are F$11 per person. Fan-cooled lodge ooms with shared facilities cost F$45/50 or singles-doubles/triples. Fan-cooled bure ave cooking facilities and fridge and cost $90 for doubles or triples; F$120 for up to ix people in a family bure. Self-caterers hould bring supplies. Meals at the restau-ant here are about F$6.50/16.50 for unch/dinner and there are backpacker spe-ials and cheap snacks at the coffee shop nd local shop. Meal plans cost from F$25 o $33.50.

The beach here is not great, however, here's a swimming pool, volleyball, tennis, iving, surfing and watersports equipment or hire. Island hopping is F$60 per person. Diving with Scuba Bula is F$90 for a two-ank dive; F$400 for an open-water course. norkelling trips with Scuba Bula are F$15. urfing trips by local boat to the reef breaks round Namotu in the southern Mamanucas ost from F$25 to $35.

Getting There & Away

rom Nadi, travel about 11km along the old Queens Road, then take a turn-off to the ight and continue for another 1.5km. Air-ort transfers using the resort minibus are $10. Local buses (Dominion Company) lepart from Nadi bus station (four times laily; one hour). There are also daily buses rom Sigatoka (20km). Taxis to Momi Bay re F$33 (45 minutes) from the airport, or $40 from Sigatoka.

NATADOLA BEACH

his gorgeous white-sand beach is the best n mainland Viti Levu. The setting is idyl-ic, but watch your valuables as there have een reports of theft. The upmarket resort pposite the beach is the only development, o far. Local villagers offer horse riding long the beach and sell coconuts and shell ecklaces.

Places to Stay & Eat

Natadola Beach Resort (☎ 721 000, fax 721 000, natadola@is.com.fj) is a cute, small-scale luxury resort. It has eight fan-cooled rooms with private courtyards, an attractive swimming pool and a landscaped garden. Prices are F$405/480 for a room/two-bedroom suite, including all meals and transfers, or F$262/337 for rooms only. The resort does not accept children under 16 years. The restaurant/bar, with Spanish-style rendered walls and open-plan courtyard, is open to the public and has an interesting menu with lunches around F$12; dinner from F$20 to $28.

Getting There & Away

Natadola Beach is fairly isolated and is a good day trip escape from Nadi. The Maro Rd turn-off heads south to Natadola off the Queens Road, 36km from Nadi just past the police post. There is a temple with a life-size goddess on the corner. Continue along the gravel road for 9.5km and turn left at a T-junction. There are no direct buses from Nadi, but there are six buses daily except Sunday from Sigatoka (the trip takes about one hour). The Coral Coast Railway runs scenic tours to this beach: see the following Yanuca entry.

YANUCA

Past the turn-off to Natadola Queens Road winds through hills and down to the coast. On the offshore island of Yanuca, about 50km from Nadi, is *Shangri-La's Fijian Resort* (☎ 520 155, fax 500 402, fijianresort@ is.com.fj), linked to the mainland by a cause-way. It has 436 air-con rooms in five differ-ent wings, all with private balconies, sea or lagoon views. Rates for standard rooms are F$355/390 sea/lagoon for singles or dou-bles. It is very family orientated: up to two children can share with parents at no extra charge, children under 12 can eat buffet-style meals for free and it has the essential kids' club, a supervised children's play area. There are five restaurants serving good food; expect to spend at least F$7/10/20 for breakfast/lunch/dinner per person a day. Nonmotorised sports are included in the

FIJI

price. Facilities include a nine hole golf course, a gym, two swimming pools, tennis courts, croquet and lawn bowls. Scuba diving is with Sea Sports – a two-tank dive costs F$132 and an open-water course costs F$487.

The **Coral Coast Scenic Railway** (☎ 520 434, fax 500 402) is on the Queens Road near the causeway. It offers scenic rides along the coast on an old diesel sugar train to the beautiful Natadola Beach. The 14km trip takes about 1¼ hours to get to the beach, departing from Yanuca at 10 am and returning at 4 pm. The ride costs F$69 per person, including a barbecue (BBQ) lunch. Children under 12 are half-price or free if under six. It is a popular trip with families, but for those on a tight budget it is probably a waste of money. Better value is a train/bus/boat day trip for F$99 combining a one-way train ride and a trip to Likuri (Robinson Crusoe Island).

SIGATOKA

Sigatoka is a small town 61km south of Nadi and 127km west of Suva. The town is near the mouth of the Sigatoka River, Fiji's second-largest river. It is predominantly a farming community as well as a service town for tourists drawn to the Coral Coast resorts.

Sigatoka Sand Dunes

This is a large formation of windblow dunes along a windswept beach near th mouth of the Sigatoka River. The dunes a about 5km long rising to about 60m at th western end. Archaeological investigatio have been carried out by the Fiji Museu and human skeletal remains and potte shards have been discovered here, sugges ing that there was a village near the easte end of the dunes in prehistoric times. Th state-owned part of the area was declared national park in 1989. It is quite spectac lar and is a great place for a walk, althoug there have been muggings at the easte end. Enter through the visitor centre on th Queens Road, 4.5km from Sigatoka. Th park entry fee is F$5. Allow about one ho each way to walk to the beach.

Tavuni Hill Fort

About 4km north of Sigatoka on the eas ern side of the river is a defensive hill fo tification, which was used in times of wa The steep limestone ridge, about 90m hig at the edge of a bend in the Sigatoka Rive was an obvious strategic location. The are a number of grave sites, *arara* (cer monial grounds) and a *vatu ni boko* (head-chopping stone). The site has bee restored and has an information centr

The Kai Colo Uprising

The last significant tribal conflict in Fiji was the Kai Colo Uprising of 1875-76. The Kai Colo (mountain people of inland Viti Levu) disagreed with the ceding of Fiji to Great Britain in 1874 and did not appreciate the imposition of the new politics and religion by the colonial regime.

The measles epidemic of 1875 destroyed about a third of Fiji's population, totally wiping out some villages. The Kai Colo interpreted this both as a deliberate effort by the European invaders to destroy them, and as a punishment from their gods for discarding the traditional ways. Any faith in the new church dissolved and they returned to the old religion and tribal warfare, descending into the Sigatoka Valley and attacking and burning villages of their traditional enemies.

This was seen by the colonial government as a direct threat to the viability of their fledgling administration. To quash this 'rebellion' and set an example to others, Sir Arthur Gordon formed a constabulary of over 1000 Fijian men under the Nadroga Chief Ratu Luki. This force ascended the valley, destroying hill forts and hanging, imprisoning or dispersing the chiefs involved. Sir Gordon's strategy was to pit Fijian against Fijian, on the one hand reinforcing the link with the new laws and, on the other, distancing the colonial government from the bloodshed.

dmission is F$3/6/15 for children/adults/ amilies, open 8 am to 5 pm daily except unday. Regular local buses departing Siga- oka bus station pass Tavuni Hill along Ka- anagasau Rd heading for Mavua seven mes daily. Taxis are about F$8 return.

laces to Stay & Eat

igatoka town is not the most interesting lace to spend a night, but it may be a con- enient stopover and base for exploring the ocal attractions. The *Sigatoka Club* ☎ *500 026)* by the river is the local hotel nd watering hole. It offers spacious simple ooms for F$24/36 for singles/doubles and five person dorm is F$11 per bed. For ice lunches, try *Le Cafe* on the main street ear the bridge. There are many cheap ateries near the market and bus station and lso two *bakeries*. Self-caterers can stock p at the *market* and the Morris Hedstrom upermarket.

Club Masa Resort (☎ *925 717)* is a surfie ang-out near the beach at the edge of the igatoka Sand Dunes. At the time of writ- ng this place was operating haphazardly nd there have been reports of knifepoint obberies at the Sand Dunes sites nearby. Nevertheless, camping is F$15 per person nd dorm beds F$22 including breakfast nd dinner.

The turn-off from the Queens Road to Club Masa is at Kulukulu Rd, about 2km outh-west of Sigatoka. It is a further 2km long the dusty road and an extra 1km hike cross the paddock to Club Masa. There are Sunbeam buses that depart from Sigatoka ous station for Kulukulu village six times daily, with fewer services on Sunday. A taxi vill cost about F$4 one way from Sigatoka.

KOROTOGO & KOROLEVU

The Queens Road between Korotogo and Korolevu winds along the shore, with scenic iews of bays, beaches, coral reefs and nountains. The Korotogo area is about 8km ast of Sigatoka, while Korolevu village is 1km east of Sigatoka. At the time of writ- ng the Outrigger Reef Resort in Korotogo vas undergoing a complete redevelopment, et to become another huge resort. This stretch of coast has a range of dormitory, self-catering and resort accommodation. Most beaches here are suitable for swim- ming and snorkelling at high tide only.

Kula Eco Park

This park (☎ 500 505, fax 520 202), north- east of the Outrigger Reef Resort, has re- cently been redeveloped into a wildlife sanctuary and educational centre for chil- dren. It has a captive-breeding program for the endangered Fiji Peregrine Falcon, and Fiji's Crested and Banded Iguanas. There are also bushwalking paths through forests. It is open from 10 am to 4.30 pm daily; admission is F$11/5.50 for adults/children.

Diving

Sea Sports (☎ 500 225) takes dive trips to some of the Coral Coast reefs and passages. A two-tank dive trip costs F$132, and an open-water course is F$487.

Organised Tours

Adventures in Paradise (☎ 520 833, fax 520 848, wfall@is.com.fj) offers day trips (F$99) to the Naihehe cave (see under Siga- toka Valley in the Viti Levu Highlands sec- tion later in this chapter), and a half-day tour (F$79) to Biausevu Waterfall, near Korolevu. Tours include a village visit and kava ceremony. Prices include lunch and transport from hotels in Nadi and on the Coral Coast. The Adventures in Paradise office is in a small group of shops just west of the Outrigger Reef Resort in Korotogo.

Mountainbikes can be hired from Adven- tures in Paradise, for F$13/25 for a half/ full-day. Independent Tours (☎/fax 520 678), has guided bike tours for groups of two to six people. A day tour of the Sigatoka area is F$79. Half-day tours to the Nausori Highlands are F$49. A three day tour of the Sigatoka Valley and Nausori Highlands, sleeping in villages, is F$299.

Places to Stay – Budget

The *Vakaviti Motel* (☎/fax 520 424, bulavakaviti@is.com.fj) is about 500m west of the Reef Resort, on the steep hillside just across the road from the beach. It has rooms opening onto a swimming pool and over-looking the ocean; F$55 for up to three people. One of the rooms is a six bunk dorm; F$12 per person. All rooms have ceiling fans, cooking facilities and private bathrooms. It also has a spacious dorm (the surf shack) with two or four-bed rooms, a sitting area and kitchen; F$15 per person.

Another good budget place is *Tubakula Beach Bungalows* (☎ 500 097, fax 340 236, tubakula@fiji4less.com) on the beachfront east of the Reef Hotel. It has 27 A-framed, fan-cooled, self-contained bungalows. Prices vary according to position: from F$50 to $68 for up to three people, plus F$10.50 per extra person. Dorm accommodation costs F$13.50 per night (three to four beds) in eight small rooms with communal cooking facilities. It also has good value, renovated 'superior' bungalows; F$70/86 for pool-side/beachfront for up to three people. It has spacious grounds, swimming pool and a minimarket. The *Crow's Nest Resort* also has a nice little elevated six bed dorm room (no cooking facilities), on top of their restaurant and pool, for F$25 per bed; see the following Places to Stay – Mid-Range entry.

The Beachouse (☎ 530 500, fax 450 200, beachouse@is.com.fj) is 7km east of Korolevu, 127km from Suva, just off Queens Road. It is a popular budget travellers' stop in the area, because of its good atmosphere and nice beach setting. It has a couple of two storey timber buildings with double rooms upstairs, and dorm rooms downstairs (maximum of five in each). Prices are F$16.50 per bed in the dorm, F$38.50 for a double room or camping F$8.80 per person. Meals at its *Coconut Cafe* restaurant cost F$3 to $5 for breakfast and about F$7 for lunch or dinner, but there is also a simple communal kitchen at the back. Buses from Suva or Nadi cost about F$5 and drivers will pick up and drop off at the gate. *Waidroka Bay Resort* also has a big eight bed dormitory bure (no cooking facilities) for F$18 per night; see the following Places to Stay – Mid-Range entry.

Places to Stay – Mid-Range

The *Crow's Nest Resort* (☎ 500 513, fax 520 354, crowsnest@is.com.fj) is 7km ea of Sigatoka town in Korotogo on the hi side across the road from the beach. It h 17 nice self-contained split-level villas wi balconies and sea views. Units have o double bed on the upper level and two si gle beds below, air-con, ceiling fans, coo ing facilities and a refrigerator. Rates a F$169 for a unit accommodating up to fo people. The resort has a swimming pool ar a sun deck next to the restaurant.

Further east past the Crow's Nest Reso is Bedarra House (☎ 500 476, fax 520 11 bedarra@is.com.fj), specialising in perso alised service. The main building, more lil a mansion than a hotel, has only four room (two family, two double), but the owne were building a new block of rooms at th time of writing. It has a swimming poo nice gardens and one of the best restau rant/bars in the area. Daily tariffs, includir breakfast, are F$132 for up to four peopl

Tambua Sands Beach Resort (☎ 50 399, fax 520 265) is approximately halfwa between Nadi and Suva, west of the Hide away Resort. The resort has 25 simple far cooled bure along a reasonably good beacl It also has a small swimming pool, but av erage services and facilities. Rates ar F$115 per bure, or F$88 in one the six gar den rooms. Meals at its restaurant will co. around F$8/9/21 for breakfast/lunch/dinne

Waidroka Bay Resort (☎ 304 605, fc 304 383, waidrokaresort@is.com.fj) is in beautifully secluded section of the coas 69km west of Suva and 4km off the Queer Road through steep hills and forest. It cater mainly for adventurous divers or surfer: Oceanfront bure with ceiling fans, tea an coffee-making facilities and verandahs t the bay cost F$99/134 for a double/tripl per night. A room in the lodge (maximum o three people in a room with shared facili ties) is F$54 per person per night. Mea packages are F$30 per day.

Two-tank dive trips inside the bay and or the outer reef are F$95 plus F$15 for equip ment rental. Boat trips to surf at Frigate Pas sage cost F$45 per person, including lunch Call ahead to organise transfers from Nad airport or from the Queens Road.

laces to Stay – Top End

he *Hideaway Resort* (☎ *500 177, fax 520 25, hideaway@is.com.fj)* is a popular reort in a nice stretch of beach in the Korovu area. The accommodation is smart, in a ell maintained garden setting. Prices start t F$215/190 for fan-cooled beachfront/ ceanview bure for up to three people. The ew, deluxe air-con villas on the beachfront re spacious, with king-size beds and freshir bathroom for F$265. Room rates include ooked breakfast. Main meals in the open-lan restaurant/bar are between F$10 and 20, and there is a five day meal plan for $120. The resort has a nice swimming ool and nonmotorised activities are inclued in the tariff. Scuba diving, windsurfing, eep-sea fishing and night tennis are also vailable; there is a right-hand surfbreak bout 100m from the shore.

Korolevu has two large resorts, both nembers of the Warwick International Motel chain and within a few kilometres of ach other. Guests can use the facilities of ither resort. *The Naviti Resort* (☎ *530 444, ax 530 099, naviti@is.com.fj)* is popular vith families and has good facilities for hildren. It has 140 air-con rooms; $275/350/650 for mountain-view/ocean-iew/suites. Rates are for doubles, and up to wo children can share with parents. Meal ackages are about F$80/55 per adult/child. he resort's restaurants also offer main neals from F$15 to $24. Some of the activties included in the price are tennis, golf, adminton, hobby cat, windsurfing, kayaking and snorkelling. There is reasonably ;ood access for disabled people.

There is a free shuttle bus (five minutes) rom The Naviti Resort to *The Warwick* ☎ *530 555, fax 530 010, warwick@is.com fj)*. With its 250 air-con rooms, it is one of the argest resorts in Fiji. Mountain-view rooms ost F$260 for up to two adults and two chil-dren; F$15 for an extra adult. Restaurants in-lude seafood dinner dining at the *Wicked Valu*, on a tiny island linked to the resort by . causeway. The resort has shops and a tour lesk, two swimming pools, tennis and squash ourts, mini golf and a kids club.

The two resorts are about 90km from Nadi airport. Taxis to the airport cost about F$65 for the 1½ hour ride; F$30 for the 20 minute drive to Sigatoka (28km).

Places to Eat

The *Bedarra House Restaurant* (☎ *500 476)* has excellent food: F$10 for lunch; F$28 for a three course dinner. *Tom's Restaurant* (☎ *520 238)*, about 5km east of Sigatoka, has seafood and good Chinese meals from F$4 to $12. The restaurant at the *Crow's Nest Restaurant* in Korotogo has a nautical theme with European and local dishes from F$6 to $16. Nearby *Le Cafe* (☎ *520 877)* has European-style food for around F$7. The small group of shops next door to Le Cafe includes a general store and inexpensive Indian eat-in or takeaway and pizzas.

The *Coconut Cafe* at the Beachouse, near Korolevu, is a nice place to stop if you are travelling along the Coral Coast. Light meals are around F$7. The larger resorts also have restaurants where visitors are welcome. *Vilisite's Seafood Restaurant* (☎ *530 054)*, between the Naviti and Warwick hotels, has a verandah overlooking the water. Seafood dishes including octopus, fish fillets and fruits are F$19.50.

PACIFIC HARBOUR

Pacific Harbour is 78km east of Sigatoka and 49km west of Suva. It is an unusual town for Fiji, planned as an upmarket housing and tourism development with meandering drives, canals and a golf course. It rains a lot here and the town itself is fairly boring, but the Beqa Lagoon offshore has world-class diving, including Caesar's Rock (see the 'South Pacific Diving' special section), and a surfbreak. It is about an hour's express bus ride from Suva and around three hours from Nadi.

Things to See

The Fijian Cultural Centre & Marketplace (☎ 450 177, fax 450 083) is about one kilometre east of the Centra Resort. The place has seen better days, now it just has a few gift shops and a restaurant. The cultural centre (closed for renovation at the time of

FIJI

writing) is OK for a quick caricature of Fijian history. Kids should enjoy the **Lake Tour** in a *drua* (old-style canoe) around the small islands that have an artificial village. The tour has a 'warrior' as skipper and guide.

Activities

The Centra Resort allows visitors to join its organised tours and to use the resort's facilities. Dinghy sailing, windsurfing or coral viewing costs F$15; and one hour horse riding is F$9/15 per adult/child. Cruises to offshore Yanuca are F$59 per person. The Golf & Country Club, with an 18 hole course, is 2km off the Queens Road.

Diving AquaTrek (☎ 702 413, fax 702 412) at the Centra Resort has the best diving operation in the area. Rates are F$165 for a two-tank dive; F$600 for open-water. Dive Connections (☎ 450 541, fax 450 539) is next to the canal at 16 River Drive opposite the Centra. A two-tank dive, including all equipment and a picnic lunch, costs F$130; F$395 for an open-water course. For snorkellers, trips are F$45, including lunch. The 33m live-aboard yacht *Nai'a* (☎ 450 382, fax 450 566, naia@is.com.fj) is based at Pacific Harbour, and has the reputation of being the best in Fiji. It has eight air-con rooms and takes up to 18 passengers.

Organised Tours

Rivers Fiji (☎ 450 147, fax 450 148, riversfiji@is.com.fj) based at Pacific Harbour, and Discover Fiji Tours (☎ 450 180, fax 450 549), based at Navua, both have trips to the Namosi Highlands north of Pacific Harbour: see the Viti Levu Highlands section later in this chapter.

Places to Stay

Coral Coast Christian Centre (☎/fax 450 178), about 1km west of Pacific Harbour, has cheap accommodation and good communal facilities. Tent sites cost F$5.50. Dorm cabins (maximum of five people in each) with fan, shared bathroom and cooking facilities are F$13/22 for singles/doubles;

F$9/5 for each extra adult/child. Alcoh and kava are not permitted here. Bring in sect repellent.

Club Coral Coast (☎ 450 421, fax 45 900) has good family rooms with a doub bed and a mezzanine with two single be for F$60/70 for singles/doubles and F$ per extra person. It also has tight bur rooms with shared facilities for F$20/30. has a lovely swimming pool and a tenn court. Coming from Nadi, turn left just b fore the Japanese restaurant, cross the can and turn left again, at Belo Circle.

The *Centra Resort* (☎ 450 022, fax 45 262, centrapacharb@is.com.fj), previous the Pacific Harbour Hotel, was built in th early 1970s. It is on the beachfront o Queens Road, about 1km west of the Fiji Cultural Centre & Marketplace. Air-cc rooms cost F$143 for singles or double F$25 for an extra adult, or up to two chi dren under 16 years old can share with pa ents free of charge. The restaurant offers a all-day menu with mains from F$12.50 t $22.50. The resort has spacious grounds, swimming pool, tennis, windsurfin snorkelling, diving, horse riding, tennis, kid's club and an OK dark-sand beach fc swimming. There are weekly fire-walkin performances.

Fiji Palms Beach Club (☎ 450 050, fa 450 025) has spacious, self-contained, tw bedroom apartments (with air-con and fans that can sleep six people. Prices are F$18 for one night or F$135 per night from tw to six nights. It has a bar and nice swim ming pool, and guests can use the facilitie at the Centra next door.

Places to Eat

If you are after good, simple, cheap food try *Kumaran's Restaurant and Milk Ba* across Queens Road from the Centra. Th *Oasis Restaurant* in the marketplace is rea sonably priced. The restaurant at Centr (see the earlier entry under Places to Stay welcomes visitors. *Sakura House* (☎ 45 300), opposite the Centra, has Japanes dishes (F$20 to $30) and European-styl steak dishes (F$10 to $15). It is open daily for dinner.

BEQA & YANUCA

Beqa and Yanuca are offshore islands south off Pacific Harbour, within the 360 sq km **Beqa Lagoon**, which is famous for its barrier reef and dive sites.

Beqa is a volcanic island about 7km in diameter, with an area of 36 sq km. It is home of Rukua, Naceva and Dakuibeqa firewalking villages. *Marlin Bay Resort (☎ 304 042, fax 304 028, george@is.com.fj)* has 19 bure on a nice beach on the western side of Beqa island, catering mostly for divers on pre-booked packages. Rates are F$370 per bure per night for a minimum of three nights; half-price for children under 10 years. Meal plans are F$110 per day. Rates include snorkelling, kayaking, unlimited shore diving and hiking. Two-tank dive trips cost F$160 and surfing trips are F$150.

Yanuca, a small island with beautiful beaches, is 9km west of Beqa. It has one small village and two surf camps. **Frigate Passage** surfbreak is nearby. Penaia at *Frigate Surfriders (☎/fax 450 801)* has a camp on a small white-sand beach. He charges F$75 per person per night in the beach hut dorm or for camping (own tent). Nonsurfers pay F$35. Prices include three meals and daily surf trips. Boat transfers are F$40 return. *Batiluva (☎ 450 202, fax 450 067)* offers accommodation and surf trips for similar prices.

VATULELE

Vatulele is 32km south of Korolevu off the Viti Levu coast, to the west of Beqa Lagoon. The 13km-long, mostly flat island has a total area of about 31 sq km. It has four villages and one exclusive resort. Vatulele is known for its **archaeological sites**, including ancient rock paintings of faces and stencilled hands, limestone caves and pools inhabited by sacred red prawns.

The exclusive *Vatulele Island Resort* (☎ 720 300, fax 720 062, vatulele@is.com.fj) is definitely one of Fiji's best top end resorts, with the price to match. The location is idyllic and the architecture stunning. The 16 bure are well spaced, each with its own stretch of white-sand beach and turquoise lagoon. Gourmet-quality meals,

beverages and alcohol are included in the rate. The minimum stay is four nights, at a nightly price of F$968/1936 for singles/doubles. Children are only accepted during family weeks (early July and late September) for F$132 each, with a maximum of two. Activities such as snorkelling, windsurfing, tennis and hiking are included. Diving is F$198 for a two-tank dive trip; F$1108 for an open-water course. The island has an airstrip, and return transfers by charter plane to Nadi (F$616 per adult; 25 minutes).

Suva

• pop 167,975

While Nadi is the tourism centre, Suva is the political and administrative capital, the major port and Fiji's educational, commercial and industrial centre. The city ranks as the largest and most sophisticated in the South Pacific and is an important regional centre, with the University of the South Pacific, the Forum Secretariat and overseas embassies.

Suva and its surrounding urban area accounts for about half of Fiji's total urban population. It is a multiracial and multicultural centre with many churches, mosques and temples.

The landscape is quite beautiful, with scenic views to the mountains across the bay, and there are some interesting old buildings, gardens and remnants of the colonial past, as well as some nondescript high-rise blocks. The climate is notorious for being hot, wet and humid, although the tropical rain (about three metres annually) often comes as refreshing change at the end of an afternoon.

History

Until the 1870s, there were few Europeans in the area. The majority of Suva's first European settlers and fortune hunters came from Melbourne, Australia, where there was an economic downturn after the gold rushes.

In 1868 the newly formed Polynesia Company agreed to clear Fiji's Chief Cakobau's inflated debts (owed to American

FIJI

settlers) in return for land, including over 9000 hectares in the Suva area, and the right to trade in Fiji. In 1870 a group of forty Australians from Melbourne arrived in what is now downtown Suva. The dense reeds were cleared for farming and they tried growing cotton and then sugar cane. Their attempts at farming on the thin topsoil and soapstone base of the Suva peninsula failed, and most of the settlers' efforts ended in bankruptcy. Two Melbourne merchants, WK Thomson and S Renwick, turned this financial ruin to their advantage by encouraging the government to relocate the capital from Levuka to Suva so as to increase land values. The government officially moved to Suva from Levuka in 1882.

In the 1880s Suva was a township of about a dozen buildings. Later, sections of the seashore were reclaimed and trading houses constructed, and by the 1920s Suva was a flourishing colonial centre with many prominent public and private buildings. Large-scale land reclamation was carried out in the 1950s for the Walu Bay industrial zone.

Orientation

Suva is on a peninsula, with Laucala Bay to the east and the downtown area facing the protected Suva Harbour to the west. Apart from the relatively flat downtown area near the wharf and market, the rest of the peninsula is hilly. There are three major roads in and out of the city: the Queens Road via Lami to the west, Princes Rd along the Tamavua ridge to the north and the Kings Road to the north-east towards Nausori.

Suva's downtown area has the GPO and business section along Victoria Parade, the main drag, which runs parallel to the waterfront. If you keep heading south you will pass the Government Buildings, Albert Park and Thurston Gardens, where Victoria Parade becomes Queen Elizabeth Drive. This then passes Government House and winds all the way around the tip of the peninsula (Suva Point). Queen Elizabeth Drive finishes on the eastern side of the peninsula at Laucala Bay, near the University of the South Pacific and the National Stadium. From Laucala Bay you can head north to

meet the Kings Road or head west back central Suva via Laucala Bay Road.

Information

Tourist Offices The best source of touri information is the FVB (☎ 302 433, fax 30 970, infodesk@fijifvb.gov.fj). Its head o fice is in Suva on the corner of Thomso and Scott Sts. It is open from 8 am to 4.3 pm weekdays, except Friday till 4 pm, ar 8 am to 12 pm Saturday.

The Tourism Council of the South Pacif (☎ 304 177, fax 301 995, spice@is.com.f has its office on the corner of Loftus St an Victoria Parade on the 3rd floor above th Dolphin Plaza Food Court – also see Touri Offices in the Regional Facts for the Visito chapter.

Money There are several money ex changes downtown as well as the Westpa bank (☎ 300 666, fax 300 275), at 1 Thom son St, and the ANZ bank (☎ 301 755, fa 300 267), at 25 Victoria Parade. Bank hour are from 9.30 am to 3 pm Monday t Thursday (Friday to 4 pm). Many of th hotels, including the budget South Seas Pr vate Hotel and the Travel Inn, will als change travellers cheques for guests at th going bank rate.

Post & Communications FINTEL, o Fiji International Telecommunication (☎ 301 655, fax 301 025), at 158 Victori Parade, provides international services, in cluding phone calls, faxes and lines to ac cess the Internet if you have your ow laptop. It is open from 8 am to 8 pm Mon day to Saturday.

Email & Internet Access The Republi of Cappuccino (☎ 300 333) on Victoria Par ade next to the Dolphin Plaza has email an Internet services. For Internet access, but n coffee, try Alpha Computer Centre (☎ 30 211, alphacomputer@is.com.fj) at 181 Vic toria Parade.

Bookshops & Libraries The Universit of the South Pacific (USP) Library, is th largest resource centre for the Pacific regio

FIJI

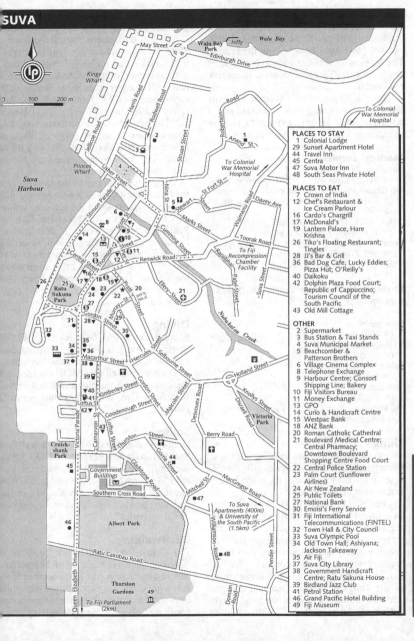

SUVA

PLACES TO STAY
1 Colonial Lodge
29 Sunset Apartment Hotel
44 Travel Inn
45 Centra
47 Suva Motor Inn
48 South Seas Private Hotel

PLACES TO EAT
7 Crown of India
12 Chef's Restaurant &
   Ice Cream Parlour
16 Cardo's Chargrill
17 McDonald's
19 Lantern Palace, Hare
   Krishna
26 Tiko's Floating Restaurant;
   Tingles
28 JJ's Bar & Grill
36 Bad Dog Cafe, Lucky Eddies;
   Pizza Hut; O'Reilly's
40 Daikoku
42 Dolphin Plaza Food Court;
   Republic of Cappuccino;
   Tourism Council of the
   South Pacific
43 Old Mill Cottage

OTHER
2 Supermarket
3 Bus Station & Taxi Stands
4 Suva Municipal Market
5 Beachcomber &
   Patterson Brothers
6 Village Cinema Complex
8 Telephone Exchange
9 Harbour Centre; Consort
   Shipping Line; Bakery
10 Fiji Visitors Bureau
11 Money Exchange
13 GPO
14 Curio & Handicraft Centre
15 Westpac Bank
18 ANZ Bank
20 Roman Catholic Cathedral
21 Boulevard Medical Centre;
   Central Pharmacy;
   Downtown Boulevard
   Shopping Centre Food Court
22 Central Police Station
23 Palm Court (Sunflower
   Airlines)
24 Air New Zealand
25 Public Toilets
27 National Bank
30 Emoisi's Ferry Service
31 Fiji International
   Telecommunications (FINTEL)
32 Town Hall & City Council
33 Suva Olympic Pool
34 Old Town Hall; Ashiyana;
   Jackson Takeaway
35 Air Fiji
37 Suva City Library
38 Government Handicraft
   Centre; Ratu Sakuna House
39 Birdland Jazz Club
41 Petrol Station
46 Grand Pacific Hotel Building
49 Fiji Museum

FIJI

(see Education in the Facts about the South Pacific chapter). The USP Book Centre and the Institute of Pacific Studies (☎ 313 900, fax 301 594) stock books about the region. The latter is a publisher with a catalogue of over 250 titles by local authors. It accepts mail orders.

The Fiji Museum in Thurston Gardens has a few interesting books for sale and a good reference library; request to visit in advance and pay a small fee/donation.

Medical Services

Boulevard Medical Centre
  (☎ 313 355, fax 302 423) 33 Ellery St, Suva.
Fiji Recompression Chamber Facility
  (☎ 850 630, fax 850 344) Amy St (Cnr Brewster St) Toorak, Suva
Colonial War Memorial Hospital
  (☎ 313 444) Waimanu Rd, Suva
Central Pharmacy
  (☎ 303 770) Shop 13 Downtown Boulevard, Suva

Emergency Some useful emergency numbers follow:

Emergency
  (☎ 000)
FVB Emergency Hotline
  (☎ 0800 721 721)
Police
  (☎ 311 222)
Ambulance
  (☎ 301 439)
Fiji Recompression Chamber Facility
  (emergency ☎ 362 172)

Things to See

The Suva Municipal Market is a must-see. It is a good place to buy kava as gifts for village visits (the unpounded roots are better) and to sample local foods.

The Fiji Museum (☎ 315 944, fax 305 143, fijimuseum@is.com.fj) has a fascinating collection of artefacts including drua, weapons, ceremonial *tabua* (the teeth of sperm whales) and kava bowls, necklaces, breastplates, tools and cooking utensils. Exhibits cover aspects of Fiji's history such as the Tongan influence, early European traders and settlers, blackbirding and Indian indenture. Admission is F$3.30; children

free. Opening hours are 9.30 am to 4 p Monday to Friday; 1 pm to 4 pm weekend

The Fiji **parliament complex** opened 1992. Its architectural aim was to integra traditional Fijian building forms and craf with a contemporary feel and modern tec nology. The complex is about 3km from th city centre – visible from Queen Elizabe Drive but the visitor's entry is off Batter Rd. The easiest way to get there is by tax otherwise take a bus along Queen Elizabe Drive and walk along Ratu Sukuna Rd f about 1km. Visiting hours are 8 am to 1 p and 2 to 4.30 pm weekdays.

The Laucala campus of the **University** **the South Pacific** (☎ 313 900, fax 301 30: is the main campus of the regional unive sity, for the 1.5 million people of 12 Sou Pacific countries. It has 11,000 studen including part-timers and distance learning The main entrance is off Laucala Bay R and is a 10 to 15 minute drive from dow town Suva. There are frequent buses fro the city centre. The taxi fare from the city about F$2.

Diving

Scuba Hire (☎ 361 088, fax 361 047), 7 Marine Drive, Lami, has dive trips to Bec Lagoon and runs Professional Associatio of Diving Instructors' (PADI) courses. Th Centra hotel in Suva also arranges dive tri with Aqua Trek at Centra Resort in Pacif Harbour.

Sailing

Honorary membership of the **Royal Suv** **Yacht Club** (☎ 312 921, fax 304 433, rsyc((is.com.fj) is given to visiting yachties. Fee are F$15 per week for solo yachts; F$30 p yacht with two or more people. Visitors ar welcome and can be signed in for weeken social activities.

Bushwalking

The **Colo-i-Suva Forest Park** (pronounce 'tholo-ee-suva') is made up of 245 hectare of forest in the hills just 11km north of Suv It is a good place for easy bushwalking an bird-watching, with three natural swimmin pools and about 6.5km of walking track

Cannibalism

Archaeological evidence from food-waste middens shows that cannibalism was practised in Viti (Fiji) from 2500 years ago until the mid to late-19th century, by which time it had become an ordinary, ritualised part of life. In a society founded on ancestor worship and belief in the afterlife, cannibalising an enemy was considered the ultimate revenge. A disrespectful death was a lasting insult to the enemy's family, particularly as cooking removed the *tabu* (sacred) quality of the body.

Bodies were either consumed on the battlefield or brought back to the village spirithouse, offered to the local war god, then butchered, baked and eaten on the god's behalf. The triumph was celebrated with music and dance. Men performed the *cibi*, or death dance, and women the *dele* or *wate*, an obscene dance in which they sexually humiliated corpses and captives. Torture included being thrown alive into ovens, being bled or dismembered, being forced to watch one's own body parts being consumed or even being forced to eat some themselves!

Priests and chiefs could not touch any kind of food as their hands and lips were considered *tabu*. They were normally fed by a female attendant who carefully avoided touching the lips, but for cannibalistic feasts they fed themselves with special long-pronged wooden forks. Considered sacred relics, these forks were individually named and kept in the spirithouse and were not to be touched by others.

Mementos were kept of the kill to prolong the victor's sense of vengeance. Necklaces, hairpins or ear-lobe ornaments were made from human bones, and the skull of a hated enemy was sometimes made into a *tanoa*, or kava drinking bowl. Meat was smoked for snacks, and the war clubs were inlaid with teeth or marked with tally notches. To record a triumph in war, bones and sometimes sexual organs and foetuses were placed as trophies in branches of trees outside the spirit houses and men's houses.

Early European visitors and settlers were obsessed with cannibalism, recording gruesome but nevertheless fascinating stories.

---

here is a security booth at the car park, but watch your belongings anyway. The Sawani bus leaves Suva bus station every half-hour, 30 minute trip). If driving, take Princes Rd ut of Suva, past Tamavua and Tacirua villages. The Visitor Information Centre ☎ 320 211) is on the left on top of the hill t the entrance to the park (entry F$5 per erson).

Places to Stay – Budget

The *Colonial Lodge* (☎/fax 300 655, 19 *nand St*) bed and breakfast, off Robertson d, is an excellent small-scale place to stay. The restored colonial home has private ooms and a nice living area and verandah pstairs with bay views. Beds in the dorm ownstairs cost F$14.50, while a twin bed n a room with shared facilities is F$25/40

for singles/doubles and an en suite room is F$35/60. Rates include a cooked breakfast. The food is good and the three-course dinners are good value.

The *South Seas Private Hotel* (☎ 312 296, fax 340 236, southseas@fiji4less.com, 6 Williamson Rd) is a classic, old, double storey weatherboard building near the Thurston Gardens. Dormitories (maximum of five people) cost F$9.50 per person; single rooms F$16; double or twin rooms F$24 and triple family rooms F$32, all with shared facilities. Double rooms with private bath and toilet are F$36. Rooms have fans and the bathrooms are clean and have solar hot water. Downstairs there is a communal kitchen/dining room, and a reading room/lounge area. Travellers cheques are accepted, but credit cards are not.

FIJI

The Travel Inn (☎ 304 254, fax 340 236, travelinn@fiji4less.com, 19 Gorrie St) is in a quiet street near the Government Buildings, and within an easy walk of the city centre. Its fan-cooled rooms are paired to share a bathroom and a small area with a table, sink and refrigerator. Singles/doubles cost F$18.50/27. There is also a communal kitchen and dining area.

Sunset Apartment Motel (☎ 301 799, fax 303 446), on the corner of Gordon and Murray Sts, is very close to the city centre. The four storey building (no lifts) has 15 self-contained apartments for F$66/77/88 for doubles/triples/quads. It also has a clean 12 bed dormitory with one bathroom, toilets, a refrigerator, lockers and small sitting area, but no cooking facilities, for F$8.70 per bed.

The new annex of the *Suva Apartments* (☎ 304 280, 17 Bau St) has good value, self-contained air-con apartments for F$50/65 for singles/doubles; however, it's about 1.5km from the city centre.

Places to Stay – Mid-Range
Suva Homestay (☎ 370 395, fax 370 947, homestaysuva@is.com.fj) on Princes Rd, Tamavua, is a great place to rest travel-weary bones. The renovated colonial house in large grounds is on the Tamavua ridge, a F$3 taxi fare from downtown. All five rooms have air-con, fans and en suites. The 'blue and white room' has a deep bath while the two large rooms upstairs both have fantastic bay views. Rates for bed and breakfast are F$115 per night in the downstairs rooms or F$130/140 for singles/doubles upstairs. An excellent breakfast is served on the terrace overlooking the pool and the bay. The place is impeccably clean, has a dog and a cat, a laundry service, and home-cooked dinners can be provided for F$25. Book in advance; no young children.

Suva Motor Inn (☎ 313 973, fax 300 381), corner of Mitchell and Gorrie Sts, is conveniently located near the Government Buildings and parks. The building is designed around a central courtyard with a swimming pool and water slide. It has 36 air-con studio units with kitchenettes for F$100 a single or double; F$20 per extra person.

There are also eight good two-bedroom apartments with kitchenette and dining area for F$170 a single or double; F$10 for each extra person, up to maximum of six people.

The 110 room *Raffles Tradewinds Hotel* (☎ 362 450, fax 361 464, Queens Road, Lami) is about a 10 minute drive west of Suva. It used to be a top end hotel but now is a bit run down. Nevertheless, it is right on the water's edge, with great views over the Bay of Islands. Rooms here cost F$102/110 for singles/doubles (but look out for special discounts) and up to two children sharing with parents are free. The hotel amenities include a floating restaurant, a swimming pool and a bar.

Places to Stay – Top End
The *Centra* (☎ 301 600, fax 300 251), previously known as the Suva Travelodge, is on Victoria Parade, on the waterfront opposite the Government Buildings. It is popular with business travellers for its proximity to the CBD. There are 130 standard air-con rooms for F$154/170.50 for singles/doubles. Renovated deluxe versions are F$225. It has a swimming pool, a restaurant and an entertainment area with a nightly house band.

Those after a more intimate scale should consider *Suva Homestay* – see the previous Places to Stay – Mid-Range entry. The closest island resort is *Toberua Island Resort*; see Toberua later in this section.

Places to Eat
Restaurants The *Old Mill Cottage* at 49 Carnarvon St, just around the corner from the Dolphin Plaza Food Court, is probably the best bet for lunch or a fruit-salad break. The Fijian, Indian and Chinese food is well prepared and very good value for around F$5.50. It's open 7 am to 6 pm weekdays to 5 pm Saturday.

A trendy place for lunch or dinner is *JJ Bar & Grill* (☎ 305 005, 9–10 Gordon St), which has a choice of air-con inside or courtyard outside. It has excellent international-style food; dishes are F$6 to $15. Another good place is *Cardo's Chargrill* (☎ 314 330), an air-con restaurant and bar in Regal Lane. It specialises in beef steaks ut also has chargrilled chicken and seafood. The steaks are not cheap (F$18.50) but are great by Fijian standards. *Tiko's Floating Restaurant* (☎ 313 626), a converted Blue Lagoon Cruiser, is anchored at the sea wall near Ratu Sukuna Park. Seafood is its speciality, with dishes from $10 to $27.50 (dinner only).

The *Hare Krishna* (☎ 314 154), on the corner of Pratt and Joske Sts, has good, cheap vegetarian meals. The air-con restaurant upstairs is open weekdays for lunch and dinner to 7.30 pm. *Ashiyana* (☎ 313 700), in the old town hall, has good Indian dishes for lunch and dinner and is open every day. The *Crown of India* (☎ 300 79), upstairs opposite the Village Cinema, has very good food and friendly staff. Curries cost from F$5 to $7.50; tandoori from $9 to $15.50.

Suva has many Chinese restaurants. Perhaps the best is the *Great Wok of China* (☎ 301 285), on the corner of Bau St and Laucala Bay Rd, Flagstaff. Though not cheap, the food is excellent. It is open daily for lunch and dinner. The *Lantern Palace* (☎ 314 633) downtown at 10 Pratt St has good value Chinese dishes for around F$8.

Pizza Hut (☎ 311 825), on Victoria Parade next to the Bad Dog Cafe, has reasonable pizzas. *Daikoku* (☎ 308 968) on Victoria Parade has quality Japanese food and steep prices.

Cafes The *Republic of Cappuccino* (☎ 300 33), on Victoria Parade at the Dolphin Plaza, has snacks, fresh juices, good coffee and Internet services. It's open from 7 am to 11 pm; 10 am to 7 pm on Sunday. The *Bad Dog Cafe*, on the corner of Macarthur St and Victoria Parade, has quality food and huge coffees; open breakfast, lunch and dinner.

Fast Food Suva has two *food courts*: one at the Downtown Boulevard Shopping Centre on Ellery St, the other at Dolphin Plaza on the corner of Loftus St and Victoria Parade. Both have a variety of takeaway outlets, including pizza, pasta, Chinese food, curries and Fijian dishes for around F$5. Otherwise, there is *McDonald's* on Victoria

Parade. *Jackson Takeaway* in the Old Town Hall building has good value Chinese for under F$3.50.

Self-Catering The *Suva Municipal Market* in Usher St is the best place for fish, fruit and vegetables. There are a couple of supermarkets downtown on Rodwell Rd facing the market and bus station. There are *bakeries* downtown, including a hot bread kitchen in the Harbour Centre.

Entertainment

Suva, with its cosmopolitan population and high number of university students, has the most diverse nightlife in Fiji. Victoria Parade on Friday and Saturday nights swarms with nightclubbers and bar hoppers. Watch out for pickpockets in the crowded discos, though. See the *Fiji Times* entertainment section for what's on.

Lucky Eddies (☎ 312 884), on Victoria Parade opposite the old town hall, has a lively disco. If you'd prefer something quieter and smaller in scale, try *Tingles* (☎ 313 626), below deck on Tiko's Floating Restaurant. *Traps Bar* (☎ 312 922, 305 Victoria Parade) and *O'Reilly's* (☎ 312 884) on the corner of Macarthur St and Victoria Parade are both popular bars with a friendly atmosphere, pool tables and music. *Birdland Jazz Club* (☎ 303 833, 6 Carnarvon St) is an underground venue offering live jazz and rhythm & blues.

The *Village Cinema complex* (☎ 311 109) is on Scott St near the Nubukalou Creek. Tickets are only F$3 to $4; see the cinema section in the *Fiji Times* for what's screening.

Shopping

The Government Handicraft Centre (☎ 211 222, fax 302 617), on Macarthur St, assists rural artisans and has good-quality reproductions, but is generally more expensive than the Curio & Handicraft Centre on Stinson Parade. The latter is interesting for a stroll. Occasionally one stall has better quality or a better deal; be prepared to bargain. Whenever there's a cruise ship in port, prices skyrocket.

FIJI

Getting There & Away

Suva is well connected to the rest of the country by air, inter-island ferry and to western Viti Levu by buses and carriers. It has an international airport at Nausori.

Air Nausori international airport is 23km north-east of downtown Suva: see the following Nausori section.

Bus & Carriers There are frequent express buses operating along the Queens Road and Kings Road. See the Getting Around section earlier in this chapter for more information.

Boat From Suva there are regular ferry services to Vanua Levu and Taveuni (Patterson Brothers, Beachcomber Cruises and Consort Shipping); to Ovalau (Patterson Brothers and Emoisi's Shipping); see the Getting Around section earlier in this chapter for details. There are also irregular boats that take passengers from Suva to Kadavu, Lau and Rotuma – see Getting There & Away in the respective sections later in this chapter.

Getting Around

It is easy to get around central Suva on foot. Taxis are quite cheap for short trips and here they actually use the meter! The busy local bus station is next to the market: just ask bus drivers or locals about timetables.

NAUSORI

The township of Nausori is on the eastern bank of the Rewa River, 23km north-east of downtown Suva. It is an important agricultural, market, transport and service centre but has little to interest travellers. There are a couple of banks and some inexpensive eateries near the market and bus station in Nausori town.

Nausori International Airport

The airport is about 3km south-east of Nausori. Air Fiji and Sunflower Airlines are the domestic carriers: see the Getting Around section earlier in this chapter for details. Air Fiji, Air Pacific and Royal Tongan Airlines have international flights that arrive here, but otherwise it is mostly used for domestic

purposes. The airport premises are sma and low key. An ANZ bank opens for inte national flights only. Taxi rides from th airport to/from Suva cost about F$17. Na sori Taxi & Bus Service (☎ 312 185 ☎ 304 178) has buses to/from the Cent Hotel for F$2.10 for most flight arrivals.

TOBERUA

Toberua is a small island just off the eas ernmost point of Viti Levu, about 30km from Suva. *Toberua Island Resort (☎ 30 356, fax 302 215, toberua@is.com.fj)* wa one of the earliest luxury resorts establishe in Fiji. It has 14 fan-cooled bure fo F$390/455 for singles/doubles; up to tw children under 16 years are free. Meal plan for adults are F$81/98 for two/three meal Activities include snorkelling, divin windsurfing, paddle boating and tours to th nearby island bird sanctuary and mar groves. Transfers involve a taxi to Nake Landing (F$14/28 from Nausori airpor Suva) and launch (F$17.50/35 per chil adult; 40 minutes). Day trips to the islar are F$120 per person including lunch ar use of a bure.

Viti Levu's Kings Road

Kings Road around northern Viti Levu, be tween Suva and Lautoka, has some beau ful scenery and is recommended for trav either by bus or car. The road is usually good condition and sealed except for abo 56km between Korovou and Dama. The are relatively few places to stay along th route. Korovou, Tavua and Ba each have simple hotel. Rakiraki has a hotel and upmarket resort and there are budget reson offshore on Nananu-i-Ra. Rakiraki 265km from Suva to Lautoka on Kin Road, compared to 221km along Quee Road.

KOROVOU & NATOVI LANDING

At Korovou, about 50km north of Suv Kings Road continues north-west throu dairy-farming country and into the hills. Another road follows the coast to Natovi Landing (about a 20 minute drive) from where there are bus/ferry services to Labasa (Vanua Levu) and Levuka (Ovalau) – see the Getting Around section earlier in this chapter.

RAKIRAKI & ELLINGTON WHARF

It's a scenic trip from Korovou across the mountains, past Viti Levu Bay and down to Ra province and Rakiraki. The road winds through hills and along the Wainibuka River, past many small villages. Rakiraki is 157km north-west of Suva and 141km north-east of Nadi. Inland from Rakiraki, about 2km off Kings Road past the sugar mill, is the township of **Vaileka**, where you will find the bus station and taxi stands, banks, a market, supermarket and a few cafes. Don't drink the tapwater in Rakiraki - it has been deemed unsafe. Heading out of Rakiraki towards Nadi, look out for **Udreudre's Tomb**, the resting place of Fiji's most notorious cannibal. It is on the left about 100m from the Vaileka turn-off.

Places to Stay & Eat

The **Rakiraki Hotel** (☎ 694 101, fax 694 45), on Kings Road 1.8km east of the Vaileka turn-off, offers rooms with fans for F$35/40 for singles/doubles, and air-con rooms for F$88/99. The rooms are musty but otherwise pretty standard and the hotel has a pool. The restaurant and bar is open to visitors; mains are F$11 to $15.

Those wanting a mid-range resort should try **Wananavu Beach Resort** (☎ 694 433, fax 694 499, wananavuresort@is.com.fj), at the northernmost point of Viti Levu. Bure here are comfortable with views from the balcony. Rates are F$165/220 gardenview/beachfront for doubles; F$20 for an extra person. Ask about walk-in deals. The restaurant has gorgeous views and good main meals for F$18.50 to $24. Visitors are welcome. There is a beach nearby, a marina, a nice swimming pool, tennis and volleyball courts, diving and snorkelling. Coming from Lautoka, continue along Kings Road

Ratu Udreudre

In 1849, some time after Ratu Udreudre's death, the Reverend Richard Lyth asked Udreudre's son about the significance of a long line of stones. Each stone, he was told, represented one of the chief's victims, amounting to a personal tally of at least 872 corpses.

> Ravatu assured me that his father eat all this number of human beings – he was wont to add a stone to the row for each one he received – they were victims killed in war he eat them all himself – he gave to none, however much he had on hand – it was cooked and recooked (by which it was preserved) until it was all consumed – he would keep it in a box so that he might lose none ... he eat but little else very little vegetable – and being an enormous eater he was able to get through a great deal.

for about 3.5km past the Vaileka turn-off and follow the unsealed (sometimes muddy) road about 3km to the resort. Transfers from Nadi airport are F$85 by taxi.

NANANU-I-RA

Nananu-i-Ra is a 350 hectare island roughly triangular in shape with steep hills, many scalloped bays, white-sand beaches and mangroves. It is a quick and inexpensive option for getting away from the Nadi area. Most locals are of European descent so don't come here looking for Fijian culture.

Diving

Ra Divers, (☎ 694 511, fax 694 691, radivers@is.com.fj), Rakiraki, will pick up from each of the budget resorts. It charges F$120 for a two-tank dive and F$450 for an open-water course. Action Diving (☎ 694 454, fax 694 829), based at Mokusigas resort, has diving lessons in German and English. Diving is F$130 for a two-tank dive; F$450 for open-water.

FIJI

Places to Stay & Eat

There are four inexpensive places to stay on the island and one upmarket resort. None of the budget places accept credit cards. Most places, with the exception of Kon Tiki Lodge, provide food, but it is a good idea to pick up some supplementary food supplies (especially fruit and vegetables). There is a small shop at Betham's that sells a few food items including bread, milk and frozen meat. Both Betham's and McDonald's have snorkelling gear for F$10 per day; kayaks and rowboats for F$5 per hour.

Three of the budget places are close together on the same beach on the south-western side of the island, so if you are not happy you can swap. Prices are competitive. *Charlie's Place* (☎ 694 676) has an eight bed dorm for F$16.50 and two self-contained cottages for F$60 a double, plus F$8 per person up to a maximum of seven. One is more spacious, good for families, with good views, but closer to the generator. Dinner costs F$10.

McDonald's Nananu Beach Cottages (☎ 694 633) has dorm accommodation with fan (maximum of six people) for F$16.50 per person, and twin rooms with shared bathrooms for F$44 for singles or doubles. Self-contained cottages sleep up to five and are F$60.50 for doubles; F$9 per extra person. Meal packages are F$24.50.

Betham's Beach Cottages (☎/fax 694 132), between Charlie's and McDonald's, has two dormitories with cooking facilities, fridge and freezer but no fan, sleeping six to 10 people, for F$16.50 per person. The four self-contained beachfront cottages are F$66 each; F$10 per extra person.

Kon Tiki Lodge (☎ 694 290 or 722 836 Nadi) is near the north-west point of the island on a lovely beach. Accommodation is for self-caterers only. There is a small shop with a few basics but we recommend you 'bring your own' (BYO) food. Camping is F$10 per tent. The dorm (up to 10 beds per room) has its own kitchen; F$16.50 per bed. Beachfront bungalows have two bedrooms and shared kitchen and bathroom; F$38.50 a double. Traditional bure with mosquito net and shared facilities are F$33 a double.

The more upmarket *Mokusigas Reso* (☎ 694 444, fax 694 404) is on a narrow steep ridge with beautiful views to the wate on both sides. It has 20 suites, each with cei ing fans and balcony, from F$260 for a max mum of three people. Rates includ breakfast and transfers. Main meals ar around F$19. Snorkelling and windsurfin are included. Action Diving has its div shop here: see the earlier Diving entry i this section.

Getting There & Away

The island is a 15 minute boat ride fro Ellington Wharf. The turn-off to Ellingto Wharf is about 5km east of Rakiraki off th Kings Road and it is then a further 1.5km t the wharf. Ferries also leave here for Vanu Levu; see the Getting Around section earlie in this chapter. Each of the resorts c Nananu-i-Ra have their own boat transfer arrange your pick-up in advance. Bo transfers are around F$17 return.

Sunbeam has regular buses along King Road: see the Getting Around section earl er in this chapter. A taxi from Vaileka Ellington Wharf is around F$8. Kontiki ha a minibus service from Nadi; F$17 one wa Alternatively, PVV Tours (☎ 700 600, fa 701 541) has daily transfers by minibu between Nadi and Ellington Wharf for F$2 one way (2½ hours) and then by boat Nananu-i-Ra (F$8.25 one way per person Sharing a taxi is another option (about F$6 to Nadi).

BA

Ba is a faily unattractive agricultural tow 38km north-east of Lautoka and 71km fro Nadi. The Ba district, with a predominant Fiji-Indian population of 12,500, is th largest in Fiji and is an expanding comme cial centre, dependent on cane growing ar the Rarawai Sugar Mill.

There is not much reason to stay her however, the *Ba Hotel* (☎ 674 000) c Bank St has gaudy but clean air-con room for F$44/55 a single/double.

Soccer is popular in the region and th local team often wins national tournament Ba also boasts the best racecourse in Fiji.

Viti Levu Highlands

The Interior of Viti Levu is one of the best places to experience traditional Fijian culture. There are small villages and settlements, which are largely self-sufficient, scattered through the hills. The Nausori Highlands have some fantastic landscapes and are good for trekking.

ABACA

The Abaca Cultural & Recreational Park (☎ 666 644, after the beep dial 1234) is part of the Koroyanitu National Park, in the mountains about 10km east of Lautoka. Abaca village, pronounced 'am-bar-tha', is at the base of Mt Koroyanitu (Mt Evans). The area has beautiful nature walks, native rainforest, waterfalls, archaeological sites and swimming. The *Nase Lodge* is about 500m from the village and has 12 bunk beds, a living area and cooking facilities. Dorm accommodation costs F$15 per person (or F$10 per person for camping). Village stays are F$30 including meals (inquire at the reception bure). Meals at the village cost F$5/7/10 for breakfast/lunch/dinner, but be sure to also take groceries with you.

Admission to the park is F$5, plus F$5 to F$10 for guided treks. Transport is by village carrier; F$8 per person each way. If driving from Nadi, turn right at Tavakubu Rd past the first roundabout after entering Lautoka, continue for about 6.5km, then turn right into the signposted Abaca Rd. It is a further 10km of gravel road up to the village, suitable for 4WD only.

NAVALA

Navala (population 800) is Fiji's most picturesque village, set in a superb landscape on a sloping site on the banks of the Ba River. While most Fijian villagers now prefer concrete block and corrugated iron construction, all of the houses in Navala are traditional bure. Obviously the chief enforces strict town-planning rules! Bure are laid out in avenues with a central promenade down to the river. The buildings are rectangular with sloping stone plinths, a timber-pole structure, woven panel walls

and hipped thatched roofs. It is a photographer's paradise but you need permission to take shots. Visitors are welcome but must present a sevusevu and a F$15 donation. The village has a radio telephone for emergencies.

Places to Stay & Eat
Bulou's Lodge & Backpacker Hostel (☎ 666 644-2116), near Navala village, is run by retired Fijian couple, Seresio and Bulou N Talili, and their son Tui. The traditional bure sleeps about six people or you can stay in their house and be part of the family; they have a cold-water improvised shower and no electricity. All meals and kava drinking are included in the F$35 per person per night fee and if you are staying three nights a lovo is included. Activities include horse riding (F$10 for a couple of hours), trips to their farm and *bilibili* (bamboo rafting) in the dry season. Take some food as a present and leave a donation for the village community centre project. Coming from Ba, the lodge is 1km past Navala and on the right about 50m before a river crossing.

Getting There & Away
There are local buses from Ba to Navala (1½ hours) daily, except Sunday. One leaves Ba at midday, returning about 1.30 pm. Only the late afternoon bus goes as far as Bulou's; ring in advance and they will pick you up from Navala. Carriers cost about F$18. The road is rough and scenic, and takes about an hour to drive the 26km from Ba. Some organised tours from Nadi visit Navala.

BUKUYA
The village of Bukuya (population 700) is at the intersection of the roads from Sigatoka, Nadi and Ba. From Nadi along the Nausori Highlands Road, it is about 1½ to two hours' drive; from Ba via Navala about 1½ hours.

Places to Stay & Eat
About the only traditional bure in Bukuya are at *Peni's* (☎/fax 700 801 Nadi) nine

The Reverend Baker

The Wesleyan Methodist missionary Thomas Baker was killed on 21 July 1867 by villagers in the isolated headwaters of the Sigatoka River. He had been given the task of converting the highlanders to the new religion.

One theory maintains that the Reverend's death was political as the highlanders associated conversion to Christianity with subservience to the chiefdom of Bau. Another story is that the local chief borrowed Baker's comb. Insensitive or forgetful of the fact that the head was considered sacred, Baker snatched the comb from the chief's hair. Villagers were furious at the missionary for committing this sacrilege and killed and ate him in disgust, sharing the flesh among neighbouring villages. One local laughingly recounted the story of his ancestors: 'We ate everything, even tried to eat his shoes'. Baker's boiled shoe is exhibited in the Museum.

MICK WELDON

thatched bure and large dining bure, built for travellers. Rates seem to be pretty arbitrary, depending how much they think you can spend! The longer the stay the cheaper the rate. Expect to pay about F$150/200 for singles/doubles for three days and two nights including meals and transport (minimum five people). Bure are small and very simple with lino over compacted earth floors and various living things making their homes in the roof. There are shared flush toilets and cold showers. Campsites are F$22 per person per night including meals, plus F$40 for return transport to Nadi.

Food is good, with plenty of home-grown fruit and vegetables. Activities may include waterfall tours, horse riding (F$15 per day), pig hunting (F$20 per person) and visits to the chief's bure, the local school and Sunday church. We have received a few letters from disappointed travellers. Try not to pay it all upfront. Do not expect anything to be strictly organised or coordinated as 'Fiji time' definitely operates here. If activities are not happening, you may have to be prepared to just appreciate the good food and get into the slow-paced village lifestyle.

Getting There & Away

All roads to Bukuya are rough and unseale Peni's carrier hurtles across the hills with h load of travellers bouncing in the back; it a bone-crunching ride, but if you're luck there may be a few bits of sponge to sit o

SIGATOKA VALLEY

The Naihehe cave, about an hour's drive u river from Sigatoka, was used as a fortres by the hill tribes and has the remains of ritual platform and cannibal oven. Adve tures in Paradise offers an interestin guided tour to this historic spot. Indepen dent Tours offers guided bike trips of th valley. For more information on these tour see Korotogo & Korolevu in the Viti Levu Queens Road (Coral Coast) section.

NAMOSI HIGHLANDS

The Namosi Highlands, north of Pacifi Harbour, has some spectacular mountai scenery with rainforest, deep river canyon waterfalls, birdlife and isolated villages.

Rivers Fiji (☎ 450 147, fax 450 148 riversfiji@is.com.fj), based in Pacific Har bour, have trips to the Wainikoroiluva Rive

FIJI

_uva Gorge) or the Upper Navua River,
oth tributaries of the Navua River. A day
ip to the Upper Navua River costs
$180; food and equipment included. It
volves a one hour road trip to
labukelevu village, followed by seven
ours by boat (rafting and punt) to
/ainadiro or Waimogi. A day trip to the
uva Gorge costs F$160 from Suva or the
oral Coast; F$175 from Nadi. This in-
olves a two hour road trip to Nakavika
illage, followed by four hours of inflat-
ble kayaking to Namuamua, 1½ hours by
otorised longboat to Nakavu or Navua.
ood, drinks and equipment are included.

Discover Fiji Tours (☎ 450 180, fax 450
49), based at Navua, has a Navua River trip
ith village visits and bamboo rafting, as
ell as two-day guided treks across Namosi
rovince, camping overnight in villages.

IADARIVATU & NAVAI

bout 3km east of Tavua, a gravel road
eads inland off Kings Road to the forestry
ettlement of Nadarivatu and across the
ighlands to Suva.

It is possible to *camp* at Nadarivatu but
irst seek permission from the Forestry Of-
ice (☎ 689 001). It can also arrange a *home-
tay* with one of the forest workers' families
r in the forest worker's dormitory. Bring
rovisions and give either some money, gro-
eries or clothing to cover your costs.

Navai is about 8km south of Nadarivatu
t the foot of Fiji's highest peak (1323m),
omanivi (Adam and Eve's place) or Mt
'ictoria. A hiking trail to Tomanivi begins
rom Navai village. Guides can be hired for
$10. Allow at least three hours for the
limb and two hours to return. The last half
f the climb is practically rock climbing and
an be extremely slippery after rain.

ietting There & Away

ocal buses depart from Tavua (opposite
ie market) at 3 pm daily (except Sunday)
o Nadrau, a village near the Monasavu
)am. The bus returns to Tavua the follow-
ng morning at about 7 am. The winding bus
rip up into the mountains takes about 1½
ours.

Mamanuca Group

The Mamanucas is a group of about 20
small islands of various shapes, sizes and
geological formations. The group is just off
the western coast of Viti Levu in a lagoon
formed between the Great Sea Reef and the
mainland.

Like the Yasawa group to the north, the
Mamanucas are very scenic with beautiful
white-sand and reef-fringed beaches. Most
of the habitable islands support a Fijian village community and/or a tourist resort.

There are only a few budget places to stay
in the Mamanucas: the backpacker hostels
on Mana, and dormitory accommodation at
Beachcomber Resort. Most resorts cater for
those willing to pay mid to top-range prices,
and guests are usually package-deal customers who have pre-arranged their trip
from overseas. Some resorts have excellent
facilities and services for families, while
others don't accept young children. In the
southern Mamanucas, the resorts on Tavarua
and Namotu cater mainly for surfers.

Dive sites along the Malolo Barrier Reef
include the famous Supermarket site (see
the 'South Pacific Diving' special section).

Getting Around

It is relatively costly to explore the Mamanuca Islands. However, most resorts run
island-hopping tours for their guests, stopping briefly at each island.

The South Sea Cruises (☎ 750 500, fax
750 501, southsea@is.com.fj) 27m fast Island Express catamaran shuttles from
Denarau Marina to the Mamanucas. One-
way rates are as follows: Castaway, Malolo
and Mana (F$41 one way), Treasure
(F$35), and inter islands between those re-
sorts (F$25). Matamanoa and Tokoriki are
linked by small launch to/from Mana
(F$66). There are coach pick-ups from ho-
tels and resorts in Nadi (free) and on the
Coral Coast (F$15). South Sea also offers
day trips to Mana (F$85) and Castaway
(F$95) including lunch, nonmotorised
sports and use of resort facilities. Children
five to 15 years pay half-price; under five
are free.

FIJI

The price of a light plane ticket is comparable with catamaran prices, and the trip by air is much quicker and more scenic. Sunflower Airlines and Air Fiji have several flights daily to Mana (F$47) and Malololailai (F$37) one way. Turtle Airways offers more expensive seaplane flights to the Mamanuca resorts, as does Island Hoppers by helicopter; see the Getting Around section earlier in this chapter. Note that weight limits apply to all flights.

Local boats are used for transporting backpackers to and from Mana and Malolo islands.

BEACHCOMBER ISLAND

Beachcomber (Tai) Island is about 20km offshore from Nadi airport. The island measures only two hectares at low tide, but has a great garden and is circled by a beautiful beach. The *Beachcomber Island Resort* (☎ 661 500, fax 664 496, beachcomber@ is.com.fj) covers the whole island. It caters for up to 200 house guests and receives lots of day trippers. While it is not a secluded oasis, it has the reputation for having the best party atmosphere in the Mamanucas and attracts a young singles crowd. Entertainment includes live music and grooving on the sand dance floor.

The new huge dorm bure sleeps 84 in two-level bunks at F$69 a bed. Alternatively, fan-cooled lodge rooms are F$165/220 for singles/doubles. There are also 20 nice beachfront bure for F$250/ 300. Children under six are free. All prices include good buffet-style meals.

Most activities cost extra, but snorkelling equipment is free for house guests. On offer is water skiing, para-sailing, giant tobogganing, windsurfing, jetskiing, island hopping and fishing trips. Subsurface (☎ 666 738, fax 669 955, subsurface@is.com.fj) has an excellent diving operation, based on the island. A two-tank dive costs F$140; open-water F$495. Diving is half-price at Beachcomber during February and March for those staying at least five nights.

Transfers are by the resort's fast catamaran *Drodrolagi* and include pick-up from the airport and Nadi and Lautoka hotels.

TREASURE ISLAND

Treasure (Levuka) Island is a short distance from Beachcomber. The six hectare coral island is covered by *Treasure Island Resort* (☎ 666 999, fax 666 955, treasureisland@ is.com.fj), catering mostly to a family clientele. There are 67 comfortable, beachfront air-con units costing F$395 for up to three adults or up to two children under 16 years with their parents. Optional meal packages cost F$62/55 for three/two meals daily.

There is nightly entertainment in the large open dining room/bar; a games room and a fresh-water pool. The resort caters well for kids, with a children's pool, playground and baby-sitting service. All non motorised activities are included in the price, plus free snorkelling trips, coral viewing and bottom line fishing. Diving trips cost F$130 for two-tank; F$520 for open-water certification.

Treasure Island Resort is serviced by South Sea Cruises; see contact details under Getting Around earlier in this section.

NAVINI

Navini, a tiny island centrally located in the Mamanucas, is surrounded by a white sand beach and offshore reef. The *Navini Island Resort* (☎ 662 188, fax 665 566 naviniisland@is.com.fj) is a good place for families or couples who want a friendly, intimate atmosphere. A one bedroom bure (maximum three people) costs F$360; duplexes with sitting rooms (maximum five people) are F$420; and honeymoon bure with verandah, private courtyard and spa cost F$495. There is a bar and small dining area and all guests eat at the same table. A meal plan is F$68/37 for adults/children. The food is good, especially the fresh fish.

All water sports and morning trips, including fishing and visiting other resorts or villages, are included in the price. Diving can be arranged with Subsurface at Beachcomber.

Most guests are picked up from Nadi or Lautoka hotels and taken by car to Vuda Point Marina, followed by a half-hour speedboat ride. Return transfers cost F$135/ 68 per adult/child.

MALOLOLAILAI

Malololailai (Plantation) Island is 20km west of Denarau Island. This is a fairly large island for the Mamanuca group (at 240 hectares), and has a good white-sand beach. Apart from two resorts, there is a time share, a marina, a dive shop, a grocery store and a restaurant near the airstrip.

Musket Cove Marina

The Musket Cove Yacht Club (☎ 662 215, fax 662 633) hosts Fiji regatta week and the Musket Cove to Port Vila yacht race. Yachts can anchor at the marina from F$36 a week and stock up on fuel, water and provisions. The club also offers a choice of charter yachts ranging in size from 6 to 32m; charter rates vary depending on duration and extent of services required.

Diving

Subsurface at Musket Cove (☎ 622 215, fax 662 633, subsurface@is.com.fj) is a well equipped dive shop, with fast dive boats and quick access to great dive sites at the Malolo Barrier Reef. A two-tank dive costs F$140; F$495 for open-water courses. Plantation Island Resort has its own diving concern: Plantation Divers. A two-tank dive is F$120 and a six-dive package is F$320.

Surfing

There is no transport to Namotu and Wilkes surfbreaks, but 'Big Johnnie' from the local village will provide boat transport to those breaks. His boat, however, does not have life jackets, radio, flares or insurance. He can be contacted at Plantation's boatshed, and rates are F$40/30/25 for one/two-three/four-five people for trips plus three hours' waiting.

Places to Stay & Eat

Plantation Island Resort (☎ 669 333, fax 669 423, plantation@is.com.fj), established in the late 1970s, was one of Fiji's first fine resorts. It caters mostly for budget-conscious families with minimal fuss, and the atmosphere can be fun, especially for children. The resort's 23 two-bedroom bure are popular: F$470/385 for garden/beachfront for singles

or doubles; or F$570/490 for six adults. Studio bure are F$280 for doubles, and air-con hotel rooms cost F$190. Up to two children under 16 can stay in the same room as their parents free of charge. Expect to get at least 25% discount off those rates in package specials or walk-in rates.

Buffet breakfast is included in the price. Expect to spend around F$10/20 for lunch/dinner. The resort has a creche and baby-sitting service, two swimming pools and a games room. Activities included in the room rate are snorkelling, volleyball, putt putt golf, canoeing and windsurfing. It also has a nine hole golf course, a tennis court, and lawn bowls.

Musket Cove Resort (☎ 662 215, fax 662 633, musketcovefiji@is.com.fj) is adjacent to the Marina. The resort is set in spacious grounds with a poolside restaurant, wide gardens, nice beachfront walking trek, and a cute island bar linked by the marina. The beach here is tidal and not as nice as at the Plantation Island Resort, however, guests from the two resorts are welcome to use each others' beaches and facilities. Musket Cove Resort caters well for families as well as for those after a quiet holiday.

Accommodation in its beachfront/lagoon bure costs F$260/372. Seaview bure with cooking facilities sleep four people and cost F$340. The double storey villas, which have a spa, two bathrooms, cooking facilities and sleep up to six people, cost F$480. Prices quoted are for double occupancy; each additional adult is charged F$15. There is no additional charge for children under 16. All units have ceiling fans. The resort also has good air-con rooms on the first floor of the administration building for F$220. Ask about low season and any other special discounts. Prices for main dinner dishes in the resort's bistro range from F$18 to $27, but there is a three course set menu for F$21.50 and meal plan for F$55. Non-motorised activities are included.

Self-caterers will be glad to know there is a well stocked supermarket 'The Trader' on Musket Cove, as well as a small general store near the airstrip near Plantation Island Resort.

Getting There & Away

Plantation Island and Musket Cove Resorts are serviced three times daily by the Malolo Cat, a fast and comfortable 17m catamaran. Return fares from Denarau Marina near Nadi cost F$75/37.50 per adult/child and take 50 minutes each way.

CASTAWAY ISLAND

Reef-fringed Castaway (Qalito) Island is 27km west of Denarau Island and has an area of 70 hectares. *Castaway Island Resort (☎ 661 233, fax 665 753, castaway@ is.com.fj)* covers about one-eighth of the island. It has 65 simple, fan-cooled bure with tapa-lined ceilings. Each bure can sleep four adults. Prices are F$515/475/445 for beachfront/oceanview/garden bure. There is a nice swimming pool/bar and a great dining terrace perched on the point overlooking the water. The all-day casual dining menu has meals for F$10 to $14 and the a la carte dinner is F$14 to $22. There is also a F$50 per day meal deal for unrestricted selection from breakfast buffet, lunch and dinner a la carte menus.

There is a creche and a children's club, which are complimentary during the day for those over three years old. Catamaran sailing, snorkelling, surf-ski paddling around the island, windsurfing, volleyball and tennis are all included in the price.

The resort's good dive operation charges F$140 for a two-tank dive. There is a small discount if you have your own equipment. Open-water courses are F$495.

Castaway Island Resort is serviced by South Sea Cruises; see under Getting Around earlier in this section.

MANA

The beautiful island of Mana is about 30km west of Denarau Island. It has grassy hills, lovely beaches and a wide coral reef, quite a spectacular site to fly over. Accommodation includes a large luxury resort and two backpacker hostels. Snorkelling is excellent, with lots of tiny colourful fish. Also check out the south beach pier at night, when the fish go into a frenzy under the lights.

Diving

There are good dive sites at the main re off Mana Island. Aqua-Trek (☎ 702 41 fax 702 412) caters for resort divers. A on tank boat dive costs F$80 including equi ment; a six-tank package is F$390, and open-water course is F$520.

Places to Stay – Budget

The two backpacker hostels are on th south-eastern edge of the Mana Resort, ne the south beach. The staff of both are us ally friendly and the party atmosphere c be fun, but it's not the place to go if yc want a quiet escape. There have bee mixed reports about both hostels. On cash is accepted and beware of theft on th beaches and in the dorms.

Ratu Kini Boko's Village Resort (☎ 6 143, 721 959 Nadi, fax 720 552) has fiv dorms of various sizes and types, from a tr ditional bure to a concrete house. Th largest takes a maximum of 16 peopl Prices are F$35 for a dorm bed and cam ing is F$22.50 per person, including mea Food is usually OK and is served buff style. The resort's activities include a BB at a 'honeymoon island' and snorkellin trips for F$5 per person for the boat pl F$5 to hire gear.

Mereani Vata Backpacker's Inn (☎ 6 099, 703 466 Nadi) has one buildin squeezing up to 24 people into bunk dorr for F$30 per person. The price includ three meals. There are also four doub rooms for F$35 per person including meal It seems that food quality and quantity he can vary. Activities include reef-fishir trips for F$5, four island sightseeing f F$20 or snorkelling, with equipment hi for F$6 per day.

The backpacker resorts charge F$30 p person each way for transfers in open boa Boats depart from Nadi's Wailoaloa Bea and the trip takes 45 minutes to 1½ hou depending on the weather and tide. Th small boat trips to the island in rou weather can be a problem. Ideally, find o about weather conditions, and avoid ove crowded boats with no life jackets or rad on board.

laces to Stay – Top End

1e Japanese-owned *Mana Island Resort* · *661 210, fax 662 713, mana@is.com.fj)*, ith its 128 bure and 32 hotel rooms, is one 'the largest island resorts in Fiji. The resort built over 80 hectares of leased land, retching between the north and south aches. Garden bure cost F$280/500 for a uble/duplex (up to six people), and spa-ous, deluxe, oceanview air-con bure are $430/720 for a double/duplex. Up to two iildren under 16 years are free. Deluxe, r-con, double hotel rooms on the northern achfront cost F$430. Resort facilities in-ude a circular pool, two tennis courts, vol-yball, games room, kids club, library and ay centre for children. All nonmotorised ater sports are included in the price.

The resort has three restaurants. The uth beach restaurant is pleasant; mains st F$15 to $26.50. There's a weekly lovo d a meke (floor show) three times a week.

etting There & Away

ana Island Resort is serviced by South a Cruises and Sunflower Airlines; see etting Around earlier in this section.

IATAMANOA

atamanoa is a small, high island north of ana. *Matamanoa Island Resort (☎ 660 1, fax 661 069, matamanoa@is.com.fj)* is a high point overlooking a beautiful ach. Bure with verandah and views to the ach cost F$400 for doubles. Each extra ult costs F$52, and there is a maximum of ur people. There are also air-con units for 180 for doubles. Matamanoa does not ter for children under 12 and is best suited couples who want a relaxing holiday. The inimum stay is three days. Rates include eakfast, and a meal plan costs F$56/28 per ult/child. The resort has a swimming pool d tennis courts; guests can trek up the hill hind the resort. Nonmotorised water orts are included in the price. Diving is th Aqua-Trek, based at Mana Island.

Matamanoa Island Resort is serviced by uth Seas' Island Express and Sunflower rlines, followed by a shuttle boat: see tting Around earlier in this section.

TOKORIKI

The small, hilly island of Tokoriki has a beautiful, long, white-sand beach facing west. *Tokoriki Island Resort (☎ 661 999, fax 665 295, tokoriki@is.com.fj)* has 27 beach-front bure with partitions; a queen-size bed and two single beds; cane furniture; fans and fridges. Deluxe versions have a similar setup, plus air-con and private open-air showers. Rates are F$430/490 for beachfront/ deluxe beachfront bure housing up to four people. Children of all ages are accepted, and breakfast is included in the price.

The resort has a pleasant dining terrace area where lunch is served for F$11 to $13; dinner costs from F$20 to $28. Activities include tennis, canoeing, sailing, reef fish-ing, diving, snorkelling, island hopping and a visit to Yanuya village. Nonmotorised water sports are included in the rate.

Tokoriki Island Resort is serviced by South Sea Cruises and Sunflower Airlines, followed by a shuttle boat: for contact de-tails, see Getting Around earlier in this section.

TAVARUA

This 12 hectare island is at the southern edge of the reef that encloses the Mama-nucas, and has great surf offshore at Cloud Break and Restaurants. *Tavarua Island Resort (☎ 723 513, fax 706 395, tavarua@ is.com.fj)* has 12 simple bure spaced among the gardens, one toilet block and a restaurant/ bar. The daily rate is F$288/412 for singles/ twins, which includes meals, transfers and boat trips to the surfbreaks. The minimum stay is one week and bookings need to be made well in advance.

NAMOTU

Namotu is a cute 1.5 hectare island next to Tavarua. *Namotu Island Resort (☎ 706 439, fax 706 039, namotu@is.com.fj)* is an intimate place, best suited to surfers and windsurfers, but also popular with divers and honeymooners. It has a verandah with a great view of the ocean and nice swim-ming pool. The two larger beach bungalows cost F$968 for up to four people and sleep two extra people for F$242 each. Double beach bungalows cost F$628 and shared rooms are F$242 per person. All meals, transfers and nonmotorised activities are included in the price. Children under 12 years are not accepted. Check in and check out is on Saturday to Saturday basis only.

Yasawa Group

The 20 islands of the Yasawa group extend in a 90km-long chain, beginning 40km north-west of Viti Levu. The group has a relatively dry climate, white-sand beaches, spectacular crystal-clear lagoons and rugged volcanic landscapes.

The high islands such as Wayasewa and Waya are great for hiking, while the reefs with brilliant hard corals are great for snorkelling and diving. It is difficult to hop between islands as transport is limited. Most places have a minimum stay and ask for payment up front.

Dangers & Annoyances

Visitors to the budget resorts travel by small boat. The trip is quite long, across an exposed stretch of water, and weather conditions can change quickly. In the past, passengers have been stranded for hours due to engine failure and in 1999 an overcrowded boat with budget resorts' guests

sank! Fortunately no-one died. Check boats have sufficient life jackets and a m rine radio.

Diving

Westside Watersports dive shop (☎ 661 46 westside@is.com.fj) on Tavewa caters f Blue Lagoon cruise passengers as well the backpacker resorts (two-tank F$11 open-water course F$390). There is also local diving operation called Dive Tre on Wayasewa. The upmarket resorts off diving to their guests.

Organised Tours

Cruises are great way to see the Yasawas. one trip you can see beautiful white-sa beaches, experience excellent snorkelling diving, go on village visits, have good fo and enjoy comfortable accommodation.

Captain Cook Cruises (☎ 701 823, f 702 045, captcookcrus@is.com.fj), Narewa Rd Nadi, offers a three night Mam nuca and southern Yasawa cruise, a fo night Yasawa cruise and a seven nig combination cruise on board the MV Re Escape. The 68m-long boat has a swimmi pool, bars, lounges, and air-con accommo dation on three decks. Prices including meals and activities, except diving, a F$1080/1285 for the three night cruise F$2268/2699 for the seven night cruise f

The Sacred Head

Prior to European contact, a Fijian's head was considered sacred, and hairdressing and face painting in Viti was an art form.

A man's hair was a symbol of his masculinity, vanity and social standing. Once initiated, men grew flamboyant, extravagant, fantastic, often massive hair-dos, dyed black, grey, sky blue, rust, orange, yellow, white or multicoloured.

Girls wore corkscrew ringlets or *tobe*, but once married their crowns were kept shaven or close-cropped. With the exception of female chiefs who could wear huge regal hair-dos, a woman's hairstyle had to be inferior to her husband's.

A chief's head was considered *tabu* and required a special hairdresser. The work could take up to two days to complete and the circumference of a chief's hair could reach more than 1.5m. Huge turbans of fine bark cloth were often worn.

Faces could be painted with striped, zigzagged, spotted, bisected or plain black, except for a red nose. There were special designs for festive occasions and war, perhaps as a disguise in conflicts against close neighbours.

ornate, colourful Swami temple in Nadi, Fiji

Preparing food in Bukuya, Viti Levu

inquisitive banded iguana

ditional *bure* (huts) in the highlands of Fiji's Viti Levu

Lindéralique cliffs, Grande Terre

Bougna, a Kanak specialty

Colourful house on Kouaoua

Mouly Beach on New Caledonia's Ouvéa Atoll

The Jean-Marie Tjibaou Cultural Centre in Noumea, New Caledo

cabin/stateroom per person, double occupancy. Children under two years are free; those up to 15 years pay F$100 per night.

Captain Cook Cruises also offers interesting sailing safaris on board the tall ship, the SV *Spirit of the Pacific*. It has three or four-day cruises to the Southern Yasawas including swimming and snorkelling trips, fishing tours, island treks, village visits, campfire BBQs and lovo feasts. Prices are F$495/599 for three/four day twin share in simple thatch bure ashore, or aboard in fold-up canvas beds below deck cabins.

Blue Lagoon Cruises (☎ 661 662, fax 664 098, blc@is.com.fj), 183 Vitogo Parade, Lautoka, offers three, four or seven-day Club Cruises to the Yasawas aboard the motor yachts: *MV Yasawa Princess* (54m, 33 cabins); the MV *Nanuya Princess* (49m, 25 cabins) or the MV *Lycianda* (39m, 21 cabins). Gold Club Cruises are aboard the luxury vessel MV *Mystique Princess* (56m, 36 staterooms). Club cruises cost from F$775/1122/3080 for two/three/six nights in twin share cabins. Seven-day Gold Club Cruise prices start at F$3332 for twin deluxe staterooms. Children under two pay 11% and those under 16 years sharing with an adult are charged from F$220 to $1100 depending on type of cruise. All accommodation has air-con and en suites, and the boats have saloons and sundecks. Transfers, cruise activities and food are included but drinks, snorkelling, diving and other equipment hire is extra. Cruises depart from Lautoka wharf. Diving is with Westside Watersports: see Diving earlier in this section.

Southern Sea Ventures (☎ 66 534 815, fax 66 534 825, cventure@midcoast.com.au) runs 11-day kayaking trips around the Yasawas between July and October. Trips cost F$2590 including meals, two-person fibreglass kayaks, camping and safety equipment.

WAYASEWA

Also known as Wayalailai (little Waya), Wayasewa has the closest Yasawa resort to the mainland. *Wayalailai Resort (☎ 669 715)* is at the base of a spectacular cliff and is run by villagers. The old Namara village

YASAWA GROUP

0   10   20 km

SOUTH PACIFIC OCEAN

Vulawalu Beach
Nanuya-i-Ra
Nanuya-i-Rata
Yawini
Muanakuasi Point
Yasawa-i-Rara
Bukumu
Yasawa
Vawa
Teci
Saunimolilevu Point
Muanabuwe Point
Nabukeru
Underwater
Cave
Sawa-i-Lau
Nacula
Tuvaka Point
Nacula
Ethel Reefs
Tavewa
Sisili
Matacawa Levu
Nanuya Lailai
Vuaki
Nanuya Levu (Turtle Island)
Matayalevu
Yaqeta
Naivalavala
Katomasulu Point
Bligh Water
Passage
Gunu
Somosomo
Soso
Marou
Naviti
Talaga Point
Drawaqa
Naukacuvu
Nanayu Balavu
Narara
Nacilau Point
Koromasoli Point
Yalobi
Wayalevu
Waya
Natawa
Wayasewa
New Namara
Kuata
White Rock
Eori
Navadra
Vanua Levu
Kadomo
Vomo
MAMANUCA GROUP
Monu
Tokoriki
Yanuya
Tavua
Lautoka
Viti Levu

1 Yasawa Island Lodge
2 Coral View Resort;
   David's Place;
   Otto & Fanny Doughty's
3 Turtle Island Resort
4 Octopus Resort
5 Wayalailai Resort

was relocated from here after a rock slide! The resort's best accommodation is in one of the five beachfront bure for F$100 per couple. It also has a 19 bed, big bure dorm for F$35 per person, a smaller eight bed dorm for F$35 and basic single rooms in the old schoolhouse for F$40. Campsites cost F$25 per person. The minimum stay is three days. All rates include three meals and mosquito nets are provided. There are flush toilets and shared cold-water showers; water supply can be restricted. Drinks and snacks can be bought at reasonable prices, and the resort has a nice deck next to the restaurant.

Wayalailai Resort has a good beach and its best snorkelling is off Kuata islet, just a short boat ride from the resort. Two-tank diving trips cost F$100. Other activities include guided hikes, volleyball, village visits and the inescapable kava ceremony. Transport to the island is by small boat (F$70 return; about 1½ to two hours; 40km), which picks up and drops off at Lautoka and Nadi hotels.

WAYA

The *Octopus Resort* (☎ 666 337, fax 666 210) on Waya is a good alternative to the busier budget places. It has a lovely beach and a good reef for snorkelling. The island has rugged hills, beautiful beaches and lagoons and four villages. You can hike to the top of Yalobi Hills to see the entire Yasawa chain. The resort has three simple standard bure, with en suites and mosquito nets. Accommodation costs F$99 for singles or doubles, and sharing a bure with a maximum of four people costs F$35 per person. Camping is F$25 per person and rates include breakfast and dinner; lunch costs F$4. Activities include village visits, island hopping, picnic or fishing trips (F$15 per person), a hiking tour (F$10), volleyball or simply hammock lounging. Diving can be arranged through Wayalailai Resort. The use of snorkelling gear and the corrugated iron kayak are included in the price. Octopus picks up its guests from Vuda Marina at Vuda Point (F$80 return; two hours).

TAVEWA

Tavewa is a small low island (about 1km wide, 3km long) with nice beaches and good swimming and snorkelling. There is no village, no chief, just three budget resorts and a dive operation. The best beach is lovely Savutu Point at the southern end of the island.

Otto & Fanny Doughty's (☎/fax 661 462) has a good dorm in a large bure (maximum of six people) for F$60 per person including meals. The two other self-contained bure can fit a maximum of three or four people. The bure near the beach is the most secluded. There are also two good new units

without cooking facilities for F$80 for do[u]bles. Three meals costs another F$50 f[or] doubles. Fanny's afternoon tea is very pop[u]lar with resort guests.

The two other budget resorts on Tavew[a] are fairly similar in quality, and both hav[e] nice spacious grounds right on the beac[h]. Ideally, pay up front for your one-wa[y] transfer only, so if you are unhappy you ca[n] check out the competition. Both resorts ar[e] popular with backpackers and have volley[-] ball, nightly music and kava sessions, fish[-] ing, beach trips to nearby islands, villag[e] visits and trips to Sawa-i-Lau caves (abou[t] F$20 per person depending on numbers[).] Canoes, snorkelling and fishing gear ca[n] also be hired.

Coralview Resort (☎ 662 648, 724 19[ ] Nadi) charges for camping (own tent) a[t] F$29 per person; F$35 a dorm bed or F$7[ ] for a double bure. All prices include thre[e] basic meals. The bure have concrete floor[s] and mosquito nets and sleep from three t[o] eight people. There is a shared facilitie[s] block with flush toilets, a kitchen and a din[-] ing hut near the beach. *David's Place* (☎/fa[x] 721 820) has camping for F$27 per per[-] son; dorm beds (up to 10 people) for F$3[ ] and accommodation in a traditional-styl[e] double bure for F$77. Prices include thre[e] simple meals a day.

Boat transfers (three hours minimum[)] from Lautoka, Viti Levu cost F$50/100 on[e] way/return.

TURTLE ISLAND

The exclusive *Turtle Island Resort* (☎ 66[ ] 889, 722 921 Nadi, fax 720 007, turtle@[ ] is.com.fj) on Turtle Island (Nanuya Levu) i[s] a privately-owned island about 2.25km lon[g] and about 900m wide. It has protecte[d] sandy beaches on the lagoon side an[d] rugged volcanic cliffs. The 1980 film *Th[e] Blue Lagoon*, starring Brooke Shields, wa[s] filmed here, as was the original 1949 ver[-] sion. There are only 14 bure, each with tw[o] rooms, spaced along the western beach[.] Prices are F$1668/2000 for a deluxe/gran[d] bure per night for doubles, all inclusive[.] Children are only allowed during specifi[c] times in July and the Christmas holidays[.]

uests can partake of deep-sea fishing, sail-
g, windsurfing, canoeing, snorkelling,
ving, horse riding and village trips. There
a six night minimum stay. Transfers are
y Turtle Airways seaplane charter, a 30
inute flight from Nadi.

ASAWA

asawa, the northernmost island of the
roup, has six small villages and the *Yasawa
Island Lodge* (☎ *663 364, 722 266 Nadi, fax
24 456, yasawaisland@is.com.fj*), a luxury
sort on a gorgeous beach. The 16 air-con
ure are spacious, with separate living and
edroom areas, sundecks and king-size
eds. The rates start at F$980 for doubles
er day, including all a la carte meals (drinks
xtra) and activities (except for diving and
ame fishing). Other pastimes include 4WD
ips, picnics on deserted beaches,
norkelling, tennis, bushwalking and use of
inghies and sailboats. There is no minium stay and children over 12 years are
ccepted for an extra F$165 per day. Trans-
rs to the resort's airstrip are by Sunflower
irlines charter that leaves from Nadi (30
inutes; F$200 per person each way).

Rotuma

pop 3000   • area 30 sq km

otuma is an isolated volcanic island, about
3km long by 5km at its widest, 470km
orth of the Yasawa Group. It is shaped like
whale with the bigger body of land linked
y an isthmus to the small tail end to the
est. The smaller islands of Uea, Hatana
nd Hofliua lie to the west. Hofliua is also
nown as 'split island' for its unusual rock
ormation. There are archaeological sites
nd the offshore islands are important
eabird rookeries.

Although Rotuma is a province of
Melanesian Fiji, its indigenous population
Polynesian – the result of Tongan inva-
ons in the 17th century. In the 1870s the
otuman chiefs ceded the island to Britain
ue to warring between religious groups.
otuma was politically joined to the Fijian
olony in 1881.

There is no bank or shopping centre.
Rotuma produces copra, which is processed
at the mill near Savusavu, but most young
people leave Rotuma to find work elsewhere. In 1988 an independence movement
was quashed by the Fijian government.

Places to Stay

For many years tourists were decidedly un-
welcome, however, the Rotuman chiefs
have recently decided to allow small numbers of visitors. Village stays in Motusa on
the Motusa isthmus with *Rotuma Island
Backpackers* (☎ *891 290*) are F$11 per
couple; extra for meals; BYO tent.

Getting There & Away

Sunflower Airlines has a twice-weekly
flight from Nadi to Suva (Nausori) and on
to Rotuma (3¼ hours). See the Fiji Air
Fares chart in the Getting Around section
earlier in this chapter. Contact Kadavu
Shipping (☎ *312 428, 311 766, Suva*) for
information on irregular passenger services
on the MV *Bulou-ni-Ceva* (F$90/130 for
deck/saloon). Yachts should obtain permission to anchor from the government station
at Ahau, Maka Bay, on the northern side of
the island near the Motusa isthmus.

Ovalau & The Lomaiviti Group

The Lomaiviti Group (409 sq km) lies off the
east coast of Viti Levu. Levuka, on the island
of Ovalau, was Fiji's earliest European settlement and the first capital. The interior of
the island has a rugged landscape of volcanic
origin. The Bureta airstrip and Buresala ferry
landing are on the western side of Ovalau,
while Levuka is on the eastern coast. There
is plenty of budget accommodation in Levuka. For most people a couple of days is
plenty of time to explore the historic town.
Add another day for hiking to Lovoni village. If you want beaches, consider the coral
islands of Leluvia and Caqelai, both of
which have budget accommodation, good
snorkelling and lovely beaches.

FIJI

LEVUKA

Levuka (population 3000) is the administrative, educational and agricultural centre for the Lomaiviti group, and one of Fiji's official entry ports.

As early as 1806 sandalwood traders were stopping here for supplies of food and water. Traders began settling in Levuka in the 1830s, and the population today is mainly of mixed Fijian and European descent. The town had its heyday in the mid to late 19th century, with the chief of Levuka encouraging traders of beche-de-mer, turtle shell and coconut oil. With 52 hotels along Beach St, Levuka developed an increasingly wild reputation. The town was a rowdy, lawless centre of the blackbirding (slaving) trade and a popular port for sailors, whalers and traders.

In the 1870s a flood of planters and other settlers came to Fiji, and the booming town had over 3000 Europeans living there. Many buildings date back to this period.

Levuka is now a slow-paced, picturesque place with buildings reminiscent of a Wild West tumbleweed town. The Department of Town & Country Planning declared Levuka a historic town in 1989 and it has been nominated for World Heritage listing.

Orientation & Information

Levuka is squeezed between the mountains and the water's edge. The Beach St oceanfront promenade is lined on its western side with historic shopfronts. This main street continues around the perimeter of the island. The modern and utilitarian PAFCO (Pacific Fishing Company) tuna cannery at the southern end contrasts starkly with the rest of the town, but it is the island's main employer.

Westpac and the National Bank, both at the southern end of Beach St, will change travellers cheques. The post office is near Queens Wharf at the southern end of Beach St. Ovalau Tours & Transport Limited (OT&T) is a useful source of information: see Organised Tours later for more information.

Levuka Hospital (☎ 440 105) is on Beach St. For an ambulance, call ☎ 440 105; for police, call ☎ 440 222.

Activities

Cycling could be a good way to explore L vuka. Mountain bikes are available for hi at F$15 per day. Inquire at OT&T tours.

Diving can be quite good, and there a some unexplored sites in the area. Speak Nobby at Ovalau Watersports (☎ 440 61 fax 440 405) behind the OT&T office. I has good gear and can give instruction English and German. Prices are F$120 f two-tank dives; PADI open-water cours are F$460. Reef snorkelling trips are F$3 There is also diving from Leluvia Island.

Organised Tours

One of Ovalau's highlights is hiking Lovoni village, uphill through rainforest ar into the crater of the extinct volcano at t island's centre. There you can visit the vi lage, have a Fijian lunch and swim in riv pools. Epi's tours cost F$20 including lunc and transport. Contact him at the Whale Tale restaurant or at The Royal Hotel.

Tabua

Tabua (whale's teeth) were once believed to be shrines for the ancestor spirits. Tabua were, and still are, highly valued and considered essential items for diplomacy. Used as a powerful *sevusevu*, a present given as a token of gratitude, esteem or atonement, their acceptance binds a chief morally and spiritually to the presenter and to their desired outcome.

A man's corpse was accompanied to the grave with a tabua, along with a war club or a musket and his strangled wives, to help defend his spirit on its hazardous journey to the afterworld.

Originally tabua were rare, obtained from washed-up sperm whales or through trade with Tonga. However, when the European traders introduced thousands of whale's teeth and replicas in whalebone, elephant and walrus tusks, these negotiation tools became concentrated in the hands of a few increasingly powerful chiefdoms.

LEVUKA

PLACES TO STAY
1 Sailor's Home
2 Mavida Guest House
6 The Royal Hotel

PLACES TO EAT
14 Whale's Tale; Taxi Stand
15 Kim's
18 Cafe Levuka

OTHER
3 Navoka Methodist Church
4 Patterson Brothers Shipping
5 Market
7 Masonic Lodge
8 Town Hall
9 Ovalau Club
10 Levuka Public School
11 Police Station
12 Sacred Heart Church
13 Marist Convent School
16 Gulabdah's & Sons (Chemist)
17 National Bank
19 Morris Hedstrom Building (Community Centre & Museum)
20 Ovalau Tours & Transport
21 Ovalau Watersports
22 Post & Customs Office
23 Air Fiji Office
24 Supermarket
25 Westpac Bank

OT&T (☎ 440 611, fax 440 405, otttours@is.com.fj), on Beach St, offers guided walking tours, day trips and overnight packages. The 'tea and *talanoa*' (have a chat) series takes you inside the homes of local residents. It's a great way to get a local perspective.

The Devokula project is a cute mock traditional village built and run by the nearby Bolakula village youth club. Visitors participate in the presentation of a sevusevu, try the local food and watch handicraft demonstrations. Overnight accommodation is fairly basic in traditional bure.

Places to Stay & Eat

Fiji's oldest hotel, *The Royal Hotel* (☎ 440 024, fax 440 174), next to the Totoga Creek, is one the best options. It has been run by the Ashley family for generations and oozes colonial atmosphere. There is a bar, billiards and a dining room. The video nights are very popular with TV-starved travellers. The fan-cooled rooms upstairs costs F$17.60/27.50 for singles/doubles. The hotel's good dormitory is in a large four bedroom building at the back. It has a common kitchen and sleeps 14 people at F$10 per person. There are also three rooms in the weatherboard cottage, with air-con, en suites and shared kitchen for F$55 per room. The new, air-con, one-bedroom cottages are very good and cost F$77 for a maximum of three.

The *Mavida Guest House* (☎ 440 477), at the northern end of Beach St near Niukaube Hill, is another good budget option. There is a dorm for four people for F$8 per person. Fan-cooled rooms with shared bathrooms cost F$12/24 for singles/doubles, or better ones in the old house are F$15/30.

Ask about the *Sailor's Home* at OT&T. It is a large, colonial weatherboard house on

FIJI

a hill, opposite the Niukaube Hill War Memorial. It has two bedrooms, kitchen, dining room, two sunrooms with views, and sleeps up to seven for F$99.

The best food in town can be had at the *Whale's Tale* (☎ *440 235)*. The cooking here is homestyle with fresh ingredients; three-course specials cost F$12 – try its fruit smoothies. *Kim's* (☎ *440 235)* is also a good inexpensive option, especially the Sunday evening buffet at F$9.90. It has a few tables on the balcony overlooking the water. There is a *produce market* near the Totoga Creek; a *supermarket* near the Community Centre and a few general stores along the main street.

Getting There & Away

Air Fiji has twice-daily Levuka/Suva flights from Nausori airport to Bureta airstrip (12 minutes). From here it's about one hour's drive by minibus (F$3 per person). The Air Fiji Travel Centre (☎ 811 188, fax 813 819) is on Beach St, opposite the Community Centre.

Patterson Brothers Shipping (☎ 440 125) has a bus and ferry service from Suva to Levuka. The office is near the market on Beach St. Emosi's Shipping (☎ 440 057) has a boat service from Suva to Levuka via Leluvia. See the Getting Around section earlier in this chapter for more information.

Getting Around

Levuka is easy to get around on foot. There is a taxi stand near the Whale's Tale restaurant. Minibuses or taxis to the airport depart from outside the Air Fiji office. A gravel road winds around the circumference of the island and is quite steep in the northern section. Another road follows the Bureta River inland to Lovoni village.

CAQELAI

This gorgeous small coral island is only a 15 minute walk around its perimeter. It has nice white-sand beaches fringed with palms and other large trees. The island is owned by the Methodist Church of Moturiki, which runs the small budget *Caqelai*

Resort. Those who are after a secluded spo and don't mind roughing it will love it here Facilities are very basic: a pump-up showe with a hand bucket, and bucket-flush toilet

Camping costs F$20 per person, dorm beds are F$25 per person and simple thatched bure are F$28 per person. Price include meals, and mosquito nets are pro vided. You can't buy any alcohol, drinks o snacks, but are welcome to bring your own

There is good snorkelling off the beach bring your own gear. Diving can be arranged with Leluvia's dive shop.

Contact the Royal Hotel to arrange trans port from Levuka by small boat (30 minutes, F$10 per person). Return transpor to/from Verata or Bau Landing, Viti Lev costs F$20, leaving at 6 am to meet the bus to Suva.

LELUVIA

Leluvia is a 7 hectare coral island with yellow-white sandy beaches. *Leluvia Island Resort* (☎ *301 584, 313 366 Suva)* has an assortment of buildings for accommodation. Beachfront bungalows with private bathrooms cost F$33/55 for singles/doubles while bure with shared facilities are F$15/30. Some bure and bungalows have cooking facilities, and a basic meal package costs F$13. Dorms cost F$12 per bed and camping is F$8 per person. Shared facilities include four showers (pumped rainwater) and four flush toilets. There is a small shop and a communal cooking area.

The dive operation Nautilus Dive Fiji is reasonably organised and offers two-tank dives for F$95, or F$390 for an open-water course. A boat trip for snorkelling at Shark Reef or Snake Island is F$15 per person including gear. Walks along the beaches reveal some fascinating rockpools.

Emosi's Shipping has an office at 35 Gordon St, Suva (☎ 313 366). The bus leaves Suva at noon daily except Sunday. It stops to shop for supplies on the way to Bau Landing from where transfers to the island take about 2½ hours by small boat. It can get choppy, with passengers and gear arriving drenched. To get to Leluvia from Levuka, ask at OT&T, Beach St, Levuka.

NAIGANI

Naigani, also known as Mystery Island, is a beautiful mountainous island midway between Ovalau and Viti Levu. It has an area of 220 hectares, with white-sand beaches, lagoons and fringing coral reefs. The island also has the remains of a large pre-colonial hillside fortification, and 'cannibal caves'.

The *Naigani Island Resort (☎ 300 925, fax 300 539, naigani@is.com.fj)* has garden and beachfront fan-cooled villas and is on the site of an old copra plantation. It is excellent value for couples, families or small groups. Two-bedroom villas cost F$218 (sleeping up to six), while double rooms are $165; ask about the reduced walk-in rates. Meal packages cost F$40/55 for two/three meals per day. The resort has baby-sitting and organises kids' camp-outs. There's a nine hole golf course, a free-form pool with swim-up bar and water slide. Nonmotorised water sports are included in the rates. Snorkelling is very good immediately offshore. Other activities include following nature trails, kayaking, windsurfing, fishing, and day excursions to Levuka on Ovalau.

Return road and launch transfers to/from Suva via Natovi Landing are F$60/30 per adult/child. It is about 1½ hours drive from Suva to Natovi plus a 30 minute speedboat ride. Naigani Island Resort has an office upstairs at 22 Cumming St, Suva.

NAMENALALA

The 44 hectare volcanic island of Namenalala is on the Namena Barrier Reef, about 40km south of Savusavu, Vanua Levu. It has lovely beaches and an old ring fortification but no longer any villages – just one upmarket resort. *Moody's Namena (☎ 813 764 or 812 366, moodysnamena@is.com.fj)* accommodates up to 12 guests in six hexagonal timber and bamboo bure with verandahs, on a ridge forested with huge trees. The all-inclusive rates are F$378 per person, with a minimum stay of five nights. Children under 16 years are not accepted.

Diving on the barrier reef is excellent and costs F$82 per tank. Windsurfing, fishing, snorkelling, beach volleyball, use of canoes and paddle boards are included in the price.

The island has a nature reserve for bird-watching and trekking. It has a giant clam farm and is home to seabirds and red-footed boobies. Turtles lay their eggs on the beaches between November and March. The resort closes for March and April.

Guests arrive by charter seaplane from Nadi (F$264 per person; one hour; minimum of two people).

Vanua Levu

● pop 139,500   ● area 5538 sq km

Vanua Levu (Big Land), Fiji's second largest island, is relatively undeveloped. The main places of interest for travellers are around Savusavu on the south-east coast. While this area has a predominantly indigenous Fijian population, the north-west has a higher proportion of Fijian Indians, concentrated around Labasa, the largest town. The island is volcanic in origin and has few sandy beaches, however, reefs offer good snorkelling and diving. The indented coastline with many bays is great for kayaking and the rainforest is good for bird-watching. The wild and rugged interior has potential for hiking, but there is little in the way of organised treks.

There are frequent ferry and flight services from Viti Levu. Both Savusavu and Labasa have airports. The road from Labasa to Savusavu is sealed but not well maintained, and most other roads are unsealed. The island's main routes are well serviced by buses, but it is also fun to explore by 4WD. Another long unsealed road around the north also links Labasa to Savusavu. It passes small villages but don't expect to be able to buy lunch or petrol.

SAVUSAVU & AROUND

Savusavu, a sleepy little place, is Vanua Levu's second largest town (population 2000). The main street, which runs parallel to the water's edge, has a market, a few shops and a yacht club. The whole of Savusavu Bay was once a caldera and the area still has geothermal activity with hot springs and vents of steam around the town.

FIJI

Locals sometimes use the springs behind the playing field for cooking. The view of Nawi Island (about 100m offshore) and beyond to the western mountain range across the bay is picturesque and sunsets can be spectacular. The port is a natural cyclone shelter and is a popular stop for cruising yachties.

Information

The ANZ and Westpac banks, opposite the bus station area, change cash and travellers cheques. The post office is at the eastern end of the town near Buca Bay Rd. The

service hub of the town is the Copra She Marina, where you can find: Eco Diver Tours; Beachcomber Cruises; Sunflowe Airlines; Air Fiji; Savusavu Yacht Clu (moorings F\$150 per month); toilet showers; a laundry service (F\$7 a bag); tw apartments and a restaurant.

Call ☎ 850 444 for the hospital or an am bulance, or ☎ 850 222 for the police.

Activities

Eco Divers-Tours (☎ 850 122, fax 850 34 ecodivers@is.com.fij) organises rainfores waterfall walks (F\$30), village trips (F\$20

VANUA LEVU & TAVEUNI

SOUTH PACIFIC OCEAN

0   10   20 km

Great Sea Reef

Kia

Ma

Nukubati Island Resort • Nukubati • Naduri Tabia

Navidamu

Yaqaga

Batiri

Mt Delaikoro (940m)

Qaloa Bay

Rukuruku Bay

• Nasarowanqa

VANUA LEVU

Nukub

Mt Seseleke (421m)

Valeni • Natua
Natuvu   Savarekare Mission

Yadua   Navunievu • Bua

Dawara   Savusavu Savusav
Bay

Bua Bay   Natovatu
• Cogea   Point

▲ Mt Navatovotu   ▲ Mt Kasi   Jean-Miche Cousteau Reso

Sawani   Dana

Wainunu   Namalata
Nasawana   Bay

Bligh Water   Nabouwalu Solevu Point

To E6 (Dive Site) &   To Viti Levu
Viti Levu (Ellington Wharf)   (Natovi Landing)   To Suva & Viti Levu

FIJI

nd a tour of copra plantations and the mill
F\$20). The company also hires out ocean
ayaks (F\$35 per day) and mountain bikes
F\$20 per day). A two-tank dive trip costs
\$143 including equipment; an open-water
ʼADI course costs F\$420. Two-hour
norkelling trips are F\$18 each for a group
f four.

Eco Divers-Tours also offers interesting
ayak expeditions of Savusavu Bay, inclu-
ling deep water passages, coastal explor-
ition and overnight stays in Fijian villages.
A six day, five night kayak expedition costs
\$699 per person in a group of six.

Places to Stay – Budget

The four-bed, fan-cooled dorm rooms at the
lower level of the Hot Springs Hotel (see
Places to Stay – Mid-Range) are good value
for F\$15. *The Hidden Paradise Guest
House (☎ 850 106)* is just past the copra
shed next door to the Shell petrol station. It
has six budget rooms with shared toilets,
cold showers and cooking facilities. Prices
are F\$15/30 for singles/doubles including
breakfast.

David's Holiday House (☎ 850 149),
near the hot springs behind the sports-
ground, has a dormitory that sleeps seven

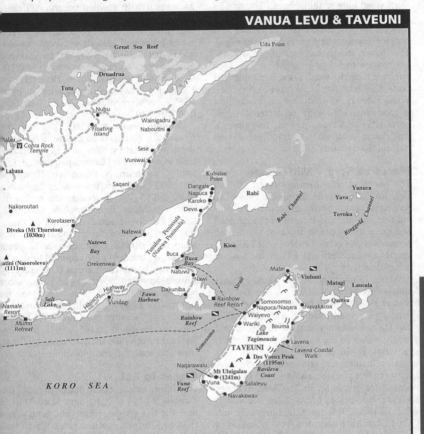

VANUA LEVU & TAVEUNI

FIJI

for F$10 per person. Campsites cost F$6. The house has a kitchen, dining area and shared bathroom. Singles/doubles cost F$14/20, including breakfast. The place is pretty basic but the atmosphere is friendly.

Mumu's Resort (☎ *850 416, fax 850 402*), about 17km east of Savusavu, is on a ruggedly beautiful site. The place is a bit run down but is still operational. It offers a variety of accommodation and camping for F$4.50/8 for singles/doubles. The dormitory, adjacent to the generator (broken down when we came past), sleeps six and costs F$14 per person. There are various shacks and bure ranging from F$40 to $50 a double. The 'dream house', perched on a rocky exposed cliff, has two rooms and cooking facilities and costs F$70 per night. The owner, Rosie, has lots of guard dogs, but beware of leaving valuables in any of the bure near the road. Food is simple and costs F$8/7/15 for breakfast/lunch/dinner. While there is no sandy beach, snorkelling is good. Take care with the currents. Local buses (F$1 to Savusavu) pass five times a day (once only on Sunday) and a taxi to/from Savusavu is F$12.

Places to Stay – Mid-Range

The four level *Hot Springs Hotel* (☎ *850 195, fax 850 430, hotspring@is.com.fj*) is Savusavu's most prominent landmark. It is built on the hill and has a swimming pool and great views out to the bay. Garden or oceanview fan-cooled rooms cost F$80 for singles or doubles; and F$125 for air-con oceanview rooms.

About 15 minutes' walk (F$1.50 by taxi) south-west of Savusavu is *Daku Garden Resort* (☎ *850 046, fax 850 334, daku@ is.com.fj*), a small resort run by the Anglican Diocese of Polynesia, with a pool and lovely views to the bay. It has six simple, fan-cooled bure for F$66/100 for singles/doubles; and self-catering villa units for up to five people costing F$110 for doubles; extra people for F$22. Children under 12 are half-price. Meals here are huge; F$8.50/12.50/20 for breakfast/lunch/dinner. Credit cards are accepted. Free transport is provided for guests to/from the airport.

Places to Stay – Top End

Jean-Michel Cousteau Fiji Islands Resor (☎ *850 188, fax 850 340, fiji4fun@is.com .fj*) is about 5km south-west of Savusavu Lesiaceva Point. It has 25 thatched-roo comfortable, fan-cooled bure with king-siz beds. Prices start at F$890 /1375 for double for gardenview/oceanfront bure. A third per son 11 to 16 years old will cost F$140 an F$190 over 17 years. Gourmet meals ar included in the price, and are served in it open-air, thatched-roof restaurant.

The resort has a swimming pool, an inter esting gift shop, a darkroom, and confer ence room with a video library. Activitie include village visits, snorkelling, kayak ing, volleyball, tennis, yoga, massage, rain forest hikes and lessons on local custom and herbal medicine. The kids' program ha fun activities and costs an extra F$80/16 for one/two or more children. Dive rates ar F$185 for a two-tank dive, with an extr F$60 for equipment rental. Scuba Certifica tion is F$720.

Namale Resort (☎ *850 435, fax 850 40* *namale@is.com.fj*) is an exclusive resort o the Hibiscus Hwy 9km east of Savusav built in a multilevel landscaped garden. It i lovely, but horribly expensive. Rates ar F$1260/1480 for singles/doubles for garde bure, and F$1700 for oceanview bure wit garden bathtubs. Prices include all meals drinks (alcoholic and nonalcoholic), trans fers from Savusavu airport and all activitie apart from diving. Children over 12 year old are accepted, but are required to stay i their own bure! The garden bure are ver private, have outdoor decks and are a shor walk from the beach. The resort has a impressive entertainment/restaurant bure guests only. Diving rates are F$370 for two-tank dive and F$1650 for a five da package. Activities include tennis, villag trips and waterfall and blowhole visits.

Places to Eat

One of the most reliable places to eat is the *Captain's Cafe* at the Copra Shed Marina near the bus station, which has good pizza (F$8 to $16 for a medium size). It's a grea spot on the outdoor deck, with beautifu views. The **Sea Breeze Restaurant** at the western end of town has good large serves of curries and Chinese for F$5. The best value curries are at **The Harbour Cafe**, two doors to the west of the customs office. The **Bula Re Restaurant** in the middle of the town upstairs has OK Chinese for F$5 to $8 and some Fijian dishes for F$6 to $9. For fine dining, book the restaurant at **Jean-Michel Cousteau Fiji Islands Resort**. For self-caterers there is the market, a small supermarket and a few grocery shops.

Getting There & Away

Savusavu airstrip is 3km south-east of the town. A trip from Nadi takes about an hour; 45 minutes from Suva. The flight over the reefs and down to Savusavu over the coconut plantations is superb. Sunflower Airlines (☎ 850 141 in Savusavu, ☎ 850 214 at the airport) has flights twice-daily from Nadi. Air Fiji (☎ 850 173 in Savusavu, ☎ 850 173 airport) has direct flights to Nadi once or twice daily, to Suva three times daily and to Taveuni three or four times daily. Refer to the Fiji Air Fares chart in the Getting Around section earlier in this chapter for prices.

Bus The bus trip from Savusavu over the mountains to Labasa, on the mostly-sealed highway, is F$4.50 (four times daily; three hours). The long route to Labasa around the north along Natewa Bay is quite scenic (departs at 9 am; 9 hours).

Savusavu to Buca Bay buses depart four times daily and cost F$3.60. From here you can catch a ferry to Taveuni: see the Ferry Suva-Savusavu-Taveuni entry in the Getting Around section earlier in this chapter.

Boat For ferry services from Suva-Savusavu, Savusavu-Taveuni and Savusavu-Buca Bay-Taveuni – see the Getting Around section earlier in this chapter.

Getting Around

Local buses pass the airport every so often, however, a taxi to/from Savusavu costs only F$2. Hot Spring Taxis' (☎ 850 226) rates are about F$15 per hour.

Avis (☎ 850 911) at the Hot Springs Hotel and Budget Rent a Car (☎ 850 700) have 4WD vehicles, which are a good way to explore the area. Eco Divers-Tours has mountain bikes for hire.

TUNULOA PENINSULA

The Tunuloa Peninsula, south-eastern Vanua Levu, is a good area for bird-watching and hiking. The scenic **Hibiscus Hwy** runs from Savusavu to Napuca and passes copra plantations, old homesteads, villages and forests. This is the habitat of the silktail, a bird on the world's endangered species list. Logging has threatened the local population of this bird.

Along the Hibiscus Hwy, the first turn-off (about 20km from Savusavu) follows the western side of Natewa Bay, an alternative 4WD route to Labasa. Instead of turning off the highway, continue to **Buca Bay**, about 65km from Savusavu (1½ hours by bus). Ferries leave from Buca Bay and cross the Somosomo Strait to Taveuni. Dive boats cross the Somosomo Strait from the Taveuni resorts to visit the famous Rainbow Reef off the south-eastern end of the peninsula.

East of Tunuloa is **Rabi Island**, home to some 4000 ethnic Micronesians. These are refugees from Banaba (Ocean Island) in Kiribati, which was devastated by phosphate mining. See the boxed text 'Rabi Island Resettlement' in the Kiribati Chapter.

Places to Stay & Eat

Buca Bay Resort (☎/fax 880 370, bucabayresort@mail.is.com.fj) has excellent thatched roof, rustic-style bure, a swimming pool, good snorkelling nearby and diving on the Rainbow Reef. The 14 bed dormitory is linked to a kitchen/bar and costs F$33 per bed. The cute waterfront bure costs F$88 a double, and the family bure is F$120 a double, plus F$10 per person up to a maximum of six. There is an external bathroom bure. A room in the main house with a share bathroom is F$88 a double. The house has a communal sitting area and porch with a view to the water. Meal packages cost F$55. Dive rates are F$120 for a two-tank dive including equipment; F$40 for snorkelling trips.

South-east of Buca Bay, on the eastern end of Vanua Levu and across the Somosomo Strait from Taveuni, is the *Rainbow Reef Resort* (☎ 880 900, fax 880 901, *rainbowreefrs@is.com.fj*). It is the closest resort to the famous Rainbow Reef. This small-scale, family-friendly resort is on a lovely white-sand beach and has comfortable beachfront cottages, each with verandah, king-size bed and open-air shower. Honeymoon cottages cost F$350/390 for doubles without/with spa, and the beachfront family suite with bedroom, sitting area and children's loft is F$420. Rates include all meals, and there is a three night minimum stay. Activities include hiking, kayaking and snorkelling. Diving and tours to Taveuni cost extra. Transfers are F$100 return, by boat from Taveuni.

Getting There & Away
The ferry landing is near the Buca Bay resort. Patterson Brothers has a bus/ferry Savusavu-Buca Bay-Taveuni service; see the Getting Around section earlier in this chapter.

LABASA & AROUND
With a population of 24,100, Labasa is the largest town on Vanua Levu. The town is on the island's north-west side, on the banks of the Labasa River. A big centre for the sugar industry in the colonial days, the district is still mainly a cane-growing area. Raw sugar and molasses, as well as timber, are exported from the port at Malau, north of the town. Labasa has a predominantly Fiji-Indian population; mostly descendants of indentured labourers brought to work on the plantations. While it is an important trade, service and administrative centre, most travellers will find the town itself pretty dull. Most shops and services can be found on the main street (Nasekula Rd). Call ☎ 811 222 for police; ☎ 811 444 for the hospital.

Places to Stay
Labasa Guest House (☎ 812 155) in Nanuku St is conveniently located but has little atmosphere. However, it does have shared kitchen facilities. Singles/double here are F$16.50/22. The *Labasa Riverview Private Hotel* (☎ 811 367, fax 814 337) is a good budget option, about a five minute walk from town past the police station along Nadawa St and the river's edge. The double storey building has 10 fan-cooled rooms and a bar with snooker tables facing the river. Rooms with fan and en suite cost F$30/40 for singles/doubles or F$45/55 with air-con. The five bed dorm upstairs with a verandah and river view, is good value for F$11 per bed.

The best mid-range option is the upgraded *Grand Eastern Hotel* (☎ 811 022, fax 814 011, grest@is.com). It has a nice courtyard with swimming pool. Standard air-con rooms are F$95 for singles or doubles, but deluxe rooms are spacious and better value for F$115.

Places to Eat
There are lots of cheap eateries along the main street. The best value Chinese-style restaurant in town is *Joe's Restaurant* (☎ 811 766). The air-con *Oriental Restaurant* on Nukusima Street, near the bus station and market, has a mixed menu. The medium-priced restaurant at the Grand Eastern Hotel is quite pleasant. There is a *hot bread kitchen* and *supermarket* near the bus station.

Getting There & Away
The airport is about 11km south-west of Labasa. It has a kiosk and a cardphone. The turn-off is about 4.25km west of Labasa, just past the Wailevu River. During the day there are regular Waiqele buses from Labasa to the airport for 55c. A taxi from Labasa costs F$6. Sunflower Airlines (☎ 812 121 airport) has four Nadi-Labasa flights daily, two Suva-Labasa flights daily, and three flights per week to Taveuni. Air Fiji (☎ 811 679 airport) has six Suva-Labasa flights daily and two Nadi-Labasa flights daily; see the Fiji Air Fares chart in the Getting Around section earlier in this chapter for prices.

There are regular buses between Labasa and Savusavu (four times daily; F$3.60).

Getting Around

Taxis are plentiful and the main stand is near the bus station. There are no written bus timetables, so just ask around. You can hire 4WD vehicles from Budget Rent a Car (☎ 811 999) and Avis (☎ 811 688).

NUKUBATI

This privately-owned island is just off the northern coast of Vanua Levu, about 40km west of Labasa. The secluded *Nukubati Island Resort* (☎ 813 901, fax 813 914) has four bungalows and three honeymoon bure for a maximum of fourteen guests at the resort. The spacious fan-cooled suites each have a private courtyard and a verandah facing a white-sand beach. Prices, including gourmet meals, nonalcoholic drinks and transfers are F$880/990 for bungalows/honeymoon bure per night per couple. Only adult couples are accepted, except for whole island bookings at F$6835 per night. The dining/bar/lounge pavilion has great views and plenty of room to find your own corner and read a book from the library.

Activities include tennis, sailing, windsurfing, snorkelling off the beach or out on the reef, and fishing. Diving is very good and costs F$185 for a two-tank dive trip. Transfers are by a one hour boat trip or by taxi along the coast past Naduri to the jetty, followed by a short boat ride.

Taveuni

● pop 12,000   ● area 435 sq km

Taveuni, also known as the 'Garden Island', is Fiji's third largest island (42km in length and about 10km wide). It is approximately 140km north-east of Viti Levu and 9km from the south-east end of Vanua Levu across the Somosomo Strait. It has a high volcanic ridge with two of the highest peaks in Fiji: Des Voeux Peak at 1195m and Mt Uluigalau at 1241m. Its rugged geography has hindered over-farming and the rainforest and wildlife are relatively intact. Taveuni is good for bird-watching. The variety and number of birds is partly due to the fact that the mongoose has not been introduced here.

Most of the coastline is rocky with some black-sand beaches. Lavena beach and Beverly beach near Matei are exceptions with white sand.

Bouma Forest Park

This national park protects over 80% of the total area of Taveuni, and covers about 15,000 hectares of rainforest and coastal forest. It has several kilometres of bush walks, including three lovely (modest size) waterfalls with natural swimming pools, not far from the reception bure. If you are a keen walker try the Vidawa Forest Walk. This is a full-day guided walk, which starts at Vidawa Village and heads up to historic fortified village sites, followed by trails into the rainforest, through river streams, then down to the Bouma waterfalls. You can buy drinks at the reception bure; park fees are F$5; F$7 for a guided waterfall tour. The Vidawa Forest Walk needs to be booked in advance. The trip runs every Friday; otherwise it can be arranged for groups (maximum of eight). It costs F$60 per person including pick-up and drop-off at accommodation around Taveuni; guides, lunch and afternoon tea; and the park fee. Inquire on ☎ 880 390, or write care of PA Bouma.

From Matei, Bouma Forest Park is 45 minutes by local bus; 20 minutes by car. A taxi costs F$15 to $20.

Lavena Coastal Walk

Lavena beach is good for swimming and snorkelling although currents can be strong here. The coastal walk entry fee (F$5 per person), payable at the reception bure, entitles you to use the beaches and the coastal walk. It is a beautiful hike along the forest edge, with the small but gorgeous **Wainibau Falls** as a reward at the end. The 5km of well marked path is mostly easy; allow at least three hours return. The only accommodation at Lavena is at the *reception bure*, which has cooking, toilet and shower facilities and a place to crash on foam mattresses in the loft. It costs F$10 per person. Camping is F$7 per person.

Lavena village is about 15 minutes' drive past Bouma. It is possible to catch the early morning bus from Naqara to Bouma, make a flying visit to the waterfalls, and catch the early afternoon bus at about 1.45 pm on to Lavena where you can either stay overnight or be picked up by a pre-arranged taxi (F$25). The early afternoon bus returns to Matei and the late afternoon bus spends the night at Lavena.

Lake Tagimoucia
This lake is in an old volcanic crater, 823m above sea level, in the mountains above Somosomo. Masses of vegetation float on the lake, and the national flower, the rare tagimoucia *Medivilla waterhouse* grows on the lake's shores. This red flower with a white centre blooms from late September to late December only at this altitude. It is a difficult walk to the lake – often very overgrown and muddy. Take lunch and allow eight hours for the round trip. The track starts from Naqara/Somosomo village. Hire a guide from the village yourself, or ask Garden Island Resort (☎ 880 283) to arrange one for you, which will cost F$40.

Diving
This area has some fantastic diving. The Somosomo Strait (the name means 'Good Water') has strong tidal currents that provide a constant flow of nutrients, ideal for soft coral growth and diverse fish life. The 32km-long Rainbow Reef off the south-west corner of Vanua Levu is world-renowned, as is the Great White Wall for drift dives.

Dive Taveuni and Aquaventure are both based in Matei, Aqua Trek at Garden Island Resort in Waiyevo and Vuna Reef Divers in southern Taveuni. The resorts on the offshore islands of Matagi and Qamea also have diving for their guests.

Organised Tours
From June to September, Keni Madden and TC Donovan of Ringgold Reef Kayaking (☎ 880 083) take kayaking and camping tours around Taveuni. Tatadra Tours, at Garden Island Resort (☎ 880 126), and some resorts in Matei have organised trips including bird-watching, rainforest walks and village visits, trips to Bouma, and the Lavena walk.

The Legend of the Tagimoucia
One day a young girl was disobedient and her mother lost her patience. While beating the girl with a bundle of coconut leaves, she told her she never wanted to see her face again. The distraught girl ran away as far as she could until deep in the forest she came upon a large *ivi* tree that was covered with vines. She climbed the vines and became entangled. She wept and wept and the tears rolling down her face turned to blood, falling onto the vine and becoming beautiful *tagimoucia* flowers. Eventually she managed to escape and returned home, relieved to find her mother had calmed down.

Accommodation
Taveuni's places to stay range from simp budget places to expensive offshore resort Power is supplied by individual generator which in most places run for a limited tim

Getting There & Away
Air Matei airport is usually open from 8 a to 4 pm and has a cardphone, kiosk and to let facilities. Sunflower (☎ 880 461) fli to/from Nadi twice daily (1½ hours), a does Air Fiji (☎ 880 062) once daily. A Fiji has flights to Nausori near Suva (5 minutes) three times daily. Refer to the Fi Air Fares chart in the Getting Around se tion earlier in this chapter for prices.

Boat The wharf for large vessels, includin the *SOFE* and *Adi Savusavu*, is about 1k north of Waiyevo (towards Matei). Smalle boats depart from Korean wharf, a bit fu ther north. Consort Shipping and Beach comber Cruises have regular Suva Savusavu-Taveuni ferries. There are als ferry/bus services to Savusavu with Patte son Brothers and aboard the *Yabula*: se Getting Around earlier in this section.

Getting Around
A gravel road hugs Taveuni's scenic coas from Lavena in the east to Navakawau i

the south. There are also a couple of other inland 4WD tracks. Getting around Taveuni involves a bit of planning, the main disadvantage being the length of time between buses. To get around cheaply and quickly you need to combine buses with walking or hitching, or share taxis with a group.

Bus Pacific Buses (☎ 880 278) depart Monday to Saturday from the Naqara depot, just south of Somosomo, to the north-east (and around the coast as Lavena) and the southwest (as far as Navakawau) at 8.30 am, noon and 5 pm (F$2.50). Beware of getting stranded at the end of the line as the last buses of the day only return the next morning. Bus transport on Sunday is restricted to one bus travelling one way only.

Car Budget Rent a Car (☎ 880 297) have 4WD vehicles. The agent is at the supermarket next to the bakery in Naqara.

Taxi Taxis are readily available in the Matei and Waiyevo areas. For destinations such as Lavena you can go one way by bus and arrange to be picked up at the end of the day at a designated time. From Matei airport expect to pay about F$12 to Waiyevo and F$25 to Vuna.

WAIYEVO

Waiyevo is the administrative centre of the island with a hospital, police station and post office (all up the hill), representatives of the *SOFE* and Patterson Brothers' ferry services. About 2.5km north of Waiyevo is Naqara, Taveuni's main shopping centre. The island's only bank, the National Bank, is here and will cash travellers cheques, but won't do cash advances. Some resorts will also change travellers cheques and the larger supermarkets and top end resorts accept credit cards. To the north of the river is Somosomo, the island's chiefly village.

The **180th meridian** passes through Taveuni, a 10 minute walk south of Waiyevo. The International Dateline actually doglegs around Fiji. **Wairiki Catholic Mission** is on the hill about 2km south of Waiyevo. In the mid-17th century an important canoe battle

took place off this beach between the Taveuni warriors and invading Tongans. The locals managed to turn back the Tongan attack and, reportedly, the dead enemies were cooked in lovo and eaten with breadfruit! The building of the Wairiki mission was a thank you to the French missionary priest who had advised the local warriors on a fighting strategy.

Places to Stay

Garden Island Resort (☎ 880 286, fax 880 288, garden@is.com.fj) has good accommodation at mid-range prices. There is no beach but a pleasant pool and restaurant/bar area looks out to the Somosomo Strait. The double storey building has sea views and air-con rooms with sliding doors to the garden or upstairs to a verandah. Singles/doubles cost F$132/168 plus an optional meal plan of F$75 per person for three meals. Two of the hotel rooms are used as dormitories (up to four people in each) for F$30 per person.

Aqua Trek Taveuni is based at the resort. It is a well equipped dive shop with good boats, Nitrox facilities and underwater photography equipment. It conducts dives of the Rainbow Reef (about 20 minutes by boat). Two dives cost F$165; six dives (three days) cost F$470 with tanks and belts only. All equipment rental is F$35/25 for one day/three or more days. PADI openwater dive courses cost F$660. The small island of Korolevu, off the resort, has beaches with good snorkelling. Trips cost F$10 per person.

Just across the Somosomo Strait from Waiyevo (about 20 minutes by boat) is the small-scale upmarket Rainbow Reef Resort on Vanua Levu: see Buca Bay in the Vanua Levu section.

Places to Eat

Outsiders are welcome at the Garden Island Resort *restaurant and bar*, but dinner needs to be ordered in the afternoon. If you find it's a bit overpriced for what's on offer, try the *Wathi-po-ee Restaurant and Cannibal Cafe* next door for cheap Chinese-style food; open from 8 am to 8 pm.

FIJI

SOUTHERN TAVEUNI

A gravel road winds along the rugged coast south from Waiyevo through beautiful rainforest, dalo and coconut plantations to Vuna village, near the end of the road. The area does not have many beaches, but the black lava rock contrasting with the turquoise water is quite beautiful. There is an impressive **blow hole** past Vuna village.

Diving and **snorkelling** on the Vuna Reef are good and can be arranged with Vuna Reef Divers at Susie's Plantation resort.

Places to Stay & Eat

There is only budget accommodation in Southern Taveuni. Those wanting contact with Fijian village life should try Salote's *Vuna Lagoon Lodge (☎/fax 880 627, bulavakaviti@is.com.fj)*. It offers simple and clean rooms, two minutes' walk from Vuna village on the edge of Vuna Lagoon. The house has a kitchen, laundry, sitting area and verandah. Some rooms have en suites and fans. Accommodation costs F$30/50 for singles/doubles in rooms or F$12 each in a four bed dorm. You can cook for yourself, otherwise home-cooked dinners cost F$10. There is a sandy beach nearby; BYO snorkelling gear.

Susie's Plantation (☎/fax 880 125), previously known as Nomui Lala Resort, was established as a copra plantation in the 1850s. The resort was operational but pretty run down at the time of writing. It has camping for F$8.50 per person and basic dorm beds for F$12 per person. Don't leave your valuables here, as the dorm building is not far from the road and robberies have been reported. The main house has a few rooms of varying size and price. Rooms sharing a bathroom are F$38 a single or double. Across the garden there are three private bure, each with self-catering facilities (no fridge, though), en suites and mosquito nets. The bure are fairly rustic but comfortable and cost F$60 to $70 a double; F$10 per extra adult. Vuna Reef Divers offers boat dives for F$60/95 a one/two-tank dive.

The Vuna area has a couple of small general stores, including one near Vatuwiri Farm and a general store in Kanacea (closed Sunday). Families grow fruit and vegetables for their own use only, so it is almost impossible to buy fresh produce.

Getting There & Away

It's about one hour by car or two hours by local bus from Matei airport to Vuna. The road is a little rough, and expect to pay F$35/25 for the taxi fare from the airport/ferry wharf, or F$5/2.60 airport/ferry wharf by bus.

MATEI

Matei is a fast-growing residential area around the airport. The freehold land is popular with Americans and other foreigners searching for a piece of tropical paradise. It has a few white-sand beaches which are OK for snorkelling.

Diving

Aquaventure (☎/fax 880 381, aquaventure@is.com.fj) is a reliable small dive shop at Beverly Beach, about 1km south of the airport. Dive trips here cost F$115 for a two-tank dive (tanks and weights only); F$20 extra per day for full equipment. Open-water courses including full equipment hire (four to five days) are F$478.

Swiss Fiji Divers (☎/fax 880 586, sfd@is.com.fj) is a new dive shop just north of Beverly Beach camp. The highlight here appears to be the equipment – high quality gear, including computer consoles, masks with underwater communication, and scooters. Two-tank dives here cost F$180 tanks and weights only, F$60 a day extra for basic equipment rental. An open-water course including all gear costs F$690.

Places to Stay – Budget

Bibi's Hideaway (☎ 880 443, 880 365) is owned and run by the amiable James Biba. He has three self-contained cottages in his large garden in a quiet and convenient location off the main road, about seven minutes from the airport towards Waiyevo. The simple cottages have spacious sitting rooms and a kitchen. The oldest cottage costs F$27.50/38.50 for singles/doubles and can accommodate up to seven people (each extra adult costs F$10). The other two bed-room cottage costs F$30 per room. The self-contained bure is F$50. All units have fridges and mosquito nets.

Karin's Garden (☎ 880 511) is across the road from Bibi's. The site is a long, narrow block of land, ending in a steep cliff with a spectacular bird's eye view down on the reef. German couple Karin and Peter have one unit with two bedrooms off a central kitchen/dining room. Rooms have en suite, wardrobe and fan, but the generator is turned off at 10 pm. Prices are F$95 per room.

Tovutovu Resort (☎ 880 560, fax 880 722) is about 20 minutes' walk east of Matei airport. The front two bure are self-contained with small kitchenettes for F$75, sleeping three in each. The two rear bure with private toilet and shower, but no cooking facilities, cost F$65 for singles or doubles. The bure have mosquito screens, and hot water, fans and power to 9 pm. The eight bed dorm and communal kitchen on the higher ground at the back costs F$15 per bed.

There are a couple of camping sites south-west of the airport. *Beverly Beach Camping* (☎ 880 684) is about 15 minutes' walk from the airport, past Taveuni Island Resort and Maravu Plantation. It accommodates a maximum of 12 people along the edge of a white-sand beach. Campsites cost F$8 per person. The camp has basic facilities, including flush toilet, shower and a sheltered area for cooking. Aquaventure living adjoins the camp. Another five minutes' walk, across the road from the Prince Charles Beach, is *Lisi's Campsite & Cottage* (☎ 880 194). It offers basic facilities for campers at F$5 per person. There is also a five bedroom cottage with shared bathroom for F$15/25 for singles/doubles.

Places to Stay – Mid-Range

Three minutes' walk east of the airport is *Coconut Grove Beachfront Cottage* (☎/fax 880 328, coconutgrove@is.com.fj). Ronna has two cute beachfront cottages and a guestroom within the restaurant/house. The guestroom has a double bed, en suite, hot water and fan for F$110. The larger free-standing cottage has a double and a single

bed, fan, fridge, cooking facilities and a private open-air shower at F$176 for up to three people. The smaller, cosier unit has a double bed, en suite, fan and verandah for F$132. There are nice views across the water to the small islets and access down through the garden to a small private beach.

There are a few good houses available for short-term rental – contact Dolores Porter (☎ 880 461, 880 299) at the airport.

Places to Stay – Top End

The long-established *Taveuni Island Resort* (☎ 880 441, fax 880 466, info@divetaveuni .com) is about 10 minutes' walk from the airstrip towards Waiyevo, on a spectacular cliff site overlooking the Somosomo Strait. The resort has a beautiful clifftop swimming pool.

The resort units have covered decks with views, king-size beds, air-con, fans, mini bar, and an outdoor shower in a private courtyard. Accommodation costs F$550/660 standard/luxury per person a night including meals, transfers and nonalcoholic drinks. Children under 15 years are not accepted. Meals are gourmet dining on the restaurant deck. A two-tank morning dive is F$220 per person per day including lunch.

On the hill across the road from Taveuni Island Resort is *Maravu Plantation Resort* (☎ 880 555, fax 880 600, maravu@is .com.fj). Standard units here have an en suite, fan, mini-bar, and verandah with hammocks. Standard units cost F$340/476/590 for singles/doubles/triples, and deluxe versions cost F$390/558/719. The resort has a pool and baby-sitting is available. Prices include meals and transfers. Organised activities include horse riding and plantation tours, as well as trips to the sites around the island. Diving is through Swiss Fiji Divers.

Places to Eat

Coconut Grove Cafe (☎ 880 328), just east of the airport, serves excellent food and is open for breakfast, lunch and dinner. It is the home of Ronna Goldstein and her well mannered doberman, Gracy. Dining is on Ronna's verandah, overlooking the water. The menu is displayed on the front door and dinner should be ordered before 4 pm. Mains are in the F$12.50 to $20 range. The restaurant is usually closed January through to March. A good place for coffee and cakes is *Audrey's Sweet Something's*, 10 minutes' walk east of the airport.

Karin's Garden (☎ 880 511) has good European-style food and is also open for breakfast, lunch and dinner. The set dinner menu is F$20 (book before 3 pm). Normally the menu doesn't cater for vegetarians. The bread and yogurt is home-made and the vegetables come from Karin and Peter's garden. Credit cards are not accepted.

The *restaurant* at Tovutovu Resort has an outdoor deck overlooking Viubani Island. The food is good value, with main courses ranging from F$7 to $15. Margaret Peterson, who sells snacks at the airport kiosk, also prepares dinner at her *house* (great food and lots of it) for F$15 per person. Let her know in advance. *Lal's Curry Place* (☎ 880 705), on the front porch of a house, has Indian food for F$10. Maravu Plantation Resort's *restaurant* is excellent but pricey: F$30/40 for the set lunch/dinner menu.

Self-Catering *Bhula Bhai Supermarket* in Matei (☎ 880 462, fax 880 050) is open from 7 am to 6 pm daily; closed on Sunday. It has a limited range of groceries, films, stationery, clothing and phonecards and accepts Visa and MasterCard (charge 10%; F$90 limit). The local cardphone and bus stop is also here.

MATAGI

Stunning horseshoe-shaped Matagi is 10km east of Taveuni. The island is only about 100 hectares in area, with steep rainforest sides rising to 130m. The *Matagi Island Resort* (☎ 880 260, fax 880 274, matagiisland@ is.com.fj) takes a maximum of 32 guests and children of any age are accepted; babysitting is available. Rates including all meals and most activities are F$332/610 828 for singles/doubles/triples for standard rectangular bure; and F$436/822/1154 for spacious circular bure. These can fit a family of four and an infant. The fantastic 'treehouses' cost F$488; for couples only. All accommodation has an en suite, ceiling fa stocked fridge and tea/coffee. The food he is very good. Activities include private pi nic lunches in the secluded bay. Dive rat are F$180 for two-tanks (plus F$40 for ge hire). The Matagi minibus meets guests Matei airport. It is a 15 minute drive Navakacoa village landing, followed by 20 minute boat ride to the island. Retu transfers to Taveuni airstrip are F$80 p person; free for children.

QAMEA

Qamea, a hilly island with a number bays, is to the east of Taveuni, off Thursto Point. It is about 10km in length and vari between 700m and 5km in width. It has s villages and an upmarket resort, the *Qame Beach Club* (☎ 880 220, fax 880 09 qamea@is.com.fj), along a lovely white sand beach. Each of the 11 rectangular bu has a ceiling fan, mini bar, tea/coffee faci ties, and a hammock on the verandah. Rate including meals and transfers, are F$82 1040/1240 for singles/doubles/triples. Chi dren under 12 are not accepted. The club new, spacious honeymoon villa is F$120 for doubles.

Diving is F$176 for a two-tank dive tri plus F$33 for full gear hire. There is exce lent snorkelling just offshore. Other activ ties include nature walks, village visits ar fish drives (where villagers form a large ci cle and entrap fish on the reef). Guests a picked up in the resort minibus from Mate Airport and driven about 10km to Navaka coa village landing to pick up a speedbo to the island (2.5km; about 15 minutes).

Kadavu

- **pop 12,000** • **area 411 sq km**

The Kadavu Group, about 100km south o Viti Levu, has Kadavu (Fiji's fourth-larges island) and a number of smaller islands. Th explorer Dumont d'Urville sailed past i 1834 and named the Astrolabe Reef after hi ship. Kadavu's highest peak is Nabukelev (Mt Washington) at 838m. There are fev roads and most transportation is by boat.

The prevailing south-easterly winds can atter the exposed side of the island. Expect ome rough weather from April to August.

The small town of Vunisea is situated on narrow isthmus between Namalata Bay to he west and North Bay to the east. It has he island's only police station, post office, elephone exchange, hospital, airstrip and a ouple of general stores. The National Bank t the post office will not change travellers heques or handle credit card transactions. Most of the resorts are a long way from 'unisea. Some do take credit cards but it nay be best to bring cash.

Activities

emote and rugged Kadavu is a great place or nature lovers, hikers and bird-watchers. he island is mountainous, especially on the astern side, with rainforest and numerous vaterfalls. Most travellers come to Kadavu or the **diving**. The famous Great Astrolabe .eef is about 50km long, wrapping around he south-eastern side of Kadavu. The veather often dictates which dive sites are uitable; the north-western side of the island s more sheltered from the prevailing winds. urf is reportedly good off an island near the emote Cape Washington. There is also surf t Vesi and Naiqoro Passages, but appar-ntly it is often blown out by the prevailing outh-east winds. The season for organised ayaking trips is from May to September: ontact Tamarillo Sea Kayaking (☎ 04-801 549 in New Zealand, fax 04-801 7349, nquiries@tamarillo.co.nz).

Dangers & Annoyances

part from being unreliable, the ferry trip to .adavu from Suva can be rough: fly instead. mall boats used for transfers to/from the irstrip often don't have life jackets or radios.

Places to Stay

f you get stranded in Vunisea, *Biana Ac-ommodation (☎ 336 010)*, on the hill near he Namalata Bay wharf (about 2km north f the airport), has reasonable rooms for $40 for singles or doubles. Thema (☎ 336 28), who runs the airport kiosk, also has omestays (F$10 per person).

Albert's Place (☎ 336 086) is on a tidal beach on the north-eastern corner of Kadavu Island. Camping is F$5.50 per person and dorm beds are F$6. There are 10 basic bure with mosquito nets for F$16/30 for singles/doubles. The two toilet blocks each have two flush toilets and one cold shower. There is no electricity in the bure. At the time of writing the owners were building a new dining and entertaining area, which will also have accommodation. Food is simple: F$25 per day or F$6/10/13 for breakfast/lunch/dinner. Self-caterers can pay F$3 to use the kitchen or have free use of the wooden stove outside. It sells basic grocery items.

You can snorkel at high tide only in front of the resort. Diving is F$95 (two-tanks including all gear) and is usually good but equipment and boats are very basic. Other activities include volleyball, hikes to a vil-lage, waterfall trips (F$15) and reef trips for F$10 per person for a minimum of four. Transfers from Vunisea airstrip cost F$60/25 for one or two persons/three or more.

On the opposite side of Ono channel to Albert's Place is *Jona's Paradise Resort (☎ 311 780, fax 303 860)* on Ono Island. This resort has been upgraded and is now run in association with Dive Kadavu. Ac-commodation is in traditional thatched bure spaced along the beachfront, with woven mats, covered coral floors and mosquito nets. There is a minimum three night stay. Prices are F$70/120 for singles/doubles. Dorm beds in the bure, with a maximum of four people, are F$50, and F$36 per person for camping. Prices include three simple meals, but bring your own snacks; there is no shop. There is an amenities block with flush toilets and hot-water showers. The all tides white-sand beach is one of the best in Kadavu, with good snorkelling directly in front of the resort. Diving is with Dive Ka-davu; two-tank morning dives cost F$90. Other activities include fishing or scenic boat trips around Ono Island for F$30/60 for a half/full day, shared between a maximum of six people. Return transfers from Vunisea airstrip are F$100 per person.

Matava, Astrolabe Hideaway (☎ 336 098, fax 336 099, matava@suva.is.com.fj) is

FIJI

Canoe Rollers

The beachcomber William Diaper visited Kadavu in 1843 with Ratu Qaraniqio of Rewa. He witnessed live captives from Nabukelevu being used as canoe rollers, to help in the dragging of the chief's enormous *drua* (old-style canoe) across the Kadavu isthmus.

managed by four young Australian guys. The beach at the front of the resort isn't great, however, a reef links it to a picturesque offshore island that makes a great snorkelling or kayaking trip. It can be windy and exposed on this side of the island, but the place has a rugged beauty and a sense of remoteness. The bure are rustic but comfortable, with timber floors and verandahs as well as solar-powered lighting. The best accommodation option is the new oceanview

bure for F$104 singles or doubles, otherwise go for the F$50 shared facilities waterfront bure, or the dorm for F$16. There spring water, 12V solar-powered electricity and gas hot water for showers. A three me package is F$41; meals are served in the verandah of the big restaurant/bar bure over looking the water through the trees.

Matava has reasonably good dive equipment, and claims to have a dive site where you can see manta rays all year round. two-tank dive is F$104 (tanks and bel only), plus F$22 daily gear hire. Other activities include: snorkelling, reef surfing kayaking, organised bushwalking and village visits. The boat trip from Vunise airstrip to Matava (50 minutes; F$25 person each way) can be a bit rough.

Dive Kadavu Resort (*☎ 311 780, fax 30 860, divekadavu@is.com.fj*) is on the western side of Kadavu, sheltered from the prevailing south-easterly winds. The lovel beach is good for swimming and snorkellin

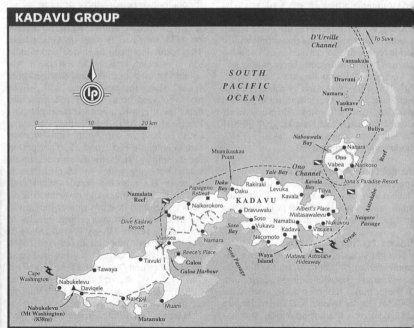

KADAVU GROUP

SOUTH PACIFIC OCEAN

D'Urville Channel — To Suva

Vanuakula

Dravuni

Namara

Yaukave Levu

Buliya

Nabouwalu Bay — Naqara

Muanikaukau Point

Ono — Vabea — Nankoso

Ono Channel

Jona's Paradise Resort

Yale Bay

Daku Bay — Rakiraki — Levuka — *Kavala Bay* — Tiliva

Papageno Retreat — Daku — Kavala

Namalata Reef — Naikorokoro — **KADAVU** — Albert's Place

Dravuwalu — Matasawalevu

Dive Kadavu Resort — Drue — Soso — Namatiu — Nukuvou — *Naiqoro Passage*

Vunisea — Vukavu — Kadavu — Vacalea

Namara — Nacomoto

Reece's Place — Waya Island — *Matava, Astrolabe Hideaway*

Tavuki — Galoa — *Soso Passage*

Galoa Harbour — *Great*

Cape Washington — Tawaya — Nabukelevu — Daviqele — Nasegai — Muani

Nabukelevu (Mt Washington) (838m) — **Matanuku**

0   10   20 km

FIJI

all tides. It has two fan-cooled, oceanview
rooms at F$260/440 for singles/doubles; and
even beachfront rooms at F$300/520 or
$220 per person with four in one room. All
rooms are well ventilated and have insect
screening and hot water. Children under 12
years are not accepted. Rates include three
meals and airport transfers. The hillside
restaurant/bar has a great view across the
water to Nabukelevu.

Dive Kadavu has an excellent setup with
good equipment and boats. Two-tank morning dive trips cost F$160 and open-water
courses are F$660. Snorkelling trips are
$30 per person. Use of windsurfers, pad-
dle boards and sea kayaks are included in
the rates. Other activities include forest
walks, village visits and a weekly lovo.

The resort is conveniently located for
travellers arriving by plane. Airport transfers are only 15 minutes by boat from Vuni-
sa airstrip.

Getting There & Away
Air Fiji has daily return flights to Kadavu from Nadi airport (1½ hours). The trip
includes one stop at Nausori airport near
Suva. Air Fiji also has two weekly services

from Nadi to Kadavu, on Monday and Saturday. Sunflower Airlines has daily flights
to Kadavu from Nadi (45 minutes). See the
Fiji Air Fare Chart in the Getting Around
section earlier in this chapter.

It is a beautiful flight from either Nadi or
Suva over stunning reefs. The approach to
Vunisea airstrip over Namalata Bay has a
spectacular view of Nabukelevu (Mt Washington), which rises steeply at the southern
point of Kadavu. The flight can sometimes
be turbulent. Ideally, have your accommodation and transfers booked in advance,
otherwise you could be stranded in Vunisea.

Ferry Suva to Kadavu on the ferry MV
Bulou-ni-ceva is F$42 per person one way.
This service is mostly for cargo and local
use, and is irregular and unreliable, taking
anything from four hours to two days! The
trip can be fine or terrible depending on the
weather you strike. Contact Kadavu Shipping in Suva (☎ 312 428).

Getting Around
Kadavu only has a few roads and small
boats are the principal mode of transport.
Book in advance to arrange transport from

The Battle of the Shark & Octopus Gods

Dakuwaqa the Shark God cruised the Fiji islands challenging other reef guardians. On hearing that a monster in
Kadavu waters was reportedly stronger than himself, he
zipped down to the island to disprove the rumour.
Dakuwaqa came across the giant octopus and
adopted his usual battle strategy of charging with
his mouth wide open and sharp teeth prepared.
The octopus, however, anchored itself to the coral
reef and swiftly wrapped its free tentacles around
the shark's body and jaws, clasping the shark in a
death lock. Dakuwaqa was rendered helpless and
had to beg for mercy. In return for lenience, the octopus demanded that his subjects, the people of Kadavu, be forever protected from shark attack. In
Kadavu the people now fish without fear and regard the
shark as their protector. Most won't eat shark or octopus out
of respect for their gods.

MICK WELDON

FIJI

Vunisea airstrip to the resorts. Transfers are expensive due to fuel costs. Most boats don't have life jackets or radios. Make sure valuable gear is covered as things can get wet. If you strike rough weather it can be a bone-crunching trip. There are no regular boats between the resorts – each has its own.

The Lau Group

The Lau group, about 57 small islands spread over 400km from north to south, is about halfway between the main islands of Fiji and Tonga. The climate in this region is drier than in most other parts of Fiji. There are no banks and little tourism infrastructure.

Because of Lau's proximity to Tonga, the islanders have been greatly influenced by Polynesian people and culture. A handful of Christian missionaries arrived in the 1830s under the protection of King George Tupou I of Tonga. After initial apathy from the locals, they eventually converted the local king, the Tui Nayau, and the rest of Lau soon followed suit.

A Tongan fleet under Enele Ma'afu invaded in 1847 to investigate the murder of a preacher, and by the mid-19th century, the region was dominated by Tongans, with Ma'afu the effective leader of Lau, Taveuni and much of Vanua Levu. Ma'afu aimed to conquer all Fiji and convert the people to Christianity; he was one of the signatories to the deed of cession to Britain in 1874.

Diving

The Lau Group is relatively unexplored in terms of diving. The Lau waters are officially protected by the Fijian government, and commercial fishing is prohibited. The up-market resorts on Vanua Balavu and Kaibu have their own dive operations, and some live-aboard dive operators take trips to Lau.

VANUA BALAVU

This beautiful island, roughly a reversed S-shape, averaging about 2km wide, has lots of sandy beaches and rugged limestone hills. The Bay of Islands at the north-western end of the island is used as a cyclone shelter by

yachts. There is a road along the easte coast that has occasional passing carrie Lomaloma, the largest village, was Fij first port, regularly visited by sailing shi trading in the Pacific. Today the people Vanua Balavu largely rely on copra a beche-de-mer for their income. There is bank on the island.

Places to Stay

There are a couple of budget guesthouses Vanua Balavu. *Moana's Guesthouse* (☎ 8 006) is at Sawana, a Tongan settlement Lomaloma. The guesthouse, built in trac tional Tongan style, has two bedrooms an living area. Rates are F$30 per person inc ding three meals. The *Nawanawa Estate* another option, closer to the airport. There no contact number, but normally they co to meet flights. Accommodation costs F$ including meals. Both places can organi boat excursions and snorkelling trips.

Just offshore from Lomaloma, on t tiny island of Yanuyanu, is the upmark *Lomaloma Resort* (☎ 895 091, fax 895 09 lomaloma@suva.is.com.fj). It caters for maximum of 22 guests in seven Tonga style bure. Rates are F$490/750 for single doubles, including all meals, drinks a transfers to/from Vanua Balavu. Snorkelli trips, nonmotorised water sports, treks a village tours are included in the rates.

Getting There & Away

Air Fiji has twice-weekly flights from Na Suva-Vanua Balavu: see the Fiji Air Far Chart in the Getting Around section earl in this chapter. There are fortnight cargo/passenger boat services from Suva the Lau Group: Saliabasaga Shippi (☎ 303 403), GPO Box 14470, Walu Ba Suva, has fortnightly trips aboard the M *Tunatuki* from Narain's Wharf, Walu Bay Lakeba, Nayau, Cicia, Tuvuca, Vanua B avu, and occasionally to Moce and Onea A one-way fare including meals is F$6 Ika Corporation (☎ 308 169, fax 312 82 Yatulau Arcade, Rodwell Road, Suva, h fortnightly trips from Suva to Cicia, Van Balavu, Lakeba, Nayau, Tuvuca and Mag A one-way fare is F$55, excluding meals

New Caledonia

tting in the south-west of the Pacific in a
gion where the lingua franca is predomi-
ntly English, New Caledonia – Kanaky to
s indigenous inhabitants – is a French-
eaking territory still partially ruled by
ance, but well on the way to independence.
In this fast-changing territory, you'll be
le to taste French culture at its best and to
perience the traditional, laid-back Kanak
e. Kanaks' tribal customs are still alive
d their culture is heavily promoted. *Gites*
group of bungalows) and homestays wel-
me travellers throughout New Caledonia.
Unlike some of its neighbours, New Cale-
nia is made up of only a handful of islands.
he main island, Grande Terre, is the largest
a lush and mountainous strip of land, sur-
unded by one of the world's biggest reefs.
latively close by are the blissfully beauti-
l Loyalty Islands and Île des Pins, and a
w uninhabited dependencies.

Noumea, the country's capital and meet-
g place, is a multicultural city with a balmy
imate and fine restaurants. But if you want
truly memorable Pacific adventure, find
e time to explore *la brousse* (everything
tside Noumea) and the islands.

Although a developed territory, New
aledonia offers a wide range of opportuni-
s to get off the beaten track: excellent div-
g and snorkelling, horse trekking in the
ountains, and idyllic and isolated spots.

acts about New
aledonia

STORY

w Caledonia was first populated by
nter-gatherers, known as Lapita, who arved from the islands of Vanuatu about
00 BC. The Lapita were named after a site
ar Koné on Grande Terre where their elab-
ate, pin-hole incised pottery was discov-
ed. Other Lapita sites include the *tumuli*
urial mounds) on Grande Terre and Île des

AT A GLANCE

Capital City (& Island): Noumea (Grand
Terre)
Population: 197,000
Time: 11 hours ahead of GMT
Land Area: 18,575 sq km (7245 sq miles)
Number of Islands: 12
International Telephone Code: ☎ 687
GDP/Capita: US$11,600
Currency: Cour de Franc Pacifique
(100 CFP = US$0.89)
Languages: French & Kanak languages
Greeting: *Bonjour* (French)

HIGHLIGHTS

- **Ouvéa** – sunset on Mouli beach

- **Île des Pins** – experience a pirogue
trip along Baie d'Upi

- **Hienghène** – overwhelming
Lindéralique cliffs

- **The Rivière Bleue Park** – explore its
wild areas

- **Scuba diving** – on Aiguille de Prony
or off Lifou

- **Kanak culture** – the Jean-Marie
Tjibaou Cultural Centre in Noumea

- **Eating** – tasting a traditional bougna
in a Melanesian *gîte*

- **Horse trekking** – through the rugged
mountains near Koné

Pins, and petroglyphs on Grande Terre. From New Caledonia, the Lapita continued to Fiji and western Polynesia; see History in the Facts about the South Pacific chapter, and the boxed text 'Lapita' in the 'South Pacific Arts' special section.

From about the 11th century AD until the 18th century, New Caledonia saw another wave of migration, this time from western Polynesian islands.

European Arrival

The English explorer James Cook spotted Grande Terre in 1774, and named this new land New Caledonia because the terrain r minded him of the highlands of Scotland which was called Caledonia by the Roman

French interest in New Caledonia w sparked 14 years later when Louis X sent Comte de La Pérouse to explore economic potential. La Pérouse and h crew disappeared during a violent cyclo in the Solomon Islands. A French sear mission, led by Admiral Bruny d'Entr casteaux, landed at Balade on 17 Ap 1793. See the boxed text 'Disaster on t Reef' in the Solomon Islands chapter f more information.

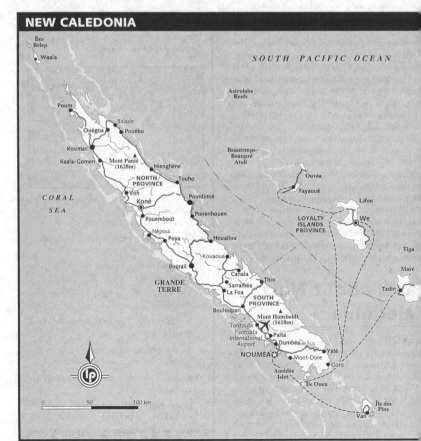

NEW CALEDONIA

In the same year, the English captain
aven sighted the southernmost of the Loy-
ty Islands, Maré.

unters, Traders & Missionaries
ritish and American whalers were the first
ommercial seafarers to land on the islands.
he whalers were followed by sandalwood
aders. Their impact on local culture was
sastrous. Most seriously, the diseases
hich European traders accidentally intro-
uced laid waste to populations of people
ith little or no resistance.

Later that century, many Kanaks were
ken to work on foreign plantations as
bourers by 'blackbirders' (essentially
avers – see History in the Facts about the
outh Pacific chapter).

Then came the men of God. Two Protes-
nt Samoan missionaries from the London
issionary Society (LMS) were the first to
rive on Île des Pins in 1841. Meanwhile
Grande Terre, seven French Marists
tablished missions at Pouébo and Balade
the north-eastern coast in December
343. Their presence profoundly changed
anak culture and daily life.

he French Colonial Order
1853, the new emperor, Napoleon III, or-
ered the annexation of New Caledonia,
ader the pretext of protecting France's
oundering Catholic missions. The French
ag was raised at Balade on 24 September
353. New Caledonia was founded as a
nal colony and the first shiploads of con-
cts arrived in May 1864 at Port-de-France
resent-day Noumea).

When settlers started to encroach on tribal
nds, hostilities between the French and
anaks began. The Revolt of 1878, led by
hef Ataï, broke out around La Foa on 25
ne and went on for seven months. The re-
ession that followed damaged the Kanak
lture and way of life forever.

Full-scale colonisation began at the end of
e 19th century. The *indigénat* (literally,
digenous) system, instituted by the French
on after the 1878 revolt, put Kanaks out-
de French common law, legally giving
em a subordinate status.

The World Wars
During WWI, 5500 Caldoche and Kanak
men were recruited to form the French Pacific Battalion, which fought in North Africa,
Italy and southern France.

During WWII, the colony's US allies
were given permission to set up a military
base on Grande Terre. From Noumea attacks were launched against the Japanese in
the Philippines and Coral Sea.

The Post-War Period
New Caledonia's status was changed from
colony to a French overseas territory after
WWII. Kanaks began to formulate their own
political and social demands. They were
given French citizenship in 1946 and the
more privileged became eligible to vote.

The first political party that was inclusive
of Kanaks was formed in 1953. Called
Union Calédonienne (UC), it was a coalition of Kanaks, small-scale landowners,
missionaries and union supporters. Their
motto was 'two colours, one people'.

The nickel boom of the 1950s and 1960s
brought prosperity but it also harvested bitter fruits. The Kanaks wanted their land
back, while the Caldoches wanted to be free
from a growing state administration run by
people they didn't know. The French
administrators' Pacific paradise and privileged life was slipping away, and the stage
was set for the violent political struggles of
the next two decades.

The Independence Movement
Having witnessed independence in Fiji
(1970) and Papua New Guinea (1975), new
political groups formed and wanted more
than the limited autonomy that the UC had
previously aspired to. With the election of
Socialist François Mitterrand to the French
presidency in 1981, Kanaks had great expectations that their right to self-determination
would be respected. But the promises remained empty. Several pro-independence
parties decided to merge to form the Front
de Libération Nationale Kanak et Socialiste
(FLNKS; Kanak Socialist National Liberation Front). The UC president, Jean-Marie
Tjibaou, was its first leader.

Between 1984 and 1986, Kanaks and whites violently provoked each other. This period of chaos is commonly referred to as Les Évènements (The Events). To calm the situation, a plan that included a referendum on independence and self-government 'in association' with France was proposed in 1985. But it was rejected by the independence movement.

The French Prime Minister decided to usher in a new program with land reforms and increased autonomy for Kanaks.

The Calm before the Storm

After the French legislative elections in May 1986, an uneasy calm prevailed as the new conservative minister in charge of the territory released his plan for New Caledonia's future. It stripped the territory's four regional councils of much of their autonomy and abolished the office that had been buying back land for Kanaks. A referendum on the question of independence was scheduled for late 1987. In 1986, the party received the official backing of the inter-governmental agency, the South Pacific Forum (SPF).

On 13 September 1987 the referendum on independence was held and boycotted by 84% of Kanaks. Of the 59% of eligible voters who cast a ballot, 98% were against independence.

The Storm

The French National Assembly approved a new plan for the territory put forward by the government in January 1987. An election was called for 24 April 1988, the same day as the first round of voting for the French presidency.

After years of their proposals being rejected by France, the FLNKS announced its 'muscular mobilisation' campaign. In April 1988, a group of militant Kanaks seized the gendarmerie (police station) on Ouvéa. Four gendarmes were killed and the rest taken hostage in a cave. Three days before the French presidential election, the military launched an assault on the cave, leaving 19 Kanaks dead. The Socialists were returned to power in France and a concerted

effort was made to end the bloodshed New Caledonia.

On 26 June 1988 the newly elect French Prime Minister, Michel Rocard, br kered the Matignon Accords. This was historic peace agreement signed at the Hôt Matignon, the Prime Minister's office, the two New Caledonian leaders, t FLNKS's Jean-Marie Tjibaou, and Jacqu Lafleur, the leader of the right-wing ruli party Rassemblement pour Calédonie da la République (RPCR; Rally for New Cal donia within the Republic).

Under the accords, it was agreed that Ne Caledonia would be divided into three r gions – the South, North and Loyalty Islan provinces. The last two would both be like to come under Kanak control in an electio The accords stated that a referendum on se determination would be held in 1998, wi all New Caledonians eligible to vote.

Towards Independence

On 4 May 1989, Jean-Marie Tjibaou and h second-in-command were shot on Ouv while attending a tribal gathering to ma the end of the mourning period for the Kanaks killed during the hostage crisis a ye earlier. Their murderers were local Kana who believed that the FLNKS leaders h sold out by signing the Matignon Accords

The assassinations ended the political vi lence in New Caledonia. As agreed in the a cords, France has been pouring money in construction and infrastructure in an attem to 'rebalance' the territory's economy a give a greater share of resources to Kanak

Right wing and many pro-independen circles are now in favour of a 'negotiate independence' and power-sharing. The id is to increase autonomy while retainin links with France. A new step was taken May 1998, when the RPCR, FLNKS ar the French government signed the Acco de Noumea (Noumea Agreement). It f cused on the gradual transfer of power fro the French State to New Caledonia and the recognition of Kanak culture. It was e dorsed by the population at a referendum November 1998. A referendum on fu independence will be held in 15 to 20 year

GEOGRAPHY

New Caledonia (18,580 sq km) is in the south-west Pacific Ocean, just north of the Tropic of Capricorn. It is made up of an archipelago comprising the main island, Grande Terre (16,350 sq km); Île des Pins (152 sq km); the Loyalty Islands (1980 sq km); and the tiny Îles Belep. Scattered round it are various dependencies totalling sq km. The highest point is Mont Panié (1628m) on Grande Terre.

In contrast to many Pacific islands, Grande Terre was not created by volcanic activity. Grande Terre broke away from eastern Australia about 140 million years ago.

CLIMATE

New Caledonia has a temperate, oceanic climate and seasons that alter little. From mid-November to mid-April it is warm and humid. Average maximum temperatures vary between 22 and 28°C, and minimums range from 11 to 17°C. February is the hottest month. The coolest period is July to August.

There is no dry season as rain is adequate year. Cyclones can affect New Caledonia from December to March.

ECOLOGY & ENVIRONMENT

Traditionally, the Kanaks had a very sensible relationship with the environment, considering it their *garde-manger* (food safe). This contrasts greatly with modern-day western attitudes and practices. Mining, smelting, urbanisation around Noumea, bushfires, and feral cats and dogs are the predominant dangers to nature in New Caledonia.

The most serious issue, opencast nickel mining, causes deforestation, erosion and water pollution. Coral reefs are damaged as run-off from the stripped mountains pours straight into the sea (coral cannot live in murky waters).

Emissions from the Doniambo nickel smelter in Noumea may be carcinogenic, and can induce asthma. Regulations forbid smelter emissions when winds are blowing towards Noumea. Instead, the emissions go out over the lagoon where they may suffocate plankton and kill the reef.

The trade in turtles is prohibited. Unfortunately this law is often flouted, with restaurants blatantly catering to tourist demands.

FLORA & FAUNA

Despite its small size, New Caledonia's biodiversity is rich. The trees you'll see include *Araucaria* pines, banyan, coconut, houp, kauri and niaouli trees. Mangrove and niaouli savannah are typical of Grande Terre's west coast.

There are an estimated 68 species of land birds. The most renowned indigenous species is the endangered *cagou* (see the boxed text 'The Cagou' in this chapter). Of the few land mammals, only roussettes (members of the fruit bat family) are indigenous. Horses, cattle, deer and feral cats have been introduced.

New Caledonia's waters are rich with around 2000 species of fish. Reef sharks, stingrays, turtles, dugongs, dolphins, gorgonian coral, sponges, sea cucumbers and a multitude of molluscs, cowrie and cone shells, giant clams, squid and the beautiful nautilus, all thrive in these waters. New Caledonia's 12 species of sea snakes are often sighted on the water's surface or on land. The most poisonous is the amphibious *tricot rayé* or striped jersey.

GOVERNMENT & POLITICS

Since the Noumea Agreement in May 1998, New Caledonia is no longer a French Territoire d'Outre-Mer (TOM) or overseas territory, but a 'special territorial entity' within the French republic. Its status will gradually change until it breaks all legal ties with France. Its inhabitants are currently French citizens. New Caledonians vote in national and presidential elections and elect three representatives to the French National Assembly in Paris.

The French government still controls many of the main sectors of society: the territory's defence and justice system, law and order, immigration, secondary and higher education, broadcasting, currency, and trade and mining regulations.

Since the signing of the Matignon Accords in 1988, New Caledonia has been governed by the 54 member Territorial Congress. It is made up of three Provincial Assemblies – the Loyalty Islands, the North and the South – which act as local parliaments with independent budgets and administrations.

The Congress elects a government that holds executive power.

There are two main political adversaries: the right wing RPCR and the pro-independence FLNKS.

ECONOMY

New Caledonia's economy centres around the mining and metallurgy industry. Grande Terre has the world's largest known nickel deposits, accounting for 30% of world reserves, and is the second-largest cobalt producer. Tourism is the second greatest money spinner, while agriculture, fishing and aquaculture contribute to a lesser degree.

France is its main trading partner and supplies half the imported consumer products – mainly food, machinery and transport equipment. On top of that, the trade balance gap is largely bridged by enormous French funding.

POPULATION & PEOPLE

The last census was carried out in 1996 and tallied the population at 196,870. Kanaks make up 44% of the population, Europeans 34%, Wallisians 9%, Indonesians 3%, Tahitians 3%, Vietnamese 1%, and ni-Vanuatu, Indians, West Indians, Arabs and others make up the remaining 6%.

The population is largely confined to the Noumea area. The total density for New Caledonia is 10.5 people per sq km.

Kanaks are Melanesians, like their neighbours in Vanuatu and Fiji, although there are some small populations of Polynesians in the country. The French are divided into two main groups – the Caldoches and the *métros* (short for *métro-poles*, meaning from metropolitan France). The Caldoches are mostly rural folk who were born in New Caledonia and whose forebears (mainly convicts) chose to stay in New Caledonia when freed. The French who come to New Caledonia to work for a few years with the benefit of high wages are called métros.

EDUCATION

A formal education is compulsory for New Caledonians between the ages of 5 and 16. Primary education is in the hands each province. Secondary schools are und state control and the teachers are most from France.

The French University of New Caledon has a campus in Noumea.

ARTS

Kanak culture and arts has been goi through a mini-renaissance in recent yea due largely to the efforts of the ADC (Agency for the Development of Kan Culture or Agence de Développement de Culture Kanak; ☎ 41 45 55, fax 41 45 5 adck@canl.nc) and to the impetus gen ated by the Jean-Marie Tjibaou Cultu Centre. Music, dance, theatre and art ex bitions are staged throughout the year. A about its program of events. See the 'Sou Pacific Arts' special section for details traditional Melanesian art forms or t boxed text 'Jean-Marie Tjibaou Cultu Centre' in this chapter.

Contemporary music includes *kaneka* blend of modern instruments with ancest harmonies and rhythms. Most songs sung in Kanak languages. They are i mensely popular with young peop throughout New Caledonia.

Dance and woodcarving are the two art tic channels, other than music, which be witness to the strength of Kanak cultu Both benefit from the tourist industry.

SOCIETY & CONDUCT
Traditional Kanak Culture

La coutume (culture) is the essential co ponent of Kanak identity and is a code living that encompasses rites, rituals and s cial interaction between and within clans. It also maintains the all-important li between Kanaks and their ancestors. Now days, politics often clashes with la coutu and, with young people leaving their cla to go to Noumea, it is under threat.

The exchange of gifts is an important e ment of la coutume as it creates a mu revered network of mutual obligations. T

Kanak Grande Case

The *grande case* (big hut) is one of the strongest symbols of the Kanak community. It is the widest and tallest *case* in each clan settlement and traditionally home to the chief. Today, the chiefs all have modern homes, called *chefferies*, located close to the grande case, where tribal gatherings and discussions still take place.

Where possible, the hut is built on a knoll above the rest of the village. The central pillar, an immense trunk of a carefully chosen tree, is erected first. It will support the entire case and symbolises the chief (in an ordinary case it represents the family's head man). A stone hearth is laid between the central pillar and the door, and is constantly alight throughout the cool months.

The entrance to the grande case is via two low doorways flanked by wide woodcarved boards. Inside, the walls and ceiling are lined with wooden posts or beams, lashed to the frame with strong vines and all of which lean against the central pillar, symbolising the clan's close link to the chief. Finally, a *flèche faîtière*, a spear-like carving that becomes home to ancestral sprits, is erected on the roof.

A chief's *case* (traditional Kanak hut), on Ouvéa in the Loyalty Islands

ne who offers a gift receives prestige from is action while placing an obligation, hich is never ignored, on the receiver to spond. In all the important stages in life, ich as birth, marriage and mourning, a gift given, symbolic offerings are made and iscussions are held.

When Kanaks enter the home of a chief, ey will offer a small token as a sign of re- ject and to introduce themselves. Food, xtiles, money or a packet of cigarettes are e traditional and contemporary offerings d, if you're given the rare privilege of eing invited to a tribal home, you should spect la coutume by bringing a gift. When

you want to camp on a clan's ground or visit a site, it's wise and courteous to intro- duce yourself to the *chef* (chief) or at least to someone in the clan.

The clan, not the individual, was *the* important element in traditional Kanak so- ciety. Some 300 clans are believed to have existed when white people arrived. The clan's activity was centred around the larg- est hut, the *grande case*, where the *chef* lived. The *chef* represents and speaks for the local community.

The most important ceremonies are for marriage, to honour the *chef* and to start the yam harvest.

The thatched round hut that's known as a *case* (see the boxed text) is the most enduring and visible artefact of Kanak culture.

French Culture

The two French groups have developed different cultural traits. The Caldoche are mostly rural folk who breed cattle. They have forged a culture of their own similar to that of outback Australia. The culture, cuisine, clothing and art of the métros, mostly in Noumea, is similar to that of urban France.

Dos & Don'ts

It is part of tribal life to greet passers-by, even if you're inside a vehicle going past pedestrians. When being introduced, Kanaks usually gently shake hands. If you are being introduced to a Kanak, you should do the same.

Do not enter villages wearing just swimwear or revealing shorts. Women should make sure their skirts or pants are of a 'decent' length and men shouldn't be bare-chested. Dressing in revealing clothes is OK around the beach suburbs of Noumea, but everywhere outside the capital it's frowned upon.

Cemeteries are the abode of the ancestors and, unless you have permission from tribal elders, you should not enter these places.

It's wise to ask permission of local people before wandering around any tribal areas.

RELIGION

Almost two-thirds of the population is Catholic. Of these, just over half are Europeans and the remainder are Kanaks and Wallisians. Protestants make up one-quarter of the population; Kanaks form the majority of followers. Other religious groups include about 4000 Muslims, generally of Indonesian descent, Mormons from Tahiti, and Buddhists, Baha'is, Seventh-Day Adventists and Jehovah's Witnesses.

LANGUAGE

French is the official language of New Caledonia. It is widely spoken and understood, unlike English, which is limited mostly to French people in the tourist industry. In addition, Tahitian, Wallisian, Indonesian and Vietnamese are also spoken, but mainly in Noumea.

An estimated 27 distinctly different Kanak languages coexist in New Caledonia but unlike neighbouring Vanuatu, Kanaks have no unifying indigenous language.

The language spoken by the largest number of Kanaks is Drehu. It comes from Lifou and is mixed with Polynesian, French and English. On Grande Terre the most spoken language is Ajië, which links clans on both coasts. The north is dominated by the Yâlayu language and the south by Xârâcùù.

For lots of useful phrases in the French language, see the appendix at the back of this book.

Facts for the Visitor

SUGGESTED ITINERARIES

Depending on the time and money you have to spend, the following itineraries could be considered:

Three Days
Spend one day in and around Noumea. Take a day trip to Amédée Islet or Île des Pins. On the final day, hire a car and go to the Parc Territorial de la Rivière Bleue or Yaté/Goro.

One Week
You could spend two days in Noumea; one day on Amédée Islet; a day in the Parc Territorial de la Rivière Bleue; one day exploring around Yaté/Goro; and two days on Île des Pins.

Two Weeks
You could have two days in and around Noumea and a day on Amédée Islet. Follow this with a hike through the Parc Territorial de la Rivière Bleue. From here you can easily take off for five or six days in a car around Grande Terre. The last six days can then be divided between the Loyalty Islands and Île des Pins.

PLANNING
When to Go

The best time to visit is from September to November when the days are not too hot or sticky and there's less likelihood of rain. June and July can also be pleasant and not overly hot.

Maps

The best map of New Caledonia is the IGN Nouvelle-Calédonie map (scale 1:500,000), which gives an overview of Grande Terre and the islands. For greater detail, IGN also publishes a four-map series of New Caledonia on a scale of 1:200,000. The Noumea tourist office gives out free-but-basic Jans Passport maps of Noumea and New Caledonia. It also sells a more detailed tourist map of the capital (100 CFP).

Marine Maps Charts can be looked at in the CNC or the capitainerie, or purchased in the Marine Corail shop. The Service Hydrographique et Océanographique de la Marine (HOM) produces excellent mariners' maps covering all New Caledonia's territorial waters. They're available from Marine Corail for 2880 CFP each.

TOURIST OFFICES
Local Tourist Offices

The Office du Tourisme de Noumea et de la Province Sud, the Office du Tourisme de la Province Nord and Destination Îles Loyauté are all based in Noumea. See Information under Noumea later in this chapter.

Tourist Offices Abroad

Some overseas addresses of New Caledonia Tourism (NCT) are:

Australia
  (☎ 02-9299 2573, fax 9290 2242,
  newcal@enternet.com.au)
  2nd floor, 30 Clarence St, Sydney, NSW 2000
France
  (☎ 01 47 03 63 23, fax 01 47 03 63 27,
  101546.1171@compuserve.com)
  370 Rue St Honoré, 75001 Paris
Japan
  (☎ 03-3583 3280, fax 3505 2873)
  Landic Nr 2, Akasaka Bldg 2-10-9 Akasaka,
  Minato-Ku, Tokyo 107
New Zealand
  (☎ 09-307 5257, fax 379 2874,
  newcal@xtra.co.nz)
  3rd floor, 57 Fort St, PO Box 4300, Auckland

New Caledonia is also represented abroad by the Tourism Council of the South Pacific (see Regional Facts for the Visitor chapter).

VISAS & DOCUMENTS

European Union and Swiss nationals and citizens of Canada, Australia and New Zealand are allowed entry into New Caledonia for three months without a visa. Citizens of Japan and the USA are allowed entry for one month without a visa.

Those travelling from New Caledonia onto other French territories – Tahiti or Wallis & Futuna – for which they need a visa should obtain it in their home country.

International Driving Permits are not required to drive in New Caledonia – a valid licence from your country will suffice.

EMBASSIES & CONSULATES
French Embassies & Consulates Abroad

New Caledonia does not operate its own embassies or consulates. Instead, the country is represented abroad by those of France. Offices around the world include:

Australia
  NSW:
  (☎ 02-9261 5779) Consulate, level 26, St Martin's Tower, 31 Market St, Sydney, NSW 2000
  Victoria:
  (☎ 03-9820 0921) Consulate, 492 St Kilda Road, Melbourne, Vic 3004
France
  (☎ 01 43 17 53 53) Ministère des Affaires Etrangères, 37 Quai d'Orsay, 75007 Paris
Japan
  (☎ 03-5420 8800) Embassy, 11-44 4 Chome, Minami-Azabu, Minato-Ku, Tokyo 106
New Zealand
  (☎ 04-384 2555) Consulate, 13th floor, Rural Bank Bldg, 34/42 Manners St, PO Box 1695, Wellington
UK
  (☎ 020-7838 2000) Consulate, 21 Cromwell Rd, London SW7 2EN
USA
  Washington DC:
  (☎ 202-944 6000) Embassy, 4101 Reservoir Rd NW, Washington, DC 20007
  Los Angeles:
  (☎ 310-235 3200) Consulate, Suite 300, 10990 Wilshire Boulevard, Los Angeles, CA 90024
  New York:
  (☎ 212-606 3689) Consulate, 934 Fifth Ave, New York, NY 10021

NEW CALEDONIA

Embassies & Consulates in New Caledonia

The following are some of the nations that are represented in New Caledonia (all offices are in Noumea):

Australia
(☎ 27 24 14) 7th floor, Immeuble Foch, 19-21 Ave du Maréchal Foch, BP 22
Indonesia
(☎ 28 25 74) 2 Rue Lamartine, Baie de l'Orphelinat, BP 26
Japan
(☎ 25 37 29) 45 Rue du 5 Mai, Magenta
Netherlands
(☎ 24 21 01) 33 Rue de Sébastopol, BP 370
New Zealand
(☎ 27 25 43) 2nd floor, 4 Blvd Vauban, BP 2219
Vanuatu
(☎ 27 26 21) 53 Rue de Sébastopol, BP 2499

CUSTOMS

Travellers arriving from Europe, America, Africa or Asia are allowed to bring in 200 cigarettes or 50 cigars or 250g of tobacco, 2L of wine, one bottle of spirits or liqueur, and a 'reasonable' quantity of perfume for personal use. Up to 50,000 French francs (or the equivalent in other currencies) can be imported without being declared.

It is strictly forbidden to bring in: firearms or ammunition, drugs, birds, cats and dogs. Animals found will be quarantined. Plants and seeds must be declared to customs.

When leaving, the export of anything that appears on the Washington Convention list (regarding the commerce of endangered flora and fauna) is prohibited. This includes rare indigenous birds, turtles and dugongs. Old objects of ethnographic interest are also not to be taken out of New Caledonia.

MONEY

Most foreign hard currencies, cash and travellers cheques can be readily changed. Automatic teller machines (ATMs) are plentiful in Noumea and away from the capital you'll find ATMs in major towns. Some post offices are also equipped with ATMs. The ATMs accept MasterCard, Visa and Eurocard. The maximum you can withdraw within sev days is 35,000 CFP.

Major credit cards are accepted by hote restaurants, big shops and airline offices Noumea, but only at the more expensi hotels outside the capital.

New Caledonia is expensive. Most of t goods are imported and are therefore price In Noumea, expect to go through abo 2000 to 2500 CFP (around US$20 US$25) per day on a budget. Even campi is pricey, with most sites charging arou 1000 CFP.

Tipping is inappropriate in New Caled nia and may cause offence.

Currency

The currency used in New Caledonia the CFP (Cour de Franc Pacifique), or P cific franc. The same currency is used French Polynesia and Wallis & Futur and although the money may have t mint mark of Noumea or Papeete, the tv are interchangeable.
Cour de Franc Pacifique banknotes cor in denominations of 500, 1000, 5000 a 10,000 CFP. Coins come in units of 1, 2, 10, 20, 50 and 100 CFP.

Exchange Rates

The CFP is tied to the French franc (FF) a fixed rate, with 1 CFP equal to 0.055F▶

country	unit		Pacific frar
Australia	A$1	=	73 CFP
Canada	C$1	=	77 CFP
Easter Island	Ch$100	=	21 CFP
euro	€1	=	120 CFP
Fiji	F$1	=	58 CFP
France	10FF	=	180 CFP
Germany	DM1	=	60 CFP
Japan	¥100	=	110 CFP
New Zealand	NZ$1	=	60 CFP
PNG	K1	=	38 CFP
Samoa	ST1	=	37 CFP
Solomon Islands	S$1	=	22 CFP
Tonga	T$1	=	75 CFP
UK	£1	=	180 CFP
USA	US$1	=	110 CFP
Vanuatu	100VT	=	88 CFP

Kids at play – Nggela, Solomon Islands

Solomon Islands hut over the water

Melanesian sunset

Sandfly Island – one of the Nggela Islands, in the Solomon Islands' Central Province

Land diving platform on Pentecost, Vanuatu

A carved *tamtam* (slit-drum) from Ambrym

Members of the Small Nambas tribe perform a yam dance at Amelboas Natsaro

ll banks handle foreign exchange. With
e exception of the American Express of-
ce in Noumea, the banks charge a 500
FP commission on cash (except French
ancs) or travellers cheque transactions.

Most banks in Noumea are open Monday
Friday from 7.20 or 7.45 am to 3.30 or
45 pm. Most are closed on weekends. In
e countryside, many banks close for lunch.

OST & COMMUNICATIONS
here are post offices throughout Grande
erre and the outlying islands. Look for the
PT (Office des Postes et Télécommunica-
ons) sign. Standard office hours are Mon-
ay to Friday from 7 am to 3 pm.

Airmail letters up to 20g and postcards
ost 105 CFP to Australia and New
ealand, 135 CFP to North America and
sia and 155 CFP to Europe.

Most post offices have a poste restante
ervice where mail sent to you can be
icked up for a 70 CFP-per-letter charge.

The phone service throughout New Cale-
onia is quite good. *Télécartes* (telephone
ards) cost 1000 CFP (25 units), 3000 CFP
0 units) or 5000 CFP (140 units) and are
vailable from post offices and a few tobac-
onists' shops in Noumea. For directory as-
stance dial ☎ 12. For emergency dial ☎ 17.
ew Caledonia's international telephone
ode is ☎ 687.

The least expensive way to make an
ternational phone call is to buy a
honecard and use a public box. The inter-
ational access code is ☎ 00. To phone Aus-
alia and New Zealand you'll be looking at
0/120 CFP per minute in off-peak/peak
me. To the USA and Canada it costs
60/240 CFP and to the UK it's 192/288
FP. Reverse charge calls can be made
om the main post office in Noumea.

A fax can be sent from post offices. The
rst page costs 600 CFP to Australia or
ew Zealand, 900 CFP to the USA, Canada
nd the UK and 800 CFP to France.

NTERNET RESOURCES
ew Caledonia Tourism's website (www
ouvellecaledonie.org) has pictures and
formation on the major attractions.

BOOKS
Les Évènements of the 1980s have led to
some very readable English-language
analyses of New Caledonia's history and
independence movement. Several books
written by Kanaks on their culture have
been published and translated into English.

Guidebooks
New Caledonia, by Mike Hosken, is a small
coffee-table book with nice photos but scant
practical or factual information.

Discover Isle of Pines, by Hilary Roots,
is a small but complete booklet covering the
island.

History & Politics
There are two excellent books that trace New
Caledonia's history from the original Kanaks
to the 1980s. *The Totem and the Tricolour*,
by Martyn Lyons, covers the history up to the
1984 crisis but not Les Évènements themselves. Alternatively, there's John Connell's
New Caledonia or Kanaky?, which covers
up to the French government's Fabius Plan.

Everlasting Hurricane, by Walter Coul-
ter, is a narrative on the escape of two convicts from New Caledonia and their
interesting journey across the Pacific. One
of the convicts was a Communard.

Politics in New Caledonia, by Myriam
Dornoy, deals with New Caledonia's contemporary political history from 1945 to
just before the start of Les Évènements.

The Kanaks of New Caledonia, by Ingrid
A Kircher, discusses the history of New
Caledonia as a colony and the growing
independence movement.

For a pro-independence account of Les
Évènements, read Helen Fraser's hardcover
Your Flag is Blocking Our Sun. This book
tells of Fraser's time in New Caledonia as a
journalist from 1981 to 1989.

Penelope's Island, by James MacNeish,
tells the story of Caldoche people living on
the north-east coast of Grande Terre at the
time of the 1984 Hienghène massacre.

People & Culture
Produced just after the Melanesia 2000
festival, *Kanaké – the Melanesian Way*, by

Jean-Marie Tjibaou was a landmark book to mark the festival. Tjibaou used colour photos, poems, legends and imagery to explain Kanak culture. The impact of modernism on his people is discussed and an outline for the future is drawn.

An enjoyable booklet offering an insight into the legends of the people of Hienghène is *Hwanfalik – Sayings from the Hienghène Valley*, by Kaloombat Tein. It's an anthology of expressions used among the people in their own dialect, with explanations in English.

Another booklet published by the ADCK is *Pue Thawe*. In this, Timothée Daahma Le We from the Tiendanite clan near Hienghène explains the myth behind the origins of traditional Kanak money.

A Swiss couple, May and Henry Larsen, produced *The Golden Cowrie*, which describes the daily life of Kanaks and settlers that they encountered in the 1950s.

NEWSPAPERS & MAGAZINES

Les Nouvelles Calédoniennes (120 CFP or 180 CFP on Thursday) is the daily newspaper. It has a pro-French viewpoint. All major French newspapers and magazines are easily found in Noumea. The only English-language newspaper sold here is the *International Herald Tribune*.

Mwa Vee is a quarterly publication devoted to Kanak culture.

RADIO & TV

TV in New Caledonia operates through Télé Nouvelle Calédonie, part of the French territories broadcasting service. At present most TV programs are dispatched directly from metropolitan France (a more regional focus is being introduced) and all are in French or dubbed into French. There is also Canal+, a French-based pay TV station.

Major radio stations are the private Radio Rythme Bleu (RRB), a private and noncommercial station, the government-run Radio Nouvelle Calédonie and Radio Djiido, the station preferred by many Kanaks.

HEALTH

The standard of medical care in New Caledonia is not as high as in Europe, the USA,

Australia or New Zealand, but it is availab and you should not hesitate to see a docte In Noumea, there are two public hospita various private clinics and many chemis Each rural town has a *dispensaire* (comm nity clinic), where you can receive eme gency first-aid.

The water in New Caledonia is safe drink, except on Ouvéa. Bottled water readily available. New Caledonia has one the highest incidences of HIV/AIDS in t South Pacific.

DANGERS & ANNOYANCES

While thefts and attacks on tourists are n commonplace, they are also not unknown Noumea. Exercise caution when walki alone at night in Noumea. Take particul care when walking back to the Hoste International (HI) hostel at night, as t route up the hill is poorly lit.

On the roads, be wary of drunk drivers New Caledonia has a high death toll fro alcohol-related road accidents.

Along the coast or in the water, be awa of the various venomous sea creatures. U derwater, stay away from the black-an beige striped jersey, whose venom is dead Luckily, they are not commonly aggressiv

When swimming or snorkelling, dor underestimate the sea's current.

Possession of marijuana is illegal New Caledonia though it's plentiful in t Loyalty Islands.

BUSINESS HOURS

Government offices and most private bus nesses are open Monday to Friday fro 7.30 or 8 am to 4 or 5 pm but close betwe 11.30 am and 1.30 pm. The exceptions a the banks in Noumea and post offices a around New Caledonia, which remain op at lunch time.

In general, shops are open weekday from 7.30 to 11 am and 2 to 6 pm, and Sa urday from 8 or 9 am to noon. Howeve some supermarkets and small convenienc stores often don't close for lunch and a open all day Saturday and Sunday mornin

Sunday is extremely quiet througho New Caledonia.

PUBLIC HOLIDAYS & SPECIAL EVENTS

New Caledonia follows France in major public holidays. In addition to New Year's Day, Easter, Ascension, Whit Monday, Labor Day, Bastille Day, Assumption Day, All Saints' Day, Armistice Day and Christmas (see the Regional Facts for the Visitor chapter for dates). New Caledonia's national day is 24 September.

Other events include:

March
Festival of the Yam
The most important Kanak festival marking the beginning of the harvest. For more information see the boxed text 'Festival of the Yam' in this chapter.

April/May
Giant Omelette Festival
Dumbéa – a huge skillet and many hands are used to make a free-for-all omelette.

Mid to late May
Avocado Festival
Nece, Maré – the island's biggest fair, to celebrate the end of harvest

La Régate des Touques
Noumea – people build decorative floats from empty oil barrels and paddle furiously in a race along Anse Vata.

Pacific Tempo
Noumea – three day music festival combining artists from Papua New Guinea, Australia and New Caledonia

Late August/early September
Foire de Bourail
Bourail – huge three day country-style agricultural fair featuring a rodeo, cattle show and sales, horseracing and a beauty pageant

October
Équinoxe
Noumea – biennial festival of contemporary theatre, dance and music

Late October/early November
Sound & Light Show
Fort Teremba, near La Foa – convict life is played out among the ruins of a former penitentiary.

ACTIVITIES
Sailing
The lagoon's calm water offers excellent sailing, while all the joys of the Pacific – reefs, atolls and deserted sandy cays – await. Sheltered anchorages can be found in the many protected bays and, for the most part, are deserted, with the exception of Amédée Islet and Île des Pins, which are popular sailing destinations for locals on weekends. The only place in the country with full facilities for yachties is Noumea.

Festival of the Yam

The Festival of the Yam takes place at harvest time, generally in mid-March, about six months after the yams are planted. However, unlike harvest festivities in many other countries, this is not a huge public affair with singing and dancing. Instead it's a calm gathering of the clan and a sharing of the blessed yam, which is treated with the reverence normally reserved for a grandfather or ancestor. Many Kanaks living in Noumea return to their villages for this event.

The elders decide when it is time for the harvest, and traditionally watch nature for signs indicating that the yam is ready. These include the appearance of certain stars, such as the Southern Cross or the flowering of a particular tree. The official start of the harvest comes when the first yams are pulled from a sacred field and presented to the older clansmen and the chief. The next day, everyone gathers in the local church (this part, of course, has occurred only since the missionaries arrived) and the pile of yams is blessed by the priest. The roots are then carried in a procession to the *grande case*, from where they are distributed among the tribe. Out of respect, the yam is never cut, but is broken like bread.

Some tribes in the Yaté/Goro region have started welcoming visitors to this festival. You'll need to ask at the tourist office in Noumea to find out dates and arrangements.

Snorkelling

New Caledonia has the world's second-largest reef. The best sites are the reefs around the Loyalty Islands and Île des Pins. In Noumea, take a day trip to Amédée Islet or arrange to go snorkelling with one of the dive clubs. Preferably, bring your own equipment and inquire with the locals about the water currents.

Diving

New Caledonia has wonderful dive opportunities that are still largely underexploited. There are internationally approved dive companies in Noumea, Népoui, Bourail, Poum, Poindimié, Hienghène, Îlot Casy and Port-Boisé on Grande Terre, and on Lifou and Île des Pins.

The sea temperature around New Caledonia peaks at a warm 29°C in February and drops to 20°C in August.

The standard price for a dive is 5000 to 6000 CFP, equipment included. CMAS and Professional Association of Diving Instructors (PADI) diving certification courses are available. Most dive locations are at the outer reef and require a minimum of a 30 minute boat ride.

Other Water Activities

Noumea's beaches catch strong sea winds and windsurfing *(planche à voile)* is enormously popular. Equipment can be rented at the main beach, Anse Vata. Catamarans, jet skis, canoes and kayaks can also be hired. Popular spots for canoeing are Dumbéa, just north of Noumea, and the Parc Territorial de la Rivière Bleue, which is east of Noumea.

For swimming, you'll find stunning white beaches on the Loyalty Islands and Île des Pins.

Hiking

During the cooler mid-year months, hiking in New Caledonia is superb. Around Noumea, Monts Koghis and the Parc Territorial de la Rivière Bleue are increasingly popular hiking areas.

Along the north-east coast, many walking paths wind up to waterfalls or lead into the mountains from river valleys. One su track is the Chemin des Arabes.

Serious hikers should visit the Directic des Resources Naturelles (☎ 27 89 51), loc ted in the Westpac building at the corner Rue Jean Jaurès and Ave du Maréchal Fo in Noumea. At this office you can pick free brochures (mainly in French but som times also in English) detailing a selecti of fascinating hikes on Grande Terre.

Horse Trekking

Horse treks will let you get to know Ca doche ways a little better and are quite po ular along Grande Terre's west coast. A tw or three day safari into the mountains can arranged at Bourail, Koné and Pocquereu near La Foa.

WORK

Only French citizens can immediately wo in New Caledonia. All other nationaliti need a work permit, and they are nigh impossible to get once you're there. Th said, people have been known to pick work on the spot if they have the right e pertise and can find an employer who willing to overlook the work permit.

ACCOMMODATION

Accommodation in hotels is pricey in Ne Caledonia, except if you buy a package de in your own country. Most hotels and re sorts are located in Noumea, but the we coast, Maré, Lifou and Île des Pins ha some good options.

If you're on a budget, stick to homestay gîtes and camping grounds. Camping is po sible almost everywhere except in Noume Official campsites with running water a showers (though only sometimes and they' rarely hot) exist around Grande Terre and the islands. Usually you'll be looking about 1000 CFP to pitch your tent.

Tribal gîtes are an authentic form accommodation that sees you staying in o of the traditional Melanesian *cases* belon ing to a local family or in a bungalow. T facilities in *cases* are basic. Bedding is eith on thin, woven pandanus mats or foam ma tresses on the floor. Expect to pay abo

00 CFP per night. Bungalows range from
:ing spartan to quite modern. The more ex-
:nsive gîtes have private shower and toilet
cilities in each bungalow. Prices range
om 1500 to 6000 CFP for one person, to
)00 to 6700 CFP for two.

New Caledonia's sole HI hostel is in
oumea.

OOD

ew Caledonia has a wide variety of
uisines, but the most common restaurants
e French, Vietnamese, Chinese and Indo-
esian. Outside the capital, restaurants are
omewhat scarce and are usually attached to
otels. Restaurants are generally open from
l am to 2 pm and from 7 to 11 pm. Very
w establishments are open on Sunday.

The best value for money is a *plat du jour*
lish of the day), which typically costs
bout 850 CFP. Better still, a *menu du jour*
ixed-price three-course meal), usually re-
:rred to simply as a *menu*, costs about 1300
FP. The cheapest type of restaurant,
nacks or cafes, serve simple dishes for
bout 850 CFP. Some takeaway specialities
iclude *nems* or Vietnamese spring rolls,
nd *salade Tahitienne*, a favourite raw-fish
alad from Tahiti. *Casse-croûtes* are popu-
ır in French cafes and consist of a half-
aguette filled with cheese, egg, meat,
eafood/salad.

In the brousse and on the islands, you'll
ave the opportunity to taste venison
along the west coast), fish, lobster, coco-
ut crab, roussette (a fruit-eating flying
ox) and various traditional Kanak food
ources, including *bougna* (see the boxed
:xt 'Preparing a Bougna' under Île des
·ins in this chapter).

The morning market in Noumea is the
iggest of its kind in New Caledonia. Super-
narkets abound in Noumea. However, in
illage shops the supplies can be limited.

DRINKS

'hroughout New Caledonia the water is
afe to drink, except on Ouvéa. Bottled
·ater is widely available. Coffee is very
opular and available in many different
orms for between 100 and 150 CFP.

The preferred alcoholic drinks are *vin*
(wine) and *bière* (beer). The favourite local
beer is Number One. French, Italian, Australian, New Zealand and Californian wines
are available in supermarkets.

On Lifou and in Noumea, kava imported
from Vanuatu is sold from private houses
called *nakamal* – look for the hand-painted
signs. See the boxed text 'Kava' in the
Regional Facts for the Visitor chapter.

ENTERTAINMENT

The local live music arena features many
Kanak bands, playing everything from
sentimental mush to reggae and kaneka
(their own brand of contemporary music).

Noumea has New Caledonia's only cinemas. All films are exclusively in French –
but may be subtitled.

Kanak and Polynesian floor shows are
staged in a few of the bigger hotels, or when
cruise ships dock.

SPECTATOR SPORTS

Cricket has been the favourite sport of
Kanak women since the missionaries introduced it to the Loyalty Islanders in the
1850s. *Pétanque*, sometimes called *boules*
(bowls), is played by men on a *boulo-
dromem*, a rough but flat gravel pitch.

As in France, football (soccer) is the most
popular sport. It is played and avidly supported throughout New Caledonia. Rugby
union is played from April to October by
about seven teams, most of which are based
in Noumea.

SHOPPING

You'll find excellent woodcarvings by
Kanak sculptors in several craft centres in
Noumea and on roadside stalls along the
north-east coast. Their works consist mainly
of *grande case*, ceremonial axe or a *bec
d'oiseau* (bird's beak club) replicas. Sandalwood is available only on Île des Pins.

Also look for cassettes and CDs of local
bands playing kaneka, sold in music shops
and supermarkets in Noumea.

There is a plethora of duty-free shops in
Noumea selling imported French perfumes,
scarves, jewellery and clothing.

Getting There & Away

AIR
Airports & Airlines
The major airlines flying into New Caledonia are Air France, Qantas Airways, Air New Zealand, Air Vanuatu and AOM. Focusing more on connections with Pacific destinations is the territory's international carrier, Air Calédonie International (Aircalin).

All international flights land at Tontouta international airport, 45km north-west of Noumea. The airport has duty-free shops, an exchange desk, a post office, car-rental outlets, a restaurant and bar, and a tourist information centre. For details on travelling between Tontouta and Noumea, and contact details for local airline offices, see Getting Around in the Noumea section.

North America
The main gateway to New Caledonia from North America is Los Angeles. You can fly with Air France or AOM to Tahiti where you can connect with an Aircalin flight to Noumea. A standard return ticket costs about US$1250.

Another option is to fly with Air Pacific from Los Angeles to Noumea via Nadi. The price is in the same range.

South America
Use an Aircalin flight to Tahiti and connect with a Lan Chile flight to Santiago, via Easter Island. A return ticket costs 154,600 CFP.

Australasia
Australia is a good jumping-off point to New Caledonia. Qantas and Aircalin flights leave from Brisbane, Sydney and Melbourne. AOM has two to three flights per week from Sydney. A return excursion fare from Sydney or Brisbane typically costs A$755/815 in low/high season.

There are three flights per week between Auckland and Noumea, either with Air New Zealand or Aircalin. The 90 day return excursion fare costs NZ$949/1079.

The Pacific
See Air Passes in the introductory Getti Around the Region chapter for several passes that include New Caledonia.

Vanuatu You can fly between Port Vi and Noumea about nine times a week (flig time one hour) with Aircalin or Air Vanuat Bought in Noumea, a standard return tick costs 42,400 CFP. Aircalin has a speci weekend deal of 31,300 CFP. Air Vanuatu represented in Noumea by Axxess Trav (see Information in the Noumea secti later in this chapter).

Fiji Aircalin flies to Nadi once or twice week (flight time two hours). A return tick costs 65,600 CFP.

Wallis & Futuna Twice a week, Aircal flies to Hihifo on Wallis Island (flight tim four hours). Once a week, a flight then co tinues to Vele on Futuna (total flight tim six hours). The return fare for either 62,900/71,100 CFP in low/high season.

Tahiti Aircalin flies to Papeete's Faaa ai port twice a week (once via Wallis Islan once via Nadi) for a return excursion fare 92,200 CFP.

Hawai'i It's possible to fly from Noumea Hawai'i via Auckland or Nadi with A Pacific. The return fare is 108,000/115,00 CFP in low/high season.

Asia
Colombo and Tokyo are the only Asia cities directly connected with New Caledo nia. The Colombo to Noumea route is se viced by AOM and the Tokyo to Noume route by Air France and Japan Airline (JAL).

Europe
Air France and AOM are the major carrie between France and Noumea, with fligh via either Japan, Australia or Sri Lanka. Se the Getting Around the Region chapter f contact details and more information abou these airlines.

EA

ruise Ships

ll cruise ships dock in Baie de la Moselle, uth of Noumea. They also drop anchor at arious spots around New Caledonia and en shuttle their passengers ashore to end a day on the beach.

P&O's *Fair Princess* and CTC's *Norwe- an Star* (departing Sydney) are the most gular visitors to these waters. Ask your avel agent for more information. In oumea, contact the Compagnie Générale Iaritime (☎ 27 01 83, fax 27 01 80) at 32 ue Galliéni.

achts

ew Caledonia welcomes about a thousand achties every year, mostly during the peak ason between August and October. The nly place in the country with full facilities or yachties is Noumea; the approach to the apital is well marked.

Noumea is the only official Port of Entry you must arrive here first and go through nmigration formalities before dropping nchor anywhere else. Ahead of arrival in oumea, use VHF Channel 67 to contact e capitainerie (harbour master's office; 27 80 95, fax 27 71 29), BP 2960, Ioumea.

The Cercle Nautique Calédonien (CNC; 26 27 27, fax 26 28 38; VHF Channel 8), BP 235, Noumea, is a yacht club on ue du Capitaine Desmier at Baie des êcheurs.

Cruising New Caledonia & Vanuatu, by lan Lucas, gives details on many natural arbours and out-of-the-way anchorages. he *Cruising Guide to New Caledonia*, by oël Marc, Ross Blackman & Marc Ram- eau, is a general yachting guide that also rovides an exhaustive list of possible an- horages around the islands. It's available French or English and costs 5400 CFP. lso see Maps in the Facts for the Visitor ection, earlier.

RGANISED TOURS

ackage deals to New Caledonia from ustralia and various countries often work ut to be cheaper than doing it on your own

and are a good option for people whose hol- idays are limited to one or two weeks.

Australia is the best place to pick up packages. Most deals include return econ- omy air fares from Brisbane, Sydney or Melbourne, accommodation in high-class hotels and the possibility of many other incentives, such as free air tickets for chil- dren, airport transfers, breakfast, casino chips, water-sports equipment and car hire.

Agents specialising in New Caledonia and the Pacific include:

Air Calédonie Holidays
　(☎ 02-9299 8854 or ☎ tollfree 1800 643 640, fax 9299 6330)
　level 12, HCF Bldg, 403 George St, Sydney, NSW 2000
Club Med
　(☎ 02-9265 0500, fax 9265 0599)
　9th floor, 55 Market St, Sydney, NSW 2000; there are two Club Med villages in New Cale- donia – the Château Royal in Noumea and Koulnoué Village near Hienghène.
Îles du Monde
　(☎ 01 43 26 68 68, fax 01 43 29 10 00)
　7 Rue Cochin, 75005 Paris, France

Getting Around

AIR

New Caledonia's only domestic airline is Air Calédonie (Aircalin). Aircalin operates out of Magenta airport in Noumea and flies to the towns of Koné, Touho, Koumac, Tontouta and Poum on Grande Terre, to Waala on Îles Belep, to each of the four Loyalty Islands and to Île des Pins.

The main office for Aircalin (☎ 28 78 88, fax 28 13 40, commercial@aircaledonie.nc) is in Immeuble Manhattan, Rue de Ver- dun, Noumea, and it has a website at www .air-caledonie.nc. It is open weekdays from 7.30 am to noon and 1.30 to 5 pm, and Sat- urday until 11 am. Aircalin agencies exist at all flight destinations.

From Noumea, the one-way fare is 9270 CFP to any of the Loyalty Islands, 6250 CFP to Île des Pins and 10,950 CFP to Koumac. Passengers carrying an international ticket can get discounted prices if they buy four tickets. Ask at the Aircalin office.

BUS

Nearly every town or large village on Grande Terre is connected by buses, all leaving from Noumea's bus station (*gare routière*; ☎ 27 82 32). On Lifou and Ouvéa, there are meagre bus systems. You'll basically have to rely on pre-arranged transport or your thumb to get around.

The most expensive fare is the ride from Noumea to Pouébo (1750 CFP).

CAR & MOTORCYCLE

Grande Terre's northern half has one road (with various names, such as the RT1, RT3, RT6 and RT7) that basically traverses the entire top end above Bourail. In the island's central portion, the two coastlines are connected by a ring road comprising two mountain crossings and the rather infamous Canala-Thio road. The latter is impassable by conventional vehicles after heavy rain. The east and west coasts are connected by just six roads, which cross the central mountains.

New Caledonia's major roads are all in sealed and good condition, but most minor roads are unsealed. As in France, driving is on the right-hand side of the road. Each town or large village will have one petrol station or at least a pump.

Rental

Car rental companies abound in Noumea, but the larger ones also have desks at the airport. Cars can also be arranged on all the islands. The tourist office in Noumea has a list of the rental companies.

Most companies charge about 2000 to 2500 CFP per day (on average) for a small sedan. In addition, there's a charge of 27 to 36 CFP per kilometre, plus daily insurance and petrol. Some companies often offer good deals with unlimited kilometres, such as one/two weeks all-inclusive rental from 40,000/62,000 CFP.

A valid driving licence from your own country is needed, and often a security deposit of 100,000 CFP.

Reviens, je t'aime (☎ 27 88 65), at Rue Jules Ferry (inside the new *gare maritime*, ferry terminal) in central Noumea, rents motorcycles and mopeds.

HITCHING

On the Loyalty Islands and Île des Pir hitching is practically the only way to g around other than hiring a car or bike, going on a tour.

BOAT
Ferry

There is a modern passenger ferry that sa regularly between Noumea and the Loya Islands or Île des Pins.

At the time of writing, a new vessel w to be launched. For more information, co tact STIL (☎ 28 50 41, fax 28 50 51). Bo tickets can be bought in Noumea at th STIL office or from Amac Tours (☎ 26 ; 38) in the Palm Beach complex at An Vata. It should sail three times a fortnight Île des Pins. A one-way ticket to Île d Pins should cost around 3200 CFP f adults and 1600 CFP for children.

The Loyalty Islands' schedule is consi erably more complicated as the route vari each day. Consult an up-to-date schedu for exact details.

The one-way fare from Noumea Lifou, Maré or Ouvéa should be arour 4900 CFP for adults and 2500 CFP for chi dren. Inter-island, the one-way fare shou be around 2400 CFP for adults and 12(CFP for children.

Yacht & Speedboat Charters

Yachts can be chartered from Nouvel Calédonie Yachting (☎ 28 21 97, fax 25 9 77), Locaux Techniques, Port Moselle, B 1068, Noumea. Pacific Charter (☎/fax 2 10 55), Locaux Techniques, Port Mosell Noumea, has 200 HP speedboats availab for hire from 30,000 CFP per day. It als has yachts such as a catamaran.

See also Yachts under Getting There Away and Sailing under Activities earlier i this chapter.

LOCAL TRANSPORT
Bus

Noumea is the only town in New Caledoni that operates an urban bus system (for moi information see Noumea's Getting Aroun section later in this chapter).

xi

xis are confined to Noumea and the larger
wns on Grande Terre. They run on a
eter, but the charge varies depending on
e time of day that you engage them.

RGANISED TOURS

ur operators in Noumea organise a host
trips to get visitors out of the capital and
to la brousse. Popular day trips, in either
conventional or 4WD minibus, include
e Yaté/Waho region, the Monts Koghis
d the Parc Territorial de la Rivière Bleue.
you want to get out onto the water, boats
il to Îlot Maître and Amédée Islet.

Outside Noumea, gîte and hotel owners
Île des Pins and the Loyalty Islands run
urs of the islands. Many of their counter-
rts on Grande Terre's northern coast also
n day tours of their local areas. Weekend
rse treks are organised at Koné, Bourail
d at Pocquereux, near La Foa.

Noumea

pop 76,000

oumea is the nerve centre of New Cale-
onia and 40% of the population have made
their home. It is also the top tourist desti-
ation in New Caledonia.

Sitting on a peninsula in the south-
estern region of the island of Grande
erre, Noumea is made up of hills and slop-
g valleys that have gradually been inte-
rated into the growing metropolis. Bay
fter bay carves the coastline, giving it the
harm of a city that opens out to the sea.

Noumea is home to the majority of New
Caledonia's Europeans. It has the flavour of
Nice in France and the Gold Coast in Austra-
ia. For tourists, it is an ideal starting point
or exploring New Caledonia. It has all the
acilities of a modern city and boasts numer-
us restaurants and long white beaches.

History

The English trader James Paddon set up on
le Nou in 1851. Three years later a French
aval officer, Tardy de Montravel, wanting
o seal France's recent possession of New

Caledonia, chose Noumea as the site for the
colony's administrative centre.

In the early 1860s, the French chose Île
Nou as the site for a convict prison. James
Paddon was given a large tract of land at
Païta in exchange for the island and in 1864
the first ship, *Iphigénie*, arrived with 248
convicts from France.

Noumea was transformed in 1875, when
gold and nickel started to be mined. However, it was many years before the provincial atmosphere of a colonial town was lost.
According to folklore, this was a time when
the *colons* (French settlers) came into town
on horseback and swaggered into cafes just
like cowboys from the American west.

The city was the USA's military headquarters during its WWII Pacific operations. Soon after it became the seat of the
South Pacific Commission (SPC) – see
Government & Politics in the Facts about
the South Pacific chapter. With the nickel
boom of the late 1960s and early 1970s,
Noumea's population grew rapidly.

During Les Évènements, violent con-
frontations erupted in the city centre. Since
the signing of the Matignon Accords, peace
has returned to Noumea. In recent years the
city has been going through a building spree
unparalleled since the nickel boom era.

Orientation

The city centre is spread along Baie de la
Moselle. A grid of ruler-straight streets lines
the centre, the heart of which is Place des
Cocotiers.

The main tourist area is at Anse Vata,
which is connected to central Noumea by
two main routes, namely the inland road,
Route de l'Anse Vata, and the picturesque
coastal route that hugs the three large bays
that carve the city's south-western edge:
Baie de l'Orphelinat, Baie des Citrons and
Anse Vata. Anse Vata ends where Ouen
Toro (132m) rises.

Noumea's central district is bordered to
the south by Ave de la Victoire. Immediately south of this busy road is the city's
small Quartier Latin (Latin Quarter). Further east is Vallée des Colons, which eventually melds into Magenta.

West of the centre, the road leads to the peninsula of Nouville, a former island that housed the colony's first convict prison.

Immediately north of central Noumea, the land is mainly industrial. A large chunk of it is occupied by Société Le Nickel's (SLN) smelter.

Information

Tourist Offices The Office du Tourisme de Noumea et de la Province Sud (☎ 28 75 80, or ☎ tollfree 05 75 80, fax 28 75 85) is the tourist office for Noumea and the South Province. Located at the northern side of Place des Cocotiers, it is open weekdays from 8 am to 5.30 pm and Saturday from 9 am to noon. The friendly staff generally speak some English.

The Office du Tourisme de la Province Nord (☎ 27 78 05, fax 27 48 87) is in Le Village shopping centre, at 35 Ave du Maréchal Foch. It is open Monday from noon to 4.30 pm, Tuesday to Friday from 8 am to 4 pm and Saturday until noon.

The Loyalty Islands information office, known as Destination Îles Loyauté (☎ 28 93 60, fax 28 91 21, destil@canl.nc), is in front of the Lantana Beach Hôtel, at 113 Promenade Roger Laroque. It is open weekdays from 8 am to 6 pm, and Saturday from 8.30 am to 11 am and noon to 5 pm.

Money Most banks have their main branch on Ave de la Victoire. The Banque Calédonienne d'Investissement (BCI) branch, on the corner of Rue du Général Mangin and Rue Anatole France, is open on Saturday morning. Most banks are equipped with an ATM.

American Express (Amex; ☎ 28 47 37, fax 27 26 36) is on the ground floor of Center Voyages at 27bis Ave du Maréchal Foch. It does not charge commission on travellers cheques or cash.

Post & Communications The main post office is at 9 Rue Eugène Porcheron. It's open weekdays from 7.45 am to 3.30 pm, and Saturday from 7.30 to 11 am.

Internet Resources Those needing an Internet fix can head to Edge Technologie, 5 Rue du Docteur Lescour in the Quart Latin. It costs 600 CFP per half-hour onli

Travel Agencies Axxess Travel (☎ 28 77), 14 Rue de Verdun, specialises in F cific destinations and is the agent for A Vanuatu. Try also Agence Jean Brock (☎ 34 39), 14 Rue Georges Clémenceau, a Nouvelles Frontières (☎ 28 27 27), 39- Rue de Verdun.

Bookshops & Libraries The 4zarts boo shop (☎ 27 38 11), 21Ter Rue Jean Jaur across Place des Cocotiers, is the best pla to go for English-language books. A go source for information on Kanak culture the médiathèque (media library) in the Jea Marie Tjibaou Cultural Centre.

Librairie Pentecost (☎ 25 72 50), 34 R de l'Alma, has a small range of contemp rary English-language novels, as well as i ternational magazines and newspapers, a maps. Librairie Montaigne (☎ 27 34 88), Rue de Sébastopol, has the entire IGN m series on New Caledonia and some region travel guides.

Laundry The HI Hostel has a washing m chine for the use of its guests. Some lau dries wash and dry a bag of dirty clothes f about 900 CFP. Lav' Services, 47 Rue Jea Jaurès in the centre, is an option.

Medical Services & Emergencie Hôpital Gaston Bourret (☎ 25 66 66), Ru Paul Doumer, is the city's main hospita Other clinics include the Polyclinique d l'Anse Vata (☎ 26 14 22), 180 Route d l'Anse Vata, and Clinique de Baie des Ci rons (☎ 26 18 66) at 5 Rue Fernand Legra There's a pharmacy at Place des Cocotier near the tourist office. In an emergency yo can call the police on ☎ 17.

Things to See

Place des Cocotiers The natural startin point for exploring Noumea is Place de Cocotiers. Named after the coconut palm that fringe the area, the square was th army's vegetable garden in the 19th cen tury. In the middle of Place des Cocotiers i

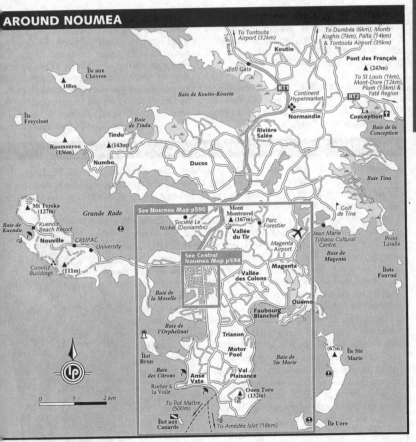

AROUND NOUMEA

To Tontouta Airport (32km)

To Dumbéa (6km), Monts Koghis (7km), Paita (14km) & Tontouta Airport (35km)

Koutio

Toll Road

Toll Gate

Pont des Français
▲ (243m)

To St Louis (1km), Mont-Dore (12km), Plum (13km) & Yaté Region

RT1

Île aux Chèvres
▲108m

Baie de Koutio-Koueta

Continent Hypermarket

RT2

La Conception

Île Freycinet

Baie de Tindu

Normandie

Baie de la Conception

Tindu
▲(143m)

Rivière Salée

Koumourou (136m)

Numbo

Ducos

Baie Tina

Mt Tereka (127m)

Grande Rade

See Noumea Map p590

Mont Montravel
▲ (167m)

Golf de Tina

Société Le Nickel (Doniambo)

Vallée du Tir

Parc Forestier

Baie de Kuendu

Kuendu Beach Resort

Nouville

CREIPAC

University

See Central Noumea Map p594

Magenta Airport

Jean Marie Tjibaou Cultural Centre

Point Lasalle

Convict Buildings
▲(111m)

Vallée des Colons

Magenta

Baie de Magenta

Îlots Fourmi

Baie de la Moselle

Ouémo

Baie de l'Orphelinat

Faubourg Blanchot

Trianon

Îlot Brun

Motor Pool

Baie de Ste Marie

(67m)▲ Île Ste Marie

Baie des Citrons

Anse Vata

Val Plaisance

Rocher à la Voile

Ouen Toro (132m)

To Îlot Maître (500m)

Îlot aux Canards

To Amédée Islet (18km)

Île Uere

0   1   2 km

---

he **Fontaine Céleste**, a fountain erected in 1892 that marks the starting point for determining road distances from the capital throughout the territory. To the east, in the op quadrant, is a renovated **bandstand** dating back to the late 1800s. On the western side, a **statue** of Admiral Olry, the colony's governor between 1878 and 1880, overlooks the city's Hôtel de Ville (Town Hall).

Bibliothèque Bernheim Bibliothèque Bernheim, on the corner of Rue de la Somme and Ave du Maréchal Foch, is the main library in Noumea. The original building on this site was constructed as the New Caledonian pavilion for the Paris Universal Exposition in 1900.

The main colonial-style building has a lovely wooden interior with large fans. Opening hours are Tuesday, Wednesday and Friday from 8 am to 1 pm, Thursday from 1 to 5.30 pm and Saturday from 9 am to 4 pm.

Musée de la Ville de Nouméa The Noumea Museum (☎ 26 28 05) was opened in 1995 and is housed in the city's old town hall on Rue Jean Jaurès, next to Place des Cocotiers. The building is a fine example of colonial architecture. It houses displays and photographs of military and penitentiary architecture, and is open Monday to Saturday from 9 am to 4.45 pm (until 7 pm on Wednesday). Admission is free.

Musée Néo-Calédonien The New Caledonia Museum (☎ 27 23 42), 42 Ave du Maréchal Foch, is an excellent place to start exploring Kanak culture.

The first room on the ground floor is de voted to a magnificent exhibition of scul tured wooden totems. Also on this floor is traditional *case* from Lifou and displays elaborate masks, ceremonial axes and a va riety of spectacular weapons. Nearby is a enormous *pirogue* (outrigger canoe), crafte by Goro's elders for the Melanesia 2000 fe tival, in 1977. The first floor is devoted masks from Papua New Guinea and Vanuatu

Jean-Marie Tjibaou Cultural Centre

Inaugurated in May 1998, the Jean-Marie Tjibaou Cultural Centre (☎ 41 45 55, fax 41 45 56, adck@canl.nc) is New Caledonia's most exciting architectural project. Dedicated to the man many remember as New Caledonia's peacemaker, this innovative and commanding piece of architecture is a testimony to the richness of Kanak culture.

Sitting on an isolated promontory at Baie de Tina, about 10km from central Noumea, this cultural centre was designed by famous Italian architect Renzo Piano (best known as one of the architects who designed the controversial Pompidou Centre, Paris). Sensitive to the Kanaks' relationship with the earth and plants, Piano worked with the Agence de Développement de la Culture Kanak (ADCK) to plan a centre that harmoniously marries contemporary architecture with deeply entrenched cultural beliefs.

Occupying some eight hectares, the centre comprises 10 *cases* (the tallest of which is 33m) that form three 'villages'. The cases are made from an African hardwood that can withstand cyclones, and they have their backs to the prevalent trade winds, which provide natural ventilation. The first three huts are designed to be a showcase of Kanak and Oceanic cultures. One hut brings together items of Kanak heritage that have been repatriated from museums around the world. Another hut houses monumental sculptures created specifically for the centre by artists throughout the Pacific. The remaining cases are home to a performing arts arena, the media library, exhibition rooms and classrooms for visiting school children. There is also a customary area, made up of three traditional Melanesian-style huts representing respectively the South, Northern Grande Terre and the Loyalty Islands.

Behind the cases weaves le Chemin Kanak (the Kanak Pathway), where a variety of trees and plants that are important to Kanaks – such as yams, taro, houp, araucaria and kaori – are interspersed with sites representing Kanak myths and customs.

The centre is open to the public from Tuesday to Sunday from 10 am to 6 pm. It has a website at www.adck.nc. There is a shop and a cafe. Entrance costs 500 CFP (add 1000 CFP if you want a guided tour in English). Take bus No 5 from the bus station.

Statue of Jean-Marie Tjibaou

JEAN-BERNARD CARILLET

Positioned along the covered walkway
ading to the outside courtyard are four
troglyphs. In the courtyard itself stands a
eautiful replica of a *grande case* from the
outh Province.

Unfortunately, all exhibit explanations
e only in French. Entry to the museum is
00 CFP for adults and 50 CFP for students
d children. It's open from 9 to 11.30 am
nd 12.15 to 4.30 pm (closed Tuesday).

hurches One of Noumea's landmarks is
: **Joseph's Cathedral**, which stands on a
ll at the end of Rue de Verdun. It over-
oks the city and is easily spotted from the
a at Baie de la Moselle. The cathedral was
uilt in 1888 by convict labour.

North of the cathedral, on Blvd Vauban,
a humble Protestant church, known as **Le
emple**, which was built in 1890.

arc Forestier The Parc Forestier (☎ 27
9 51) is on Route Stratégique, just below
e summit of Mont Montravel. It was
tablished in 1972 and is a botanic garden
nd fauna park. This peaceful place is the
nly place in New Caledonia where you
re guaranteed to see New Caledonia's en-
angered national emblem, the cagou (see
e boxed text 'The Cagou' later in this
hapter).

The reserve boasts many other species of
irds endemic to either New Caledonia or
ther Pacific nations. Also present are *rous-
ettes* (flying foxes or fruit bats), butterflies
nd coral and shell displays.

It's about 4km north-east of the city cen-
e; the *Petit Train* and organised tour buses
top at the gate but no public buses pass this
vay. The closest that a public bus (No 12)
vill drop you off is at the orange-and-white
ousing complex at Montravel. From here
's a 1.25km uphill walk along a road that
ets little traffic.

The park is open Tuesday to Sunday from
0.15 am to 5.45 pm (between May and
ugust until 5 pm). Admission is 300/100
FP for adults/children.

Doniambo Nickel Smelter You cannot
niss the huge metallurgical factory owned

by SLN, sitting just north of the city centre.
This multi-chimney eyesore has operated
since 1910 and employs 1700 workers.
Nickel and cobalt extracted from mines
around Grande Terre are processed here.

Noumea Aquarium The aquarium (☎ 26
27 31) on Route de l'Aquarium at Anse Vata
was created in 1956. It's one of the most natural aquariums in the Pacific. The display
tanks contain rare and unusual species of
marine life, including sea snakes, sharks and
eels, all in a coral environment.

The aquarium has plans to expand in the
next few years. For now, it is open daily
from 10 am to 4.45 pm (closed on Monday). Admission is 650/210 CFP for adults/
students and 115 CFP for children. There
are English, Japanese and French explanations. Bus No 6 stops out the front.

Le Petit Train *Le Petit Train* is a miniature
train that slowly chugs from Anse Vata to
the city centre, up to the Botanic Garden,
and then back along Baie de Ste Marie. It
completes this circuit four or five times a
day, en route picking up and dropping passengers off at selected points around town,
including the Palm Beach complex at Anse
Vata and the tourist office in the city centre.
A ticket that's valid for the whole day costs
800/500 CFP for adults/children and can be
bought from Amac Tours, Palm Beach complex, Anse Vata. For more information call
☎ 28 98 78.

Nouville The hilly peninsula of Nouville
rises to the west of central Noumea. A few
convict buildings still stand, including the
old hospital, which is located halfway along
the peninsula's southern flank.

About 1.5km further is Noumea's smallest, most picturesque beach, **Baie de
Kuendu**. It is sheltered by Mont Tereka
(127m). At the top are sunken stone walls,
which are all that remain of a fort built in
1878, and four cannons mounted in the late
1890s to defend the colony.

Mont Tereka is reached by winding up
the 1.5km-long dirt road that starts on the
right just before the Kuendu Beach Resort.

NOUMEA

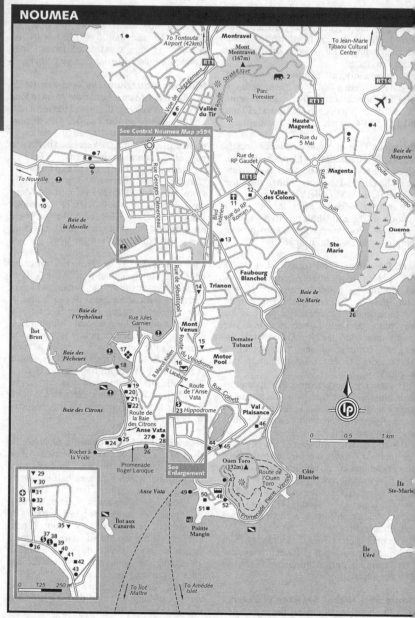

NOUMEA

PLACES TO STAY				
12	Paradise Park Motel	34	L'Amédée	17 Les Marinas Shopping Complex; CTC
19	Marina Beach Hotel	35	Tex Mex Restaurant; Liberty Station	18 Cercle Nautique Calédonien (CNC)
20	Hôtel Ibis; Teppanyaki Restaurant; Hôtel de la Baie	40	Jullius	22 Monte Cristo
24	Le Surf Novotel; Casino Royal	41	San Remo Pizzeria; Bambino	23 Westpac Bank
31	Hôtel Le Lagon; Pick Me Up Nightclub	45	Le Miretti	25 Noumea Aquarium
39	Lantana Beach Hôtel	**OTHER**		26 Public Toilets
42	Nouvata Parkroyal	1	Société Le Nickel (Deniambo)	27 Secretariat of the Pacific (SPC)
44	Motel Anse Vata	2	Parc Forestier	28 ORSTOM
46	Motel Le Bambou	3	Magenta Airport	32 Globe Trotteurs
50	Club Med Château Royal	4	University of South Pacific	33 Polyclinique de l'Anse Vata
51	Le Méridien	5	Magenta Stadium	36 Plages Loisirs Kiosk
		6	Cricket Ground	37 BNP Bank
PLACES TO EAT		7	Customs Office	38 Destination Îles Loyauté
14	La Bastide Restaurant	8	Maison des Métiers	43 Palm Beach Complex
16	Calypso Restaurant	9	Old Gare Maritime	47 Boulodrome
21	Jade Palace; La Saladière	10	Nouville Plaisance	48 Swimming Pool
29	Snack Ulysse	11	Église St Jean Baptiste	49 Club Med Jetty
30	La Dolce Vita	13	Maison Célières	52 Grand Casino
		16	Anse Vata Post Office	

Island Escapes

Amédée Islet This small coral islet, about 20km south of Noumea, is a marine reserve, noted for its clear water, its popularity as a day trip destination and the 56m-high lighthouse that rises from its centre.

The only commercial operator is Mary D (☎ 26 31 31) and it has an office in the Palm Beach complex at Anse Vata. It's open weekdays from 7.30 am to noon and 1 to 6 pm, and on Saturday morning. Tickets can be bought here or from one of the many tour operators around town. Its plush vessel reaches the island in 30 minutes, leaving at 8.15 am from Port Moselle or 8.45 am from the Club Med jetty at Anse Vata, and returning by about 4.30 pm. Tickets cost 5750/5000 CFP for adults/children. Lunch is included. Snorkelling equipment can be rented for 1500 CFP.

Other Islands & Islets The Plages Loisirs kiosk at Anse Vata has a watertaxi for ferrying people to any of the offshore islets in the morning and picking them up again in the afternoon. A return trip to Îlot aux Canards, just off Anse Vata beach, costs 1500 CFP (minimum three people); to Îlot Maître, further south, is 6000 CFP; and to

Îlot Larégnère, way out to the west, is 12,000 CFP.

Walks & Views

A good vantage point is **Ouen Toro** (132m) at Anse Vata. It's reached by a road that winds 1.5km to the summit, where two cannons stand guard. These are leftovers from an Australian artillery unit stationed on Ouen Toro for seven months during WWII.

The most comprehensive view you can get of Noumea is from **Mont Montravel** (167m). You can't climb to the top, but the view from the road that runs along the crest, known as Route Stratégique, is good enough.

Beaches

Anse Vata and **Baie des Citrons** are the two most popular tourist beaches. Nicer is Baie de Kuendu (see the previous Nouville entry), which is the favoured weekend haunt for many locals.

Diving

Noumea has some excellent offshore dive spots, including the famous Passe de Boulari, Passe de Dumbéa and the wreck of *La Dieppoise*. There are several internationally recognised diving clubs based in the city, including Alize (☎ 26 25 85, fax 27 86 33), based at the Nouvata Parkroyal Hotel, and Amédée Diving Club (☎ 26 40 29, fax 28 57 55) at 28 Rue du Général Mangin.

Other Water Activities

The Plages Loisirs kiosk, open daily from 8 am to 6 pm, on the beachfront at Anse Vata, hires equipment by the hour, half-day or day. Catamarans cost 3000 CFP per hour, sailboards cost 1200 CFP, two-person canoes cost 1500 CFP and single kayaks cost 1000 CFP. Windsurfing is popular at Anse Vata, Côte Blanche in Baie de Ste Marie, and in Baie de Magenta.

Language Courses

The CREIPAC school (☎ 25 41 24, fax 25 40 58) at Nouville teaches French to tourists and visiting students.

Organised Tours

Several English-speaking operators run minibus tours of Noumea, usually lasting three hours, with pick-ups from your hotel.

A few companies include:

Agence ORIMA
  (☎ 28 28 42) 1st floor, 27bis Ave Maréchal Foch
Amac Tours
  (☎ 26 38 38) Palm Beach complex, Anse Vata
Globe Trotteurs
  (☎ 28 32 22) 153 Route de l'Anse Vata, Anse Vata

Places to Stay – Budget

The cheapest place to stay in Noumea is the *Auberge de Jeunesse* or HI Hostel (☎ 27 58 79, fax 25 48 17, Route Château d'Eau). It has a fantastic location, perched behind St Joseph's Cathedral, and with a wide view of Baie de la Moselle. The large, four storey building is very clean and has both double rooms and dormitory-style rooms for four people. There's a big kitchen with excellent cooking facilities. Luggage can be stored in the office for a few days, and mail and faxes can be sent here. Breakfast is not provided.

The hostel charges a rate of 1200/1400 CFP per member/nonmember in a four bunk room or 2900/3100 CFP for a double

room with two single beds. Membership cards are available for 1400 CFP. Most of the rooms have large, lockable metal wardrobes. Office hours are Monday to Saturday from 7.30 to 10 am and 5 to 7.30 pm, and Sunday from 6 to 7.30 pm. Outside these times you can drop off luggage but you can't check into a room. Those arriving late at night should reserve a bed. Credit card is accepted.

The *Hôtel Caledonia* (☎ 27 38 21, fax 27 81 45) is a cheapie located on the corner of Rue de Sébastopol and Rue Auguste Brun in the Quartier Latin. It is on a busy intersection and street-front rooms get direct traffic noise. A bland double without/with shower costs 4500/5000 CFP. A continental breakfast is served for 400 CFP.

The nicest and most central hotel in this bracket is *Hôtel Lapérouse* (☎ 27 22 51, fax 25 90 37, 33 Rue de Sébastopol). It has 21 simple rooms, all adequate and clean but with nothing to rave about. Prices start at 4200/4600 CFP for a single/double with communal shower/toilet and no TV. Rooms on all the lower floors have TVs. Rooms with shower, toilet and air-con cost 6200 CFP. Breakfast is 600 CFP. Credit card is accepted.

In Baie des Citrons, try *Hôtel de la Baie* (☎ 26 21 33, 5 Route de la Baie des Citrons), next to Hôtel Ibis. This is a scruffy place catering mainly for long-term rentals, but overnighters are welcome if there's a vacancy. Rates are cheap enough at 3000/4000 CFP for a double room without/with kitchenette. The reception is at the counter of the downstairs Chez Alban restaurant.

The *Motel Le Bambou* (☎ 26 12 90, fax 26 30 58, 44 Rue Spahr) in Val Plaisance is the best option for budget accommodation after the HI Hostel. Set in a residential area, the motel is quiet and clean. There are 16 compact and homey studios. Each has a small balcony, fan and excellent cooking facilities. A studio for one or two people costs 5500 CFP. The motel is 1km from Anse Vata beach. Bus Nos 3 and 6 stop a block north of the motel on Rue Gabriel Laroque.

Another good budget option is the friendly *Motel Anse Vata* (☎ 26 26 12, fax

5 90 60, cirypierre@offratel.nc, 19 Rue
abriel Laroque). Rooms in this motel are
ean and have mosquito screens. Singles or
oubles are 6000 CFP. All have air-con (500
FP extra per day), TV and a kitchenette.
us Nos 3 and 6 stop out the front.

Places to Stay – Mid-Range

the city centre, the large and uninspiring
*Hôtel Le Paris (☎ 28 17 00, fax 27 60 80,
7 Rue de Sébastopol)* has 48 rooms with
ll the creature comforts but little atmos-
here. Singles or doubles are 6500 CFP.
irectly below the hotel, Café de Paris re-
ains open until midnight and the noise can
arry up to the rooms.

In Baie des Citrons, the *Marina Beach
Hotel (☎ 28 76 33, fax 26 28 81, 4 Rue A
age) has attractive studios with TV, air-
on and sparsely equipped kitchenettes. It
osts 8000 CFP for two people and breakast costs an extra 800 CFP. There's a small
wimming pool out the back.

A hotel that's popular with Japanese on
ackage deals is the beachfront *Hôtel Ibis
☎ 26 20 55, fax 26 20 44, 7 Promenade
oger Laroque)*. The rooms have modern
urnishings, though the hotel itself looks a
ttle tired. Facilities include a cafe, Japanse restaurant and small swimming pool.
tandard rooms for one or two people are
800 CFP, and a triple is 9800 CFP. Rooms
t the front with a view cost an extra 1000
FP. Breakfast costs 800 CFP.

In Anse Vata, the *Lantana Beach Hôtel
☎ 26 22 12, fax 26 16 12, 133 Promenade
oger Laroque)* is in the heart of Anse Vata,
cross the street from the beach. The hotel
as all the necessary amenities but it is
lightly drab. There are 35 rooms, some
ith a balcony and view. The price for a
ingle/double/triple is 7200/8200/9200
FP. Continental breakfast is available for
50 CFP.

Places to Stay – Top End

he beach-side Anse Vata has the pick of
Joumea's top end hotels. The *Hôtel Le
agon (☎ 26 12 55, fax 26 12 44, 143 Route
e l'Anse Vata)* is a serenely-decorated five
torey hotel. There are 59 rooms, all with

kitchenette. The 'studio' rooms for two
people cost 10,000 CFP and breakfast costs
an extra 900 CFP. The hotel has a bar. It's
about a two minute walk to the beach; bus
No 3 stops out the front.

*Le Surf Novotel (☎ 28 66 88, fax 28 52
23, 55 Promenade Roger Laroque)*, Anse
Vata, has rooms for one or two people with-
out/with a view for 10,000/12,000 CFP,
while suites cost 20,000 to 24,000 CFP. The
American buffet breakfast costs 1200 CFP.
There is also a French restaurant and the
Casino Royal.

*Nouvata Parkroyal (☎ 26 22 00, fax 26
16 77, 123 Promenade Roger Laroque)*,
Anse Vata, has been renovated and has luxury double rooms spread in two buildings.
Prices cost from 19,000 to 62,000 CFP. The
hotel has all the facilities you'd expect
including a swimming pool.

Le Méridien (☎ 26 50 00, fax 26 51 00)
is draped around Pointe Mangin at the far
end of Anse Vata beach. This five star hotel
is New Caledonia's top resort. Opened in
1995, it boasts 253 luxury double rooms that
cost 26,000 CFP. It also has a range of more
expensive suites. The resort has everything
that's needed for a splurge of this kind.

There are also several options around
Noumea's outskirts, including the *Escapade
Island Resort (☎/fax 28 53 20)*, which is
about 3km offshore from Anse Vata. This resort is built on small Îlot Maître, a beautiful
islet bordered by sandy beaches. Some 46
bungalows are dotted around the resort. The
bungalows have either garden or beach views
and cost 20,000/24,000 CFP respectively.
The resort offers a wide range of water activities, and transport to and from the island is
provided from Port Moselle or Anse Vata.

*Kuendu Beach Resort (☎ 24 30 00, fax
27 60 33)* in Nouville is 6.5km west of central Noumea and has bungalows divided into
three categories – new pillared huts, older
garden huts and beachfront huts. All have a
kitchen, TV and air-con. The bungalows
situated in the garden costs 12,000 CFP for
one or two people. The equivalent by the
beach costs 14,000 CFP. A thatched bungalow built on pillars over the water costs
32,000 CFP for two. Resort facilities include

CENTRAL NOUMEA

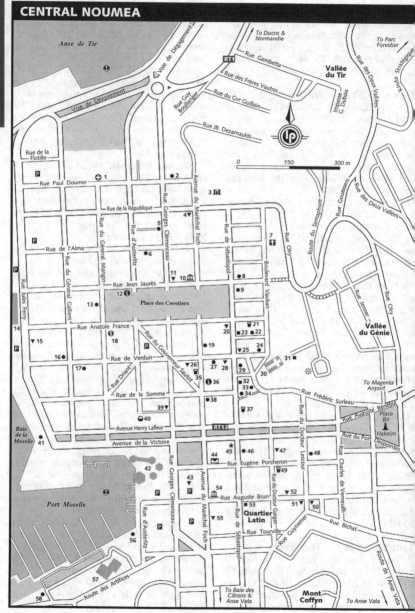

CENTRAL NOUMEA

PLACES TO STAY
23 Hôtel Lapérouse
31 Auberge de Jeunesse (HI Hostel)
32 Hôtel Le Paris; Café de Paris
53 Hôtel Caledonia

PLACES TO EAT
4 Self Foch
11 Café La Luna
15 Casino/Johnston Supermarket
20 Le Saint-Hubert
25 Café Le Flore
26 Hameau II
29 Kim Leng
39 SAVAH Supermarket
42 Market
43 Food Vans
47 Quán Nhó
50 El Cordobes
51 Le Maité
52 Restaurante El Salvatore
55 McDonald's

OTHER
1 Hôpital Gaston Bourret
2 Bureau des Étrangers
3 High Commission of the Republic
5 Agence Jean Brock
6 Librairie Pentecost
7 Le Temple
8 Lav' Services (laundry)
9 Librairie Montaigne
10 Musée de la Ville de Nouméa
12 Office du Tourisme de Nouméa et de la Province Sud
13 Hôtel de Ville (Town Hall)
14 New Gare Maritime
16 Compagnie Générale Maritime
17 Axxess Travel
18 BCI Bank
19 American Express; Agence Orima; Centre Voyages
21 Deep 501
22 AOM
24 Immeuble Manhattan; Air Calédonie International; Nouvelles Frontières

27 Qantas Airways
29 Air France
30 St Joseph's Cathedral
33 Aircalin)
34 City (cinema)
35 Route 66
36 Le Bilboquet; Office du Tourisme de la Province Nord
37 Hotel San Francisco
38 Bibliothèque Bernheim
40 Gare Routière
41 STIL (passenger ferry to the islands)
44 Main Post Office
45 Commissariat Central (Main Police Station)
46 Plaza (cinema)
48 Edge Technologie
49 Relais de la Poste
54 Musée Néo-Calédonien
56 Capitainerie
57 South Province Headquarters
58 Nouvelle Calédonie Yachting & Pacific Charter

swimming pool, two restaurants and water-sports equipment for hire. The resort provides free transport for its guests to and from central Noumea, several times a day.

Places to Eat

A multitude of restaurants compete for the appetites of tourists and locals alike, offering French, Vietnamese, Indian, Chinese and Japanese cuisines, among others. French and seafood restaurants are the most expensive. Unless otherwise stated, all the cafes and restaurants mentioned here are closed on Sunday and on public holidays.

City Centre You'll find numerous small and inexpensive *snack/cafes* in the 'little Chinatown' area near the bus station.

A consistently popular choice with workers is *Hameau II* (☎ 28 48 32, 32 Rue de Verdun). The quality is pretty good for the price – a plat du jour will cost 750 CFP and a sandwich about 300 CFP. It is open weekdays from 6 am to 6 pm. On Saturday it closes at about noon.

The *cafe* inside the market is open daily from 5 am and serves croissants, coffee and freshly squeezed orange juice.

Café Le Flore (☎ 28 12 47, 39 Rue de Sébastopol) has a 850 CFP plat du jour that's only available at lunch time. Breakfast costs 500 CFP.

Self Foch (☎ 28 37 77, 8 Avenue du Maréchal Foch) is a cafeteria-style place with a plat du jour for 900 CFP, pre-made salads for 450 CFP and sandwiches from 280 CFP. It's open daily except Sunday from 6 am to 5.30 pm.

Le Saint Hubert (☎ 27 21 42, 44 Rue Anatole France) is where the locals have for decades passed the time reading the newspaper or chatting over coffee. A plat du jour is 950 CFP, a sandwich is 380 to 530 CFP and a beer is 300 CFP. Or you can order pizzas, starting at 700 CFP. The cafe opens at 6.30 am for breakfast and remains open until midnight.

The other Noumean institution is *Café de Paris* (☎ 28 20 00, 45 Rue de Sébastopol), a favourite spot for off-duty soldiers. It serves snacks and has a range of meals for lunch and dinner starting at 700 CFP. This is one of the few places open on Sunday.

Cafe La Luna (☎ 27 22 23, 37 Rue Jean Jaurès) is a trendy bar-restaurant that serves inexpensive dishes. Pastries cost from 120 to 140 CFP and a coffee is 140 CFP. A plat du jour will set you back about 950 CFP. Live bands play occasionally.

Le Bilboquet (☎ 28 43 30, Ave Foch), Le Village shopping centre, serves pasta, salads and meat dishes. You'll pay 900 CFP for a plat du jour. Daily, except Sunday, it remains open until 11.30 pm.

Kim Leng (Rue de Verdun) has good Chinese and Vietnamese fares, including soups starting at 400 CFP and a plat du jour at 700 CFP for lunch. It is also open on Sunday evening.

Quartier Latin One of the best value eateries in this area is *Le Maité (☎ 27 45 74, 12 Rue du Docteur Lescour)*. This cosy little restaurant has an enclosed courtyard where you can eat a good menu du jour (lunch only) for 1350 CFP. A la carte meals include a North African couscous for 1800 CFP or a Spanish paella for 1750 CFP.

Nearby, *Restaurante El Salvatore (☎ 27 11 3615, Rue Auguste Brun)* has a plat du jour for 1000 CFP that includes dessert. Pizzas cost from 1200 CFP and pasta from 1300 CFP.

Quán Nhó (☎ 28 56 72, 5 Rue du Docteur Guegan) is a tiny, unpretentious little diner serving a range of Vietnamese dishes costing from 820 to 1080 CFP.

El Cordobes (☎ 27 47 68, 1 Rue Bichat) is one of the many restaurants competing for Noumea's highest honours. It is open for lunch and dinner, and serves gourmet French food with a la carte mains costing from 1950 to 2500 CFP. There is a good value menu du jour at 1800 CFP.

Mont Venus & Trianon Tucked away south of Trianon near Motor Pool is *Calypso (☎ 26 37 16, 3 Rue Michel Ange)*. There is not a wide range of dishes on the menu but the seafood is excellent. Mains cost from 750 to 5400 CFP.

Baie des Citrons The *Jade Palace (☎ 2 42 15)* is halfway along the bay and serve Chinese soup for 550 CFP, steamed por with taro for 1400 CFP and mains from 1000 CFP. Open daily for lunch and dinne (including Sunday) but for dinner only o Monday and Tuesday.

Nearby is *La Saladière (☎ 26 35 95, 2 Route de la Baie des Citrons)*. Salads cos from 1200 to 1800 CFP. The house specia ities are also crêpes, *gaufres* (waffles) an liqueur sorbets, but all are quite pricey.

For authentic Japanese cuisine tr *Teppanyaki (☎ 26 20 55)* in the Hôtel Ibi It has a lunch menu from 1500 CFP, a pla du jour for 900 CFP and a range of set din ners from 2200 CFP.

Anse Vata The only relatively inexper sive restaurant here is *La Dolce Vita (☎ 2 24 41, 3 Rue Tabou)*. The food is good an the clientele is a mixed bag of tourists an locals. Pasta dishes start at 850 CFP an (ultra thin) pizzas from 850 CFP.

L'Amédée (☎ 26 10 35, 153 Route d l'Anse Vata) represents solid value. Seafoo is the speciality and the 1500 CFP menu d jour is superb.

San Rémo Pizzeria (☎ 26 18 02, 11 Promenade Roger Laroque) is open dail and is highly recommended. Small pizza start at 900 CFP and large ones (ample for a average appetite) from 1300 CFP. You ca also order spaghetti, meat dishes and salad

The *Tex Mex Restaurant (☎ 24 96 17, Ru Louis Blériot)* is popular and bookings ar often required. It serves main courses fc about 1000 to 1500 CFP and is one of the fe places in Noumea that also caters for vegetar ians. It's open daily from 11 am to midnigh

The intimate little *Le Miretti (☎ 26 1 82, 24 Rue Gabriel Laroque)* specialises i cuisine from France's Périgord regior Main courses start at 1800 CFP. It is ope on Sunday.

Fast Food A number of beachfront *snac* bars have spawned along Baie des Citron in recent years. All serve similar fare you'll be looking at about 300 to 400 CF for a half-baguette sandwich.

In Anse Vata, close to Hôtel le Lagon, the est bet is *Snack Ulysse*, which is open even days. It serves burgers from 380 CFP, ishes from 650 CFP and sandwiches for 80 CFP. At *Jullius* and *Bambino*, on romenade Roger Laroque, you can get amburgers for 500 CFP, a *croque monsieur* oasted cheese and ham sandwich) for 250 FP, a large plate of chips for 400 CFP and aufres for 250 CFP.

A popular takeaway source is the contin-ent of minivans that gathers in the large arpark on Rue Georges Clémenceau, next the market. Simply called *the vans*, these ehicles line up every evening, including unday, from about 6 pm, and serve an rray of cold salads, drinks, cakes, nems nd piping hot meals such as chicken or eef curry with rice and bread for 560 CFP. hey operate until about 11 pm.

elf-Catering Noumea's *market* is oppo-te the bus station and next to Port Moselle. is well worth a look and opens daily from round 5 to 11 am.

In addition, you'll find several well ocked supermarkets, including the *AVAH*, opposite the bus station, and the *asino/Johnston*, on the corner of Rue natole France and Rue Jules Ferry, near e new gare maritime.

ntertainment
ick up the free, monthly *NoumeaScope* om hotels or the tourist office for a run-own on entertainment listings.

The *Plaza (65 Rue de Sébastopol)* and *ity* cinemas are on the same street and reen current releases. Admission is 750 FP.

If you're looking for a disco, head for aie des Citron's *Monte Cristo*. There is no ver charge but you'll have to order a rink. The cheapest one is 500 CFP. In the ity centre, the *Deep 501 (46 Rue Anatole rance)* has occasional bands on Friday and aturday night. There's a 1000 CFP cover arge on weekends, which includes a drink.

Noumea's longest standing watering hole *Le Saint Hubert (44 Rue Anatole rance)*. There is a band on Saturday nights. Just down the road, *Café de Paris* is the hang-out for lonely, bored soldiers.

A nice hang-out is the bar at *Hôtel San Francisco (55 Rue de Sébastopol)*. This place is decorated with American parapher-nalia and cowboy music drifts from the darkened bar. It is open every night until 1 am and later on Friday night when a band usually plays. On this night, a drink costs 500 CFP.

An interesting pub in the Quartier Latin is the *Relais de la Poste*, on the corner of Rue du Docteur Guegan and Rue Eugène Porcheron, where many of the more bohem-ian French hang out.

In central Noumea, *Route 66* on Ave du Maréchal Foch has mural paintings and is difficult to miss. A draught beer costs 300 CFP. Consider also the very hip *Cafe La Luna* on Rue Jean Jaurès.

Another nightspot in town is *Liberty Sta-tion*, next to the Tex Mex restaurant on Rue Louis Blériot, Anse Vata. This big American-style bar is open nightly until 2 am.

If you're interested in gambling, head for Casino Royal, in the Surf Novotel, or the Grand Casino, on Le Méridien's grounds at Anse Vata.

Shopping
Duty-free shops specialising in French goods – clothing, lingerie and shoes – are dotted along Rue de Sébastopol and Rue de l'Alma.

Curio and Pacific artefact shops are also abundant, particularly along Rue Anatole France and Ave du Maréchal Foch. You can try L'Atelier des Femmes de Nouvelle-Calédonie (☎ 88 87 81) on Place des Co-cotiers at the corner of Rue Sautrot and Rue Anatole France. Also try the Association des Sculpteurs de Nouvelle-Calédonie.

Getting There & Away
Air All international flights arrive at Tontouta airport, where passengers must pass through customs and immigration. For more information see the Getting There & Away section in this chapter. For infor-mation on air travel within New Caledonia see the Getting Around section.

Major airlines in Noumea include:

Air Calédonie International (Aircalin)
(☎ 26 55 11) 8 Rue Frédéric Surleau
Air France
(☎ 25 88 00) 41-3 Rue de Sébastopol
AOM French Airlines
(☎ 24 12 12) 1 Rue d'Ypres
Qantas Airways
(☎ 28 65 46) Rue de Verdun

Bus The main bus station is at the end of Rue d'Austerlitz. Buses bound for destinations around Grande Terre leave from the left of the main building, as you're facing the market. There is a small kiosk where you can get bus schedules and buy tickets.

Car & Motorcycle Cars, camper vans and motorcycles can be hired from the various rental companies in Noumea. The Office du Tourisme de Noumea et de la Province Sud (☎ 28 75 80, fax 28 75 85) has a list of car rental companies.

Boat Most cruising yachts anchor at Port Moselle. A passenger ferry connects Noumea with Île des Pins and the Loyalty Islands – for more information see the Getting Around section earlier in this chapter.

Getting Around
Tontouta Airport Tontouta international airport is 45km, or 40 minutes by car, north of Noumea. It is serviced by buses and minivan operators. When leaving Noumea, you can arrange to be picked up at your hotel, motel or the HI Hostel.

Agence ORIMA (☎ 28 28 42), 27bis Avenue du Maréchal Foch, operates minivans. The owner will send someone to pick you up at your hotel or the HI Hostel on request. It's 2500 CFP one way to the airport. SCEA (☎ 43 31 41) is a large bus company that drops off and picks up passengers from all major hotels and the HI Hostel about two hours before departure time. The normal one-way fare is 2000 CFP.

The public buses, called blue bus, are the cheapest way of getting to and from the

airport. At Tontouta, they wait outside the arrival hall, to the left as you exit the building. In Noumea, they depart from the main bus station. The long journey takes about an hour and 10 minutes either way. A one-way fare is 400 CFP (420 CFP on weekends). From Noumea, they run hourly on weekdays between 5.30 am and 5.30 pm, leaving on the half-hour. On Saturday the buses are hourly from 5.30 to 11.30 am, and there are additional buses at 1, 3 and 5 pm. On Sunday there is a bus every two hours (on the hour) between 7 am and 5 pm. From Tontouta buses run hourly from 6 am to pm on Sunday, leaving on the hour.

Taxis charge for a return trip even if you are going only one way because they are not guaranteed passengers once they reach the airport. The fare is 8000 CFP for up to four persons.

Magenta Airport The domestic airport at Magenta is 4km east of the city centre and is easily reached by public transport. Bus No 7 leaves every 15 minutes from the main bus station in Noumea and will drop you at the doorstep. The fare is 120/140 CFP on weekdays/weekends. The ride to the airport takes 20 minutes; the return trip is about 10 minutes longer with a short side-trip.

Taxis from Place des Cocotiers charge about 800 CFP.

Bus All buses leave from the gare routière, the main bus station, at the southern end of Rue d'Austerlitz. You pay the driver as you get on. En route, buses stop at the blue-and-white signs – if you want to get on at one of these stops you must flag it down.

On weekdays, buses run from 5 or 5.30 am to 6.15 or 6.30 pm. On weekends and public holidays they start later, finish slightly earlier and are less frequent. Fares are 120/80 CFP for adults/children except on Saturday afternoon, Sunday and public holidays, when an extra 20 CFP is levied. For more information on bus routes, pick up the free *Interlignes* guide from the tourist office. For Anse Vata, take bus No 3 or 4; for Magenta airport take bus No 7; and Nouville is serviced by bus No 13.

axi The main taxi rank is at Place des Coco-
ers, though you can also hail a cab from vir-
ually anywhere around Noumea. Taxis
perate 24 hours a day, seven days a week.

icycle & Moped Around Noumea bicy-
les can be rented from Reviens, je t'aime
 Come back, I love you'; ☎ 27 88 65), Rue
les Ferry, inside the new gare maritime. It
ents both mountain bikes and mopeds. A
ountain bike costs from 1000 to 1500 CFP
er day. Mopeds are 1950 CFP per day.

Plages Loisirs kiosk, on Promenade
oger Laroque in Anse Vata, rents bikes at
00 CFP for an hour and 1000/1500 CFP
r half-day/full day.

Grande Terre

pop 145,000   • **area 18,580 sq km**
rande Terre is a cigar-shaped mountainous
land, 400km long and 50km wide, en-
ompassed by a barrier reef.

SOUTHERN GRANDE TERRE

outhern Grande Terre is made up of three
istinct regions: the rugged and diverse
outhern tip; the west-coast plain dotted
ith Caldoche towns and cut by the only
ad heading north; and the east-coast min-
g towns inhabited by Kanak people.

The Southern Tip

eading east from Noumea along the RT2,
ou'll come across the villages of La Con-
eption and St Louis. Soon after is the turn-
ff to Mont-Dore, Plum and Prony. The
eal' southern tip around Baie de Prony is
ccessible by conventional vehicles. **Prony**
 a former convict settlement and later a
ining village. It offers some interesting
lics of its bygone eras, as well as spec-
cular views of the surrounding reef and
aie de Prony with its sole islet, Îlot **Casy**,
ccessible by boat.

Following the RT2, you'll arrive at the
estern end of the vast and artificial **Lac de
até**, which offers wide panoramas and
me superb areas for nature lovers, inclung the massive **Parc Territorial de la Rivière**

Bleue (Blue River). This recreational park
is a fully protected nature reserve of about
90 sq km that is home to many bird species
including New Caledonia's national bird,
the cagou. It is open daily, except Monday,
from 7 am to 5 pm, with the last cars allowed in at 4 pm. There's a small entry fee.
The entrance is 2.5km from the RT2 turn-
off (it is signposted). Bring food supplies as
there are no shops. The park office has plot-
ted several hikes, detailed in its brochure.
With your own tent, it's possible to camp at
many points along the Rivière Bleue. There
are also two basic refuges in the park where
you can stay overnight, but bring your own
bedding.

The **Plain of the Lakes** encompasses the
heart of Grande Terre's southern tip and is
a fascinating area of shrubland, water holes
and marshes. The main dirt road into this
region leads off from the RT2 at Pernod
Creek in the north, 20km past the turn-off
to the Parc Territorial de la Rivière Bleue.
About 11km into the journey you'll pass
close by the area's most famous sight, the
Chutes de la Madeleine, a small waterfall
that cascades over a ridge of iron rock into
a popular weekend swimming hole. The
road up to the falls is accessible (in dry
weather) with conventional vehicles. It is
signposted.

A few kilometres after the road leading
off to Chutes de la Madeleine is the turn-off
to the **Yaté Dam**. Built in 1959, this 45m-
high *barrage* (dam), spanning about 200m,
is part of a hydroelectric scheme that supplies power to Noumea and some other
areas of Grande Terre. After passing the
dam turn-off and crossing the last *col*
(mountain pass), the sea suddenly comes
into view. The road descends sharply until,
just before the Yaté bridge, a turn-off to the
left leads to Yaté village and Unia, while the
road over the bridge heads to Wao and Goro
to the south. The **Wadiana Falls** are a kilometre past Goro. The road passes right next
to the falls, which cascade from a rocky
cliff and form a natural pool at the bottom
where you can swim. From Goro, you can
go as far as Port-Boisé by car, some 120km
from Noumea.

Île Ouen sits just off the tip of Grande Terre. It is a large, sparsely vegetated, mountainous island, covering 116 sq km. The **Aiguille de Prony** (Prony Needle), in Baie de Prony, is also off the southern tip of Grande Terre and offers superb diving.

Diving is offered at Hôtel Casy (☎ 28 39 81) on Îlot Casy and at gîte Kanua (☎ 46 90 00) at Port-Boisé. Both operators have the outstanding Aiguille de Prony on their list of dive sites.

Places to Stay & Eat The *Gîte IYA* (☎ 46 90 80, 46 42 23) is about 3km south of Wao. It has three airy, clean bungalows, each with a shower, that overlook the cove and a small beach squeezed between the low coral cliffs. The two smaller bungalows cost 5000 CFP per night. The bigger bungalow costs 6000 CFP. Camping in a pleasant coconut grove costs 1500 CFP per tent per night. Set menus cost between 1500 CFP and 3000 CFP.

Next up is *Gîte St Gabriel* (☎ 46 42 77), 3km past Touaourou. It has a superb beachfront location set amid coconut palms. There are five bungalows, each with toilet and shower. They cost 4500 CFP or 5500 CFP. Camping is 1500 CFP per tent. It has a restaurant that serves a standard plat du jour for 1200 CFP. A crab or lobster meal costs 2500/3500 CFP but you'll have to ask for it a day or so in advance.

At Port-Boisé, the *Gîte Kanua* (☎ 46 90 00, fax 46 41 72) is an excellent place. It has four comfortable bungalows near the beach that cost 6000 CFP per night for two people. The restaurant serves meals for 2000 CFP. It is also possible to camp for 1500 CFP per tent. Various tours can be organised and there are rental mountain bikes and canoes.

The tranquil little *Hôtel Casy* (☎ 28 39 81, ☎/fax 26 47 77 in Noumea) is a popular little island getaway for holidaying Noumeans. Situated on Îlot Casy in Baie de Prony, the hotel is surrounded by lush forest and towering araucarias, and has 15 comfortable rooms, a restaurant, swimming pool and a small pier. Single/double/triple rooms cost 6500/7500/8500 CFP. Transfers can be arranged from Prony (1000 CFP).

Day trips from Noumea are also on offer f 7500 CFP.

Another getaway place is *Le Cruso* (☎ 28 53 62, fax 24 18 00), on Île Ouen. A bungalow costs 5000/7500 CFP o weekdays/weekends. Set meals cost 290 CFP and breakfast is 800 CFP. Transfers ca be arranged from Noumea or Plum. Day trij and weekend packages are also available.

Getting There & Away The bus to Ya (550 CFP), Wao (550 CFP, 1¾ hours Touaourou (650 CFP), Gîte St Gabriel (7C CFP) and Goro (1000 CFP, 2½ hour leaves from the Noumea bus station, Moi day to Saturday at 11.30 am.

The Road North

Known as the Route Territoriale 1 (RT1), tł road north traverses the island's western coa all the way to Poum, a journey of 424km. E route it skirts the mountain range of tł interior. In places you'll see a nickel min while much of the interior is like that of th west coast with open expanses, cattle station and a distinctly Caldoche atmosphere.

Two northbound roads lead out ● Noumea. The more direct is the to (péage) road, starting at Koutio and ru ing for just 17km. The other road north the RT1, which winds past the **Mon Koghis**, 14km north of Noumea. The ar● is popular for hiking, with trails rangir from 30 minutes to six hours. **Dumbéa** a sleepy town and is 18km north Noumea. If you want to arrange canoe ● kayak trips in the area, contact Ter Incognita (☎/fax 41 61 19).

Païta, part of Greater Noumea, is a sma town 26km north-west of Noumea on tł RT1. **Tontouta**, or La Tontouta as it's fo mally known, is the site of New Caledonia international airport and little else. Along tł RT1 through Dumbéa and Païta it's 45km.

Bouloupari sits on the plain several kil● metres from Mont Ouitchambo, an almo perfectly shaped conical mountain risir 587m to a fine tip, just north of the tow The area is mainly rural and undevelope About 1km north of the town centre is tł junction for the RT4 to Thio.

About 110km from Noumea, **La Foa** is a historic settlement with some old homes that are still in good nick. The Kanak revolt of 1878 ignited when Kanaks attacked the gendarmerie in La Foa and killed those inside.

The tiny studio of Remy Weiss (☎ 44 31 26), a **woodcarver** who does sculptures inspired by traditional Melanesian art, is about 1.5km from the town centre, on the road towards Bourail.

Petit Couli is a small tribal village famed for the beautiful, 80-year-old *grande case*, standing at the end of a double row of araucarias, on the main road just past the Sarraméa turn-off.

Situated in a side valley off the RT5bis, **Sarraméa** is like a cool oasis after the open plains and dry country preceding it. The area is greened by forests and occasionally interrupted by meadows with tall blackwood trees.

Horse trekking is available at Pocquereux Randonnées (☎ 77 32 54 in La Foa or ☎ 43 81 50 in Noumea). It is a 1500 hectare cattle and sheep property situated 12km inland in the valley of the same name. The property has set up a rough camp from

SOUTHERN GRANDE TERRE

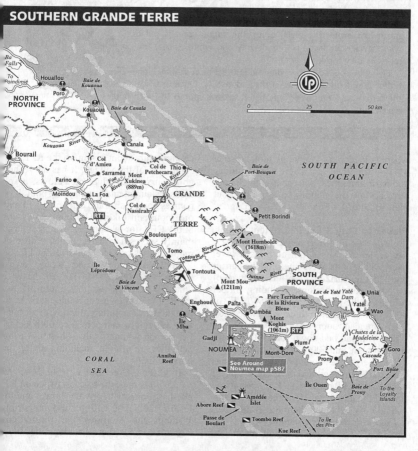

The Cagou

A stocky, flightless bird, the *cagou (Rhynocetos jubatus)* is New Caledonia's national bird. Sadly, it is now an endangered species, owing to dogs and feral cats hunting it, and wild pigs disturbing its habitat.

A successful breeding program has been carried out in the Rivière Bleue, east of Noumea, where numbers are slowly rising. However, you're unlikely to see one in the wild. The best place to see one is at the Parc Forestier in Noumea.

Standing 0.5m tall, this plump nocturnal bird has soft, silky-grey plumage, red eyes and an orange beak. It is most noted for its cry, which is reminiscent of a dog's bark and is only made in the early morning. When startled or protecting their young, the cagou spreads out its wings, which are laced with dark-grey-and-white stripes, and raises its silky top-knot crest.

Living in isolated pairs in damp rainforest or at slightly higher altitudes, they feed on worms, snails and insects. Once or twice a year, the female lays one egg. Typically, it takes a month to hatch, after which both parents raise the baby.

JACQUI SAUNDERS

where guided tours – either by foot, horse or 4WD – are organised. There is a dormitory and basic amenities. You can also pitch your tent. Follow the signposted turn-off about 3km south of La Foa.

Places to Stay & Eat In the Mont Koghis, the *Auberge du Mont Koghi* (☎ 41 29 29, *fax 41 96 22)* sits 476m above sea level overlooking parts of Noumea and the barrier reef on the horizon. It offers a range of accommodation options, including timber refuges in the forest, priced at 4500 CFP or 6000 CFP (maximum three to four people). There are also roomy chalets at the Auberge where you can bed down for 7500 CFP for the first night and 6000 CFP for extra nights. The Auberge's restaurant serves specialities from the Savoy region in the French Alps for about 2600 CFP per person. It is open at any time of the day for a refreshment or snacks.

The only accommodation in Boulouparis is *Les Paillottes de la Ouenghi* (☎ 35 17 35, *fax 35 17 44)*, which is a golf resort and country club, about 2.5km off the RT1, 5km south-east of the village. It has an 18 hole golf course, individual bungalows, a spacious restaurant and a swimming pool. It organises horse riding and canoeing, and rents out mountain bikes. The bungalows cost 8000 CFP for a couple. The restaurant mainly serves a la carte meals, with most main courses priced around 1500 CFP.

Between Boulouparis and La Foa, you can stop at *Convivia* (☎ 46 90 90), based at Ouano Beach. The signposted turn-off from the RT1 is 22km west of Boulouparis. A nice and modern camping ground with all facilities welcomes campers for 500/800 CFP per person without/with a shelter. Various activities are offered, including diving and horse riding.

In La Foa, *Hôtel Banu* (☎ 44 31 19, fax 44 35 50) is opposite the post office on RT1 and has rooms with private shower and toilet for 4200/5000 CFP for a double/triple. Without the facilities the rooms cost 3200/4800 CFP (there's an amenities block

:arby). Behind this building are five com-
rtable bungalows, all with TV, air-con and
rivate facilities. These are priced at
)00/6800 CFP for a double/triple. There is
so *Naïna Park Hotel* (☎ *44 35 40, fax 44*
9 35), which is 1.5km south of La Foa. It
:nts fine bungalows with private bath for
)00 CFP (up two people) and 4 rooms
haring an amenities block for 3500 CFP.

You can eat at Banu or Naïna Park, or
ead for *Flo Pizzeria*, on the main road,
hich has a good range of pizzas starting
om 550/850 CFP. Next to the Flo Pizzeria
the *Restaurant L'Hermitage*, which fea-
ures a cool terrace where lunch and dinner
served daily – the menu du jour costs
600 CFP. There is a supermarket in town.

In Sarraméa, the *Évasion 130* (☎/fax 44
2 35) is 4km from the Petit Couli turn-off.
iurrounded by dense forest, the hotel has
quare bungalows, all with shower and toi-
.t, but no cooking facilities. They are OK
you can forego creature comforts. Rooms
ost 4000/5000 CFP for one/two people.
he hotel's restaurant offers menus du jour,
arying in price from 2500 to 3000 CFP.

etting There & Away The Monts
oghis area is not easily reached without
rivate transport. The turn-off to the
iuberge is 14km north of central Noumea
n the RT1 to Dumbéa. From here, it's an-
:her 5km through rainforest and then up
:eep bare slopes to the auberge.

Dumbéa is easily reached by Noumea-
aïta buses (220 CFP one way). Any bus
eading from Noumea along the west coast
r going up to the east coast will drop you
ı Bouloupari. The fare is 700 CFP and it
ikes an hour. Daily buses connect Noumea
ı La Foa (800 CFP).

he Mining Towns
idden by the central mountain chain,
»uthern Grande Terre's east-coast mining
•gion, which includes the towns of
»uaoua, Poro, Canala and Thio, tends to
ave travellers in a mixed state of awe and
nease. Most peoples' lives are dedicated to
ork in the opencast nickel mines that scar
ıe mountains.

Other than the landscape, which can be
stunning, with waterfalls and deep bays, the
main attraction in the area is the **Musée des
Mines** (Mine Museum). Located in Thio,
which was a nickel-mining centre for several decades, the museum displays local
photographs from the early 1900s as well as
a collection of minerals. It is open weekdays from 7.30 to 11.30 am and 1 to 4 pm,
and weekends from 9 am to noon. Entry
costs 100/50 CFP for adults/children.

West of Thio, Canala sits at the end of a
long, wide waterway, the Baie de Canala.
The town and surrounding area is backed by
steep, scrubby mountains from which the
mighty **Ciu waterfalls** cascade. Situated in
an inland valley, they offer wide views over
the valley and the start of the deep bay. The
falls can be reached along a small dirt road
to the right, about 1.5km from Canala, on
the road towards Thio. The turn-off is unmarked. From here it's about 4km to the top
of the falls. A sign reading 'cascades' marks
the path from the road to the falls.

Places to Stay & Eat The most pleasant
place to stay around Thio is *Gîte Ouroue*
(☎ *44 50 85)*, which is on the beachfront
4.5km from town, off the road to Canala.
You can camp here for 1000 CFP per tent or
stay in one of four sparsely furnished
bungalows, which have views of coconut
palms and the water. The bungalows cost
3000 CFP for up to three people. A fish dinner costs 1500 CFP. The gîte is signposted.
From the turn-off, it's 1.5km to the beach.

In Thio, *La Fiesta* (☎ *44 51 81)* is near
the museum and is a tiny but cosy room
where lunches are dished up for 800 CFP,
and meat or chicken meals for 950 CFP. It
may or may not be open for dinner.

Getting There & Away Buses from
Noumea travel the RT4 to Thio, leaving once
a day from Monday to Sunday (900 CFP, 2
hours). To Noumea, there is also one bus a
day Monday to Sunday. There are no buses
from Thio to Canala. By car, Bouloupari is
47km away, roughly an hour's drive, along
the good but winding RT4 over the Col de
Nassirah (350m).

From Noumea, there is also at least a daily bus to Canala. By car, the Canala-Thio road (26km) includes a 13km single-lane dirt road, open to traffic from either direction at alternate hours, which snakes up and around a steep hill eventually to cross Col de Petchecara (435m).

THE NORTH-WEST COAST

Much of the north-west coast has been cattle country since the early colonial days, when settlers claimed the land and the Kanaks were moved onto reservations. Everything here – the landscape, climate, people and atmosphere – is different from that across the mountain range to the east. The scenery can be quite monotonous, the rounded brown hills stretch down to grassy plains. This scene gives way to coastal mangrove swamps and shallow bays, where the beaches are nothing to get excited about. In the far north, beyond Koumac, is niaouli savannah, while around Népoui the hills have been sliced open for nickel mining.

The RT1 is a good sealed road, skirting the mountains all the way from Noumea to Poum in the north. There are just three roads leading off from the north-west across the mountains to the east – one road from

Bourail, the second from Koné and the thi from Koumac.

Bourail
- pop 4350

Bourail is New Caledonia's second-large town and has a strong Caldoche comm nity. It sits on the plain 162km on the ca ital. It was founded in 1867 as a penitentia and had the typical array of convict faci ties. Bourail grew to a large settlement 400 families but in 1897, when the flow convicts stopped, the town stagnated a became just like any other rural village.

Before arriving in the town from th south you'll pass the **Cimetière d Arabes**, which is between the Népoue a Nassoudi creeks, about 12km south Bourail. The origins of those buried he date back to the 1871 Berber insurrectio in the former French colony of Algeria. number of rebels were deported to Ne Caledonia and at the end of their pris terms, some chose to stay, settling arou Nessadiou. About 2.5km further, als flanking the RT1 and about 9.5km south Bourail, the **New Zealand Pacific W Cemetery** is the resting place for 212 so diers killed in the Pacific during WW

Nickel

Nickel has been mined in New Caledonia since 1875. It is the third-largest nickel-producer in the world, after Canada and Russia. The last nickel booms were in 1963 and from 1969 to 1971, after which the industry went into crisis, largely due to Russian oversupply. New Caledonia has enough reserves for mining to continue well into the 21st century.

Mining for nickel is open cast, as it lies between the base rock and the scraped-off layer of top earth. Bulldozers generally work on the tops of mountains and the ore is carted down by trucks or conveyor belts (which are often several kilometres long) to the coast, from where it's shipped to the Doniambo smelter in Noumea or exported to Japan, France and Australia.

Visiting Grande Terre, you'll see numerous ochre scars disfiguring the mountains. The largest mine sites are around Thio, Poro and Kouaoua on the east coast and Koumac, Koné and Nepoui on the west coast. There are about a dozen mining centres, variously owned by: Société Le Nickel (SLN); wealthy families such as the Pentecost family; and the Société Minière du Sud Pacifique (SMSP).

Nickel mining is of vital economic importance for the Territory, but it is also central to environmental concerns. Indeed, opencast mining is responsible for deforestation, erosion, reef damage, and river and stream pollution.

he majority of the New Zealand troops
rived in 1942 to train for jungle warfare
gainst the Japanese.

Travellers will find bank, supermarket and
ost office facilities in Bourail. About 800m
uth from the town centre, the **Bourail Mu-**
eum focuses on the early settlers of Bourail
nd displays a few artefacts used by the
anaks from around Bourail. There is also a
ase at the back. The museum is open
/ednesday, Friday, Saturday and Sunday
om 8 to 11 am and 1 to 5 pm. Admission is
00/50 CFP for adults/children, and there are
me English explanations.

The nearby coast has the renowned **La**
Roche Percée (The Pierced Rock) landmark
and sandy **Plage de Poé** beach. La Roche
Percée is the north-west coast's only unusual rock formation and as a result it features on every tourist brochure in the
region. It's 7km from the RT1 turn-off, en
route to Plage de Poé, which is an 18km
stretch of white sand. From the RT1 turn-off
near Bourail, it's 15.5km to the start of the
beach. Off Bourail, **La Faille de Poé** (see the
'South Pacific Diving' special section) is a
magnificent dive. Diving is offered at Sub
Loisirs (☎ 44 20 65), located at the Base

NORTHERN GRANDE TERRE

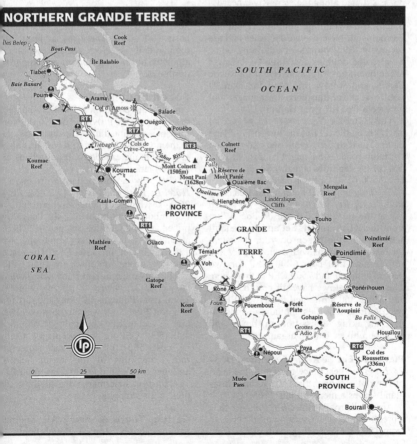

Nautique de la Roche Percé. The Faillé de Poe is regularly scheduled.

If you are interested in **horse trekking**, contact Marcel Velayoudon (☎ 44 14 90) between 7 and 8 pm.

Places to Stay Bourail's closest official *camping ground* (☎ 44 14 10) is at Plage de Poé, 15.5km from the Néra Bridge turn-off. It's a nice spot on the beachfront and it has plenty of shade. Camping costs 800 CFP per tent for the first night (500 CFP following nights).

Hôtel El Kantara (☎ 44 13 22, fax 44 20 33) is situated along the Néra River near La Roche Percée. This slightly Moorish-style hotel has a swimming pool and restaurant. Its rooms all have private facilities and are set out in long blocks of adjoining units. Singles and doubles cost 4800 CFP. To get to the hotel, turn off to the left at La Roche Percée and follow this road for 1km. If you're stuck for transport, the manager will arrange a free lift from Bourail.

The *Hôtel La Néra* (☎ 44 16 44, fax 44 18 31) is on the RT1 at the turn-off to Plage de Poé, next to the Néra River and right on the main road. It has eight rooms, all with TV, private facilities and air-con. The rooms cost 5500/6500 CFP for one/two people.

The only upmarket hotel in the area is the *Poé Beach Resort* (☎ 44 18 50, fax 44 10 70) at the far end of Plage de Poé, 17km from the RT1 turn-off. Set amid a tranquil setting, with the beach on your doorstep, the resort has rooms with a shower, TV and refrigerator that cost 6800 CFP for two people with fan and 7500 CFP with air-con. The six bungalows have air-con, bath, TV and fridge and are rented for 8700 CFP for two. Various activities, including windsurfing, kayaking, glass-bottom boats and mountain bikes, can be organised.

Places to Eat *Le Relais Gourmand* (☎ 44 23 23) is the best place to dine in the heart of Bourail. At lunch time, Le Relais Gourmand serves a menu du jour (1680 CFP).

Across the road is the *Ch'ti Bar*, which is a breezy pizzeria/bar serving pizzas costing from 1000 CFP or other main dishes from

1300 CFP. It's open daily until 10.30 p You'll also find several *snacks* and *Champion* supermarket in town.

Outside Bourail, *Hôtel La Néra* a *Hôtel El Kantara* each have a restaurant. Plage de Poé, *L'Eden Roc* (☎ 44 22 90) a restaurant/bar with a large terrace an lovely timbered interior. Salade Pacifiq including seafood costs 1200 CFP. Me dishes start at 1200 CFP.

Finally, *Poé Beach Resort* has a resta rant that overlooks the pool and the water. serves expensive a la carte dishes; a men du jour for 2000 CFP (2400 CFP for dinne

Getting There & Away By bus, the 2 hour trip between Noumea and Boura costs 1000 CFP. There are at least thr regular daily services, usually continuin along the north-west coast or crossing to t north-east.

Pouembout

Pouembout (population 1190) is home the Hôtel de la Province du Nord (Nor Province Administrative Headquarters), ju to the north on the road to Koné. It is also gateway to the east coast. It has a bank an a supermarket.

The only accommodation in town *Hôtel Le Bougainville* (☎ 47 20 60, fax 29 84), which is at the southern entry Pouembout. The hotel has six bungalow priced at 5800 CFP for two people. There also a line of six basic but clean rooms, wi TV and air-con, for 5500 CFP. The resta rant serves a menu du jour for 1650 CFP.

The only other option is the *Gîte Tamac* (☎ 47 90 22, ☎/fax 47 27 26), which 13km from Pouembout along the dirt ro to Fôret Plate. It's well signposted. The are 3 rectangular bungalows rented 4000/5000 CFP for one/two people. Cam ing costs 500 CFP per person. Horse a foot excursions of the region can arranged. A menu du jour costs 1600 CF

A *Uniprix* supermarket has all the esse tials in the shopping centre.

Getting There & Away All Noume Koumac buses stop at Pouembout. A

...ses bound for Koné leaving Noumea also ...op at Pouembout.

...oné
pop 4000

...oné is a fairly large town, surrounded by ...e rolling hills of the Massif de Koniambo ...d flat cattle pastures. Like Pouembout to ...e south, it has grown significantly in re-...nt times, due to its new status as capital ... the North Province.

...Koné is probably most noted for its ex-...llent **horse trekking** opportunities. Koné ...déo (☎ 47 21 51), run by Patrick Ardi-...ani, organises various treks into the un-...med regions around town. The stables are ...m north of town, down a dirt road to the ...ght, and should be signposted. You can ...so contact Eric Tikarso (☎ 47 23 68).

...aces to Stay & Eat *Gîte d'Ateu* (☎ 47 ...13) is 12km north-east of Koné. This ...e welcomes campers for 500 CFP per ...rson and has toilets and showers for visit-...s. Meals are available for about 1300 ...P. Ring in advance.

The cheapest rooms in town are at the *L'Escale de Koné* (☎ 47 21 09), which is across from the post office. It is a double storey block of eight small rooms, all with private facilities that sleep two people and cost 4000 CFP. It offers a variety of plats du jour for 980 CFP.

The next rung up the price ladder is the *Hôtel Le Joker* (☎ 47 37 07, fax 47 35 09), which is next to the Westpac bank. It has four rooms at the back of the main building, priced at 4000/5000 CFP for one/two people. A menu du jour amounts to 1450 CFP.

Another option is *Hôtel Koniambo* (☎ 47 39 40, fax 47 39 41), which is opposite the airport on the RT1 about 3km north of the centre. There's a row of motel rooms rented at 5500 CFP for one person and 500 CFP for each extra person. A menu du jour costs 1650 CFP.

Koné's top end accommodation option is the welcoming *Monitel L'Hibiscus* (☎ 47 22 61, fax 47 25 35). It's a modern hotel at the southern entry to town with single/double rooms for 5000/5500 CFP (6500/7000 CFP for rooms next to the swimming

A mural painted on a building in Koné tells a tale from local history.

JEAN-BERNARD CARILLET

pool). It can organise excursions around Koné. A menu du jour is 1600 CFP (at lunch time and on weekdays only).

There's a **Heli** supermarket on the main road.

Getting There & Away Koné has an airport. There are flights between Noumea and Koné (9820 CFP one way) and between Koné and Koumac (6430 CFP).

Noumea-Koumac buses stop in Koné.

Koumac

Sitting on the edge of a sprawling plain, is Koumac (population 2640). It's 368km away from Noumea and is not really geared for tourism; most of the hotels are filled with business people and sub-contractors. It has banks, a post office and a hospital.

The barrel-shaped **Église Ste Jeanne d'Arc** was constructed in 1950 out of an aircraft hangar. It has beautiful stained-glass windows and an impressive array of wood-carvings inspired by traditional Kanak art and incorporating Christian symbolism.

Koumac's seldom-visited limestone **caves** are 7km east of town at the base of a large escarpment, near a tributary of the Koumac River – this area is very difficult to reach without your own transport. Take a torch if you intend to go exploring.

Ranch La Crinière (☎ 47 66 51) offers **horseriding**.

If you want to meet a local **sculptor**, contact Léonce Weiss (☎ 47 65 32), whose studio is in Koumac's industrial zone, on the main road 2.5km south of town.

Places to Stay & Eat The cheapest place to stay is the shady beachfront **Camping de Pandop**, 2km south of town, towards the marina. It costs 500 CFP to pitch your tent.

The most central place is **Hôtel Le Grand Cerf** (☎ 47 61 31, fax 47 60 16), which is just north of the roundabout. It has nine bungalows, a bar, restaurant and swimming pool. Each bungalow has a TV and private facilities, and costs 5400 CFP for one person plus 600 CFP for each extra. The restaurant is rather cheerless, but the lunch-time menu du jour is cheap enough at 1550 CFP.

Alternatively, there's **Le Passiflore** (☎ 62 10) on Ave Georges Baudoux. Simpl rooms, in a row at the back of the comple cost 3500 CFP without a private shower, 4500/5000 CFP for single/double w shower. There's a small bar and restaura

The **Monitel Koumac** (☎ 47 66 66, fax 62 85) is south of the roundabout and Koumac's most modern lodging. An asso ment of well kept bungalows, all with t necessary private facilities, have been bu around a large swimming pool. A bungalc costs 6500/7000 CFP for one/two peop The restaurant is large and serves a menu jour for 1650 CFP.

There is also a couple of **snacks**, sever well stocked **supermarkets** and tv **boulangeries** (bakeries).

Getting There & Away Koumac has small airport. There are only three flights week between Koumac and Noumea (10,9 CFP, 1½ hours), each via Koné (6430 CF 20 minutes). Some flights then contin from Koumac to Îles Belep (8190 CFP, minutes). There is one flight per week fro Koumac to Touho (8190 CFP, 25 minutes

Koumac's bus station is 450m south the roundabout. There are regular buses b tween Noumea and Koumac (1550 CFP, 5 hours) and less frequent services to Pou and east to Ouégoa, and over to the ea coast village of Pouébo.

Koumac to Boat-Pass

On leaving Koumac, Grande Terre tape into a narrow peninsula that is carved many bays. The terrain becomes windswe and the soil is dry, overtaken by niaouli s vannah. About 8km north of Koumac, t RT7 turns eastwards off the RT8 a crosses the tip of Grande Terre, throu, beautiful country over the Cols de Crèv Cœur, to Ouégoa and later the east coast

About 20km north of Koumac and easi visible from the RT1, the **Tiébaghi mi** was once the largest and richest chrom mine in the world. The old mine is now d funct and the village that rose around it i ghost town. Visits can be arranged throu, Koumac's town hall (☎ 47 61 08).

Poum marks the end of the RT1, 56km orth of Koumac. Only a rough dirt road 5km before Poum) continues north, ending : Pointe Nahârian. This is the tip of Grande erre and is also known as **Boat-Pass**, vhich is the name of the channel separating e Baaba from the mainland. It's a hilly ter- ain that's exposed to the sea, with sandy eaches bordered by araucarias, palms and rassland. There's a gîte 3km before the op. The road is rough and very slippery hen wet.

laces to Stay & Eat The luxurious *Ialabou Beach Resort (☎ 47 60 60, fax 47 0 70)* is built along Baie de Nehoue, about 5km south of Poum. A collection of square ungalows and luxury suites with all facil- ies dot the peaceful grounds. A bungalow or up to three adults costs 9600/10,600 'FP in low/high season. The suites cost 8,000 CFP. A wide array of activities can e arranged through the resort. The restau- nt offers a menu du jour for 2800 CFP and ther a la carte specialities.

About 400m north of Malabou Beach is a rn-off to the left to *Camping Golone ☎ 47 90 78)*. This tranquil and isolated site, bout 4.5km from the main road, is bordered y two nice beaches. Campers are charged 00 CFP per person. The only bungalow is riced at 3000 CFP (up to two people). Pad- le-boats and kayaks can be rented.

ietting There & Away Just north of the 1alabou Beach Resort, 15km south of oum, is the region's only airstrip. Aircalin as just one flight per week from Noumea, ia Touho to Poum (14,160 CFP, 1½ hours). his flight returns to Noumea via Koné 9070 CFP, 25 minutes).

There are infrequent bus connections be- veen Koumac and Poum.

es Belep
his remote archipelago is 50km north-west f the northern tip of Grande Terre. At its ntre is Île Art, the group's largest island. ist north is Île Pott, also inhabited, while the south are the small Île Niénone and e two Daos (north and south) islets.

The Belep Islands are home to 920 Kanaks. The islands are rarely visited by tourists as there are only a couple of flights and boats per week, and there is no tourist accommodation.

THE NORTH-EAST COAST
Scenery and people make the north-east coast Grande Terre's most impressive re- gion. The area is characterised by lush forests, streams, waterfalls and coastal coco- nut groves. There are fascinating rock formations in the vicinity of Hienghène, as well as New Caledonia's highest peak, Mont Panié (1628m). To the north of the region's hub, Poindimié, there are nice beaches.

The north-east coast is home to numerous Kanak clans but few Europeans, most of whom left prior to or during Les Évène- ments, in the mid-1980s.

Getting There & Away
Three main roads span the central mountain chain: the RT6 between Bourail and Houaïlou; the partly sealed Koné-Tiwaka road, in the far north; and the RT7 linking Koumac-Ouégoa-Balade.

In contrast, just one main road covers the entire north-east coast: the RT3 meanders the 210km between Houaïlou and Pouébo. To reach the area, you need to cross moun- tain passes, including Col des Roussettes (381m) and Col d'Amoss.

Air Touho has the only regional airport. There is at least one flight daily from Noumea to Touho (9820 CFP, 1½ hours) and back to Noumea. Most days these flights go via Koné. The Touho-Koné leg costs 5440 CFP and takes 20 minutes. There are also flights between Touho and Tontouta (9820 CFP, 35 minutes), between Touho and Poum (9070 CFP, 30 minutes), and from Koumac to Touho (8190 CFP, 25 minutes).

Bus Buses to this coastline are much less frequent than to destinations along the north-west coast. In general, there are two or three per day from Noumea. However, one bus goes only as far as Houaïlou, and an- other terminates at Poindimié. Only one bus a day goes all the way to Hienghène, stopping en route at all major villages and towns.

Buses depart from Noumea for Hienghène (1550 CFP) at least once daily. To Poindimié (1350 CFP) and Houaïlou (1150 CFP), there's a daily bus.

In addition to these buses, there are a couple of services between Pouébo and Poindimié, stopping at Hienghène and Touho, and between Pouébo and Hienghène.

Pouébo, Balade and Ouégoa are infrequently serviced by buses from Koumac.

From Houaïlou to Poindimié

Houaïlou, 68km north-east of Bourail and 230km from Noumea, is the first coastal village you'll come to after descending from the mountains on the RT6. It's built along a river of the same name and is set in lush and beautiful surroundings.

The **Ba Falls** are 13.5km north of the Houaïlou bridge. The track leading to the falls is on the left, directly after a large bridge. It is a 10 minute walk.

Ponérihouen is a small village, 46km north-west of Houaïlou, a couple of kilometres inland on a bend in the Nabai River.

Places to Stay About 7km north of Ponérihouen, near the village of Tiakan, there's a lovely beachfront *camping ground* set amid a large palm grove. It's on the right-hand side, down a dirt track leading off the RT3, and is well signposted. To pitch your tent for the night costs 1000 CFP. There is a small *épicerie* (grocery store) just 100m down the road.

Poindimié
● pop 4340
About 308km from Noumea, Poindimié is the administrative centre of the north-east coast and serves as an excellent point for exploring the region. It's a place with great atmosphere, stretched along a rocky coastline. It has all the necessary services, such as inexpensive accommodation, good restaurants, supermarkets, banks, a hospital and a post office.

Tiéti beach is in front of the municipal camping ground and is one of the finest sandy beaches of the area.

For **scuba diving**, contact Tiéti Diving (☎ 42 72 73), based at the Monitel de Tiéti. You'll explore the outer reef, about 30 minutes away by boat.

Places to Stay & Eat The *municipal camping ground* at Tiéti beach, next to the Monitel de Tiéti, is a nice enough spot. However, reports of theft from this camp site are rife.

More secure is the beachfront at the Monitel itself. You can camp here for free provided you buy at least a drink (or dine) at the hotel during your stay.

Hôtel Le Tapoundari (☎ 42 71 11) is set beside the Poindimié River, just below the main bridge. Rooms without air-con cost 4500/5000 CFP for one/two people, while renovated rooms with air-con and cooking facilities are 5500/6000 CFP. Its restaurant has a variety of snacks plus, on weekdays (at lunch time only), a 1600 CFP menu du jour.

The large, multistorey *Hôtel de la Plage* (☎ 42 71 28), near Tiéti beach to the north, has a popular restaurant and bar. A single or double room with private amenities cost 5500 CFP. The restaurant has a weekday menu du jour for 1800 CFP, or a fancier *menu touristique* (tourist menu) for 2200 CFP.

Almost directly across the road from the Hôtel de la Plage is the *Monitel de Tiéti* (☎ 42 64 00, fax 42 64 01), a luxury beachfront complex with private bungalows, rooms, a restaurant, swimming pool, bar and dive centre. It has four modern bungalows, all with air-con, TV, a sea view and shower/toilet. The bungalows cost 7500/8500 CFP for one/two people. Behind the bungalows is a row of five rooms priced at 7500/8500 CFP for a single/double. The Monitel has a large, elegant restaurant that opens to a poolside terrace. Mains vary in price from 1500 to 2000 CFP.

Bar/Snack Les 3A (☎ 42 71 10) is a spacious terrace restaurant with a spectacular view of the sea and distant islands. Chinese cuisine is the house speciality. Expect to pay about 1000 CFP for a beef or meat dish.

The *Gîte de Napoémien* (☎ 42 74 77) in a beautiful valley in the tribal village of the same name. The clan has three houses at it rents for 1500 CFP per person per ght. Both have kitchen facilities. The vil-ge is 4km inland from Poindimié, along sealed road that hugs a fast-flowing eek.

oindimié to Hienghène

nce you leave Poindimié, the scenery be->mes more dramatic, with lush, mountain-us countryside and distant waterfalls. bout 5km north of central Poindimié is ie beginning of the **Amoa River valley**, ith dirt roads leading into the valley along ther river bank. The **Tié Mission** was built 1866 and is 500m further. Around 8km ist the mission you'll cross the wide Ti-aka River and immediately come across ie turn-off for the Koné-Tiwaka road.

Touho is built on a bay that curls around Cap Colnett and is protected from the sea y the Mengalia Reef and nearby islets.

Touho Mission was established by two larists who came down the coast from alade in 1853. The church was built in 889, seven years after a military post was stablished nearby. The mission was built lose to the beach, about 2.5km west of elais Alison. Simply continue past the endarmerie until the first turn on your ght, which leads 800m down to the iurch.

The Touho-Hienghène section is the most)ectacular of the north-east coast. From ouho, the RT3 closely hugs the water's lge. About 9km before Hienghène, the :enery dramatically changes to black cliffs)wering over startling green water.

laces to Stay & Eat The focal point of ouho is a small hotel/restaurant called *Re-iis Alison (☎ 42 88 12)*. It has five clean, ir-con rooms, each with a shower, costing 500/5000 CFP for one/two people. It has a ienu du jour for a pricey 2000 CFP. The :staurant is closed on weekends.

The cheapest place to stay in Touho is *amping Leveque (☎ 42 88 19)*, opposite elais Alison. Though pretty run-down, this lace has bungalows and open land for set-ng up tents next to the beach. The camp-g fee per night is 500 CFP. A bungalow

costs 1500 CFP, however, there are no sheets or blankets.

You can camp for free at *Camping Gastaldi*, a calm spot dotted with coconut palms on the mouth of a small river west of Touho. It's about 3.5km from Touho's cen-tre to the signposted turn-off (to the right off the RT3). The campsite is another 1km away, just beyond one of Gastaldi's two grocery shops.

You can also head 15km west of Touho to the picturesque *Gîte Mangalia (☎/fax 42 87 60)*. Overlooking the large Mengalia reef, it's a lovely place, located just off the RT3. Double/triple bungalows cost 4000/5000 CFP. Its restaurant serves either a la carte or menus du jour.

Hienghène

Hienghène (population 2200) is known throughout New Caledonia for two signifi-cant reasons. Firstly, its coastline is carved with the most fascinating rock formations that New Caledonia can offer.

In a more sober vein, Hienghène was also the scene (in 1984) of one of New Caledonia's most brutal modern-day mas-sacres. This event has made the village a symbol of the liberation struggle. This spirit was personified by former Hienghène mayor and assassinated FLNKS leader, Jean-Marie Tjibaou, whose tribal commu-nity of Tiendanite lies about 20km south-west of Hienghène.

There is a post office, but no banks. A small tourist office (☎ 42 43 57) is located behind the town hall. It can organise various tours and accommodation in tribal gîtes. It's open weekdays and Saturday morning.

Goa Ma Bwarhat Cultural Centre is a multi-faceted cultural centre (☎ 42 81 50) situated on the right just before the bridge into Hienghène. It contains a one room mu-seum (admission is 100/50 CFP for adults/ children) that exhibits various artefacts. The centre is open Monday to Saturday; closing time 3.30 pm).

Lindéralique Cliffs are dramatic black limestone cliffs that start about 9km south of Hienghène, near Club Med, and continue to the bay of Hienghène. Rising abruptly out of nowhere, they stretch in places to 60m and are topped by jagged, razor-sharp edges. The most famous of the rock formations is Le Poulet, or the Brooding Hen – a high, rocky slab rising from the centre of Hienghène bay. Slightly north-west is the Sphinx, another of nature's masterpieces. These two are best viewed from the **lookout**, 1.5km south of the cultural centre. A signpost marked 'Point de Vue' shows you the way.

The **Base Nautique** (☎ 42 82 05), on the beach below the gendarmerie, rents kayaks, canoes and mountain bikes.

For **scuba diving**, contact Koulnoué Dive Centre (☎ 42 83 59), based at Club Med. George Schools, the dive instructor, will make you discover the outer reef, including Tidwan, Tombant des Papillons, Donga Hiengha, Pointe aux Cachalots. Pelagics, including numerous sharks, and schools of fish are commonly seen at these sites.

Places to Stay & Eat You can camp at the *Base Nautique* (☎ 88 27 37 weekdays only) for 250 CFP per tent plus 150 CFP per person. There are shower and toilet facilities in the centre. It also has one grungy studio room with five beds and an ultra-basic kitchenette. It's very rough around the edges, but cheap enough at 800 CFP per person.

Gîte Ka Waboana (☎/fax 42 47 03) is perched on a hill opposite the wharf. It has three nice bungalows for 6000 CFP for one or two people and three self-contained units for 6500 CFP. The menu du jour costs 1800 CFP.

About 7.5km north-west of Hienghène is *Gîte Weouth* (☎ 42 45 16). It's just off the RT3, to the right – a hand-painted sign points the way. The accommodation consists of two very basic cement bungalows, which cost 1800 CFP per person. Both have a rough shower and toilet. A typical meal costs around 1800 CFP. You can also camp for 800 CFP per night. Boat trips can be organised.

Club Med's *Koulnoué Village* (☎ 42 81 66, fax 42 81 75) is stretched out along a coconut-palm-lined beach and overshadowed by the Lindéralique cliffs. There's a pool, a massive bar and a restaurant. The reception has facilities for exchanging cash as

well as all travellers cheques. The comple[x] has luxury bungalows priced at 960[0-] 10,600 CFP per night in low/high season[.] The village runs various tours and ren[ts] mountain bikes. Club Med's restauran[t,] which is open to nonguests, prepares a cop[i-] ous buffet daily at lunch (1800 CFP) an[d] dinner (2700 CFP). The turn-off to Club Me[d] is 8.5km south of Hienghène on the RT3. It[']s then another 1.25km from the main road.

Hienghène to Pouébo

On this road, you cross numerous bridge[s] between the sea and fast-flowing rivers an[d] creeks. Kanak huts and stalls dot the side[s] of the road and powerful waterfalls tumbl[e] down from the Massif du Panié.

Ouaïème Bac is New Caledonia's la[st] surviving river ferry. It takes vehicles acros[s] the Ouaïème River, 17km north-west [of] Hienghène. The ferry runs 24 hours a day.

The **Tao waterfalls** are in the mountain[-] ous Massif du Panié, which dominates th[is] section of the coast. The walking path up [to] the falls starts about 7km north of th[e] Ouaïème River ferry, at a cottage just aft[er] a bridge. The falls can easily be seen fro[m] the centre of this bridge. An entry fee of 20[0] CFP per person is levied on those walkin[g] up to the falls.

Mont Panié (1628m) is New Caledonia['s] highest peak. It is possible to climb th[e] mountain from a trail starting near Tao fall[s] but the return trip takes the best part of [a] day. There is a refuge on the mountain ([at] 900m) where hikers can stay overnight.

Places to Stay & Eat After *Gîte Weou[th]* (see Hienghène's Places to Stay & Eat se[c-] tion, earlier), there are two tribal sites wher[e] you can pitch a tent and, further on, a gî[te] that has both bungalows and campin[g] space.

The first site is *Chez Théo & Maria* [at] Wâjik (formerly spelt Ouenguip), which i[s] 10.5km north of Hienghène. It should b[e] signposted. You can pitch a tent among th[e] beachfront coconut palms for 800 CF[P.] There's a pit toilet and one cold commun[al] shower.

About 3km north of the Ouaïème Riv[er]

rry, at the base of Mont Panié, is the ameless beachfront *camping de Panié*. It's n the right-hand side as you're heading orth and, set between the road and the each, is immediately obvious. There's no nower here, and the overnight charge is 00 CFP per tent and 200 CFP per person.

Finally, there's *Gîte Galarino* where you an stay in 2 bungalows overlooking the ea – it's the last place as you head north on ne north-east coast. It's 19km north of ꭇuaiemé (or 26km south of Pouébo) in the lan of Colnett, set in a picturesque loca-on. The five cement bungalows with natched roofs have one double bedroom nd a kitchen. They're not flash but they are ufficient. Expect to pay 3000 CFP for one erson plus 500 CFP for each extra, and ou can camp on the beachfront for 1000 ꭇFP. Boat trips to the reef can be arranged.

ꭇouébo

ꭇouébo (population 2350) is 63km north-vest of Hienghène and is the last village ettled close to the sea (about 2km inland) n the north-east coast. The first Europeans ꭇ arrive in Pouébo (in July 1847) were ꭇatholic missionaries who had come down rom Balade, in the north.

Pouébo Mission Church still stands on ne original mission site. Its interior is ramed by splendid kauri timber beams eaching a height of 12m. **La Salette** is a mall chapel, 2km north of Pouébo's small ridge. It was constructed in 1876 by ꭇrother Reboul.

ꭇalade

ꭇalade is 11km north of Pouébo's mission hurch and is more an historical site than a illage or community. Set amid dry hills, ꭇoastal mangrove plains and niaouli trees, nis coastal area was the first place that ꭇuropean explorers set foot on New Cale-onian soil. Captain Cook landed at Koul-oué M'Balan beach in September 1774.

There are no administrative services or hops in Balade. Ten kilometres north-west f Balade, *Camping d'Amoss* is on the eachfront at the foot of Col d'Amoss. It's delightful spot, and there are showers and

---

Roadside Stalls

Roadside stalls are found only along Grande Terre's north-east coast. Seasonal fruits, shells collected from the beach, lo-cally made woodcarvings and soapstone figurines are the standard wares. The stalls are generally humble affairs, consisting of a few lengths of bamboo strung together to form a sturdy lean-to and a thatched canopy (or sheet of corrugated iron) for shelter from the rain.

Some stalls will offer one bunch of green bananas and three shells, while others are laden with seasonal fruits such as avoca-dos, coconuts, pawpaws and lemons. North of Hienghène, soapstone and wood carvings are popular and sell for much less than in Noumea.

The price might be marked on a scrap of paper tucked underneath an item or written straight onto the fruit's skin. All the stalls have an honesty box, usually a little tin or a clam shell, placed nearby for the money. However, just because it's an honesty sys-tem, it doesn't mean that nobody's watch-ing. More often than not, the stall owner heard your car pull up and is keeping an eye on things from behind the tropical foliage.

---

a toilet block. It charges 500 CFP for a tent. The site is signposted 1km off the RT3.

Balade to Ouégoa

After leaving Balade you'll notice the scenery becomes desolate, dry and some-what disappointing after the spectacular countryside to the south. About 9km from Balade, the main road turns south and in-land towards Col d'Amoss.

Ouégoa is an outpost town and the only significant north-east village that is not set-tled close to the sea. There is little for visit-ors to do.

The hotel/restaurant *Le Normandon* (☎ 47 68 28) is the only place in town where you can bed down for the night. Five very basic rooms cost an exorbitant 3000/4000 CFP a single/double. The restaurant serves a simple menu du jour for a pricey 2000 CFP or sandwiches for 500 CFP.

The Loyalty Islands

The Loyalty Islands consist of four raised coral atolls, about 100km off the east coast of Grande Terre. From south to north they are Maré, Tiga, Lifou and Ouvéa. Totalling 1980 sq km, they are roughly 50km apart and have their highest point (138m) on Maré. There are no rivers, though fresh water is found in numerous deep caverns and *trous* (holes) in or under the coral platform. While nature is not as diverse here as on Grande Terre, the Loyalty Islands' eroded limestone coastlines are very impressive. Towering araucarias look down on the most sublime beaches that New Caledonia can offer.

Traditional Kanak society has been best preserved in these islands. Ancient traditions remain strong and lifestyles centre around community concerns.

For those looking for an authentic taste of island life, tribal gîtes and *logements chez l'habitant* or homestays are dotted around the islands.

History

Melanesians have inhabited the Loyalty Islands for millennia, but hundreds of years ago, seafaring Polynesians arrived, dominating and ultimately mingling with the Melanesians.

Bruny d'Entrecasteaux is supposedly the first European to have spotted Ouvéa before landing on Grande Terre in April 1793. In 1827, Dumont d'Urville was officially sent to chart the islands. Whalers and sandalwood traders were the next arrivals, followed by evangelist Tongan teachers from the London Missionary Society (LMS) as early as 1841.

The Catholic missionaries started to set up their own missions in the Loyalty Islands in 1856, but were unable to convert all of the islanders. Caught between the two factions, the social structures of the clans on the three islands broke down and wars broke out. The wars raged until 1864, when the colony's Governor Guillian officially took possession of Lifou and Maré. Ouvéa followed the next year.

In the second half of the 1800s, islander from Maré and Ouvéa were taken by black birders to Australian sugar cane plantation to work.

After blackbirding came to an end, the two world wars and the appeal of the lucrative mining industry saw many more islander leave their homes. In more recent decade they have been followed by students needing to gain a secondary or tertiary education, and people in search of a job.

The population of the four Loyalty island is 98% Kanak, with only a handful of French. A large proportion of the islands population live or work in Noumea.

MARÉ
- **pop 6900**   • **area 650 sq km**

Maré is a lush island with a magnificent steep coastline dropping into the big blue of the Pacific. It is the second largest of the Loyalty Islands and its coral cliffs are the group's highest, rising abruptly to 140m While only a few beaches interrupt the cliff lines, those that do are intensely beautiful.

Maré's population encompasses about 20 clans divided into three chiefdoms. The clans all speak Nengone.

Things to See

The west-coast port town of **Tadin** is the island's administrative centre and port. This was the home town of Yeiwene Yeiwene, the second in command of the FLNKS, who was assassinated on Ouvéa in May 1989 He is buried here, by the sea.

The village has no beach. There is a clinic, BCI branch, post office (open standard hours) and a gendarmerie. At the T-junction close to the sea, a monument is dedicated to the people who drowned on an inter island trader, *Monique*, in 1953. At least 126 people were on board and no trace of the ship, which disappeared between Maré and Lifou, was ever found.

Between Tadin and Cengeite is an **aquarium naturel**, a round, naturally carved rock pool fed from underground. Its clear translucent water is home to a variety of fish. The aquarium is on the right-hand side, roughly 3km from the Tadin gendarmerie, just before a slight rise in the road and the start of small cliffs to the left.

Cengeite and the contiguous village of **Wabao** are probably the best examples of paradise in all of New Caledonia. This picturesque south-west corner of Maré is sprinkled with coconut palms and, nearby, has the purest of beaches. Cengeite starts about 8km south of Tadin, which boasts the island's only top end hotel, Nengone Village. Wabao is home to two lovely gîtes that

lie between the main road and a smaller coastal road, which leads off to the right as you arrive from Cengeite.

From Nengone Village it's an easy and very enjoyable 3km walk to **Baie de Pede**, on the northern side of Cap Wabao. A well signposted track starts at the hotel and runs parallel to the waterfront. Near Cap Wabao, the track veers inland and meanders through a forest before ending at Baie de Pede.

At the south-western end of the island, about 9km from Cengeite, **Medu** and **Eni** are two adjoining villages. Medu has a large Catholic church, set well back from the

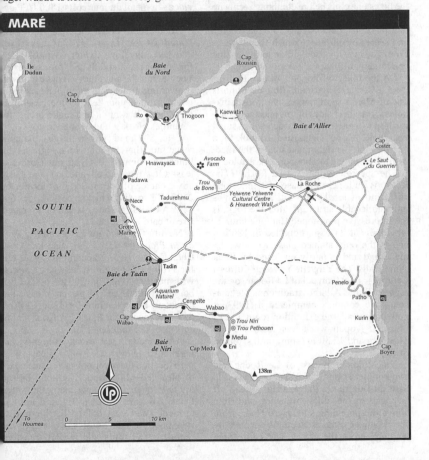

MARÉ

Île Dudun

Baie du Nord

Cap Roussin

Cap Machau

Ro — Thogoon — Kaewatin

Baie d'Allier

Cap Coster

Le Saut du Guerrier

SOUTH

Hnawayaca — Avocado Farm

PACIFIC

Padawa

Trou de Bone — Yeiwene Yeiwene Cultural Centre & Hnaenedr Wall — La Roche

Nece — Tadurehmu

OCEAN

Grotte Marine

Baie de Tadin — Tadin

Penelo

Patho

Aquarium Naturel — Cengeite — Wabao

Cap Wabao

Trou Niri
Trou Pethouen
Medu

Kurin

Baie de Niri — Cap Medu — Eni

Cap Boyer

▲ 138m

To Noumea

0   5   10 km

road, which was built as part of a mission in 1886. A few hundred metres down the road is Eni's small Protestant church.

Before arriving at the villages, there is a spectacular trou (sinkhole) called **Pethoen**. It's about 500m before Medu, on the road's final curve. A foot track winds its way over the limestone floor for 100m to a deep cavern, where stalactites drip into cool, green, saline water.

Going north from Tadin, the road winds along a spectacular coastline of limestone rock until Nece, 8km north of Tadin. After Nece, the road continues close to the base of the limestone cliffs before climbing steeply up the plateau to the village of **Padawa**. A tranquil place, it's dominated by a white church and separate bell tower, which face the sea. From Padawa, it's about 10km to the fishing community of Ro, a very sleepy village.

On the road to Thogoon, about 3km off the La Roche-Tadin road, **Trou de Bone** is one of Maré's most impressive trous (sinkholes). The sheer sides of this enormous cavity drop to a lush tropical garden with a small waterhole. It's not signposted, so look for a guardrail on the right-hand side of the road, as you're heading to Thogoon, or ask a local.

The spacious village of **La Roche** (The Rock) is built near the base of a limestone cliff, known locally as 'Titi'. La Roche's most noticeable structure, after the rock, is the impressive pink-toned Catholic church, which sits at its base. Founded in 1866, it boasts the only stained-glass windows on the island and is partly enclosed by thick stone walls. The **Yeiwene Yeiwene Cultural Centre** is about 2km out of La Roche, on the road to Tadin. A large, traditional Melanesian-style complex completed in 1993, it now houses a large exhibition room and library. It's open weekdays from 7.30 to 11.30 am and 12.30 to 5 pm (until 4 pm on Friday).

Nine kilometres east of La Roche and two kilometres north of Wakone village is **le Saut du Guerrier** or the 'Warrior's Leap'. It is a gap in the cliffs, 5m wide and 30m above the pounding surf. Here Hnor, from the Hnathege clan, escaped his enemies by leaping across the abyss. The entire area

around Wakone is rugged, with splendi rock formations and crevasses.

Places to Stay & Eat

Wabao's three accommodation options s almost side by side across the road from blissful beach. They have splendid views o the water and reef.

The *Yedjele Beach* (☎/fax 45 40 47) ha four immaculate bungalows nestled in shady forest setting that costs 6000/650 CFP for singles/doubles. Each bungalow ha a small attic, TV, large terrace and a goo kitchenette. On request, meals can be pro vided – a menu du jour costs 1800 CFP an breakfast is 750 CFP. Credit card is accepted

About 200m down the road is *Gîte Si Hmed* (☎/fax 45 41 51). It has seve thatched bungalows, which cost 4000 CF for one person and 500 CFP for each extra They're not flash but they all have a privat shower and toilet, and a fan. Alternatively you can pitch your tent on the beachfron for 1200 CFP a night and make use of th amenities block with hot showers.

Gîte Si-Hmed has a large, thatche restaurant that is open to nonguests fo lunch and dinner (but you must order a least a few hours in advance). There's usu ally a choice of coconut crab or lobster fo 2700 CFP; or fish, chicken or pork for 160 CFP. A traditional bougna can be prepared Credit card is accepted.

Next to Gîte Si-Hmed is *Camping Far de la Plage* (☎ 45 42 24), also known a Chez Celine. Here you can pitch your ten for 1100 CFP a night. It also has a *snack* with meals costing from 700 to 1600 CFP. A bougna is 1000 CFP per person. It has a fev mountain bikes for hire for 1200 CFP pe day and canoes for 350 CFP. Chez Celin acts also as a *snack*.

At Cengeite, the two star *Nengone Vil lage* (☎ 45 45 00, fax 45 44 64) boasts a su perb location that overlooks a pristine beac of bleached-white sand. The hotel has at tractive square bungalows along the water front. All have air-con, TV and a smal terrace. They cost 8500 CFP for one o two people. The hotel can arrange ca rental, island tours and airport transfers

here's a pool right next to the restaurant. Bikes can be rented for 500 CFP (half day). At lunch or dinner, you can order the menu u jour (2500 CFP) or various a la carte options. Credit card is accepted.

Chez Léon Dunhara (☎ 45 43 70) is right in the heart of the Eni community, between he Medu and Eni churches. The one basic hatched *case* has mattresses and pandanus mats spread over the floor. Sleeping here costs 1500 CFP per person; with your own tent you can camp for 1000 CFP. There's an attractive *fare* (meeting house) for relaxing nd dining – breakfast is 500 CFP and a meal or bougna costs 1500 CFP. An amenities block was under construction at the time of writing. Airport transfers cost 4000 CFP return for up to two people, and island tours nd guided walks can be organised.

In the Kaewatine community, set in a large clearing, *Gîte Xaada Sa Nord* (☎/fax 45 43 85) is a family-run place with a row of four rooms for 5000 CFP (the rooms can accommodate up to three people). Its restaurant serves a plat du jour for 800 CFP and breakfast for 200 CFP. From the gîte you can walk (45 minutes one way) through a cool forest to Plage de Utila. As the track is quite rough you'll need a guide – ask at the gîte. Airport/wharf transfers cost 2000/3000 CFP return. Credit cards are accepted.

Getting There & Away

The airport is at La Roche, a village 22km north-east of Tadin and 1km from the village itself. There is at least one direct daily flight between Maré and Noumea's Magenta airport. It takes 35 minutes and costs 8410 CFP one way. Irregular inter-island flights connect Maré with Tiga (2900 CFP, 15 minutes), Lifou (5650 CFP, 25 minutes) and Ouvéa (8270 CFP, 1½ hours).

See the Getting Around section earlier in this chapter for more information about the passenger ferry that services the Loyalty Islands from Noumea.

Getting Around

Maré has no public transport. Transfers to and from the airport at La Roche, or the ferry wharf at Tadin, are organised by most accommodation places. It's best to arrange it when you book your visit. You'll be looking at 2400/1000 CFP for a return transfer to the airport/wharf from Cengeite.

Cars are available for 6500 to 7500 CFP per day (unlimited kilometres) from the following people: Yeiwene Jean-Pierre (☎ 45 43 95) in Tadin; Deiradane Nemia (☎ 45 43 75) and Kawa André (☎ 45 42 67) in Nece; and Wiako Jacques (☎ 45 43 85) in Kaewatin. Cars will usually be delivered to your hotel or gîte, or you can pick them up at the airport on arrival.

Most accommodation places rent bikes from 500/1000 CFP per half/full day.

Tours of the island are organised by the hotels and gîtes, and cost between 2200 CFP and 2500 CFP per person. You can also contact Jean-Pierre Yeiwene (☎ 45 43 95).

Kayaks can be hired from Camping Fare de la Plage (☎ 45 42 24) next to Gîte Si-Hmed, in Wabao.

TIGA

• pop 380   • area 10 sq km

The tiny island of Tiga, just 6km by 2km in size, sits midway between Maré and Lifou, roughly 30km from the closest point of both. Like its neighbours, Tiga is a raised coral atoll, 76m at its highest point and encircled by a fringing reef.

The Tokanod clan inhabits the north-west corner, where Tiga is least exposed and the reef most accessible. There's a post office, church, clinic and small supply store, but no accommodation.

Getting There & Away

The island is connected to the outside world by just four inter-island flights per week. From Maré (2900 CFP one way) the flight takes 15 minutes; from Lifou (3640 CFP) it's a few minutes longer. Should you want to fly directly from Noumea to Tiga (8410 CFP one way), Monday's inter-island flight has direct links.

LIFOU

• pop 10,000   • area 1196 sq km

Lifou is the largest of the Loyalty Islands and is bigger than Tahiti. A peculiar shape, this raised coral atoll is geographically diverse with wonderful limestone caves, bleached-white sand and rich sea life amid the coral reefs.

Lifou is the most populated Loyalty Island. Four-fifths of the population actually live on the island, while the other 2000 reside in Noumea. The island has three chiefdoms. The local language, Drehu (pronounced 'day-hoo'), is actually the indigenous name for Lifou.

Things to See & Do

We & North of Lifou We is Lifou's largest town, home to the provincial headquarters, the island's only bank and clinic, as well as the main gendarmerie and post office. It is curled around the Baie de Châteaubriand, a wide sandy bay cut by a reef and dotted with rocky outcrops. The small CEMAID (☎ 45 00 32) office, attached to the *mairie* (town hall), hands out island maps as well as brochures. It's open weekdays from 7.30 to 11.30 am and 12.30 to 5 pm. It has a desk at the airport that's open at each arrival. You can change money at the BNP on the main road (open weekdays from 7.20 am to 3.45 pm) or at the BCI, next to Aircalin office. BCI has an Automatic Teller Machine (ATM or DAB). The post office (which is open standard business hours) is behind the provincial headquarters.

North of town, well hidden in thick vegetation, is **Grotte d'Avio**, a huge cavern with 4m-long stalactites and a pool of jade water. Ask for a guide at the CEMAID office.

Three kilometres south-east of the airport, **Hnathalo** is the home of the *chef* of Wetr. There is a *grande case* that's surrounded by a wooden palisade and set in a garden. It's behind the chief's concrete house, which is next to the church. It's the only *grande case* on Lifou that you can visit without seeking permission.

Jokin (Doking in French) is Lifou's northernmost village. It's a sublime spot, sitting high on the cliffs overlooking a magnificent bay. It has one of the most attractive *cases* in all New Caledonia. In very calm weather, the bay is magnificent for snorkelling. Next to

the *case* is a footpath leading down to a little limestone cove.

Easo is a small coastal village, sitting peacefully on a cliff above the wide Baie du Santal. The road west of Easo church leads to the **Chapelle Notre Dame de Lourdes**, a small chapel topped by a large statue perched on a hill above the sea at the end of Easo Peninsula. It is the destination of some 200 pilgrims who gather annually from around Lifou.

Xepenehe is another coastal village, 5km east of Easo, overlooking Baie du Santal.

Peng is a blissful, secluded sandy beach on Baie du Santal, 3.5km off the We-Drueulu road along a dirt road. Before 1925 a tribe lived here, but the whole village packed up and moved 4km south-east to Hapetra during an outbreak of leprosy. The beach is calm and a fantastic spot for relaxing.

About 20km west of We, **Drueulu** lines the small Baie de Drueulu, part of the larger Baie du Santal. There's a lovely beach. From Drueulu you can take the long southern road through several tribal communities to Mu and Xodre in the south-east of the island.

For **scuba diving**, contact Lifou Fun Dive (☎/fax 45 02 75), located near the Drehu Village hotel. There are three main dive sites, all noteworthy for their abundance of soft corals, gorgonians and sharks.

South of Lifou Eight kilometres southeast of We is the village of **Traput**, followed two kilometres further by **Jozip**, a quiet coastal settlement where there is a wooden sculpture workshop.

Continuing south, 26km from We, **Luengoni** boasts the most beautiful beach in New Caledonia. Protected by a barrier reef, the turquoise lagoon is idyllic for swimming.

Eleven kilometres south of Luengoni is Lifou's southernmost village, **Mu**. The southern road comes to a final halt at the settlement of **Xodre**, which is a desolate spot close to the rugged coastline.

Places to Stay & Eat

Lifou has quite a diverse range of accommodation options, conveniently spread over the island.

LIFOU

Cap Escarpé

Baie de Jokin
Jokin

Grotte du Diable
Hnacaôm
Tingeting
Cap Bernardin

Vanilla Farm
Siloam
Hunëtë

Easo
Pte Aimé Martin
To Ouvéa
Chapelle Notre Dame de Lourdes
Xepenehe
Kumo
Hnathalo

Nang
Cila
Kirinata

Baie du Santal

District de Wetr

Luecila
Baie de Châteaubriand
We
Traput
Jozip

Baie de Drueulu
Peng Beach
Pte Lefèvre
Hapetra
Drueulu
Wedrumel

District de Gaica
Hnadro

District de Losi
Inagoj
Hmelek
Huipatromë
Kejëny Kedeigne
Luengoni
Joj
Cap des Pins
To Île Nié (5km)
Mu
Huiwatrui
Xodre
Enefëji

SOUTH PACIFIC OCEAN

▲ 104m

To Noumea
Cap de la Flotte
To Noumea

0   5   10 km

We North of town, *Chez Rachel* (☎ 45 12 43, fax 45 00 78) is set back 150m off the beach, in a nice verdant setting. It's an easy 10 minute stroll into We's centre. The motel has eight large bungalows with cooking facilities, refrigerator and private bathroom with hot water. They cost 6500 CFP for one person and 500 CFP more for each extra guest. In addition, there are four small studio rooms with kitchenette and private facilities costing 6000/6500/7000 CFP for one/two/three people. Camping costs 800 CFP per person per night. Motel Chez Rachel charges 1900/1000 CFP for a lift to and from the airport/wharf. It has a restaurant that serves good food, charging 2000 CFP for a standard meal. Credit card is accepted.

We's upmarket abode is *Drehu Village* (☎ 45 02 70, fax 45 02 71, drehuvil@ canl.nc). Along the beachfront, it has all the trimmings of a relaxing tropical retreat, including a swimming pool. The hotel's design and decor are identical to that of Nengone Village at Cengeite on Maré, except here the bungalows are built in pairs, making them a little less private. Guest facilities are also the same, as are accommodation prices (for more information see Places to

Stay & Eat under Maré, earlier). It has a restaurant that serves various dishes costing between 1400 CFP and 2200 CFP. Bougna is 1800 CFP and breakfast amounts to a hefty 1200 CFP. Transfers to the airport cost 1500 CFP. Credit cards are accepted.

The *Motel Le Grand Banian (☎ 45 05 50, ☎/fax 45 04 71)* is up on a plateau (about 1km from the main road; it is sign-posted) north of We and has a wonderful view over Baie de Châteaubriand. There are three adjoining studios, each with kitchenette, that cost 6500 CFP per night for one person and 500 CFP for each extra. Return transfers to the airport/wharf are 1900/1400 CFP. It has a small restaurant overlooking the bay, where you can get a standard meal for 1600 CFP. Credit cards are accepted.

All of the above restaurants are open to nonguests but you would be wise to book. *Snack Madinina*, close to the Protestant church on the main road, is a pleasant, waterfront eatery with an open-air *fare*. It serves fried fish or coconut milk chicken for 950 CFP and sandwiches for 400 CFP. It's open everyday except Sunday for lunch and dinner.

Snack Wenehua, across the road from the provincial headquarters, has lunch-time menu du jour for 1000 CFP, or there's a main dish for 850 CFP. It is open weekdays.

For self-caterers, the *Impac* supermarket and the *Lifou Center* are the best options.

North of the Island *Gîte Le Servigny (☎ 45 12 44, fax 45 00 28)* is close to the turn-off to the airport and is in the community of Kumo. This place offers two clean studio rooms (5000 CFP for two people) overlooking Lifou's biggest swimming pool, and three bungalows with air-con for 6500 CFP. There is also one traditional *case* (2000 CFP per person and 1000 CFP each extra person) that is in good condition and has a clean, tiled floor and raised beds and a TV. The owners serve local dishes and the food has a good reputation. Transfers to the airport are free, but cost 1000 CFP to We's wharf. For clients only, the gîte offers car rental for 6500 CFP per day.

In Jokin, *Fare Falaise (☎ 45 02 01)* ha a *case* in the centre of the compact ground and two bungalows, perched on the ver edge of the cliff. The view of the sea is fan tastic. The bungalows have private facilitie and cost 5500 CFP (up to three). There is a third at 4000 CFP, but it's set back an shares a communal toilet and shower block Inside, it's acceptable. You can pitch you tent for 1500 CFP a night. In the *case*, i costs 1500 CFP per person. Airport/whar transfers cost 1600/2000 CFP both ways Lunch or dinner starts at 1000 CFP. Credi card is accepted.

In Easo, you'll find *Chez Benoît Bonue (☎ 45 01 43)*. Though basic, this place ha a scenic location overlooking Baie de San tal. Campers pay 1000 CFP per night. A rudimentary bungalow costs 1500 CFP fo up to three persons. There is an amenitie block. A bougna serving is 1000 CFP and a simple meal is 600 CFP.

There is an eatery in Easo called *Chez Simone (☎ 45 02 17)*, which is about 150m on the right after the cement cross on the road to Xepenehe.

South of the Island In Traput, you'll find homestay accommodation at *Chez Marce & Suzanne (☎ 45 15 69)*. It has one *case* set aside for visitors and a separate amenities block (cold showers). Marcel is welcoming and it's a nice place to stay if you don't need creature comforts. In the *case* you'll pay 3000 CFP per person including all meals. Camping costs 500 CFP per person. A sim-ple meal amounts to 700 CFP. Return trans-fers to the airport or the wharf at Xepenehe cost 2000 CFP, and 1000 CFP to the wharf at We.

In Baie de Luengoni, the first place you'll come to as you're heading south is *Chez Noël Pia (☎ 45 03 09)*. Situated on the edge of the raised coral, this humble but welcom-ing homestay offers one *case* for 1500 CFP per person. Alternatively you can pitch your tent for 1000 CFP and 50 CFP for each per-son. Meals can be ordered but Noël prefers guests to cook their own food in a *fare* equipped with cooking facilities. Breakfast is 500 CFP. Noël arranges reputable norkelling excursions to the nearby reefs or 1000 CFP per person and takes guided walks to inland caves for 1000 to 1500 CFP er person.

Just 500m down the road, but set back rom the beach, is the basic but acceptable *Chez Jeanne Forrest* (☎ 45 16 56). Jeanne as one traditional *case* with a mattress, vhich she rents out for 1500 CFP per peron. A more comfortable bungalow-style *ase* with a bed costs 2000 CFP. Camping vill set you back 1000/1500 CFP for ne/two persons. Simple meals start at 1000 CFP and breakfast is 350 CFP. Bougna osts 1500 CFP.

Gîte Neibash (☎ 45 15 68) has perhaps he most idyllic beach setting of any gîte on Lifou. The road to Gîte Neibash leads off to he left, if you're coming from We, at Lungoni's church – look for the sign nailed to a tree. The gîte comprises a cluster of three quare bungalows and two round and basic *paillottes* (straw huts). The bungalows are nodern and comfortable, with shower, and ost 6000/6500/7500 CFP for a single/ double/triple. The paillottes cost 3500 CFP or each and 1000 CFP for each extra peron. There is also a traditional *case* that osts 2500 CFP per person. Beachfront camping is 1500 CFP per tent. Transport to nd from the airport/wharf costs 1800/1000 CFP. The gîte's restaurant serves a menu du our for 1800 CFP or a bougna for 2000 CFP per person. Credit card is accepted.

Mu's only accommodation is *Chez Waka Gaze* (☎/fax 45 15 14). It's on the main road next to the beach. The prices start at 1500 CFP per person in the *case* and goes up to 2500 CFP for a basic bungalow or a room in a house (1500 CFP for each extra person). Campers pay 1000 CFP per tent. Meals can be prepared and cost from 1200 to 2000 CFP. Transfers to and from the airport or the wharf cost 2000 CFP.

In Druelu, the *Gîte Kelemen Qassangy* (☎/fax 45 51 58) is close to the beach, behind the white cross. You'll pay 1000 CFP to sleep in the *case* and 500 CFP to pitch your tent (plus 50 CFP per person).

In the Wedrumel community, inland and south-east of Druelu, the gîte *Hnaxulu –*

Chez Loulou Qaeze (☎ 45 19 19) is on the main road. It offers two *cases* and two basic bungalows, with a toilet and shower block. The price to stay here is 1500 CFP per person in a *case* or 3500 CFP (up to three persons) in a bungalow. The gîte's humble restaurant serves meals for 1500 CFP and breakfast is 500 CFP. Airport/wharf transfers cost 1800/1200 CFP return.

You'll find groceries with limited supplies in each village.

Getting There & Away

Lifou's Wanaham airport terminal is 20km north of We, close to the village of Hnathalo. Aircalin has a desk at the airport as well as a modern main office (☎ 45 11 11) on the main road in We. Both offices are open weekdays from 7.30 to 11.15 am and 1.30 to 5 pm, and Saturday from 7.15 to 10 am.

At least three direct flights each day connect Lifou and Noumea's Magenta airport. The trip takes 35 minutes and costs 8410 CFP one way. Irregular inter-island flights go from Lifou to Ouvéa (3690 CFP, 20 minutes), Tiga (3640 CFP, 15 minutes) or Maré (5650 CFP, 25 minutes).

See the Getting Around section earlier in this chapter for details about the passenger ferry that operates between Noumea and the Loyalty Islands.

Getting Around

The airport is 2.5km from the intersection of the Xepenehe-We road. To get to it, there is one public bus on the island but it only connects with the first incoming flight of the day. The bus leaves Xodre at 5 am and travels via We to the airport. It then returns to Xodre.

The passenger ferry docks at We and Xepenehe. Most accommodation places will provide transfers to and from the wharves and the airport, but you'll need to book this when you reserve your accommodation.

There's only one bus reserved for the public. It travels from Xodre to We twice a day – once via the coastal road and once along the inland route – leaving Xodre at 6.35 am and again at 12.30 pm. From We it departs at 10 am and 4 pm. The fare is 200 CFP.

Cars can be hired from several private operators on the island, including Avenod (☎ 45 11 42), Akwaba (☎/fax 45 03 20) and Avis (☎/fax 45 13 15). Prices range from 6500 to 8000 CFP per day.

In We, Motel Chez Rachelle rents bikes for 1000 CFP per day.

Island tours are organised by Someltrans (☎ 45 14 78) and most of the accommodation places. Half-day tours, which usually cover either the south or north, or a bit of both, cost 2000 CFP per person.

OUVÉA ATOLL
- **pop 4000**　　　　● **area 160 sq km**

A 35km-long coral atoll, Ouvéa comprises two large masses of limestone joined by a thin, natural causeway only 400m wide at its narrowest point. On one side of this sliver of land is a 14km-long strip of unbroken white beach lapped by the aqua-coloured waters of an enormous lagoon. On the other side, a fringing reef and coral cliffs break the Pacific's mighty swell.

Seventeen clans live on Ouvéa. Many of the inhabitants are of Polynesian origin – the island's name comes from Uvea, the original name of Polynesian Wallis Island, and the Wallisian language Faga Uvea is spoken at both ends of the island.

Fayaoué, the island's capital, is little more than a very long village. There a BCI bank on Ouvéa, but it is open Tuesday to Thursday only.

The Pléiades Islands are a chain of 21 tiny, uninhabited coral islets surrounding Ouvéa to the west like a necklace. The unspoilt Beautemps-Beaupré Atoll is 15km north of the Passe d'Anemata.

Things to See
North of the Island Stretching 3km along the lagoon, Ouvéa's largest village, **Fayaoué**, offers essential services, food, accommodation and a seemingly never-ending beach. Take a look at the Protestant church and its larger, twin-towered Catholic neighbour. Next up is the post office, where there's a public telephone. The clinic is on the road to the airport.

About 5km east of Fayaoué, **Cong Hulup**

JEAN-BERNARD CARILLET

Catholic church in Fayaoué, Ouvéa

(in French, Cong-Ouloup) is a cave directly aligned with the airstrip and is set in a high cliff wall that obstructs the ocean view. To go to the cave you need to ask permission from No-No, the owner of the area, who lives in the house by the football field, just east of the airport. He will guide you in return for some gift or a 1000 CFP fee.

Hwaadrila Hwaadrila (Wadrilla in French) is the first real village north of Fayaoué. I has the unfortunate distinction of being the site where Jean-Marie Tjibaou and Yeiwene Yeiwene were killed, as well as having the memorial for the 19 Kanaks who died during the hostage crisis.

The long thin neck of land joining Ouvéa's two land masses starts just after Hwaadrila and continues for 15km, almost to St Joseph. Its western coastline is fringed by small pockets of sand broken by large tracts of rock.

About 9km north of Hwaadrila is a large round hole with the most amazing royal blue water, the **Trou d'Hahawa**. To find it take the dirt track off to the left when the road curves abruptly to the right (ask permission from the people living in the house

OUVÉA

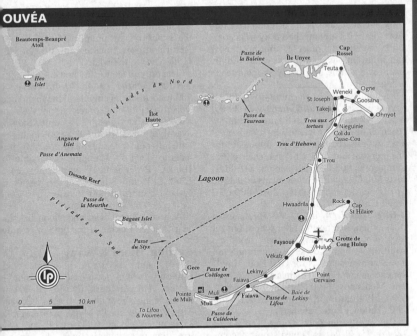

Beautemps-Beaupré Atoll

Heo Islet

Passe de la Baleine

Île Unyee

Cap Rossel

Teuta

Pléiades du Nord

Weneki

St Joseph

Ogne

Goosana

Takeji

Ohnyot

Îlot Haute

Passe du Taureau

Trou aux tortues

Nieguinie
Col du Casse-Cou

Anguene Islet

Passe d'Anemata

Trou d'Hahawa

Trou

Douade Reef

Lagoon

Passe de la Meurthe

Pléiades du Sud

Bagaat Islet

Hwaadrila

Rock

Cap St Hilaire

Passe du Styx

Fayaoué

Hulup

Grotte de Cong Hulup

Vékatr

(46m)▲

Gece

Passe de Coëtlogon

Lekiny

Point Gervaise

Faiava

Pointe de Muli

Muli

Faiava

Passe de Lifou

Baie de Lekiny

Passe de la Calédonie

To Lifou & Noumea

0   5   10 km

---

lose by). Follow this track for 100m to a clearing, from here an overgrown footpath to the right leads through the bush to the hole.

St Joseph St Joseph is Ouvéa's northern hub. Several tribes live in the vicinity and their language is of Wallisian origin. As you enter, there's a *chefferie* (traditional house of the chief) surrounded by a wooden palisade. One kilometre on is the Catholic mission church, founded in 1857.

From St Joseph, the road veers east, through the tribal settlement of Weneki, to Ouvéa's northernmost clan, the Teuta (Teputa), 5km north of Weneki. To the east, the main road continues through neighbouring Goosana to Ohnyot (also written Ognat), 7km from Weneki.

South of the Island About 9km south of Fayaoué along the coastal road is **Baie de Lekiny** (also spelt Lékine), where a 100m-wide channel separates Ouvéa's main island from the nearby tiny island of **Faiava** (also called Fayawa) and the southern island of Muli. From the bridge, the view around here is almost surreal, with the white sand contrasting sharply against the different shades of brilliant blue water. The bay is protected by coral cliffs, formed long ago when the atoll was pushed up.

Ouvéa's southernmost village, **Muli** (also Mouli or, in French, Mouly), is 6km south-west of the Lekiny bridge, along a road with little sign of life. The village is made up of huts scattered amid a coconut grove. Just north of Muli is a coconut fibre cooperative where strong hand-spun rope is made. Visitors are welcome.

After Muli, the beach gives way to coral rocks, while a road meanders along the peninsula's last 3km to **Pointe de Muli**. Here two rocky outcrops are separated by a small beach. Snorkelling here is excellent, but be aware if the strong currents.

Places to Stay & Eat

Only Fayaoué and Muli offer tourist services. Eateries are attached only to accommodation and you must let your host know half a day in advance if you want to dine. There is a couple of grocery shops in each village.

In Ouassadieu community, north of Fayaoué, *Gîte Bougainvillier* (☎ 45 72 20) is set back several hundred metres from the beach. It has three Melanesian-style bungalows with shared facilities for 3000 CFP for one person and 500 CFP for each extra. Camping is 800 CFP per person. Breakfast costs 500 CFP, while other meals cost 1300 CFP. Return airport transfer costs 800 CFP (1600 CFP to the wharf).

Gîte Ireital (☎/fax 45 70 56), also in Ouassadieu, just north of the school but set back about 100m from the road, has three traditional bungalows. Accommodation prices are the same as for Gîte Bougainvillier except camping, which is 1000 CFP per tent. Meals cost 1100 CFP and breakfast is 400 CFP. Return airport transfer costs 800 CFP (1600 CFP to the wharf).

The family-run *Gîte Beaupré* (☎ 45 71 32, fax 45 70 94) is Ouvéa's best accommodation, north of the village. The place is relatively modern and has three wooden bungalows with a shower for 6050 CFP for one or two people. Basic studio rooms cost 4000/4500 CFP for one/two people. Bikes are available for 1500 CFP per day. Gîte Beaupré prepares a simple but generous meal for 1980 CFP. Return airport transfer costs 1000 CFP (1600 CFP to the wharf). Credit card is accepted.

Gîte Iris (☎ 45 71 95) is inland, close to the medical centre. There is one decent but small fare with private bath for 5000 CFP for two people but the place has nothing appealing and it is well away from the beach. The owners have a basic *snack* close by where simple meals are served for 1200 CFP. Sandwiches cost about 500 CFP.

Camping de Lekine (☎ 45 71 62, 45 73 16) boasts a wonderful location, right in front of Baie de Lekiny. You can pitch your tent for 1000 CFP or rent one for 1500 CFP.

Add 200 CFP if you want to use the cooking facilities. Simple meals can be served in the *snack* on the premises for 1000 CFP. Return airport transfer costs 1200 CFP (1500 CFP to the wharf).

The only place to stay and eat in Muli is the *Le Cocotier* (☎ 45 70 40), which is 500m north of the church on the main road. This tribal gîte-cum-*snack* has one *case* and a *fare* that can sleep 10 people. Staying overnight costs 4000/5000 CFP including half/full pension, but there are only thin mats to sleep on. Camping is possible for 1000 CFP per tent. A simple meal costs 1500 CFP and 3000 CFP for lobster or bougna. Return airport transfers cost 2000 CFP (2500 CFP to the wharf).

A luxury hotel was under construction near Baie de Lekine at the time of writing.

Getting There & Away

Ouvéa's small airport at Hulup (also spelt Houloup) is 5km north-east of Fayaoué. It has an Aircalin desk (☎ 45 70 22) in Hwaadrila. Direct daily flights between Ouvéa and Noumea's Magenta airport take 35 minutes and cost 8410 CFP one way. Irregular inter-island flights do connect Ouvéa with Lifou (3690 CFP; 20 minutes), Tiga (6410 CFP; 1 hour 20 minutes) and Maré (8270 CFP; 1½ hours).

Ouvéa's wharf is at the centre of the island and 6km north of Hwaadrila. For more information about the passenger ferry that services the Loyalty Islands from Noumea, see the Getting Around section earlier in this chapter.

Getting Around

A blue bus is supposed to meet incoming flights and then head to Fayaoué (50 CFP). You can also try to hitch a ride into Fayaoué. All gîtes will pick you up and take you back to the airport or the wharf at Wadrila if you're arriving on the passenger ferry, but you should arrange this when you reserve your room. The one-way price is usually about 800 CFP.

The island's one bus does a run from St Joseph to Muli and back once a day (not on Sunday) in the morning. It leaves St Joseph

5.15 am, picking up passengers en route,
d departs from Muli at 7 am. From
yaoué to St Joseph it's 200 CFP, while it's
20 CFP to Muli.

Gîte Ireital and Gîte Cocotier rent cars.
ou can also contact Aben Julien (☎ 45 72
), M. Henere (☎/fax 45 70 56) or Kaouma
runo (☎ 45 72 65). The cars are about
00 CFP per day.

Gîte Beaupré hires bikes for 1500 CFP a
y. At Gîte Ireital, Camping de Lekine and
Cocotier, the rental price is 1000 CFP.

With a minimum of eight people, Gîte
eaupré will conduct an island tour for
00 CFP per person, including a lunch at
e gîte. Island tours and boat tours can also
arranged with Le Cocotier for 2500/3500
FP per person.

le des Pins

pop 1670   • area 152 sq km

his beautiful island boasts sublime
aches and bays. It was given its contem-
orary name by English explorer Captain
ook, inspired by the araucaria trees that
ne the island's shore. To its indigenous in-
abitants it is known as Kwênyii or Kuni
ronounced 'koo-nee-yeh').

Fifty kilometres south-east of Grande
erre, Île des Pins extends 17km from north
south and is 14km wide. The island is
ore or less circular in shape, with a low
bleland sweeping around the 60km
astal perimeter. Île des Pins' south-west
gion is dominated by Pic N'Ga (262m),
e island's highest peak.

The eight main clans living on the island
ave been able to maintain a traditional
ay of life. In early times, the Kunies were
e only people in New Caledonia who
avelled by sea and could navigate by the
ars. They sailed on pirogues, great double
trigger canoes that carried more than 40
ople.

Administratively, Île des Pins is part of
ew Caledonia's South Province, gov-
ned from Noumea. The island's chief is
cally elected as the mayor. The small is-
nd's economy is based on the export of
(diminishing) edible forest snails, sandalwood, some fruit and tourism.

History

The island's original settlers were the Kunies, people of Austro-Melanesian stock
who lived peacefully on the island until the
early 17th century, when they were conquered by a warring tribe from Lifou.

In 1774, James Cook sighted and named
the Île des Pins. In the first half of the
1800s, traders rushed from Sydney to harvest the island's sandalwood.

The traders were soon followed by missionaries from the London Missionary Society who, in 1841, attempted to establish
themselves on the island's northern tip, but
weren't successful. The French managed to
annex the island on 29 September 1853. By
this time the Kunies' Catholic conversion
was well underway due to the influence of
French Marist missionaries.

Following the death of the Kunie leader
Vendegou in 1855, tribal wars erupted. This
was due in part to the succession of his
daughter, Queen Hortense.

In 1872, Île des Pins became a convict
settlement for Communards, political prisoners from the Paris Commune uprising in
France. Also incarcerated were 750
Kanaks who had staged the great 1878 uprising against colonial settlers in the La
Foa area. Not until 1911 was the Île des
Pins prison finally closed. The colonial
administration then handed the island back
to the Kunies.

Information

Pick up brochures from the Office du
Tourisme de Noumea et de la Province Sud
(for details see Information in the Noumea
section earlier in this chapter).

Île des Pins' only post office is in Vao. It
also has one of the island's few public telephones. Another is at the airport. There is
one bank on the island (in Vao), but some of
the gîtes accept credit cards.

Topless and nude bathing is not permitted
on any beach or islet of Île des Pins. Wearing a swimsuit on the roads or in the township of Vao itself is also not tolerated.

ÎLE DES PINS

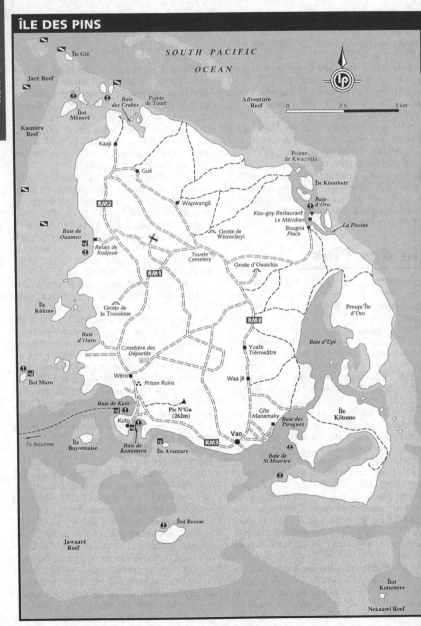

SOUTH PACIFIC
OCEAN

Île Gié

Jaré Reef

Adventure
Reef

0   2.5   5 km

Kasmira
Reef

Îlot Ménorë

Baie
des Crabes

Pointe
de Tuurè

Pointe
de Kwacivita

Kaaji

Île Kônubutr

Gué

Baie
d'Oro

Wapwangä

Kou-gny Restaurant
Le Méridien

La Piscine

RM2

Grotte de
Wêmwânyi

Bougna
Place

Baie de
Ouameo

Relais de
Kodjeue

Touete
Cemetery

Grotte d'Ouatchia

RM1

Île
Kûûmo

Grotte de
la Troisième

Presqu'Île
d'Oro

Baie d'Upi

Baie
d'Ouro

Cimetière des
Déportés

Yuate
Trémwâtre

Île
Kôtomo

Îlot Moro

Wèro

Prison Ruins

Waa jë

Baie de Kuto

Pic N'Ga
(262m)

Gîte
Manamaky

Baie des
Pirogues

To Noumea

Kuto

Île
Bayonnaise

Baie de
Kanumera

Île Aventure

RM3

Vao

Baie de
St Maurice

Îlot Brosse

Jawaaré
Reef

Îlot
Kotumere

Nekaawi Reef

etting There & Away

here are at least three flights per day to Île
s Pins (6250 CFP, 20 minutes) from Manta airport in Noumea, and considerably
ore on weekends. Flights can still be fully
oked by day-trippers so you'd be wise to
ake a reservation. Île des Pins' airport is
km north of Kuto.

Aircalin has an office at Kuto (☎ 46 11
) or the airport (☎ 46 12 46). The Kuto
fice is open weekdays from 7.30 to 11 am
d 2 to 5 pm, and Saturday until 11 am.

For information about the passenger ferry
at connects Île des Pins and Noumea, see
etting Around earlier in this chapter.

etting Around

here is no public transport on Île des Pins.
he gîtes provide airport transfers if you
ve booked accommodation (1200 to 1600
FP both ways).

The island's 60km of asphalt can be ex-
ored by car. Cars can be rented from Re-
is de Kodjeue, Gîte Nataiwatch and Hôtel
ou-Bugny. You'll be looking at 5500/8000
FP for a half day/full day.

Bikes can be rented from Gîte Natai-
atch, Hôtel Kou-Bugny and Gîte Mana-
aky for 1500 CFP a day.

All the gîtes have minivans in order to
n tours. They cover the island's most im-
ortant sights in a space of two or three
urs. On average they charge from 1300 to
500 CFP per person – ask at your gîte
ception for details.

Tours on one of Île des Pins' famous out-
gger canoes can be arranged through your
otel or gîte. The most popular is the trip to
e stunning translucent waters of Baie
'Upi on the east coast, followed by a short
alk across the narrow neck of the
resqu'Île d'Oro and a bougna lunch. All
e gîtes charge 2500 CFP per person for
is trip; the bougna or lunch at the restau-
nt is an extra 2000 to 2500 CFP.

AO

ao is located on the island's southernmost
p and is the only real village on Île des
ins. It is home to the *chef* and has most of
e administrative facilities.

JEAN-BERNARD CARILLET

Woodcarving in Vao

The BCI (☎ 46 10 48) in Vao, 100m from
the church, changes travellers cheques and
will do cash advances for major credit
cards. It's open weekdays from 7.30 am to
noon and 1.30 to 4 pm.

Vao's **Mission Church**, in the village centre, was built in 1860. It was established by
the Marist priest Father Goujon, who managed to convert the entire island in just over
30 years from his arrival in 1848. About
500m from Vao church, the **Baie de St Maurice** was the site of the first Catholic service
held on Île des Pins. As a tribute, the locals
have encircled a statue of St Maurice, who
stands high upon a coral platform, with tree
trunks carved as totems.

Baie des Pirogues, also referred to as
Baie de St Joseph, is a lovely bay often dotted with outrigger canoes, about 2km north-
east of Kuto, near Gîte Manamaky.

Places to Stay & Eat

Overlooking Baie des Pirogues, about
1.5km from Vao's church (follow the main

northbound road until you see the sign-post), *Gîte Manamaky* (*☎/fax 46 11 11*) is the only place where you can eat and sleep in the vicinity of Vao. It has four comfort-able and beautiful bungalows, which cost 5500/6500 CFP for two/three people. All the rooms have private facilities, a fridge and TV. Two other units, with shared bath, will set you back 4000/5000 CFP for two/three people.

The gîte has a restaurant. A simple menu du jour (most of the time this means fish) costs 1800 CFP and breakfast is 600 CFP.

KUTO AREA

Six kilometres west from Vao, this lovely area of white sand, coral and araucaria pines is Île des Pins' tourist hot spot. Here you'll find the bulk of gîtes, restaurants and stun-ning beaches. But even with all this, the area remains quiet. There's excellent swim-ming at **Baie de Kuto** and good snorkelling around **Baie de Kanumera**; be warned that the striking coral outcrop just off the Kanu-mera beach is strictly off limits.

The **ruins of the prison** that held some of the deportees are just opposite the Wèro bakery, about 1.5km north of Kuto beach, towards the airstrip. The main building comprises two enormous cells with thick stone walls. To the rear stand the ruins of individual cells that were home to mentally unstable deportees.

The **Cimetière des Déportés** is about 700m north from the Wèro bakery, 600m off the main road on the right (it is signposted). It contains the remains of some 240 depor-tees from the Paris Commune who died in exile on the island between 1871 and 1880. Twelve rows of graves line the ground, sim-ply marked by rectangles of stones.

You can also climb **Pic N'Ga**. It is a 45 minute (steady) hike to the top of this 262m-high peak, and the vista from the top is superb. The path to the summit begins near Gîte Kuberka, about 100m south of a house with four pine trees in front of it.

Places to Stay

Camping Camping is at its most sublime at *Gîte Oure* and *Gîte Nataiwatch*. You can pitch your tent in front of the white sa beach. The nightly rate is 750 CFP per p son at Gîte Oure. It is 1000/1400 CFP one/two people at *Gîte Nataiwatch*. The are shower and toilet facilities. *Relais Kuberka* also accepts campers and as 800/1000 CFP for one/two people.

Gîtes The cheapest place to stay on Île Pins is *Gîte Oure* (*☎ 46 11 20*), sometim called Chez Christine. It is ideally situal on the waterfront at the eastern end of Ba de Kanumera. Its four square bungalows, with shower and toilet, can each accomm date three people and cost 3000/3700/45 CFP for one/two/three persons.

In a property adjacent to the previc one, *Gîte Nataiwatch* (*☎ 46 11 13, fax 46 29*) is an excellent address. It is about 15(from the water, set under coconut trees a tall ferns, towards the eastern end of Baie Kanumera. It has well built bungalows, sp in half to accommodate two lots of visito All have private shower and toilet, and c(5100/5700 CFP for one/two people. The are also four old bungalows, called 'tra tionals', which cost slightly less but do have private facilities (the campers' ame ties close by are excellent). They ha cooking facilities.

Relais Le Kuberka (*☎ 46 11 18, fax 11 58*), on the main road through Ku has a row of eight modern rooms (behi the restaurant), all with immaculate p vate toilet/shower facilities and fridge It's set back about 350m from Kuto beac Rooms cost 4800/5800 CFP for one/tw people.

The *Hôtel Kou-Bugny* (*☎ 24 92 80, f 24 92 81, resbugny@canl.nc*), across t road from the beach, is the Kuto area's t place to stay. Its forest-like setting is s perb. The hotel's architecture is appealin with *buni*, *houp* and *kohu* trunks used pillars for the buildings. It has a sma swimming pool and offers bungalows 16,500 CFP (up to five people) or bung lows, each with a mezzanine, for 19,5(CFP.

All these places to stay can arrange isla tours.

aces to Eat

l Kuto's restaurants are attached to gîtes hotels and all accept nonguests. Through-t Île des Pins, it is a good idea to place or-rs at gîtes a few hours in advance to allow e staff time to plan the meal.

Wèro Bakery is about 800m north of the rcalin agency and acts as Kuto's general ore. It's open Monday to Saturday from 30 to 10.30 am and 4 to 6 pm. There's no eshly-baked bread on Thursday.

On the north side of Kuto is *Snack dey*, a small but busy snack-cum-shop, nich is open daily from 7 am to 6 pm. It s cold beers (250 CFP), sandwiches (300 FP) and simple meals (950 to 1050 CFP), d also does takeaway fare.

The friendly, relaxed restaurant at *Gîte ure* has sandwiches (500 CFP) all day or ou can order a three course chicken (1500 FP) or lobster meal (3000 CFP) at lunch dinner. Its bougna are made with either sh or chicken (2000 CFP per person). eakfast is 500 CFP.

Neighbouring *Gîte Nataiwatch* has a ore formal-style restaurant but with a sim-ar menu. A basic three course lunch or din-r costs 1800 CFP. It also serves the and's forest snails for 3000 CFP. A dine-bougna made with chicken or fish costs 00 CFP. Breakfast is 800 CFP. This staurant is closed on Sunday.

Gîte Kuberka specialises in seafood and rves a seafood plate for 4000 CFP. There e also four menus, costing from 1500 to 00 CFP, and a la carte dishes starting at 0 CFP.

Hôtel Kou-Bugny has an all-you-can-eat 00 CFP lunch buffet, as well as a lobster snail menu for 3500 CFP. In addition, ere are a la carte dishes.

opping

nong the few people who speak English on e island are Albert and Cleo (Hilary Roots), e owners of the boutique/workshop Créa-ns Île des Pins (☎ 46 12 68), located be-de the gendarmerie. Here they sew and nd-paint T-shirts and *pareos* (brightly-corated sarongs), as well as sell postcards d copies of Cleo's books.

Preparing a Bougna

Of all the Melanesian dishes you try dur-ing your travels in New Caledonia, the *bougna* will stick in your mind for months after you return home. Meant for times of sharing – such as during tribal festivals, weddings or after Sunday mass – the bougna combines all the traditional fare of Melanesia into one meal. It's a combina-tion of delicious chunks of yam, taro, sweet potato and banana, with pieces of chicken, crab, lobster or other meat. All this is mixed in coconut cream then wrapped in banana leaves, tied tightly with palm fronds and baked or steamed on hot coals, or in an earth oven, for about two hours.

Most Melanesian-run *gîtes* or homes-tays on Île des Pins, the Loyalty Islands or Grande Terre can prepare a bougna but you have to give a day's notice. Ex-pect to pay from 1500 CFP to 3000 CFP per person. Lobster bougna is the most expensive.

GROTTE DE LA TROISIÈME

This freshwater cave has a name carried over from the penal era, when the local district was known as the Third *(la Troisième)* com-mune – you'll also see it written as Grotte de la 3ème. It's a cave, 8 to 10m deep, where highly experienced scuba divers can dive among stalactites and stalagmites.

The cave is hard to find as there are no signposts. Basically, it's about 6km north of Kuto, down a track to the left off the main dirt road towards Kaaji.

BAIE DE OUAMEO

Not quite as pristine as Kuto and Kanumera bays, this isolated bay is the departure point for divers going to Kaaji, which is a 20 minute boat ride to the north.

Diving

All diving on Île des Pins is arranged through the Kunie Scuba Centre (☎ 46 11 22), based at Relais de Kodjeue at Baie de

Ouameo. There is a rich variety of sites at Kaaji, especially Vallée des Gorgones. Divers will enjoy both the vision of soft and hard corals and a profusion of sea life, including eagle rays and leopard sharks.

Places to Stay & Eat

The only place to stay in the north is **Relais de Kodjeue** (☎ *46 11 42, fax 46 10 61*), which is on the calm waterfront of Baie de Ouameo. It has 27 bungalows, some of which have terraces built out over the beach. It has a TV and fridge, and some have cooking facilities. You'll pay from 6700 to 16,000 CFP for one or two people. Cheaper still are the six small studio rooms, each with bathroom, which cost 4800 CFP for one or two people.

The hotel has a swimming pool and a tennis court. You can hire snorkelling equipment for 1000 CFP a day. Car and bicycle rental is also possible, and airport transfers and island tours can be arranged.

The hotel also has a restaurant. A simple meal of salad, main course, bread and dessert costs 1800 CFP.

KAAJI

Kaaji (spelt Gadji in French), the northernmost community on the island, was formerly the capital of Kunie, where the *grands chef* (grand chiefs) had their power base. From here, Chef Vendegou waged war on the tribes of Grande Terre; the Kunies would cross the waters in their pirogues and feast on their prisoners back at Kaaji.

Here too the first sandalwood traders and evangelists made landfall in New Caledonia, the latter in 1841.

WAPWANGÂ CASE

About halfway between Kaaji and the airport is Wapwangâ Case, built by the community at Wapwangâ (also spelt Wapan) as an example of a traditional *grande case*, albeit a very low and squat one. Situated on the eastern dirt road from Kaaji, the craftwork on the building is very impressive.

GROTTE DE WÈMWÂNYI

Grotte de Wèmwânyi (also called Grotte d'Oumagne or Grotte de la Reine Hortense) is Île des Pins' most famous and frequen visited cave. It was here that Queen Ho ense supposedly hid for several months tween 1855 and 1856, during the tribal wa

Entered from a cool forest with tall t ferns, the cave contains a makeshift shr featuring a statue of the Virgin Mary drap in torn strips of cloth. The floor is flat a there is a high ceiling, with large mo covered stalactites. A little stream ru through the interior, disappearing, like few tiny bats, into the depths of the cave

The cave is east of the airport, or 2.5 south of Wapwangâ Case. Coming fr Vao, it's about 13km – you need to turn along a dirt road (to the right) just befo the main road swings steeply up and arou and continues on to the airport. Follow dirt road, which eventually leads to W wangâ and Kaaji, for about 300m until y see a sign for the grotte. It's another 50 from the sign. Admission costs 200 CFP

GROTTE D'OUATCHIA

Another cave worth exploring, though much less frequented by tourists, is Gro d'Ouatchia (also written as Waacia), wh is off the main Vao-airport road in the Te ete region. The trail to this cave beg about 1km south of the turn-off to B d'Oro, near a cross on top of a hill. I about a 40 minute walk and may not easy to reach without directions from the cals. The cave itself has a long, narrow p sage that goes underground past splen rock formations. Unless you have previ caving experience, it is better to have guide. Guides can be found around the h at the turn-off to Baie d'Oro.

BAIE D'ORO

This remote bay, halfway up the islan east coast, is the island's jewel. It is sh tered behind two islands, which create natural causeway. At high tide, the s rushes in and covers the sandy causew with knee-deep water. Hours later, it em ties, leaving just one pool of wat coloured the most exquisite turquo imaginable. Towering over all this proud araucarias.

Dependencies of New Caledonia

New Caledonia's four dependencies are scattered around the perimeter of the territorial waters, hundreds of kilometres from Grande Terre. They range from reefs with barely emerged coral cays and islets like the Chesterfield and Entrecasteaux groups, to larger outcrops such as Walpole and the volcanic Matthew and Hunter islands. All are uninhabited but have enormous ecological importance because of their rich variety of bird and marine life.

Some 600km west of the northern tip of Grande Terre in the Coral Sea, the **Chesterfield group** lumps together the Sable and Chesterfield island groups, Caie de l'Observatoire and the Bellona Reefs. The land surface totals just 1 sq km. These scraps of land are essential seabird rookeries and turtle nesting areas.

The **Récifs d'Entrecasteaux** are aligned with Îles Belep and Grande Terre's mountain axis. They sit about 220km to the north-west, separated by the Grand Passage, and are made up of a few atolls, which have a surface area of 65 hectares.

Walpole, 150km east of Île des Pins, is a raised coral island 3km long and 400m wide. It is exposed and inhospitable, without any beach or protecting reefs. It is a veritable 'Citadel of the Ocean', with its raised 70m-high limestone cliffs hiding numerous caves and shafts – popular nesting spots for various seabirds.

As for **Matthew** and **Hunter** islands, these two tiny volcanic islands have been the centre of a territory dispute between Vanuatu and New Caledonia (ie France) since 1929. They are closer to Vanuatu than to Grande Terre, but 1929 the French authorities included the islands in newly drawn maps of New Caledonia despite customary claims to the islands by Vanuatu's Anatom people. A plaque was erected by the French on Hunter in 1975, only to be removed by Vanuatu's government in 1980 and replaced by its flag. In turn, France pulled down the Vanuatu flag and raised the tricolour. It was then guarded by a French military contingent for seven years until the personnel were withdrawn.

What exactly is the fight all about? Basically, the islands are incidental, the dispute has much more to do with each country trying to increase its territorial waters. Hunter and Matthew islands are of little interest to New Caledonians, sitting 450km and 525km respectively east of the southern tip of Grande Terre.

The only people really interested in the islands are the Anatom islanders and the odd yachtie, en route to Fiji or Tonga, looking for a shelter for the night.

No tribe lives permanently at Baie d'Oro these days as there's no fresh water. In earlier times, the local Touete tribe survived here by carving hollows into the spine of coconut trees to collect rainwater. However, this led to plagues of mosquitoes so the practice was abandoned.

The only way to get to Baie d'Oro, other than on a tour, is to walk, cycle or drive along the white coral road, which starts opposite the Touete tribe's cemetery, about 9km north of Vao, on the main road to the airport. For more information about organised tours see Getting Around earlier in this chapter.

Place to Stay & Eat

Opened late 1998, the *Meridien* (☎ *26 50 00, fax 26 51 00*) is nested in a vast forest of araucarias. This top resort is rated five star and is certainly the most luxurious place to stay in New Caledonia together with its counterpart in Noumea. It boasts superb bungalows and luxury rooms. You'll pay 33,000 CFP for a deluxe room, 41,000 CFP for a garden bungalow and 46,000 CFP for a beach bungalow for up to two people. The restaurant has a menu du jour at 4500 CFP or a la carte dishes that cost anything from 400 CFP for a snack to 2800 CFP for

NEW CALEDONIA

a lobster bougna. All watersports and tours can be organised.

The modest *Restaurant Kou-gny (☎ 46 10 65 in Touete)* is situated right on the beachfront on the southern side of the two small islands. Meals here are typically made up of seafood combined with local fare, but you must book the day before.

Alternatively, you can organise for a bougna lunch to be prepared by the group women who cater for the day-tripper tra at *Chez Regis (☎ 46 10 32)*, but you mu give them a day's warning. It will cost y 2000/2500/3000 CFP per person for chicken/ fish/lobster bougna to be eaten the beach, or 3500/4000/5000 CFP for takeaway bougna – enough food for three four people.

Solomon Islands

...me of the islands of the Solomons are ...ge with densely forested mountain interi-...s and fast flowing rivers, while others are ...y, low-lying coral atolls that encircle stun-...ng lagoons. The archipelago is the South ...cific's third largest and is inhabited by a ...ried population of mostly Melanesian ...ople. Most live in small villages, clinging ...a subsistence lifestyle that has barely ...anged for centuries. Shark calling and ex-...anging *kastom* (custom) money can still be ...en, as can sacred skull shrines – macabre ...d fascinating reminders of the old days.

It's hard to believe the friendly, easy-...ing islanders were perhaps the world's ...ost violent and dangerous people until the ...30s. Killing, cannibalism and skull wor-...ip were central elements of traditional ...lture. These days the islanders are a lot ...ore relaxed.

The Solomons is a famous dive destina-...n, but snorkellers too can enjoy the ex-...ordinary fish life and colourful corals in ...e calm, tropical waters of the world's ...rgest lagoons. There are hundreds of ...nken war wrecks to explore and WWII ...bris is strewn across the islands. Fishing ...ns and surfers are coming in increasing ...mbers.

Little tourism infrastructure exists ...ound the country, and there are few ...staurants or high-class hotels. But if ...u've ever wanted to get away from it all ...d have a beach to yourself, ride motor-...noes and immerse yourself in warm trop-...al waters and friendly Melanesian culture, ...en you will love the Solomons.

Facts about the Solomon Islands

HISTORY

...bout 25 million years ago the first of the ...lcanic Solomon Islands rose from the ...ean depths.

AT A GLANCE

Capital City (& Island): Honiara (Guadalcanal)
Population: 400,000
Time: 11 hours ahead of GMT
Land Area: 27,540 sq km (10,740 sq miles)
Number of Islands: 992 (347 inhabited)
International Telephone Code: ☎ 677
GDP/Capita: US$610
Currency: Solomon Islands dollar (S$1 = US$0.20)
Languages: About 90 indigenous languages plus Pijin
Greeting: *Halo* (Pijin)

HIGHLIGHTS

- **Honiara** – spending a few days in bustling Honiara with its shops, restaurants and hotels

- **Guadalcanal** – wartime memorials and sites

- **Diving** – (and snorkelling) in waters that teem with fish, exquisite corals and WWII wreckage

- **Western Province** – magnificent aerial views of Roviana and Marovo lagoons (a proposed World Heritage Site)

- **Malaita** – the artificial islands of Langa Langa and Lau lagoons

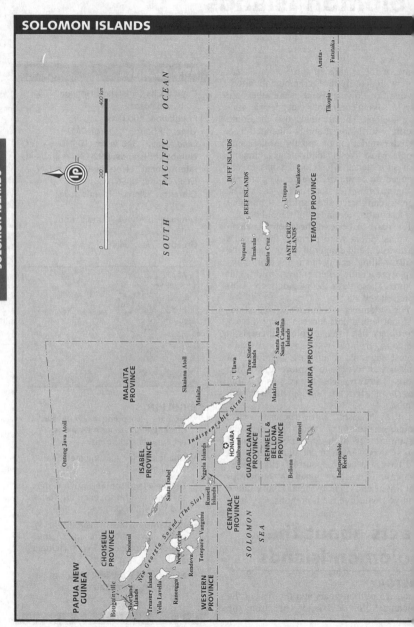

SOLOMON ISLANDS

By 25,000 BC, Papuan-speaking hunter-
therers from New Guinea were settling
southern and eastern Solomon Islands.
lese were the first people to settle the
cific, and the only people for many thou-
nds of years. Austronesian-speaking
oto-Melanesians began arriving in the
chipelago around 4000 BC. Lapita people
ee the boxed text in the 'South Pacific
ts' special section) appeared between
00 and 1600 BC.

Most people lived in small villages on
bal lands. They practised shifting cultiva-
n, fishing, hunting, carving, weaving and
noe building. Rule was by kastom as re-
lled by clan elders. Ancestors were wor-
ipped and blood feuds, head-hunting and
nnibalism were common.

Polynesian settlers from the east settled
e outer islands like Rennell and Bellona,
d Ontong Java between 1200 and 1600
D. The Polynesian settlements suffered
ids from Tonga between the 14th and 18th
nturies.

panish Exploration

on Alvaro de Mendaña y Neyra left Peru
th two ships in November 1567. On 7
bruary 1568, he saw and named Santa
abel, and settled there. On 11 August,
ter six months of conflict, the expedition
t sail for Peru.

Mendaña returned in 1595 with four
ips and 450 would-be colonists. He came
on and named Santa Cruz, and estab-
hed a settlement there. Mendaña died of
alaria. After two months, the settlement
as abandoned and the survivors limped
ck to Peru.

Mendaña's chief pilot from 1595 was the
rtuguese Pedro Fernandez de Quirós, who
ft Peru with three small ships on 21 Dec-
aber 1605 and reached the Duff Islands
rly in 1606 (see the boxed text 'Pedro Fer-
ndez de Quirós' in the Vanuatu chapter).

rther Exploration & Early
ading

ere was almost no further contact until
e late 18th century. Captain Philip
rtaret, a Briton, came upon Santa Cruz in

1767 and then Malaita. British, French and
American explorers followed.

Whalers started arriving in 1798. Sandalwood traders followed between the 1840s
and late 1860s, buying pigs, turtle shell,
pearl shell and beche-de-mer. The sandalwood traders were cruel to the islanders, and
brought European diseases that caused them
to die in their thousands. Resentment towards European treachery and diseases led
to the murder of a number of missionaries.

The Solomons was the most dangerous
place in the Pacific, and foreigners were
routinely killed. Although they were very
active elsewhere in the Pacific, churches
moved cautiously in the Solomons.

In the 1860s, sailors traded iron and steel
tools, calico, tobacco, beads, fish-hooks and
guns. Firearms produced an explosive
growth in head-hunting and slave raids.

Blackbirders (slavers – see History in the
Facts about the South Pacific chapter) took
over 29,000 Solomon Islanders to work on
sugar cane plantations in Australia and Fiji.

The Protectorate

In the 1890s, about 50 British traders and
missionaries were in the Solomons, and
Germany was active in New Guinea, the
Shortlands, Choiseul, Santa Isabel and
Ontong Java. On 6 October 1893, Britain
proclaimed a protectorate over the archi-
pelago's southern islands, which was ex-
tended in 1897 and again in 1898. In 1899,
Britain relinquished claims to Western
Samoa, and Germany ceded the Shortlands,
Choiseul, Ontong Java and Santa Isabel to
Britain.

Charles Morris Woodford became the
first resident commissioner in 1896. Missionaries sought to eradicate local culture
declaring customs and ceremonies to be
evil. Sorcery and head-hunting diminished,
but people died in huge numbers from
European diseases.

The Kwaio Rebellion on Malaita in
1927 was a rejection of European values
(see the boxed text 'Kwaio Rebellion'). In
1928 several Kwaio rebels were hanged in
the then capital, Tulagi. Basiana, the defi-
ant rebel leader, declared before his death,

'Tulagi will be torn apart, and scattered to the winds', and 14 years later it was.

WWII

In April 1942, the Japanese seized the Shortland Islands. Three weeks later Tulagi was taken and the Japanese began building an airstrip on Guadalcanal.

US troops began landing on Guadalcanal in August 1942. In the early hours of 9 August, while landings were in progress, a Japanese naval force left Rabaul in New Guinea to attack the US transports at Red Beach before they unloaded. This, the Battle of Savo, was one of the US navy's heaviest defeats – 1270 Allied sailors were lost.

The US forces gradually gained the upper hand, but at a tremendous cost of life on both sides. After six months the Japanese withdrew to New Georgia. During the Guadalcanal campaign, six naval battles were fought and 67 warships and transports

sunk. Over 7000 Americans were killed a nearly 40,000 Japanese soldiers were lo on land and at sea.

As 1943 progressed, more islands we recovered by the Allies and by the year's e only Choiseul and the Shortlands remain in Japanese hands. The Allies recover them after the Japanese surrender in 1945

Thousands of islanders, mainly Mala tans, went to Guadalcanal to work at t huge US supply base at Honiara. T Americans (some black skinned) treated t islanders as equals, as their colonial maste had not. This, and the mass-materialism a profligacy of the US war effort, gave rise cargo-cultism.

Postwar Recovery

Tulagi had been gutted during the war, a the Quonset-hut township of Honiara x placed it as the capital. The economy was ruins.

A nationalist movement sprang up Malaita. Called Marching Rule, it was self-reliant movement opposed to any c operation with the British authorities, w had been restored after WWII. Its membe were regimented into coastal villag dependent on community-based agricultu The Marching Rule was also cargo-culti believing that US goods would be deliver to islanders by those US forces remaini behind in the Solomons after WWII. Ma arrests of followers by the British autho ties in 1947 and 1948 caused the moveme to wane, and it died out after the last of t US forces left in 1950. Britain began to s the need for local government, and region assemblies were introduced.

There was an elected governing coun in 1970. The British Solomon Islands Pr tectorate was renamed the Solomon Islan five years later and independence w granted on 7 July 1978.

Independence

Bougainville's attempts to secede fro Papua New Guinea (PNG) have strain relations between the Solomons and larger neighbour. The Bougainville Revo tionary Army (BRA) became active

The Kwaio Rebellion

On 4 October 1927, District Officer William Bell was in Kwaio territory (Malaita) to collect tax and confiscate rifles. With him were 14 Malaitan constables. A Kwaio called Basiana killed Bell, and in the ensuing melee all but one of the constables were killed.

The reaction in Tulagi, the capital, was immediate – and rather excessive. European volunteers boarded the Australian cruiser HMAS *Adelaide*, which sailed from Sydney. The cruiser shelled all the villages it could find and Kwaio gardens were poisoned. Consecrated ritual objects, ancestral relics, slit drums and sacrificial stones were defiled or destroyed. The Kwaio claim 1246 people were killed and that 59 villages, 538 shrines and 1066 gardens were destroyed.

Six Kwaio were hanged at Tulagi (including Basiana), and 30 others died in jail. This ruthless action subdued the Kwaio but left a long legacy of ill feeling towards government and Europeans.

88, and the PNG defence force responded blockading the province in 1990. The is- d was embroiled in civil war for 10 years t in 1998 a truce was brokered and a frag- peace has been maintained.

Shortland Islanders have close family d cultural connections to Bougainville d have provided support to the rebels. ternational incidents have occurred with G forces pursuing BRA rebels into lomons' territory, and lives have been st. Bougainvillian refugees are numerous Western Province.

EOGRAPHY

e islands of the Solomons are a scattered uble chain that extends 1667km south- st from Bougainville in PNG. The third- gest archipelago in the South Pacific, the lomons cover over 1.35 million sq km of a. The total land area is 27,556 sq km.

Of all the 992 islands, 347 are populated. e largest islands are Guadalcanal, alaita, New Georgia, Santa Isabel, Makira d Choiseul. The country's highest peak, t Makarakombu (2447m), is on Guadal- nal. There are active volcanoes, and rthquakes are common.

LIMATE

om late May to early December – the dry ason – south-easterly trade winds produce easantly mild weather. Rainfall is light d rain periods are usually several days art.

From mid-December to mid-May, mon- on winds come from the west or north- st and bring the wet season. This is a ne of higher temperatures, humidity and nfall. Short, sharp, torrential rains are lowed by bright sunshine. A recent spate droughts has been attributed to the last El ño.

Honiara's annual rainfall is about 54mm, but it is drier than most of the rest the country. Some parts, like Guadal- nal's south coast, can receive 12.5m! Cyclones can blow up between January d April. Daytime coastal temperatures ry through the year from 21 to 32°C. At ght the temperature falls to around 19°C.

The humidity can be oppressive and is high- est in the morning, regularly reaching 90%.

ECOLOGY & ENVIRONMENT

Much of the Solomons is covered with dense rainforest, with mangrove swamps occurring along parts of the coast. Most islands are fringed with coral reefs and lagoons. Many have formed around initial volcanic cones and become overlaid with terraces of coral rock. Other islands are former reefs lifted high out of the water by volcanic activity. Rennell is the most striking example of an uplifted coral atoll in the Pacific.

Tropical rainforest covers 79% of the country. Timber accounts for over half of all export earnings, and trees have been felled at an unsustainable rate – at current levels the country's forestry resources will be exhausted in just eight to 10 years. Successive governments have failed to honour pledges to reduce timber quotas, but the current prime minister, Bartholomew Ulufa'alu, has dramatically reduced timber exports and resisted the soft touch of the meddling Malaysian logging companies.

Efforts to add value to the Solomons' natural resources are on the rise – fish canneries, small-scale logging and timber milling by local landowners are examples. Large-scale gold mining was established at Gold Ridge on Guadalcanal in 1997, and there are other known deposits.

Eco-tourism resorts in the Marovo Lagoon have been sponsored by the Worldwide Fund for Nature (WWF) and the World Heritage Committee (a UNESCO body). Marovo is the largest island-enclosed lagoon in the world and has been proposed for World Heritage listing.

The majority of people live by the sea, and the predicted rise in sea levels due to global warming (see the 'Global Warming' boxed text in the Facts about the South Pacific chapter) could have a huge impact – many low-lying atolls would disappear.

FLORA & FAUNA
Flora

The Solomons has over 4500 plant species, including 230 varieties of orchid. Many

SOLOMON ISLANDS

plants and trees are valued by islanders as sources of traditional building materials, food, medicine or cloth.

A common evergreen is the *sumai* tree, which blossoms at night. Sumais are recognisable by the large number of dark-green, box-shaped, fallen and unopened fruit littering the adjacent ground.

The American vine was introduced from the southern states of the USA for use as a fast-growing camouflage in WWII. It has since spread unrestrainedly in north-eastern Guadalcanal, choking indigenous vegetation.

Honiara is a good place to see the many hibiscus varieties, including whites, yellows, oranges, pinks and reds. You'll also find white and pink-flowered frangipanis, red ginger plants, colourful bougainvilleas and many other varieties around the country.

The large, purple-veined *nalato* leaf causes a nettle-like rash. Another toxic plant is the *hailasi*: its bark and sap can produce blisters. The *loya*, or lawyer, cane has hooks on the end of its leaves, and some varieties also have barbs on their stems. Take care what you grab hold of when going up or down a hill.

Fauna

Birds The Solomons is home to 173 bird species including hawks and eagles, pigeons, parrots, kingfishers and starlings. Among their names are the dollar bird,

marbled frogmouth, buff-headed couc, midget flowerpecker and spangled drong

Around 40 species are unique to t Solomons, including the cardinal lory – familiar sight around Honiara and els where. Some species live only on one land, such as the Rennell fantail and t slaty flycatcher of Vanikoro.

Frigate birds – blackish males, whi breasted females – are important to isla folklore, as are megapode birds and t brown-plumaged Sanford's eagle.

Insects & Arachnids Most of the hu variety of insects in the Solomons live the upper reaches of the rainforest. Amo those found lower down are butterfli moths, wasps, beetles, mosquitoes, cen pedes, scorpions and caterpillars.

More than 130 butterfly species a found locally, and 35 are endemic. The t largest forms – the Queen Victoria birdwi and the blue mountain birdwing – ha spans of over 25cm.

The 1.2cm Solomons' fruit wasp is co mon in Bellona.

Mammals There are four rat types larg than a domestic cat! The largest ne underground in Choiseul and Guadalcan eating nuts, fruit and insects. The islar are also home to the Polynesian rat and common brown rat.

JANE HART

A male frigate bird in a courtship display

The cuscus, or marsupial phalanger, is und on the larger islands. Ranging in lour from pure white to nearly black, it's nsidered a delicacy, and its teeth are used traditional currency. Fruit bats make pular village meals, and their teeth are llected for bride price.

eptiles & Amphibians Compared with ands further east, the Solomons harbour a ge variety of reptilian life.

akes There are eight sea-snake species in lomons' waters. They're venomous, but t aggressive. The black-banded sea krait lso called the coral snake) is common. ake Te'Nggano on Rennell is home to the eshwater *tugihono* snake. It's extremely isonous, but placid.

There are also seven land species, three which are nonvenomous. The *typhlina* is prownish-red burrowing snake up to 35cm ng. The 2m tree boa is limited to Temotu. he ground boa is a similar length and eyish-brown. Guppy's snake is the most gressive of the four venomous land akes, but rarely bites. A brown tree snake also found in the Solomons.

zards The 1.5m monitor lizard is plenti-l on Rennell and in the Three Sisters ands off Makira. The giant prehensile-led skink is about 75cm long.

ocodiles The dangerous saltwater croco-le is the short-mouthed, wide-bodied ast that is often up to 4m long. The long-outhed crocodile is a slim, freshwater riant 1m to 2m long. It eats mainly fish, t can take dogs, pigs or small children.

Freshwater crocodiles favour clear rivers e north Malaita's waterways and the Ulo iver area of Vella Lavella. Saltwater croco-les live in many of the country's mangrove vamps and tidal estuaries, though they're pable of travelling far inland up muddy, w-lying rivers. Beware of coastal rivers, arshes, tidal flats and mangrove swamps.

ogs & Toads The Solomons has several ecies of frog and toad. Cane toads were introduced in WWII and are now a pest – any animal eating a cane toad can expect to die from poisoning within an hour.

Marine Creatures Whales are rare visitors to the Solomons, but dolphins often play around inter-island boats. People in Malaita and Makira/Ulawa hunt dolphins – their flesh is eaten and their teeth are used for bride price.

Green and hawksbill turtles nest on many islands from November to February.

Sharks Shark attacks are rare, but seek local advice before taking to the water. Islanders usually consider themselves safe when they're inside a reef or swimming from a white-sand beach. Black sand is generally volcanic in origin, and there's usually no protective reef.

GOVERNMENT & POLITICS

The Solomon Islands became an independent country on 7 July 1978. It's a parliamentary democracy with a single legislative assembly. The British Crown, as leader of the Commonwealth, is head of state, with the governor general, chosen by parliament, acting as the monarch's representative.

The judicial system is British: it has a high court, court of appeal and magistrates' court. Local courts are conducted by village elders and there's a customary land appeal court.

The Solomon Islands is a member of the UN, the World Bank, two of the European Union (EU) subgroups, the Commonwealth, the South Pacific Forum and the Secretariat of the Pacific Community.

National Government

The 47-seat parliament is in Honiara. The 1997 election installed Bartholomew Ulufa'alu as prime minister. He formed a coalition government known as Solomon Islands Alliance for Change (SIAC).

The parties are not strongly differentiated – members regularly cross the floor to attach themselves to emerging personalities. Elections are held every four years. All citizens over 18 may vote. The logging lobby is a powerful influence in national politics, but

SOLOMON ISLANDS

Ulufa'alu has been reducing timber exports, and this has made him some enemies and substantially reduced government revenues.

Regional Assemblies

Each province has its own provincial government that sits for a four year term and is headed by an elected premier. Provincial assemblies have some autonomy, but depend on the national government for finance.

ECONOMY

The country's main natural resources are its trees and its fisheries. The Solomons has allowed these assets to be exploited by foreign companies who pay the government low taxes and take profits abroad.

In recent years, there's been diversification from copra into cattle, oil palms, cocoa and spices. There are deposits of bauxite, phosphates, gold, silver, copper, manganese and nickel.

The Solomons' approximately 35,000 employed people earn an average of S$4168 annually, yet the per-capita income is only S$134 per year because 75% of Solomon Islanders live as subsistence farmers.

Government finances are in a mess and the recent collapse of the timber trade has brought an inevitable financial crisis.

The Solomons' exports go to Japan (39%), the UK (23%), Thailand (9%), Australia (5%) and the US (2%). Imports come from Australia (34%), Japan (16%), Singapore (14%) and New Zealand (9%).

Agriculture

About 30% of land is cultivable, but only in small parcels. The only expansive area of good agricultural soil is the Guadalcanal plains. Gardens, fishing and livestock supply basic village needs, plus earn a modest cash income.

Palm-oil output continues to expand, though world prices are very low. New oil-palm plantations are often a ruse for clear-felling timber.

Land Use & Ownership

Around 88% of Solomons' land is under customary tenure. Neither the government nor expatriates may own it. The other 12 is registered land; the government ow over half, the rest belongs to kastom ow ers. Foreigners may lease land for 75 yea the life of a coconut tree.

Traditionally, land belongs to people, institutions, and often it is inherited ma linearly. Other people may only use la with the consent of those who have inheri rights to it. Land transfers beyond memb of the same family require payment of co pensation. In some areas this involves fea ing and the exchange of shell money.

Legal wrangles over land sought by m ing and timber interests are common, as litigation between islanders.

Mining

Gold prospects in the Shortlands, Santa abel, Choiseul, Vella Lavella, Mbava a Marovo Lagoon remain unexploited. Co mercial mining has started at Gold Ridge Guadalcanal and there'll soon be a nic mine in Santa Isabel. Offshore oil expl ation is beginning in earnest.

Fishing

The waters of the Solomons are rich w tuna. Fish – skipjack, yellowfin tuna a albacore – are caught and the bulk of catch is frozen and exported. Commerc fishing is the Solomons' second-bigg earner.

Japanese-owned Solomon Taiyo Ltd a cannery at Noro that operates at full ca acity yet reports annual losses and pa negligible taxes.

The Solomons proclaim a 200 nautic mile (376km) exclusive fishing zone, bu is difficult to police and foreign boats ha been caught fishing inside it (including US boat, causing an incident that led to expensive embargo on Solomons tuna the USA).

Tourism

Of the 12,000 yearly visitors only 4000 tourists. Over 36% of visitors come fro Australia, 12% from New Zealand and 8 from PNG. Events that attracted visitors 1998 were the Brisbane to Honiara Ya ace, the Melanesian Art Festival and the completion of the new Henderson airport. Governments have regarded tourism as something to be developed by the private sector and so have put few resources into it. Infrastructure will help open up the Solomons to 'soft adventure' travellers, but currently only the Western Province and the capital, Honiara, have any real tourist industry. Low-impact eco-lodges are a very popular idea among land owners, and Village Stay resorts in Marovo Lagoon have been sponsored by the New Zealand government and UNESCO.

POPULATION & PEOPLE

The Solomons' population is about 400,000. Melanesians represent 95% and Polynesians number about 15,000, or 3.75%. There are also about 4500 Microesian settlers from Kiribati – still called Gilbertese – and a smattering of expatriate residents and Asians.

Legendary People

Whether Kakamoras have ever lived, or still do, nobody knows. Little is known of the fierce Mumutambu from the Nggela Islands, the Sinipi of Choiseul, or the Mongoes of Santa Isabel.

The first Polynesians are said to have come across the Hiti people on Rennell and Bellona. They had furry skin and lived in caves and forests. The Hiti were not dangerous, but made off with the women. They had beautiful gardens and taught the Polynesians how to cook certain plants. There are still sightings of Hiti on Bellona.

Islanders tell of a pygmy, pre-Melanesian people called the Kakamoras, who still hide in mountain caves on Makira, Santa Isabel, Choiseul, Guadalcanal, Vanikoro and Santa Cruz. There have been numerous sightings – they're said to be short with very long, straight hair, sturdy legs and pointy teeth. Kakamoras can run fast and hop across rocks and boulders, and each is as strong as three men.

The Solomons' population density of 14.5 people per sq km is one of the Pacific's lowest. The population has increased annually by 3.5% since the early 1970s. Death rates and infant-mortality rates are falling, and life expectancy is now over 70 years (having risen from only 54 in the late 1980s).

About 75% of the population lives in villages but urban drift is causing Honiara's population to grow by 7% per year.

Melanesians

The variation in the physical appearance and traditions of the Solomons' Melanesian people is considerable. You can often tell where people are from by their appearance: the darkest-skinned people live in the western areas and are ethnically related to Bougainville Islanders in PNG; the people from Malaita are lighter and often have blond hair (and distinctive facial engravings).

Melanesian life is more democratic than the aristocratic system prevailing in Polynesian islands. Although there's plenty of intermarriage there are occasional tensions too.

Polynesians

Some Polynesians, particularly those from Sikaiana, have slim, Asiatic features, due to a Micronesian mixing in the 19th century.

Gilbertese

Between 1955 and 1971, Micronesian settlers came from the Gilbert Islands (now Kiribati) under a British resettlement scheme. Their overcrowded islands had been exhausted by drought. They were resettled on Ghizo, Shortland and Wagina, and some moved to White River village in Honiara and to Red Beach just east of Henderson airport.

Asians

The small Chinese community lives mainly in Honiara's Chinatown. There are Chinese stores in Gizo, Auki and Kirakira, but Tulagi's large pre-war Chinatown has gone. Japanese and Koreans work for the Noro-based Solomon Taiyo fishing company.

SOLOMON ISLANDS

SOLOMON ISLANDS

Expatriate Residents

European residents, known as expats, are mostly based in the capital. In contrast, most overseas volunteers work outside Honiara. The majority of expats are Britons, Australians, New Zealanders and Americans, who hold jobs in medicine, teaching, technical trades or water supply.

ARTS

There are strong carving and artefact-making traditions in the Solomons, but sadly many art forms were lost with the onset of Christianity and with the introduction of new goods and materials. Pottery, once made in the Shortlands, Simbo, Wagina and Kolombangara, is now only produced in northwestern Choiseul. Tapa cloth is still occasionally made and worn as ceremonial regalia.

Carving

Carvings incorporate human, bird, fish and other animal motifs, often in combination; and they frequently represent deities and spirits. Traditionally, only the best reproductions of a god's image could ensure success in war, fishing, gardening and healing. Carvings are often inlaid with nautilus or trocchus shell. Carvings of *nguzungu* (canoe figureheads, also carved in min ture) and various animals are skilfully fa ioned in Western Province, using keros wood and ebony (ebony is now rare a very expensive – beware of inferior timb blackened with stain). Decorated bowls widely available.

Weaving

Bukaware baskets, trays, table mats a coasters are made in many parts of Solomons and are woven from the v tough *asa* vine. Whack your bukaw against a rock to get rid of any dirt a loose fibres – you'll have less grief w customs when you're going home.

Gilbertese make sturdy, brown sleep mats out of pandanus leaf. Finely wov shoulder bags are produced on Rennell a Bellona, and in the Reefs.

Music & Musical Instruments

Bamboo bands have between three and ei performers. Bamboo pipes are common most of the larger islands, and are tied gether as panpipes or used singly like flu

When the music first developed in 1920s, the ends of the larger bamboo tu

---

Nguzunguzu

The carvings called *nguzunguzu* (pronounced 'noo-zoo-noo-zoo') used to adorn the prows of war canoes. The nguzunguzu warded off water spirits, guided the craft through jagged reefs and protected the warriors aboard. The figurehead rests its chin on two clenched fists (for war), a human head (head-hunting) or on a dove (peace). The best are made of ebony and inlaid with pieces of pearly nautilus shell, making a striking contrast with the smooth, jet-black timber.

Although native to Western Province, the figurehead has been taken up as a kind of national symbol and embossed on the one dollar coin. Nguzunguzu are widely available in Western Province.

The shell-inlay work used to be done with an adhesive paste made from a nut called *tita*, but these days glues like Supa Glue and epoxy resin (like Araldite) are used and keenly sought. Stow a few tubes in your luggage – carvers trade for them.

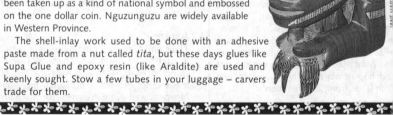

ere struck with coconut husks to make a
ne. The trusty thong (flip flop) is used
wadays, and the queer resonances within
e tube make an unusual sound.

Stamping drums are made in Ontong
va, Malaita and Vanikoro. Dance sticks
e made in Malaita and Santa Ana. Slit
ums are made and played across the
lomons, and vary in size.

Stringband music is popular and played
ith guitars and a ukulele. It's loosely
sed around a 12-bar blues structure, but
ringband music can be deceptively com-
ex and subtle. Gilbertese men sit around
plyboard box thumping out the dirge
ythm with their hands. The harmonies ac-
mpanying their traditional dance perfor-
ances are wonderful.

raditional Dance
here are regular dance performances
ch week at the major hotels and around
e towns. Independence Day is a day of
lebration.

Villagers may invite you to watch kastom
nces. They'll expect you to watch and not
rticipate unless specifically invited. Re-
ect their rules – there is still much *tabu*
sociated with traditional dancing.

Grass skirts are rarely seen now except at
nces and ceremonies. They're made from
tel leaf or hibiscus bark, or these days
om brightly coloured synthetic fibres.

attoos
any tattoo patterns are traditional mark-
gs that confirm a person's age and social
sition. Some Polynesians from Ontong
va and Anuta are still heavily tattooed.
ttooing is more common among fairer-
inned peoples.

Facial engraving is practised on Malaita.
grooved, unpigmented design is made
ing a scraper bone against the skin.

In northern Malaita, men are tattooed
low the eye and women decorate their
easts. Ontong Java's people have their
reheads tattooed, and in the Reef Islands
e back of a woman's thigh is a common
ace for a tattoo. Chests are tattooed in
kopia, and in Rennell and Bellona.

Ornaments
Shell-money necklaces are used as personal
decoration in Malaita and Western
Province, and oyster-shell pendants are
traditional to Choiseul, Malaita and Guadalcanal. *Kapkaps* are forehead discs – open-
worked turtle shell over a clam-shell disk –
and come from Nggela, Malaita and the
New Georgias. Other ornaments are made
from the teeth of porpoises, dogs, possums
and flying foxes.

In Malaita, belts of red, black and white
shell money are worn as armbands, and
some people wear fancy ear ornaments.

Currency
Kastom mani is used for paying bride price
and other special transactions. Shell money
is used in Malaita, while in the Temotu Islands red-feather coils are still used.

Literature
*Ples Blong Iumi – The Solomon Islands,
the Past Four Thousand Years* (USP & the
Solomon Islands College of Higher Education, Suva & Honiara, 1989), by Sam
Alasia and others, contains contributions by
14 Solomon Islanders.

Zoleveke – A Man from Choiseul (USP,
Suva, 1980) by Gideon Zoleveke recounts
the story of a Choiseul man who became a
Cabinet minister. *From Pig-Theft to Parliament – My Life Between Two Worlds* (USP
& the Solomon Islands College of Higher
Education, Honiara, 1989) by Jonathan Fifi'i, translated and edited by Roger Keesing,
tells of the author's childhood in Malaita,
the Marching Rule movement and parliamentary life. *Kanaka Boy* (USP, Suva &
Honiara, 1985) by Sir Frederick Osifelo is
the autobiography of the first Solomon Islander to be knighted.

SOCIETY & CONDUCT
Solomon Islanders' obligations to their clan
and village chief bigman are eternal and enduring, no matter whether they live in the
same village or have moved to another
country. The *wantok* system is observed
here like in most Melanesian cultures (see
the boxed text 'Wantok').

SOLOMON ISLANDS

SOLOMON ISLANDS

The Wantok System

Fundamental to Solomons' culture and common to many Melanesian societies is the idea of *wantok*. In Pijin, wantok simply means 'one talk', and your wantoks are those who speak your language – your clan and family. All islanders are born with a set of obligations to their wantoks, but they're also endowed with privileges that only wantoks receive.

Within the village, each person is entitled to land and food, and to share in the community assets. And any clanspeople, whether in Honiara or Hanoi, are expected to accommodate and feed their wantoks until they can make more permanent arrangements.

For most Melanesian villagers it's an egalitarian way of sharing the community assets. There's no social security system, and very few people are in paid employment, but the clan provides economic support and a strong sense of identity.

The wantok system affects everything – if you are tendering out a construction project and a wantok bids, you give the contract to the wantok. If your bus driver is a wantok you won't have to pay. And if you have a wantok in the judiciary maybe you won't go to jail.

Transferred to the political and public-affairs arenas, however, the wantok system translates as nepotism and corruption. It undermines democratic institutions and hampers the country's development.

Traditional Culture

There are about 90 indigenous languages and dialects in the Solomon Islands. Beliefs, ceremonies, systems of authority and proclamations of status often differ from island to island.

Kastom Villagers refer to their traditional ways, beliefs and land ownership as kastom (custom), and it's bound up in the Melanesian systems of lore and culture that are discussed in Society & Conduct in the Facts about the South Pacific chapter.

Dances, songs and stories celebrate war, hunting, and the harvesting of crops. Some islanders still believe in magic. In Malaita the spirit of a dead person can live in a shark; the shark is offered gifts and is worshipped.

Village Life About 75% of Solomon Islanders live in villages. Most settlements are coastal and close to freshwater springs. Each family has a small coconut plantation for copra production and cash income, and a few scattered vegetable plots.

The nearby bush provides foods like nuts, ferns and fruits; materials for leaf-house and canoe construction, rope and basket making;

and firewood. Traditional crops such as tar are cultivated in village plots.

Dos & Don'ts

Solomon Islanders are very tolerant of ou siders' unintentional errors, but they do ex pect their rules to be observed. If yo accidentally breach a rule apologies a usually sufficient. Land ownership and foo growing are extremely delicate matter however, so stick to the road when passi through a village. Don't pick flowers grow ing by the road – they belong to someon

In remote areas people may wear few no clothes, and men or women may be bar chested or naked. Despite this, foreigne dressed in scant swimwear can cause negative reaction. Nude bathing and skimp swimwear should be avoided, for either se

Men often hold hands with their ma friends, and female friends do likewise. B local men will not touch women in publi It's OK for western couples to do this, wi restraint. It's disrespectful to step over seated person's outstretched legs.

Tabu Village life is beset with taboos *(tab* and rural women's lives are particular fraught with them. They may not sta

gher than a male, nor can they step over a
re, as its smoke may rise higher than a man.

Men may not deliberately place them-
lves below women. So, walking under a
oman's clothesline or swimming under
er canoe is forbidden.

Villages have areas set aside for men-
ruating women and childbirth that are
bu for men. Women must enter confine-
ent during their pregnancy, and cannot
ok or work the garden.

Women are barred from going near men's
bu places, such as skull shrines, but boys
ay visit these once they're initiated.

Bad manners are very rare in Melanesia,
nd most locals will do nothing at all if you
reak a rule, unspeakingly forgiving you for
ot knowing.

astom Fees Villagers charge kastom
es for access to some sites. Visiting a col-
ction of ancestral skulls or a cavern, ther-
al area, war site or island may incur a
astom fee. Prices as high as S\$50 are oc-
sionally asked, but S\$10 is more com-
on. Suggest what you're prepared to pay
the price is too high. Commissioning a
cal guide may help.

ELIGION

bout 96% of the population are Christians.
f these, 35% are members of the Anglican-
filiated Church of Melanesia and 20% are
oman Catholics. A further 18% belong to
e South Seas Evangelical Church, 11%
elong to the Uniting Church, and 10% are
eventh Day Adventist. Christian sects in-
ude the Baha'is, Jehovah's Witnesses and
e Methodist Christian Fellowship
hurch.

Islanders still practise pre-Christian reli-
ions in a few remote areas, and in others
aditional beliefs are observed alongside
hristianity.

ANGUAGE

he national language of the Solomons is
olomon Islands Pijin, or Pijin for short.
owever, there are 67 officially listed inigenous languages and about 30 dialects in
e Solomon Islands, most of which belong

to the Austronesian language group. Another 15 are much-older Papuan languages.

Pijin Blong Solomon

It's quite common for people from villages
only a few kilometres apart to speak mutually unintelligible languages, so people
who aren't wantoks communicate in Pijin.
People who have received some education
generally speak English so you can get by
in the Solomons without learning any Pijin.
However, English is perceived to be a 'serious' language – if you're able to converse in
Pijin, people lose their shyness and really
open up to you.

Lonely Planet's new *Pidgin* phrasebook
has a large section on Solomon Islands
Pijin, with guides to grammar and pronunciation and many more useful words and
phrases than we have space for here.

Pijin Basics

Hello.	*Halo.*
Good morning.	*Gud moning.*
Good afternoon.	*Gud aftanun.*
Good night.	*Gud naet.*
See you later.	*Okei/Lukim iu.*
How are you?	*Hao iu stap?*
I'm well (thanks).	*Mi orait (tanggio).*
Please.	*Plis.*
Thanks (very much).	*Tanggio (tu mus).*
You're welcome.	*No waris/No sek sek/Hem oraet.*
Yes.	*Ya.*
No.	*No/Nating.*
I (don't) understand.	*Me (no) savi.*
Do you speak our language (Pijin)?	*Iufala save toktok languis blong Solomon?*
What's your name?	*Watkaen nem blong iufala nao?*

Facts for the Visitor

PLANNING
When to Go

The coolest months are June to September.
Humidity levels are lowest from October to
December. Cyclones can occur from Janu-
ary to April.

June to August is the time of public holidays and festivities. Seven provinces have their annual holiday at this time, and the Queen's Birthday and Independence Day are in June and July respectively.

Maps

Ordnance Survey maps are available at Ministry of Lands & Housing offices in each provincial centre. The Honiara branch (☎ 21511) has all of the Solomons' survey maps. Hema produces a map (1:1.2 million) of the Solomons that is widely available.

What to Bring

Light cotton summer clothing is suitable for day and night-time all year round, and the style for men and women is casual.

Lightweight poncho-style rainwear that will cover your backpack and double as a groundsheet is recommended.

You will need sandals, sneakers or diving boots for walking over reefs. Plastic sandals are ideal for canoe travel, but sturdy shoes are best for walking through the bush and light trousers will protect your legs.

Beachwear should be conservative. A sleeping sheet is useful if you are staying in villages and a mosquito net is essential.

Other useful items include candles, matches, a flashlight (torch), a water bottle and a Swiss Army knife.

Tampons, sanitary pads, nappies and condoms can be bought in Honiara and other main towns. Slide film is not available in the Solomons.

Bring your own snorkelling gear.

TOURIST OFFICES
Local Tourist Offices

The Visitor Information Bureau (☎ 22442), PO Box 321, is in Honiara. Limited information is provided in Gizo and Auki – see the Western Province and Malaita sections.

Tourist Offices Abroad

See Tourist Offices in the Regional Facts for the Visitor chapter for offices of the Tourism Council of the South Pacific (TCSP), which represents the Solomon Islands abroad. In Australia and New

Zealand, travel agents will give you usef information.

VISAS & DOCUMENTS
Visas

Every tourist has to have a valid passpo onward ticket and adequate funds.

In theory, entry visas are not required f any tourist, as a visitor's permit for a stay up to three months is granted on arriva However, the guidelines are ambiguous fe nationals from former or continuir communist countries, the Indian subcon nent, Nauru and Kiribati. Airlines ma refuse to allow people from these nations board Solomons-bound planes without visa, which can only be issued from Hon ara. These nationals should seek advic from a Solomon Islands' embassy befor travelling.

Visitor's permits can be extended for further three months at the Immigration O fice (☎ 22585) in Honiara. The extensic costs S$30 for each month.

EMBASSIES & CONSULATES
Solomon Islands Embassies & Consulates

The Solomon Islands' diplomatic represen tation abroad includes:

Australia
    High Commission:
    (☎ 02-6282 7030, fax 6282 7040)
    PO Box 256, 1st floor, JAA Building, Unit 4/19, Napier Close, Deakin NSW 2600
    Consul General:
    (☎ 07-3221 7899)
    GPO Box 850, Brisbane QLD 4001
    Consulate:
    (☎ 02-9361 5866, fax 9361 5066)
    Level 5, 376 Victoria St, Darlinghurst NSW 2010
European Union
    Embassy:
    (☎ 02-732 7085, fax 732 6885)
    Ave de L'yser 13, Bte 3, 1040 Brussels, Belgium
Japan
    Honorary Consulate:
    (☎ 03-5275 0515, fax 222 5959 5960)
    16-15 Hirakawa-cho, Z-Chome, Shiyoda-ku, Tokyo

ew Zealand
  Honorary Consulate:
  (☎ 09-373 4676)
  PO Box 21360, 3rd floor, Kean's Building,
  35 High St, Auckland
apua New Guinea
  Honorary Consulate:
  (☎/fax 213051)
  PO Box 419, Kund WY No 3, P/L Port
  Moresby
Jnited Kingdom
  Honorary Consulate:
  (☎ 020-8296 0232, fax 8946 1744)
  19 Springfield Rd, London SW19 7AL,
  England
JSA & Canada
  Mission to the UN:
  (☎ 212-599 6193, fax 661 8925)
  Suite 800, 820 2nd Ave, New York, USA

Embassies & Consulates in the Solomon Islands

All foreign embassies are in Honiara. The British high commission (☎ 21705), PO Box 676, is adjacent to the Telekom office. Nearby, in Mud Alley St, is the Australian high commission (☎ 21561), PO Box 589. The PNG high commission (☎ 20561), PO Box 1109, is in the Anthony Saru building, the New Zealand high commission (☎ 21502), PO Box 697, is in the Y Sato building, and the Japanese embassy (☎ 22953), PO Box 560, is in the NPF building. The Taiwanese embassy (☎ 22187) is 2km away at Lenggakiki. Applications for US visas can be routed through Keithie Saunders (☎ 22393) of BJS Agencies, Mendana Ave.

CUSTOMS

Customs officials meet every international flight at Henderson airport, as well as staffing offices at other ports of entry to the country. If you're over 18, you may bring into the Solomons 200 cigarettes, 250g of tobacco or 50 cigars. You can also bring in 2L of spirits.

Fruit and vegetables need an import permit issued from the quarantine section (☎ 36014) in the Ministry of Agriculture & Fisheries in Honiara. Police permits are required for weapons, and pornographic materials and drugs are prohibited.

MONEY
Currency

The local currency is the Solomon Islands dollar (S$). There are S$2, S$5, S$10, S$20 and S$50 notes, S$1 coins and 5, 10 and 20c coins. Cash in small denominations is useful outside the towns, at markets and for bus rides.

Exchange Rates

country	unit		dollars
Australia	A$1	=	S$3.30
Canada	C$1	=	S$3.50
Easter Island	Ch$100	=	S$0.96
euro	€1	=	S$5.30
Fiji	F$1	=	S$2.60
France	10FF	=	S$8.10
Germany	DM1	=	S$2.70
Japan	¥100	=	S$4.80
New Zealand	NZ$1	=	S$2.60
Pacific franc	100 CFP	=	S$4.50
PNG	K1	=	S$1.70
Samoa	ST1	=	S$1.70
Tonga	T$1	=	S$3.40
UK	£1	=	S$8.30
USA	US$1	=	S$5.10
Vanuatu	100VT	=	S$4.00

Exchanging Money

The National Bank of the Solomon Islands (NBSI), Westpac and ANZ are the commercial banks, and they will change money in most major currencies. They all offer similar rates of exchange, but it's good to support the local business (NBSI). No commission is charged, but Westpac charges S$20 to cash cheques. Major hotels will change money at a poorer rate. There are banks in Gizo, Auki, Munda, Kirakira, Lata and Tulagi. There are no automatic teller machines (ATMs).

Travellers Cheques Stick to the name brands – Visa, American Express and Thomas Cook.

Credit Cards Credit cards are accepted by businesses in Honiara, Gizo and Munda, including hotels, car-rental agencies, airlines, and tour and dive operators. Elsewhere it's strictly cash. Payment by credit card often incurs a 5% surcharge. ANZ and Westpac give cash advances on credit cards; NBSI does not.

Costs

It's possible to travel cheaply in the Solomons. If you stay in budget accommodation and self-cater with local fruit, fish and vegetables you can get by on about S$60 a day. Inter-island transport is cheap by boat and domestic air fares are moderate. In villages you should give some cash, food or goods for accommodation.

Honiara, Gizo and Munda offer higher priced accommodation, restaurants and resorts. Diving, tours and car hire will also push costs up considerably.

Tipping & Bargaining

Tipping is not practised in the Solomons, and visitors are asked to respect this. Melanesians consider that giving creates an obligation on the receiver to reciprocate.

Bargaining is not a natural thing in Melanesian cultures; shops and market traders have set prices. It's becoming more common to ask for a 'second price' for handicrafts, but protracted haggling is considered rude.

Taxes

There's a 10% government tax on hotel and restaurant prices. More basic places often don't charge it. All prices given in this book are *inclusive* of tax.

POST & COMMUNICATIONS
Post

The only postal delivery is to post office boxes or to poste restante. The international postal rate is only S$2.00 for postcards and S$3.90 for letters; domestic letters go for S$1.00. Airmail takes about a week to Australia and New Zealand; surface mail can take two months. Items to Europe and North America take twice as long.

Telephone

There are 6000 telephone subscribers in the country, and a teleradio (radio telephone) network connects isolated communitie Public phones are becoming common towns. Phonecards are widely availabl There are no area codes.

International calls can be made from a over the country. They can be expensiv from hotels but are cheaper from publ phones with a phonecard.

The Solomons' international telephor code is ☎ 677.

Fax

Faxes can be sent via Telekom offices. Tl charge is S$6.25 nationally and S$18.7 internationally per page (minimum tw pages). Your hotel might do it cheape Faxes can also be received by Teleko (S$3.15 per page) where they are collecte by the customer.

Email & Internet Access

Telekom provides a very slow, unreliabl and expensive connection to the Internet, s much so that local subscribers use email ex clusively. Email is becoming popular amon businesses, but there are no public facilitie

INTERNET RESOURCES

There is limited information on the Interne about the Solomon Islands, but a search en gine will reveal all related sites. Solomons dive operators, resorts and major hotel have an advertising presence on the web.

BOOKS
Guidebooks & Travel

Dirk Seiling's *Solomon Island Cruisin Guide* is the definitive yachties' guide. It' self-published but brand new and ver comprehensive. Contact Dirk (☎/fax 60199 solchar@welkam.solomon.com.sb) at Solo mon Charters, care of Gizo Post Office.

The annual *Solomon Islands Trade Di rectory* is full of information. It's publishe by BJS Agencies (☎ 22393, fax 21017), P(Box 439, Honiara.

History & Politics

The Search for the Islands of Solomon 1567-1838 by Colin Jack-Hinton record the history of the European exploration o e Solomons. Judith Bennett's *Wealth of e Solomons* is a history of the archipelago om 1800 to 1978.

Passage, Port and Plantation by Peter orris recounts the blackbirding days. Hector Hothouse's *White Headhunter – The xtraordinary True Story of a White Man's ife among Headhunters of the Solomon Is-nds* tells the story of Scotsman John Renon, who lived from 1868 to 1875 in Malaita.

Lightning Meets the West Wind – The Malaita Massacre by Roger Keesing & Peter orris is the story of William Bell, a district fficer killed by Kwaio tribesmen in 1927. *he Maasina Rule Movement* edited by Hugh aracy (USP, Suva, 1983) is about a noncoperation movement in Malaita after WWII.

WWII There are many books about the Guadalcanal campaign and coastwatch acivities. They include Eric Felot's *The Coast Watchers*, H Macquarie's *Vouza and the Solomon Islands*, Richard F Newcomb's *avo*, and *Guadalcanal Diary* by war correspondent Richard Tregaskis.

The Big Death – Solomon Islanders Remember WWII by Geoffrey M White and thers is a collection of stories told by islanders who took part in WWII.

James Jones' *The Thin Red Line* (1963) has been made into a film. The grim WWII tory is fictional but set in Guadalcanal.

General

Naismith's Dominion by Peter Corris is set n a fictional British protectorate and has parallels to the events of 1927 in Malaita.

Grass Roots Art of the Solomons – Images and Islands edited by John & Sue Chick s a good book on Solomons' art.

NEWSPAPERS & MAGAZINES

The mostly widely read newspaper is the daily *Solomons Star* (S$2). It's unusual with ome inventive grammar and local features. The *Solomons Voice* (S$2.50), out every Friday, devotes more space to world news.

RADIO & TV

Local radio (SIBC) broadcasts programs in English and Pijin on MW (1035kHz) and SW (5020kHz), with local and overseas features and news. The Australian Broadcasting Corporation (ABC) is at 630kHz MW.

There's no local TV. Hotels with satellite TV can pick up CNN and Australian TV, and movie channels are offered at some.

PHOTOGRAPHY

The best times for photography are before 9.30 am and after 4 pm. If your camera is automatic it may overcompensate for the Solomons' strong light, causing dark-skinned faces to come out shadowy. Manual settings are better for such pictures.

Most people are happy to be photographed, and won't expect money in return. Get permission before photographing kastom sites (which may incur a fee).

Bring enough film for your entire trip. Film prices are high and print film is only available in a few towns. In Honiara 36-exposure 100 ASA film is about S$30. Slide film is not available *anywhere*. Print film can be developed quickly in Honiara.

TIME

Clocks are set to GMT plus 11 hours, one hour ahead of Australia's Eastern Standard Time. Local time is the same as in Vanuatu, but one hour behind Fiji and New Zealand. There is no daylight saving.

ELECTRICITY

Power and lighting are provided in urban centres. The current is 230/240V AC, 50Hz, and Australian-style flat three-blade plugs are used. In rural areas, medical clinics, businesses and resorts have generators.

WEIGHTS & MEASURES

The old imperial system dies hard in the islands. The official system is metric but market people still talk in terms of pounds. People outside the capital mostly talk in miles and motor-canoe fuel is measured in gallons.

HEALTH

Care should be taken against malaria everywhere, including Honiara. National malaria rates are dropping thanks to the

World Health Organization-sponsored education programs.

Water purity cannot always be relied on, and hookworm is endemic in the countryside and along beaches.

Health-Care Facilities

Basic medical services are free at hospitals and medical clinics. There are hospitals in each of the main towns, plus 130-odd medical clinics and aid posts spread throughout the country.

Dental care is available at Honiara, Auki and Gizo. The two chemists are in Honiara, where malaria tablets are available without prescription. The optician is also in the capital.

WOMEN TRAVELLERS

It's not usual for local young women to be out at night by themselves. Exercise normal caution in Honiara – after dark take a taxi and stay in busy areas. Female tourists swimming or sunbathing alone at isolated beaches might attract unwanted attention.

Foreign women travelling solo around remote villages are very rare. In villages male travellers are sometimes accommodated in structures that are *tabu* for women, so it might not be possible for couples to sleep together. There may be other areas that women are not allowed to see (and areas *tabu* for men). This should be respected.

It is still *tabu* for females to show their thighs in public, so shorts should be knee-length and swimwear should be modest. Rape and sexual assault are rare.

DANGERS & ANNOYANCES

Criminal activity has recently increased in Honiara. It's usually associated with alcohol and unemployment. Thieves occasionally steal money from parked cars and break into houses, but the Solomons is a very safe country to travel through, and violence or hostility towards expats or visitors is uncommon.

Honiara has been the scene of some ethnic tensions between the Guadalcanal Islanders and Malaitans. This resulted in riots in early to mid-1999. Civil disobedience, associated with the ethnic tensions, included

some hold ups of travellers on Guadalcanal outside the capital (see the boxed text 'Guadalcanal Revolutionary Army' in the Honiara section). Seek advice from your hosts or from staff at your hotel or resort about travel on Guadalcanal outside Honiara.

BUSINESS HOURS

Banking hours in Honiara are from 8.30 am to 3 pm Monday to Friday; some branches outside the capital close for lunch between noon and 1 pm. Government offices are open from 8 am to noon and 1 to 4 pm Monday to Friday. Private businesses close half an hour later, and operate on Saturday until noon.

Shops in town open from 8.30 am to pm Monday to Friday and until noon Saturday, though some open longer, including on Sunday. There are a few 24-hour stores.

PUBLIC HOLIDAYS & SPECIAL EVENTS

As well as New Year's Day, Easter, Whit Monday and Christmas, annual holidays in the Solomons include:

Queen's Birthday	June
Independence Day	7 July
National Thanksgiving Day	26 December

Airplanes and ships from Honiara are always full around Christmas time.

Independence Day celebrations in early July are the Solomons' most important annual festival. There are provincial festivities that include sporting events, a military parade and kastom dances.

There are parades in Honiara on Whit Monday, when war veterans march, and on the Queen's Birthday, when the police march.

Listen out for festivals and ceremonies in the villages.

Provincial Holidays

Each province has its own holiday:

Central	29 June
Choiseul	25 February
Guadalcanal	1 August

abel	8 July
Makira/Ulawa	3 August
Malaita	15 August
ennell/Bellona	20 July
emotu	8 June
Western	7 December

ACTIVITIES

The Solomons offer bushwalking, canoeing, mountain and volcano climbing, scuba diving, snorkelling, swimming, surfing, fishing, shell collecting, bird-watching and caving. For the less active there are beaches to laze on and archaeological sites and ancient customs to observe. There are war wrecks to see and scenic drives near the capital.

Bringing an ocean kayak or a mountain bike would be worthwhile and provide an interesting perspective on village life. Golf, squash and tennis are played in Honiara and almost every village has a soccer field.

Bushwalking

The Solomons is probably too hot and humid for extended bushwalks. The cooler midyear months are most suitable. There are beaches, mountains, craters, waterfalls, hot springs, caves and lakes to see. Islands like Choiseul have tracks from one side to the other. Always watch the weather – heavy rains can cause sudden floods. Carry water, food, money and insect repellent.

Volcano & Mountain Climbing

There are accessible volcanic peaks on Simbo, Savo and Vella Lavella. Climbing either Rendova or Kolombangara requires a two day hike, but their summits offer magnificent views over Western Province.

Surfing

There are good waves at Pailongge on Ghizo, Poro on Santa Isabel and Tawarogha on Makira. Surf has also been reported at Beaufort Bay in southern Guadalcanal; Malu'u, Manu and Fakanakafo Bay in northern Malaita; Nemba, Byron and Kala bays on Santa Cruz; and between Nifiloli and Fenualoa islands in the Reefs group. Surfers should seek permission at the village before entering water.

Fishing

Sailfish, marlin, shark, tuna, barracuda and wahoo are caught in New Georgia waters and charter boats are available. Most of the larger islands have fast-flowing rivers, but beware of saltwater crocodiles in coastal rivers and swamps. Always ask before fishing over a reef or in a river.

Diving

The Solomon Islands are among the world's top few diving destinations. The extensive coral and fish life alone are as good as anywhere in the world, but there are also hundreds of sunken WWII wrecks. Most wrecks are accessible and have been undisturbed for 55 years, with objects in situ. Every region in the Solomons offers a variety of diving locations. See the 'South Pacific Diving' special section.

There are registered scuba operators in Honiara, Tambea, Gizo, Uepi, Munda and Pigeon Island in the Reefs. Details and prices are quoted in the regional sections.

Water temperatures in the Solomons are among the warmest in the world, but wear something (at least a T-shirt) to protect your skin against grazes. Many divers bring their own gear, but Solomons' dive operators rent all equipment.

Underwater visibility is usually good to around 30m.

Live-Aboard Dive Craft Bilikiki Cruises (☎ 20412, fax 23897), PO Box 876, Mendana Ave, Honiara, does scuba trips (seven to 10 days) around the country, often through the Russell Islands. The charge per person is US$445/296 a day for single/twin occupancy on the MV *Bilikiki*, and from US$296/225 on the MV *Spirit of Solomons*. The company also has a US office (☎ 800-663 5363), and a website (www.bilikiki.com).

Blue Lagoon Cruises (☎ 25300, fax 39377), PO Box 1022, Honiara, charges from US$285 per day for similar trips on the MV *Solomon Sea*.

Dive Holidays Many divers pre-arrange their stay in the Solomons. Specialist companies organise package dive tours, and

Australia-based companies include Dive Travel Australia (☎ 02-9970 6311) and Dive Adventures (☎ 02-9299 4633, or ☎ toll free 008 22 2234).

Snorkelling

Snorkelling in the Solomons is excellent. The warm, clear water of the still lagoons and the countless colourful fish and corals make it a real treat. It's a good idea to bring your own gear, although resorts and hotels have rental equipment.

ACCOMMODATION

Honiara, Gizo and Auki provide a range of accommodation options, but elsewhere accommodation is basic. In villages there's usually simple short-term shelter available in leaf huts. Book your accommodation ahead. It will secure your bed and enable your host to meet you at the airfield or port – useful where there's no public transport.

Camping

Camping is rare, and campers may feel a little vulnerable in the bush in a jazzy high-tech tent. There's almost always somewhere simple to stay in the villages, and in accordance with Melanesian hospitality, it's incumbent upon your hosts to look out for you. If you have a large group it may be worthwhile bringing a tent, but seek the landowner's permission before pitching it, and if you want a fire, ask before collecting wood.

Staying Overnight in a Village

Most villages have a leaf house, which are built for wantoks and other islanders, but foreigners can use them. The charge is usually nominal. If there isn't a leaf house, you may be able to use the local school or clinic.

Villages rarely have electricity. The water supply often comes from a stream or communal tap. The toilet is a hole in the ground, or a reserved place in the bush or over the reef. Bring enough food to share around – tinned meat or tuna, tea, coffee, sugar and fresh bread are useful.

Upon arrival, see the chief and ask permission to stay. It's good to have modest gifts to offer – tobacco sticks, betel nut and

rice are suitable. T-shirts, fishing gea[r] knives, lighters and candles are also goo[d] For isolated villages send a radio messag[e] ahead.

Organised Village Stays Village sta[ys] can be pre-arranged with locals who ha[ve] an idea of what tourists want and expe[ct] Visiting on this basis is highly recom mended – it is a wonderful experience f[or] the traveller and it puts money into loc[al] communities.

The World Heritage Committee and t[he] WWF have been active around Marovo L[a]goon, helping to set up eco-tourist lodges [in] villages (see Marovo Lagoon in the Weste[rn] Province section of this chapter).

Solomons Village Stay (☎ 22442, f[ax] 23986), PO Box 321, Honiara, arranges sim ilar village accommodation in Guadalcana[l] Malaita, Ghizo, Kolombangara, Vella La[v] ella and the Nggelas. The A\$50 daily charg[e] (A\$25 for children) includes accommoda tion, meals and village-based activities.

Resthouses & Hostels

These comprise church hostels, provinci[al] government resthouses and private res[t] houses. Most have fans, shared washin[g] facilities and a communal kitchen. The[y] generally charge around S\$35 per pers[on] per night. Most of your fellow guests wi[ll] be islanders. Drinking and smoking a[re] often forbidden.

Hotels & Resorts

Comfortable, tourist-class hotels only exis[t] in Honiara, Gizo, Munda and Auki. The[y] generally have rooms with or without pri vate shower and air-con, depending on ho[w] much you're prepared to pay. A telephon[e] TV and tea/coffee-making facilities may b[e] provided. Some have restaurants and bar[s] Resorts are found away from towns, usuall[y] in idyllic locations.

FOOD

Unless you're eating in hotel restaurant[s] and resorts, food is not likely to be the hig[h] point of your visit to the Solomons. Only [a] few towns have restaurants.

ocal Food

egetables you'll encounter are cassava, *umara* (sweet potato), taro and yams; rice a staple. Most locals prefer tinned tuna ver the abundant fresh fish. Tinned meats re also popular – a legacy of WWII. Cassava starch can be processed into tapioca, which is used in puddings. A portion of fish nd kumara chips makes a terrific lunch.

Vegetarian

1ost islanders are unfamiliar with végetarnism and it's considered rude to decline ood that's offered to you. In Honiara vegearian foodstuffs and restaurant meals are vailable, but elsewhere they are rare.

Self-Catering

Markets sell coconuts, bananas, pawpaws, umara, taro and yams. In some parts of the ountry you'll find breadfruit, cabbage, edile ferns, nuts, limes, oranges, pineapples, nangoes and sugarcane. Tomatoes, beans, hillies and capsicums are often on sale in ne town markets, as is fresh fish.

Town stores stock a variety of goods, but illage trade stores stock mostly tinned fish nd rice.

Betel Nut

A popular legal high is chewing betel nut. 1ost islanders – including debating Provinial Assembly members – enjoy the occasion chew. See the boxed text 'Betel Nut' in ne Federated States of Micronesia chaper for more information about this Asia-'acific delicacy.

DRINKS

Nonalcoholic Drinks

own tap water is generally not safe to rink and should be boiled or treated. Rainvater is collected and bottled water is availble. The Solomons Brewery produces xcellent bottled soft drinks (S$2.50), and n restaurants you can get a refreshing glass f bush lime and water.

Alcoholic Drinks

he Solomons produces its own beer – an xcellent German-style lager called

Solbrew. It and the slightly stronger SB cost around S$4 a bottle. Australian-brewed Victoria Bitter (VB) is also available.

The only bars in the Solomon Islands are those attached to clubs and hotels. Solbrew costs around S$8 in such places. Many of Honiara's restaurants are also licensed to sell alcohol.

ENTERTAINMENT

Except for in Honiara, where there are discos and casinos, there's little nightlife in the Solomons. There are regular film screenings in Honiara, Auki, Munda and Gizo, and they show action videos on large-screen TVs. Traditional music and dance is performed at the hotels on weekend evenings.

SHOPPING

The only specialised handicraft shops are in Honiara, though hotels and resorts also sell local crafts. Artefacts can often be purchased directly from the makers (see Arts in the earlier Facts about the Solomon Islands section of this chapter). Shops in major towns generally close for an hour or two in the middle of the day.

Getting There & Away

AIR

Airports & Airlines

The Solomons' only international airport is Henderson airport (air code HIR), 11km east of Honiara. In 1996, as part of a Japanese-financed S$60 million upgrade, a new terminal building was constructed and other facilities provided.

All international flights to the Solomons are code-shared between Solomon Airlines, Qantas, Air Pacific, Air Nauru and Air Niugini. This means two airlines sell tickets for the same flight, and the plane has a different flight number for each airline. Solomon Airlines flights are prefixed 'IE'.

There are few direct flights to the Solomons. Only eastern Australia and a few South Pacific neighbours offer direct connections and flights from there are expensive. See Air Passes in the introductory Getting Around the Region chapter for information on combining the Solomons with other Pacific destinations.

Departure Tax

A S$40 airport tax is charged on international flights. The only exemptions are transit passengers who don't leave the customs and immigration area at the airport, and children under two years old.

Australia

Solomon Airlines and Qantas code-share flights direct from Brisbane to Honiara every Monday, Thursday and Saturday, with the return flight leaving the following day. The fare is A$691/839 one way/return. The Solomon Airlines office is in Brisbane (☎ 07-3229 0000, fax 3229 1399); tickets are also sold in Melbourne, Sydney, Canberra and Adelaide.

New Zealand

On Tuesday Solomon Airlines flies from Auckland to Honiara, including a 50 minute transit stop in Port Vila. The flight returns in the afternoon. The one-way/return fare is NZ$986/1376. World Aviation Systems (☎ 09-308 9098) in Auckland represents Solomon Airlines. From the South Island it would be cheaper to fly via Brisbane (Australia).

The Pacific

Solomon Airlines has offices in Nadi, Fiji (☎ 722 831) and Port Moresby, PNG (☎ 325 5724). It also has sales agents in Suva, Fiji (☎ 315 755); Noumea, New Caledonia (☎ 286 677); and Port Vila, Vanuatu (☎ 23878).

Fiji Air Pacific and Solomon Airlines share a service twice a week between Honiara and Nadi (western Fiji), routed via Port Vila (Vanuatu). The one-way/return fare is F$813/1046.

Papua New Guinea Solomon Airlines and Air Niugini code-share on the service

from Port Moresby to Honiara on Wedne day and Sunday mornings. Excursion far cost K475 one way and K618 return. T normal return fare is K619.

Vanuatu Services to Honiara from Ne Zealand and Fiji are routed through Vanu tu's capital, Port Vila. From there to Hor ara costs 34,800VT (46,400VT return).

Asia

The most direct route to/from Asia is via Po Moresby in PNG, though depending on yo starting point, connections may be more fr quent and cheaper going via Brisban Garuda connects Indonesia to Australia east coast (Brisbane, Sydney or Melbourne The low season, one-way fare to Sydney A$765 from Jakarta and A$646 from De pasar, with a free stopover allowed.

Qantas can get you from eastern Austr lia to Singapore during the low season f A$839 one way or A$1129 return; it som times has cheaper one-off deals.

For tickets purchased in Honiara, Solo mon Airlines charges S$4766 to Manil S$6387 to Hong Kong, S$5939 to Singapor and S$5578 to Seoul and four Japanese ai ports, including Tokyo. These destinatio involve connecting flights with other airlin and all flights are routed via Brisbane.

Europe

See the introductory Getting There & Awa chapter for details about reaching the Pac fic from Europe.

The cheapest return fares are via Austr lia. A charter flight from London to Me bourne, Sydney or Brisbane could cost little as £500 return, but there may be lo of restrictions. Scheduled flights start around £600 in the low season.

Travelling west via the USA and Fiji also a possibility. London-Los Angele costs about £300 return; then you can pic up Air Pacific's flight to Nadi.

A round-the-world (RTW) airline ticke may work out cheaper than a return ticke In the low season, a RTW fare includin Brisbane could cost under £700, ont which you could add Honiara as a side trij

Solomon Airlines' office (☎ 01959-0737) in Kent, England, sells Air Pacific kets.

orth America

r Promotions Inc (see North America under r in the Getting There & Away chapter) is e US agent for Pacific-based airlines, inclung Solomon Airlines. The best route be-een the USA and the Solomons is via Fiji ing a regional air pass (see the Fiji chapter d Air Passes in the introductory Getting round the Region chapter).

EA

ruise Ship

ruise ships occasionally visit Honiara – eck with your travel agent for details.

argo Ship

's still possible to book passage on a cargo ip with the help of an experienced travel ent in a major port. See the introductory tting Around the Region chapter.

acht

he Solomons is a favourite destination for chties, with many taking refuge in the untry's lagoons during cyclone season. long with Honiara, Korovou (Shortland Is), izo, Ringi Cove, Yandina, Tulagi Island d Graciosa Bay are official ports of entry to the country.

In Honiara, yacht owners leave 'crew anted' notices up at the Point Cruz Yacht lub (☎ 22500) behind the Visitor Infor-ation Bureau. See Yacht in the Sea section f the introductory Getting Around the Re-ion chapter for more pointers about travel-ng the Pacific by yacht. Also see the olomon Islands Cruising Guide under ooks in the earlier Facts for the Visitor ction of this chapter.

ustoms, Immigration & Fees Yachts ould clear customs and immigration at an fficial port of entry. The officials will want know your planned port of departure om the country. There's a S$100 fee (plus 0c a tonne) for yachts sailing in Solomons' aters.

ORGANISED TOURS

Package tours are ideal for those with limited time. A pre-arranged holiday (or component) can be cheaper than a budget trip with some comforts thrown in. Packages sometimes include car hire, subsidised hotel prices, restaurant vouchers, tours and activities.

Several travel agents in Australia and New Zealand specialise in the South Pacific; the Pacific Island Travel Centre in Sydney (☎ 02-9262 6555, fax 9262 6318) is one. Scobie's Walkabout Tours (☎/fax 049-570458), PO Box 43, Newcastle 2300, Australia, takes groups to Marovo Lagoon and Rennell Island.

Getting Around

Getting around the Solomons can be a challenge and a pleasure. Air services usually stick to their timetables, but with any other transport 'Solomons time' kicks in and everything relaxes. A truck or a boat might leave earlier than expected or considerably later – nobody cares too much. Generously allow for unexpected delays in getting back if you venture off from the main towns. Around Christmas much of the country is on the move, so reserve seats well in advance.

AIR

Flying is a great way to get around. The Solomons' lagoons and islands look fantastic from above, and in small planes you're always close to a window. On some legs the planes cruise at only 1000m and can you see plenty of detail on the ground.

The only domestic flyer is Solomon Airlines. It services over 20 airfields around the country. Nearly all flights originate in Honiara. Domestic air fares are cheap and bookings can be changed without penalty. You can make reservations without paying up front, but they will be cancelled if payment is not received by the time it is due. Solomon Airlines has stopped offering air passes and discounts for international travellers after complaints of unfairness from locals. Students get a 25% discount: this is only supposed to apply to trips to/from college, but rural agents may give it anyway if you flash an International Student Identification Card.

The baggage allowance is the standard 20kg per person.

BUS

Public minibuses are only found in and around Honiara. The flat S$1.50 fare will take you anywhere on the bus's route, which is written on a placard behind the windscreen. In Malaita and parts of Guadalcanal, people pile into open-backed trucks.

CAR & MOTORCYCLE

There are 1300km of motorable roads in the Solomons, mainly in Guadalcanal, Malaita and Western Province, and about 1500km of secondary plantation and forestry roads. The roads are generally in dreadful condition, although roadwork gangs are hard at work in Honiara. International driving permits are accepted, as are most current national driving licences. People drive on the left-hand side. Rental cars and 4WD vehicles are only available in Honiara.

BICYCLE

Bikes are a popular local form of transport and the Solomons would be very suitable for a mountain bike. There are no bike rental facilities.

HITCHING

If you want a ride through the countryside, flag down a passing vehicle and ask the driver the cost of a lift. Many will give you a free ride, but others may ask between 10c and 20c a kilometre. Most vehicles double as public transport.

BOAT

Boats are a fun way to get around but they are slow and prone to delays. Air transport carries 50,000 internal passengers a year, yet ships move this number every seven weeks. Shipping services to remote areas are irregular. Wharves are uncommon in the outer islands and canoes are used to ferry cargo and people to shore.

Those that are primarily passenger boats, such as the *Ocean Express*, tend to stick to their timetables, but others can be unpredictable. Details of shipping movements are posted in company offices at main ports and announced over the radio.

Inter-Island Ships

For longer trips hire a cabin if you can. Cabins below deck get hot, but the cabins on the upper deck are cooled by breezes. No-one will enter your cabin uninvited, but an open door at night is an invitation for others to sleep on the floor, so keep your door closed. Cabins have mattresses but you'll need a sleeping sheet, and a mat if you're going deck class.

There's usually drinking water and a kitchen with water on the boil. You'll need cutlery, a cup, a plate and a cooking pot. Bring a fishing line and enough food for the entire trip. If you have too much, give some away. The crew trail lines astern and when a large fish is caught everyone gets some.

Most shipping organisations have offices near Honiara's main wharf. The largest is National Shipping (☎ 25939, fax 26039), PO Box 1766, with eight ships (rarely all in service). It services Lata/Reef Islands, Makira, Malaita and Choiseul fortnightly and Temotu, Rennell and Bellona, and Malaita's atolls monthly.

Malaita Shipping (☎ 23501, fax 23503), PO Box 584, has two ships, *Ramos I* and *Ramos II*, and goes to Malaita and Western Province. Its monthly schedules are advertised in the *Solomon Star*.

The Commodities Export Marketing Authority (CEMA; ☎ 22528, fax 21262) transports cargo and goes to all provinces. Florida Shipping (☎ 20210) goes frequently to the Nggelas. Tavuilo Shipping (☎ 21445) runs between Honiara and Auki.

The Isabel Development Company (☎ 22122, fax 22009) sends two ships to its namesake province, and Universal Shipping (☎ 25119, fax 24868) goes to Temotu, Rennell and Bellona, and Ontong Java. Wing Shipping (☎ 22811), PO Box 9, at the eastern end of Hibiscus Ave, services Western Province, Malaita, Makira and Isabel.

Paddle-driven canoes are routinely used on remote islands where fuel supplies are uncertain.

Ocean Navigation (☎ 24281, fax 24280), PO Box 966, operates the *Ocean Express*, visiting Auki, Buala and Kirakira on a weekly basis. This is a fast ship, but it rolls in rough seas.

Canoe

Motor-canoes (fibreglass-hulled canoes fitted with an outboard motor) are everywhere. They sometimes cover considerable distances in choppy seas, but they're better suited to protected lagoons.

Dress for wet weather in a motor-canoe. There'll be a dry area in the bow for cargo, but everything else gets wet.

Safety is a consideration, especially outside the lagoons in foul weather – Solomon Islanders are skilled mariners, but every year lives are lost in motor-canoe accidents. Flares, life jackets and fire extinguishers are conspicuously absent. Don't get into a motor-canoe that doesn't also have a paddle. Motor-canoes supply goods to stores all over the Solomons and locals pay a fare to travel aboard. These canoes can be unreliable and

infrequent – start asking around as soon as possible and be prepared to wait.

Canoe charters cost from S$50 per day up to S$150. This will include the canoe and driver, but probably not fuel (which can cost S$4 a litre in remote areas).

LOCAL TRANSPORT
Taxi

Taxis are only plentiful in Honiara, but there are small fleets in Gizo and Auki. They don't have meters, so agree on the price before you set off – the price may be slightly higher at night. Tipping is not expected.

ORGANISED TOURS

Tour operators are based in Honiara, Munda and Gizo. they usually have a set programme of excursions, but given the small scale of most operations, it's often possible to arrange a tailor-made tour based on your own special interests. From Honiara, tours of WWII battlefields are popular. In Gizo, tours sometimes combine diving with local land-based attractions.

Guadalcanal

● **pop 100,000**   ● **area 5302 sq km**
Guadalcanal is the largest island in the Solomons' group and a province in its own right. Honiara and Guadalcanal Island are administered separately.

History

A cave on the Poha River, north-east of Honiara, was occupied 6000 years ago, and again around 1000 BC. On 9 April 1568 the crew of the Spanish skiff *Santiago*, part of Mendaña's fleet, were the first Europeans to

sight Guadalcanal. The commander, Ga[...]lego, named the island Wadi-al-Canar af[...] his home village in southern Spain. T[...] name became Guadalcanal in the 19th ce[...]tury. The Spaniards searched for gold in t[...] rivers and left after two months. Guada[...]canal had no more European contact f[...] over 200 years.

A British expedition sailed by in 178[...] and later the French admiral Bruny d'Entr[...] casteaux had a look around. By the 1890[...] a few traders and missionaries were livin[...] on Guadalcanal Island. On 6 October 189[...] the British proclaimed a protectorate ov[...]

GUADALCANAL

st of the Solomon Islands, including
adalcanal.

The events of 1942 changed everything.
e panic-stricken departure of colonial
ropeans was followed by the arrival of
panese forces on 8 June. Then an immense
S fleet appeared, followed by the landing
US marines at Red Beach on 7 and 8
gust. Six months of fighting followed
til the Japanese withdrew from Cape
pérance in February 1943. The Guadal-
nal campaign was pivotal to the war in the
uth Pacific. Japanese fleet commander
dmiral Tanaka said, 'On that insignificant

shore, inhabited only by islanders, Japan's
doom was sealed'.

Once WWII was over, Honiara replaced
Tulagi as the national capital. Honiara owes
its life to the huge US supply depot between
Kukum and Point Cruz in 1943. The capital
has spread inland over nearby ridges, many
of which were WWII battlefields.

Climate

Honiara's rain falls mostly from December
to April. Morning humidity levels reach
89% in March, although afternoons are
more comfortable. Average maximum and

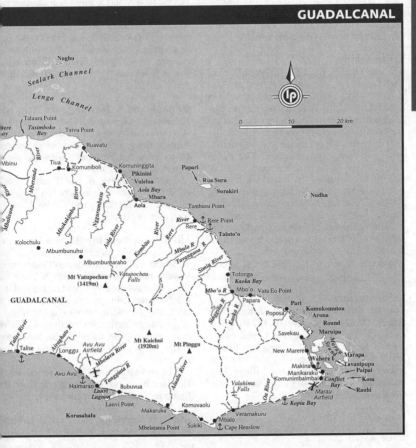

GUADALCANAL

minimum temperatures are 31 and 21°C. The south coast averages 5000mm of rain a year.

HONIARA
• pop 40,000

Honiara is the centre of government, commerce and tourism. The national museum is here and excursions can be made to WWII relics and other sights. Tours are available and diving in Iron Bottom Sound, over the wreckage of the South Pacific's most fierce WWII fighting, is a highlight. There are hotels, restaurants, cafes, bars, markets and handicraft shops, as well as gridlock traffic jams on the one main road. On first impression Honiara appears a dusty, uneventful small town, but after a while in the provinces it seems like a metropolis.

Orientation

The central area from the Solomon Kitano Mendana Hotel (usually shortened to Mendana Hotel) to Chinatown can be covered in a 20 minute stroll along Mendana Ave, the town's main strip. In this compact sector are the central market, government offices, the port complex, shops, embassies, banks, hotels, restaurants and churches. The 12km urban sprawl has the settlements of Rove and White River to the west, while eastwards are Mataniko Village, populated by Ontong Javans, and Chinatown. Beyond them are Kukum and industrial Ranadi.

New settlements like Lenggakiki on the ridge overlooking Honiara and Iron Bottom Sound offer breathtaking views.

Several shops sell Hema maps of the Solomons (S$20).

Information
Tourist Offices The Visitor Information Bureau (☎ 22442, fax 23986), PO Box 321, is beside the Mendana Hotel, and opens from 8 am to 4.30 pm Monday to Friday and 9 am to noon Saturday. The bureau has information about Solomons Village Stay accommodation and can radio isolated locations to make bookings.

Money The NBSI, ANZ and Westpac banks have branches in Mendana Ave. The NBSI and Westpac also have Chinatow branches. Major hotels will change forei currency and travellers cheques, but poorer rates than the banks.

Post & Communications The main p office, just off Mendana Ave, opens from am to noon and 1 to 4.30 pm Monday to F day and Saturday mornings. There's a phi telic bureau around the corner. There's a post office in Ranadi.

Solomon Telekom, on Mendana Ave, h a fax and telex service, as well as card a coin telephones. It's open from 8 am to 4. pm weekdays and 8 am to noon Saturday

Travel Agencies Guadalcanal Travel S vices (GTS; ☎ 22587, fax 26184), PO B 114, in the Y Sato building, is the only int national travel agency in the Solomons, fering hotel and flight bookings, plus tou and itineraries.

Bookshops & Newsagents Acor St tioner, by Solomon Airlines on Menda Ave, sells newspapers, including the Briti *Weekly Telegraph*. Newspower in the A thony Saru building has Australian new papers and paperbacks.

The University of the South Paci (USP) in Kukum sells texts on the Solomo and the Pacific, and there's a bookshop the Honiara Hotel.

Libraries & Reading Rooms The pub library, near Mataniko Bridge, is open fro 10 am to 5.30 pm Monday to Friday, fro 9 am to noon Saturday and from 2 to 5 p Sunday; it's closed Wednesday. Behind it the National Library, open from 10 am noon and 1 to 4.30 pm weekdays. It has large Pacific reference section, includi many out-of-print titles on the Solomor USP's library has material from all ov Oceania.

The embassies and high commissions Honiara have reference materials on t Solomons and foreign newspapers.

Medical Services The Central Hospit (☎ 23600) in Kukum, known as Nambanae

umber nine), provides free medical care.
he Honiara Dental Centre (☎ 22029) is on
endana Ave and the Bartimaeus Vision
are Centre (☎ 24040) is on Chinatown Ave.

mergency

mbulance	☎ 25566
›lice	☎ 22266
re	☎ 20235
arine rescue	☎ 21611
mergency	☎ 999

angers & Annoyances Honiara is the
ace you're most likely to encounter crime
the Solomons. It's not dangerous, and
avellers needn't take any more precau-
ons here than in any other city. However,
›u should be aware that there is tension on
oniara's streets, which were the scene of
ter-racial feuding between Guadalcanal
landers and resettled Malaitans in mid-
399. Seek advice before travelling on
uadalcanal outside Honiara (see the boxed
xt 'Guadalcanal Revolutionary Army').

oint Cruz
n 12 May 1568, Mendaña and his men
rected a cross at a spot called Kua, renam-
ig it Point Cruz. They said prayers and
aimed for Spain their discoveries in the
olomons. A tree beside Point Cruz's pub-
c toilets allegedly marks the site.

Parliament
This unusual building on the hill above
Ashley St opened in 1993. There's a public
gallery and the sergeant at arms will give
you a tour. The building cost US$5 million
and was funded by the USA.

National Museum & Cultural Centre
The National Museum (☎ 22309) is opposite the Mendana Hotel and opens from 9
am to noon and 1 pm to 4.30 pm Monday to
Friday and from 9 am to 1 pm Saturday.
Entry to the museum is S$2. There are dis-
plays on dance, body ornamentation,
currency, weaponry and archaeology. Behind it are eight traditionally constructed
houses, each from a different province.

Central Bank
This building beside the police station dis-
plays woodcarvings from Rennell and
Makira, and traditional currencies including
Santa Cruz red-feather money, Malaitan
dolphin-teeth and shell money, *mbarava*
(white clam-shell carvings) from New
Georgia, and Choiseul clam-shell money.

National Art Gallery
Opposite the Central Bank is the new
National Art Gallery, which exhibits con-
temporary works by the country's leading

SOLOMON ISLANDS

Guadalcanal Revolutionary Army

In and around Honiara there's been some trouble. Inter-racial tension between Guadalcanal
islanders and settlers from Malaita boiled over into riots in Honiara in 1999.

In WWII many Malaitans came to work at the huge US base on Guadalcanal, and after
the war, this Quonset-hut township became the national capital. Guadalcanal islanders, many
resentful of Malaitans' success, are demanding compensation for the positioning of the
national capital on their tribal lands. The federal government has given A$750,000 in com-
pensation to the Guadalcanal Provincial Government.

In June 1999, Guadalcanal elements in politics and logging interests were provoking civil
disobedience. An alliance called the Guadalcanal Revolution Army (GRA) or the Isatambu
Freedom Fighters, started intimidating people of the capital.

Although travellers were embroiled in incidents at Tavanipupu and Tambea, they are not
targets of GRA hostility. Honiara is safe, but at the time of writing, travel on Guadalcanal outside the capital was considered unwise. The situation might soon settle down, so seek advice
from your accommodation venue.

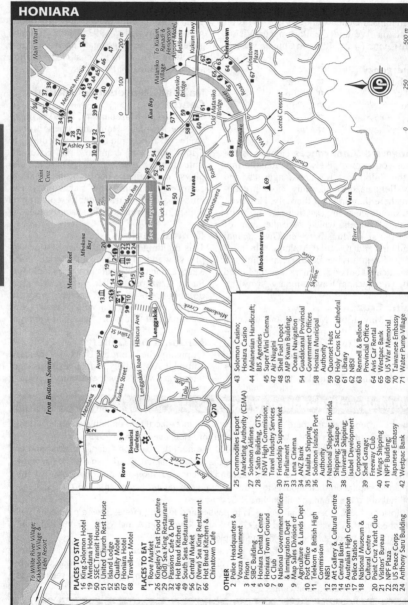

HONIARA

SOLOMON ISLANDS

PLACES TO STAY
16 King Solomon Hotel
19 Mendana Hotel
50 SSEC Transit House
51 United Church Rest House
52 Island Lodge
55 Quality Motel
67 Honiara Hotel
68 Travellers Motel

PLACES TO EAT
1 Rove Market
26 Kingsley's Fast Food Centre
29 (Old) Sea King Restaurant
32 Passions Cafe & Deli
46 Hot Bread Kitchen
49 South Seas Restaurant
56 Central Market
57 (New) Sea King Restaurant
66 Hot Bread Kitchen &
   Chinatown Cafe

OTHER
2 Police Headquarters &
  Vouza Monument
3 Prison
4 SIBC Building
5 Honiara Dental Centre
6 Honiara Town Ground
7 G Club
8 National Government Offices
9 Immigration Dept
  & Labour Division of
  Agriculture & Lands Dept
10 Post Office
11 Telekom & British High
   Commission
12 NBSI
13 Art Gallery & Cultural Centre
14 Central Bank
15 Australian High Commission
17 Police Station
18 National Museum &
   Cultural Centre
20 Point Cruz Yacht Club
21 Visitors' Bureau
22 NPF Plaza
23 US Peace Corps
24 Anthony Saru Building

25 Commodities Export
   Marketing Authority (CEMA)
27 Solomon Airlines
28 Y.Sato Building, GTS;
   NSW High Commission;
   Travel Industry Services
30 Friendship Supermarket
31 Parliament
33 Lena Cinema
34 ANZ Bank
35 Malaita Shipping
36 Solomon Islands Port
   Authority
37 National Shipping; Florida
   Shipping; Sasape
38 Universal Shipping;
   Isabel Development
   Corporation
39 Shell Garage;
   Freeway Club
40 Wings Shipping
41 NPF Building;
   Japanese Embassy
42 Westpac Bank

43 Solomon Casino;
   Honiara Casino
44 Melanesian Handicraft;
   BJS Agencies
45 Super Mini Cinema
47 Air Niugini
48 Shell Fuel Depot
53 MP Kwan Building;
   Ocean Navigation
54 Guadalcanal Provincial
   Government Offices
58 Honiara Municipal
   Authority
59 Quonset Huts
60 Holy Cross RC Cathedral
61 Library
62 NBSI
63 Rennell & Bellona
   Provincial Office
64 Avis Car Rental
65 Westpac Bank
69 US War Memorial
70 Taiwanese Embassy
71 Water Pump Village

ROWAN MCKINNON

The US War Memorial in Honiara

tists. Entry costs S$5. In the pleasant ounds are some traditional leaf houses.

otanical Gardens
eside the SIBC building a track leads past e prison to the botanical gardens. The gar-ns has a herbarium, an orchid garden and cascading creek. They are always open, it the herbarium and orchid greenhouse en office hours only.

xyline Drive
nis was a wartime jeep track running 5km tween Honiara and Valeatu. The road pro-des commanding views over town. The 5 War Memorial was unveiled on 7 Aug-t 1992, the 50th anniversary of the US ach landings. It's a hot 20 minute walk up om Mendana Ave.

hinatown
nis is immediately east of the Mataniko ver. Chinatown's main street, Chung ah Rd, has some colourful stores and teresting old colonial buildings. To the est of Chung Wah Rd is New Chinatown.

ukum
ukum is east of the Mataniko River. oniara's Central Hospital is known as ambanaen. Its wartime name was 9th Sta-n, hence the Pijin name. Opposite is the ge Church of Melanesia Cathedral of St irnabas, where there's a small memorial Bishop Patteson, killed in the Reef Is-nds in 1871.

Sporting Centres & Clubs
Kukum has an Indoor Sports Centre. Out-side are tennis courts; contact the Honiara municipal authority (☎ 21133). The Honi-ara Golf Club (☎ 30181) at Ranadi has the only golf course in the Solomons. Green fees are S$50. The Honiara Squash Club is on Chinatown Ave, Kukum. The charge is S$10 per hour.

Diving & Snorkelling
The water temperature at Honiara's dive sites is 28°C and visibility is usually good to 30m. Solomon Sports Diving (☎ 22103, fax 21493), based in the Mendana Hotel, and Let's Go Diving (☎ 20567, fax 20577), in the King Solomon Hotel, offer compre-hensive diving trips and instruction. Resort courses are available, as is full PADI certi-fication. Dive operators can also arrange excursions on live-aboard boats.

Mendana Reef, only 250m from the Men-dana Hotel, is a good place to learn diving. Iron Bottom Sound is littered with sub-merged war wreckage, including the popu-lar Japanese wrecks *Bonegi I* and *Bonegi II*.

Swimming
Honiara's beaches are disappointing. There's a small stretch of sand in front of the Men-dana Hotel and Point Cruz Yacht Club, but the water is murky. Ranadi and Kakambona, 4km east and 6.5km west respectively, have good black-sand beaches.

Organised Tours
GTS (☎ 22586, fax 26184) runs tours of the battlefields, Tambea, Vulelua and Savo from S$100 per person. Destination Solomons (☎ 26091, fax 26092) covers much the same ground, and offers bush-walking to Tenaru and Mataniko Falls and a Savo Island tour (S$400).

Heli Solomons (☎ 36033) can arrange excursions by helicopter.

Places to Stay – Budget
The *SSEC Transit House (☎ 22800)* charges S$25 per person, or S$40 for cou-ples. There's a kitchen and lounge; smoking and drinking are forbidden.

The *United Church Resthouse* (☎ 20028), up Cluck St, has a good view from the terrace. It's clean and charges S$33 per bed. *Island Lodge* (☎ 23139), near Cluck St, has singles/doubles for S$66/88. *Travellers Motel* (☎ 25721) is near the old Mataniko Bridge. No alcohol is allowed. The prices rise from S$66 per person.

Places to Stay – Mid-Range

The *Quality Motel* (☎ 25150, fax 25277, PO Box 521) overlooks the central market and Iron Bottom Sound. There's a balcony, and meals are available. Twin or double-bed rooms cost from S$159. Family units cost from S$277.

The *Honiara Hotel* (☎ 21737, fax 23412, PO Box 4) has budget singles/doubles for S$115/128 and a range through to executive rooms at S$363/380. There's a pool, bar and restaurant; it's comfortable and good value.

The *Airport Motel* (☎ 36446, fax 36411) has singles/doubles for S$165/198. The owners also offer beachside bungalows for S$198/231.

Places to Stay – Top End

The *Mendana Hotel* (☎ 20071, fax 23942, PO Box 384, kitano@welkam.solomon .com.sb), Mendana Ave, fronts the water. There's a pool, restaurant and open bar area. Singles/doubles with TV and air-con cost from S$253/286.

The *Iron Bottom Sound Hotel* (☎ 25833, fax 24123, PO Box 1892), a 10 minute westward walk from town, has rooms for S$292/309 per single/double.

The seaside *Lelei Resort* (☎ 20720 or ☎ 22970, PO Box 235), 3km west of Honiara, has six smart rooms (without TV) for S$308/352. Each room has two double beds.

The *King Solomon Hotel* (☎ 21205, fax 21771, PO Box 268), Hibiscus Ave, has a bar, restaurant, pool and a funicular lift. Double rooms with TV and air-con cost from S$376.

Places to Eat

Hotel & Club Restaurants The *Point Cruz Yacht Club* (☎ 22500) offers reasonable pub-style lunches and dinners from S$20.

The major hotels offer the best dinir
Seafood dishes – including chilli crab
prawns and grilled fish – are well prepare
Cuts of beef in the Solomons are poor, a
though imported Vanuatu beef is goc
Lunches cost S$20 to $40 and dinners u
wards of S$35.

King Solomon Hotel serves pizza ar
good a la carte dishes with an occasion
Thai twist. The restaurant at the *Mendar*
is good and has a menu of authentic Japa
ese dishes.

The *Tomoko Restaurant* in the Lelei R
sort is excellent, although a little mo
pricey. The best is the restaurant at t'
Honiara Hotel where Jacques cooks exce
lent French food. It also has an extensi'
winelist (rare in the Solomons).

Chinese Restaurants Several Chine
restaurants open for lunch and dinner. T'
South Seas Restaurant (☎ 22363), Clu'
St, is pretty good. Noodle dishes cost S$
and mains are S$25 or more.

The old *Sea King Restaurant* (☎ 2362
in Ashley St has mains from S$22, ar
serves hamburgers for S$10. The new *S*
King Restaurant (☎ 23678) near MataniP
Bridge is plush and more expensive.

Cafes *Passions Cafe & Deli* (☎ 26507), b'
hind the Y Sato building, is popular f'
lunch. It also imports some finer foods th'
are not available in the supermarkets.

Fast Food Lots of vendors sell fish ar
chips at around S$4. NPF Plaza has *foe*
stalls where you can eat cheaply, and the
is food served from snack bars all over tow

Kingsley's Fast Food Centre, Ashley S'
opens from 7.30 am to 7.30 pm weekda'
and 8 am to 5.30 pm weekends, and you c'
fill up for under S$10. On Chung Wah R'
is *Chinatown Cafe* with S$7 noodles ar
S$12 rice dishes.

Self-Catering *Wings Supermarket*, NF'
Plaza, is open to 6 pm on weekdays and to'
pm on Saturday. *Friendship Supermarke*
Ashley St, keeps longer hours. *ELO 24* o'
Cluck St is one of several 24-hour stores.

The *Hot Bread Kitchen*, open from 6 am 8 pm daily, has branches on Mendana 'e, Chung Wah Rd and Kukum Hwy.

The *central market* trades Monday to turday and has fruit, vegetables and fish. *ve market* is opposite the prison, and ere's also *Kukum market*. The *Salo fresh 'h market* is opposite Kukum's SDA urch.

ntertainment
ars & Clubs There's a happy hour at the *int Cruz Yacht Club (☎ 22500)* on ednesday evening. Frequented by expats, chties and well-heeled islanders, it's a easant place to enjoy a Solbrew (S$5.50) d the sea breeze. The *G Club (☎ 20796)*, the west, is a little seedy.

The bars at Honiara's major hotels are ways popular.

The *Freeway Club*, Hibiscus Ave, opens m 9 pm to 2 am, Thursday to Saturday. s popular with expats and islanders, and ere's a S$20 cover charge.

nemas *Lena Cinema*, opposite the ANZ nk, has screenings daily for S$5. Various inicinemas show videos on large TV reens.

asinos Honiara has four casinos. *lomon Casino* and *Honiara Casino*, ighbours on Mendana Ave, are open from am to 3 am daily. *Club 88*, on Chinatown 'e, is open from 9 pm to 3 am Wednesday Saturday and 6 pm to 3 am Sunday.

hopping
ere are souvenir shops on Mendana Ave d in the NPF Plaza. Islanders sell their ares outside the Mendana Hotel. Mela-sian Handicraft is opposite the Shell fuel pot and has reasonable prices. The shop the National Museum has some good tefacts and the central market sells jewel-ry and shell money.

etting There & Away
r Nearly all flights to the provinces orig-ate at Henderson airport. See the main tting There & Away section earlier in this chapter for details about international flights. All international flyers have offices in Mendana Ave: Air Niugini (☎ 22895), Solomon Airlines (☎ 20031) and Western Pacific (☎ 36533). Travel Industry Services (☎ 36533), next door to GTS, is the agent for Air Pacific and Qantas.

Boat Shipping operators are listed in the Getting Around sections. Routes are covered in the regional sections. Motor-canoes travel around Guadalcanal and to neighbouring islands, and they gather beside the Point Cruz Yacht Club and at the central market.

Getting Around
To/From the Airport The standard taxi fare into town is S$35. Minibuses also do the 15 minute run into town for S$2 – wait under the trees by the main road. Going to the airport, take minibuses marked CDC 1, 2 or 3 going through town every 15 min-utes. Major hotels do airport transfers for around S$20 per person.

Minibus Honiara's minibuses are cheap, frequent (in daylight hours) and an interest-ing way to rub shoulders with the locals. Minibuses travel between King George VI School (KGVI or KG6 on their signs) and Rove, and some turn inland at Kukum. Just flag one down. The flat-rate fare around town is S$1.50.

Car Car rental is expensive. Phoenix (☎20444, fax 25357), near the central mar-ket, and Budget (☎ 23205, fax 23593), by the Visitor Information Bureau, have cars from S$190 per day (including insurance and tax). Avis (☎ 24180, fax 23489) is on Chinatown Plaza and in the Mendana Hotel.

Taxi Honiara taxis don't have meters, so agree on a fare before getting aboard. Around S$3 per kilometre is reasonable. Taxi companies include Bounty Taxi (☎ 36444), Sombagi (☎ 24333) and Vine-yard Cabs (☎ 39333).

Hiring a taxi by the hour or day may be better than hiring a car. The standard hourly rate is S$40.

AROUND GUADALCANAL

Guadalcanal outside Honiara was considered unsafe at the time of writing due to inter-racial tension between Guadalcanal Islanders and resettled Malaitans (see the boxed text 'Guadalcanal Revolutionary Army' earlier in this chapter). Seek advice from your place of stay.

Many of the sights along Guadalcanal's north coast are accessible as day trips from Honiara.

Getting Around

Air Guadalcanal has three airfields on the south coast: Mbambanakira, Avu Avu and Marau. They are serviced weekly.

Bus There are regular minibuses between Kakambona and White River to the west of Honiara, and Henderson, Mbaravuli, Nini and Karoururu to the east. Infrequent minibuses go to Tambea, and trucks leaving from Honiara's central market carry passengers farther afield; fares are about S$1 per 10km. Ask around.

Along the south coast, the provincial government runs tractors that take passengers.

Private vehicles often stop if you flag them down.

Boat The Guadalcanal Provincial Government (☎ 20041) has two ships that go around the island on a weekly basis in opposite directions. Inquire at the shipping division in the Honiara offices. The *Ocean Express* stops at Manikaraku (Marau Sound) on its run to Makira.

Guadalcanal's all-weather anchorages are at Rere Point and Makina on the north coast, and Wanderer Bay, Ghoverighi Harbour, Kopau Bay, Tiaro Bay and Lambi Bay in the south.

East of Honiara

Mataniko Falls This waterfall thunders down a cliff into a cave. This cavern and others nearby were hide-outs for Japanese soldiers. It's a two hour walk from Honiara. At Tuvaruhu, cross the river and follow it south. Find a guide after Tuvaruhu and expect to pay kastom fees.

Mt Austen Road The Solomons PeaMemorial Park has a large memorial bu by Japanese war veterans in 1981. There a magnificent view over Honiara and wards Savo and the Nggela Islands. T road passes several significant WWII si up to the summit of **Mt Austen** (410m).

Betikama About 6km from Honiara is t turn-off south to the Betikama SDA M sion about 1.5km away. There's a lar carving shop with a collection of WW debris, and a saltwater crocodile in a p behind the shop.

Henderson Airport A memorial at t airport honours US forces and their Paci Islander allies. About 100m to the west the terminal is the US WWII control tow

Red Beach On this beach a Japanese g points forlornly out to sea. The *Tenav Country Club* (☎ 31174), with tennis cou and a bar, opens from 4 to 10.30 pm weekdays and from noon on weekends.

Hell's Point There's a monument at He Point. It's a poignant site for Japanese vis ors. Colonel Kiyono Ichiki and 800 m died there on 20 August 1942. The large l troopship *John Penn* was bombed and su 4km offshore. It's 40m under water.

Vulelua Island Vulelua Island is 68k east of Honiara, and only 250m in diamet *Vulelua Island Resort* (☎/fax 29684, I Box 96) is a retreat that's popular w Honiara's expats. Vulelua has excelle snorkelling. It's a 75 minute drive fro Honiara. The 3km boat ride to Vulelua free as long as you eat or stay at the reso GTS and Discover Solomons offer d tours to Vulelua including lunch for S$2

Marau Sound

This lagoon at the island's eastern tip ha large expanse of fringing reef, clusters of lands, reefs, shoals and coral garde Particularly dazzling are Paipai and Aarite amo reefs, which enclose tiny islands – diving is superb. There's an airfield at Mar

ASTRID WITTE & CASEY MAHANEY

Villagers wait outside a traditional leaf house in Makaruka on Guadalcanal.

Manikaraku This village has government offices, stores and a clinic. *Gower Resthouse* (☎ 29055) charges S$50 per person.

Tavanipupu Island Tavanipupu is a 20 minute canoe ride through the lagoon from Marau airfield. The *Tavanipupu Resort* (☎/fax 29043, PO Box 236) is owned by expat Denis Bellotte, and it is plush and stylish. Accommodation is in six high-roofed *vale* (traditional houses) with solar power. Excellent meals are included. There are sandy beaches and mangroves, and the snorkelling is fantastic. The nightly cost is S$412.50 per person.

West of Honiara

There are countless WWII wrecks along this stretch of coast.

Poha A 1.5km trail along Poha River's eastern bank comes to a steep cliff and cave shelter. This is the **Vatuluma Posori Cave**. Petroglyphs on walls were carved around 1000 BC, and other remains date from 4000

BC. There are 26 wall carvings, including fish, snakes, a skull and a woman in childbirth. The cave is protected by the Poha villagers and the National Museum. Ask the museum's help if you want to see it.

Vilu A turn south off the coastal road 25km from Honiara brings you to the **Vilu War Museum**. There are US and Japanese memorials, and war relics. Entry costs S$10.

Aruligo One kilometre farther along the main road is the International Centre for Living Aquatic Resources Management (ICLARM; ☎ 29255). It farms giant clams to repopulate the reefs, and it exports juveniles and produces pearls. It's open to visitors from 9 am to 4 pm daily and charges S$5.

Cape Espérance Named by D'Entrecasteaux in 1793 after the *Espérance*, it was here that the Japanese evacuated most of their 13,000 starving men at the end of the Guadalcanal campaign in January 1943.

West is **Vila**, a good place to find a canoe ride to Savo Island. Bishop Epalle, murdered on Santa Isabel in 1845, is buried at the Catholic mission at nearby **Visale**.

Tambea *Tambea Holiday Beach Resort (☎ 23629, fax 20376, PO Box 4)* has 24 self-contained bungalows that are fan cooled and comfortable. Singles/doubles/triples cost S$225/295/340; ask about the divers' dorm and backpacker discounts. There's a restaurant, bar, pool, volleyball court and barbecue (BBQ) area. A monument next to the swimming pool commemorates 200 Japanese soldiers who are buried there. Day-trippers are welcome. The resort has its own dive shop and the nearby diving and snorkelling are excellent. Horse riding and fishing trips are offered, and Savo tours for two or more cost S$180 per person.

The Weather Coast

The southern shore's poor weather conditions have discouraged human settlement: the villages along the south coast have small populations.

Beaches extend eastwards from Viso, broken by occasional wide alluvial rivers. Fast-flowing creeks spill down jagged mountain sides, some in a chain of small cascades.

A journey on foot would require a guide and careful planning.

Central Province

Central Province is 1000 sq km and is made up of the Nggela (or Florida) group, Savo and the Russells. The province is one of the country's poorest, with most of the population engaged in subsistence farming..

THE NGGELA ISLANDS

● pop 10,500   ● area 391 sq km

Initially called Flora, and later the Florida Islands, by the Spanish in 1568, the Nggela group consists of four larger islands and about 50 others between Guadalcanal and Malaita. Tulaghi is a small island half a kilometre from the south of Nggela Sule Island.

The two main islands are divided by Mboli

Passage. Nggela Sule (or Big Gela) is west the passage and Nggela Pile (Small Gela) east. On the western edge of the Ngge group are the two other sizable islands, San fly and Buena Vista. There are long whit sand beaches and mangrove swamps.

History The population of the Nggela I lands declined rapidly in the 19th centur as islanders resettled, waged war on eac other and succumbed to European disease and slavery. In two months in 1867 ov 100 men were forcibly carried off by blac birders and another 18 were murdered.

Tulagi was established as the Britis Solomons' capital in 1897.

Most Europeans fled before the Japane invaded in May 1942. US forces recaptur Tulagi in August, but the Japanese dug in c nearby Ghavutu and Tanambogo island Tulagi was ruined after WWII and the cap tal was moved to Honiara.

Getting There & Away There are no o erational airfields in the Nggelas. Flori Shipping's *Florida II* runs between Honia and the Nggela Islands (S$20) each wee day. Sasape Shipping's *Thomas E*, a larg boat, regularly does similar trips.

There are bays and anchorages throug out the Nggelas. In addition to Tulag Wharf and Sasape, Tulaghi Island has t National Fisheries Developments Tula Base. There are anchorages at Leitong Ghavutu, Siota, Tanatau Cove, Mbike Islar and Hanesavo Harbour.

Getting Around There are walking pat. around Tulaghi, along Nggela Sule's nor coast and in Nggela Pile. Otherwise trav is by canoe.

Nggela Sule

Most people live along the north coast Nggela Sule Island from Rara to Mboli Pa sage. The villages on the south coast inclu Halavo, the subprovincial headquarters ar former Australian WWII seaplane bas There are various WWII relics.

There's a water pipe running out fro the shore at the bottom of Mboli Passag

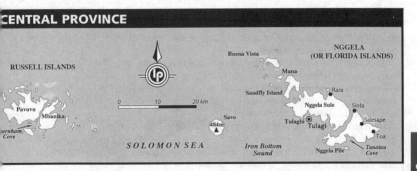

CENTRAL PROVINCE

uilt by US forces to supply their ships ith drinking water, it runs 12km from an nderground stream. The pipe leads up the iff face to **Watering Hole Cave**. A nearby vern, **the Cathedral**, is alive with bats and alactites, and extends 500m to a sinkhole.

Mana
Taravagi Resort (☎ 29065) on Mana Island as leaf-style rooms with shower and toilet; ghting is by hurricane lamp. Meals are in- uded in the daily charge of S$150. Canoe ansfers per person are S$50 from Honiara S$25 from Tulagi. There are snorkelling d diving spots and kastom sites nearby.

ggela Pile
he eastern tip of Nggela Pile Island has ves and rock shelters. You'll need a guide see them and permission from the own- s at Salesape and Ghole.

ulaghi Island
ulagi town is at the south-eastern end of ulaghi Island (same pronunciation, differ- t spelling). The large National Fisheries evelopment Tulagi Base was formerly a sh cannery; now it's a boat-maintenance ntre.

rientation & Information Tulagi occu- es the shoreside area from the main wharf the east of the Cutting (dug by pre-war isoners), and north to the National Fish- ies Developments Tulagi Base. Immedi- ly to the west of the Tulaghi Wharf is the sape Marine Base II slipway.

Bokolonga has provincial government offices, and a post office, NBSI branch, li- brary and hospital (☎ 32008). The Telekom office (☎ 32185, fax 32180) is south of the Cutting.

Things to See & Do Dominating the south is Nambawan Haos, where CM Woodford established himself as the first resident com- missioner. There are magnificent views from the path in front of the house.

Behind the Bokolonga sports ground is another relic left by US marines – a naked woman fashioned in concrete on a rock. You'll need help to find it.

A two hour walk takes you around the island.

Places to Stay & Eat The *Central Province Resthouse* beside the Bokolonga sports ground charges S$30 per person, with shared facilities. The provincial government office (☎ 32100, ext 18) takes bookings. There are two stores and a mar- ket near the sports ground.

Vanita Accommodation (☎ 22246, fax 32186) in Tulagi has eight twin-bed rooms at S$80 per room. There's a bar and restau- rant, but no kitchen.

Next door is the *Tulagi Bakery* and there's a tiny market across the road.

Offshore Islands
In pre-war days, nearby **Makambo Island** was the British logging company Levers Brothers' national headquarters and the Solomons' commercial centre.

SOLOMON ISLANDS

Megapodes

Known in Pijin as *skrab dak* or *scrab faol*, these chicken-sized birds, with yellow beaks and stocky, orange legs, are unusual.

Each night hundreds of females come to the megapode field. They dig 90cm holes and bury their eggs where the temperature is 33°C – an ideal temperature at which to incubate the eggs (the heat is generated by nearby underwater volcanic fissure). After eight or nine weeks the young hatch, fully developed. They peck their way out of their shells, and scratch up to the surface through the soft sand. The young can run immediately, fly shortly afterwards and need no maternal care.

The field is divided into family plots. The villagers harvest the eggs and eat them.

KATE NOLAN

The Japanese made a last-ditch stand at **Ghavutu** and its tiny neighbour **Tanambogo**, to which it is joined by a narrow causeway. Once the USA began using Ghavutu as a seaplane base, the Japanese bombed it repeatedly. Wrecked US warplanes litter the wharf.

SAVO
● pop 2300 ● area 31 sq km

Savo Island, 14km north of Guadalcanal, is an active volcano with hot springs, mud pools and a population of megapodes. Savo's people speak an old Papuan tongue.

Information
Mbonala is the island's subprovincial headquarters. The piped water isn't drinkable without boiling and there's no electricity. Visiting the megapode field and hot springs may incur kastom fees.

Hot Springs & Thermal Areas
Ground temperatures rise to nearly 85°C (185°F), and mud boils in Savo's centre. Thermal sites ring the main crater. The largest is **Fisher Voghala**, churning out hot, sulphurous water day and night. Nearby **Mbiti Voghala** is an area of boiling mud, and **Voghala** has spectacular mud pools and geysers. Three small hot springs – Reok Mbulika and Tavoka – are near Sesepi.

Organised Tours
GTS and Destination Solomons do Sa tours from Honiara (see the Honiara C ganised Tours section). Tambea Resort al does Savo tours.

Places to Stay
The *Legalou Nature Site Village* is 6k south-west of Mbalola. There are tw rooms with four beds, and the price is S$ per person. Meals are available.

Getting There & Away
Canoes travel regularly between Mbal and Port Vila (north-western Guadalcana A shared ride is about S$15 and takes hour. From Honiara to Mbalola by shar canoe is about S$25 and takes 1¾ hours; i quire beside the Point Cruz Yacht Club or the central market.

There are anchorages at Kaonggele a Alialia (both exposed to easterlies).

THE RUSSELL ISLANDS
● pop 5000 ● area 210 sq km

There are two main islands in the Russ group – Pavuvu and Mbanika – and smaller islets. About a third of the residents are Tikopians imported to work the plantations and tend cattle. There are also many Malaitans and Gilbertese.

Information Much of the Russell Islands is owned by Russell Islands Plantation Estates Ltd (RIPEL) so you should arrange somewhere to stay before you arrive. Contact RIPEL via the Honiara office (☎ 22528, fax 23494), or the Yandina head office (☎ 29039, fax 21785), where the company resthouse is located.

Diving Live-aboard dive boats such as the MV *Solomon Sea* and MV *Bilikiki* do trips around the Russell Islands. There are submarine caverns and prolific reef growth in the area, and many sunken war wrecks. The two inlets either side of Lever Point are excellent dive sites, with a vast number of war relics lying in 24m of water.

Getting There & Away Yandina is serviced by air from Honiara twice a week and the fare is S$115. The Solomon Airlines agent (☎ 21779) in RIPEL's Yandina offices can arrange transport to/from the town.

Yandina is the first stop from Honiara for Gizo-bound boats; the fare on *Ramos I* is S$40 for Honiara-Yandina and S$70 for Yandina- Gizo.

Yandina is one of the Solomons' main deep-water ports and has customs facilities but no immigration. Crews need permission to stop at Yandina's wharf. There are also wharves at Nukufero and Telin Island, and anchorages at Wernham Cove, Renard Sound, Nono Bay, West Bay, Samata and Baila Island.

Getting Around The longest stretch of road is between Lever Point and White Beach on Mbanika. You can hitch a ride with plantation vehicles. Access to the neighbouring islands is restricted, so inquire before making plans to visit.

Mbanika
Separating Mbanika from Pavuvu is the deep Sunlight Channel. Yandina, on Mbanika Island's east coast, is the Russell Islands subprovincial headquarters and RIPEL's company town. RIPEL's *resthouse* is 500m from the wharf. It charges S$35 per person. Guests can use the facilities at the Mbanika Club.

Pavuvu
Pavuvu, the largest island in the Russell Islands, has been aggressively logged by a Malaysian-owned timber company.

Western Province

Pristine lagoons, spectacular diving and snorkelling, lush forests and skull shrines are just some of what makes the New Georgia region of Western Province essential to visit. It's about the only place in the Solomons besides Honiara that has any tourist infrastructure, so travelling in this region is not nearly the challenge that it is elsewhere.

The many lagoons look exquisite from the air: the green tree-covered islands, white sand bars and beaches, light-blue coral shallows and dark-blue seas come together in a breathtaking vista out the window of a 20-seater plane.

Western Province included Choiseul and Wagina until they became a new province in 1991. The local speciality in the 19th century was head-hunting, and people lived on defendable ridges. The ruins of inland settlements – defensive walls and house foundations – are common throughout the area. The New Georgia interior has reverted to thick forest and people now live in shoreside villages.

Munda, Gizo and Marovo Lagoon provide the backbone of the country's tourist industry, and the province has accommodation and transport options to suit all travellers.

Many local landowners are opting for low-impact eco-tourism over logging, but the logging lobby is very strong and concessions have been issued for vast tracts of forest.

Over 2500 Micronesians were resettled in Western Province from the Gilbert Islands

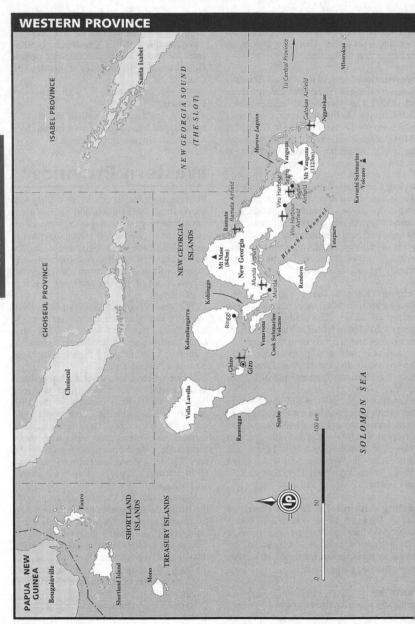

WESTERN PROVINCE

now Kiribati) between 1955 and 1964. their overcrowded islands had been exausted by drought.

History

Head-hunting, cannibalism and warfare were the ways of the people from Western Province, and the islanders from New Georgia, Ranongga and Simbo were particularly erce. War canoes travelled 250km each way in raids on southern Guadalcanal, anta Isabel and Choiseul. Raiding parties eturned with male heads and female capves; some were eaten and others enslaved.

Americans Read and Dale aboard the *Alance* came upon Ghizo, Ranongga and ella Lavella in 1787, and Captain John hortland saw the Shortland group in 1788 om the *Alexander*. Traders and blackbirds were regular visitors in the next century, nd the introduction of guns caused an exlosion of head-hunting and inter-tribal arfare.

In 1892 the British deployed HMS *Roylist* to suppress head-hunting and every illage in Roviana Lagoon was levelled. he following year the Protectorate was roclaimed over much of the Solomons, ncluding New Georgia. Christianity and British law slowly put an end to headunting and cannibalism, but the Ranongans made raids on Choiseul and Santa Isael until 1936.

The Shortlands were the first islands in he Solomons to be occupied by the Japanse in WWII. The Japanese then occupied ella Lavella and Ghizo. There was fierce ighting around Munda: the Japanese were riven out in October 1943 by the Allies fter more than a year's occupation.

Climate

New Georgia's average annual rainfall is 552mm. It rains seven days in every 10, nd morning humidity rises to 90% from anuary to September. Temperatures vary etween 22°C and 32°C.

Getting There & Away

Air The major settlements are well serviced y aircraft. Gizo – the provincial capital – has several flights per day. There are three airfields on New Georgia Island, two on Kolombangara and Vella Lavella, and one each on Shortland, the Treasuries, Ramata, Vangunu and Nggatokae.

Boat Wings Shipping's *Iuminao* makes a return journey twice a week through the New Georgias from Honiara to Gizo. Western ports visited are Mbili Passage, Marovo Lagoon, Viru Harbour, Rendova, Munda and Ringgi in Kolombangara. This fantastic journey takes 28 hours or more. Malaita Shipping's *Ramos I* leaves Honiara for the Western ports fortnightly.

Getting Around

Motor-canoes are the main mode of travel.

GHIZO ISLAND
- pop 6000 - area 37 sq km

Ghizo is 11km long and about 5km wide, and its main town, Gizo (same pronunciation, different spelling), is the second largest town in the Solomons.

Diving and snorkelling fans are well served here. War wrecks and coral gardens provide some of the Solomons' best dive sites.

Gizo
- pop 4500

Gizo is a nice place – a bit like Honiara in miniature. It's hot and dusty with a waterfront main road – pedestrians give way to the town's few cars. There's an array of accommodation options, and all sorts of activities and excursions are offered by tour operators.

Orientation Small boats line the wharf and the town is spread 1km along the waterfront Middenway Rd. In the hills above and behind the harbour are residential areas and many of the places to stay, most with spectacular views.

Information The Ministry of Culture & Tourism (☎ 60251, fax 60154), PO Box 36, on Middenway Rd is hopelessly underresourced. It's open from 8 am to 4.30 pm

SOLOMON ISLANDS

weekdays. It may have copies of the excellent *Gizo Guidebook* (ask at the Gizo Hotel also), which has information about local history and arts, a walking tour and day trips. The police station (☎ 60111) is opposite.

The Immigration Office (☎ 60214) is near the Catholic church. Branches of the ANZ bank and NBSI are on Middenway Rd, as is Telekom (☎ 60127, fax 60128). There's a small public library across from the football field, and the post office is by the market. There's also a large hospital (☎ 60224) at Gizo.

Monuments There are two monuments front of the police station. One honours Ca tain Ferguson, who traded between Ne Georgia and Shortland, but was killed 1880 on Bougainville. Another commem rates Captain Woodhouse, a long-time trad from 1876 – he died in Gizo in 1906.

Activities The 'South Pacific Diving' sp cial section lists just two of the several ma nificent dive sites near Gizo. There are tv outfits that organise **diving** and **snorkelli** trips, and other excursions. Friendly Dan and Kerrie Kennedy run Adventure Spor

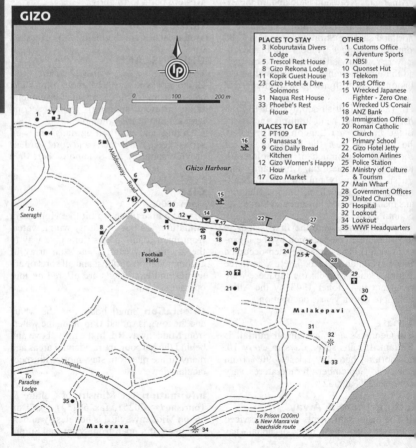

GIZO

PLACES TO STAY
3 Koburutavia Divers Lodge
5 Trescol Rest House
8 Gizo Rekona Lodge
11 Kopik Guest House
23 Gizo Hotel & Dive Solomons
31 Naqua Rest House
33 Phoebe's Rest House

PLACES TO EAT
2 PT109
6 Panasasa's
9 Gizo Daily Bread Kitchen
12 Gizo Women's Happy Hour
17 Gizo Market

OTHER
1 Customs Office
4 Adventure Sports
7 NBSI
10 Quonset Hut
13 Telekom
14 Post Office
15 Wrecked Japanese Fighter - Zero One
16 Wrecked US Corsair
18 ANZ Bank
19 Immigration Office
20 Roman Catholic Church
21 Primary School
22 Gizo Hotel Jetty
24 Solomon Airlines
25 Police Station
26 Ministry of Culture & Tourism
27 Main Wharf
28 Government Offices
29 United Church
30 Hospital
32 Lookout
34 Lookout
35 WWF Headquarters

Ghizo Harbour

To Saeraghi

Middenway Road

Football Field

Malakepavi

To Paradise Lodge

Timpala Road

To Prison (200m) & New Manra via beachside route

Makerava

60253, fax 60297, divegizo@welkam
.solomon.com.sb), PO Box 21, at the western end of town, and theirs is the longest
established business. Adventure Sports
quotes in Australian dollars and charges
A$65 for a dive including all equipment,
and offers resort courses for A$85. Full PADI
certification costs A$400. Dive Solomons
(☎ 60324, fax 60137), PO Box 30, is in the
Gizo Hotel.

Both companies can arrange **fishing**
trips, as can Solomon Charters (☎/fax
60321, solchar@welkam.solomon.com.sb),
which also offers **sailing**.

Wilson Hisu, a local character, takes
people on half-day **bushwalks** up Voruku
Hill. These take in kastom sites and Wilson's commentary on culture and history.
The price is S$35 per person, and you can
book through Adventure Sports.

Places to Stay Thirty-five dollars buys a
lot in Gizo. The family-run **Gizo Rekona
Lodge** (☎ 60296) is spick and span throughout, with a kitchen and balcony views. Fan-
cooled rooms cost S$35 per person. It's
central and accessible by the footpath from
football ground. The **Naqua Resthouse**
(☎ 60012) charges S$35 per person with a
kitchen, and balcony views. Nearby
Phoebe's Resthouse (☎ 60336) has cooking
and laundry facilities *and* good balcony
views for S$35. **Trescol Resthouse**
(☎ 60090), Middenway Rd, has a kitchen
and beds for S$35, or you could try **Kopik
Guest Haus** (☎ 60374).

Koburutavia Divers Lodge (☎ 60257) is
clean and comfortable with shared facilities. It's well located at the town's western
end and is popular with divers.

Paradise Lodge (☎ 60021, PO Box 60)
has an ocean view with downstairs backpacker beds for S$38.50; there's a kitchen.
Upstairs rooms are comfortable with
shower and toilet. The smaller rooms sleep
two and cost S$143, the larger ones sleep
four and cost S$196. Meals are served.

The **Gizo Hotel** (☎ 60199, fax 60137, PO
Box 30, gizohtl@welkam.solomon.com.sb),
beside the harbour, offers a range of rooms
with their own shower/toilet, fan, telephone,

fridge and tea/coffee-making facilities.
Dorm-style quads are S$86.90 per bed.
Double rooms cost S$247 and deluxe air-
con rooms are S$341. The hotel has a pool,
restaurant and bar.

Places to Eat There are several snack bars
around town that are open until about 5 pm,
and fish and chips are available at the market. The **Gizo Women's Happy Hour**, run
by a local women's cooperative by the market, opens for lunch weekdays and some
Saturdays. A plateful costs S$8.

Trescol Island Restaurant, part of the
Trescol Resthouse, serves local, western
and Chinese food for S$7 to S$15.

PT109, attached to the Koburutavia
Divers Lodge, serves some of the best food
in the Solomons. Two evening choices are
offered, and for around S$40 you get three
courses. It's licensed.

The **Paradise Lodge Restaurant**, also licensed, serves three meals a day. Main
evening dishes cost around S$35.

The **Gizo Hotel Restaurant** serves breakfast, lunch and dinner in a large leaf-style
building. There's a good choice of evening
dishes from about S$30.

Self-Catering There's fresh bread at the
Gizo Daily Bread Kitchen. **Gizo market**
sells fresh fish, fruit and vegetables daily
except Sunday. The **Western Fishermen's
Co-op** sells fresh fish on weekdays and Saturday morning. There are limited groceries
in the trade stores.

Entertainment The bar at the **Gizo Hotel**
is popular, and there's an occasional disco.
Video films are shown in a minicinema in
a Quonset hut. Daily screenings are at noon
and 7 pm. Adults pay S$3; children S$1.50.

Shopping Carvers display their work at
the Gizo Hotel. Riverstone carving is a
local speciality, and nguzunguzu and other
carvings are available also. Adventure
Sports has carvings and souvenirs for sale.

Getting There & Away Gizo is well serviced by air and sea.

SOLOMON ISLANDS

Air Gizo's airfield is on Nusatupe Island. Three flights a day go to Honiara (S$330) and call at Munda (S$105) and Seghe (S$140) en route. Solomon Airlines flies to Choiseul (S$170), Ballalae (S$170) and Ramata (S$105) several times a week, and the region's remote strips are serviced weekly.

Boat The *Iuminao* plies between Honiara and Gizo twice a week (the Gizo Hotel is a ticket agent). The one-way fares are S$100/125/160 for economy/1st class/cabin. The *Ramos I* travels between Honiara and Gizo fortnightly. Gizo's daily market generates regular motor-canoe traffic between the neighbouring islands.

Around Ghizo Island

The main road out of Gizo skirts the shore to Saeraghi at the island's north-western end. **Titiana**, Ghizo's main Gilbertese village, is pronounced 'si-**si**-ana'. About 500 Micronesians came to Titiana and New Manra between 1955 and 1962 from drought-stricken Manra Island in eastern Kiribati.

Pailongge, 6km from Gizo, is a neat village that features 2m surf. Surfers are welcome provided they act respectfully. **Saeraghi**, 11km from Gizo, has one of the Solomons' most beautiful beaches, about half a kilometre before the village.

Nusatupe Nusatupe Island is just big enough for its airstrip, which services Gizo, 2km west. The ICLARM clam farm (☎ 60022) is also on the island and for S$10 staff will show you around. Snorkelling over the giant clams in the ocean is fantastic – some clams are as big as armchairs. Motor-canoes that meet flights cost S$10 each way.

Kennedy Island Kennedy Island, 7km south-east of Gizo, is where John F Kennedy and 10 shipmates swam ashore after their patrol boat PT *109* was sunk by the Japanese destroyer *Amagiri* in August 1943.

Olasana This sand-surrounded island has terrific snorkelling and is a favourite picnickers' spot. Adventure Sports does a great

beach BBQ here each week for S$25 per person.

OTHER ISLANDS NEAR GHIZO
Kolombangara

Kolombangara (Nduke) Island is a classic cone-shaped volcano. It's 685 sq km in size 30km across and rises to 1770m. Kolombangara's 4000 people live along its south western shore.

The *KFPL Guest House* (☎ 60230) Ringgi charges S$60/80 for singles/double most rooms have private shower.

Vila Point was an important WWII Japanese base and there are still guns in the bush

A cache of shell-money rings, now in the Honiara museum, was found at **Vanga Point** in the 1970s.

Simbo

Simbo Island, 8km south of Ranongga and 31km south-west of Ghizo, is home to 130 people. Two volcanic cones in the south cause thermal activity where **megapodes** nest. The island was one of the first in the Solomons to welcome foreigners, with European traders living there permanently from the 1840s. It was a port of call between eastern Australia and the Chinese coast by the 1860s. Simbo was a notorious head-hunting centre in the 19th century.

There's a **skull site** at Pa Na Ghundu with 12 coral-stone reliquaries containing skulls and clam-shell money. There's another at Pa Na Ulu and a third at Gurava. Some are centuries old. Righuru has two **petroglyph sites**, and another at Vareviri Point.

Lake Ove is deep green because sulphur drains into it from the nearby hillside. There's a hot spring where villagers cook megapode eggs in the naturally heated waters. **Ove Crater**, on the western edge of the 335m Mt Matindingi, is yellow and sulphur covered. There are **megapode** hatcheries on the mountainside.

A shared canoe ride from Gizo market may be possible; expect to pay about S$3 each way. Seas can be very rough between Ranongga and Simbo so don't risk the trip in blustery conditions. Gizo tour operators do day trips to Simbo.

anongga

anongga Island is 28km long, and narrow.
s high west coast falls into deep water,
hile the east coast is lower, with terraces
d onshore reefs. Its 3900 people live
ong the south-east coast. A **hot-spring site**
es 500m south of Mondo. Villagers bathe
 thermally heated water and use it to cook
eir food.

ella Lavella

ella Lavella Island is wooded and moun-
,inous and has 7500 Papuan-speaking
eople. Mt Tambisala is 790m high, yet its
rater floor is close to sea level. Bird and in-
ct life is prolific. There are **megapodes** in
e Ulo River area, and parrots and butter-
ies everywhere. Snakes and crocodiles are
so plentiful.

There's a large **thermal area** around Ulo
iver.

etting There & Away Vella Lavella has
vo airfields. Barakoma has weekly con-
ections to Gizo (S$105) and Choiseul Bay
S$150). Geva is serviced weekly from
izo (S$110).

Gizo-based boats sometimes make the
ip. There's a passenger speedboat on Mon-
ay and Friday; fares from Gizo are S$25 to
.ambulambu and S$30 to Mboro.

In 1965, one WWII Japanese soldier was
ocated still hiding in the bush, and there
ave been other sightings since, including
ne in 1989.

NEW GEORGIA ISLAND

pop 19,000   • area 2145 sq km

he area around the island of New Georgia
ncludes the islands of Vonavona, Ko-
inggo, Rendova and Tetepare. Munda, on
New Georgia itself, makes a suitable base
or exploring this part of the province.

New Georgia Island, the largest in the
New Georgia group, is 85km long and
1km wide. The island, named by Short-
and in 1788, is fringed by lagoons and
heir many tiny islets. New Georgia's
oast is mainly swamp. New Georgia's
ast coast borders the magnificent Marovo
.agoon.

Munda

New Georgia Island's largest settlement is a
collection of villages strung 6km along the
shore from Ilangana to Kindu. They are collectively called Munda.

The Munda area saw frenetic WWII activity. It was an important Japanese base of
4500 troops. When the Americans captured
Munda they lengthened the airfield, laid
roads and built many Quonset huts. Munda
is also known for its pink and blue orchids
and shoreside freshwater pools.

Information Lambete village, in the centre of the string of villages, has the airport
terminal, government offices, an NBSI
branch, a police station (☎ 61135) and some
stores. There's a Telekom office (☎ 61149,
fax 61150) next to the post office. Helena
Goldie hospital (☎ 61121) is 3km west, near
Munda Point.

East of Lambete There are freshwater
pools at **Ndunde** containing turtles and fish,
and a small crocodile farm (S$3 entry).

Kiambe Island is 100m from the shore,
near Kia. Behind it is a US dump – landing
craft carrying jeeps were scuttled here in the
shallow water. More accessible, behind **Kia**
is a huge pile of war material rotting in the
bush. It's known as the **American Dump**.
Amid thick trees are rusting aircraft parts,
trucks, Japanese guns and US landing craft.
It's a 20 minute walk from Agnes Lodge
and worth the S$20 kastom fee.

West of Lambete Two aircraft lie in shallow water off **Lokuloku**, and a Japanese
Nelly bomber lies in 4m of water, 600m
from shore.

A long rusty pipeline leads north from the
shallows at **Munda Point** to Kokenggolo.
WWII tankers unloaded 3000 tonnes of fuel
per day here.

Nearby Islands You can visit nearby islands from Munda by canoe. **Hombuhombu**
is 3km south of Munda. There's a sunken
motorised pontoon in shallow water just beyond the island's small jetty. It's complete
with driver's cab and colourfully encrusted

in coral. **Kundukundu** is 4km west and has a long, white sand bar and coral gardens. Turtles lay their eggs at nearby **Kokohle**.

Activities Solomon Sea Divers (☎ 61224) operates from Agnes Lodge and offers **diving** over numerous wall, wreck and reef sites. It quotes in Australian dollars. The basic price is A$65/100 for one/two dives, though equipment hire could add A$40. PADI certification costs A$425 and a resort course is A$90. **Snorkelling** trips cost A$30.

Mountain **hiking** and **mountain bike riding** are offered by Go West Tours.

Organised Tours Go West Tours (☎ 61133) is also based in Agnes Lodge. For three or more people, tours to see Roviana Island's Dog Stone together with Piraka Island's skull shrine cost S$80 per person. Roviana Lagoon has many attractions – long empty beaches, WWII relics, tidal rivers and kastom sites.

Places to Stay *Sunflower House* (☎ 61072) in Lambete is preparing two inexpensive rooms attached to the famous restaurant by the water (see the following Places to Eat section). *Sogabule's Lodge* in Lambete, also called Soba's Lodge, has three rooms and shared washing and cooking facilities for S$35 a night. It has fans and a small lounge.

Agnes Lodge (☎ 61133, fax 61230, PO Box 9), by Munda Wharf in Lambete, has a choice of rooms. Three-bed backpacker rooms are S$38.50 per person. Doubles with private shower/toilet are S$192.50; large rooms start at S$242 per person. Eight self-contained cottages go for S$330. The lodge can get busy and noisy. There's a bar and restaurant.

Hopei Island has self-contained cottages. Bring your own food. The cost is S$180 per night, which includes canoe transfers. Inquire at Agnes Lodge.

Nusa Roviana Resort is part of the Solomons Village Stay (☎ 22442, fax 23986) network, PO Box 321, Honiara. The nightly cost is A$50 and includes meals and activities.

Places to Eat By the airport terminal is *Harovo Coffee Shop*, which has fish and chips and snacks. In the same block is a *Hot Bread Shop* and a 24-hour store.

The *Agnes Lodge Restaurant* serves reasonable food. Evening dishes start at S$35. Lunch specials chalked on the board start at S$20; breakfast is priced from S$6.

Sunflower House (☎ 61072) is open in the evenings only (lunches on request) and does a selection of excellent pizzas, pasta, vegetarian and seafood dishes as well as Thai dishes and curries for S$30 to $50.

Shopping Highly polished nguzunguzu are made at Munda. Sharks and dolphins are also carved, and pendants, earrings, bracelets, hair ornaments, pandanus-leaf handbags and floor mats are also made for sale.

Getting There & Away Munda is well serviced by air and sea.

Air The airport terminal has a customs and immigration office and a Solomon Airlines counter (☎ 61152).

Solomon Airlines connects Munda with Honiara (S$290), Gizo (S$105) and Seghe (S$105) daily. Twice a week, flights go to Ramata (S$105) and Viru Harbour (S$105).

Boat The *Iuminao* and the *Ramos I* make stops along the south coast of New Georgia Island. From Honiara, the Wings Shipping economy/1st-class fare is S$73/103 to Viru Harbour, S$81/110 to Munda and S$82/11 to Noro. From Munda, it's S$47/74 to Viru, S$48/74 to the Marovo Lagoon stops and S$46/74 to Gizo.

Anchorages around New Georgia include Munda, Canaan, Kalena Bay, Viru Harbour, Seghe, Lever Harbour, Paradise, Valuli Point, Rice Harbour, Mbaeroko Bay, Noro, and Mbuini Tusu, Vakambo and Keru islands.

Getting Around The only roads in New Georgia are the US-built crushed-coral tracks around Munda. There's a new road from there to Noro, and a logging route

rom Viru Harbour to Kalena Bay. Elsewhere transport is by motor-canoe, small
opra launches or on foot.

Around Munda

Molupuru Falls This 10m waterfall is just
north of the bridge over the Mburape River.
Below the waterfall is a 3m swimming hole.

Mt Bau Stones and pillars stand on raised
platforms deep in the bush atop Mt Bau,
representing ancestral spirits. The site is
about 9km inland from the coast at Ilangana
on a very overgrown bush trail towards
Enoghae Point. You will need a guide and
should expect to pay a kastom fee.

Noro Noro, 16km north-west of Munda, is
where the pole-and-line boats operating in
Western Province are based. There's a large
Solomon Taiyo cannery here that employs
hundreds of people. Noro has banks, a police station, a bakery and piped water. The
Noro Lodge (☎ 61238) charges S$35 per
person in shared rooms. Standard rooms are
S$125 and studio rooms are S$180.

Roviana Lagoon The notorious headhunter Ingava ruled from a coral-walled
fortress on **Nusa Roviana** until it was destroyed in 1892. His tribe had a dog, Tiola,
as its totem and worshipped at a rock carved
in its likeness before going head-hunting.
Remains of the **Dog Rock** are still there. The
fortress was up to 30m wide, and 500m of
coral walls still remain. There's a giant's
cave nearby. Kastom fees are charged at both
sites. Nusa Roviana is 4km east of Munda.

Roviana Lagoon extends 52km eastwards from Munda to Kalena Bay, and has
many small islets. **Nusa Hope Island** has a
crocodile farm (S$10 entry).

Viru Harbour, 30km south-east, was an
important WWII Japanese base. It's now a
saw-milling centre. In the 19th century, five
coral-stone bastions protected the sea entrance from head-hunters. Three ancient
fortresses are close to **Tombe**, and another
is near **Tetemara** on the harbour's western
side. Stone monoliths and coral-rock platforms stand on nearby ridge tops.

New Georgia's North Coast

Attractive **Vakambo Island** is a good access
point for visits to the sand-fringed **Tatama**
and **Kotu Kuriana** islands. About 13km
north is **Mondomondo Island**. The small
bay on the eastern side of this island is
noted for its fishing. **Ramata Island** and airfield are 18km north-west.

Paradise is a large village that welcomes
outsiders. It's in an attractive position behind a string of reefs, on the southern bank
of the Maerivi River. Paradise is the centre
of a religion known as Etoism, a Christian
church formed on kinship lines.

Vonavona

Vonavona Island (also called Wana Wana
or Parara) is a flat 70 sq km coral-limestone
island west of New Georgia; beautiful
Vonavona Lagoon separates it from neighbouring Kohinggo. Vonavona has about
3500 people. Local fisherfolk make nets
from bush vines. A juice in the vine stuns
the fish making them easy to catch.

Vonavona Lagoon

This lagoon extends for 28km between the
Blackett Strait islets and Nusaghele. Most
of the inner Blackett Strait islets are surrounded by white beaches, and you can
walk between some at low tide.

Skull Island The tiny islet at the tip of
Kundu Point (Vonavona) has a skull house,
or reliquary, containing the skulls of many
chiefs and warriors. They're between 70
and 300 years old. The skull house is a
small casket also containing clam-shell
valuables. The kastom owners live at Kum-
bonitu on Vonavona. They charge a S$10
fee to see the skulls.

Lola The *Zipolo Habu Resort (☎/fax
61178, PO Box 165, Munda)* on Lola Island
is very popular. Joe and Lisa Entrikin rent
leaf-house cottages with kitchens for
S$138/195/220 a single/double/triple. There
are palms, a white-coral beach and excellent
fishing – fishing and snorkelling gear can be
rented. Bring your own food if you want to
cook; however, the excellent meals package

Ancient chiefs on well-named Skull Island

is S$139 per day. The 30 minute canoe ride from Munda is S$96 return.

Rendova

Rendova Island (400 sq km) lies due south of New Georgia's Roviana Lagoon. It's 40km long and home to 3000 people. Rendovans perform war dances at cultural festivals.

The Japanese had more than 20 large anti-aircraft guns at Rendova Harbour, but the harbour was still taken by US marines in June 1943. Rendova Harbour became a US naval base for 20 PT boats, including PT *109* with crew member John F Kennedy.

Rendova Peak (1063m), also called Mt Longguoreke, dominates the island. Climbing it takes two days return, and requires a guide. **Egholo Cove** is a large inlet with a rusting war wreck on the shore at its southern entrance. A US two-seater warplane lies in 10m of water near **Randuvu**.

There are no proper resthouses on Rendova, though village accommodation is available.

Lumbaria

Quiet Lumbaria Island is a resort off th[e] north coast of Rendova with lots of nearb[y] sandy beaches. The snorkelling over sunke[n] war remains and large fish is excellent. Th[e] **John F Kennedy Museum**, beside whe[re] Kennedy lived in between naval action[s,] has an unimpressive collection of WW[II] objects.

The *Lumbaria Island Resort* has tw[o] houses providing 14 beds at about S$3[?] each, or S$100 with meals. Cooking faci[li]ties are available – bring your own foo[d.] Make arrangements with Ketily Zonga, P[O] Box 27, Munda. Rides from Lumbaria t[o] Munda cost about S$70 by chartered moto[r] canoe.

MAROVO LAGOON

Marovo Lagoon, on New Georgia Island[']s eastern edge, is the world's largest island[-] enclosed lagoon and has been proposed fo[r] World Heritage listing. It nearly surround[s] Vangunu Island (itself 520 sq km) and end[s] with Nggatokae Island. James Michene[r] reckoned it the eighth wonder of the worl[d.]

The lagoon, flecked with reefs and sand[y] cays, is protected along its north-easter[n] side by narrow barrier islands. Many o[f] these have golden, sandy shores and san[d] bars. Marovo has exquisite beaches an[d] coral gardens, and only 20 of the lagoon['s] many islands are inhabited.

The volcanic rims of Mt Mahimb[a] (821m) and Mt Hungu (605m) dominat[e] New Georgia's eastern shore, descendin[g] into mangrove swamps near Njai Passage[.]

Vangunu Island is volcanic, with Mt Van[-]gunu's 1123m-high crater in the south ofte[n] shrouded in clouds. In the north-east i[s] 520m Mt Reku, whose rocky pinnacle[s] tower over the Mbareke Peninsula, wher[e] most of the island's 4000 people live. Th[e] swampy Nggevala River forms a divisio[n] between the island's two parts.

Information There are clinics at Seghe (o[n] New Georgia Island), Chea and Mbatun[a] (Vangunu) and Penjuku (Nggatokae). Ther[e] are no telephones nor any electricity apar[t] from private generators. Water comes fro[m]

ASTRID WITTE & CASEY MAHANEY

SOLOMON ISLANDS

nks or communal taps and should always
: boiled before drinking.

UNESCO's World Heritage Committee
is assisted the establishment of seven vil-
ge-level eco-tourist lodges. They are built
i traditional style, using bush materials,
it tourist comforts are considered. Village
osts show visitors cultural aspects of tra-
tional life.

World Heritage lodges are at Horena,
Matikuri, Mbili Passage, Tachoava, and
ombiro, and there are two at Telina. All
ave radios, which makes bookings
raightforward through the Visitor Infor-
ation Bureau in Honiara.

etting There & Away Air Solomon Air-
nes flies into Seghe from Honiara (S$240)
aily, and continues on to Munda (S$105)
nd Gizo (S$140).

The *Iuminao* and the *Ramos I* pass
arough Marovo Lagoon weekly. From
loniara, the Wings Shipping economy/1st-
lass fare is S$65/96 to the Mbili Passage
nd S$69/99 to Patutiva. Economy fares
om Patutiva are S$28 to either Chea or
Gasini.

For yachts, there are anchorages at
hemoho, Mbatuna, Mbale (all on Vangunu
land), Matikuri Island, Mbili Passage, and
t Penjuku and Kavolavata on Nggatokae.

etting Around There are no roads and
w paths. Travel is by canoe.

eghe

WII hero Donald Kennedy's coastwatch
ase near Seghe was only 18km south of the
apanese stronghold at Viru Harbour, but
ae Japanese never found it. Seghe, a sub-
rovincial headquarters on New Georgia's
outh-east coast, has grown up around the
IS-built airfield. There's a P-38 Lightning
ghter at the end of the runway under 6m
f water.

The *Seghe Resthouse*, near the airfield,
harges S$35 per bed. It's has a kitchen.

Horena Lodge is on a tiny islet near
Mbareho Island in the Nono Lagoon, seven
ninutes by canoe from Seghe. The cost is
$40 per person, and there's a kitchen.

Matikuri

Matikuri Island and the area around it has
many kastom sites to visit, attractive
beaches, good fishing and excellent
snorkelling. *Matikuri Lodge* has four leaf-
houses costing S$45 per person. There are
cooking facilities but you need your own
food. Transfers from Seghe are S$20 per
person each way.

Vanua Rapita

Vanua Rapita Lodge is on tiny Michi Island
off Vangunu Island. Beds in leaf huts cost
S$40; meals are available or you can self-
cater. Transfers from Seghe are S$25 each
way. Bookings can be made through WWF
in Gizo or GTS in Honiara.

Uepi

Uepi (pronounced 'oo-py') Island has shallow lagoon waters to the west and the deep
waters of New Georgia Sound to the east.
This is a prime **diving** centre, and the reefs
around Uepi offer superb **snorkelling**. In
just 30cm of water at Uepi's jetty you can
look down a spectacular 30m submarine
wall with a garden of giant clams.

The diving is exceptional at The Elbow,
Uepi Point, Charopoana Island (a drift dive
through teeming fish) and Landoro Island,
with its drop-off and beautiful coral gardens. There are also cave dives and enormous gorgonian fans.

The resort has a full dive shop. Island-
based dives cost S$145; more distant sites
incur additional fees. Snorkelling gear is
S$25. A resort course costs S$195, and full
certification courses are available. The **fishing** is also good, and boat and equipment
hire costs S$65 per hour. **Sailboarding** is
free. Overnight **sea-kayaking** excursions in
the lagoon can be arranged, as can river tours
and visits to woodcarvers' villages. Day-
trippers are welcome (no notice required).

The *Uepi Island Resort (PO Box 920,
Honiara)* quotes in Australian dollars, and
offers a divers' dorm lodge for A$59 per
person and bungalow accommodation with
electricity, king-size bed, fridge and private
shower/toilet for A$83 per person. The
compulsory meals package is excellent and

SOLOMON ISLANDS

worth the A$55 per person. Seghe airstrip canoe transfers are A$39 return. All rates are reduced for children. There's a bar and a few other comforts.

Book through Tropical Paradise Pty Ltd (☎ 03-9787 7904, fax 03-9787 5904, email info@uepi.com), PO Box 149, Mt Eliza, Victoria 3930, Australia. In Honiara speak to GTS or Roco Ltd (☎/fax 26076), PO Box 920.

Marovo
Sasaghana on Marovo Island's western side has many woodcarvers. On its eastern shore is Chumbikopi, where there's a war canoe on display (S$10 kastom fee). Chea is where the Honiara-Gizo boats stop. Villagers sell fine carvings.

Telina
Many modern carving styles have spread from Telina Island, and its woodwork is highly regarded. Opposite the island, on Vangunu, is *Kajoro Sunset Lodge*, owned by local legend John Wayne, who also carves. His narratives on tribal history and excursions to *tabu* sites are very interesting. Beds are S$35 each, and evening meals are S$12, though there are cooking facilities.

West across the bay is *Lagoon Lodge*, which charges S$30 per bed and S$15 for dinners. There's a kitchen, and excursions are offered.

Vangunu
On Vanguni Island, Muven Kuve's *Hideaway Lagoon* is 2km west of **Cheke** village. He has four rooms at S$30 per bed with simple cooking facilities. Three local-style meals a day are provided for S$20 per day.

Islands near **Chemoho** have dazzling beaches, while Chemoho itself has an *SDA resthouse*.

Tachoava
Tiny Tachoava Island, east of Vangunu, is good for bird-watching and snorkelling, and monitor lizards can be seen. *Tachoava Lodge*, run by Mirinda Choko, provides beds for S$35 and evening meals for S$15. Canoe transfers cost S$30 to Mbatuna and S$20 to Sombiro.

Nggatokae
Nggatokae (pronounced 'gat-oh-kye') I land is a large volcanic cone that reaches i 887m peak at Mt Mariu's narrow crater rir There's an area of raised reef near Peava. the past, Nggatokae war canoes raided far as Choiseul, 200km away. Now, many the island's 1700 people are carvers.

The airfield is at **Sombiro**, where there also an *SDA resthouse*. A 20 minute wa from the airfield is *Ropiko Lodge*, run b Piko Riringi. He does excursions to nearby Japanese plane wreck, and othe sites. The lodge has ocean views and kitchen. Beds are S$35 and dinner is S$1.

A spit of land reaches up to **Mbili Pas sage**, the first shipping stop from Honiar Adjoining it is Mbili village, on the lor Minjanga Island. *Tibara Lodge* can accom modate eight; beds are S$35 and dinner S$15. It has a kitchen, and there's goo snorkelling nearby.

THE SHORTLAND ISLANDS
- pop 3500   • area 340 sq km

The scattered Shortland Islands make up th Solomons' north-western tip only 9km fror PNG. The main island is Shortland (Alu Its principal neighbour is Fauro. Copra pro duction and logging are the main industrie and the people are fiercely independent.

Information Korovou has an immigratio office. The only proper resthouse in the re gion is on Faisi Island. Gizo-based dive op erators can organise diving/land package to Nila and Ballalae.

Getting There & Away Solomon Airline services Ballalae twice a week with con nections to Choiseul Bay (S$105), Gizc (S$170) and Mono in the Treasury Island (S$105). The Honiara-Ballalae fare i (S$440).

Some Gizo-based boats, such as *Western Queen*, *Parama* and *Vele*, make infrequen trips to the Shortlands.

Anchorages are at Korovou, Nuhu Ghaomai, Harapa and Kamaleai Two or Shortland, and Kariki and Toumoa in Fauro Faisi Island and Nila both have a jetty.

It's possible go to/from Bougainville in NG by motor-canoe across the Western Entrance. Although the situation in Bougainville has dramatically improved in recent years, the crossing is illegal, and it's not a good idea to make it. Breaches of this international boundary by BRA rebels, their many Shortland Islander wantoks and journalists covering the Bougainville war have become a very sore point over the years.

Getting Around There are lots of motor-canoes at Korovou and Nila, although fuel is expensive here. A network of logging tracks dissects the flat terrain in eastern Shortland Island.

Shortland Island

Shortland is 22km long by 16km wide. Shortland's north-western side is dotted with reefs and islets. **Harapa** was the original Gilbertese settlement in these islands, settled in 1962, and there are other Micronesian settlements at nearby Kamaleai Point, Kamaleai Two and Laomana Island. Bird life is abundant on the small islands in **Maliusai Bay**. **Korovou** is the local sub-provincial headquarters.

Across the channel is **Poporang Island**, where Nila village has a store. Near **Maleai**, on a tiny island in Shortland Harbour, is a store (with beer), which doubles as the Solomon Airlines agency.

Faisi

Faisi Island was the first place in the Solomons to be seized by the Japanese, in April 1943. The *Faisi Resthouse* has two rooms where beds are S$30 each. There's a kitchen and sometimes electricity.

Ballalae

Ballalae Island receives the region's domestic flights. Three Japanese Betty bombers are in the thick bush beside the airfield.

THE TREASURY ISLANDS
● pop 1000   ● area 80 sq km

Mono and Stirling are the only substantial members of the Treasury Islands group, 29km south-west of the Shortlands.

Mono airfield on Stirling Island receives one Solomon Airlines flight per week from Gizo (S$170).

Choiseul Province

● pop 18600   ● area 3294 sq km

Choiseul (pronounced '**choy**-zul') became a province in its own right when it split from Western Province in September 1991. Lying along a north-west to south-west axis are 161km-long Choiseul Island and its neighbours.

Only 200m from Choiseul, across the Nggosele Passage, is the (almost) unoccupied Rob Roy Island. Wagina Island, 8km farther east, has a Gilbertese population of about 2000.

History

Mendaña's 1567 expedition reported sighting a large island north-west of Santa Isabel, which they named San Marcos. This was probably Choiseul Island.

Two hundred years later Louis de Bougainville named the island after Choiseul, the French foreign minister. In the 19th century, head-hunting and slave-raiding parties from New Georgia regularly attacked the island. In the 1870s Liliboe, a Choiseul bigman sought revenge, leading raids westwards, he also made forays against neighbouring Wagina until it became totally uninhabited.

Negotiations between Britain and Germany granted Choiseul to Germany in 1886, and then to Britain in 1899. In 1916 there were ferocious tribal wars on Choiseul that were finally subdued by a peace treaty in 1921.

The Japanese occupied Choiseul from early 1942 and some remained there until the end of WWII. The Allies made brief landings at Voza, Sanggighae and Choiseul Bay in late 1943.

Climate

Choiseul Bay receives 3559mm of rain annually. Temperatures range from 23°C to 31°C throughout the year. Morning humidity

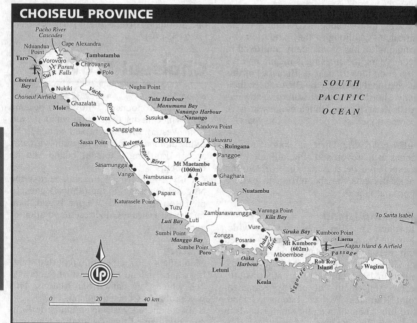

CHOISEUL PROVINCE

levels reach 90% for three months a year, while afternoon humidity averages 79% or less.

Information

Taro, on tiny Taro Island in Choiseul Bay, is the provincial capital. There is a satellite telephone connection to the Telekom office in Taro (☎ 0061-145 110 203). Each medical clinic has a radio.

Taro, Sasamungga and Mole Island have hospitals and there are clinics at Papara, Posarae, Panggoe, Susuka, Polo, Voza and Chirovanga, and at Kukutin on Wagina Island.

Gizo-based dive operators can organise packages to Choiseul. The only proper rest-houses are in Taro and Sasamungga.

Getting There & Away

Air Choiseul airfield is on Taro Island. Solomon Airlines flies to Choiseul twice a week from Honiara (S$440), via Gizo

(S$170), and once a week via Ballala (S$105).

Kagau airfield is on a tiny island o Choiseul Island's east coast, a 15km cano ride from Wagina.

Boat National Shipping goes to Choise Bay from Honiara (S$90) every two week Gizo-based cargo boats sometimes mak the trip to Choiseul.

Getting Around

There's a road on Choiseul between Vang and Sanggighae, and footpaths connect th villages. Motor-canoes are the main mod of transport.

CHOISEUL ISLAND & AROUND

Choiseul people, like the Shortland Is landers, have strong ties with PNG' Bougainvillians. Choiseul Island is long narrow and densely wooded. The interior i cut by rugged ridges and deep gorges. M

Maetambe, a volcanic cone, rises to 1060m. The shoreline consists of long beaches, some bordered by large freshwater marshes.

Taro

A 1972 survey found that Taro Island, off Choiseul's north-west coast, was unfit for human habitation because of its poor water supply and many mosquitoes. A settlement sprang up anyway and now it's the provincial capital. Taro has government buildings, a hospital, a school, Telekom and Solomon Airlines offices, a post office, a bakery and several stores.

The *Provincial Government Resthouse* has six double rooms for S$35 per bed. There are overhead fans and good shared facilities. And there's sometimes electricity.

Choiseul Bay

The **Parasi Falls**, on the Sui River, are worth a visit. Go there by canoe. **Vorovoro** is 6km north of Choiseul Bay. Beyond, at **Nduandua Point**, there's a large collection of *kesa* (shell money) and ancient carvings. There are numerous archaeological and *tabu* sites around.

Sasamungga

Sasamungga, on the west coast, is Choiseul Island's largest village and has a mission *resthouse*. Radio if you want to stay. Canoes travel far up the **Kolombangara River** to the high grasslands at its headwaters.

ROB ROY & WAGINA ISLANDS

Also known as Vealaviru Island, **Rob Roy**, off Choiseul's south-east coast, is owned by an expatriate who is the island's only resident.

Jean de Surville aboard *St Jean Baptiste* came upon **Wagina** in 1769. Late in the 19th century, the Melanesian population fled after being decimated by disease and New Georgian head-hunters. The island was repopulated by Gilbertese in the 1960s.

Isabel Province

Isabel Province is dominated by Santa Isabel, the Solomons' longest island at 200km long and 30km wide. Other islands include San Jorge, smaller islands in the Western and Arnarvon groups, and Ramos to the east.

Isabel Province has 16,500 people in an area of 4014 sq km. Logging is a major activity. The island is rich in minerals, but commercial mining is just beginning. Fishing and copra production are supplemented by coffee growing and cattle, and harvesting trocchus shell and beche-de-mer.

The province receives very few foreign visitors.

History

Mendaña sighted and named Santa Isabel on 7 February 1568. Relationships between Spaniards and islanders were initially friendly but soon deteriorated and violence ensued. The Spaniards were disgusted by cannibalism and lizard worship and left after only two months.

Frenchman Jean de Surville showed up in 1769 and captured a young boy to 'display' in Paris. French missionary Bishop Jean-Baptiste Epalle went ashore unarmed in 1845 and was mortally wounded.

In the mid-19th century, Isabel people suffered at the hands of head-hunters from Simbo, New Georgia and Malaita. Epidemics of European diseases also took a terrible toll. The people of Santa Isabel's south coast were wiped out.

Isabel, initially under German control, was transferred to Britain in 1899.

In 1929, Richard Fallowes, a British missionary, supported the local people's right to autonomy and pressed for a Santa Isabel parliament. This call soon spread as far as Nggela. Fallowes was deported in 1934. He returned in 1939 to reorganise his campaign called the Chair & Rule Movement. Fallowes was expelled again in 1940.

In 1942, the Japanese occupied Santa Isabel, establishing a large base at Suavanao in Rakata Bay.

Information

Buala, the provincial capital, has a hospital. There are clinics at Nodana, Poro, Tatamba, Vulavu, Guguha, Kalenga, Kolomola, Kolotubi, Susubona, Samasodu, Kia, Bolotei and

SOLOMON ISLANDS

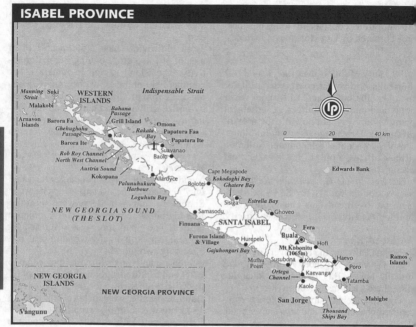

ISABEL PROVINCE

Baolo. Malaria is widespread, especially in Kia and Santa Isabel's south coastal villages.

Buala has the only formal accommodation in the province.

Getting There & Away

Air Solomon Airlines flies from Honiara to both Fera (Buala; S$165) and Suavanao (S$215) in the north-west weekly. There is a Solomon Airlines agent (☎ 35015) in Buala.

Boat The Isabel Development Corporation runs the *Ligomo IV* or *Ligomo V* between Isabel and Honiara weekly. Fares range from S$48 (Sepi) to S$62 (Kia); to Buala it costs S$54.

The *Ocean Express* runs between Honiara and eastern Isabel each week.

There are wharves at Buala, Tatamba, Kaevanga, Allardyce and Kia. Santa Isabel also has anchorages at Cockatoo Island, Thousand Ships Bay, Susubona, Gajuhongari Bay, Furona, Finuana Island, Samasodu,

Loguhutu Bay, Palunuhukuru Harbou[r], Kokopana Island, Suavanao and Kokodog[hi] and Estrella bays.

Two channels in the province require pa[r]ticular care: Ortega Channel is usual[ly] navigable to a minimum depth of 2.4m[.] North West Channel is exceptionally na[r]row and can be very turbulent.

Getting Around

To/From the Airport Fera airfield is o[n] Fera Island, 3km from Buala. A canoe rid[e] with the Solomon Airlines agent is S$10.

Boat Transport around the province is ea[s]iest by motor-canoe; however, Isabel[']s shores are exposed to rough weathe[r.] Motor-canoe journeys are expensive. Th[e] cheapest charters are through Buala['s] provincial fisheries (☎ 35108).

Tractor There are 22km of tractor routes i[n] the province, 17km between Kaevanga an[d]

olomola. There's also a track between Ka-
aosi and the sea at Kasera, another be-
ween Buma and Visena, and logging roads
round Allardyce.

ANTA ISABEL
pop 16,000 • **area 3380 sq km**
alled Mbughotu in the local language, this
rge volcanic island has sheer-sided moun-
in ranges dissected by river valleys. Man-
rove and freshwater swamps are common
the lowlands.

Inland villages in south-eastern Santa
abel were built high on ridges (up to
00m) for defence against head-hunters.

Buala
bout 2000 people live in Buala, a very
uiet little town spread along 2.2km of the
tractive Maringe Lagoon. Buala hugs a
arrow littoral strip between the Maringe
agoon and Tirotonga Hill's very steep
des. Forests and coconut plantations cling
recariously to the rugged escarpment,
hich climbs to 800m.

nformation Buala has the provincial
overnment offices, a hospital (☎ 35016), a
olice station (☎ 35063), a post office,
BSI and Solomon Airlines agencies, a
harf, and a Telekom office (☎ 35040).

laces to Stay The *Provincial Assembly
esthouse* (☎ 35031, ext 212), in Buala,
harges S$20 for a bed in one of four fan-
ooled double rooms with shared facilities.
he friendly *Mothers' Union Resthouse*
☎ 35035), in Jejevo, charges S$35 a night
ith shared facilities. It has a card phone.

Near the Church of Melanesia headquar-
rs is its *Diocesan Resthouse* (☎ 35011),
harging S$35 per bed.

See also Eco-Tourist Villages later in this
ection.

Maringe Lagoon
ive small islands face Buala across the
alm lagoon waters. The largest is Fera,
ith golden sand along its northern edge.
era is connected by a 9km-long fringing
eef to Vaghena and Juakau islands.

Eco-Tourist Villages
Three bush villages behind Buala are designed for eco-tourist visits – part of a project that also promotes honey production and
sustainable logging. The charge is S$100 per
day, which includes accommodation, meals
and activities. Contact William Feitei
(☎ 35119), Isabel Sustainable Forest Management Project, PO Box 7, Buala Station.

South-Eastern Santa Isabel
There's a long, sandy beach at **Poro** and
sometimes 2m surf. **Tatamba** is the island's
subprovincial headquarters. Nearby is
Tanabuli Island, a WWII coastwatch site,
and **Lighara**, which has a white-sand beach.
The Lumasa Seseo Cave at **Lokiha** is 1km
north-west of Mboko Point.

Chiefs Bera and Soga are both buried at
Sepi and skull houses are nearby. Another
is 1km inland from **Tinoa** and there's a 19th
century *toa*, or fortress. The remains of
Bera's main fortress are near **Mboula
Point**.

The sheltered **Thousand Ships Bay** was a
19th century traders' anchorage. It was also
used by the Japanese fleet in 1942 prior to
its Tulagi assault. There are attractive coral
gardens on its south-eastern side.

Kaevanga is one of Santa Isabel's more
fertile and populated areas.

North-Western Santa Isabel
The north coastline is convoluted with
swampy bays and a few sandy beaches
separated by rugged promontories and
cliffs. **Cape Megapode** is named after the
incubator birds that nest there.

Although Mendaña reported that this area
was heavily populated, 19th century head-
hunting left it with only six settlements
north-west of Maringe Lagoon.

Over 1000 people live in **Kia**, a large village with stores, a fisheries centre and a police station. Many of Kia's houses are built
on stilts over the water.

SAN JORGE
• **pop 500** • **area 200 sq km**
The province's second-largest island was
named Ysla de Jorge by Mendaña, but the

island's inhabitants knew it as Moumolu-Naunitu. The largest of its four villages is **Kaolo**, the subprovincial headquarters.

THE WESTERN & ARNARVON ISLANDS

● pop 0   ● area 432 sq km

Many of the Western Islands and the Arnarvon Islands barely protrude above the water and none are inhabited. The Arnarvon Islands are one of the world's largest nesting grounds for the endangered hawksbill turtle.

There are attractive lagoons throughout the Western Islands, notably Austria Sound and Rob Roy Channel.

Rennell & Bellona Province

Rennell and Bellona islands, traditionally known as Mu Nggava and Mu Ngiki respectively, are Polynesian outliers. Both are uplifted-coral atolls and extremely rocky. Rennell is unique – raised five times and with separate stages clearly visible on its cliff face. East Rennell is a national wildlife park and has been a World Heritage Site since 1998. South of Rennell are the Indispensable Reefs, which extend over 123km of sea.

History

Lapita people occupied Bellona initially around 1000 BC, and subsequent settlements date from 130 BC. The present-day Polynesian inhabitants claim ancestorship from Uvea (Wallis Island) – their ancestors landed around 1400 AD. The islanders waged bloody war on each other well into the 20th century.

Captain Benjamin Boyd, aboard the *Bellona*, was the first European to see the islands, in 1793. Afterwards there was barely any European contact until Bishop Selwyn's short stay in July 1856. Missionaries came in 1910, and three Melanesians stayed on, only to be killed after a sudden epidemic caused many deaths.

The Protectorate authorities closed th islands, and they remained isolated unt 1934, when mission ships arrived to recru villagers for religious instruction. Tw years later the recruits came back and the i landers slowly stopped fighting and took u Christianity.

There was murderous violence betwee newly converted Christians and traditiona ists who revered Semoana. Then a pictur of Jesus was seen to speak, and rituals, god and traditions were abandoned for funda mentalist Christianity.

Climate

The average annual rainfall is 4250mm. Jar uary, February and March are the onl months in which it doesn't rain almost daily

Flora & Fauna

The Rennellese orchid is particularly strik ing with multiple mauve veins on a whit flower, with a pale-yellow undersurface.

A number of bird species are endemic t Rennell, including the Rennell fantail an the rare Rennell white spoonbill. At leas eight subspecies that have evolved dis tinctive features have been identified o Rennell.

Lake Te'Nggano attracts circling flock of frigates, cormorants and boobies, espe cially at dawn and dusk.

The *tugihono* is a freshwater snake foun only in Lake Te'Nggano. It's deadly, bu very docile.

Language

People in Rennell and Bellona speak Polynesian language closely related t Samoan.

Information

The Rennell and Bellona Provincial Offic (☎ 24251), PO Box 1764, is in Honiara' Chinatown. Staff will help organise trips t the province, including booking accommo dation by radio.

There are no telephones on the islands but you will be able to make satellite tele phone contact with Telekom on Rennell Is land (☎ 0061-145 11 272).

etting There & Away

ir From Honiara, Solomon Airlines flies
Rennell (S$220), via Bellona (S$205),
vice a week. The Bellona-Rennell sector
ests S$105. Rennell airfield is known
cally as Tinggoa.

oat Boat services are very infrequent. Na-
onal Shipping makes the 24-hour trip from
oniara once a month at best. Universal
hipping and the Church of Melanesia visit
ery occasionally. The fare is around S$80.
Rennell's only anchorage is at Lavanggu,
ough ships also wait offshore at Tuhung-
anggo and Mangga Utu.
Vessels calling at Bellona moor about
00m offshore at Potuhenua.

etting Around

o/From the Airport One of the island's
ree tractors meets the planes at Tinggoa
rport.

ractor The 32km tractor trail between
inggoa and Lavanggu has been extended
8km through to Lake Te'Nggano. The
umpy ride through dense rainforest from
inggoa airfield to the lake takes at least
ur hours.
Tractors are available for charter at S$20
er hour. Anyone can catch the tractor and
et off anywhere on its route by paying
$1.

RENNELL ISLAND
pop 1500   • area 629 sq km
ennell is 202km south of Guadalcanal
cross the Solomon Sea; it's 80km long and
4km wide. Rennell's coast is comprised of
mestone cliffs (up to 200m) covered by
ense bush. Reef surrounds the island. The
orth coastline is straight; Kanggava Bay is
deep inlet in the undulating south coast.
rom the island's raised rim, the land sur-
ace gradually sinks to nearly sea level in
ennell's central basin.
At 130 sq km, Lake Te'Nggano, in the
outh-east, is the South Pacific's largest ex-
anse of fresh water. Both the east-central
nd far-western parts of Rennell are unin-
abited wildernesses of towering trees.

Information
There are clinics at Tinggoa and Te'
Nggano. The island is malaria-free. Electricity is provided by private generators.
Rainwater tanks and wells provide drinking
water. The few stores on the island sell limited goods.

Places to Stay
Moreno Guesthouse, near Tinggoa airfield,
is clean and has kitchen facilities. Beds cost
S$25 per night. The *Airport Lodge* by the
airfield has similar facilities and charges the
same price.
Tahamatangi Resthouse on the western
shore of Lake Te'Nggano offers beds for
S$40 per person. There are basic kitchen
facilities, and meals are available. Canoe
transfers from Tebaitahe cost S$40. The
Lakeside Lodge on the northern shore is
similarly priced; canoe transfers are S$10
per person.

Lake Te'Nggano
The brackish 130 sq km Lake Te'Nggano is
27km long, up to 9km wide and is surrounded by lofty cliffs. Its western end has
200-odd coral islets and swamps where taro
grows. Four large villages hug the shore:
Te'Nggano, which is the subprovincial headquarters, Tebaitahe, Niupani and Hutuna.
The lake has stilt-houses over the water
and coral limestone hills behind. Bird life is
abundant. Marine life includes freshwater
prawns and giant eels, and the reedy shores
provide cover for monitor lizards.
Motor-canoe charters for lake trips are
pricey at around S$200 per day including
fuel, while guided rainforest walks cost
S$10 per person per hour. Octopus Cave on
the northern shore is a popular excursion.

BELLONA
• pop 1000   • area 15 sq km
Bellona Island is densely populated, with a
fertile interior. It's 180km south of Guadalcanal and surrounded by forest-covered cliffs
rising 30m to 70m high. Bellona's cliffs are
often easy to climb, unlike Rennell's.
Since the 1970s many Bellonese people
have reacted against the dominance of

fundamentalist Christianity. Many have deserted the large church-dominated villages and returned to their traditional lands. Bellona is pock-marked with caves. There are beaches at Ahanga and One.

Information

Bellona Island's only clinic is at Pauta. As on Rennell, drinking water here is always scarce. Bellona is free of malaria.

Western Bellona

Bellona Island's most sacred ancient rituals took place at the Nggabengga site in **Matahenua**. Around here are caves where early Bellonese settlers lived. They were occupied right up to the 1930s. **Angu Cave** is about 450m to Matahenua's south-east.

Eastern Bellona

The Tapuna and Saamoa **caves** are 1km to the north of Matangi. Tradition says the Hiti people lived in stone buildings inside them. Some stone remains can still be seen in **Tapuna Cave**. About 300m south of the road at Ahenoa is the **Teahaa Cave**.

The Hiti Walls at **Ou'taha** are a weathered line of coral rocks, the remains of an uplifted reef. Traditionally, the Hiti people are said to have built these huge coral structures before the first Polynesians arrived.

Places to Stay

The friendly *Suani Resthouse* at Tangakitonga charges from S$35 per person. It has a kitchen, and meals are available. Bicycle hire and bushwalking/snorkelling trips with lunch can be arranged.

The beautifully situated *Aotaha Cave Resort* on the east coast enjoys cool sea breezes. Beds are S$40 and cave tours and bike hire are available. It has a kitchen, and meals are available on request.

Getting Around

A tractor trail runs from Potuhenua in the north-west, Bellona's only anchorage, and continues to the south-eastern tip at Ana'otanggo. The island's one tractor meets every flight and ship. It shuttles passengers anywhere along it's route for S$1.

Malaita Province

The province's 96,000 people make it th most densely populated part of the countr They are all Melanesian except for 20(Polynesians who live on the far-flung ato of Ontong Java and Sikaiana.

Malaita Island and its immediate neigh bour, Maramasike (sometimes called Sma Malaita), occupy 98% of the 4243 sq k province. Together they are 191km long ar 47km wide.

MALAITA ISLAND

● **pop 89,000**   ● **area 3840 sq km**

Malaita's rugged highland interior rises 1303m at Mt Kolovrat. Deep valleys, shar ridges and fast-flowing rivers have ol structed cross-island movement and Mala tans speak many different languages. Fierc inter-tribal fighting stopped in the 1920s.

Islanders from the central and south eastern parts still worship ancestral spiri and live almost entirely by shifting cultiva tion and barter.

The artificial islands in Langa Langa ar Lau lagoons are built in the shallows wit coral boulders taken from the nearby ree On these islands the tradition of shark wo ship still lingers.

History Oral histories of the Kwaio peopl – the most fierce, traditional and indeper dent of the islanders – from Malaita's eas central mountains, claim ancestors that g back 150 generations to about 1400 BC. Ar chaeological remains from Kwara'ae vil lages date back to 440 AD.

On Malaita, life was dominated by inte tribal fighting, head-hunting and fea Raiders came from as far away as Santa Isa bel, and villages were heavily fortified Langa Langa and Lau lagoons' artificia islands and cliff-top houses in the interio are relics of very violent times.

Blackbirders raided Malaita Island to and 'recruited' 9000 islanders between 187 and 1903 – often against their will. As a re sult, Malaitans distrusted all white peopl and routinely killed those who visited. Th British government retaliated with force.

There was sporadic fighting between the British Protectorate authorities and the islanders between 1880 and 1911. In 1909, a district office was opened in Auki. Things began to settle until 1927 and the Kwaio Rebellion (see the boxed text 'The Kwaio Rebellion' in Facts about the Solomon Islands earlier in this chapter).

The cruelty of pre-war expatriate plantation managers led to a movement of noncooperation, which, after WWII, became the Marching Rule movement. Many Malaitans went to Guadalcanal to work at the huge US base. The postwar Marching Rule movement united Malaita and Maramasike islanders in opposition to the restored British Protectorate government (see History in the Facts about the Solomon Islands section).

Climate Auki gets 3271mm of rain per year over 236 days. January to March is the wettest period. Morning humidity reaches 90% and temperatures range from 23 to 30°C.

Information Kastom fees and canoe rides can be expensive in Malaita, and locals

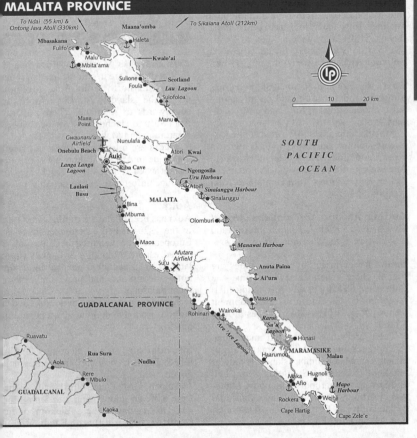

MALAITA PROVINCE

To Ndai (55 km) & Ontong Java Atoll (330km)

To Sikaiana Atoll (212km)

Maana'omba

Mbasakana
Fulifo'oe
Malu'u
Mbita'ama
Haleta
Kwalo'ai

Sulione
Foula
Scotland
Lau Lagoon
Sulofoloa

Manu
Point
Manu

Gwaunaru'u
Airfield
Onebulu Beach
Nunulafa
Atori Kwai

Auki
*Langa Langa
Lagoon*
Riba Cave
Ngongosila
Uru Harbour
Atoifi
Sinalanggu Harbour
Sinalanggu

Laulasi
Busu
Bina
Mbuma
MALAITA

Olomburi

Maoa

Afutara
Airfield
Su'u
Manawai Harbour

Anuta Paina
Ai'ura

Kiu
Maasupa

GUADALCANAL PROVINCE
Rohinari
Wairokai
*Raroi
Su'u
Lagoon*
Hunasi

*SOUTH
PACIFIC
OCEAN*

0   10   20 km

Ruavatu

Rua Sura
Nudha

Aola
Rere
Mbulo

GUADALCANAL

Kaoka

'Are 'Are Lagoon

Haarumou
MARAMASIKE
Malau

Maka
Afio
Hugnoli

Rockera
Weihli
Cape Hartig
*Mapo
Harbour*

Cape Zele'e

might claim to be landowners and demand fees that they're not entitled to. A guide might help with these negotiations.

Malaita has hospitals at Kilu'ufi (near Auki) and at Atoifi. There is a dentist at Kilu'ufi.

Auki has places to stay, but elsewhere on Malaita the options are limited. There's simple accommodation in Malu'u, Atoifi, Foula, Maoa and on Kwai and Ngongsila islands. *Solomons Village Stay* (see Accommodation under Facts for the Visitor earlier in this chapter) has a place in the north of Malaita Island and another south of Auki.

Getting There & Away Air All flights into Malaita come from Honiara. Solomon Airlines flies daily to Auki (twice most days; S$130), and twice a week to Parasi (S$165) on Maramasike Island. There's a Solomon Airlines office (☎ 40163) in Auki.

Boat From Honiara, National Shipping runs a monthly boat to Auki and on to Ontong Java; another goes to Su'u and on to Sikaiana Atoll.

Malaita Shipping's MV *Ramos I* plies between Honiara and Auki (S$37) twice a week, and goes every second week to Malaita's northern and southern ports. The *Ocean Express* goes from Honiara to Auki weekly (S$42).

Getting Around To/From the Airport Gwaunaru'u airfield is 10km from Auki and a S$20 ride in the Solomon Airlines bus.

Boat Charter prices of motor-canoes are higher here than elsewhere in the Solomons; S$150 per day (excluding fuel) is common. The Fisheries Development Centre (☎ 40161) in Auki charges around S$100.

There are wharves at Auki and Foula. Anchorages include Mbita'ama, Malu'u, Haleta (on Maana'omba Island), Kwalo'ai and Scotland islands, Sulofoloa, Atori, Uru and Sinalanggu harbours, Olomburi, Manawai Harbour, Ai'ura Island, Maasupa, Maka, Wairokai, Rohinari, Waisisi Harbour, Kiu, Mbuma and Laulasi.

Artificial Islands

A feature of Malaita is the large number o artificial islands, particularly in Langa Langa and Lau lagoons. They're built or sand bars or reefs by piling up boulders.

A few islands date from the 1550s, anc new ones are built each year. The bigges are more than 1 sq km in size and some are surrounded by a coral wall. Most, however, are very small and consist of a few houses on stilts.

An island takes around a year to build Stones from the lagoon floor are collected and canoed or rafted to the site, and piled up 2m above the high tide mark. Sand is spread around, houses are built and coconuts palms are planted.

Cars & Trucks Most of Maliata Island 325km of road are in chronic need of repa Roads run north from Auki to Foul across the island to Atori and Atoifi, ar southwards to Asimana. There's a trac from Su'u to Hauhui, and another betwee Haarumou and Maka.

Trucks are infrequent. The best place get a ride in Auki is at the wharf or nearb market when a ship calls in. Trucks are slo and uncomfortable, but reasonably price

Auki

Auki has been Malaita's capital since 190 In the 1920s it had a perimeter fence ar Europeans who ventured beyond took a armed escort. Auki, the Solomons' third largest town, has 4000 people, and shop hotels, restaurants and provincial gover ment buildings.

There are good views over Auki and it harbour from a high point 200m behind th prison.

Information There's a Secretary for Cu ture & Tourism (☎ 40059) in the provincia government.

Auki has ANZ and NBSI banks, ope from 8.30 am to noon and 1 to 3 pm Mor day to Friday. The Telekom offic (☎ 40152, fax 40220) is on Batabu Rd.

Auki often has periods of the day without
~~ter. Treat or boil tap water before drink-
~ it.

The hospital is at Kilu'ufi (☎ 40272),
~km north of town.

~waibala River There's a good swimming
~ot in the Kwaibala River near the pump
~use on the road to Ambu. Jack Sibisoa at
~ pump house can guide you up to the
~ve waterfall nearby. Near the river's
~uth a house stands midstream on two
~ncrete stilts.

~ki This 80m-wide artificial island is 1km
~m town and home to two families. It
~s, at one time, the home of shark wor-
~ippers and there are kastom areas con-
~ining ancestral skulls. Men can visit
~se sites with permission, but they're
~bu for women. Ask before you photo-
~aph anything. Auki Island people have
~en known to ask S$50 landing fees from

those wishing to see their island. It's not
worth that much money.

Canoes go to or past the island from the
Auki Wharf, Lilisiana and Ambu.

Lilisiana This very friendly village is
1.2km walk from the wharf. It has houses
on stilts over the water and women make
shell money and necklaces here, polishing
them on special work benches.

Lilisiana has a long golden-sand spit beside coral shallows. Ask permission to
swim or sunbathe there.

Beside the beach is Osi Lagoon.

Places to Stay The *SSEC Transit House*
(☎ 40173) is clean and quiet. It has three
rooms with eight beds and charges S$35 a
person. The kitchen is communal, and there
are shared showers and toilets.

Auki Travellers Motel (☎ 40395) is comfortable and good value. It's on the 1st floor
and charges S$45 per bed or S$90/100 for

SOLOMON ISLANDS

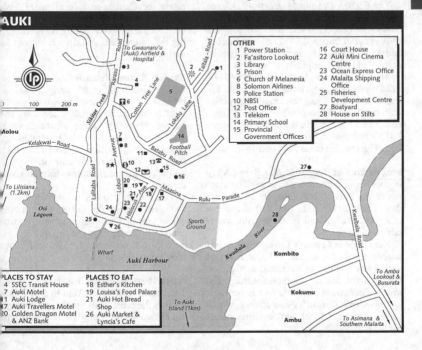

AUKI

0   100   200 m

Molou

Kelakwai—Road

To Lilisiana
(1.2km)

Osi
Lagoon

Sibeue Creek

Kirarau Road

To Gwaunaru'u
(Auki) Airfield &
Hospital

Road

Talala—Road

Cotton Tree Lane

Lokafu Lane

Lalitaba Road

Loboi

Avenue

Football
Pitch

Batabu Road

Hibiscus Ave

Maasina

Rulu — Parade

Sports
Ground

Wharf   Auki Harbour

Kwaibala River

Kombito

Kwaibala Road

To Ambu
Lookout &
Busurata

Kokumu

To Auki
Island (1km)

Ambu

To Asimana &
Southern Malaita

OTHER
1 Power Station
2 Fa'asitoro Lookout
3 Library
5 Prison
6 Church of Melanesia
8 Solomon Airlines
9 Police Station
10 NBSI
12 Post Office
13 Telekom
14 Primary School
15 Provincial
    Government Offices
16 Court House
22 Auki Mini Cinema
    Centre
23 Ocean Express Office
24 Malaita Shipping
    Office
25 Fisheries
    Development Centre
27 Boatyard
28 House on Stilts

PLACES TO STAY
4 SSEC Transit House
7 Auki Motel
11 Auki Lodge
17 Auki Travellers Motel
20 Golden Dragon Motel
   & ANZ Bank

PLACES TO EAT
18 Esther's Kitchen
19 Louisa's Food Palace
21 Auki Hot Bread
   Shop
26 Auki Market &
   Lyncia's Cafe

Shark Calling

Laulasi islanders traditionally worshipped sharks. In ceremonies that are rare these days, sharks are summoned to the shore by villagers beating stones together underwater and baiting it with pig meat. The dramatic ritual ends with a young boy astride a large shark, riding around the lagoon.

The shark worshippers believe that their ancestors and those of the shark are connected. Black and red are *tabu* (taboo) on Laulasi – black is associated with pig skin, and red with blood. Pick between the rest of your wardrobe when visiting.

a single/double with private shower/toilet. Good, inexpensive meals are served in the pleasant dining room.

The *Auki Motel* (☎ 40014), next to Solomon Airlines, has singles/doubles for S$90/100 and shared rooms at S$45 per bed.

The *Golden Dragon Motel* (☎ 40113) has beds available from S$35 per person. Twins or doubles cost S$90 and larger rooms with shower/toilet cost S$120. There's a kitchen and a lobby area. If no-one is there, inquire at the Auki Store opposite.

The top place is *Auki Lodge* (☎ 40131, PO Box 171). Rooms have showers and toilets, and there's a bar, restaurant and lounge with satellite TV. Fan-cooled singles/doubles cost S$90/130, standard air-con rooms are S$120/140 and deluxe rooms cost S$160/200. The restaurant serves good food.

Places to Eat The *Auki Hot Bread Shop* is open from 6 am to 8 pm daily. The store under the Auki Motel is open 24 hours a day. The *market* sells fish and chips and other snacks, as well as fresh fruit, vegetables and fish.

Next door is *Lyncia's Cafe*, which offers simple meals for under S$10, and opens until 5 pm Monday to Thursday, 8.30 pm on Friday night, and till noon on Saturday. *Esther's Kitchen* on Hibiscus Ave is similar.

Opposite is *Louisa's Food Palace*, which serves excellent lunch and evening meals for around S$20.

The *Auki Travellers Motel* serves thr good meals a day. The evening mains *Auki Lodge* are very good and start around S$35; it's licensed.

Entertainment The *Auki Mini Cinema* in Hibiscus Ave. Entry costs S$4.

Around Auki

A tough one hour walk east of Auki is D wasi and the **Riba Cave**. The kastom fee around S$20 and you'll need a guide an torch (flashlight).

Onebulu Beach, at the mouth of the l River 9km north of Auki, is the best in area.

South-Western Malaita Island

Langa Langa Lagoon Langa Langa l goon, just south of Auki, is famous for artificial islands, particularly Laulasi a Alite. Tours of the lagoon can be arrang in Auki – ask at your hotel or see the Se retary for Culture and Tourism. JT Ente prises (☎ 40197), Hibiscus Ave, Auki, c take people to visit Busu for S$150, inclu ing the canoe, fuel and driver, but not ka tom fees.

Laulasi & Busu Islands Laulasi is an ar ficial island built in the early 1600s, a Busu is the larger island immediately sou west. Separated from public areas are spi houses where the skulls of ancestors a dead enemies are housed. Only males m enter these areas. Because of recent la disputes, Laulasi is not currently open tourists, but Busu welcomes foreign visite for a fee.

You can get to Busu by taking a S truck ride to Talakali, 16km from Au where you can arrange return transport l canoe. If you organise the trip through yo hotel you'll be sure of costs and kasto fees before you set out.

Northern Malaita Island

The 'north road' from Auki to Lau Lago follows the coast from Sisifiu to Silolo, pr viding sea views. Long stretches of whit sand beach line the shore.

bita'ama Mbita'ama is 65km along the rth road. A **marine cave** at nearby waiorua Point called Mana Ruuakwa netrates inland, terminating in a deep le in the ground. Islanders say sharks me here to sleep. Shell money is made in bita'ama.

basakana Beautiful Mbasakana Island ronounced 'mbatha-**ka**-na') is 2km long d 1km wide. Surrounded by reef and nite-sand beaches, this flat landmass is out 1.5km from Fulifo'oe on Malaita's rth coast. The friendly Mbasakana villgers can show you an interesting cave arby.

alu'u This friendly subprovincial head-arters is a good stop on the 'north road' tween Auki (five hours over 82km of eadful road) and Lau Lagoon at the 'head ad' two hours away. There's a good beach re, and another round the point to the st. Malu'u has a monument to Malaita's st missionary, who arrived in 1894. The wn has stores, electricity and piped water.

A 4km hilltop trail behind Malu'u leads **A'ama**, where there's a *biu* (a treehouse r initiated boys). One kilometre farther is **ala**, where there's a skull house.

Malu'u Lodge, above Tang's store, has phone – make bookings by radio. There e kitchen and bathroom facilities, and the st is S$40 per person.

Ask around for Ishmael & Florence Ila-nia who offer a very clean room in their ouse behind town for S$20 per person. here are views over the bay to Mbasakana land.

Malu'u is a very religious community d none of the trade stores sell beer.

au Lagoon This 35km-long lagoon con-ins more than 60 artificial islands. It retches from the shallows between **Uru-u** and **Maana'omba**, where there are arti-cial islands, down to **Lolowai** (see the xed text 'Artificial Islands' earlier in this apter).

There's a strong tradition of shark call-g, especially on **Funaafou**, and people practise animism merged with elements of Christianity.

Central & Eastern Malaita Island
There's a road across the mountainous interior to the east coast around Atori that is washed out in the midyear wet season. The route begins near Dala, and it's most scenic spot is at Nunulafa, where it crosses over the Auluta Gorge.

Atori, 61km east of Auki, is a subprovincial headquarters. There's surf in **Fakanakafo Bay** and at **Manu**, 14km north.

MARAMASIKE
• pop 7000   • area 700 sq km

Small Malaita, as Maramasike Island is often called, is separated from Malaita Island by the 20km-long Maramasike Passage. In places it's less than 400m wide and only 4m deep, but plenty of coastal shipping passes through. There are simple *resthouses* at **Haunasi** and at the school at **Rokera**.

There's a large archaeological site at **Hugnoli** – you'll need permission from the kastom owners at **Weihii** to visit.

SIKAIANA ATOLL
• pop 300   • area 2 sq km

The triangular atoll of Sikaiana lies 212km north-east of Malaita Island. The atoll's lagoon has three small, raised islets on its western side, and Sikaiana Island, built up from an extinct volcano, to the east.

ONTONG JAVA ATOLL
• pop 1700   • area 12 sq km

The Solomons' northernmost point is Ontong Java, also known as Lord Howe Atoll. Its Polynesian inhabitants often call it Luaniua.

Ontong Java is just south of the Equator and 258km north of Santa Isabel; it's 50km from north to south and 57km wide. Its huge 1400 sq km lagoon contains 122 islands. Except for three rocks, nothing is higher than 13m above sea level. Most islets are barely 2m high and very vulnerable to rising sea levels.

The only sizable populations are in **Luaniua** and **Pelau**.

Makira/Ulawa Province

Makira, the province's main island, is 3188 sq km, 139km long and 40km wide. Ulawa is 75km to the north. The province's 28,000 people are renowned for their traditional dancing and carving.

History

Lapita pottery from around 1400 BC has been found at Pono'ohey on Makira Island.

The region was violent, but there were also long periods of peace. Ceramics were made, and trade flourished between Makira and Ulawa. There was fighting between coastal and bush people. Mercenaries from Santa Ana attacked the Makiran coast and professional assassins were active until the 1920s. Human flesh was essential for feasting and ancestor worship was practised.

Hernando Henriques, one of Mendaña's expeditioners, sighted Makira Island in May 1568. The Spaniards took hostages to exchange for food and 93 war canoes attacked the expedition at Waiae Bay.

Jean de Surville came in 1769, John Shortland in 1788 and Alexander Ball two years later. Nineteenth century whalers made the first lasting contacts, trading at Makira Harbour by 1849. European traders settled on Ugi and Santa Ana islands.

The first Marist missionaries came in 1846 – those who weren't eaten fled.

Climate

Makira Island receives 3601mm of rain a year over 235 days. Morning humidity levels reach 95% in February. Temperatures range from 31 to 20°C; August is coolest.

Fauna

The Makiran mountain rail is a 25cm-long, flightless bird that lives in Makira's highlands above 650m. The red-throated fruit dove on Ugi and Makira islands has a snow-white head and chin.

There are more saltwater crocodiles in this province than in any other part of the country.

MAKIRA/ULAWA PROVINCE

The very rare Pacific Ridley turtle ne$ on Makira Island's coast.

Getting There & Away

Air Solomon Airlines flies from Honia into Kirakira's airfield at Ngorangora Makira three times a week; the fare S$215. On Monday it goes on to Santa A Island (S$275, or S$105 from Kirakira) a on Saturday to Santa Cruz (S$535, S$360 from Kirakira).

Boat The *Ocean Express* leaves Honia every Thursday at 8 am and arrives at K rakira at 6 pm, returning the followi morning. National Shipping and Isabel D velopment Corporation vessels come eve few weeks; from Honiara to Kirakira/San Ana costs S$72/80 in economy class.

There's a small jetty at Na Mugha, a anchorages at Kirakira, Maoraha Islan Waimasi and Hada bays, Makira a Marunga harbours and Mwaniwowo.

Getting Around

To/From the Airport The 4km ride fro Ngorangora airfield into Kirakira in th Solomon Airlines vehicle costs S$5.

at & Car There's 48km of unsealed road ing the north coast of Makira Island. A km track goes westwards from Nukukasi the Wainuri River. Most travel is by tor-canoe.

AKIRA

op 22,500   • area 3188 sq km

endaña's name for Makira Island was San istobal, which is still sometimes used. vo-thirds of Makira's people live on the rth coast. Makira's mountains form a ine down its centre, reaching 1040m and lling steeply into the sea along the south. vers cut the island and there are swamps and, some 80m above sea level.

Makira Islanders traditionally worship arks. Many carvings and traditional nces feature shark themes.

formation Kirakira, the provincial cap-l, has a hospital, and there are 13 clinics ound the island. Kirakira tap water needs be boiled before drinking.

Very few tourists come to Makira and rakira has the only proper resthouse.

irakira

government station was established at rakira in 1918, and since then it has be-me home to 3200 people.

formation Kirakira has a hospital, a post fice, a police station, a library, a Solomon rlines branch, a Telekom office and an 3SI bank.

ings to See & Do There is an old build-g up the main street that was the district ficer's residence in colonial times and is id to be a **haunted house**. A girl hanged rself there after an unhappy affair with a strict officer. Her ghost is very beautiful, d very friendly … then she gets nasty!

The **kastom house** by the football field s murals, a leaf roof and carved house-sts. There's a good **sandy beach** 1km to e east.

Ngorangora airfield is 4km west of Kira-a. The coral shore at the eastern end has me small blowholes. A further 2km west

is a small **copra mill** that you're welcome to look around.

Places to Stay & Eat The *Provincial Government Resthouse* has eight double rooms with communal kitchen and washing facilities. The charge is S$30 per person.

There are several stores in town, includ-ing a *Hot Bread Shop*. The stores opposite the hospital sell beer. There's a small *mar-ket* by Puepue Creek, and the adjoining store sells fish.

North-Western Makira

The north-west coast of Makira Island is rugged and sparsely inhabited. Thickly wooded hills reach down to the waterline. The island's mountainous spine is often cloud-covered. Outrigger canoes are built at **Maro'u**.

The crew of the Spanish galleon *Santa Is-abel* landed near the headland 750m east of **Pamua** in 1595, after becoming separated from Mendaña's second expedition. A hill-top fortress and 16th-century Spanish pot-tery were discovered there, but there's nothing to see now.

The Solomons' most protected anchorage, **Makira Harbour**, was a favourite of whalers. It has a narrow inlet and a wide lagoon.

South-Eastern Makira

Maroghu and Marunga harbours both have black-sand beaches interspersed with man-grove swamps. About 20km south of Kira-kira is **Hauta**, which receives occasional visitors who walk along the river. It's a good area for bird-watching but visits must be pre-arranged. Contact Soltrust in Honi-ara (☎ 30947).

Tawarogha, on the east coast, has good surf between May and July.

There's a kastom house with impressive carvings at **Wosu** on the Surville Peninsula.

SANTA ANA

Santa Ana has 1600 people and is very fer-tile. Also known as Owa Rafa, it's a raised coral atoll up to 143m in height. The island has beaches on its western side, and turtles lay eggs north of Mary Bay.

At **Ghupuna** there are many carvers. There's an ancient Polynesian track over the hill to **Nataghera** where two kastom houses contain ancestral skulls, bones and war canoes, some of them 500 years old.

THE THREE SISTERS ISLANDS

Also known as the Olu Malau group, the Three Sisters lie about 20km east of Ugi. They're low-lying raised coral atolls that are home to 100 people. There's good swimming, diving and fishing.

ULAWA

Although geographically and culturally closer to southern Malaita, 65 sq km Ulawa Island is administered with Makira, and has 2600 inhabitants.

The thickly forested interior is cut by ravines. The west coast is lined with low coral-limestone cliffs, while the eastern seaboard is generally coral sand. Ulawa is administered from **Hadja**.

Temotu Province

Formerly called the Eastern Outer Islands, Temotu Province is the most easterly part of the Solomons. The islands are a widely dispersed archipelago and are separated from the rest of the country by the 6000m-deep Torres Trench.

Three island groups make up the province: the volcanic Santa Cruz Islands – Santa Cruz (Nendo), Tinakula, Utupua and Vanikoro; the nearby Reef Islands, low coral terraces and sandy atolls; and the Duff Islands – Tikopia, Anuta and uninhabited Fatutaka – which are extinct volcanoes and extremely remote.

Temotu's islands cover 926 sq km, scattered over a huge 150,000 sq km of sea. Vanuatu's Torres and Banks groups, 173km to the south-west, are the closest neighbours, while the nearest Solomons' land mass is Makira/Ulawa 400km west.

There are 19,600 mainly Melanesian people living on the larger islands, with Polynesians living on the small coral cays and isolated volcanic islands.

History

Melanesians from New Guinea settled Santa Cruz around 1500 BC to 1400 E The Lapita people left their distinctive m on Tikopia, the Reef Islands, the Duffs a Anuta Island from around 1000 BC to € BC.

Melanesians settled the Duffs in 1 A but were overrun by Polynesians in the m 15th century. Polynesians began arriving Tikopia around 1200 AD and gradua eliminated the pre-existing people. Tonga raided the region regularly and wiped whole populations. Tongan nobles came rule Tikopia and dominate the region (cept for Santa Cruz), but warriors fr Uvea (present-day Wallis Island), Rotu (now part of Fiji) and Niue made sorties the islands.

Warfare was domestic also: land pr sures were great and caused inter-tri bloodshed.

In the early 18th century, Tikopian for raided Vanikoro, 240km to the north-w and slaughtered all the Melanesians Tevai Island. Melanesians then drove Tikopian colonists out.

The first European contact was made Mendaña on his return to the Solomons 1595.

On 7 September he found and nam Santa Cruz. The Spaniards had a testy re tionship with the islanders. They buil camp at Pala in Graciosa Bay, but aba doned it after just a few weeks, by wh time nearly 50 settlers had perished at hands of islanders or from malaria (incl ing Mendaña).

In 1606, Quirós set out to rediscover Sa Cruz but found the Duff Islands inste Philip Cartaret in the HMS *Swallow* ca upon Santa Cruz in August 1767, but hos islanders drove him away after a few day

In 1797, Captain Wilson in the missi ary ship *Duff* named this island group a his vessel.

The first substantive European cont with Tikopia Islanders was in 1813, wh Irishman Peter Dillon stopped by in *Hunter*. He landed three passengers at th request – a Prussian doctor called Buckha

his Fijian wife, and an Indian sailor. He
urned in 1826 to pick them up.

Bishop Patteson visited Nukapu in the
ef Islands in 1871, shortly after Aus-
ian blackbirders had shot or kidnapped
eral locals. Patteson and two of his ship-
tes were battered to death, and in return,
kapu was shelled by a British warship.
Mission ships, traders and blackbirders
osed the islanders to new European dis-
es and population numbers plummeted.
A major WWII sea action, the Battle of
nta Cruz, was fought offshore in October
42.

imate
nta Cruz gets 4325mm of rain per year.
ere's rain most days, especially in Feb-
ry and March. Average temperatures are
°C from December to February, and
.5°C in August. Morning humidity levels
ch 90% in March and April.

Tikopia has about 4000mm of rainfall a
year; heaviest between October and March.
Cyclones occasionally strike. Year-round
temperatures range from 25 to 29°C.

Fauna
The Pacific tree boa is very common in the
Reefs. The very rare Santa Cruz ground pi-
geon is found in only three places in the
world: Tinakula, Utupua and Espiritu Santo,
Vanuatu's largest island.

Language
The people of the Santa Cruz Islands and
the majority of the Reef Islands are Papuan-
speaking Melanesians like the Papuans of
PNG. Elsewhere Polynesian languages are
spoken.

Getting There & Away
Lata, on Santa Cruz Island, has the
province's only airfield. Solomon Airlines
flies from Honiara (S$535) twice a week.
Once a week it goes via Kirakira.

SOLOMON ISLANDS

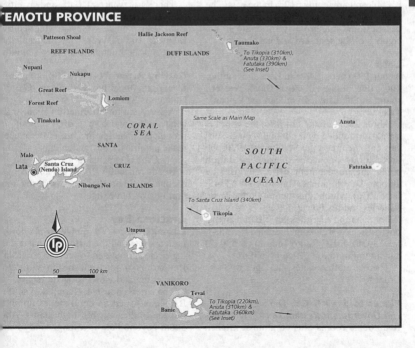

TEMOTU PROVINCE

There are very few boat services to Lata. National Shipping sails once or twice a week from Honiara. Universal Shipping sometimes makes the trip.

Getting Around

Boats are the only way to get around, and delays are frequent. Boats to Lata from Honiara usually continue to the Reef Islands, but a full tour of the Temotus only happens once every month or two.

Yacht crews should report to immigration at Lata. However, boats heading north from Vanuatu sometimes call at outer islands without clearing customs in Lata.

SANTA CRUZ ISLAND

● pop 10,300   ● area 660 sq km

Officially called Nendo, Santa Cruz is 44km long and 25km wide. The island's western end is composed of a fertile 180m-high coral plateau. The rest of Santa Cruz has few people and is largely undeveloped. It's volcanic, reaching 517m in the east. The north coast is rocky, with some narrow beaches, and mangroves proliferate in the lagoons of the southern and east coasts.

Lata

About 1500 people live in Lata and another 4000 live along Graciosa Bay's western shore. In the distance you can see volcanic Tinakula.

About 200m up the hill from the wharf is a park surrounded by modern buildings. Locals call the area Lata Station. In 1970, the Protectorate opened a district substation here. The government offices house the Temotu Development Authority (☎ 53145, fax 53036), which runs the provincial farm, fisheries and resthouse.

Lata Station also has an NBSI bank, a post office, a Telekom branch (☎ 53034, fax 53036), SIBC Radio Temotu (☎ 53047) and an immigration office (☎ 53061).

There are often water shortages in Santa Cruz.

Places to Stay & Eat The basic *Provincial Government Resthouse* (☎ 53145) has five double rooms plus communal kitchen and washing facilities. It charges S$30 night, but it's always full during the Prov cial Assembly sessions held every weeks.

Just beyond the jetty at Freshpoint *Paul Brown's Resthouse*, charging S$30 night. The best accommodation is at *Lue Resort* (☎ 53144), near the wharf to south. There are 12 double rooms at S$ per person. They're small but have fa and there's a pleasant verandah.

The only sit-down eatery is the *PLC snack shop*, offering simple rice dishes a fish and chips. There's also a *hot bre shop*.

Getting There & Away See the Getti There & Away information for Temo Province for details of scheduled air a sea services.

Motor-canoes travel the 78km to Lo lom in the Reefs for S$50, but the four ho trip there is dangerous in rough seas.

There's a wharf at Lata and a jetty Nanggu. There are anchorages at Kala Ba Big Bau'Venga, Nea, Mbonembw Lueneki Bay, Byron Bay, Lueselem Nepa and the Luembalele River's mouth

Getting Around National Shipping's fa from Lata to either Kala Bay, Gaito Nanggu is S$30.

Ask around for information about shar canoe rides, and be prepared to wait. T provincial fisheries in Lata is the place make inquiries about charter canoes. Fuel Santa Cruz is expensive.

Roads run south from Lata and there a a couple of Forestry roads making loc north-east from Noipe.

Graciosa Bay

Luowa Luowa is 15 minutes' walk north Lata and beyond the airfield. It has a dar ing circle surrounded by smooth coral sla Beyond is a pleasant beach with go snorkelling and views of **Malo Island**.

The chief's house at **Nepu**, 2km south Banua, is raised on coral stones up on hillside, indicating his high status. Abe 500m beyond **Pala** is a long, sandy bea

st inland from here is the pumping sta-
n. Mendaña's settlement was 10m west
the track to the pumping station. About
0m beyond the pumping station turn-off
Luembalele River.

‿ound Santa Cruz Island

‿u'll need a guide to walk to **Nemya Bay**.
‿ndabu and **Naiavila** are abandoned vil-
‿es on the 220m-high knoll, 1.5km south-
st of Pala. A cargo cult emerged at
‿ndabu in the early 1930s.

A coral road runs along Santa Cruz's
‿st coast passing coral walls and friendly
‿lages. A track begins by Lata's radio tow-
‿s, and leads southwards across Santa
‿uz's western plateau before turning east.

New Nea, 10km south of Lata, a foot-
‿th leaves the track and heads southwards
‿shoreside **Nea**.

Nemya Bay has good snorkelling and
‿rfing.

‿UPUA

‿op 740 • area 69 sq km
‿upua Island lies 70km south-east of
‿nta Cruz. The island is 11km across, and
‿ Melanesian population mostly lives
‿und **Nembao**.

VANIKORO

• pop 800 • area 190 sq km

Banie Island and its small neighbour Tevai
are jointly known as Vanikoro. Rainfall is
heavy, with an annual average of 5100mm.

A crater rim forms the tallest peak at Mt
Banie (923m). Three other mountains beside it are subsidiary volcanoes, with traces
of lava flow still visible. A reef surrounds
most of the coastline, which is largely covered by mangroves. The slaty flycatcher, a
small grey bird, is endemic to Vanikoro.

The main centre is **Emua**, on Banie Island, with traditional ellipse-shaped houses,
a sandy beach and coral gardens. Outrigger
canoes are plentiful at **Muruvai**.

In **Paeu**, close to the Laurence River, is
the spot where La Pérouse's survivors built
their doomed getaway vessel. A museum
houses relics from the two sunken French
vessels. Along the coast is **Ramboe Bay**.
The memorial to La Pérouse and his crew is
on this inlet's northern side.

THE REEF ISLANDS

• pop 6000 • area 78 sq km

The Reef Islands lie 78km north of Santa
Cruz. These 16 small landforms are spread
over 4000 sq km of ocean.

SOLOMON ISLANDS

Disaster on the Reef

‿ French expedition, led by Jean-François de Galaup, Comte de la Pérouse, was wrecked at
‿anikoro in a cyclone in 1788. Frigates *Boussole* and *Astrolabe* were lost. La Pérouse's ship,
‿he *Boussole*, sank so quickly that few escaped.

Most of the crew of the *Astrolabe* got ashore at Paeu. They built a two-mast vessel from
‿alvaged material and all but two sailed away into the blue oblivion – their fate is not known.

The two survivors were nearly rescued several times. Captain William Bligh, after the
‿ounty mutiny in 1789, reached Vanikoro in an open boat with his 18 loyal crew. He didn't
‿and, pressing on to reach Timor. Captain Edwards sailed past Vanikoro in 1791 on his mis-
‿ion to capture the *Bounty* mutineers. The French government dispatched Admiral Bruny
‿'Entrecasteaux in 1791 to search for the lost ships. But he also sailed right past the island.

An Indian sailor called Joe visited Vanikoro in 1820 and met the now elderly French sur-
‿ivors. In 1826, the story reached Irishman Peter Dillon on Tikopia, who set off to rescue the
‿nen. He found the remains of the *Astrolabe* but no survivors; one had died and the other
‿ad left Vanikoro.

Two years later, the French explorer Dumont d'Urville heard Dillon's story in Tasmania. He
‿ailed to Vanikoro and built a memorial to La Pérouse at Ramboe Bay.

The Reef Islands are split into two groups – the Outer Reefs and the Main Reefs. The Outer Reefs consists of five very small, low-lying, sandy islets only a few metres above sea level. They feature coral-debris beaches, scrub and coconut vegetation, and surrounding reefs. The population is Polynesian. The most distant islets are Nupani and Nalongo, about 71km north-west of the main group. Closer, but still 28km away, is Nukapu. Makalom and Pileni are closer to the Main Reefs.

The principal islands are in the Main Reefs group. These are Nifiloli, Fenualoa, Ngalo, Ngawa, Nanianimbuli, Gnimbanga Temoa, Gnimbanga Nende, Nola, Ngatendo, Pigeon and Matema.

The Main Reefs

Lomlom Lomlom is the collective name for Ngalo (or Ngambelipa), Ngawa and Nanianimbuli islands. Lomlom is the main centre for the Reefs, with 3800 people. There are coral cliffs and marine caves, only accessible by canoe.

Nifiloli & Fenualoa Islands Nifiloli has beaches at its northern end. The remainder is raised coral, thickly covered with coconut palms. Stretching westwards from Nifiloli village is the 25km-long Great Reef. Dazzling coral and colourful fish make this a favourite dive site.

At low tide you can walk from Nifiloli to Fenualoa Island. Its 1200 people live along its western shore.

Pigeon Island There are no pigeons on this tiny raised-coral islet, just lots of parrots. It's opposite Ngatendo in Mohawk Bay. Accommodation is available at the *Ngarando Resort*. The island has a small store and two houses, each with shower, toilet, kitchen facilities and satellite TV. Prices in Australian dollars are A\$66/99 for singles/doubles. Contact the resort by teleradio from Honiara or Lata. Meals are also served.

The resort organises boat and fishing trips, and provides free snorkelling gear. There's a full dive shop with rental equip-

Red-Feather Money

Santa Cruz red-feather money, or *touau* is still used in parts of Temotu for brid price. Brown pigeon feathers are boun together to form the basis of a long coi which is covered with the red head an breast feathers of the scarlet honey-eate (found only in Temotu). For each red feather coil, 600 birds are trapped plucked and released alive.

Bride price is between five and 24 coils plus cash. After the currency exchange th father of the newly-wed daughter an nounces he has red-feather coils for sale for S\$400 each, to any men with marriag on his mind.

This custom was widespread through out the province but now is only seen o the Duffs.

ment – dives cost A\$60, including equ ment. Underwater visibility is usually go to at least 30m.

The Outer Reefs

The tiny islets of the Outer Reefs are ho to Polynesian people. Some of the 100-o from **Nupani** tend gardens on volca **Tinakula**.

A large, idyllic lagoon surrounds ti **Nukapu**, which is home to 150 people monument commemorates Bishop Pat son's violent death.

Over 200 people live on **Pileni**. Ma epic Polynesian sea voyages w launched from here. Pileni people ca from Tuvalu, and have closer cultural c nections to islanders on Sikaiana and C tong Java, than to Temotu's Polynesians

THE DUFF ISLANDS
● pop 400   ● area 14 sq km
The 28km-long Duff Islands are a sc tered line of eleven small rocks and islan 150km north-east of Santa Cruz. **Tauma** rises to 280m but it's less than 6km lo

Duff Islanders speak a Polynesian l guage, but they're physically and cultura

re like Melanesians – the result of cen-
ies of intermarriage.

The Duff Islands are still ruled by hered-
ry chiefs. Some islanders believe in an-
tral spirits and consult witch doctors.
nta Cruz red-feather money is still used
e the boxed text 'Red-Feather Money').
Taumako Island is tall with cliffs that drop
aight into the sea. More than 200 people
tightly packed on tiny **Tahua Island**, an
ificial island that Quirós called Venecia.

KOPIA
op 1000　　　● **area 5 sq km**

kopia Island is 2km wide, 3.5km long,
380km south-east of Santa Cruz, and
s white-sand beaches along ·its south-
stern shore. The culture and language of
people are distinctly Polynesian.

The island is an extinct single-cone volcano, Mt Reani (380m). Te Roto is a crater
lake below the summit, which is ideal for
swimming.

Tikopia is extensively cultivated, with
gardens and coconut groves extending high
up Mt Reani's slopes. The island has been a
stronghold of Polynesian culture – and
tyranny over neighbouring islands – since
1200 AD when Tongans invaded. Hereditary chiefs rule Tikopia and there are many
archaeological sites to see.

Boat services are monthly at best.

ANUTA
Anuta Island is only 400 sq m in area, and
lies 450km east of Santa Cruz. Its nearest
populated neighbour is Tikopia, with which
it retains close traditional ties.

Vanuatu

Vanuatu's name, pronounced 'van-**wah**-too', means 'Our Land' – the word for land *(vanua, fanua* or *fenua)* is one of the widest-spread of Pacific words. The country's people are called Ni-Vanuatu, meaning 'Of Vanuatu'.

Prior to independence from the UK and France in 1980, this long archipelago of mainly small islands was known as the New Hebrides. James Cook gave it this name during his explorations in 1774 – the dark, rugged islands reminded him of the Hebrides group, off Scotland's western coast.

The national capital, Port Vila, or Vila as it is usually called, is the friendly hub of the country's tourist trade. Most visitors confine themselves to the main island, Efate, and perhaps do a quick trip to see the active volcano on Tanna. Relatively few get to experience the other islands, which between them have a number of outstanding highlights. These include Ambrym's twin volcanoes, Pentecost's land-diving ceremony, Malekula's diverse culture and the scuba-diving sites of Espiritu Santo (also called Santo).

Until recently it was official government policy to restrict tourism to just a few areas of the country. This has now changed, and village-based enterprises such as tours and basic, island-style guesthouses have sprung up in many places that previously saw few visitors. However, high costs and a lack of infrastructure, particularly transport, are a great handicap to these new developments.

Facts about Vanuatu

HISTORY

The first humans to reach Vanuatu crossed the sea from the Solomon Islands to Vanuatu's northern islands in about 1500 BC. People of the Lapita culture (see the boxed text 'Lapita' in the 'South Pacific Arts' special section) are some of the ancestors of

AT A GLANCE

Capital City (& Island): Port Vila (Efate)
Population: 182,000
Time: 11 hours ahead of GMT
Land Area: 14,760 sq km (5755 sq miles)
Number of Islands: 80
International Telephone Code: ☎ 678
GDP/Capita: US$1085
Currency: Vatu (100VT = $0.77)
Languages: Bislama, English, French & over 100 Melanesian languages
Greeting: *Alo* (Bislama)

HIGHLIGHTS

- **Tanna** – the unforgettable fireworks display at night on Mt Yasur volcano

- **Espiritu Santo** – a mind-blowing dive on the SS *President Coolidge*, the world's largest accessible shipwreck

- **Pentecost** – the remarkable and unbelievable *naghol* (land-diving) ceremony

- **Tanna & Pentecost** – traditional Vanuatuan culture in *kastom* villages

- **Efate** – quaffing kava at a *nakamal*, then devising your own gastronomic tour of Vila's many good restaurants

- **Malekula** – the fascinating ancient traditions of Malekula's diverse cultural groups

- **Epi** – donning goggles and swimming with the dugong at Lamen Bay

VANUATU

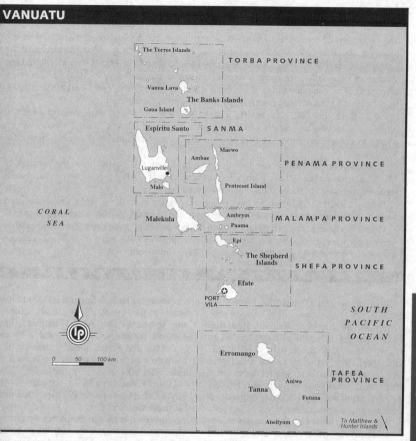

...anuatu's modern Melanesian population. ...fter the Lapita moved on to New Caledo-...a and Fiji, subsequent settlers moved ...uth through these islands, inter-marrying ...ith their predecessors.

Between the 11th and 15th centuries AD, ...wave of Polynesian settlers sailed in from ...e central Pacific. A number of Vanuatu's ...aditions tell of culture heroes arriving ...ound this time from islands to the east.

...ncient Vanuatu

...s is the case today, Ni-Vanuatu lived in ...ainly small, clan-based villages on the land that their ancestors had occupied on arrival. The archipelago's rich cultural diversity reflects the fact that these villages were often separated by significant physical barriers, such as difficult mountain terrain.

Everyone lived in the shadow of their ancestors' spirits. Some spirits were benevolent, but others were often hostile – famines, cyclones, enemy attack and other misfortunes could result if they became seriously displeased. Magic was the main defence against angry spirits. On the other hand, sorcery was automatically suspected when anyone suffered a misfortune.

Pedro Fernández de Quirós

The chief pilot of the second Mendaña expedition, which had discovered and named the Solomon Islands in 1595, was Pedro Fernández de Quirós, a Portuguese in the service of the Spanish Crown. For 10 years Quirós petitioned the Spanish king, Pope Clement VIII and the Viceroy of Peru to finance another expedition to the islands. Finally in 1605 he was given command of an expedition to find the missing southern continent, *Terra Australis Incognita*, to colonise it for Spain and convert its people to Roman Catholicism.

On 21 December 1605 Quirós left Callao in Peru with three small ships. Aboard were 130 adventurers serving as soldiers and sailors, plus 10 monks. Quirós' indecision over which course to sail and his enthusiasm for religion soon brought his rough-and-ready crew close to mutiny.

After stops in the Tuamotus and northern Cook Islands, the lookout spied the tall peak of Mere Lava, one of the Banks Islands in northern Vanuatu. After a brief and initially well-received stopover at nearby Gaua, Quirós pressed on.

In May 1606, the small Spanish fleet sailed into Big Bay in northern Santo. Quirós believed he had at last found the great southern continent and named it 'Austrialia del Espirito Santo'.

Quirós declared Santo and *all* lands south of it to be under Spain's rule, and attempted to make a permanent settlement at Big Bay. The fledgling colony lasted a mere 54 days before it was abandoned following the desertion of Quirós' mutinous crew.

Inter-island trade networks were well established, with large sailing canoes venturing as far afield as New Caledonia. Otherwise the different villages tended to regard their neighbours with deep suspicion, particularly if they spoke a different language. Interclan wars, which were commonplace, usually arose over such matters as the theft of coconuts or other crops, trespassing and suspected sorcery.

Sometimes, however, the attackers' aim was simply to kill or capture one or two males, whom they would carry off to eat. Generally, only men of certain rank were allowed to consume human flesh. (In cannibal areas it was considered a friendly gesture to present a neighbouring village with an arm or leg ready for cooking!) Naturally the victim's relatives would mount a reprisal raid. Once commenced, such hostilities often continued indefinitely.

Explorers

The first Europeans to visit Vanuatu, in May 1606, were members of the Spanish expedition led by Pedro Fernández de Quirós (see the boxed text), who was convinced that in Santo he had found the fabled Great Southern Continent, *Terra Australis Incognita*. It was not until May 1768 that Louis Antoine de Bougainville sailed between Malekula and Santo, thereby proving that Vanuatu's largest island was not Terra Australis after all.

James Cook arrived in Vanuatu on 1 July 1774, on his second Pacific expedition. He drew the first charts of the region and gave his own names to the places he visited. Many of these names are still in use today, including Tanna, Erromango, Ambrym and the Shepherd Islands.

In 1789 William Bligh sailed through the northern Banks group in his longboat shortly after the famous mutiny on the *Bounty*. He sighted several previously unrecorded islands, and returned three years later to confirm his discoveries.

Sandalwood

In 1825 the Irish explorer-trader Peter Dillon discovered a treasure trove of sandalwood trees on Erromango. Other traders, eager to satisfy the insatiable demands of the Chinese market, soon found stands is aromatic softwood on several other lands. The archipelago's sandalwood ade only lasted 40 years – it ceased when e last accessible stands were removed.

See History in the introductory Facts out the South Pacific chapter for more formation about the sandalwood trade.

issionaries

he first Christian missionary on the scene as the Reverend John Williams, from the ondon Missionary Society. In 1839 he epped ashore on Erromango, and was omptly killed and eaten. After this inauscious beginning the Church decided to nd Polynesian teachers from Samoa, ping that they would be more acceptable an Europeans. However, a number of em were also killed, or died of malaria.

In 1848 the Reverend John Geddie arrived Aneityum and made it the headquarters r the Presbyterian mission in Vanuatu. esbyterianism eventually became the ajor Christian denomination, particularly the islands from Efate south. The Anglin Diocese of Melanesia followed in 860 and became influential in the northern lands, while Catholicism arrived in 1887.

The Protestants in particular took an unmpromising stand against many aspects Ni-Vanuatu culture. On the positive side ey put a stop to such practices as cannialism and warfare, but more benign cusms such as ancestor worship, kava inking and dancing were also discouraged.

Although a steady stream of converts nerged, Ni-Vanuatu often mingled this ew doctrine with their traditional beliefs. lany rejected Christianity altogether, prerring to stick with their age-old customs. oday around 90% of the population is at ast nominally Christian. Most of the reainder are Jon Frum cultists or adherents indigenous religions.

pidemics & Catastrophe

s was the case elsewhere in the Pacific, e indigenous peoples of Vanuatu were ecimated by the diseases Europeans rought with them. Some estimates put anuatu's population at about one million

in the early 19th century. By 1870 the number was down to 650,000, and in the next 20 years it fell to around 100,000. This gloomy trend continued until 1935, when only 41,000 Ni-Vanuatu remained.

European Settlement

Although a trading post was established on Aneityum in 1844, the first true European settler was a cattle rancher who arrived 10 years later. Others followed, particularly in the 1860s when the high price of cotton during the American Civil War lured settlers from Australia.

Neglected by the British government, which didn't want to be involved in the archipelago, most of the new settlers were soon near bankruptcy. Many sold their land to French interests, who were also busy buying up land from Ni-Vanuatu. By the mid-1880s, French settlers outnumbered the British by three to one.

Intense rivalry existed between the two groups, and brawls were commonplace thanks to the absence of law and order. At the same time there were frequent clashes between settlers and Ni-Vanuatu, who resented the loss of their land. The Anglo-French Joint Naval Commission was established in 1887 in an unsuccessful attempt to curb this disorder.

The Condominium

In 1906 the Anglo-French Condominium of the New Hebrides was created as a response to German expansionism in the region. The agreement established Vanuatu as an area of equal influence for the two colonial powers, with neither having exclusive sovereignty. British and French nationals had equal rights, and retained their home country's citizenship, but Ni-Vanuatu were officially stateless.

Cynics called the Condominium the Pandemonium, as the dual administration produced a bizarre duplication of authorities that were seldom effective. For example, there were two education systems, two police forces and two currencies. Traditional Anglo-French rivalry reached new depths of farce in Vanuatu.

WWII

Japan's lightning advance through the Pacific had reached the Solomon Islands by early 1942, when US forces arrived in Vanuatu. They began to construct bases, first at Havannah Harbour and Vila on Efate, then a much larger one in south-eastern Santo.

With Japan's defeat in 1945, the US Forces withdrew leaving behind huge quantities of surplus equipment. Some of this was sold at bargain-basement prices and the remainder was dumped into the sea near Luganville.

Cargo cults appeared on several islands as villagers sought to secure the kind of wealth they'd seen being so wantonly discarded – they believed that if they acted like Europeans then 'cargo' would automatically come their way. Most of these movements waned when the riches failed to materialise.

Towards Self-Rule

Land ownership had become Vanuatu's major political issue by the mid-1960s. It was the spark that spurred the country to take the path to independence.

At this time white settlers 'owned' about 30% of the country's land area, with about half of that having been developed for agriculture. The Ni-Vanuatu, who contended that all undeveloped land was exclusively theirs, protested when the settlers began clearing new land for cattle ranching.

Consequently, a *kastom*-oriented movement called Nagriamel (kastom ownership is the traditionally acknowledged ownership of a piece of land – see the glossary at the back of this book for more details) sprang up under the leadership of the charismatic Jimmy Stevens. Operating from Santo, its aims were to protect Ni-Vanuatu claims to their traditional land. By the late 1960s, Nagriamel had expanded to other islands in northern Vanuatu.

In 1971 the New Hebrides National Party, later called the Vanua'aku Party, was formed by an Anglican minister, Father Walter Lini. It drew its support from English-speaking (Anglophone) Protestants, whereas Nagriamel was identified with French interests.

The UK supported early independence fo the archipelago. However, Francophone wanted the Condominium either to remain as it was or to be replaced by French rule

As Vanuatu became more politicised the Condominium authorities agreed to hold the country's first general election. This took place in November 1979, with the Vanua'aku Party being clear winners. Independence was fixed for mid-1980.

Independence

Serious threats of secession were being made on Santo and Tanna in early 1980, but as usual Britain and France couldn't agree on how to react. Late in May matters came to a head. An insurrection on Tanna split the island between government supporters and rebels. On Santo, secessionists seized Luganville and hoisted the flag of the Independent Republic of Vemarana.

Several other northern islands proclaimed their own secessions during June They merged and announced a Provisional Government of the Northern Islands, under Jimmy Stevens.

France and Britain despatched a joint military force to restore order in Luganville but the troops had no power of arrest and failed even to prevent looting. Following independence on 30 July, the new government brought in soldiers from Papua New Guinea. They quickly restored order and arrested the secessionist ringleaders, after which the rebellion collapsed.

The New Nation

Since independence the Vanuatu government has generally attempted to ensure that development benefits everyone equally, while preserving the new nation's age-old culture. It has established diplomatic relations with over 70 countries signed the General Agreement on Tariffs Trades (GATT), and declared the country nuclear-free zone.

Land ownership has remained a major political issue. Differences of view over the matter have produced factionalism within the Vanua'aku Party, with several major figures either leaving to form breakaway

vements or mounting dramatic leader-
ip challenges. Indeed, a constitutional
isis in 1988 led to the dismissal and tem-
rary detention of Vanuatu's first presi-
nt, Ati George Sokomanu.

EOGRAPHY

anuatu is a Y-shaped chain of islands ex-
nding 1176km in a north-south direction
tween the equator and the tropic of Capri-
rn. Its nearest neighbour is the Solomon
lands, just over 170km to the north. The
pital, Port Vila, is 1900km north-east of
risbane, Australia.

Vanuatu covers 860,000 sq km, of which
,760 sq km is land. This is made up of
out 80 islands, 12 of which are significant
terms of economy and population. The
rgest are Espiritu Santo (4010 sq km),
alekula (2069 sq km), Efate (980 sq km)
d Erromango (900 sq km).

Most islands are either mountainous or
eeply undulating. Generally, the steeper
untry is covered with forest and secon-
ry growth, while agriculture dominates
e coastal plains. Santo boasts the coun-
y's highest peak: 1879m Mt Tabwe-
asana. Ambae, Ambrym and Tanna also
ve peaks over 1000m high.

olcanoes & Earthquakes

anuatu lies squarely on the Pacific Ring of
re, where the action of the Pacific tectonic
late being forced up and over the Indo-
ustralian plate causes frequent earth
emors. Much of the country experiences
ontinual uplift (2cm per year in some
reas), while other parts are subsiding.
here are nine active volcanoes (seven on
nd), and fumaroles and thermal springs
re found throughout the archipelago.

LIMATE

anuatu's climate varies from wet tropical
the north to subtropical in the south. The
ry season – from May to October inclu-
ve – is dominated by fine, warm days and
easantly cool nights. November to April
the wet season, when higher tempera-
res, heavy rains and occasional cyclones
re experienced.

Temperature

Mean maximum temperatures in Luganville
and Port Vila range from 27°C in July to
30°C in January – Lenakel (on Tanna) is a
degree or two cooler. Mean minimum temperatures are eight or nine degrees below
the mean maximums in all three areas;
winter nights in Vila can drop below 12°C.

Rainfall

January to March are the wettest months;
March averages 21 days of rain, contrasting
with 13 in August (the driest month).
Luganville receives 2300mm per year on
average, with Vila a little drier.

The eastern slopes are the wettest areas –
those of the north-eastern islands receive
more than 4000mm of rainfall per year,
while those in the south get about half that
amount. The driest rain-shadow areas are on
the north-western slopes of the higher
ranges.

Cyclones

An average of 2.5 cyclones strike Vanuatu
each year – any given point is devastated by
a cyclone every 30 years or so, and receives
some damage every year from wind and
rain. Cyclones can occur any time between
November and May, but the usual season is
December to March inclusive.

FLORA & FAUNA

Vanuatu has rather fewer bird species than
its northern neighbours and very little in the
way of native mammals. However,
snorkellers will often be enthralled by the
abundance of marine life around the country's numerous fringing reefs. Here you'll
find around 300 species of coral and over
450 species of reef fish.

Flora

About 75% of the country is covered by
natural vegetation including rainforest and
rain-shadow grasslands. Most of the forest
has been heavily disturbed by cyclones, logging and subsistence farming, but the more
pristine areas are botanical wonderlands.

The lord of most forests is the banyan
tree, a huge fig whose crown can be 70m or

VANUATU

The Gentle Dugong

Also called the sea cow, the dugong *(Dugong dugon)* is the world's only herbivorous marine mammal. It feeds almost exclusively on sea grass, which commonly grows in the calm, shallow waters of bays and off the sheltered sides of coastal islands and coral reefs. On this diet, plus an occasional meal of marine algae, it grows to 3m long and weighs up to 420kg.

Dugongs inhabit the warm (18°C or above) tropical and subtropical coastal waters of the Indian and south-west Pacific oceans, with Vanuatu forming the easternmost limit of its distribution. As deep water occurs just off most of Vanuatu's islands, suitable habitat is generally limited here.

Worldwide, populations of these inoffensive creatures are declining due to overhunting, drowning in fishing nets, pollution and loss of food resources. As a result, the species is considered vulnerable to extinction. According to the results of an aerial and postal survey in 1988, however, Vanuatu's dugong population is stable and may even be increasing.

There are thought to be several hundred dugongs distributed throughout the archipelago. The 1988 survey revealed that they occur in nearly 100 localities, from Aneityum, in the south, to Hiu, in the Torres Islands. Futunà is one of the few islands that doesn't have them. Over half the groups recorded consisted of one or two animals, while herds of more than 10 animals were rare.

Dugongs are occasionally hunted for food on several islands, particularly northern Epi, Efate and the Maskelyne Islands off south-eastern Malekula; some villagers on Pentecost and Santo also hunt them. Most dugongs are killed by spearing. Others are shot, netted or caught when falling tides leave them stranded.

As with many *kastom* activities in Vanuatu, dugong hunting is accompanied by strict *tambu*. At Lamen Bay, on Epi, women are forbidden to swim in the sea for two months before a dugong hunt, which occurs during the March full moon at the time of the yam harvest. During the same period men are not allowed to throw stones or spears, or shoot arrows, into the sea.

Ironically, Lamen Bay is one of the few places in Vanuatu where you have a good chance of seeing a dugong. A herd of nine or 10 animals lives in the area; one of them – a large male – allows humans to swim close and observe it feeding on the bottom. Another good place is Port Resolution, on Tanna, although here there's only a solitary male.

ore across – there are many large speci-
ens in and around Vila. Forests of large
kauri trees are found on Erromango, while
oud forests dripping with moss and mois-
re are a magnificent feature of many high-
nd areas.

auna

ats, dogs, cattle, horses, pigs and goats
ere all introduced to Vanuatu and have now
one wild. Rats are the bane of village life
nd do much damage to the copra industry.

Thanks largely to the relative youth and
olation of the islands, the native land
nammals are restricted to four species of
ying fox and eight of bats. Only one of
ese – the white flying fox – is endemic.
he country's largest resident mammal is the
ugong, or sea cow, which is at the eastern-
nost limit of its range in Vanuatu.

irds Vanuatu's 121 bird species include
2 seabirds. Santo has the richest bird
auna, with 55 species including all seven
f the country's endemic species. Of these
ne Santo mountain starling is rarest, being
ound only in the higher mountains of the
sland. In contrast, the endemic white-eye
s widespread and common throughout
anuatu.

One very interesting species is the mound-
uilding, fowl-like megapode (*namalao* in
islama). It normally uses the heat generated
rom rotting vegetation to incubate its eggs.
3ut in actively volcanic areas such as here
nd in the Solomon Islands (see the boxed
ext 'Megapodes' in that chapter) it simply
ays its eggs in the hot soil. Megapode num-
ers are believed to be falling because of
abitat destruction and over- harvesting of
ggs.

eptiles There are 19 native lizards, all
mall skinks and geckoes, and one land
nake – the harmless Pacific boa, which
,rows to 2.5m. While the yellow-bellied
nd banded sea snakes are both extremely
enomous, their small mouths and teeth
ren't at all suitable for savaging humans.

The saltwater (or estuarine) crocodiles
hat appear from time to time around the
northernmost islands have probably swum
down from the Solomons after losing their
bearings during cyclones.

Conservation Areas

Vanuatu has three official conservation
areas: Vatthe and Loru in north-eastern
Santo, and the Happy Lands kauri reserve
on Erromango. See Useful Organisations in
the Facts for the Visitor section of this chapter for more information.

Local chiefs and kastom landholders
often proclaim conservation areas as a
means of protecting some valuable resource, such as turtles or coconut crabs,
from over-exploitation.

GOVERNMENT & POLITICS

Vanuatu has a Westminster-style constitution. The country's single legislative chamber, or parliament, sits in Vila and its 52
members are elected for a four year term.
The cabinet, or executive, consists of the
prime minister and members of the council
of ministers. All ministers must be members
of parliament.

Vanuatu's head of state is the president,
who is elected by an electoral college composed of members of parliament and the
presidents of the six provincial governments. A national council of chiefs – the
Malfatu Mauri – advises parliament on all
constitutional matters relating to traditional
customs.

ECONOMY

Vanuatu's economy is essentially agricultural. Most of the population is engaged in
subsistence farming and cash cropping of,
in particular, copra, cocoa, kava and vegetables. There are several large copra producers on Malekula and Santo.

Other significant income is derived from
tourism, beef production, logging and the
country's role as a tax haven. Mining, fishing and manufacturing are only of minor
importance.

The value of Vanuatu's imports exceeds
that of its exports by a factor of three. The
principal imports are consumer goods, in
particular rice, clothing, processed food,

VANUATU

electrical goods and motor vehicles. Copra, cocoa and beef are the major export earners; Vanuatu's export income totalled 3565VT million in 1997 (2551VT million in 1995).

The gross domestic product (GDP) for 1995 was 26,633VT million (US$235 million), a 6.9% increase on the previous year. The GDP per capita that year was 158,200VT (US$1200).

Agriculture
Vanuatu's fertile volcanic soil is among its greatest assets. Forty per cent of the land area has at least reasonable agricultural potential and about half of this has been developed, mainly for subsistence farming and coconuts. Agriculture earns 85% of the country's export income.

Forestry
Although rainforest covers about 35% of the country, its value in economic terms is limited by steep terrain, lack of commercial species, small tree sizes and the damage caused by cyclones and shifting agriculture.

There is little government control on the way Vanuatu's dwindling timber resources are being exploited. Fortunately, however, the country has been spared the large-scale environmental destruction that has occurred in Papua New Guinea and the Solomons. The export of unprocessed logs is banned.

Tourism
Tourism is the country's largest foreign exchange earner after agriculture. In 1997 almost 50,000 visitors arrived by air and stayed an average of nine days. That year there were visits from 30,500 cruise ship passengers – a slump of almost 50% on 1995 and 1996. Most cruise ship visitors spend only a day or two on land.

Over 50% of Vanuatu's tourists come from Australia, with another 14% from New Zealand and 12% from New Caledonia. The busiest period is the southern winter (June to August).

Overseas Aid
With its recurrent trade deficit, Vanuatu's economic survival depends on aid donations

from other countries – although increasing these contributions are in the form of exp tise rather than cash. The most generous a donors have been Australia, the Europe Development Fund, France, New Zeala and the UK.

POPULATION & PEOPLE
Vanuatu's population in 1998 was estimat at 182,000, of which all but 3500 were N Vanuatu. (Although some islands have strong Polynesian heritage, the Ni-Vanua population as a whole is overwhelming Melanesian.) The 'others' included abo 1500 Europeans, with the remainder bei mainly Asians and other Pacific Islanders

Two-thirds of the population lives (Efate, Santo, Malekula and Tanna, ar around 80% lives in rural areas, mostly villages of less than 50 people. On mo islands the population is concentrated alon narrow coastal strips, or on offshore islet A recent trend is the drift into towns, pa ticularly Vila, by young Ni-Vanuatu in usually vain search for jobs. Vila's popul tion doubled to 36,000 in the 10 years 1998.

ARTS
The most common subject material f Vanuatuan arts is the human form and tra itional interpretations of what ancestral fig ures looked like. The most importa artefacts are made for *nimangki* grade taking ceremonies (see Nimangki und Society & Conduct later in this section) the best examples come from areas whe this is still an integral part of village life.

Some ritual objects, such as *Rom* cos tumes (see the section on Ambrym Island are believed to be taken over by malevole spirits during or after the ceremony. For th reason, such artefacts are usually destroye as soon as the ceremony is completed.

Carvings
While wood is the main carved materia objects are also made from tree fern, ston and coral. The majority of carvings are dec orated with a stylised human face or a rep resentation of an ancestral spirit. Seriou

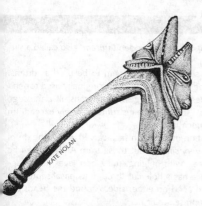

Carved clubs such as this are used to kill pigs during *nimangki* grade-taking rituals.

arving is almost entirely created for traditional ceremonies; items for sale to tourists re usually small copies of the real thing.

lubs & Weapons Bows and arrows and eremonial spears are still carved, as are lubs. War clubs are made to traditional deigns that seldom vary from generation to eneration, let alone carver to carver. To lter a basic shape is considered a breach of astom, especially as the design is often atibuted to a culture hero.

Another type of club is used for ritual pig illing. This is shaped like a mattock, with vo carved stylised faces – one on either ide.

owls Large platters and bowls are used to ound yams and kava in, or to serve *laplap* he Vanuatu national dish). Some, such as ose from the Shepherd Islands, are carved depict birds or fish.

ree Fern Figures Statues made from ee ferns are made on Ambrym and lalekula. They represent both male and male ancestral figures and are carved for imangki ceremonies. Tree fern statues are ften painted in several different colours, e choice depending on the grade being ken. There are plenty of examples ound Vila.

Traditional Dress
These days the great majority of Ni-Vanuatu wear European clothing as their normal daily attire. However, they usually exchange this for traditional dress when taking part in clan ceremonies.

Local Variations In kastom-oriented parts of Tanna and Pentecost, men still wear *nambas* (penis wrappers) every day, while women dress in grass skirts. On Santo, the men wear *mal mal* (genital-covering cloth T-pieces) and women wear grass skirts or an apron of leaves.

On Malekula, the Small Nambas women traditionally wore raffia skirts woven from banana tree fibres. Women from the Big Nambas tribe of Malekula wore nothing more than a long purple headdress made from dried pandanus leaves.

Men on Futuna traditionally wore long kilts made from tapa. It's the only part of Vanuatu where this typically Polynesian practice prevailed.

Masks The wearing of elaborate headgear is a major aspect of traditional ceremonies, especially on Ambrym, Ambae, Maewo and Malekula. Masks, which represent the faces of demons and ancestral spirits, can be made from tree fern material or constructed out of clay reinforced with coconut fibres and layered onto a wickerwork frame. On Pentecost and Vao, masks are carved from hardwood.

South-western Malekulan clay masks are decorated with paint, feathers and carved pigs' tusks. Several masks from this area are on permanent display in Vila's Cultural Centre.

Musical Instruments
Panpipes, usually complete with seven small bamboo flutes, are found all over Vanuatu. Ambrym people play a long, geometrically carved musical pipe, while in Santo a simple three-holed flute is used.

On many islands, large triton shells are blown as a means of communication. Unlike Polynesians farther east, Ni-Vanuatu make a hole in the side of the shell and use that to blow through.

VANUATU

Tamtam

Vanuatu's most striking musical device is the huge, carved wooden *tamtam*, also called a slit-gong or slit-drum, from Malekula and Ambrym.

Tamtam are carved logs with hollowed-out slits that enable them to be used as drums. They're usually stood at an angle to make playing easier. Tamtam were originally used to send coded messages as well as forming drum orchestras. The largest could transmit a message 30km downwind – the original 'bush telegraph'. Today, these instruments rarely exceed 3m in height, although in earlier times they were much larger.

The typical tamtam has a stylised representation of a human face carved above the drum part. Faces on Malekulan drums are generally very simple, but those from Ambrym can be extremely ornate. The latter have up to 12 faces, with bulging 'full moon' eyes and exaggerated noses being common features. Each face has a hole cut through its nasal septum to allow cycad leaves to be passed through and draped on either side. Around the heads are lines of indents that look like dogs' teeth but represent hair.

Tamtam are traditionally made from the breadfruit tree, which isn't the best hardwood but does give the best sound for passing messages. In the old days they were carved with adzes of human bone, stone or shells, and the end result smoothed off with shark skin or an abrasive seaweed. The hollowed centres were created by placing heated stones in the slit so that the wood became charred. The burnt layers were then scraped away with an adze.

The tools used today are more efficient, of course, but creating a tamtam is still a slow task requiring much patience and skill. As an example, it takes about 160 hours to produce a 2.5m-high tamtam with a single face. While chisels and hatchets have taken over from hot stones and primitive adzes, the carver still uses a pencil made from a rolled-up green kava leaf to mark out the rough shape.

On Ambrym, specific tamtam designs belong to particular families. If a carver from outside that family wants to use its design he must pay a fee. A design can be recognised by such characteristics as the number of heads, the way they're facing, and the shape of eyes and other features. The lines of 'dogs' teeth' indicate the owner's social status: the more lines, the greater the status.

The tourist trade and the local demand for decorative Ambrym tamtam have resulted in some carvers producing copies in Vila. This practice is against *kastom* (custom), and Ambrym chiefs are always on the lookout for such transgressors. They are no longer executed for this offence, as in earlier times, but they are fined.

The *tamtam* is Vanuatu's most interesting musical device – see the boxed text for more information.

Visual Arts

Painting Petroglyphs and rock paintings are the country's most ancient forms of pictorial art. The former are common and widespread, though their meanings have been lost and their main significance these days is to archaeologists. Several islands have caves whose walls are decorated with hand stencils and simple paintings of animals.

Sand Drawing On several northern islands villagers use elaborate sand drawings to recount legends, songs and ceremonies, or just to leave messages. The artist first draws the foundation design, usually a sequence of squares or rectangles, in the sand. Then he or she begins to circle with a finger, making many delicate loops and circles without raising the finger until the design is finished.

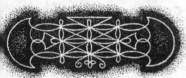

KATE NOLAN

Sand drawings can be used to illustrate local legends or leave messages.

Pottery

This was once a widespread industry and many finds of ceramics dating back to around 500 AD have been made. Today, however, the only remaining traditional potters live in two isolated villages, Wusi and Anduri, in south-western Santo. The craft is restricted to women.

Weaving

Baskets and mats are made throughout the country. Fish, bird and shellfish traps are also manufactured, as are items such as Panama-style hats. Weaving is done mostly by women, with pandanus leaves and *burao* (wild hibiscus) stalks being the most favoured materials. Wicker, coconut leaves and rattan are used when a more robust item is required.

SOCIETY & CONDUCT

There is immense variety in Vanuatu's culture and customs. Dances, funerals, weddings, initiations, status and systems of authority, artistic styles, and animal and crop husbandry all differ from island to island, and often from one district to another on the larger islands. Yet there are common themes, particularly the acceptance of the obligation to pay for all services rendered.

Village Life

Virtually the entire rural population is engaged in subsistence farming. The forests are a major resource, providing medicine, food, firewood, building materials and timber for boat-building and artefacts. Fresh water is often in short supply and in some cases must be collected from other islands or distant streams.

Women can spend up to 10 hours a day away from home in the family garden. Men spend about the same amount of time in such activities as fishing, hunting, boat-building, artefact carving and discussing council matters.

While the women prepare the evening meal, the men typically sit around drinking kava and talking about the day's events. Generally, it's the woman's responsibility to attend to the gardening, cooking, cleaning, childcare and water collection.

The average Ni-Vanuatu female can expect to live a shorter, and usually harder working, life than her male compatriots. This is largely because of the high birth rate – an average of six children per family – that prevailed until very recently, and the associated heavy workload.

Tabu (Tambu)

Village life is beset by *tambu* (the plural form of *tabu*) in the more kastom-oriented areas. Many of these relate to traditional ceremonies. Women and uninitiated men are barred from seeing parts of certain ceremonies, while others are restricted to women.

Women in particular must endure some rather unusual *tambu*. For example, in some areas a woman may not stand higher than a male. Nor may a woman step over a smouldering fire, as while she's standing in its smoke it may rise higher than a man.

Menstruation and birth are surrounded by all sorts of restrictions. Most traditional villages have an area set aside for women to go to during menstruation and childbirth. For a woman living in a kastom-oriented village to continue gardening and cooking while menstruating is a serious breach of rules.

Dances & Ceremonies

Traditional dances in Vanuatu involve either impersonation or participation. Impersonation dances require more rehearsal as each dancer pretends to be an ancestor or legendary figure. Because the character being represented is not human, the dancer's actions and dress are similarly nonhuman. This allows the participants to wear elaborate masks or headdresses, such as in the Rom dances of Ambrym.

VANUATU

In participatory dances, several people – or even several villages – take part to enact traditional themes such as hunting, war or death. These events serve to bring villagers together, as team rehearsals are often needed, as in the Nekowiar festival of Tanna (see the Tanna section of this chapter for details of the Nekowiar).

Chiefs

Women can attain much status in their communities, but only men can become chiefs. A Ni-Vanuatu chief acts as a justice of the peace and as a delegate to speak for the people of the village. His word is law in most villages. Even senior bureaucrats and politicians must do what the chief says when they're visiting their home villages.

In most northern areas chiefs achieve their rank by holding a series of lavish feasts. In contrast, chiefs from the Shepherd Islands southwards either inherit their titles or are elected. While a chief puts fellow villagers in his debt when they consume his food at a feast, he faces the sack if he fails in his responsibilities.

The Nimangki

From Epi northwards, status and power are earned by taking grades through the nimangki system. In this process men earn respect by publicly disposing of their wealth in a series of elaborate ceremonies.

Each step up the village social ladder is accompanied by the ritual killing of pigs. Because a boar takes between six and seven years to grow a good set of tusks (the prized article) only men wealthy enough to own a large number of pigs can hope to reach society's highest levels.

Southern Malekulan males can take up to 35 grades, while on Ambae only four are required. Women from southern Malekula also take grades, though far fewer than their menfolk.

The Nakamal

In most parts of north and central Vanuatu, the *nakamal* is a two-roomed hut used as a men's clubhouse and clan museum. Elsewhere it's just the place where men meet at sunset to talk and drink kava – it may be an open-ended hut, or a space under a large tree.

A traditional nakamal must never be entered without the permission of one of its members. They are usually strictly *tabu* to women, including tourists, particularly in kastom-oriented areas.

Marriage

In the past a man might have paid up to 100 pigs, as well as scores of mats and shells, for a wife. Nowadays the maximum bride price for the entire country has been set at 80,000VT, or the equivalent value in pigs. The groom also has to pay compensation to his mother-in-law of up to 20,000VT for the loss of a worker.

LANGUAGE

Vanuatu claims the highest concentration of different languages per head of population of any country in the world. There are at least 105 local languages as well as Bislama (the national lingua franca), English and French. Most of the population speaks at least some Bislama, while English is also widely spoken. Villages with Roman Catholic missions tend to be Francophone. For a list of useful French words and phrases see the French language appendix at the back of this book.

Bislama Basics

Hello.	*Halo.*
Hello. (two people)	*Halo tufala.*
Hello. (three people) (from English 'all together')	*Halo trifala/olgeta.*
Hello. (more than three)	*Halo olgeta.*
Good morning.	*Gud morning.*
Good afternoon.	*Gud aftenun.*
Good night.	*Gud naet.*
How are you?	*Olsem wanem?*
Thank you (very much).	*Tangkiu (tumas)/T...*
Do you speak English?	*Yu save tok tok long Inglis?*
I'm sorry but I only understand a little bit of Bislama.	*Sore, be mi no save tumas Bislama ye...*

What's your name?	*Wanem nem blong yu?*
My name is …	*Nem blong mi …*
I come from …	*Mi kam long …*

Facts for the Visitor

SUGGESTED ITINERARIES

With only eight or nine days to spend in Vanuatu, the average visitor is content to spend their time in and around Vila, plus to a two or three day trip to Tanna. Two weeks are easily filled if you add (for example) a scuba-diving trip to Santo, a visit to the Small Nambas people of north-eastern Malekula or a bushwalking tour on Ambrym or Erromango. Allow three weeks or more if you want to do all these things.

PLANNING
When to Go

The most pleasant time to visit is during the dry season from May to October. Visitor numbers peak over the Australian school holiday periods in June/July and September.

Maps

The Department of Land Surveys (☎ 22892), on Montfort St in central Vila, has ordnance survey maps covering most of the country.

What to Bring

Summer clothing is generally suitable year round. However, Efate and islands to the south can have cool nights between May and September, so make sure to pack at least a light pullover. Warm clothing can be useful after diving, for sea travel and for travelling in the open backs of 4WD taxis – a light raincoat may also come in handy. Clothing styles are almost always casual.

TOURIST OFFICES
Local Tourist Offices

The National Tourism Office (NTO; ☎ 22515 or ☎ 22685, fax 23889), PO Box 209, in central Vila, has friendly staff and a range of brochures etc. Contact it well in advance of your booking date if you want to be sent information – or check its website (www.vanuatu.net.vu).

Tourist Offices Abroad

The NTO is represented abroad by Air Vanuatu, which has offices in:

Australia
  NSW:
    (☎ 02-9299 9737) 1st floor, 160 Clarence St, Sydney, NSW 2000
  Queensland:
    (☎ 07-3221 2566) Level 5, Bloomberg Corporation Bldg, 293 Queen St, Brisbane, Qld 4000
  Victoria:
    (☎ 03-9417 3977) Level 6, 126 Wellington Pde, East Melbourne, Vic 3002
New Caledonia
    (☎ 28 6677) Axxess Travel, Lot 36 Rue de Verdun, Noumea
New Zealand
    (☎ 09-373 3435) Level 2, West Plaza Bldg, Cnr Customs and Albert Sts, Auckland 1

Vanuatu is also represented oversea by the Tourism Council of the South Pacific, whose offices are listed under Tourist Offices in the Regional Facts for the Visitor chapter.

VISAS & DOCUMENTS
Passport

Every visitor must have a passport that is valid for at least four months from the date of arrival, as well as a return or onward ticket. Immigration staff may also ask for proof that you have sufficient funds to support yourself while in the country.

Visas

Entry visas are not required by nationals of British Commonwealth and European Union countries, Fiji, Norway, the Philippines, South Korea, Switzerland and the USA.

Nonexempt visitors can obtain entry visas either from UK consulates, local prefectures in France, or the Principal Immigration Officer (☎ 22354, PMB 092 in Port Vila). Application forms are available from the overseas offices of Air Vanuatu (see earlier).

VANUATU

Permission to stay is initially granted for 30 days, but this can be extended one month at a time for up to four months within a 12-month period. Visa extensions can only be applied for at the Department of Immigration in Port Vila and Luganville.

Other Documents

For driving licence requirements see Car & Motorcycle in the Getting Around section, later in this chapter.

EMBASSIES & CONSULATES
Vanuatuan Embassies & Consulates

Vanuatu's honorary consuls include:

Australia
   (☎ 02-9597 4046)
   Mr William Longwah; 54 Eden St, Arncliffe, NSW 2205
France
   (☎ 01-40 53 82 25)
   Mr Daniel Martin; 9 Rue Daru, 75008 Paris
Japan
   (☎ 03-3238 5535)
   Mr Bunnosuke Yoshioka; The Forum 4-1, Kioi-Cho, Chiyoda-ku, Tokyo

Contact details for other honorary consuls can be obtained from the Department of Foreign Affairs (☎ 22913), PMB 051, Port Vila.

Embassies & Consulates in Vanuatu

All the diplomatic representations to Vanuatu are in Port Vila.

Australia
   (☎ 22777) Australian High Commission, PO Box 111, KPMG House, Rue Pasteur St
France
   (☎ 22353) Ambassade de France, PO Box 60, Kumul Hwy
New Zealand
   (☎ 22933) NZ High Commission, PO Box 161, Prouds Bldg, Kumul Hwy
People's Republic of China
   (☎ 23598) PMB 071, Rue d'Auvergne St
UK
   (☎ 23100) British High Commission, PO Box 567, KPMG Hse, Rue Pasteur St

CUSTOMS
Concessions

Visitors aged over 15 may bring in 200 cigarettes, 100 cigarillos, 50 cigars or 250g of tobacco. You may also bring in 2L of wine and two bottles of spirits (maximum 1.5L), 250mL of *eau de toilette*, 100mL of perfume and other items up to a value of 20,000VT.

Restrictions

All plants, fruit, seeds, meat, fish, shellfish and dairy and poultry products must be declared on arrival. No firearms or ammunition may be brought into the country.

MONEY
Currency

Vanuatu's currency is the *vatu*, abbreviated to 'VT'. Vatu means 'stone' in many languages of Vanuatu – and traditionally large stones were a symbol of permanence. There are 200, 500, 1000 and 5000VT banknotes and coins worth 1, 2, 5, 10, 20, 50 and 100VT.

There are no limits on the amount of money you may bring into or take out of the country. However, the vatu isn't a familiar currency overseas, so leftover funds may be heavily discounted when you come to change them at your local bank.

Exchange Rates

country	unit		vatu
Australia	A$1	=	84VT
Canada	C$1	=	88VT
Easter Island	Ch$100	=	24VT
euro	€1	=	140VT
Fiji	F$1	=	65VT
France	10FF	=	210VT
Germany	DM1	=	69VT
Japan	¥100	=	120VT
New Zealand	NZ$1	=	66VT
Pacific franc	100 CFP	=	110VT
PNG	K1	=	43VT
Samoa	ST1	=	42VT
Solomon Islands	S$1	=	25VT
Tonga	T$1	=	85VT
UK	£1	=	210VT
USA	US$1	=	130VT

xchanging Money

anuatu's commercial banks (ANZ, West-
c, Banque d'Hawaii and the National
ank of Vanuatu (NBV)) have their main
fices on Kumul Hwy in central Vila. All
ve branch offices in Luganville; the NBV
s branches in most of the main centres.

There are private moneychangers in Vila
d Luganville (see the sections on these
wns for details).

ash & Travellers Cheques The main
aty-free shops and hotels in Vila accept
avellers cheques in major international
urrencies. However, the few hotels outside
e capital may only be willing to accept
ustralian or US dollars.

Always take plenty of vatu when travel-
ng in rural Vanuatu as you won't be able
change foreign currencies in villages.
arry a good reserve of coins and smaller
nomination notes for such things as taxi
res and small purchases.

redit Cards The major international
edit cards (American Express, Master-
ard, Visa and, to a lesser extent, Diners
lub) are accepted by the larger tourist-
iented businesses in Vila and Luganville,
ut don't expect to be able to use them
sewhere.

osts

ila is not a cheap place to visit, particu-
rly if you eat out a lot and stay in a
asonable hotel. Even if you're in budget
lf-catering accommodation it's easy to
end 4500VT a day without doing much
all; take a day tour or enjoy a three-
urse meal at a good restaurant and you
n expect that amount to double.

While accommodation can be relatively
eap in rural Vanuatu, travel costs are nor-
ally high regardless of whether you're
ing by air, speedboat or taxi.

Always check that hotel and restaurant
ices, in particular, include the 12.5% VAT.

ipping & Bargaining

pping and bargaining are not customary
actices in Vanuatu and may cause offence.

POST & COMMUNICATIONS

Post

Vanuatu has no street postal delivery service, so you must write to a post office box
– the poste restante service is said to be
very inefficient. All major rural administrative centres have post offices.

Telephone & Fax

A microwave network connects all major
islands. In addition, HF and VHF teleradio
services are provided to many isolated communities. Public telephones are widely
available, although are few in number.

Calls within Vanuatu To use the HF teleradio network, dial ☎ 22759 in Vila; for the
VHF network, dial ☎ 22221 in Vila and
☎ 36248 in Luganville. When making such
a call it's a good idea to have a Bislama
speaker on hand to help you out.

The most convenient (and sometimes the
only) way to pay for calls from public telephones is with a phonecard from Telecom
Vanuatu. When using coins, the minimum
charge for a local telephone call is 20VT;
for a teleradio call it's 40VT. The cheapest
rates are between 6 pm and 6 am Monday
to Friday and all weekend.

There are no area codes in Vanuatu.

Service Messages Villages without telephone or teleradio services can usually be
contacted by sending a service message
over Radio Vanuatu (☎ 22999 in Vila, or
☎ 36851 in Luganville).

International Calls The code for international calls from Vanuatu is ☎ 00. Vanuatu's international telephone code is ☎ 678.
Public international telephone, telex, telegraph and fax facilities are available at the
Vila general post office (GPO) and the
Telecom Vanuatu office in Luganville.
International calls can be made from any
public telephone.

Email & Internet Access

Telecom Vanuatu's public Internet access
service allows you to send or receive email
for 75VT per minute. Its office is behind the

grandstand at Independence Park, in central Vila.

BOOKS

Lonely Planet's Pisces series includes *Diving & Snorkeling Vanuatu*, which has a full description of 30 dive sites.

There are many books on Vanuatu and the following is a very small selection.

History

To Kill a Bird with Two Stones (Vanuatu Cultural Centre Publications, Vila), by Jeremy MacClancy, is an exceptionally good history of Vanuatu. It takes the country from its earliest beginnings through the Condominium period (the 'two stones' of the title) right up to independence.

Also recommended is *Ethnology of Vanuatu – an early twentieth century study*, by Felix Speiser (Crawford House Press, Bathurst NSW). This impressive, well-illustrated work contains the results of a scientific expedition to the country in 1910-12 by Dr Speiser, a professor at the University of Basel, Switzerland.

Arts & Customs

Arts of Vanuatu (Crawford House Publishing, Bathurst, NSW), edited by Joel Bonnemaison et al, is an essential reference. This lavishly illustrated work explores the rich diversity of Vanuatu's unique cultural identity, looking at it in both historical and contemporary contexts.

Flora & Fauna

Heinrich Bregulla's detailed *Birds of Vanuatu* (Anthony Nelson, Oswestry, UK) is required reading for bird-watchers. The book contains good general information as well as specifics on the country's 121 bird species, but is too large to be carried in the field.

NEWSPAPERS & MAGAZINES

There are two modest national newspapers: the government's trilingual *Vanuatu Weekly Hebdomadaire* and the privately published English-language *Trading Post*. Both are published twice weekly and cost 100VT.

RADIO & TV

The government-owned Radio Vanuatu provides trilingual FM, AM and SW services throughout the country. All services operate continuously from 6 am to 10 pm and offer international and local news bulletins on the hour.

Local TV is available on a single channel from around 4.30 pm to 11.30 pm daily.

TIME

Vanuatu time is GMT/UMT plus 11 hours which is one hour ahead of Australian Eastern Standard Time. Noon in Vila is 1 am in London, 8 pm in New York and 11 am in Sydney. Local time is the same as in New Caledonia, but one hour behind Fiji and New Zealand.

WEIGHTS & MEASURES

Vanuatu uses the metric system. Petrol and milk are sold by the litre, fish and fruit by the kilogram. Distance is measured in metres, and speed limits are in kilometres per hour (km/h). Temperatures are measured in degrees Celsius. If you need help with metric conversion, turn to the tables on the inside back cover of this book.

HEALTH

The major medical facilities are in Port Vila and Luganville, both of which have good sized hospitals and well-stocked pharmacies – Vila has the country's only dental surgery and optician. Many remote rural areas have no health facilities apart from aid posts, if that.

Water

Domestic water supplies in main urban centres are normally quite safe for drinking, although in some areas (eg Luganville and Lamap) it should be boiled towards the end of a long dry season.

In rural areas, drinking water obtained from springs is generally OK. Water from other sources should be purified before drinking.

Mosquito-Borne Diseases

Malaria is Vanuatu's major health risk, only tiny Futuna Island is considered free of e disease and dengue is also wide spread. See Health in the Regional Facts for the Visitor chapter.

USEFUL ORGANISATIONS
Vanuatu Cultural Centre
The curator of the Vanuatu Cultural Centre (☎ 26590, kaljoralsenta@vanuatu.gov.vu), PO Box 184, in Vila, can give advice on independent travel in remoter areas. He may also be able to arrange for guides.

Vanuatu National Council of Women
The Vanuatu National Council of Women (VNCW; ☎ 23108), PO Box 975, in Vila can advise you on all cultural matters relating to women. It can also tell you about contact people, accommodation and transport in remote areas. Women intending to travel by themselves to the outer islands should definitely contact the VNCW first and discuss likely problems.

Conservation Areas
For information on official conservation areas contact the Environment Unit (☎ 25302, fax 23565), PMB 063, in Vila, or its Luganville office (☎ 36153).

Other
If all else fails, the various provincial government offices can often give useful information about travel matters in their areas. However, you may find it very difficult to get through on the telephone. The Ministry of Home Affairs, at Independence Park in Vila, can give you up-to-date contact details.

Also worth trying are the church offices in Vila and Luganville. They can tell you about their missions throughout the country.

DANGERS & ANNOYANCES
Your belongings will normally be quite safe in your hotel room. However, petty theft is on the increase and you should never leave any valuables, wallets or handbags lying about unattended. Clothing, footwear, snorkelling gear and other useful items are also at risk from thieves.

BUSINESS HOURS
Government offices open Monday to Friday from 7.30 to 11.30 am and 1.30 to 4.30 pm, and sometimes Saturday morning. Most businesses operate during the same hours but will generally stay open until 5 pm.

Shops normally begin trading at 7.30 am. In true Gallic style, many close between 11.30 am and 1.30 or 2 pm, but then remain open until 6 or 7 pm. Saturday shopping generally ceases between 11.30 am and noon, although Chinese stores tend to remain open all weekend. Most cafes, restaurants and bars in Vila open daily.

PUBLIC HOLIDAYS & SPECIAL EVENTS
In addition to New Year's Day, Easter, Ascension Day, Assumption Day and Christmas (see the Regional Facts for the Visitor chapter for dates), Vanuatu celebrates:

Kastom Chiefs' Day	5 March
Labour Day	1 May
Children's Day	24 July
Independence Day	30 July
Constitution Day	5 October
National Unity Day	29 November
Family Day	26 December

Independence Day festivities are Vanuatu's most important annual event. Other notable events of cultural interest include:

February
Jon Frum Day
Sulphur Bay, Tanna; includes festivities, dancing and parades

April/May/June
Land Diving
Occurs in several villages in southern Pentecost. See the boxed text in that chapter.

August to November
The Toka
Clan alliance dance, held on Tanna over a period of three days every year

ACTIVITIES
Water Sports
Swimming Vanuatu has hundreds of safe swimming beaches, many with brilliant

VANUATU

white sand fringed by coconut palms. However, sharks, stonefish and strong currents are a danger in some areas. Always seek local advice before plunging in.

Diving Vanuatu's many scuba sites include several world-class dives. Many are listed in Lonely Planet's *Diving & Snorkeling in Vanuatu* (see Books, earlier in this section), and some are spotlighted in the 'South Pacific Diving' special section, earlier in this book. Vila probably has the best range of underwater topography in a small area, while Santo has the best wreck, coral and fish dives. Visibility is normally excellent throughout.

For contact details of specialist dive-tour operators in Vila and Luganville, see the sections on Efate and Santo later in this chapter.

Bushwalking

The country has many fine walks, including strenuous overnight treks. Frank King Tours in Vila and Butterfly Tamaso Tours in Luganville have some good walks on offer, as do most rural guesthouses. This chapter includes a number of options for independent trekkers.

When walking on jungle paths always wear long pants to protect yourself from stinging plants – ignore this advice at your peril. Sandals and joggers are not suitable for jungle trekking or volcano climbs.

Before leaving any public road or path and heading off by yourself, you should check that it's OK to do so. Guides are generally required for walks off the beaten track – hiring one will cost anything from a smile of thanks to 2500VT per day.

ACCOMMODATION

If you like comfort with an element of luxury, there's a good selection of hotels in and around Vila and, to a much lesser extent, Luganville. Several places in these towns can claim to be of backpacker standard, but very few charge backpacker prices.

Camping

Vanuatu doesn't have official camping grounds, but some guesthouses will allow you to pitch your tent in their grounds. The local chief may give approval if you want camp on some out-of-the-way beach.

Village Leaf Houses & Nakamal

Rudimentary thatched huts (called 'le houses') and nakamal are the country most basic form of visitor accommodatic – just about every rural village has a le house set aside for visitors' use. Fleas c be a problem here (take insecticide and pe sonal insect repellent), and food etc shoul be secured against rats.

It may cost up to 250VT to stay in a le house, depending on its standard. Otherwis you could say 'thank you' with a small gi such as a tin of beef or packet of cigarette

Hostels & Guest/Resthouses

Places in the 1000VT to 2500VT range in clude church hostels, guesthouses and govern ment resthouses. The last are mainly fo government workers, but you can stay in the if there's room. This style of accommodatic varies enormously in standard, and rats can b a problem here as well. Although rural place are often very basic – washing and toilet faci ities are invariably primitive, electricity a almost unheard-of luxury – most do provid clean bedding and mosquito nets.

All government resthouses have commu nal cooking facilities, although once aga these can be extremely basic.

Resorts, Hotels & Motels

A handful of generally basic motels in Vil and Luganville charge under 6000VT for double or twin room. Most have cookin, facilities, and air-con or fans.

If you'd prefer something a little mor sophisticated – although price is no guaran tee of sophistication – a number of place charge between 7000VT and 10,000VT fo two people in a studio or one-bedroon apartment.

Rates at Vanuatu's international-standar hotels and resorts start at around 17,000V for a double or twin room.

FOOD & DRINK

Vila is well known in the Pacific for its in ternational cuisine, and boasts one of th gion's more famous restaurants (Rossi's). The main supermarkets all carry a good range of local and imported food and drink, including alcohol. There are no takeaway liquor sales on Saturday afternoon or Sunday.

Restaurants are scarce outside Vila and Luganville, although most rural guesthouses provide basic island-style meals. The larger villages have general stores, but their choice of grocery lines is often limited. Some also have markets where you can buy cheap, fresh local produce.

Kava drinking is an evening ritual throughout the country – it's available in most villages, and there are plenty of kava bars in Vila and Luganville. You can even buy dried kava to take home. See the boxed text 'Kava' in the Regional Facts for the Visitor chapter.

SHOPPING
Duty-Free Shopping

Vila is the country's only duty-free port. When making duty-free purchases you must produce your passport and onward or return ticket. The shop will deliver the goods to you on departure at the airport or main wharf.

Handicrafts

Vanuatu offers a wide range of traditional and contemporary handicrafts and artefacts. In terms of wood carvings, northern Ambrym has the best reputation for quality and artistry. The major handicraft outlets are in Vila, where examples of all the nation's art forms are available. Elsewhere, purchasing is usually by direct contact with village artisans.

Objects must be fumigated if they are made from tree ferns, have soil or feathers on them, or have fresh borer holes. If necessary you can arrange this yourself at one of the country's two quarantine stations: near the airport in Vila (☎ 23130) and at Luganville's main wharf (☎ 36728). The process takes a minimum of 24 hours and costs up to 800VT.

You'll need an exemption form for objects made of tree ferns or parts of animals, including shell and coral. Applications for these 'CITES' exemptions can be made at the Environment Unit (☎ 25302) in the Georges Pompidou Building in central Vila.

Restrictions on Exports

The export of all magic stones and antiques – that is, artefacts more than 50 years old – is banned. If your purchase could possibly be taken for a restricted item, make sure to obtain a certificate proving that it's been made recently.

Getting There & Away

AIR

Aircalin (Vila ☎ 22019) and Air Vanuatu (Vila ☎ 23838) are the only international airlines providing direct services to Vanuatu. Air Pacific, Qantas and Solomon Airlines have code-sharing arrangements with Air Vanuatu. Various air passes (see the Getting Around the Region chapter) connect Vanuatu with other Pacific islands and Australasia.

Airports

Vanuatu's major international airport, Bauerfield, is 6km from Port Vila (air code VLI). Processing by customs and immigration is generally quick and efficient. Staff at the information desk speak English and French.

Departure Tax

A 2500VT airport tax is charged to all international passengers leaving Vanuatu except travellers who transit within 24 hours. Remember to keep sufficient vatu in reserve if this tax isn't included in your ticket price.

Travel Agencies

Vila's out-bound operators are South Pacific Travel (☎ 22836 or ☎ 22705, fax 23583, spts@vanuatu.com.vu) and Surata Tamaso Travel (☎ 22666, fax 24275, tamaso-aliatwitours@vanuatu.com.vu).

Both are on Kumul Hwy in central Vila. They can arrange and confirm bookings on any airline around the world.

Australia

Brisbane The cheapest fare between Australia and Vila is an excursion return from Brisbane on either Aircalin or Air Vanuatu.

Air Vanuatu has three outward and inward flights per week along this route, while Aircalin has a weekly service out of Brisbane via Noumea – it may be possible to include a stopover in Noumea for the same cost. There's a five or 10 day minimum stay with these fares, depending on which airline you choose.

Melbourne & Sydney Air Vanuatu has one direct return flight per week between Melbourne and Vila, and five per week between Sydney and Vila.

New Zealand

Air Vanuatu's Vila -Auckland service operates twice a week in both directions.

The Pacific

Fiji Code sharing with Air Pacific, Air Vanuatu has three return flights between Nadi in Fiji and Vila.

In addition there's a triangle fare with either Air Pacific or Aircalin that connects Nadi, Vila and Noumea in New Caledonia. The only rule is that you have a stopover in each country lasting at least 24 hours.

New Caledonia Tontouta, Noumea's international airport, is Vanuatu's closest international destination. Air Vanuatu and Aircalin have a total of nine return flights per week between Vila and Noumea, with a minimum/maximum stay rule of three/30 days.

Air Vanuatu is proposing a direct service between Tanna and New Caledonia.

Papua New Guinea & the Solomon Islands Solomon Airlines (code sharing with Air Vanuatu) offers a weekly connection to/from Port Moresby via Honiara in the Solomons. It also has return flights twice a week between Honiara and Vila.

SEA
Cruise Ships

Vila hosts a cruise ship on average once twice a fortnight. Cruise lines visiting Vanuatu on a regular basis from Sydney a P&O Lines (Sydney office ☎ 02-93 2619); and the Norwegian Capricorn Lin (Sydney reservations ☎ 1300 364 699).

Cargo Ships

South Pacific Shipping in Vila (☎ 22387, fa 23529) will know of any passenger-carryin freight lines that visit Vanuatu. It's the loc agent for Bank Line, which operates from Europe to the Pacific via Singapore – i vessels can carry eight passengers.

Yachts

The best source of general information o yachting matters is the Vanuatu Cruisin Yacht Club (☎ 24634), PO Box 1252, Po Vila. Touring yachts are not permitted t make landfall in or depart from Vanuat until they have cleared customs and imm gration (either in Vila or Luganvill There are hefty fines for disobeying tha rule.

Getting Around

All the major islands receive scheduled a services from Vila or Luganville. While th national road network continues to grow many remote areas can only be reached b footpath or boat.

AIR

Vanuatu's domestic air carrier, Vanair, ha scheduled flights into 28 airfields using i fleet of 20-seat Twin Otters. You can chec schedules and prices at its head offic (☎ 22643, fax 23910), on Kumul Hwy i central Vila. The service is generally reli able, although delays of an hour or more ar common.

Vanair allows children between two an 12 years of age to fly half-price. Student are granted a 25% discount on presentatio of satisfactory proof such as an Inter national Student Identity Card (ISIC).

Always book your seat well in advance, particularly on the more popular routes such as Vila to Luganville and Tanna. Don't despair if you're told that the plane is booked out: if you turn up at the airfield just prior to departure there's at least a 50% chance of finding a vacancy.

If you're just going to be in a place for a couple of days it's a good idea to confirm your onward booking on arrival. Another wise precaution is to watch while freight is unloaded at bush airfields en route to check that your baggage isn't taken off by mistake. As well, always make sure that it gets off when you do.

Finally, few of Vanair's bush terminals have toilet facilities. In most cases you'll have to make do with a nearby clump of bushes – if there is one!

Charters

You can arrange a charter with the Helicopta Kompani (☎ 24424, fax 24693), Sea Air (☎/fax 27044) and Air Club Vila (☎/fax 22514), all based in Vila.

Discover Vanuatu Pass

Vanair's Discover Vanuatu Pass, which is only available offshore, allows you to fly a combination of sectors within 30 days for US$270. The specified destinations are Craig Cove on Ambrym, Norsup on Malekula, Luganville and Tanna.

BUS

Public minibuses carrying up to 14 passengers operate in Vila, Luganville and, to a much lesser extent, eastern Santo and north-eastern Malekula. You'll know them by the red 'B' fixed to their number plates.

These vehicles are a little like taxis, only much cheaper. In the towns they don't run fixed routes, but zoom all over the place at the whim of their passengers. You simply flag them down by the roadside, and they'll stop if there's a spare seat.

TAXI

Most islands with roads have taxis. In Vila and Luganville these are mostly conventional sedans, while in rural areas they're 4WD

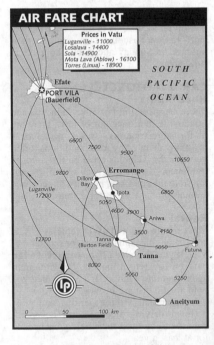

AIR FARE CHART

Prices in Vatu
Luganville - 11000
Losalava - 14400
Sola - 14900
Mota Lava (Ablow) - 16100
Torres (Linua) - 18900

trucks or utilities. Taxis and public transport trucks have a red 'T' on their number plates.

The minimum charge in urban areas is 100VT, and for a straight point-to-point charter you can expect to pay around 100VT per kilometre. However, in some rural areas, such as south Pentecost, you'll be charged a lot more than that.

Taxis in Vila and Luganville should have their meters on for trips within the town area. If the meter is off, ask that it be switched on. For longer journeys you can negotiate a price with the driver, but, having agreed on the fare, make sure you stick to it. Some drivers will try to add extra at the end of the trip, while others will pretend to have no change!

A day charter will generally cost between 6000VT and 10,000VT depending on factors such as road conditions and distance. In addition, you may be expected to provide lunch for the driver. Always ask your hotel to recommend someone rather than take pot luck down at the taxi rank.

At bush airfields, the best source of information on local taxis is the Vanair clerical staff. Taxis are usually conspicuous by their absence on Sunday and public holidays in rural areas.

CAR & MOTORCYCLE
Road Rules
There's a speed limit of 50km/h in Vila and Luganville, but once out of town there are no formal restrictions – speed in rural areas is usually dictated by road conditions (often very rough). Vehicles drive on the right, as in France. Always give way to traffic coming from the right, and be wary of people or animals on the road in rural areas.

Rental
You can hire cars and 4WD vehicles in Vila and Luganville, and mopeds (or scooters) in Vila. If you're under 23 you can't rent a car, but you can rent a moped. The minimum age for renting a moped is 17, provided you hold a valid driving licence.

International driving permits and most national driving licences are accepted. However, you must have held your licence for at least a year.

BOAT
For adventurous travellers with plenty of time, the cheapest way to get around the archipelago is with the small cargo vessels that operate out of Vila and Luganville. Conditions on these craft are invariably spartan at best and you may need to bring everything with you, including food, drinking water and bedding. Still, while it may be uncomfortable, travelling by this method is a great way to meet local people.

Inter-Island Shipping Services
The major operators are Ifira Shipping Agencies (☎ 24445) and Toara Coastal Shipping (☎ 22370), both in Vila. Neither company has schedules as such, but they do work to a pattern. In Ifira's case, the 115 tonne MV *Saraika* does a round trip of a fortnight from Vila, servicing ports on Epi, Paama, Ambrym, Pentecost, Maewo, Ambae and Santo. Then it does a three day

southern loop to Tanna and Erromango be fore heading north again.

Toara provides a similar service with i 100 tonne MV *Aloara*; its 15 tonne M *Marata* visits Epi and the Shepherd Islan from Vila. Dinh Shipping (☎ 22735) visi all the islands south of Efate.

Ask at BP Wharf in central Vila abo other craft – such as the MV *El Shadd* and MV *Rosalie* – that may be operatir between Vila and Luganville.

Canoes & Speedboats
When Ni-Vanuatu talk of speedboats, the mean outboard-powered dinghies or sma work-boats. Canoes are simply dugout cra with outriggers, usually powered by pa dles. Except on the shorter routes, speed boats have generally replaced canoes a commuter craft.

Regular speedboat services connect som areas, such as Epi with Lamen Island. Th charges are invariably much, much cheape if you wait for the scheduled departure rath than ask the boatman to make a special tri Speedboat prices can be very high, and longish journey on which you're the onl passenger can really damage the budget.

ORGANISED TOURS
There's a wide variety of tours on offer, par ticularly on Efate and Santo. These includ traditional culture, yacht cruises, scuba div ing, bushwalking, bus tours and sceni flights. See later sections in this chapter fo details.

Between them, the major inbound tou operators (all in central Vila) have details c most tours throughout the country.

The Adventure Centre
    (☎ 25155 or ☎ 22743, fax 27763,
    sailaway@vanuatu.com.vu)
Adventures in Paradise
    (☎ 25200, fax 23135,
    paradise@vanuatu.com.vu)
Island Safaris
    (☎ 23288, fax 26779,
    islands@vanuatu.com.vu)
Tamaso Aliat Wi Tours
    (☎ 25600 or ☎ 25225, fax 24275,
    tamaso-aliatwitours@vanuatu.com.vu)

VANUATU

fate

● **pop 50,000**   ● **area 915 sq km**

mes Cook named this island after Lord
ndwich, the British patron of his voyage.
owever, the islanders' own name for it,
ate (pronounced 'ef-**art**-ay'), has pre-
iled. Efate has two of the country's best
ep-water anchorages (Vila Bay and
avannah Harbour) as well as the principal
rport and its largest town, Port Vila.

Havannah Harbour was the site of the
st European settlement on Efate. For a
ne it was the island's commercial centre,

but in the 1880s most of its malaria-ravaged
residents decamped for the healthier climate
of Vila Bay. In 1906 Vila was declared the
seat of the newly proclaimed Condominium
government and thus became the national
capital.

PORT VILA
● **pop 36,000**

Built around horseshoe-shaped Vila Bay,
Vila climbs steep hillsides that offer stunning views over the bay and Iririki and
Ifira islands. This is one of Oceania's most
attractive towns.

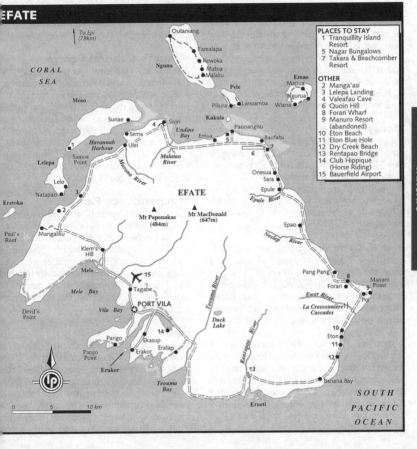

EFATE

PLACES TO STAY
1 Tranquillity Island
   Resort
5 Nagar Bungalows
7 Takara & Beachcomber
   Resort

OTHER
2 Manga'asi
3 Lelepa Landing
4 Valeafau Cave
6 Quoin Hill
8 Forari Wharf
9 Manuro Resort
   (abandoned)
10 Eton Beach
11 Eton Blue Hole
12 Dry Creek Beach
13 Rentapao Bridge
14 Club Hippique
   (Horse Riding)
15 Bauerfield Airport

VANUATU

Orientation

Most of Vila's commercial buildings and its main shopping precinct are concentrated along the shore in an area measuring only about 1km by 250m, so it's easily explored on foot. Kumul Hwy, the chaotic main street, winds along parallel to the waterfront – its name honours Papua New Guinea's Kumul Force, which mopped up the Santo Rebellion in 1980. Cruising yachts and charter boats usually line the seawall near the Waterfront Bar & Grill, while inter-island copra boats moor at the Burns Philp (BP) Wharf.

Information

Tourist Offices The National Tourism Office (☎ 22515 or ☎ 22685), off Kumul Hwy near the GPO, is the logical first stop in Vila. It has quite a bit of tourist information, and if its staff don't know about a place they can direct you to someone who does. It opens during normal business hours as well as on Saturday mornings.

Money Foreign exchange is handled by the major commercial banks as well as two or three privately owned money exchanges. See Money in the Facts for the Visitor section earlier in this chapter.

Goodies Money Exchange, on the corner of Kumul Hwy and Rue Pasteur St, generally gives the best rates. It opens daily including public holidays.

Post & Communications Vila's GPO is open from 7.30 am to 4.30 pm, with a two hour break for lunch, Monday to Friday, and from 7.30 to 11.30 am on Saturday. It has a poste restante service and a stamp counter. Public phone boxes (both coin and card) are outside; private phone and fax booths are inside.

Libraries The National Library, across from Goodies, has French and English-language lending sections, a Vanuatu reference section and a newspaper reading room. Ask the duty librarian if you want to read the reference books. The library opens from 9 am to 6 pm weekdays and from 8 to 11.30 am on Saturday.

The Alliance Française behind the Fren Embassy has a library where you can read t major French newspapers and magazin Similar facilities are available at the Austi lian and New Zealand high commissions.

Vanuatu's best source of scientific refe ence books on the region is the Orstom I brary, upstairs from Trader Vic's, behind Gecko Restaurant in central Vila. It ope Monday to Friday during normal busine hours.

Medical Services Vila's Central Hospi has a dentist, several private practitione and a dispensary; its outpatient departme is open during normal business hours. / well, you'll find three well-stocked pharm cies in central Vila.

Vanuatu Cultural Centre

The Vanuatu Cultural Centre on Rue d'A tois St has a small museum containing variety of cultural artefacts. Of particul interest are a display of traditional potte and a variety of ceremonial headdresses there's an extraordinary example from t Naluan society of south-west Malekula.

The museum opens from 8 am to 4 p weekdays and from 8 am to noon on Satu day; the entry fee is 400VT.

Independence Park

On Winston Churchill Ave above centr Vila, this large area of lawn and shady tre was at the heart of the colonial administra tion. The French and British governme residencies were nearby, and checks we often made to ensure that the Union Jac and Tricolour flew at the same height. N wonder their attempts at dual governme were often laughable.

Iririki

Little Iririki Island, 300m from Vila's wate front, is connected to the mainland by a fre 24-hour ferry service. The walk around takes you through lush tropical bushlar and is easily accomplished in 30 minute Pedaloes, catamarans, windsurfers etc ai for hire at a little swimming beach ju south of the resort. You can enjoy a coc

ink up at the restaurant, where there's a
arvellous view of Vila.

wimming
la has little to offer apart from the small
vimming beaches on Erakor and Iririki
lands. The most popular spots near town
e Black Sand Beach (beside the golf club)
d Mele Beach opposite Mele (Hideaway)
land.

iving & Snorkelling
nere are a number of good dive sites near
la including wrecks, coral reefs, deep
op-offs, chasms, caverns and swim-
roughs. Scuba sites close to Vila include
e *Star of Russia* and Black Sand Reef (see
e 'South Pacific Diving' special section).
The specialist dive-tour operators based
and around town include:

deaway Island Dive
(☎ 26660, fax 23867,
hideaway@vanuatu.com.vu)
on Hideaway (Mele) Island
utilus Scuba
(☎ 22398, fax 25255,
nautilus@vanuatu.com.vu)
in central Vila
o Dive Vila
(☎/fax 23010, prodive@vanuatu.com.vu)
on Iririki Island
anquillity Dive
(☎ 25020, fax 22979,
drewco@vanuatu.com.vu)
on Moso Island

lso check out the various yacht charters as
ey generally offer scuba diving as an extra.
 Some dive sites can be snorkelled, and if
u'd rather do this than scuba you can join
tour for around 1200VT, inclusive of kit.
ne cost of a single boat dive generally
arts at around 3800VT if you have your
vn gear.

orse Riding
lub Hippique (☎ 23347), 8km from cen-
al Vila, has trail rides through the tropical
inforest and coconut plantations above
nden Lagoon. It charges 2300/3500VT
r a one/two hour ride. A minibus from
wn costs 200VT.

Sporting Centres & Clubs
Between them, Korman Stadium, on the
eastern outskirts of town, and the old Stadium, north of central Vila, have facilities
for a wide range of sports. You can get a
program from the Department of Youth &
Sport (☎ 25106) in central Vila.

The Port Vila Tennis Club (☎ 22437) is
beside the old Stadium. It has five hard
courts, two squash courts and a gymnasium,
and holds aerobics classes. Vanuatu's only
lawn tennis courts are at the White Sands
Country Club, 16.5km from Vila.

The Port Vila Golf Club (☎ 22564) and
the White Sands Country Club have 18-hole
courses. Otherwise there are small golf
courses at Le Meridien and Le Lagon
Parkroyal (see Places to Stay later in the
Port Vila section).

Organised Tours
Sea Trips There's a good choice of glass-
bottom boat trips and yacht cruises, with
several operators vying for your vatu. Expect to pay upwards of 3000/6000VT for a
half/full day cruise, not including dives.
Sunset cruises with or without night coral
viewing are around 3000VT including wine
and nibbles.

Cutting Edge Adventures (☎ 22176) has
guided day and overnight kayaking trips
around the Efate coast. Self-paddle and
guide-paddle options are available. On day
trips (3500VT) you paddle around Erakor
and Eratap islands near Vila; longer excursions take you to the islands of north Efate.

Bus Tours Most inbound operators offer
bus tours. You'll pay upwards of 4400VT
for the round trip of Efate, a short day tour.
Progress is normally fairly slow because of
the road conditions, so you may only stop
four or five times en route.

Cultural Tours The Melanesian feast nights
held in villages near Vila cost upwards of
3000VT. They're a good opportunity to
sample kava and traditional cooking, listen
to string bands and watch kastom dancing.
The feast night at Ekasup is particularly
good.

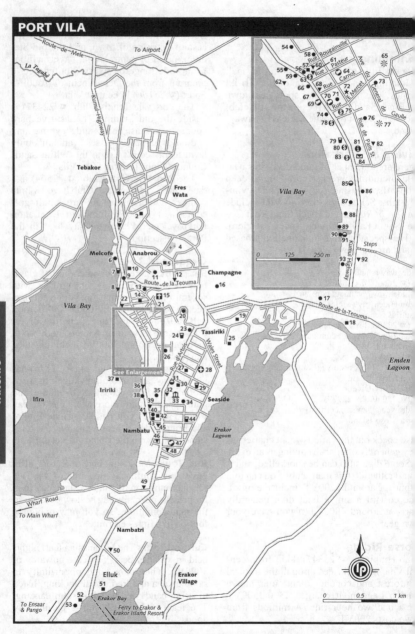

PORT VILA

PORT VILA

PLACES TO STAY
1 Coral Motel
2 VNCW Guesthouse
5 Emman & Imalo Motel
10 Luron Guesthouse
14 Tafea Guesthouse
18 Vila Chaumières
19 Holiday Motel
25 Le Meridien
27 Sutherland House
30 Ah Tong Motel
37 Iririki Island Resort
42 The Melanesian Port Vila
43 Kaiviti Motel
51 Le Lagon Parkroyal
52 Pacific Lagoon Apartments
57 Iririki Centre Ville Hotel; Ezy
   Wash Laundrette

PLACES TO EAT
3 Harbour View Restaurant
8 Food Stalls
12 Les Delicés Patisserie
22 The Office Pub
32 Bamboo Royal Restaurant;
   Ebisu Restaurant
36 Waterfront Bar & Grill;
   Vanuatu Cruising Yacht Club
39 Le Bistrot
41 The Galley Bar & Bistro
45 Regal Restaurant
46 Au Bon Marché
48 L'Houstalet
49 La Cabane
50 Golden Dragon Restaurant
60 Trader Vic's Pizza & Takeaway;
   Orstom Library (upstairs)
61 El Gecko Restaurant & Cafe
62 Rossi Restaurant

68 Ma Barker's Restaurant;
   Mamu Bar
82 Club Vanuatu
92 Harbourside Café Restaurant

OTHER
4 Cemetery
6 Connie's Art Blong Yumi
7 Trader Vic's Bar
9 Surata Tamaso Travel
11 Stadium
13 Georges Pompidou Building
15 Porte du Ciel Roman Catholic
   Church
16 University of the South Pacific
   (USP)
17 Korman Stadium
20 Supreme Court
21 Roman Catholic Sacre Coeur
   Cathedral
23 Vanuatu Society For Disabled
   People
24 PJ's Nakamal
26 Independence Park
28 Central Hospital
29 Red Light Nakamal
31 Taxi & Bus Centre
33 Cultural Centre; VNCW
34 Chiefs' Nakamal
35 Parliament House
38 Nautilus Scuba
40 Cine Hickson
44 Ronnie's Nakamal
47 People's Republic of China
   Embassy
53 Michoutouchkine & Pilioko
   Foundation Art Gallery
54 Radio Vanuatu
55 Fung Kuei

56 The Adventure Centre
58 Chew Store
59 Air Calin
63 Goodies Money Exchange;
   Olympic Take Away
64 UK High Commission;
   Australian High Commission
65 WWI Memorial
66 National Library
67 Island Safaris
69 New Zealand High Commission (upstairs); Stop Press
70 French Embassy
71 Alliance Française; Maison du
   Combattant
72 Police Station
73 Town Hall
74 Immigration (upstairs)
75 National Bank of Vanuatu
76 Air Vanuatu
77 Lookout Point
78 Banque d'Hawaii
79 Le Flamingo
80 Westpac Bank
81 National Tourism Office
83 ANZ Bank
84 General Post Office; Proud's
85 Taxi Rank
86 Constitution Building (includes
   Customs)
87 Covered Market
88 Fish Market
89 Burns Philp (BP) Wharf
90 Iririki Wharf
91 Taxi Stand
93 Helikopta Kompani; Le Café
   du Village

VANUATU

Probably the best cultural tour on Efate is ²e Ekasup Cultural Village, where Futunan ªlanders demonstrate and talk about vari-ᵤs aspects of their traditional lifestyle. The ᵥo hour tour costs 3200VT.

ᵤshwalking Tours Frank King Tours ⁷ 22808) has an interesting 15km day ªlk for around 4000VT. Frank can also ʳange more strenuous treks, such as the ᵥo day walk across Efate's rugged centre ᵒm Onesua to Bauerfield airport. ªmaso Aliat Wi Tours (☎ 25600) has a ⁻lection of walks including a 25km ªrathon.

Places to Stay – Budget
Hostels & Guesthouses There are a number of hostel-style places in Vila, but the situation is fluid in terms of standards. The ones listed here have basic, generally shared kitchen, shower, toilet and laundry facilities, and provide bedding.

In Anabrou, about 15 minutes walk from town, the friendly *Vanuatu National Council of Women's Guesthouse* (☎ 26964) charges 1500VT for a bed and 700VT to camp in the grounds. This place is very clean and usually quiet.

The *Luron Guesthouse* is handy to the northern end of the central business district.

It has a good kitchen and most bedrooms have ceiling fans. Its cheapest beds (1000VT) are in a cramped two-bunk 'dorm'; other beds cost 1500VT (2000VT with breakfast).

Also close to town, the spartan *Tafea Guesthouse* (☎ 27787) has bunk beds for 1500VT and single/double rooms for 2500/3000VT. Some rooms don't have windows and can be on the stuffy side. It's about 150m east of the Vanuatu National Provident Fund building on Ave Andre Ballande.

Most upmarket of Vila's hostel-style accommodation is the *Emman & Imalo Motel* (☎ 23927), about 10 minutes walk north from town. It offers rooms with private or shared facilities at 2000/3000/4500VT for singles/doubles/ triples, and free pick-ups from the airport.

Motels On Kumul Hwy north of central Vila, the *Coral Motel* (☎ 23569) has 13 fan-cooled units with kitchen facilities, as well as a two-bedroom house. The units, which sleep up to five and have knockout colour schemes, cost from 5400/5900/6400VT for doubles/triples/quads.

East of the city, and overlooking the golf course at Le Meridien, is the very pleasant *Holiday Motel* (☎ 23527). Its air-conditioned studios and apartments cost from 4800VT for doubles.

Places to Stay – Mid-Range
Right in the centre of town, the *Iririki Centre Ville Hotel* (☎ 23388, iririki@vanuatu .com.vu) is favoured by visiting business-folk. Its double/triple rates are 8100/10,300VT for standard rooms, 9000/11,200VT for studios, and 11,200/13,400VT for apartments.

The Melanesian Port Vila (☎ 22150, whivila@vanuatu.com.vu), on Kumul Hwy about 1km south of central Vila, has two restaurants, three bars and a swimming pool, as well as 85 air-con or fan-cooled studios and apartments. Rooms with cooking facilities cost 12,800/18,600VT for doubles/ triples, while apartments sleeping up to six cost from 17,900VT for doubles plus 5800VT for each extra person.

Next door, and also with a bar and swim-ming pool, the *Kaiviti Motel* (☎ 24684) is down-at-heel but much friendlier place. I 28 fan-cooled studios sleep four and co 8000/9000/10,000VT for doubles/triple quads; also sleeping four, its two-bedroo apartments cost 11,500/12,500/13,500VT

Places to Stay – Top End
The *Iririki Island Resort* (☎ 2338 iririki@vanuatu.com.vu) is the most centr of Vila's principal hotels. Its 72 luxu bungalows – some over the water – slee four and cost upwards of 19,000VT f doubles. Other attractions include gre views, a swimming pool, water sport restaurant, bar and regular floor shows.

A 20 minute walk east of central Vila, *I Meridien* (☎ 22040) has 150 air-con roo and 10 over-water bungalows near the t of Erakor Lagoon. Most of its rooms slee three people and start at 21,250VT for do bles. Among its facilities are a swimmi pool, private beaches, a nine-hole go course, water sports and casinos. Its ba and restaurants are among Vila's best.

Le Lagon Parkroyal (☎ 2231 lagonres@vanuatu.com.vu) is on the sho of Erakor Lagoon about 3km south of cer tral Vila. Its 141 air-conditioned room suites and bungalows start at 16,800V twin-share. The resort is popular with far ilies (a 'kid's club' operates daily), and i cludes a private beach, water sports and 12-hole golf course.

Places to Stay – Vila's Outskirts
About 3.5km south of central Vila, *Paci Lagoon Apartments* (☎ 23860) has 12 con fortable apartments at the mouth of Erak Lagoon. These sleep up to six people an cost from 6800VT to 9800VT per unit.

The *Erakor Island Resort* (☎ 2698 erakor@vanuatu.com.vu) opposite Le Lago Parkroyal has 18 self-contained waterfro bungalows costing from 12,500VT for do bles, which is pricey for the standard. Bu beds in a spartan dorm cost 2500VT.

About 3.5km east of central Vila, Emden Lagoon, is *Vila Chaumièr* (☎ 22866). Its four self-contained bungalov

ep up to three people each and cost from
,200/12,200VT for doubles/triples. Chil-
en under 16 years are not accepted here.
Up on the hillside near the Bellevue
antation, *Les Alizes (☎ 23594)* is a very
endly place in peaceful rural surround-
gs. Its five comfortable, fan-cooled
ngalows sleep four and cost from
00VT for doubles, including breakfast.
e trip to town costs 150VT by bus and
0VT by taxi, or you can walk there in 30
inutes.

laces to Stay – Out of Town

yet another tropical island setting, the
pretentious *Hideaway Island Resort
☎ 26963, hideaway@vanuatu.com.vu)* is
at past the airport, 10km from town.
ere's a range of styles, including dorm
ds for 2400VT and basic rooms with
ared facilities for 5300/7000VT for
ngles/doubles. While all rooms have ceil-
g fans, the electricity is turned off be-
een 11 pm and 7 am.

On Moso Island, the *Tranquillity Island
esort (☎ 25020, fax 22979, drewco@
nuatu.com.vu)* has rooms from 7425VT
r person. Both Hideaway and Tranquillity
dive trips.

On the south coast about 15.5km from
la, the *Tamanu Beach Club (☎ 27279)*
joys a very good reputation among lo-
ls. It has luxury accommodation in
ench colonial-style bungalows, plus a
od restaurant.

A kilometre farther along the coast is the
*hite Sands Country Club (☎ 22090,
hitesan@vanuatu.com.vu)*, which has 11
n-cooled bungalows costing 8000/
,000VT for doubles/families. There's a
imming pool, 18-hole golf course, lawn
nnis courts and a courtesy bus to Vila.

Continue on about another 4km and you
me to the *Blue Water Island Resort
☎ 27588)*. Its 50 fan-cooled, self-contained
ngalows sleep up to four people and cost
om 9200VT for doubles, including a
ght breakfast and transfers to and from
wn. Activities here include tennis,
lleyball, water sports, horse rides and
shwalks.

Places to Eat – Vila

Takeaways & Cheap Eats A number of
restaurants and cafes do takeaways. Probably the best is the *Olympic Take Away*,
next to Goodies – fish and chips cost from
600VT and hamburgers from 350VT.

If you like white rice, Vila's cheapest
place for lunch is a small group of *food
stalls* just beyond the Office Pub. Other
places worth mentioning are *Club Vanuatu*,
on Rue de Paris St, and *Trader Vic's Pizza
& Takeaway*, on Rue Bougainville St.

Cafes The classiest and most popular of
central Vila's cafes are: *El Gecko Restaurant & Cafe*, next to Goodies; the *Harbourside Café Restaurant*, diagonally opposite
the Helikopta Kompani; and *Le Café du
Village*, on the waterfront behind the Helikopta Kompani. At all three, cooked
breakfasts start at around 450VT, large
sandwiches are upwards of 400VT; they
also have restaurant-style meals.

Restaurants On the waterfront in the centre of town, the *Rossi Restaurant* is one of
Vila's dining institutions. It's open daily for
breakfast, lunch and dinner, and is famous
for its seafood. Go there at sunset for a marvellous view of Vila Bay.

Close by are *El Gecko Restaurant &
Cafe* and *Ma Barker's Restaurant*, both of
which offer lunches and dinners starting at
around 1200VT. The *Mamu Bar* adjoining
Ma Barker's sells cheaper pub meals, as
does the *Office Pub* farther north.

Also in central Vila, the island-style
Waterfront Bar & Grill is open daily for
lunch and dinner. A large steak or piece of
fresh fish, plus as much as you can eat from
the salad bar, costs from 1600VT.

With one of the most imaginative menus
in town, *L'Houstalet* offers a French provincial atmosphere and fare such as frogs' legs,
snails, flying fox and green pigeon. It's diagonally opposite Au Bon Marché supermarket in Nambatu.

Up by the Cultural Centre, the *Ebisu
Restaurant* specialises in Japanese cuisine.
Mains cost from around 1000VT. Next door,
the *Bamboo Royal Restaurant* is generally

VANUATU

considered the best of the local Chinese restaurants.

Between them, the resorts and major hotels have a number of bars and restaurants offering a range of styles.

Places to Eat – Vila's Outskirts

'Laid back' best describes the **Hideaway Island Resort**, where you eat beachcomber style at shaded tables. Its restaurant opens between 7 am and 8 pm daily, with meals costing from 800VT.

Open daily for lunch and dinner, **Vila Chaumières** has a wonderful atmosphere. Also in this general area, **Les Alizes** and the **Tamanu Beach Club** farther out both have highly regarded French restaurants.

Entertainment

On a wet day, there's not much to do in Vila except visit the Cultural Centre, go shopping, browse in a library, and take a long lunch. It's much the same story after dinner, although a couple of small casinos and discos might tempt you.

Casinos The **Palms Casino** in Le Meridien is open daily from noon until early morning for blackjack, roulette, baccarat and poker machines. You'll also find poker machines at **The Melanesian Port Vila** and **Club Vanuatu**.

Discos Vila's cheapest night spots are the Ni-Vanuatu discos scattered about town. If you want to visit one, take ear plugs and preferably go with someone who knows the ropes. L'Houstalet (see Places to Eat earlier in the Port Vila section) has the best of these. It's open nightly, except Friday, from 9 pm.

By far the classiest disco in town is **Le Flamingo**, in central Vila. It opens from Tuesday to Saturday at 5 pm and closes late.

Private Clubs In Rue de Paris St, the **Club Vanuatu** offers a range of facilities including a bistro, bars, snooker, darts, satellite TV and live bands on weekends. It's open daily from 10 am to midnight and overseas visitors are welcome; short-term visitors gain entry by signing the visitor book.

Behind the French Embassy, the **Mais du Combattant** is a French-language soc club open for coffee and light snacks betwe 9 am and 6 pm, with a two hour break f lunch. In the same building, the **Allian Française de Port Vila** has a variety of ent tainments and activities including bushwal and plays. Once a month it organises a ga tronomic tour of local French restaurants.

Kava Bars Vila has well over 100 ka bars (so-called nakamal), with most bei little more than iron sheds or open shelte The sunset kava cup, served in a cocor shell or glass bowl, is a ritual for many Vila's expats as well as Ni-Vanuatu.

Kava bars popular with expats inclu **PJ's Nakamal** on Ave Edmond Colardea **Ronnie's Nakamal** in Nambatu, and t **Red Light Nakamal** near the hospital. T going rate is 50VT for a small shell (abc 150mm) and 100VT for a larger one.

Cinemas **Club Vanuatu** has film nights b the material is usually of the head-bangi Rambo variety. The **Cine Hickson**, next The Melanesian Port Vila, shows Fren language and subtitled films nightly exce Thursday.

Shopping

Chinatown Rue Carnot St in central Vila lined with Chinese shops, and there a more round the corner in Rue de Paris . Many seem to sell everything from Japane stereos and watches to straw hats and Cl nese cigarettes. Prices are often a lot cheap here than on the main street, so have a go look around before you start spending.

Market Vila's public market is on t waterfront near the GPO. Except on Su day, it's normally filled with tables and m piled with fresh produce. Food prices he are rock-bottom; coconuts, pawpaws a huge grapefruit normally start at arou 30VT, and you could pay as little as 150V for a generous slab of laplap. However, prices of souvenirs can increase drama cally on cruise ship days, so compare the with those in the shops before you buy.

As with all Melanesian commerce, ere's no bargaining. Prices are fixed and early marked, so if you feel the price is reasonable, just keep moving to the next ll. No-one ever hassles you to buy anyng you don't want.

andicrafts The best selection of handiafts in town is at Connie's Art Blong Yumi, the way to the airport. There's plenty of od quality stock on display, and you can tch the wood carvers in action out the back. Goodies, in central Vila, has a variety of efacts and handicrafts, particularly carvgs, with most islands represented. Only a w of its artefacts are on display, so ask if u're interested in seeing the real thing.

uty-Free Stores Most of the duty-free tlets are concentrated on Kumul Hwy in ntral Vila. By far the best range of goods offered by Fung Kuei – its prices are very mpetitive, too.

Proud's, next to the GPO, is a very attracve shop specialising in French perfume d cosmetics, jewellery (including South a pearls) and Lladro porcelain.

etting There & Away
e the main Getting There & Away and etting Around sections earlier in this chapr for details of airline and shipping serces to and from Vila. See also the Vanuatu r Fares Chart in the main Getting Around ction earlier in the chapter, and Getting ere & Away sections for individual desations later in this chapter.

etting Around
/From the Airport Airport shuttle ses charge 400VT to or from Vila, and xis 1000VT shared. Alternatively, if you n't have much luggage, you can catch a inibus for 100VT.

inibus The cheapest way around Vila is minibus (see Bus in the main Getting ound section earlier in this chapter). The in routes are usually thick with minibuses tween 6 am and 7.30 pm; fares are a uni-rm 100VT within the wider town area.

Car & Motorcycle Vila's car-hire companies are Avis (☎ 24690), Budget (☎ 23170), Discount Rentals (☎ 23242), Hertz (☎ 25700) and Thrifty (☎ 22244 or ☎ 22533). Avis, Hertz and Thrifty have desks at the airport, while Budget and Discount Rentals have courtesy phones.

Competition is fierce, with different packages and freebies on offer, so it's best to sit down and study the figures. Little things to check for include: delivery and collection charges, if any, and whether extra amounts are charged to cover government charges and VAT. As an example of costs, a one or two day hire of Hertz's cheapest four seater costs 9700VT per day inclusive of VAT, collision damage waiver and distance travelled.

Nautilus Scuba (☎ 22398) rents motor scooters, charging 2800/4100VT for a half/full day.

Taxi There are over 200 taxis operating in Vila, and as there's sufficient work for only 70 or so the service tends to be very competitive (see Taxi in the main Getting Around section earlier in this chapter).

The main taxi stands in central Vila are beside the market and Iririki Wharf. The Taxi Association & Bus Service Centre (☎ 25135) in Nambatu offers a 24 hour service.

Walking Traffic drives on the right, so Brits, Aussies and Kiwis should look carefully before stepping into the street. Most of Vila's streets are poorly lit at night, and some of the potholes are like tank traps. Carry a torch if you're going to be out late.

AROUND PORT VILA
Just outside Vila are several easily accessible places that are definitely worth visiting. Distances are from the GPO in Vila.

Erakor (4.5km)
At the mouth of Erakor Lagoon lies Erakor Island, one of the jewels of Vila. The island's southern half, which is like a natural botanic garden of infinite variety, is a tantalising glimpse of what many other islets in the archipelago are like. There's a small swimming beach at the resort, which takes

up the island's northern half. A free, 24-hour ferry service links the resort to a small jetty just south of Le Lagon Parkroyal.

Michoutouchkine & Pilioko Foundation Art Gallery (5.5km)

This Oceanic art gallery and artists' studio is about 1km past the turn-off to Le Lagon Parkroyal. You may wander around the gallery's beautiful private garden and display between 10 am and 5 pm daily (admission free).

The centre is named after its two resident artists, Nicholas Michoutouchkine and Aloi Pilioko. It houses a fascinating collection of Pacific bric-a-brac and memorabilia, including ornate carvings and masks produced by the master craftsmen of southern Malekula. Interspersed among these are stunning batik cotton prints and embroideries.

Pango Point Area

Pango (6.5km) Continue past the Michoutouchkine & Pilioko Foundation Art Gallery to get to Pango. This village gets its name from the Samoan missionaries who arrived here in the 1840s – they came from Pago Pago (pronounced 'pa-ngo pa-ngo') in American Samoa.

A sign says that outsiders who wish to swim or enjoy the privacy of the beaches in this area must pay 100VT per vehicle. Just beyond the village, several tracks cut northwards through the thick bush. One of these crosses the peninsula to **Paradise Cove**, a popular sunbathing and snorkelling spot for charter boat groups.

Other Destinations

Port Vila Golf Club (8.4km) The club house for Vanuatu's principal golf course is on the main road to Mele about 4km past the Tagabe roundabout, where the airport road turns off. Visitors are welcome, and you can also use nearby **Black Sand Beach**, a popular swimming spot.

Mele (Hideaway Island; 9.5km) On the left as you head along the main road, a dirt road leads down to **Mele Beach**. Barely

200m across the water is the Hideaway Island Resort, with a free ferry plying ba and forth during the day. The entry fee 500VT is payable at the bar.

The dense vegetation covering the island two hectares is punctuated by the resor beachfront bungalows. Just offshore is t best snorkelling close to Vila; on the edge the reef you'll find a bewildering variety corals, as well as swarms of colourful fish

You can hire snorkelling gear at the di shop, or take a ride over the reef in a glass bottom boat. Kayaks and catamarans c also be hired. On the downside, the sma coral beach in front of the restaurant ge very crowded on busy days – such as wh a cruise ship is in port.

A trip from town to Mele Beach cos 200VT by minibus and 1500VT by taxi.

Mele-Maat Cascades (10.5km) Th attractive spot, which features a 20m-hi waterfall shaded by rainforest, is right the bottom of **Klem's Hill**. You can easi spend a couple of hours here swimmin exploring, and admiring the scenery. Ent costs 250/500VT per child/adult, and if y want a guide it'll be 200VT extra.

AROUND EFATE

Puncture repair facilities and fuel statio are scarce in rural Efate. If you're hiring car to get around, check the spare tyre, jac ing equipment and wheel brace before lea ing town.

Roads outside Vila are invariably rou and occasionally washed out. When w the steep climbs in the island's north-w are impassable to conventional vehicl travelling in a clockwise direction.

The following distances are clockwi from the Port Vila post office. Major poi of interest closer than 11km to Vila are d scribed in Around Vila earlier in this chapt

Klem's Hill (11km)

The road leaves the coastal plains aft Mele-Maat and climbs sharply to 20C above sea level. Near the top, a parking b offers a superb view over extensive cocor plantations towards Vila and Mele Island

VANUATU

Seven kilometres farther, you crest an-
her steep hill to see **Eretoka**, **Lelepa** and
oso islands and **Havannah Harbour**
retching before you.

elepa Landing & Lelepa Island
2km)

ne small, open landing area is where you
n get a speedboat ride across to Lelepa
land. This will cost you around 3000VT
turn. If there's nobody around, sound your
r horn or bash on the gas cylinder that's
ing up in a tree for that purpose. Hope-
lly the villagers will hear you across the
ater and come over.

Worth seeing is **Feles Cave**, a large cav-
n on Lelepa's south coast. It's believed to
e the deathplace of Roy Mata, a legendary
olynesian chief who united the villages of
fate and the Shepherd Islands under his
le in the 1250s. You can visit the cave
ith Sailaway Cruises, which has a particu-
rly good commentary.

amoa Point (28km)

he north-west corner of Efate has many
ndy coves interspersed with rocky head-
nds, one of which is Samoa Point. Used in
WII as a US seaplane base, it has pleas-
t swimming off a small sandy beach.
here's good snorkelling in shallow water
the Vila side of the point.

lei (30.5km)

ronounced 'oo-lie', this village is on the
te of the former Havannah Harbour settle-
ent. During WWII, US warships grouped
the harbour's protected waters prior to
e critical Battle of the Coral Sea in mid-
42. Later, the USA used the area as a
val base. On the seaward side of the road
ar central Ulei is the **American Pool**, a
oncrete reservoir that served as a water
urce for visiting warships.

iviri (40km)

side road bears northwards to Siviri vil-
ge. Just before the village is **Valeafau**
ave, a small cavern with many interesting
nestone formations and a freshwater lake.
he entry fee is 100VT.

There are magnificent views from Siviri
across **Undine Bay** towards the tall, steep
outlines of **Nguna**, **Pele** and **Emao** islands.
There is good walking over extinct volcanoes on all of these islands. At low tide you
can use the onshore reef in front of the village to walk across to Moso Island, but
watch out for stonefish.

About 1km past the Siviri turn-off, a road
leads down to a **picnic area** on the shore,
with more marvellous views of the islands.
The headquarters of **Undine Bay Plantation**
– Efate's largest coconut plantation – is a
little farther on.

Paonangisu (51.5km)

This village is probably the best place to
find a speedboat ride across to Nguna, Pele,
Emao and **Kakula** islands – Nagar Bungalows will arrange this if you're staying
there. At high tide you can snorkel in the
marine reserve around Kakula Island.

Although run down, *Nagar Bungalows*
(☎ 23221) has very attractive grounds right
on the waterfront. Six fan-cooled bungalows (some self-contained) sleep up to five
for 3000/4000VT for singles/doubles, including breakfast. Alternatively, for 500VT
per person, you can pitch a tent in the
grounds. The restaurant has basic meals and
a pleasant alfresco setting.

Getting There & Away The taxi fare from
Vila is about 4000VT, or you may be able
to get a ride with a tour coach. Otherwise
the resort may be able to arrange a lift.

Return speedboat rides cost 3000VT to
Kakula Island, 4000VT to Pele Island and
6000VT to Nguna Island. All rides should
be arranged in advance to suit the tides.

Takara (56km)

Although a windswept spot, Takara is fairly
popular with Vila residents on weekends.
From the beach there's a fine view of
nearby **Emao Island**, where **Mt Sokometa**,
an extinct volcano 416m high, makes a
tempting target for walkers.

Looking beyond Emao you can see
towering, pinnacle-shaped **Mataso Island**
with smaller **Wot Rock** (Etarik Island) on

the right. In the distance are the beckoning, misty outlines of the rest of the **Shepherds** group.

Set on the waterfront, the basic *Beachcomber Resort* (☎ 23576, beachc@vanuatu .com.vu) has a bar, a restaurant and fan-cooled brick bungalows sleeping up to five.

Getting There & Away Access details are as for Nagar Bungalows, earlier. Speedboat rides to Wiana on Emao cost 6000VT return, but you need to arrange them in advance.

Sara (59km)

The village has a minimarket selling garden produce, processed foods and handicrafts. You can use the small swimming beaches here for 200VT per person.

Some of Efate's best scenery lies along the road between Sara and Forari. One minute you're passing close to small sand beaches and coral rock, the next you're driving through overgrown coconut plantations and enormous banyans that overhang the road.

Epao (69km)

There's a rest stop here selling refreshments and handicrafts. On the roadside, a sign advertising a visit to **Pounarup Cave** for 200/500VT per child/adult promises 'an adventurous chance that you should never miss'.

Forari (81km)

A manganese mine operated at Forari from 1961 to 1978. On the shore is a huge ship-loading **gantry** which conveyed ore into the holds of waiting ships. It was turned into a heap of twisted scrap by cyclone Prima in 1992.

Manuro Point (87km)

Two kilometres past the old wharf, a turn-off takes you east past the village of **Poi** to Manuro Point. From here a track heads south to an abandoned resort near a lovely sandy beach; check at Poi as to whether or not you can camp there.

Eton (90.5km)

Just before the village is a small sand bea and a swimming area surrounded by co rock. There's usually a villager on hand collect the entry fee of 500VT per car.

Past Eton you enter cattle country. Fr here almost to Vila much of the forest a coconut plantations have been cleared make way for lush pasture.

Dry Creek (96km)

Also known as **Banana Beach**, this is ideal spot for a picnic in calm weather. a public beach, so you don't have to a permission or pay a fee.

Rentapao River (111km)

The bridge here has a hazardous approac so take it slowly. Some **cascades** upstre of the bridge are being developed as tourist attraction.

Three kilometres past the bridge is t Blue Water Island Resort – see the earli section on Port Vila.

Teouma River (129km)

Efate's largest river drains from rugged **MacDonald** in the north. Just before t bridge is the turn-off to the **Teouma Vall Tropical Park**, which has kastom houses, n tive plants and animals, bush walks, po rides and other attractions. Guided tou cost 1900VT.

From the bridge, central Vila is abo 9km away.

Epi

- pop 4500   • area 444 sq km

Epi is extremely steep and rugged exce along the western coastal strip, which h several large coconut plantations in coloni times. The west coast is predominant palm-fringed with small beaches inte spersed with rocky headlands and onsho reefs.

Getting There & Away

Air Epi has airstrips at Lamen Bay a Valesdir. Vanair's 'milk run' flies thr

es a week between Vila and Santo, land-
g at Lamen Bay, Paama, Ambrym, and
rsup on Malekula. Valesdir is visited four
es each week from Vila via Emae and
ngoa, both in the Shepherd Islands. Fares
m Valesdir are 3100VT to Emae,
50VT to Tongoa and 5400VT to Vila.

at Ifira Shipping charges 4500VT from
la to Lamen Bay, while Toara Coastal
ipping charges 3200VT.

etting Around
xi A taxi truck from Lamen Bay costs
00VT to Nikaura and 6000VT to Vales-
. We've received several reports of rip-
s here, so make sure the fare is firmly
gotiated before you start out and don't
y more than the agreed price.

at Speedboats connect Lamen Island
th the mainland. See the following infor-
tion under Lamen Island.

AROUND EPI
Western Epi
The following distances are from Lamen Bay.

Lamen Bay There's excellent swimming
off the beach, and plenty of shallow coral
for snorkelling. The bay is home to several
dugong, including a large male that sometimes allows snorkellers to swim with him.

The guesthouse has several tours, including a full day **waterfall** trip by truck and
foot, and a visit to a **subsistence garden**
high up in the hills. Tasso, the friendly
owner, has a speedboat and can arrange
fishing, snorkelling and sightseeing excursions around the coast, including a visit to
Lopevi.

The basic *Paradise Sunset Bungalows*
(☎ 28204) is on the beachfront a short walk
from the airfield terminal. It provides dinner, bed and breakfast for 5900/7800VT for
singles/doubles, and there's a cheaper self-
catering option.

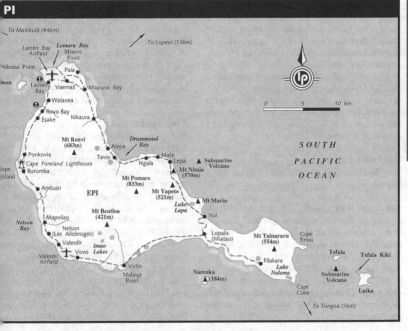

PI

To Malekula (44km)
To Lopevi (13km)

Lamen Bay Lomaru Bay
Airfield   Morevi
               Point
Nduana Point
              Paia
nen
      Lamen Vaemali   Mapuna Bay
      Bay
        Walavea
      Rovo Bay   Nikaura
    Esake

        Mt Renvi   Drummond
        (683m)   Bay
Ponkovia   Alepa
                Tavio   Mate
Cape Foreland Lighthouse   Ngala   Lepa Submarine
ape Burumba   Mt Nitaia Volcano
eland   (570m)
      Anduan   Mt Pomare
                      (833m)   Mt Yapeto
             EPI   (521m)   Mt Mariu
                      Lake
        Mt Beutloa   Lapa
        (421m)   Nul
Nelson
Bay   Mapvilao
      Nelson   Lopalis   Mt Tainaruru
      (Les Allobroges) (Miatao) (554m)   Cape
      Valesdir   Erina
Valesdir Vovo Imao   Tefala Tefala Kiki
Airfield   Lakes   Filakara
             Votlo   Lake
           Malingi   Namuka Nalema   Submarine
           Point   (184m)   Volcano
                             Cape   Laika
                             Cone
                          To Tongoa (7km)

SOUTH
PACIFIC
OCEAN

0   5   10 km

VANUATU

Lamen (2km by canoe) This small (1.25 sq km), beautiful, relatively flat island is a striking contrast to the mountainous mainland. Its 600 inhabitants all have their gardens on the mainland, so traditional coconut palm-leaf sail canoes and modern speedboats shuttle back and forth throughout the day.

The normal speedboat fare – if you're happy to wait until one is available – is about 300VT, while a special charter is at least 1500VT. Otherwise the guesthouse at Lamen Bay can arrange a visit.

Rovo Bay (5.5km) This is Epi's administrative centre. It has a government *resthouse (council office ☎ 28258)* where beds cost 1500VT.

Valesdir (27km) Valesdir Plantation, which produces copra, beef cattle and kava, gives you an opportunity to sample life on a working plantation. If that palls there's horse riding among the coconut palms and snorkelling along a private coral reef. Other tours and activities include kastom dances at nearby **Vovo** and guided walks to the **Imao Lakes**. For some real excitement you can join the locals on a pig hunting expedition on foot using dogs.

The *Valesdir Plantation Guesthouse (☎ 23916)* has bungalows costing 4000VT for twin-share, and a dormitory block with cooking facilities for 1500VT per person. Meals are also available – a three-course dinner is around 1400VT.

Eastern Epi
The following distances are from Lamen Bay.

Mapuna Bay (5km) A white sand beach and some attractive coral gardens are the main attractions here. En route to Nikaura are fine views of the rugged coastline in front, and the Ambrym and Lopevi volcanoes to the north and north-east.

Nikaura (9km) This large, attractive village has a co-op store and a self-catering *guesthouse*.

Tanna

● pop 20,700   ● area 565 sq km

Tanna is the most densely populated Vanuatu's larger islands, while the northe interior has one of the country's most pr ductive agricultural areas. In contrast, mu of the south is mountainous. Two peaks Mt Melen and Mt Tukosmera – rise to ov 1000m.

Traditional Vanuatu is easy to find Tanna, where you can visit full-kastom v lages and watch age-old ceremoni There's also the fascinating Jon Frum c (see the boxed text 'The Jon Frum Mov ment' in this chapter). Tanna is reputed have Vanuatu's strongest kava, and if you lucky you'll be able to sample it at a tra tional kava ceremony – it's considered honour to be invited to one.

Tanna's major drawcard is its active v cano, Mt Yasur (361m). This is one of t world's most accessible volcanoes ar when it's really firing, a visit to it is unf gettable (see the boxed text 'Visiting Yasur' in this chapter). While it's possible fly in and out of Tanna and see Mt Yasur in one day, the volcano is most spectacu at night. For this reason a stay of at least tv days is recommended. There are seve mainly basic guesthouses and resorts, me in south-eastern Tanna and around Lenak the island's commercial centre.

The Nekowiar
Everyone describes the Toka as one Vanuatu's major cultural events. Howev it is only one stage of a huge, three-day gi exchanging ceremony called the Nekowi whose main purpose is to renew allianc between neighbouring villages. There c be as many as 2000 participants in Nekowiar. All try to outdo each other wi the quality of their gifts, the colour a stylishness of their make-up and decor tions, and the skill of their dancing.

The first day features the Napen-Nape which represents the women's toil in t fields. It's a spectacular ceremony, wi women of all ages arrayed in red, yello blue, green and mauve grass skirts.

TANNA

The Toka – a men's ceremony – begins
the next morning and reaches its frenzied
climax late that night. This is the main event
and the men have been training in the jungle for weeks. It's a serious matter, as the
purpose of the dance is to increase the pro-
ductiveness of their gardens.

On the third day, following the Nao ceremony (the host village's dance), dozens of
pigs together with a great quantity of kava
roots, woven mats, grass skirts and laplap
are brought out. The hosts club the pigs to
death, then present everything to their
guests. This marks the climax of the

Nekowiar. Everyone inspects the display to
assess the hosts' generosity, after which the
pigs are cooked and a huge feast begins.

There's usually at least one Nekowiar
held between August and November, but
the actual date is often only announced a
few days in advance. You may need to camp
out, like the villagers, and will have to pay
up to 5000VT to watch; there's an extra fee
of 10,000VT to video the proceedings.

The main booking agents are the National Tourism Office (see the Port Vila section
earlier in this chapter) and Island Safaris
travel agency (see Organised Tours in the

The Jon Frum Movement

By the early 20th century considerable resentment had built up among Tannese people over the rigid rules of the Presbyterian Church. Eventually, a home-grown religion called the Jon Frum movement emerged as a form of resistance to the missionaries' teachings. It blossomed to such an extent that by the end of WWII it was one of Tanna's three main religious groups, the others being Presbyterians and *kastom* people. Although widely regarded as simply another cargo cult, it is in fact a hybrid of Christianity and traditional beliefs in which cargo (or wealth) is secondary. However, it's this aspect of the cult that has most appeal to tourists.

In the Beginning

In 1936, people in western Tanna began talking about a mysterious person called Jon Frum who, it was claimed, was the brother of the god of Mt Tukosmera. The story said Jon Frum had come from the sea at Green Point and announced himself to some kava drinkers there. He told them there would be an abundance of wealth and no more of the epidemics that had killed so many people. However, all Europeans had to leave the island before this could happen.

The Pacific War

Soon after Jon Frum's appearance, US troops landed on Efate and Santo. Many Tannese went to work for them, including a number of Jon Frum worshippers. They saw that the troops had huge quantities of steel ships, jeeps, aircraft, refrigerators and radios as well as endless supplies of Coca-Cola and cigarettes. But most of all, the Tannese saw how generous the US

---

main Getting Around section of this chapter), both in Vila.

Organised Tours

Most accommodation places on Tanna offer package deals from Vila. A typical package includes return air fares, airport transfers, two nights' accommodation, all meals and visits to Mt Yasur and a kastom village for upwards of 35,000VT.

With the guesthouses, check what sort of tour transport they use if you don't want to rough it. You may not enjoy bouncing around in the rear of a 4WD truck, particularly if it starts to rain.

Most day tours incorporating Port Resolution, a kastom village and Mt Yasur cost upwards of 17,000VT leaving from the west coast. Similar tours departing from the Mt Yasur area may seem much cheaper on the face of it, but you need to take into account transfer charges from the airport.

If you're staying in or near Lenakel you can organise your own tour by hiring a taxi. The daily rate is at least 8000VT excluding

entry fees – it costs 2000VT per person ju to visit Mt Yasur. Remember that some kas tom villages only accept visitors b arrangement.

Getting There & Away

Air Tanna's new airport is 10km north o Lenakel. Vanair has return services betwee Vila and Tanna at least once daily, an there's a service twice a week linking Vil with Tanna, Aniwa, Aneityum, Futuna an Erromango. See the Vanuatu Air Fare Chart in the main Getting Around sectio earlier in this chapter.

Boat Ifira Shipping and Toara Coasta Shipping charge 4500VT from Vila t Lenakel and Port Resolution – it take *Saraika* about 18 hours to get from Vila t Lenakel. Both charge 2250VT betwee ports on Tanna and Erromango.

Getting Around

To/From the Airport There's usually a least one taxi truck to meet each incomin

The Jon Frum Movement

servicemen were, especially the African-Americans, who were surely Tannese in disguise. Jon Frum must certainly be from the USA.

Shortly after WWII, dozens of small red crosses were erected all over Tanna. To the islanders, the Red Cross sign, seen often during the war, meant expert medical treatment, free of charge. So villagers began putting up red crosses, hoping this would bring free medical attention to their island too. Nowadays they remain a feature in Jon Frum villages.

Europeans explained there was no Jon Frum, but this was interpreted to mean that they were still trying to deprive the Tannese of their rightful wealth. For a long time after the Pacific War, cultists would examine any plane they saw in case Jon Frum was inside. Any Americans they met were asked if they had any messages from him.

Waiting for Jon Frum

Over the years Jon Frum supporters, keen to hear his message, have made imitation radio aerials out of tin cans and wire. Others have built an airfield in the bush and constructed wooden replica aircraft to entice his planes full of cargo to land. Still others have erected wharves where his ships can berth.

Some cultists recommend a return to a totally traditional lifestyle, including wearing *nambas*. Others continue to wear European clothes, feeling this will be more to their Messiah's liking and therefore hasten his arrival.

When will he come? His followers have waited since the 1930s and nothing has happened yet. 'How long have Christians waited?' they ask. 'Nearly 2000 years, yet we've waited only 65!'

light from Vila. The fare to Lenakel is 000VT, shared.

axi A number of taxis – mostly open-tray WD utilities with no rear seats – operate ut of Lenakel. The best place to find one is utside the Tafea Cooperative Association tore; ask the store manager for assistance f you want a quote. A one-way charter from enakel to Port Resolution will cost around 000VT.

Tanna is another good place to be ripped ff by taxi drivers (see Taxi in the main jetting Around section earlier in this hapter).

Walking You can walk across the island rom Lenakel to Port Resolution by following the main road. This 41km route limbs some steep hills, particularly in the entral range. You'll find a leaf house at nost villages along the way, and there's the likity Guesthouse just before Dip Poin see the Loanialu Lookout section later in his chapter).

A more pleasant and challenging alternative for experienced bushwalkers is the forest path over the range from Yakel to Lake Isiwi and Sulphur Bay, near Mt Yasur. This walk takes five or six hours.

AROUND TANNA
South-Western Tanna

The following distances are from Lenakel.

Lenakel Around 1000 people live in Lenakel. There are several stores, the largest and best stocked of which is the Tafea Cooperative Association Store (TCAS), at the northern end of town. It sells fresh bread, processed food and alcohol, as well as clothing and hardware.

Across from the store, the covered market is open Monday, Thursday afternoon and Friday. A smaller open market near the wharf is open on the same days.

Places to Stay & Eat Behind the TCAS is the basic, self-catering ***Tanna Ocean View Guesthouse*** (☎ 68695). Its dorm beds cost

1500VT and private rooms are 2500/3100/4600VT for singles/doubles/triples; pedestal fans are available. There's a reasonable kitchen, but the toilet and shower facilities are hopelessly inadequate if there's even a hint of a crowd.

At the other end of town, the **Uma Guesthouse** (☎ 68768) has small, stuffy twin rooms for 2000VT per person, including breakfast. Alternatively, you can camp under the trees for 500VT. The owners will prepare meals for you (700VT), or you can share their kitchen.

There are some simple eat-out options in Lenakel. Next door to the TCAS, the grandly named **Tanna Ocean View Restaurant** has rice meals for lunch (250VT) and dinner (500VT). You have to book for breakfast and dinner, as well as all meals on Sunday.

Other cheap places are the **stalls** across from the covered market, and the little **Amaniam Restaurant** down the road towards the wharf. Both serve rice lunches daily except Sunday.

You can also eat at the **Tanna Beach Resort** (see the later Ebul Bay section), which reputedly has Tanna's best restaurant. A taxi from town costs 500VT.

Isangel (2km) The administrative centre for Tanna and Tafea province, Isangel has about 1200 residents. There's a regular market here on Wednesday, with villagers setting up their stalls the previous afternoon.

The self-catering government **resthouse** (provincial office ☎ 68638) charges 2000VT per head. We've had several reports of uncleanliness and lack of maintenance here.

Ebul Bay (3km) The island-style **Tanna Beach Resort** (☎ 68626) has Tanna's most upmarket accommodation. Styles range from guesthouse rooms for 4400/6200VT to self-contained bungalows from 10,200VT for singles and doubles. Extra people are charged 2700VT in all rooms.

Yakel (8.5km) Kastom reigns supreme at Yakel, a town which is one of Tanna's main tourist attractions. Villagers wear only nambas and grass skirts, and the chief refuses allow girls to attend school, or to trav hoping that they'll keep to the old ways. seems to be succeeding, as you see lit sign of the modern age anywhere here. T most-visible exceptions are the village tru and the odd soccer ball.

Yakel has a population of about 80 peop As it's central to six other villages, up 600 people share the open-air nakama which is under a huge banyan tree. All t buildings here are made in the tradition fashion – most have roofs of coconut that and walls of woven pandanus, and abo half are on stilts. Each household has a da to-day dwelling as well as a cyclone shelt built into the ground nearby.

North-Western Tanna
The following distances are from Lenake

Imanaka (9km) There are Jon Fru dances here on Friday night. Visitors a welcome but should accompany a tour; t entry fee is 3000VT.

Continue along the coastal track pa the new airport to **White Grass Bunge lows** (☎ 68688), where self-containe bungalows cost 6200/7200/7700VT f singles/doubles/triples. It has a bistro, a b and a lovely view over the sea in front.

Eastern Tanna & Yasur Volcano
The following distances are from Lenake

Loanialu Lookout (22km) The looko on top of the main range on the road fro Lenakel to Port Resolution offers a fi view of the Yasur volcano. On a clear da Aniwa and Futuna islands can be seen to th north-east and east respectively.

Near the bottom of the main range yc pass the **Nikity Guesthouse** (☎ 68616 which has basic rooms costing 150(3000VT per couple/family. It is often su jected to a prolonged rain of fine as which makes it difficult to keep thing clean here. There's a market here on Frida and a small store nearby selling a limite range of tinned goods.

New Futuna

About 70km east of Tanna, the people of Futuna Island have Polynesian ancestors who migrated here in canoes 1400km from the island of Futuna, in the modern French territory Wallis & Futuna.

Just as James Cook was to apply a British name (the New Hebrides) to this whole region a thousand years later, the Futunans named the new island after *their* old home in the east.

❋ ❋ ❋ ❋ ❋ ❋ ❋ ❋ ❋ ❋ ❋ ❋

White Sands (32km) There's a health centre, a mission, an education centre, two stores and a card phone here. A warm spring runs across the sand at the northern end of the beach, which has good swimming. The *mission* has guest rooms for 1500/2000VT and can provide meals.

On the beachfront about 3km north of White Sands, the *Friendly Bungalows* (*Tanna booking agent ☎ 68676*) is owned and managed by French expats Stephane and Muriel Orreindy. It's one of the few places in Tanna to give real value for money.

There are five self-contained bungalows built in the Melanesian fashion, but with French style and class – costing 5000/6000VT for doubles/triples. Twin rooms with shared facilities are 1200VT per person. Naturally, there's a very good licensed restaurant specialising in French cooking.

The tours available here are very reasonably priced. For example, you can walk to the volcano without a guide (two hours) and be picked up by transport for the ride home for 2800VT, including the entry fee. Its half-day tour to Port Resolution, Imayo kastom village and Mt Yasur (day and night) costs 6400VT all inclusive.

Sulphur Bay (33.5km) This village is the centre of the Jon Frum cult. A good time to visit is Friday evening, when cultists come from nearby villages to dance; the entry fee is 500VT.

Jon Frum's day is celebrated on 15 February, the date he is expected to return

bringing the wealth he has promised. Prayers and flowers are offered, followed by a flag-raising ceremony and military parade. The 'soldiers', armed with bamboo rifles and with 'USA' painted on their bare backs, march under the command of village elders dressed like US Army sergeants.

Jon Frummers believe that by acting like white people they'll attract the magic that gives them their wealth. They try different things (eg holding military parades and building bamboo aircraft) in the hope that one will do the trick. See the boxed text 'The Jon Frum Movement' earlier in this section.

Ash Plain (31km) Towering above the still waters of **Lake Isiwi**, Mt Yasur darkens the sky with great clouds of ash-laden smoke. Over the centuries this gritty material has smothered the vegetation, reducing the landscape to a grey moonscape. In the background, the volcano with its stark flanks resembles a huge, smoking sand dune.

Imayo (38km) This kastom village, one of several in the area, is visited by tours from the guesthouses in south-eastern Tanna. The impressive **Imayo Waterfall** lies deep in the rainforest, but only serious trekkers can get there – ask at the Yasur Guesthouse at nearby **Loanengo** about guides.

You can do a number of other walks from Loanengo, including Mt Yasur (1½ hours), and Port Resolution (two hours) along the road. Shorter guided walks take you to a **bat cave**, full-kastom villages, and Lake Isiwi. A small **botanic garden** is being developed near the guesthouse.

The basic *Yasur Guesthouse* (*Tanna booking agent ☎ 68676*) at Loanengo is the closest accommodation to the volcano – there's a good afternoon view of it from the ridge above the guesthouse. Staying here will cost you 3600/4300/6450VT for a single/double/triple including a light breakfast; a simple island-style lunch or dinner costs 1000VT. There are four spartan rooms, each sleeping four.

Yasur Volcano (41km) In the local language Yasur means 'old man'. South-eastern

Visiting Mt Yasur

The level of activity within Yasur fluctuates between downright dangerous and relative calm. This is what you may experience when the mountain is flexing its muscle.

Stumbling up the rough path from the car park to the crater rim, your introduction to the turmoil within consists of whiffs of sulphur accompanied by whooshing and roaring noises. Then you're on the barren ash rim looking down into a dark central crater about 300m across and 100m deep.

At the bottom, three vents seem to be taking it in turns to spit showers of molten rock and smoke, like monstrous Roman candles. When the biggest one blows there's an ear-splitting explosion that causes heads to disappear into collars. The earth trembles and a fountain of fiery magma soars skywards above the rim. After this come progressively smaller roars until eventually all is quiet, except for the sound of rocks thudding back into the crater. At night you can see glowing boulders as big as trucks somersaulting back down into what looks like the embers of a vast campfire.

Then, just when you're getting used to it, you hear a great 'gasp' as of indrawn breath, followed by an almighty *bang* as if a blockbuster bomb has gone off at your feet. The ground underfoot shakes like a jelly. Great lumps of red-hot magma shoot high overhead as black smoke boils upwards in a dense, writhing column.

After these cataclysmic events you may hear lava bombs landing behind you, a reminder of the rocks you passed on the way up. There are no hard hats, of course – there isn't even a guard rail. Mind you, a hard hat wouldn't be much good if a decent-sized rock landed on your head. Neither would a guard rail if the lookout point decided to shake loose and fall into the crater.

Common sense dictates that you go at night when Yasur is really firing – not only are the fireworks more spectacular then, but you can see the lava bombs coming and thus have a chance of avoiding them. That said, in 1995 two guides and a Japanese tourist were killed in two separate incidents when, while standing on the crater's rim, they were struck by flying lava.

Still game? Take a good torch and a warm pullover, and do have your personal affairs sorted out before you go.

Denis O'Byrne

Tannese believe that the volcano is the originator of the universe, and that it's where a person's spirit goes after death. Jon Frummers will tell you that Jon Frum lives in the volcano along with a huge army of spirits.

This place is so accessible that 4WD vehicles can easily get to within 150m of the crater rim. However, the rough path from the car park to the summit requires surefootedness, particularly at night – you'll need eyes like a cat if you haven't brought a good torch.

It can be windy on top, so take long trousers and a long-sleeved shirt to protect yourself from flying ash.

The entry fee of 2000VT per perso[n] helps local villagers buy food when the as[h] rain ruins their crops.

Port Resolution (43km) Named b[y] James Cook in 1774, Tanna's best anchor age for yachts is the home of a solitar[y] male **dugong**. He'll allow you to swin[m] with him, but you need to be careful – h[e] can be aggressive towards males and ma[y] try to shepherd females away from shore[.] Maybe he's just lonely! The entry fee o[f] 750VT, payable at the yacht club, isn't re[-] funded if the dugong fails to show, whic[h] often happens.

The *Port Resolution Yacht Club (Tanna booking agent ☎ 68676)* is set among coconut palms on a cliff top, with a marvellous view over the bay to rugged **Mt Melen**. Its nine traditional-style bungalows sleep up to four people with one/two people costing 5150/6300VT, including breakfast and dinner. Alternatively, you can camp in the grounds for 1500VT.

Erromango

pop 1600   • area 975 sq km

A mountainous, mainly forested island, Erromango is one of the largest, but least developed and most sparsely populated, members of the Vanuatu group. Its people live in a few villages scattered around its generally rugged coast.

By the 1840s Erromango had a well-earned reputation as a dangerous place for Europeans. The villagers had a penchant for warfare and cannibalism, and didn't hesitate to attack the whalers, sandalwooders, missionaries and blackbirders who landed on their shores. Five white missionaries were murdered here between 1839 and 1872. Today, Erromangans will tell you that the dramatic depopulation of their island from 10,000 people in the 1820s to less than 400 a century later) was God's punishment for killing the missionaries.

Not many tourists visit Erromango, and those that do mainly have walking in mind – another reason is to see the island's giant kauris, which in itself requires some hard walking. June to August can be cool and wet, particularly in upland areas, so it's wise to take appropriate clothing.

Getting There & Away
Air The island's airfields are at Dillons Bay in the north-west and Ipota in the south-east. Vanair has two weekly return flights from Vila to Tanna via Ipota and two via Dillons Bay. See the Air Fares Chart in the main Getting Around section of this chapter.

Boat Toara Coastal Shipping and Ifira Shipping charge 4500VT from Vila to Dillons Bay, Elizabeth Bay and Cook's Bay. Coming the other way from Tanna costs 2250VT.

Dihn Shipping's fortnightly service from Vila to Erromango goes on to Tanna and other islands in Tafea province.

Getting Around
To/From the Airport The truck service between Dillons Bay and the airfield costs 600VT.

Taxi There are few roads on Erromango. One is the 9km road between Dillons Bay and the airfield. The others are old logging routes from Dillons Bay to Port Narvin (usually impassable) and from Ipota into the southern forests.

Boat Speedboats can be hired at Dillons Bay, Port Narvin and Ipota. It costs upwards of 10,000VT for a charter from Dillons Bay to Port Narvin.

AROUND ERROMANGO
North-Western Erromango
Dillons Bay Also called Unpongkor, this village of 500 people is by the coast on the Williams River's northern bank. It's Erromango's largest settlement.

In a small **cemetery** on the river bank opposite the village are the burial sites of three of the murdered missionaries (the other two were eaten) and that of another missionary who died of natural causes. Nearby are examples of the **sandalwood** trees that were once so plentiful on the island. Also nearby is a large **rock** that villagers say shows the outline of John Williams, the first missionary to be killed on Erromango. His murderers laid his body on the rock and chipped around it prior to cooking it.

You can do several guided walks from Dillons Bay, where the island's giant kauris are the main attraction. The guesthouse owners can arrange speedboat rides and/or guides for the trip via Happy Lands to the **kauri reserve**. They have options to see big kauris closer to Dillons Bay, but be warned – we've received reports of visitors who thought they were being taken to a mature kauri forest,

VANUATU

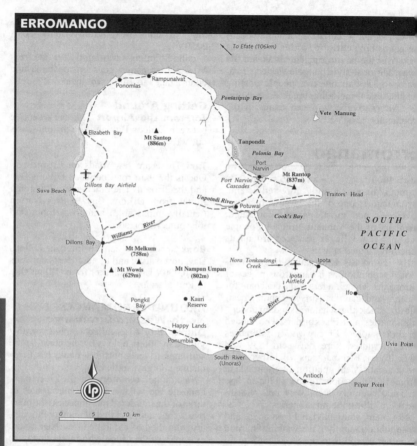

ERROMANGO

only to find themselves at a single young tree. Make sure there is no confusion about this before you leave Dillons Bay.

Meteson's Guesthouse (☎ *68677*) is a comfortable little place charging 3000VT for dinner, bed and breakfast. The owner, William Mete, is an affable and obliging fellow who'll be happy to give advice on all your travel plans. As a bonus, his wife and daughter-in-law are great cooks.

South-Western Erromango

The walk from Dillons Bay to Ipota via **South River** (Unoras) takes three to four days allowing for some interesting si[de] trips. You may be able to hire a guide in D[il]lons Bay for the entire route, or you m[ay] have to engage one for each section – expe[ct] to pay 1500VT per day, and supply th[e] guide's food.

The path as far as South River main[ly] takes you along the top of high coast[al] cliffs, with many magnificent views. Th[is] section is generally easy apart from sever[al] steep drops and gruelling climbs in and o[ut] of deep, fjord-like valleys. It takes abo[ut] five hours to walk from Dillons Bay [to] Happy Lands and another three from the[re] o South River. Weather permitting, you can shorten the walk with a 1½ hour speedboat ride from Dillons Bay to **Pongkil Bay** for 5000VT. It's an hour's walk from Pongkil Bay to Happy Lands.

Both Pongkil Bay and Happy Lands Umponyelongi) have a *nakamal* where you can spend the night. If you have the time, spend a day at Happy Lands on a side trip to the kauri reserve. Here you'll find a huge diversity of plant life – the most impressive being kauri trees as high as 40m growing on the steep slopes below *Mt Vampun Umpan*. It's a moderately difficult two hour walk from the village and you can usually camp there; a guesthouse is proposed for the reserve.

South River has a *nakamal* where you can sleep, a general store and a HF radio. If you want to be met by a taxi from Ipota, this is the obvious spot to arrange it.

From South River to Ipota takes about a day. There's a choice of two routes, both of which eventually meet up with the logging road network outside Ipota. One path follows the South River, with much boulder-hopping required and shallow fords to be crossed – this track meets the road first, so it's the one to take if you're meeting a taxi. The other, which climbs the scarp and crosses higher country, comes out near the Ipota airfield.

Across Erromango & Down the Coast

The 25km logging road from Dillons Bay to Port Narvin crosses undulating country covered with an interesting mix of rainforest and low scrub, with some fine views en route. Allow a full day for the walk.

Port Narvin This pleasant village of 250 people has a long black sand beach with good surf. There are some **cascades** 1km inland that are worth seeing.

Towering over the village, and 4km to the east, is 837m **Mt Rantop**. From the top – it's a stiff climb – is a fine view of Erromango's east coast. Below Mt Rantop, and on its southern side, is a white sand beach with coral shallows.

Port Narvin to Ipota (18km) The path south from Port Narvin heads up a short, steep gradient just beyond the village. Soon afterwards the terrain flattens out and then it's mostly level walking as far as **Cook's Bay**.

After you've crossed the **Unpotndi River** at Cook's Bay, follow the shore for 12km on to Ipota. It's an interesting walk with some nice coastal scenery, but the rugged going makes for slow progress in places.

Ipota The village and its airstrip were built by a French logging company in 1969, and today 150 people live there. You'll probably have no difficulty finding a place to sleep either in the *nakamal* or one of the old *logging quarters*.

Aneityum

● **pop 700**   ● **area 162 sq km**

Aneityum Island, which rises to 852m at Mt Inrerow Atahein, is mountainous and thickly wooded. Its flora is different to the rest of Vanuatu, being more akin to that of Australia and New Caledonia. The island was a centre for sandalwood logging in the 1840s, but only kauri has been exported in this century – large specimens of this species have virtually disappeared as a result of unrestrained logging.

Scattered around the island are rocks decorated with petroglyphs, including representations of the sun, stars, people, birds and fish as well as spirals and other geometrical designs. Islanders claim these are the work of an earlier people. There are also many old irrigation channels, which indicate that the island had a much higher population in the past. In fact, an estimated 12,000 people lived here before the arrival of Europeans.

Aneityum has several attractive beaches as well as a reef that surrounds three-quarters of the island, making it an ideal spot for snorkellers and scuba divers. It's on the itinerary of cruise ships, which call in at tiny Inyeug Island (Mystery Island) every three weeks or so.

ANEITYUM

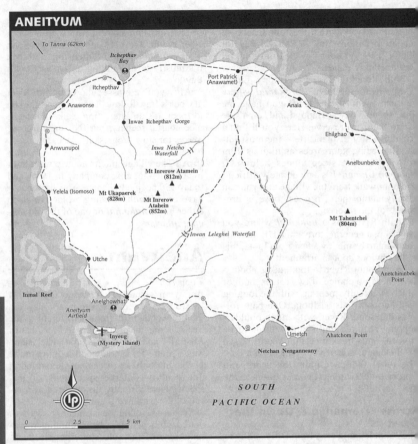

To Tanna (62km)

Itchepthav Bay

Itchepthav

Port Patrick (Anawamet)

Anawonse

Anaia

Inwae Itchepthav Gorge

Inwa Netcho Waterfall

Anwunupol

Ehilghao

Anelbunbeke

Mt Inrerow Atamein (812m)

Yelela (Isomoso)

Mt Ukapaerek (828m)

Mt Inrerow Atahein (852m)

Mt Tahentchei (804m)

Inwan Leleghei Waterfall

Utche

Inmal Reef

Anetchininbeke Point

Anelghowhat

Aneityum Airfield

Inyeug (Mystery Island)

Umetch

Ahatchom Point

Netchan Nenganneany

SOUTH

PACIFIC OCEAN

0   2.5   5 km

VANUATU

Getting There & Away

Air Aneityum's airfield is on Inyeug Island. Vanair operates two return trips per week connecting Vila, Tanna, Futuna and Aneityum. See the Vanuatu Air Fares Chart in the main Getting Around section of this chapter.

Boat Dihn Shipping charges 7500VT from Vila and 2000VT from Tanna.

Getting Around

To/From the Airport A speedboat connects Inyeug Island with the mainland at Anelghowhat for about 500VT.

Walking The 51km footpath around Aneityum is mainly easy going except for the south-eastern section, which is steep and rough. Here it repeatedly detours into the bush away from high cliffs. The best option is to walk around the west coast from Anelghowhat to Port Patrick, then return through the middle of the island. This will take two to three days.

All around the west coast you'll find lots of beautiful picture-postcard scenery — white beaches, waving palms and turquoise water. The walking is easy, being mainly on the beach, and there is good drinking water in the streams you cross en route. Along the way you can explore old irrigation channels and village sites in the fringing grassy hills. Some of the channels are still used for the cultivation of water taro.

The 14km cross-island footpath from Port Patrick to Anelghowhat crosses the rugged central range and is difficult in places. As compensation, the scenery is often magnificent, with large kauris and high waterfalls along the way. The orchids in the forest (there are 84 species) bloom all year but are at their best in October and November.

Ask at Anelghowhat about guides for walking on the island.

AROUND ANEITYUM

The following distances are clockwise from Anelghowhat.

Anelghowhat

This is a popular anchorage for cruising yachts as it offers a secure shelter from all but the west wind. The village is Aneityum's largest, and boasts a fine swimming beach. There's good snorkelling on a couple of sunken wrecks (a trawler and small cargo vessel) in the bay. The impressive Inwan Eleghei Waterfall is in thick bush about 5km inland.

The Presbyterian minister John Geddie built a stone church here that could seat a thousand people, but devastating epidemics of measles and dysentery in 1861 ensured it could never be filled. A tsunami in 1875 left the church a ruin, now overgrown.

Places to Stay There's a self-catering guesthouse in the village with beds for 500VT. You can contact the manager by ringing ☎ 22759 in Vila and asking for telex-dio Aneityum. The manager probably won't be there, so arrange to ring back when he's available to speak to you.

Inyeug (1.5km by boat)

This beautiful sandy islet is surrounded by broad sandbank and dazzling coral. In 1844 the very succesful James Paddon built a trading post here that became the first permanent European presence in Vanuatu.

The Aneityumese didn't mind – they believed it to be the home of ghosts and would not live there.

A self-catering guesthouse charges 2000VT per person – contact details are as for the guesthouse in Anelghowhat. Except on cruise ship days, you'll usually have the island to yourself.

Anawonse (12km)

This area was the centre for Vanuatu's 19th century whaling industry, and some huge rusting cooking pots, once used for melting whale blubber, still lie hidden in the thick bush. Ask at Anelghowhat about a guided whaling tour.

Port Patrick (Anawamet; 20.5km)

Port Patrick is Aneityum's only village of any size outside the south-west. From here you can see Inwa Netcho Waterfall, 4km inland. The local people have created a marine sanctuary in an attempt to protect the numerous turtles that gather to feed along the reef – unfortunately the turtles are still being hunted elsewhere around the island.

Umetch (42km)

Looking south-east from here on a clear day you can sometimes see the thick black smoke that issues from the volcano on distant Hunter Island.

There are hot springs about 3km along the track towards Anelghowhat, and another spring 2km farther. Anelghowhat is 4km beyond this.

The Central Mountains

Aneityum's centre is dominated by several mountains, including two extinct volcanoes: Mt Inrerow Atahein (852m) and Mt Tahentchei (804m). In island tradition the former is the husband of its near neighbour Mt Inrerow Atamein (812m). Climb Inrerow Atahein and you'll get an excellent view into the crater on top.

From the summit you can also see over most of Aneityum as well as the islands of southern Tafea.

Malekula

● pop 24,000   ● area 2023 sq km

Malekula is Vanuatu's second-largest island. On a map it looks like a sitting dog, with two highland areas connected by a narrow section often called 'the dog's neck'. The northern part of the island is 'the dog's head'.

More than 30 different languages are spoken on Malekula, which is Vanuatu's most linguistically and culturally diverse island. It is home to two similarly named but completely distinct cultural groups. In the north-west are the Big Nambas, while other Malekulans are generally grouped under the title Small Nambas.

Vanuatu's last known cannibal feast took place on Malekula in 1969 (the culprits were Big Nambas). Today, though, just about everyone has been Christianised and human flesh is *tabu*. Apart from the handful of small villages that remain in the rugged interior, Malekulans are now a coastal-dwelling people.

The coastal waters of Malekula often look inviting, but swimming can be risky. There are a number of hot spots for shark attack, so check with villagers before plunging in.

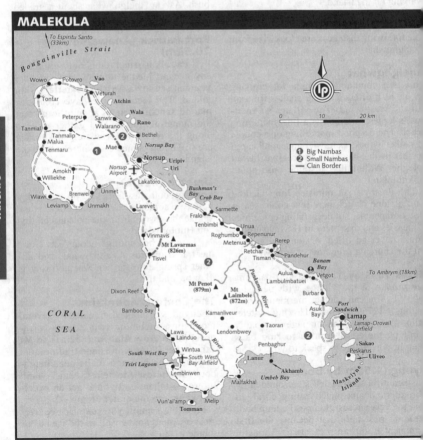

MALEKULA

① Big Nambas
② Small Nambas
— Clan Border

etting There & Away

ir Vanair flies via Norsup at least twice a ay on its Vila-Luganville run; these flights o via Lamap and South West Bay three mes a week. A flight twice a week between uganville and Vila links Norsup with Am-ym, Paama, and Lamen Bay on Epi.

oat The only regular shipping service is e little MV *Rosalie*, which calls into ports ong the east coast and around to South 'est Bay most weeks. It charges 1350VT om Luganville to Lakatoro, and 5400VT om Vila.

etting Around

o/From the Airport The Norsup airport 3km from Norsup and 4km from Laka-oro. It's 300VT by taxi and 100VT by inibus into both towns.

ir Vanair has Norsup-Lamap and Norsup-outh West Bay flights three days a week, ith tickets costing 3900VT and 3700VT espectively. There are no regular flights etween Lamap and South West Bay.

Minibus Public minibus and truck ser-ices operate along the east coast, charg-g 200VT from Norsup to Veturah, pposite Vao Island, and 800VT to amap. They depart fairly frequently from akatoro for the north, but only once a ay for Lamap. The loop run around the dog's head' departs once a day from akatoro for 500VT.

As a rule, the island's roads are empty of ublic transport on weekends and public olidays. Make prior arrangements for a harter if you want to go anywhere at these mes.

axi There are taxis in Norsup, Lakatoro nd Lamap, although they can be hard to ind on weekends. A charter from Norsup osts 3000VT to Veturah and Unmet, and round 8000VT to Lamap.

Boat The lack of roads in southern and vestern Malekula makes speedboats the nain form of transport there.

AROUND MALEKULA
North Coast

The northern Malekulan coast is one of Vanuatu's most densely populated areas. The heaviest concentrations of people live on small islands along the north-eastern seaboard between Vao and Lakatoro.

The following distances are from the township of Norsup.

Norsup With around 1000 residents, unat-tractive Norsup is Malekula's largest town. During the Condominium it was the centre for French administration in northern Malekula, and is still mainly French-speaking. Its commercial activities revolve around the Plantations Réunies de Vanuatu (PRV) company, whose coconut plantations border the town on three sides. This is Vanuatu's largest copra producer.

Norsup has a hospital, two general stores, a bakery and a post office. There's a market every day except Sunday.

Things to See & Do Only 300m beyond the airport terminal is sandy **Aop Beach**, whose palms and turquoise water make it the prettiest spot around Norsup. It's much more appealing to wait here for your plane than at the grotty terminal. A long stretch of beautiful coral reef extends southwards from Aop Beach to **Litslits**, the main port for this area.

Places to Stay & Eat The basic and run-down government ***resthouse*** *(☎ 48491 weekdays)* charges 1500VT for a bed. Most days you can get cheap rice meals at the *food stalls* opposite the market.

Getting Around The 7km journey between Norsup and Lakatoro costs 400VT by taxi and 100VT by bus.

Sanwir (15.5km) More generally known as Wala Mainland, this village is the place to find a canoe or speedboat across to **Wala Island**.

Peter Fidelio, of the Wala Island Resort (see the following Places to Stay & Eat section), can arrange a number of tours and

VANUATU

activities at this end of Malekula. One is a demanding half-day return walk (1800VT) to a Big Nambas cannibal site deep in the forest behind Sanwir – it has a stone fireplace, stone tables where corpses were dismembered, and many bones. Another is a two day trek across the rugged 'dog's head' from Sanwir to **Malua**, on the west coast, where you pick up transport for the return.

There's been a cultural revival in several places among local Small Nambas and Big Nambas people. Peter can arrange kastom dancing at restored *natsaro* (dancing grounds) on **Rano Island** and near Sanwir (both Small Nambas), and at **Unmet** (Big Nambas). There's more dancing at **Bkaier** (see the later section on Amokh), these days the most traditional of the Big Nambas villages.

Places to Stay & Eat Set on the beachfront on Wala Island, the basic ***Wala Island Resort*** (☎ *48488*) has thatched bungalows costing 5400/7700VT for singles/doubles, including breakfast. The meals are usually good, with traditional and European styles costing 1400VT each for lunch and dinner.

This is a very friendly and welcoming place with a good atmosphere; it's among the best of Vanuatu's village guesthouses.

Getting There & Away From Norsup to Sanwir costs 200VT on the scheduled minibus service and 1500VT for a charter. If you take the former option, ask the driver to drop you at the boat landing – otherwise there are many tracks and you will probably get lost.

A boat charter across to Wala Island costs around 1000VT, shared.

Atchin Island (31km & 0.3km by canoe) Tiny Atchin covers only 0.8 sq km yet has a population of over 1000 people, making it one of Vanuatu's most densely populated islands. Atchin Islanders own three shipping companies and are regarded as the wealthiest people on Malekula.

While swimming isn't an option (too many sharks!) you can visit to look around and buy handicrafts. The islanders' specialities are masks and carved model canoes, complete with stylised frigate-bird figure heads and sails.

Amelboas Natsaro

The primeval throbbing of a *tamtam* shattered the quiet as I walked along the jungle path to Amelboas Natsaro. I was with Peter Fidelio, manager of the Wala Island Resort, and we were on our way to see something of the ancient traditions of the Small Nambas people.

Suddenly we broke out of the trees at the edge of a large, fenced clearing lined with thatched shelters and carved *nimangki* figures. Chief Emile, 'bigman' of this particular *natsaro*, stepped forward with a smile of welcome. He was a young man resplendent in yellow body paint, and wearing only a *namba*, a headdress and a pig's tusk. The latter hung around his neck as a symbol of his chiefly status.

Once the greetings had been made we settled down to watch the show. A small group of older men started up the drum orchestra opposite. On a signal, about 20 painted male dancers, each wearing a namba, ankle rattles and tall feather headdress, came into the natsaro to begin the canoe dance. More modestly dressed in pandanus skirts, the same number of women and girls made an appreciative audience on the side.

Forming a canoe shape, the men cleaved the air with brightly coloured paddles as they stamped and chanted in perfect rhythm up and down the clearing. Peter said they were telling the story of travels to Ambae, Ambrym and other islands to buy pigs for grade-taking ceremonies.

The drummers were producing a complex mixture of notes using tall tamtam and small logs, which were beaten with sticks. Chief Emile's father – the master of ceremonies – sat with a coconut in each hand facing the two largest tamtam. His left hand held a green coconut with which

Vao (36.5km by canoe) Traditional customs have survived on Vao Island better than elsewhere in north-eastern Malekula; nimangki grade-taking is still practised in the natsaro. With a population of 1350 in an area of only 1.3 sq km, spare land on Vao has become extremely scarce. For this reason, as at Atchin, the islanders have their gardens on the mainland opposite.

There's a very interesting walk around the island, which has several old natsaros bordered by stone monoliths up to 3m high.

Vao Islanders make wooden masks in addition to clubs, ceremonial bowls and other carved objects. You can purchase some excellent work here at much lower prices than in Vila.

Tanmial (59.5km) Near Tanmial is a large and spectacular **cavern** with a hole in its roof. The Big Nambas used to bury their dead chiefs here, believing the spirits would rise up to the sky through the vent. Handprints high up on the ceiling are said to have been put there by the spirits as they passed out of the cavern. There's an entry fee of 200VT per person.

A kastom owner dispute was going on at the time of writing, and visits weren't recommended. Check the situation with Peter Fidelio or the provincial government office in Lakatoro.

Tenmaru (73km) Big Nambas culture is still fairly strong here, and kastom dancing is popular entertainment. Just north of the village, the **Lekan Spirit Cave** is another traditional burial place for Big Nambas chiefs. It's almost as large as the one at Tanmial and also has handprints on its walls. You must ask the chief for permission to enter, which costs 400VT.

The Amokh Road

You may be able to hire a 4WD truck in Unmet or Brenwei to take you up to Bkaier. Alternatively, the return taxi fare from Norsup is about 4000VT.

Distances are from Norsup.

Unmet (19km) The residents of Amokh – the last full-kastom village of the Big Nambas – have all moved to Unmet and neighbouring **Brenwei**, where missions have

Amelboas Natsaro

he beat time on one tamtam. In his right hand he held a dry coconut, which, when pounded on the second drum, produced a deeper booming note that indicated changes in pattern. His skill was the secret of the dancers' perfect timing and choreography.

I spent three fascinating hours at the natsaro watching dances, and learning about grade-taking and the different ranks of chiefs. There were also demonstrations of cooking and fire lighting. Finally, after I'd eaten my fill of chicken *laplap* and delicious fruit, all the dancers lined up and I was asked to give a small *tankyu* speech. My Bislama wasn't really up to the task, but they seemed pleased with my poor effort – at least they applauded on its conclusion. Next time I'll study my Lonely Planet phrasebook and give it a better shot.

Denis O'Byrne

DENIS O'BYRNE

VANUATU

converted them to Christianity. Ask at either of these two villages, or farther along the coast at Unmakh or Wiawi, if you need a guide for the interior. Alternatively, the Wala Island Resort arranges tours in the area.

Hoping to raise a few vatu, the Big Nambas have built a kastom nakamal at Unmet for tourists to visit. This village is one of the best places to see traditional Big Nambas dancing.

Amokh (42km) Now overgrown, this village was abandoned in the late 1980s following the chief's death. By the roadside, tall tamtams mark the edge of the old natsaro.

Bkaeir, just north-west of Amokh, is the most kastom-oriented of the Big Nambas villages; it's a good place to see traditional houses and watch dancing. You can walk here from **Wiawi** on the coast, but the trek is hard going and takes about four hours. Guides can be hired in Wiawi, where there's a small *guesthouse* charging 1500VT for a bed.

East Coast

Eastern Malekula's coastal plain was one of Vanuatu's first areas to be settled by Europeans. Coconut plantations reach from the shore right up to the foothills of the densely forested interior.

Distances are from Lakatoro.

Lakatoro Set at the foot of a tall ridge, Malampa province's administrative capital is quite an attractive place, with many shady trees. Its compact tidiness contrasts markedly with nearby Norsup.

Lakatoro has a population of about 700. It was the island's British government centre during Condominium days, so is mainly English-speaking. There are two general stores, a branch of the NBV and a bakery.

Places to Stay & Eat Lakatoro's government *resthouse (government office ☎ 48491)* is in the town's upper level. It's basic but reasonably well-equipped, and charges 1500VT for a bed.

Down by the school, the ***Sato Kilman Guesthouse*** *(☎ 48401)* charges 2500/3000/3500VT for singles/doubles/triples. The

units are cramped, but each has a private to[ilet], shower and cooker. The manager liv[es] about 600m down the road towards Norsu[p].

There are two eateries. The very bas[ic] ***Commercial Centre (LCC) Restaura[nt]*** opens on weekdays for breakfast, lunch a[nd] dinner. The licensed ***Maxi Restaurant*** [at] the nearby Malekula Distributor Cent[re] (MDC) Store is open the same hours, a[nd] you can book for weekend meals. Goo[d] sized mains cost from 250VT to 1600VT.

There are several *nakamal* in Lakato[ro] where you can drink kava.

Uripiv (1km & 4km by boat) The ma[in] attraction on Urpiv Island is a **marine san[c]tuary** that completely encircles the islan[d]. This has everything for the snorkeller [–] beautiful coral, small colourful fish, turtl[es] and many other varieties of marine lif[e]. There's more good snorkelling on nearb[y] **Uri Island**.

Places to Stay & Eat Run by the loc[al] women's club, the ***Ngaim Orsel Gues[t]house*** *(☎ 48564 or ☎ 48566)* is a ve[ry] friendly place set in the middle of an o[ld] natsaro. There are only two beds, but t[he] ladies will soon arrange more if require[d]. They charge 1000VT for a bed and an ext[ra] 500VT if you want to cook your own mea[l].

Getting There & Away You can get to t[he] island by canoe or speedboat from the jet[ty] at Litslits. There are plenty of canoes goin[g] across between 4 and 4.30 pm, when it cos[ts] 100VT for a ride. Otherwise, a speedbo[at] charter is 1000VT.

Pankumu River (31.5km) There are sev[-]eral river crossings prior to the Pankum[u] River, which is Vanuatu's longest wate[r]course outside Santo. Over the centuries [it] has repeatedly changed course betwee[n] Metenua and Retchar, leaving a large we[t]land of isolated oxbows and bayous. Th[is] area, downstream from the stony crossin[g], is a great spot for bird-watching.

Vetgot (53km) This village of about 10[0] people is right on the shore of **Banam Ba[y]**

here's good swimming near the guesthouse, and guided walks into the hills to
waterfalls and a wet cave.

The main attraction here is Small Nambas **kastom dancing** – one of the men's
dances features Rom-like costumes (see the
Ambrym section of this chapter). A program of eight dances costs 3000VT per person (minimum charge 4500VT).

**Places to Stay & Eat Banam Bay Beach
Bungalows** is right by a sandy beachfront
with large, shady trees. Book through Island
Safaris travel agency in Vila, or contact
John Eddie Saitol, the manager, by teleradio
– they listen out on weekdays between 8.10
and 9 am and again at 4.10 pm.

The guesthouse has two traditional-style
bungalows sleeping three and a large,
thatched building with four single bedrooms. Singles/doubles are 5000/7000VT
including substantial island-style meals. The
facilities include hot-water showers from a
drip heater – a rarity in rural Vanuatu.

Getting There & Away A taxi to Vetgot
costs 3500VT from the Lamap airport and
at least 6000VT from Lakatoro. If you wait
for public transport it costs 300VT from
Lamap and 500VT from Lakatoro. See the
Getting Around information for Malekula
Island earlier and Lamap later in this chapter.

Lisuk Bay (61km) Villagers bathe in the
river rather than in the sea for fear of
sharks. If the road to Lamap is closed you
may be able to find a speedboat here to
take you across to the Port Sandwich
wharf, near Lamap.

South-East Coast
The following distances are from Lamap.

Lamap During the Condominium, when it
was the principal French government centre
on Malekula, Lamap was Vanuatu's third-
largest town. Today it's a derelict shadow of
its former self.

Lamap's facilities include two small
stores, a post office, a government *resthouse*

(apparently very run down) and a branch of
the NBV. To be on the safe side, tap water
should be boiled or otherwise treated before
you drink it.

Getting Around Taxis and speedboats can
be hired in Lamap. The 5km taxi ride from
the airport costs 500VT.

Public transport for Lakatoro generally
leaves Lamap just once a day, and that's
very early in the morning. Ask at the stores
for information about getting a ride.

Port Sandwich (3km) Malekula's safest
anchorage was named by James Cook after
his patron, the Earl of Sandwich, a former
British prime minister.

It's a pleasant 45 minute walk from
Lamap to the wharf on Port Sandwich. En
route you pass several villages including
Merivar. At the wharf a small golden beach
may tempt you in for a swim. Don't do it!
This is one of the worst places in Vanuatu
for shark attacks.

The *Karuma Guesthouse (☎ 48594)* in
Merivar has three twin bungalows for
3500VT per person, including meals and
transfers to/from the airport. As a bonus, the
local store sells cold beer.

Point Doucere (7km) The road from
Lamap ends at a pleasant sandy beach, with
a nice view across the water to **Sakao Island**.
This is a major landing for canoes and
speedboats travelling to and from islands in
the **Maskelyne** group. You may be able to
find transport across to the islands here, or
you can hire a speedboat in Lamap.

It takes about 20 minutes to walk through
the coconut plantations from the airport to
the beach. If you're stuck waiting for a
plane this is a much nicer alternative to the
terminal.

South-West Bay Area
Small Nambas culture is better preserved in
south-western Malekula than elsewhere on
the island. Indeed, a cultural revival is taking place here, with nakamal and dancing
grounds being reopened and grade-taking
on the increase.

Despite their long-held fear of malaria, most highland people have abandoned the interior and now live around South West Bay. There are six language groups in the immediate area, making it the most interesting culturally in Malekula.

The following distances are from Wintua.

Wintua On the shores of South West Bay, Wintua is the regional administrative centre. From here you can do a day walk into the hills to three mainly kastom villages: **Looranba'an**, **Veremboas** and **Mendua**. Their chiefs, dressed in the kastom fashion, will demonstrate or tell you about various kastom activities and traditions, and there's dancing by arrangement. You can also purchase handicrafts and artefacts, enjoy lovely scenery and meet some great people.

There's a safe swimming beach off the western end of the airstrip, a short walk from the guesthouse. You can also do a canoe trip into nearby **Tsiri Lagoon**. A fairly easy three hour walk takes you into the rainforest to an impressive **waterfall** with a deep plunge pool, the home of large eels.

Places to Stay & Eat The *Alo Lodge (community phone ☎ 48466)* is near the airport terminal – George Thompson, the manager, is the Vanair agent, so he meets most flights. The guesthouse is a basic European-style building with four bedrooms and better facilities than most of its type. George charges 6000/8000VT, including all meals.

Lawa (6km) In the hills behind the settlement is an old **village site** with broad coral paths, dry-stone walls, burial places, sacred stones and ceremonial sites. You can visit it with Chief Alben Reuben of Lawa, whose very interesting tour includes a traditional nakamal and natsaro – this is bounded by standing stones up to 2m high.

You can walk to Lawa quite easily from Wintua in 1½ hours, or pay 1000VT for a speedboat charter. Lawa is the gateway to the interior, with several walking tracks starting here. George at the Alo Lodge in Wintua (see that section earlier) can tell you about them.

Tomman

This is an extremely attractive island, w an abundance of coral gardens and gole sand. Although the local people retain ma of their ancient traditions, the practice binding small boys' heads to give them elongated cranium has died out.

Melip, on the mainland 3km east Tomman, is said to have one of the pretti beaches in Vanuatu – it's in the bay to east of the village. You can check throu George at the Alo Lodge whether or not chief at Melip will let you camp there.

Getting There & Away The 17km spe boat trip from Wintua to Tomman is arou 8000VT for a half-day return. Alternative there's a fairly easy walk from Wintua Melip (the villagers say this takes arou six hours), where you can hire a canoe speedboat to take you across.

Ambrym

- pop 8000   • area 680 sq km

Ambrym's main feature is its twin vol noes Mt Marum and Mt Benbow. The have erupted seven times this centu whole villages were lost in 1913, 1929 a 1950, while lesser events occurred in 19 1946, 1979 and 1993. Drifting ash of creates serious problems by disrupting fruiting of food plants and increasing s acidity.

Most islanders live in coastal villages the north, south-west and south-east. T relatively few inland villages are built hills or ridges because, in the event of eruption, only the higher ground is sa from the molten lava.

Local Customs

In Vanuatu, magic is said to be strongest islands with active volcanoes, so Ambry is generally considered the country's s cery centre. A powerful *man blong ma* (sorcerer) is treated with great respect by islanders – they've seen too many une plained happenings to regard them w anything but awe.

ie Rom Dance This, the island's most
iking ceremony, takes place over several
·eks every August in the north as part of
·ade-taking ceremonies. It was in danger
· dying out in the south-west, but is being
·vived as an annual event for tourists.

The Rom costume consists of a tall, con-
·al, brightly painted mask, and a cloak of
·nana leaves that conceals the wearer's
·dy. Because the dancer represents a spirit,
·ch costume is burned after the dance in
·se any of the spirit's power remains – oth-
·wise it will take the costume over and
·unt or impersonate the dancer. Conse-
·ently, very few Rom outfits exist for pos-
·ity, although the Cultural Centre in Vila
·s one.

·etting There & Away
·r Ambrym's airfields are at Craig Cove in
·e south-west and Ulei in the south-east.
·Vanair calls in to Craig Cove five times
·ch week on its Vila-Luganville run and

once on a return loop from Vila. Three of
these services, including the latter, call in to
Ulei. Three flights connect Craig Cove with
Norsup (Malekula), and three with Paama
and Lamen Bay (Epi).

Boat Ifira Shipping charges 4800VT between Vila and Craig Cove, and 1100VT
between Ambrym and its immediate
neighbours.

You can travel by speedboat from north
Ambrym to south-west Pentecost for upwards of 6000VT.

Getting Around
The terrain along the sparsely inhabited
west coast is very rough, with no established path. You can travel between Craig
Cove and Ranvetlam by speedboat, but this
is expensive if there's only one or two of
you – the charter costs 10,000VT. The
cheapest option is a trading vessel, which
will probably charge less than 1000VT.

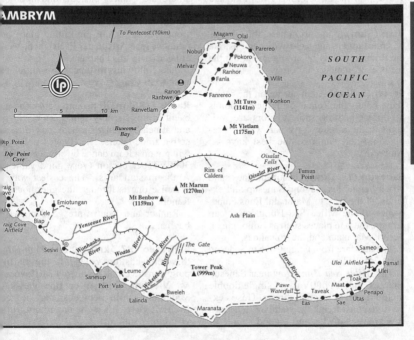

AROUND AMBRYM
South-Western Ambrym

The 4WD road from Craig Cove to Endu winds along the coast through small villages, coconut plantations and patches of jungle. Numerous paths lead down to the shore, and there are some fine views from the higher points.

The following distances are from Craig Cove.

Craig Cove The commercial centre at Craig Cove is opposite the wharf, a short walk from the airfield. It has an NBV agency, and a general store.

Places to Stay The self-catering *Craig Cove Guesthouse (Vanair agent ☎ 48620)* was in poor shape at the time of writing, but its renovation was said to be imminent. Beds will cost 1500VT when it's been fixed up; you can collect a key from the nearby store.

The Presbyterian Women's Club at **Wuro**, near the airfield, has *guest quarters* you can use for 500VT per person.

Biap (6km) Inland from here, the villages of **Emiotungan** and **Lele** will demonstrate the Rom ceremony by arrangement, but the fee is exorbitant.

Sesivi (9.5km) A hot spring on the rocky shore below the Roman Catholic mission is a popular bathing spot. Visitors are welcome at the mission kava bar, which is reputed to sell some of the best kava on Ambrym.

Sanesup (13.5km) A beautiful black sand beach begins just beyond Sanesup and extends all the way to Maranata. Enos Falau, owner of the Milee Sea Bungalows, can arrange tours to places such as Emiotungan, Sesivi, Maranata and the volcanoes.

The taxi fare from Craig Cove to Sanesup costs 2500VT.

The *Milee Sea Bungalow* near Sanesup charges 6500/9000VT a single/double including breakfast and dinner. This is expensive considering the standard, but Enos is a great character and a good source of

information on the whole island. Make boo ings through Island Safaris in Vila, or lea a service message through Radio Vanuatu.

Lalinda (19.5km) The chief at Lalinda the kastom owner of the southern access the volcanoes and charges a small fee visit them. This is where you collect yo guide for the walk, which normally starts a vehicle drop-off point about 5km away the **Woketebo River**.

You may be allowed to sleep at either t *school* or the *Presbyterian Women's Clu* which will certainly be a much cheap alternative to Sanesup's guesthouse.

The taxi fare to Lalinda is 3000VT fro Craig Cove and 500VT from Sanesup.

Northern Ambrym

Most of Ambrym's northern coast is e. tremely rocky – only Olal, Magam, Parer and Ranon have beaches, all of which a OK for swimming. Northern Ambrym where the island's customs and traditio have been least affected by the mode world, and where its best carvings con from. These feature pig-killing clubs an tamtams (see Arts under Facts about Van atu earlier in this chapter).

The following distances are anticloc wise from Craig Cove.

Ranhor (85km) Rom dances are an annu event in this friendly semi-kastom villag and at nearby **Neuwa**, where most men a active grade-takers. The villagers at Ranh will put on a Rom dance by arrangement f 3000VT per person (very good value t Ambrym standards). The easiest way organise one is through the guesthouse Ranon.

Ranhor and Neuwa are good places buy carvings.

Fanrereo (87.5km) Set on a high ridg this semi-kastom village is the startin point for the climb up nearby **Mt·Tuvo** an **Mt Vletlam**. Both offer fine views Malekula, while Pentecost can be see from Mt Tuvo. It's a one day return trip visit either summit.

anon (88.5km) This village – another
arving centre – has the best swimming
each in northern Ambrym. Speedboats can
e hired here.

Laan Douglas, the owner of Solomon
ouglas Bungalows, can arrange Rom
ances, guided walks to the volcanoes and
1ts Tuvo and Vletlam, and village walking
urs. He can also arrange speedboat rides
 Craig Cove and across to Pentecost. To
ontact Laan direct, ring the Lolihor
evelopment Council (☎ 48405) in nearby
anvetlam and arrange to call back. They'll
ass the message for him to be there at the
ppointed time.

Most days there are carvers at work near
1e guesthouse, and you're welcome to
vatch.

laces to Stay & Eat The very basic
olomon Douglas Bungalows charges
000/6000VT, including all meals. A fea-
ure of this place is the huge, island-style
1eals cooked by Laan Douglas' mother –
ou'll need the fuel as most of the walks in
1is area are steeeeep.

he Volcanoes
he dark, brooding outlines of Mt Benbow
nd Mt Marum are 1km or so apart, with Mt
1arum, the highest by a hundred metres,
sing to 1270m. Usually shrouded in
noke and cloud, they dominate the vast,
esolate 'ash plain' that lies within the old
aldera. At night, the sky above them glows
ed from the lava in their craters.

Columns of white smoke pour from Mt
enbow's central crater, while molten rock
nd dense black smoke spew from the vents
n Marum. In 1999 the authorities were
ecoming increasingly concerned that it
vas about to blow its top again. Evacuation
lans had been worked out, just in case.

ccess Points The best starting points for
alks to the volcanoes are Lalinda in the
uth and Ranvetlam in the north.
Vhichever way you go, you'll need to
llow two days if you want to climb both
olcanoes. To climb one requires a reason-
bly long day from both ends.

Walking Conditions Starting from either
end, the path takes you up dry riverbeds
and steep slopes, with thick jungle that tears
at your skin. There's no shade on the barren
ash surfaces in the caldera, where the heat
can be terrific. Skin protection (including a
broad-brimmed hat) and plenty of drinking
water are essential.

The slopes around both volcanoes have a
dry slippery crust. Soft-heeled shoes such as
joggers are not at all suitable for this type of
surface – you might end up using your back-
side to toboggan down a very high, steep
ridge when your feet slip from under you.

Organised Tours The Lolihor Development Council in Ranvetlam (☎ 48405; ask
for Chief Isaiah Bong) does a guided walk
from Ranvetlam to Craig Cove, climbing
both volcanoes and spending a night on the
ash plain.

Alternatively, you can do a day walk from
Ranvetlam to either volcano. This costs
around 5500/7000VT for one/two people if
you're doing it through Solomon Douglas
Bungalows. The guides live in Ranvetlam,
where there's a small *guesthouse* charging
2000VT per person including meals.

Starting from the south you can, if you're
fit, do the return walk to one of Mt Marum's
external vents and climb to the summit of
Mt Benbow in a day. The cost for this
through the guesthouse in Sanesup is
9500/15,000VT for one/two people, including transport to the drop-off point.

Espiritu Santo

• pop 30,000   • area 3677 sq km

Although officially named Espiritu Santo –
Spanish for the Holy Spirit – Vanuatu's
largest island is called Santo by almost
everyone. To add a little confusion, Luganville, the island's principal settlement, is
also generally referred to as Santo.

Santo has Vanuatu's four highest peaks:
Mt Tabwemasana, Mt Kotamtam, Mt
Tawaloala and Santo Peak, all over 1700m.
They rise from the mountainous spine that
runs almost the full length of the island's

VANUATU

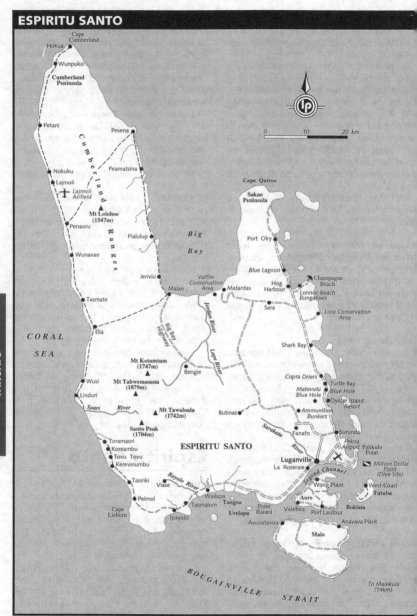

ESPIRITU SANTO

Cape Cumberland
Hokua
Wunpuko
Cumberland Peninsula

Petani
Pesena
Peamatsina
Nokuku
Lajmoli
✚ *Lajmoli Airfield*
▲ Mt Lolohoe (1547m)
Penaoru
Pialulup
Wunavae
Jeriviu
Malao
Tasmate
Elia

Cumberland Ranges

CORAL SEA

Wusi
Linduri
Soari River
▲ Mt Tabwemasana (1879m)
▲ Mt Kotamtam (1747m)
Bengie
▲ Mt Tawaloala (1742m)
Butmas
▲ Santo Peak (1704m)
Toramaori
Koreambu
Tovu Tovu
Kerevinumbu
Tasiriki
Pelmol
Cape Lisburn
Ipayato
Viase
Bayolo River
Wailapa
Tasmalum
Tangoa
Point Ratard
Urelapa
Vatebea

ESPIRITU SANTO

Big Bay
Vatthe Conservation Area
Matantas
Jordan River
Big Bay Highway
Lape River

Cape Quiros
Sakao Peninsula
Port Olry
Blue Lagoon
Hog Harbour
Champagne Beach
Lonnoc Beach Bungalows
Sara
Loru Conservation Area
Shark Bay
Copra Driers
Matevulu Blue Hole
Turtle Bay
Blue Hole
Oyster Island Resort
Ammunition Bunkers
Fanafo
Sarakata River
Surunda
Pekoa Airport
Palikulo Point
Luganville
La Roseraie
Million Dollar Point (Dive Site)
Wong Plant
West Coast
Tutuba
Aore
Bokissa
Port Lautour
Avunatavoa
Anavava Plant
Malo

Second Channel

To Malekula (14km)

BOUGAINVILLE STRAIT

0   10   20 km

VANUATU

st coast. In contrast, the much flatter
uthern and eastern coastal strips have
en largely developed for cattle grazing
d plantations. This is where most of the
pulation lives.

Santo is still an important centre for ni-
angki grade-taking ceremonies. Although
eryone living along the southern and east-
n seaboards wears European clothing, in
her parts many people still dress as kastom
mands.

During WWII, south-eastern Santo was
rned into a huge US forward military
se. All up over half a million military per-
nnel, including John F Kennedy and
mes Michener, were stationed here prior
heading off to battle elsewhere in the Pa-
fic. At times there were as many as 100
ips moored off Luganville.

Santo is an extremely interesting and at-
ctive island with plenty of potential for
sitors. There's no shortage of good walk-
g, some great beaches, kastom villages,
d several world-class scuba dives. Most
the island's tourist facilities are concen-
ted in and around Luganville, where
ere are several hotels, motels and restau-
nts. Much of the eastern half has a fairly
od network of unsealed roads, but else-
here you either take a boat ride or walk.

formation

urist Offices To find out what's avail-
le, ask at your hotel/guesthouse or check
th Surata Tamaso Travel or the Natangora
fé in Luganville.

ctivities

iving & Snorkelling There are at least
worthwhile dive sites in the channels
thin 20km of Luganville. Most reefs are
itable for snorkelling, as is **Million Dol-
Point**, but the wrecks are out of reach for
e divers. The 'South Pacific Diving' spe-
al section describes the SS *President
olidge* (Vanuatu's most famous dive),
llion Dollar Point, and Tutuba (Tutuba
and). Other sites include the following.

N Henry Bonneaud This former coastal trading
vessel sits upright in 30 to 40m of water. It

makes an excellent introduction to both wreck
and deep diving, and is said to be one of the
world's great night dives.

Bokissa Bommie The main attraction here is fish.
A dozen whaler sharks live here and are the
focus of shark feeding. If you're into thrills
this shouldn't be missed.

Tubana This drop-off dive near Urelapa Island
off Tangoa Landing, about 20km south-west of
Luganville, has depths ranging from 5 to 70m.
Here you can see huge gorgonia sea fans, black
coral trees and swarms of fish.

Organised Tours

Several tour operators have main street
premises in Luganville. The rural resorts at
Lonnoc Beach, Matantas and Oyster Island
all offer a variety of tours.

Land Trips The principal operators are
Butterfly Tamaso Tours (☎ 36537) and
Sandy's Hibiscus Tours (Aore Resort
☎ 36705). They offer a range of minibus
tours including the so-called Santo full
circle, which visits Fanafo, Matantas,
Champagne Beach and the Matevulu Blue
Hole for 4000VT. They also arrange
guided walks including major treks into
the mountains.

Alternatively, you can hire a taxi and
arrange your own tour. A day trip to the
Matevulu Blue Hole and Champagne
Beach will cost around 8000VT shared,
plus entry fees. If you just want to go for a
swim in the blue hole you'll pay around
3000VT shared.

Man Bush Eco Tours (☎ 36175) has a
very good half-day tour for 3000VT that
includes adventure caving and a visit to a
kastom village. It also offers cave diving for
certified divers.

Scuba Diving Local dive tour operators are:

Aquamarine
  (☎/fax 36196, aquamrne@vanuatu.com.vu)
  on Main St, Luganville;
  www.aquamarine-santo.com
Bokissa Island Dive
  (☎ 36911, fax 36912,
  pdsanto@vanuatu.com.vu) on Bokissa Island
Santo Dive Tours
  (☎/fax 36822) on Main St, Luganville

VANUATU

Santo Dive Tours does shore dives only, concentrating on the *President Coolidge* and Million Dollar Point. For a broader range of dives you need to contact Aquamarine, which does boat and shore dives, including the *President Coolidge*, and Bokissa Island Dive, and which specialises in boat dives.

Getting There & Away

Air Santo had five operational airfields during WWII, but of these, only Pekoa, 6km from Luganville, remains in use; wartime pilots knew it as Bomber Two. The island's only other commercial strip is at Lajmoli, on the north-west coast.

Pekoa is the main feeder airport for the northern islands. There are at least two, and usually three, return flights daily between Santo and Vila, with tickets costing 11,000VT one way.

Sea Ifira Shipping and Toara Coastal Shipping charge around 7000VT from Vila to Santo. The MV *Rosalie* operates between Luganville and Vila every fortnight, and does a weekly trip along the east and south coasts of Malekula. It charges 6800VT to Vila, taking 19 hours for the trip.

Several small trading boats ply the northern routes from Luganville and their skippers may be prepared to take you on as a passenger. You can check by asking around at the Chinese stores, starting with the LCM Store on Blvd Higginson (Main St).

Getting Around

To/From the Airport The minibus fare between Pekoa airport and Luganville is 200VT, while taxis charge from 500VT shared.

Air Vanair has one flight each week from Luganville to Lajmoli airfield in the island's north-west.

Minibus Regular minibus services connect Luganville and Port Olry. The best way to catch a ride is to stand by the roadside before 7 am if you're heading in and after 5 pm on the outward run. The fare is 500VT each way.

Truck & Taxi There are plenty of taxis and public transport trucks – open-backed 4WD trucks with a red 'T' fixed to their number plates – operating around Luganville. As in Vila, competition is fierce and tourists are fair game for some operators.

Car You can hire cars and light 4WDs in Luganville at Surata Tamaso Travel and the Hotel Santo, both on Main St. The former is the Hertz agent.

LUGANVILLE

Before WWII, Luganville was a scattered collection of modest buildings separated by coconut plantations. Then the Americans came and changed its face forever. Today the main town area sprawls along several kilometres of waterfront. It's a sleepy, dilapidated sort of place, with numerous ageing Quonset huts, rusting steel sea walls and empty concrete slabs remaining as evidence of busier times.

Information

Money The country's four commercial banks have branch offices on Main St (see Money in the Facts for the Visitor section of this chapter). The Santo Sports Club, also on Main St, has a private money exchange.

Post & Communications The post office has postal services only. If you want to make a telephone call, go along to Telecom Vanuatu's office in Rue La Pérouse – it has the town's public telephone, telegram, fax and telex facilities, and there's usually quite a queue waiting to use the phones. It's closed on weekends.

Medical Services The hospital (☎ 3634) is perched above the town in Le Plateau. There's a pharmacy at the hospital and two smaller ones on Main St.

Market

Villagers come from all over southern and eastern Santo to sell their garden produce and handicrafts at the busy Luganville market, on Main St, near the Saraka Bridge.

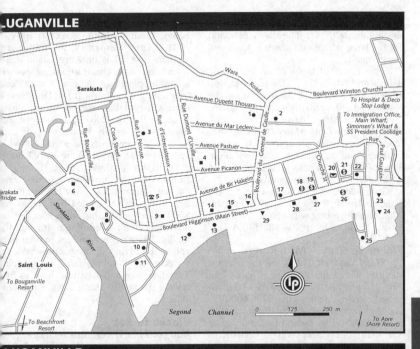

LUGANVILLE

PLACES TO STAY
4 Natapoa Motel
6 Riviere Motel
9 Unity Park Motel
14 Hotel Santo
27 New Look Motel
28 Asia Motel

PLACES TO EAT
16 Santo Sports Club
23 Santo Chinese Restaurant
24 The Coolidge Bar

29 Natangora Café

OTHER
1 University of the South Pacific
2 Radio Vanuatu (Studio 5 NOT)
3 Cine Hickson
5 Telecom Vanuatu
7 Fish Market
8 Covered Market
10 Women's Handicraft Centre
11 Chiefs' Nakamal
12 Unity Park
13 Santo Dive Tours
15 LCM Store
17 Vanair
18 Westpac
19 National Bank of Vanuatu
20 Post Office
21 Banque d' Hawaii
22 Surata Tamasu Tours
25 BP Wharf
26 ANZ Bank

VANUATU

The market is open more or less continuously from Monday afternoon through to Saturday evening.

Places to Stay – Budget

Most popular of the town's cheaper places the 13-room **Unity Park Motel** (☎ 36052). It has share kitchen and bathroom facilities, with fan-cooled rooms from 1320/1980/2310/3080VT per single/double/triple/quad. Larger upstairs rooms sleep three people and cost 2750VT per room.

Also good value is the **Riviere Motel** (☎ 36782), between the market and the Sarakata Bridge. It has similar facilities and while its bedrooms are small and dingy, the place is clean; its rooms sleep up to three and cost 1200/1800/2700VT a single/double/triple. There's a nakamal out the back where you can buy kava and cheap meals.

In the centre of town is the very basic *Asia Motel* (☎ 36323). This place has no kitchen, and in terms of standards it's at the bottom end of Luganville's cheaper motels.

Just up the street above the New Look Store, the *New Look Motel* (☎ 36440) has rooms (some with air-con) with private facilities and shared kitchens for 2800/ 3900/ 5000VT. It offers a good standard and is popular with long-stay guests.

Also in demand with long stayers is the *Natapoa Motel* (☎ 36643), off Ave Picanon. It has pleasant rooms with cookers, fans and private facilities for 3800/4800/5300VT.

Places to Stay – Mid-Range

The *Hotel Santo* (☎ 36250) has the smartest lodgings within the town area. Its air-con rooms cost 9000/ 9500/10,300VT while fan-cooled singles/doubles cost 5200/6000VT. There's a swimming pool, bar and restaurant.

High on the ridge behind Luganville, and with a fine view over Segond Channel to Aore Island, the *Deco Stop Lodge* (☎ 36175) has basic dorms sleeping up to eight for 2800VT, including a light breakfast. Its double/twin rooms cost 4900/6600VT. All rooms have fridges and safes, and there's a licensed eatery selling Australian-style meals.

On the southern outskirts of town, the friendly *Beachfront Resort* (☎ 36881) has pleasant, airy rooms sleeping up to three from 5000/7000/9500VT, and family rooms sleeping five for 11,000VT. Its private swimming beach and cool, shaded lawns make it a nice place to relax on a warm day. A licensed restaurant sells snacks and bar meals.

Places to Stay – Outside Luganville

About 4km from the centre of town, the *Bougainville Resort* (☎ 36257) boasts a lovely garden setting with views over Segond Channel. Its 18 attractive, fan-cooled bungalows cost 9500/10,700/ 12,900VT, and there's a bar, swimming pool

and the most sophisticated restaurant Santo. A minibus from town costs 100VT

The *Aore Resort* (☎ 36705, aore vanuatu.com.vu) is on Aore Island acro from Luganville. This is a relaxing spot w a coconut plantation out the back and go snorkelling on coral in front. However, basic self-contained bungalows seem ove priced at 9500/11,200VT, including a lig breakfast. Its family rooms sleep five f 21,000VT. Speedboats leave from BP Wha several times a day, charging 400VT retur

On Bokissa Island, about 10km fro Luganville, the *Bokissa Island Reso* (☎ 36913) is run down, but boasts an idy lic setting. Its fan-cooled bungalows c 8000VT per person, including transfers a all meals, with a minimum stay of tv nights. There's a bar and swimming poo and scuba diving, fishing, bushwalks a visits to neighbouring islands are availabl Transfers take about half an hour to/fro town – the launch leaves from Simonsen Wharf.

Places to Eat

Budget Eats The cheapest places to eat Luganville are the *food stalls* beside t market and at the western end of Uni Park. They sell simple rice meals for 250V a serve – ask for more 'sauce' if you' served a pile of rice and little else.

The *Santo Sports Club*, not to be co fused with the Sports Club nearer the Hot Santo, has basic meals from 300VT.

Cafes & Restaurants The *Santo Chine. Restaurant* is open daily for lunch a dinner, with large mains starting at 800V Next door, the *Coolidge Bar* is a good sp for pizza and drinks.

On Main St, the friendly *Natangora Ca* opens daily except Sunday and specialis in breakfasts, hamburgers and home-ma pastries and cakes.

The *Bougainville Resort* is open dai for lunch and dinner, with the à la carte di ner menu starting at 1500VT for mains. specialises in French cuisine and seafoo and offers one of Santo's few opportuniti for a gourmet experience.

ntertainment

he only nightlife other than the handful of
rs and restaurants is *Cine Hickson*, which
s evening film shows starting at 7.30 pm.
's open nightly except Monday and shows
ench-language or subtitled films.

Open daily, the Santo Sports Club has
ker machines and satellite TV coverage of
ternational news and major sporting events.

ava Bars Luganville has over 30 licensed
va bars. Most will welcome your custom.

hopping

he best place to buy handicrafts is the
omen's Handicraft Centre, at the western
d of Unity Park.

etting Around

inibus You'll have no difficulty finding
minibus between 7 am and 5.30 pm, but
s a different story outside these hours.
he standard rate anywhere around town is
0VT.

xi The minimum cab fare is 100VT. Taxis
d public transport trucks can be found at
e market (on market days) or cruising up
d down Main St. The market is the best
ace to find them after 5.30 pm.

alking The most dangerous aspect of a
sit to Luganville is walking around the
reets at night. Carry a torch so you can see
e potholes!

ROUND ESPIRITU SANTO

ll distances are from the Luganville post
fice. See the special section 'South Paci-
Diving' for more about the first two dive
es.

outh-East Santo

President Coolidge (7.5km) Take
e track on your right about 400m past the
wmill. Just out in the channel from the
all parking area, a couple of floats mark
e wreck.

illion Dollar Point (8.5km) Just
ere the main road turns to the north, a

good track runs southwards to the beach.
In front of the automatic lighthouse is the
jetty where US military equipment was
dumped. At low tide you'll find metal objects littering the beach for 1km in either
direction. It's a great snorkelling spot on a
calm day.

Club Nautique (12km) Turn right to
Palikulo Point at the road junction about
4km beyond Million Dollar Point. Just
north of the intersection is Club Nautique,
a popular swimming and picnic spot and an
anchorage for yachts – a small fee is
charged to use its modest premises. The taxi
ride from town costs around 1200VT, but
getting back to town can pose a problem.

Santo Golf Club (15.5km) Back at the
junction before the Club Nautique, the road
heads north-west to Surunda. Passing the
overgrown remains of the wartime **Bomber
One** airstrip, you come to the Santo Golf
Club by Palikulo Bay. The club is mainly
active on weekends and visitors are welcome – it costs 500VT to play and the same
to join the club.

Roman Catholic Cemetery (4.9km)
The inland road from Luganville to Surunda
travels through coconut plantations, which
continue for most of the way to Turtle Bay.
Golden-brown Limousin cattle graze beneath coconut palms in this rustic paradise.

About 400m before the Fanafo turn-off is
an interesting cemetery with several Vietnamese tombs.

Surunda (10km) The road via Palikulo
Point joins up with the main inland route at
Surunda, the site of a wartime camp for US
and New Zealand forces.

Just past the village on the coast road, and
on your left, an old bitumen road climbs the
hill to the site of a wartime hospital. Down
at the plantation headquarters, on the right,
an iron cottage shelters under a huge tree on
the beachfront. This was Bloody Mary's
brothel, of *Tales of the South Pacific* fame.
Local legend has it that convalescing soldiers would walk down from the hospital to

the brothel, where they'd test their fitness before returning to the war.

Matevulu Blue Hole (20.5km) The track on the left takes you up the former US wartime airstrip, Fighter One. About a quarter of the way along it, and on the left, you pass the wreckage of a **Grumman Avenger** torpedo bomber.

The main track turns left towards the Matevulu Agricultural College about halfway along the strip, but you continue up the strip to the end. Here you swing left and follow the track around to the crystal-clear Matevulu Blue Hole. This is the largest such feature on Santo, being about 50m across and 18m deep. Not surprisingly, it's a great spot for swimming and scuba diving.

Oyster Island Resort (20.9km) The track on your right heads down to a landing area where you catch the boat across to nearby Oyster Island. This beautiful spot, more correctly called Malwepe (or La Pérouse) Island, is one of several islets that shelter behind the raised coral structure of Mavea Island.

The friendly *Oyster Island Resort* (☎ 36283) has eight self-contained, breeze-cooled bungalows in a beautiful waterfront setting. While the two older units are cramped, they're generally good value at 4500/5500/6500/7000VT, including a light breakfast. It's well known for its licensed à la carte French restaurant, which serves magnificent seafood (it's wise to book).

Getting to Oyster Island from Luganville costs 300VT by minibus or 1500VT by taxi. To summon the boat across, either sound your car horn or call out from the beach.

Blue Hole River (23.1km) The road crosses this pellucid, spring-fed stream over an unusually solid bridge built by the US Army in WWII. Look out for speed bumps (called 'sleeping policemen') on the approaches.

Copra Driers (26km) Here you drive through the headquarters of the huge NCK Plantation by Turtle Bay. On the left is a bank of copra driers, while the ramshackle

structures on the right are the worke quarters.

North-East Santo
Shark Bay Blue Hole (29.6km) T spectacular, crystal-clear spring is about 3(across and 15m deep. It's an excellent s| for snorkelling – when you look up from reasonable depth, the fish appear to be swi ming in the sky. The entry fee is 500VT.

Loru Conservation Area (47.7k| Covering 220 hectares, this new park cc tains one of the last patches of lowland fc est remaining on Santo's east coast. Ther an information centre, several nature wall many **coconut crabs** and a bat cave, whi the villagers use as a cyclone shelter. T entry fee is 500VT.

Lonnoc Beach (55km) With its beauti coastal setting, the *Lonnoc Beach Bung lows (☎ 36141)* is a great spot to drop c in for a few days. Its traditional-sty bungalows (basic shared facilities only) a lined up along the beachfront and cc 3000/4000/5500VT, including breakfa Allow 3000VT per person per day for me and drinks.

The resort has a bar and restaurant, a there's a sandy swimming beach and a stu ning view of **Elephant Island** out the fro It runs a daily return bus service to Luga ville for 500VT each way; tours include 5000VT day trip to the Vatthe Conservati Area (see the Matantas section for infc mation about the Vatthe itself).

Champagne Beach (56km) The ro past the Lonnoc Beach resort stops Champagne Beach, which is as lovely the brochures say it is. Cruise ships drop a chor here every four weeks or so betwe May and October but otherwise you likely to have it to yourself.

There is, of course, the inevitable kast(fee, except in this case there are two of th(– you must place 500VT per car in each the honesty boxes on the way in. Two lo(men claim to be the beach's rightful kast(landholder, and each wants payment for |

ht to use it. Usually the claimants, who
e nearby, go straight to their box to collect
money. If you haven't paid, watch out!

ue Lagoon (58km) A parking area by
road marks the start of a short track to
another spring-fed blue hole. As you
scend through the rainforest you might
tice pieces of coconut fixed to the ground.
ese are bait to catch coconut crabs.

Between here and Port Olry you pass
olden Beach and Longar Beach, both of
hich are open to visitors (the entry fee is
0VT). Golden Beach is the more attrac-
e of the two.

uganville to Fanafo

he road initially follows the inland route
wards Surunda, turning off just past the
oman Catholic Cemetery.

anyans (13.1km) Look in the grove of
l trees on the right; you'll see how some
ung banyans, having become established
the trunks, have sent down roots to reach
e ground. It's a slow process, but eventu-
y they'll strangle their hosts and take
er completely.

mmunition Bunkers (16km) The
WII bunkers and ammunition roads on
her side were part of a huge complex, but
u can't see much from the road.

Turn right at the Y-junction at 21.4km. To
to Fanafo, turn left at the T-junction at
.4km – turn right to continue straight on
Matantas.

anafo (23.8km) You can call in un-
nounced to visit this interesting group of
llages, but it's best if you make prior
rangements – that way you can be sure to
e everything. When you arrive, ask for
ief Tabou Rusa and he'll detail someone
act as guide.

Fanafo was the centre of the Nagriamel
cessionist movement and many of its res-
ents were followers of Jimmy Stevens, its
under. One of the things you'll be shown
re is Stevens' grave, as well as various
lics associated with him. The grave has

been only partially filled in so that his spirit
can escape to complete his work.

Chief Tari Buluk's basic *guesthouse* in
Fanafo makes a good base for a day-return
walk to **Butmas**, a kastom village up in the
hills – a number of Stevens' supporters went
to live there after his death. Chief Tari's father was heavily involved in the Nagriamel
movement, and he can tell you some interesting stories about those days.

Fanafo's Christians wear ordinary
clothes, while kastom-oriented males of all
ages are naked except for their mal mal.
You may also see small girls wearing
leaves, and older females in grass skirts.

Fanafo to Matantas

The road from Fanafo to Matantas is fairly
adventurous because of its narrowness and
the lack of traffic and human habitation.
There are some straight stretches at first,
but the road winds about with many tight
turns and roller-coaster sections once it
reaches the uplands.

The following distances are from Fanafo.

Big Bay Hwy (26km) Opened in 1994,
this road takes you to Malao village in the
south-west corner of Big Bay. There is a
truly magnificent panorama of the rugged
Cumberland Range as you wind down to
the fast-flowing **Lape River**, 13km from the
intersection. There are some large holes to
cool off in at the causeway, and a nice picnic spot on the western bank.

Matantas (53km) This village is split
into two parts, with one being Baha'i and
the other Seventh-Day Adventist. The former is the first part you come to. Here,
Chief Moses welcomes visitors and will
arrange for a guide to show you around.

In the centre of the village is a cemetery
surrounded by a low, square, mortared stone
wall. There's a theory that it was used as a
fortified camp by Quirós in 1606, but it's
more likely to have been built by a French
missionary or trader in the 1860s.

Vatthe Conservation Area This is one
of Santo's highlights for anyone who likes

VANUATU

trees, birds and bushwalks. Covering about 45 sq km, it stretches along the coast from north of Matantas to the **Jordan River**, and inland to the top of a 400m-high limestone scarp. Half of it is covered by Vanuatu's largest reasonably intact alluvial lowland forest – the main reason for its protection.

Forest walks are the major attraction, with bird-watching second; you can see 82% of Vanuatu's native land and freshwater bird species here. Various walks are available, including a two day trek that includes the highest point on the scarp – 449m **Mt Wimbo**. You get superb views of the Cumberland Peninsula right along the scarp. Puriti Tavue, the guesthouse manager, can arrange guides as well as kastom dancing, coconut crab hunts and other activities

Places to Stay & Eat The *Vatthe Lodge* has several small island-style bungalows sleeping two people for 2800/3500VT a single/double, including breakfast. This place has no running water (they're hoping for an aid grant) but it's clean and friendly, and the meals are very good. You can pitch your tent for 500VT per person either at the lodge or down on the sandy beach.

Getting There & Away A transport charter from Luganville costs 5000VT, but if there's a truck going out that way it will cost only 500VT per person. To find out about this, contact the Vatthe office (☎ 36153) at the Sanma provincial government centre in Luganville.

South Coast

Distances are from central Luganville.

Lambue Airfield (6km)

The turn-off to **Nambel** is about 4.5km from the Luganville post office. On the way in you cross the disused Lambue wartime airfield, formerly Bomber Three.

There's a small coconut-oil factory at the back of the house on the left about 1km past the old strip. This operates most days except weekends and Mondays, and expat Aussie manager Ron Hawkins will be happy to show you around. If you buy

some samples of his fragrant skin-care products he'll probably let you in for free. It's an interesting enterprise and well wort the detour.

Point Ratard (13.5km)

This scenic spo has a large, inviting sandbar about 150m offshore. You can snorkel around the cora reef and see hundreds of WWII ammunitio boxes – but watch out for the current pas the sandbar.

This is where you catch a speedboa across to **Malo Island**.

Tangoa Landing (28.5km)

You'll usu ally find outrigger canoes and speedboa moored here, so if you're prepared to wa you should be able to get a ride over t Tangoa Island.

The landing has a 1km-long black san beach – while this looks like a nice place fo a swim, several people and many dogs hav been taken by tiger sharks in recent year There's often a local market under the b trees on the beachfront.

Tangoa (28.5km & 0.3km by boa

Traditionally, Tangoa Island was the fir stage in an ancient trade route that ran be tween southern Santo, Malo and nort western Malekula. The usual product wa pandanus leaves, which were in great d mand in north-western Malekula for ma ing clothing and mats. Today, Tango houses a Presbyterian Bible college. Th island was settled by missionaries in 188 making it probably the first Europea foothold on Santo.

Wailapa (39km)

This village, just befo the Wailapa River, is a good spot to see ka tom fire dances (ask at Surata Tamaso Tou in Luganville). The crossing marks the e of the road for conventional vehicles.

Beyond Tasmalum (48.5km)

Pa Tasmalum the 4WD road continues **Tasiriki** via Ipayato. The coast north Tasiriki boasts some of the most scenica rugged country in Vanuatu. Here, toweri cliffs and steep, jungle-clad mountai

lunge straight down to black sand beaches.
These qualities, together with the deeply in-
ised streams, usually remind Kiwis of their
wn spectacular Fiordland.

Santo Peak
South-west Santo has Vanuatu's highest
mountains: Mt Tabwemasana (1879m), Mt
Kotamtam (1747m), Mt Tawaloala (1742m)
nd Santo Peak (1704m).

You'll need to organise an expedition to
limb Mt Tabwemasana, but Santo Peak is
simpler proposition. From Tasiriki the
oing is very steep and slippery when wet,
which is most of the time, and there is no
well-defined path – you follow the guide as
e hacks through the vegetation with his
ush knife! The return 'walk' takes two to
ree full days.

The route from Ipayato is said to be easi-
r. It takes two days to walk up a path that
enerally follows a spur to the summit.

Apart from the feeling of achievement at
e end, Santo Peak's major reward is its
ossy cloud forest, which begins at about
00m. While the views from the top are
agnificent, you normally can't see them
ecause of cloud.

Regardless of which village you start from,
low at least a full day there to organise your
uide (for advice on guides ask at the provinial government office in Luganville). Carry
arm clothing, a sleeping bag and a tent as
's invariably cold and wet on top.

Pentecost Island

pop 13,000 • **area 438 sq km**
ugged, traditional Pentecost Island is
est known for its amazing *naghol*, or
nd-diving ceremony, which takes place
ere each year – see the boxed text later in
is section.

Getting There & Away
ir Pentecost has two airfields: Sara in the
orth and Lonorore in the south-west.
anair has three return flights each week to
oth airports from Vila and Luganville via
mbae.

Boat Ifira Shipping charges 5900VT from
Vila to Melsisi (on the west coast) and
4500VT from Luganville; Toara Coastal
Shipping charges 5000VT and 3200VT respectively. Both charge around 1100VT if
you're just travelling between Pentecost
and Maewo or Ambrym.

A speedboat charter across Patteson
Strait between north Pentecost and south
Maewo is around 4000VT. To get from Bay
Martelli in the south to Olal in northern
Ambrym will cost about 6000VT.

Getting Around
Pentecost has a number of 4WD taxis scattered about at various villages, but the fares
are high. Salap is the best place to find a
guide if you want to walk across the southern mountains to Bunlap.

AROUND PENTECOST
South-Western Pentecost
The following distances are from Lonorore
Airfield

Lonorore Airfield There's a public card
phone in the airport terminal and a post office nearby. Each year the men of Bunlap
supervise the building of a **land-dive tower**
on a hill near the southern end of the runway.

Panas (6km) The large **crucifix** outside the
village co-op store commemorates a small
boy who was taken by a shark in 1984. One
or more **land-dive towers** are erected annually on the hills between here and nearby
Wali.

The Melten Women's Council's *guesthouse* charges 1500VT per person including
three meals. You can leave a message for the
manager, Evelyn, by calling the provincial
government office in Pangi on ☎ 38327.

Salap (10.5km) You can hire taxis and
speedboats in this village, which is by the
shore of **Bay Homo**. The 14km 4WD road
across the island to Ranwas makes a
memorable ride in the back of a truck.

If you're organising your own land-dive
tour, Chief Willy Orion of Salap is probably
the person to talk to. He can be contacted by

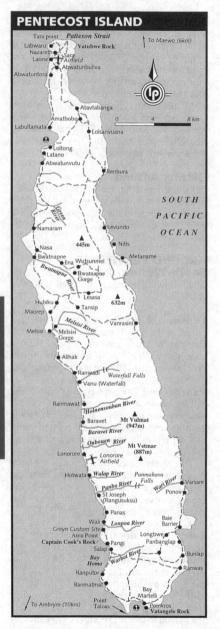

PENTECOST ISLAND

ringing the provincial government office
Pangi (☎ 38327) and arranging to call bac

If you're very fit you can hike from Sal
to Bunlap via small **kostom villages** in t
mountains, spend a night at Bunlap, th
return along the road from Ranwas. Con
tions in the bush are often difficult a
strenuous, with steep, slippery slopes a
many roots to trip over. Chief Willy w
arrange guides and tell you about options
route – some villagers may not want to
bothered by tourists.

Places to Stay Just south of the villag
Chief Willy's island-style ***Nagol Bung
lows*** has twin rooms costing 5000/8000V
a single/double, including all meals, and
much cheaper camping option. There are
couple of pit toilets, but no showers – yo
can wash in the sea or the nearby river.

Getting There & Away A speedboat ri
from Salap costs 2500VT to Bay Marte
and 4000VT to Ranwas. By taxi it's 4000V
to Ranwas and 3000VT to the airport.

South-Eastern Pentecost
The following distances are from Salap.

Ranwas (14km) This very attractive v
lage is perched on a high ridge overlooki
the sea. From here a slippery footpath hea
north to Bunlap, the walk taking about
minutes.

Bunlap (16km) Situated on a steep slop
this large, full-kastom village lines bo
sides of a central path. At the Ranwas en
are three nakamal and two natsaros ring
with coral stones. All around are traditio
ally designed leaf houses, built so low the
roofs just about touch the ground.

Traditions are strictly preserved in Bu
lap and attempts to introduce Christiani
which recently succeeded at neighbouri
Baie Barrier, have failed. Here most v
lagers wear nambas and grass skirts all t
time. There are no schools – although t
children can attend schools elsewhere – a
the women are generally forbidden to spe
Bislama.

Land Diving

In April, as soon as the first yam crop begins to emerge, the villagers begin building tall wooden towers at various sites in the far south of the island. These towers are usually 18 to 23m high, but can reach to 27m.

On one or two chosen days from April to early June, men and boys dive from these rickety looking structures with only two long, springy *lianas*, or vines, tied to their ankles to break their fall. Villagers believe that this ritual 'leap into oblivion' is required to guarantee a bountiful yam harvest the following year. The aim is for the diver's hair to brush the ground, which is loosened beforehand, thus ensuring the fertility of the next crop.

Incredibly, no-one is killed in these dives, although minor injuries do occur. The only known fatality occurred during a dive held out of season for Queen Elizabeth II in 1974 – apparently the vines were springier than they would have been at the usual time.

It's *tabu* for a woman to see the towers being built, even though legend has it that the first land-diver was female. She'd lured her husband – who she must have hated with a great passion – to the top of a banyan tree and dared him to follow her when she leapt off. She jumped and so did he, but unbeknown to him she'd tied vines between her ankles and the tree. So while he hit the ground and was killed, his wife was pulled up short by the vines.

Land diving occurs at a number of places, including Lonorore airfield. Two sites in the hills behind Bay Homo are set aside mainly for the entertainment of tourists, with villagers from surrounding areas taking turns to perform there. Commercial dives take place one day a week (usually Saturday) during the season.

Any of the major inbound and charter yacht or aircraft operators in Vila can arrange visits for you to see a naghol. It won't be cheap – the 1999 entry fee was set at 20,000VT per person, with transport and accommodation on top of that. If you've got some time you can save quite a bit by arranging your own tour.

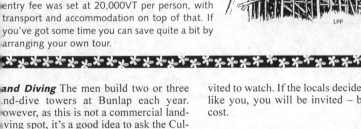

LPP

Land Diving The men build two or three land-dive towers at Bunlap each year. However, as this is not a commercial land-diving spot, it's a good idea to ask the Cultural Centre in Vila whether you'll be allowed to visit during the season. Remember that your presence at the time of a land dive is no guarantee that you'll be invited to watch. If the locals decide that they like you, you will be invited – but it will cost.

Places to Stay & Eat The village has a *leaf house* with beds for six people, but no mattresses or bedding. It costs 2000VT per person per night, including food.

Ambae

- **pop 10,000**
- **area 405 sq km**

Ambae rises steeply to 1496m at Mt Lombenben, the highest point on the rim of a semiactive volcano. Its upturned-boat shape gave James Michener, who was based on Santo during WWII, his vision of what the mysterious island of Bali Hai looked like in *Tales of the South Pacific*.

There are several legends about the mountain and its three crater lakes. One tells how Tagaro (the island's main traditional god, and probably the Tangaroa of Polynesian mythology) took fire from Mt Lombenben to Ambrym, then drowned its vents by filling them with water. The largest of these – Manaro Lakua and Vui – represent Lombenben's eyes. The summit is sacred and the whole area is beset with *tambu*, which can inhibit access.

The people of Ambae exhibit some distinct Polynesian characteristics including language and physical features – many ha[ve] light-brown skin and straight, dark ha[ir]. Most of the population lives along th[e] south-west and north-east coasts.

Ambae's main village, Saratamata, is th[e] administrative centre for Penama provinc[e] which incorporates Ambae, Maewo an[d] Pentecost islands.

Getting There & Away

Air Ambae's airfields are at Longana in th[e] north, Redcliff in the south-east and Wala[ha] in the west.

Vanair has return flights three times [a] week between Vila and Luganville v[ia] Longana and Walaha, as well as Sara an[d] Lonorore on Pentecost. There are also tw[o] return flights each week between Luga[n]-ville and Maewo via Longana, Redcliff a[nd] Walaha.

Boat Ifira Shipping calls in to ports alo[ng] the west coast on its regular Vila-Luganvi[lle]

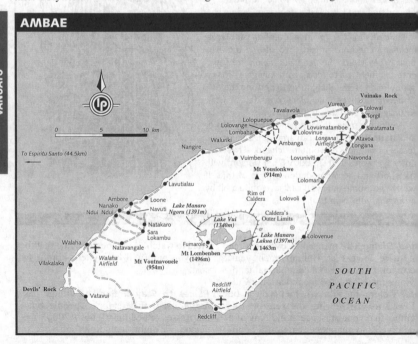

AMBAE

run. Tickets from Lolowai in northern Ambae cost 1100VT to Maewo, around 1500VT to northern Pentecost, 2300VT to Luganville, and 6800VT to Vila. Toara Coastal Shipping is a little cheaper.

Getting Around
Except for an 18km stretch of footpath on the rugged north-western coast, you can drive right around the island. There are a few taxis on Ambae, and you can hire speedboats at most of the larger coastal villages.

AROUND AMBAE
Western Ambae
The following distances are from Devils' Rock.

Devils' Rock The spirits of recently deceased people are believed to come here, where they leap into the sea and turn into sharks. This is the local explanation for the large number of shark attacks that have occurred in the area (and of course if someone is *killed* by a shark they add to the problem).

Walaha (5km) The *guesthouse (☎ 38330)* at Halalulu village, about 1km from the airfield, charges 1000VT per person. A speedboat from Walaha to **Ndui Ndui** (the commercial centre of western Ambae) costs 1000VT.

Nanako (11km) The very basic *Nanako Guesthouse (☎ 38345)* has cooking facilities and costs 1000VT per person, as does the government *resthouse (teleradio ☎JT419)* at nearby **Ambore**.

Nangire (22km) Taremulimuli, an important chief in Ambae's past, is buried on the cliff top at Nangire. His 300 sq m **burial enclosure** is marked by several tall stones and has an inner section shaped like a boat.

Vureas (40km) The **black sand beach** just beyond the secondary school is one of Ambae's best swimming spots. The school ☎ 37378) has quite a good *guesthouse* with cooking facilities costing 1000VT per person.

Eastern Ambae
The following distances are from Lolowai.

Lolowai The high rock just beyond the inlet is called **Vuinako**, which Ambae people believe to be the female companion of Gwala, or Devils' Rock. Originally they lived together near Vureas. However, they fell out one day over a pig, and Gwala fled to the western tip of Ambae to escape Vuinako's wrath.

Lolowai contains Vanuatu's principal centre for the Anglican Diocese of Melanesia. The village has a post office, hospital, small *guesthouse*, wholesale store and NBV agency.

Saratamata (3km) The village has a provincial government *resthouse (provincial office ☎ 38348)*, which charges 1000VT per person. Alternatively, the *Tausala Guesthouse (☎ 38348)* at nearby **Longana** offers a reasonable standard for 1000VT per person self-catering or 2500VT with meals. Gladys Bani, the manager, can arrange fishing excursions and walks to various places, including the crater lakes.

The taxi fare from Saratamata to Longana airstrip is 1200VT.

Trekking to the Lakes
Mt Lombenben is often blanketed by mist and rain, which has helped create some of Vanuatu's finest cloud forest. While the craters are interesting, their contours are softened by jungle so don't expect anything dramatic. The views from the top are restricted by trees and clouds.

The water levels in the two larger lakes drop considerably in the dry season. This exposes a beach at **Manaro Lakua** which – if you can ignore the frogs – makes an excellent camping spot. The lakes are the only sources of drinking water on the mountain. Villagers sometimes make the trek up to the lakes to catch prawns, but because of their fear of devils they don't like spending the night there.

The usual routes to the top are from Redcliff, Ambanga in the north and the Natakaro area in the west. There is some confusion as to which village is the rightful kastom owner of the western approach, so check this with the Cultural Centre in Vila. Guides are required for all walks.

Once you get onto the mountain proper all routes are gruelling, with steep slopes climbing endlessly upwards through the damp, misty jungle. Allow three days for the return walk if trekking from Ambanga – it's about seven hours each way – and at least two from the other take-off points. Campsites are extremely limited on top.

Banks & Torres Islands

Forming the province of Torba, the 13 inhabited islands of the Banks and Torres groups are administered from Sola on Vanua Lava, in the Banks Islands. There are four airfields in the province, but little in the way of tourist accommodation and roads. Despite its considerable beauty and fascinating culture, very few visitors make it to this part of Vanuatu – particularly the Torres group.

THE BANKS ISLANDS
• pop 7700   • area 746 sq km
This 144km-long chain of mainly tall, rugged islands has two active volcanoes: Mt Garet on Gaua and Mt Sere'ama on Vanua Lava. Both islands cover around 330 sq km and are by far the largest of any in the Banks or Torres groups.

Getting There & Around
Air There are airstrips at Sola on Vanua Lava, Lembot on Gaua, and Ablow on Mota Lava. Vanair flies twice a week to all three, with one flight calling in to the Torres group. A ticket from Luganville costs 6700VT to Gaua and 7700VT to both Sola and Mota Lava. From Sola it's 2700VT to Mota Lava, 3300VT to Gaua and 5700VT to the Torres group.

Boat Copra boats from Luganville call irregularly and infrequently at the various

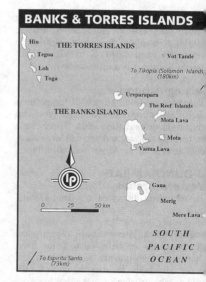

BANKS & TORRES ISLANDS

THE TORRES ISLANDS
Hiu
Tegua   Vot Tande
Loh
Toga   To Tikopia (Solomon Islands
                                        (180km)

                              Ureparapara
                                    The Reef Islands
THE BANKS ISLANDS
                                    Mota Lava
                                    Mota
                          Vanua Lava

                                    Gaua

                                    Merig

                                    Mere Lava

0   25   50 km

SOUTH
PACIFIC
OCEAN

To Espiritu Santo
(73km)

Banks Islands ports. Ask around at Lugan ville's Chinese stores for news of forth coming departures.

As a guide to speedboat fares, it cos 12,000VT return from Sola to Tasmate, c Mota Island, and 8000VT one way to V on Mota Lava. The seas are often to choppy for safe travel between the island

Gaua
Gaua is a roughly circular island abo 20km across. In its centre is an ancien caldera with 797m Mt Garet and 7km-lon Lake Letas on its floor. The lake curls pa way around the volcano and drains out vi the Mbe Solomul River, which passe through a breach in the old crater rim. E route to the sea the river tumbles over th narrow, 120m-high Siri Falls, Vanuatu largest waterfall.

Most of Gaua's population lives alon the north-east coast.

History Gaua had an estimated 20,00 people prior to the 1860s, but a series c devastating epidemics (culminating wit influenza in 1935) killed thousands, even tually slashing the population to 700. It wa

ly in the late 1970s that the population
gan to increase again.

tone Relics Although inland Gaua is
rgely uninhabited, the evidence of more
opulous times is everywhere. Most obvious
e long stretches of dry-stone walls, and
uilding foundations made of large rocks.
's said that stone foundations can be seen
Lake Letas. Stone platforms and obelisks
ter the bush; you'll often find stone bowls
led up at the bases of large banyan trees.

Stones about 1.5m high were sometimes
rved, and these were treated as powerful
ods. One of the island's more famous relics
a particularly large monolith about 2m
ross. Apart from its size, the remarkable
ing about it is the rich variety of petro-
yphs that cover almost the entire surface.
's in the south of the island, a three to four
our walk from the airport.

ekking to the Scenic Centre You can
sit **Siri Falls**, **Lake Letas** and **Mt Garet** on
hard two day walk from Lembot (where
e airport is) to Lambal. Starting at the
irstrip it's 40 easy minutes to a **huge
anyan tree** – the path winds for 35m
rough its roots, with the stone foundations
f an old nakamal on one side.

Coming from Lambal, to the east, you ar-
ve at Lake Letas just south of the overflow
to the Mbe Salomul River, where there's
ood camping on the sandy shore. A dugout
anoe is left here so your guide can paddle
ou across to the volcano – it's a fairly easy
imb from the lake up to the volcano.

laces to Stay Less than five minutes
alk from the airport terminal, the very
asic *Wongras Bungalows (☎ 38502)* has
vo bedrooms and cooking facilities for
300/4300VT, including breakfast. Don't
e too shocked if breakfast completely fails
eventuate!

etting Around A road runs down the
oast from the airfield at Lembot to near the
outh of the Mbe Salomul River at Mbare-
t. The 14km drive costs 1500VT by taxi.
ootpaths link villages in the north-east

with Lake Letas and Siri Falls. You can hire
a guide at the Wongras Bungalows for
2500VT per day.

Vanua Lava

The highest point of mountainous Vanua
Lava Island is 946m **Mt Tola**. Just 25m
lower, the semiactive volcano **Mt Sere'ama**
gives off clouds of steam that can be seen
from Sola, 14km away. However, Vanua
Lava's most dramatic sight is said to be **Sara
Falls** – twin cataracts that tumble over the
cliff into a large pool by the sea.

Once you could hunt saltwater crocodiles
on Vanua Lava, but the 1972 cyclone devastated the population and only two remain –
one is estimated to be 6m long, and the other
2m. Islanders say the crocs' ancestors were
brought here by Bishop Patteson in the
1860s. They escaped, but Patteson commanded them to refrain from eating humans.
So far they're doing as instructed, although
there have been some close escapes.

Sola The provincial capital is a strung-out
sort of place boasting government offices, a
fishery base, co-op store, post office and
NBV branch.

From here you can do a three day return

KATE NOLAN

Headdress from the Northern Islands

VANUATU

walk around the south coast to Sara Falls, overnighting at **Vureas Bay** where there's a small guesthouse. This is where you pick up a guide for the walk to the falls. Villagers say Sara Falls is a reasonably easy, day return walk from Vureas Bay, so aim to spend two nights with them. It's a half day walk from Sola to Vureas Bay.

Places to Stay & Eat Sola's extremely basic government *resthouse (provincial office ☎ 38550)* has beds for 1000VT. Nearby, the slightly more upmarket *Leumerous Guesthouse* has small thatched bungalows costing 3900/5700VT for singles/doubles, including all meals. Alternatively, you can camp for 500VT per person.

Getting Around A taxi from the airport to Sola costs 600VT, otherwise it's a 40 minute walk.

Mota Lava
At the south-western end of Mota Lava Island, 243m **Mt Tuntog**, also known as Sleeping Mountain, offers a magnificent panorama to the south from the Reef Islands around to Mota. The view is worth the effort, but not the 5000VT entry fee that the kastom owners were planning to charge in 1998.

At low tide you can walk across to Mota Lava's beautiful but tiny neighbour, Ra Island – ask the villagers to point out the underwater footpath.

Ra Island
Ra has some huge rocks at its southern end, the highest of which offer marvellous views of the surrounding islands. Down below

there's an old 'devil cave', once used fo storing shell money, whose resident spiri was exorcised by an early missionary. Prio to that, any 'unqualified' person who en tered the cave was doomed.

The Harry Memorial Guesthouse ca arrange a kastom **Snake Dance** for 3600V per person. This is a colourful performanc but you should first ask how many dancer there will be and how long the demonstratio lasts. It would be wise not to pay in advanc

Places to Stay & Eat On the beachfro with a fine view across the water to Vanu Lava, the basic and rather dilapidate *Harry Memorial Guesthouse* charge 4400/ 5800VT for singles/doubles, inclu ding all meals. It would be a good idea t bring some extra food, just in case.

Getting There & Away You can fly int Ablow and take a taxi for 2600VT t Ngerenigman, on the mainland opposite R A dugout ride across to the guesthouse cos 100VT.

Alternatively, you can charter a spee boat from Sola on Vanua Lava to Ra fo 8000VT one way.

THE TORRES ISLANDS
● pop 600   ● area 105 sq km
This small archipelago stretches for 42km and consists of six main islands, four o which are populated.

Dazzling white sand beaches are the gen eral rule. Surfing is particularly good, espe cially when the south-east trade winds ar blowing. Loh and Toga are good places t see megapode birds, known locally as scru hens, which lay their eggs in the warm sand

MICRONESIA

Micronesia

Largely overshadowed by the more famous Polynesia and Melanesia, the third region of the Pacific, Micronesia (Small Islands), is well named. Although there are a handful of higher volcanic islands, most of the region's 2000-odd islands are tiny low-lying coral islands and atolls.

Micronesia was first settled by an Asian people who arrived in the western Caroline Islands from the Philippines about 3000 years ago. Subsequent settlers came from not only the Philippines but also north from the islands of Melanesia and north-west from Polynesia. Although settled by different cultures, ancient Micronesia was more integrated than other regions of the Pacific. Micronesian navigators voyaging between the islands knew their area intimately.

Guam was the point of the first contact between Pacific islanders and Europeans. Magellan's landed there in 1521, setting the scene for later contact between European and Pacific races by killing seven locals in a dispute about theft.

After this momentous occasion, Micronesia slipped into relative obscurity. I small resource-poor islands were unable hold the attention of European traders, wh were plundering the rest of the Pacific f beche-de-mer and sandalwood.

Spain and Germany competed for own ership of the islands of Micronesia in th 19th century, with Germany eventually winning control of most of the region. A the outbreak of WWI, Japan, wghich wa allied with Britain, easily seized control the whole of Micronesia. Japan had a lon history of economic ties with the regio, and quickly moved a large number Japanese settlers, administrators and busi ness ventures into the Micronesian island

The region leapt to world attention i WWII when some of the Allies' fiercest ba tles against Japan were fought here. Rem nants of the war, in the shape of rustin tanks on land and sunken ships beneath th sea, are haunting reminders of those time for modern visitors.

WWII locked much of Micronesia into a
-year long relationship with the USA,
th the UN's postwar establishment of the
ust Territory of the Pacific Islands. The
ist brought to Micronesia both prosperity
in the shape of massive investment and
onomic assistance – and tragedy, with
cial disruption and nuclear testing.
Since the 1970s, almost all of the states
Micronesia have assumed independent
le, although the past members of the
ust Territory are still heavily dependent
US money. Only the island state of
uam, and a handful of almost-uninhabited
olls, remain US territories.
Guam is the most popular tourist desti-
ation in the region – about two-thirds of
e Pacific's annual three million tourists

head to either Guam or the Northern Mariana Islands. However, many of Micronesia's other islands are rarely visited.
Tourist infrastructure and transport options
are sparse in these islands, whose isolation
is part of their charm.

Travellers come to the region to sample
traditional island life, such as on the islands
of Yap, to check out the beautiful scenery
and to investigate the fascinating ancient
drowned city of Nan Madol on the tropical
paradise of Pohnpei.

More than anything else, though, tourists
come to Micronesia for the spectacular diving and snorkelling opportunities. The region's most famous diving spots are Palau,
Bikini, Yap and Chuuk, with the Blue Corner dive in Palau one of the world's best.

Federated States of Micronesia

The Federated States of Micronesia (FSM) consists of the four states of Kosrae, Pohnpei, Chuuk (formerly Truk) and Yap. All are part of the Caroline Islands and share colonial histories under Spain, Germany, Japan and the USA. Even so, the four states have distinctive cultures, traditions and identities. Chuuk is renowned for its diving, Yap for its traditional culture, Kosrae for its preponderance of true believers and Pohnpei, the capital, for its lush landforms and ancient ruins.

Facts about the Federated States of Micronesia

HISTORY
Some FSM islands are believed to have been settled around 200 AD.

Medieval Pohnpei was ruled by the Saudeleurs, a tyrannical royal dynasty who reigned from Nan Madol, an elaborate city of stone fortresses and temples. By 1400 stratified Kosrae was unified under one paramount chief, or *tokosra*, who ruled from the island of Lelu. While the commoners lived on the main island, then called Ualang, the royalty and their retainers lived inside more than 100 basalt-walled compounds on Lelu and nearby islets. With its canal system and coral streets, the fortressed island of Lelu would have rivalled its medieval counterparts in Europe.

The first Europeans arrived in Yap and Ulithi Atoll around 1526. The Spanish, arriving later, claimed sovereignty over the Caroline Islands until 1899, when it sold its holdings to Germany.

Pohnpei's infamous 1910-11 Sokehs Rebellion was sparked when a Pohnpeian working on a labour gang on Sokehs Island was beaten by a German overseer. Pohnpeians killed the overseer – and the revolt

AT A GLANCE

Capital City (& Island): Palikir (Pohnpei)
Population: 114,000
Time: 10 hours ahead of GMT (Chuuk, Yap); 11 hours ahead (Pohnpei, Kosrae)
Land Area: 695 sq km (271 sq miles)
Number of Islands: 607
International Telephone Code: ☎ 691
GDP/Capita: US$1930
Currency: US dollar
Languages: English & state languages
Greeting: *Kaselehie* (Pohnpeian)

HIGHLIGHTS

- **Diving** – the manta rays of Yap, the wrecks of Chuuk and the whirling variety of marine life on Pohnpei and Kosrae

- **Ancient ruins** – you can paddle through the sunken ruins of Nan Madol on Pohnpei or explore Kosrae's ancient kingdom of Lelu on foot

- **Traditional culture** – no island group holds so strongly to its old ways as Yap, well known for its giant stone money and its Bechiyal Cultural Center

- **Hiking** – the lush volcanic swells of Pohnpei and Kosrae offer numerous scenic hiking options

The Saudeleurs' Demise

The most common story of the demise of the Saudeleurs tells of conquests from Kosrae. The Thunder God, who had been severely punished for having an affair with the wife of a Saudeleur on Pohnpei, set out for Kosrae in his canoe. The canoe sank, but the Thunder God was able to continue on when a floating taro flower changed into a needlefish and guided the god to the island. On Kosrae he made a woman of his own clan pregnant, and the child, Isokelekel, was raised on the stories about the cruel Saudeleurs back on Pohnpei. After reaching adulthood Isokelekel gathered an army of 333 men and went to Nan Madol. He conquered the Saudeleurs and became a district chief.

as on. The Germans promised revenge, ter blockading Kolonia and sending lelanesian troops charging up Sokehs idge. The uprising was suppressed and 17 bel leaders were executed and thrown into mass grave. The Germans exiled 426 okehs residents to Palau and then brought her islanders to settle on Sokehs.

In 1914 the Japanese navy took control of e islands and their population dwarfed at of the locals. Chuuk's huge, sheltered goon became the Japanese Imperial leet's most important central Pacific base, impenetrable that it was called the jibraltar of the Pacific'.

On 17 February 1944, the US navy airombed the Japanese fleet docked in the goon and sank some 60 ships, which lie n the bottom today.

After the war, when the USA took over d the Trust Territory was set up, Kosrae as included in the Pohnpei district, but in 977 Kosrae broke away from Pohnpei and ter became a separate state.

In July 1978, the Trust Territory districts f Pohnpei, Kosrae, Chuuk, Yap, the Marall Islands and Palau voted on a common onstitution. The Marshalls and Palau rected it and went on to establish separate

countries. What was left became, by default, the Federated States of Micronesia.

In October 1982 the FSM signed a 15-year long Compact of Free Association with the USA, which guaranteed annual funding to the islands in exchange for granting the USA exclusive military access to the region. The compact was officially implemented in November 1986. In 1991 the FSM was admitted to the United Nations.

While the compact pretty much gives the US military carte blanche in the FSM, the end of the Cold War kept military development essentially at nil.

GEOGRAPHY

The FSM's islands spread for more than a million square miles across the Pacific. Pohnpei has nearly half the land area. Rugged Kosrae, the easternmost island of both the FSM and the Caroline Islands chain, is the only state with no outer islands. Pohnpei, high and volcanic, holds the FSM's highest peak, 2595 foot Ngihneni.

Chuuk State includes 192 outer islands in addition to the 15 main islands and more than 80 islets of Chuuk Lagoon. The rolling hills of Yap Proper, 515 miles south-west of Guam, consist of the four tightly clustered islands of Yap, Tomil-Gagil, Map (pronounced 'mop', and also spelt Maap) and Rumung. Some 134 outer islands are out to the east.

CLIMATE

Temperatures on all the FSM islands average 80 to 81°F year-round. Rainfall is heaviest on Pohnpei, whose interior gets a whopping 400 inches annually (though Kolonia gets less than half of that). The wettest months are in late spring and summer. Yap is the driest island. The FSM islands are all outside classic cyclone tracks, though they are not immune from them.

GOVERNMENT & POLITICS

The FSM has three levels of government: national, state and municipal. The FSM congress is unicameral, with 14 senators. Each state elects one senator-at-large, plus five from Chuuk, three from Pohnpei and

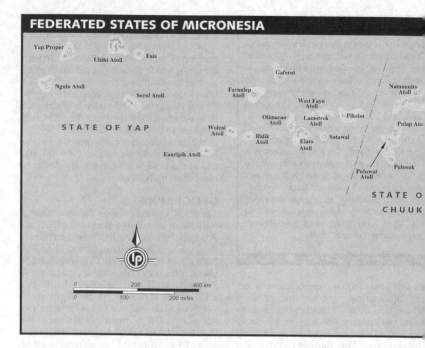

FEDERATED STATES OF MICRONESIA

one each from Kosrae and Yap. The president and vice president, who cannot be from the same state, are elected by congress from among its members. Each state elects its own governor and a state legislature. Traditional village leaders can play an active role in municipal government, particularly on Yap, by selecting candidates and influencing opinion.

ECONOMY

The FSM economy is still heavily reliant on US money. As the 15-year compact – in which the USA gave the FSM more than US$1.3 billion – winds down in 2001, there is mounting anxiety about renegotiation. There's little except waste and continued trade imbalance to show from the compact funding. Chuuk in particular has been accused of misappropriation of the funding.

The waters around the FSM are some of the world's most productive tuna-fishing grounds. The US$18 to $24 million t▮ FSM collects each year as fishing fees fro▮ Chinese and Taiwanese boats is its large▮ source of income following US aid.

Among more creative forms of reven▮ gaining, the FSM began selling its intern▮ domain name (.fm) to radio stations (ear▮ ing about US$150,000 in 1998).

Sakau (kava) crops have become a maj▮ cash crop in recent years. Tourism remai▮ only a minor source of income.

POPULATION & PEOPLE

Chuuk has 57,300 people, Pohnpei 36,90▮ Kosrae 7700 and Yap 11,900. As the com▮ pact permits FSM citizens 'habitual res▮ dence' in the USA, 7000 FSM citizens hav▮ decamped to Guam, 3000 to the Norther▮ Mariana Islands (CNMI) and about 5000 t▮ the US mainland.

The people of the remote Pohnpeian i▮ lands of Nukuoro and Kapingamarangi a▮ the only Polynesians in the FSM.

FED STATES OF MICRONESIA

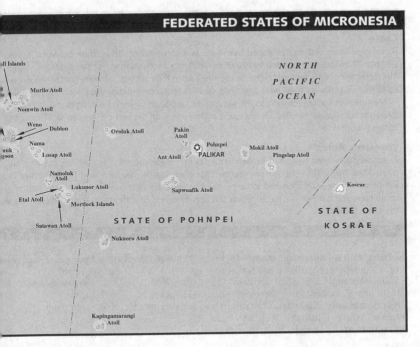

FEDERATED STATES OF MICRONESIA

NORTH
PACIFIC
OCEAN

all Islands

Murilo Atoll

Nomwin Atoll

Weno — Dublon

Nama

uuk Losap Atoll
goon

Oroluk Atoll

Pakin
Atoll

Pohnpei
PALIKAR

Ant Atoll

Mokil Atoll

Pingelap Atoll

Kosrae

Namoluk
Atoll

Lukunor Atoll

Etal Atoll

Mortlock Islands

Sapwuafik Atoll

STATE OF
KOSRAE

Satawan Atoll

STATE OF POHNPEI

Nukuoro Atoll

Kapingamarangi
Atoll

ARTS

All the FSM states have beautiful handicrafts and dances. Pohnpei is known for the wood carvings, of dolphins and sharks, created by the Kapingamarangi people. In terms of traditional architecture, Pohnpei has traditional ceremonial buildings called *nahs*, while Yap has *pebai* (community meeting houses) and *faluw* (men's meeting houses). The most noteworthy form of indigenous money is the Yapese stone money, called *rai* or *fae*.

SOCIETY & CONDUCT

On Kosrae when you talk about society, you talk about religion; everything closes on Sunday, when church, held at 10 am, is the *only* activity.

Clans remain strong throughout the FSM. On Chuuk, other islanders are often obliged to present the clan leader with some token of respect, such as the fruits from the first harvest. On all islands, it's best if visiting

women wear long, loose skirts; this is particularly true on Chuuk and Yap. The Yapese, more than any other Micronesian peoples, have been reluctant to adopt western ways – it's especially important to ask permission before walking on private land or into buildings on Yap.

RELIGION

On Kosrae, about 85% of people are Congregationalists. Pohnpei and Chuuk residents are fairly evenly divided between Protestant and Catholic faiths, while on Yap Catholicism predominates. On all islands, you'll find small groups of Mormons, Jehovah's Witnesses, Baha'i and followers of other religions.

LANGUAGE

English is the official government language for inter-island communications, but the islands have their own indigenous languages as well. On Kosrae it's Kosraean;

Yapese Society

Caste

A complex caste system developed over time as a consequence of warfare between Yapese villages. The victors demanded land ownership rights and patronage of the defeated village. The defeated people retained rights to use the land in their village but were compelled to perform menial tasks for their new landlords, such as road construction and burial of the dead.

Members of a village belong to the same caste, although their rank within that caste varies. Every plot of land in the village has a name and a rank, with the highest-ranked plot belonging to the village chief.

Women's Roles

Traditionally women have had subservient roles in Yapese society. They did the cooking and tended the fields, harvesting from one plot for male family members and from another for the females. The food then had to be prepared in separate pots over separate fires. Not only could men and women not eat together but also members of different castes could not share the same food.

---

on Pohnpei it's Pohnpeian, though Mokilese, Pingelapese, Ngatikese and Nukuoro-Kapingamarangi are also spoken. On Chuuk it's Chuukese, but there are also several minority dialects. On Yap it's Yapese, while Ulithian, Woleaian and Satawalese are spoken by outer islanders.

Kosraean Basics

Hello.	Lotu wo.
Goodbye.	Kut fwa osun.
How are you?	Kom fuhkah?
I'm well.	Nga ku na.
Please.	Nunakmuna.
Thanks.	Kulo ma lunhlhp.
Yes.	Aok.
No.	Moohi.

Pohnpeian Basics

Hello/goodbye.	Kaselehie.
How are you?	Ia iromw?
I'm well (thanks).	I kehlail (kalangan).
Please.	Menlam.
Thanks.	Kalahngan.
Yes.	Eng.
No.	Soo.

Chuukese Basics

Hello.	Ran annim.
Goodbye.	Kone nom.
How are you?	Ifa usum?

I'm well (thanks).	Ngang mei pochokur (kilisou).
Please.	Kose mwochen.
Thanks (very much).	Kilisou (chapur).
Yes.	Wuu.
No.	Apw.

Yapese Basics

Hello.	Mogethin.
Goodbye.	Kefel.
How are you?	Ke us rogom buoch?
I'm well.	Kab fe'l rogog, kam magar.
Please.	Wenig ngom.
Thanks.	Mogethin.
Yes.	Arrogo'n.
No.	Danga'.

Facts for the Visitor

SUGGESTED ITINERARIES

As all islands except Pohnpei are accessed by only two international flights a week it's best to plan a trip with the individual islands in mind, rather than the entire FSM. If you have only one week, Yap, with its traditional culture and excellent diving, is a worthwhile choice; it is a free stopover on the way to Palau on Continental Airlines.

On the other side of Guam, Chuuk, Pohnpei and Kosrae are sequential stops on Continental's island-hopper. Spending three days on each provides a varied sample of FSM life.

TOURIST OFFICES
Each state within the FSM has a tourist office in the district centre.

VISAS & EMBASSIES
Passports are not required of US citizens – but it's a good idea to have one anyway. Each of the states has its own immigration process so you automatically get a new entry permit, good for up to 30 days, each time you fly into a new district centre. Entry permits can be extended through the immigration offices for a total stay of up to 90 days, or up to 365 days for US citizens.

FSM Embassies & Consulates
The following are FSM embassies and consulates abroad:

Fiji
  Embassy:
  (☎ 304 180)
  Box 15493, Suva
Guam
  Embassy:
  (☎ 671-646 9154, fax 649 6320)
  PO Box 10630, Suite 613, Tamuning, Guam 96931
USA
  Consulate:
  (☎ 808-836 4775, fax 836 6896)
  3049 Ualena St, Suite 408, Honolulu, Hawai'i 96819
  Embassy:
  (☎ 202-223 4383, fax 223 4391)
  1725 N Street NW, Washington DC 20036

Embassies in the FSM
The following foreign embassies are in Pohnpei:

Australia
  (☎ 320 5448)
USA
  (☎ 320 2187)

MONEY
The US dollar is the currency throughout the FSM; see Exchange Rates under Money

in the Regional Facts for the Visitor chapter. Pohnpei and Chuuk each have one ATM. Credit cards are accepted at most top-end hotels and many dive shops.

POST & COMMUNICATIONS
The FSM uses the US postal system – letters should be addressed 'via USA'. Postal codes are: Chuuk 96942, Kosrae 96944, Pohnpei 94941 and Yap 94943.

Each state has a 24 hour telecommunications centre where you can place international calls, send and receive faxes and check the Internet. By purchasing an FSM phonecard to use in the telecommunications centre, you avoid the three-minute minimum charge otherwise added to international calls. Calls between FSM states cost US$1 per minute from 6 am to 6 pm weekdays and 50c a minute at other times. International rates are discounted 25% from 6 pm to midnight and 50% from midnight to 6 am.

The FSM's international telephone code is ☎ 691.

INTERNET RESOURCES
Check for information at www.fsmgov.org.

BOOKS & MEDIA
Lonely Planet's Pisces series includes *Diving & Snorkeling Chuuk Lagoon, Pohnpei & Kosrae*, and *Diving & Snorkeling Guam & Yap*.

Kosrae and Yap have no TV services.

ELECTRICITY
The electricity supply is 110/120V AC, 60Hz; plugs are US style with two flat blades.

WEIGHTS & MEASURES
The FSM uses the imperial system of measurement. See the conversion table at the back of this book.

HEALTH
Tap water must be boiled before drinking in all four states.

DANGERS & ANNOYANCES
While other islands are placid tropical backwaters, Chuuk has idle flotillas of

young men lining the streets who harass western women. More details are in the Chuuk section.

BUSINESS HOURS

Business hours are from around 8 am to 4.30 pm on weekdays; banking hours are typically from 10 am to 3 pm Monday to Thursday and 10 am to 5 pm on Friday. On Kosrae, government cutbacks have reduced the working week to Monday to Thursday.

PUBLIC HOLIDAYS & SPECIAL EVENTS

The Micronesian games take place every four years and will be in Pohnpei in 2002; they feature everything from running events to classic Micronesian-style events, such as outrigger canoe races.

All islands celebrate New Year's Day, Easter Sunday and Christmas. Other national holidays are:

FSM Constitution Day	10 May
United Nations Day	24 October
FSM Independence Day	3 November

State Holidays

Holidays particular to individual states include the following:

Yap Day	March
Yap State Constitution Day	24 December
Kosrae Constitution Day	11 January
Kosrae Liberation Day	8 September
Sokehs Rebellion Day (Pohnpei)	24 February
Cultural Day (Pohnpei)	31 March
Liberation Day (Pohnpei)	11 September
Pohnpeian Constitution Day	8 November
Chuuk State Constitution Day	1 October

ACTIVITIES

All four islands have sensational diving – Chuuk with its underwater wreck museum of 60 Japanese ships, Yap with prolific manta rays, and Kosrae and Pohnpei, with varied marine life and good underwater visibility, plus a few wrecks. Some dive prefer the latter two islands, away from t crowds of Chuuk and Yap.

Chuuk has only one major dive sho Blue Lagoon Resort. The other distr centres have several small operations (e cept the larger Manta Ray Divers on Ya Particularly on Pohnpei, obtaining equi ment can be a challenge – bring your o if possible. Two popular live-aboard di boats are based in Chuuk; see the Activiti section under Chuuk for details. Snorkelle will find good reefs on all islands. Trolli and kayaking are possible on most islan

ACCOMMODATION

Camping is not customary as all land is p vately owned, but there are exceptions see the respective states for details. Ea island has a good range of accommodatio Traditional-style hotels, one each on Ya Kosrae and Pohnpei, allow visitors to st in pleasant open-air thatched roof cottage All top-end hotels accept MasterCard a Visa, though budget hotels may not.

FOOD & DRINK

Fish – usually tuna – and rice are staple also common is breadfruit, taro and ban nas. Western foods like hamburgers, san wiches, fried chicken and steak are ofte found, as is fresh sashimi, teriyaki ar ramen. Local drinks include *tuba* (cocon wine) on Yap and sakau (the intoxicatir drink usually called kava; see the boxed te in the Regional Facts for the Visitor cha ter) on Pohnpei. Chuuk is officially dry (b isn't) and Kosrae ostensibly requires drin ing permits (see under Places to Eat in th Kosrae section later in this chapter).

Getting There & Away

AIR

Chuuk, Pohnpei and Kosrae are stopove on Continental's island-hopper ticket b tween Guam and Honolulu, and can be pa of a Circle Micronesia or Visit Micrones

r pass. See the introductory Getting
round the Region chapter for details.

Yap lies between Guam and Palau; in
her words, to get to Yap from other FSM
lands you must stop in Guam.

Continental is the only international car-
er for Chuuk, Kosrae and Yap. Pohnpei is
so served twice a week by Air Nauru,
hich flies to Nauru (with connections to
ustralia, Tarawa and Fiji) in one direction,
ad to Guam and Manila in the other. Airline
ffice details are given under Getting There
 Away in each section later in this chapter;
e the introductory Getting Around the
egion chapter for home office numbers.

eparture Tax

eparture taxes are: US$5 from Pohnpei,
S$10 from Chuuk and US$10 from Kos-
e. Yap has no departure tax.

EA

achties will find regulations detailed
der specific island sections. Note that you
ust obtain clearance at an official port of
try for each state that you visit. Getting
earance for Kosrae does not allow you
e movement within Pohnpei or Chuuk.

You can apply for a vessel entry permit
rior to entering the FSM from the Division
f Immigration and Labor (☎ 320 2605, fax
20 7250, ImHQ@mail.fm), Pohnpei.

Ports of entry are Lelu and Okat harbours
 Kosrae, Kolonia in Pohnpei, Weno
achorage in Chuuk and Tomil harbour and
lithi anchorage in Yap.

RGANISED TOURS

number of US-based dive operators come
 the FSM, particularly Chuuk and Yap.
ee under Organised Tours in the Palau
apter for details.

Getting Around

ap and Pohnpei both have local carriers
at fly to the outer islands.

Chuuk and Pohnpei have excellent
ared taxi systems; Kosrae and Yap have
all private taxis.

All islands have rental car agencies;
prices typically start around US$45 per day
with unlimited mileage.

Hitching is simple on Kosrae, culturally
inadvisable on Yap, definitely discouraged
on Chuuk and difficult on Pohnpei, where
the taxis will pick you up.

Field-trip ships connect the islands
every few months; but their schedules are
unreliable.

Kosrae

● pop 7700   ● area 43 sq miles

Unspoiled Kosrae (pronounced 'ko-
shrye') Island is a casual, unpretentious
backwater, where people consistently return
a smile. A high volcanic island whose
peaks are draped in lush tropical greenery
and sometimes shrouded in clouds, Kosrae
is rich in natural beauty. It has an interior
of uncharted rainforests, a pristine fringing
reef, a coast that mixes sandy beaches with
mangrove swamps and an ancient ruined
city. Religion remains the dominant cultural force.

Information

The tourist office (☎ 370 2228, fax 370
2066, kosrae@mail.fm), housed in a traditional-style Kosraean building in Tofol, is
open from 8 am to 4 pm Monday to Thursday. The post office and the island's two
banks, the Bank of the FSM and the Bank
of Hawaii, are in Tofol.

Local and long-distance telephone calls
can be made from the 24 hour FSM
Telecommunications building in Tofol.
Internet use is US$4 per hour. The island's
small hospital (☎ 370 3012) is in Tofol, as
is the police station (☎ 370 3333, or ☎ 911
in emergency).

Things to See & Do

Tofol The one-room **Kosrae Museum**, up
the dirt road by the farmer's market, has ancient basalt food pounders, adzes made
from giant clam shells, an outrigger canoe
made from a breadfruit and the ship log
from the 1874 wreck *Leonora*.

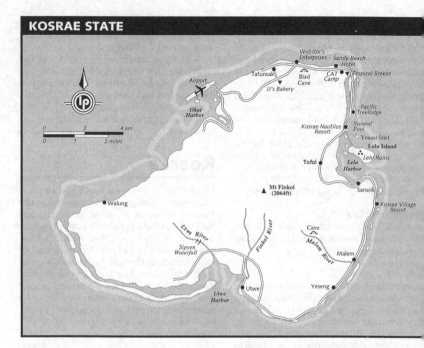

KOSRAE STATE

Webster's Enterprises
Sandy Beach Hotel
Tafunsak
Bird Cave
CAT Camp
Tropical Breeze
Airport
JJ's Bakery
Okat Harbor
Pacific Treelodge
Kosrae Nautilus Resort
Natural Pool
Yenasr Islet
Lelu Island
Lelu Ruins
Tofol
Lelu Harbor
Sansrik
Mt Finkol (2064ft)
Kosrae Village Resort
Walung
Cave
Malem River
Utwe River
Finkol River
Malem
Sipyen Waterfall
Utwe
Yeseng
Utwe Harbor

0   2   4 km
0   1   2 miles

Lelu Lelu Island (also spelled and pronounced 'Leluh') is connected to the rest of Kosrae by a causeway. The early Kosraeans artificially extended Lelu by piling stones and packing coral upon the surrounding reef. Lelu Hill, the island's high point, has caves and tunnels used by the Japanese during WWII.

Lelu Ruins Dating back at least to 1400 AD, and probably as early as 1250 AD, this royal city and feudal capital covered the entire lowland area of Lelu Island. Its ruins, hidden from the road, still cover one-third of the island.

Still extant are the dwelling compounds of some of the high chiefs, two royal burial mounds, a few sacred compounds and numerous large walls of huge hexagonal basalt logs that have been stacked log-cabin style.

To enter the Lelu Ruins, take the driveway between a store and the Lelu Elementary School. Follow the path to the graveyard site

and continue straight ahead through the com plex. Just before crossing the channel tal the stone footpath on the right to get to th impressive **Kinyeir Fulat**, which has stack prismatic basalt walls reaching 20 feet hig and is believed to have been both dwellin compound and meeting house.

The compounds opposite Kinyeir Ful are called **Pensa**. The walls at Pensa a mostly of medium-sized round basalt stone The high chief's feast house occupied th south-eastern compound and the adjace areas of Pensa, used for food preparatio still contain about 20 pounding stones.

Bat is the large dwelling compou across the canal from Pensa. Its high basa walls are thought to be among the newes town, dating from around 1600 AD.

The **Finbata Compound**, to the south Bat, contains the remains of a feast hous while **Lurun**, a high-walled dwelling co pound, offers another example of impressiv stacked prismatic architecture. **Insruun,**

northern end of the complex, is thought
have originally been a dwelling compound
at was later converted for other uses.

Insru and **Inol** contain mounded tombs
at served as temporary resting places for
ceased royalty. It was a sacred area,
used to commoners except for a group of
ailing female mourners who, from the
ne the king was laid in the crypt, kept a
ntinuous watch over his tomb and decay-
g body. After the king's flesh decom-
sed, the bones were ceremoniously
rried to Yenasr Islet and dropped into a
ep, natural hole in the reef.

In 1910 a German excavation found a
ale skeleton in one of the tombs, presum-
ly Lelu's last buried king.

eeping Lady Looking southwards across
lu Harbor towards Tofol you'll see the
gged profile of the 'Sleeping Lady' moun-
n range. To view the profile, imagine a
oman lying on her back facing south-east,
th her hair flowing out behind her head.
ae pointy 'breasts' are easy to spot.

According to legend, the gods were angry
th a woman so they laid her in the sea in
sleeping position and turned her into the
and of Kosrae. That the woman was then
enstruating accounts for the rich red soil
und in the jungle between her 'thighs'.
osraean men used to trek into the interior
gather the red soil from this sacred place
d use it to make a paint for their canoes.

alem Malem, five miles south of Tofol at
e mouth of the Malem River, is Kosrae's
ird-largest village.

Behind the municipal building there's a
all stone monument honouring the island's
0 WWII dead.

The first road to the right past the munici-
l building goes up to a small dam that
arks the beginning of a short, overgrown
ail leading to the old Japanese command
st. The commander's cave-bunker is a few
inutes walk up the right side of the river.

twe Five miles past Malem at the mouth of
e Finkol River, the pleasant village of Utwe
lso called Utwa) houses the **Utwe-Walung**

Marine Park (☎ 370 2321, fax 370 2322,
marinepark@mail.fm), a conservation area
extending between Utwe and Walung; the
office can organise cultural shows and
guided tours.

There's a pretty 45 minute walk from
Utwe up the Finkol River to some nice
pools; ask anyone in Utwe how to get
started. If you want to go all the way up Mt
Finkol you should ask for a guide.

Tafunsak Tafunsak, which stretches along
the entire western flank of Kosrae, includes
the remote Walung village, Okat Harbor,
the airport and Tafunsak village.

Tafunsak Gorge The steep 70 foot gorge in
Tafunsak Village makes for good exploring. The gorge is extremely narrow so be
wary of its flash-flood potential.

To get there, take the path south-east
from Stop n Shop at the crossroads in
Tafunsak Village. It's a 45 minute walk up
the gorge, following an old steel water pipe.

Walung Kosrae's circle road will eventually connect Walung on the west coast with
the rest of the island. Home to just a few
hundred people and lined with lovely sandy
beaches, Walung is the island's most traditional village and rather enjoys its isolation,
though visitors are welcome. The village,
which has the foundations of an old mission, is cut by tidal channels that are
spanned by log footbridges.

You can hike Walung following the southern coast; a guide is essential for the all-day,
arduous trip. It's far preferable to journey by
outrigger canoe, which the tourist office or
the Utwe-Walung Marine Park can arrange
(US$35 return). Alternatively, ask at the
Okat Marina dock about a private speedboat
ride (15 minutes). The tourist office can
arrange homestays on Walung.

Activities
Diving Kosrae has unspoiled coral reefs,
varied marine life and visibility up to 200
feet in summer. Lelu Harbor holds a US
PBY search plane, a 300 foot Japanese
freighter skip-bombed during WWII and

the remains of a whaling ship. Other good spots include the Blue Hole in Lelu, Hiroshi's Point, a drift dive to the south over beautiful soft coral, and the area between Utwe Harbor and Walung.

Kosrae Village Resort (☎ 370 3483, fax 370 5838, kosraevillage@mail.fm), a five-star PADI dive operation, amply accommodates single and handicapped divers. Two-tank dives cost US$80. Open water certification and referral courses are available.

The Australian-run Kosrae Nautilus Divers (☎ 370 3567, fax 370 3568, nautilus@mail.fm) also caters to English speakers. A two-tank boat dive costs US$90. A Blue Hole shore dive costs US$45.

Snorkelling & Swimming The snorkelling and swimming are usually good between Malem and Utwe in winter, though treacherous currents and rogue waves surrounding Malem itself are not uncommon. In summer try near Tafunsak. Also, the north-eastern side of the airport runway is a favourite snorkelling spot, with 15 to 20 foot walls, lobsters, giant clams, stingrays and good visibility, but beware of channel currents.

Snorkellers are often taken to Walung's coral gardens. The Utwe-Walung Marine Park (☎ 370 2321) can arrange mangrove-channel snorkelling trips.

Kayaking & Canoeing A trip through the mangrove channels on the eastern (by kayak) and south-western (by canoe) fringes of the island is magical. Kosrae Village Resort offers guided kayaking tours for US$39. Kosrae Nautilus Divers rents kayaks (US$15 a day) and arranges canoe rentals (US$20). The Utwe/Walung Marine Park (☎ 370 2321) organises nice four to six-hour canoe trips (US$35).

Hiking The hike up the Tafunsak Gorge makes for a pleasant little afternoon outing. The Japanese caves are another, more novel option. The challenging day-long hike from Utwe to the top of Mt Finkol culminates in an incredible view. Call Hanson Nena (☎ 370 5230) of Utwe, who charges US$50 for guiding.

Places to Stay

A tax of 5% is included in the rates list below. All hotels accept Visa; most acce MasterCard.

The only hotel in Tofol is the *Cocon Palm Hotel (☎ 370 3181, fax 370 308* above the post office, with three straig forward but clean rooms with des minifridge and air-con. It's a good value US$37/42 for singles/doubles.

Sandy Beach Hotel (☎ 370 3239, fax 3 2109), on the beach between Tafunsak a Lelu, has a restaurant and 13 adequa rooms with air-con, a desk, minifridge a an oceanfront porch. Rates are US$55/70 smaller cottage is US$35/50.

Pacific Treelodge (☎ 370 2102, fax 3 3060), half a mile north of Kosrae Nauti Resort, has modern rooms with air-cc carpeting, phone and refrigerator in dupl cottages spread around a mangrove por Ask if the restaurant has reopened.

The upmarket Australian-run *Kosr Nautilus Resort (☎ 370 3567, fax 370 356 nautilus@mail.fm)*, a few minutes walk fro the Lelu causeway, has comfortable, mode and clean rooms with minifridge, bath, a con and VCR. Rooms cost US$90/109; ext people are charged US$25.

A few miles south of Tofol, *Kosrae V lage Resort (☎ 370 3483, fax 370 58. kosraevillage@mail.fm)* has pleasant bung lows tucked between the mangrove chann and the ocean. Each bungalow, construct with native materials, has a queen and a si gle bed with mosquito netting, minifridg coffee-maker and ceiling fans and is whee chair accessible. Rooms cost US$70/95; extra bed (US$25) can be added.

Places to Eat

Visitors officially need a drinking permit purchase alcoholic beverages in Kosrae though enforcement waxes and wane Both Kosrae Nautilus Resort and Kosr Village Resort have restaurants that ser alcohol and can issue diners the permit f US$3.

Bill's Restaurant, a Tofol local favouri has good, cheap food; try the sashimi wi rice (US$3.25).

The **Kosrae Nautilus Resort** has a pleasant noke-free restaurant. At lunch, burgers with ies cost up to US$5. Dinners include aghetti, grilled or chicken teriyaki om US$6 to US$10.50. Side-orders of local ods are available; save room for the house ssert, a scrumptious *crepe a la mode* JS$4).

The thatched-roof, open-air restaurant at osrae Village Resort serves some of the land's best food at reasonable prices. The g, healthy mangrove crabs are a worthwhile at. Hungry vegetarians should try the tasty getarian burrito (US$5.50). The seafood lads, made with tuna and mangrove crab, ve a reputation as the island's best.

The bakery at **Tropical Breeze**, on the astal road near the US military Civil Ac-n Team (CAT) Camp, makes tasty ba-na bread, turnovers and other treats. hocolate-frosted donuts (40c) are a relia-e morning find.

All stores (and non-hotel restaurants) close Sunday, so stock up on bottled water and unchies beforehand. **Webster's Enterprises** Tafunsak and **Thurston's Enterprise** in lu are Kosrae's largest general stores.

Fresh fish, live lobster and mangrove abs are sold at the little dock at **Okat Har-r**, by the causeway to the airport. Sashimi-vers should stop at the **FSM Aquaculture enter** on the causeway to Lelu, which sells ant clams the size of mangoes.

The **farmer's market** opposite the tourist fice in Tofol opens on weekday mornings.

hopping

pical Kosraean crafts include wooden ro pounders, carved wooden canoes, oven bags and purses and wall hangings fibres and shells. The Community evelopment Office, behind the old court-use, has a plethora of reasonably priced ndicrafts, including coconut spears, taro ounders, outrigger canoes and head reaths made of shells.

etting There & Away

ere's a Continental office in Tofol (☎ 370 24, fax 370 3112) and at the airport 370 2024).

SeAir Transportation irregularly takes passengers on its Pohnpei-Kosrae cargo runs.

Yachties should notify the Department of Public Works (☎ 270 3011) or the dock (☎ 370 2154) of their intended arrival date. Lelu and Okat are official ports of entry.

Getting Around

Car DJ Car Rental (☎ 370 2308) has cars for US$39 and US$49, the cheapest in town. TE's (Thurston's Enterprise) Car Rental (☎ 370 3991) and Webster George Car Rental (☎ 370 3116) have cars from US$45.

Taxi Thurston Taxi (☎ 370 3991), Kosrae's sole taxi service, has a four-taxi fleet. Prices are very reasonable – it's US$1 from Tofol to Kosrae Village Resort and US$3 to Malem. In general, it's much cheaper to rely on taxis and hitching than to rent a car.

Hitching It's quite easy to get rides around Kosrae; people will often go out of their way to drop you off.

Pohnpei

● pop 36,900   ● area 133 sq miles

Lush Pohnpei Island's abundant rainfall feeds a multitude of streams, rivers, tumbling waterfalls and a spongy, uninhabited rainforest interior. Pohnpei's boldest landmark is the steep, scenic cliff face of Sokehs Rock. The ancient stone city of Nan Madol, abandoned on nearly 100 artificial islets off the south-eastern coast, is Micronesia's best known archaeological site. Outside small-town Kolonia, Pohnpei is unspoiled and un-developed, with just a smattering of small villages.

Activities

Diving & Snorkelling Pohnpei has pretty coral reefs, manta rays and lots of fish. It's also possible to dive Nan Madol.

While snorkelling is not good on Pohnpei Island itself, small nearby atolls have good coral and marine life. Ant and Pakin atolls are favourite diving spots – the former for its schools of barracuda and reef sharks, the latter, for its virgin reefs with gorgonian fans and abundant marine life. Spring, summer and autumn are the best times for diving.

Dive Shops Phoenix Marine Sports (☎ 320 5678, fax 320 2364) is an excellent Japanese dive operation. Two-tank boat dives cost US$65 inside Pohnpei reef, US$75 outside. For Ant or Pakin, add US$10. Snorkelling tours including a visit to Nan Madol and Kepirohi Waterfall cost US$55.

The Village Hotel (☎ 320 2797, fax 320 3797, thevillage@mail.fm) also runs a nice dive operation; rates vary with the number of people and scuba gear is about US$20. Iet Ehu (☎ 320 2958, fax 320 2958) is a local operation that's short on equipment but otherwise friendly. Two-tank boat dives within Pohnpei reef cost US$65, to Ant and Pakin US$85. Iet Ehu does not rent out scuba equipment.

Kayaking Nan Madol, along with Pohnpe[i] mangroves, makes a relaxed kayaking lo[ca]tion. The Village Hotel (☎ 320 2797) re[nts] out single/double kayaks for US$25/35.

Hiking & Other Activities The two ma[in] hikes around Kolonia are on Sokehs Isla[nd;] one is an easy hike up the ridge and [the] other a difficult one up the rock face. B[oth] offer great views. Hikes into the inter[ior] need a guide.

Trolling, bottom fishing and spearfishi[ng] trips can be arranged through most to[ur] companies or dive shops.

KOLONIA
● **pop 3258**

Not to be confused with Yap's Colon[ia,] Kolonia has a slow, frontier-like feel. Do[gs] laze on the side of the roads and every ya[rd] seemingly contains a pen of squealing p[igs] – though the main street allegedly fills w[ith] 'rush hour' traffic.

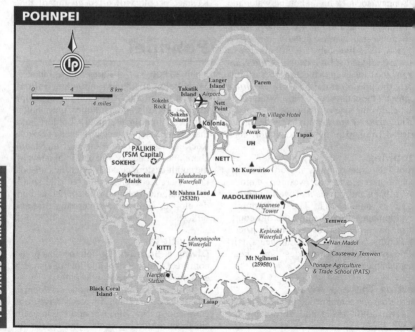

POHNPEI

Information

Tourist Office The tourist office (☎ 320 421, fax 320 6019), on Main St, is supplemented by the equally helpful nonprofit Pohnpei Visitors Bureau (☎ 320 4851, fax 320 4868, pohnpeivb@mail.fm), in the old Agricultural Station just south of town.

Money The Bank of Guam and the Bank of Hawaii occupy a small complex just off Main St. A 24-hour ATM is outside.

Post & Communications Pohnpei's main post office is on Main St. Local and long-distance calls can be made from the 24 hour FSM Telecommunications building on Main St. Faxes can be received free (fax 320 745) and sent for the price of a phone call. Internet access is US$4 per hour.

Medical Services & Emergency The hospital is on the main road heading down the east coast, a mile from Kolonia. It's a rudimentary if inexpensive facility.

For nonemergencies, try the clean Pohnpei Family Health Clinic (☎ 320 5777, fax 320 2229, khni@mail.fm), a few hundred metres from the US embassy and up a short dirt road.

For police emergencies dial ☎ 320 2221; for medical emergencies dial ☎ 320 2213.

Things to See & Do

Pohnpei Lidorkini Museum Displays at this one-room museum near the baseball field include shell adzes, coral pounders, pottery shards and beads found at Nan Madol. There are also weavings and a few rusted WWII items.

German Tower & Spanish Fort Pohnpei's original Catholic mission, founded in the late 19th century by Capuchin missionaries, got its bell tower from the Germans in 1907; the tower survived the WWII bombing raids.

Also in this area are the moss-covered remains of 1887 Spanish stone walls.

Cemeteries Cemeteries in north-western Kolonia hold the Sokehs Rebellion dead.

The overgrown German cemetery, behind the church near the South Park Hotel, has the remains of sailors from the German cruiser *Emden* who died fighting the Sokehs rebels.

The mass grave for the executed Pohnpeian rebels is in a residential area northeast of the German cemetery. Look for the unmarked cement enclosure at the left edge of the dead-end road.

Kapingamarangi Village This village, on the western side of town, is home to the Polynesians who moved to Pohnpei from Kapingamarangi and Nukuoro atolls following cyclone and famine disasters early in the 1900s. They live a more open and outdoor lifestyle than other Kolonia residents (in raised thatched homes) and are known for their excellent craftwork.

Sokehs Island To get to Sokehs Island, take the road to the right at the fork past the Palm Terrace Store. Once you cross the causeway onto the island the road divides and both ways come to a dead-end rather than circle around.

It takes a half-day to walk around Sokehs Island. The northern part is the road the Germans built with forced labour in 1910, an incident that touched off the rebellion. After the rebellion, all Pohnpeians living on Sokehs Island were exiled and the land resettled by people from the Mortlocks in Chuuk and from Pingelap, Mokil and Sapwuafik atolls.

The 900 foot **Sokehs Ridge**, loaded with anti-aircraft guns, naval guns, pillboxes and tunnels, has an excellent view of Kolonia and the surrounding reef as well as nesting tropicbirds and fruit bats. The easy 45 minute trail starts on a 4WD road behind the municipal office.

The sheer, challenging climb up 498 foot **Sokehs Rock** yields a great view. After crossing the causeway, take the road to the right; the trail begins shortly before the end of the road, near the church. A guide is advisable – ask at the municipal office.

Around Pohnpei Island A 54 mile road circles Pohnpei. Close to two-thirds of it is

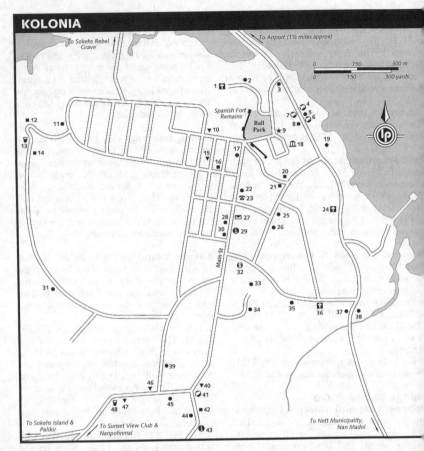

KOLONIA

To Sokehs Rebel Grave

To Airport (1½ miles approx)

Spanish Fort Remains

Ball Park

Main St

To Sokehs Island & Palikir

To Sunset View Club & Nanpohnmal

To Nett Municipality, Nan Madol

paved; the remaining third, on the island's southern rim, is a very rutted dirt road and can easily harm a rental-car belly. It takes about 1½ hours to travel the 22 miles from Kolonia clockwise to the Madolenihmw municipal building, and about four hours to go around the entire island. You'll see a good cross-section of village life: men walk along carrying stalks of bananas or a baskets of yams and children play at the roadside.

There are several magnificent waterfalls off the circle island drive – the 50 foot **Liduduhniap Waterfall** in Nett, a 15 minute

drive from Kolonia; the 70 foot **Kepirol Waterfall** further along in Sapwehrek; an close to Palikir, the 30 foot **Lehnpaipoh Waterfall** with a good swimming hole. As for directions.

An easy trail up the high volcanic cone Pwusehn Malek **Chickenshit Mounta** starts by the telephone pole on the rig side, just over 1½ miles south of the Palik capital complex. Legend says this form tion was created during the defeat of Poh pei's Saudeleur dynasty: Palikir's rul became a giant rooster, flew to Nan Mad and left behind a huge mound of dropping

KOLONIA

PLACES TO STAY
8 Sea Breeze Hotel
12 South Park Hotel
14 Cliff Rainbow Hotel
16 Joy Hotel
20 Nara Gardens
21 Yvonne's Hotel
42 Penny Hotel

PLACES TO EAT
10 Cafe Ole; Ambros Store
15 Joy Restaurant
40 Sei Restaurant
46 Palm Terrace Store
47 China Star Restaurant

OTHER
1 Catholic Church
2 German Bell Tower

3 Iet Ehu Tours
4 Japanese Embassy
5 Ponape Coconut Products
6 Chinese Embassy
7 Australian Embassy
9 Police Station
11 German Cemetery
13 Across the Street
17 SeAir Transportation
18 Pohnpei Lidorkini Museum
19 Public Market
22 Budget Rent-A-Car
23 FSM Telecommunications
24 Protestant Church
25 Kolonia Town Hall
26 GP Car Rental; Tennis Courts
27 Post Office
28 Pharmacy

29 Tourist Office
30 J&T Store
31 Kapingamarangi Village
32 Banks; Travel Agencies
33 State Legislature
34 Pohnpei Supreme Court
35 College of Micronesia
36 Kosrae-Kolonia Congregational Church
37 Pohnpei Cinema
38 Ace Hardware
39 Coin Laundry
41 US Embassy
43 Agricultural Station; Pohnpei Visitors Bureau
44 Pohnpei Family Health Clinic
45 Library
48 Jungle Bar

At **Palikir**, the 135 acre FSM capital complex, built in 1989, incorporates traditional Micronesian architectural designs. Note the Kosraean traditional-style roofs, the black pillars resembling Nan Madol's basalt columns and the beam ends resembling Japanese rai and Chuukese outrigger canoes.

Nan Madol An important political, social and religious centre built during the Saudeleur dynasty, Nan Madol was a place for ritual activity and the homes of royalty and servants. Nan Madol is comprised of 92 artificial islets, extending for a mile, built on the tidal flats and reef off the south-eastern side of Pohnpei, near Temwen Island.

Wide basalt pillars, up to 25 feet long, formed naturally into hexagonal columns. They were quarried on Pohnpei Island and hauled to the site by raft, then stacked horizontally around the islets as retaining walls. The resultant twisting canals have been dubbed the 'Venice of Micronesia'. On the level surfaces were temples, burial vaults, meeting houses, bathing areas and pools for turtles, fish and eels. The eastern half, Madol Powe (upper town), had priests and rituals. The western half, Madol Pah (lower town), was the administration section.

Nan Madol's construction began between 1100 and 1200 AD and continued for another 200 to 300 years. Nan Madol was uninhabited, though recently abandoned, when the first westerners arrived in the 1820s.

The tourist office keeps a helpful brochure of Nan Madol. It's best to visit Nan Madol by boat at high tide, which allows you to easily navigate the twisting mangrove-lined channels and to see the majority of the islets – don't try going by the car-scraping road. Tour companies provide boat tours from Kolonia for US$40. You can also arrange to kayak or canoe through Nan Madol.

See the boxed text 'Nan Madol' in the 'South Pacific Arts' special section.

Organised Tours
For tours try Iet Ehu Tours (☎ 320 2958), Micro Tours (☎ 320 2888, fax 320 5528) or ask at the Village Hotel.

Places to Stay
Camping can be arranged on the uninhabited islands of Ant and Pakin atolls; ask the tourist office to help with arrangements.

Pohnpei has a 6% hotel tax. Almost all of the hotels accept MasterCard and Visa and a few take American Express. Unless otherwise noted, all hotels have air-con, TVs, phones, refrigerators and private bathrooms.

FED STATES OF MICRONESIA

Yvonne's Hotel (☎ 320 5130, fax 320 4953) has six pleasant rooms in an apartment building. It's a few minutes walk from town centre and is reasonable value at US$50/56 (tax included). A room-car package is US$80.

The 18-room *South Park Hotel* (☎ 320 2255, fax 320 2600, southparkhotel@ mail.fm) has a fine hillside location on Kolonia's western side. The new wing has pleasant rooms, each with tile floors and verandahs with a view of Sokehs Rock. Rates are US$75/85. The old wing (US$40/ 45) is also nice but lacks phones.

The *Cliff Rainbow Hotel* (☎ 320 2415, fax 320 5416, cliffrainbow@mail.fm), near the South Park Hotel, has singles from US$40 to $85 and doubles from US$48 to $95. The cheaper rooms are in an older section that's quite ordinary but clean and adequate.

Another reasonably priced option is the *Sea Breeze Hotel* (☎ 320 2065, fax 320 2067), on the harbour road near the Australian embassy. Rooms are good-sized with a single and a double bed. It charges US$50/60 for ocean-view rooms and US$10 less for rooms without the view. In addition to tax, the hotel has a 5% service charge.

Joy Hotel (☎ 320 2447, fax 320 2478, joy_ponape@mail.fm) is a town hotel with 10 nicely-furnished rooms with balconies. Rooms cost US$69/74 and it's US$90 for rooms with two beds (tax included).

The popular *Village Hotel* (☎ 320 2797, fax 320 3797, thevillage@mail.fm) has 20 native-style thatched cottages on a hillside five miles south of Kolonia. Rooms have two queen waterbeds, wicker furniture, private baths and ceiling fans but no air-con, TVs or phones. Rates cost from US$80/90; prime views cost a bit more. Additional guests are charged US$10; children under 12 stay for half-price. Airport transfers cost US$8.

Places to Eat

Cafe Ole, a simple cafe beside Ambros Store, has coffee for 75c, good toasted sandwiches, burgers with fries from US$3 to $5 and plate lunches from US$5; try the sashimi platter (US$5.25).

Joy Restaurant, on the northern side Kolonia, is a perennial favourite with e cellent Japanese food. Fresh fish is the sp cialty, though there are beef and chick dishes. The popular 'Joy Lunch' of fri tuna, rice, sashimi, soup and salad is ju US$5.50. It's open for lunch only from Su day to Friday.

PCR Restaurant, on the way to Soke is popular for its great waterfront setti and consistently excellent food. Its famo Napolitan spaghetti sizzles with fish, oc pus and green capsicum (US$6.50).

The popular *South Park Restaurant* at t South Park Hotel has a nice view of Soke Rock through glass louvered windows. T varied menu includes *oyako donburi* a various fish, chicken and pork dishes. lunch, opt for the fish set (US$5.50).

Outside Kolonia, the open-air thatch restaurant at the *Village Hotel* has an u beatable hillside setting, with a view t wards Sokehs Rock. It's a good breakfa (or Sunday brunch) stop for those headi around the island – try the Pohnpei h cakes topped with thick fruity syr (US$3.50). Dinners include seafood a meat specials (US$14 to $20).

A *public market* is along the waterfro road in Kolonia by the Chinese embas: The modern *Palm Terrace Store* is the land's largest grocery store.

Entertainment

Across the Street is a large open-a thatched-roof bar opposite Cliff Rainbo Hotel with a great hilltop view of Soke Rock. Also try *Rumors*, beside the marir and the *Jungle Bar* beyond the Pen Hotel. A bit more genteel is the *Tattoo Irishman* at the Village Hotel, which ha breathtaking view. Have a tropical drink the thatched gazebo.

Sakau bars are prolific but inconspicuo – ask the locals for the scoop. Within Kol nia people tend to bring flasks to fill and g rather than sit and drink.

Pohnpei's cultural centres offer sho with ritual sakau making, grass skirt wea ing, dances and native food makir Performances can be arranged either

lling Nett Municipality directly (☎ 320
22) or the Pohnpei Visitors Bureau
320 4851). The price is US$50 for one
four people.

hopping

hnpei's fine handicrafts are made by
apingamarangi islanders resident in Kolo-
a. Most common are dolphins, sharks with
al shark teeth, turtles and outrigger canoe
odels with woven sails, all carved of man-
ove or ironwood. There are also manta rays
d dolphins carved from ivory palm nut.
y the Carving Spot Handicraft Shop or the
apingamarangi Gift Shop in Kapingama-
ngi Village. Traditional Micronesian handiafts are sold at Joy Restaurant.

etting There & Away

ir The Continental office (☎ 320 2424) is
the airport, as is the Air Nauru office
320 5963). Village Travel (☎ 320 2777,
x 320 3797) in Kolonia is helpful. See the
etting There & Away section earlier in this
apter for flight details.

oat SeAir Transportation (☎ 320 2865,
x 320 2866) sends irregular boats to Kos-
e and sometimes to Chuuk and Yap.
Kolonia Harbor is Pohnpei's official port
entry. Yachties should notify the port
thority (☎ 320 2793) in advance. The Ru-
ors Marina yacht club is a good place to
lk to local yachties.

etting Around

hnpei's plentiful shared taxis charge
S$1 to go anywhere within greater Kolo-
a, or US$2 to the Village Hotel. Wave
wn the taxis or call Waido (☎ 320 5744)
Lucky 7 (☎ 320 5859).
Rental car companies include GP Car
ntal (☎ 320 5648), Budget (☎ 320
05/8760), H & E (☎/fax 320 2413) and
nny Rent-A-Car (☎ 320 5770); prices
rt at around US$45.

LANDS IN POHNPEI LAGOON

lm-lined Langer Island and Black Coral
and, both a 15 minute boat ride from
hnpei Island in the lagoon, have nice

snorkelling day-trip spots and have very
simple overnight accommodation. Contact
Jerry Barbosa (☎ 320 2769) for Langer and
Dakio Paul (☎ 320 4869) or the dive companies for Black Coral.

OUTER ATOLLS
Ant Atoll

With a palm-fringed lagoon, this atoll lies a
few miles south-west of Pohnpei Island. It
has pristine white-sand beaches, abundant
coral and fish that make for good diving,
and a large seabird colony, including brown
noddies, great crested terns, sooty terns and
great frigate birds.

Pakin Atoll

This atoll is 25 miles off Pohnpei Island's
north-western coast. It is a popular dive spot.

Mokil Atoll

A popular whaling spot of old, this atoll has
friendly people, a pretty lagoon and a 1000
foot airstrip.

Pingelap Atoll

This is known for *kahlek*, a kind of night
fishing (done January to April) that uses
burning torches to attract flying fish into
hand-held nets. Kahlek means 'dancing'
and refers to the way the men holding the
torches have to sway to keep their balance
when they're standing up.

Sapwuafik Atoll

This atoll is well known for its outrigger
sailing canoes, made from breadfruit logs
and assembled using wooden pegs and
coconut fibre twine.

Places to Stay & Eat

Caroline Islands Air (☎ 320 8406) can
arrange a simple *homestay* on Mokil or
Pingelap if given advance notice. Otherwise,
contact the mayor of the island you intend to
visit; the Office for Island Affairs (☎ 320
2710) can help track him down.

Getting There & Away

The only airstrips on Pohnpei's outer atolls
are on Mokil and Pingelap. Caroline Islands

Air (☎ 320 8406) flies to Mokil/Pingelap on Monday and Friday for US$50/65 one way.

The government field-trip ship *Micro Glory* has spotty service; for details contact the Office for Island Affairs (☎ 320 2710).

Chuuk

• pop 57,300   • area 49 sq miles

Chuuk (formerly Truk) is colourful, lively and rough. On hot days village women sit bare-breasted in streams doing laundry and young children run naked around brightly painted houses. Chuuk's sunken wrecks – an entire Japanese fleet – draw enthusiastic divers from all over the world. Most wrecks lie off the islands of Dublon, Eten, Fefan and Uman, and together they represent the largest naval loss in history.

Activities

Diving On the bottom of Chuuk Lagoon rest about 60 Japanese ships, including oil tankers, submarines, cruisers, tugboats and cargo ships, as well as scores of US and Japanese planes. They lie just as they sank in 1944 – some upright, some intact, some in pieces strewn across the lagoon floor. The holds are full of guns, trucks and fighter planes, the dining areas are littered with

WARNING

Despite its dive charms, Chuuk poses a danger to travellers. A high unemployment rate, combined with general languor and sufficient black-market alcohol, has volatile young men idling on the streets all day. Foreign women walking alone will experience constant verbal harassment. It's much better to take taxis, go around with a man or, best yet, don't go out at all. Male and female travellers alike should under no circumstances venture out after dark. Recently a carload of doctors driving at night between Blue Lagoon Resort and Weno's town centre had their car stoned and one man's glasses shattered into his eye.

dishes, silverware and sake bottles. T crews' skeletal remains lie 'buried' at sea

The wrecks have become artificial re for hundreds of vividly coloured cora sponges and anemones. The water is war about 85°F, and visibility is generally 50 100 feet. The wrecks have been declared underwater historical park and can't visited without a guide.

The largest wreck in the lagoon is t *Heian Maru*, a 535 foot passenger a cargo ship. Divers can see the ship's nar and telegraph mount on the bow, as well large propellers, periscopes and a torpe The *Fujikawa Maru*, an aircraft ferry t landed upright in 40 to 90 feet of water, one of the most popular dives. Underwa photographers are drawn to the the ha destroyed munitions freighter *Sankis Maru* for its excellent soft coral formatio

Dive Shops The Blue Lagoon Dive Sh (☎ 330 2796, fax 330 4307, bldiveshop mail.fm), the larger of Chuuk's two d operations, has one-tank/two-tank/nig dives for US$60/90/65. Many US-bas dive companies have package tours; see t companies listed under Organised Tours the Getting There & Away section in t Palau chapter. The smaller Sundance Tou & Dive Shop (☎ 330 4234, fax 330 445 sundance@mail.fm) is beside the Truk St hotel. Two-tank dives cost US$70.

Dive Boats Two popular live-aboard di boats are based in Chuuk Lagoon. The 2 passenger SS *Thorfinn* has a seven-d diving package with up to five dives a d for US$2195. A longer option is a 14 d diving tour of the islands between Chu and Yap for US$4295, which combines c tural exploration with diving. Contact Se ward Holidays (☎ 330 3040, fax 330 425 seaward@mail.fm) for reservations.

The *Truk Aggressor II* (☎ 330 2198, f 329 2629), the reincarnated *Palau Aggre sor*, has week-long trips with 5½ days diving for US$2295. Reservations can made through Live/Dive Pacific (☎ to free 800 344 5662, fax 808-329 262 livedive@compuserve.com) in the USA.

From Truk to Chuuk

To outsiders, the name change from Truk to Chuuk may be confusing, but Chuukese have always called the islands in the main lagoon 'Chuuk' when speaking in their native language. The pronunciation of 'Truk', a Germanic corruption of the name, was used only when speaking in English. Chuuk means 'mountain'.

norkelling Boat trips for snorkellers usually include a visit to the *Dainihino Maru*, small coral-encrusted transport ship that es on its starboard side in 40 feet of water ff Uman.

The Blue Lagoon Dive Shop charges S$55 for its snorkelling tour. Sundance as snorkelling trips for US$50. Both dive ops rent out snorkel sets for US$10.

VENO

pop 15,250   ● **area 7 sq miles**
Veno Island, formerly Moen, is the capital nd commercial centre of Chuuk. It is the agoon's second largest island, and the rgest urban area in the FSM. Many outer landers come to Weno in search of the few b opportunities and end up living in ensely populated poverty.

nformation

he Chuuk Visitors Bureau (☎ 330 4133, x 330 4194, cvb@mail.fm) is tucked ehind the post office. It has a one-room thnographic Centre with love sticks, reck artifacts from the *Fujikawa Maru* nd an *ulong*, a special food bowl that as used to present the season's first harest to the high chief; admission is just S$1.

The Bank of Guam, with a 24-hour ATM, next to Shigeto's Store. Chuuk's only post ffice is in the centre of Weno. Telephone alls and faxes can be made from the 24-our FSM Telecommunications building, ast of the airport. Local calls and faxes ceived (fax 330 2777) are free; Internet cess is US$4 per hour.

The hospital (☎ 330 2216) is in the centre of Weno, up from the government offices. For police emergencies dial ☎ 330 2223; for medical emergencies dial ☎ 330 2444.

Things to See & Do
When the legendary Sowukachaw arrived on Chuuk he stuck a lump of basalt rock on the summit of **Mt Tonaachaw** and built a meeting house from which he ruled all of Chuuk Lagoon.

The steep-sided, 754 foot mountain is the backdrop for the airport and harbour. A trail goes to the top of Mt Tonaachaw from the CAT camp. It's about 30 minutes to the top, where there's a Japanese bunker, one tree and good panoramic views.

East of the airport, the Jesuit-run **Xavier High School**, Micronesia's first and best four year high school, opened in 1953. Originally the site of a German chapel, the land was taken by the Japanese in 1940 and a fortress-like wartime communications centre was constructed. The main building, with 2-foot-thick reinforced concrete walls and vault-like steel doors and windows, miraculously survived two direct hits by US bombers. Visitors can climb the roof for a panoramic view of Chuuk Lagoon and walk around the grounds, provided they don't disturb classes.

An even better view is from the 1930s **Japanese lighthouse** nearby; contact the property owner, Rively Walter (☎ 330 2222), who can arrange a trip for US$10 (and add on Xavier).

Organised Tours
Land tours of Chuuk are rarely inspiring because there's little to see. Try Truk Land & Sea Tours (☎ 330 2438) or Sundance Tours & Dive Shop (☎ 330 4234); land tours are US$20, boat tours US$50. The visitors bureau can also arrange a guide.

Places to Stay
Avoid camping on Weno for safety reasons. Divers with Blue Lagoon can join an overnight excursion to Blue Lagoon's shelters on Fananang Island (Blue Lagoon Island), a 20 minute boat ride from Weno.

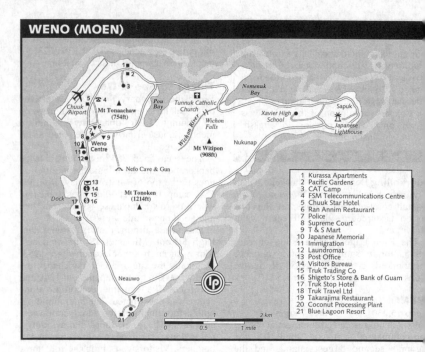

WENO (MOEN)

1 Kurassa Apartments
2 Pacific Gardens
3 CAT Camp
4 FSM Telecommunications Centre
5 Chuuk Star Hotel
6 Ran Annim Restaurant
7 Police
8 Supreme Court
9 T & S Mart
10 Japanese Memorial
11 Immigration
12 Laundromat
13 Post Office
14 Visitors Bureau
15 Truk Trading Co
16 Shigeto's Store & Bank of Guam
17 Truk Stop Hotel
18 Truk Travel Ltd
19 Takarajima Restaurant
20 Coconut Processing Plant
21 Blue Lagoon Resort

Add a 10% room tax and, for larger hotels, a US$30 late checkout fee (if your flight leaves late). Unless otherwise noted, rooms have TV, phone, air-con and private bathrooms. The large hotels often meet arriving flights.

Kurassa Apartments (☎ 330 4415, fax 330 4355), three-quarters of a mile east of the airport, is the best budget option with pleasant, safe, kitchenette-equipped apartments for US$48 (tax included). A room and car package is US$80.

Pacific Gardens (☎ 330 4639, fax 330 2334), a local hotel opposite Kurassa Apartments, is OK but not special. Rooms cost US$55/65.

The **Chuuk Star Hotel** (☎ 330 2040, chuukstar@mail.fm) is a clean, (approaching) upmarket hotel just south of the airport; it charges US$70.50 (singles or doubles; tax included). There's a good restaurant on site.

Truk Stop (☎ 330 4232, fax 330 2286, trukstop@mail.fm) is a popular 23-room

hotel about a mile south of the airport. Rooms are spacious, comfortable and clean with two double beds, minifridges and large showers with good water pressure. Oceanfront/standard units are US$99/9 there's a fax and email service.

The **Blue Lagoon Resort** (☎ 330 2727, fax 330 2439, bldiveshop@mail.fm), at the island's southernmost point, is Weno's only beachside hotel. A pleasantly landscaped hotel for divers, it has well-furnished rooms in two-storey wood buildings, each with a balcony facing the lagoon. Given the safety situation on Chuuk, this may be the best place for divers – you don't have to drive anywhere. Rooms without TV cost US$100/11 add US$3 for TVs. Diving packages are available; airport transfers are US$5.

Places to Eat

Most restaurants offer a combination of American and Japanese foods, while the main street stalls offer traditional Chuukese ms. The unmarked **Ran Annim Restaurant**, in the same shack as the bakery near the power plant, is a simple, inexpensive favourite of Peace Corps volunteers; go for the French toast (US$1.50) or the fried fish (US$4). It's open for breakfast and lunch only. The **Truk Stop Restaurant** serves the island's only pizza (US$9.50 to US$10.50) and has a pleasant lagoon view. **Takarajima** **Restaurant**, near the Blue Lagoon Resort, has Weno's best Japanese food. The *oyakodon*, sweetened chicken and egg atop rice is one of the better deals at US$6.50; most other dishes, like mangrove crab and lobster, are pricier. The **Blue Lagoon Resort** has good food, a pleasant atmosphere and terrific lagoon-side views of the Uichuks, Fefan and Dublon. Dinner ranges from chicken *yakita* for US$7 to black-pepper steak for US$18.

Truk Trading Co, **Shigeto's Store** and **KS Mart** are Chuuk's largest grocery stores.

Entertainment
Though Weno is officially dry, you'd never know it. Beer sells for US$3 a can at the **Blue Lagoon Resort** and at a number of restaurants and small shops with signs saying 'Cold Beer Here'.

Go out at your own risk in Chuuk, where raucous bars can become bottle-hurling scenes in a flash. Stick to the tamer hotel bars at the **Truk Stop Hotel** and the Blue Lagoon Resort.

Shopping
For love sticks and other traditional souvenirs, check Yumi's Handicrafts, opposite the airport.

Getting There & Away
Continental's island-hopper connects Weno with Pohnpei and Guam. Continental's office (☎ 330 2424) is at the airport.

Visiting cruise ships should request an application for entrance from the Chuuk Immigration and Labour Department (☎ 330 2335) and submit it to the FSM Immigration and Labor Division in Pohnpei (☎ 320 4844).

There is no harbour fee on Weno, but contact Chuuk's harbour master (☎ 330 2592) in advance. Weno and Puluwat have the best anchorage and channels in Chuuk.

Getting Around
For car rentals try the Truk Stop Car Rentals (☎ 330 4232) and Kurassa Apartments (☎ 330 4415). Cars cost US$45 to $55.

Licensed or unlicensed, practically every other car declares itself a 'taxi' on Chuuk. Wave them down or try calling Mo's (☎ 330 2668), though its pickup is impressively sluggish. It's 50c for rides in central Weno.

Chuukese Love Sticks

In the days of thatched houses, love sticks were used by courting males to get a date for the evening. These slender sticks of mangrove wood were each intricately notched and carved in a design unique to its owner.

A young man would show his love stick to the object of his desire, so she would be able to recognise the carving at the appropriate time.

If all went well the suitor would wait until the young woman had gone to bed and then push the love stick in through the side of the thatched house and entangle it in her long hair. She would be woken by his gentle tugging, feel the carving to determine who was outside and, if tempted, would sneak out into the night for a secret rendezvous.

MICK WELDON

ISLANDS IN CHUUK LAGOON
Dublon
Both the Germans and Japanese made **Dublon** (population 3000) their administrative centres, but intense US bombings left the Japanese military headquarters in ruins. Most WWII relics are on the island's western side; seeing them generally costs a bit of cash.

Overgrown vegetation in **Sapou Village** partly conceals a ruined city. A former **Japanese naval hospital** can be explored for US$2. Driving counterclockwise from Sapou to the southern side of Dublon, you'll see a large Japanese dome-like **concrete bunker**; the protruding iron pipe served as an air vent. Ahead, take the road's right fork to a **fortified Japanese building** with heavy metal doors and windows and, further on, an old **Japanese seaplane base**. Other island sites include a small **Japanese memorial** and a massive Japanese **cement tunnel**.

Eten Island
From a distance Eten looks like a huge aircraft carrier which, in effect, it was. The Japanese used Chuukese labour to tear down the mountaintops and carry away half the island to turn Eten into an airfield. The island's points of interest include a massive two-storey **concrete structure**, which islanders say was hit by 15 to 20 bombs; one room is amazingly still intact. Nearby are three more two storey Japanese buildings with 2-foot-thick concrete walls and vault-like steel windows and doors. There's a demolished **tower** and a big gun on top of the hill as well as wrecked planes in the water around the island.

Fefan
Fefan Island is known for its abundance of fresh produce and high-quality basketry woven of banana and hibiscus fibres. Mangrove swamps line much of the shoreline, while the forested interior reaches an elevation of 984 feet. Pieces of pottery found in archaeological digs on Fefan date back 1500 years. On Fefan, kids come up and touch you to see if you're for real. They smile, ask your name, follow you around for a minute or two and then go back to whatever they were doing. Most **war reli** are inland on the hills and difficult to reac

Faichuk Islands
The Faichuk Islands, in the western part Chuuk Lagoon, include Tol, Polle, Pat Udot, Eot, Ramanum and Fanapanges. T gether they have one-third of Chuuk population. **Tol**, the largest and most pop lated, is a one hour boat ride from Weno a has Chuuk's tallest peak (Mt Tumuita 1453 feet). Tol's high jungle forest is t sole habitat of the rare Truk greater whit eye. In the 1970s, most Faichuk islande wanted Chuuk to opt for commonweal status with the USA, but a veto by t FSM's president quashed the movemer though it still festers.

Picnic Islands
There are numerous small uninhabit coral islets, many with white-sand beach and good snorkelling, scattered around t lagoon.

For **Falos**, contact the *Falos Beach R sort (☎/fax 330 2606)*, which keeps simp cottages with shared outdoor toilets ar showers for US$45/55, plus tax and bo fare. Bring your own food.

Getting There & Away
Commuter boats and private speedboa leave the main lagoon islands for Weno weekday mornings and return in the ear afternoons – a bit backwards for anyo planning a day trip from Weno. Blue L goon Dive Shop (☎ 330 2796, fax 33 4307, bldiveshop@mail.fm) sometim takes divers to Dublon but more often go to Blue Lagoon Island for camping.

CHUUK'S OUTER ISLANDS
Outside Chuuk Lagoon are the far-flur Mortlocks (south-east of Chuuk Lagoon Hall Islands (north of Chuuk Lagoon) a Western Islands (the most traditional ar nearest to Yap's outer islands). All are fl coral formations, while some are just wis of sand. All maintain a traditional lifesty a day's work might include fishing, cul vating the taro patch or preparing copra.

Accommodation is easiest to find in the ortlocks, where Binte and Reiko Simina ave four simple cottages on a white-sand each on Ta Island for US$30/40, plus S$10 for meals. Call Binte in Weno at 330 4469.

The only way to reach Chuuk's outer isnds is by boat. Two field-trip ships, the *icro Trader* and the *Micro Dawn*, tother make about 40 to 50 week-long trips year. Treat the schedule, available from e transportation office (☎ 330 2592) with epticism. Also call the *Truk Queen 7* ☎ 330 4151) or Chee Young's Family ore (☎ 330 2015).

ap

pop 11900 • **area 46 sq miles**

ap, the land of giant stone money, is the SM's most traditional district. Some men d boys wear brightly coloured loincloths d some women wear only woven hibiscus irts. Everyone has a bulge of betel nut in eir cheek. Out in the villages, which are onnected by centuries-old stone footpaths, *law* (meeting houses for men) are still built the elaborate, traditional style of wood, atch, rope and bamboo. It's a society where e caste system survives and village chiefs ill hold as much political clout as elected ublic officials. The Yapese are a shy yet roud people. For the traveller who treads ently, Yap is a rare place to experience.

AP PROPER

he major islands of Yap, Map and Tomiliagil are all tightly clustered and connected by bridges. Yap Island is the esternmost and largest island, with half of ap Proper's land area and two-thirds of its eople. Rumung is separated from the rest f Yap Proper by Yinbinaew Passage and an only be reached by boat; outsiders need n invitation.

nformation

he Yap Visitors Bureau (☎ 350 2298, fax 50 7015, yvb@mail.fm) is just north of e bridge. The Bank of Hawaii changes

A Land Called Wa'ab

According to one story, when early European explorers first arrived, the natives paddled out to meet them. The explorers pointed and asked the name of the island but the islanders, with their backs to the shore, misunderstood the point. Holding up their paddles they replied '*yap*' – which was their word for paddle. Ever since, the islands that the local residents call Wa'ab have been known to those outside its shores as Yap.

travellers cheques and foreign currencies and does cash advances. Yap Proper's only post office is on the northern side of Chamorro Bay. Long-distance phone calls can be made from the 24-hour FSM Telecommunications building up the hill in Colonia. Faxes can be sent and received (fax 350 4115); Internet access is US$4 an hour.

There's a public hospital (☎ 350 3446) on Colonia's northern side. For police emergencies dial ☎ 350 3333 or ☎ 911.

Things to See & Do

Colonia Colonia (population 1188), on Yap Island in Yap Proper, is the state capital, the business and administrative centre and the only part of Yap that is vaguely modern. Even so, it has the feel of a rustic village. Colonia wraps around Chamorro Bay, named for the Chamorro labourers imported from Saipan to build the transpacific cable station during the German era. For exploring, try the stone footpath across town or a walk to the rai bank and men's house in the nearby village of Balabat. Note the Japanese *torii* (pillared gate) near the state legislature.

A lovely, shaded traditional **stone footpath** starts opposite the waterfront just south of Ocean View Hotel. When the path splits, take the left fork and you'll come out to the paved road just above the Catholic school.

Turn right and go up the road for about 20 feet. A second path, heading down to Chamorro Bay, begins between a dumped car and a pigpen. This path is not as well-lined

YAP PROPER

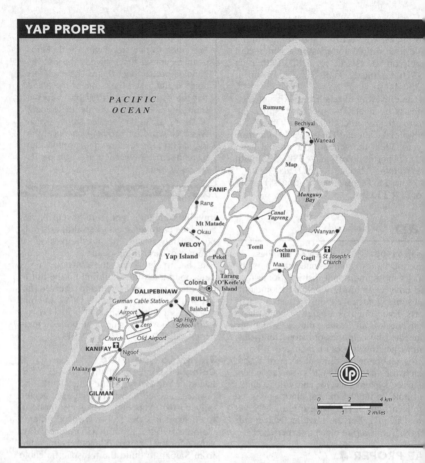

with stones as the first, but it does offer some glimpses of taro patches and village houses.

The mile-long walk to **Balabat village** is a convenient way to see a traditional men's house and rai bank. The road starts at Colonia's petrol station near the bridge. You'll pass Madrich, once the site of a Spanish trading station, and continue along the waterfront to the **Rull municipal office**, where the road is lined with rai; expect to pay US$2.50 to enter. Take the road curving to the right, and two-tenths of a mile along look on the left for a wide dirt road. It's just a couple minutes down to more rai and a **seaside faluw**. The main road ends at two raised **stone platform** used for community gatherings.

German Cable Station & Japanes Zeroes One mile west of the airport, on a unmarked dirt road leading to the left, the old **German Cable Station**, built i 1905, that linked Shanghai through Gua and the Philippines and, nearby, tw **Japanese Zeroes**.

Okau Village Okau village in Weloy ha one of Yap's best fulaw and rai banks at th end of a very pleasant stone footpath.

Yapese Stone Money

Legend has it that ancient navigator Anagumang set sail in search of the ideal stone to be used as Yapese currency. On Palau's Rock Islands he found a hard crystalline limestone that the Yapese then quarried into huge flat discs. Holes were carved in the centre so logs could be slipped through and the stones were then lugged down to barges and towed by canoe 250 miles to Yap.

With their weighty cargo, entire expeditions were sometimes lost in storms at sea. The most valuable stones were not necessarily the largest, but those that were transported at the highest cost of human lives. These stones commonly bore the names of the lost mariners.

Stone money, which the Yapese call *rai*, can range up to 12 feet in diameter and weigh as much as five tons. The Japanese civilian government counted 13,281 coins in 1929.

Most stone money is kept in 'banks' lined up along village pathways. The money is not moved, even when ownership changes. Stone money remains in use today for some traditional exchanges, although the US dollar settles most commonplace transactions.

From Colonia head west towards the airport, but instead of turning left with the main paved road take the right fork onto the side dirt road, which is three-quarters of a mile from the west-side bridge on Chamorro Bay. When the road forks again, bear right, continuing on the wider road. The stone pathway, just over three miles from the airport road, starts on the right opposite a stone platform and just before two small houses and a bridge. The large pebai, about 10 minutes down the pathway, is built on a raised stone platform. Nearby are several thick rai.

Wanyan To get to Wanyan, across Tomilsagil Island, bear left at the fork three-quarters of a mile after the academy, on the road paralleling the power lines. Yap's largest piece of rai is on Rumung Island, but as it's closed to visitors you'll have to settle for number two, in the centre of Wanyan village. Past the fulaw are two huge rai standing along the ocean side of the road. The piece on the left is Yap's second largest. One of Yap's most accessible beaches is Wanyan Beach, at the end of the road, with thatched picnic shelters, restrooms and showers. Expect to pay US$2. Swimming is best at high tide; kayaks can be rented.

Bechiyal Cultural Center Bechiyal is a special place, a friendly beachside village at the northern tip of Map that has a low-key cultural centre. The swimming is good if you wade out for 10 minutes. Visitors are welcome to use the beach in front of the men's house, though the beaches just beyond the village are even nicer and more secluded. For US$10 to $15, snorkellers can be taken out by boat to the channel, where the manta rays feed.

Bechiyal's pebai is the largest on Yap, while its faluw is one of the island's oldest. Inside the faluw are dried turtle skulls and a carved wooden figure that represents the *mispil*, which in times past was a woman captured from a neighbouring village and used as the mistress for the faluw.

The entrance fee to Bechiyal is US$2.50. Video cameras are restricted, though not still photography. Meals, US$3 to $4 each, should be arranged a day in advance. Dinner might well be a hearty Yapese meal of fish or crab, breadfruit, taro and fried banana. Bechiyal's *tuba* has a great reputation. A handicraft hut in Bechiyal sells locally made woven bags, baskets, pandanus placemats, betel-nut bags and toy bamboo rafts.

To get to Bechiyal, drive or take a taxi (US$10) to the end of the Map road (take the lefthand fork). Park and head across the log footbridge. The mile-long path passes through two traditional villages with many rai along the way. Continue straight across when you intersect another road.

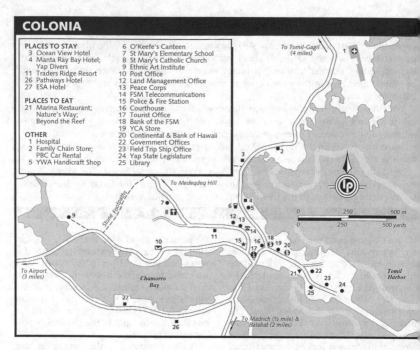

COLONIA

PLACES TO STAY
3 Ocean View Hotel
4 Manta Ray Bay Hotel;
   Yap Divers
11 Traders Ridge Resort
26 Pathways Hotel
27 ESA Hotel

PLACES TO EAT
21 Marina Restaurant;
   Nature's Way;
   Beyond the Reef

OTHER
1 Hospital
2 Family Chain Store;
   PBC Car Rental
5 YWA Handicraft Shop
6 O'Keefe's Canteen
7 St Mary's Elementary School
8 St Mary's Catholic Church
9 Ethnic Art Institute
10 Post Office
12 Land Management Office
13 Peace Corps
14 FSM Telecommunications
15 Police & Fire Station
16 Courthouse
17 Tourist Office
18 Bank of the FSM
19 YCA Store
20 Continental & Bank of Hawaii
22 Government Offices
23 Field Trip Ship Office
24 Yap State Legislature
25 Library

To Tomil-Gagil (4 miles)

To Medeqdeq Hill

Stone Footpaths

To Airport (3 miles)

Chamorro Bay

0   250   500 m
0   250   500 yards

Tomil Harbor

To Madrich (½ mile) &
Balabat (2 miles)

Activities

Diving & Snorkelling Yap has good diving, including virgin reefs with excellent coral, vertical reefs, sea caves, channel drifts, schools of grey sharks and barracuda, sea turtles and a couple of shipwrecks. The reef off Gilman at the southern tip of Yap Proper slopes gently with extensive branching corals, huge lettuce corals and spectacular coral heads. Yap's most novel attraction, however, is its manta rays – gentle creatures with wingspans of up to 12 feet. In winter, they swim through the channel as divers cling to a ledge 30 feet below.

Dive Shops The five-star PADI Yap Divers (☎ 350 2300, fax 350 4567), at Manta Ray Bay Hotel, is Yap's largest dive shop. Two-tank dives are US$95. Beyond the Reef Charters (☎ 350 3483, fax 350 3733, beyondthereef@mail.fm), in the Marina Restaurant, is a friendly alternative dive company with one-tank/two-tank boat dives

for US$60/90. Nature's Way (☎/fax 35 3407, naturesway@mail.fm) has an Englis speaking Japanese dive instructor; one/tw three-tank dives are US$60/90/125. Bo Nature's Way and Beyond the Reef offer one day introductory scuba course and b ginner dives; all three offer night dives f US$50; and snorkellers can join the boat f US$35 to $45.

Swimming & Fishing The most accessib beaches are Wanyan Beach in Tomil-Gag and the beach at Bechiyal Cultural Center Map. Women should cover up on the beac All the dive shops offer fishing trips.

Organised Tours

Guided sightseeing tours cost, on averag US$35 to $45 for a half-day and can b arranged through the hotels and the div shops. Nature's Way and the Pathway Hotel are the best; also try Ocean View an ESA Hotel.

FED STATES OF MICRONESIA

Betel Nut

Everyone, but everyone, in Yap chews *buw*, as betel nut (the nut of the areca-palm) is called. Betel nut is also popular in Palau, in the Solomon Islands, where it's known as *bia blong Solomon* (Solomons' beer), and indeed across South-East Asia and on the Indian subcontinent.

Techniques vary, but in the Pacific the nut is split open while green, then chewed with crushed coral lime and pepper leaves. Together, the three components produce a mild intoxication that lasts about 10 minutes.

The process produces masses of saliva, which is turned vivid-red by the betel nut. It stains the teeth red and will eventually cause them to go black. The lime is highly caustic and, over time, can cause serious mouth ulcers and cancers.

Expatriates (and dentists) regard betel-nut chewing as rather disgusting, but in the Solomons, Yap and Palau, most islanders enjoy a quiet chew. Seeing a foreigner chewing betel nut will bring broad smiles to the faces of locals, and you'll immediately make friends.

Are You Game?

Take the husked nut between your back teeth and crack it near the stem end. Prise it open and pluck the nut out. The technique from then on varies according to where you are.

In Micronesia, the nut is sprinkled with crushed coral lime, wrapped in pepper leaves and then the whole package is chewed. In Yap they sometimes like to combine their vices by adding tobacco, or tobacco soaked in vodka, to their betel nut!

In the Solomons, the nut is chewed alone until it's properly smashed (just keep chewing!). Only then is the rolled-up pepper leaf roll added and masticated, then lime is added and also chewed.

Your chewing technique will largely determine the effectiveness of the betel nut, and you may be underwhelmed by your first try. Watch how others do it. Chew the nut in the back of your mouth to one side. Your saliva will turn bright red and it tastes dreadful!

Be warned that until you're well practised, the voluminous red spit is likely to escape your mouth, run down your chin and stain your favourite T-shirt.

Magical Uses

Betel nuts are widely thought to have magic properties and figure in many folklore stories. According to old timers in Yap, even ghosts chew betel nut. If a sailing canoe was to stop for no obvious reason in the middle of a lagoon the sailor would prepare a special betel nut mixture, wrap it in extra leaves and tie it up tightly with many knots. He would then throw it overboard and sail away easily, while the ghost who'd been holding his canoe was busy untying the knots.

MARTIN HARRIS

Places to Stay

Camping & Homestays *Bechiyal Cultural Center* in Map can accommodate campers (US$5 per person).

The tourist office maintains a list of Yapese families offering *homestays*. Advance notice is preferred but sometimes homestays can be arranged on the spot. They cost about US$20 per person, meals included.

Cyprian Mugunbey (☎ 350 3344, fax 350 7074, cmugunbey@mail.fm) keeps a glorious stilted *bungalow* place near Wanyan Beach – it costs US$25/35 for singles/doubles including one meal.

Bechiyal has a simple stilted wood-and-bamboo *cottage* for overnight guests, who get a mattress, sheets, mosquito nets and lanterns. It's US$20 per person (plus meals). Overnighting at the men's house (women allowed) is US$10 for floor-mat space. Reserve through Chief John Tamag (☎ 350 2939).

Hotels Yap has a 10% hotel tax, which is added to all hotel rates.

The *ESA Hotel* (☎ 350 2139, fax 350 2310, esayap@mail.fm), an older motel-style place overlooking Chamorro Bay, has clean but plain rooms with refrigerators, phones and TVs. It charges US$96.50/104.50 including tax; rooms in the older wing go for US$38.50/49.50.

The *Ocean View Hotel* (☎ 350 2279, fax 350 2339), on the north-eastern side of Colonia, is clean, cheap and unexciting. Rooms have air-con, a small Japanese-style bathroom and minifridge. Singles or doubles are US$44 (including tax). Airport transfers cost US$2. Credit cards are not accepted.

The *Pathways Hotel* (☎ 350 3310, fax 350 2066, pathways@mail.fm), one of the region's best hotels, consists of freestanding hillside cottages that balance modern comforts with traditional Yapese aesthetics. Each cottage was built with native materials and has pleasant sitting verandas, many with a clear view of Chamorro Bay, surrounded by a garden-like setting. Rooms have ceiling fans, air-con and minifridge. The rate is US$115/125, which includes a continental breakfast and airport transfers.

Catering largely to divers, the three storey *Manta Ray Bay Hotel* (☎ 350 2300, fax 350 4567, billacker@mail.fm) has large rooms with modern conveniences, including VCR, air-con, telephone, minibar, and ground-floor water beds. Rooms start at US$132/167, including airport transfers. The hotel has its own dock, dive shop, restaurant and bar.

A new upmarket hotel called *Traders Ridge Resort* (☎ 350 6000, fax 350 4279, tradersridge@mail.fm) was going up on the hill just behind Colonia's post office at the time of writing (US$175).

Places to Eat

There are no restaurants outside Colonia. A great place to dine is the *Marina Restaurant*, a casual, open-air eatery on the waterfront beside the marina. A fresh fish sandwich costs US$2.50 and a hearty fish or chicken dinner with taro, breadfruit, rice, fruit and a drink costs from US$6 to $ (lunch) or US$10 (dinner).

The *Pathways Hotel's* little open-air courtyard makes a nice setting for any meal, whether it's a breakfast muffin and coffee or a plate of fresh fish. Popular seafood dishes go for US$8. Tuesday and Saturday are buffet nights, complete with *tuba* (US$25 for all-you-can-eat; reservations required).

The *Manta Ray Grill*, on the third floor of Manta Ray Bay Hotel, has a nice bayside view and tasty, if pricey, American fare. At lunch, a fish sandwich with fries cost US$8.50; entrees like vegetarian pasta or chicken coconut curry cost from US$10 to $22. The cheese pizza (US$9.50 to $14.50) is Yap's best.

YCA is Yap's biggest general store; it closes early on Sunday.

Entertainment

Colonia's nice open-air bars include the *Marina Restaurant*, which has the cheapest drinks; the *Pathways Hotel*; the *Manta Ray Bar & Grill*; and *O'Keefe's Canteen*.

Maa Village, on Tomil-Gagil Island, opens up to tours on request, with traditional dancing by costumed boys and girls village stroll along a stone footpath and a sampling of local fruits. The two-hour tour (US$45) can be arranged by the hotels.

Shopping

Yap has fine native handicrafts. *Lava-lava* skirts hand-woven of cotton or hibiscus and banana-tree fibres can make attractive wall hangings; also consider handbags or betelnut pouches.

You can buy crafts directly from the artists at the Ethnic Art Institute of Micronesia on Colonia's western side; also try Yap Art Studio and Gallery.

Getting There & Away

Yap is a free stopover on Continental's flights between Guam and Koror (twice weekly in each direction). Continental offices are in the YCA complex (☎ 350 2127) and at the airport (☎ 350 2788).

Yap does not have a harbour or dockage fee for visiting yachts, though this is because they haven't hosted very many. Contact FSM Immigration in Pohnpei (☎ 320 5844, fax 320 5488) prior to your visit.

Getting Around

The island's main paved road begins at the airport, curves through Colonia, and continues through Tomil to the north-east end of Map. Most other roads on the island are packed dirt, though in fairly good condition.

For car rentals try ESA Hotel (☎ 350 2139), PBC Car Rental (☎ 350 2266) and Islander Rentals (☎ 350 2566, fax 350 2555). Prices are from US$40.

Yap's meterless, radio-dispatched taxis cost up to 75c around Colonia and US$2 to the airport. Try Wanyo Taxi (☎ 350 2120) and Savway Taxi (☎ 350 2120).

OUTER ISLANDS

Yap's outer islanders are some of the most isolated people on earth. It's believed that their islands were settled independently of Yap Proper. Yap's easternmost islanders and Chuuk's westernmost islanders have more physical, cultural and linguistic similarities with each other than with either of their district centres.

Most outer islanders live the same way they have for centuries, wearing *thu* and lava-lavas, living in thatched huts and subsisting on fish and farming. Some of the elderly men still have elaborate body tattoos.

Ulithi Atoll, with a huge lagoon, has the most land and the most people (over 1000) of any of the outer islands. It's also the most 'developed' of the outer islands. A 14-room hotel is scheduled to open on Ulithi in July 1999.

A close second to Ulithi in land size and population, **Woleai Atoll** was fortified by the Japanese, and wrecked ships and planes, old tanks, bunkers, field guns and monuments surround its islands. Even the airfield is a former Japanese fighter airstrip.

Fais (population 300) is a single island of raised limestone with a partial fringing reef, sandy beaches, cliffs and sea caves. Its women are known for their skilled weaving of lava-lavas, many of which are created during their stays in the village menstrual house.

Permission to Visit

You should make a request to the Yap Visitors Bureau at least one month before your visit to the outer islands. If the island's chief approves your visit, you will get an authorised pass stating your length of stay. You can then purchase a ticket from either the field-trip ship or Pacific Missionary Aviation (PMA).

Upon landing the pass must be presented

Mau Piailug

Tiny Satawal Island (population 450) is the home of some of the Pacific's most skilled traditional navigators and sailors.

Local hero Mau Piailug found fame when he navigated the *Hokule'a* canoe 4250km from Hawai'i to Tahiti in 1976.

Piailug, who now teaches navigation in Hawai'i, is the hero of Stephen Thomas' book *The Last Navigator*. His recent journeys include New Zealand to Rarotonga (2400km) on the *Te Aurere* in 1992 and Hawai'i to the Marshall Islands (3700km) aboard the *Makali'i* in 1999.

to the island chief, along with a visitor fee of US$20. Bring cigarettes or canned food for your host family.

Getting There & Away

PMA (☎ 350 2360, fax 350 2539) flies a nine-passenger plane a few times a week to Ulithi (US$60 one way), Fais (US$75) and Woleai (US$110).

The field-trip ship *Micro Spirit* does a 14 day (approximately) trip monthly between Yap Proper and all populated outer islands.

Get permits to disembark from the Offi of Outer Islands Affairs in the governme offices complex. Book through the Offi of Sea Transportation (☎ 350 2403, fax 35 2267), on Colonia's eastern side.

For yachties, the best facilities are c Ulithi, Woleai, Ifalik, Elato, Lamotre Sorol and Ngulu. You must get special pe mission from the Council of Tamol (☎ 35 2343, fax 350 4271) to visit the outer i lands and must enter the main island – Ya Proper – before proceeding onwards.

Guam

Guam, an unincorporated US territory, is Micronesia's largest, most populous and most developed island. The Japanese come by the planeload (almost a million per year) to scoop up the duty-free items available at Guam's innumerable malls, while Micronesians from nearby islands haunt the enormous Kmart.

Tumon Bay and Tamuning are terribly overcommercialised, but further out, along the 50 mile circular drive, Guam becomes a kaleidoscope of sleepy villages, stunning waterfalls and pristine beaches.

The US military presence is palpable, with large naval and air force bases closed to casual visitors.

In a push to reassert its heritage, Guam's indigenous Chamorro population is lobbying to return the pre-Spanish names to all of Guam's villages. The name of the capital city, Hagåtña, has just been changed from Agaña, and the rest of the villages may soon follow.

Facts about Guam

HISTORY

The ancient Chamorro were probably from Indonesia and inhabited the Mariana Islands at least as early as 1500 BC.

Their society was stratified and organised in matrilineal clans. Only *matua* (nobility) could become warriors, sailors, artists and fishermen.

The highest-ranking district noble, the *chamorri*, was in charge of local affairs. With no single island-wide leader, interdistrict fights were frequent.

The first western contact with the Pacific islands was on 6 March 1521, when Ferdinand Magellan's *Trinidad* sailed into Guam's Umatac Bay. Magellan named the chain of islands Islas de las Velas Latinas (Islands of Lateen Sails) but retained Guam's local name, Guahan (We Have).

In 1668 the Jesuit priest Diego Luis de Sanvitores established a Catholic mission in Hagåtña. The Chamorro rebelled until

1890, when bloodshed, smallpox and influenza had reduced their population by a staggering 95% to 5000.

In 1898, after the Spanish-American war, the Treaty of Paris ceded Guam to the USA.

813

GUAM

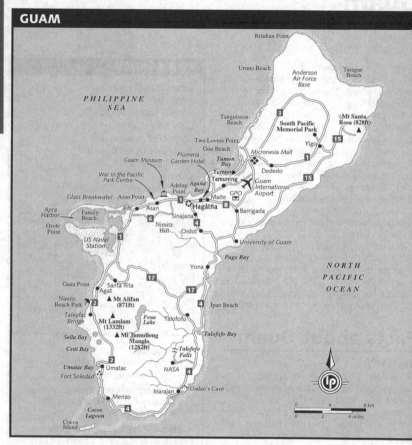

In February 1941, US president Franklin D Roosevelt ordered Guam off limits except to navy-approved visitors – a 'Coconut Curtain' which remained in place until 1962.

Japanese bombers attacked Guam from Saipan on 8 December 1941 and two days later Guam surrendered.

On 12 July 1944 the Japanese military command herded the Chamorro into concentration camps on the eastern side of the island – an ominous move that actually saved lives by keeping the Chamorro away from the US pre-assault bombings on the opposite coast.

The US invaded on 21 July 1944 and se cured Guam on 10 August after heavy cas alties: 17,500 Japanese and 7000 American Hagåtña was a city in ruins, and 200,00 American servicemen moved in to prepar for the invasion of Japan.

When the war ended the US bases be came permanent facilities, and were use later in the Korean and Vietnam wars.

GEOGRAPHY & ECOLOGY

Guam, the southernmost island in the Mar ana Islands chain, is about 30 miles lon and nine miles wide. It is surrounded b

The Spanish Reduction

The villages of Merizo and neighbouring Inarajan were founded in 1695, largely as resettlement sites for Chamorro who were forced to move from the Northern Mariana Islands to southern Guam under a Spanish policy known as 'reduction', intended to more effectively convert and 'Hispanicise' the natives by centralising them on one island. To this day, many inhabitants of Merizo and Inarajan can trace their lineage to the still-uninhabited islands of the Northern Marianas that their ancestors had been forced to abandon.

ef and its highest point rises to 1334 feet. orthern Guam is a raised limestone lateau with some steep vertical cliffs. The outh has high volcanic hills and valleys arved by rivers and waterfalls.

In 1993, Guam was rocked by an earthuake that registered 8.2 on the Richter cale – the worst to hit the region in a cenary. The quake originated deep in the Marina Trench, where seismic activity is ommon, although its effects are usually uffered by the world's greatest ocean epth.

Supertyphoon Paka

Though in the centre of Micronesia's 'typhoon alley' (cyclone zone), Guam has seen nothing like Supertyphoon Paka, which struck on 16 December 1997. Instruments at Anderson Air Force Base in southern Guam recorded wind gusts of 235.7mph (146km/h) – the highest wind speed ever recorded. Miraculously no-one died, but thousands of homes and businesses were wrecked. Guam was immediately declared a disaster area, with damages near US$500 million. The 1997 Christmas season was full of neither joy nor light – especially since the electricity was out for several weeks after the storm.

CLIMATE
Guam's dry season is from January to April.

Guam lies in the path of typhoons (cyclones) and strong tropical storms, which occur most frequently in the last half of the year but can occur in any month.

GOVERNMENT & POLITICS
Guam is an unincorporated territory of the USA. Guamanians cannot vote in national elections and have one non-voting representative in the US Congress. Guam has its own 15 seat legislature. It is trying to change its status from unincorporated territory to US commonwealth, like the Northern Mariana Islands, but Washington will have none of it.

ECONOMY
Despite the Cold War's end, Guam continues to have a heavily militarised economy, as the US pullout from bases in the Philippines has kept up defence spending on Guam.

The tourism industry, a pillar of the economy, has been hard hit by the Asian financial crisis. Towards the end of 1999, the lack of government funds resulted in the retrenchment of hundreds of government employees. 'Non-essential' government services, such as health, were cut drastically.

POPULATION & PEOPLE
The Chamorro are Guam's largest ethnic group (43%), followed by Filipinos (23%) and Caucasians (15%). The population of 153,000 includes about 6300 US military personnel (4000 from the navy), who support 6700 dependents.

ARTS
Indigenous singing, dancing, chanting and cooking are showcased at Guam's many colourful fiestas. Guam has few indigenous handicrafts to speak of, aside from those sold in Hagåtña's Chamorro Village.

RELIGION
Over 90% of Guam's Chamorro population is staunchly Roman Catholic, and the Spanish influence is especially evident in Guam's fiestas.

GUAM

COURTESY OF GUAM VISITORS BUREAU

Warriors and commoners in an ancient Chamorro village in the Mariana Islands

LANGUAGE
Spanish never completely replaced the Chamorro language, even though an estimated 75% of modern Chamorro words come from Spanish; for example 'good morning' is *buenas dias*. Some older residents – and many younger shopkeepers – speak Japanese.

Chamorro Basics
Hello.	*Håfa adai.*
Goodbye.	*Adios.*
How are you?	*Håfa tatamanu?*
I'm well.	*Maolek.*
Please.	*Pot fa bot.*
Thanks.	*Si yu'os ma'åse'.*
Yes.	*Hunggan.*
No.	*Ahe'.*

Facts for the Visitor

SUGGESTED ITINERARIES
Whether you have one day or one week, it's vital to get out of the Tumon Bay/Tamuning area. Guam's sights are individualised and scattered, so you can see a beach one day (Ritidian Point), a waterfall (Talofofo Falls) the next day, then a cultural attraction (Inarajan) the next day, and so forth.

TOURIST OFFICES
Local Offices
The Guam Visitors Bureau (☎ 646 5278, fax 646 8861, guaminfo@visitguam.org in Tumon just south-east of the Hilton, open daily to 5 pm.

Overseas Offices
USA
(☎ tollfree 800-873 4826) 1336-C Park S Alameda, CA 94501

VISAS & EMBASSIES
Guam is under US embassy jurisdiction.

All non-US citizens need a US visa t visit Guam, except Canadians and those eli gible for Guam's visa waiver program. Vis waivers allow citizens of the followin countries to enter Guam visa-free for 1 days maximum (no extensions): Australia Brunei, Burma, Hong Kong, Indonesia Japan, Malaysia, Nauru, New Zealand Papua New Guinea, Singapore, Solomo

ands, South Korea, Taiwan, UK, Vanuatu
d Western Samoa.

USTOMS

sitors to Guam can bring duty-free goods
orth up to $1000. US citizens returning
om Guam are permitted US$800 worth of
uty-free items (compared to the usual
S$400).

MONEY

uam's currency is the US dollar; exchange
tes are listed under Money in the Regional
acts for the Visitor chapter. Credit cards
e widely accepted and automatic teller
achines (ATMs) abound.

The Bank of Guam and the Bank of
awaii together have about 20 branches
ound Guam.

OST & COMMUNICATIONS
ost

uam is included within the US postal ser-
ice and uses US stamps. Post restante
general delivery) mail for Guam must be
icked up at the General Post Office (GPO)
n Route 16 in Barrigada. Mail should be
ddressed care of General Delivery GMF,
arrigada, Guam 96921.

The post office has branches in Hagåtña
nd Tamuning.

elephone

uam's international telephone code is
1-671, and its largest long-distance car-
er is IT&E (☎ 646 8886). IT&E's main of-
ce is along Marine Drive near the
amuning Plaza Hotel. From here you can
all internationally. IT&E also has offices in
Dededo, Harmon, Agat, and Sinajana. It is
ignificantly cheaper to call the USA from
uam than from surrounding islands.

mail & Internet Access

uam's public library has two overcrowded
nternet terminals. Try the Coffee Beanery,
n Tumon's Fountain Plaza along Route 14,
r Crystal Sand Multimedia Services in
amuning (take Route 30 past Shirley's and
urn right at the stop sign). Both charge
JS$8 per hour.

INTERNET RESOURCES

The Guam Visitors Bureau website
(www.visitguam.org) has some useful
tourist information, and the government
website (ns.gov.gu) is useful too.

BOOKS

Lonely Planet's *Diving & Snorkeling Guam
& Yap* has descriptions and underwater
photographs of Guam's best dive sites. *Destiny's Landfall – A History of Guam* (University of Hawai'i Press, Honolulu; 1995),
by Robert F Rogers, comprehensively and
articulately traces Guam's history from Magellan's landing to the present day, with good
attention to Chamorro cultural heritage.

MEDIA

All hotels have cable TV including CNN.
Guam's excellent daily newspaper, *Pacific
Daily News*, carries local, US and international news.

WEIGHTS & MEASURES

Like the USA, Guam uses the imperial system of measurement (feet, miles and degrees Fahrenheit). Use the table at the back
of this book to convert to metric.

HEALTH

Guam's tap water is safe to drink.

The main civilian hospital is the Guam
Memorial Hospital (☎ 647 2330, or ☎ 647
2489 in emergencies) in Tamuning. For routine issues, try the Seventh Day Adventist
Clinic (☎ 636 0894).

There's a 24-hour decompression chamber (☎ 339 7143) at the naval base.

EMERGENCY

For police, fire or ambulance emergencies,
dial ☎ 911. The non-emergency police number is ☎ 472 8911.

PUBLIC HOLIDAYS & SPECIAL EVENTS

On US holidays, government services
close; on Guam holidays, banks shut but
most federal services remain open.

Guam's holidays include: New Year's
Day, Martin Luther King Day, Easter, US

Independence Day, Columbus Day, Veterans' Day, Thanksgiving (see Regional Facts for the Visitor for these dates), and Christmas. Other holidays are:

President's Day	3rd Monday in February
Guam Discovery Day	First Monday in March
Memorial Day	Last Monday in May
Liberation Day	21 July
Labor Day	1st Monday in September
All Souls Day	2 November
Immaculate Conception	8 December

Each of Guam's 19 villages has an annual fiesta honouring its patron saint; the largest fiesta is held in Hagåtña on 8 December.

ACTIVITIES
Diving & Snorkelling
Divers are drawn to Guam's war wrecks and rich marine life. There are several popular dive spots clustered around Apra Harbor. Two of the best sites in Guam, the *Tokai Maru* in Apra Harbor, and the Blue Hole, at the end of Orote Peninsula, are highlighted in the 'South Pacific Diving' special section.

Good snorkelling spots include Gun Beach in Tumon, Ypao Beach next to the Hilton, Outhouse Beach north of Apra Harbor, and the Piti Bomb Holes.

The five-star PADI Micronesian Divers Association (MDA; ☎ 472 6321, fax 477 6329, islands@mdaguam.com), opposi▮ the Piti Bomb Holes, is the region's large▮ dive operation and caters to English spea▮ ers. MDA offers a range of boat div▮ (US$40 for two tanks). Also try Real Wor▮ Diving Co (☎ 646 8903, fax 646 495▮ two-tank dives cost US$95. Check the website (www.mdaguam.com) for details▮

The tourist office keeps lists of other di▮ shops; most court Japanese speakers.

The calmest swimming waters are alo▮ the west coast; Tumon Bay has the busie▮ beaches. Surfing conditions are betwe▮ December and June.

Hiking
Guam has many excellent hikes. Dav▮ Lotz's booklet *The Best Tracks on Gua▮* available in the Bestseller bookshop in M▮ cronesia Mall, gives a good overview.

The Department of Parks & Recreatio▮ (DPR) sponsors guided bushwalks (US$▮ on most Saturday mornings. Call ☎ 47▮ 8197 for the current schedule.

Other Activities
Guam's myriad 18-hole golf courses charg▮ up to US$170/130 on weekends/weekday▮ Contact the tourist office for listings.

The 65 foot *Atlantis* submarine (☎ 47▮ 4166) dives Gab Gab Reef II in Apra Ha▮ bor (US$96 including hotel pick-up). Th▮ semi-submersible *Nautilus Guam* (☎ 64▮ 8331) also tours Apra Harbor (US$25; ski▮ the US$55 hotel pick-up rate).

Brown Tree Snake

The brown tree snake, native to the Solomon Islands, was accidentally introduced to Guam with military cargo in the late 1940s and has wiped out virtually all of Guam's forest birds. Nine of the island's endemic species, including the Guam flycatcher and the Guam broadbill, are now extinct, and others survive in precariously low numbers.

Meanwhile millions of brown tree snakes live without predators on Guam, roaming the forest trees at night and polishing off birds and eggs. With so few birds left to eat, the snakes are resorting to chicken eggs, rodents and lizards.

Adult snakes can reach up to eight feet in length but pose little danger to humans (other than infants), as their venom is mild and is injected through chewing rather than a strike.

Other Pacific island nations worry that the snake may slink onto their islands via cargo from Guam.

Getting There & Away

AIR

Guam's modern international airport is near Tamuning. There are direct flights to Guam from Honolulu, Australia, Indonesia, New Caledonia, the Philippines, South Korea, Taiwan and most Japanese cities. Guam is also a hub for flights to other Micronesian islands.

Continental is the main carrier for Guam (and Micronesia), but there are also flights on Northwest (to Japan, and to Hong Kong via Tokyo), Asiana Airlines (Korea), Air Nauru (Pohnpei, Manila), Japan Airlines (Japan) and All Nippon Airways (Japan).

Two small commuter airlines, Freedom Air and Pacific Islands Aviation, fly between Guam and the Northern Mariana Islands (see that country's chapter for details).

Continental services Indonesia (three days a week), Hong Kong (via Saipan; twice a week), Manila (daily), Taiwan (four times a week), Cairns, Australia (twice a week) and numerous Japanese cities (daily). Its prices peak from June to August, and mid-December to mid-January.

From Guam, Continental flights radiate out to other Micronesian destinations in three directions: To Yap and Koror; to Saipan; and to Chuuk, Pohnpei, Kosrae, Kwajelein, Majuro, Johnston Island (for military personnel only) and Honolulu, a flight known as the island-hopper.

As Continental has a virtual monopoly on Micronesian routes, flights are quite expensive. To Koror (Palau), for example, it's US$365/730 one way/return, including a stopover in Yap.

From Guam to Honolulu via the island-hopper it costs US$700 one way; this allows open stopovers on all islands (except Johnston) in between. Purchasing individual segments of the island-hopper route is much more expensive. Continental also flies nonstop daily between Honolulu and Guam (US$825 return). If you want to island-hop one way and return on a direct flight, you

must piece together two one-way tickets – or opt for one of Continental's money-saving Micronesia air passes (see Air Passes in the Getting Around the Region chapter).

The following airlines have offices in Guam:

Air Nauru	☎ 642 4253
All Nippon Airways	☎ 642 5555
Asiana Airlines	☎ 646 9131
Continental	☎ 647 6453
Freedom Air	☎ 649 2294
Japan Airlines	☎ 646 9195
Northwest Airlines	☎ 649 1665
Pacific Island Aviation	☎ 647 3600

SEA

Apra Harbor is the only port of entry for Guam. Yachties should contact the Marianas Yacht Club (☎ 477 3533) at Apra Harbor.

Getting Around

It's virtually impossible to get around Guam without a car. Hitching is uncommon and dangerous.

BUS

Guam Mass Transit Authority (☎ 475 7433) operates a limited public bus system serving central Guam. The most useful route runs from Hagåtña to Tamuning, Tumon Bay and the Micronesia Mall. Rides cost US$1. Shuttle buses run regularly between the malls and major Tumon Bay hotels.

CAR

Budget (☎ 647 1446), Hertz (☎ 649 6283), National (☎ 649 0110), Toyota (☎ 642 3200), Avis (☎ 646 8156) and Nissan (☎ 632 7300) have booths on the airport baggage claim level. Prices start at around US$50 with unlimited mileage.

Collision damage waivers (CDW) are an additional US$16.

TAXI

Taxi fares start at US$1.80 flagfall. From Tumon Bay it costs about US$10 to the airport. A 10% tip is customary. Try Hafa Adai Taxi Service (☎ 477 9629) or City Taxi (☎ 646 1155).

ORGANISED TOURS

A score of tour companies provide all sorts of sightseeing tours, but most are expensive and in Japanese only. Discover Guam (☎ 649 8687, fax 649 3487) has English-speaking tours for US$45 to $85 per person; ask the tourist office about other English-speaking tours.

Around Guam

HAGÅTÑA

● pop 1400

The capital city of Hagåtña (pronounced 'hag-**aht**-ni-ya'; formerly called Agaña) has been the main centre of Guam since the Spanish period. It has pleasant parks, bridges, historic sites and the Chamorro Village.

Plaza de España & Surroundings

Plaza de España in central Hagåtña is a peaceful refuge of Spanish-era ruins, old stone walls and flowering trees. Later the Japanese used it as a seat of government.

Buildings once surrounded the central park area and included priests' quarters, the governor's residence, a military compound, arsenal and town hall, but only a few buildings survived the US pre-invasion bombings in 1944.

Among those that remain is the **Garden House**, which was formerly a storage shed. A minute's walk north is the **Chocolate House**, a white circular building with a pointed tile roof, where the wives of Spanish governors served guests hot chocolate and other refreshments.

Immediately west of the Chocolate House are the foundation of **Casa Gobierno**, the Governor's Palace. The three storey arches date from 1736 and were originally part of the arsenal.

There's a 10½ foot roadside **statue** of Pope John Paul II north of the plaza on the site where he conducted Mass during 1981 visit. Uniquely, this pope revolves making one complete turn every 24 hours. Near the statue is a **war memorial** honouring Guamanians killed during the Japanese invasion of 10 December 1941.

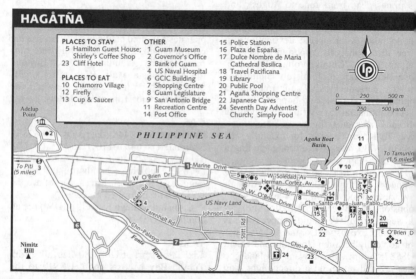

HAGÅTÑA

PLACES TO STAY
5 Hamilton Guest House; Shirley's Coffee Shop
23 Cliff Hotel

PLACES TO EAT
10 Chamorro Village
12 Firefly
13 Cup & Saucer

OTHER
1 Guam Museum
2 Governor's Office
3 Bank of Guam
4 US Naval Hospital
6 GCIC Building
7 Shopping Centre
8 Guam Legislature
9 San Antonio Bridge
11 Recreation Centre
14 Post Office
15 Police Station
16 Plaza de España
17 Dulce Nombre de Maria Cathedral Basilica
18 Travel Pacificana
19 Library
20 Public Pool
21 Agaña Shopping Centre
22 Japanese Caves
24 Seventh Day Adventist Church; Simply Food

The nearby **Dulce Nombre de Maria Cathedral-Basilica** was built in 1669, although the current building dates from 1958. Chief Quipuha, who was Hagåtña's highest-ranking chief when Guam's first mission was built and was Guam's first baptised adult, is buried beneath the floor.

Above the main altar is a 12 inch statue Santa Marian Camarin, which has human hair and an ivory face. Local lore has it that in the early 1800s, two gold crabs with lighted candles between their claws guided the figurine ashore.

Latte Park & Surroundings

The *latte* stones in Latte Park, at the base of Asamata Hill, are thought to be house pillars from about 500 AD and were moved here from south-central Guam.

Latte Stones

Latte stones are the most visible remains of early Chamorro culture. The upright posts were quaried from limestone; the rounded-top capstones were of either limestone or brain coral. Historians believe the stones were used as foundation pillars for mens' houses and the homes of nobility. Latte stones vary from a few feet high to as tall as 20 feet.

NED FRIARY

Numerous Japanese-era **caves**, built by forced Chamorro labour, sprinkle the hillface at the park and farther west along O'Brien Drive.

San Antonio Bridge & Surroundings

Back downhill on W. Soledad Ave, the San Antonio Bridge was built in 1800 to cross an artificial branch of the Agaña River. The bridge survived WWII bombing raids but during Hagåtña's reconstruction, the canal it spanned was filled and the river diverted. However, the bridge still stands and its park-like setting with its seasonal flame trees is attractive.

Paseo de Susana

Paseo de Susana, north of central Hagåtña, occupies an artificial peninsula created during the Hagåtña reconstruction. Today it's a popular park and recreation centre, as well as the site of Hagåtña's **Chamorro Village**, a market with food vendors, produce sellers and a few handicraft artists.

Surveying the traffic-flow stands a **statue** of Chief Quipuha; he donated the land for Guam's first Catholic church, where the basilica sits now.

Guam Museum

This worthwhile little museum, built on an open-air Spanish plaza, stands atop a gorgeous ocean overlook on Adelup Point, not far south of central Hagåtña. Historical displays include an outrigger canoe, portraits of Chamorro chiefs, and traditional fishing equipment.

The museum is open weekdays to 4 pm, Saturdays to 2 pm. Admission is US$3.

TUMON BAY (TOMHOM)

Tumon Bay is Micronesia's most developed resort area and is largely geared towards Japanese package-tourists – which translates to high prices. Gorgeous white-sand beaches are lined with hotels, duty-free shops and restaurants.

Gun Beach, one-third of a mile down the road by the Hotel Nikko, is popular with snorkellers and divers.

Sirena the Mermaid

Overlooking the pool at San Antonio Bridge is a statue of the mermaid Sirena. According to legend, Sirena, a young girl from Hagåtña, went swimming instead of gathering coconut shells as her mother had asked. When she didn't return on time the mother cursed her daughter saying, 'If the water gives Sirena so much pleasure I hope she turns into a fish!' Sirena's godmother overheard the curse and intervened in time to add, 'Let the part that has been given to me by God remain human.' Sirena thus became a mermaid – half fish, half human.

KATE GALBRAITH

NORTHERN GUAM
Two Lovers Point

Two Lovers Point tops a 410 foot limestone cliff just north of Tumon Bay. Head north on Route 1, turn left onto a small road just before the Micronesia Mall and follow the signs.

As the story goes, two young Chamorro lovers entwined their hair and jumped to their deaths to escape a Spanish captain who sought the girl in marriage.

Accessing the actual clifftop point – a platform with a fabulous view jutting out beyond a steep coastal dropoff – costs US$3.

The Point, open until 8 pm daily, [ ] picnic tables, a snack bar and a good s[ ] set view.

Ritidian Point

Ritidian Point, a former coconut plantati[ ] turned into a national wildlife refuge at [ ] northernmost tip of Guam, is a prist[ ] sandy beach that's gorgeously empty [ ] weekdays and filled with picnickers we[ ] ends. It's dangerous and swimmers sho[ ] stick very close to shore.

The refuge is open daily until 5 p[ ] camping is prohibited.

South Pacific Memorial Park

This park on Route 1 in Yigo, a WW[ ] memorial site, has a 30 foot sculpture [ ] large white hands folded in prayer s[ ] rounded by Japanese plaques. A sm[ ] chapel is staffed by Buddhist monks.

Steps lead down the hill from the mo[ ] ment to four caves that served as the [ ] Japanese army command post. On 11 A[ ] gust 1944, US soldiers detonated seve[ ] 400-pound blocks of TNT at the opening [ ] the caves. When the caves were reopene[ ] few days later more than 60 bodies were [ ] moved, including that of the Japanese co[ ] mander, Lieutenant General Hideoyos[ ] Obata, who had taken his own life. T[ ] caves are surrounded by a bamboo for[ ] that creaks in the wind and is spoo[ ] enough to conjure up images of restle[ ] spirits.

The park is open from 8 am to 5 pm dai[ ]

SOUTHERN GUAM
War in the Pacific Park

Further south on Route 1 in Asan, the W[ ] in the Pacific National Historical Park h[ ] an interesting visitor-centre-cum-WW[ ] museum. There are period photos, milita[ ] paraphernalia and a film on the US retaki[ ] of Guam. You can also request to see an[ ] thing in the extensive library of tape[ ] which are in four languages; call ahead [ ] schedule a viewing time. Subjects inclu[ ] Guam's brown tree snakes, Chamorro h[ ] tory and culture, environmental issues a[ ] war battles around the Pacific.

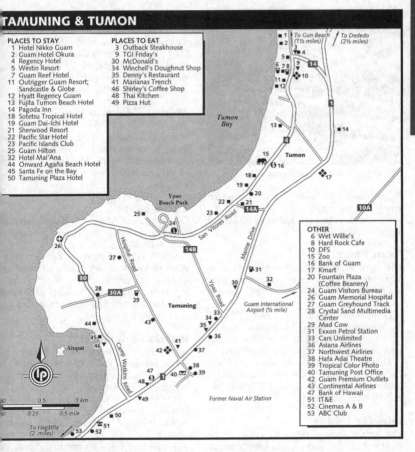

TAMUNING & TUMON

PLACES TO STAY
1 Hotel Nikko Guam
2 Guam Hotel Okura
4 Regency Hotel
5 Westin Resort
7 Guam Reef Hotel
11 Outrigger Guam Resort;
   Sandcastle & Globe
12 Hyatt Regency Guam
13 Fujita Tumon Beach Hotel
14 Pagoda Inn
18 Sotetsu Tropical Hotel
19 Guam Dai-Ichi Hotel
21 Sherwood Resort
22 Pacific Star Hotel
23 Pacific Islands Club
25 Guam Hilton
32 Hotel Mai'Ana
44 Onward Agaña Beach Hotel
45 Santa Fe on the Bay
50 Tamuning Plaza Hotel

PLACES TO EAT
3 Outback Steakhouse
9 TGI Friday's
30 McDonald's
34 Winchell's Doughnut Shop
35 Denny's Restaurant
41 Marianas Trench
46 Shirley's Coffee Shop
48 Thai Kitchen
49 Pizza Hut

OTHER
6 Wet Willie's
8 Hard Rock Cafe
10 DFS
15 Zoo
16 Bank of Guam
17 Kmart
20 Fountain Plaza
   (Coffee Beanery)
24 Guam Visitors Bureau
26 Guam Memorial Hospital
27 Guam Greyhound Track
28 Crystal Sand Multimedia
   Center
29 Mad Cow
31 Exxon Petrol Station
33 Cars Unlimited
36 Asiana Airlines
37 Northwest Airlines
38 Hafa Adai Theatre
39 Tropical Color Photo
40 Tamuning Post Office
42 Guam Premium Outlets
43 Continental Airlines
47 Bank of Hawaii
51 IT&E
52 Cinemas A & B
53 ABC Club

The centre (☎ 472 7240) is open from 9 am to 4.30 pm Monday to Friday and from 9 am to 5 pm on weekends. Admission is free, as are the brochures that map out the various battle sites around Guam.

A number of separate parcels of land that were WWII battlefields are part of the park's historical holdings and some of them are easily visited.

A mile further south, **Asan Point** was one of the major July 1944 US invasion sites. An octagonal marble monument flanked by coconut trees was erected on the beach in 1994 to mark the invasion's 50th anniversary. The area is now a favourite kite-flying and picnicking spot. On the south-west side of the park, a 15 minute loop trail takes in a cave and a couple of Japanese gun emplacements.

Piti Bomb Holes

The Piti bomb holes, carved in the reef about 100 yards offshore, are ideal for beginner divers. No, they're not bomb craters – they're natural sinkholes.

The largest bomb hole contains a new, environmentally controversial underwater observatory called **Fish Eye Marine Park**.

WWII coastal guns

Portholes 30 feet down give good close-up views of fish, coral, and scuba divers. It's open weekdays to 5 pm and costs US$20/10 for adults/children.

Gaan Point

The park at Gaan Point, on Route 2 in Agat, was one of the main landing sites for the July 1944 US invasion of southern Guam.

From their coastal caves and pillboxes the Japanese cut down Americans jumping from their landing crafts. It took the Americans three days to secure the beachhead.

There's an 8 inch naval coastal defence gun, an anti-aircraft cannon and intact bunkers as well as a diveable US WWII amtrac 50 feet underwater.

Taleyfac Bridge

The best-preserved Spanish bridge is in Agat at Taleyfac, just beyond **Nimitz Beach Park**, on the ocean side of the road and a few hundred feet from Route 2. The picturesque 36 foot bridge has twin stone arches that span a narrow river.

Umatac (Humåtak)

Unspoiled Umatac commemorates Magellan's 1521 arrival in Umatac Bay each March with four days of activities, including a landing re-enactment. There's a tall **monument** to Magellan in the village centre. Attractions include the decorative **Umatac Bridge** and a diveable Japanese Zero **fighter-plane wreck** in the bay.

Fort Soledad

Fort Nuestra Senora de la Soledad, built the Spanish in the early 1800s to prote their Manila galleons from pirates, offer lovely hilltop view of Umatac Bay; tu right on the ironwood-lined road aft crossing the Umatac Bridge.

Merizo (Malesso')

The courtyard of San Dimas Church Merizo, Guam's southernmost villag holds a **monument** to 46 Chamorro w were executed by the Japanese in the Me zo hills in July 1944, one week before t US invasion.

Cocos Island

Offshore from Merizo is Cocos Island, 1½-mile-long atoll with good beaches a calm waters.

Cocos Island Resort (☎ 828 8691) is popular Japanese day-trip destination a offers every conceivable water sport (co ing from US$25 to $80). Boats go to Coc from the Merizo Pier between 9 am and pm (US$40).

Inarajan (Inalåtak)

Sleepy Inarajan along the south-east coa holds **Salugula Pool**, a natural saltwa pool, with diving platforms and arch bridges now in disrepair.

The body of Chamorro priest Jesus Ba Duenas, beheaded by the Japanese WWII, is buried in Inarajan's **Saint Joseph Church**.

The waterfront **Chamorro Cultural V lage** is a complex of thatch shelters whe coconut candy making, weaving and oth Chamorro crafts are demonstrated in th morning (US$8).

Talofofo Falls

Talofofo Falls is a lovely two-tier cascad A gondola ferries visitors down the ste grade from the parking lot to the falls and small museum nearby.

A 10 minute trail through the jung leads to the **Yokoi Caves**, where a Japane soldier, Corporal Yokoi Shcoichi, subsist for 28 years after WWII.

To get there, take the marked turn-off
m Route 4, turn right about 1½ miles
wn (just before the NASA station) and
low the signs. Admission is US$13/5 for
ults/children.

ACES TO STAY
mping

mping is uncommon but many parks
ow it. Visit the DPR (☎ 475 6288) in
yan in Barrigada to get a US$2 per head
rmit; shelters cost US$10 more.

otels

e high-rises lining Tumon Bay contain
st of Guam's 8700 hotel rooms. All ho-
s, except for a few budget ones, accept
sa and MasterCard, and most top-end
tels charge US$15 return for airport
nsfers. All hotel rooms have air-con TV,
one, refrigerator, private bathroom, and
e subject to 11% tax unless otherwise
ted. Some Guam hotels, including the
amilton Guest House, have 'hourly' rates;
nerally these are sleazier establishments.
Hotel prices are liable to rise once the
sian economies rebound.

udget The spacious *Guam Garden Villa*
☎ 477 8166) is Guam's only B&B. It's in
pleasant family setting in Ordot, about
ree miles from Hagåtña. The house is spa-
ous, with a porch and garden, and two
est rooms with shared bathroom. The rate
$40/50 for singles/doubles (tax included);
is includes a hearty breakfast. It's usually
oked up – call far in advance to reserve.
Tamuning Plaza Hotel (☎ 649 8646, fax
9 8651, tphotel@kuentos.guam.net), near
e Ben Franklin store in Tamuning, has
rge rooms and is well maintained. It has a
undromat on site, free airport transfers,
d restaurants aplenty nearby. Rates are
S$60/70 for singles/doubles (subtract
S$20 if the economy is bad).
Hamilton Guest House (☎ 477 6701, fax
77 6700) is a bit tired but clean and con-
nient to central Hagåtña (as well as to the
irley's downstairs). The price is US$40
r person (tax included). Airport transfers
e unavailable.

Harmon Loop Hotel (☎ 632 3353, fax
632 3330) has 61 rooms above a small shopping centre on Route 16 across from Mc-
Donald's, about two miles east of the airport.
Rooms are straightforward but modern. The
location's not special but if you're just there
to sleep it's good value at US$50/55. Airport
transfers are usually unavailable.
The popular *Plumeria Garden Hotel*
(☎ 472 8831, fax 477 4914, plumeriagh@
kuentos.guam.net), on Route 8 in Maite, has
nice rooms flanking a courtyard swimming
pool. Rooms cost US$55.50/61 (tax inclu-
ded); there's a 20% weekly discount.
Hotel Mai'Ana (☎ 646 6961, fax 649
3230, maiana@ite.net), quarter of a mile
west of the airport, has rooms with kitchenettes, and a pool and sauna. Rates begin
at US$88/99 for a studio/one-bedroom unit
(tax included).
The pleasant *Regency Hotel* (☎ 649
8000, fax 646 8738), a 10 minute walk from
the beach, is great value for Tumon (US$85
per room).

Top End The plush *Guam Hilton* (☎ 646
1835, fax 646 6038, gumhilt@ite.net), at the
quieter end of Tumon Bay beside Ypao
Beach, has a swimming pool and lighted
tennis courts. Rates begin at US$185/215
for singles/doubles.
The 455-room *Hyatt Regency Guam*
(☎ 647 1234, fax 647 123) is among Tumon
Bay's swankiest, with a grand pillared
lobby, beautifully landscaped grounds and
rooms with oceanfront balconies, soaking
tubs and voicemail. It has a nonsmoking
floor and excellent restaurants. Rates begin
at US$210/225 for singles/doubles.
The immaculate *Sherwood Resort* (☎ 647
1188, fax 647 1166, sherwood@hafa.net.gu)
in Tumon may not have a beach backyard
but it still manages an air of grandeur. For a
luxury hotel, the rates are reasonable
(US$150 for singles and doubles).
The 600-room *Outrigger Guam Resort*
(☎ 649 9000, fax 647 9068) is among
Tumon's top resorts, with rates from
US$240 to $700.
Contact the tourist office (☎ 646 5278)
for a list of Tumon's other resorts.

PLACES TO EAT

Guam has a rainbow of different cuisines to choose from. Restaurants at the resort hotels excel in Japanese food and Sunday brunch.

A tip of 10 to 15% is generally expected.

Budget

Chamorro Village, Hagåtña's public market, is the best place for a cheap and tasty local meal. Numerous tidy huts sell plate lunches of local favourites such as spicy chicken *kelaguen* (minced chicken with lemon, onions, pepper and shredded coconut) and barbecued spareribs with red rice for US$3 to $5. In Chamorro Village, *Jamaican Grill (☎ 472 2000)* is a popular stop for a sit-down or take-away meal; try the scrumptious Paseo Vegetarian, a colourful plateful of grilled tomato, eggplant and onion on a heaping bed of rice. Also in Chamorro Village, *Carmen's* serves up excellent Mexican food (US$4 to $10). For Chamorro food, get a Fiesta Plate (US$5) from *Terry's*. Chamorro Village is also the best place to find fresh fruits and vegetables.

Shirley's Coffee Shop, a Guam institution renowned for great food and mammoth servings, has a branch on Route 30 in Tamuning that's open 24 hours on weekends. The endless menu includes omelettes, steak, cashew dishes, crepes, pasta, chop suey and burgers (most items well under US$10). Shirley's has branches in Harmon, Mangilao, Hagåtña and the airport.

Fabulous Thai food is served at *Thai Kitchen*, in a droopy office complex on Marine Drive in Tamuning. If you're driving from Hagåtña, it's on the left just past Pizza Hut. Pink tablecloths, low lighting, and soft music create a romantic setting; main dishes are priced at US$7 to $12.

McDonald's, Wendy's, Burger King, Pizza Hut, Subway, Winchell's and *Denny's* are ubiquitous.

Top End

Among Guam's umpteen steakhouses, the standout is *Outback Steakhouse*, just north of Planet Hollywood along San Vitores Road in Tumon Bay. The Bloomin' Onion

appetiser – a small forest of marvellou crispy, spicy onion sticks – can fill you Steaks cost about US$20.

Firefly, on Martyr St in Hagåtña, is upscale bistro serving gourmet me seafood and pasta dishes. Pepper-crust tuna (US$18) is a perennial favourite. It' good refuge from the tumult of Tumon B

La Mirenda (☎ 546 3463) at the Hy has a good buffet lunch (US$15) that cludes a dessert table of fresh fruit a tempting cakes and pies. There's also popular seafood buffet Wednesday and F day evenings; make reservations.

Worth a splurge is *Roy's Restaura (☎ 646 3193)* in the Guam Hilton, whi serves superb Pacific Rim cuisine. The go cheese in filo with roasted red capsic (bellpepper) and eggplant salad makes a n starter at US$6. For dessert, the hot choc late souffle (US$7) is a rare treat.

ENTERTAINMENT

For local flavour, try the *Chamorro Villa* in Hagåtña on Wednesday evening. Starti at 6 pm, the village bursts into a colour mini-fiesta with bands, dances, craft sta and barbecued Chamorro food.

Planet Hollywood, the *Hard Rock Ca* and the snazzy, multi-theme-room *Globe* Tumon's Sandcastle Entertainment whopping US$30 cover) are wildly popu with the younger crowd.

On a mellower note, there's a great su set view from the wraparound windows the *Salon del Mar* in the Guam Ho Okura. *Sante Fe on the Bay*, a new hotel Tamuning between Shirley's and Onwa Agaña Beach Hotel on Route 30, is a nice but pricey (margaritas cost US$6.5 Guam has several cinemas.

SHOPPING

Most Guam souvenirs are trinkets made the Philippines; opt for the handicraft fro the stalls at Chamorro Village in Hagåti For supplies, make a pilgrimage to Guam massive Kmart, a few miles south of t Micronesia Mall. Should you need design clothes, Guam has three major malls a countless duty-free shops.

US Territories

...ce the 19th century, the USA has claim... several small islands in the North Paci-... Most are narrow coral reefs, and most ...re claimed under the 1856 Guano Islands ...t – see the boxed text – in the heyday of ... phosphate hunt.

...Some territories, like Palmyra and King-...n, are privately owned. Jarvis Island is ...imed by the Marshall Islands, and Kiri-...ti has recently asked the USA for How-...d, Baker and Jarvis so that it can extend ... Exclusive Economic Zone (EEZ).

...With the exception of Palmyra, none of ...se islands is open to visitors; many are ...dlife refuges and none have the facilities ...support visitors en masse. For information ...the national wildlife refuges, contact the ...h & Wildlife Service (FWS) in Honolulu ... 808 541 1201, fax 808 541 1216).

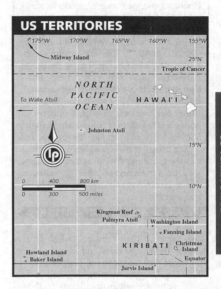

...owland Island

...eeless and barren, the uninhabited ...ldlife refuge of Howland is home to ...ds, turtles, and other animals that can live ...its harsh environment. There is no fresh-...ter and only scrub vegetation. Howland ...s mined for phosphate until 1878.

...Howland is most famous as the intended ...uelling stop for US aviator Amelia ...rhart on her round-the-equator trip in 1937. An airstrip was built in 1937 in an-ticipation of her landing, but Earhart and her navigator Fred Noonan never made it. It appears that they could not locate the island and instead came down elsewhere in the Pacific. Her fate remains unknown, but theories abound – the most dramatic being that she was captured by the Japanese dur-ing WWII and taken to Mili Atoll in the Marshall Islands. The most recent hypoth-esis is that her bones were found on Niku-maroro, in Kiribati's Gilbert chain – see the boxed text 'Was Earhart Found?'

Baker Island

Like Howland, uninhabited and barren Baker Island belongs to the Phoenix Island group. At its highest point, Baker reaches 27 feet. The island has a fringing coral reef and is a breeding area for pelagic birds and stop for migrating shorebirds; it also has marine turtles.

Guano Islands Act of 1856

'... Whenever any citizen of the United ...tates discovers a deposit of guano on any ...sland, rock or key, not within the lawful ...urisdiction of any other government and ...ot occupied by the citizens of any other ...government, and takes peaceable posses-...ion thereof, and occupies the same, such ...sland, rock, or key may, at the discretion ...f the President, be considered as apper-...aining to the United States ...'

Was Earhart Found?

The mystery of Amelia Earhart and Fred Noonan's disappearance en route to How-land Island may finally have been solved.

British soldiers discovered two sets of bones and shoes on remote Nikumaroro (Kiribati) in 1941. The remains were pro-nounced by a British doctor to be the bones of two European men. In late 1998, how-ever, the doctor's notes were re-examined, leading modern specialists to conclude that the doctor was wrong – that one set of bones belonged to a Caucasian female, 5'7" or 5'8" tall – just like Amelia Earhart.

The bones, meanwhile, have long since vanished, though it is suspected that they may be somewhere in the Fiji museum. The museum has commenced an exhaus-tive search.

In the mid-19th century, whalers fre-quented Baker and Howland for provisions. Phosphate was mined in the 19th century. In 1935 the US government planted a few colonists to strengthen its claims to the is-land, but they were evacuated in 1942 when the Japanese attacked. The next year, 2000 US troops arrived and built an airstrip. Baker became a national wildlife refuge in 1974 and refuge employees visit a few times a year.

Jarvis Island

Jarvis' nearest neighbour is Kiribati's Christmas Island. Like Christmas, Jarvis is part of the Line Islands group and its dry climate stifles all but grasses and small shrubs. Migratory birds, however, abound. Like Palmyra, the island is also an impor-tant green turtle nesting spot.

Phosphate mining operations com-menced in 1858. The next inhabitants were colonists, sent by the US government in 1936 to firm up the US territorial claim. They were evacuated in 1942 and the island remains uninhabited. In 1974 the island be-came a national wildlife refuge. The FWS visits every few years.

Palmyra Atoll

Palm-lined Palmyra comprises 52 islets su rounding three lagoons. Americans aboa the ship *Palmyra* first discovered the at in 1802, but it was not until 1862 th Hawai'i claimed it. The USA also (sep ately) claimed the atoll around that ti under the Guano Islands Act. Howev when the USA annexed Hawai'i in 1898 annexation act specifically exclud Palmyra from the state of Hawai'i becau it turned out to have no guano and had th been unlawfully claimed.

In 1922, Hawai'i's Fullard-Leo fam bought Palmyra for US$15,000 and h owned it ever since, though the navy bu an airstrip and some buildings there duri WWII. Since the mid-1990s, however, t family has appeared willing to sell it. T first major bidder, a New York corporatio was on the verge of purchasing it for $ million, but its plans to use Palmyra as a r clear waste dump sparked an outcry fro across the Pacific. The most recent like purchaser to emerge is the Nature Cons vancy, a major US conservation group th would turn Palmyra over to the FWS.

Currently, one couple lives on the isla which has large WWII rainfall cachmer and is relatively fertile. The boat pier a wide harbour makes Palmyra an attracti stop for visiting yachts, but you must ask p mission first. Contact the Palmyra Develo ment Company (☎ 1-808-942 7701, fax 9 5429). The Fullard-Leo family permits catc and-release fishing, snorkelling and diving

Kingman Reef

Treeless, triangular Kingman, with a ma mum elevation of just 3 feet, is little mo than a 5000 sq foot coral head surround by a massive reef. Like Palmyra 35 miles the south, Kingman Reef is owned by t Fullard-Leo family. Kingman was disco ered in 1798 by a US whaler, but nam after Captain WE Kingman of the US ve sel *Shooting Star*, who came by in 1853. was claimed under the Guano Islands A

hough subsequently it was discovered to
ntain no phosphate.

In 1934, Kingman was placed under the
ntrol of the US Navy, and it remains
der navy jurisdiction.

Vake Atoll

ake Atoll consists of three small islands
eale, Wake and Wilkes) with a total land
ea of 2.5 square miles. Wake is named
ter a British captain who landed there in
'96. The USA officially claimed it about a
ntury later when a US ship heading to the
ilippines during the Spanish-American
ar planted the US flag on Wake in 1898.

Originally intended as a cable station,
ake served as a refuelling base for trans-
acific flights during the 1930s; a 48-room
otel supported the base and its 9800 foot
rstrip. After WWII, the US Navy adminis-
red Wake until 1962. Now, the US Army
ace and Strategic Defense Command
SDC) controls Wake and keeps 300 people
ere. The Marshall Islands has laid claim to
e atoll on the grounds that it's part of the
atak chain. On the US side there is some
lk of making Wake a national wildlife
fuge. For now it is off limits.

ohnston Atoll

hnston Atoll consists of two natural coral
lands (Sand and Johnston) and two artifi-
al islets, North and East (Akau and Hik-
a). The reef that encloses the islands is
out 21 miles in circumference. Viewed
om the air, Johnston Island has a most un-
ual shape, its shoreline extending out in
ard straight lines. This is because soil was
ooped up from the lagoon during WWII
d used to lengthen the runway.

Johnston's other geographic distinction is
s isolation. It's 717 nautical miles south-
est of its nearest neighbour, Hawai'i, which
akes it a useful refuelling stop for Conti-
ntal Airlines flights bound for Micronesia.

In 1796, Captain Johnston of HMS *Corn-
allis* came ashore. Johnston was claimed

by the USA and Hawai'i in 1858 – Hawai'i
arrived three months after the USA, ripping
down the US flag and putting up the
Hawai'ian flag. When Hawai'i became a
US state in 1898, the USA separately annexed Johnston Island. The atoll's limited
phosphate deposits were mined until the
early 20th century. In 1926, Johnston became a national bird refuge. However, its
peace was interrupted in 1934 when it came
under navy control and was used as a submarine refuelling base and air base. The air
force took over the islands in 1948, and the
North and East islets were created over the
next 15 years.

Since 1990, Johnston Island has served
as a disposal site for weapons – one of nine
US sites devoted to this purpose. Over 1200
US military and contract workers live on
Johnston and are busy destroying 6% of the
world's weapons arsenal – including mines,
missiles, mortars, rockets, bombs and VX
nerve gas – all stored on Johnston. According to the most recent report, 77% of Johnston's weaponry has been destroyed
including all the volatile sarin nerve gas.

Continental uses Johnston as a refuelling
point, but passengers without permission
from the US military cannot disembark.
Yachts are not permitted within 3 miles of
Johnston Island.

Some Wildlife Refuge!

Johnston Island is the Dr Jekyll-and-Mr Hyde
of the Pacific. While infamous as a chemical
weapons cleanup site, it is simultaneously a
national wildlife refuge. Thousands of birds,
including boobies, shearwaters and terns,
use it as a migratory or nesting stop. All told,
Johnston has over 300 species of fish, 20
species of native and migratory birds and 32
species of coral, as well as green sea turtles,
dolphins and humpback whales. If the US
military finishes its operations in 2001 as
planned, Johnston will be turned over in full
to the Fish & Wildlife Service to run as a national wildlife refuge. Then – at long last –
Johnston may slowly return to nature.

Kiribati

The Republic of Kiribati (pronounced 'Kiribas') encompasses the Gilbert, Phoenix and Line islands. Measured by land size Kiribati is a tiny nation, but its 33 atolls span 3.5 million sq km of ocean.

The passing centuries have had little impact on Kiribati's outer islands, where people still subsist on coconuts, giant prawns, octopuses and fish. Even on the main island, Tarawa, most people live in thatched huts – though cars, litter and even the Internet give notice of mounting western influence.

The I-Kiribati revel in their rich natural resources. Small, wide-eyed children chirp a bold *mauri* (hello) to passing strangers, while their elders spend afternoons relaxing in thatched *maneaba* (village meeting houses). Traditional singing and dancing remain integral to everyday life.

Facts about Kiribati

HISTORY
The first settlers, most likely from the Caroline and Marshall islands, came to the Gilbert Islands and Banaba over 3000 years ago. The Phoenix and Line islands never supported permanent settlements, though archaeological evidence suggests occasional pre-European landings.

The early Gilbertese settled in distinct *kainga* (hamlets). Except in northern Butaritari and Makin, where centralised chiefs governed, each kainga had a maneaba. Most communities also had a *bangota*, a shrine to ancestral gods. The I-Kiribati were fierce warriors, known for their sharp shark-tooth spears.

Due to its isolation, Kiribati was bypassed by the Spanish and Germans and saw just a scattering of whalers, traders, blackbirders and missionaries in the 19th century. On 27 May 1892, British captain EHM Davis of the HMS *Royalist* declared the Gilbert & Ellice islands a British protectorate (the Ellice Islands are present-day

AT A GLANCE

Capital: Tarawa Atoll
Population: 86,800
Time: 12 hours ahead of GMT (Tarawa)
Land Area: 811 sq km (315 sq miles)
Number of Atolls: 33
International Telephone Code: ☎ 686
GDP/Capita: US$545
Currency: Australian dollar (A$1 = US$0.65)
Languages: English & Gilbertese
Greeting: *Mauri*

HIGHLIGHTS

• **Traditional dancing** – colourful, vibrant and easy to arrange – just get yourself invited to a *maneaba*

• **Homestays** – relaxing with a fresh coconut in one of North Tarawa's houses on stilts over the aqua lagoon

• **War relics** – enormous WWII guns from the bloody 1943 Battle of Tarawa

• **Outer islands** – life moving at a relaxed pace, locals salting clams or weaving thatch

• **Christmas Island** – bonefishermen and birdwatchers unite!

Tuvalu). Three years later, Tarawa became the administrative capital.

In 1900, geologist Albert Ellis of the Pacific Islands Company discovered the

Rabi Island Resettlement

After WWII ended, widespread destruction on Banaba made it impossible for the hundreds of deported Banabans to return, so they agreed to resettle for two years on the island of Rabi (pronounced 'ram-bi'), off the coast of Fiji's second-largest island, Vanua Levu. Rabi had been bought for £25,000 in 1942 by the British Phosphate Company with Banaban phosphate trust money. The first Banabans arrived on 15 December 1945 and within two years voted to remain on Rabi. Now citizens of Fiji, the Banabans on Rabi have become a separate community, closed to tourists and accessible only by sporadic ship. (To get there you must obtain permission from the Banaba Island Council on Suva.) They have one representative in the Kiribati parliament.

claimed Banaba, not far from Tarawa, was loaded with high-grade phosphate – 20 million tons of it. Mining operations swiftly commenced. The British folded Banaba into the protectorate in 1901 and moved the administrative capital there in 1908 (though Tarawa later regained its status as the capital). In 1916, the protectorate became a full-fledged colony and the Union Islands (modern-day Tokelau) were incorporated (they were off-loaded to New Zealand in 1925). Christmas Island and other Line Islands were added in 1919, and the Phoenix Islands joined in 1937.

In December 1941, Japan bombed Banaba (Ocean Island) and also took Butaritari, Makin and Tarawa. In mid-1942, US marines raided Butaritari to distract the Japanese from their Guadalcanal thrust. Japanese reprisals against both Gilbertese and Europeans were harsh, and they fortified Betio, one of Tarawa's islets.

In November 1943, US marines attacked Betio and, after three days of bloody fighting, gained control of the island. While the battle had no lasting strategic import, it did demonstrate the utility of amphibious tractors – amtracs.

Road to Independence

Kiribati's independence movement heated up in the 1960s, simultaneously with those of the Solomon Islands and Fiji. A series of governing structures were gradually instituted, culminating in an elected House of Representatives (1967) and a House of Assembly (1974).

On 12 July 1979, a year after the secession of the Ellice Islands (see the boxed text 'Independence for Tuvalu' in the Tuvalu chapter), the Republic of Kiribati, consisting of the Gilbert, Phoenix and Line islands and Banaba (whose secessionist movement had been quashed) became an independent nation, ending 87 years of British rule. It was a cruel – perhaps calculated – irony that the new nation's independence coincided with the exhaustion of Banaba's rich phosphate reserves. Before independence, phosphate mining on Banaba accounted for 45% of Kiribati's GDP and 85% of its exports.

GEOGRAPHY & ECOLOGY

Kiribati's oceans stretch 3870km east to west. The country is composed of three main island groups: the 16 atolls of the Gilbert Islands chain, north of Fiji; the eight atolls of the Phoenix Islands, south-east of the Gilberts; and the Line Islands chain, even further east. Banaba, 400 kilometres west of the Gilberts, is a raised coral atoll. The other islands are flat coral atolls with central lagoons and long, spindly islands. The Line and Gilbert Islands are split by the equator, whereas the Phoenix Islands lie just south of it.

Rising sea levels have mildly eroded some atolls. See the boxed text 'Global Warming' in the Facts about the South Pacific chapter.

CLIMATE

Butaritari in the north consistently has the highest annual rainfall (318cm in 1998), followed by Tarawa. Because of Kiribati's proximity to the equator, it is out of the path of typhoons (cyclones).

GOVERNMENT & POLITICS

Kiribati is a member of the British Commonwealth, was admitted to the UN in

KIRIBATI

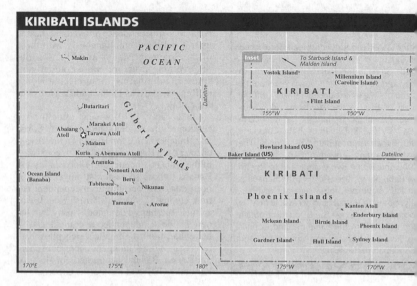

KIRIBATI ISLANDS

PACIFIC OCEAN

Makin

Butaritari

Gilbert Islands

Abaiang Atoll
Marakei Atoll
Tarawa Atoll
Maiana
Kuria Abemama Atoll
Aranuka
Nonouti Atoll
Ocean Island (Banaba)
Beru
Tabiteuea
Nikunau
Onotoa
Tamana Arorae

Dateline

Howland Island (US)
Baker Island (US)

Dateline

KIRIBATI

Phoenix Islands

Kanton Atoll
Enderbury Island
Mckean Island Birnie Island Phoenix Island
Gardner Island Hull Island Sydney Island

Inset

To Starbuck Island & Malden Island

Vostok Island
Millennium Island (Caroline Island)

KIRIBATI

Flint Island

155°W 150°W

170°E 175°E 180° 175°W 170°W

1999, and operates on a Westminster-style parliamentary system. The 41-member Maneaba ni Maungatbu (House of Parliament) is popularly elected every four years, as is the President (Beretitenti). The Maneaba convenes in a traditional maneaba.

Island councils control local government; they work closely with the *unimane* (old men), the traditional village elders.

ECONOMY
Most I-Kiribati maintain a largely subsistence lifestyle. Copra (dried coconut meat), Kiribati's principle export, earns A$4 million annually; almost all goes to Bangladesh where it is used in the manufacture of cosmetics.

Kiribati's principal asset is the 3.5 million sq km Exclusive Economic Zone (EEZ), which earned Kiribati A$42,464,000 in 1998 from foreign fishing licences. About 1700 I-Kiribati seamen work on foreign (mostly German) vessels and send back money to their families. Tourism is marginal except on Christmas Island.

POPULATION & PEOPLE
With an average of 4.5 children per family, Kiribati's population pressure is severe. An internal resettlement program is trying shift people from overcrowded South Tara to the Phoenix and northern Line Islands.

ARTS
Typical I-Kiribati crafts include wood baskets, mats and conical fishermen's h made from pandanus, carved outrigger o noes, woven bags and purses, and neckla of fibres and shells. Most are made on t outer islands and shipped in to Tarawa.

Kiribati's colourful, rhythmic chants a dances are one of the highlights of Mic nesia. Dancing remains an important part local culture, and the largest hotels in ea district centre – the Captain Cook Hotel Christmas Island and the Otintaii Hotel Tarawa – both have regularly schedul dance performances.

SOCIETY & CONDUCT
If you are invited to enter a maneaba, y will be expected to participate by giving speech and/or singing a song; prepare yo best patriotic melodies.

The I-Kiribati are split fairly evenly b tween the Roman Catholic Church and t (Congregationalist) Kiribati Protesta

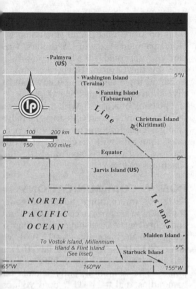

KIRIBATI

Maneaba

Found throughout Kiribati, *maneaba*, or traditional meeting houses, have sloping thatched roofs and locally woven mats. Typically the largest building in the village, inside the maneaba is an environment of respect and strict social hierarchy. By design, the pointed roof of the maneaba drops below a normal person's height, so you must duck respectfully to enter.

The *unimane*, or old men, sit cross-legged in the maneaba centre and conduct the meeting; they are always served food before everyone else. So respected is the sanctity of the maneaba that if a man commits a crime against another person, his best option is to run to the nearest maneaba where he will be protected from the wronged family's vigilante justice.

hurch. Other faiths, including Baha'i, are presented, and there are a small number of ormons.

ANGUAGE

iglish is the official language of Kiribati, at the indigenous language, Gilbertese, edominates. Even on South Tarawa, many cals know only a smattering of English.

The most dificult aspect of pronouncing ilbertese words concerns the letters 'ti' at e end of a word; they should be pro-unced 's' – which is why Kiribati is pro-unced 'kiri-bas'.

The name Kiribati is a transliteration of iilberts', after a British captain who spot-d the islands in 1788. Locals still some-nes refer to the Gilbert chain as 'Tungaru'.

ilbertese Basics

ɔllo.	*Ko na mauri.*
ɔodbye.	*Tia bo.*
ɔw are you?	*Ko uara?*
n well (thanks).	*I marurung (ko raba).*
ease.	*Taiaoka* or *bubuti.*
nanks.	*Ko raba.*
s.	*Eng.*
ɔ.	*Tiaki.*

Facts for the Visitor

SUGGESTED ITINERARIES

If you have one week it's best to tour the war relics on South Tarawa, the main island, and then head for Abaiang (the only outer island readily accessible by boat) or to rustic North Tarawa. Those with more time and flexibility might consider Butaritari. From Honolulu, Christmas Island is a one-week trip.

TOURIST OFFICES

See Information in the Tarawa and London sections for local tourist offices.

Kiribati is represented abroad by the Tourism Council of the South Pacific (see contact details in the Regional Facts for the Visitor chapter).

VISAS

Citizens of Britain, Canada and New Zealand can enter visa-free for a 28 day maximum stay.

Citizens of other countries, including the USA and Australia, need visas (A$40 single-entry, A$70 multiple-entry). Send a completed application, your passport, one passport photo and the payment to a Kiribati diplomatic mission (see later in this section). Visas can be granted upon entry, but it's best to notify the immigration authorities prior to arrival. Upon arrival, you will get a one-month visitor permit that can be extended three times.

Travellers to Christmas Island can get visas immediately before departure, as Kiribati's Honorary Consul in Hawai'i shows up at the Honolulu airport just before the weekly flight.

If you notify the Kiribati immigration authorities that you are doing anthropological work or other 'research', you will be charged astronomical immigration fees.

EMBASSIES & CONSULATES
Kiribati Embassies & Consulates
Kiribati's diplomatic representation abroad includes:

Australia
  (☎ 02-9371 7808, fax 9371 0248)
  Honorary Consul-General; 33 Dover Rd, (PO Box 376) Rose Bay, NSW 2029
New Zealand
  (☎ 09-419 0404, fax 419 1414)
  Honorary Consul; 3 Gladstone Rd, Northcote (PO Box 40205 Glenfield), Auckland
UK
  (☎/fax 1873-840 375)
  Honorary Consul; The Great House Llanddewi, Rhydderch Monmouthshire NP7 9UY
USA
  (☎ 808-521 7703, fax 521 8304)
  Honorary Consul; 850 Richard St, Suite 503, Honolulu, HI 96813

Embassies & Consulates in Kiribati
High commissions in Bairiki, Tarawa, are:

Australia
  (☎ 21 184, fax 21 440)
New Zealand
  (☎ 21 400, fax 21 402)

MONEY
Kiribati's currency is the Australian dollar (denoted A$; exchange rates are listed under Money in the Regional Facts for the Visitor chapter), although a few transa[c]tions on Christmas Island (including M[ ] Hotel payments) are in US dollars. Cre[dit] cards are accepted (for a hefty commissi[on] only by the Otintaai Hotel, the bank a[nd] Tobaroai travel agency on Tarawa and t[he] dive shop on Christmas Island.

The bank of Kiribati, with three branch[es] on Tarawa and one on Christmas Island, [ex]changes cash foreign currency for a poo[r] rate than it will exchange travell[ers] cheques. Kiribati has no Automatic Te[ller] Machines (ATMs).

POST & COMMUNICATIONS
Kiribati's international telephone code [is] ☎ 686; there are no area codes. Only Tara[wa] and Christmas Island have more than o[ne] telephone; North Tarawa (☎ 027 100), M[ari]ana (☎ 027 101), Abaiang (☎ 027 102) a[nd] Marakei (☎ 027 103) each have one te[le]phone. The remaining outer islands ha[ve] ham radios; dial ☎ 21 411 to book your ca[ll.]

INTERNET RESOURCES
Kiribati's government website (www.ts[ ].net.ki/kiribati) has links to some use[ful] tourist information.

BOOKS
For a good history, particularly of t[he] Gilbert & Ellice Islands' failed marria[ge,] try Cinderellas of the Empire – Towards [a] History of Kiribati and Tuvalu (Australi[an] National University Press, Canberra, 198[2] by Barrie Macdonald.

Atoll Politics – The Republic of Kirib[ati] (Macmillan Brown Centre for Pacific Stu[d]ies, 1993), edited by Howard Van Trease, [is] a collection of informative essays by lea[d]ing I-Kiribati politicians and scholars.

A Pattern of Islands by Arthur Grimble [is] a charming, if sometimes a bit patronisin[g] account of the islands during the era [of] British colonialism.

MEDIA
Kiribati has no television stations; Rad[io] Kiribati airs brief Australian news broa[d]casts. A weekly news leaflet, Uekera, is [in] English and Gilbertese.

Millennium

The International Dateline has moved many times since early European circumnavigators of the globe complained of losing a day on the trip.

The Dateline used to split Kiribati down the middle – until January 1, 1995, when the Republic of Kiribati (quite legally) shifted part of the Dateline eastward. The stated purpose of the move was to unite Kiribati's dispersed atolls on the same side of the Dateline. Previously, when it was Friday on Christmas Island, it was already Saturday on Tarawa.

This move propelled tiny Kiribati onto the cutting edge of global millennium fever. Recently, many countries recognised the tourist potential in being the first to welcome the 'new millennium' at the start of 2000. Tonga, Fiji, New Zealand and Kiribati all launched massive promotional campaigns. Even being the last to see the old millennium was worth a tourist buck.

Being so far east, Kiribati's Line Islands simultaneously start each new day (and each new year) one full hour before anyone else. However because of the earth's tilt, they don't always see the first sunrise. The first spot of land to see the sun rise each New Year's morning is near Victor Bay on the Antarctic coast. Caroline Island (recently renamed Millennium Island), one of Kiribati's uninhabited southern Line Islands, is the second land to see the sunrise. The first *inhabited* land is Pitts Island in the Chathams (New Zealand). The only land actually crossed by the 180° line (apart from the Russian mainland and Antarctica) are a handful of Fijian islands. The last sunset of the year (not counting Antarctica) is at Falealupo in Samoa.

Competition for the top spot has been fierce. Critics have claimed that Kiribati's massive kink in the Dateline, as well as Fiji and Tonga's temporary introduction of daylight-saving time, are somewhat artificial. But they're no more artificial than the choice of 180° longitude (as far from London as possible) or New Year's day (the feast of the Roman god Janus) or counting years since the theoretical birth of Christ.

Of course the pedants amongst us have known all along that the new millennium doesn't start till 1 January 2001.

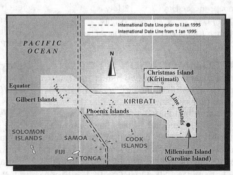

KIRIBATI

TIME

The time on Tarawa is GMT + 12; Christmas Island is GMT + 14.

ELECTRICITY

Electricity is 240V AC, 50Hz, and an Australian-type three-slot plug is used. On Christmas Island, some plugs are US two-prong style and voltage may also differ.

WEIGHTS & MEASURES

Kiribati uses the metric system.

HEALTH

Kiribati has periodic outbreaks of dengue fever. Boil all tap water before drinking.

BUSINESS HOURS

Typical hours are weekdays from 8 am to 4.30 pm, while banks are open from 9.30 am to 3 pm; anticipate a leisurely lunch break.

PUBLIC HOLIDAYS

Kiribati's holidays include New Year's Day,

Cutting Toddy

Kiribati's local brew is *kaokioki*, or sour toddy; it fills the niche of the kava drunk on othe[r]
Pacific islands. Essentially it's fermented sap tapped from the coconut tree. The syrupy 'swee[t]'
toddy' skips the fermentation stage.

'Cutting toddy,' as the extraction procedure is called, is done by I-Kiribati men and require[s]
technique and skill. First, the man shimmies up a coconut palm and wraps a rope rightl[y]
around the branch. He ties on a container to catch the sap, which is collected twice dail[y]
Most men cut their toddy twice a day, in the mid-morning and again in mid-afternoon
Particularly on the outer islands, men sing merry adulations of their girlfriends or wives a[s]
they cut toddy.

Sour toddy is ubiquitous but you won't find it in restaurants or bars. Instead, just ask [a]
local to point you to the nearest toddy purveyor. A word of caution: toddy is often dilute[d]
with tap water, which is not likely to be boiled.

When walking along the road, glance up at the coconut trees for the innocuous glass bottles

Easter, Christmas, Boxing Day, plus the following:

Health Day	9 May
Independence Day	12 July
Youth Day	1 August
Human Rights Day	12 December

ACCOMMODATION & FOOD

Christmas Island has two hotels and Tarawa has a handful; none are very luxurious. More pleasant and traditional are the homestays and bungalows on North Tarawa.

Each of the outer islands has a resthouse run by the island council, with generator electricity and mosquito netting. Quality varies but the price is usually A$25 per night.

Coconuts, fish and rice are traditional foods. Sour toddy, made from coconut sap, is the local alternative to Victoria Bitter.

Getting There & Away

AIR

Only Tarawa and Christmas Island are serviced by international flights. Air Nauru flies from Nauru to Tarawa to Fiji and back on Tuesday and Thursday; from Nauru you can continue to Melbourne or Brisbane or to Pohnpei and Guam. Buy the ticket as far [in] advance as possible to get a low-fare sea[t]

Air Marshall Islands flies twice-week[ly] between Majuro and Tarawa for A$2[ ] each way.

An Aloha Airlines 737 chartered by A[ir] Kiribati has a weekly service betwe[en] Honolulu and Christmas Island.

Departure Tax

Tarawa and Christmas Island each have [a] A$10 departure tax.

SEA

Supply ships occasionally go to Fiji a[nd] Tuvalu (see Getting There & Away in t[he] Tarawa section).

Fanning and Christmas islands are pop[u-] lar with yachties. Visiting yachts must cle[ar] customs on Banaba (Ocean Island), Tara[wa] or Christmas (Kiritimati) Island before pr[o-] ceeding to their destination. Tarawa, Fa[n-] ning and some of the outer Gilberts ha[ve] good channels and harbour facilities; s[ee] those respective sections for details, or [di-] rect questions to the Ministry of Info[r-] mation, Communications, and Transport [in] Tarawa (☎ 26 003). Policy with respect [to] yachts tends to evolve fairly rapidly.

ORGANISED TOURS

Most tourists to Christmas Island go [on] package sportfishing or diving tours; s[ee]

the Christmas Island section for details. Valor Tours (☎ 415-332 7850, or ☎ tollfree 500 842 4504, fax 415-332 6971) in the USA, which specialises in WWII history, can help arrange a trip to Tarawa.

Getting Around

AIR

Air Kiribati flies to most outer Gilberts at least once a week. Its planes are occasionally grounded for lack of fuel or encounter some other trouble, so it's wise to allow a bit of extra time if you're planning a visit to one of the outer islands. There are no flights to the Phoenix or Line islands (except the Aloha plane from Honolulu to Christmas Island).

BOAT

Most of the outer Gilberts are serviced by supply ships from Tarawa every month or two, and ships go very occasionally from Tarawa to Christmas, Fanning and Washington. There is an almost daily boat to Abaiang, the closest of the outer islands.

BUS, CAR & MOTORCYCLE

Tarawa has an efficient minibus service, while Christmas Island's fledgling service has a one-bus fleet. On both islands car rentals are available; on the outer islands you may be able to rent a bicycle or a motor scooter or get a boat ride, but there likely won't be many trucks.

Driving is on the left side of the road.

Tarawa Atoll

pop 33,300   **• area 64 sq km**

Triangle-shaped Tarawa is divided into North Tarawa and South Tarawa; the south the locus of all government activity and services, while the rural north approximates an outer-island experience. South Tarawa is home to more than a third of Kiribati's population. Most live on the islet of Betio at the westernmost tip. Betio was the site of a bloody victory over the Japanese by US

marines, and still has huge guns along its beaches and rusting tanks just offshore. Bairiki, in South Tarawa between Bikenibeu and Betio, has most of the government buildings.

Information

Tourist Offices The helpful tourist office (☎ 26 157, fax 26 233, commerce@tskl .net.ki) is on a small dirt road behind Betio's shipping storage facilities.

Money The Bank of Kiribati in Bairiki has branches in Bikenibeu and Betio.

Post & Communications The central post office is in Bairiki; branches are in Betio and Bikenibeu.

International telephone calls can be made from the Telecom Services Kiribati Limited (TSKL) office in Bairiki, which has an Internet terminal (A$30 per hour).

Emergency The hospital (☎ 28 100) is near the airport. For police emergencies dial ☎ 992; for medical emergencies dial ☎ 994.

Things to See & Do

Cultural Centre The new cultural centre in Bikenibeu, open weekdays, has a smattering of local artefacts, including coconut-fibre torso armour.

War Relics Relics from the 1943 US invasion of Betio are still scattered through the atoll. Toward the end of the Betio causeway are large **eight-inch guns** easily visible from the road.

Further along, the **cemetery**, on the left side of the road, is speckled with bunkers, some quite large. There's also a moving **memorial** to 22 British slaughtered by the Japanese on 15 October 1942.

An **eight inch gun** occupies Betio's western tip, and another gun emplacement guards the aptly named **rubbish tip**. A nearby **Japanese memorial garden** has a Shinto shrine, a Korean shrine and an anti-aircraft gun. Just beyond are Red Beach One and Red Beach Two, where the marines landed.

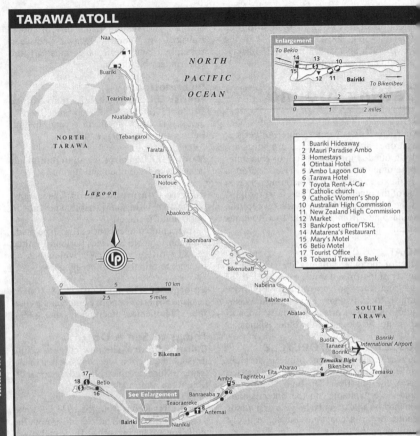

TARAWA ATOLL

NORTH PACIFIC OCEAN

Naa

Buariki

Tearinibai

Nuatabu

NORTH TARAWA

Tebangaroi

Taratai

Taborio
Notoue

Lagoon

Abaokoro

Tabonibara

Bikenubati

Nabeina

Tabiteuea

Abatao

SOUTH TARAWA

Buota
Tanaea
Bonriki

Bonriki
International Airport

Temaiku Bight
Bikenibeu

Temaiku

Abarao

Tagintebu Eita

Ambo

Banraeaba

Teaoraereke

Antemai

Nanikai

Bairiki

Betio

Bikeman

Enlargement

To Bekio

Bairiki

To Bikenibeu

1. Buariki Hideaway
2. Mauri Paradise Ambo
3. Homestays
4. Otintaai Hotel
5. Ambo Lagoon Club
6. Tarawa Hotel
7. Toyota Rent-A-Car
8. Catholic church
9. Catholic Women's Shop
10. Australian High Commission
11. New Zealand High Commission
12. Market
13. Bank/post office/TSKL
14. Matarena's Restaurant
15. Mary's Motel
16. Betio Motel
17. Tourist Office
18. Tobaroai Travel & Bank

See Enlargement

KIRIBATI

Turn left at Peter & Sons store and proceed towards the sea wall; a **Sherman tank** is visible at low tide, as is a light **Japanese tank**.

On Betio's back roads, small guns and bunkers intermingle with pigs and children.

John Brown of Molly's Tours (☎/fax 26 409) gives a fantastic war relics tour culminating in a 15-minute battle video; his wife Molly then takes over for a cultural tour (A$30).

Diving Mauri Paradise Ambo (☎ 21 646, fax 21 416, mp@tskl.net.ki) runs Tarawa's only dive operation. Usually divers stay few nights at Mauri Paradise's idyllic gues house in North Tarawa, a 1½ hour ride b outrigger canoe from South Tarawa; se Places to Stay later for details. For guests, two-tank dive costs A$88, a night dive A$6 scuba/snorkel set rental A$22/10. Diving da trips from South Tarawa are pricier.

Other Activities Expat John Thursto (☎/fax 28 661) charters his Trimara *Martha* for A$400 per day – good for visi ing the outer islands or North Tarawa.

Canoe racing and soccer are popular.

aces to Stay

uth Tarawa Add a 10% tax to the rates
low. Call ahead for airport transfers.

Foreign business travellers stay at the
erpriced *Otintaai Hotel* (☎ 28 084, fax 28
5) in Bikenibeu, the A$70 to $80 singles
clude continental breakfast. Rooms have
r-con, private bath, refrigerator, phone
d reliable hot water. *Mary's Motel* (☎ 21
4), in Bairiki at the start of the causeway
Betio, has two nice new rooms with air-
n, refrigerator, shower and clean bath-
oms (singles/doubles A$77/85). Skip the
n-down older rooms (A$55/66). *Tarawa
otel* (☎ 21 445), just north of the Ambo
agoon Club, has six basic but decent
oms with ceiling fans (no air-con), shared
ilet and shower areas and kitchen facili-
es for A$25/35. *Betio Motel* (☎ 26 361,
x 26 048) in Betio has plain rooms with
r-con and private bath for A$45/65 (tax
cluded). It's friendly if not immaculate
d the bar has satellite TV.

orth Tarawa Some of North Tarawa's
ost pleasant *homestays* are on Abatao, just
short canoe trip away from the end of the
outh Tarawa bus line. Raion Bataroma has
couple of gorgeous *bungalows* on stilts
ver the lagoon, just across the canoe pas-
ge (A$25/30 for singles/couples). Susan
arrie at Tobaroai Travel (☎ 36 567) in Betio
as a *resthouse* in North Tarawa for A$35
er person including breakfast and dinner.

A few hours by canoe, at the far end of
orth Tarawa, is the new *Buariki Hide-
vay* (☎ 26 695 or ☎ 30 222, fax 26 250,
uariki@tskl.net.ki), a group of well-kept
ungalows owned by Swiss-German trans-
ant Mike Strub. Small/large bungalows
ith kitchen equipment go for A$20/40;
eals, snorkelling, fishing, and boat and
ke hire can be arranged. Canoe transport
osts A$20 return.

Mauri Paradise Ambo (☎ 21 646, fax 21
16, mp@tskl.net.ki) keeps two bungalow-
yle houses in North Tarawa. The cost is
$80 per person per night, including tasty
cal meals. The 1½ hour ride costs A$122
eturn. See the Activities section earlier for
ve prices.

Places to Eat

Most of Tarawa's food comes from Australia at monthly intervals. The main *market* in
Bairiki has drinking coconuts, and fish.
Amms and *One-Stop*, both with branches
just south-east of Mary's Hotel in Bairiki,
are Tarawa's largest stores.

The small *shopping arcade* opposite the
market has two cheap, clean local eateries
where a hearty plateful of chicken or fish
with rice costs from A$1.50. Behind
Amms store in Betio is a small *restaurant*
serving cheap fish, chicken and pork
dishes. Good food at reasonable prices is
served at the outdoor tables at *Mary's
Motel* in Bairiki, but the service is
leisurely; try the Tarawa chicken tropical,
dipped in breadcrumbs, cheese, bacon and
pineapple (A$9.50).

Matarena's Restaurant, next door to
Mary's, does an excellent job with fish; try
the crispy fish in chilli sauce (A$7.50) –
four tender chunks of fried fish with rice or
chips. The *Otintaai Hotel* serves good but
more expensive dishes; go Friday for
'cheap cheap night,' when all mains cost
A$5.50. They also have a barbecue twice
a week.

Entertainment

Any number of wild local bars cluster in
Betio. *Ambo Lagoon Club* is an expat
favourite with a pool table and plenty of Victoria Bitter (VB); visitors must purchase a
temporary membership (A$5.20). The *Otin-
taai Hotel* has local dancers at its Thursday
night barbecue. Transport could be a problem as minibuses stop running at 8 or 9 pm.

Shopping

To purchase I-Kiribati crafts, try the
Catholic Women's Training Centre between
Bairiki and Bikenibeu. The choicest items
are traditional swords with shark-tooth
spikes and giant prawn tentacles extending
from a coconut-wood shaft (from A$18).

For I-Kiribati music, bring a blank cas-
sette to the Kiribati Broadcasting office in
Bairiki, where the staff will make you a tape
of local favourites (A$9.40).

Mauri Paradise has good postcards.

KIRIBATI

Getting There & Away

Air Tarawa's airport is in Bonriki, about a 50 minute drive from Betio. Tobaroai Travel Agency (☎ 26 567, fax 26 000) in Betio handles Air Nauru bookings. Air Marshall Islands (☎ 21 577, fax 21 579) has an office in Bairiki. For flight information see the Getting There & Away section earlier in this chapter.

Boat Kiribati Shipping Services (☎ 26 195, fax 26 204) sends ships to Fiji, Tuvalu and Suva every two months.

Visiting yachts can anchor in Tarawa's Betio Harbour. Tarawa is currently the only island in Kiribati with harbour dues, but Island Councils elsewhere may require a fee.

Getting Around

Tarawa's one main road extends the length of South Tarawa, which is connected by causeways, and into the southern tip of North Tarawa; from there you can take catch the canoe ferry to North Tarawa (a five-minute canoe paddle). North Tarawa's islets are connected by causeways or accessible by canoe. Private boats sometimes motor back to South Tarawa; ask around.

Tarawa's bus system is excellent; minivans sporting a cardboard 'BUS' sign whiz by between 6 am and 8 or 9 pm (A$1.50 maximum fare). There are no real stops; flag down a bus and holler when you want to get off.

Toyota Rent-A-Car at Tarawa Motors in Bairiki (☎ 21 090, fax 21 451) has cars for A$50 a day, as does the Otintaai Hotel (☎ 28 084).

Call your hotel ahead of time for airport transfers (generally free).

Other Islands

Beyond Tarawa, packaged western products are a rarity and life is relaxed. People live off fish and coconuts, and occasionally earn revenue by selling copra abroad. Women sit by thatched huts weaving pandanus or salting clams to send to Tarawa. Rarely are there more than a few trucks (except on more developed Christmas Island).

The outer Gilberts are inhabited and a[c]cessible by Air Kiribati (see later in th[is] section). The Phoenix Islands, except f[or] Kanton's 30 people, are uninhabite[d]. Among the Line Islands to the east, on[ly] Fanning, Washington and Christmas Isla[nd] are inhabited.

Getting There & Away

Air Air Kiribati (☎ 21 550 or 21 227, f[ax] ☎ 21 188), with an office in the Bairi[ki] shopping arcade in Tarawa, flies to m[ost] outer Gilberts at least weekly. There is no a[ir] service to the Phoenix Islands or the Li[ne] Islands (except to Christmas via Honolul[u]; see the Christmas Island section later for d[e]tails). The following list indicates one-wa[y] prices and the number of weekly flights:

destination	flights weekly	one way ($A)
Abaiang	3	29
Abemama	3	45
Beru	1	116
Aranuka	1	49
Arorae	1	116
Butaritari	3	61
Kuria	1	48
Maiana	3	28
Makin	1	68
Marakei	3	35
Nikunau	1	124
Nonouti	2	76
Onotoa	1	116
Tabiteuea North	3	94
Tabiteuea South	1	104
Tamana	1	136

Boat To ride one of the sporadic supp[ly] ships from Tarawa to the outer islands, as[k] at Kiribati Shipping Services (☎ 26 195[,] WKK Shipping Line (☎ 26 352) or Fe[?] Store (☎ 26 596).

Yachties might consider Fanning, 1[?] days from Christmas by boat, which ha[s] wide, deep channels and a good natural ha[r]bour. Docking costs A$1 per passenger.

Of the outer Gilbert Islands, only Ab[a]iang, Maiana, Tabiteuea South, Onotoa an[d] Abemama have lagoons that can handl[e] large boats. Island councils may require [a] fee from visiting yachts.

BAIANG ATOLL

pop 4360 • area 17.5 sq km

ur hours by boat or 15 minutes by plane m Tarawa, Abaiang is the most accessi- e of Kiribati's outer islands but proffers a pically remote experience. The island uncil's pleasant resthouse, *Hotel Nikuao*, s four thatched cottages surrounding a acious dining area. Meals are fish, spongy *bai* (taro) cake and pancakes made from conut cream. There's good **swimming** at gh tide but don't venture too far out. hose in good shape can rent a bicycle bout A$5) and cycle 15km to Koinawa, hich houses the **Catholic church**.

UTARITARI ATOLL

pop 4900 • area 13.5 sq km

ith abundant rainfall, Butaritari is Kiri- ati's greenest island. Butaritari saw heavy ghting between the USA and Japan in 942 and 1943. An annual celebration on 20 ovember called the Remembrance of nderground Cave Openings commemo- tes the day the USA won and the village lders emerged from their cave hideouts.

In addition to the usual island resthouse, ere's the family-owned *Pearl Shell Rest- ouse*, which fronts a good **swimming** and norkelling area (A$25 a night). Linda Uan nd John Anderson (☎/fax 21 629, irivid@hotmail.com) on Tarawa can rrange your stay.

Near Butaritari is **Makin**, the northern- nost of the Gilbert islands. At the northern p of Makin is **Nakaa's Beach**, the tradi- onal departure point for I-Kiribati spirits eading to the underworld. See also the oxed text 'Gateway to the Underworld' in e Samoa chapter.

BANABA (OCEAN ISLAND)

pop 344 • area 6.3 sq km

anaba, Kiribati's only uplifted limestone sland, rises to 78m above sea level. In 900 a British company discovered rich hosphate reserves on the then-unclaimed sland. Mining commenced immediately nd continued until 1979, the year of Kiri- ati's independence. The Japanese occupied anaba during WWII and deported most

Banabans to other islands. Only two of the 160 Banabans remaining on the island sur- vived after a brutal kill-the-natives order was issued in August 1945. During the post- war years Banaba, inspired by nearby Nauru, agitated unsuccessfully for indepen- dence. Equally without success, the Bana- bans tried to get money from the British to rehabilitate their lands. Banaba today has four villages, and rusting mining equipment.

To stay on Banaba, obtain a government permit from the Home Affairs office (☎ 21 092) in Bairiki on **Tarawa**; there are no flights.

FANNING ISLAND (TABUAERAN)

• pop 600 • area 34 sq km

Ring-shaped Fanning, one of the northern Line Islands, was the site of a 1902 cable station that was part of the first trans-Pacific cable, running from Australia to Fiji to Fan- ning and through to Vancouver. In 1916, a German cruiser flying a French flag cut the cable but it was later restored. A small WWII six-inch gun sits between the airport and the cable station.

The island council runs a small *resthouse* on the south side of the harbour entrance. A nicer option are Tabia Baraniko's three thatched *bungalows*, which face the lagoon and are ventilated by the trade winds (A$20 to $25, meals included).

CHRISTMAS ISLAND (KIRITIMATI)

• pop 3570 • area 388 sq km

With 48% of Kiribati's total land area, pincer-shaped Christmas Island is the world's largest coral atoll. It is home to 18 seabird species and a dazzling variety of fish. The whole island, accessible by plane from Honolulu, is a wildlife sanctuary. Christmas, also known as Kiritimati, was a nuclear testing area for British and US forces from 1957 to 1962, but the high- altitude tests have had no obvious long-term effects on the island.

American sportfishermen are mes- merised by the large bonefish that lurk in Christmas Island's coral flats, and Christ- mas' tally of 1650 annual visitors far ex- ceeds Tarawa's slender tourist numbers.

KIRIBATI

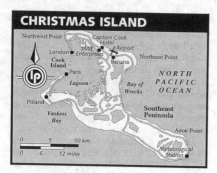

CHRISTMAS ISLAND

Northwest Point
Captain Cook Hotel
London
JMB Enterprises
Airport
Cook Island
Northeast Point
Banana
Paris
NORTH PACIFIC OCEAN
Lagoon
Bay of Wrecks
Poland
Southeast Peninsula
Vaskess Bay
Aeon Point
Meteorological Station
0   5   10 km
0   6   12 miles

Information

Most government services are in London, at the tip of Christmas Island's northernmost pincer. The Captain Cook Hotel in Banana is a half-hour ride from London.

There's a tiny tourist office (☎ 81 198) in London, as well as a post office and telecommunications centre. There's a bank too, but you'll get better rates if you change money at JMB Enterprises. The Fish & Wildlife Service (FWS; ☎ 81 217), in the building marked Ministry of Line and Phoenix Development, issues permits to visit Christmas Island's four restricted areas (A$10), though you'll have to pay for a guide and transport as well.

Things to See & Do

Across the channel from London, the lazy metropolitan hub of Christmas, is Cook Island, a mecca for nesting **seabirds**. Even if you decide not to land on Cook Island (guide and permit needed), you can swing by on a boat and marvel at the thicket of birds.

South of Cook Island, across another channel, is Paris. Both channels are prime **diving** spots.

Captain Cook Hotel, built atop the remains of British barracks used during the 1957 to 1959 nuclear tests, is a 30 minute drive clockwise from London.

Continuing south past the airport is the undiveable **Bay of Wrecks**, named after some ill-fated 19th century square-riggers.

At the southeastern tip of Christmas Island, two hours from Captain Cook Hotel,

is the **Korean wreck**, with picnic tables a a beach. Nearby is a meteorological stati used during the nuclear tests.

Christmas Island's interior consists large of desolate flats where the legendary bon fish abound. It is very easy to get lost in t flats; do not venture in without a guide.

Dive Kiribati (☎/fax 81 139, divekiribati juno.com), run by Californian transpla Kim Anderson, has package deals or wal in dives for US$75/100/120 per on two/three-tank dive. The FWS also assess an A$35 fishing and diving permit, payab at the airport upon arrival. Divers will see good variety of fish.

The abundance of bonefish makes **spo** fishing quite popular; see Getting There Away later in this section for details.

Places to Stay & Eat

Christmas Island's two hotels tend to fill in January and February. Add a 10% tax the rates below.

Captain Cook Hotel (☎ 81 230, fax 8 425), about halfway between the airport a London, has adequate, clean rooms ar bungalows, each with a mini-refrigerato and telephone (upon request). Single doubles in air-con rooms are A$89/11 bungalows cost A$95/105. Independe travellers are strongly advised to agree c the price beforehand. Fixed-menu **meals** a served to sportfishing guests. For indepe dent travellers, the price is hefty: breakfa is A$10, lunch A$13 and dinner A$20; will probably be more for the Saturda night luau. The fish is fresh and excellent

The friendly **Mini Hotel Kiritimati** (☎ 8 371, fax 81 336) has four basic, clea dorm-like rooms with shared toilet an shower. There's no air-con but a there is ceiling fan and kitchen. Singles/double cost US$40/50. The **restaurant** is ope upon advance request.

Father Bermond (☎ 81 365 or ☎ 81 251 a resident French priest, runs the plain kitchenless, one-room **Fare Tony Hostel** b the Catholic church in London; the price about a A$20 church donation.

There's a dingy **Fish Restaurant** i London. Snack items are available at JM

KIRIBATI

nterprises near the Captain Cook Hotel, *ojin* in London and the *Mini Store* at Captain Cook Hotel.

etting There & Away

n Aloha Airlines jet chartered by Air Kiribati (☎ 888-800 8144 or ☎ 808-839 6680, x 808-839 6681), in the USA, has a eekly service from Honolulu to Christmas land (US$750 return). The airport is a 15 inute drive from Captain Cook Hotel and 45 minute drive from London.

Most visitors to Christmas Island come a a sportfishing or diving package. Froners (☎ 800-245 1950, fax 724-935 5388, fo@frontierstrvl.com), in the USA, is the rgest; sportfishing trips with accommodaon at the Captain Cook Hotel start at $1785, and diving packages start at $1600. Not included are air fare and alcoolic beverages. Royal Journeys (☎ 888-33 5495 or ☎ 425-483 5495, fax 425-402 300), in the USA, has comparable packzes. A bit cheaper is Christmas Island

Outfitters (☎ 800 694 4162, fax 717-281 7121), which operates from the Mini Hotel.

Christmas' shallow channels cannot support large boats.

Getting Around

Compared to other islands in Kiribati, Christmas Island is huge – driving from one end to the other would take more than two hours. A van from Captain Cook Hotel meets arriving flights, while Mini Hotel charges US$10 for air transfers each way. There's a lone minibus between Banana (near Captain Cook Hotel) and London (A$1); flag it down. JMB Enterprises (☎ 81 501, fax 81 505) rents vehicles to nonfishermen/fishermen for US$60/95 per day (fishermen have a poor driving record on the island). Rates at Dojin store (☎ 81 110, fax 81 321) in London are A$50 per day for a pick-up truck (plus A$15 insurance). Mini Hotel (☎ 81 371) also has pick-ups for US$60 to $80 per day. Otherwise, hitching is possible.

Marshall Islands

The Marshall Islands consist of more than a thousand slender, flat coral islands. Their people, long reliant on the sea, are expert fishers and navigators. The two main atolls have quite different characters. Majuro, the capital, is quite westernised. Kwajelein, Continental Airlines' other Marshall Islands stop, is leased to the US military for missile testing. Kwajelein's non-military visitors are shuttled to nearby Ebeye, where wall-to-wall tenements house the Marshallese who work on the base. Most of the outer islands, however, still retain the pristine feel of the tropical Pacific.

After WWII the USA used the isolated islands for 67 powerful nuclear bomb tests. Though the bombing is long over, the Marshallese still grapple with the lingering effects of radiation, and entire communities have been resettled.

Facts about the Marshall Islands

HISTORY
The Marshalls were never unified under one leader, though at times the entire Ralik chain came under the rule of a single chief. Chiefs had absolute authority and depended on loyalty and tribute payments.

Because their islands are so widely scattered, the Marshallese developed some of the Pacific's finest canoe-building and navigational skills. Little visited by early European explorers, the islands were named after the English sea captain John Marshall, who, in 1788, sighted several atolls and docked at Mili. Traders and whalers came in the early 1800s, but violent attacks by the Marshallese repelled them.

Germany annexed the Marshalls in 1885, but until the German administrators arrived in 1906, the islands were run by Jaluit Gesellschaft, a group of powerful German trading companies. The Japanese, who took

AT A GLANCE

Capital City (& Atoll): Delap-Uliga-Darrit (Majuro)
Population: 60,000
Time: 12 hours ahead of GMT
Land Area: 180 sq km (70 sq miles)
Number of Islands: Five high islands, 29 atolls
International Telephone Code: ☎ 692
GDP/Capita: US$1145
Currency: US dollar
Languages: Marshallese & English
Greeting: *Yokwe yuk*

HIGHLIGHTS
- **Diving Bikini** – the newly accessible wrecks from Bikini's nuclear debacle are a fabulous underwater spectacle.

- **Outer island experience** – innumerable atolls accessible by air retain their traditional ways.

- **WWII relics** – some of the outer Marshall atolls, covered end to end with Japanese relics, make excellent exploring.

control in 1914, developed large base throughout the Marshalls.

The first Micronesian islands captured b the USA in WWII were at Kwajelein Ato in February 1944. Majuro Atoll was take next. From here the USA staged attacks o the Japanese-controlled Caroline Islands

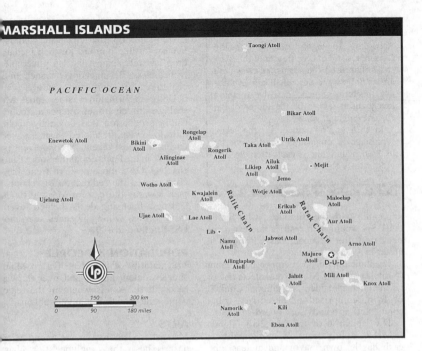

MARSHALL ISLANDS

PACIFIC OCEAN

Taongi Atoll

Bikar Atoll

Enewetok Atoll

Bikini Atoll

Rongelap Atoll

Utrik Atoll

Taka Atoll

Ailinginae Atoll

Rongerik Atoll

Ailuk Atoll

Likiep Atoll

Mejit

Jemo

Wotho Atoll

Ujelang Atoll

Wotje Atoll

Kwajalein Atoll

Maloelap Atoll

Erikub Atoll

Ujae Atoll

Lae Atoll

Aur Atoll

Ralik Chain

Ratak Chain

Lib

Namu Atoll

Jabwot Atoll

Arno Atoll

Ailinglaplap Atoll

Majuro Atoll

D-U-D

Jaluit Atoll

Mili Atoll

Knox Atoll

Namorik Atoll

Kili

Ebon Atoll

0   150   300 km

0   90   180 miles

fter the war, the USA immediately moved
, resettled islanders and commenced
omic bomb experiments on Bikini and
newetok atolls. Kwajalein Atoll was later
stablished as a missile testing site. Some of
e islanders who were directly exposed to
llout, or lived on contaminated land, have
nce died from radiation-related ailments,
hile others have lingering health problems.

Aspiring to political independence, the
Marshallese boldly withdrew from the Con-
ress of Micronesia in 1973. The ploy
orked, and their constitution became ef-
ective on 1 May 1979.

GEOGRAPHY & ECOLOGY

Almost all of the Marshalls' 1225 islands
nd islets are part of 29 coral atolls. The
tolls run roughly north-south for 800 miles
n two nearly parallel chains about 150
hiles apart. The eastern chain is Ratak,
which means 'Towards Dawn' and the
vestern chain is Ralik (Towards Sunset).

Although only 70 sq miles of total land
area, the Marshalls spread across 750,000
sq miles of ocean. The widest island, Wotje,
is less than a mile across; the highest elevation, just 34 feet, is on Likiep.

CLIMATE

On Majuro, daily temperature averages
81°F (27°C). The northern Marshalls are
quite dry, but some southern islands get up
to 160 inches of rain a year. Majuro's wet
period is September through November. A
severe drought caused the Marshallese
government to declare their country a disaster area in March 1998, but the island is
recovering. Full-blown tropical storms or
cyclones are rare.

GOVERNMENT & POLITICS

Like other Trust Territory districts, the Mar-
shallese signed a 15 year Compact of Free
Association with the USA, which sought
Kwajelein as a missile testing site. Though

MARSHALL ISLANDS

Bikini

According to legend, Bikini was the favourite island of Loa, creator of the Marshalls. Loa used the words *lia kwe!* (you are a rainbow!) to describe Bikini. Eventually the term grew to describe anything lovely and is said to be the source of the current greeting, *yokwe*.

In case you're wondering, the bikini swimsuit was originally named *atome* by its French designer, a year after the first atomic tests at Bikini.

unpopular with the Bikinians, who feared the USA would then restrict nuclear compensation, the Compact passed and took effect in 1986.

The unicameral 33 member parliament (Nitijela) meets in Majuro and elects one of its members president. A national Council of Iroij, comprised of hereditary tribal chiefs, acts as an advisory board.

The Republic of the Marshall Islands (RMI) is divided into 24 municipalities; each has its own mayor and at least one senator in the Nitijela.

ECONOMY

US funding drives the Marshallese economy. Payments connected with the US$4 billion missile project on Kwajelein Atoll provide about US$30 million annually over 30 years. The 15 year compact, moreover, will have funnelled nearly US$1 billion to the Marshalls by 2001. However, the Marshalls badly overspent their compact money early on, sinking it into poor business investments. Among myriad other scrimping measures, the government cut salaries by 12.5% in 1998.

When compact renegotiation begins in 1999, the Marshalls stand a good chance of renewing, or even increasing, their allotment because they hold a trump card – Kwajelein. Although the USA technically can extend its rights to Kwajelein until 2016 without financial obligation, it's unlikely that the USA would leave its landlords in

the cold. The US Congress also allocat US$240 million to compensate victims nuclear testing in return for their pledge drop lawsuits against the US governme Nonetheless, Bikinians may launch an a peal to recover additional money.

US cash infusions aside, most Ma shallese still rely on subsistence agricultu Copra production was down by about third following the altered weather patter during the most recent El Niño event (s Climate in the Facts about the South Paci chapter). On a more positive front, the Niño caused the redirection of schools tuna towards the eastern Marshalls. Th and new licensing deals, helped reven from foreign fishing licences soar abo US$4 million in 1998.

POPULATION & PEOPLE

The majority of islanders live on Maju and Kwajelein atolls, and over 95% a Marshallese. As elsewhere in the regio population growth is a huge problem.

ARTS

Marshallese handicrafts are among Micr nesia's best; they include stick char carved models of outrigger canoes and i tricately woven items such as baskets, wa hangings and purses made from pandan leaves, coconut fronds and cowrie shells.

SOCIETY & CONDUCT

Marshallese society has always been strat fied, and despite increasing westernisatio social status still derives from kinshi Chiefs continue to wield a great deal of a thority. Although most clothing worn no is western-style, women and girls dre modestly; you may see older women wea ing loose-fitting, floral-printed *muu-mu* dresses.

RELIGION

Most Marshallese are Christians – eith Protestant or Catholic.

LANGUAGE

Marshallese is the official language, b English is taught in schools and is wide

Stick Charts

The low elevation of the Marshalls and the distances between the atolls make them particularly difficult to sight from the sea. In travels between islands, early inhabitants learned to read the patterns of the waves by watching for swells that would show when land was ahead.

Stick charts were used to teach the secrets of navigation. They were made by tying flat strips of wood together in designs that imitated the wave patterns. Shells were then attached to these sticks to represent the islands.

Three kinds of charts were used. The *mattang* showed wave patterns around a single island or atoll and was used first to teach the basic techniques. The *medo* showed patterns around a small group of atolls and the *rebillit* mapped an entire chain, showing the relationships between the islands and the major ocean swells.

All the information contained on the stick charts was memorised and the charts themselves were not actually taken on journeys. Not many present-day Marshallese understand how to read stick charts, though due to their popularity as souvenirs many islanders can still make them.

understood. The islanders' gentleness is reflected in their traditional greeting *yokwe yuk*, which means 'love to you'.

Marshallese Basics

Hello/goodbye.	*Ko na mauri.*
How are you?	*Ejet am mour?*
I'm well (thanks).	*Emman (komomol tata).*
Please.	*Joij.*
Thanks.	*Komomol tata.*
Yes.	*Aet.*
No.	*Jab.*

Facts for the Visitor

SUGGESTED ITINERARIES

The charm of the Marshall Islands is the outer atolls, but if you have only a few days, you'll have to stay on Majuro because Air Marshall Islands generally serves outer atolls just once a week.

Mili Atoll is a good first choice for an outer island to visit, or Wotje or Maloelap for WWII buffs. Divers, of course, should visit Bikini. Ebeye is only for very keen divers.

VISAS & EMBASSIES

Visas are not required. Upon arrival visitors will be issued a 30 day entry permit that can be extended twice, for a maximum stay of 90 days, for US$10 per extension.

RMI Embassies & Consulates

The republic's diplomatic representation abroad includes:

Fiji
(☎ 387 899, fax 387 115)
41 Borron Rd, Box 2038, Suva
USA
(☎ 202-234 5414, fax 232 3236)
2433 Massachusetts Ave NW, Washington DC 20008

Embassies & Consulates in RMI

The only consulate in Majuro is that of the USA (☎ 247 4011), Airport Rd.

MONEY

The Marshall Islands uses the US dollar (see Exchange Rates in the Regional Facts for the Visitor chapter). Credit cards are increasingly accepted on Majuro and have limited use on Ebeye, where you should expect a surcharge. Tipping is customary in the high-end restaurants but not elsewhere.

POST & COMMUNICATIONS

Majuro uses the US postal system. The postal codes are 96960 (Majuro) and 96970 (Ebeye). The Marshall Islands international telephone code is ☎ 692; there are no area codes. Calling Kwajelein Island from other RMI islands is like making an international call to the USA. To make an international call, dial ☎ 011.

MARSHALL ISLANDS

INTERNET RESOURCES

The Marshalls' official website (www
.rmiembassyus.org) has good links; www
.bikiniatoll.com is another interesting site.

MEDIA

Majuro gets cable TV; Ebeye gets US military TV, a unique combination of news, soaps and military propaganda. Majuro's weekly *Marshall Islands Journal* has good coverage of the islands.

ELECTRICITY

The Marshalls' electricity supply is at 110/120V AC, 60Hz. Plugs and sockets are US style with two flat blades.

WEIGHTS & MEASURES

The Marshalls use the imperial measurement system. See the table at the back of this book if you need to convert to the metric system.

HEALTH

Don't drink unboiled tap water.

BUSINESS HOURS

Most businesses and government offices are open Monday to Friday from 9 am to 5 pm.

ACTIVITIES

The Marshall Islands have excellent diving and snorkelling; the former is particularly good on Bikini, Kwajelein and some of the other outer islands.

PUBLIC HOLIDAYS & SPECIAL EVENTS

Public holidays in the Marshalls include New Year's Day, Easter Sunday and Christmas (see the Regional Facts for the Visitor chapter for these dates). Also:

Nuclear Victims' Day	1 March
Constitution Day	1 May
Fisherman's Day	First Friday in July
Labor Day	First Monday in September
Culture Day	Last Friday in September
Independence Day	21 October
President's Birthday	17 November
Gospel Day	First Friday in December

On Constitution Day, Majuro's Outrigg
Hotel hosts the Outrigger Marshall Islan
Cup races, which feature inter-atoll can
races, handicrafts and local food.

Getting There & Away

AIR

Kwajelein and Majuro are free stopovers
Continental's 'Circle Micronesia' isla
hopper between Honolulu and Guam. (S
the introductory Getting Around the Regi
chapter for air passes and all airline conta
details.)

Air Marshall Islands has a twice-week
service from Majuro to Tarawa, Kiribati, f
US$180 each way.

Aloha Airlines flies weekly from Hon
lulu to Majuro/Kwajelein for US$800/9
return.

Departure Tax

Majuro has a US$15 airport departure ta

SEA

Before visiting any of the outer Marsha
Islands, yachties must check in with Majuro
Port Authority (☎ 625 8269), which issues
US$50 entrance fee, and obtain a permit fro
the Ministry of Internal Affairs (☎ 625 8240

The only atolls with suitable docks a
Jaluit, Likiep and Bikini. Arno, Mili, Jalui
Ailinlaplap, Namu, Aur, Maloelap, Likie
Wotho, Rongelap and Bikini all have sa
passages for entry into the lagoon. Som
charge entrance fees (up to US$100).

ORGANISED TOURS

Some USA-based fly-fishing and divin
tours go to Majuro; the RMI website (se
Internet Resources under Facts for the Visi
or) usually has good links.

Getting Around

Air Marshall Islands flies to most of th
Marshalls' inhabited atolls once a week an

as a frequent service between Majuro and
wajelein.

State-run boats travel irregularly to the
uter atolls, but private boats go with more
equency.

Shared taxis are abundant and cheap in
entral Majuro and there are some on
beye. Cars can be rented on Majuro for
round US$45 per day.

Majuro Atoll

pop 30,000 • area 3.8 sq miles

val-shaped Majuro Atoll, with 53 islets
rcing in a slender 67 mile-ribbon, is the na-
on's political and economic centre. The
arger islets are connected by a 35-mile long
aved road. When Robert Louis Stevenson
isited Majuro in 1889 he called Majuro
Pearl of the Pacific'. Though heavily west-
rnised and the most populated of the Mar-
halls' atolls, Majuro still keeps a simple
sland flavour.

Information

Tourist Offices The helpful Marshall Islands Visitors Authority (☎ 625 6482, fax

625 6771, tourism@ntamar.com) is in the
Small Island section of D-U-D.

Money Majuro has the Bank of Guam,
Bank of the Marshall Islands and a Bank of
Hawaii is beside Gibson's department store.
There's an ATM in Uliga's RRE grocery
store.

Post & Communications Majuro's main
post office is next door to the RRE grocery
store in Uliga. For international calls and
faxes try the National Telecommunications
Authority building in Delap (open 24
hours). Call ahead (☎ 625 3363) to schedule a radio call to the outer islands. Tourist
Trap near Gibson's has two Internet terminals for US$6 per hour.

Medical Services Majuro's relatively
modern hospital (emergency ☎ 625 4144,
switchboard ☎ 625 3399) is in Delap.

Things to See
D-U-D Municipality D-U-D – comprised
of Delap, Uliga and Darrit (Rita) islands –
has the greatest concentration of commercial services.

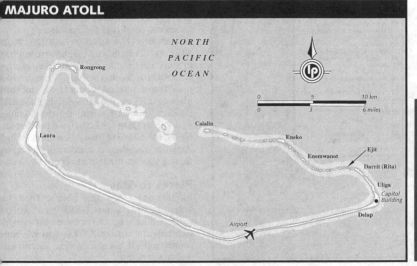

MAJURO ATOLL

NORTH
PACIFIC
OCEAN

Rongrong

Laura

Calalin

Eneko

Enemwanot

Ejit

Darrit (Rita)

Uliga
Capitol
Building

Delap

Airport

0   5   10 km
0   3   6 miles

MARSHALL ISLANDS

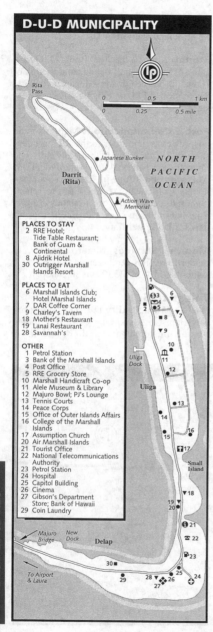

D-U-D MUNICIPALITY

Rita Pass

0   0.5   1 km
0   0.25   0.5 mile

Japanese Bunker

NORTH PACIFIC OCEAN

Darrit (Rita)

Action Wave Memorial

PLACES TO STAY
2 RRE Hotel;
   Tide Table Restaurant;
   Bank of Guam &
   Continental
8 Ajidrik Hotel
30 Outrigger Marshall
   Islands Resort

PLACES TO EAT
6 Marshall Islands Club;
   Hotel Marshal Islands
7 DAR Coffee Corner
9 Charley's Tavern
18 Mother's Restaurant
19 Lanai Restaurant
28 Savannah's

OTHER
1 Petrol Station
3 Bank of the Marshall Islands
4 Post Office
5 RRE Grocery Store
10 Marshall Handicraft Co-op
11 Alele Museum & Library
12 Majuro Bowl; PJ's Lounge
13 Tennis Courts
14 Peace Corps
15 Office of Outer Islands Affairs
16 College of the Marshall
   Islands
17 Assumption Church
20 Air Marshall Islands
21 Tourist Office
22 National Telecommunications
   Authority
23 Petrol Station
24 Hospital
25 Capitol Building
26 Cinema
27 Gibson's Department
   Store; Bank of Hawaii
29 Coin Laundry

Uliga Dock

Uliga

Small Island

Majuro Bridge   New Dock   Delap

To Airport & Laura

MARSHALL ISLANDS

Government offices are spread arour Delap; particularly noticeable is the moc ernistic, glass-encased US$9 million **capito building**. In Uliga is the **Alele Museum Library**, with small but good quality exhibi of early Marshallese culture, including stic charts, model canoes and shell tools.

People commonly wade across the reef the islands north of Rita at low tide. Th pleasant beaches of **Enemwanot**, beyon Rita, are popular for weekend picnics an snorkelling; contact Kirtley Pinho (☎ 62 0155) about boat transport.

Laura Laura, a quiet green refuge 30 mile from D-U-D, is the atoll's agricultural cer tre. Its tip is fringed with a gorgeous white sand beach. Majuro's finest, the beach popular for weekend picnics. The Japanese built **Majuro Peace Park** has a memorial t those who died in WWII.

Activities

Tropical fish, white-tipped and grey ree sharks and a few wrecks make Majuro fine dive spot. A popular dive is the Calali Channel (also known as Shark Alley). Th water gets clearer farther from Rita. Enem wanot has good snorkelling and Calalin even better, but beware of current; Snorkellers without boat transport will fin a shallow coral reef at Laura Beach.

Marshalls Dive Adventures (MDA; ☎ 62 5131 ext 215, fax 625 3505, rreadmin@ ntamar.com), run by the RRE Hotel, charge US$90/110 for a two-tank dive in Ma juro/Arno Atolls; add about US$25 for com plete gear. There is a 10% discount for RRI (Robert Reimers Enterprises) Hotel guests Snorkel sets rent for US$10 a day. Matthew Holly (☎ 625 3669) of Marshall Island Aquatics also does some diving. For sport fishing contact the tourist office.

Places to Stay

Majuro has a few fine hotels. There's hotel tax of 8% plus US$3 per room pe night. Call ahead and most hotels provid free airport transfers. All have private bath rooms and all but the Ajidrik accept Visi and MasterCard.

Places to Stay – Budget

The *Ajidrik Hotel* (☎ 625 3171, fax 625 712) in central Uliga has 15 run-down, basic, air-con rooms with mini-refrigerators and TV. Singles/doubles cost US$40/50. Nicer by far is the new *Hotel Marshall Islands* (☎ 625 3002, fax 625 3004, journal@ntamar.com), above the Marshall Islands Club in Uliga. Immaculate, modern rooms have TV, mini-refrigerator and phone (local calls 25 cents). Rooms are US$68/83 (tax included). The newly refurbished *RRE Hotel* (☎ 625 3250, fax 625 3505, rreadmin@ntamar.com, Box 1) in central Uliga is deservedly popular with business travellers. Singles/doubles are from US$75/80. Past its peak but still nice is the *Royal Garden Hotel* (☎ 247 3701, fax 247 3705), two miles west of D-U-D across the Majuro bridge. Rooms have TV, bathtub, phone, air-con, carpeting, refrigerator and ocean views. The sprawling, 150-room *Outrigger Marshall Islands Resort* (☎ 625 2525, fax 625 2500, outrigger@ntamar.com), about a quarter of a mile west of Gibson's, is comfortable and has all expected amenities – tub, TV, phones and usually a marvellous lagoon-side beach view. Singles and doubles are US$125; add US$25 for an extra bed.

Places to Eat

Budget The excellent *DAR Coffee Corner*, located behind the museum in Uliga, is simple, clean, cheap and smoke-free. Fluffy 25c pancakes are an unbeatable morning starter, and local food served buffet-style later in the day is excellent. Also cheap and nonsmoking is *Mother's Kitchen*, next to Momotaro's store at Small Island. Recommended are the grilled tuna and the teriyaki chicken plate, each US$4. *The Deli* attached to the RRE store in Uliga has ordinary burgers and sandwiches from US$2 to US$3. *Savannah's*, a new eatery next to Gibson's that's popular with locals and expats, is a good place for a steak-and-egg or fish-and-rice meal.

Of the numerous grocery stores in D-U-D, the best are *Gibson's* and the *RRE Store*.

Top End *Tide Table Restaurant*, upstairs at the RRE Hotel, is a popular place with excellent food and fine lagoon views. Lunch features burgers and sandwiches (US$4) and hot dishes for a bit more. Full seafood and steak dinners cost US$10 to $15. The *Lanai Restaurant*, on the lagoon at Small Island, has a varied menu of tasty Chinese food. At lunch everything on the menu is US$5, including satay beef, Peking stir-fry and chicken curry; dinners are US$10 to US$13. *Enra Restaurant*, downstairs at the Outrigger Hotel, has fine food to accompany a wonderful lagoon view. The menu is an impressive array of steaks, seafood, and salads, all reasonably priced. Lunchtime pizzas are from US$7. The Outrigger also offers pricey dinner cruises (US$38 before drinks).

Entertainment

The locally popular *Marshall Islands Club* in Uliga brews its own golden ale, called Whiteball. Other local hang-outs include *PJ's Lounge*, above Majuro Bowl in Uliga and *Charley's Tavern* in central Uliga. *Lanai Restaurant* morphs from restaurant to disco on weekends. Expats patronise the bar at the *Tide Table Restaurant* in the RRE Hotel.

Shopping

Excellent Marshallese handicrafts include stick charts, carved models of outrigger canoes and intricate weavings such as baskets, wall hangings and purses made from pandanus leaves, coconut fronds and cowrie shells. Try the Marshall Handicraft Co-op, where you can also watch women weaving, and the Alele Museum next door.

Getting There & Away

The Continental office (☎ 625 3209) is in the RRE Hotel building. Air Marshall Islands (☎ 625 3733, fax 625 3730) has an office near the Lanai Restaurant. For flight details see the Getting There & Away section earlier in this chapter.

Getting Around

Majuro has inexpensive shared taxis. It's 50 cents to go anywhere within the D-U-D, where most taxis operate. Taxis will meet arriving flights; most hotels will provide airport transfers if you call ahead. To Laura, catch a minivan from the RRE Hotel carpark (US$2), which leaves when full.

Car rental agencies include DAR (☎ 625 3174, fax 625 3344), next to the eponymous coffee shop, which charges from US$50 a day or US$7.50 an hour. The RRE Hotel (☎ 625 3250, fax 625 3505) rents cars for US$47, insurance included. Other companies include the Royal Garden Hotel (☎ 247 3701, fax 247 3705) and Deluxe Car Rental (☎ 625 3665, fax 625 3663).

Kwajelein Atoll

- pop 10,000   - area 6.5 sq miles

Nowhere in Micronesia is the US military presence so pronounced as on Kwajelein Atoll, a US$4 billion space tracking and missile defence facility operated by the US Department of Defence. Measured by lagoon size, Kwajelein is the world's largest coral atoll. Its 97 islands, just 6.5 sq miles in land mass, surround an immense 1100 sq mile lagoon. The lagoon, sometimes called 'the world's largest catcher's mitt', is the target and splashdown point for intercontinental ballistic missiles (ICBMs); many come from the Vandenberg Air Force Base in California, 4200 miles away. The Kwajelein Missile Range (officially called US Army Kwajelein Atoll, or USAKA) includes Kwajelein Island to the south, Roi-Namur Island in the north and some smaller islands between the two.

KWAJELEIN ISLAND

About 2700 US civilian contract workers and their families live on Kwajelein Island ('Kwaj'). Kwaj is US suburbia transplanted, with a golf course, two swimming pools, baseball diamonds, tennis courts and a nice, air-conditioned Marshallese Cultural Center. For food, try the *Three Palms* snack bar beside the Bank of Guam, which has classic American fare – burgers, pizza and ice cream – and pastries. Many services, including the Continental office (☎ 355 1013), are on Kwajelein. WWII relics include a

well-preserved bunker and a manicure Japanese cemetery, site of the mass grave f Japanese soldiers defending Kwajelein.

Getting There & Away

For unofficial visitors, Kwajelein Island off limits except as a transit point to neigh bouring Ebeye. To overnight on Kwaj, yc must have an official 'sponsor' who ca arrange for your stay. Day passes, howeve are not difficult to obtain. Go to the Ebey police station at about 7.30 am to arrange next-day pass. The next morning, take th ferry to Kwaj and your day pass will available for pick-up in the Kwaj dock wai ing room at 8 am (return by 2 pm).

EBEYE

Over 1300 Marshallese labourers work o Kwajelein Island and live on 78 acre (3 hectare) Ebeye Island, three miles to th north. They support about 12,000 mor relatives and friends in one-room shack and lean-tos of plywood, tin and plasti sheeting, jammed together in tenement con ditions with little water (islanders hav water from Kwaj) and spotty electricity.

Needless to say, Ebeye is not a big touri spot, but the people are very friendly, espe cially the children.

Information

Ebeye has a post office, a Bank of the Ma shall Islands and a Bank of Guam. A 24 hour National Telecom Agency (NTA) towards the southern end of the island; fc calls to Kwaj, go to the Kwaj dock (it' much cheaper). Air Marshall Islands has a office in Ebeye (☎ 329 3036) near Triple Variety store.

Diving

Kwajelein's lagoon contains more than 3 WWII-era Japanese ships. The highlight the wreck of the German pocket battleshi *Prinz Eugen*, which served as an escort t the *Bismarck* during its legendary WWI battle against the British *Hood*. Dive-maste Steven Gavegan of Ebeye-based Kwajelei Atoll Dive Resort (☎/fax 329 3297) has twc tank dives for US$95 (add US$45 for gear

laces to Stay & Eat

ll of Ebeye's hotels are overpriced and verbooked – you need to call weeks in advance for a cheaper room. Add US$2 plus 0% tax. Relatively nice is the two storey **nrohasa Hotel** (☎ 329 3161, fax 329 248), whose rooms have air-con, refrigertor, phone and TV. Older rooms go for S$65; newer rooms are from US$85. A inimum US$100 deposit is required. The nly palatable budget option is the **DSC lotel** (☎ 329 3194), which has seven passble rooms with double bed, TV and refrigrator for US$52. **Bob's Island Restaurant**, block from the Anrohasa Hotel, has a vater view, good prices and Ebeye's best ood. The **Anrohasa Hotel Restaurant** has varied menu with US-style food and Chiese and Japanese dishes. If you're desperte (and you will be), the accessible **snack ar** at the Kwaj dock serves fresh pastries the morning, plus cheap sandwiches and nported fruit.

Triple J Variety Store near the Ebeye ock has groceries.

etting There & Away

o get to Ebeye you'll need to go via Kwa-lein Island – you'll be issued a temporary ase pass at the airport and told to take a xi (or get a ride) to the ferry terminal. On eturn, you must show your ticket at the wajelein dock before you can proceed to e airport; if you have an open ticket, ob-in a printout of your flight times.

Outer Islands

the quiet, traditional villages away from Majuro and Kwajelein, everyone is friendly nd usually a few speak English. Although ome outer islanders still use the *korkor* (a ug-out fishing canoe made from a bread-uit log), *boom-booms* (motorboats) are eadily gaining in popularity. Both kinds of oats are used for frequent *jambos* (trips or icnics) to uninhabited islands of the atoll.

Accommodation & Food

lthough many atolls do not have formal arrangements for visitors, the Marshallese are generally hospitable. Only a few atolls have guesthouses – Mili, Likiep, Arno and Bikini. Otherwise, you will need to radio ahead to the mayor of the island you wish to visit, and arrange for something to be set up, possibly in an island council rest-house or schoolhouse.

Most outer islands lack electricity, running water and flush toilets.

Expect to eat fresh local foods like bread-fruit, pumpkin, taro and fish prepared by your hosts. Usually a few stores stock rice, flour, tea and canned meats. Most outer islands are alcohol-free.

Getting There & Away

Air From Majuro, AMI flies once a week (rarely more) to all other inhabited atolls, including the ones listed above. Some flights hop across a couple of islands at a time.

As AMI flies nearly daily between Kwa-jelein and Majuro, you can generally go to one of the outer islands from Kwajelein or Majuro.

Boat The Marshalls have two field trip ships, *Micro Pilot* and the MV *Juk Ae*, which service the outer islands about once a month, dropping off supplies and picking up copra. Scheduling information is available from the Transportation Office (☎ 625 3469, fax 625 3486) at Uliga Dock in Majuro. Also ask at the RRE Store, which sends boats occasionally to Mili, Jaluit and Kili; charters can be arranged any time to Arno, Maloelap and Likiep.

Yachties should radio ahead from Majuro before visiting outer islands and should check-in with the mayor of each atoll upon arrival in the lagoon.

Getting Around

The outer islands have few land vehicles but usually at least one motorboat. Trips to other islands within the atoll can generally be negotiated for a reasonable price. It should also be fairly easy to get someone to take you fishing, lobstering or coconut-crab hunting.

MILI ATOLL

• pop 850   • area 6.1 sq miles

Friendly and accessible with good beaches, Mili is a good choice for visiting an outer atoll. As a major WWII Japanese base, Mili has abandoned weapons, Japanese and US war planes and bombed-out buildings still scattered around. The whole lagoon side of Mili Island is trimmed with sandy white beaches. At low tide, walk along the reef to the neighbouring islands.

Places to Stay

Majuro-based MDA maintains several thatched *cottages* on Wau Island as part of the Wau Island Giant Clam Farm. Each has a private bathroom, running water and solar power. A week's trip is US$750, which includes air fare from Majuro, dives, food and accommodation (six person minimum). Shorter stays may be possible.

MALOELAP ATOLL

• pop 800   • area 3.8 sq miles

Taroa (Tarawa) Island, in Maloelap Atoll, was the main Japanese airbase in the eastern Marshalls during WWII. There are numerous twisted wreckages of Zeros and Betty bombers, pillboxes, guns as well as the remains of an airfield, narrow-gauge railroad and a radio station. The southern tip of the island has coastal defence guns, including a 127mm anti-aircraft gun and a Howitzer on wheels. Many relics are hidden under thick jungle foliage, so it's useful to have a guide.

Off Taroa's lagoon beach the Japanese freighter *Toroshima Maru* lies half submerged where it was sunk by US bombers. Periscopes and the mast can still be seen, but it's pretty well stripped, except for some live depth charges.

ARNO ATOLL

• pop 1700   • area 5 sq miles

Arno, with 133 islands, is the closest atoll to Majuro, just nine miles away. The Longar area in Arno is famous for its 'love school' where young women were once taught how to perfect their sexual techniques. The waters off Longar Point are known for superb deep-sea fishing, where yellowfin tuna, marlin, mahi-mahi and sai fish abound.

RRE's Black Pearl Farm Island has tw *cottages* on Arno's northern tip. The Arn House is on Arno Island, the closest to M juro Atoll, and the Enedrik Island House on Enedrik Island, in the eastern part of t atoll. Contact the RRE Hotel in Majuro f information on all three places.

LIKIEP ATOLL

• pop 480   • area 4 sq miles

Likiep is made up of about 60 islands arour a shallow lagoon. Its houses are built semi-western style with porches and railing

In 1877, during the German era, Jose d Brum, a Portuguese harpooner who arrive aboard a US whaleship, and Adolf Capell a German trader, bought Likiep Atoll fro the high chief. They both married Ma shallese women and settled in, startir profitable copra and ship-building comp nies. Their descendants still own Likiep ar operate it as a copra plantation. The sale the island remains a source of contention, current traditional leaders claim the doc ment of sale was written in a foreign la guage that the high chief wasn't able to rea

The brand new *Likiep Plantation Hot* has 10 rooms and a restaurant. Arrang stays through the tourist office on Majur

WOTJE ATOLL

• pop 650   • area 3.2 sq miles

Wotje, the main island in Wotje Atoll, covered end to end with WWII remnan Large portions of the island were one paved in concrete, and machinery, fu tanks and all sorts of unidentifiable w junk stick out everywhere. In the centre the village there is a large Japanese gun th can still be moved on its pivot. The lago is also full of wreckage, including a fe ships. The lagoon beaches of Wotje Islar are quite beautiful and relatively clean.

MEJIT

• pop 450   • area 0.8 sq miles

Beautiful, coconut-lined Mejit is a sing coral island, about three-quarters of square mile. Mejit has a small freshwat ke, a rarity in the Marshalls, which even tracts a few wayward migrating ducks in e winter. It also has lots of seasonal tuna, well as lobster and octopus and, unlike her islands, no poisonous fish.

ALUIT ATOLL

pop 1700   **• area 4.4 sq miles**

raditionally Jaluit was the home of the gh chief of the southern Ralik islands.

Jaluit's main island, Jabwor, became the erman capital. When the Japanese took ver they fortified the islands and started a shing industry; the ruins of Japanese uildings and bunkers still remain. You can so see the wreck of the ship *Alfred* still on e reef at Jabwor Pass where it sank in 899. Jaluit Atoll's planes and shipwrecks ake some of the Marshalls' best diving.

laces to Stay & Eat

he *Sawaj Hotel* (☎ *625 3829 in Majuro, eccorp@ntamar.com*) run by Marshall lectric Company has four air-con, double-ccupancies units with two shared bathrooms. *etto's Store* has two small units; contact An-ri Jason (☎ 625 3450) on Majuro. Both harge US$50 per night per person.

IKINI ATOLL

pop 10   **• area 2.3 sq miles**

ome to the earliest known habitation in licronesia, Bikini was selected by Presi-ent Truman as the site for the first peace-me explosion of the atomic bomb.

Early in 1946 the US military governor f the Marshalls met with the fervently re-gious Bikini islanders to inform them that heir islands were needed for 'a greater ood'. After deliberations, Bikini's Chief da – still awed by the US firepower that ad recently defeated the Japanese Imperial avy – responded that if the USA wanted to se Bikini for the 'benefit of all mankind' s people would go elsewhere.

Bikini's 161 residents were relocated on e assurance that they could move back once e tests were over. A few months later the SA exploded a nuclear device 500 feet over ikini's lagoon, the first of 23 nuclear tests at would leave the islands uninhabitable.

The Bikinians were first moved to Ron-gerik Atoll, a place of ill omen in Mar-shallese legend. They got sick from eating poisonous fish in the lagoon and nearly starved from inadequate food supplies. Two years later they were moved to Kwajelein Atoll and then later to Kili Island.

In the 1970s the Bikinians were told it was safe to move back home and a resettle-ment program began. Although two entire islands had been blown away and the others were treeless and debris-covered, the is-landers remained on Bikini and tried to get their lives back in order.

In 1978 US tests showed that by eating food grown in the caesium-contaminated soil the Bikinians had collected huge levels of radioactivity in their bodies, so they were moved back to Kili again. It was later re-ported that the return program was a US bumble: the islanders were supposed to have been put on Eneu Island, the other main island in Bikini Atoll, not on Bikini Is-land, which is eight times more radioactive.

The final cleanup of Bikini will require replacing all the current topsoil with im-ported soil. The cost of that procedure alone is about US$200 million, nearly double the amount of money allocated to the entire cleanup project. Eneu, which the cleanup workers are using as a base, is currently considered safe.

Diving

Thanks to its ominous nuclear history, newly-opened Bikini is one of Micronesia's premier dive spots. One highlight is the USS *Saratoga*, the world's only diveable aircraft carrier, which still holds visible planes and racks of bombs. Another memorable dive is the *Nagato*, a Japanese battleship from whose deck Admiral Yamamoto ordered his warplanes to attack Pearl Harbor. Grey reef sharks abound, and spotting a silvertip on the wrecks is not uncommon.

Sportsfishing (mostly catch and release) on Bikini is quite good, with skipjack, yellowfin and trevallys.

MDA also has a one week trolling pack-age, similar to the diving package, for US$3750, and flyfishing for US$2750. If you want to take a dive package but substitute a day's trolling or flyfishing, arrange with MDA in advance.

Places to Stay

MDA in Majuro operates the eight-unit *Bikini Atoll Resort* on Bikini. Rooms are simple but have air-con from generator electricity. There's hot and cold water and a recreation room with a VCR, pool table and table tennis. The price for one week is US$2750, which includes 12 dives, lodging and meals on Bikini and one•night at the RRE Hotel in Majuro. The AMI air fare (US$215 one way) between Majuro and Bikini is not included.

ENEWETOK ATOLL

● pop 715   ● area 2.3 sq miles

Enewetok islanders were evacuated to Ujelang Atoll before atomic bomb tests began in 1948. Over a 10 year period, 43 atomic bombs were detonated from Enewetok.

In 1980, after a US$120 million cleanup program, the islanders were allowed to return to Enewetok Island, in the southern part of the atoll.

A 9.8 megaton hydrogen bomb that exploded in 1958 on Enewetok blasted a mile-wide, 200-foot-deep crater in the lagoon and fractured the rock to a depth of 1400 feet beneath the crater's surface.

RONGELAP ATOLL

● pop 0   ● area 3.1 sq miles

The immensely powerful hydrogen bom 'Bravo' that exploded on Bikini on 1 Marc 1954 sent clouds of deadly radioactivi towards inhabited Rongelap Atoll, 10 miles to the east. The fallout came down a powdery ash six hours after the blast.

Signs of radiation sickness includin nausea, hair loss and severe burns occurre within hours, yet it wasn't until three da after the blast that the US military evac ated the 82 inhabitants of Rongelap to Kw jelein. The Rongelapese were returned their atoll in 1957.

The Rongelapese have continuing heal problems – almost 75% of the people wh were under the age of 10 on the day of t blast have had surgery for thyroid tumour

In 1985 the Greenpeace ship *Rainbo Warrior* moved the Rongelapese to a ne home on Mejato Island in Kwajelein Ato 110 miles to the south. In 1995, after tes mony by atomic energy officials reveale that the day before the bomb test a warnin from US meteorologists of a wind shift the direction of Rongelap had been ignore the US established a US$45 million tru fund for the Rongelapese. Rehabilitation the island began soon after; now infrastru ture is being constructed, a precursor resettlement.

Nauru

The people of the tiny, potato-shaped island republic of Nauru were once among the world's richest. Nauru's vast phosphate deposits, discovered in 1900, supplied Australia with abundant fertiliser for almost a century. Nowadays, however, phosphate supplies are rapidly dwindling, leaving the island's interior a treeless moonscape of coral pinnacles.

Facts about Nauru

HISTORY

Nauruan society was divided into 12 matrineal tribes, though two died out in the 20th century. Little else is known about pre-European Nauruan society, which was scrubbed away first by missionaries and later by the focus on phosphate.

First sighted by Europeans in 1798, Nauru quickly became a regular whaler port. In 1878, armed with European guns, Nauru's tribes began a 10 year deleterious civil war that reduced the island's population to 900 people. In 1886, Germany assumed control of Nauru, and German administrators and missionaries helped quash the civil war. Thirteen years later Nauru was folded into Germany's Marshall Islands Protectorate and Nauru remained under German control until WWI.

In 1900, Albert Ellis, a geologist with the London-based Pacific Islands Company, discovered that his doorstop, a stone from Nauru, was actually high-grade phosphate; mining operations commenced on erstwhile tranquil Nauru in 1907.

The British controlled Nauru during WWI and auctioned off the Germans' shares of the British Phosphate Corporation in London for £600,000. At the war's end, Australia, New Zealand and Great Britain assumed joint trusteeship of Nauru, eyeing its phosphate potential. To accommodate soaring postwar phosphate demand, Nauru's first cantilever was built in the late 1920s.

Capital City: None
Population: 11,300
Time: 12 hours ahead of GMT
Land Area: 21 sq km (8 sq miles)
Number of Islands: One
International Telephone Code: ☎ 674
GDP/Capita: US$2805
Currency: Australian dollar
  (A$1 = US$0.65)
Languages: English & Nauruan
Greeting: *Mo yoran*

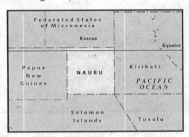

HIGHLIGHTS

- **Coral moonscape** – a fascinating, bizarre bleached-white moonscape which will remain long after the phosphate's gone

- **Phosphate works** – a chance to inspect the mammoth machinery that once made Nauru's people among the richest in the world

The Germans shelled the phosphate works early in WWII and damaged the cantilever, causing phosphate operations to halt until after the war. In August 1942 the Japanese vanquished the island and the following year deported 1200 Nauruans to the island of Truk (now the state of Chuuk in the Federated States of Micronesia). The Japanese held onto Nauru until 1945; only 737 deportees survived to return in 1946.

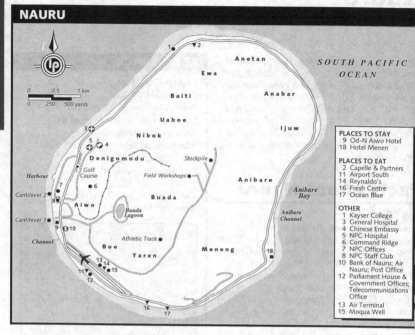

NAURU

SOUTH PACIFIC
OCEAN

Anetan

Ewa

Anabar

Baiti

Uaboe

Nibok

Ijuw

Denigomodu

Stockpile

Golf
Course   Field Workshops

Harbour   Anibare

Cantilever 2   Anibare
                                                    Bay
Aiwo   Buada
              Lagoon   Anibare
Cantilever 1   Channel

Channel   Athletic Track

        Boe   Meneng

    Buada

Yaren

PLACES TO STAY
9 Od-N Aiwo Hotel
18 Hotel Menen

PLACES TO EAT
2 Capelle & Partners
11 Airport South
14 Reynaldo's
16 Fresh Centre
17 Ocean Blue

OTHER
1 Kayser College
3 General Hospital
4 Chinese Embassy
5 NPC Hospital
6 Command Ridge
7 NPC Offices
8 NPC Staff Club
10 Bank of Nauru; Air
    Nauru; Post Office
12 Parliament House &
    Government Offices;
    Telecommunications
    Office
13 Air Terminal
15 Moqua Well

After the war, Nauru, with its local population decimated, became a UN Trust Territory. The phosphate works were repaired and another cantilever built in 1961.

Independence

As it groped toward independence in the mid-20th century, Nauru entertained a series of local governing structures: a Council of Chiefs was formed in 1927, replaced in 1951 by the Nauru Local Government Council. Though neither had real power, the symbolism of self-government resonated with the people.

Nauru gained independence on 31 January 1968, shortly after the Nauru Phosphate Corporation (NPC) bought the rights to Nauru's phosphate industry from the British Phosphate Corporation for US$21 million.

GEOGRAPHY & CLIMATE

Forty-two kilometres south of the equator, with a land area of just 21.3 sq km, Nauru is a stunning sight from the air – an isolate blot of land with an interior of blazing white coral pinnacles.

The mining industry has wreaked havoc on Nauru's tropical climate. The interior rock exposed by deforestation reflects the sun's rays back upwards and chases away the clouds and rain. Deforestation combined with this 'oven effect' is killing many indigenous birds, including frigate bird and Nauru's beloved noddies (see the boxed text 'Noddy Hunting' later in this chapter

GOVERNMENT & POLITICS

Nauru has been a Special Member of the British Commonwealth since 1968. It has one of the world's smallest parliaments (1 members), elected every three years, which in turn elects a president from its members As turmoil grows over Nauru's uncertain future and economic failures, no-confidence votes that spur a change of government have become common: in 1997, Nauru

Mining Devastation

For all the wealth brought by phosphate, mining has left Nauru physically a wreck. Trees have been removed, and much of the interior – topside – consists of lifeless, grey-white coral pinnacles. With this in mind, Nauru filed a 1989 suit in the Hague-based International Court of Justice against Australia for the damages caused by mining while the island was under Australian jurisdiction. In 1993, the suit was settled out of court for A$109 million; part of the agreement binds Australia to assist Nauru with rehabilitation and development. Ironically, Nauru itself has stayed the course of physical destruction, and mining operations, on a reduced scale, are expected to continue until the phosphate runs out in about 10 years.

turned through four presidents in as many months. In recent years, Nauru has had one female MP, Ruby Dediya, but she was voted out of office in 1997.

Nauru was admitted to the UN in 1999.

ECONOMY

Since the beginning of the 20th century, phosphate exports have been Nauru's only source of revenue. Nauru's people became some of the richest in the world (with a GNP of US$21,000 per capita) as annual phosphate exports reached two million tons. In the early 1990s, however, Nauru's exports fell to 500,000 tons. At more than A$60 a ton, phosphate remains a tremendously lucrative industry. Nonetheless, Nauru's phosphate supplies will likely be exhausted within 20 (or even ten) years. Most disturbingly, the government of Nauru's investment of the mining proceeds has been a case study in financial mismanagement, causing much of the Nauruan people's savings to evaporate.

In March 1999, the government began a program of retrenchment, laying off over 500 workers as part of a cost-cutting operation. It is also scrambling to diversify Nauru's economy by expanding fishing operations. The tourism industry is, as yet, nonexistent.

POPULATION & PEOPLE

Ethnic Nauruans, with a mix of Polynesian and Micronesian ancestry, account for 70% of Nauru's population. The balance comprises other Pacific Islanders, Asians (predominantly Chinese and Filipinos) and a few Europeans. I-Kiribati (Gilbertese) and Tuvaluans make up the majority of unskilled workers in the phosphate industry.

ARTS

Most traditional customs, dances and crafts have been completely subsumed by Nauru's all-encompassing focus on phosphate. No-one on Nauru knows how to make handicrafts anymore, except for a few of Nauru's most aged citizens.

Phosphate carving, however, has morphed into a craft of sorts – see the Shopping section for details. .

SOCIETY & RELIGION

Nauruans are fanatical about Australian Rules football and weightlifting.

Nauruan houses are modern by Micronesian standards. Most Nauruans are Christians, with fairly even numbers of Catholics and Protestants.

LANGUAGE

Although English is used for official government transactions, Nauruan – a language with both Polynesian and Micronesian influences – dominates conversation. Because of the large numbers of mine workers from other Pacific islands, you will hear a smattering of other Pacific languages as well.

Nauruan Basics

Hello.	*Mo yoran.*
Goodbye.	*Tarowang.*
How are you?	*Wo reit ed?*
I'm well.	*Mmo kor.*
Please.	*Magada.*
Thanks.	*Tubw.*
Yes.	*Em.*
No.	*Keo.*

Facts for the Visitor

SUGGESTED ITINERARIES
One day, or at most two, is plenty to see Nauru – visit the phosphate works and dramatic interior coral pinnacles, as well as Command Ridge.

VISAS & EMBASSIES
Visas for up to 30 days can be granted to visitors upon arrival in Nauru; if possible, bring a letter showing a pre-arranged hotel booking, though they'll undoubtedly let you in so long as the hotels have vacancies. Upon arrival visitors must give their passports to the immigration authorities; pick it up from the immigration office the next working day.

None of the above applies to transit passengers, who can stay on Nauru until their departure.

Nauruan Embassies & Consulates
Nauru's representation includes:

Australia
    Consulate:
    (☎ 02-9922 7722, fax 9923 1133)
    Box 1303, 47 Falcon St, Crows Nest, Sydney NSW 2065
    Consul General:
    (☎ 03-9653 5709, fax 9654 4738),
    Nauru House, 80 Collins St Level 50, Melbourne VIC 3000
UK
    (☎ 020-7235 6911, fax 7235 7423)
    Nauru Government Office; 3 Chesham St, London SWIX 8ND

MONEY
Nauru's official currency is the Australian dollar (exchange rates are listed under Money in the Regional Facts for the Visitor chapter). Only Air Nauru and the hotels accept credit cards.

The cash-strapped Bank of Nauru has difficulty changing money and travellers cheques, so bring sufficient Australian dollars into the country. The catch is that to carry over A$1000 in cash out of the country, you must obtain authorisation from the Bank of Nauru.

POST & COMMUNICATIONS
There is no postal code. The international telephone code is ☎ 674 and there are no telephone area codes. Public internet terminals are unavailable.

MEDIA
Nauru has two television stations. One plays mostly live CNN and the other is a sports network.

ELECTRICITY
Electricity is 240V AC, 50Hz and plugs are Australian style with three prongs.

WEIGHTS & MEASURES
Nauru uses the metric system.

HEALTH
Do not drink unboiled tap water. Nauru is subject to periodic typhoid outbreaks.

PUBLIC HOLIDAYS
Nauru celebrates New Year's Day, Easter (Sunday, Monday and Tuesday), and Christmas. Also celebrated are:

Independence Day	31 January
Constitution Day	17 May
Angam Day	26 October

ACTIVITIES
Diving is not good due to the sharp drop-off of Nauru's reef, and there are no dive shops anyway. Swim only with great caution in the harbour, Gabab Channel and the Anibare Channel north of the Menen Hotel.

Nauru has one nine-hole golf course where you can play free. For sportfishing contact the Oppenheimer family at Capell & Partner (☎ 555 6333, fax 555 6477) which charters a boat for A$90 an hour.

ACCOMODATION & FOOD
Nauru has two hotels. All restaurants on Nauru are Chinese; the myriad backdoor establishments sprouting up every 200m are good and cheap (A$2.50 for a meat-and-rice plate), but if there's typhoid circulating it best to stick to the licensed restaurant (listed in the Places to Stay & Eat section)

Noddy Hunting

Grilled noddy is a Nauruan delicacy, and hunting black noddy birds is a popular pastime in the Topside area. Hunters don camouflage clothing and head out after dark. In earlier centuries they would make noddy-like whistles to attract the birds; these days they bring stereos with pre-recorded noddy songs. The hunters then snag the noddies with a net attached to a long bamboo stick.

ren ankiwi – sashimi in coconut juice – is a speciality you'll find at most small Chinese shops (though not at the listed restaurants).

Getting There & Away

The only real way to get to Nauru is by air. Yacht facilities are almost nonexistent and the country is – not surprisingly – absent from luxury cruise-liner itineraries.

Nauru has a clean, modern airport. The reliable Air Nauru, the only airline serving the island, is a link to other Pacific destinations as well as Australia. Its one plane, a Boeing 737-400, flies to Fiji via Tarawa, Melbourne via Brisbane, and Manila via Pohnpei and Guam. The Air Nauru office (☎ 444 3141) in town, open weekdays, accepts American Express.

Getting Around

To/From the Airport

Both hotels send vans to meet arriving planes. Hotel Menen owns Nauru's only two taxis; it's A$16 around the island. Hotel Menen has two rental cars (A$50 a day). Also ask Kinza Clodumar (☎ 444 3856) about rentals. Hitching is possible.

For tours around Nauru ask your hotel, or the tourist office, which keeps a booklet entitled *Nauru – Educational Visits Guide*, which lists a range of tours (mostly free) of the island.

Around Nauru

Orientation

A paved 18km road circles the island; a road into the interior branches off near the NPC buildings. Across the runway from the airport are the government offices, though you'll have to circle around the runway to get there. Most services cluster just north of the runway.

Information

The office of Culture and Tourism (☎ 444 3292, fax 444 3791) in the government complex is unaccustomed to tourists.

The Bank of Nauru, in 'town' north of the runway, gives slow service and has little cash. Next door is the post office, which has two international phones and a fax machine; receive faxes (A$2 per page) at fax 444 3201. International calls can be made 24 hours a day from the Telecommunications building, across the runway from the airport.

Nauru has two hospitals; opt for the NPC Hospital (☎ 555 4155). The police emergency number is ☎ 110. For an ambulance dial ☎ 118.

Things to See

Numerous WWII **Japanese bunkers** line the coast. Other major WWII relics are on **Command Ridge**, Nauru's highest point. Drive as far up the dirt road as you can and angle left on foot at the three large water tanks. Just beyond on the right is the first rusted gun. Further along is a bunker that you can enter with a lantern, and further still are two enormous guns.

Back in town, check out the copious WWII relics at the excellent **NPC museum**, and the nearby **Arts & Crafts Centre** for its heaps of stone tools, old fishing nets, grass skirts and other handicrafts; both are closed but the tourist office has the key.

It's well worth a drive into the interior to see the **phosphate mining operations** and the resulting moonscape of coral pinnacles.

NAURU

Coral Pinnacles

Nauru's interior is a parched white sea of jagged coral pinnacles, some towering up to 15m high, that were created when the phosphate was extracted. Removal of the pinnacles may provide an opportunity for secondary mining, as there is up to 10% more phosphate lurking in the troughs between – too deep for the mining machinery to scoop.

Ask the NPC offices (☎ 555 4209) if they'll give you a brief tour. Back on the coast, the two giant **cantilevers** built offshore to expedite ship loading are an impressive sight; only one still works today.

Places to Stay

The government-owned *Hotel Menen* (☎ *444 3300, fax 444 3595)*, on the coast 4km east of the airport, has immaculate, spacious rooms with wooden desks, air-con, glass-enclosed shower, porch, phone, TV and tea-making set. Standard singles/doubles cost A$85/120, ocean-view rooms A$115/140, and suites are A$230. Major credit cards are accepted.

The concrete-block *Od-N Aiwo Hotel* (☎ *444 3591, fax 555 4555)*, located right in town, has 30 clean but plain rooms with refrigerator and air-con. There's a restaurant on site. Singles/doubles/triples cost A$45/

60/70. American Express and Diners Club are accepted (5% surcharge).

Places to Eat & Drink

The largest grocery store is *Capelle and Partners*, on the island's north side. Fast food is served up at a booth next door. The *Fresh Center*, between the airport and the Hotel Menen, for imported fruit. *Ocean Blue*, a clean eatery half a kilometre from the runway toward Hotel Menen, has scrumptious Chinese food. An excellent choice is the fish slices in black bean sauce (medium size is plenty at A$8). Right beside the airport, *Reynaldo's* also has tasty Chinese food for about the same prices, as does *Airport South*, across the runway from the airport. For drinks, the *Hotel Menen* has two bars. For a more local scene there's the spacious and pleasant *NPC Staff Club* in the building behind the tennis courts; it's not 'Members Only'. Wildly popular *Bingo Night* is Wednesday and Friday at pm sharp in Aiue Boulevard.

Shopping

Nauru has no traditional handicrafts on sale but there are excellent phosphate souvenirs. Phosphate rock, carved to resemble a map of Nauru and embedded in glossy native *tomano* wood (also in the shape of Nauru) is available at the NPC's engineering office near the second cantilever. These souvenirs come as paperweights (A$20) or as plaques (A$50); ask for a free inscription.

The Northern Mariana Islands

As a US Commonwealth, the Northern Mariana Islands (the CNMI) has closer political ties with the USA than other Micronesian island groups. Saipan, the largest island with 90% of the population, gets most of the tourist trade and Chamorro culture lies buried beneath American fast food, ubiquitous casinos and sex shops. But quiet, friendly Rota has just one paved road and Tinian is also a peaceful backwater, if you overlook the glittery new casino-hotel at one end of the island.

The Northern Marianas was the scene of some of the Pacific War's most devastating battles and today makes global headlines because of unsavoury labour practices associated with Saipan's billion-dollar garment industry.

Facts about the Northern Mariana Islands

HISTORY

The islands of the Northern Marianas were settled around 1500 BC by Chamorros that were culturally akin to Guam's indigenous people; see the Guam history section for details on early Chamorro culture.

First named the Islas de los Ladrones (Islands of Thieves) by Ferdinand Magellan in 1521, the Mariana Islands were renamed as Marianas upon the arrival of the Spanish priest Luis Diego Sanvitores, in honour of the Spanish queen Maria Ana of Austria. In the 1690s, the Spanish rounded up the Chamorros and brought them to Guam to convert them more effectively to Christianity. On Rota several hundred Rotanese managed to hide in the hills and avoid capture. After Spain gained sovereignty over the Marianas in 1885, the now Hispanicised Chamorros were encouraged to move back to the Northern Marianas from Guam,

AT A GLANCE

Capital City (& Island): Garapan (Saipan)
Population: 58,846
Time: 10 hours ahead of GMT
Land Area: 472 sq km (184 sq miles)
Number of Islands: 14
International Telephone Code: ☎ 670
GDP/Capita: US$8370
Currency: US dollar
Languages: English, Chamorro & Carolinian
Greeting: *Haf adai* (Chamorro)

HIGHLIGHTS

- **Fiestas** – music, dancing and Chamorro food feasts at these festive church-centred events

- **The Grotto, Saipan** – Saipan's most unique and exciting dive – for the experienced only

- **Suicide Cliff, Saipan** – another place to reflect on the tragedies of WWII

- **North Field, Tinian** – the massive, utterly deserted runways from which the bombers carrying the atomic bombs to Hiroshima and Nagasaki took off

- **Rota** – a friendly, peaceful island where everyone waves holds intriguing natural wonders, such as the bird sanctuary or the taga stone quarry

NORTHERN MARIANAS

Farallon de Pajaros

Maug Islands

Asuncion

*PHILIPPINE
SEA*

Agrihan

Pagan

Alamagan

Guguan

0   50   100 km
0   25   50 miles

Sarigan

Anatahan
          Farallon de
          Medinilla

GARAPAN   Saipan

Aguijan   Tinian

*NORTH
PACIFIC
OCEAN*

Rota

GUAM

Mariana Trench

though some Carolinians, who had mov
to the Marianas in the 1820s, had taken t
best coastal land. Germany bought t
Northern Marianas from Spain in 1899, a
the Japanese took the Northern Marian
from Germany at the beginning of WV
and set up flourishing sugar cane plant
tions. At the outbreak of WWII there we
over 45,000 Japanese and immigrant wor
ers in the Northern Marianas – more than
times the number of Micronesians.

Operation Forager, a massive US inv
sion with 127,000 soldiers, captured t
Mariana Islands in June and July 1944. L
pre-invasion bombing attacks included t
first-ever wartime use of napalm. A wild a
fight known as the 'Marianas Turkey Shoo
took place just west of the Marianas.

US troops immediately extended t
Japanese airbase on Tinian, using it to sta
air raids on Japan, including the atom
bomb drops on Hiroshima and Nagasaki.

The fierce fighting between the US a
Japan had reduced whole towns to rubb
and in the years following the war the US a
ministered the islands by providing han
outs rather than by encouraging econom
development. In 1948 the CIA closed off ha
of Saipan to islanders and outsiders alike a
used the northern part of the island for cov
military manoeuvres. In 1962 the CI
moved its operations out of Saipan and t
Northern Marianas were finally opened
visitors. The UN Trust Territory administr
tion then moved its headquarters to Saipa

In 1961 Saipan and Rota petitioned t
US government to become integrated wi
Guam, but Guam voters rejected this in
1969 referendum. In June 1975 the Northe
Marianas voted to become a US Commo
wealth, and became the first district to wit
draw from the Trust Territory. Under t
commonwealth agreement, which becan
fully effective in 1986, the Northern Ma
ianas retained the right to internal se
government and its people became US ci
zens, while the USA controls foreign affai

GEOGRAPHY & ECOLOGY
The Northern Mariana Islands divide t
Pacific Ocean and the Philippine Sea. Th

stal-clear waters and rock arches in Palau's fabled Rock Islands

An aerial view of the Rock Islands in Palau – a mecca for divers

Painted *bai* (men's house)

Cocktails in the sun – a picnic villa at a resort in Yap

Just one of Palau's many magnificent island resorts

Mariana Trench

The Mariana Trench is an underwater canyon extending 1835 miles along the ocean floor east of the Mariana Islands. Formed by the Pacific tectonic plate diving beneath the neighbouring Philippine Sea plate, the trench contains the world's greatest known ocean depth – 36,201 feet (11,034m).

Forced upwards by the clash of the two tectonic plates, the Mariana Islands are but the emerged tips of massive underwater mountains. And they can claim another record – if measured from their bases deep in the Mariana Trench, the islands would tower 10,000 feet over Mt Everest.

comprise 14 of the 15 islands in the Mariana archipelago, which arcs 400 miles northward from Guam, the chain's southernmost island. All the islands are high, of either volcanic or limestone formation, though Tinian is the lowest, reaching just 590 feet. The highest point in all of Micronesia is in the Marianas – 3166 feet on the remote island of Agrihan. Saipan is 47 sq miles, Tinian is 39 sq miles and Rota is 32 sq miles. Micronesia's only active volcanoes are here – the most recent eruption was in 1981 on the outer island of Pagan.

CLIMATE

Saipan's temperature averages 81°F (27°C) year-round, with a dry season from December to May. Like Guam, the islands lie directly in the typhoon track, which most commonly occur from August to December.

GOVERNMENT & POLITICS

The Commonwealth of the Northern Mariana Islands (CNMI) has its own governor and lieutenant governor, plus a legislature with nine senators – three each from Saipan, Tinian and Rota, and 15 representatives – 13 from Saipan, one from Tinian and one from Rota. Each district centre has its own mayor.

Although CNMI residents are US citizens, they don't vote in US elections and are exempt from US income taxes. CMNI representation in the US Congress is limited to observer status.

FLORA & FAUNA

After WWII Saipan was so deforested that tangan plants were aerially seeded to prevent erosion. These plants now predominate the northern end of the island and have choked up the natural ecosystem. Hibiscus, banana and coconut trees are everywhere, as are flame trees that flower in May and June.

ECONOMY

The USA has heavily subsidised development in the CNMI, where the government remains the largest employer. Tourism is an important industry, with a significant proportion of tourists arriving from Japan. However, the recent Asian economic crisis has impacted on tourism and the economy (nearly 1800 businesses closed in 1998!). The CNMI minimum wage, just US$3.05 an hour, is the lowest of any territory under US jurisdiction. Unemployment and poverty rates among the Chamorro population are high, as 90% of private-sector jobs are held by low-paid Asian workers.

POPULATION & PEOPLE

With a 4.2% growth rate, the Northern Marianas' population more than tripled from 1980 to 1995. The vast majority of people live on Saipan (approximately 52,698 people) and a few thousand live on Rota and Tinian. Slightly more than half of the total population are resident aliens, mostly from the Philippines, China and Korea. Of the native population, roughly 75% are Chamorro and the remainder are Carolinian.

ARTS

Authenticity is hard to come by in the CNMI, particularly on Saipan, where Chamorro culture has been almost buried by heavy commercialisation and western values. Though Tinian and Rota are much less developed than Saipan, handicrafts are still not readily available and those seeking out cultural relics or performances must look quite hard.

NORTHERN MARIANAS

Shady Labour Practices

Under the commonwealth covenant, the CNMI government retains its own immigration controls. In the 1980s many US companies set up factories in Saipan to take advantage of the tens of thousands of low-paid Filipino and Chinese workers, and the duty-free access to the USA. These infamous US$1.2 billion 'garment industry' factories turn out designer clothing tagged 'Made in the USA' and Saipan benefits from over US$2 million in annual taxes.

The industry is an economic pillar of Saipan. However, there are huge problems with the treatment of foreign workers, some of whom claim they have been beaten, locked into factories and forced into abortions. Others claim that they must work up to 14 hours a day, seven days a week.

These complaints coalesced into a US$1 billion class-action lawsuit filed in the late 1990s by California and Saipan-based human rights groups. The lawsuit named 18 high-profile US retailers as defendants, including big names like Tommy Hilfiger, J Crew and Gap.

On the political front, US President Clinton has strongly criticised the CNMI's labour practices and immigration policies. There are strong indications that Congress will reassume control of these policies early within the next decade, which would effectively extinguish the garment industry: new Congressional legislation would raise labour and immigration standards to federal levels and other legislation would end Saipan's 'Made in the USA' labels and revoke Saipan's duty-free shipping status, which amounts to US$200 million in lost federal tax revenue.

SOCIETY & CONDUCT

The local Chamorro culture is a hybrid of native and Spanish colonial influences, with a powerful overlay of popular American trends.

RELIGION

Roman Catholicism predominates, especially among the Chamorro population and Filipino immigrants.

LANGUAGE

English is the official language, while Chamorro (also spoken on Guam) and Carolinian are native tongues. See the Guam chapter for a few basic Chamorro words and phrases.

Facts for the Visitor

SUGGESTED ITINERARIES

All three major CNMI islands can easily be visited within one week or 10 days. Peaceful and friendly Rota makes a fine getaway for a few days and is only a short trip, via commuter flight, from Guam. Saipan has good diving and historical points that could easily absorb a few days, if you can ignore the casinos and strip-joints. Tinian is an historical treasure-trove, but most of its accommodation options aren't quite up to par.

TOURIST OFFICES

See Internet Resources and Information under Saipan later in this chapter.

VISAS & EMBASSIES

The CNMI uses US embassies. US citizens need no visa (or passport) and can stay as long as they like. Non-US citizens can stay visa-free for up to 30 days. Tourists can get an extension of up to two months (US$100

MONEY

The CNMI uses US dollars (see Exchange Rates under Money in the Regional Facts for the Visitor chapter). Credit cards are widely used on Saipan and are becoming more common on Rota and (more slowly) Tinian. Saipan has numerous ATMs, while Rota and Tinian have one each.

Prices quoted in this chapter, particularly hotel prices, will probably rise once the Asian financial crisis lifts.

POST & COMMUNICATIONS

Mail is handled by the US postal service. Postal codes are: Saipan (96950), Rota (96951) and Tinian (96952); the Marianas' abbreviation is 'MP', but write 'via USA', so you would address mail to: name, address, island, postal code, MP via USA.

The CNMI's international telephone code is ☎ 670 and there are no area codes. Dial ☎ 411 for directory assistance. Internet access is possible on Saipan but not Rota or Tinian.

INTERNET RESOURCES

Check out the tourist office website (www.visit-marianas com).

MEDIA

The *Marianas Variety* is published six days a week and the *Saipan Tribune* five days a week. All islands have access to cable TV.

ELECTRICITY

The Marianas' electricity is single phase 60Hz, 115/230 volts AC, with two-prong US-style plugs.

WEIGHTS & MEASURES

The CNMI, like the USA, uses the imperial system. See the table at the back of this book for conversion to metric.

HEALTH

Water on Saipan and Tinian should be boiled before drinking, though Rota's water is good to drink. There is a hospital on each of the main islands, although Saipan's is the best.

BUSINESS HOURS

Most Saipan and Tinian businesses are open weekdays from 8 am to 5 pm. On Rota, hours are earlier: 7.30 to 11.30 am and 2.30 to 4.30 pm is typical. Banking hours are typically Monday to Thursday from 10 am to 3 pm and Friday from 10 am to 6 pm.

PUBLIC HOLIDAYS & SPECIAL EVENTS

Public holidays in the Northern Marianas include New Year's Day, Easter, US Independence Day, Columbus Day, Veterans Day, Thanksgiving and Christmas (for these holiday dates, see the Regional Facts for the Visitor chapter). Other public holidays are:

Commonwealth Day	9 January
President's Day	3rd Monday in February
Covenant Day	24 March
Memorial Day	Last Monday in May
Labor Day	1st Monday in September
Citizenship Day	4 November
Constitution Day	8 December

Most villages have an (alcohol-free) annual fiesta honouring their patron saint: Rota has two, Tinian one and Saipan six. In Saipan they're in San Vicente (early April), San Antonio (mid-June), Mt Carmel Cathedral in Chalan Kanoa (mid-July), San Roque (mid-August), Tanapag (early October) and Koblerville (late October). Rota's fiestas are in Songsong Village (mid-October) and Sinapaulo (mid-March). Tinian's San Jose fiesta is held during late April or early May.

All three islands have sporting events year-round; Saipan's Tagman triathlon (☎ 234 1001) is especially popular.

ACTIVITIES

All islands have good diving. A junkyard of WWII equipment lies just off Tinian, Rota has some new 'wrecks' and Saipan has the challenging Grotto. Saipan and Rota have golf courses.

ACCOMMODATION & FOOD

Rota has the region's first youth hostel. Saipan has numerous resorts and Rota has one. Most food is western-style, though you can sometimes find Chamorro dishes; see the boxed text in the Guam chapter for an overview of Chamorro food.

Getting There & Away

AIR

Continental Airlines serves Saipan via Guam from Japan, Hong Kong and Taipei. Northwest Airlines and Japan Airlines

(JAL) fly directly from Tokyo and JAL services other Japanese cities. Continental connects to more destinations, including Chuuk, Koror, Yap, Bali, Manila and Honolulu. For details see the Getting There & Away section in the Guam chapter. Saipan can be visited relatively cheaply with Continental's Visit Micronesia or Circle Micronesia passes – see Air Passes in the Getting Around the Region chapter for details. The cheaper CNMI-based commuter airlines Freedom Air and Pacific Island Aviation also fly to Guam from Saipan.

SEA

Yachties will be charged from US$62 for an entrance fee plus US$56 dockage on Saipan, though the fee may be waived altogether for pleasure boats. You can go straight to Rota (rather than going through Saipan), though its harbour facilities are worse than those of Saipan or Tinian; call Rota's seaport at ☎ 532 8489 in advance.

Getting Around

AIR

Pacific Island Aviation (PIA) and Freedom Air fly daily between Saipan and Guam, some flights stop through Rota. Both also make the 15-minute hop from Saipan to Tinian daily. Flights are frequent, cheap and reliable.

CAR & HITCHING

Only Saipan has taxis, but they're so expensive that it's more economical to rent a car. All three islands have major car rental agencies, prices start around US$40 per day for unlimited mileage. Hitching is dangerous on Saipan, but Rota and Tinian are safer.

Saipan

- pop 52,698   • area 47 sq miles

Only Guam rivals Saipan in its crush of Japanese tourists. Much of the island's Micronesian character has been overshadowed by fast-food chains and poker houses, as tourists and alien workers now outnumber the Saipanese. Still, outside flashy Garapa Saipan has gentle beaches on its weste and southern coasts, a rugged and rocl eastern coast, a hilly interior and dramat cliffs on the northern coast.

Information

Tourist Offices The Marianas Visito Authority (☎ 664 3200, fax 554 3237, mva saipan.com) is on the inland side of Bea Rd, south of Garapan.

Money The Bank of Guam and the Bank Hawaii have branches in Garapan a Susupe. There are abundant ATMs. T American Express (Amex) representative located at the MITA travel office on Bea Rd on Garapan's south side.

Post & Communications You can pi up general delivery mail from the main po office, which is in Chalan Kanoa.

Local and long-distance calls can made from pay phones and most hote Dial ☎ 411 for directory assistance. Inte national calls can be made via IT&E pho booths around the island and at an office

Suicide Attack

The quiet village of Tanapag was the site of one of the most fanatical attacks of WWII On the night of 6 July 1944, about 4000 Japanese soldiers hurled themselves in a *banzai* attack upon US forces, which were lined up along Tanapag Beach. Some of the Japanese had guns, but most were armed just with clubs, bayonet sticks, bamboo spears and grenades. The Japanese, honour-bound to die one way or another in the face of defeat, were intent on taking as many Americans with them as possible. As wave after wave of Japanese soldiers rushed down in the surprise attack, the Americans were pushed out into the water, across Tanapag Harbor and all the way back onto the reef, firing all the while at the unrelenting enemy. By the next morning it was al over and 5000 men were dead.

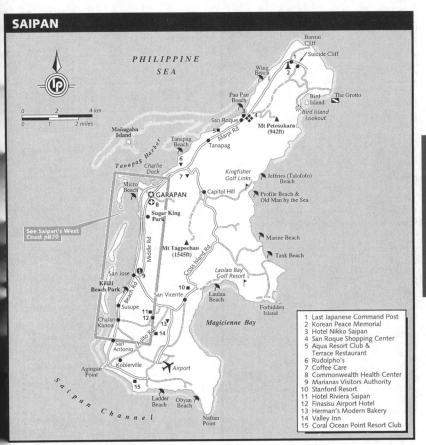

SAIPAN

PHILIPPINE SEA

Banzai Cliff
Suicide Cliff
Wing Beach
Pau Pau Beach
Bird Island
The Grotto
Bird Island Lookout
San Roque
Mt Petosukara (942ft)
Mañagaha Island
Tanapag Beach
Tanapag
Marpi Rd
Tanapag Harbor
Charlie Dock
Kingfisher Golf Links
Jeffries (Talofofo) Beach
Micro Beach
GARAPAN
Sugar King Park
Capitol Hill
Profile Beach & Old Man by the Sea
See Saipan's West Coast p870
Middle Rd
Marine Beach
Mt Tagpochau (1545ft)
Cross Island Rd
Laolao Bay Golf Resort
Tank Beach
San Jose
Kilili Beach Park
Beach Rd
Susupe
San Vicente
Laulau Beach
Forbidden Island
Chalan Kanoa
Magicienne Bay
San Antonio
Isito Rd
Koblerville
Airport
Agingan Point
Saipan Channel
Ladder Beach
Obyan Beach
Naftan Point

1 Last Japanese Command Post
2 Korean Peace Memorial
3 Hotel Nikko Saipan
4 San Roque Shopping Center
5 Aqua Resort Club & Terrace Restaurant
6 Rudolpho's
7 Coffee Care
8 Commonwealth Health Center
9 Marianas Visitors Authority
10 Stanford Resort
11 Hotel Riviera Saipan
12 Finasisu Airport Hotel
13 Herman's Modern Bakery
14 Valley Inn
15 Coral Ocean Point Resort Club

0   2   4 km
0   1   2 miles

NORTHERN MARIANAS

San Jose; faxes can be sent and received (fax 234 8525) here for 50 cents a page. Try the library for Internet access or look around Garapan, where Internet venues tend to come and go.

Libraries Saipan's modern public library is near the Joeten Shopping Center in Susupe and is closed Wednesday and Sunday.

Medical Services & Emergency For police, fire and ambulance emergencies, dial ☎ 911. Saipan's modern hospital, the Commonwealth Health Center (☎ 234 8950), is on Middle Rd in Garapan. For typhoon, storm or medical evacuation emergencies, call ☎ 322 9274. For weather info dial ☎ 234 5724.

Garapan
● pop 15,000

The Japanese developed Garapan, their Marianas administrative centre, into a little Tokyo, with public baths, sake shops, Shinto shrines and Japanese schools and office buildings. Garapan was completely leveled by US bombers during WWII and it wasn't until the 1960s that the Saipanese began to resettle the area. These days Garapan is

NORTHERN MARIANAS

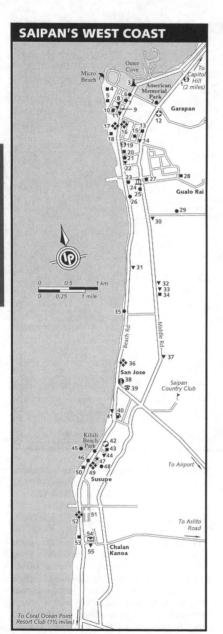

SAIPAN'S WEST COAST

SAIPAN'S WEST COAST

PLACES TO STAY
4	Hyatt Regency Saipan – Gilligan's & Kili Terrace; Windsurfing Saipan
5	Dai-Ichi Hotel
10	Remington Club
13	Oriental Hotel; Shirley's Coffee Shop
15	Holiday In Saipan
18	Hafadai Beach Hotel
20	Saipan Ocean View Hotel
28	Sugar King Hotel
34	Garden Motel
43	Sun Inn
46	Saipan Diamond Hotel
50	Saipan Grand Hotel
53	Pacific Gardenia Hotel; Sunset Bar & Grill

PLACES TO EAT
8	Chamorro House
9	Figueroa's
11	Bobby Cadillacs; Winchell's
14	Mom's Round Two
22	Canton Restaurant
30	La Filipina
31	Thai House Restaurant
32	Pizza Hut
33	Kung Chun
37	McDonald's
41	Oleai Beach
44	Island Farmer's Market
55	Saipan Farmers' Market

OTHER
1	Bank of Hawaii
2	Public Tennis Courts
3	Court of Honor Memorial
6	Fire Station
7	Saipan Scooters
12	Commonwealth Health Center
16	DFS Galleria
17	Hafadai Shopping Center
19	Bank of Guam
21	MITA Travel Office
23	Horiguchi (Federal) Building
24	CNMI Museum
25	Japanese Jail
26	Abracadabra
27	Sugar King Park
29	Stingray Divers
35	Japanese Tank
36	Hakubotan
38	Marianas Visitors Authority
39	IT&E Office
40	24 Hour Petrol Station
42	Philippine Consulate
45	American Tanks (offshore)
47	Police Station; Library
48	Nauru Building
49	Joeten Shopping Center
51	Mt Carmel Cathedral
52	Town House Shopping Center
54	Main Post Office

booming, thanks again to the presence of the Japanese – this time as tourists.

Micro Beach is Saipan's most attractive white sand beach. It's travel poster material, with brilliant turquoise waters and a good view of Mañagaha Island and the sunset. Wade out to the deeper water for good swimming.

American Memorial Park stretches north along the coast from the Hyatt hotel, with ublic tennis courts, beachside picnic rounds, restrooms and two large **memori-ls** honouring Americans who died in the JS invasions of Saipan and Tinian during VWII.

Sugar King Park, on the east side of Midlle Rd, features a steam-powered engine nce used to haul sugar cane from fields in he Marpi area and a botanical garden. The 934 bronze statue in the park centre is of Iaruji Matsue, responsible for developing he sugar industry in the Marianas. At the ar end of the park a red, riverless bridge eads to a **Japanese shrine**. The steps behind he shrine lead to a 15-minute loop trail that asses a hexagonal prayer temple that's ledicated to WWII Japanese soldiers.

The ruins of the old **Japanese hospital**, lirectly across Middle Rd from Sugar King ark, have become the small **CNMI Mu-eum**, holdings include some trinkets reovered from the 17th century wreckage of he Spanish galleon *Concepcion*.

A bit further south on Middle Rd is the ntact and intriguing old **Japanese jail**.

North of Garapan

The northern tip of the island, called Marpi, as most of Saipan's WWII tourist attracions and its prettiest scenery. The northern nd of **Pau Pau Beach** in San Roque is pleasntly undeveloped, with soft sand, a picnic helter and good snorkelling and swimming luring high tide, take the paved road just iorth of the Nikko. A bit over a mile north long Marpi Rd and then down an unmarked oad to the left after the country club swimning pool, is **Wing Beach**, which is also andy and good for snorkelling.

About 7½ miles north of Garapan is the (orean Peace Memorial. Take the turnoff opposite the memorial to **Banzai Cliff**, where iundreds of Japanese civilians jumped to heir deaths as the Americans took the island n 1944. Whole families lined up in order of ige. Each child was pushed over the edge by he next oldest brother or sister, until the nother pushed the oldest child and the faher pushed his wife before running back-vards over the cliff himself. Plaques and nemorials commemorate the spot.

At the **Last Command Post** the troops of the Japanese Imperial Army readied themselves for their final desperate battle against US invasion forces. Lieutenant General Yoshitsugo Saito, acknowledging defeat, asked his remaining soldiers to each take seven American lives for the emperor, triggering the *banzai* (literally 'hurrah') suicide attack at Tanapag Harbor. Saito then faced north-west toward Japan and committed *harakiri* (belly cutting suicide). Guns, torpedoes and tanks are below the command post bunker, cleverly concealed in a rock face. You can climb inside the bunker.

Half a mile beyond the Last Command Post, bear right and then right again, and then travel 2 miles up to **Suicide Cliff**. Runners sometimes take the paved roadside path up in the evenings. The 820 foot sheer rock face, with a great view, was the site of Japanese suicides, similar to Banzai Cliff.

The Grotto, Saipan's most unique dive, is a collapsed limestone cavern with a pool of cobalt-blue seawater filled by three underwater passageways. Sometimes the Grotto is calm and at other times filled with powerful surges of water. Steep concrete stairs lead down to the water, as tiny stalactites and massive spider webs hang overhead. To reach the Grotto, turn left quarter of a mile past the Suicide Cliff turn-off. The same turn-off leads to the **Bird Island lookout**. Bird Island is a rocky limestone islet that's a wildlife sanctuary for brown noddies and other seabirds.

Cross-Island Road

The Cross Island Rd heads north from Garapan, turns inland to Capitol Hill, circles Mt Tagpochau, goes south through San Vicente and then heads back to the west coast, ending up on Beach Rd in San Jose.

Capitol Hill holds most CNMI government offices. The CIA built the complex in 1948 to train Nationalist Chinese guerrillas to fight against Mao Zedong. You can drive to the top of 1545 feet **Mt Tagpochau**, Saipan's highest point, which affords excellent views. Take the crossroad opposite Capitol Hill's convention centre, drive through the housing project and turn right. Continue a few hundred yards beyond the

COURTESY OF THE GUAM VISITORS BUREAU

NORTHERN MARIANAS

Latte stones are thought to be pillars that once supported ancient buildings. Many such stones still stand in the Mariana Islands today – although the buildings are long gone.

civil defence buildings and take the dirt road heading down to the right.

South of Garapan

A decade of development has turned Beach Rd into a nearly continuous strip of nightclubs, restaurants and shopping centres. **Ladder** and **Obyan** are two south coast beaches off the tourist track. Go around the runway's south-west tip and the road to Ladder Beach comes in on the right, quarter of a mile after the turn-off to Koblerville. More appealing is pretty white Obyan Beach, with a turn-off 1½ miles beyond Ladder Beach. Near Obyan are a large WWII concrete bunker and eight *latte* stones (foundation pillars that were used to support ancient Chamorro buildings) carbon dated to around 1500 BC.

Mañagaha Island

Small, uninhabited Mañagaha, 1½ miles north-west of Micro Beach, is covered with a fringing white sand beach and has Saipan's best snorkelling, with colourful tropical fish and abundant coral. Rusting war relics include a pair of coastal cannons along the beach near the boat landing. On the other side of the island is a colourful statue and a small monument marking the burial site of the Yapese chief Aghurubw, who in 1815 led a group of settlers from the Satawal atoll in the Yap chain and established a Carolinian settlement on Saipan.

Mañagaha fills with Japanese tourists on day trips and prices are high: US$15 will rent a set and US$21 buys a barbecue lunch. There are covered picnic tables and changing rooms (US$2 to $3). The 15 minute boat ride to Mañagaha begins at Saipan's new Outer Cove marina, boats depart generally between 10 am and 3 pm and cost US$35 to $45.

Activities

Diving & Snorkelling Saipan's most unusual and exciting dive is the Grotto. For experienced and fit divers only, it features a 30m cavern that's accessible by concrete stairs. Turtles, sharks and sometimes a manta ray can keep company with divers. The currents can be quite tricky, so get a thorough briefing beforehand. Other popular dives include war wrecks in Tanapag Harbor, caves and garden eels at Obyan each and a huge coral head offshore from the Saipan Grand Hotel.

Saipan's best snorkelling is at Mañagaha Island. Pau Pau, Laulau and Wing beaches have reasonably good snorkelling. You can also try snorkelling the US Army tanks off Susupe's Kilili Beach.

Among Saipan's few English-speaking operations is Abracadabra (☎ 233 7234, fax 33 7235, ejcomfort@saipan.com) on Beach Rd, south of Garapan. Two-tank wreck dives are US$65, and a Tinian trip is US$90. Gear costs US$45, but you don't have to re-rent the gear for consecutive days. Stingray Divers (☎ 233 6100, fax 234 6709) is at Gualo Rai (if you're driving south from Garapan, turn left off Middle Rd when you see the Honey Motel and hang the first left). Another American-run operation, Stingray has beach dives from US$30 and boat dives from US$40 to $45 per tank. Gear rents from US$20 to $35 and intro dives cost US$60. They'll go to Tinian upon request.

Other Activities Windsurfing is popular along Micro Beach, contact Windsurfing Saipan (☎ 234 6965) on the beach near the Hyatt, where equipment costs US$40/60 for a half/full day. Snorkel sets rent for US$8 and kayaks for US$15 an hour. Groups go to Mañagaha for US$20 a head.

Joggers and roller-bladers can enjoy the new 2½ mile Beach Pathway along the coast north to Garapan from Kili Beach Park. Saipan has four 18-hole golf courses and one nine hole course, ask the tourist office for a listing. Many first-class hotels have tennis courts for their guests.

Places to Stay

Rates for all tiers of hotels are likely to rise significantly when the CNMI's economy returns to normal. Most budget and mid-range hotels provide free airport transfers, while top-end hotels are likely to charge. Unless otherwise noted, the hotels have air-con, cable TV, phones, mini-fridges, private bathroom and a 10% room tax.

Saipan lacks camping grounds and sufficient crime makes it inadvisable.

Budget Though inland, the *Valley Inn* (☎ 234 7018, fax 234 7029) near the airport has a cheerful staff and pleasant rooms. Compact but cosy studios have a separate kitchen area (US$45, tax included). The *Garden Motel* (☎ 234 3729) along Middle Rd is another small, family-run hotel with a comfortable atmosphere. Watch carefully for the sign, which is partially obscured by trees. Rooms with the usual amenities and a VCR go for US$39 (tax included).

The Korean-owned *Sun Palace Hotel* (☎ 234 3232, fax 235 6062), behind the baseball field in Susupe, has large rooms for US$30. Though you can sometimes smell cigarette smoke and the air-con might not be really cold, it's cheap, safe and convenient. The Japanese-owned *Remington Club* (☎ 234 5449, fax 234 5619) is a pension-style hotel in Garapan and is just a minute's walk from Micro Beach. Rooms are straightforward but quite adequate and considering its prime location, it's a good value at US$55/72 for singles/doubles.

Mid-Range The locally owned *Pacific Gardenia Hotel* (☎ 234 3455, fax 234 3411) is on Beach Rd at the north end of Chalan Kanoa. Despite its poker-dotted setting, it stands on a gorgeous white-sand beach. The 14 rooms, along an atrium-like hallway, are large and well furnished, and most have kitchens. It's US$54/60 for singles/doubles, including continental breakfast and one free drink. *Finasisu Airport Hotel* (☎ 235 6524, fax 235 8013, finasusuhotel@saipan.com), near the airport, is a large, condo-like complex where units have a full kitchen, living room and two bedrooms (US$60). The *Holiday In Saipan* (☎ 234 3554, fax 235 5023), a couple of blocks inland from Beach Rd in Garapan, has decent rooms for US$50 for singles/doubles, plus pool (airport transfers US$10 each way).

The Chinese-owned *Oriental Hotel* (☎ 233 1420, fax 233 1424, orientalhotel@saipan.com) is on Middle Rd, opposite the Commonwealth Health Center and a 10 minute walk from Micro Beach. It has decent rooms right atop Shirley's Coffee Shop. Singles/doubles cost US$54/60.

NORTHERN MARIANAS

Top End The seven-storey *Hyatt Regency Saipan* (☎ 234 1234, fax 234 7745), right on Micro Beach, has 325 rooms with balconies and ocean views. Rates start at US$275 and prices in the newer south wing and the regency wing are higher. The grounds are pleasantly landscaped and there's a pool, lit tennis courts, a fitness centre and excellent restaurants. Airport transfers are US$15 each way.

The *Aqua Resort Club* (☎ 322 1234, fax 322 1220), on the beach in Tanapag, is among the top Japanese-oriented resorts. Casual yet classy, it has a pleasant open-air lobby that incorporates some Micronesian touches, a fabulous beachfront setting and large swimming pools. The rooms have verandas (most with ocean views). The rates start at US$270, airport transfers are US$15 each way.

Contact the tourist office for a further listing of Saipan's resort hotels.

Places to Eat

A 10% tip is expected at most restaurants.

Budget *Bobby Cadillacs* (☎ 234 3976), near Winchell's in Garapan, is all things to all people. Some swear by its US$4 pancakes, others by its pizzas and still others by its killer meat sandwiches. Call ahead for takeout. *Herman's Modern Bakery*, on the airport road, is a local eatery with cheap breakfasts, sandwiches and lunch specials. It opens at 6 am daily; come early for the freshest bread. *Shirley's Coffee Shop*, in the Oriental Hotel, is a small branch of the beloved Guam restaurant. Here it's more a quick-stop than a restaurant, but you can still get good coffee and a hearty meal (sandwiches, curry, seafood and steak, most dishes cost US$6 and up).

Mid-Range *Coffee Care*, half a mile up the Capitol Hill Rd, is run by a former Peace Corps worker and is a favourite expat watering hole. Besides cappuccinos and espressos, you can get light meals at reasonable prices and good beer in the evenings. The US$10 focaccia sandwich is pricey but popular. Dinner specials such as pasta or Thai food cost about US$10.

Rudolpho's, opposite the turn-off to Capitol Hill, has good, reasonably priced Mexican and Italian food. The bar's outdoor seating draws expats. You can get a taco, burrito or enchilada with rice and beans for around US$8. Seafood, chicken and steak meals are US$10 to $17. It has great evening specials like US$1 pizza or discount margaritas.

Thai House Restaurant on Beach Rd at the south end of Garapan has good Thai food at moderate prices. Pad Thai, red or green curries and other dishes are US$7 to $8; order mild – hot is *hot*. Frosty 18-ounce (600mL) mugs of Steinlager on tap cost US$3.50. *Kung Chun* (☎ 234 1249), a Korean restaurant on Middle Rd, is popular for its friendly service and cheap, tasty barbecue buffet (US$8 at lunch, US$10 at dinner).

Chamorro House is in the Micro Beach area and serves local food, though prices are un-locally high as it caters to the Japanese crowd. Their best deal is lunch, when Chamorro dishes such as *tinaktak katni* (beef strips in coconut milk) and *kelaguen mannok* (grilled chicken and fresh shredded coconut in a light lemon sauce) go for US$7.50. Dinner prices are about double.

Top End The Aqua Resort Club's *Terrace Restaurant* (☎ 322 1234) has an Austrian chef and Saipan's best-value buffets. Friday nights feature fresh oysters, shrimp and other seafood (US$20). On Saturday there's Black Angus prime rib buffet. Other days have a 'light and easy' luncheon buffet (US$12). The Hyatt's *Kili Terrace* is a reasonably good lunch buffet – you can sit out in the pleasant open-air terrace beside the pond and eat your fill of *mahimahi*, sushi, *soba*, spare ribs, breads, soup, salads and desserts for US$20. The Hyatt's new and popular *Giovanni's*, just inside from Kili Terrace, serves excellent Italian food.

Self-Catering *Saipan Farmers' Market*, the 'Co-op of the Hardworking People', is a simple fruit and vegetable market opposite the post office in Chalan Kanoa. Supermarkets in Saipan are modern and well stocked. Try the *Hafadai Shopping Center* and *Joeten Shopping Center*.

Entertainment

The open-air ***Sunset Bar & Grill*** is behind the Pacific Gardenia Hotel in Chalan Kanoa and is a fabulous sunset locale on a white sand beach. ***Gilligan's***, in the Hyatt, hosts dinner shows and then turns into a dance floor. It's open nightly except Mondays and has a US$5 cover charge. There's a movie theatre in Chalan Kanoa.

Shopping

Saipan's largest shopping centres are the upmarket DFS Galleria in Garapan and Hakubotan in San Jose. Another large shopping centre, San Roque, is opposite the Hotel Nikko Saipan.

Getting There & Away

See the Getting There & Away section earlier in this chapter for flight and ship details.

Continental's ticket office (☎ 234 6491) is in the Oleai Center in San Jose and is open from 9 am to 5 pm Monday to Saturday. Other airlines centre their operations at the airport. The MITA travel agency on Beach Rd handles business for Northwest, Continental and Japan airlines. For Freedom Air dial ☎ 234 8328 and for PIA dial ☎ 234 3601.

Getting Around

Shuttle Buses Saipan has no public bus system. However, three shuttle buses – La Fiesta San Roque (☎ 322 0998), Gray Line Island Shuttle (☎ 234 7148) and Sugar King (☎ 322 8778) run regularly between Saipan's major hotels and shopping centres (US$3).

Taxi Saipan's metered taxis are very expensive. It typically costs US$25 to get from the airport to Garapan and Micro Beach, and US$15 from Garapan to Susupe. Try Bo's Boys (☎ 322 3822).

Car Hertz (☎ 234 8336), Dollar (☎ 288 5151), Budget (☎ 234 8232) and Tropical (☎ 288 0373) share a hut at the airport, walk up to each window and compare prices. You can expect to pay from US$40 to $45 minimum.

Tinian

• **pop 2,631** • **area 39 sq miles**

Tinian is a peaceful one-village island 3 miles south of Saipan and is historically notorious as the take-off site for the aircraft that dropped the atomic bombs on Hiroshima and Nagasaki. The second largest island in the Northern Marianas, Tinian is also the least mountainous. It's an attractive island with ancient latte stones, grazing cattle and secluded sandy beaches. The Japanese levelled Tinian's forests and turned the island into a chequerboard of sugar cane fields. The US captured the island in 1944 and developed it into a huge airbase. They named the roads Broadway, 42nd St and 8th Avenue for a New York Commander – though 86th St now seems a bit strange for an island with such little traffic! After the war Tinian reverted to cattle ranching. The US military has sole access to northern Tinian and leases the

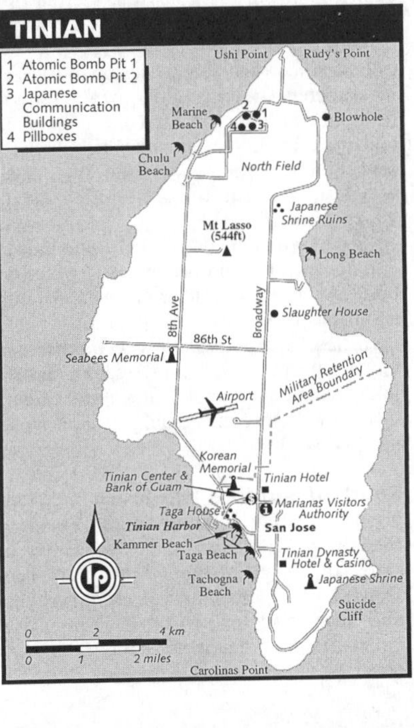
TINIAN
1 Atomic Bomb Pit 1
2 Atomic Bomb Pit 2
3 Japanese Communication Buildings
4 Pillboxes
Ushi Point
Rudy's Point
Marine Beach
Blowhole
Chulu Beach
North Field
Japanese Shrine Ruins
Mt Lasso (544ft)
Long Beach
8th Ave
Broadway
Slaughter House
86th St
Seabees Memorial
Military Retention Area Boundary
Airport
Korean Memorial
Tinian Center & Bank of Guam
Tinian Hotel
Marianas Visitors Authority
Taga House
Tinian Harbor
San Jose
Kammer Beach
Taga Beach
Tinian Dynasty Hotel & Casino
Tachogna Beach
Japanese Shrine
Suicide Cliff
0 2 4 km
0 1 2 miles
Carolinas Point

NORTHERN MARIANAS

middle third, though Tinian is only occasionally used for military exercises.

Information

The helpful Marianas Visitors Authority (☎ 433 9365, fax 433 0653) is on Broadway. There's a Bank of Guam with a 24-hour ATM machine. Tinian's post office is open weekdays from 9.30 am to 3 pm and Saturday until noon. At the Tinian Center you can place international calls (40c a minute to the USA).

For emergencies dial ☎ 911. The police and fire station can be reached at ☎ 433 9222 and the Tinian Health Center at ☎ 433 9233.

Things to See

San Jose Small, quiet San Jose, where most of Tinian's residents live, was once the site of an ancient village of 13,000 Chamorros. The current population is partly comprised of a group of Chamorros who had been living on Yap since the German era and were resettled in San Jose after WWII.

Taga House is an impressive collection of latte stones, with capstones up to five feet in diameter. They are said to be the foundations of the home of Taga the Great, legendary king of the ancient Chamorros. A few minutes' walk east is the **Taga Well**, which in ancient times supplied spring water to the island.

Kammer Beach, also called Jones Beach, is a nice white sand beach east of the harbour and an easy walk from the town centre. It has coconut palms, pavilions, picnic facilities, restrooms, showers and a nice view. During WWII, Americans staged a fake diversionary landing at Kammer Beach just hours before the actual invasion on the north-west shore.

South of San Jose **Taga Beach Park**, with good swimming, is a mile south of town on Broadway. The clifftop is accessible by steps and has a striking view. **Tachogna Beach Park**, immediately beyond the beach and also good for swimming (and snorkelling), has a broad white sand beach. Both beaches can be reached by foot from San Jose by following a coastal walkway th starts by Kammer Beach. The best-preserve **Japanese shrine** on the island is in the hil above Taga Beach and the Dynasty, but di ections are excruciating so it's best to as the tourist office for help.

To get to **Suicide Cliff**, follow the roa inland from Taga Beach another 4 mile bearing right first at the crossroads an then at the fork. In the hills above the clif are the natural and soldier-dug caves th were the last defence position and hide-ou for the Japanese military. Most of the 400 Japanese defenders that are still missing ar assumed to have committed suicide insid the caves. A peace memorial remember the Japanese civilians who leapt from th cliffs.

North of San Jose You can make an inter esting tour of the island by heading nort from San Jose along Broadway and then re turning via 8th Avenue. About 4 miles fron the airport turn-off, a large **Shinto torii** (gate on the left is visible from the road and mark the entrance to the site of a former Japanese shrine. Just ahead, the road circles a round about that has another old Japanese shrine ir its centre. The four corners are Japanese lanterns. Turn right just after the Japanese Shrine roundabout and you'll come to a choice between the Atomic Bomb Pits and the **Blow Hole**. The latter has towering, pleasant sprays, though heed the fences, which warn of unexploded ordnance.

The main road loops around **North Field**, which is a massive network of landing fields and criss-crossing roads that once comprised the world's largest military airbase. Airstrips built by US Seabees, each 1½ miles long, were take-off sites for firebomb raids on Japan and later for the planes that carried the atomic bombs to Hiroshima and Nagasaki. Once inside the field, there's a confusing, huge maze of roads, airstrips and overgrown crossroads.

From the main road circling North Field, a road to the **atomic bomb loading pits** is on the left, about three-quarters of a mile beyond the turn-off to **Ushi Point** and 4½ miles from the Japanese shrine roundabout.

Little Boy & Fat Man

In the early evening of 5 August 1945 a uranium bomb code-named 'Little Boy' was loaded aboard the *Enola Gay*, an American B-29 aircraft. The 4 ton bomb had been brought to Tinian from San Francisco aboard the heavy cruiser *Indianapolis*.

The *Enola Gay* and its 12 man crew took off from Tinian at 2.45 am on 6 August and headed for Hiroshima, 1700 miles away. The bomb was dropped at 9.15 am Tinian time. It exploded in the air above the city, forming a fireball that quickly mushroomed into a dark-grey cloud 3 miles wide and 35,000 feet high. More than 75,000 people perished that day from the explosion, beginning the age of atomic warfare, and the final death toll reached an estimated 200,000.

The second atomic bomb loaded on Tinian was a 4½ ton plutonium bomb named 'Fat Man'. It was dropped on Nagasaki on 9 August 1945, immediately killing 75,000 of the city's 240,000 residents; another estimated 75,000 people have since died from the effects of radiation.

Go south a few hundred yards from the loading pits until the road splits and turn left, then take the first right and the first right again onto a runway. Continue on the runway until you notice a small overgrown road to the right going into the complex. Hidden, straight ahead, are a larger two-storey former **communications building** and low concrete **pillboxes** with gun holes.

From the Japanese buildings turn right, back onto the runway, and at the end of the road turn left, then take the next right to get to **Chulu Beach**. A little to the north of Chulu Beach is **Marine Beach**. These attractive white sand beaches, dubbed White Beach I and II by US forces, are where more than 15,000 US troops landed in July 1944. Archaeological excavations at Chulu Beach have uncovered three layers of Chamorro civilisation, ranging from 1500 BC to the Latte Period of 1000 AD to 1500 AD.

About 1¼ miles south on 8th Avenue, a side road leads east to the 544 foot **Mt Lasso**, northern Tinian's highest point.

Seven miles south of Chulu Beach on 8th Avenue, turn inland onto a grassy path lined with palm trees. Not far from the road is a **Korean WWII memorial**, built on the back of a carved stone turtle, honouring Koreans who died during WWII. Honeycombed into the nearby hills are caves where the Japanese hid from US forces.

Activities

Tinian has clear waters, a sloping ocean bottom and a number of good dive sites close to San Jose. One of the most popular is Dump Coke, a huge dumping ground for WWII junk including small Japanese tanks, jeeps, trucks and shell casings.

Sea Quest Dive Shop (☎ 433 0010) is Tinian's only dive shop. A one-tank beach dive is US$45 and a two-tank boat dive is US$90. Introductory beach dives are US$75 and hour-long snorkelling tours cost US$35. Diving equipment rents for US$40 a day, snorkel sets for US$15. Most Saipan dive shops will go to Tinian, see Saipan's Activities section earlier this chapter.

The best snorkelling near shore is at Tachogna Beach. Fuji Marine Sports (☎ 433 0648) is based there and rents snorkel sets for US$10 and has snorkelling trips for US$35 (including equipment).

Places to Stay

Camping facilities are good and no permission is needed to camp on public beaches. Try Kammer Beach or Taga and Tachogna beach parks – all have showers. Chulu Beach on the north-west coast is more remote.

Besides the Dynasty, Tinian has a few small hotels, all in San Jose. Rooms in all have private bathrooms, cable TV, air-con and small refrigerators, but no phones or ceiling fans. A 10% tax is added to the room rates here.

The locally owned *Lori Lynn's Hotel* (☎ *433 3256, fax 433 0429*) has decent rooms costing US$35 for singles or doubles (including tax). There's a good restaurant and airport transfers on request. The renovated *Tinian Hotel* (☎ *433 7000, fax 433 7700*), across Broadway from the Tinian Center, is San Jose's best deal, with nice rooms from US$33 (tax included). Besides Dynasty, it Tinian's only hotel to accept major credit cards and have in-room phones.

The finest – albeit least local – place to stay is the 412 room, US$140 million *Tinian Dynasty* (☎ *328 2233, fax 328 1133, casino@saipan.com*), Saipan's new casino-hotel complex. Exquisite soft pink rooms come complete with minibar, safety box and other amenities. It's US$70 plus tax, but if the economy improves this will quickly jump.

Places to Eat

All restaurants are in San Jose or the Tinian Dynasty. *Rosie's Gazebo* has a pleasant outdoor dining area, a bar, good food and an extensive multiethnic menu. A variety of western-style breakfasts cost US$5. There are beef or chicken dishes for US$7 and fancier 'cook's specials' for around US$12. *JC Cafe* has a varied menu that includes tasty chicken, beef, fish, squid and mussel dishes averaging US$8 to $9. Sandwiches are US$3.50 and plate breakfasts average US$6. *Lori Lynn's Restaurant*, at the hotel of the same name, serves western and Japanese dishes and is known for its good Chamorro food. Lunch and dinner average US$7 to $12. *Broadway*, the upscale Italian/Pacific restaurant in the Dynasty, has a nightly buffet for US$25. Lunch is US$20 and breakfast US$12.

The island has several small grocery stores, including *Kim's*, *Tinian Center* and *Fleming's*. The *Farmers' Market*, near the harbour, has a sparse selection of seasonal fruit.

Entertainment

When you tire of the 400 slot machines and 80 gaming tables at the *Dynasty*, there's the cover-free disco called *Club De Macau*, open nightly until 2 am. For more local flavour, *Rosie's Gazebo* has a billiards room and *J C Cafe* has karaoke.

Getting There & Away

Air Between Saipan and Tinian, Freedom Air (☎ 433 3288) flies 12 times daily and PIA (☎ 433 3600) flies twice. Both charge US$25 for the 10 minute hop.

Boat The Dynasty-owned *Tinian Express* (☎ 234 9157) chugs over from Saipan six times daily. Reservations are unnecessary but call in advance (☎ 287 9933 on Saipan, ☎ 433 3075 on Tinian) to verify departure times. It is free going to Tinian and US$20 coming back. Hint: take the boat there and fly back!

Getting Around

Budget (☎ 433 3104), Avis (☎ 433 2847) and Islander (☎ 433-3025) have booths at the airport. Budget also hides out in the Dynasty. Cars start at about US$39 a day. Credit cards are accepted. It's often possible to hitch from the airport to San Jose, though outside San Jose the lack of traffic hampers hitching. Sea Quest Dive Shop (☎ 433 0010) rents bicycles for US$15 a day.

Rota

• pop 3509   • area 32 sq miles

Oblong Rota, halfway between Guam and Saipan, gets some overflow tourists but retains a distinctively slow pace, with good spring water and fiery orange sunsets. Rota has earned the moniker 'The Friendly Island', as all drivers wave to each other in passing. Songsong, which means 'village' in Chamorro, is the island's business centre, while Sinapalo, just south of the airport, has rapidly grown into the island's second village. Despite efforts to lure tourists, Rota remains pristine. Where else can you swim right in town and still have the beach all to yourself?

Information

The Marianas Visitors Authority (☎ 532 0327), is up the hill across from the fire

tion. The modern Bank of Guam changes
rrency, cashes travellers cheques (Amex
ly) and issues commission-free credit
rd cash advances. An ATM is outside. The
st office is in central Songsong.

For international phone calls and faxes,
ad to GTE (☎ 532 3499, fax 532 0101),
hich is on the north-east side of town, a
ock from the tourist office. It's open
eekdays only.

hings to See

ongsong Village Quiet Songsong Village,
tending along a narrow neck of land on
ra's south-west peninsula, has a scenic
ackdrop in the 469 foot Mt Taipingot,
hich is nicknamed Wedding Cake Moun-
in for its layered appearance. Songsong has
n abundance of latte stones, some adorn the
brary, while others landscape front yards.

entral & Northern Rota A turnoff near
he airport leads to the Taga Stone Quarry
nd the Bird Sanctuary. The **Taga Stone
Quarry** has nine latte shafts and seven cap-
tones still sitting in the trenches where they
vere being quarried before being inexplic-
bly abandoned. The early Chamorros

quarried the latte stones without metal
tools, possibly by building fires in trenches
around the stones and then using basalt
stone adzes to cut into the softened limestone. According to legend, the ancient
Chamorro king Taga the Great jumped from
Guam to Rota to establish a kingdom here.
He then put the island's inhabitants to work
quarrying these latte stones, which he used
as foundation pillars for royal buildings.

At Rota's **Bird Sanctuary**, down a 1½ mile
dirt road, a clifftop wooden walkway is wonderful for watching and photographing sea
and shorebirds. Sunrise or sunset are best.

East of Songsong Village Along the
bayside road east of Songsong Village are
scenic views and tropical jungle canopies.
About 1½ miles east of the village is a fun
tropical zoo featuring coconut crabs, iguanas, fruit bats and other tropical animals
(admission is US$5). Another mile east-
ward, a **Japanese cannon** points straight out
to the harbour and to Mt Taipingot from its
concrete shelter. Just over a mile past the
cannon, there's an open grassy field on the
right side of the road, which slopes down to
Pona Point, a wind-whipped rocky outcrop

NORTHERN MARIANAS

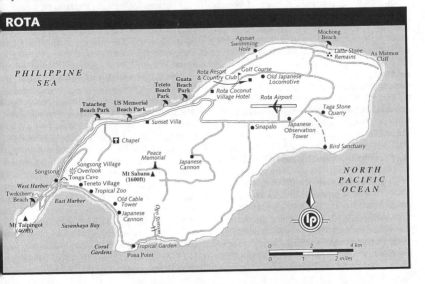

ROTA

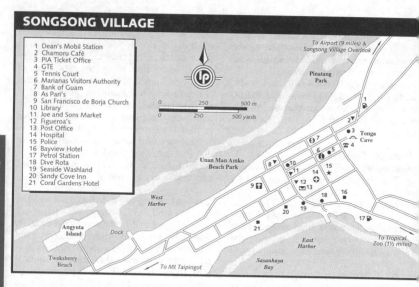

SONGSONG VILLAGE

1 Dean's Mobil Station
2 Chamoru Café
3 PIA Ticket Office
4 GTE
5 Tennis Court
6 Marianas Visitors Authority
7 Bank of Guam
8 As Pari's
9 San Francisco de Borja Church
10 Library
11 Joe and Sons Market
12 Figueroa's
13 Post Office
14 Hospital
15 Police
16 Bayview Hotel
17 Petrol Station
18 Dive Rota
19 Seaside Washland
20 Sandy Cove Inn
21 Coral Gardens Hotel

To Airport (9 miles) &
Songsong Village Overlook

Pinatang Park

Tonga Cave

Unan Man Amko Beach Park

West Harbor

Angyuta Island   Dock

Tweksberry Beach

To Mt Taipingot

Sasanhaya Bay

East Harbor

To Tropical Zoo (1½ miles)

with a good view and excellent cliff fishing. A bit further east is a **tropical garden** (☎ 532 3394), which is a great place to learn to identify tropical fruit trees. For US$10, one of the workers will lead you through the plantation's innumerable groves of bread-fruit, coconut, papaya, banana, star-apple, and other trees. If you're lucky, he might pluck a bagful of take-home fruit samples. Call ahead to schedule a tour time.

Activities

Diving Rota diving stands out for its ex-cellent visibility, on normal days you can see 100 feet down. Cave and tunnel dives, and now two sunken wrecks, complete the scene. Dive Rota (☎ 532 3377, fax 532 3022) is a small personalised dive operation operated by Mark and Lynne Michael. Boat dives cost US$50/80 for one/two tanks, night dives are US$60. Snorkel sets rent for US$5. The new Japanese-run S2 Dive Shop (☎ 532 3483, fax 532 3484), just east of Songsong village, has higher prices. For snorkelling, Teteto Beach has large coral formations just below the surface. Closer to town, the entrance to Sasanhaya Bay boat harbour has soft corals and tropical fish.

Places to Stay

Many of Rota's public beach parks allow camping, but be aware of crime. The Sandy Cove Inn also plans a camping area. A 10% tax is added to all room rates.

The new *Sandy Cove Inn* (☎/fax 532 2683), on the bay in Songsong, is the bud-get backpacker's dream come true. Beds go for US$10 a night, a room with kitchenette costs US$18.50 and two comfortable single rooms are US$25. Breakfast is included.

The *Coral Garden Hotel* (☎ 532 3201, fax 532 3204) commands a gorgeous ocean-view vista in Songsong Village. Rooms are neat and compact with whitewashed walls, cable TV, air-con, refrigerators and ocean-front balconies. It's good value at US$45/50 for singles/doubles and has a car rental deal.

Three miles north of Songsong, the new *Sunset Villa* (☎ 532 8445, fax 532 8458, sunsetv@gtepacifica.net) is right on the water and offers sparkling rooms with TV, phone, refrigerator, air-con and minibar. Sin-gles/doubles are US$45/65 (including tax).

A good upper-end choice is the *Rota Coconut Village Hotel* (☎ 532 3448, fax 532 3449), which has 10 duplex cottages with an island motif of peaked roofs, rattan

Coral Detonation

The apex of Rota's diving used to be Coral Gardens, in Sasanhaya Bay. Besides having huge platter corals, the area was home to the wreck of the *Shoun Maru*, a Japanese freighter sunk by an aerial torpedo during WWII. The wreck, containing coral-encrusted trucks, bathtubs and bicycles, lay offshore with two other Japanese boats, about 90 feet underwater in Sasanhaya Bay.

But the US navy decided that the wreck contained hazardous, unexploded ordnance and in 1996, to the outrage of divers, the Navy blew up the three wrecks and ruined Coral Gardens.

The story doesn't end there. In 1998 the US Marshalls office sold two illegal Chinese smuggling boats to Rota. The cost was US$2 ($1 each). That June, the Navy sank the two boats offshore in Sasanhaya Bay – debatably as compensation for the chagrined divers.

furnishings and small Japanese-style soaking tubs that fill tiny bathrooms. Singles/doubles cost US$85/95. If you're driving from the airport, go past the turnoff to the country club and watch for a small, unmarked dirt road leading sharply right along the coast at the bottom of the hill.

The *Rota Resort & Country Club* (☎ 532 1155, fax 532 1156), situated magnificently atop an 18 hole golf course with a view to the sea, is Rota's clear luxury choice. Beautiful two-and four-bedroom suites with all the amenities start at US$250 for two people (breakfast included). Call beforehand to negotiate a lower rate. Additional persons in the suite are US$40. There's a swim-up bar for you and an activity station for the kids.

Places to Eat

Restaurants in Rota tend to be more expensive than you might expect but the food is hearty and usually quite good. Besides the spots listed below, the large hotels have nice restaurants.

As Pari's restaurant and bar, on the main road in Songsong, is a perennial favourite, with well prepared food and reasonable prices (US$8 to $10). For wholesome food, the restaurant at *Sandy Cove Inn* is an excellent choice. An order of home-caught reef fish or a large, thick-crust pizza is US$10.

Figueroa's is a popular bar and grill next to Songsong's post office. It's American-owned, with a Budweiser basketball, graffiti on the walls and peanuts everywhere. Entrees – a smorgasbord of fajitas, seafood, steaks and burgers – cost from US$12 to $15.

One of the best stocked of Songsong's numerous grocery stores is *Lucky Store*, around the corner from the Sandy Cove Inn. It has cheap platefuls of food (US$2 to $3) in the late mornings.

Getting There & Away

Rota's small airport is 9 miles north-east of Songsong Village. PIA (☎ 532 0420) and Freedom Air (☎ 532 3801) have six flights daily to Saipan and four to Guam, altogether. One-way prices to Saipan are US$57 to $65.

Getting Around

Rota's one paved road runs between the airport and Songsong Village, though Songsong Village is slowly getting paved. Otherwise most of the island's road system is packed coral or dirt.

Rota has four car rental agencies. There's Islander Rent-A-Car (☎ 532 0901, fax 532 0902), Paseo Drive Car Rental (☎ 532 0406) and Budget (☎ 532 3535), and prices start around US$40. Coral Rent-A-Car (☎ 532 1996) has an excellent room-and-car package with the Coral Garden Hotel for US$68. Otherwise the cars start from US$38. All but Budget have booths at the airport. All take major credit cards and offer optional collision damage waivers (US$12.50).

For those who are fit, bicycling is a wonderful way to see Rota. You can rent bikes from Sandy Cove Inn for US$15 per day.

The Rota Coconut Village Hotel has full-day sightseeing tours for US$38/58 for half/full day. The Rota Resort & Country Club has tours from US$15 to $60, children get discounts. You can probably also find someone in Songsong to take you for a spin.

Palau

The Republic of Palau features Micronesia's richest flora and fauna, both on land and underwater. Exotic birds fly around the islands, crocodiles inhabit the mangrove swamps and the sea holds an incredible spectrum of coral, fish and other marine life, including quarter-ton giant clams.

Palau's crown jewels are the gloriously green, mushroom-shaped Rock Islands, whose waters offer some of the world's finest snorkelling and diving. Though mildly set back by a bridge collapse and the Asian economic crisis, this young country, more than any other in Micronesia, epitomises tropical paradise.

Facts about Palau

HISTORY

Carbon dating has established that the Rock Islands were settled by at least 1000 BC. Palau's culture was matriarchal and matrilineal: property was inherited by women, who had the power of the purse. Villages usually comprised seven to 10 clans.

It wasn't until 1783, when English Captain Henry Wilson was wrecked off Palau's Ulong Island, that there was significant contact between Palauans and westerners. The influence of British traders was largely negative, weapons supplied by them to the Palauans sparked fierce inter-tribal warfare. Spain finally expelled the Brits in 1885, and the Germans took control in 1899. By then Palau's population had been reduced from 40,000 to 4000 by disease.

The Japanese occupied Palau from 1914. After 1922 all of Japan's Pacific possessions were administered from Koror, which the Japanese developed into a bustling modern city of paved roads, electricity and piped-in water. Out of 30,000 residents, only about 20% were Palauan. In the late 1930s, Japan closed Palau to the outside world and fortified the islands. Toward the end of WWII, US aircraft bombed military

AT A GLANCE

Capital: Koror
Population: 17,225
Time: 9 hours ahead of GMT
Land Area: 500 sq km (196 sq miles)
Number of Islands: 10
International Telephone Code: ☎ 680
GDP/Capita: US$7390
Currency: US dollar
Languages: Palauan & English
Greeting: *Alii* (Palauan)

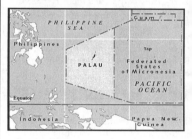

HIGHLIGHTS

- **Kayaking or diving the Rock Islands** – a maze of divinely green, mushroom-shaped islands

- **Babeldaob** – Micronesia's second-largest island, with powerful waterfalls and traditional *bai* (mens' houses)

- **Snorkelling** – sharks, mantas and other underwater treasures

- **Peleliu** – a WWII-ravaged island which is now a tranquil retreat

- **Seafood** – feast on mangrove crab, lobster or exquisite sushi in one of Palau's many outstanding restaurants

installations on Malakal Island and Airai or Babeldaob, but Palau's major battles took place in September 1944, when the USA stormed Peleliu and Angaur islands.

In administering Palau after the war, the USA hoped to spin off Palau with the rest of Micronesia into a single political entity. Palauans, however, voted in July 1978 against joining the Federated States of Micronesia (FSM) and in July 1980 Palauans adopted their own constitution, with Koror the provisional capital.

Palau's 'nuclear free' constitutional clause sparked a stand-off with the USA, which wanted Palau as a fallback base in case they lost the Philippines. The USA then drew up a Compact of Free Association that allowed it to bring nuclear weapons into Palau and also gave it eminent domain over virtually all Palauan territory. In exchange, Palau was offered millions of dollars in aid. After years of heated debates and referenda, Palauan voters approved the Compact – hoping, so far correctly, that the Cold War's end would make US military installations unlikely.

On 1 October 1994 Palau officially became an independent nation, ending 47 years as a Trust Territory.

Post-Independence

Palau's struggle to emerge as a new nation had a troubled beginning. Palau's first president was assassinated in 1985; three years later his successor was found shot dead in an apparent suicide. The situation has since stabilised.

Implementation of the Compact and the new western style of government triggered a power struggle between elected officials and Palau's traditional authorities; these disputes are slowly being litigated. Concerned about their own compact management, Palauans are hawkishly watching the FSM and the Marshall Islands, which squandered much of their compact money early on and are up for compact renegotiation.

The albatross around Palau's neck is infrastructure. In 1996, Palau's 700 foot reinforced concrete bridge, called the K-B Bridge, collapsed after undergoing repair work. Palau got US$17 million from the construction companies, and a temporary floating bridge now links Koror and Babeldaob. A new Japanese-funded bridge was due to be in place by 2000.

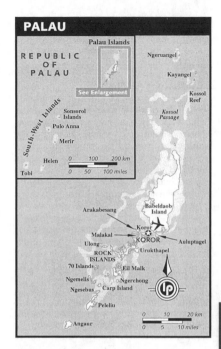

GEOGRAPHY & ECOLOGY

Palau, which is part of the Caroline Islands, is the westernmost part of Micronesia. The tightly clustered Palauan archipelago consists of the high islands of Babeldaob, Koror, Peleliu and Angaur; to the north of which are the low coral atolls of Kayangel and Ngeruangel; and south are the more than 200 limestone Rock Islands. Palau encompasses the 'South-West Islands' – six small, isolated islands that extend 370 miles south-west from Koror. Thickly jungled Babeldaob is Micronesia's second-largest island, three-quarters the size of Guam, with a land area of 153 sq miles. Environmental problems include erosion, overfishing and litter. Palau has reacted by designating new conservation areas around the Rock Islands and on Babeldaob.

CLIMATE

In Koror, the average daily high is 87°F (30°C) and the average daily low is 75°F

(24°C). February and March are the driest months, and June to August is wettest. Palau lies outside the main cyclone zone but occasionally gets hit.

FLORA & FAUNA

Tropical forest covers much of the islands, though there is also mangrove forest. Palau has 50 species of resident birds including seabirds, land and wetland varieties. The spectacular marine environment boasts over 1,500 species of fish, over 700 species of coral and anemones and even saltwater riparian crocodiles. Rare species such as giant tridacna clam and dugongs are also found here.

Palau also has a few snakes – the Pacific island boa in forests, the Palau tree snake in small trees and shrubs and the dog-faced water snake in mangrove swamps. None pose a threat to adults.

GOVERNMENT & POLITICS

Palau's national congress is a 30 seat bicameral legislature, called the Olbiil Era Kelulau (Meeting Place of Whispers). The House of Delegates has 16 members, one from each state. The Senate, which is based on proportional representation, has 1 members. Legislators and the president a elected for four-year terms.

ECONOMY

Despite its political independence, Palau r mains heavily dependent upon US ai Palau's compact with the USA entitles it US$450 million in funding over 15 year until 2008. Palau's GDP of around US$70C per capita is one of Micronesia's highes but the government remains the largest en ployer. Tourism, an important industry Palau, suffered mildly from the Asian cris after a mid-90s boom.

POPULATION & PEOPLE

Palau's population is approximately 17,20 which includes an estimated 4500 foreig workers, who are mostly Filipino.

ARTS

Traditional Palauan arts are more con monly found outside built-up Koror. Intr cately carved storyboards make wonderf souvenirs. Traditional dancing is no long as strong in Palau as of yore.

Palauan Money

The early Palauans developed an intricate system of money that was used as a mode of exchange and as gift offerings at traditional events. Beads, called *udoud*, were the most common type of Palauan money. The beads were made of clay or glass and were usually yellow or orange in colour.

Common round beads were used for daily transactions, while beads which were oval, faceted or cylindrical were more prestigious and valuable. The beads were not made in Palau and although no-one today knows exactly where they came from, it is thought that they may have originated in Indonesia or Malaysia.

One legend, however, says they came from a mysterious Yapese island called Kablik. Kablik was said to be so magical that stones thrown from the island toward the sea never touched the water, but returned instead to the thrower.

The beads still have value but are in limited use today, exchanged mainly at times of birth, marriage and death. Strings of udoud are worn as necklaces (called *iek*) by high-ranking women on special occasions and it's common to see Palauan women wearing a single bead on a black cord as an heirloom necklace.

Another kind of traditional Palauan money is *toluk*, made by steaming hawksbill turtle shell and pressing it into a wooden tray-shaped mould. The shell is hardened into the shape of an oval plate; the larger and lighter coloured the toluk, the more value it has.

OCIETY & CONDUCT

ough Palauans are among Micronesia's ost westernised people, family and kin- p ties remain strong. Chiefs command a minishing but still-important role in the cial hierarchy. Betel nut chewing and tting has a hefty Palauan following; see e boxed text in the Yap section of the FSM apter for details.

RELIGION

he Catholic and Protestant churches are ell established. Many Palauans still hold me traditional beliefs, based on nature irits, clan-ancestral worship and village ities.

LANGUAGE

lauan is spoken at home, while English is ore common in business and government; th are official languages. South-West Is- nders speak Sonsorolese and Tobian lan- ages, which are more closely related to pese or Chuukese (see the Federated States Micronesia chapter) than to Palauan.

alauan Basics

ello.	*Alii.*
oodbye.	*Mechikung.*
ow are you?	*Keuangerang?*
m well (thanks).	*Ak mesisiich (sulang).*
ease.	*Adang.*
nanks.	*Sulang.*
es.	*Choi.*
o.	*Diak.*

acts for the Visitor

UGGESTED ITINERARIES

you have just a few days in Palau, it's best stay on Koror and see the Rock Islands. you have weeks, you should do the same ing! For variety, consider exploring abeldaob's *bai* (traditional men's houses) d waterfalls, camping on the Rock Is- nds or spending a few days on Peleliu.

OURIST OFFICES

he following is a Palau Visitors Authority presentative abroad:

USA
  (☎ 808-591 6599, fax 591 2933)
  Limtiaco Company, 1210 Auahi St, Suite 208, Honolulu, Hawai'i 96814

VISAS & EMBASSIES

All tourists may visit Palau for 30 days without requiring a visa; this visit may be extended for two 30 day periods (US$100 per extension).

Palauan Embassies & Consulates

Guam
  (☎ 671-646 9281, fax 646 5322)
  Palau Consulate Office, 540 Marine Dr, ITC Bldg, Tamuning, Guam 96911
Northern Marianas
  (☎ 670-235 6804, fax 235 6809)
  Palau Consulate Office, Joeten Shopping Cen- ter, Box 7984, Saipan, MP 96950
USA
  (☎ 202-452 6814, fax 452 6281)
  Embassy of the Republic of Palau, 2000 L. St, NW, Suite 407, Washington DC 20036

Embassies & Consulates in Palau

The USA's consulate (☎ 488 2920) is in Topside, Koror.

MONEY

Palau's currency is the US dollar (for ex- change rates see Money in the Regional Facts for the Visitor chapter). There are sev- eral ATMs on Koror and credit cards are widely accepted.

POST & COMMUNICATIONS

Palau uses the US postal system but has its own stamps. Palau's postal code is 96940. Its international telephone code is ☎ 680; there are no area codes. For directory assis- tance, dial ☎ 411. To reach an international operator, dial ☎ 0.

BOOKS

Diving & Snorkeling Palau (from Lonely Planet's Pisces series) gives an excellent overview of Palau's best dive spots.

MEDIA

Palau gets US cable TV. Guam's *Pacific Daily News* is sold in some shops.

PALAU

WEIGHTS & MEASURES

Palau uses the imperial system of measurement (feet, miles and degrees Fahrenheit). Use the table at the back of this book if you need to convert to metric measurements.

HEALTH

Palau's water should always be boiled before drinking.

BUSINESS HOURS

Most businesses stay open weekdays from 8 am to 5 pm. Banking hours are (conservatively) 9.30 am to 2.30 pm Monday to Thursday and to 5 pm Friday.

PUBLIC HOLIDAYS & SPECIAL EVENTS

Palau celebrates New Year's Day, Easter Sunday, Thanksgiving and Christmas. Also:

Youth Day	15 March
Senior Citizens' Day	5 May
President's Day	1 June
Constitution Day	9 July
Labor Day	6 September
Independence Day	1 October

Peleliu and Angaur have a 'WWII Memorial Day' commemorating the respective US landings.

ACCOMMODATION & FOOD

Palau's Rock Islands are excellent camping spots, and camping is possible at other islands outside Koror. Homestays are possible on Babeldaob and Kayangel (see those sections, later). Koror's top-end hotels are excellent. Fresh fish – tuna, crab, lobster and sushi – are served at Palau's excellent restaurants. There are no restaurants outside Koror and Babeldaob's Airai State.

Getting There & Away

AIR

Continental (☎ 488 2448 in Koror) has daily flights to and from Guam (some with a stop in Yap) and to Manila (Philippines). Eastern Air Transport (☎ 488 3931 in Ko has twice-weekly flights from Taipei (wan). Other connections are through Gu Palau can be reached on the Circle Mi nesia and Visit Micronesia air passes the Getting Around the Region chapter).

The airport is in Airai State, in south Babeldaob, a 25 minute drive from cen Koror.

Departure Tax

There's a departure tax of US$20.

SEA

Visiting yachts should notify the immigra office (☎ 488 2498) and the harbour ma (☎ 488 5789) before arrival. Baggage, e and line handling fees will be applied.

ORGANISED TOURS

Palau is one of the South Pacific's prem tour destinations, and going by tour n save you a bit of money. In the USA, Trip-N-Tour (☎ tollfree 800 348 0842, 760-724 9897, info@trip-n-tour.com), wh also handles live-aboards; World of Adv ture Vacations (☎ tollfree 800 900 76 fax 310-322 5111, info@worldofdiv .com); Tropical Adventures (☎ 206- 3483, or ☎ tollfree 800 247 3483, fax 2 441 5431, dive@divetropical.com); or PADI Travel Network (☎ tollfree 800 7234, fax 949-858 7234, ptn1@padi.co

For a snorkelling and cultural tour c tact San Francisco-based Oceanic Soci Expeditions (☎ tollfree 800 326 7491, 415-474 3395).

Getting Around

Most hotels provide airport transport guests who call ahead. There are taxis car rentals at the airport. Around Ko taxis are abundant if not cheap. Hitchin uncommon but possible.

State boats run twice weekly betwe Koror, Angaur and Peleliu and much regularly and frequently between Koror Palau's outer islands.

oror State

op 12,299 • area 7 sq miles

ror, the relaxed economic centre and
ital of Palau, contains 12,000 people al-
st two-thirds of the country's population.
ror State consists of the inhabited islands
Koror, Malakal and Arakabesang, all of
ich are connected by causeways. The
and of Koror is also connected to neigh-
uring Babeldaob Island via a floating
dge, the temporary replacement for the
B Bridge, which collapsed in 1996.

n pre-war Japanese days Koror was
imed with geisha houses, Shinto shrines,
nono tailors and public baths, and if you
k closely you'll often find architectural
nnants of a more traditional past sitting
ngside the newer structures.

The greater Koror area is worth a day of
loration, but after that it's best used as a
se for trips to the Rock Islands, Peleliu,
gaur and Babeldaob.

Information

Tourist Offices The helpful Palau Visitors
Authority (☎ 488 2793, fax 488 1453,
pva@palaunet.com) is on the west side of
town. Its website is www.visit-palau.com.

Money The Bank of Hawaii and the Bank
of Guam are on Koror's main road and both
have 24-hour ATMs outside.

Post & Communications Palau's only
post office, with poste restante and attractive
postage stamps, is in central Koror. International phone calls can be made 24 hours a
day from the Palau National Communications Corporation (PNCC) building near the
airport. More convenient (but closed weekends and evenings) is the PNCC office in
central Koror. Faxes can be sent and received
from here (fax 488 1725) free of charge.

The Rock Islands Computer Institute, in
the IA building near the tourist office, has
internet access for US$20 per hour.

KOROR STATE

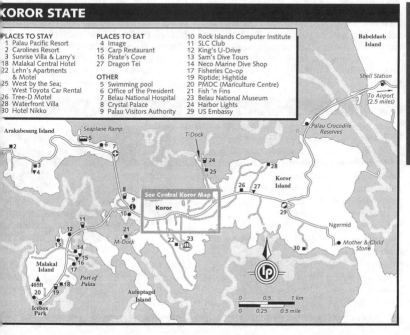

PLACES TO STAY
1 Palau Pacific Resort
2 Carolines Resort
3 Sunrise Villa & Larry's
18 Malakal Central Hotel
22 Lehn's Apartments
   & Motel
25 West by the Sea;
   West Toyota Car Rental
26 Tree-D Motel
28 Waterfront Villa
30 Hotel Nikko

PLACES TO EAT
4 Image
15 Carp Restaurant
16 Pirate's Cove
27 Dragon Tei

OTHER
5 Swimming pool
6 Office of the President
7 Belau National Hospital
8 Crystal Palace
9 Palau Visitors Authority

10 Rock Islands Computer Institute
11 SLC Club
12 King's U-Drive
13 Sam's Dive Tours
14 Neco Marine Dive Shop
17 Fisheries Co-op
19 Riptide; Hightide
20 PMDC (Mariculture Centre)
21 Fish 'n Fins
23 Belau National Museum
24 Harbor Lights
29 US Embassy

Babeldaob Island

Shell Station

To Airport (2.5 miles)

Arakabesang Island

Seaplane Ramp

T-Dock

Palau Crocodile Reserves

Koror Island

See Central Koror Map

Koror

Ngermid

Mother & Child Stone

M-Dock

Malakal Island

405ft

Port of Palau

Icebox Park

Auluptagel Island

0   0.5   1 km
0   0.25   0.5 mile

PALAU

Medical Services Dr Yano's clinic, Belau Medical Clinic (☎ 488 2688) in Koror centre, is recommended for non-emergency medical attention.

The Belau National Hospital (☎ 488 2558) on Arakabesang Island is just over the causeway from Koror and has a decompression chamber.

Emergency The police emergency number is ☎ 911; the non-emergency number is ☎ 488 1422. For an ambulance or the fire department dial ☎ 488 1411.

Things to See

Belau National Museum Follow signs off the main street to the small Belau National Museum. Besides the intricate story-board above the door, displays include tortoise shell money, as well as local artefacts and crafts (admission US$3).On the museum grounds is a beautiful carved wood-and-thatch bai; it depicts Uab, whose body created the Palauan islands.

Eastern Koror For a superb **Rock Islands view**, especially at sunrise, head to the Hotel Nikko. At the hilltop are two anti-aircraft guns. Near the beginning of the hotel driveway there's a rebuilt Japanese **Shinto shrine**.

The **Palau Crocodile Preserves** is on causeway island between Koror and Babeldaob (US$3 for adults, US$2 for children; photos cost extra).

Malakal Island Malakal Island, across causeway from Koror, has the Fisheries C op, the deep-water commercial port, sm boat docks and other marine businesses.

At the southern tip of the island is grass Icebox Park. The **Palau Maricultu Demonstration Center** (PMDC; ☎ 4 3322), at the end of the road on Malakal land, has long shallow tanks of giant clam and sea turtles (US$2 admission). Luc clams get replanted in Palau's reefs; u lucky ones become sashimi.

Activities

Snorkelling The beach fronting the Pal Pacific Resort has some of Koror's be snorkelling. Its clear, calm waters ho colourful tropical fish, platter and mus room corals, and giant tridacna clams w iridescent mantles. It's US$25 for nongue to use the beach. Snorkelling is also good Icebox Park and the PMDC grounds Malakal Island. But no-one really comes Palau to snorkel in Koror. The real action in and around the Rock Islands.

Information on diving in Palau, and

Giant Clams

Micronesia's endangered giant tridacna clams (*Tridagna gigas*) regularly grow more than four feet in length and can weigh more than 500 pounds (225kg), making them the world's largest bivalve mollusc. Their fleshy mantles have intriguingly mottled designs of browns, greens and iridescent blues. Some live more than a hundred years.

Palauans have long eaten the meat of the clams, sold the huge shells to tourists and ground up the smaller shells for lime powder to chew with betel nut.

The main threat to the clams, however, comes from outside poachers, mainly from Taiwan who are wiping out the tridacna on coral reefs around the Pacific, overharvesting to a point where few are left for breeding. The poachers often take only the profitable adductor muscle of the clam, which is prized as a delicacy in Asia, while the rest of the clam is left to rot

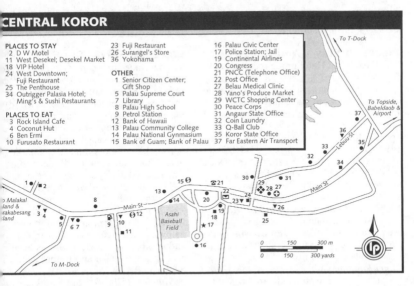

CENTRAL KOROR

PLACES TO STAY
2 D W Motel
11 West Desekel; Desekel Market
18 VIP Hotel
24 West Downtown;
   Fuji Restaurant
25 The Penthouse
34 Outrigger Palasia Hotel;
   Ming's & Sushi Restaurants

PLACES TO EAT
3 Rock Island Cafe
4 Coconut Hut
6 Ben Ermi
10 Furusato Restaurant

23 Fuji Restaurant
26 Surangel's Store
36 Yokohama

OTHER
1 Senior Citizen Center;
   Gift Shop
5 Palau Supreme Court
7 Library
8 Palau High School
9 Petrol Station
12 Bank of Hawaii
13 Palau Community College
14 Palau National Gynmasium
15 Bank of Guam; Bank of Palau

16 Palau Civic Center
17 Police Station; Jail
19 Continental Airlines
20 Congress
21 PNCC (Telephone Office)
22 Post Office
27 Belau Medical Clinic
28 Yano's Produce Market
29 WCTC Shopping Center
30 Peace Corps
31 Angaur State Office
32 Coin Laundry
33 Q-Ball Club
35 Koror State Office
37 Far Eastern Air Transport

To T-Dock

To Topside,
Babeldaob &
Airport

To Malakal
Island &
Arakabesang
Island

To M-Dock

Main St

Lebuu St

Asahi Baseball Field

0   150   300 m
0   150   300 yards

---

ive shops based in Koror, is given later in the Rock Islands section. Most large dive shops rent snorkel sets for US$10 per day.

ther Water Sports Ocean kayaking is ideal in the Rock Islands. Planet Blue Guided Kayak Tours (☎ 488 1062, fax 488 1003, planetblue@palaunet.com), a subsidiary of Sam's Tours, does trips with half-day/full-day/overnight options priced at US$55/85/130. Also try Splash Kayak Center (☎ 488 2600, fax 488 1741, splash@palaunet.com), based at the Palau Pacific Resort, and Adventure Kayaking of Palau (☎ 488 1694).

Sportfishing is becoming more popular. International Anglers (☎ 488 5305, fax 488 1003), a branch of Sam's, does offshore trolling from US$350 to $550 for a half day. Prices at Fish 'n Fins (☎ 488 2637, fax 488 3418, fishnfin@palaunet.com) are a bit better – half/full days are US$300/475. You need a fishing license (US$15), available from any dive shop or the Visitors Authority.

Places to Stay

Central Koror holds most low and middle-range hotels, but all top-end hotels, except the Outrigger Palasia, are a bit out of the centre. All rooms, unless otherwise noted, have private baths, air-con, mini-fridge and 10% tax. Almost all accept credit cards. Budget hotels generally provide free airport transfers upon request. Most mid-range and upper end hotels have good package deals with Koror's dive companies; contact the hotels or dive companies for details.

Places to Stay – Budget

The **Tree-D Motel** (☎ 488 3856, fax 488 4584), in Topside, is a friendly, simple, clean family-run hotel. Rooms are US$45 for singles and couples, US$55 for twin beds.

Lehns Apartments & Motel (☎/fax 488 1486, lehns.motel@palaunet.com) is tucked away from Koror's main road but still central. Driving from the airport, take a left just past the post office; when the road curves left, turn right. Adequate budget rooms are small and basic, with hall bathrooms and shower. They go for US$38.50 (including tax). Larger rooms go for US$66.50 and include kitchen equipment, cable TV and private bath.

The **DW Motel** (☎ 488 2641, fax 488 1725) has 17 tired but adequate rooms in central Koror. There's a TV in the guest

PALAU

lounge and a laundry on site. Rooms are US$35/45 a single/double.

Places to Stay – Mid-Range

The West Plaza Hotel group (central booking ☎ 488 2133, fax 488 2136, west .plaza@palaunet.com) has several separate locations. All rooms have air-con, cable TV, mini-fridges, telephones with free local calls and airport transfers. A four-day sportsfishing tour package with Fish 'n Fins is US$420, a seven day package is US$820. *West by the Sea (☎ 488 2133)* near T-Dock is US$70, or US$90 with kitchenettes. More conveniently located is *West Desekel (☎ 488 2521, fax 488 6043)*, with relatively spacious rooms above the Desekel Market grocery store. Singles and doubles are US$70; kitchenette suites are US$80. *West Downtown (☎ 488 1671, fax 488 5521)* in the town centre has adequate rooms from US$70. The *West Hotel Malakal (☎ 488 5291, fax 488 5290)*, not far from downtown Koror, has nice rooms for US$70; suites with one/two bedrooms go for US$90/100.

The tawny new *Waterfront Villa (☎ 488 2904, fax 488 4904, waterfront.villa@ palaunet.com)* is the best deal around but slightly out of the way. Coming from Babeldaob, turn right at the petrol station after the Dragon-Tei, turn right again at the first four-way intersection after the school, go about quarter of a mile and take a left at the first stop sign. Follow this paved road until it ends. Comfortable, immaculate rooms with phones and tubs are about US$60/75 in low/high season. Suites with kitchenette are US$75/95.

The renovated *Airai View Hotel (☎ 587 3530, fax 587 3533)*, on Babeldaob near the airport, has rich mahogany wood floors and a grand lobby decorated with the island's largest storyboard. Its standard rooms (US$80) are straightforward yet elegant, with TV and wooden furniture. Deluxe rooms (US$100) have huge balconies.

The pleasant *VIP Hotel (☎ 488 1502, fax 488 1429)* is above the Continental office in Koror. The rooms, each with TV and balcony, are spotlessly clean and the atmosphere quite personable. Singles/doubles cost US$65/85; there's a surcharge credit card payments.

Places to Stay – Top End

The new nine-story *Outrigger Palasia Ho (☎ 488 8888, fax 488 8800, outrigge palaunet.com)* in central Koror has all the sort amenities (except a beach backyard) business centre, swimming pool, excell restaurants and duty-free shops. All roo have a phone, TV and mini-fridge. There nonsmoking floors and the building wheelchair accessible. Rooms start US$200/270 during low/peak seasons.

The rustic *Carolines Resort (☎ 4 3754, fax 488 3756, carolines@palau .com)*, on a hill on the way to Palau Paci Resort, offers clean and comfortable b galows with air-con, private bathroom, and minibar for US$150. Guests have f access to the beach and to the facilities the Palau Pacific.

Sunrise Villa (☎ 488 4590, fax 4 4593), on a hill on Arakabesang Island, posh, huge, comfortable rooms with f views over the lagoon, as well as carpetin TVs, refrigerators, and phones. Sing double rooms are US$130/160. The fa tastic presidential suite (with a 180° vie is US$295. The hotel has an excelle restaurant, a pool, and a cozy bar ove looking the bay.

The *Hotel Nikko (☎ 488 2486, fax 4 2878, nikko@palaunet.com)*, once Pala premier hotel, is still coveted for its g geous hillside setting overlooking Pala northernmost Rock Islands. Standard roo have a refrigerator and phone but no TV a cost US$150. Some rooms are quite a hi uphill from the reception area.

Palau Pacific Resort (☎ 488 2600, f 488 1606, ppr@palaunet.com), a 20 minu drive from Koror on Arakabesang Island, one of the region's finest resort hotels. I the only hotel in Palau located on a beach, protected strand that's the best in Kor Rooms have rattan furniture, tile floors, cei ing fans and private lanais (verandas). Rat start at US$280/250/215 for a garden vie in peak/high/low season; it's US$340/29 250 for an ocean view, while suites a

cier (add tax plus 5% service charge).
ere's a beachside swimming pool, tennis
rts, a fitness centre and a dive shop. Air-
t transfers are US$15 round-trip.

ces to Eat

dget *Ben Ermii*, a burgers-on-wheels
parked opposite the high school, is Mc-
nald's Palau-style. Burgers cost between
$2.75 and US$5, milkshakes are US$3,
d a side order of fries is US$1. It's open
(until 2 am Wednesday to Saturday) and
ves to Airai's baseball field (Babeldaob)
Sundays. The clean, deli-style *Coconut*
t (☎ 488 2124), adjacent to the Rock Is-
d Cafe, has cheap takeaway burgers and
ndwiches. It's closed Saturdays. *Furu-*
o Restaurant, next to the Bank of
waii, is another popular, good-value
ery. Curry rice, noodle or *oyako domburi*
US$5. *Yokohama* on Lebuu Street is a
al restaurant with generous portions at
nest prices. Sandwiches cost around
$2, sashimi or ramen US$3.

id-Range The *Rock Island Cafe* in
wntown Koror is a favourite among ex-
ts for its excellent pizza, good seafood
d steaks, and relaxed atmosphere. A small
pperoni pizza or fresh sashimi costs
$5, pasta and Mexican food are US$5 to
and a good burger with fries is US$5.
Larry's at the Sunrise Villa is a pleasant
ot with a fine hillside lagoon view and
od food at surprisingly reasonable prices.
lunch, grilled chicken or fried fish with
e or fries costs US$6.75. Lunch and din-
r specials run to about US$14.
Pirate's Cove, near the Fisheries Co-op
Malakal Island, has a water view and
ell-prepared food. Dishes range from
aghetti in fish sauce for US$6.75 to
riyaki steak with rice and salad for
$12. It's closed Sundays.

p End The popular *Fuji Restaurant*, in
e same complex as West Downtown
otel, is a good upmarket place for seafood
d Japanese dishes. Sweet and sour fish or
pork cutlet cost US$8 while the set dinner
th sashimi, land crab and various side

Storyboards

Palau's most unique art form is the storyboard, a smaller version of the carved legends that have traditionally decorated the
beams and gables of *bai* (men's meeting
houses). The carving style was suggested
in 1935 by Japanese anthropologist
Hisakatsu Hijikata, who viewed the smaller
boards as a way to keep both the art form
and legends from dying out. Today, many
of the storyboard scenes depicted have an
element of erotica.

NED FRIARY

dishes costs US$25. It's open for dinner
only on Sundays.

The general consensus is that the Japanese run *Dragon Tei (☎ 488 2271)* in Topside serves the best food in Palau –
Okinawa with a touch of Palau. Specialities
include coconut crab and a tasty Napoleon
fish sauteed in white wine. Most dishes are
priced between US$6 and US$8. There's a
teppanyaki grill used to make huge
okonomiyaki, dubbed 'Japanese pizza'.

Ming's Restaurant on the second floor of
the Outrigger Palasia Hotel is a pleasant,
airy restaurant with gorgeous dripping chande-
liers and fantastic Chinese cuisine prepared
by a Shanghai chef. Many of the entrees,
from the popular sweet-and-sour options to
seafood, cost from US$9.50 to $32.

PALAU

Just down the hall, the Outrigger's small *Sushi Restaurant* has great food and is a comfortable place to eat alone. The best deal is a US$10 'special set' which comes with miso soup, rice, fruit and a delicious or meat fish entree.

Self-Catering The *WCTC Shopping Center* has a large, modern supermarket with reasonable prices and an ATM in the lobby. Next door, *Yano's Produce Market* is a great place to buy local produce and freshly cooked Palauan food – fried fish, teriyaki squid, turtle with coconut milk and fried bananas.

Entertainment
All bars close by Koror's midnight curfew. Red Rooster, the local beer, is widely served.

The open-air *Riptide* on Malakal Island is a favourite expat hangout. Its sister, *High-tide*, is just across the way.

The beach bar at *Palau Pacific Resort* is a fine upmarket place for a sunset drink, as is the outdoor covered bar above the pool at *Sunrise Villa*. For the local scene try the *SLC Club* on the road to Malakal, with dancing and live bands, or *Harbour Lights*, where foreigners are occasionally spotted. Billiards players mob the *Q-Ball Club* on Lebuu St (closed Monday). Ask around for the faddish karaoke joints. Koror's only disco, *Crystal Palace*, is a late-evening spot popular with both locals and expats.

Shopping
Palauan storyboards make excellent, albeit pricey, souvenirs. A good place to find quality storyboards is at the shop in Koror's jail. At the Senior Citizen Center near the DW Motel, local craftspeople sit in an open-air bai-like shelter and weave hats, baskets and purses. The affiliated gift shop has excellent crafts. The museum gift shop sells storyboards, books about Palau, T-shirts and woven baskets and purses.

Getting There & Away
See the section at the beginning of this chapter for details on flights to Palau.

Getting Around
Taxis are plentiful in Koror and can be flagged down. The fare from central Koror to the Palau Pacific Resort is US$5; to the airport it's between US$15 and US$25. Try City Cab (☎ 488 1394) or Koror Tax (☎ 488 1519).

The following car rental agencies have booths at the airport as well as offices in Koror: West Toyota Car Rental (☎ 488 5599), I-A Rent-A-Car (☎ 488 1113), King's U-Drive (☎ 488 2964, fax 488 3273 and Budget (☎ 488 6233). Rates start at US$30 to $35 per day.

If you're driving deep into Babeldaob it's best to rent a high-riding vehicle that can handle the rough road. Driving is on the right.

The Rock Islands

More than 200 rounded knobs of limestone totally covered with green jungle growth dot the waters for a 20 mile stretch south of Koror. The bases of these famous Rock Islands have been undercut by water erosion and the uniquely shaped islands are often likened to emerald mushrooms rising from a turquoise-blue sea.

The waters surrounding the Rock Islands contain some of the most abundant and varied marine life in the world. The islands also have crocodiles and fruit bats and are rich with bird life. Most of the islands are too undercut for boat landings and are off limits to visitors, but a few (your guide will know which ones) have white beaches and are accessible. Ancient rock paintings can be found on **Ulong Island** and half-quarried Yapese stone money can be seen in a **limestone cave** near Airai Channel. Other islands have caves with dripping stalactites, rock arches and underground channels.

The Rock Islands hold about 80 marine salt lakes, former sinkholes now filled with saltwater. Variations in algae give them different colours and some have soft corals, fish, sponges or jellyfish. The heavily forested island of **Eil Malk** contains **Spooky Lake**, which has stratified layers of

ankton, hydrogen sulphide and gases, and
Jellyfish Lake, filled with jellyfish that have
lost the ability to sting.

Visitors must pay a US$15 Rock Island
permit fee, which goes toward conservation
and is usually not included in your dive
shop fee. Once purchased, the permit is
valid for 30 days; carry it along on all Rock
Islands trips.

Diving & Snorkelling

Palau is one of the world's truly spectacular dive spots. If coral reefs, blue holes,
WWII wrecks and hidden caves and tunnels
aren't enough, consider the more than 60
vertical drop-offs.

The Rock Islands' waters teem with over
500 varieties of reef and pelagic fish.
There are immense tabletop corals, interlocking thickets of staghorn coral and soft
corals of all types and colours. Divers can
see manta rays, sea turtles, moray eels,
giant tridacna clams, grey reef sharks and
sometimes even a sea snake, rare dugong or
chambered nautilus. The sea temperature
averages about 82°F (27°C) and visibility
extends over 100 feet along drop-offs.

Three of Palau's most magnificent dives
are spotlighted in the 'South Pacific Diving'
special section, earlier in this book: the
Ngemelis Wall, also called the 'Big Drop-
off', is widely considered the world's best
wall dive; while **Blue Corner** is Palau's
most popular dive. The Wall is also good for
snorkelling, but Blue Corner is for experienced divers only.

Both the **German Channel** and **Turtle
Cove**, near Peleliu, offer good novice dives;
the latter has good snorkelling.

Dive Shops Dive boats generally leave
Koror at around 9 am and return around 4
pm, breaking for a Rock Island picnic
lunch. Lunch, tanks and weights are generally included in prices. Trips to Peleliu typically cost US$15 to $20 extra. Snorkellers
generally pay US$55 to $60 to go out on a
dive boat.

Splash (☎ 488 2602, fax 488 1601), a
well-regarded PADI five-star dive centre at
the Palau Pacific Resort, has two-tank boat

dives/night dives for US$105/70. Novice
dives and certification courses are available.

Neco Marine Corp (☎ 488 1755, fax
488-3014, necomarine@palaunet.com), at
a marina on Malakal Island, is one of
Palau's largest operations. It costs US$65/
98/133 for a one/two/three-tank dive,
night dives are US$65. There is no charge
for a trip to Jellyfish Lake after the second
dive. Snorkelling tours, boat charters,
PADI courses and introductory courses
can be arranged. Neco also runs a good
dive shop.

Fish 'n Fins (☎ 488 2637, fax 488 5418,
fishnfin@palaunet.com) keeps a tidy shop
on M-Dock in Koror. A two-tank dive costs
US$95. Fish 'n Fins has a good four day
(US$470) or seven day (US$820) accommodation and diving package with the West
Plaza hotels. Three-day certification and introductory dive courses are available.

Sam's Tours (☎ 488 1062, fax 488 5003,
samstour@palaunet.com), is a large, popular five-star PADI dive operation. One/two-
tank dives cost US$65/99.

A smaller operation favoured by Peace
Corps volunteers is Dive Palau (☎ 488
3548, keithpda@palaunet.com), headed by
long-time Missouri transplant Keith Santil-
lano. Two/three-tank dives cost US$90/120;
night dives are US$55. Introductory one/
two-tank dives cost US$60/130.

Live-Aboard Dive Boats Three live-
aboard dive boats ply Palauan waters. All
prices are double occupancy and include
meals and diving.

The 106-foot long *Palau Aggressor II*
(paggressor@palaunet.com) has eight
luxurious cabins. The cost is US$2295, with
a US$200 discount if you also book with
Truk Aggressor in Chuuk. Reservations are
made through Live/Dive Pacific (☎ 808-
329 8182, or ☎ tollfree 800 344 5662, fax
808-329 2628, livedive@compuserve.com)
in the USA. On Palau, contact Neco Marine
Dive Shop (☎ 488 1755).

The 138 foot *Sun Dancer II* has 10 lav-
ish double cabins. The week-long cruise is
US$2195; add US$50 port charges plus a
US$25 dive fee. Trips from late July to

PALAU

mid-October get a US$400 discount. Reserve through Peter Hughes Diving (☎ 305-669 9391, or ☎ tollfree 800 932 6237, fax 305-669 9475, dancer@peterhughes.com) in the USA.

A smaller vessel is the 60 foot *Ocean Hunter* (☎ 488 2637, fax 488 5418, ocean .hunter@palaunet.com) operated by Fish 'n Fins. Its seven to 14 day trips start at US$2295 per week.

Day Trips The dive shops can drop you off on a Rock Island beach in the morning and pick you up after their last dive, usually for the same price as a snorkelling tour.

Palau Diving Center (☎ 488 2978, fax 488 3155) and Neco Marine Dive Shop usually take you to their own islands, Carp Island and Neco Island respectively. Carp Island is the more scenic choice, while the snorkelling is better at Neco. A trip to Carp is US$35 return, to Neco it's US$50.

Places to Stay
The Rock Islands are an amazing camp spot and the star gazing is tremendous. Some of the islands have shelters and picnic tables, though none have water and you'll need bug protection. Make drop-off and pick-up arrangements with a dive shop. For a guided camping/kayak outing, try Planet Blue Kayaking (see Activities under Koror in this chapter).

The only guesthouse is the *Carp Island Resort*, booked through Palau Diving Center (☎ 488 2978, fax 488 3155, carpcorp@ palaunet.com). A variety of grossly overpriced accommodation is geared mostly toward Japanese divers. Dormitory-style accommodation is US$65/55 for high/low season; add US$20 for the plain cottages. Generator electricity comes on at night. Meals are expensive; it's better to bring your own food and use their kitchen. Campers can stay for US$10.

Getting There & Away
Most visitors see the Rock Islands via boat trips run by the dive shops (for contact details see Diving & Snorkelling earlier in this section).

Other Islands

BABELDAOB
● **pop 4600**   ● **area 153 sq miles**
High, volcanic Babeldaob, or Babelthaup has 10 states. Babeldaob's freshwater Lake Ngardok is the region's largest natural lake. Parts of the island's dense jungle interior remain virtually unexplored. There are beautiful stretches of sandy beach on the east coast, and mangroves along the west coast. Many villages are connected by ancient stone footpaths. A paved US$149 million 53 mile road around the island, planned for construction soon, will make the island much more accessible to tourists. But things on Babeldaob have a reputation for being slow – Melekeok State was constitutionally designated as Palau's future capital, but the grandiose plans have yet to be effected.

In Ngarchelong State, at the northernmost point of Babeldaob, is an open field with rows of large basalt monoliths known as **Badrulchau**. There are 37 stones in all, some weighing up to five tons.

At the southern end of Babeldaob, **Airai State**, just across the bridge from Koror, holds Palau's famous **bai** (mens' houses). To reach them, continue past the airport to the bombed-out shell of a Japanese administration building 1¼ miles beyond. Behind the main ruins is another old wartime building, as well as a Japanese tank and a few rusting guns. Continue down the main road for about 200 yards to a security gate; just past that the road splits. Turn left to reach the new bai, which is on the right.

Just beyond, turn left at the T-junction – the road will end at Palau's oldest bai. The century-old bai has a steeply pitched 40 foot roof. It was constructed without nails using native materials of wood and thatch on a stone platform. Entry is about US$2; US$10 if you want to photograph the bai (US$50 for video cameras). Also in Airai State is **Metuker ra Bisech**, a quarry for Yapese stone money, about 20 minutes by boat from Koror.

Places to Stay
Homestays are possible in Ngarchelong State (☎ 488 2871), Ngardmau State

488 1401 or ☎ 488 2683), and Ngchesar ate (☎ 488 2636). It's about US$25 to 35. Boat or car transport will be an additional expense. Three spacious new Babeldaob *guesthouses* are operated by Lazarus odep (☎ 654 1001 or ☎ 488 2728, fax 654 003), the governor of Melekeok. Constructed out of beautiful dark wood, they have 24-hour power, showers and excellent kitchen equipment; it's US$40 a night (plus tax) and transport is US$25. *Ngaraard raditional Resort (☎ 488 1788, fax 488 725, jdean@palaunet.com)* has three traditional cottages with outdoor toilets and evening electricity in a natural beach setting in Ngaraard. It's US$45/55 for singles/doubles, and US$10 for small children. Meals are US$33. Tours of northern Babeldaob, including the stone monoliths of Badrulchau, can be arranged. The Airai View Hotel is also on Babeldaob; see Places to Stay in the Koror section.

Getting There & Away

Private speedboats, fishing boats and state motorboats to Babeldaob leave from Koror's T-Dock or the Fisheries Co-op; ask at the state offices or go down to the docks and ask around. Ngaraard Traditional Resort can arrange a private speedboat from Koror to Ngaraard (one hour) for US$100 per boatload return. Guided tours of Babeldaob can be arranged from Koror, but they tend to be expensive, averaging about US$65/100 per person for a half /full day. Try Palau Island Adventures (☎ 488 4511, fax 488 1843, pia@palaunet.com).

You can drive from Koror to the bai in Airai in a sedan, but beyond that you'll need a 4WD vehicle.

PELELIU

● pop 600   ● area 5 sq miles

Peleliu hosted one of WWII's bloodiest battles: more than 15,000 men were killed, not much less than Palau's entire current population. The USA attacked because of its fear, ultimately ungrounded, that the Japanese on Peleliu could thwart US efforts to retake the Philippines. During the fighting Peleliu's forests were bombed and razed, but today jungle growth blankets the battle scars; watch for the occasional pillbox, rusting tank or memorial.

Many war remnants cluster north of the airport amidst a confusing criss-cross of roads. It's helpful to have a guide. The island still has a scattering of live ammunition, so take care if you go off the road and don't be tempted to take 'souvenirs', no matter how small. Most good beaches are to the south.

Around the Island

A small temporary **war museum** containing war artefacts, munitions and period photos is adjacent to the school. Ask for the key at the nearby governor's office. A multistorey bombed-out **Japanese communications centre** lies in the village centre, tangled with vegetation and encircled by homes. There's a small **US military monument** opposite Keibo's Store.

The first US forces came ashore at **Orange Beach** on 15 September 1944. Despite the Japanese barrage, 15,000 US soldiers

---

The Last Japanese Stragglers

In the late 1950s, a Japanese soldier who had been hiding in the jungle was discovered by an elderly woman as he entered her garden. Crouching low to see who had been stealing her tapioca, the woman froze and then screamed, thinking she was seeing a ghost. The man's uniform was torn into shreds, his hair matted and teeth streaked black. Koror police hunted the straggler down, bound him with rope and paraded him around for everyone to see. In that inglorious manner, the last WWII soldier left Peleliu.

However he was not the last soldier fighting the Pacific war. In 1972, Corporal Yokoi Shcoichi, surrendered after hiding for 27 years in the jungles of Guam.

made it ashore the first day. Today Orange Beach is a quiet picnic spot with a sandy beach and calm, clear waters too shallow to swim. Just before the beach are two **WWII monuments**. On the beach, look south to spot a Japanese defence bunker partially concealed by the rocks. Behind **Camp Beck Dock** you'll find a huge pile of mangled WWII plane engines, cockpits, pipes, tubing, fuselages, anchors and who knows what, all compacted into blocks of twisted aluminium and steel.

At Bkul Omruchel, on the island's southwest tip, is **Peleliu Peace Memorial Park**. **Bloody Beach** is a calm circular cove with a nice sandy strand. Just north is the **Ngerewal picnic area**. North-east of the airport is **Honeymoon Beach**, with good seasonal surf. Heading back from the eastern tip of the island, off a grassy road to the right, there's a refreshing little **swimming hole** of half-salt, half-freshwater that rises and falls with the tides. A metal ladder hangs down the side.

Diving & Snorkelling
The Peleliu Wall, south-west of Peleliu, is one of the world's finest dives, an abrupt 900 foot drop with sharks, hawksbill sea turtles, black coral trees, mammoth gorgonian fans, and fish. White Beach, Bloody Beach and Honeymoon beach have coral and good snorkelling.

Peleliu Divers (☎/fax 345 1058, pdivers@palaunet.com), a small operation beside the Storyboard Resort, charges US$85 for a two-tank dive. Dive shops from Koror come out to Peleliu frequently.

Places to Stay & Eat
Camping is easy (and acceptable) on Peleliu. Some beaches have open-air shelters, tables, barbecue pits and outhouses, but you'll need to take drinking water, plus bug protection. Notify the governor's office (☎ 345 1071 on Peleliu) of your plans. Try Ngerewal picnic area, Honeymoon Beach or Orange Beach. Hotels have a 10% hotel tax and no daytime electricity.

The *Wenty Inn* (☎ 345 2967) is a five-room guesthouse (US$15 per person) on a

nice beach. Meals are US$27 per day. *Mayumi Inn*, Mayumi Keibo rents th plain rooms with a shared outdoor bat room/shower and air-con behind Keibo Store. It's US$22 per person (includi tax); meals are US$7 to $12 each.

Storyboard Beach Resort (☎ 345 10 fax 345 1058, pdivers@palaunet.com Peleliu's nicest accommodation, has s simple but clean A-frame concrete cottag on the beach near Keibo's Store (US$85 p cottage). The cottages have hot showe lanais and ceiling fans.

Getting There & Away
The state boat, *Peleliu Islander*, runs twi weekly between Koror and Peleliu; call t governor's office (☎ 345 1071) for depa ture times (US$12 return). Some dive con panies will take their midday break o Peleliu and give land tours for an additior fee.

Getting Around
For vehicle rental, check at Mayumi In which rents an old van for US$49.50; or a around. Wenty Inn rents bicycles f US$10. An excellent tour of the island given by Tangie, Peleliu's resident 'histc ian'. It's US$77 for one to four people; a for Tangie at the Mayumi Inn. Also t Peleliu Divers (☎/fax 345 1058).

ANGAUR
● pop 193   ● area 3 sq miles

Angaur, seven miles south-west of Peleli is outside the protective reef that surround most of Palau's islands. Open ocea pounds the north coast where the sea e plodes skyward through small blowhole The calmer southern end is fringed wit sandy beaches. There's good diving arour Angaur between January and July, but th rest of the year the water's too rough. Ther are no dive shops and few Koror dive con panies go to Angaur.

Camping can be complicated; try t make arrangements for guesthouses at th Angaur governor's office (☎ 488 5282 i Koror, or ☎ 277 2967 in Angaur) befor you go. Electricity and water are onl

npei dancer

Local kids leaning on *rai* (stone money) in Yap

nding roots to make *sakau*, an intoxicating drink, at a cultural centre on Pohnpei

A Yapese woman

The lory, Pohnpei's state bird

A magnificent flame tree

Statue of Guam's Chief Gad

Ruins of an ancient city – Nan Madol's artificial islands, Pohnpei, F

Angaur Monkeys

Angaur has thousands of crab-eating macaques, descendants of a couple of monkeys brought to the island by the Germans in the early 1900s to monitor air quality in Angaur's phosphate mines. Accidentally released, the monkeys took well to Angaur's jungles, despite attempts to eradicate them. As the macaques occasionally raid crops, many islanders consider them pests.) While their export to other Palauan islands is officially prohibited, they are prized as pets and you may occasionally spot one in Koror.

ailable for part of the day. *Island Villas*, anaged by Leon Guilbert, has a spacious, odern house on the beach with a kitchen d a wraparound oceanview deck, two drooms and a couple of rooms capable of commodating larger groups. It costs S$20/30 for singles/ doubles. Meals are S$23 a day. Car and bike rentals are ailable (though you can walk around Anur by foot). A new four room *guesthouse* ar the dock has rooms for US$35 or $45. tchen facilities are available but they do t prepare meals. Ask for Kasiano, the ner.

Call the state office in Koror to inquire out the state boat's twice-weekly depares for Angaur. Private speedboats make e trip only occasionally, because the chan-l is rough.

KAYANGEL
- pop 124   • area 1 sq mile

Kayangel, 15 miles north of Babeldaob, is a picture-postcard coral atoll, with sun-bleached beaches, a well protected aqua-blue lagoon and just one small traditional village.

Kayangel plans to open its reef up to sportfishing in late 1999; until then the reef is a restricted preservation area. After the restrictions are lifted, Kayangel hopes to welcome more controlled fishing and visitation in the area. Some companies will be allowed to bring tourists; check with the governor's office or the Visitors Authority for the latest.

Tourists need a permit to visit – the Kayangel governor's office in Koror (☎ 488 2766) will issue you one for US$8 to $20. They – or the Kayangel office (☎ 876 2967) – will also help to arrange camping or homestays (US$20 to $50). Take rice, coffee, betel nut, baked goods or other provisions as gifts. The fortnightly state boat takes two hours and costs US$20.

SOUTH-WEST ISLANDS
- pop 72   • area 2½ sq miles

The South-West Islands comprise half a dozen small islands, each less than 1 sq mile. They are related culturally to the central Caroline Islands, especially Yap and Palau; and maintain a very traditional lifestyle. People are friendly and may speak some English. Boats run every month or two; contact the Sonsorol governor's office (☎ 488 1237) or the Tobi governor's office (☎ 488 2218), both in Koror, for details.

PALAU

ahu – raised altar or chiefly backrest found on ancient *marae* (Polynesia)

'aiga – Samoan for *kainga*

'ainga – see *kainga*

aitu – spirit, ghost (Polynesia)

Anglophone – any English-speaking person; as opposed to a *Francophone* (New Caledonia, Solomon Islands, Vanuatu)

ariki – (also *aliki, ali'i, ari'i*) widespread term for the paramount chief or members of a noble family

atoll – low-lying island built up from successive deposits of coral. The classic atoll is circular, enclosing a shallow lagoon, and sitting on a submarine volcanic peaks surrounded by deep ocean.

atua – Polynesian word for god or gods

aualuma – society of unmarried women (western Polynesia)

aumanga – (spelled *aumaga* in Samoa) a society of untitled men who do most of the fishing and farming (Polynesia)

Austronesians – people or languages from Indonesia, Malaysia and the Pacific islands

'ava – Samoan for *kava*

babai – Kiribati word for *taro*

bai – men's meeting house (Palau)

banyan – a huge fig tree

barrier reef – (or offshore reef) a long, narrow coral reef lying offshore and separated from the land by a lagoon of deep water that shelters the land from the sea (see also *fringing reef*)

beche-de-mer – (also known as a *trepang* or *sea slug*) lethargic, bottom-dwelling sea creature highly prized by Asian chefs

betel nut – round, greenish-orange nut of the Areca palm chewed for its narcotic effect (Solomons, northern Vanuatu, FSM, Palau)

bigman – Melanesian expression for chief (Solomons, Vanuatu)

bilo – vessel made from half a coconut shell and used for drinking *kava* (Fiji)

biu – treehouse for initiated boys (Solomons)

blackbirding – a 19th century recruitme scheme little removed from outright slave

bonito – blue-fin tuna

bougna – traditional *Kanak* meal of ya taro and sweet potatoes with chicken, fi or crustaceans, wrapped in banana leav and cooked in coconut milk in an earth ov (New Caledonia)

boulangerie – bakery (French territori

breadfruit – large, starchy fruit with coarse green skin. It can be boiled mashed, or fried like chips.

bula – Fijian greeting

bure – thatched dwelling (Fiji)

cagou – New Caledonia's national bird

caldera – large crater formed by the e plosion or subsidence of a volcano

Caldoche – white people born in Ne Caledonia whose ancestral ties go back the convicts or the early French settlers

cargo cults – religious movements who followers hope for the imminent delivery vast quantities of modern wealth (carg from either supernatural forces or the inha itants of faraway countries (eg the USA)

case – French word for traditional *Kan* houses (New Caledonia)

cassava – edible, starch-yielding root

CFP – the cour de franc Pacifique (al called the Pacific franc); the local curren in France's three Pacific territories

Chamorro – the indigenous people of t Mariana Islands

chef – French word for the customa leader of a clan (New Caledonia)

ciguatera – a type of food poisoni caused by eating infected tropical fish

clan – another term for tribe, a clan is grouping of people with a real or repute descent from a common ancestor.

CNMI – Commonwealth of the Northe Mariana Islands

coconut crab – a huge, edible land crab

Commonwealth – usually referring to t Commonwealth of Nations, or Briti Commonwealth

pra – dried coconut kernel from which
is extracted; once an important export
m the Pacific

ral – rock-like structure composed of the
ad, calcified remains of many generations
tiny sea creatures called coral polyps

coutume – French for custom, see the
planation for *kastom* (New Caledonia)

êperies – eating establishment specialis-
in pancakes (French territories)

stom – see *kastom* and *la coutume*

lo – Fijian for *taro*

pal – women's meeting house (Yap, FSM)

ateline – see *International Dateline*

op-off – diving term for a steep drop in
ocean floor

ua – double-hulled canoe (Fiji)

gong – (also called a manatee) a her-
vorous mammal which lives in the west-
Pacific

Z – exclusive economic zone. Waters out
200 nautical miles offshore which are
wned' by a country.

– (also *lei*) necklace (Cook Islands)

Niño – a weather phenomenon that
ings wet weather to the eastern Pacific
d droughts to the west (also see *La Niña*)

demic – plants, animals or diseases pe-
liar to a localised area

pat – short for expatriates; Europeans
sident in the islands

afafine – see *fakaleiti*

fine – see *vahine*

kaleiti – (*fa'afafine* in Samoa, *mahu* in
ench Polynesia) a man who dresses and
es as a woman (Tonga)

ka [culture] – (or *fa'a*) according to [a
lture's] customs and tradition For exam-
fa'a Samoa or *faka Pasifika*

le – (also *fare* or *vale*) traditionally a house
th thatched roof and open sides, but often
ed to mean any building (widespread)

le fono – meeting house, village hall or
rliament building (widespread)

le umu – kitchen huts (widespread)

luw – men's meeting house (Yap, FSM)

nua – Samoan for *fenua*

re – see *fale*

fenua – (*vanua* in Melanesia, *fanua* in
Samoa) widespread Pacific word for land

fiafia – dance performance (Samoa)

fono – governing council (Polynesian)

Francophone – someone who speaks
French; as opposed to an *Anglophone* (New
Caledonia, Solomons, Vanuatu)

French Territories – French Polynesia
(including Tahiti), Wallis & Futuna and
New Caledonia

fringing reef – (or onshore reef) coral reef
along the shore of an island without enclosing a lagoon (see also *barrier reef*)

FSM – Federated States of Micronesia

fumarole – a small volcanic or thermal fissure in the ground from which steam,
smoke or gas arises

fusi – cooperative stores (Tuvalu)

GDP – gross domestic product, or total
value of goods and services produced by a
nation in one year

gîte – a group of bungalows used for tourist
accommodation (French territories)

global warming – refers to the warming of
the Earth due to the greenhouse effect, which
is likely to render some Pacific nations uninhabitable within the next 100 years

GMT – Greenwich Mean Time, or the time
in London, England, which is used as a
standard across the rest of the world; essentially identical to Universal Time (UTC)

grade-taking – the process by which
Melanesian men progress through a series
of castes – proving their worth through
feasts and gifts (see *nimangki*)

guano – sea bird manure and dead bodies,
rich in phosphate and nitrates; once used as
fertiliser

heilala – Tonga's national flower

hôtel de ville – see *mairie*

i'a – see *ika*

ika – (or *i'a*) fish (widespread)

I-Kiribati – a native of Kiribati

I-Matang – foreigner (Kiribati)

International Dateline – the 'line'
approximately following 180° longitude.
Countries on the eastern side of the Dateline
are one day earlier than those on the right.

iroij – chief (Marshall Islands)

ISIC – International Student Identity Card

jambos – picnics or trips (Marshall Is)

kai – widespread Pacific word for food

kaiga – see *kainga*

kainga – (also *kaiga*, *'aiga* or *'ainga*) Polynesian word for the extended family

kaleve – see *kaokioki* (Tokelau)

Kanaks – indigenous New Caledonians (from the Polynesian words *kanaka*, *tanata* or *tangata*, meaning 'people')

kaokioki – (*kaleve* in Tokelau, *tuba* in the FSM) a beer-like fermented coconut drink, also known as sour toddy (Kiribati)

kastom – custom (Solomons, Vanuatu) Rules relating to traditionl beliefs. *Kastom ownership* is traditional ownership of land, objects or reef. Sometimes owned by a family or clan. Permission must be asked before trespassing on *kastom* land See also *la coutume*

kava – (also *'ava* or *sakau*) a mud-coloured, mildly intoxicating drink made from the roots of the *Piper methysticum* plant and drunk throughout Polynesia and in many parts of Melanesia and Micronesia

kirikiti – (also *kilikiti*) a Polynesian form of cricket with many players on each side. The game is played in French Polynesia, Samoa, Tokelau, Tuvalu and Wallis & Futuna.

korkor – a Marshallese dugout fishing canoe made from a breadfruit log

kumara – (also *kumala* or *'umala*) sweet potato; originated in South America and taken across the Pacific by Polynesian voyagers.

kuri – (or *kuli*) dogs (widespread)

lagoon – shallow area of water between the land and the ocean, sealed off by a network of reefs or islands

lanai – a Hawai'ian word commonly used in Micronesia to refer to a veranda

La Niña – weather pheneomenon related to (and often following) *El Niño* which brings wet weather to the western Pacific and droughts to the east

Lapita – the ancestors of the Polynesians

latte stones – the stone foundation pillars used to support ancient Chamorro buildings in the Mariana Islands

lava-lava – (also *pareu* or *sulu*) a saron type garment. A wide piece of cloth worn a skirt by women and men (widespread).

leeward – on the downwind side, shelter from the prevailing winds

lei – see *ei*

LMS — London Missionary Society; first group of missionaries to arrive in Pacific – Protestant

lovo – traditional feast (Fiji)

mahu – French Polynesian word for *fakale*

maire – an aromatic leaf (Cook Islands)

mairie – (or *hôtel de ville*) French term fo town hall (French Polynesia, New Caledon

makatea – the geological term for a rais coral island. In the Cook Islands the sa term refers to a coral coastal plain arou an island.

mal mal – a *T-piece* of cotton on *tapa* clo worn by male dancers in Vanuatu

malo – Polynesian greeting

mana – personal spiritual power (wid spread, particularly in Polynesia)

maneaba – (or *maneapa*) a tradition community meeting house (Kiribati)

maneapa – Tuvaluan for *maneaba*

mangrove – a tropical tree that grows tidal mud flats and extends looping roo along the shoreline

Maohi – (or Maori) the name for the i digenous people of the Cook Islands a Society Islands

marae – (also *malae* or *me'ae*) in weste Polynesia, the marae is a community v lage green; in eastern Polynesia it is a p Christian sacred site.

matai – (*mataiapo* in the Cook Islands) p litical representative of a family (Samc Tokelau and Tuvalu)

mataiapo – see *matai*

matrilineal – relating to descent and/or i heritance along the female line

meke – a dance performance that enac stories and legends (Fiji)

Melanesia – islands of the western Paci comprising Papua New Guinea, t Solomons, Vanuatu, New Caledonia and F The name is Greek for 'Black Islands'.

métro – someone from France (Ne Caledonia)

icronesia – islands of the north-western
cific including Palau, the Northern Mari-
a Islands, Guam, FSM, Marshall Islands,
uru and Kiribati. The name is Greek for
mall Islands'.

oa – chicken (widespread)

oai – a large stone statue (Easter Island)

uu-muu – (also called a Mother Hubbard
mission dress) a long, loose-fitting dress
roduced to the Pacific by the missionaries

waramwars – head wreaths of flowers
d fragrant leaves (FSM)

otu – widespread term for an island or islet

ghol – land-diving ritual (Vanuatu)

hnmwarki – a district chief in Pohnpei

hs – a traditional ceremonial house on
hnpei

kamal – men's clubhouse (New Cale-
nia, Vanuatu)

mba – penis-wrapper or sheath worn by
ry traditional Vanuatuans

tsaro – traditional dancing ground
anuatu)

guzunguzu – carved wooden canoe
gurehead (Solomons)

mangki – status and power earned by
king a series of *grades* (Vanuatu)

pa palm – a palm tree whose foliage is
ed for thatching and basketry

u – widespread Pacific word for coconut

i-Vanuatu – people from Vanuatu

ddy – a tropical tern, or aquatic bird,
ith black and white or dark plumage

ono – annoying small gnats or sandflies
und on many beaches of French Polynesia

ku – (or *nu'u*) village (Polynesian)

u'u – see *nuku*

utrigger – a float mounted parallel to the
ll of a canoe to make it more stable

a'anga – the currency of Tonga

ADI – Professional Association of Dive In-
ructors, the world's biggest diving group

ae pae – paved floor of a *marae*

alangi – (also *palagi*) widespread Polyesian term for a white person

andanus – a common plant whose
vord-shaped leaves are used to make mats,
skets and *tapa*

Papuans – ancient people who are among
the ancestors of modern Melanesians

pareu – (also *parpar* or *pareo*) word for
lava-lava in the Cook Islands, French Polynesia, New Caledonia and Vanuatu

pâtisserie – pastry shop (French territories)

pawpaw – (or *papaya*) sweet-tasting fruit
eaten in many parts of the Pacific

pebai – a Yapese community meeting house

peka – (*beka* in Fiji, *pe'a* in Samoa) widespread term for a bat or a small bird such as
a swallow

pelagic – creatures living in the upper waters of the open ocean

petroglyph – a design carved in stone

pilou – a Kanak dance, performed for important ceremonies or events

pirogue – a dugout canoe

Polynesia – the huge triangle of ocean and
islands bounded by Hawai'i, New Zealand
and Easter Island. Includes the Cook Islands, French Polynesia, Niue, Pitcairn Island, Samoa, Tokelau, Tonga, Tuvalu and
Wallis & Futuna. The name is Greek for
'Many Islands'.

Polynesian Outliers – the islands of eastern Melanesia and southern Micronesia
which are populated by Polynesians

poste restante – (or general delivery)
mail sent care of a particular post office and
collected there by the adressee

puaka – (or *pua'a*) pig (Polynesia)

pulenuku – (or *pulenu'u*) head man or village mayor (Polynesia)

purse seine – a large net generally used
between two boats that is drawn around a
school of fish, especially tuna. Boats that
use this method are called purse seiners.

quonset hut – WWII military storage
shed made from corugated iron

rack rates – normal walk-in room rates
without discounts

rae rae – French Polynesian word for
fakaleiti

rai – huge stone money (Yap, FSM)

rangatira – (*ragatira* in Samoa, *ra'atira* in
Tahiti) Polynesian word for a chief or the
nobility

ratu – chief (Fiji)

reef – ridge of coral, rock or sand lying just below the sea's surface; see *barrier reef* and *fringing reef*

RFO – Radio France Outre-Mer; the overseas arm of the French broadcasting service

RTW – round-the-world ticket

sa – sacred or forbidden; also the holy day or a holy time (Samoa and Tuvalu)

sakau – see *kava*

sake – Japanese rice wine

Saudeleur – a tyrannical royal dynasty which ruled ancient Pohnpei

sea slug – see *beche-de-mer*

seka – a narcotic, ceremonial drink similar to *kava* (FSM)

sevusevu – a presentation of a gift as a request for certain favours (Fiji)

siapo – Samoan for *tapa*

skrab dak – (or *scrab faol*) megapode bird (Solomons)

snack – cheap cafe (French Territories)

sour toddy – see *kaokioki*

SPF – South Pacific Forum, an intergovernmental association which meets annually to discuss regional matters

sulu – Fijian for *lava-lava*

swim-through – diving term for a hole or tunnel large enough to swim through

tabu – see *tapu*

tagimoucia – national flower of Fiji

tambu – the plural form of *tabu* (Vanuatu)

tamtam – slit-gong or slit-drum, made from carved logs with a hollowed-out section (Vanuatu)

tanoa – multi-legged wooden bowl used for mixing *kava* (Wallis & Futuna)

ta'ovala – distinctive woven pandanus mats worn around the waist in Tonga

tapa – bark cloth made from the paper mulberry tree (widespread)

tapu – (also *tabu* or *tambu*) sacred or prohibited, the source of the English word 'taboo'; either a noun or an adjective

taro – (*dalo* in Fiji, *babai* in Kiribati) a plant with green heart-shaped leaves, cultivated for both its leaf and edible rootstock

taulasea – traditional healer (Samoa)

taupo – ceremonial virgin (Samoa)

taupou – title bestowed by high-ranking

chief upon a young woman of his fam (Polynesia)

thu – a loincloth worn by Yapese ma and by outer island Chuukese (FSM)

tiki – carved human figure (Polynesia)

tivaevae – colourful intricately sewn a plique works (Cook Islands)

tokosra – paramount chief (FSM)

to'ona'i – Sunday lunch (Samoa)

T-piece – small piece of cloth coveri only the groin area (Solomons, Vanuatu)

trade winds – the near-constant winds t blow from the north-east in the North Pac and from the south-east in the South Pac

trepang – see *beche-de-mer*

tridacna clam – the giant clam, *Tridag gigas*; the largest known bivalve mollus

trochus – a shellfish commercially h vested for its shell and flesh

tuba – Yap word for *kaokioki*

tufanga – (*tufaga* in Samoa, *tahua* Tahiti) priest or expert (Polynesia)

tui – (*tu'i* in Tonga) central Pacific term a paramount king

umu – widespread Pacific term for a sto oven in the ground

umukai – a feast of foods cooked in an *u*

unimane – respected old men or village ders (Kiribati)

USP – University of the South Pacific R gional university based in Fiji

va'a – see *vaka*

vahine – (*fafine* in Samoa) Polynesi word for woman

vaka – (or *va'a*) canoe (widespread)

vale – Fijian for *fale*

vanua – see *fenua*

wantok – literally 'one talk'; the weste Melanesian concept that all those wh speak your language are allies (Solomon

windward – the side of an island whi faces the prevailing; the opposite of *leewa*

World Heritage Site – a site chosen for unique natural or historical values

yam – starchy tuber which is a staple foc in the Pacific

yaqona – see *kava* (Fiji)

Appendix 1 – Climate Charts

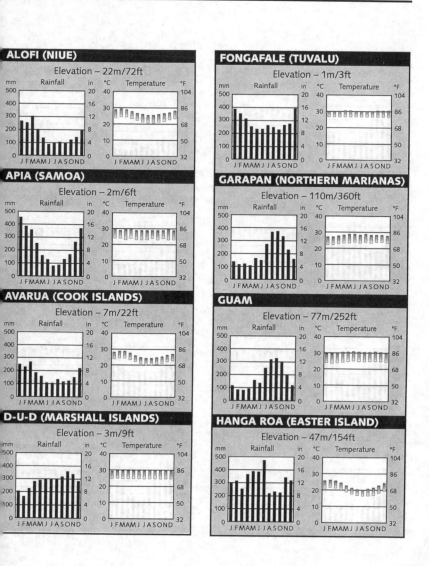

ALOFI (NIUE)
Elevation – 22m/72ft
Rainfall / Temperature

APIA (SAMOA)
Elevation – 2m/6ft
Rainfall / Temperature

AVARUA (COOK ISLANDS)
Elevation – 7m/22ft
Rainfall / Temperature

D-U-D (MARSHALL ISLANDS)
Elevation – 3m/9ft
Rainfall / Temperature

FONGAFALE (TUVALU)
Elevation – 1m/3ft
Rainfall / Temperature

GARAPAN (NORTHERN MARIANAS)
Elevation – 110m/360ft
Rainfall / Temperature

GUAM
Elevation – 77m/252ft
Rainfall / Temperature

HANGA ROA (EASTER ISLAND)
Elevation – 47m/154ft
Rainfall / Temperature

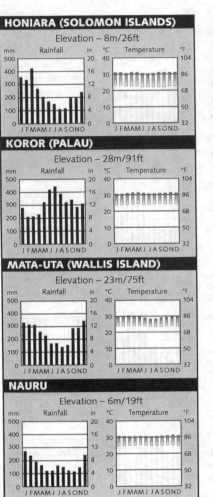

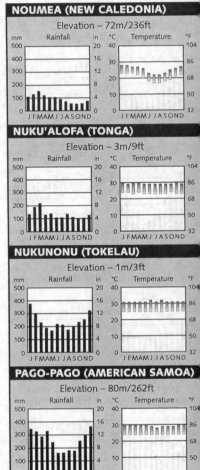

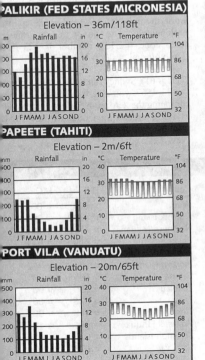

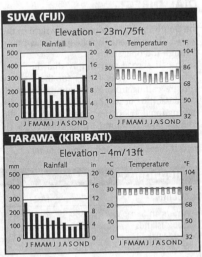

Appendix II – Telephones

DIAL DIRECT

You can dial directly from most countries in the South Pacific to almost anywhere in the world. This is usually cheaper than going through the operator.

To call abroad you simply dial the international access code (IAC) for the country you are calling from (most commonly ☎ 00 in the Pacific but see the following table), the international telephone code (ITC) for the country you are calling, the local area code (if there is one, and usually dropping the leading zero if there is one) and then the number.

If, for example, you are in the Cook Islands (international access code ☎ 00) and want to make a call to the USA (international telephone code ☎ 1), San Francisco (area code ☎ 212), number ☎ 123 4567, then you dial ☎ 00-1-212-123 4567.

To call from Fiji (IAC ☎ 05) to Australia (ITC ☎ 61), Sydney (area code ☎ 02), number ☎ 123 4567, you dial ☎ 05-61-2-1234 5678 (dropping the zero from Sydney's area code).

There are no area codes in any of the countries of the South Pacific except for New Zealand.

Telephone Codes

Country	ITC	IAC	Country	ITC	IAC
American Samoa	☎ 684	☎ 00	Niue	☎ 683	☎ 00
Cook Islands	☎ 682	☎ 00	Norfolk Island	☎ 6723	☎ 00
Easter Island	☎ 56-32	N/A	Northern Marianas	☎ 1-670	☎ 011
FSM	☎ 691	☎ 011	Palau	☎ 680	☎ 011
Fiji	☎ 679	☎ 05	Papua New Guinea	☎ 675	☎ 05
French Polynesia	☎ 689	☎ 00	Pitcairn Islands	☎ 872-144-5372	
Guam	☎ 1-671	☎ 011	Samoa	☎ 685	☎ 00
Hawai'i	☎ 1-808	☎ 011	Tokelau	☎ 690	☎ 00
Kiribati	☎ 686	☎ 00	Tonga	☎ 676	☎ 00
Lord Howe Island	☎ 61-2	☎ 0011	Tuvalu	☎ 688	☎ 00
Marshall Islands	☎ 692	☎ 011	Wallis & Futuna	☎ 681	☎ 19
Nauru	☎ 674	☎ 00	Solomon Islands	☎ 677	☎ 00
New Caledonia	☎ 687	☎ 00	Vanuatu	☎ 678	☎ 00
New Zealand	☎ 64	☎ 00			

Other countries' International Telephone Codes (ITC) include: Australia ☎ 61, Canada ☎ 1, France ☎ 33, Germany ☎ 49, Hong Kong ☎ 852, Indonesia ☎ 62, Japan ☎ 81, Malaysia ☎ 60, Singapore ☎ 65, South Africa ☎ 27, UK ☎ 44, USA ☎ 1

ITC – International Telephone Code (to call *into* that country)
IAC - International Access Code (to call abroad *from* that country)

Appendix III – French Language

ench is the major non-indigenous language
French Polynesia (including Tahiti), New
ledonia and Wallis & Futuna. It will also
ove useful in Vanuatu.

There are a few peculiarities of French
onunciation you should remember: **ai** is
onounced as the 'e' in 'pet', **eau/au** as the
u' in 'caught', **ll** as the 'y' in 'yet', **ch** as
h', **qu** as 'k', and **r** as a rolled 'r'; conso-
nts at the end of words are usually silent;
hen **n** or **m** occur at the end of a word they
dicate nasalisation of the preceding vowel.

ssentials

ello/Good morning.	*Bonjour.*
ood evening.	*Bonsoir.*
oodbye.	*Au revoir.*
ow are you?	*Comment allez-vous?*
m fine (thanks).	*Je vais bien (merci).*
'hat's your name?	*Comment vous appelez-vous?*
1y name is ...	*Je m'appelle ...*
es	*Oui.*
lo.	*Non.*
lease.	*S'il vous plaît.*
'hank you (very much).	*Merci (beaucoup).*
'ou're welcome.	*Je vous en prie.*
xcuse me.	*Excusez-moi.*
'm sorry (Forgive me).	*Pardon.*
understand.	*Je comprends.*
don't understand.	*Je ne comprends pas.*
'ould you please write that down?	*Est-ce que vous pouvez l'écrire?*

'etting Around

When does ... eave/arrive?	*À quelle heure part/arrive le ...?*
the bus	*le bus*
the boat/ferry	*le bateau/le bac*
Where is ...?	*Où est ...?*
the bus station	*la gare routière*
the bus stop	*l'arrêt d'autobus*
the ticket office	*le guichet*

I'd like to hire ...	*Je voudrais louer ...*
a bicycle	*un vélo*
a car	*une voiture*
a guide	*un guide*
I want to go to ...	*Je voudrais aller à ...*
How do I get to ...?	*Comment peut-on aller à ...?*
Is it near/far?	*Est-ce près/loin d'ici?*
(Go) straight ahead.	*(Allez) tout droit.*
(Turn) left/right.	*(Tournez à) gauche/ droite.*

Around Town

Where is ...?	*Où est ...?*
I'm looking for ...	*Je cherche ...*
a bank	*une banque*
the hospital	*l'hôpital*
the police	*la police*
the post office	*le bureau de poste*
a telephone box	*une cabine téléphonique*
the tourism office	*l'office de tourisme*
What time does it open/close?	*Quelle est l'heure d'ouverture/ de fermeture?*
How much is it?	*C'est combien?*
bookshop	*la librairie*
chemist (pharmacy)	*la pharmacie*
clothing store	*le magasin de vêtements*
laundry	*la laverie*
market	*le marché*
newsagency	*l'agence de presse*
breakfast	*le petit déjeuner*
lunch	*le déjeuner*
dinner	*le dîner*
set dish of the day	*le plat du jour*
bakery	*la boulangerie*
butcher	*la boucherie*
cafe-style snack bar	*la brasserie*
food shop	*l'alimentation*
grocery store	*l'épicerie*

Emergencies

Help!	*Au secours!*
Call ...!	*Appelez ...!*
a doctor	*un médecin*
an ambulance	*une ambulance*
Call the police!	*Appelez la police!*
Go away!	*Vas t'en!*
I've been robbed.	*On m'a volé* (m)/ *volée* (f)
I've been raped.	*J'ai été violée.*

restaurant	*le restaurant*
shop	*le magasin*
supermarket	*le supermarché*

I'm a vegetarian.	*Je suis végétarien* (m)/ *végétarienne* (f).

Accommodation

I'm looking for ...	*Je cherche ...*
a youth hostel	*une auberge de jeunesse*
a camping ground	*un camping*
a hotel	*un hôtel*

I'd like ...	*Je voudrais ...*
a bed	*un lit*
a single room	*une chambre simple*
a double room	*une chambre double*

How much is it ...?	*C'est combien ...?*
per night	*par nuit*
per person	*par personne*

Times & Dates

At what time?	*À quelle heure?*
What time is it?	*Quelle heure est-il?*
When?	*Quand?*
today	*aujourd'hui*
tonight	*ce soir*
tomorrow	*demain*
yesterday	*hier*

Monday	*lundi*
Tuesday	*mardi*
Wednesday	*mercredi*
Thursday	*jeudi*
Friday	*vendredi*
Saturday	*samedi*
Sunday	*dimanche*

Health

I need a doctor.	*J'ai besoin d'un médecin.*
Where's a hospital?	*Où est l'hôpital?*
I'm diabetic/ asthmatic.	*Je suis diabétique/ asthmatique.*
I'm pregnant.	*Je suis enceinte.*
I'm allergic to ...	*Je suis allergique ...*
antibiotics	*aux antibiotiques*
penicillin	*à la pénicilline.*

antiseptic	*l'antiseptique*
aspirin	*l'aspirine*
condoms	*des préservatifs*
contraceptive	*le contraceptif*
diarrhoea	*la diarrhée*
medicine	*le médicament*
nausea	*la nausée*
sanitary napkins	*des serviettes hygiéniques*
sunscreen	*de la crème haute protection*
tampons	*des tampons*

Numbers

1	*un*
2	*deux*
3	*trois*
4	*quatre*
5	*cinq*
6	*six*
7	*sept*
8	*huit*
9	*neuf*
10	*dix*
20	*vingt*
30	*trente*
40	*quarante*
50	*cinquante*
60	*soixante*
70	*soixante-dix*
80	*quatre-vingts*
90	*quatre-vingt-dix*
100	*cent*
1000	*mille*
2000	*deux mille*

ON THE ROAD

Travel Guides explore cities, regions and countries, and supply information on transport, restaurants and accommodation, covering all budgets. They come with reliable, easy-to-use maps, practical advice, cultural and historical facts and a rundown on attractions both on and off the beaten track. There are over 200 titles in this classic series, covering nearly every country in the world.

 Lonely Planet Upgrades extend the shelf life of existing travel guides by detailing any changes that may affect travel in a region since a book has been published. Upgrades can be downloaded for free from **www.lonelyplanet.com/upgrades**

For travellers with more time than money, **Shoestring** guides offer dependable, first-hand information with hundreds of detailed maps, plus insider tips for stretching money as far as possible. Covering entire continents in most cases, the six-volume shoestring guides are known around the world as 'backpackers bibles'.

For the discerning short-term visitor, **Condensed** guides highlight the best a destination has to offer in a full-colour, pocket-sized format designed for quick access. They include everything from top sights and walking tours to opinionated reviews of where to eat, stay, shop and have fun.

CitySync lets travellers use their Palm™ or Visor™ hand-held computers to guide them through a city with handy tips on transport, history, cultural life, major sights, and shopping and entertainment options. It can also quickly search and sort hundreds of reviews of hotels, restaurants and attractions, and pinpoint their location on scrollable street maps. CitySync can be downloaded from **www.citysync.com**

MAPS & ATLASES

Lonely Planet's **City Maps** feature downtown and metropolitan maps, as well as transit routes and walking tours. The maps come complete with an index of streets, a listing of sights and a plastic coat for extra durability.

Road Atlases are an essential navigation tool for serious travellers. Cross-referenced with the guidebooks, they also feature distance and climate charts and a complete site index.

LONELY PLANET

ESSENTIALS

Read This First books help new travellers to hit the road with confidence. These invaluable predeparture guides give step-by-step advice on preparing for a trip, budgeting, arranging a visa, planning an itinerary and staying safe while still getting off the beaten track.

Healthy Travel pocket guides offer a regional rundown on disease hot spots and practical advice on predeparture health measures, staying well on the road and what to do in emergencies. The guides come with a user-friendly design and helpful diagrams and tables.

Lonely Planet's **Phrasebooks** cover the essential words and phrases travellers need when they're strangers in a strange land. They come in a pocket-sized format with colour tabs for quick reference, extensive vocabulary lists, easy-to-follow pronunciation keys and two-way dictionaries.

Miffed by blurry photos of the Taj Mahal? Tired of the classic 'top of the head cut off' shot? **Travel Photography: A Guide to Taking Better Pictures** will help you turn ordinary holiday snaps into striking images and give you the know-how to capture every scene, from frenetic festivals to peaceful beach sunrises.

Lonely Planet's **Travel Journal** is a lightweight but sturdy travel diary for jotting down all those on-the-road observations and significant travel moments. It comes with a handy time-zone wheel, a world map and useful travel information.

Lonely Planet's eKno is an all-in-one communication service developed especially for travellers. It offers low-cost international calls and free email and voicemail so that you can keep in touch while on the road. Check it out on www.ekno.lonelyplanet.com

FOOD & RESTAURANT GUIDES

Lonely Planet's **Out to Eat** guides recommend the brightest and best places to eat and drink in top international cities. These gourmet companions are arranged by neighbourhood, packed with dependable maps, garnished with scene-setting photos and served with quirky features.

For people who live to eat, drink and travel, **World Food** guides explore the culinary culture of each country. Entertaining and adventurous, each guide is packed with detail on staples and specialities, regional cuisine and local markets, as well as sumptuous recipes, comprehensive culinary dictionaries and lavish photos good enough to eat.

OUTDOOR GUIDES

For those who believe the best way to see the world is on foot, Lonely Planet's **Walking Guides** detail everything from family strolls to difficult treks, with 'when to go and how to do it' advice supplemented by reliable maps and essential travel information.

Cycling Guides map a destination's best bike tours, long and short, in day-by-day detail. They contain all the information a cyclist needs, including advice on bike maintenance, places to eat and stay, innovative maps with detailed cues to the rides, and elevation charts.

The **Watching Wildlife** series is perfect for travellers who want authoritative information but don't want to tote a heavy field guide. Packed with advice on where, when and how to view a region's wildlife, each title features photos of over 300 species and contains engaging comments on the local flora and fauna.

With underwater colour photos throughout, **Pisces Books** explore the world's best diving and snorkelling areas. Each book contains listings of diving services and dive resorts, detailed information on depth, visibility and difficulty of dives, and a roundup of the marine life you're likely to see through your mask.

ONELY PLANET

FF THE ROAD

urneys, the travel literature series written by renowned travel
thors, capture the spirit of a place or illuminate a culture with a
urnalist's attention to detail and a novelist's flair for words. These
e tales to soak up while you're actually on the road or dip into as
at-home armchair indulgence.

e range of lavishly illustrated **Pictorial** books is just the ticket for
th travellers and dreamers. Off-beat tales and vivid photographs
ing the adventure of travel to your doorstep long before the journey
gins and long after it is over.

nely Planet **Videos** encourage the same independent, tough-
nded approach as the guidebooks. Currently airing throughout the
rld, this award-winning series features innovative footage and an
iginal soundtrack.

s, we know, work is tough, so do a little bit of deskside dreaming
th the spiral-bound Lonely Planet **Diary** or a Lonely Planet **Wall
alendar**, filled with great photos from around the world.

RAVELLERS NETWORK

nely Planet Online. Lonely Planet's award-winning Web site has
sider information on hundreds of destinations, from Amsterdam to
mbabwe, complete with interactive maps and relevant links. The site
so offers the latest travel news, recent reports from travellers on the
ad, guidebook upgrades, a travel links site, an online book-buying
otion and a lively travellers bulletin board. It can be viewed at
ww.lonelyplanet.com or AOL keyword: lp.

anet Talk is a quarterly print newsletter, full of gossip, advice,
ecdotes and author articles. It provides an antidote to the being-
-home blues and lets you plan and dream for the next trip. Contact
e nearest Lonely Planet office for your free copy.

omet, the free Lonely Planet newsletter, comes via email once a
onth. It's loaded with travel news, advice, dispatches from authors,
avel competitions and letters from readers. To subscribe, click on the
omet subscription link on the front page of the Web site.

Lonely Planet Guides by Region

Lonely Planet is known worldwide for publishing practical, reliable an
no-nonsense travel information in our guides and on our Web site. Th
Lonely Planet list covers just about every accessible part of the worlc
Currently there are 16 series: Travel guides, Shoestring guides, Condense
guides, Phrasebooks, Read This First, Healthy Travel, Walking guides, Cyclin
guides, Watching Wildlife guides, Pisces Diving & Snorkeling guides, City Maps, Road Atlases, Out t
Eat, World Food, Journeys travel literature and Pictorials.

AFRICA Africa on a shoestring • Botswana • Cairo • Cairo City Map • Cape Town • Cape Town City Map
East Africa • Egypt • Egyptian Arabic phrasebook • Ethiopia, Eritrea & Djibouti • Ethiopian Amharic phrase
book • The Gambia & Senegal • Healthy Travel Africa • Kenya • Malawi • Morocco • Moroccan Arab
phrasebook • Mozambique • Namibia • Read This First: Africa • South Africa, Lesotho & Swaziland • South
ern Africa • Southern Africa Road Atlas • Swahili phrasebook • Tanzania, Zanzibar & Pemba • Trekking in Ea
Africa • Tunisia • Watching Wildlife East Africa • Watching Wildlife Southern Africa • West Africa • World Foc
Morocco • Zambia • Zimbabwe, Botswana & Namibia
Travel Literature: Mali Blues: Traveling to an African Beat • The Rainbird: A Central African Journey • Song
to an African Sunset: A Zimbabwean Story

AUSTRALIA & THE PACIFIC Aboriginal Australia & the Torres Strait Islands •Auckland • Australia • Australia
phrasebook • Australia Road Atlas • Cycling Australia • Cycling New Zealand • Fiji • Fijian phrasebook • Health
Travel Australia, NZ & the Pacific • Islands of Australia's Great Barrier Reef • Melbourne • Melbourne City Map
Micronesia • New Caledonia • New South Wales • New Zealand • Northern Territory • Outback Australia • Out t
Eat – Melbourne • Out to Eat – Sydney • Papua New Guinea • Pidgin phrasebook • Queensland • Rarotonga
the Cook Islands • Samoa • Solomon Islands • South Australia • South Pacific • South Pacific phrasebook • Sydne
• Sydney City Map • Sydney Condensed • Tahiti & French Polynesia • Tasmania • Tonga • Tramping in New Zealar
• Vanuatu • Victoria • Walking in Australia • Watching Wildlife Australia • Western Australia
Travel Literature: Islands in the Clouds: Travels in the Highlands of New Guinea • Kiwi Tracks: A New Zealan
Journey • Sean & David's Long Drive

CENTRAL AMERICA & THE CARIBBEAN Bahamas, Turks & Caicos • Baja California • Belize, Guatemal
& Yucatán • Bermuda • Central America on a shoestring • Costa Rica • Costa Rica Spanish phrasebook • Cub
• Cycling Cuba • Dominican Republic & Haiti • Eastern Caribbean • Guatemala • Havana • Healthy Trave
Central & South America • Jamaica • Mexico • Mexico City • Panama • Puerto Rico • Read This First: Centr
& South America • Virgin Islands • World Food Caribbean • World Food Mexico • Yucatán
Travel Literature: Green Dreams: Travels in Central America

EUROPE Amsterdam • Amsterdam City Map • Amsterdam Condensed • Andalucía • Athens • Austria • Balti
States phrasebook • Barcelona • Barcelona City Map • Belgium & Luxembourg • Berlin • Berlin City Map
Britain • British phrasebook • Brussels, Bruges & Antwerp • Brussels City Map • Budapest • Budapest City Ma
• Canary Islands • Catalunya & the Costa Brava • Central Europe • Central Europe phrasebook • Copenhage
• Corfu & the Ionians • Corsica • Crete • Crete Condensed • Croatia • Cycling Britain • Cycling France • Cypru
• Czech & Slovak Republics • Czech phrasebook • Denmark • Dublin • Dublin City Map • Dublin Condense
• Eastern Europe • Eastern Europe phrasebook • Edinburgh • Edinburgh City Map • England • Estonia, Latvi
& Lithuania • Europe on a shoestring • Europe phrasebook • Finland • Florence • Florence City Map • Franc
• Frankfurt City Map • Frankfurt Condensed • French phrasebook • Georgia, Armenia & Azerbaijan • German
• German phrasebook • Greece • Greek Islands • Greek phrasebook • Hungary • Iceland, Greenland & th
Faroe Islands • Ireland • Italian phrasebook • Italy • Kraków • Lisbon • The Loire • London • London City Ma
• London Condensed • Madrid • Madrid City Map • Malta • Mediterranean Europe • Milan, Turin & Genoa
Moscow • Munich • Netherlands • Normandy • Norway • Out to Eat – London • Out to Eat – Paris • Paris
Paris City Map • Paris Condensed • Poland • Polish phrasebook • Portugal • Portuguese phrasebook • Pragu
• Prague City Map • Provence & the Côte d'Azur • Read This First: Europe • Rhodes & the Dodecanese
Romania & Moldova • Rome • Rome City Map • Rome Condensed • Russia, Ukraine & Belarus • Russia
phrasebook • Scandinavian & Baltic Europe • Scandinavian phrasebook • Scotland • Sicily • Slovenia • South
West France • Spain • Spanish phrasebook • Stockholm • St Petersburg • St Petersburg City Map • Sweden
Switzerland • Tuscany • Ukrainian phrasebook • Venice • Vienna • Wales • Walking in Britain • Walking i
France • Walking in Ireland • Walking in Italy • Walking in Scotland • Walking in Spain • Walking in Switzer
land • Western Europe • World Food France • World Food Greece • World Food Ireland • World Food Italy
World Food Spain **Travel Literature:** After Yugoslavia • Love and War in the Apennines • The Olive Grove
Travels in Greece • On the Shores of the Mediterranean • Round Ireland in Low Gear • A Small Place in Ital

Lonely Planet Mail Order

L onely Planet products are distributed worldwide. They are also available by mail order from Lonely Planet, so if you have difficulty finding a title please write to us. North and South American residents should write to 150 Linden St, Oakland, CA 94607, USA; European and African residents should write to 10a Spring Place, London NW5 3BH, UK; and residents of ther countries to Locked Bag 1, Footscray, Victoria 3011, Australia.

IDIAN SUBCONTINENT & THE INDIAN OCEAN Bangladesh • Bengali phrasebook • Bhutan • Delhi Goa • Healthy Travel Asia & India • Hindi & Urdu phrasebook • India • India & Bangladesh City Map • Indian imalaya • Karakoram Highway • Kathmandu City Map • Kerala • Madagascar • Maldives • Mauritius, Réunion Seychelles • Mumbai (Bombay) • Nepal • Nepali phrasebook • North India • Pakistan • Rajasthan • Read his First: Asia & India • South India • Sri Lanka • Sri Lanka phrasebook • Tibet • Tibetan phrasebook • Trekking the Indian Himalaya • Trekking in the Karakoram & Hindukush • Trekking in the Nepal Himalaya • World ood India **Travel Literature:** The Age of Kali: Indian Travels and Encounters • Hello Goodnight: A Life of Goa In Rajasthan • Maverick in Madagascar • A Season in Heaven: True Tales from the Road to Kathmandu • Shopng for Buddhas • A Short Walk in the Hindu Kush • Slowly Down the Ganges

MIDDLE EAST & CENTRAL ASIA Bahrain, Kuwait & Qatar • Central Asia • Central Asia phrasebook • Dubai Farsi (Persian) phrasebook • Hebrew phrasebook • Iran • Israel & the Palestinian Territories • Istanbul • Istanbul ity Map • Istanbul to Cairo • Istanbul to Kathmandu • Jerusalem • Jerusalem City Map • Jordan • Lebanon • Middle ast • Oman & the United Arab Emirates • Syria • Turkey • Turkish phrasebook • World Food Turkey • Yemen ravel Literature: Black on Black: Iran Revisited • Breaking Ranks: Turbulent Travels in the Promised Land • he Gates of Damascus • Kingdom of the Film Stars: Journey into Jordan

NORTH AMERICA Alaska • Boston • Boston City Map • Boston Condensed • British Columbia • California • Nevada • California Condensed • Canada • Chicago • Chicago City Map • Chicago Condensed • Florida • eorgia & the Carolinas • Great Lakes • Hawaii • Hiking in Alaska • Hiking in the USA • Honolulu & Oahu ity Map • Las Vegas • Los Angeles • Los Angeles City Map • Louisiana & the Deep South • Miami • Miami ity Map • Montreal • New England • New Orleans • New Orleans City Map • New York City • New York ity City Map • New York City Condensed • New York, New Jersey & Pennsylvania • Oahu • Out to Eat – San rancisco • Pacific Northwest • Rocky Mountains • San Diego & Tijuana • San Francisco • San Francisco City Map • Seattle • Seattle City Map • Southwest • Texas • Toronto • USA • USA phrasebook • Vancouver • Vanouver City Map • Virginia & the Capital Region • Washington, DC • Washington, DC City Map • World Food ew Orleans **Travel Literature**: Caught Inside: A Surfer's Year on the California Coast • Drive Thru America

NORTH-EAST ASIA Beijing • Beijing City Map • Cantonese phrasebook • China • Hiking in Japan • Hong ong & Macau • Hong Kong City Map • Hong Kong Condensed • Japan • Japanese phrasebook • Korea • Korean hrasebook • Kyoto • Mandarin phrasebook • Mongolia • Mongolian phrasebook • Seoul • Shanghai • South-West China • Taiwan • Tokyo • Tokyo Condensed • World Food Hong Kong • World Food Japan ravel Literature: In Xanadu: A Quest • Lost Japan

SOUTH AMERICA Argentina, Uruguay & Paraguay • Bolivia • Brazil • Brazilian phrasebook • Buenos Aires • uenos Aires City Map • Chile & Easter Island • Colombia • Ecuador & the Galapagos Islands • Healthy Travel entral & South America • Latin American Spanish phrasebook • Peru • Quechua phrasebook • Read This First: entral & South America • Rio de Janeiro • Rio de Janeiro City Map • Santiago de Chile • South America on a hoestring • Trekking in the Patagonian Andes • Venezuela **Travel Literature:** Full Circle: A South American Journey

SOUTH-EAST ASIA Bali & Lombok • Bangkok • Bangkok City Map • Burmese phrasebook • Cambodia • ycling Vietnam, Laos & Cambodia • East Timor phrasebook • Hanoi • Healthy Travel Asia & India • Hill Tribes hrasebook • Ho Chi Minh City (Saigon) • Indonesia • Indonesian phrasebook • Indonesia's Eastern Islands • ava • Lao phrasebook • Laos • Malay phrasebook • Malaysia, Singapore & Brunei • Myanmar (Burma) • Philipines • Pilipino (Tagalog) phrasebook • Read This First: Asia & India • Singapore • Singapore City Map • outh-East Asia on a shoestring • South-East Asia phrasebook • Thailand • Thailand's Islands & Beaches • Thaind, Vietnam, Laos & Cambodia Road Atlas • Thai phrasebook • Vietnam • Vietnamese phrasebook • World ood Indonesia • World Food Thailand • World Food Vietnam

ALSO AVAILABLE: Antarctica • The Arctic • The Blue Man: Tales of Travel, Love and Coffee • Brief Encounters: tories of Love, Sex & Travel • Buddhist Stupas in Asia: The Shape of Perfection • Chasing Rickshaws • The ast Grain Race • Lonely Planet ... On the Edge: Adventurous Escapades from Around the World • Lonely Planet Jnpacked • Lonely Planet Unpacked Again • Not the Only Planet: Science Fiction Travel Stories • Ports of Call: A Journey by Sea • Sacred India • Travel Photography: A Guide to Taking Better Pictures • Travel with Children Tuvalu: Portrait of an Island Nation

Index

Abbreviations

Text

Bold indicates maps.

Boxed Text

MAP LEGEND

BOUNDARIES

.... International
.... State
.... Disputed

HYDROGRAPHY

.... Coastline
.... River, Creek
.... Lake
.... Intermittent Lake
.... Salt Lake
.... Canal
.... Spring, Rapids
.... Waterfalls
.... Swamp

ROUTES & TRANSPORT

.... Highway
.... Major Road
.... Minor Road
.... Unsealed Road
.... City Freeway
.... City Highway
.... City Road
.... City Street, Lane

.... Pedestrian Mall
.... Tunnel
.... Train Route & Station
.... Tramway
.... Cable Car or Chairlift
.... Walking Track
.... Walking Tour
.... Ferry Route

AREA FEATURES

.... Building
.... Park, Gardens
.... Cemetery
.... Reef

.... Market
.... Beach, Desert
.... Urban Area

MAP SYMBOLS

❂ **CAPITAL**	National Capital	✈	Domestic Airport	☀ ...... Lookout
◉ **CAPITAL**	State Capital	✈	International Airport	⚐ ...... Monument
● **CITY**	City	⚓	Anchorage	▲ ...... Mountain or Hill
● Town	Town	⁘	Archaeological Site	)(...... Pass
● Village	Village	⛉	Bar	★ ...... Police Station
○	Point of Interest	☂	Beach	▣ ...... Post Office
		⌒	Cave	⤬ ...... Shipwreck
▪	Place to Stay	⊞ ✚	Church	❖ ...... Shopping Centre
⚑	Camping Ground		Cliff or Escarpment	▭ ...... Swimming Pool
⛺	Caravan Park	◪	Dive Site, Snorkelling	☎ ...... Telephone
⌂	Hut or Chalet	◲	Embassy	❶ ...... Tourist Information
		⚑	Golf	▣ ...... Tomb
▼	Place to Eat	ⓤ	Hindu	◖ ...... Transport
⛾	Pub or Bar	✛	Hospital	⛪ ...... Museum

Note: not all symbols displayed above appear in this book

LONELY PLANET OFFICES

Australia
Locked Bag 1, Footscray, Victoria 3011
☎ 03 8379 8000 fax 03 8379 8111
email: talk2us@lonelyplanet.com.au

USA
150 Linden St, Oakland, CA 94607
☎ 510 893 8555 TOLL FREE: 800 275 8555
fax 510 893 8572
email: info@lonelyplanet.com

UK
10a Spring Place, London NW5 3BH
☎ 020 7428 4800 fax 020 7428 4828
email: go@lonelyplanet.co.uk

France
1 rue du Dahomey, 75011 Paris
☎ 01 55 25 33 00 fax 01 55 25 33 01
email: bip@lonelyplanet.fr
www.lonelyplanet.fr

World Wide Web: www.lonelyplanet.com *or* AOL keyword: lp
Lonely Planet Images: lpi@lonelyplanet.com.au